THE
CONCISE CAMBRIDGE HISTORY OF
ENGLISH LITERATURE

THE
CONCISE CAMBRIDGE HISTORY OF
ENGLISH LITERATURE

THE CONCISE CAMBRIDGE HISTORY OF ENGLISH LITERATURE

BY

GEORGE SAMPSON

THIRD EDITION
REVISED THROUGHOUT AND WITH
ADDITIONAL CHAPTERS ON
THE LITERATURE OF THE
UNITED STATES OF AMERICA
AND THE MID-TWENTIETH-CENTURY
LITERATURE OF THE
ENGLISH-SPEAKING WORLD
BY
R. C. CHURCHILL

CAMBRIDGE
AT THE UNIVERSITY PRESS
1970

Published by the Syndics of the Cambridge University Press
Bentley House, 200 Euston Road, London N.W.1
American Branch: 32 East 57th Street, New York, N.Y.10022

Standard Book Numbers:
521 07385 5   clothbound
521 09581 6   paperback

First edition 1941
Reprinted 1941 1942 1943 1944 1945 1946 1949 1953 1957 1959
Second edition 1961
Reprinted 1965
Third edition 1970

Printed in Great Britain
at the University Printing House, Cambridge
(Brooke Crutchley, University Printer)

CONTENTS

CHAPTER I

FROM THE BEGINNINGS TO THE CYCLES OF ROMANCE

CHAPTER II

THE END OF THE MIDDLE AGES

CHAPTER III

RENASCENCE AND REFORMATION

CHAPTER IV

PROSE AND POETRY: SIR THOMAS NORTH TO MICHAEL DRAYTON

CHAPTER V

THE DRAMA TO 1642: PART I

CHAPTER IX

FROM STEELE AND ADDISON TO POPE AND SWIFT

CHAPTER X

THE AGE OF JOHNSON

CHAPTER XI

THE PERIOD OF THE FRENCH REVOLUTION

CHAPTER XII

THE NINETEENTH CENTURY: PART I

CHAPTER XIII

THE NINETEENTH CENTURY: PART II

CHAPTER XIV

EMPIRE AND AFTER: FROM THE NINETEENTH TO THE TWENTIETH CENTURY IN BRITAIN AND OVERSEAS

CHAPTER XV

THE LITERATURE OF THE UNITED STATES OF AMERICA FROM THE COLONIAL PERIOD TO HENRY JAMES

CHAPTER XVI

THE AGE OF T. S. ELIOT: THE MID-TWENTIETH-CENTURY LITERATURE OF THE ENGLISH-SPEAKING WORLD

The first thirteen chapters of this book are based on the corresponding volumes of *The Cambridge History of English Literature*. "Each chapter", as the late George Sampson wrote in the Preface to the First Edition, "takes for its subject matter the volume that bears its title, and reference to the parent work is therefore easy. Paragraphs and sentences in their original form have been incorporated into the narrative when such treatment seemed desirable and practicable... The writer of an epitome must respect his terms of reference, but he is entitled to move freely within them. He may not transform his matter, but he may add or amend; and so, while this volume presents, in the main, the views of the parent *History*, it includes certain modifications necessitated by the fact that some of the original chapters were written over thirty years ago."

A further period of almost the same length has now elapsed since Sampson wrote these words in 1941. Further modifications are therefore necessary. In preparing this Third Edition, I have proceeded on much the same lines as my predecessor. I have not transformed the matter, but I have added, amended or omitted, according to the literary climate of 1968, which differs from that of 1941 by as wide a margin as 1941 differed from 1907. The first thirteen chapters retain their original titles and the majority of their original text, but while not seeking to trespass on the preserves of George Watson's *Concise Cambridge Bibliography of English Literature* I have borne in mind that this is an age of scholarship and education and I have therefore met the needs of students, without affecting the convenience of the general reader, by including a few of the main works of modern scholars and biographers under the authors and periods to which they belong. I have provided more cross-references than Sampson thought necessary. And I have taken the opportunity of a new edition to rewrite entirely the sixth section of chapter XIII, which Sampson had already expanded, and to put Gerard Manley Hopkins where he belongs in life, in the Victorian age, instead of placing him, as in both the First and Second Editions of this book, in the twentieth century when he was first published.

The fourteenth chapter has required more drastic revision. Sampson brought it up to date originally in 1941 by adding to "The Nineteenth Century: Part III" some further material under the heading of "Post-Victorian Literature". I have kept to the same general plan, at this further stage of literary development, but having regard to the increasing importance of the literature of the Commonwealth and other former colonial countries I have increased the length of this chapter by rewriting and expanding the sections on Indian, Canadian, Australasian and South African literature, giving the chapter the new and appropriate title of "Empire and After: From the Nineteenth to the Twentieth Century in Britain and Overseas".

This is a long chapter, covering an important and revolutionary period in the development of many aspects of literature in the English language, both in the British Isles and abroad. But one omission will immediately strike the reader.

If the emphasis is now to be on "literature in the English language" rather than on "English literature" in its original national meaning, it is surely fitting that the United States of America, which has its own most vigorous and important literature, should be included. I have therefore added a new chapter, chapter xv, covering the literature of the United States from the Colonial Period to Henry James, giving particular attention to the relations between American and British literature, the way each has influenced the other.

The original chapter xv in the First Edition of this book was where George Sampson parted company with the parent *History* and added his own new chapter on "Late-Victorian and Post-Victorian Literature". It was felt in 1960 that this chapter had outlived its usefulness, that it should be replaced by a new modern chapter more in harmony with the critical opinion of the mid-twentieth century. I was commissioned to write this new modern chapter, which I entitled "The Age of T. S. Eliot" after the great Anglo–American writer who is admitted to be both the leading poet and the leading critic of the period *c.* 1920–60. This new modern chapter appeared in our Second Edition in 1961.

In this Third Edition I have retained the title for the last chapter, which is now chapter xvi, because the name of Eliot is even more appropriate than it was in 1960, now that we have decided to include the literature of his native country as well as the literature of the country of his adoption. But I have rewritten and expanded this final chapter throughout, in accordance with its new sub-title: "The Mid-Twentieth-Century Literature of the English-Speaking World". Ending with a section on the literature of the West Indies and the new African states, this final chapter closes a book which now takes the reader from early Anglo–Saxon times to the late nineteen-sixties and in terms of space from England itself to "regions" (to paraphrase Cowper) which neither Caesar nor Shakespeare ever knew. I believe that the author of *English for the English*, with his great love of English literature wherever it is found, would have welcomed this expansion of his original Cambridge plan and I hope that readers and students in all parts of the English-speaking world will welcome it too.

Sampson ended his Preface to the First Edition by paying a tribute to the work of his predecessors in the parent *History*, scholars like George Saintsbury, W. P. Ker, H. M. Chadwick, Sir Herbert Grierson, Harold Child, Charles Whibley, J. Dover Wilson, W. P. Trent, D. Nichol Smith, Émile Legouis, Pelham Edgar, and the editors Sir Adolphus Ward and A. R. Waller, many of whose original chapters are still among the best introductions to their authors and periods and still often consulted by scholars and critics. "Much learning", he wrote, "has gone into the volumes represented by the present chapters; and the author, now that his long day's task is done, turns to offer a parting salute of respect to the scholars whose work he has here sought to bring home 'to the great Variety of Readers'".

This Third Edition addresses an even greater Variety than the First Folio of Shakespeare whose preface Sampson was quoting or than his own First Edition. I should like to end this Preface by paying, in my turn, a respectful tribute to George Sampson himself. Anyone who doubts the great literary skill and immense scholarly patience which went into his "long day's task" has only to read, for example, the first volume of the parent *History*, and afterwards the equivalent chapter of this book, to realize both the magnitude of the task and how admirably equipped he was to undertake it. I can only hope that I have expanded him in time and space without too much cosmopolitan deviation from his original Johnsonian virtues.

R.C.C.

St Leonards, Sussex
March 1968

CHAPTER I

FROM THE BEGINNINGS TO THE CYCLES
OF ROMANCE

I. THE BEGINNINGS

The history of a national literature, however much destined to be international, is part at first of the national story; but it is a separable part, for man is older than his songs, and passed through many stages of development before he found his way into the kind of self-expression that we call literature. Nothing definite remains of the songs or stories possessed by the Britons whom Caesar found in southern England, and next to nothing of the literature possessed by the Britons during the centuries of the Roman occupation. Though echoes from Celtic Britain must have lingered in men's minds, English literature begins, at least, by being English.

The earliest forms of English literature, like the earliest forms of other national literatures, have perished. We know nothing whatever of Old English poetry in its rudest shape. The fragments we possess are not those of a literature in the making, for the poets of *Beowulf* and *Widsith*, of *The Ruin* and *The Seafarer* knew what they wished to say, and said it without any trace of struggle for word or form. Whether what survives is the best we have no means of knowing. *Beowulf* comes down to us in a single manuscript. Three other ancient volumes, the Exeter Book, preserved in the Cathedral library at Exeter, the Vercelli Book, strangely washed up out of the wrecks of time into a Lombard haven at Vercelli, and the Junian manuscript given to Oxford by Dujon, a friend of Milton, contain nearly all the rest of the Old English poetry we know. That is to say, if four damaged or precariously preserved old books had gone with the rest into destruction, Old English poetry would have been merely something to guess at.

Our earliest literature has much to do with life and journeys that were a constant struggle against a grim and pitiless element. The shadow of long nights by waters wild with storm or fettered by frost falls darkly upon our first poems. The sea of our forefathers was not a gracious Mediterranean washing with blue water the steps of marble palaces, but an ocean grey and tumultuous beating upon dismal shores and sterile promontories. The very land seems as cruel as the sea. No song of lark or nightingale gladdens life for these shore-dwellers; their loneliness is made more terrible by the scream of sea birds crying about the cliffs or by strange sounds that mingle with the moan of the wind across the meres. With rude implements they scratch the soil, and, in hope of the harvest, greet the earth in lines like those below, perhaps some of the oldest in our language:

> Hal wes þu, folde, fira modor,
> beo þu growende on godes faeþme;
> fodre gefylled firum to nytte.

Hale be thou Earth, Mother of men!
Fruitful be thou in the arms of the god.
Be filled with thy fruit for the fare-need of man!

We quote the modern version by the Victorian scholar Stopford Brooke.

II. RUNES AND MANUSCRIPTS

When the aboriginal English still lived by the northern seas they shared with their kindred an alphabet of "runes". We need regard here only the alphabetical value of these symbols and ignore tradition that ultimately made "Runic rhyme" develop into a stock term for mystery or incomprehensibility. The runic alphabet naturally took a form that lent itself easily to rough carving, and certain famous inscriptions upon stone, metal or bone still remain. Each rune had its own name, which was also the name of some familiar thing. Thus the symbol þ, which degenerated into an initial y, was the "thorn."

Runes went out of use in the ninth and tenth centuries. Their place had, however, been usurped long before that period by the Roman alphabet which the English received from the early Irish missionaries. The missionary and the Roman alphabet travelled together, and it was the Christian scribe who first wrote down what heathen memories had preserved. A school of Roman hand-writing was established in the south of England by Augustine and his missionaries; but its existence was brief, and little evidence of its activity survives. The most powerful influence came from Ireland, to which manuscripts in the Roman "half-uncial" hand had been brought by missionaries perhaps in the fifth century. When Northumbria was Christianized by the Irish, the preachers taught their disciples to write the Word in characters more pleasing to God than the runes of heathendom. Thus the English learnt the exquisite penmanship of the Irish and were soon able to give such striking evidence of their skill as the magnificent *Lindisfarne Gospels* of about 700, in the rounded half-uncial.

After the Conquest the native hand disappeared, the only traces left being a few characters to express peculiarly English sounds, ρ (wynn) and þ (thorn), and the later symbols ȝ (yok) and ð (eth). The ρ was replaced in the thirteenth century by *w*, and disappeared; the French *qu* replaced cρ. The two signs þ and ð were interchangeable and represented the two sounds of *th*. Of these the first long survived (later in the form of initial y) and is still met with in the semi-humorous archaism "ye" for "the". The symbol ȝ (a form of *z*) was variously used. It stood for *z*, for *y* in ȝeer (year) and daȝe (day), and in such forms as kniȝt and rouȝ represented the Old English *h* (*gh*), in *cniht* and *ruh*.

The writing materials of medieval England included the old *boc* or wooden tablet, coated with wax, and written upon with a style of bone or metal. Parchment and vellum were used for writings meant to endure. The scribes were monks or nuns who wrote with truly religious patience in the chilly cloisters or the cells of the monasteries, only the fortunate few having a special *scriptorium* or writing room for their task. Gradually, however, a professional class of scribes came into existence, working either for, or actually in, the monasteries.

III. EARLY NATIONAL POETRY

The first English poet known to us by name (or nickname) is "Widsith", the "Wide Wanderer", a *scop* or itinerant minstrel of the sixth century, who gives us glimpses of his own life in a poem of about 150 lines (Exeter Book). The many allusions in *Widsith* are as puzzling to us as a catalogue of names from some ancient gazetteer or genealogy, and arouse no emotion higher than an impulse towards research; but they had each a thrill for the primitive hearers. What the modern reader catches in *Widsith* is a glimpse of a poet's joy and grief appealing humanly across the centuries.

Deor's Lament (Exeter Book), a poem unique in its time for a strophic form with a constant refrain, "þæs ofereode: þisses swa maeg", "That was lived through, so can this be", is a song of the poet's own misfortunes, illustrated by the equally hard lot of others who once were happy. *Deor* has a lyric note.

The Wanderer (Exeter Book), a moving elegy of 115 lines, is the lament of a man who has lost his protecting lord, and wanders over the waters to find a resting place. In dreams his vanished happiness shines on him again, but day brings back the grey sea and the driving snow and the desolation of the earth. *The Seafarer* (Exeter Book) is usually read as a dialogue between an old man who knows the joyless life of the sea and a young man who will not be deterred from maritime adventure by the melancholy tale of the old seaman. But it may be the monologue of a man who, hating the hardships and cruelty of the sea, knows that for him there is no other life. Among modern versions and paraphrases, that of the American poet Ezra Pound, first published in *Ripostes* (1912), is notable:

> List how I, care-wretched, on ice-cold sea,
> Weathered the winter, wretched outcast
> Deprived of my kinsmen;
> Hung with hard ice-flakes, where hail-scur flew...

Among the fragmentary poems in the Exeter Book there is one short piece commonly called *The Ruin*, remarkable because it takes us away from the sea and describes the downfall of some great palace or rich city—possibly Bath. The imperfection of the Exeter manuscript makes this poem difficult to read and adds to the obscurity of other short pieces like *The Wife's Complaint* and *The Husband's Message*.

The fullest revelation of the hard, heroic and joyless lives led by our old English forefathers is to be found in *Beowulf*, a narrative poem of 3183 lines transmitted in a tenth-twelfth century manuscript, now safely preserved in the British Museum after many damaging adventures. Like the epics of Homer, *Beowulf* has been subjected to a close critical examination that has produced almost as many opinions as there have been critics. Some hold that its home is the Baltic shore, and that it was brought to England by the invading Northmen. Others designate England as the place of composition and the Yorkshire coast as the scene of the story. The fact should be noted that, not only in *Beowulf*, but in all our early national poetry, the allusions are Continental or Scandinavian: no reference can be found to persons who are known to have lived in Britain.

There is general agreement that the West Saxon dialect in which *Beowulf* now exists is not that in which it was originally composed, and that the lays out of which it was fashioned belong to pre-Christian times, although in its present form it contains many passages of distinctly Christian character. What may be called the "stuff" of *Beowulf* is essentially heathen; the sentiment and reflections are Christian. The mixture indicates that the poem is a heathen legend which received its present expression from a Christian poet. The resemblance between the deeds of Beowulf and those of other heroes do not point to imitation, but rather to the tendency of primitive heroes to become each the centre of stock adventures. Naturally, few heroes in any early romance have escaped a combat with a monster. The story of *Beowulf* is so generally familiar that it need not be told here. The poem is interesting both as a heroic lay and as a national document. It is the earliest, as it is the finest, of the northern hero-poems, and in places it attains a very moving quality. The song of the fight at Finnsburh, the description of the monster-haunted mere, and the story of Beowulf's death and burial have the note of great literature. The poem gives us glimpses of the communal life of our ancestors in the hall of their lord, and tells of the emotions that moved them. They were brave; but they were terror-haunted. Against the beasts they could fight; against the dim, impalpable unknown they were helpless. The long nights of the northern winter harrowed them with fear and wonder. The Homeric heroes are the playthings of the gods; but their life is more joyous than that of the Wyrd-haunted heroes in the hall of Hrothgar. Perhaps because it has no sense of joy or light or colour, the greatest of Old English poems has never really entered into the being of the Englishman, who has turned for his heroes to the Mediterranean and not to the Baltic. We do not know who first assembled the stories of *Beowulf* into a continuous narrative, nor when they were thus assembled. There is a modern prose translation by Clark Hall and C. L. Wrenn, with an introduction by J. R. R. Tolkien.

Apart from *Beowulf*, the only surviving remains of early national epic poetry are a fragment (50 lines) of *Finnsburh* (MS. now lost) and two short fragments (63 lines together) of *Waldere* (MS. at Copenhagen). The *Finnsburh* story, though obscure to us, must have been popular, for it is the subject of a long episode in *Beowulf* (ll. 1063–1159), and three of the characters are mentioned in *Widsith*. The full story of *Waldere* is available in several other sources. The fragments begin with praise of the sword Mimming, the master-work of Weland the smith, which Waldere is to wield against Guthhere (Gunther).

Few traces remain of heathen religious poetry. What we have are popular "charms" or incantations for securing fertility of the fields or immunity from witchcraft, and even these have plainly felt the influence of later Christianity. It is probable that they were not written down until they had ceased to be part of a heathen ceremonial and had become part of peasant folk-lore.

Old English verse takes, as a rule, one general form, the particular character of which is discussed in a later section. The verses were made for oral delivery, the alliteration itself probably marking the strong chords or clashes of whatever noises accompanied the voice. Possibly the nearest approach we have to Anglo–Saxon verse is the "pointing" of the Psalms in the Church service, i.e. the fitting of verses with no fixed number of syllables to a form of chant with a fixed number of accents. The general style of Old English verse is ejaculatory—the style of men who draw their images from the strife of the elements. Old English literature is the literature of men, not of women. We need not doubt that there were songs of other kinds—common songs and comic songs, songs about women and songs about drink; but such songs had a purely oral life and perished because they were never recorded. The Germanic tribes were decorous in their lives, but they were not unnatural ascetics and did not suffer from abnormal repressions.

The poems named in the early pages of this chapter are a selection from the pieces, not all of literary interest, that survive in Old English transcriptions made in the tenth century or later. There are no "original manuscripts". Song and saga existed before scribes and script. Some communities have regarded writing as the enemy of man's most precious possession, his memory. Law would be recorded before lyric. In Wagner's *Ring*, the pact with the giants is carved on the shaft of Wotan's spear; no one records the songs of the Rhine Daughters.

IV. OLD ENGLISH CHRISTIAN POETRY

Roman-British Christianity, which gave Britain its first martyr and its first heretic, left no recorded trace upon the course of English literature. The invading barbarians from Germany overwhelmed British religion as well as British poetry. But in Ireland the faith preached by St Patrick still held its ground. The re-Christianizing of England, first by Celtic missionaries from Ireland through the western islands of Scotland, and next by Augustine and his monks sent hither from Rome itself, changed much in the matter and feeling of English poetry, but left its form and general machinery unaltered. The bleak mists of the unknown enshrouding primitive life dissipate as light breaks into the heathen darkness. The subject of the poets' song is now the story of Christ and the deeds of saintly heroes. The dim and inexorable Wyrd gives place to an all-seeing Father; and grace, hope and mercy begin to lighten the darkness of lives once terror-haunted. The form of the verse and the shape of the poems remain unchanged. The heroism of Judith is sung in the measure that had chanted the deeds of Beowulf, and God and the angels, or Christ and the apostles, take something like the form of an English chief with a shining host of unconquerable clansmen.

The new spirit in English poetry came from Christianity, but not from that alone. English poetry did not change because a Kentish king was baptized by a Roman monk. In 597 St Augustine landed at Ebbsfleet; but St Columba was already at Iona in 563, and from Iona came St Aidan to Lindisfarne in 635. St Augustine brought a theological system to the south; St Aidan brought religious grace to the north. The missionaries who carried Christianity into the Anglian kingdoms came not merely from the island of St Patrick but from the island of Deirdre, and it was in a monastery ruled by Celtic, not Roman, usage that Caedmon found his gift of song. Thus northern English literature came to be touched by an influence that people have agreed to call Celtic. The effect was to make English poetry subjective rather than objective, lyric rather than epic.

The first English poet clearly known to us by name is Caedmon (fl. 670), who, as Bede tells us in a beautiful passage of his *Ecclesiastical History*, dwelt till middle age in the monastery ruled by the Abbess Hild at Streoneshalh (Whitby). Then in a vision he was called by name, and bidden to sing of God the Creator. He made his verses, and, when he awoke, remembered them and made others like them. Bede, a careful and exact historian, tells us that Caedmon turned into song the story of Genesis and Exodus, the settlement of the chosen people in the promised land, the life and death of the Saviour, and the revelation of the judgment to come. Now it happens that in what is called the Junian manuscript at Oxford there are poetical versions of *Genesis*, *Exodus* and *Daniel*, together with three *Christ* poems (or three parts of one *Christ* poem)—*The Fallen Angels*, *The Harrowing of Hell* and *The Temptation*. These were naturally assumed to be the Caedmon poems described by Bede; but critical research has proved the ascription to be impossible. Perhaps the Caedmon songs were used by later singers and left their spirit in the poems that remain; but of the originals described by Bede we have no trace. The Caedmonian *Hymn* itself, possibly the oldest surviving piece of English poetry composed on English soil, is all that we possess of the first known English poet. It is quoted by Bede. We may be sure that if Caedmon had been a "secular" poet and not a "sacred" poet, his name would not have been recorded.

The most interesting of the Junian poems is *Genesis*, a narrative of nearly 3000 lines. After singing the praises of the Creator in the Caedmonian manner, and describing the fall of the angels, the poet proceeds with the Bible story from the Creation to the frustrated sacrifice of Isaac. At l. 235, however, begins a repetition of the story of the rebel angels told in a style unlike that of the rest. No one had questioned the unity of the poem till 1875, when the German scholar Eduard Sievers conjectured that ll. 235–851 were (*a*) an interpolation and (*b*) a translation of an Old Saxon paraphrase of the Old Testament (long lost), by the author of the Old Saxon paraphrase of the New Testament, commonly known as the *Heliand*. In 1894 the discovery in the Vatican Library of a manuscript containing fragments of the Old Saxon original (ninth century) confirmed the brilliant conjecture of Sievers. The main body of the poem is now generally known as *Genesis A* and the interpolation as *Genesis B*. Who made the translation from Old Saxon and why it was inserted in an Old English work will probably never be known; but the incident is worth noting as a very early example of literary intercourse between England and Germany. The author of *Genesis A* follows the scriptural story very closely, even though, like the early Italian painters, he represents the main incidents, especially the battle-scenes, in terms of contemporary life. But the Christian poet is apparent in softer descriptions than could have found a place in *Beowulf*. The Old Saxon poet of *Genesis B* was of a more daring order. He gave his imagination wings, and his picture of the unconquerable Satan thrust out of heaven into the murk of hell, and there pursuing his strife with the Almighty by seeking to destroy the newly-created race of man, irresistibly suggests the proud fiend of *Paradise Lost*.

Exodus relates the escape of the Israelites and the destruction of the Egyptians in the Red Sea. It is boldly and vigorously written, and has the older epic note. *Daniel* is a tame and homiletic rendering of the opening chapters of the Scriptural book. The story of the three children in the furnace is better told in a short poem called *Azarias* transmitted in the Exeter codex. The *Christ* poems, especially *The Harrowing of Hell*, endure comparison with later treatment of their matter. They have a primitive note, and it has been suggested that they are possibly nearer to the Caedmonian originals than any of the other poems in the Junian codex.

All the old religious poems that were not assigned to Caedmon were invariably given to Cynewulf (fl. 750). As Caedmon was the accepted poet of the Junian manuscript, so Cynewulf was the accepted poet of the Exeter Book. Modern scholarship has taught us to be more discriminating. Dim as the figure of Cynewulf is, we are surer of him than of Caedmon, if only because in two poems of the Exeter Book and two of the Vercelli he has inserted runic characters that have meaning in the verses and form the name Cynewulf or Cynwulf. The general conclusion of scholars is that, though the poems are transmitted in a West Saxon version, Cynewulf was a Northumbrian or Mercian who wrote towards the end of the eighth century. His work represents an advance in culture upon the more primitive Caedmonian poems. Much of it shows acquaintance with Latin originals and seems to exhibit a more conscious effort to attain artistic form. The most notable of the Cynewulf poems is the *Christ* (not to be confused with the Caedmonian poem of the Junian manuscript), a trilogy, to the first and third parts of which the Cynewulfian authorship has been denied. Each part can be traced to Latin sources, but the poet is as original as Milton, and voices in eloquent language a personal vision of life. The description of the Last Judgment and the joys of the blessed are the work of a true poet. Immediately after the *Christ* in the Exeter Book comes *Juliana*, which, like the *Christ*, is signed in runes. The poem derives from the *Acta S. Julianae* and describes the life and death of the virgin martyr. But the intrinsic merit of the poem is small; and this must be said, too, of the Vercelli *Fates of the Apostles*, also signed in runes. *Andreas* (Vercelli Book), the Cynewulfian authorship of which is doubtful, though it was once considered part of *The Fates of the Apostles*, is a great poem. It is a story of the missionary labours of St Andrew, divinely sent to save St Matthew from Ethiopian cannibals; but in essence it is a tale of sea adventure. The poem shows the author's close acquaintance with the moods of the sea, which he renders with great power. *Elene* (transmitted in the Vercelli Book) is Cynewulf's masterpiece, and carries his runic name. Besides being a poem of original power, it is a document illustrating the new *cultus* of the Cross. Constantine's celebrated vision before his victory at the Milvian Bridge (312) inspired his mother Helena to set out in quest of the Cross itself; and, guided by a vision, she found it buried unbroken. The iconoclastic movement in the eighth and ninth centuries against idolatrous attachment to images contributed to an increased reverence for this arch-symbol of the Christian faith, and the two festivals, the Invention (or finding) and the Exaltation (or recovery) of the Cross, were both observed in the Old English church. The story of Helena as told in the *Acta Sanctorum* gave Cynewulf the basis of his poem. It is in fourteen "fitts" or cantos, and tells with true poetic inspiration the story of a quest involving many adventures and conflicts on land and sea.

With *Elene* we may fitly consider *The Dream of the Rood*, a poem of some

150 lines in the Vercelli Book, forming part of the Cynewulf apocrypha. In beauty of language and in ecstasy of devotional feeling, it is among the finest of English religious poems. In a dream the poet sees the Cross, "a gallows tree, but not of shame", decked with gold and jewels. But as he looks, the Cross streams with blood, and, gifted with a divine voice, it begins to speak, and tells of the dreadful day when the skies were darkened and the rocks rent as the King of Heaven was uplifted in mortal agony.

Guthlac, a poem of 1370 lines, the latter and better part of which is probably Cynewulf's, narrates the oft-told life and death of the Mercian saint. The finest lines are those that describe the passing of the holy man, joyously departing to bliss amid the harmony of heavenly voices and the streaming of the Northern Lights.

The Phoenix, a poem of 677 lines in the Exeter Book, is remarkable not merely as an elaborately descriptive poem, but as a successful attempt to replace the Northumbrian landscape by an imaginative and ideal world. In its artistic achievement of pure description *The Phoenix* shows a notable advance in English poetic technique.

Among the minor remains of Old English poetry we may mention an incomplete *Bestiary*—*Whale*, *Panther* and *Partridge*—an allegorical moralized description of animals, very popular in all languages during the Middle Ages; an *Address of a Lost Soul to the Body*, and an *Address of a Saved Soul to the Body*, the first a common and the second a rare theme; a group of four short homiletic poems, the *Gifts of Man*, the *Fates of Man*, the *Mind of Man* and the *Falsehood of Man*; and a *Rhyming Poem*, the sole surviving example of the use of end-rhyme and alliteration together in one piece.

Many poetical riddles are transmitted in the Exeter Book. Some of them are good pieces of description as well as interesting sidelights on popular beliefs. The proverbs, of which the Exeter Book contains a collection, possibly represent heathen utterances Christianized in transmission. Moral poetry is represented by *A Father's Instruction* containing ten admonitions in ten times as many lines. The didactic dialogue, familiar in several literatures, is exemplified in Old English by *Salomon and Saturn*, found in a Cambridge manuscript. The fact that so much of Old English literature is religious or didactic does not mean that there were no secular poets. It must be constantly remembered that we have to deal, not with what existed, but with what was written down. The monastic scribes would never waste hard labour and precious material on vain and amatorious poems. Even the old took a new shape as it passed through their hands, and in *Beowulf* itself we can discern the wild Teutonic spirit touched here and there by the spirit of Roman Christianity.

V. LATIN WRITINGS IN ENGLAND TO THE TIME OF ALFRED

Much of the older literature of Christian England is written in Latin. That universal language prevailed, indeed, into the age of Harvey and Newton. Some of the more interesting matter has been industriously translated by scholars like J. A. Giles (1808–84); some still remains almost unknown to general readers. The historian of English literature has a difficulty in deciding which of the earliest Latin writings by natives of Britain fall within his province. It is outside the scope of this work to survey the various scattered documents of British origin which were produced outside Britain. Among the writings thus excluded from consideration may be mentioned the remains of Pelagius (i.e. Morgan, early fifth century), who seems to have been actually the earliest British author, as well as our first heretic, and the two famous epistles of St Patrick, the *Confession* and the *Letter to Coroticus*, which, in spite of their barbaric style, are among the most attractive monuments of ancient Christianity.

The first works that call for notice are the book of Gildas and the anonymous *Historia Britonum*. Gildas Sapiens, "Gildas the Wise", appears to have been born about 500, to have written his *De Excidio Britanniae* before 547, and to have died abroad about 570. His work, variously named in the manuscripts, is entitled by the German scholar Theodor Mommsen, "Of Gildas the Wise concerning the destruction and conquest of Britain and his lamentable castigation uttered against the kings, princes and priests thereof." Gildas is essentially a prophet; he makes little claim to historicity: "If there were any records of my country," he says, "they were burned in the fires of the conquest, or carried away on the ships of the exiles, so that I can only follow the dark and fragmentary tale that was told me beyond the sea." One-quarter of his work is occupied by a narrative that begins with the Romans and comes down to forty-four years after the battle of Mount Badon (516), when the descendants of Ambrosius Aurelianus—the hero of that field and a dim foreshadowing of the mythical Arthur—had forsaken the ways of their great ancestor, and, together with the rest of Britain, had departed from God and fallen into the vilest degradation. Gildas is specially interesting as a specimen of the Romanized Briton. "Our tongue" for him is Latin, and his eyes, in changing times, are fixed tragically on the great Roman past.

The *Historia Britonum* is more important as history than as literature. The probable date of the original compilation is somewhere about 679. Of several later recensions the most important is that made in the ninth century by Nynniaw (Latin, Nennius) a Welshman whose version is not fully extant. Into the complicated question of authorship we are not called upon to go; but we should note that one main source of the *Historia* is Gildas. In manner it somewhat resembles the Old Testament *Chronicles*, with their mixture of genealogy and legend. Its chief legacy to later generations is the story of Vortigern. Within a few years of the death of Gildas, *ultimus Britannorum*, came the mission of St Augustine to Kent, and England passed once more under definite, if different, Roman influences. Attributed to Gildas is a metrical prayer or charm, the *Lorica*, i.e., cuirass or breastplate. A similar piece in Irish is claimed for St Patrick. In the enumeration of parts of the body it uses an extraordinary vocabulary, even more abundantly employed in *Hisperica Famina*, a strange work of over 600 lines with a primitive metrical structure. That the author was either Irish or had some connection with Ireland is clear. Similar in its use of Hisperic Latinity is the alphabetic hymn *Altus prosator* attributed to St Columba.

The first important English writer of Latin is Aldhelm, Bishop of Sherborne, who died in 709. A tradition represents him as skilled in singing to the country people English songs of his own composing; but of these, unfortunately, not a trace remains. What does remain is a large body of Latin compositions—verses, a discussion of metre, riddles, letters, and a treatise on virginity, written first in prose and then in hexameters. Though Aldhelm could be simple, he preferred to be elaborate in style and fantastic in his choice of words, like the Hisperic compositions. Interesting as he is historically, the loss of all his writings would leave the world of letters no poorer. The known followers and imitators of Aldhelm were not many, and hardly concern the student of English literature.

Aldhelm and his followers were men of the south. The two greatest of our early English Latinists were northerners scarcely touched by the literary influence of Aldhelm. Bede and Alcuin both enjoyed a European reputation, but the fame of the former was more genuinely literary. He is, indeed, in spite of his chosen idiom, among the best of English writers, with a sweet lovable personality radiating from every page. He was born at Monkwearmouth about 673, and died in 735 at Jarrow, where almost the whole of his life was spent. His industry was enormous and his works are too numerous even for bare mention here. Many of them are theological, but the others cover a wide range of knowledge. Bede's enduring fame for us depends chiefly upon his historical writings. The *Martyrology*, expanded by later hands, was a highly popular summary of ecclesiastical biography. The short work *De Temporibus*, dealing, among other things, with the calculations connected with the observance of Easter, not only touched upon a cause of division between the Celtic-English and the Roman-English churches, but let the dry light of mathematics into religious controversy. The tract ends with a brief chronicle of the events in the six ages of human history. This chronicle plays a much more important part in the longer work *De Temporum Ratione*. Bede was the first chronicler to give the date from Christ's birth in addition to the year of the world. Bede's best and greatest work is the Latin *Ecclesiastical History of the English Race* in five books, parts of which are now among the national legends. Every schoolboy knows the story of Gregory and the Angles and the calling of Caedmon. Those older than schoolboys cannot read unmoved the passage in which the nameless noble at the Northumbrian court, touched by the preaching of Paulinus, likens the life of man to the flight of a bird out of the winter night into a warm and lighted hall and thence into the dark again. The miraculous visit of Drythelm to the world beyond death, narrated in Book V, is an admirable exercise in the kind of medieval literature that we have learned to call Dantesque. The whole work is written with the transparent sincerity of a beautiful mind and the matter is appropriately presented in prose that has no trace of the Aldhelmian affectations. Although he wrote in Latin, Bede rendered to English letters the high service of popularizing a direct and simple narrative style. The metrical life of St Cuthbert is interesting as Bede's most considerable effort in verse. The *Letter to Egbert* shows that, cloistered as he was, the soul of Bede ranged far beyond the walls of his abbey and concerned itself eagerly with the whole state of the English people. First and last it is the personality of Bede that fascinates us; and we rejoice to think that the affecting story of his death, as told in his pupil Cuthbert's letter to Cuthwin, is so exquisitely in tune with the beauty of a gentle and beneficent life.

The paradox of Alcuin (735–804) is that he is of European rather than of English importance. A famous passage proclaims his debt to the library, as well as to the teachers, in the great school of York; but though he was himself master there in 778, his fame rests on the fact that he left England for ever to become the apostle of education in the empire of Charlemagne. Most of his works were written abroad and could have no effect in England because the raids of the Scandinavians extinguished the learning and literature of Northumbria and paralysed intellectual effort all over the land. The ninth century, to the historian of our Latin literature, is almost a blank.

The remaining Latin writings of the eighth and ninth centuries—mainly lives of saints—are not of great importance. Felix, author of the *Life of Guthlac*, was plainly fascinated by the tales of the demon hordes that haunted the lonely hermit of the fens, and has portrayed them in language which, whether directly or not, was reproduced in vernacular poetry not many generations later. Other visions of the world to come, like that of Drythelm recorded by Bede, occur in the extant literature. Saints' lives were really "tales of wonder".

The century from 690 to 790 is marked by the rise of two great schools, those of Canterbury and York, and by the work of one great scholar. The south of England produced works characterized by a rather affected and fanciful erudition. It was the north that gave birth to Bede, the only writer of that age whose works are of first-rate value, and to Alcuin, whose influence was supreme in the schools of the Continent.

VI. ALFRED AND THE OLD ENGLISH PROSE
OF HIS REIGN

The glory of Alfred's reign is Alfred himself (849–901). Not only was he preeminent as scholar, soldier, law-giver and ruler: he had in abundance the gift that Englishmen never fail to value, in the end, far beyond cleverness or attainments, namely, character. The hunted and patiently victorious king of Wessex has become a national legend and fully deserves the halo of sanctity bestowed by centuries of popular admiration. Though never king of England, he was a thoroughly English king, making his narrow plot of ground in Wessex the model of what a kingdom should be. The culture of Northumbria, where Caedmon had sung and Bede had taught, went down to destruction in the viking raids that had begun before Alcuin left York on his educational mission. So lost was learning that, at the date of his accession (Alfred tells us), no scholar could be found, even south of the Thames, able to read the Latin service-books. But what England had given England might borrow, and Alfred turned for help to the Frankish empire. He filled the growing monasteries with competent teachers and began himself to translate Latin works into the Wessex tongue. A certain preliminary *Handbook* of extracts from the scriptural and patristic writings seems to be lost, and the first book of Alfred's, therefore, that calls for notice is a translation of the *Regula* or *Cura Pastoralis*, written in the sixth century by Gregory the Great. Obviously a revival of learning had to begin among the clergy, and in Gregory's work, designed to guide the priest in his holy life, Alfred found a suitable primer of instruction and stimulus. The Preface from the king's own hand is specially important, as it is, in effect, a preface to all his subsequent translations. In it Alfred describes the desolation of learning in England, and his own resolve to attempt a restoration. One of Alfred's next works (the precise order cannot be determined) was a free version of the *Historia adversus Paganos*, an ethico-historical treatise by the fifth-century Spanish ecclesiastic Paulus Orosius. Ignoring its value as controversy, Alfred seized upon and rendered its merit as history and geography, omitting much and making additions of great value. Thus, he inserted accounts of the voyages of Ohthere and Wulfstan, taken down from the direct narration of the adventurers themselves, who had explored the Baltic and sailed into the White Sea.

An abbreviated but close rendering of Bede's *History* is attributed to Alfred by long and respectable tradition from Aelfric onwards; but a lack of distinction in the rendering together with certain linguistic peculiarities have led some scholars to question the authorship. Much more important, and among the best of Alfred's works, is the version of Boethius' *De Consolatione Philosophiae*. This famous and once consolatory treatise, written in a Roman prison (525) by the martyred minister of Theodoric, entered deeply into the moral life of medieval Europe, until its stoical fatalism was supplanted by the warmer doctrines of the *Imitation*. It has been translated into English by a great sovereign and an equally great poet. Alfred's version is a paraphrase rather than a translation and is entitled to an existence of its own. He expands and alters with sensible freedom. The concluding prayer is a moving utterance by a noble mind. Upon Alfred's Code of Laws we need not dwell here. The last work attributed to him is an adaptation of St Augustine's *Soliloquia*, which some identify with the *Handbook* and some reject altogether, though the case for his authorship is strong.

The most notable work inspired though not written by Alfred is the *Old English Chronicle*. In some monasteries casual notes of important events had been made; but under Alfred's encouragement we get, for the first time, a systematic revision of the earlier records and a larger survey of West Saxon history. The *Chronicle*, as known to us, is a highly composite piece of work, consisting of various recensions. The original nucleus belonged to Winchester, the capital of the West Saxon kingdoms. The Alfredian version comes down to 892 only, at which date the first hand in the manuscript ceases, and of this portion Alfred may be supposed to have acted as supervisor. The *Chronicle* is remarkable both as the first continuous history of a western nation in its own language and as the first great book in English prose. The account of the years 893–7, covering the struggles with the Danes in southern England, is a masterpiece of historical narrative.

The most important source of information about the king's life is a short biographical sketch attributed to Asser (d. 909), Bishop of Sherborne, whom Alfred called from Wales to aid him in the re-establishment of learning. The authenticity of the work has been hotly disputed and vigorously defended; but the matter is hard to settle, as the unique manuscript was almost entirely destroyed in the fire which decimated the Cottonian Library in 1731 and the early printed editions are not trustworthy. It is appropriate that the first biography of an English layman should be devoted to a great ruler who, besides raising England from the dust and giving it a naval tradition, helped also to create a worthy English prose, and expressed his own strong and appealing personality in works designed with simple sincerity to enlighten his people.

VII. FROM ALFRED TO THE CONQUEST

Alfred died in the first year of the tenth century, a date that forms a landmark in history. A king of Wessex presently becomes ruler of all England; a Danish sovereign governs a northern empire from an English throne; and the first Norman influences begin to be felt. Meanwhile the *Chronicle* proceeds. Begun, as we have seen, under the inspiration of Alfred, it lasts into the changed times of two and a half centuries later, when the last English king had been dead for nearly a hundred years, and the English language had vanished from court and curia, from school and society. The history of the *Chronicle* is as complicated as its literary merits are various. Six recensions still exist, together with two fragments of which no notice need be taken here. To follow the resemblances and differences the reader must consult such an edition as Thorpe's, which sets the six versions in parallel columns. Any brief description would be more confusing than helpful. The recensions vary greatly in length. Some begin at 60 B.C., the date assigned by Bede to the invasion by Julius Caesar. The longest of all contains, near the end, the famous passage describing the horrors of the reign of Stephen, when men said openly that Christ and his saints slept. Sometimes we have nothing but a bare date and event, and sometimes we have passages of strong and moving narrative. With all its falterings and defects the *Chronicle* is a wonderful national possession of which Englishmen should be proud, and of which they should know much more. Reference to the verse fragments contained in it will be made later on.

The plight of the church was too desperate to be remedied in the reign even of an Alfred. Successive ravages of heathen invaders continued to destroy much that had been raised up. The Continent itself was in the shadow of the Dark Ages of barbarism; but the reformation which Europe owes to the Benedictines touched England with its influence and brought us once again into the growing light of Continental culture. In the reign of Edgar, first king of England, there was a marked revival led by Dunstan (924–88) and Aethelwold (908–84), Bishop of Winchester. By the king's command Aethelwold not only adapted and explained the Benedictine rule in Latin to the new monasteries, he translated it into English for the many still ignorant of Latin, and upheld before English novices the ideal of a life combining labour, culture and service. The revival in religious zeal expressed itself in other forms, and during the years between 960 and 1000 there was great activity in the production of homilies. The nineteen *Blickling Homilies*, part narrative, part sermon, date from this period. They are somewhat "primitive" in their appeal to the terrors of judgment, but they are vigorous and sincere. They voice the almost universal belief that the world would end in the year 1000.

In Aethelwold's school at Winchester the greatest of English homilists was growing up. Aelfric (955?–1022?) wrote three series of homilies, which tell the sacred stories now familiar to later generations, but then unknown and even unknowable by the illiterate many, save through oral exposition. Aelfric uses a poetical manner with a sing-song alliterative rhythm which must have made his discourses immediately attractive, and, in the fullest sense, memorable. But Aelfric was educationist as well as homilist, and wrote for the novices at Winchester a Latin grammar (based upon Priscian), a Latin-English vocabulary, and the familiar *Colloquy* designed to instruct the young scholars in the daily speech of the monastery. The *Colloquy* is a conversation between a teacher, a novice and others who represent the usual occupations of life. Its human touches are vivid and appealing, and, as a method of instruction, it is thoroughly enlightened. The original Latin has an English gloss, perhaps not Aelfric's.

Very different from Aelfric in manner was the fiery, vehement Wulfstan (d. 1023), Archbishop of York in the troubled days of Aethelred. Of fifty-three homilies described in the Bodleian MS. Junius 99 as *Sermones Lupi*, though they are in English, very few are indisputably his. The most famous is the address known as *Sermo Lupi ad Anglos*, delivered in the time of the Danish persecutions. Like a true patriot Wulfstan does not shrink from telling his hearers that their sins have deserved heavy punishment. Wulfstan uses an alliterative rhythmic style intended to impress his matter upon the memory of the unlettered listener.

Besides the homilies there were composed in the tenth century three notable English versions of the gospels. The *Lindisfarne Gospels*, a great vellum quarto now in the British Museum, is one of the most beautiful of manuscripts. It was written about 700; but it concerns us here because, about 950, a Northumbrian priest Aldred added to the Latin script an interlinear gloss in his own dialect. The *Rushworth Gospels*, in a slightly differing Latin text, has both a tenth-century Mercian gloss and a South Northumbrian, similar to that of the *Lindisfarne Gospels*. A late tenth- or early eleventh-century West Saxon version of the Gospels exists in several manuscripts.

Eastern legends still had their fascination for the English people. Cynewulf's *Elene* had told the story of the finding of the Cross. A tenth or eleventh century prose *Legend of the Holy Rood* tells with moving grace and charm the story of the growth of the Cross from three seeds of cypress, cedar and pine. In addition to the sacred legends there are the secular (and apocryphal) *Letter from Alexander to Aristotle*, *The Wonders of the East* and *Apollonius of Tyre*. The first two have as hero an entirely legendary Alexander the Great, who was soon to figure largely in medieval romance. The third, coming like the others from Greek through Latin, is specially noteworthy, because its story of the incestuous monarch's riddle reappears in *Gesta Romanorum* and in Gower's *Confessio Amantis*, whence it was borrowed for the partly Shakespearean *Pericles*, in which Gower figures as Chorus.

As will be seen from the foregoing paragraphs, the age of Alfred and Aelfric was an age of prose. Prose of excellence is a flower of less rapid growth than poetry; but in such compositions as the *Colloquy*, the English language does really seem to be moving towards the great prose virtues of lucidity, ease and exactness. That development was suddenly checked by the Norman Conquest, with its introduction of a foreign idiom, and the whole slow process had to be gone through again. But the Aelfric tradition endured, and English prose attained once more the point it had reached in the last fine utterances of the *Chronicle*. The collapse of Old English poetry was much more complete and much less explicable. The alliterative rhetorical verse had already begun to deteriorate and was being replaced by the "sung" or four-beat metre of the popular ballad. The *Chronicle* offers some examples. The first poem occurs under the year 937 in celebration of Aethelstan's victory at Brunanburh. It is admirable both as patriotism and as poetry, and has attracted many translators from Tennyson onwards. It adheres, however, to the ancient alliterative line. The first poem in "sung" verse occurs under the year 959, and celebrates the accession of Edgar. The general effect is roughly like that obtained later by Layamon; the poetic merit is small; but the run of the verse shows a clear departure from the old traditional form. This is true of some other verses in the *Chronicle*. That the metrical scheme is obscure may be due to imperfect transmission by the scribes. The writing down of popular songs cannot have been easy to the monkish chroniclers.

Of the *Chronicle* poems only that on Brunanburh has any real poetic merit, and this one exception appears to have derived its inspiration from the epic fragment, *Judith*, of which some 350 lines have survived in the British Museum manuscript Cott. Vitell. xv containing *Beowulf*. This was at one time attributed to Caedmon and to Cynewulf, but the general assent of scholars places it much later (*c.* 918), and finds in it a tribute to Aethelflaed, the Lady of Mercia. It is a great achievement, in the front rank of Old English verse. The same high patriotic feeling inspired, doubtless, by the same poem, can be found in the tragic lines describing the last stand of Byrhtnoth and his men before Northern invaders at Maeldune (Maldon, Essex) on the banks of the Panta (Blackwater) in 991. In the tragedy of its matter and its reticent dignity of narrative *The Battle of Maldon* enshrines a spirit that we like to think is essentially English.

The most interesting among the miscellaneous poems of the period is *Be Domes Daege*, a free and enlarged version of the Latin *De Die Judicii*. This is the kind of "vision-poem" typical of medieval literature. It tells how, as the author sat lonely within a bower in a wood, where the streams murmured among pleasant plants, a wind suddenly arose that stirred the trees and darkened the sky, so that his mind was troubled and he began to sing of the coming of death. Then, in a highly imaginative outburst, he describes the terrors that accompany the Second Advent. The poem ends with a passage, partly borrowed from the Latin, on the joys of the redeemed. The translation is one of the finest in Old English. It is more powerful than its Latin original, and many of the most beautiful passages are new matter put in by the translator. A gloomy poem, *The Grave*, made familiar by Longfellow, is perhaps of later date. After 1100, English poetry ceased to be written down for nearly a century; but the "sung" rhythm never died out amongst the common folk, and, lingering specially in the distant north, found new life in the ballads.

VIII. THE NORMAN CONQUEST

The invasion of English literature by French influence did not begin on the autumn day that saw Harold's levies defeated by Norman archers on the slopes of Senlac. It had begun in the time of Edward the Confessor, who was the grandson of a Norman duke and had spent his years of exile in Normandy. Nevertheless, the year 1066 is a crucial point, because, from that date, the language of the ruling classes was no longer English. As the preservation of letters depended on scholars of foreign extraction, English was not written down. Formal manuscripts are neither English nor French, but Latin. The Normans were not apostles of culture, and very little of the vernacular literature of France was transplanted to English soil at the Conquest; but the language came, and with it came a change in the orientation of our polite literature. When the Normans landed, Taillefer, the *jongleur*, came first, as Wace tells us, and sang of Roland and Roncesvalles. The invasion of England by Taillefer and his song of Roland is as important as the invasion of England by William and his knights. It was the coming not, indeed, of romance, for we had that before; but it was the coming of Romance. In the end it was the English language that conquered; but in conquering it suffered a sea-change. The asperities of the Northern Ocean and the Baltic were softened by the waters of the Mediterranean and the English poets turned their eyes from the North to the South.

It is useless to speculate upon the probable course of English letters had there been no Norman Conquest; but at least we are entitled to say that the facts presented in the foregoing pages should prevent a gloomy view. The darkest period of the tenth century was the age of Aelfric, of Dunstan, of the *Old English Chronicle*, of *Judith* and *The Battle of Maldon*. The poetic spirit of the English people never died, and the wonderful assimilative capacity of the language was soon to reveal itself. The gain to English literature that accrued from the Norman Conquest was immense. The language was enriched by the absorption of a Romance vocabulary; methods of expression and ideas to be expressed were multiplied; and the cause of learning was strengthened by the coming of great scholars and by the associations that were later to bind Paris and Oxford. Learning and literature further gained by the intercourse with the Continent that made our wandering scholars aware of the wisdom of the East. Harun-ar-Rashid was a contemporary of Alcuin, and he and his successors made Baghdad and the cities of Spain centres of knowledge and storehouses of books.

The Christian learning of the West received fresh impetus in the middle of the eleventh century at the hands of Lanfranc, who made the monastic school at Bec famous for its teaching, and who, when he came to England, to work for church and state, did not forget his earlier care for books and learning. Lanfranc's successor in the see of Canterbury was his fellow-countryman and pupil Anselm, perhaps less of a statesman, but a greater genius, and a more profound thinker. Writers in English were at school under the new masters of the land, whose cycles of romance provided material for translation. We do not know what we lost; but we do know what we gained. Norman art may have been stolid, but Norman building was at least solid. Native speech—the true life of any language—continued to flourish and develop outside of "officialdom". When the language had lost its more rigid inflections and had gained by additions to its ornamental vocabulary, the new singers were able to give fuller expression to their creative impulses. They were preparing the way for the coming of Chaucer. Meanwhile the Latin chroniclers were busy at their labours.

IX. LATIN CHRONICLERS FROM THE ELEVENTH TO THE THIRTEENTH CENTURY

The revival of learning which followed the coming of the Normans and reached its zenith under Henry II gave us many gifts, but none greater than the Latin chronicles compiled during the twelfth and thirteenth centuries. Some few of these are real literature, and all of them, whether written by native Englishmen or by Normans domiciled in England, reflect the united patriotic sentiment which it was the design of later Norman statesmanship to foster. Though composed in Latin, the chronicles are histories of England, and are written from a national English standpoint. They embody English traditions. No other country produced, during that period, any historical compositions to be compared with the English chronicles in variety of interest, wealth of information and amplitude of range.

Apart from national incentives, there were external influences which stimulated at this time the study and writing of history. The Norman settlement in England synchronized with a movement that shook Western Christendom to its foundations. The Crusades not only stirred the religious feelings of Europe, they quickened the imagination and stimulated the curiosity of the Western world as nothing had done for centuries. Intercourse with the East, and the mingling of different tribes in the crusading armies, brought about a "renascence of wonder" as far reaching in some of its effects as the great Renascence itself. Modern romance was born in the twelfth century. The institution of chivalry, the mystic symbolism of the church, the international currency of popular *fabliaux*, the importation of oriental stories of magic and wizardry—all these made their contribution of strangeness, fantasy and remoteness to the sober tales of the historians and the wilder inventions of the poets. Though many of the chroniclers were monks, they were not all recluses. Some of them lived in close intercourse with public men, who visited the monasteries and gave first-hand material for the records.

It is naturally in the region of Bede that we find the most ancient school of Anglo-Norman history. The first notable chronicler in the twelfth century is Simeon of Durham, who used Bede's history and the lost annals of Northumbria. His work was continued by two priors of Hexham, the elder of whom, Richard of Hexham, wrote the *Acts of King Stephen and the Battle of the Standard*. John of Hexham brought the narrative down to 1154. The first important Latin chronicler of the south is Florence of Worcester (d. 1118) whose *Chronicon ex Chronicis* is, as its name implies, a compilation. It ended with the year 1117, but was continued by others elsewhere to the close of the thirteenth century. Simeon and Florence were merely conscientious annalists. Literature of a richer colour and history of a higher order are to be found in the writings of two contemporaries, one an Englishman and the other a Norman of English birth. Eadmer (d. 1124), friend and follower of Anselm, wrote in six books a history of his own time down to 1122, *Historia Novorum in Anglia*, as well as a life of his master. Ordericus Vitalis (1075–1143), a Norman born in Shropshire, was more ambitious and wrote a lengthy *Historia Ecclesiastica* in thirteen books from the beginning of the Christian era to 1141. Orderic was a shrewd and curious observer, and is one of the standard authorities for the Norman period. His style is sometimes rhetorical and even fantastic, but he is always readable.

A much greater historian and far more attractive writer is their contemporary, William of Malmesbury (d. 1143), of whom Milton has said that both for style and judgment he is the best of all. William aspired to be a historian in the manner of Bede. His chronicle is in two parts, five books called *De Gestis Regum Anglorum* which tell the national story from the coming of the English in 449 to 1127, and three books called *Historia Novella* narrating the events from 1125 to 1142. He wrote much else that hardly concerns us. William of Malmesbury had learning, industry, judgment and a wide knowledge of the world; and to these general gifts he added a disinterested love of history and an engaging fondness for anecdote, digression and quotation. His graphic account of the First Crusade has a spaciousness and a wealth of colour which all but rival the glowing periods of Gibbon.

Henry of Huntingdon (1084–1155), author of *Historia Anglorum* (55 B.C.–A.D. 1155), is less important. He prided himself on his skill in verse, and frequently drops into poetry during the course of his facile and perfunctory narrative. A much better authority for his period is the anonymous chronicler who wrote the *Acts of Stephen* (*Gesta Stephani*). Though the king's partisan (and possibly his confessor), he writes with conspicuous fairness, and not even William surpasses him in vividness and power.

The historian Geoffrey Arthur, or Geoffrey of Monmouth, Bishop of St Asaph (1100–54), has been called the Father of English Fiction. William of Malmesbury had sought to fill the gap between Bede and Eadmer. Geoffrey proposed to go back farther and describe the kings who lived in Britain before the Incarnation of Christ. As there appears to be no material for this, the *History of the Kings of Britain* (*Historia Regum Britanniae*) is usually considered more remarkable for its fancies than for its facts. Geoffrey filled the blank spaces of pre-Christian and early Christian history with delightful stories alleged to have been derived from a "most ancient book in the British tongue" providentially supplied to him by Walter, Archdeacon of Oxford. The fact that no such book is now forthcoming proves nothing; and it is a narrow view of history that considers Geoffrey an unabashed inventor. He caught and embodied many traditions of the Celtic West which we should have lost without him. To Geoffrey we owe our acquaintance with Brutus the Trojan King of Britain, with Lear and Cymbeline, with Bladud and King Lud, with Locrine and Sabrina, with Merlin and Arthur. That he was denounced by duller chroniclers is a tribute to his charm, not an indictment of his veracity. The *History* was completed about 1139 and became the most popular production of its time. Even before Geoffrey's death Wace had begun to translate it into French verse.

Geoffrey would probably have been content to exchange the approbation of historians for the affection of the poets. To be praised by Chaucer, Spenser, Drayton and Wordsworth, and to have given stories, directly or indirectly, to Milton and Shakespeare should be enough fame for any man. Geoffrey's dissemination of the Arthurian stories will be dealt with in later pages.

One of Geoffrey's severest critics was William of Newburgh (1136–98) who, in a preface to his *Historia Rerum Anglicarum*, which extends from the Conquest to 1198, denounces the genial romancer as one who had profaned the duties of a historian. This preface has gained William of Newburgh the praise of some historians; but the *Historia* itself is little more than an ordered and critical statement of affairs in the time of Stephen and Henry II. The final judgment is that Geoffrey is still read; William of Newburgh is sometimes consulted.

Richard Fitz-Neale, or Fitz-Nigel (d. 1198), is perhaps the author of the most authoritative chronicle of the reign of Henry II generally ascribed to Benedict of Peterborough (d. 1193), but he is more certainly entitled to fame as author of the celebrated *Dialogus de Scaccario*, or Dialogue about the Exchequer, which is one chief source of our knowledge of constitutional principles in pre-Charter England. The so-called Benedict Chronicle forms the foundation of the *Chronica*, an ambitious compilation by Roger of Hovenden (d. 1201), extending from 732 to 1201 and including a fairly comprehensive history of Europe during its special period, the reigns of Henry II and Richard I. Roger may be called the last of the northern school. The *Imagines Historiarum* of Ralph of Diceto (fl. 1180), Dean of St Paul's, a sober, straightforward chronicler, and a shrewd judge of character, ranges from 1148 to 1202 and makes judicious use of important contemporary documents.

King Richard's Crusade has been described by many chroniclers, but by none more vividly than Richard of Devizes (fl. 1190), whose *De Rebus Gestis Ricardi Primi* (1189–92) is a brief but brilliant treatment of its theme. His chronicle gives a striking picture of the social conditions of England in Richard's reign. But social conditions, especially the interior economy of the monasteries, are revealed to us most delightfully in the brief and fascinating *Chronica* (1173–1203) of Jocelin of Brakelond (fl. 1200), whose account of the Abbot Sampson at St Edmundsbury was made widely known by the eulogies of Carlyle in *Past and Present*.

The thirteenth century is the golden age of monastic historians, and at their head stands Matthew Paris, greatest of all our medieval chroniclers. At St Albans the Abbot Simon established a regular office of historiographer. The first occupant of this office was Roger of Wendover (d. 1236), whose *Flores Historiarum* (from the Creation to 1235) is an excellent compilation, the nature of which is indicated by its title; but its best part is the writer's original narrative of events from 1216 to 1235. It may be observed that the title *Flores Historiarum* was appropriated in the fourteenth century to a compilation based on the chronicle of Matthew Paris. The work was long ascribed to one "Matthew of Westminster"; but no chronicler of that name ever existed. Roger is remarkable for the fearless candour of his personal and moral judgments. He was succeeded by Matthew Paris in 1236, who, in his *Chronica Majora*, continued the work of his predecessor down to his own death in 1259. Courtier and scholar, monk and man of the world, Matthew Paris was, both by training and position, exceptionally well qualified to undertake a history of his own time. Moreover, he had the instinct, the temper and the judgment of the born historian. He took immense pains in the collection and the verification of his facts, and appears to have been in communication with many correspondents at home and abroad. Indeed, his work reads like a stately journal of contemporary European events. But Matthew is much more than a mere recorder. He is a fearless critic and censor of public men and their doings. His narrative style and his sense of order give his *Chronicle* a unity and a sustained interest possessed by no other English medieval history.

Great as Matthew was, much in the reign of Henry III would be obscure were not his *Chronicle* supplemented by the great work of Henry of Bracton (d. 1258), *De Legibus et Consuetudinibus Angliae*. In addition, Henry of Bracton compiled a notebook containing some two thousand cases taken from the plea rolls of his time, with comments of his own. This work is not only the most authoritative English law-book of the time, but (as Pollock and Maitland say in their *History of English Law*) "the crown and flower of English medieval jurisprudence". There were numerous other chroniclers, whose names hardly call for mention in a summary. The writings of scholars, such as John of Salisbury, Peter of Blois, Gervase of Tilbury, Nigel Wireker, Gerald of Wales (Giraldus Cambrensis) and Walter Map, illustrate the life and habits of their time and form a valuable supplement to the considered annals of the chroniclers.

X. ENGLISH SCHOLARS OF PARIS AND FRANCISCANS OF OXFORD: LATIN LITERATURE OF ENGLAND FROM JOHN OF SALISBURY TO RICHARD OF BURY

It was fortunate for England that her connection with France became intimate at a time when Paris was about to rise to intellectual dominance over Europe. The university of that city owed its origin to the cathedral school of Notre-Dame. Here, and afterwards at Sainte-Geneviève, taught the eloquent, brilliant, vain, impulsive and tragically unfortunate Abelard (d. 1142). The fame of his teaching made Paris the resort of many scholars, whose presence led to its becoming the home of the Masters by whom the university was ultimately founded. The first important English pupil of Abelard was John of Salisbury, who studied at Paris and Chartres from 1136 to 1148, and returned to England about 1150. He became secretary to Theobald, Archbishop of Canterbury, entered the service of Becket in 1162, shared his master's troubles, and was said to have been "sprinkled with the blood of the blessed martyr" in the cathedral of Canterbury on the fatal 29 December 1170. Six years later John became Bishop of Chartres. His works include an encyclopaedia of miscellanies, in eight books, called *Policraticus* or *De Nugis Curialium et Vestigiis Philosophorum*, *Metalogicus*, a defence of the method and use of logic, and *Entheticus*, an elegiac poem of 1852 lines. John's Latin has been praised for its classical elegance and correctness. He was a humanist, two centuries in advance of his time.

Walter Map, or Mapes, was born about 1137 on the marches of Wales, and studied in Paris from about 1154 to 1160. He became one of the king's itinerant judges and was appointed Archdeacon of Oxford in 1197. He was no longer living by 1209. Map was the author of an entertaining miscellany in Latin prose, *De Nugis Curialium*, a work in a far lighter vein than that with a similar title by John of Salisbury. But, even in his lighter vein, Map has often a grave moral purpose. To Map are ascribed certain poems in rhymed Latin verse, notably the *Apocalypse*, the *Confession* and the *Metamorphosis* of Bishop Golias, who is taken as a type of clerical vice. From the *Confession* come the familiar lines beginning "Meum est propositum in taberna mori", set to music as a drinking-song. There is very little reason for believing that Map wrote any of these verses, and in any case they were written as satire and without any jovial intention. Map is persistently credited in certain manuscripts with the author-ship of the "original" Latin of the great prose romance of *Lancelot du Lac*, including the *Quest of the Holy Grail* and the *Death of Arthur*; but no such "Latin original" has yet been found. Could Map be proved the author of all the works attributed to him he would certainly be the greatest of English writers before Chaucer.

Only the briefest mention can be made of Gervase of Tilbury, author of *Otia Imperialia* (1211), a miscellany of legendary tales and superstitions, and of Nigel Wireker (d. 1200), witty author of *Speculum Stultorum*, a poem on the adventures of the donkey Brunellus (or Burnellus)—a "donkey-in-particular" as opposed to the "donkey-in-general" of the abstract philosophers. The Nun's Priest's delightful tale of the Cock and the Fox makes an appropriate allusion to "Daun Burnel the Asse".

Chief among Latin authors of the time is the fascinating and excessive Gerald of Barry or Gerald the Welshman (1146?–1220?) who studied in Paris. Gerald helped Baldwin, the Archbishop of Canterbury, to preach the coming Crusade. He was appointed to write its history in Latin prose, and the archbishop's nephew, Josephus Iscanus, or Joseph of Exeter, to write it in verse. Joseph had already composed an epic *De Bello Trojano*, England's solitary Latin epic, and he celebrated the Crusade in his *Antiocheis*, now represented by a solitary frag-ment alluding to the *flos regum Arthurus*. Gerald neither fought nor wrote. The earliest of Gerald's works, the *Topographia Hibernica*, is a first-hand authority on medieval Ireland. The *Expugnatio Hibernica*, a narrative of the attempt at a Norman conquest of Ireland (1169–85), is more properly historical in matter, and more sober in manner. His *Itinerarium Kambriae* not only has topographical and ecclesiastical interest, but shows us Gerald deeply interested in languages. The companion *Descriptio Kambriae* ascribes many high intellectual accomplish-ments to Welshmen and preserves some specimens of current English. *Gemma Ecclesiastica* (the author's favourite work) presents a vivid picture of the state of morality and learning in Wales. In *De Principis Institutione* Gerald not only dis-cusses the duties of a prince but tells the story of the finding of King Arthur's body at Glastonbury. His latest work, *Speculum Ecclesiae*, depicts the principal monastic orders of the time in violent language. Gerald may be a vain and garrulous writer; but he was among the most learned of a learned age, and had an engaging personality which he successfully transmitted in everything he wrote.

The almost legendary Michael Scot (d. 1236?), a Lowlander (like his great namesake), was another product of Paris. He learned Arabic at Palermo, where he lived at the brilliant court of Frederick II, and returned to that city after a long sojourn at Toledo. There is no evidence that he was ever at Oxford. To his knowledge of medicine and the stars is due his fame as a magician, referred to by Dante, Boccaccio and Walter Scott. His great service to learning was that his familiarity with Arabic enabled him to make known certain physical and metaphysical works of Aristotle existing in that tongue when Greek was still unknown to the West. Michael Scot's legendary power to read the stars may be taken to mean that he had learned from the great Arabian teachers of mathematics more of that science than any Europeans could give.

The education of Europe might have long remained in the hands of the secular clergy but for the rise of the new orders of the Franciscans and the Dominicans in the second decade of the thirteenth century. The old monastic orders had made their homes in solitary places; the aim of the Franciscan order was to work in the densely crowded towns. The Franciscan order was founded at Assisi in 1210, the Dominican at Toulouse in 1215; and, at an early date, both orders resolved on establishing themselves in the great seats of education. The Dominicans fixed their headquarters at Bologna and Paris (1217), besides settling at Oxford (1221) and Cambridge (1274); while the Franciscans settled at Oxford and Cambridge in 1224, and at Paris in 1230. When once these orders had been founded, all the great schoolmen were either Franciscans or Dominicans. In Paris, the greatest Dominican teachers were Albertus Magnus (1193–1280) and his favourite pupil, the great St Thomas Aquinas, *Doctor Angelicus* (c. 1225–74), who brought scholasticism to its highest development by harmonizing Aristotelianism with the doctrines of the church. St Francis, who was "all seraphic in ardour", and felt no sympathy whatsoever for the intellectual and academic world, nevertheless counted among his followers men of academic, and even more than academic, renown. Foremost of these were Alexander of Hales, Roger Bacon, Duns Scotus and William of Ockham.

Alexander, a Gloucestershire man, was a student at Paris and became one of the leading teachers there. Innocent IV entrusted him with the preparation of a *Summa Theologiae*, which remained unfinished at his death, but which earned him the name of the *Irrefragable Doctor*. Roger Bacon, nevertheless, spoke of his work with contempt. When the first little band of Franciscans settled in Oxford, their chief friend and adviser was Robert Grosseteste, who became Bishop of Lincoln in 1235. His numerous writings include treatises on theology, essays on philosophy and a practical work on husbandry. The most interesting of his works, however, is the *Chasteau d'Amour*, a poetic allegory of 1757 lines in praise of the Virgin and her Son, originally written in "Romance" for those who had "ne letture ne clergie", and translated into Latin and English. Wyclif ranked him above Aristotle, Gower hailed him as "the grete clerc", Roger Bacon praised his knowledge of science, and Matthew Paris saluted him in a succession of honourable titles from "rebuker of popes and kings" to "preacher of the people".

Roger Bacon (1214–94), *Doctor Mirabilis*, greatest of the Oxford Franciscans and one of the greatest of Englishmen, was born near Ilchester. Under the influence of Grosseteste Roger entered the Franciscan order. He was ordained about 1233, left for Paris about 1245, and returned to England in 1250. His liberal opinions brought him into trouble, and he was kept in strict seclusion for ten years. But Clement IV favoured him and pressed for an account of his researches. Thereupon, in the wonderfully brief space of some eighteen months, the grateful and enthusiastic student wrote three memorable works, *Opus Majus*, *Opus Minus* and *Opus Tertium* (1267). These were followed by his *Compendium Studii Philosophiae* (1271–2) and a Greek grammar. Roger was condemned in 1278 for "suspected novelties of opinion" and again endured restraint. He was released before writing his *Compendium Studii Theologiae* (1292) and died at Oxford. The *Opus Majus*, which remained unknown till it was edited by Jebb in 1733, is called by Sandys the *Encyclopédie* and *Novum Organon* of the thirteenth century. *Opus Minus*, first published (with portions of *Opus Tertium* and *Compendium Studii Philosophiae*) by Brewer in the Rolls Series, discusses the six great errors that stand in the way of the studies of Latin Christendom. Only a fragment, equivalent to some 80 pages of print, has been preserved in a single manuscript in the Bodleian. *Opus Tertium*, though written later, is intended to serve as an introduction to the two previous works. The three compositions, even in their fragmentary form, fill as many as 1344 pages of print; and it was these three that were completed in the brief interval of eighteen months. In science Roger Bacon was at least a century in advance of his time, and, in spite of the long and bitter persecutions that he endured, he was full of hope for the future. His repute was so great that he developed into a popular myth as alchemist and necromancer. Like Virgil, he was supposed to have used a "glass perspective" of wondrous power, and, like others in advance of their time, to have constructed a "brazen head" that possessed the faculty of speech. His speculations, as we know, included the possibility of flight, the properties of the magnet and the nature of Greek fire. The popular legend was embodied in *The Famous Historie of Fryer Bacon* and in Greene's *Friar Bacon and Friar Bungay* (c. 1587). Roger Bacon presents the tragic figure of a strong, daring and originating personality in the garb of a mendicant friar under narrow discipline. Sixteen volumes of his works hitherto unprinted, amounting to about four thousand pages, have been published under the editorship of Robert Steele (1909–40).

John Duns Scotus (1265?–1308?) was a Franciscan of Oxford. It is not certainly known whether he was born in England, Scotland or Ireland. He wrote very copiously, and steadily opposed the teaching of St Thomas Aquinas; but he was stronger in the criticism of the opinions of others than in the construction of a system of his own. Duns Scotus gradually lost his authority, though as late as the Victorian age the *Doctor Subtilis* was described by the Jesuit poet Gerard Manley Hopkins as

> Of realty the rarest-veinèd unraveller; a not
> Rivalled insight, be rival Italy or Greece...

The teaching of Aquinas was opposed not only by the realist Duns Scotus, but by the nominalist William of Ockham, the *Invincible Doctor* (1280–1349), who had a stirring life. William's great principle, that entities must not be unnecessarily multiplied—"Occam's razor", as it was called—cut at the root of "realism", with its belief in the real existence of "universals". William of Ockham was the last of the greater schoolmen. We need not mention the lesser, not even Thomas Bradwardine, named by Chaucer with Boethius in the Nun's Priest's tale, probably for the sake of a rhyme to "Augustine". The last of the medieval Latinists whom we need consider, Richard of Bury (1281–1345), Bishop of Durham, is appropriately famous as a great lover of books. The ascription of his *Philobiblon* to the Dominican Holkot need not be taken seriously. Holkot probably "wrote" it as the bishop's amanuensis. Richard's love of letters breathes in every page of his work, and few writers have transmitted more convincingly the peculiar ecstasy of the true book-lover.

In the course of this very brief survey, we have observed, in the age of Abelard, the revival of intellectual interests which resulted in the birth of the University of Paris. We have watched the first faint traces of the spirit of humanism in the days when John of Salisbury was studying Latin literature in the classic calm of Chartres. Two centuries later, Richard of Bury marks for England the time of transition between the age of scholasticism and the revival of learning.

XI. EARLY TRANSITION ENGLISH

The century from 1150 to 1250 shows us many changes in the native language. Inflections vanish, pronunciation is modified, the verse develops into new forms, and the very script passes to a modification of the Latin alphabet used by French scribes. While monks were compiling their chronicles and scholars their treatises in the learned language, the popular tongue lived on in songs and verses that have not survived. The material of romance began to assume an English habitation and a name. Legends of Weland and Wade persisted, and we begin to discern the gay and gallant figure of Robin Hood. The modern reader must not expect too much from the earliest attempts to write down native verse. The four lines of the *Canute Song* (*c.* 1167), recorded by a monk of Ely, cannot be called successful poetry, but they represent an effort to produce a quatrain with rhyme, assonance and a regular rhythm:

> Merie sungen muneches binnen Ely,
> Tha Cnut chyning reu ther by;
> Roweth, cnihtes, noer the land,
> And here we thes muneches sang.

In a verse of Godric (d. 1170?), pedlar, pirate and palmer before he turned hermit, we find more symptoms of success:

> Sainte Marie, Cristes bur,
> Maidenes clenhad, moderes flur,
> Dilie mine sinne, rixe in min mod,
> Bring me to winne with the self God.

The *Paternoster*, belonging to the same period, is a homiletic treatment of the Lord's Prayer in a poem of some 300 lines, exhibiting the first known consistent use of the rhymed couplet, as well as a regular pattern of accents. Perhaps some

French poem or Latin hymn gave the model. The slightly later *Poema Morale*, parallel to *Be Domes Daege* mentioned earlier (see p. 15), has more intrinsic interest, and numerous manuscripts indicate its popularity. The verse is specially interesting. Here, for the first time in English, is found the rhymed "fourteener" line—even though (as usual at all times) the fourteens are often fifteens:

> Ich em nu alder thene ich wes awintre and a lare;
> Ich welde mare thene ich dede, mi wit ahte bon mare.

This metre is attractive for its own sake; it is also important as an adumbration of the ballad stanza.

The so-called *Old English Homilies* are twelfth-century transferences from the Aelfric period, though in some are discernible certain new and foreign influences. The fragmentary *Old Kentish Sermons* (before 1250) come almost directly from French texts. Both sets exhibit firm command of sound, efficient prose and show that the Aelfric tradition endured. It will be observed that during this early period the note of literature is religious or didactic. As we have seen from the preceding section, theology engaged the attention of the greatest minds in the land, and new religious enthusiasm was kindled by the coming of the friars. But religious and ecclesiastical interests did not occupy the minds of all the people all the time. Human nature in those days as in these craved for imaginative creations that would give it something the world of difficult living could not provide. That in this early period there is very little light literature does not prove that light literature did not exist; it merely proves that light literature was not recorded. There were few hands to hold the pen, and those few were not likely to waste time and material on trifles. Religious manuscripts were meant for hard, constant professional use. They were, in a sense, tools. The literature of recreation was left to the memory. We must be constantly on our guard, therefore, against the temptation to date the beginning of a form or note in literature from its first appearance in manuscript. Songs and stories may exist for centuries without any kind of written record. The Arthurian legend, which at this period begins to colour popular literature, is an instance. Somewhere in the minds of many generations the stories of Arthur grew. They were ancient stories when Geoffrey of Monmouth gave them the first popular written circulation of which we know anything. Now, again for the first time of which we know anything, they were to be enshrined in the English verse of Layamon's *Brut*. The desire for romance was further gratified by a new kind of love-poetry. France, in the eleventh and twelfth centuries, had been swept by a wave of popular love-poetry which brought in its wake the music of the troubadours. Germany, in the twelfth century, produced the Minnesingers. The contemporary poets of Italy were also love-poets, and, at a slightly later date, Portugal, too, possessed poets of the same kind. This general inspiration, originating in France and passing over the frontiers on the lips of the troubadours, reached England soon after 1200. Though it failed at first to affect English secular poetry, it imparted a note of passion to religious writings, which may be divided into four groups according to the aims they have in view. The purpose of the first is to teach Biblical history; of the second to exhort to holier living; of the third to encourage the religious life of women; of the fourth to express the ecstasies of devotion, especially a passion for the person of Jesus and of his Mother.

In bulk the most considerable attempt at a literary exegesis of Scripture is the *Ormulum*, which an Augustinian brother named Orm or Ormin (fl. 1200), living somewhere in the east Midlands, conscientiously wrote to expound for English hearers the gospels of the ecclesiastical year. Though the scheme was not carried out completely, the poem is 20,000 lines long, according to the numbering in White's text, or 10,000 if the two short lines are counted as one. Orm is totally devoid of originality or fancy, and even his theology is antiquated. Yet one cannot help admiring the passionless and scrupulous sincerity of this obscure, God-fearing man as he pursues his endless and pious task. By his method of doubling every consonant immediately following a short vowel, Orm furnishes most valuable evidence about vowel-length at a critical period of the language. He was not a premature phonetician. He was anxious to transmit his teaching in an orthographical notation that would leave no doubt about delivery. Every line of his poem contains exactly fifteen syllables of exactly the same metrical pattern, without rhyme or alliteration. As the earliest example of phonetic spelling the poem is fascinating; as literature it is naught.

The second group, containing the hortatory pieces of the period, needs but short consideration. There are *Genesis and Exodus* lines (*c.* 1250), not to be confused with the Old English poems described earlier, and shorter pieces, *The Passion of our Lord* and *The Woman of Samaria*. The satirical *Sinners Beware* is noticeable for its use of a six-line stanza, and *The XI Pains of Hell* for its rhyming couplets. In *The Vision of St Paul* we get a specimen of the medieval literature that Dante was then raising to incredible heights—a visit of the apostle to hell under the guidance of St Michael. Allegory was employed in *An Bispel* (i.e. a parable), *Sawles Warde* and a *Bestiary*. *Sawles Warde* (in prose) presents Wit as lord of a castle, and Will, his capricious wife, with an allegorical equipment of daughters (Virtues) and servants (Senses). The *Bestiary*, in verse, symbolizes spiritual and moral truth, in a time-honoured way, by the habits of certain animals. *Vices and Virtues* (*c.* 1200) is noticeable for its use of the prose dialogue form—a Soul's confession of its sins, with Reason's description of the virtues. The prose pieces are quite efficiently written.

Interest in the religious life of women is the note of the next group of writings, for the golden age of monasticism witnessed also an increased sympathy with convent life. But *Hali Meidenhad*, an alliterative prose homily, presents ideals of chastity with a crudeness likely to provoke hostility in the modern reader. Certain saints' lives, narrating the stories of St Margaret, St Katherine and St Juliana in rhythmical alliterative prose, will probably be found less repellent, though the note is still hard. The *Ancren Riwle* (*c.* 1200) is more attractive. Its purpose is to give guidance to three anchoresses who, after a period of training in a nunnery, dedicated themselves to a religious life outside. Its originality, its personal charm, and its sympathy with all that is good in contemporary literature, place the *Ancren Riwle* apart as the finest English prose work of the time. The writing exhibits astonishing security and ease. This is accomplished, not tentative, prose.

Remarkable for their feminine note are those works that belong to the Virgin cult and those that are touched with erotic mysticism. The writings in this group are the outcome of the chivalrous ideals which had dawned in the twelfth century, and represent some of the allegorical tendencies of which Dante was the culmination. The best known English examples are the *Lofsong of ure Lefdi* (in prose), *On God Ureisun of ure Lefdi* (in rhyming couplets), *The Five Joys of the Virgin* (in eight-line stanzas), and *A Prayer to our Lady* (in four-line stanzas). The fullest success in this blending of the physical and the mystical is attained in the *Luve Ron* of Thomas de Hales (c. 1240) in eight-line stanzas, designed to exhibit the perfect love that abides with Christ. One stanza has interrogations that remind us of those in Villon's most famous Ballade, two centuries away. The note of moral interrogation is heard also in a striking poem of 1275 found in the Bodleian MS. Digby 86, under the heading *Ubi sount qui ante nos fuerount?* —"Were beth they biforen us weren." Three prayers in alliterative prose belong to the same category as the *Luve Ron*: *The Wohung of ure Lauerd*, *On Lofsong of ure Louerde* and *On Ureisun of ure Louerde*. The modern reader will possibly find their physical—indeed almost sexual—ecstasy a little disconcerting, but they have beauty of a kind.

An important part of thirteenth-century literature is that which forsakes theology altogether, and turns to romance for romance's sake. The greatest (and longest) work of this kind is the *Brut* written early in the thirteenth century by Layamon—more correctly written Laghamon, i.e., "Lawman"—a priest of Ernley (Arley Regis) on the river Severn. He proposed to tell the history of Britain from the time of the Flood, but he begins with the story of the Trojan Brutus and comes down to the death of Cadwalader, A.D. 689. His main source can be simply indicated; the minor sources are confused and need not be discussed here. The ever popular *History* of Geoffrey was almost immediately versified by the Norman Wace of Jersey as *Li Romans de Brut* (1155) in octo-syllabic couplets. Layamon read Wace in some version, and in his own poem paraphrased and expanded the matter freely. His form is specially interesting. Layamon shows us English verse almost in the very act of change. The poem has alliteration, free movement, syllabic strictness, rhyme and assonance all in turn. Layamon was, in fact, writing with two tunes in his head; he was adapting French syllabic couplets while still thinking of free accentual English verse; and so we get octosyllabic lines neighboured by others that suggest the Old English recitative. Layamon's *Brut* is interesting as a store of legends from which later writers freely drew. Apart from the Arthurian adventures, here for the first time in English we have the story of Lear and Cymbeline, Cloten and Locrine. Layamon's most resonant lines, like those of his literary ancestors, deal with the conflict of warriors or the strife of the elements. Strange and remote as the poem may look to the eye of the modern reader, it has true English quality and feeling. The *Brut* is the work of the first poet of any magnitude in Middle English, and, standing at the entrance to that period, Layamon may be said to look before and after. He retains much of the Old English tradition; he is the first to make extensive use of French material; and in the place of a fast-vanishing native mythology, he endows his countrymen with a new wealth of legends.

The Owl and the Nightingale, in the Dorset dialect, is gaily serious and not theological. It contains 1794 lines and belongs probably to the very beginning of the thirteenth century. The author and sources are alike unknown, for Nicholas of Guildford, named in the poem, and John of Guildford, a recognized verse-writer, cannot be certainly credited with the authorship; and though it embodies the spirit as well as the structure of Old French models, it is not a copy of any known one. It is a "debate", conducted poetically, yet with almost humorous legal formality, each opponent undertaking the defence of his nature and kind. Here the nightingale represents the world, and the grave owl the cloister. The poem is specially interesting as a long and successful English exercise in octosyllabic couplets, used with great metrical skill and delicate charm. The vignettes of natural scenery are far away from the wilder aspects of nature which had appealed to the primitive English poets. Alike in form, matter, accomplishment and outlook, *The Owl and the Nightingale* testifies to the genuine life of native poetry at the beginning of the thirteenth century. It is a delightful poem.

XII. THE ARTHURIAN LEGEND

The mystery of Arthur's end is not darker than the mystery of his beginning. While the ancient tradition is everywhere, the facts and records are nowhere. The earliest English Arthurian literature is singularly meagre and undistinguished. The romantic exploitation of "the matter of Britain" was the achievement, mainly, of French writers, and, indeed, some critics would have us attach little importance to British influence on the development of the Arthurian legend. The "matter of Britain" very quickly became international property—a vast composite body of romantic tradition, which European poets and story-tellers of every nationality drew upon and used for their own purposes. Arthur was non-political and could be idealised without offence to any ruling family. The British king himself faded more and more into the background, and became, in time, but the phantom monarch of a featureless "land of faëry". His knights quite overshadow him in the later romances; but they, in their turn, undergo the same process of denationalization, and appear as natives of some region of fantasy, moving about in a golden atmosphere of illusion. The course of the story is too obscure to be made clear in a brief summary which must necessarily ignore the hints and half-tones that count for much in the total effect, and which can take no account of French, German and Italian contributions to the legend. Old English literature, even the *Chronicle*, knows nothing whatever of Arthur. To find any mention of him earlier than the twelfth century we must turn to Wales, where, in a few obscure poems, a difficult prose story, and two dry Latin chronicles we find what appear to be the first written references, meagre and casual, but indicating a tradition already ancient. The earliest is in *Historia Britonum*, which, as we have seen (p. 9), dates from 679, though the existing recension of Nennius was made in the ninth century. The reference of Nennius to Arthur occurs in a very short account of the conflict that culminated in Mount Badon, usually dated 516, though some would put it as early as 470. Gildas, who was a youth in 516, also mentions Mount Badon; but the only hero he names is "Ambrosius Aurelianus". In Nennius the hero has become "the magnanimous Arthur", who was twelve times victorious, last of all at Mount Badon; but he is a military leader, not a king—or perhaps, as the anthropologist Lord Raglan thinks, "a god of war".

The poems of the ancient Welsh bards have been discussed almost as fiercely as the poems of Ossian; yet there is no doubt that together with much of late and doubtful invention they contain something of indisputably ancient tradition. But the most celebrated of the early Welsh bards know nothing of Arthur. Llywarch Hên, Taliesin and Aneirin (sixth or seventh century?) never mention him; to the first two Urien, Lord of Rheged, is the most imposing figure among all the native warriors. There are, indeed, only five ancient poems that mention Arthur at all. The reference most significant to modern readers occurs in the *Stanzas of the Graves* contained in the *Black Book of Caermarthen* (twelfth century): "A grave there is for March (Mark), a grave for Gwythur, a grave for Gwgawn of the Ruddy Sword; a mystery is the grave of Arthur." Another stanza mentions both the fatal battle of Camlan and Bedwyr (Bedivere), who shares with Kai (Kay) pre-eminence among Arthur's followers in the primitive Welsh fragments of Arthurian fable. Another Arthurian knight, Geraint, is the hero of a poem that appears both in *The Black Book of Caermarthen* and in *The Red Book of Hergest* (fourteenth century). One of the eighteen stanzas just mentions Arthur by name. *The Chair of the Sovereign* in *The Book of Taliesin* (thirteenth century) alludes obscurely to Arthur as a "Warrior sprung from two sources". Arthur, Kai and Bedwyr appear in another poem contained in *The Black Book*; but the deeds celebrated in the almost incomprehensible lines of this poem are the deeds of Kai and Bedwyr. Arthur recedes still further into the twilight of myth in the only other old Welsh poem where any extended allusion is made to him, a most obscure piece of sixty lines contained in *The Book of Taliesin*. Here, as Matthew Arnold says, "the writer is pillaging an antiquity of which he does not fully possess the secret". Arthur sets out upon various expeditions over perilous seas in his ship Pridwen; one of them had as its object the rape of a cauldron belonging to the king of Hades. Ancient British poetry has nothing further to tell us of this mysterious being, who is, even at a time so remote, a vague, impalpable figure of legend.

The most remarkable fragment of the existing early Welsh literature about Arthur is the prose romance of *Kulhwch and Olwen*, assigned by most authorities to the tenth century. It is one of the stories that Lady Charlotte Guest translated from *The Red Book of Hergest* and published as *The Mabinogion* (1838). Of the twelve "Mabinogion", or stories for the young (the word has a special meaning but is loosely used), five deal with Arthurian themes. Two, *Kulhwch and Olwen* and *The Dream of Rhonabwy*, are British; the other three are based on French originals. In *The Dream of Rhonabwy*, Arthur and Kai appear, Mount Badon is mentioned, and the fatal battle at Camlan with Mordred is referred to in some detail. The Arthur of *Kulhwch and Olwen* bears little resemblance to the mystic king of later legend, except in the magnitude of his warrior retinue, in which Kai and Bedwyr are leaders. Arthur, with his dog Cavall, joins in the hunt for the boar Twrch Trwyth through Ireland, Wales and Cornwall, and his many adventures are clearly relics of ancient wonder-tales of bird and beast, wind and water. The wild and even monstrous Arthur of this legend is equally remote from Nennius and from Malory; but the charm of the story is something that the long-winded Continental writers could not achieve.

The serious historian William of Malmesbury, who wrote a few years earlier than Geoffrey of Monmouth, refers to Arthur as a hero worthy to be celebrated in authentic history and not in idle fictions. He adds, "The sepulchre of Arthur is nowhere to be seen, whence ancient ballads fable that he is to come." Plainly, Arthur was already a popular tradition. The transformation of the British Arthur into a romantic hero of European renown was the result of contact between British and Norman culture. No doubt the Normans got their first knowledge of Arthurian story from Brittany; but the real contact was made in Britain itself, where the Normans had succeeded in establishing intimate relations with the Welsh. Thus the true father of the Arthurian legend is Geoffrey of Monmouth. How much he derived from ancient sources we shall probably never find out; but we can reasonably assume that he did not invent the fabric of the story, however fancifully he embroidered it. And, after all, the real point is not how much he invented, but how he used his matter, historical or legendary. Geoffrey had the art of making the improbable seem probable, and his ingenious blending of fact and fable not only gave his book a great success with readers, but made Arthur and Merlin the romantic property of literary Europe. So it has been urged that we should take Geoffrey's compilation, not as a national history, but as a national epic, doing for Britain what the *Aeneid* did for Rome, and finding in the mythical Brutus, great-grandson of Aeneas, the name-giving founder of the British state. In such a story all the legends have their natural place. Geoffrey's *History* is thus the first *Brut*—for so in time the records of early British kings with this mythical starting-point came to be called. The first few books of *Historia Regum Britanniae* relate the deeds of Arthur's predecessors. At the close of the sixth book the weird figure of Merlin appears on the scene, and romance begins to usurp the place of sober history. Arthur is Geoffrey's hero. He knows nothing of Tristram, Lancelot or the Holy Grail; but it was he who, in the Mordred and Guenevere episode, first suggested the love-tragedy that was to become one of the world's imperishable romances.

In the Latin *Life of Gildas* written at about the time of Geoffrey's death there is a further interesting allusion. Arthur is described as being engaged in deadly feud with the King of Scotland, whom he finally kills; he subsequently comes into collision with Melwas, the wicked king of the "summer country" or Somerset, who had, unknown to him, abducted his wife Guenevere, and concealed her in the abbey of Glastonia. This seems to be the earliest appearance of the tradition which makes Melwas (the Mellyagraunce of Malory) an abductor of Guenevere. Some of the Welsh traditions are used in Peacock's delightful story *The Misfortunes of Elphin*, Melwas and the abduction both appearing.

The value of the Arthurian story as matter for verse was first perceived in France; and the earliest surviving standard example of metrical narrative or romance derived directly or indirectly from Geoffrey is *Li Romans de Brut* by Wace, who, born in Jersey, lived at Caen and Bayeux, and completed his poem in 1155. Some of the matter is independent of Geoffrey's *History*. Thus, it is Wace, not Geoffrey, who first tells of the Round Table. The poem, 15,000 lines long, written in lightly rhyming verse and in a familiar language, was very popular. Wace's *Brut*, possibly in some form not now existing, or in some blend with other chronicles, provided the foundation of Layamon's *Brut*, the only English contribution of any importance to Arthurian literature before the fourteenth century; for, so far, all the matter discussed is in Welsh or Latin or French. Layamon added something personal to the essentially English character of his style and matter, and he gives us as well details not to be found in Wace or Geoffrey. Thus, he amplifies the story of the Round Table and narrates the dream of Arthur, not to be found in Geoffrey or Wace, which foreshadows the treachery of Mordred and Guenevere, and disturbs the king with a sense of impending doom. Layamon's enormous and uncouth epic has the unique distinction of being the first celebration of "the matter of Britain" in the English tongue.

Not the least remarkable fact about the story of King Arthur is its rapid development as the centre of many gravitating stories, at first quite independent, but now permanently part of the great Arthurian system. Thus we have the stories of Merlin, of Gawain, of Lancelot, of Tristram, of Perceval, and of the Grail. A full account of these associated legends belongs to the history of French and German, rather than of English, literature, and is thus outside our scope. In origin Merlin may have been a Welsh wizard-bard, but he makes his first appearance in Geoffrey and quickly passes into French romance, from which he is transferred to English story. Gawain is the hero of more episodic romances than any other British knight; when he passes into French story he begins to assume his Malorian (and Tennysonian) lightness of character. He is the hero of the finest of all Middle English metrical romances, *Sir Gawayne and the Grene Knight*, and, as Gwalchmai, he plays a large part in the story called *Peredur the Son of Evrawc*, included in the *Mabinogion*. Peredur is Perceval, and the story comes from French romance. The love of Lancelot for Guenevere is now a central episode of the Arthurian tragedy, but Lancelot is actually a late-comer into the legend, and his story is told in French. The book to which Chaucer refers in *The Nun's Priest's Tale* and Dante in the famous passage of *Inferno* VI is perhaps the great prose *Lancelot* traditionally attributed to Walter Map (see p. 21). The Grail story is another complicated addition to the Arthurian cycle. Out of the quest for various talismans, no doubt a part of Celtic tradition, developed the story of Perceval, as told in French and German romances; and the "Grail", a primitive symbol, proved capable of semi-mystical religious interpretation, and came to be identified with the cup of the Last Supper in which Joseph of Arimathea treasured the blood that flowed from the wounds of the Redeemer. The story of Tristram and Iseult is probably the oldest of the subsidiary Arthurian legends, and we find the richest versions in fragments of French poems and fuller German compositions. The English literature of Tristram is very meagre. The whole story bears every mark of remote pagan and Celtic origin. Finally, as an example of how independent legends were caught into the great Arthurian system, let us note the Celtic fairy tale of *Lanval*, best known in the lay of Marie de France (*c.* 1175), a fascinatingly obscure personality who, possibly English, wrote in French. And as a postscript we may note that the sceptical twentieth century has nevertheless not lagged behind the

Middle Ages or the Victorians in its devotion to King Arthur, as witness the Arthurian trilogy *Merlin, Lancelot* and *Tristram* (1917–27) by the American poet Edwin Arlington Robinson, the reshaping of the Grail legend in John Cowper Powys's *Glastonbury Romance* (1933), Charles Williams's *Taliessin through Logres* (1938) and *The Region of the Summer Stars* (1944), and T. H. White's trilogy *The Once and Future King* (1958) which inspired the American stage and film success *Camelot.*

Through all the various strains of Arthurian story we hear "the horns of Elfland faintly blowing"; and it is quite possible that, to the Celtic wonderland, with its fables of the "little people", we owe much of the fairy-lore which has, through Shakespeare and poets of lower degree, enriched the literature of England. Chaucer, at any rate, seemed to have no doubt about it, for he links all that he knew, or cared to know, about the Arthurian stories with his recollections of the fairy world:

> In th' oldë dayës of the King Arthoúr,
> Of which that Britons speken greet honóur,
> Al was this land fulfild of fayerye;
> The elf-queen with hir joly companye
> Dauncëd ful ofte in many a grenë mede.

So let us believe with the poets, and leave the British Arthur in his unquestioned place as the supreme king of Romance.

XIII. THE METRICAL ROMANCES. I

> Men speke of romances of prys,
> Of Horn Child and of Ypotys,
> Of Beves and Sir Gy,
> Of Sir Libeux and Pleyn-damour;
> But Sir Thopas—he bereth the flour
> Of royal chivalry.

Thus wrote Chaucer in *Sir Thopas,* that perfect parody of the metrical romances, with their monotony of matter, their flabbiness of metre and their poverty of style. The great change from Old to Middle English story-telling is hard to explain. *Beowulf* and *Waldere* have style and courtliness; *Horn* and *Havelok* have little of either. The Norman Conquest degraded English to the rank of a vehicle for stories suited to the vulgar; but, oddly enough, there is the same kind of degradation at much the same period in Denmark, Sweden, Germany and the Netherlands, where there was no Conquest. A widening of the world and a broadening of taste must be reckoned as factors. A larger public, and especially a larger female public, demanded popular art. In all the Teutonic countries, though not at the same time in all, there was a change of taste and fashion which rejected old epic themes and native forms of verse for new subjects and rhyming measures. This meant a great disturbance and confusion of literary principles and traditions; hence, much of the new literature was experimental and undisciplined. The nations were long in finding a literary standard. The Germans attained it about 1200; the English in the time of Chaucer; the Danes and Swedes not until long after the close of the Middle Ages.

In a world without printing, where books were laboriously written by hand and therefore few in number, however often copied, popular literature was a matter for the ear rather than for the eye. The functions of editor, publisher, circulating library, and sometimes of author, were combined in the minstrel, who, with his moving tales of accident by flood and field was sure of welcome from the assembled company in hall or bower or market-place, according to his rank and skill. In a heroic age the *scop* or gleeman, far-travelled like Widsith, delighted his warrior hearers with tales of battle and strange lands; in a softer age and clime the ambitious troubadour at the court of Raimon or Eleanor disseminated his elaborate lyrics by the mouth of the itinerant *joglar*. *Beowulf* and *The Battle of Maldon* were story poems appropriate to heroic and primitive times. With the development of social amenities, arose the demand for a new kind of story-poem—something, as we should say now, a little more sentimental. What kind of poem pleased the English in the reign of Harold Godwinsson or of Henry I nothing remains to show. Between *The Battle of Maldon* and Layamon's *Brut* there is a great gap of two centuries. In France, these centuries are rich in storybooks still extant; and the English metrical romances depend very largely upon them.

The English language was the tongue of a subject nation, and, save for the moral compositions of the godly, nothing in it appears to have been committed to writing. The songs of the people, whatever they were, lived on the lips of those who sang them, and have perished with them. Twelfth-century France, however, was the home of lyric and romance. The old national epics, the *chansons de geste*, were displaced by a new romantic school, which triumphed over the old like the new comedy of the Restoration over the last Elizabethans. The *chansons de geste* were meant for the hall, for Homeric recitation after supper; the new romances were intended to be read in my lady's bower; they were for summer leisure and daylight. The new romances were, in fact, the nearest approach to popular novels that could exist in the days before printing. In the production of such literature, England was a long way behind France. When France had achieved style and form, England was still content with easy, shambling verse, haphazard spelling and a low literary standard. In fact, it was not until the time of Chaucer that English reached the level of Chrétien's French, of Wolfram's German, of Dante's Italian.

A striking peculiarity of many medieval romances must be mentioned. The Virgin cult referred to in an earlier page was a symptom of civilization—of a romantic interest in women. In the secular world this was represented by the doctrine of courtly love with its elaborate laws and ritual. Love, as the troubadour lyrists understood it, was homage paid to a liege lady, who might be remote and even non-existent. This religion of love passed from the lyrics into the stories. It was the duty of every knight to have a lady for whom his deeds were done and to whom his homage was offered. Don Quixote of La Mancha with his peerless Dulcinea del Toboso, though drawn much later, and drawn too, with kindly laughter, embodies this ideal love in its extremes of fantastic devotion and fantastic absurdity. The rhetorical love interest of much modern literature can be traced to the literary fashion set by eleventh-century troubadour poetry. The English were naturally less interested than the French in the lengthy and elaborate rhetoric of courtly love, and English versions of French romances therefore tend to abbreviation as surely as the German versions tend to expansion. The English liked the minstrels to cut the reflections and come to the incidents. Of course there was not one literary public then any more than now; the available literature had its long range from tragedy to trash, and the minstrels themselves, who were not merely the singers and actors, but the journalists and gossips of their day, resembled the modern "professional" in extremes of success and seediness.

The general subject-matter of romance has been summed up for us in one of the happy indispensable phrases of history. Jean Bodel, at ll. 6–7 of his *Chanson des Saisnes* (Saxons) or *Guiteclin de Sassoigne* (thirteenth century), declares that

> Ne sont que iij matières à nul home antandant,
> De France et de Bretaigne et de Rome la Grant.

The "matter of France" was found in stories of Charlemagne and the Twelve Peers and the subsidiary or contending figures—Roland, Oliver, Ferumbras, Ogier the Dane, Huon of Bordeaux and the Four Sons of Aymon. The "matter of Britain" was, briefly, the Arthurian legend. The "matter of Rome the Great" was all classical antiquity, as far as it was known—stories of Troy (like *Troilus and Cressida*), stories of Thebes (like *Palamon and Arcite*), stories out of Ovid —the author of *Ars Amatoria* being a favoured figure in the days of courtly love —and, above all, stories of Alexander, who usually figures as a feudal sovereign. But there were other stories that cannot be ranged under the three "matters" —stories from the East, like *Flores and Blancheflour*, *Barlaam and Josaphat* and *The Seven Sages*, the story of *Roberd of Cisyle* (familiar in two modern poems), and the wildly unhistorical *Richard Cœur de Lion*. It is true that the variety of scene and costume does not always prevent monotony; but that objection can equally be made to the romances of every age. In fact, all heroes tend to be monotonous. Briefly and roughly, the history of the English romances might be put in this way: about the year 1200, French literature came to dominate the whole of Christendom, especially in the matter of stories; not only sending abroad the French tales of Charlemagne and Roland, but importing plots, scenery and so forth, from many lands, Wales and Brittany, Greece and the further East, and giving new French forms to them, which were admired and, as far as possible, borrowed by foreign nations, according to their several tastes and abilities. The English took a large share in this trade. Generally speaking, their taste was easily satisfied. What they wanted was adventure—slaughter of Saracens, fights with dragons and giants, rightful heirs getting their own again, innocent princesses championed against their felon adversaries. Such commodities were purveyed by popular authors, who adapted from the French what suited them and left out what the English liked least. The English romance writers worked for common minstrels and their audiences, and were not particular about their style. They used, as a rule, either short couplets or some variety of that simple stanza which is better known to most readers from *Sir Thopas* than from *Horn Childe* or *Sir Libeaus*.

The far East began very early to tell upon Western imaginations, not only through the marvels of Alexander in India, but later through the Crusades. One of the best of Eastern stories, and one of the first, as it happens, in the list of English romances, is *Flores and Blancheflour*. *The Seven Sages of Rome* may count among the romances, though it is an oriental group of stories in a setting, like *The Arabian Nights*, a pattern followed in *The Decameron*, in *Confessio Amantis*, and in *The Canterbury Tales*. *Baarlam and Josaphat* is the story of the Buddha, and *Robert of Sicily*, the "proud king", has been traced back to a similar origin. *Ypotis* (rather oddly placed along with *Horn* and the others in *Sir Thopas*) is Epictetus: *The Meditations of Childe Ypotis* is hardly a romance, it is more like a legend; but the difference between romance and legend is not always very deep; and one is reminded that Greek and Eastern romantic plots and ideas had come into England long before, in the lives of the saints.

The varieties of style in the English romances are very great, under an apparent monotony and poverty of type. Between *Sir Beves of Hamtoun* and *Sir Gawayne and the Grene Knight* there is as wide an interval as between (let us say) Monk Lewis and Scott. As regards verse, there are the two great orders, rhyming measures and unrhymed alliterative lines. Of rhyming measures the most usual are the short couplet of octosyllabic lines, and the stanza called *rime couée*, *rithmus caudatus* or "tailed rhyme". *King Horn* exemplifies one stage in the development of English metre—the half-way stage between Layamon and regular octosyllabic couplets; for though the poem is certainly in couplets, the syllables vary abruptly and quite anomalously in number. As long as the rhymes are reached, the poet seems not to mind how he reaches them; one feels all the while that in the back of his mind the Old English tune is running, and that he is unconsciously making, not couplets, but pairs of half-lines. In *Havelok the Dane*, the couplet, though sometimes a little rough, is not unsound; *Ywain and Gawain* is nearly as correct as Chaucer; and *The Squire of Low Degree* is one of the happiest examples of this verse in English.

Besides the short couplet, different types of common metre ("eights and sixes") are used; very vigorously, with full rhymes, in *Sir Ferumbras*, and as "fourteeners", without the internal rhyme, in *The Tale of Gamelyn*, the verse of which has been so rightly praised. Chaucer's *Sir Thopas* gives what may be called the standard form of *rime couée* or *rithmus caudatus* or tailed rhyme. *Sir Thopas* itself shows several variations, and there are others, which Chaucer does not introduce. In the stanza of *Sir Thopas* quoted at the head of this section, the main lines contain eight syllables, and rhyme in pairs; the two *caudae* or "tails" contain six syllables and rhyme together. But the length of line and stanza and the arrangement of rhymes and "tails" vary greatly in other poems. One of the romances of *Octavian* is in the old Provençal and old French measure which, by roundabout ways, came to Scotland, and was used in the seventeenth century to celebrate Habbie Simson (see p. 415), the piper of Kilbarchan, and, thereafter, by Allan Ramsay, Fergusson and Burns. The French originals of these English romances are almost universally in short couplets, the ordinary verse for all subjects, after the *chansons de geste* had grown old-fashioned. *Rime couée* is later than couplets, though the couplets last better, finally coming to the front again and winning easily in *Confessio Amantis* and *The Romaunt of the Rose*. There are many examples of rewriting; tales in couplets are sometimes rewritten in stanzas. Thus, *King Horn* is in couplets, *Horn Childe* in the *Thopas* stanza. New forms are employed at the close of the Middle Ages, such as rhyme royal (e.g. in *Generydes*) and the heroic couplet (in *Clariodus* and Sir Gilbert Hay's *Alexander*); still, for simple popular use, the short verse proved the most suitable.

Unrhymed alliterative verse suddenly reappeared in the middle of the fourteenth century as a vehicle for romance. Where the verse came from is not known clearly to anyone. The new alliterative verse was not a battered survival of the old English line, but a regular and clearly understood form. It must have been hidden away somewhere underground—continuing in a purer tradition than happens to have found its way into extant manuscripts—till, at last, there is this striking revival in the reign of Edward III. Plainly more went on in the writing of poetry than we know, or shall know, anything about. What the verse could do at its best is nobly shown in *Sir Gawayne*, and, later still, in *Piers Plowman*.

"Breton lays" meant for the English a short story in rhyme, like those of Marie de France, taken from Celtic sources. Some of these were more "artistic" (as we should say) than spun-out efforts like *Sir Beves of Hamtoun* and *Sir Guy of Warwick*; moreover, there is something in them of that romantic mystery which is less common in medieval literature than modern readers generally suppose. The best examples in English are *Sir Orfeo* and *Sir Launfal*. *Sir Tristrem* is a great contrast to *Sir Gawayne*, though both works are ambitious and carefully studied. The author of *Sir Gawayne* took some old wives' fables and made them into a magnificent piece of Gothic art; the author of *Sir Tristrem* had one of the noblest stories in the world to tell, and translated it into thin tinkling rhymes. Tristram and Iseult have hardly yet found their inspired poet in England. *The Tale of Gamelyn* may count for something on the native English side against the many borrowed French romances. It is a story of the younger son cruelly treated by his tyrannical elder brother, and coming to his own again by the help of the king of outlaws. Thomas Lodge made a novel out of it, and Shakespeare improved upon Lodge. *The Tale of Gamelyn* is *As You Like It*, without Rosalind, Touchstone or Celia.

XIV. THE METRICAL ROMANCES. II

The metrical romances began with the twelfth-century revival in literature; they were part of the medieval world; and they ceased when the last feudal king fell betrayed at Bosworth Field. Disregarding Bodel's traditional classification, we can see that they fall into four groups: Carolingian or Old French, Classical, Oriental and Celtic. Among the stories in the French group, we find in *Sir Otuel* a Saracen emissary who insults Charlemagne, is challenged by Roland, and finally converted. *Roland and Vernagu* deals with Charlemagne's exploits in Spain, Vernagu being a black giant from Babylon. *Sir Ferumbras* tells the story of the capture of Rome by Saracens, and its relief by Charlemagne. Ferumbras is indeed none other than the redoubtable Fierabras, whose name will be familiar to readers of *Don Quixote*.

In the earlier romances directly springing from English soil, the viking atmosphere is prevalent. True, the raiders who make an orphan of Horn are called Saracens, but they are obviously Norsemen. *Havelok the Dane* tells how a Danish prince and English princess, defrauded by wicked guardians, come to their own again. The ponderous but popular *Guy of Warwick* is a tedious expansion of a stirring English legend relating how Sir Guy saved England by his victory over Colbrand the Dane. *Sir Beves of Hamtoun* is the best example of the ordinary popular tale, the medieval book of chivalry with all the right things in it. The hero's father is murdered, like Hamlet's; the hero is disinherited, like Horn; he is wooed by a fair Paynim princess; he carries a treacherous letter, like Hamlet again; he is separated from his wife and children, like Sir Eustace or Sir Isumbras; and exiled, like Huon of Bordeaux, for causing the death of the king's son. The horse Arundel is like Bayard in *The Four Sons of Aymon*, and the giant Ascapart is won over like Ferumbras. In the French original there was one conspicuous defect—no dragon. But the dragon is supplied, most liberally, and with great success, in the English version.

Other romances borrow from classical antiquity and appear to be inspired by the piety that attributed the foundation of Britain to Brutus of Troy. The *Gest Hystoriale of the Destruction of Troy* tells the ancient story with the apparatus of medievalism. But most interesting of all in the Troy narrative are those elements of the story of Troilus and Criseida taken from Benoît de Sainte-More's *Roman de Troie* and subsequently moulded into one of the world's greatest stories. *King Alisaunder* presents the conqueror of the East as a legendary person performing legendary exploits in a legendary world. *Richard Cœur de Lion* shows us a differently named hero of the same kind, doing the same kind of thing.

The East has touched other romances to an issue unlike that of *King Alisaunder*, as in the love story of *Flores and Blancheflour*. In *The Seven Sages of Rome* we have a story-sequence of the true oriental line. But the most remarkable of the Eastern romances in substance and history is *Barlaam and Josaphat*. This is indeed a curiosity of literature, for the saintly hero of an apparently Christian story current in Europe for several centuries is none other than the Buddha himself. The story found its way into the *Vitae Sanctorum*, and thence into *The Golden Legend*, from which it was translated into later English by Caxton. The identification of Josaphat with Buddha was first made by a Portuguese in 1612, but the suggestion remained unnoticed, and was not fully established till the nineteenth century.

The influence derived from Celtic sources is possibly the most important of all. The stories called Arthurian seem to embody some features of the others— the English names of the places, the combats of the Carolingian heroes, the magnification of the dimly discerned overlord, together with the romantic love-scenes and ever-present magic and mystery of the Eastern tales. *Sir Tristrem* contains all the facts of its wonderful story, and is quite ambitious, though the singer's thin and tinkly lines never rise to the level of their theme. *Sir Launfal* takes us into fairyland, and is a variant of an old theme, the love of a fairy for a mortal. *Sir Orfeo*, a genuinely successful poem, translates the theme of Orpheus and Eurydice most successfully into the terms of Celtic fairy story. *Lai le Freine,*

translated from Marie de France, is a charmingly told short story of two pairs
of twin children, one infant having been hidden, for destruction, in a hollow
ash tree. *Emaré* is the story of a mysteriously beautiful maiden, persecuted by
unnatural parents. In *Sir Degare* we find a hero who is the son of a fairy knight
and a princess of Britain. *Sir Gowther* is the story of the passions that worked
in the son of a mortal woman and her "demon lover". Best of all the fairy
stories is the delightful *Thomas of Erceldoune*, telling how Thomas the Rhymer
was carried away into fairyland by a fay with whom he dwelt, and who saved
him from the devil by bringing him again to Eldone tree. *Golagros and Gawayne*
introduces to us the Arthurian figure who long remained the pattern of knightly
virtues. Gawain figures, too, in *The Awntyrs of Arthure at the Terne Wathelyne*.
Ywain and Gawain tells the story of two knights who fight until a long delayed
recognition ends the combat. In *The Wedding of Sir Gawaine* the hero saves the
life of Arthur by marrying a loathsome hag, who providentially turns into a
beauteous maiden. *Libeaus Desconus* has a story like that of Gareth and Lynette.
In *The Avowing of Arthur* we have four adventures of Sir Gawain, Sir Kay, Sir
Baldwin and the King. *Le Morte Arthur* (in rhyming stanzas and not to be confused with the alliterative *Morte Arthure*) tells for the first time in English poetry
the tragic story of Lancelot and Elaine. The alliterative *Morte Arthure*, a fine
poem, takes us to the last dim battle of the west and the end of all the Arthurian
chivalry.

Any attempt to group the many extant romances will always leave a few
unclassified. Five may be considered as studies of knightly character. *Ipomedon*
shows us the traditional knightly lover, fighting disguised, and winning, after
protracted labours, the queen whom he might have had at once. *Amis and
Amiloun* is a moving story of sublime friendship. In *Sir Cleges* we find a familiar
theme—a poor knight bringing a gift to court and being refused admission by
greedy officials till he has promised to give them half of what he gets. He asks
for twelve strokes, and they get a full share. *Sir Isumbras* varies another familiar
theme, the proud, rich man suddenly brought to humiliation and repentance
by loss of lands, goods, wife and children. *The Squire of Low Degree* is a delightful, and mercifully brief, story of a humble wooer's toilsome but finally happy
winning of a high-born lady. Three more, *Sir Triamour*, *Sir Eglamour of Artois*
and *Torrent of Portugal* belong to the "reunion of kindred" type which appealed
to Chaucer and still more to Shakespeare in his latest period.

It is not possible in a brief space to name the multitude of romances, much
less to describe them. The very multitude of stories indicates the extent to which
they fed an existing appetite. Such volumes as the Thornton and Auchinlech
MSS. (now our sole authorities for certain pieces) show us *Sir Tristrem* or *Sir
Octavian*, *Thomas of Erceldoune* or *Morte Arthure* laboriously copied out and
treasured up, with recipes, charms, prayers, and other domestic necessities, as a
permanent part of a family's reading. If ever there was a fiction that took men
"out of themselves" and gave a gorgeously coloured relief to the boredom of
current existence, it was the mass of literature that formed the light reading
(or hearing) of our ancestors for two centuries. Four remarkable general
characteristics may be briefly noted: (1) the medieval romances, like the
medieval cathedrals, are anonymous; (2) they describe a Utopian society in

which everything appears to be anybody's and in which there is no consciousness of patriotism or nationalism, but only a sense of universal Christendom at
war with the powers of darkness; (3) they indicate a passion for external beauty
and ceremonial, for colour and pageantry, for marvels and magic and mystery;
and (4) they have their being in a world of abstractions in which there seems to
be no definite place or time or politics or problem of existence. Their complete
detachment from the life of man, together with their defects of shapelessness,
monotony and interminable length, produced the inevitable reaction. Better
criticism than the eternally adorable *Don Quixote* was never penned by man,
though it was prose and not metrical romance that fuddled the wits of the hero.
But Cervantes was still far away. Nearer to hand was another great humanist
and humorist. Chaucer catches almost every fault of the romances in *Sir
Thopas*, which is, indeed, such a likeness of what it caricatures, that for general
readers it has become almost as hard to enjoy as the dullest of its victims. There
is no need to catalogue the shortcomings of the old stories. People in all ages
are easily amused. It is not for the consumers of crime-novels, thriller films or
television serials to cast stones at the medieval romances.

XV. *PEARL, CLEANNESS, PATIENCE* AND
SIR GAWAYNE

The remarkable revival or emergence of alliterative verse during the fourteenth
century has already been mentioned. This sudden apparition of an ancient form
is strange and almost disquieting. We long to ask questions, and there is no one
to answer. In comparison with the jog-trot movement of the rhyming romances
the best alliterative verse has extraordinary grip and power; yet it has no effect
on the main current of English poetry, which continues to develop along the
lines now familiar. The greatest productions of the alliterative revival are contemporary with Chaucer; but he writes as if they had no existence, and would
have written no differently had he known them.

William of Palerne or *William and the Were-Wolf* is one of the earliest poems
in the revived form. It was translated from the French about 1350. The heir to
the Spanish throne is changed by his step-mother into a werewolf, and in that
shape he protects William, the young prince of Palermo. It is a good story,
rather lengthily and tamely told in lines that flow pleasantly.

Morte Arthure, a very striking poem, which occurs only in the Thornton MS.,
has been attributed to Huchoun of the Awle Ryale. Though ostensibly based on
Geoffrey's *History*, it makes clear allusion to contemporary affairs, especially the
wars of Edward III. This touch of allegory is very unusual in medieval romances.
A specially striking passage of the poem is that near the end of its 4500 lines
describing the king's disquieting vision of those "that whilom sate on top of
Fortune's wheele".

But the most moving artistic product of the alliterative revival is a group of
four poems contained (with some alien matter) in the small volume in the
British Museum known as MS. Cott. Nero A x. They are generally called
Pearl, Patience, Purity (or *Cleanness*) and *Sir Gawayne and the Grene Knight*. Not

a line of these poems has been found in any other manuscript. They have been attributed to Huchoun, but no definite authorship can be established. *Pearl* is a lovely poem of 1212 lines, combining rhyme and alliteration, with a "catchword" system that makes the first line of each twelve-lined stanza repeat a word in the last line of the stanza before. The poem is possibly, but not certainly, an allegory of a dead child. This precious pearl has been lost in the ground, and the "joyless jeweller" wanders in sorrowful search. He at last sees the figure of a maiden, in raiment of dazzling white covered with pearls, who shows him a vision of the celestial city. But the vision passes, and he wakes to find himself once more on the hillside alone. *Patience*, which is a versified account of Jonah, takes us to the sea and gives us an excellent storm. *Purity* (or *Cleanness*) is a lengthy review of the scriptural stories that illustrate the vices opposed to "clannesse".

The masterpiece of this manuscript is the story of *Sir Gawayne and the Grene Knight* told in 2530 lines, broken irregularly by a short refrain. This "jewel of medieval romance" has extraordinary strength and power, and moves on its appointed way with artistic determination from its strange beginning to a noble end. The elements of the plot are as ancient and unreasonable as are to be found in any mythology. No precise original has been found; but the chief adventure, the beheading game proposed by the Green Knight to the reluctant courtiers of Arthur, occurs in other stories. *Sir Gawayne* is one of the most singular works of the fourteenth century. The author was an excellent artist, getting the utmost out of his wild story, and turning its very impossibilities, as Shakespeare turned the magic of *The Tempest*, to moral ends, without abating any of his art. The poem is in no sense easy, but it amply rewards the effort it demands.

Nothing whatever is known about the author of these poems. There is no certainty, even, that they are all from the same hand, though W. P. Ker considers it "probable". In 1838 Edwin Guest, the historian of English rhythms, set up a claim for Huchoun of the Awle Ryale (see p. 61), and to him have also been assigned various other alliterative poems, namely, *The Wars of Alexander, The Destruction of Troy, Titus and Vespasian, The Parlement of the Thre Ages, Wynnere and Wastoure, Erkenwald,* and the alliterative rhyming poem *Golagros and Gawane*; but the claims cannot be established. It is safer to consider all these compositions as the literary remains of several alliterative poets who flourished somewhere in the north-west during the second half of the fourteenth and the early years of the fifteenth century.

XVI. LATER TRANSITION ENGLISH: LEGENDARIES AND CHRONICLES

The approaching triumph of English over French and a growing recognition of the needs of the middle and even of the lower classes can be discerned in the fact that, for two generations before Chaucer, some of the chief contributions to literature take the form of translations from Latin and Norman-French, made expressly for those who could read nothing but English. We can divide this literature into two main classes, the first religious, including homilies, saints' lives and scriptural paraphrases, the second historical, including the chronicles and political songs: but they are alike in this, that the homilies point their morals with legends, and the histories adorn their tales with exhortations.

The two chief chroniclers of the period are Robert of Gloucester and Robert Mannyng of Brunne. To the chronicle known as Robert of Gloucester's more than one hand contributed. The work dates from the end of the thirteenth century, and plainly embodies the narratives of eyewitnesses. Some passages seem to derive from folk songs; others are probably based on popular oral tradition. The form of the *Chronicle* is no less interesting than its theme. The metre is an adaptation of the two half-lines of Old English poetry into one long line, and the rhymes help to emphasize a surging movement well suited to narrative verse. The whole work shows that writers of English were becoming sure masters of sustained metrical form. A fine sense of historical narrative is exhibited not only in the old stories from earlier chroniclers, but in the contemporary passages that describe the town and gown riot at Oxford in 1263 and the tragedy of Simon's death at Evesham.

The South English Legendary is a collection of versified lives of the saints written in the dialect and metre of the Gloucester *Chronicle*, and belonging to the same time and place. Of the saints' lives therein contained, none has greater attraction than the story of St Brendan, who is one of the legendary navigators, a sort of Christian Ulysses or Sindbad, with the latter of whom he has strong affinity. Half-remembered legends of ancient adventures on the sea are here represented as the voyage of a Christian saint in search of an earthly paradise.

While the monks of Gloucester were thus busy with history and hagiology, writers of the north were composing literature more directly hortatory. A cycle of homilies in the octosyllabic couplet was written, possibly at the beginning of the fourteenth century, covering all the Sundays in the ecclesiastical year. The gospel for the day is turned into English and then expounded; and, in addition to this, there is a *narracio*, or story, to illustrate the lesson and drive the moral home. The stories are quite memorable. A very attractive and well-ordered work of the godly kind is the encyclopedic book of scriptural story, *Cursor Mundi*, "the Course of the World", a poem of some 24,000 lines, mainly in the octosyllabic couplet, composed in the early part of the fourteenth century. It was expressly intended to displace the romances of chivalry and to edify by amusing. Men, says the author, are attracted by stories and take delight in their "paramours"; but the best lady of all is the Virgin Mary. Therefore the poet will compose a work in her honour; and because there is much in French, but nothing for those who know only English, he will write it for him who "na French can". He then proceeds to describe the "course of the world", beginning with the Creation. The unknown poet was an accomplished scholar, well-read in medieval literature. His work, admirably written, with a note of sympathetic humanity, is a storehouse of legends, not all of which have been traced to their original sources. The numerous manuscripts show that it was popular.

The most skilful story-teller of his time was Robert Mannyng of Brunne (i.e. Bourne in Lincolnshire) who, between 1303 and 1338, translated into his native tongue two poems written in poor French by English clerics, William of Wadington's *Manuel des Péchiez* and a chronicle composed by Peter of Langtoft,

a canon of the Augustinian priory of Bridlington. In *Handlyng Synne*, a version
in 12,000 octosyllabic lines of Wadington's *Manuel*, Mannyng declares that
his purpose is to benefit ignorant men who delight in listening to stories. He
therefore offers them stories that will edify and instruct. It is interesting to find
this moralist banning both tournaments and religious plays as occasions of sin.
Only two kinds of plays should be allowed, those on the Nativity and the
Resurrection, and they must be played within the church. Mannyng excels in
all the qualities of a narrator. He combines, in fact, the *trouvère* with the homilist,
and shows the way to Gower's *Confessio Amantis*. Apart from its literary qualities,
Handlyng Synne has considerable value as a picture of contemporary manners.
In his attacks on tyrannous lords, and his assertion of the essential equality of
men, Mannyng resembles the author of *Piers Plowman*, and in words that may
not have been unknown to Chaucer, he draws the picture of the ideal parish
priest. Mannyng's other work, the *Chronicle of England*, adapted from Wace
and Peter of Langtoft, is less attractive, though its use of octosyllabic couplets
and rhymed alexandrines may attract the student of prosody.

The literary activity of the south-east of England during this period was less
remarkable than that of the west and north; nevertheless three writers call for
mention. Adam Davy's *Five Dreams about Edward II* (*c.* 1310), a poem of 166
lines in octosyllabic couplets, is something of a curiosity, if only in its deliberate
and gloomy obscurity; but it has not much literary importance. Dan Michel's
Ayenbite of Inwit (i.e. The "Again-biting" or Remorse of Conscience) translated, about 1340, from the popular French treatise, *Somme des Vices et des Vertus*,
is, like the *Ormulum*, philological rather than literary in its interest. It is an excellent
example of the Kentish dialect, most carefully spelt. William of Shoreham, so
known from his birthplace at Shoreham, near Sevenoaks, is, from the literary
point of view, a much more interesting person than Adam or Michel. Though
his seven fairly long religious poems deal with the favourite themes of the
medieval homilist, they are written in skilfully varied lyrical stanzas, and are not
unfavourable specimens of sacred poetry.

Very different from Davy's gloomily patriotic *Dreams* are the cheerfully
patriotic poems of Laurence Minot, written in the northern dialect during the
period 1333–52. Minot's theme is the famous victories of Edward III, from the
battle of Halidon Hill (1333) to the capture of Guisnes (1352). There are eleven
poems, all straightforward and vigorous in the style of a patriotism that sings
quite unabashed, "my country, right or wrong". Minot essayed a variety of lyric
measures with success, though his touch is not that of a master. He is decisive;
he is not delicate. The song to Edward III beginning "Edward our cumly king"
shows the kind of thing he did well. Minot is most interesting, not as a lyric
poet, but as the first singer of a militant patriotism that had, by his time, become
definitely English.

XVII. LATER TRANSITION ENGLISH: SECULAR AND SACRED LYRICS, TALES, SOCIAL SATIRE

The abiding qualities of English poetry are clearly apparent in the general body of Middle English lyric verse. "Spring, the sweet spring" is as fickle, as enchanting, and as provocative, to the singer in the thirteenth century as to the singer in the twentieth. And with this joy in the general wonder of things we find, too, the Englishman's characteristic resentment of injustice and his tendency to voice his social and political discontent in song. Nor is there wanting a sense of personal, rather than collective, religion. The fourteenth-century Englishman would make a song against the Church, but not against the Faith.

We may observe with pleasure that almost the first successful English lyric we know is one that is sung to this day. *Sumer is icumen in* exists, indeed, rather as song than as poem, for the only manuscript is a piece of music, the famous Reading Rota or Round, in which four equal voices sing in strict imitation (canon at the unison), each voice entering four measures after the preceding. There is, as well, a "burden" held by two additional voices, also in imitation. The tune itself is joyous and delightful. Obviously this cannot be an isolated miracle of music: there must have been more which has not survived. The preservation of this leaf of manuscript is probably due to the piety that wrote a decorous (and clumsy) Latin alternative under the gay words and notes of the English song.

The progress of our early lyric poetry cannot be clearly traced. In the surviving remnants of Old English poetry there is scarcely anything with the lyrical form and spirit. By the thirteenth century, however, lyric poetry was being written with complete success. How far it developed out of native songs and carols and how far its growth was stimulated by French and Latin examples we do not know. By the thirteenth century there was regular intercourse with the south of France, the home of troubadour poetry; but the earliest English lyrics are not Provençal in matter or manner. What French influence there was came through the north. Latin hymns and songs in rhyme clearly influenced some early poems. "Stond wel, moder, under rode" (in several versions) has the six-lined stanza which was popular in the twelfth century and which was to find its most endearing expression in "Stabat mater dolorosa". But the best English songs are really English. A few early fragments survive in casual scribblings here and there in various documents. Of several manuscript collections the best known is the British Museum MS. Harley 2253, written during the first decades of the fourteenth century, and containing transcriptions of various pieces, English, French, Latin and "macaronic", by unknown writers from the thirteenth century to its own time. Some of the songs in slightly differing versions occur in other manuscripts. *Early English Lyrics* (Chambers and Sidgwick), Carleton Brown's *English Lyrics of the XIIIth Century* and *Religious Lyrics of the XIVth Century*, various volumes in the Early English Text Society's publications and the collections of Thomas Wright contain many beautiful English poems, far too little known, though they are as easy to read as the songs of Burns. The secular lyrics are frank, free and unashamed in their rejoicing and take their place in the chain that links Catullus with the Caroline poets. A view of sacred and profane love is given in a pair of lyrics, each beginning, "Lutel wot it anymon", the one considering how "He bohte us with is holy blod" and the other dwelling on the love of woman. In the sacred lyrics of this time we find instinctive, natural poetry often touched with mysticism; but there is no diversion of human feeling into such byways as the laudation of conventual celibacy or erotic ecstasies about the person of Jesus. The note of stern serious-ness is often heard. Few short poems of any age are more impressive than the lines beginning "The lif of this world Ys reuled with wynd" (Harley 7322).

The Harley manuscript (2253) also contains the shrewd and homely *Proverbs of Hendyng*, which appear to have been collected in their present form at the close of the thirteenth century or the beginning of the fourteenth. Their main interest lies in the form of the verse, as they offer a very early use of the *rime couée* or *Sir Thopas* stanza, with an extra line containing the proverb, and a concluding "tag", *Quoth Hendyng*.

Thomas Wright's valuable collection, *The Political Songs of England from the Reign of John to that of Edward II* (1839), shows us national discontent expressing itself in song. Of the thirteenth and fourteenth century poems preserved, some are in Latin, some in French, and some in English. A few combine two languages, e.g. the *Song against the King's Taxes* (as Wright calls it) in French and Latin (temp. Edward II). The unknown singers denounce the venal bishops, the church and the favoured foreigners of Henry III's rule, and hail Simon de Montfort as a national hero or mourn his loss as a martyr. Not the least unpopular person of the time was Henry III's brother, Richard, Earl of Cornwall, who had been elected titular king of the Romans and crowned at Aix-la-Chapelle. The stanzas of a vigorous song made against him end with the refrain, "Richard, thah thou be ever trichard, tricchen shalt thou never more". The song of the husbandman, beginning "Ich herde men upo mold make muche mon", illustrates, in its matter, the ordinary man's feeling against the war-like adventures of Edward I, and, in its manner, the persistence of alliteration in popular song. The general indignation against foreigners and foreign wars, however, did not preclude popular sympathy with the Flemish burghers in their struggle against France. A powerful *Song of the Flemish Insurrection* (as Wright calls it) was composed soon after the battle of Courtrai (1302). *A Song against the Retinues of Great People* (Wright) expresses popular discontent in vigorous rhymes and extrava-gant words, some of which defy interpretation. *A Song on the Times* (Wright) resorts to parable, and presents its characters in the form of animals—wolf, fox, ass and lion.

We meet the familiar animals of fable again in a much longer verse story of the thirteenth century, *The Vox and the Wolf*, which relates, in bold and firm couplets, the familiar story of the escape of Reynard from the well at the expense of the wolf Sigrim. The poem is an admirable example of comic satire, perhaps the best of its kind before the days of Chaucer. Social satire can also be found in the few Middle English examples of the *fabliau* still extant. The short and broad verse-tale probably appealed to the Englishman as strongly as to the Frenchman; but very few English examples have survived, and even those are of foreign origin. The deceived husband and the lascivious cleric are almost stock figures of the plot. The capital story of *Dame Siriz* (or *Sirith*) was put into English, after many wanderings through other languages, about the middle of the thirteenth century, and is excellently told in verse that varies between the octosyllabic couplet and an arrangement of lines approximating to the *Thopas* type. The story resembles the twenty-eighth of *Gesta Romanorum*, a famous collection of brief tales in Latin prose, each designed to point a moral, compiled about the end of the thirteenth century. The purpose was edification; but if the "morals" are ignored, the work becomes, as in fact it did become, when translated into English, a popular story book; and it provided plots for many later writers. The title is a singular misnomer, for not a few of the tales are oriental. There were other collections, such as the *Summa Praedicantium* by John de Bromyarde (fourteenth century), a Dominican friar. This was the age of tale-sequences, for the middle of the fourteenth century gave us the most famous of European collections, the *Decamerone* of Boccaccio.

Those who were familiar enough with the "romances of prys" to enjoy parodies of them were amused by such salutary tales as *The Turnement of Totenham*, which describes, with excellent command of burlesque, a countryside wedding preceded by the mysteries of a medieval tournament. The spirited octosyllabic couplets of *The Land of Cokaygne* depict a Utopia of gluttony and idleness, a kitchen-land, not where it was "always afternoon", but where it was always feeding-time. The walls of the monastery are built "al af pasteiis" with pinnacles of "fat podinges", and geese already roasted fly to it crying "All hot!".

Nearly all the degrees between gravity and gaiety can be found in the abundant anonymous songs of the thirteenth and fourteenth centuries. What we should like to have is more knowledge of the tunes to which the earliest secular songs were sung. But the history of early English music is a difficult subject, and beyond our purpose.

XVIII. PROSODY OF OLD AND MIDDLE ENGLISH

In form Old English poetry resembles the poetry of other early Teutonic and Scandinavian languages. This form may be described as a long line divided into two halves (or as a couple of short lines) rhythmically connected by alliteration and stress. Generally there are four stressed syllables in each line (or two in each half-line), and of these at least three should be alliterated:

> Wenian mid wynnum. Wat se þe cunnað.

Around the stressed syllables can be grouped a varying number of unstressed syllables; and attempts have been made to classify the variations. Actually we do not know whether there were any rules at all, or whether there was freedom to use any number of syllables that could be held together by the main stresses. The "sprung rhythm" of Gerard Manley Hopkins is a modern revival of free syllabic writing. What should be remembered as important is first, that this freedom in number of syllables is a persistent characteristic of Old English poetry, and next, that apparent irregularities are no more irregular than the blank verse of Shakespeare in his latest plays. In fact, the bulk of Old English poetry is very regular, with the natural variations of rhythm characteristic of all accomplished verse. The lines are consecutive, as in *Paradise Lost*; that is, there is no attempt at any stanza form; though, as we have noted, the lines of *Deor* are broken at irregular intervals by a kind of refrain. Whether this is a more primitive or a more developed form cannot be profitably discussed through sheer lack of evidence. In Old English poetry the lines do not rhyme, save by the accidental occurrence of similar inflections. The one important exception is found in *The Rhyming Poem* of the Exeter Book. Further, there is no evidence that, though rhyme was eschewed, assonance was deliberately sought, as it is in the *Chanson de Roland*. Except in nursery rhymes assonance has never become acclimatized in England, and even modern attempts read like mistakes. Asson-ance makes what we call a "lower class" rhyme, as when the old song matched "In and out the *Eagle*" with "Pop goes the *weasel*". The educated English ear demands not assonance, i.e. similarity of vowels, but true rhyme, i.e. similarity of consonants, and will tolerate "love" and "move" as rhymes, even though the vowel sounds are dissimilar. To these general characteristics of Old English verse we may add one more, a quasi-trochaic rhythm which dominates it, which sometimes retreats, but which always comes back. By the tenth century, the Old English line showed a tendency to break into two halves, and become an unrhymed couplet, with four stresses, strong or weak, in each line. One early —and rather rough—example of this is the "Edgar" poem that begins under the date 959 in the *Old English Chronicle*. Whether the change happened by design or by decay—whether it was the development of a new technique or merely a breakdown of the old—cannot be discussed here. The fact must be accepted that, before the Conquest, "sung metre", i.e. the regular metre of song, was beginning to replace the large freedom of the Old English recitative.

After the Conquest there is a gap of nearly two centuries in the recorded evidence. During that period the Normans had diffused in England not only a new language, but a new scheme of verse, the rigid syllabic system, characteristic of French poetry. Now just as the English ear has never tolerated assonance as a system, so it has never tolerated syllabic regularity as a system. The *Ormulum* is intolerable because it goes on and on in line after line of exactly fifteen syllables arranged with maddening monotony. Layamon's *Brut*, on the other hand, is specially interesting, because the poet knew a little of both tunes, English and French. Much of the *Brut* reads like Old English verse written by a man who had lost the secret of its composition; but constantly there creeps in something resembling the rhyming French octosyllabics.

In *Poema Morale* the fifteen-syllabled line tends, by the frequency of feminine endings, to become fourteen, and to break up, thanks to its rhymes, into the ballad metre of eight and six; moreover, its lines (like those of Robert of Glou-cester) are elastic, not rigid. The Middle English *Genesis and Exodus* (c. 1250) anticipates, in the freedom of its octosyllabic lines, the *Christabel* metre which Coleridge thought he invented more than 500 years later. Happily, the Old English tradition of a pair of half-lines, especially when broken into "sung metre", offered no obstacle to the acclimatization of French stanza-forms; and soon (late thirteenth century) we get, as in Hendyng's *Proverbs*, the *rime couée* which Chaucer ridicules in *Sir Thopas*. By the time we reach the lyrics and romances at the end of the thirteenth century and the beginning of the fourteenth we are moving among familiar English metres. A curious fact is that although five-foot or five-stress lines emerge, no one seems to have used them consecutively and constructively in a poem. For the triumph of the five-stress couplet we had to wait till Chaucer; for the triumph of five-stress blank verse we had to wait till Surrey.

The re-emergence in the fourteenth century of the Old English alliterative line, altered, rhymed, and even used for elaborate stanza-arrangements, is one of those historical literary curiosities of which there are many ingenious but few convincing explanations. The old line blazed with glory in *Sir Gawayne*, touched its height in *Piers Plowman*, and then vanished for ever. Thereafter English verse continues to be metrical, rhymed, and to use alliteration only for a separable and casual ornament, and not as a constituent or property. And, tenaciously, from first to last, English verse clings to syllabic freedom, and refuses to be a slave to French syllabic regularity. In later centuries the trisyllabic foot, as a variant, seemed to vanish, and the eighteenth century frowned upon it as an impediment to "numbers" and "smoothness"; but it came back, and with it returned the characteristic flexibility of the English line.

XIX. CHANGES IN THE LANGUAGE TO THE DAYS OF CHAUCER

The three Germanic peoples—the Jutes from Jutland, the Angles from Schleswig and the Saxons from Holstein—who in the fifth and sixth centuries made themselves masters of southern Britain, spoke dialects so nearly allied that they could have had little difficulty in understanding each other. There was no name for their common race and common language. The Britons called all the invaders Saxons; St Gregory had to call them Angles for the sake of his famous pun; but an emperor called the Anglian king of Northumbria *rex Saxonum*. Though Bede sometimes speaks of *Angli sive Saxones*, his name for the language is *sermo Anglicus*. Alfred, a West Saxon, calls his language *Englisc*. Actually the Anglian name was appropriate, for the history of southern English is largely concerned with the spread of Anglian forms. When Camden used *lingua Anglosaxonica* for pre-Conquest English, he meant not a blend of Anglian and Saxon, but simply "English Saxon" as distinguished from "German Saxon". The term, though misunderstood, tended to survive. The German philologist Jakob Grimm introduced the practice of dividing a language into its Old, Middle and Modern periods, and so the term Old English came into use. There is, of course, no precise point at which people ceased to speak "Old English" and began to speak "Middle English". The terms are merely philological conveniences. However, we may regard the form of language we call Middle English as having emerged about 1150, and as having ceased about 1500, when the printing press conquered the *scriptorium*.

Old English retained its inflectional system; but in course of time the inflections tended to be assimilated. Thus in the declension of Gothic *guma*, a man, there are seven distinctive forms in the eight cases of singular and plural; in the declension of Old English *guma* there are only three. The almost universal substitution of *-es* for the many Old English endings of the genitive singular and nominative and accusative plural began before the Norman Conquest; and in the fourteenth century the English of educated Londoners had lost most of its Southern characteristics and had become a Midland dialect. Chaucer's plurals and genitives end in *-es*, the number of exceptions being hardly greater than in modern English. The dative disappeared from Midland English in the twelfth century. Southern English (Kentish and West Saxon) was much more conservative. The forms of the Old English pronouns of the third person in all dialects were very similar in pronunciation—the pairs *him* and *hoem*, *hire* and *heora*, being easily sounded alike. The ambiguity was got rid of by a process very rare in the history of languages, the adoption of foreign forms. It is from the language of the invading Danes that we get such forms as *they*, *their*, *them*. But the older forms persisted. Chaucer used *her* for *their* and he always has *hem* for *them*. The Old English *ic* became *I* early in the thirteenth century; but in the South *ich* was general. The Old English inflections of adjectives and article, and with them the grammatical genders of nouns, disappeared early in Middle English. In these respects Orm and Chaucer are almost alike. All these changes were once generally believed to have been brought about by the Norman Conquest; but the spoken language had travelled far towards the Middle English stage before 1066. Of course the Norman occupation had influence; the new political unity and development of intercommunication tended to diffuse grammatical simplifications; but if we except such effects as the use of *of* instead of a genitive inflection, and the polite substitution of plural for singular in the second person, hardly any specific influence of French upon English grammar can be traced.

As we have said in an earlier page, the runic alphabet of the heathen English was superseded, under Christian influence, by the Latin alphabet of twenty-two letters, to which were added the runic letters ƿ (called *wynn*), þ (called *thorn*) and ð (called *eth*). The last two were used indifferently and did not represent voiced and unvoiced *th*. The vowels were sounded nearly as in modern Italian, except that *y* was like French *u* and *ae* like *a* in *pat*. The consonants had much the same sound as in modern English. The greatest change in the written language came after the Conquest, and was chiefly a matter of spelling. Children had ceased to read and write English, and were taught to read and write French. When, later, a new generation tried to write English, they spelt in French fashion. The changes in pronunciation are too intricate for summary. How different was the course of development in different parts of the country can be seen in the fact that the English pronunciation *home* and *stone*, and the Scottish *hame* and *stane* both derive from the Old English long *a* as in *father*. The "Zummerzet" pronunciation of initial *f* and *s* as *v* and *z* was common all over the south and is exactly recorded in the Kentish *Ayenbite of Inwit* (1340).

The Norman Conquest had a profound influence on vocabulary. A few French words came in before the Conquest; after that event the number steadily increased. Chaucer is quite wrongly accused of having "corrupted" English by introducing French words. It cannot be proved that he made use of any foreign word that had not already gained a place in the English vocabulary. Very sad is the total loss of many Old English words. In the first thirty lines of Aelfric's homily on St Gregory, there are twenty-two words which had disappeared by the middle of the thirteenth century. The fourteenth century alliterative poets revived some of the ancient epic synonyms for "man" or "warrior" —*bern, renk, wye, freke*; but they did not last.

Only a few peculiarities of dialect can be mentioned here. The use of a dialect, of course, did not indicate an inferior education. Writers employed for literary purposes the language they actually spoke. Chaucer would not have found it easy to read the Kentish *Ayenbite of Inwit* and the North-western *Sir Gawayne* would have puzzled him. The diversity of the written language in the different parts of the country during the fourteenth century may be indicated briefly thus: *they say* = Kentish *hy ziggeth*, South-western *hy siggeth*, East Midland *they seyn*, West Midland *hy* (or *thai*) *sayn*, Northern *thai sai*; *their names* (in the same distribution) = *hare nomen, hure nomen, hir names, hur namus, thair names*. The ultimate triumph of the East Midland dialect was largely due to the fact that it *was* midland, i.e. midway between *hy ziggeth*, and *thai sai*. The fact that Oxford and Cambridge were linguistically in this area had an influence. The London English of Chaucer and the not dissimilar Oxford English of Wyclif became, in fact, the literary language of England.

XX. THE ANGLO-FRENCH LAW LANGUAGE

A special case of the influence of the Conquest upon vocabulary is offered by the Anglo-French law language. The Act of 1362 tried to substitute English for French as the oral language of the courts, but it could not disestablish French as the language of the law itself. Arguments might be conducted in English; the pleadings remained French; and we find Roger North exclaiming, "Really, the Law is scarcely expressible properly in English." This seems a strange utterance from an Englishman living in the age when Berkeley and Bolingbroke, Pope and Swift were writing. But, actually, the law was not expressible properly in English until that language had appropriated to itself scores of French words. The lawyers had made a language as highly technical as that of the chemist or the mathematician; and the result, with that touch of paradox which seems never absent from English affairs, is that the law remained English because it was French. In the critical sixteenth century the national system of jurisprudence which showed the stoutest nationalism was a system that was hardly expressible in the national language. Being in a foreign (technical) language it was tough and impervious to foreign (external) influence. It was protected from the meddlers of many ages; and Roman law did not triumph here as it did in Germany.

Many of the words that once "lay in the mouths" of our serjeants and judges —words descriptive of logical and argumentative processes—were in course of time to be heard far outside the courts of law; "to allege, to aver, to affirm, to avow, to except, to demur, to determine", are a few among them. Old French allowed a free conversion of infinitives into substantives, and so we have "a voucher, a disclaimer, a merger, a tender, an attainder". We need not dwell upon "assize", but may call attention to the strange word "asset", which is no other than *assez* (*asetz*) in disguise—*asetz* being taken as a plural, and giving us the coined and modern singular "asset". In the days when there was little science and none of it popular science, the lawyer mediated between the abstract Latin logic of the schoolmen and the concrete needs and homely talk of gross, unschooled mankind. Law was the point where life and logic met.

CHAPTER II

THE END OF THE MIDDLE AGES

I. *PIERS PLOWMAN* AND ITS SEQUENCE

The anonymity of many poems in Middle English is no cause for regret. We do not greatly care who wrote *Poema Morale* or *King Horn*, and we are even content to let the authorship of the numerous lyrics remain an unanswered question. Almost the only veil we should like to raise is that which hides from us the remarkable poet who wrote *Sir Gawayne*. But we now come to a poem or group of poems more deeply appealing than anything we have yet considered; and we are a little troubled when we find that the author is scarcely even a name. Few English poems of the Middle Ages have had more influence than those grouped under the general title of *The Vision of William concerning Piers the Plowman*. Eagerly read in the latter half of the fourteenth century, the time of their composition, they remained popular throughout the fifteenth century, were regarded by reformers in the sixteenth as an inspiration, and, in modern times, have been cited as a vivid picture of contemporary life and as a stern exposure of social and religious abuses. In all ages they have been read as poetry, that is, as "something more philosophic and of graver import than history". But of the author we know almost nothing.

Let us consider the main facts. We have what appears to be one long poem in alliterative verse of the old form, divided into numerous "passus" or "books", and extant in several versions differing considerably from each other. So popular was the poem that some fifty or sixty manuscripts are still in existence, though, rather strangely, it remained unprinted till 1550. Skeat, its major editor, distinguishes three principal versions or texts, the A text, B text and C text. The A text contains three visions that come to the writer as he is sleeping by a stream-side among the Malvern Hills. From various clues, some internal, some external, the following reconstruction has been made: The author was William Langland (or Langley) born in 1331–2 somewhere near the Malvern Hills. He was educated in the school of the Benedictine monastery at Malvern and probably took minor orders, but never rose in the church. By 1362 he was in London, poor, and writing his poem. He began with the vision of Lady Meed (prologue and passus I–IV), went on to the vision of Piers the Plowman (passus V–VIII), and presently added the vision of Do-well, Do-bet, Do-best (passus IX–XII). This constitutes the A text—twelve passus containing 2567 lines. Moved by indignation at the evils of the age he took up the poem again in 1377 and expanded it to nearly thrice its original length. The existing lines were very little changed, but many insertions were made; passus XII was cancelled and replaced by nine new passus. This is the B text. Total: twenty passus, 7242 lines. About 1393 (or 1398) the author took up the poem again and redistributed the B text with some alterations. This makes the C text, very like B, but arranged in twenty-three passus, containing 7357 lines. About 1399 he began (according to Skeat) another poem called *Richard the Redeless*, dealing with the last years of Richard II. It is a fragment containing a prologue (without its beginning) and four passus (the last a fragment). That, apparently, was the end of his work. The reader must not suppose that there is anything at all improbable in these periodical enlargements and reconsiderations of a long poem by its author during his life. The nineteenth century *Festus* (for example), by Philip James Bailey, was for fifty years the steadily enlarged receptacle of the author's opinions.

The inferences and conjectures of Skeat were challenged in 1908 by the American scholar J. M. Manly in the second volume of the *Cambridge History*. Relying upon differences of diction, matter and method (some of them generally admitted and attributed to change or development in the poet) Manly distinguished five separate authors. He held that failure to recognize the presence of these different hands had led to a mistaken charge of vagueness and obscurity, and had contributed to a misunderstanding of the objects and aims of the satire contained in the poems separately and collectively. These views led in turn to many rejoinders, the most important of which were published by the Early English Text Society in 1910 under the title *The Piers Plowman Controversy*. Generally speaking, Manly's views found little favour with later scholars and were rejected outright, for example, by George Kane (editor of the A text in 1960) in his *Piers Plowman: The Evidence for Authorship* (1965). As Nevill Coghill puts it: "Reason that could convince was never shown and critics have now ceased to saw the poet asunder". What Ifor Evans well calls "the plastic surgery of scholarship" has put William Langland together again.

Piers Plowman should be read as a great poem, and not as material for the higher criticism or as a text-book of social discontent. Its fervent adoption by reformers, ecclesiastical and economic, has tended to obscure the absolute poetic greatness by which alone, like Dante's *Divina Commedia*, it endures in the heart. Its grave and moving music, its creative charity, its vivid pictures of person and place, and its imaginative criticism of life, make it one of our greatest long poems. It is, in one sense, a beacon light of farewell. In it the Old English alliterative line, strangely rekindled, blazes up to a glorious end, and is seen no more.

In a Cambridge MS. of the B text occurs the poem which Skeat called *Richard the Redeless* from a phrase in the first line of the first passus. An old note indicates that it was known as *Mum, Sothsegger* (Hush, Truthteller). Nothing was known of it but the Cambridge fragment, which contains 857 lines; but in 1928 a manuscript was casually discovered, apparently part of the same poem, adding another 1750 lines. The whole is now published as *Mum and the Sothsegger*. The attribution to Langland is no longer accepted. In the poem there is no vision as in *Piers Plowman*, but there is plenty of allegory or symbolism to express its criticism of Richard II's weakness and the misdeeds of his friends.

Two very interesting poems, *The Parlement of the Thre Ages* and *Wynnere and Wastere* (see p. 40) may have preceded *Piers Plowman*. Like the greater poem they are moral and critical. Both employ the popular machinery of a vision, and both have considerable power and interest. To 1393 or thereabouts belongs the remarkable poem called *Peres the Ploughmans Crede*. The versification is imitated from *Piers the Plowman*, and the theme, as well as the title, was clearly suggested by it. It is, however, not a vision, but an account of the writer's search for someone to teach him his creed. The poem is notable both for the vigour of its satire and the vividness of its descriptions. With the *Crede* is associated the pseudo-Chaucerian poem in stanzas known as *The Ploughman's Tale*, attributed to the same author. Part of the piece as existing was written during the controversies of the sixteenth century, but it may contain genuine stanzas of a fourteenth-century Lollard original. Three other associated pieces, *Jacke Uplande*, *The Reply of Friar Daw Thopias* and *The Rejoinder of Jacke Upland* are vigorous examples of popular religious controversy, but they have no merit as literature.

The influence of *Piers the Plowman* lasted, as we have seen, for several centuries. Interest in the poem and in its central figure was greatly quickened by the supposed relations between it and Wyclifism. The name or the figure of the Plowman appears in numerous poems and prose writings, and allusions of many kinds abound. He became a symbol and set the pattern of social and religious criticism in his own age, and is not without significance, even in this.

The fourteenth century, which has for beginning the accession of Edward II and for ending the deposition of Richard II, can hardly be called glorious, even when the barren exploits of Edward III and the Black Prince are favourably considered. Nevertheless the century of the Black Death comprises within its limits the beneficent and salutary lives of Chaucer, of Wyclif, and of others less known, or known not at all, who fought for mercy, justice, and the light in the mind and the soul. Not least among these were the authors of *Piers Plowman* and the poems that cluster round it.

II. RELIGIOUS MOVEMENTS IN THE FOURTEENTH CENTURY

As we have seen, it is difficult to identify individual writers in the Middle Ages. Both the general disposition and the literary habits of the time tended to hide the traces of individual hands. The importance now attached to personal authorship would have been incomprehensible to the medieval mind. No one wrote for gain; nor could there be anything like property rights in books until printing multiplied them and made them marketable; and even then, what was sold was the work of the printer, not the work of the author. When books were still literally written, several hands sometimes contributed to a lengthy manuscript; and works of special appeal were widely copied and imitated, often with changes, designed or accidental, that make text and authorship uncertain. So it happens that the work of one man may be attributed to a school or collection of similar thinkers, or the work of such a school may be attributed to one man. We have already seen that all alliterative poems of a certain type were attributed to the author of *Piers Plowman*, just as all Flemish paintings of a certain type used to be attributed to Van Eyck; we have now to observe two further examples of the same tendency, namely, the attribution to Richard Rolle and John

Wyclif of all the mystical or controversial works composed under their inspiration.

Richard Rolle of Hampole (1300?–49?), "Richard Hermit", as he was called, left Oxford at nineteen, eager, for his soul's health, to live the life of a recluse. He took with him into retirement the usual knowledge of religious philosophy and a great love for the Scriptures. He settled finally at Hampole near Doncaster, where he was regarded as a saint. He stood aloof from life academical, ecclesiastical or civil, and sought the closest knowledge of God. He spread his doctrine, first by preaching, and next by writing. His works, with their intense personal feeling, sympathy and simplicity, give him a high place among those who have recorded religious convictions and experiences. In form Rolle marks a stage of transition, for he makes extensive use of alliteration in prose and in verse, whether Latin or English. His Latin works, some of which have autobiographical interest, hardly concern us, though they had considerable influence on the Continent. His works in English give us a clear view of his mind and feelings. An English Psalter contains, with much that is experimental, some excellent renderings, and with Lollard additions and interpolations had a wide circulation. *Meditations on the Passion* may suggest the prose ecstasies of an earlier period (see p. 27), but there is clear gain in lucidity. Rolle's few lyrics resemble his prose, which seems constantly at the point of breaking into song. For a recluse at Ainderby he wrote or translated in prose *The Form of Living*, the finest of his English works, and for a nun of Yedingham he wrote his beautiful *Ego dormio et cor meum vigilat*, also in prose. Both contain passages of verse. It is hard to distinguish between the work of Rolle and that of his followers. Much was attributed to him that he could not have written. Rolle was a practical mystic. Recognizing that, for most people, life must be active, he tried to teach the spirit in which that life may be lived. *The Pricke of Conscience*, a summary of medieval theology in nearly 10,000 lines of octosyllabic couplets, was generally attributed to Rolle; but the evidence is against his authorship. Rolle is among the best prose writers of his time, achieving often an ease and conciseness rare among writers of his special character.

Like Rolle, John Wyclif (1320–84) was a Yorkshireman, born near Richmond. He spent much of his life at Oxford, where he lectured on theology and incurred the first suspicion of heresy. No place was more democratic than a medieval university. Thither all classes came, and the ideas born in a lecture room at Oxford were soon carried to distant places in England and in countries abroad. Bohemian scholars like Jerome of Prague made Wyclif's teaching familiar in central Europe, where his most famous follower was John Hus. Wyclif, though bound by the methods of scholastic philosophy, made his own strong personality felt. We can scarcely discern this in Latin works which had for medieval students a force that we cannot recapture; nevertheless it is there. But Wyclif, great scholar though he was, turned naturally to the native tongue, and in his preaching touched the hearts of a larger public. His doctrines owed something to William of Ockham, but even more to Grosseteste and FitzRalph, Archbishop of Armagh. From the latter he drew the doctrine of dominion or lordship, to which a special meaning came to be attached. Wyclif's expression "dominion is founded in grace" was applied later in a material way not originally intended by him or his master. Wyclif cannot be claimed as a fourteenth century anticipation of Karl Marx or as a preacher of the dictatorship of the proletariat. He was the last of the English scholastic philosophers, not the first of English political agitators. His theological views aroused much discussion and he became skilful in controversy. These intellectual combats with opponents helped to make widely known his firm belief that endowments were the root of all evil in the church and that it was the duty of civil power to enforce reformation by seizing church property. The years 1366-7 saw the resistance to the tribute paid by England to Rome and the growth of a strong court party favourable to the taxation of the church and hostile to the employment of ecclesiastics in political office. Wyclif's views were welcomed by this party, and John of Gaunt asked him to London to preach on the anti-clerical side. His activities aroused many enemies, and Rome endeavoured to silence his teaching. One of his larger Latin works *De Veritate Sacrae Scripturae* belongs to this time. The Great Schism arising from the election of "anti-pope" Clement VII (1378) in opposition to Pope Urban VI made Wyclif definitely anti-papal. Henceforth for him the Pope was "Anti-Christ", not in any mystical sense, but as the enemy of Christ's teaching. Wyclif no longer confined himself to the criticism of abuses; he questioned the righteousness of every part of the ecclesiastical system. The one feature of church life with which he had sympathy was the poverty and the popular preaching of the friars. This feeling led him to institute his "poor priests", who began their itinerant preaching about 1377. Wyclif's preachers at first were priests; but later many of them were laymen, and, as happens sometimes with enthusiastic disciples, they hardened his teaching into general hostility to all social and ecclesiastical institutions. Wyclif stimulated public opinion, but he must not be held responsible for the excesses of the later Lollards.

The Scriptures were the rock upon which Wyclif built, and his constant appeal to them gained him the title of *Doctor Evangelicus*. There is a strong tradition that he translated the whole Bible into English: but the extent of his participation is not actually known. There are two Wyclif versions, one earlier in date, stiff, uneasy, and afraid to leave the safe anchorage of Latin, the other later, bolder and daring to be English. Both were made from the Vulgate. As we have seen, versions and paraphrases of various parts of the scriptures had been made from early times. The obscure history of pre-Wyclif translations, some made for special reasons, cannot be discussed here. The Wyclifite versions, however, had a much wider purpose, and were meant for the whole general public. The numerous manuscripts are an indication that the aim was achieved. With Wyclif worked Nicholas Hereford and John Purvey. One manuscript containing part of the earlier version directly attributes the translation to Hereford. The revised version ascribed to Purvey is, however, manifestly superior in all respects. But no doubt several hands contributed to the great task. The translation, widely known as it was, assisted the development of English prose as a means of expression. Some parts are uneasy, and there are few touches of the almost miraculous felicity that was to establish later versions in the hearts of the people; nevertheless, there are equally few lapses into the mire of formlessness that makes some of the pseudo-Wyclif or Lollard utterances a heavy trial to the endurance. Whatever part was played by Wyclif himself in the actual translation, he was the moving spirit of the work. It came as the reply to his demand that the written source of the faith should be available for all in the language most familiar to them. The version may not be Wyclif's; but it is Wyclifite, and it was the first complete rendering of the Bible into English.

The last few years of Wyclif's life were marked by the controversy that followed his teaching against transubstantiation—the fundamental basis of priesthood. He denounced the doctrine as a philosophical impossibility; he made no attack on the sacrament as a ceremony. A council at Blackfriars (1382) condemned Wyclif's teaching, but there seems to have been no attempt at restraint of person, for after censure of his doctrines at Oxford he retired to Lutterworth, where he died on the last day of 1384. The work he produced in Latin and English towards the end of his life is enormous in bulk and uncompromising in spirit. The writings in Latin, such as the *Opus Evangelicum* and the *Trialogus*, with its three interlocutors, are more important than those in English. One effect of the universality of Latin in medieval times is that this great Englishman has left no original English book by which he can be remembered. The collected volumes of Wyclif's English works contain numerous brief sermons or expositions and controversial tracts, but from this mass of plain, pedestrian writing nothing emerges to arrest the attention of later readers unconcerned in the party politics of theology. Two tracts in English, *De Officio Pastorali* and *De Papa*, contained in the Early English Text Society's volume (1880), will give a favourable idea of the Wyclifite manner. There can, however, be no certainty that the English is Wyclif's own. Much that used to be attributed to Wyclif cannot be his; but his influence was very widely spread, and he was, perhaps, the first writer in English to make an appeal to his countrymen of all ranks, districts and dialects as one united body. Wyclif had always been moved by the warmest national feeling. It is shameful, therefore, to have to relate that, at the bidding of the Council of Constance in 1415, the bones of a great Englishman were dug up and burnt and the ashes cast into the water of the Swift. Hus was burnt alive. Wyclif is one of those who give rise to great movements and are lost in the life they have created. To us his writings are remote and obscure, and the man himself dim as a shadow on the heaving waters of ecclesiastical controversy; but his work abides, transmuted into the freedom of faith and thought which he helped to win for us.

III. THE BEGINNINGS OF ENGLISH PROSE

The triumph of English over French is attested by certain facts that can be briefly noted. Three successive parliaments (1362–4) were opened by speeches in English from the Chancellor. A statute of 1362 ordered legal proceedings to be conducted in English on the ground that French was no longer sufficiently understood. After the Black Death, English instead of French was used as the medium of instruction in schools. Trevisa, writing in 1385, tells us that this vital reform was the work of John Cornwall and his disciple Richard Pencrich. By the end of the fourteenth century it could no longer be assumed that French and Latin were familiar to all lettered persons. The pseudo-Mandeville wrote in French for gentlemen who had no Latin, and was able to steal his matter from Latin works without detection. Books of information had therefore to be put into English, and among those translated were *De Proprietatibus Rerum* by Bartholomeus Anglicus, the *Polychronicon* of Ranulf Higden, and *The Travels of Sir John Mandeville*. These translations became recognized authorities among the reading public of the fifteenth century, and they may be regarded as the beginning of popular readable English prose. All were accepted as veracious. The geography of Mandeville, the science of Bartholomew, and the legends of Higden were taken as literally as their citations from Holy Writ.

The first of our great translators, John Trevisa (1326–1412), was a contemporary of Wyclif at Oxford and suffered ejectment in 1379, probably for Wyclifite leanings. Ranulf Higden (d. 1364) had written his *Polychronicon* about 1350, beginning (as usual) with the Creation, and coming down to his own time, taking all the legends of all the known histories by the way. Trevisa's version was completed in 1387, and by 1398 he had finished a translation of *De Proprietatibus Rerum*, the author of which, known as Bartholomew the Englishman (Bartholomew de Glanville, fl. 1250), was a minorite friar and theological professor in the university of Paris. His work is an encyclopedia of universal knowledge in nineteen books, and in the later version of "Batman upon Bartholomew" was current in Elizabethan times, although much of its information was at least a thousand years out of date. The section on birds includes bees, and its picture of these industrious and orderly creatures was the immediate origin of the innumerable apologues that adorn the literature of the time. Trevisa was no pedant. He did not care how far he strayed from his Latin as long as he gave Englishmen good English to read. He is expansive, and he is fond (as we all are) of the doublet. Thus, *limites* becomes "the meeres and the marke", and *antiquitas* is stretched into "long passynge of tyme and elde of deedes". A point of special interest in the translation of Bartholomew is the rendering of Scriptural quotations. These Trevisa puts forth in a version certainly not Wyclif's, and probably his own. Always simple and picturesque, these passages cause regret for the loss of that translation of the Bible which, according to Caxton, Trevisa made.

The Travels of Sir John Mandeville had been a household word in eleven languages and for five centuries before it was ascertained that Sir John never lived, that his travels never took place, and that his alleged personal experiences were compiled out of all the authorities back to Pliny. Ostensibly the book is a guide and itinerary for pilgrims to the Holy Land (with diversions to Tartary and China), but actually it is a collection of tales and legends and oddities of natural history admirably put together from many sources. The author takes no account of time, for though his references to Hungary are up to date, some of his observations on Palestine are three centuries out. In his convincing presentation of fiction as fact, he anticipates Defoe. The "plot" of the story is simple. A certain John de Mandeville, knight of St Albans, left England in 1322 to make the pilgrimage to Jerusalem. He travelled all over the world, and on his return in 1343 was taken ill at Liège, where he was attended by a doctor who persuaded him to alleviate his sufferings by writing an account of his travels. It is probable that the real author was an industrious compiler of books, Jean d'Outremeuse, whose *Myreur des Histors* contains the story of an old man who confessed to Outremeuse on his death-bed that he was John de Mandeville, Earl of Montfort, etc., who had been compelled to live in disguise because he had killed a man of rank. Outremeuse adds other details, none of which can be confirmed. Whoever the author was, Jean d'Outremeuse or another, he carried out the most successful literary fraud ever known in one of the most delightful books ever written. No less than 300 MSS. are said to be in existence, and there are at least three distinct English versions. The unknown translators of Mandeville made a genuine contribution to English literature. The prose moves steadily and smoothly without the lavish colloquialism of Trevisa or the uncouthness of the Wyclifite sermons. In a sense it was a new venture in our literature, a prose work which, thinly disguised as a manual for pilgrims, was written as a book of pure amusement. Prose, which had maintained a high level in homiletic compositions, had hitherto been associated with edification. True, "Sir John" is at times soberly instructive; but we like to think of him as the unknown benefactor who added the Lady of Lango, the Lady of the Sparrowhawk, the Great Cham and Prester John to general mythology.

IV. THE SCOTTISH LANGUAGE: EARLY AND MIDDLE SCOTS

In the fourteenth century, the language of Barbour's *Bruce*, written in Aberdeen, is closely akin to the language of *The Pricke of Conscience*, written in Yorkshire. The differences are almost negligible. To Barbour and his successors their tongue is not "Scots" but "Ynglis". In its original application "Scots" is the speech of the Scottish settlers in Alban, that is, Celtic of the Goidelic group, the ancestor of the present Scottish Gaelic. Later the name was applied to the language of the entire area north of the line joining the estuaries of Forth and Clyde. In the thirteenth century, "Ynglis" is the speech of the "Scottish" court and of the surrounding Anglian population in the Lothians and Angus, and "Scots" the speech of the northern and western provinces. Even at the close of the fifteenth century "Scots" is the name for the Gaelic speech of north and west. By Lothian writers this "Scots" is referred to as the speech of savages; they themselves, Scots, subjects of the king of Scots, and proud of their Scotland, are careful to say that the language they speak is "Ynglis". It is not until the sixteenth century that what was called "Ynglis" becomes "Scots" and what was called "Scots" becomes "Ersch" or "Yrisch" (Irish). This break with the family name indicates a change in the language itself, resulting from the gradual cessation of intercourse with England after the War of Independence, and the change is discernible from the middle of the fifteenth century. Though the names are open to objection, it is convenient to adopt the following terms for the stages of language: before 1300, Northumbrian or Early Northern English; 1300–1450, Early Scots; 1450–1620, Middle Scots. The typical examples of Early Scots are Barbour's *Bruce* and Wyntoun's *Chronicle*; of Middle Scots the writings of Henryson, Dunbar, Douglas and Lyndsay. For the sake of exactness, we may distinguish an Early Transition Scots (1420–60), typified by *The Kingis Quair*, and *Lancelot of the Laik*; but the language of these poems represents no type, literary or spoken; it is a bookish fabrication, containing southern and pseudo-southern forms derived from Chaucer.

The greater Middle Scots writers used what was in some respects an artificial language, a language which was not the spoken language of any people. They were conscious literary artists, delighting in "aureate" mannerism, and seeking to "illumine" the vernacular with "fresh, enamelled terms". The chief modifying causes at work in the language were English, Latin and French. The English influence, which is the strongest, came from Chaucer, from religious and controversial literature, and from the political and social relations with England before and after the accession of James VI. In poetry Chaucer's influence is the most important, and it led to an increase in the Romance elements of the language. Not only was the vocabulary influenced, but fantastic grammatical forms, unknown and impossible to the northern dialect, were borrowed. In prose the political and religious influences are most important. The language of nearly all religious literature from the middle of the sixteenth century is either southern or strongly anglicized. Until the publication of the Bassandyne Bible (1576–9), all copies of the Scriptures were imported from England, and the Bassandyne, as authorized by the Reformed Kirk, is a close transcript of the Geneva version. Knox himself is the most English of Scottish prose writers, and the Catholic pamphleteers girded at the Protestants for their southernism. The going of the court to England in 1603 ended the artificial Middle Scots. All the poets, Alexander, Drummond and the rest, became "Elizabethan" in language and sentiment. When Scottish literature revives a century or more later, its language is the spoken dialect of the Lothians and the west.

The influence of French has been exaggerated. The French element in Middle Scots represents three stages of borrowing: first the material incorporated during the process of Anglo-French settlements in the Lothians; next the Anglo-French material drawn from the English of Chaucer and the Chaucerians; and third, the material adopted from central French during the close relations between France and Scotland. The last influence, once supposed to be the most powerful, is actually the least. Nearly all the Romance elements in Middle Scots which cannot be traced to English (i.e. Anglo-French) influence, are of Latin and not of French origin; and even supposed Gallicisms of grammar such as the adjective plural and the postponement of the adjective (e.g. *inimy mortall*) are relics of Latin syntactical habit. The long tradition of legal and theological Latin must not be forgotten in any consideration of linguistic peculiarities. Latin itself was important in the moulding of Middle Scots. Such different authors as John of Ireland, a writer of vernacular prose, Gavin Douglas, the accomplished poet, and the author of *The Complaynt of Scotlande* give direct testimony to the need they felt of drawing from Latin; but they are silent about French. The influence of Celtic is questionable, and in any case small.

V. THE EARLIEST SCOTTISH LITERATURE

Of a Scottish literature before the War of Independence there is no trace. It is difficult to believe that no such literature existed; but, as the dialect of Scotland was not yet clearly differentiated, a Scottish literature could hardly be identified, save by clear local allusions. The earliest poetry extant appears in the few pathetic verses on the death of Alexander III (1286). It is with Barbour, whose poem *The Bruce* is a triumphant chronicle of the making of the new kingdom by Robert and Edward Bruce and the great "James of Douglas", that Scottish literature begins. John Barbour (1320–96) was a typical prosperous churchman, who must have been between fifty and sixty when he finished his poem. *The Bruce*, like other national epics, mingles fancy with fact, for it begins by confusing Robert the Bruce with his grandfather, and treats the principal actors as heroes of romance. But though Barbour is an ardent patriot, he does his best to be fair. He can hardly be called an inspired poet. He was a God-fearing churchman and statesman, who sought to put on record the story of his country's deliverance, before it should be forgotten. What he attempted he achieved. He writes easily—too easily, for he finds the octosyllabic couplet so facile that at times he falls into the merest commonplace. The battle of Bannockburn occupies a disproportionate space in the poem; but Bannockburn was a famous victory, and the account of it is the poet's masterpiece. If Barbour has not the highest qualities of an epic or narrative poet, he is at least rapid, simple, sincere and unpretentious. To Barbour have been attributed other pieces—*Lives of the Saints*, a lengthy work in couplets, adapted from various Latin sources, *The Stewartis Oryginalle*, which carries the genealogy of the Scottish kings back to the builder of Nineveh, a fragmentary *Siege of Troy*, found in a Cambridge MS., and *The Buik of Alexander*. The last is a good poem; but Barbour's claims to the authorship of these works need not be discussed; it is by *The Bruce* that he endures.

Lasting popularity was secured by another national epic, Blind Harry's *Wallace*, which, in a modernized version, was a popular volume up to the nineteenth century. The hero, being more genuinely a Scot than Bruce, and more certainly a tragic figure, appealed to the popular imagination. The poem departs even further from historical fact and chronology than Barbour's. *Bruce* is in the main a chronicle; *Wallace* is a patriotic poem with all the defects of its kind. Next to nothing is known of the author. He seems to have been a wandering minstrel, blind from birth, and to have lived between 1460 (the probable date of the poem) and 1492. There is not much conviction in the argument that he could not have been blind because he has descriptive passages and borrows freely from Barbour and Chaucer, for blind persons can imitate descriptions and borrow from authors read to them. The main charge against the poem is that it is unhistorical and unoriginal. The character of Wallace is, in fact, a combination of Barbour's Douglas and Chaucer's knight. There is only one manuscript, which may have been written down from the author's dictation. Regarded as a late traditional romance, *Wallace* has merit: it is quite good minstrel work. The decasyllabic couplet is well used, and there is no lack of verve in the battle scenes.

George Neilson, who has closely examined the borrowings from Barbour, is severe upon it. "As history," he says, "the poem is the veriest nightmare. As literature it requires an almost deranged patriotism to accept as worthy of the noble memory of Sir William Wallace so vitiated a tribute."

One incident in *Wallace* is borrowed from *The Buke of the Howlat*, a poem written about 1450 by Sir Richard Holland in an elaborate lyrical stanza (found in other pieces) composed of thirteen alliterative rhyming lines, nine long followed by four short, rhyming *ababababcdddc*. It tells the familiar tale of the bird in borrowed plumes, a tale at least as old as *Barlaam and Josaphat*, and it had some historical application not clearly intelligible. Incidentally it gives a version of the journey undertaken by Douglas with the heart of Bruce. This is the Douglas version and differs from the account in Barbour's *Bruce*. Indeed, much of the piece is occupied with Douglas matters, not now interesting, though it is the source of the traditional Douglas epithets, "tendir and trewe".

Like this poem in form, but of an earlier date, is a series of romances which cluster about the name of "Huchoun of the Awle Ryale", one of the most mysterious figures in our early literature. The earliest mention of him is to be found in Wyntoun's *Orygynale Cronykil*, written about 1420. Wyntoun, in describing King Arthur's conquests, remarks that "Huchoun of the Awle Ryale, In til his Gest Hystoriale" has treated this matter; and in a spirit of admiration mentions other works by him—*The Gret Gest of Arthure*, *The Anteris of Gawane* and *The Epistill als of Suete Susane*. The identity of Huchoun has never been clearly established, in spite of ingenious efforts and vigorous discussion. All we need say is that there seems good evidence for the existence of a Scottish poet called Huchoun in the middle of the fourteenth century, and that he may be the statesman Sir Hew of Eglintoun, who was an older contemporary of Barbour. The "Awle Ryale" is the *Aula Regalis*, and would be an appropriate addition to the name of one who had served as justiciar. But no less a person than Henry Bradley believed it to be Oriel College. The next difficulty is the identification of the poems attributed to Huchoun in Wyntoun's lines. *The Gret Gest of Arthure* has been identified with the alliterative *Morte Arthure* of the Thornton MS. at Lincoln (see p. 39). The *Anteris* (adventures) *of Gawayne* is perhaps *The Awntyrs of Arthure at the Terne Wathelyne*, or *Golagros and Gawayne* or even *Sir Gawayne and the Grene Knight* (see pp. 36, 40). The *Epistill of Suete Susane*, which occurs in several versions, is a versified form of *Susanna and the Elders* from the Apocrypha, a story which, as many paintings prove, appealed to the medieval mind. It is written in twenty-eight *Howlat* stanzas, but with a "bob" of two syllables like *Tho thare* or *So sone* at the ninth line. The *Awntyrs of Arthure* tells a good story in fifty-five *Howlat* stanzas. *Golagros and Gawayne* contains a hundred and five stanzas of the same type. As no manuscript is known—the piece surviving in a printed pamphlet of 1508—little can be inferred about its date.

The popular and amusing *Rauf Coilyear* passes from Arthur to Charlemagne. The story describes how Charles, lost in a snowstorm, finds a night's lodging in the house of Rauf, a collier or charcoal-burner. The inevitable complications of royalty *incognito* take place, and the blunt, honest Rauf, as usual, shows up well, and the good fellow is made knight and marshal of France. It is almost a parody on the old romances; but the tale has plenty of movement and, what is lacking in other romances, plenty of humour. Two other stories, mentioned by Gavin Douglas, are *John the Reeve*, clearly an English work, and *The Tale of Colkelbie's Sow*, as clearly Scottish. This animal is sold for three pennies, each of which has a great adventure. The story was obviously very popular, but it makes a sorry end to the old romances.

But the Scots of the fourteenth and fifteenth centuries did not spend all their leisure in hearing or reading romances or Barbour's *Lives of the Saints*. They had an equal interest in the chronicles. *Scalacronica*, compiled in Norman French by Sir Thomas Gray (*c.* 1355) and *Scotichronicon* compiled in Latin by John of Fordun and his continuator Walter Bower or Bowmaker (*c.* 1384–1449) hardly concern the student of English literature. Even Andrew of Wyntoun (d. 1420?), who wrote *The Orygynale Cronykil* in Barbour's couplet and in the Scottish tongue, is merely a chronicler with no claim to be received as a poet. The name of his work means that he went back to the beginning of things, as do the others; but Wyntoun surpasses them in beginning with a book on the history of angels. The most famous of his stories tells of Macbeth's meeting with the weird sisters and the coming of Birnam wood to Dunsinane. Into his perversions of history for patriotic purposes we are not required to enter.

VI. GOWER

The work of John Gower (1325–1408), apart from its intrinsic merit, deserves special notice as indicating the faint doubt with which educated men of his time regarded the English language. If a fourteenth-century poet wished to do justice to himself and a noble theme, in what language should he write? He had the choice of French, Latin and some form of English, and was probably capable of using all three with equal facility; but if he wanted to appeal to a large, rather than to a select audience, he found himself almost bound to write in English, and equally bound to find the best English to write in. Dante had felt a similar difficulty a century before, and wrote *De Vulgari Eloquentia* in Latin to prove that a poet could write in Italian. But the *Divina Commedia* was a stronger argument than any treatise. Gower solved the difficulty about the three languages of England in a way of his own: he wrote in all of them. His first work of any magnitude was the French poem *Speculum Meditantis*, or *Speculum Hominis*, or *Mirour de l'Omme*, long lost and not discovered till 1895. His next venture was in Latin; and it was not till the last decade of the century that he adopted English as the vehicle of literary expression. That he was acquainted with Chaucer is clear from the conclusion of *Troilus and Criseyde* in which that poet directs his book to "moral Gower" and "philosophical Strode".

The literary work of Gower is represented chiefly by those three books upon which the head of his effigy rests in Southwark Cathedral, the French *Speculum Meditantis*, the Latin *Vox Clamantis*, and the English *Confessio Amantis*. In his own Latin note the poet tells us why he wrote each of these works. The first, in French, was designed to teach the way by which sinners could return to a knowledge of the Creator. The second, in Latin, was intended to point the moral of Richard II's misdoings. The third, in English, marks out the time from Nebuchadnezzar onwards, tells how Alexander was instructed by the discipline of Aristotle, but relates chiefly the infatuated passion of lovers. Thus Gower was consciously didactic, though his books have a higher literary quality than is found in most works of edification.

Speculum Hominis or *Speculum Meditantis*, the French work, placed first by Gower, ranks first in order of time. It has come down to us in a single copy, under the French title *Mirour de l'Omme*. For several centuries it disappeared and was supposed to have perished. In it we get the familiar allegory of Sin, daughter of the Devil, giving birth to Death. The poet then discusses the moral history of mankind and declares that we must approach God and Christ through the help of Mary, whose life he proceeds to narrate. The poem is a true literary work with a due connection of parts, and not a mere string of sermons; but the poet, unfortunately, says everything at such length that he becomes wearisome. The most remarkable feature of the work is the mastery which the writer displays over the language and the verse. The rhythm is both French and English, being strictly syllabic as well as accentual. Chaucer's verse also depended upon this combination of the French syllabic principle with the English accentual principle—a combination so alien to English traditions that it could not survive the changes caused in the language by the loss of weak inflectional syllables; and therefore, in the fifteenth century, English metre showed signs of collapse. In Chaucer's verse we see only the final results of the French influence; in Gower we see both the French and the English tendencies.

The very interesting social material of the *Mirour de l'Omme* is used again in Gower's next work, the Latin *Vox Clamantis*. Here, however, a great political event is made the text for his criticism of society. The Peasants' Rising of 1381 seemed a fulfilment of the prophecies contained in the *Mirour*, and it made a strong impression upon Gower, whose native county of Kent was deeply affected. The poem is in Latin elegiac couplets, and extends to about ten thousand lines. The first book, about one-fifth of the whole, contains a graphic account of the insurrection. In general, the *Vox Clamantis* is an indictment of human society; and so the picture, which appears in several manuscripts, of the author aiming his arrows at the world fairly represents its scope. There is no need to dwell upon the poetical style of Gower's Latin poems. Judged by the medieval standard, *Vox Clamantis* is fairly good in language and in metre, but many couplets and longer passages are borrowed from other writers.

In *Confessio Amantis* Gower partly abandons his former determined morality, and, admitting frankly that he was not born to set the world right, proceeds to tell stories about Love, which, after all, is a main motive in the world of men. Accordingly we have in *Confessio Amantis* more than a hundred stories of varying length and of very diverse origin, from Ovid to the Bible, told in a pleasing and simple style by one who clearly had a gift for story-telling, though without the large humanity which makes the stories of Chaucer unique in the literature of his time. The plan of the work is not ill-conceived; but, unfortunately, Gower had no sense of proportion in execution and no control over his fatal weakness for digressions and dissertations. The influence of Chaucer is apparent in the opening and concluding scenes, and something was clearly derived from the *Roman de la Rose*. But to say this is not to accuse Gower of wanting originality. No previous writer, either in English or in any other modern language, had versified so large a collection of stories or had devised so ingenious and elaborate a scheme of combination. Gower's style of narration is simple and clear. In the actual telling of a story he is neither tedious nor diffuse. But he has no humour and no command of character. Yet he has definite poetic qualities of a kind. The descriptive touches indicate that he had observed as well as meditated. It is unfortunate that most readers know him by one of his less happy efforts, the long story of Apollonius used by the author of *Pericles*, in which Gower appears appropriately as Chorus. The language, like that of Chaucer, indicates the development of a cultured English speech replacing the once prevalent French as the language of polite literature. The most marked feature of Gower's English verse is its great regularity and the extent to which it uses inflectional endings for metrical purposes. It shows, like his French verse, an almost complete combination of the accentual with the syllabic principle.

The other works of Gower do not call for notice. In French we have the series of ballades commonly known as *Cinkante Balades*, dealing with love according to the conventions of the age, in a graceful and poetical fashion. In Latin, the author sets forth his final view of contemporary history in the *Cronica Tripertita*, a poem in leonine hexameters. Early in the reign of Henry IV he became blind, and, like a more famous poet, makes in one place a touching allusion to his affliction.

That Gower, through the purity of his English style and the easy fluency of his expression, exercised a distinct influence upon the development of the language cannot be questioned. But though he may fairly be joined with Chaucer as one of the makers of standard English, his mind was narrowly medieval and shows nothing of Chaucer's creative imagination.

VII. CHAUCER

Chaucer is not merely the greatest English poet of medieval times, he is one of the greatest English poets of all times. Yet we are still without definite knowledge about parts of his life. We possess no autograph manuscript of any of his works; we have no more than a conjectural knowledge of the order in which he wrote his poems; and we were long in ascertaining what constitutes the genuine Chaucerian canon. We are now so accustomed to clearly published and advertised authorship that we forget the cheerful anonymity of medieval literature and the tendency of older writers to abandon their literary children as soon as the pangs of birth were over. Gower tells us something definite about his major works. Chaucer tells us a little, but that little is casual and incomplete; and he made no attempt to collect his writings, or to catalogue them, or even to finish them. What we do know of Chaucer is that he inherited the high courtly tradition of French poetry, and that, with all his Italian acquirements and his English spirit, he was French in the grace and skill of his technique. He led a useful public life, enduring personal and general misfortune with courage, and never lost faith in truth, beauty and goodness. He took a large, sagacious, charitable view of mankind, and (like another poet) travelled "on life's common way in cheerful godliness".

Geoffrey Chaucer (1340?-1400), born in London, was connected in some official capacity with the royal court. In 1359 he was taken prisoner in the French wars, and was ransomed in 1360. Apparently he was in France again in 1369, abroad somewhere on royal business in 1370, in Italy during 1372-3, abroad again somewhere in 1376, in France and Flanders in 1377, and in Italy once more in 1378. He died in his own house at Westminster, and was buried in the Abbey, his place of interment being the chapel of St Benedict, thereafter named Poets' Corner. These foreign visits naturally contributed to his literary education by enlarging his knowledge both of men and of books. He may have met Froissart. He may have met Petrarch, who died at Arqua in 1374; and he may have met Boccaccio, who died a year later. Dante had been dead for over half-a-century. But whether Chaucer met any of the Italian writers in the flesh is less important than the fact that the Italy of his time was filled with their spirit. French and Italian poetry in the fourteenth century were accomplished when English poetry was still tentative; and from them Chaucer drew the stimulus and example that make him the first English poet who is a first-rate literary artist, the first English poet who takes by absolute right a place in the hierarchy of the world. Statements like these must be read intelligently. No influence, general or specific, can convert a mere literary artisan into an artist; but where there is a native instinct for artistry, persuasive example may save a long laborious process of trial and error. It is often forgotten that, since the Renascence, nearly all great English poets, from Spenser to Swinburne, have been disciplined in their art by the works of the classical writers. The French and Italians were to Chaucer what the Greeks and Latins were to later poets; and they helped him to such mastery that English poets of his own century and of the next hailed him as their chief. Occleve has left us a portrait of his "maister dere and fader reverent" illuminated in the margin of one of his manuscripts. Nevertheless, nearly three hundred years had to pass before a sound edition of *The Canterbury Tales* (Tyrwhitt 1775) replaced the old prints of Caxton (1478? and 1484?), Wynkyn de Worde (1498), Pynson (1493? and 1526), Thynne (1532), Speght (1598 and 1602), and Urry (1721). These old editions included works now assigned to other hands, but at least they presented the material out of which later scholarship—notably by W. W. Skeat (1897) and by J. M. Manly and Edith Rickert (1940)—has been able to construct the accepted Chaucerian canon.

We have seen that, in his youth and early manhood, Chaucer was much in France, that in early middle life he was not a little in Italy, and that he apparently spent the whole of his later days in England. Now if we take the generally authenticated works, we shall find that they sort themselves into three fairly well-defined groups. The first consists of work translated or imitated from the French, and couched in forms mainly French in origin—*The Romaunt of the Rose*, the three *Complaints*, *The Book of the Duchess*, the minor *Ballades*, etc. The second consists of pieces traceable to Italian originals—*Troilus and Criseyde*, *The Legend of Good Women*, *The Knight's Tale* and perhaps a few more of *The Canterbury Tales*. The third includes the best and most characteristic of the *Tales*, which are purely and intensely English. Such a grouping is neither completely accurate nor completely indicative of the substance and form of Chaucer's work; it is useful merely as an intimation of his progress as a craftsman. He did not adopt a French manner and drop it to adopt an Italian manner: he was always himself. The division of any man's work into "periods", whether the man be Shakespeare or Beethoven, must not be mechanically applied as a formula. Nevertheless it is clear that Chaucer, like Beethoven, laboured at his art, and passed, like Shakespeare, from one kind of writing into another, and thence into yet another.

The English version of *Le Roman de la Rose* represents only a small part of the great original of Guillaume de Lorris (thirteenth century) and Jean de Meun or Jean Clopinel (*c.* 1250-1305). What became of Chaucer's own translation we do not know. Modern scholarship definitely denies to Chaucer the existing translation as a whole and allows only a very doubtful probability that a part may be his. But at least it is worthy of Chaucer and of the delightful original. The first author and his continuator were writers of different spirit, but their English translator has shown himself equal to every requirement, with a mastery that only a consummate man of letters could display. The metre is that of the original—the octosyllabic couplet—and it is admirably handled. There is nothing among the numerous verse translations of the time which approaches this in poetry, wit, charm and courtly grace.

The dating of Chaucer's compositions is a hazardous speculation. First of the three considered earliest, *The Book of the Duchess* or *The Death of Blanche* (*c.* 1369), is a poem of more than 1300 lines in octosyllables, not quite so smooth as those of *The Romaunt*, but rather more adventurously split up. The much shorter *Complaint unto Pity* has for its special interest the first appearance in English of the great stanza called "rhyme royal", that is to say the seven-lined decasyllabic stanza rhymed *ababbcc*, which held the premier position for serious verse in English poetry till the Spenserian dethroned it. Its "royalty" derives from the use made of it by James I in *The Kingis Quair*. The third piece, *Chaucer's ABC*, adapted from the French of Deguileville, is in the chief rival of rhyme royal, the octave *ababbcbc*. In *The Complaint of Mars* and *A Complaint to his Lady*, metrical exploration is pushed even further, as a reference to the works will show. These evidences of experiment are most interesting and nearly decisive as to date; but none of the pieces can be said to have high poetical value. In *Anelida and Arcite* and *The Parliament of Fowls* this value rises very considerably. Both are written in the rhyme royal. The first named is still a "Complaint", but it escapes the artificiality of the earlier poems. *The Parliament of Fowls*, with its memorable opening, is the first poem in which we meet the true Chaucerian qualities—the happily blended humour and pathos, the adoption and yet transcendence of medieval commonplaces (the dream, the catalogue of trees and birds, the classical digressions, and so forth), as well as the faculty of composition which makes the poem a poem, and not a mere copy of verses.

In *Troilus and Criseyde*, Chaucer has entirely passed his apprentice stage; indeed, in its own line, he never did better, though he was to do very different things and to do them superbly. The story is one of those developments of the tale of Troy which, unknown to classical tradition, grew up in the Middle Ages. Criseyde or Cressida is, in origin, the girl Briseis, cause of the wrath of Achilles.

Probably first sketched in the curious and still uncertainly dated works put
forth with the names of "Dictys Cretensis" and "Dares Phrygius" (fourth or
fifth century?), the story had been worked up into a long legend in the *Roman
de Troie* of Benoît de Sainte-More, a French *trouvère* of the late twelfth century.
Thence it had been adapted a hundred years later in the prose Latin *Historia
Troiana* of Guido delle Colonne. On this, in turn, Boccaccio, somewhat before
the middle of the fourteenth century, based his poem of *Il Filostrato* in *ottava
rima*; and from the *Filostrato*, Chaucer took the story, and told it in rhyme royal
stanzas, excellently fashioned. Not more, however, than one-third of the
actual *Troilus and Criseyde* is, in any sense, translated from Boccaccio. The piece
is too long; it has too many digressions; there is too much talk and too little
action. But these were faults so ingrained in medieval literature that even
Chaucer could not entirely avoid them. Nevertheless, from the fine opening
to the finer close, the poem rarely falls below the level of its opportunities. It
happens to be in verse, but it is the first English psychological novel.

Troilus was followed somewhere about this time by *The House of Fame*, *The
Legend of Good Women* and *The Knight's Tale*. *The House of Fame* is a reversion
—in metre to the octosyllable, in plan to the dream-form, and in episode to the
promiscuous classical digression. The beginning is itself a digression, the real
subject not appearing till we reach the second book. Though the poem exhibits
both a full command of the metre and a richer skill in ironic humour, it failed,
apparently, to satisfy the author, as he left it unfinished, and did not use the
octosyllabic couplet again.

For the substance of *The Legend of Good Women*—stories of famous and
unhappy ladies of old—Chaucer had precedents in two of his favourite authors,
Ovid and Boccaccio; and to tell his tales he took a metre which had not been
regularly used in Middle English, which had been largely used in France, and
which he had himself employed with facility at the end of each stanza of *Troilus*
—the great decasyllabic or heroic couplet, the supplanter of the octosyllabic
couplet as a staple of English verse, the rival of the stanza for two centuries, the
tyrant of English prosody for two more, and still one of the greatest of English
metres for every purpose but the pure lyric. The *Prologue* to the *Legend* is the
most personal, varied and complete utterance that we have from Chaucer. The
transitions of mood are remarkable. In particular that rapid shifting from the
serious to the humorous, which puzzles readers not to the English manner born,
pervades the whole piece. Both in the *Prologue* and in the stories themselves the
metre is handled with a mastery that Chaucer did not excel till he came to write
The Canterbury Tales. But perhaps because he found the stories of these fair martyrs
of love becoming monotonous, he abandoned the whole project, and turned to
The Canterbury Tales, in the large humanity of which he found himself at home.

The plan of collecting tales and uniting them by a central idea is one of the
stock methods of the world. *The Arabian Nights* and *The Decameron* are two of
the most famous examples. The more compact collection known as *The Seven
Sages* had been known to Englishmen long before Chaucer's time. It is unnecessary, therefore, to seek for either a special or a general original of *The
Canterbury Tales*. The thing was in the air of the time, when tales had to be told
and pilgrimages were many. Chaucer's work is incomplete, both as a whole

and in parts. It is sketched out but not filled in. The only clear string of connection from first to last is the pervading personality of the Host, who gives a unity of character to the whole work, inviting, criticizing, admiring, denouncing, but always keeping himself in evidence. It is conjectured that the pieces in couplets were written or rewritten directly for the work, and that those in other metres and in prose were the adopted part of the family. What is certain is that the couplets, especially of the *Prologue*, are the most accomplished, various, thoroughly mastered verse that we find in Chaucer himself or in any English writer up to his time; nor are they exceeded by any foreign model, unless it be the *terza rima* of Dante.

The ever present humour of the work cannot be missed; and the exquisite and unlaboured pathos which accompanies it has been acknowledged even by those who have failed to appreciate Chaucer as a whole. The stories cover nearly the whole ground of medieval poetry. *The Knight's Tale* is high romance on a full scale, told in heroic couplets. The tales of the Reeve and Miller are examples of the *fabliau*, the story of ordinary life with a farcical tendency. *The Man of Law's Tale* returns to romance, but it is pathetic romance, told in rhyme royal. The Prioress's beautiful story is an excursion into hagiology—romance with a difference; and its neighbour, Chaucer's own tale of Sir Thopas, is a burlesque of all the weakness of the romances put into the weakest of the romance verse forms. *The Tale of Melibeus* illustrates the extraordinary appetite of medieval hearers for long, serious and (to our minds) boring and unremunerative prose narrative. Chaucer, in some respects as modern as Dickens, is here medieval. The pilgrims, it should be observed, are neither bored by Melibeus nor shocked by the Wife of Bath. *The Monk's Tale*, objected to by the Knight on the score of its lugubriousness, may be intended as a set-off to the frivolous description of that ecclesiastic in the *Prologue*. After the admirable *fabliau* of the Cock and the Fox told by the Nun's priest, the Wife of Bath's delightful prologue, the diablerie of the Friar's tale, and the story of Griselda told by the Clerk, romance comes back in the "half-told" tale of the Squire, the "story of Cambuscan bold". The romantic tone is kept up in *The Franklin's Tale*, one of the most poetical of all, and specially interesting in its portrayal—side by side with an undoubted belief in actual magic—of the extent of medieval conjuring. With *The Canterbury Tales* we reach, for the first time in this story, the literature of everyman, that is to say, the kind of work that belongs to the same world as the work of Shakespeare and Dickens. It is idle to suppose that such expressions of the medieval mind as *Cursor Mundi* or even *Confessio Amantis* will ever be widely enjoyed. The best of *The Canterbury Tales* can be enjoyed by the people who enjoy *Pickwick Papers* and *The Tempest*.

The two separate prose works, a translation of Boethius and a short unfinished *Treatise on the Astrolabe* (an instrument for observing the positions of the stars), show Chaucer's ability to deal successfully with vastly different subjects. The main attraction of the *Astrolabe* treatise is the additional evidence it gives of Chaucer's interest in astronomy or astrology, an interest which kept its hold on English men of letters as late as Dryden. The translation of Boethius is interesting as one in a long sequence of English versions of this author. An earlier translation, by King Alfred, has already been noticed (p. 12); a later by John Walton (*c.* 1410) was to come. Chaucer's version is specially interesting because he has translated into prose, not merely the prose portions of the original, but the metres or verse portions. These necessarily require a more ornate style of phrase and arrangement than the rest; and so we have here, for the first time in Middle English, deliberately ornate prose, aureate in vocabulary, and rhythmical in cadence. In his rendering, Chaucer shows the freedom which all great translators have used. But we should be ready to admit that, plain or adorned, the prose of Chaucer is far below his verse, not only in artistic quality, but in sheer efficiency of statement. The medieval Englishman with something to say said it either in Latin prose or in English verse. English prose was uncharted territory in which he was liable to lose his way.

Chaucer was one of those who (like Shakespeare) extract the maximum of personal nourishment from reading. He knew the usual Latin authors, especially Ovid, always one of the most important in medieval literature; he was familiar with French and Italian literature, and he knew the English romances which he parodied in *Sir Thopas*. He was a man of originating genius, and this gift, combined with his reading, enabled him to bring to ripeness the art of writing, which had been slowly developing during the two centuries before his time. Chaucer is no oddity. He comes as naturally as Shakespeare in the line of progress. His humour, like Shakespeare's, is kindly and never cruel. It is broad and unashamed; but it never sides with evil or mocks at good. The charity of Chaucer is immense. He is, further, a great artist in verse. Earlier poets tended to stumble between English syllabic freedom (spaced by accent) and French syllabic rigidity (spaced by caesura). Chaucer took an unfaltering way between both. He made an English dialect into a first-rate literary medium. The old charge against him of Frenchifying English has been disproved, and he is so far modern, that though he wrote over five centuries ago, his language presents few difficulties to intelligent readers of to-day. His power to communicate poetic grace, and charm, and that large comprehension of humanity which we may call a criticism of life is clear beyond any controversy. And he really understood people and their place in the world, and so could bring his crowd of pilgrims together with complete success. To the development of English as the means and matter of creative art he rendered true service, and he has fully earned his traditional title of father of our literature.

VIII. THE ENGLISH CHAUCERIANS

The influence of Chaucer upon English poetry of all dialects during the century (and more) after his death is almost unparalleled in literature. But the admiration he called forth was not very critical and was too generously extended. One of his disciples, Lydgate, was elevated (with Gower) to equal rank with the master, and awarded an excess of praise that later judgment feels bound to mitigate. We know little of Lydgate's life, beyond the facts (or inferences) that he lived somewhere between 1370–1450, that he was baptized John and called Lydgate from his Suffolk birth-place, that he was a monk of Bury St Edmunds, that he spent some time abroad and perhaps had personal acquaintance with Chaucer.

He was a lamentably prolific writer. The antiquary Joseph Ritson, who in 1802 catalogued an enormous number of his compositions, calls him, with characteristic violence, "a voluminous, prosaic and drivelling monk", and each epithet of that summary judgment can be defended. Lydgate shows some traces of Chaucerian humour, largely diluted, but none of Chaucer's vigour, pathos and vivacity. His enormous *Pilgrimage of the Life of Man* translated from Guillaume Deguileville stands in some remote relation to *The Pilgrim's Progress*, but has nothing of Bunyan's command of vigorous language, character and shrewd wisdom, though its vast extent (over 20,000 lines) includes a greater and more varied assortment of adventure. Lydgate's *Troy Book*, translated from Guido delle Colonne's *Historia Destructionis Troiae*, extends to 30,000 lines of heroic couplets, and is duller than the *Pilgrimage*; but it seems to have been read, for it was twice printed in full during the sixteenth century. *The Falls of Princes or Tragedies of John Bochas*, translated at second hand from Boccaccio in rhyme royal, is longer still, and was to have later, as we shall see, connection with another famous work. *Reason and Sensuality* in octosyllabic couplets, dimly related to *The Romaunt of the Rose*, has been found livelier than other of his compositions. *The Temple of Glass* and *The Assembly of Gods* are in similar allegorical vein. The best and most poetical passages in Lydgate's vast work are to be found in the rhyme royal stanzas of *The Life of our Lady*. Of several lives of the saints the best is the *Saint Margaret*. The beast-fable had something in it peculiarly suitable to Lydgate's kind of talent, and this fact is in favour of his *Aesop*, and of the two poems (among his best) known as *The Churl and the Bird* and *The Horse, the Sheep and the Goose*. *The Complaint of the Black Knight*, long assigned to Chaucer, is tolerable, though it has Lydgate's curious flatness. The remainder of the minor poems includes his most acceptable work: *London Lickpenny* (denied to him by later criticism), the *Ballade of the Midsummer Rose*, *The Prioress and her Three Suitors*, the poet's *Testament*, and the sincere "Thank God of all". To him is attributed the popular versified instruction in manners known as *Stans puer ad mensam*. Lydgate seems to us a dull, long-winded and metrically incompetent poet. He rarely rises above sheer flatness of diction, the dull, hackneyed, slovenly phraseology, emphasized by occasional aureate pedantry, which makes the common commoner and the uncommon uninteresting. But we must not forget that he was greatly admired by contemporary poets and by successors as late as Hawes and Skelton, and that our first printers produced him for a public that evidently wanted him. He is certainly the fullest example we have of the medieval mind in poetry.

The inseparable companion of Lydgate in literature is Thomas Occleve or Hoccleve (*c.* 1368–*c.* 1450). He received much less attention than Lydgate from the early printers, and the extent of his work is still uncertain. The most important of his known compositions is *De Regimine Principum* or *Regiment of Princes*, addressed to Henry Prince of Wales (i.e., Henry V), and extending in all to some 5500 verses. It is partly political, partly ethical, partly religious, and based on a blending of Aristotle with Solomon. The long introductory passage contains his famous tribute to Chaucer and Gower. Next to this in importance come two verse-stories from *Gesta Romanorum*, *The Emperor Jereslaus's Wife* and *Jonathas*, and a really fine *Ars Sciendi Mori*, the most dignified and the most poetical thing that Occleve has left us. In one curious poem, *La Male Regle*, he confesses to a long course of not very violent dissipation. Self-revelation, indeed, is one of Occleve's personal tendencies. His main attraction is that he has something to communicate about himself and his feelings; and so, in spite of his technical shortcomings, he is refreshing; for it is better to read about good fellowship or even about personal infelicities, than to be confronted with extensive moral commonplaces expressed without mitigation of earnestness.

Other writers of the group include Benet or Benedict Burgh (d. 1483) who continued Lydgate's pseudo-Aristotelian *Secrets of old Philosophers* (*Secreta Secretorum*) and wrote on his own account *Aristotle's ABC*, *A Christmas Game* and the *Great* and *Little Cato*, the first version of the distichs of Dionysius Cato. Of the poems (mainly didactic) written by, or attributed to, George Ashby and Henry Bradshaw little need be said, except that they illustrate the complete loss of grip that had come upon English verse. Certain of the Chaucerians have a kind of attraction because they followed up the alchemical interest exhibited in *The Canon's Yeoman's Tale*. The two chief are George Ripley and Thomas Norton. Ripley's *The Compound of Alchemy or the Twelve Gates* (1471), in varied and insecure stanzas, is a curiosity of "poetic science". Thomas Norton's *Ordinall of Alchemy* (1477), in exceedingly irregular couplets, is even less a poem, but his greater discursiveness may make his work more interesting to some readers.

The most attractive part of the period is that which gives us the poems at one time attributed to Chaucer. *The Tale of Beryn* or *The Second Merchant's Tale*, a story of commercial adventure in foreign parts, has clear merits as a narrative and fully deserves reading, though it is long and complicated. *La Belle Dame sans Merci*, ascribed to Sir Richard Ros (*c.* 1450) and translated from Alain Chartier, is dull and pretentious, and indisputably post-Chaucerian. Very much better is *The Cuckoo and the Nightingale*, also called *The Book of Cupid God of Love*, attributed to Sir Thomas Clanvowe (early fifteenth century), which is at least Chaucerian in date. Numerous as are the pieces which deal with May mornings and bird songs, this may keep its place with the best of them. *The Assembly of Ladies* and *The Flower and the Leaf*, both in rhyme royal, and both perhaps by the same author, are alleged to be written by a woman. *The Assembly* is the usual kind of allegorical piece, peopled by personified abstractions. *The Flower and the Leaf*, also allegorical, with the Flower as a symbol of the gay and passing and the Leaf as a symbol of the (comparatively) enduring, is much finer, and shows a certain grace of choice, arrangement and treatment of subject. Out of Chaucer it is difficult to find anything of the time better done. There is a singular brightness over it all, together with a rare power of Pre-Raphaelite decoration and of vivid portraiture. *The Court of Love*, by a Cambridge "clerk", shows the rhyme royal competently handled, and made the vehicle of genuine poetry. The poem contains some excellent episodes, and ends with a charming, if not entirely original, bird chorus to the initial words of favourite psalms and passages of Scripture. If *The Court of Love* is to be placed within the sixteenth century, we must regard it as the latest piece of purely English poetry which exhibits strictly medieval characteristics. It is the last echo of the music, the last breath of the atmosphere, of *The Romance of the Rose*, that perfect song and essence of medieval allegory.

IX. HAWES

The close of the fifteenth century and the opening of the sixteenth found the English language still unstable. The final *e*, influential for much that is good in Chaucer, had fallen into disuse in the spoken language, and the accentuation, especially of words borrowed from foreign tongues, was uncertain. It was difficult for the men of Henry VIII's reign to understand the speech of another shire or the English of an earlier age. The matter and the manner as well as the language of medieval literature belonged to the past. Popular poetry and morality plays flourished, history written in English made tentative beginnings, the newly printed prose books were read, but the courtly poetry of the Chaucerian tradition had become antiquated, and found its last exponent in Stephen Hawes, who, amid the men of the new age, has the forlorn air of a survivor from another era. He felt his solitariness, and in his most important work, briefly known as *The Pastime of Pleasure*, lamented that he remained the only true votary of poetry. And if we remember that his idea of poetry was that of Gower and Lydgate, namely, something elaborately allegorical and didactic, we must admit that he had good cause for his lament, even though our sympathy may be slight. Stephen Hawes (1474–1523) was a Suffolk man, educated at Oxford. Besides *The Pastime* he wrote *The Example of Virtue* (1510), *The Conversion of Swearers* (1509), *A Joyful Meditation of the Coronation of Henry VIII* (1509) and *The Temple of Glass* (1505?). The dates are those of the first-known printed texts. His other pieces are unimportant. With the exception of one episode, which is in decasyllabic couplets, *The Pastime* is in rhyme royal, and contains about 5800 lines divided into forty-five chapters. It is an elaborate allegory in the true medieval fashion, which Hawes naturally defends, praising "morall Gower" briefly, and Chaucer and Lydgate at length. Having reached his long delayed end, Hawes apologizes for his "lacke of scyence", prays that "wronge Impressyon" may not spoil his scansion, and laudably aspires "bokes to compyle of morall vertue" after the fashion of his "mayster Lydgate".

Hawes had really very little to say, and put into *The Pastime* much that he had already written, with slight variation of form. *The Example of Virtue*, his most important work after *The Pastime*, was written earlier. It is a complete allegory of the life of man from Youth to Age. *The Conversion of Swearers* contains an exhortation from Christ to princes and lords to cease swearing by His blood, wounds, head, and heart. The metre of this, as of *The Example*, is the seven-line Chaucerian stanza, except a fantastic passage in form as follows:

> Se
> > Ye
> > > Be
> > > > Kind
> > > > > Again
> > > > > > My payne
> > > > > > > Reteyne
> > > > > > > > In Mynde;

and so on the metre goes, increasing to lines of six syllables and decreasing again to words of one syllable. It is an early example of "shaped" verses, which in later days take the form of wings, crosses, altars, and pyramids, as in some poems of George Herbert. In choice of theme, in method of exposition and in mode of expression, Hawes was limited by his fixed ideal of poetry. He repeatedly insists that every poet should be a teacher. Living though he did at the opening of a new age, he still shows the characteristic marks of medievalism. His writings abound in long digressions, debates, appeals to authority, and prolix descriptions. He employs all the familiar medieval machinery and firmly believes that all poetry is allegory. What Hawes did feebly in *The Pastime of Pleasure* and *The Example of Virtue* was to be done nobly in *The Faerie Queene*. That Spenser had read Hawes and even learned something from him may be considered possible; but certain supposed resemblances are nothing but the likenesses bound to occur in all allegorical representations of life.

The verse of Hawes is disconcerting to modern readers, perhaps because we try to fit his lines to a tune he did not intend. Dryden tried to fit Chaucer to Dryden's own tune, and, failing, declared that Chaucer was a faulty metrist. The eighteenth century thought the tune of the old ballads wrong, because it lacked "smoothness" and "numbers". We are wrong when we try to extort from *The Pastime of Pleasure* the mellifluous ease of *The Faerie Queene*. We might remember more often, in reading the fifteenth-century poets, the liberties of the ballads and the nursery rhymes. Hawes himself certainly believed that his verses had a tune, or he would hardly have prayed to be delivered "Frome mysse metrynge, by wronge Impressyon". He has immortalized himself in one couplet, at least. Death, says the epitaph in Chapter XLII of *The Pastime*, is the end of all earthly joys; "after the day cometh the derke nyght",

> For though the day be never so longe,
> At last the belles ryngeth to evensonge.

X. THE SCOTTISH CHAUCERIANS

It is customary to describe the fifteenth century in Scotland as "the golden age of Scottish poetry", and to say of James I, Henryson, Dunbar and Gavin Douglas that they, rather than Lydgate or Occleve, were the true descendants of Chaucer. That is part of the truth, for intrinsically these Scottish writers were far better poets than Lydgate and Occleve. What may be overlooked is that the success of the Scottish Chaucerians was very deliberately obtained. The alliterative tradition and chronicle-romances like Blind Harry's *Wallace* and Wyntoun's *Chronicle* lasted later in the north than in the south; but with James I and the "makaris" there is a change—an adoption of the medieval artifice outworn in the south but new to the north, and a moulding of the language to suit the purpose. Thus, though the "new" Scottish poetry is more modern than the old, it looks backwards rather than forwards. There is no revulsion from medievalism, no anticipation of the Renascence. The Scottish Chaucerian poetry succeeded because, in a sense, it was behind the times.

The herald of this change in Scottish literary habit is the love-allegory of *The*

Kingis Quair, or *King's Book*, ascribed to James I (1394–1437), the atmosphere of which is that of *The Romance of the Rose*. Upon that poem it was probably modelled, and Scottish literature was fortunate in being introduced to the new genre in a piece of such literary competence. Not only is *The Kingis Quair* superior, in literary craftsmanship, to any poem by Chaucer's English disciples, but in happy phrasing and in the retuning of old lines it is hardly inferior to its models. *The Kingis Quair* (which runs to 1379 lines, divided into 197 "Troilus" or rhyme royal stanzas) may be described as a dream-allegory dealing with two main topics—the "unsekernesse" of Fortune and the poet's happiness in love. It uses the medieval machinery of the dream and the allegory and manages them deftly. At the conclusion, the writer refers to his masters Gower and Chaucer with more than the usual appropriateness, for he was Chaucerian by assimilation, not by imitation. Indeed, it is the power of assimilation—a symptom of original talent—that discriminates the Scottish Chaucerians generally from such blundering imitators as Lydgate and Occleve. The story of the poem is James's capture in March 1405, his imprisonment by the English, and his wooing of Joan Beaufort. Whether it was actually written by James and whether its date is 1423 or some years later are matters still in dispute. The period of his captivity would have given the king ample opportunity for a study of the great English poet whose name as yet was unknown in the north. The influence of Chaucer is hardly recognizable in any of the other works which have been ascribed to James. The "popular" poems *Peblis to the Play* and *Christis Kirk on the Grene* belong to a genre in which there are no traces of southern literary influence.

Of Robert Henryson (*c.* 1425–*c.* 1500), in some respects the most original of the Scottish Chaucerians, we know very little. Henryson's longest and most accomplished work is his *Morall Fabilis of Esope*, written in the rhyme royal stanza. Unlike Lydgate, he clearly separates story and moral and gains thereby freshness and humour of presentation. He is traditional in his general attitude to nature, but his particular descriptions of some of the animal characters are delightfully vivid and appealing. *Orpheus and Eurydice*, based on Boethius, resembles the *Fables* in type and in literary quality. It contains some lyrical passages of considerable merit, notably the lament of Orpheus. In *The Testament of Cresseid*, Henryson essays boldly to continue the story told by "worthie Chaucer glorious". His theme is the later tragedy of Cresseid, when, cast off by Diomede, she becomes a leper, and passes to a living death in the spital. The poem is deeply moving and deserves to take rank with its model. Thirteen shorter poems which have been ascribed to Henryson are varied in kind and verse-form. The majority are reflective, and deal with the topics that are the delight of the fifteenth-century minor muse. Two of the poems, the pastoral dialogue of *Robene and Makyne* and the burlesque *Sum Practysis of Medecyne*, deserve special mention. The *estrif* between Robene and Makyne develops a familiar sentiment, expressed in the girl's own words:

> The man that will nocht quhen he may
> Sall haif nocht quhen he wald.

These pieces are almost entirely non-Chaucerian, and represent a strain of the older popular poetry which persisted into a later period. It is uncritical to suppose that because King James and Henryson wrote lofty and serious poems they were incapable of the rougher, racier pieces. Sir Walter Scott (to say nothing of Shakespeare) is a sufficient answer to such objections.

William Dunbar (*c.* 1460–*c.* 1520) has generally held the place of honour among the Scottish "makaris" and, on the whole, his position is secure. Like all the greater Scottish poets of the time, with the exception of the schoolmaster Henryson, he was of good birth and connected with the court. This must be remembered when the courtly and non-popular character of the Scottish Chaucerian verse is considered. Dunbar became a Franciscan, but seems to have had no clear call to the ascetic life. In Paris (we may suppose) it was not the Sorbonne, but the wild life of the faubourgs and the talent of Bohemians like François Villon (whose poems had just been printed posthumously) which had the strongest claims upon the restless friar. Dunbar's poems fall into two main divisions, the allegorical and the occasional. Both show the strength of the Chaucerian tradition, though it must be remembered that he wrote as a courtier for the court. What is outstanding in Dunbar is not, as in Henryson, the creation of new genres or fresh motives. Compared with Henryson, Dunbar shows no advance in broad purpose and sheer originality—in fact, he is more artificial; but he had genius, and not only gave new rhythms to old movements, but added original life and humour to the old matter. *The Goldyn Targe* has the simple allegorical motive of the poet's appearance (in a dream) on a conventional May morning before the court of Venus. A similar theme appears in his short poem *Sen that I am a prisoneir* (sometimes known as *Beauty and the Prisoner*). In *The Thrissil and the Rois* the familiar machinery of the dream poem is used to celebrate the marriage of James IV and Margaret Tudor. In Chaucer's simpler narrative manner we have the tale of *The Freiris of Berwik*, dealing with the old theme of an untrue wife caught in her own wiles. *The Tretis of the Twa Mariit Wemen and the Wedo* echoes the gossip of the Wife of Bath, but it speaks with the freedom of colloquial satire of Dunbar's native Scots speech.

The satirical and occasional poems constitute at once the greater and more important part of Dunbar's work. His humour is unlike Henryson's in lacking the gentler and more intimate fun of their master. Dunbar's satirical powers are best seen in *Tidings from the Session*, an attack on the law courts, in the *Satire on Edinburgh*, denouncing the filthy condition of the capital, in his verses on the flying friar of Tungland who came to grief because he had used hens' feathers, in the fiercer invectives of the *General Satire* and *The Epitaph on Donald Owre*, and in the vision of *The Dance of the Sevin Deidlie Synnis*. The last is one of the very best examples of Dunbar's realism and literary cunning in suiting the word and line to the sense. In all, but especially in the *Dance*, there is not a little of the fantastic ingenuity which appears in his more purely comic sketches. And these again, though mainly "fooleries", are not without satirical intention, as in his *Joustis of the Tailyeour and the Sowtar* and his *Black Lady*, where the fun is a covert attack on the courtly craze for tourneys. Of all the pieces in this category, the *Ballad of Kynd Kittok* best illustrates that elfin quality which relieves his boisterous strain of ridicule. Its conclusion recalls the close of Burns's *Address to the Deil* and *The Dying Words of Poor Mailie*. The reach of Dunbar's fancy is at its greatest in the "interlude" of the *Droichis* (dwarf's) *part of the play*

—the "banns" or "crying" of an entertainment—in which he gains a triumph of the grotesque. In his *Flyting of Dunbar and Kennedie* (his poetic rival Walter Kennedy) we have a Scottish example of a widely-spread European genre in its extremest form. It remains a masterpiece of scurrility. *The Lament for the Makaris* is a poem on the passing of human endeavour. The solemn effect of the burden *Timor mortis conturbat me* and a sense of literary restraint give the piece high distinction. Its historical interest is great because Dunbar tells us much about his own contemporaries. He names his greater predecessors, and properly puts Chaucer first on the roll. Dunbar has been called the Scottish Skelton as well as the Scottish Chaucer; but if there had been borrowing it must have been Skelton's from him. The two are alike in their unexpected turns of satire, their Rabelaisian humour, their intellectual audacity, their metrical boldness, and their wild orgies of words. To dismiss all this as "doggerel" is to forget that it is an extension of the range of poetry in one direction, as high-flown phrase and "aureation" are an extension in another. Both are right—when they succeed.

Like Dunbar, Gavin or Gawain Douglas (1475?–1522) was of good family and a cleric; but he had influence and fortune which made him a bishop when the ex-friar was running about the court and writing complaints to his empty purse. He was the third son of "Bell-the-Cat", Archibald, fifth earl of Angus. His later history is exclusively political. *The Palice of Honour*, Douglas's earliest work, is an example of the later type of dream poem, and carries on the tradition of Chaucer's *Hous of Fame*. Of *King Hart* the same may be said, though it is a better poem, better shaped as an allegory, and better tuned in verbal music. Douglas's translation of the twelve books of the *Aeneid* (and of the thirteenth by Mapheus Vegius) begun in 1512, is the most interesting of his works, with special attractions in the thirteen prologues and supplementary verses. A picture of a Scottish winter introduces book VI, another of May, book XII, and another of June, book XIII. A *tour de force* in the popular alliterative stanza, not without suspicion of burlesque intention, is offered as a preface to the eighth book. The opening homage to Virgil is instructive, but Chaucer is not really far away. Douglas names him ere long, and loads him with the old honours, though he places him second to Virgil. But his Virgil is, for the most part, the Virgil of the dark ages, part prophet, part wizard. The language of the translation is specially interesting. No other Scot has built up such a diction, drawn from so many sources. Douglas has been inexplicably denied the honour due to him as a fine Scottish poet. His *Eneados* is a noble effort, and is memorable as the first translation of a great classical poet into English, northern or southern. The minor poets mentioned in Dunbar's *Lament for the Makaris*, Douglas's *Palice of Honour* and Lyndsay's *Testament of the Papyngo* add nothing to our notion of Middle Scots poetry and need not be discussed.

The discipleship of the Scottish Chaucerians, though sincere, was by no means blind. They imitated well because they understood with discrimination; and, being less addicted than Lydgate and his like to finding a moral in everything, they could give their attention to poetry for its own sake.

XI. THE MIDDLE SCOTS ANTHOLOGIES

Strong as was the Chaucerian influence on the Scottish poets during the fifteenth and sixteenth centuries, it by no means suppressed or transformed the native habit of Scottish verse. The Chaucerian influence came from the courtly side. The movement was begun by the author of *The Kingis Quair*, and may be rightly regarded as part of the general European effort to dignify the vernaculars and make them a fitting vehicle of great poetry. We have now to consider the non-Chaucerian matter and especially the anonymous poems preserved in anthologies of the sixteenth century made by antiquaries who had no literary axe to grind. These collections are (1) the Asloan MS. written *c.* 1515 by John Asloan, and formerly in possession of the Boswell family; (2) the Bannatyne MS., written in 1568 by George Bannatyne, and now in the National Library of Scotland; (3) the Maitland folio MS. compiled *c.* 1580 by Sir Richard Maitland of Lethington, and now in the Pepysian Library (Mag. Coll., Camb.); and (4) the Maitland quarto MS., written by Maitland's daughter in 1586 (Pepysian Lib.). Collections of less importance are the Makculloch MS. (1477) and the Gray MS. (*c.* 1500). Chepman and Myllar's prints, produced separately in 1508 by Walter Chepman and Andrew Myllar, the earliest extant specimen of Scots printing, are bound together in a unique volume in the National Library. A clear account of these various collections and their contents will be found in *Specimens of Middle Scots* by G. Gregory Smith, a most useful volume for the general reader. That this indigenous literature was really familiar and appreciated is made clear by the record of poets in Dunbar's *Lament for the Makaris* and by the allusions in a familiar passage of Douglas's *Palice of Honour*.

The two best-known examples of this popular literature are *Peblis to the Play* and *Christis Kirk on the Grene*, attributed to James I. Their theme is the rough fun of a village festival; and they afford valuable evidence of the abiding rusticity of the northern muse and of its metrical habit. Not less important is the complicated verse form, which supplies a link in the transition from the older northern romances to the later northern ballad. From the long irregular stanza of *Sir Gawayne and the Grene Knight* through the thirteen-lined stanza of *The Buke of the Howlat* and the eleven-lined stanza of *Sir Tristrem* to the pieces under discussion we find, not imitation, but simple continuity. The habit of these "popular" fifteenth and sixteenth century poems—the alliteration, the rhyme, and, above all, the breaking away in the "bob"—is an effect of antiquity. This form represents the native element which is obscured for a time during the Chaucerian ascendancy; but this is the permanent element—it is the courtly manner of the "golden age" that is the exception and accident. History confirms this; for when aureation and other fashions had passed, the reviving vernacular broke forth anew in the old forms. The actual form of the *Christis Kirk* stanza (eight lines with "bob" and refrain) lived on, and persisted as the medium for the narration of rustic frolic. Another example of the same type is *Sym and his Brudir*, a good-humoured satire on church abuse. In *The Wyf of Auchtirmuchty* we have the familiar story of the labourer who thinks the housewife's work is easy till he tries it and comes to disaster. *The Wowing of Jok and Jynny* is Burns's *Duncan Gray* some centuries earlier.

But there are pieces of a different kind—the supernatural treated more or less humorously. The brief *Gyre Carling* is a burlesque tale of what happened to a flesh-eating witch. Another comic love-tale of fairyland is told in *King Berdok*. In *The Laying of Lord Fergus's Gaist* there is some attempt at a parody of the old romance style. A third variety of popular verse is the bacchanalian—an intimation that Burns's preoccupation with "Scotch drink" was not peculiar to him or to his time. The best of all the Middle Scots convivial verse is Dunbar's *Testament of Mr Andro Kennedy*. The anonymous *Quhy sowld nocht Allane honorit be?* is a sprightly "ballat" on "Allan-a-Maut", alias John Barleycorn. Another piece anathematizes the bad brewing and praises the good. *Fabliaux* are less numerous, one of the best being the old, old tale of *The Dumb Wyf* made to speak by her husband's request, and his bitter repentance. Of historical and patriotic verse there is little. The purely poetic quality is highest in the love lyrics, which combine something of the popular directness with the aureate style of the courtly "makaris". The best is *The Murning Maidin*.

The Asloan MS. contains a number of passages which are among the earliest remains of Scotch prose, other than official documents. They belong to the fifteenth century, when Latin had long been the prose medium, but they show no trace of conscious attempts at style. Their literary merit is inconspicuous. Early in the sixteenth century, Murdoch Nisbet wrote out his Scottish version of Purvey's recension of the Wyclifite translation of the New Testament. This anticipates the Bassandyne Bible by half-a-century but it does not appear to have been generally circulated.

XII. ENGLISH PROSE IN THE FIFTEENTH CENTURY. I

The work of creating a sound written idiom of communication in English was a slow process. We may take it as a sign of advance that books of simple utility as well as of high endeavour began to be written and circulated. Instruction in manners and in cookery, service books and didactic essays, as well as old romances copied and modernized, and chronicles growing briefer and simpler, helped to familiarize the middle class with books and with written prose as an instrument of communication. Dictionaries, such as the *Promptorium Parvulorum*, indicate the spread of study, and many letters and business papers survive to show that soldiers, merchants, servants and women were learning to read and write with fluency. The House of Commons and the King's Council conducted their business in English; and politicians in the fifteenth century, like Wyclif in the fourteenth, sought to appeal to the sense of the nation in short tracts. The art of prose writing, in the creative sense, advanced no further. The translations of Mandeville mark the high tide, for *The Master of Game*, the Duke of York's elaborate treatise on hunting, was, save for the slightest of reflections, purely technical. The learned still used Latin as the formal medium; and so, of the chronicles compiled during the fifteenth century, nearly two dozen were written in Latin, with a bare seven in English.

John Capgrave (1393–1464), the learned and travelled friar of Lynn in Norfolk, was the best-known man of letters of his time; but the bulk of his work is in Latin. Nevertheless, he composed in English, for the unlearned, a life of St Katherine in verse and one of St Gilbert of Sempringham in prose, as well as a guide for pilgrims to Rome, and a *Chronicle of England*, presented to Edward IV. The chronicle attracts attention by the terseness of its style—he called it an "Abbreviacion of Cronicles" rather than a book. Capgrave, who had no sympathy with heroes of the "left" like Wyclif and Oldcastle, has been harshly judged by socialistic editors like Furnivall. But even a chronicler is entitled to his convictions.

The most striking figure in fifteenth century prose is Reginald Pecock (1395?–1460), a brilliant, vain and too clever thinker, who managed to get himself ground between the upper and nether millstones of York and Lancaster, and of Church and Lollardy. Pecock's laudable aim was to overcome the heresies of the Lollards by persuasion, and he therefore issued many books or pamphlets to answer those which the heretics were pouring forth. In 1444 he was made Bishop of St Asaph, and translated to Chichester in 1450. His main writings fall roughly between 1444 and 1456. He was so anxious to be reasonable that all parties united in rejecting him and calling him a heretic. His best-known work, *The Repressor of Over Much Blaming of the Clergy*, which its author thought would destroy Lollardy and prevent further criticism of the hierarchy, brought about his ruin. Yorkist politicians accused him of Lancastrianism, ecclesiastics accused him of heresy, and he had to choose between recantation or the stake. After a vain attempt to obtain protection from the papacy, Pecock was committed in 1458 to a dreary imprisonment for life in Thorney Abbey; and there he died. Like Roger Bacon, Reginald Pecock was an unlucky man. He appealed to reason in an age when neither bishops nor Lollards had any intention of being reasonable; what each party wanted was something that we now call "totalitarianism". One charge the ecclesiastical authorities made against him was that he wrote on great matters in English, and another that he set the law of nature above the Scriptures and the sacraments. These crimes have now the complexion of virtues. Pecock was not a deep thinker, but he sought earnestly to give currency to such thought as was available to him. His lesser works, *The Reule of Cristen Religion*, *The Donet* with its later *Folewer* (i.e. sequel), and *The Book of Feith* deserve as much attention as *The Repressor*, because in them a careful writer was attempting a rendering of technical theology into the kind of English which should not be too learned for general reading and which should not descend to the slovenliness of Lollard tracts. Pecock writes so clearly that his achievement is hardly realized at first in its magnitude. His wide command of words shows that he had studied the poets as well as the theologians. That Pecock will ever be generally read is not to be expected; but he should at least be remembered as an intrepid writer, shrinking (and who shall blame him?) from the last extremity of the stake. Further, though he was in no sense a literary artist, he is one of our first writers of an ordered, reasonable prose which does not sprawl, and lose itself in its own writhings, and which can therefore be used for the clear presentation of abstract argument.

Sir John Fortescue (1394–1476?), an intrepid chief justice and constitutional lawyer, wrote much in Latin to justify the claims of the house of Lancaster. Tewkesbury field left the Lancastrians without a cause, and Fortescue could only bow to the inevitable and lay before the new sovereign *de facto* his last treatise upon his favourite subject. It is in English, and is sometimes entitled *Monarchia*, and sometimes *The Difference between an Absolute and a Limited Monarchy*. It was probably finished about 1471. Its connection with literature may seem slight, but it served a literary purpose, for, being accepted as an authority, it was freely quoted in controversy, and so helped the diffusion of a rational English prose.

The devotional, as distinguished from the controversial, religious literature of the age derived from the school of Richard Rolle. The chief writer is Walter Hylton (d. 1396), an Augustinian canon of Thurgarton in Nottinghamshire, whose beautiful *Ladder of Perfection* supplied both system and corrective to Rolle's exuberance of feeling. Hylton's works are far more modern than Rolle's, both in matter and expression. They were favourites with the early printers and have retained their interest to the present time. The lofty thought, the clear insight, the sanity and the just judgment of *The Ladder of Perfection* and the anonymous *Cloud of Unknowing* (sometimes attributed to him) are not more striking than the clarity of the style. Probably there was much more devotional literature which was literally read out of existence. Only fragments survive. The best-known work after Hylton's is the *Revelations of Divine Love*, by the anchoress Juliana of Norwich (*c.* 1342–1442), an utterance of fervent piety, showing acquaintance with Hylton. A fascinating addition was made both to religious literature and to fifteenth century prose when the manuscript of Margery Kempe's autobiography, hitherto known only in brief extracts, was discovered and printed first in 1936, and more exactly in 1940, five centuries after it was written down at her dictation. She confesses her bodily and spiritual difficulties with complete frankness and narrates her pilgrimage to the Holy Land with attractive detail. Margery, like Capgrave, belonged to Lynn. She had read Rolle and Hylton and visited Juliana at Norwich. In her personal experience of religious ecstasy she was so full of tears and outcries as to make herself heartily disliked, but in her public dealings she exhibits the fearless conviction of divine inspiration that we find later in George Fox's Journal, though she was neither heretic nor Lollard, but more orthodox than the orthodox. *The Book of Margery Kempe*, the first autobiographical confession of its kind in English, is a moving addition to the literature of religious experience. It shows English prose as clearly written in the fifteenth century as in the century of Fox and Bunyan.

Wholly different in kind are the moralized skeleton tales, by no means always moral in themselves, of the famous *Gesta Romanorum* (see p. 45), the great vogue of which is witnessed by the fact that the book was being continually copied in the fifteenth century, and that an English translation then appeared, giving this source-book of future literature equal popularity with the English *Legenda Aurea*—*The Golden Legend*—which, half original, half translation, belongs to the same period. Gravely studied by thoughtful men was another old classic of the Middle Ages, *Secreta Secretorum* (see p. 71), three prose translations of which were executed in the fifteenth century. This is a work which ranks high among medieval forgeries, for it professed to be no less than an epistle on statesmanship addressed by Aristotle to his pupil Alexander the Great.

In historical writing little of importance was accomplished. The *English Chronicle* (1347–1461) made by a monk of Malmesbury or Canterbury, the staid *Cronycullys of Englonde* and the more scholarly *Chronicle* of the Lancastrian John Warkworth (d. 1503) need no more than bare mention. Far more important than any contemporary chronicle is the collection of letters and business papers preserved by the Paston family and first printed in 1787 with an addition in 1789. The much enlarged edition of James Gairdner, published in 1904 and the subject of one of Virginia Woolf's essays in *The Common Reader*, has superseded the old quartos. *The Paston Letters*, written during the fifteenth century, give a detailed picture of three generations of a well-to-do Norfolk family, their friends and enemies, their dependants and noble patrons, and form an inexhaustible treasure of personal, domestic and historical information about the period.

During the fifteenth century there was a steady increase in the production of books. The monasteries had long ceased to supply the market, and professional scribes produced copies as professional typists do now. The Stationers' Guild, in existence much earlier, was incorporated in 1403 and had a hall in Milk Street. "Paternoster Row" was already known. Prices of materials were stable and costs for ordinary transcription varied from a penny to two-pence a page, according to size. Of course elaborately illuminated books were luxuries, paid for at luxury rates. Ordinary people, then as now, had ordinary books, but were naturally more careful about them. Several of the Pastons owned books and were chary of lending them. Written literature, once the hand-maid of theology, now ministered to rational amusement. The reading public had grown. What was needed was a way of increasing the production of books.

XIII. INTRODUCTION OF PRINTING INTO ENGLAND

The fifteenth century is one of the pauses in history. If ever the life of England seemed to stand still it was during the years from the usurpation of the first Lancastrian to the death of the last Yorkist at Bosworth. The smoke of sacrifice that went up from Lollards in England and from St Joan in France showed the determination of ecclesiastical, dynastic and feudal powers to keep their possessions exempt from any contagion of novelty or change. The known world was small. The Mediterranean was almost literally its centre, as the earth was the centre of the universe. And then, upon the outworks of obstinate medievalism, rang out a series of hammer-strokes that shook the old world to pieces. About 1455 the great printed Bible of Gutenberg appeared at Mainz. In 1453 Constantinople fell before the conquering Turk, and the leaven of classical thought and literature began to spread more rapidly through Europe. In 1492 the New World was discovered. In the same year the last of the Spanish Caliphs left the Peninsula. In 1498 Vasco di Gama reached India by sea.

The coming of print is the most important event of the fifteenth century. As the pen is mightier than the sword, so the press is mightier than the pen. It was

4

soon after the year 1455 that the new art showed its possibilities in Germany. Its progress was rapid. It reached Italy in 1465, Switzerland in 1467, France in 1470, Austria and the Netherlands in 1473, and Spain in 1474. Printers were at work in seventy towns and eight European countries before Caxton set up his press at Westminster. Neither in quality nor quantity does early English printing rank high, but in one respect it is superior to all. The first products of the foreign presses were in Latin; the English press produced books in English, and produced them, not for scholars, but for general readers. So it happens that the greatest literary figure in fifteenth century England is not an author but a printer. William Caxton (1422?–1491) was born in Kent, and lived abroad in Flanders and Burgundy. During a visit to Cologne in 1471, he saw, for the first time, a printing press at work. He determined to practise the new art, and about 1475, in the city of Bruges, the first printed book in English made its appearance. It was *The Recuyell of the Historyes of Troye*, translated out of French by Caxton himself. Indeed, Caxton was something of an author. Nearly all his literary work was in the form of translations, but to most of his publications, he added prologues or epilogues which have a pleasant personal touch, and show us that he had one valuable possession, a sense of humour.

In 1476, Caxton returned to England and set up his press at Westminster. His first productions were small books such as Lydgate's *Temple of Glass* (1477), two editions of *The Horse the Sheep and the Goose* (1477), and *The Churl and the Bird* (1477), two editions of Burgh's *Little Cato*, Chaucer's *Anelida and Arcite* and *The Parliament of Fowls* (1478), Boethius (1478), and the *Stans puer ad mensam* (1479). From what we know of Caxton's tastes, these are just the kind of books that he would be anxious to issue, and there may have been others. The first two large books from his press were *The History of Jason* (1477) and Chaucer's *Canterbury Tales* (1478). In November 1477, was finished the printing of the *Dictes or Sayengs of the Philosophres*, the first dated book issued in England.

It is unnecessary to make here a catalogue of Caxton's productions. The most outstanding of his works are Trevisa's *Polychronicon* of 1387 with a continuation by Caxton himself (1482); another edition of *The Canterbury Tales* (1484); *Confessio Amantis* (1483); *The Golden Legend*, Caxton's most important translation (1483); and Malory's *Le Morte d'Arthur* (1485). One manuscript of *Le Morte d'Arthur* has been found. It differs from the printed text. Caxton revised the compilation, adding a prologue, which is the printer's best piece of writing as well as a sound criticism of Malory's romance. The *Eneydos*, translated in 1490, and printed about the same time, is not in any way a translation of the *Aeneid*, but the version of a French romance. The printer's preface is specially interesting, for in it Caxton sets out his views of the English language, its changes and dialects. One other translation by Caxton remains to be noticed, the *Metamorphoses* of Ovid, which he mentions himself, but of which no printed copy of his own time is known, though part of a manuscript, "translated and finished by me William Caxton", is in the Pepysian library at Cambridge. Caxton deserves special esteem for his sound sense. He gave the public both what it wanted and what he thought it ought to want. He was a great admirer of Chaucer, and expressed in print his appreciation of the poet and placed a memorial to him in the Abbey. England was fortunate in its first printer.

Presses were set up at Oxford in 1478, and about 1479 at St Albans. Both produced learned rather than popular works. The last book from the latter press is well known under the title of *The Book of St Albans* (1486). It contains three treatises, the first on hawking, the second on hunting, and the last on coat-armour or heraldry. Much has been written about the authorship of this book, which is probably not all from one hand. A reference in one place to "Dam Julyans Bernes" has led to a ridiculous attribution of the book to a prioress, Julyana Berners; but no woman, certainly no prioress, wrote any of it. "Julyana Berners" is a Mrs Harris.

The first printing press in London itself (as distinct from Westminster), set up in 1480 by John Lettou (i.e. the Lithuanian), produced only two Latin books. Lettou entered into partnership with William de Machlinia (i.e. of Mechlin) and produced law books. Their typographical work was better than Caxton's. It was not until about 1483, when Machlinia was at work by himself, that books in English were printed in London. One of his best was the curious *Revelation how a Monk of Evesham was rapt in spirit* (1485), treating allegorically the pilgrimage of a soul through Purgatory to Paradise. Caxton's successor, Wynkyn de Worde (d. 1534?) an Alsatian, and Machlinia's successor, Richard Pynson (d. 1530) a Norman, were efficient printers, not literary amateurs like Caxton. It will be noticed that the immediate post-Caxton printers were not English. Pynson's record of publications includes Lydgate's *Falls of Princes* (1494), Mandeville's *Travels* (1496), a version of the *Imitatio* (1503), Barclay's *Ship of Fools* (1509), Fabyan's *Chronicles* (1516)—first of the series of modern chronicles —and Berners's translation of Froissart (1523). Wynkyn de Worde's list includes Trevisa's *Bartholomew* (1495), *The Pastime of Pleasure* (1509) and other poems by Hawes, a *Canterbury Tales* (1532), and many romances. But the demand for religious and educational books kept the printers busy on less literary work.

Soon after Caxton's death various Antwerp printers began to issue books for the English market. One of these, known as Richard Arnold's *Chronicle* (*c.* 1502), unexpectedly includes among its commercial and antiquarian entries the famous ballad (really a dramatic lyric) generally called *The Nut Brown Maid*. Nothing whatever is known about the poem, and this inappropriate book is its best source. The appearance of Tindale's New Testament at Worms in 1525 marks an entire change in the character of English books printed abroad. After this time, the foreign presses issued nothing but the works of refugees whose religious or political opinions had made them outcasts. The Reformation dealt a heavy blow at books of entertainment.

During its first fifty years the English press apparently did little for contemporary writers. Skelton seems to be very poorly represented. But it is unsafe to make general charges. Very few early books of any kind survive; and the probability is that small books of poems and stories were read to pieces. A notable survival, like Malory's *Le Morte d'Arthur*, representative of a mass of translation and compilation, should prevent a hasty judgment that the seventy years between Skelton's satires and *Tottel's Miscellany* were a barren period of book production. The early history of the book trade and the reading public can be read in H. S. Bennett's *English Books and Readers, 1475 to 1557* (1952) and its sequel (1965) covering the Elizabethan period.

XIV. ENGLISH PROSE IN THE FIFTEENTH CENTURY. II

The course of English reading, for a long time, was determined, not by an author, but by a printer. Unlike his fellow-craftsmen abroad, Caxton made no attempt to issue religious texts; and, unlike his fellow-readers at home, he had small interest in the old metrical romances. He preferred to satisfy the chivalric-romantic taste of the court and lettered middle-class by prose translation from French works of already established repute. That *The Four Sons of Aymon* or *Paris and Vienne* had small intrinsic value in no way lessens their importance as a step in the progress of English literature. Books such as these handed on material not disdained by Spenser. They formed a link between medieval and modern romance, and from among them has survived an immortal work, Malory's *Le Morte d'Arthur*.

There is no evidence that Caxton's enthusiasm for Chaucer created any demand for books of verse on a large scale, and Lydgate was the only other poet he printed. *Piers Plowman* would not have appealed to Caxton's patrons, and he did not touch it. The greater part of Caxton's output took the form of prose translation; and his translations, like his press, must be reckoned as having the stamp of his authority, though other hands undoubtedly helped. A comparison of his editions of *The Golden Legend* and *Polychronicon* with the original English versions leaves the older prose easily first; and in his interesting prefaces we see how it was that he sometimes went wrong. When he had no French example to guide him, he wrote, so to speak, beyond his means. In desiring to avoid a low style he went too high and became involved. When he is content to be plain he is almost as vigorous as Latimer; when he tries to build an elaborate paragraph he loses himself. In this power of writing with a naïve vivacity, while deliberately striving after a more ornate manner, Caxton belongs to his age. His claim to have embellished the older authors and his quiet pride in his own authorship are of the new world, not of the old. Henceforth, not the substance alone, but its form will challenge attention. Prose, like poetry, becomes conscious literature.

Caxton's largest and most popular book, *The Golden Legend*, was translated anew from the French and is not a version of the old English edition. The far-away thirteenth century Latin original of Jacopus de Voragine (1230–98) is much altered, as in all translations. The book is a cyclopaedia of sacred legend and instruction, and the public evidently preferred it to Malory or Chaucer, for it went through edition after edition. A blend of religion and entertainment in book or play is perennially popular.

Like *The Golden Legend*, *Le Morte d'Arthur* looks back to the Middle Ages. Though in substance a mosaic of translated quotations, it is, nevertheless, a single literary creation such as no work of Caxton's own can claim to be, and it is the earliest prose book in English to form part of everyman's reading. Author and printer came together at the perfectly right moment. Sir Thomas Malory has been identified with an actual person of the same name; but the identification tells us nothing we need to know. The author of a book so remote and impersonal should remain the shadow of a name, mysterious as the Arthur of his imagination. The book belongs to no age and no condition of normal life, and this "bodiless creation" is an element in its immortality. These tireless champions of the helpless, these eternal lovers and their idealized love, are as remote from time and place as the forests and the fields among which they travel. Medieval stories were, naturally, negligent of causes in a world where the unaccountable so constantly happened. The atmosphere of magic places Malory's characters outside the sphere of criticism, since, given the atmosphere, they are consistent with themselves and their circumstances. Most admirable is the restraint in the portrayal of Arthur, who, as here depicted, is Malory's own creation. He is neither human nor superhuman, but the strong though elusive centre of the magical panorama. The prose in which is unfolded this barely Christianized fairy-tale is almost childlike, but, unlike mere simplicity, it never becomes tedious. Malory, who reaches one hand to Chaucer and one to Spenser, escaped the stamp of a particular epoch and bequeathed a prose epic to literature. He was a poet who wrote in prose, and his lively speech, which is both epic and lyrical, is so simple in its sincerity that it has baffled all the literary imitators.

Tudor prose owes its foundations to three men of affairs who took to literature late in life. Next to Caxton and Malory stands Sir John Bourchier, Lord Berners (1467–1533). It was partly to solace his anxieties while captain of Calais, as well as "to eschew idleness, the mother of all vices" that he executed the series of translations which secure to him the credit of a remarkable threefold achievement. Berners was the first to introduce to our literature the famous figure of Oberon, the fairy king; he was the first to attempt successfully in English the ornate prose style which shortly became fashionable; and he was the first to give our historians a new source-book and a new model in his famous rendering of Froissart. He made this work an original adaptation rather than a translation. Though in his hands history is still akin to heroic romance, he taught Tudor historians the value of well-proportioned detail and occasional quotation of witness in impressing the sense of actuality. If Hall and Holinshed borrowed little from Berners in style, they learned from him the way and shape of an enduring chronicle.

In *Arthur of Little Britain* (1555) and *Huon of Bordeaux* (1534), Berners took up the extravagant prose romance of the ordinary medieval type. Huon reminds us of the ignobly born simpleton heroes of German peasant story. Auberon (Oberon) is half-way to being the fairy of poetry, the child of a fairy "lady of the isle" and a mortal father, Julius Caesar, who in the Middle Ages had the same magical reputation as Virgil. The English of *Huon* is extremely straightforward, and bears hardly more trace of the graceful fluency of the *Froissart* than of the fantastic prose its translator was next to attempt. To a modern reader it appears strange that the most popular work by the translator of Froissart should have been his rendering of a verbose didactic book by the Spanish secretary of Charles V, Antonio de Guevara, an author whose involutions of language rapidly captivated fashionable taste in Spain, France and England. One writer whom he sophisticated was Marcus Aurelius. Berners first introduced Guevara and his style to English readers in *The Golden Boke of Marcus Aurelius* (1535), which so much delighted the polite world that it went through fourteen editions in half a century. The desire to make prose an art in itself was beginning to be felt; and Berners may be called an initiator of the manner which was to receive its epithet from its most perfect example, *Euphues*. What he lacked was the power of giving his intentions artistic realization. He lacked the art which conceals art. A comparison of his *Golden Book* with North's version, *The Dial of Princes* (1557), makes obvious the defects of his self-conscious fantastication.

XV. ENGLISH AND SCOTTISH EDUCATION: UNIVERSITIES AND PUBLIC SCHOOLS TO THE TIME OF COLET

When the twelfth century drew to its close, Paris was the English academic metropolis. There were already masters and students in Oxford; but what drew them to that town it is not possible to say. Modern research points to the year 1167 as the date at which Oxford became a *studium generale*. By the end of the twelfth century the number of scholars had grown very large. In 1209, when certain Oxford clerks were hanged by King John on suspicion of complicity in the death of a woman, the Oxford masters proclaimed a suspension of studies, and three thousand scholars dispersed, some to Reading, some to Paris, and some to Cambridge. By the end of the twelfth century, Cambridge was a town of importance; but it is not till early in the thirteenth century that genuine history records the presence there of a concourse of clerks. In 1229 a riot in Paris led to a similar migration of scholars from the metropolitan university, and Cambridge shared with Oxford the benefit of the exodus. Thenceforward, Oxford and Cambridge advanced on parallel lines, Oxford having a start of fifty years.

When the irruptions of the barbarians burst upon western Europe, learning had taken refuge in the monasteries. The Benedictines preserved humane culture, and their schools were long in high repute. But the Benedictine scheme of education was directed exclusively to the requirements of the religious life. Though they had schools in Oxford and Cambridge before the rise of the two universities, it was not until after the coming of the mendicants that they were roused to play an active part in English university life. In 1217, within two years after the foundation of their order, the Dominicans planted a settlement in Paris; in 1221 they invaded Oxford; in 1274 they were in Cambridge. They were followed at Oxford in 1224 by the Franciscans, who, at the same time, appeared at Cambridge. Entering in the guise of mendicants, they soon became possessed of valuable property, and their magnificent buildings astonished the scholars of both universities. Other orders followed. It was not their studies but their ambition which lost to the mendicants the favour of the medieval universities. Beginning as assailants of the abuses of the older orders, within a very few years they furnished to the world a still more striking spectacle of moral degradation. They had outstayed their welcome in both universities a full century before Chaucer launched at them the shafts of his humour, Piers Plowman lashed them with invective, and Wyclif poured out on them the vials of his vituperation.

The bulk of the students who thronged the streets of a medieval university were poor, though there were some who were able to set a scandalous example by a display of finery. The poorest resorted to menial or manual tasks to get their daily bread. Others were supported by wealthy friends, patrons, or institutions. Benefactors, even before the college era, endowed loan-chests or founded "exhibitions". The latter half of the thirteenth century is marked by two notable events in university history, the foundation of Walter de Merton's College at Oxford in 1274, and the foundation of what is now Peterhouse at Cambridge in 1284. The college, as the endowed home of students who lived under a rule that was not monastic, was found to be a desirable and practical institution. Before the year 1400 there had arisen in Cambridge six of the present colleges. In Oxford the college of Merton had rivals in six of the existing colleges. In 1411 the Bishop of St Andrews, Henry Wardlaw, was inspired to found a university in his cathedral city, and this, the first of the Scottish universities, was followed in 1451 by the foundation of the University of Glasgow, in 1494 by Aberdeen, and in 1582 by Edinburgh. Trinity College, Dublin, dates from 1591.

To William of Wykeham (1324–1404) is due a further development of the educational conception of both university and college. He was inspired to establish in Oxford a college which should outrival the most splendid foundation of the university of Paris. The "New College" was to combine the features of a society of learning with those of a collegiate church. William also conceived the idea of linking his college with a particular preparatory institution, and, by the creation of "Seint Marie College at Winchester", became the founder of one of the first English public schools. His purpose was quite narrowly vocational. All members of his society were required to proceed to priests' orders. It was as a direct imitator of Wykeham that Henry VI, in 1440–1, founded the allied institutions of King's College, Cambridge, and "the College Roiall of oure Ladie of Eton beside Windsor". Half the fellows and scholars of Winchester were transferred to Eton to constitute the nucleus of the royal school, of which William Waynflete (1395?–1486), the Winchester schoolmaster, became an early provost.

The studies of the medieval university were based on the seven liberal arts. Three of these, grammar, logic and rhetoric, constituted the *trivium*; the bachelor passed on to the *quadrivium*—arithmetic, geometry, music and astronomy—his conquest of which was denoted by the licence or degree of master of arts. To these seven arts, the thirteenth century added the three philosophies—natural, moral, and metaphysical. Of written examinations the medieval student knew nothing whatever; his progress was secured by the reading of set books and enforced attendance at assigned lectures, by frequent "posing" and debate, and, lastly, by the necessity of himself delivering lectures after attaining the baccalaureate. The education offered to the young student in the Middle Ages was essentially utilitarian: he was trained for a particular kind of service. A few rules of grammatical expression, some elementary calculations, geometry, some ill-informed geography, music enough for the singing of a mass, and Ptolemaic astronomy, directed to the correct determination of Easter—these, with skill in argument, constituted the ripe fruit of the course in *trivium* and *quadrivium*. But though the medieval universities offered their scholars nothing resembling an education in the large humanities, they were the centres of intense, if narrow, intellectual enthusiasm, and their worst products would have compared favourably with some of the pass men who adorned Oxford and Cambridge in the Victorian days of Cuthbert Bede's character Mr Verdant Green.

XVI. TRANSITION ENGLISH SONG COLLECTIONS

Though the surviving manuscripts are few, many English songs of this period have been preserved, some evidently much earlier than the date of transcription and showing the influence of folk-song. The characteristics of folk-poetry are, as to substance, repetitions, interjections, questions, and refrains; and, as to form, a verse accommodated to the dance. The refrain is so generally employed that a song without it is the exception. The interjections ("Troly, loly", "Hey, ho", and so forth) were perhaps stamping rhythms, with sounds imitated from some musical instrument. Some of the songs have preserved refrain, interjection and repetition as well, as in the familiar piece of which each stanza begins with "I have twelve oxen", includes "With hey, with how", and ends with the refrain, "Saweste not you myn oxen, you litill prety boy?" This is the kind of song that can still be heard in children's games, when individual singers in turn detach themselves from the chorus to perform some ritual of dancing or counting or touching. A delightful fragment of repeated question and answer is that beginning, "Maiden in the moor lay"; and pure repetition is the characteristic of the well-known "Adam lay ibowndyn". Frequent ecclesiastical denunciations testified to the prevalence of communal singing in medieval England; but so much more potent are custom and cult than authority, that women, dressed in the borrowed costumes of men, continued to dance and sing in wild chorus within the very churchyards, in unwitting homage to the old heathen deities.

The carol was originally a dance-song. It scandalized the clergy, and both words and motions were, in time, made respectable. Carols were sung at any festive season; but Christmas, being a time of traditional rejoicing to mark the lengthening days, became the chief occasion of carols, and they have generally the repeated refrain, "Noël". Some of them, in their metres, lean for support on Latin hymns, and use, as refrains, actual phrases or lines from the canticles, sequences, and graduals in missal or breviary. Christmas carols deal either with sacred themes suggested by the Nativity, or with secular themes appropriate to rejoicing. Charming are the songs of ivy and holly which were sung in connection with some little game or ceremony of the season. "Holly and his mery men" were matched in friendly contest with "Ivy and her jentyll women". But whatever the song may be, the conclusion of the matter is that "Holly must have the mastry". Related to the Christmas carols are the spiritual songs: some simple cradle songs, some dialogues between mother and babe, and some anticipations, by one or the other, of the coming Passion. They are deeply affecting. From "Lullay, by by, lullay" to "Stond wel, moder, under rode", these old songs carry us, with their moving simplicity, from Crib to Cross.

Growing out of the simple religious songs we find hortatory and reflective poems that reprove sin and counsel good deeds; and these, in turn, become worldly-wise and didactic. The perennially sly warnings against women are, of course, to be found. Some are counterparts of the brawling scenes in the old plays, and bid for laughter by representing the goodman defeated and driven out by a shrewish and voluble wife. Of all popular poems, the convivial songs, with their festivity and their rollicking spirits, are the most engaging. Some drinking songs are daring parodies of hymns, justifications of drinking by the Sacrament, *credos* of wine, women and song. These were already venerable in the fifteenth century. Drinking songs are early types of communal verse, and the folk-element is apparent in many of them, especially in that which has for its refrain: "But bryng us in good ale."

The song of the death dance is represented in several manuscripts by a most melancholy and singularly powerful poem, beginning "Erthe out of erthe is wondirly wroghte." In all its repetitions of phrase it holds the hearers' minds relentlessly to the contemplation of that which must come.

Love songs range from the saucy and realistic songs of the clerks to the ornate and figured address of the gallants. The French types which were translated or imitated without material modification include the address, the *débat*, the *pastourelle*, and the *ballade*. The address is a poem in stately and formal language wherein the poet addresses his lady. Though the *débat* has a variety of themes in French lyrics, in English it is usually restricted—save for the debate of holly and ivy—to contentions between the lover and his lady. Of the type of *pastourelle* in which a gallant makes love to a rustic maiden, the one sung by Henry VIII still survives in a popular modern form:

> Hey, troly loly lo, maide, whether go you?
> I go to the medowe to mylke my cowe.

A more primitive type of *pastourelle* is that in which a shepherd laments the obduracy of a shepherdess. Light-foot measures, such as the *lai* and the *descort*, exerted a noteworthy influence upon the late transition lyrics. A French type which has influenced several English songs without being exactly imitated in any is the *aube*, or complaint of the lover at the envious approach of morn, a theme to be immortally transfigured in the farewell of Romeo and Juliet. Similar to this is the *chanson à personnages*. Though English songs furnish no complete example of the *chanson à personnages* as it existed in France, there are various songs in which the poet represents himself as chancing upon a maiden or a man who is lamenting an unrequited love or the treachery of a false lover. The form easily lent itself to the presentation of overheard ribaldry. The *chansons à personnages* shade into the English May poems, the refrain of a *chanson* sometimes being taken from popular English verse. The May poems that follow the English tradition all breathe the blithe, out-of-doors spirit. Of kindred spirit are hunting songs, songs of the "joly fosters" who love the forest, the bow, and the horn, and desire no other life. All the songs, delightful in themselves, are important as part of the national history, for they tell us that the Elizabethan lyric was no sudden coming of a new thing into English literature.

XVII. BALLADS

The word ballad is used rather loosely. Sundry shorter poems, lyrics, hymns, "flytings", political satires, mawkish stories, last confessions of malefactors, and so forth, have gone by the name of ballad. Ballad societies have published a vast amount of street-songs, broadsides and ditties, which are not ballads in any sense. The genuine ballad has these special marks of character: (1) it is a narrative poem without any discernible indication of personal authorship; (2) it is strong, bare, objective, and free from general sentiments or reflections; (3) it was meant originally for singing, and, as its name implies, was connected at some time with dancing; (4) it has been submitted to a process of oral tradition among unsophisticated people fairly homogeneous in life, habit and outlook, and below the level at which conscious literary art appears. Conditions favourable to the composition of such poetry ceased to be general after the fifteenth century; and though ballads were both preserved and produced after that date in isolated rural communities, the instinct that produced and the habit that transmitted them were survivals from a vanished age. In the process of oral transmission ballads tended to lose their dramatic, mimetic, and choral character, and to become narrative or epic; and thus many have failed to keep their once essential refrains; but they have kept both the impersonal note and the freedom from all trace of deliberate artifice. No verse of this sort can be produced under the conditions of modern life, and the three hundred and five ballads represented by some thirteen hundred versions in F. J. Child's collection (1882–98) set the patterns which later revivals or recoveries tended to follow.

Misunderstanding the references of certain chroniclers, people have assumed the existence of a body of early "ballads" now lost. But not a single specimen can be produced. The surviving heroic poetry, from *Beowulf* to *The Battle of Maldon*, is not ballad poetry. Early lyric verse is not ballad poetry. The earliest recorded piece of English verse with signs of the ballad upon it is the *Canute Song* (see p. 24). This fragment is of great historical value, for it is not only one of the first known pieces of English poetry to break away from the uniform stichic order of Old English metres, but it is in the rhythm which belongs to the best English and Scandinavian ballads of tradition. Whether the resemblance is merely accidental no one can say. There is nothing like it for many years after.

The "ballad question" has been fiercely debated. Opinions have ranged between the extremes of the "original artist" theory and the "communal composition" theory. Nothing can be proved, but some probabilities are clear. It is certain that the English and Scottish ballads were not made, preserved or transmitted by professional minstrels, though later minstrels may have sung versions of some of them, as Victorian street-singers sang what they supposed to be the words and tunes of old songs. Such poems as minstrels are known to have made do not resemble the genuine ballads. The old ballads were not made and sung *for* the people, they were made and sung *by* the people. As in children's singing games, performers and audience were one. Ballads were not produced in a final form (there is no "final form") either by individual artists or by communal committees earnestly anxious to create genuine "folk-poetry" for later admiration. Someone suggested, improvised or made something for a particular or general occasion, and, after that, many others made that something over again for their own particular or general occasions. Whatever was made lived, so to speak, a mouth-to-ear existence for several generations; and so the surviving ballads exhibit evolutionary processes of adaptation, accretion and attrition. All genuine poetry of universal appeal is, in a sense, miraculous; the ballad is not singularly and specially miraculous. It differs from other poetry in the conditions under which it was made and the agency by which it was transmitted. From this difference there arise two important exceptions to the ordinary rules of literary investigation: it is useless to hunt for an "original" version, and it is useless to lean too strongly upon chronology, for one of the latest recorded ballads may be older in form than another written down in a much earlier manuscript. The ballad may not be specially miraculous; but the circumstances of composition and preservation make it an independent poetic species. A choral throng, with improvising singers, is the almost certain origin of the ballad as a poetic form. It is to singing and improvisation that one turns for origins, and it is to tradition that one turns for the growth and spread of the versions themselves. Origin made the ballad something suited for group-acting, group-singing and group-dancing; oral preservation and transmission gradually changed it into something suited for narration, with a tendency towards the epic, the chronicle, the story, the romance. We may note, as a parallel, that among children the "action song" gradually becomes the "recitation", as they grow older.

The ballads fall into two main classes. One, demonstrably the older in structure, tends in form to the couplet with alternating refrain or burden, and in matter to the rendering of a single situation. A dominating feature here, often recorded and always to be assumed, is repetition, in a form peculiar to balladry. When, however, the "action poem" began to move towards narrative, the ballad was lengthened in plot, scope, details, and was shorn of its now useless refrain. Thus arose a second class, the long ballad, recited or chanted to a monotonous tune by a singer. Instead of the short singing piece, steeped in repetition, we have deliberate narrative, without the old repetitions and refrains, and dealing with progressive situations, sometimes at length. By a happy chance, this epic process can be followed into its final stage. We have numerous ballads which tell different adventures in the life of Robin Hood; and we have an actual epic poem, formed upon these ballads or their very close counterparts, which embodies the adventures in a coherent whole. Between the style of *The Gest of Robyn Hode*, however, and the style of the best Robin Hood ballads, there is almost no difference at all; and these may well represent the end of the epic process of balladry. In metrical form, they hold to the quatrain made up of alternating verses of four and three measures, which is not very far from the old couplet with its two alternating verses of the refrain. The well-known opening of *Robyn Hood and the Monk* shows the change in form and the new smoothness of narrative:

> In somer, when the shawes be sheyne
> And leves be large and long,
> Hit is full mery in feyre foreste
> To hear the foulys song.

After another similar stanza, the story begins with a dialogue between Little John and Robin, passes into the third personal narrative, and so tells its tale with a good plot and plenty of incident.

Old as it is by record, this Robin Hood ballad seems far more finished, familiar, and modern than a ballad recovered centuries later from oral tradition in Scotland, short, intense, abrupt, with communal song for every other line of it from beginning to end, a single dominant situation, a dramatic and choral setting. The refrain is repeated with each stanza:

> There were three ladies lived in a bower,
> *Eh vow bonnie,*
> And they went out to pull a flower
> *On the bonnie banks o' Fordie.*

It is plain how near this is to the choral throng and the action of taking hands and turning; the speeches of individuals and the collective refrain all point to a singing and moving body of people. The refrain of the throng is constant; and the action advances, not by continuous narrative, but by a series of repetitions, each repetition containing an increment, a new phrase or word, to match the new posture of affairs. This incremental repetition is the main mark of the old ballad structure, and retained its importance long after the choral conditions which created it had been forgotten. Only in the long narrative ballads does this incremental repetition fade away. A ballad known in English as *The Maid Freed from the Gallows* had an astonishing vogue throughout Europe. Finland, alone, has fifty versions of it. In the English version a girl faces death on the gallows and appeals vainly to all her relatives in turn to save her, the climax coming with her last appeal—to her true love. A noticeable feature of this ballad is its adaptability to a crowd of any size, the list of relatives being as long or as short as need arises. Of course, few ballads remain in this initial stage. They pass into oral tradition, and are sung as stories rather than presented as action.

We may thus summarize the facts of ballad progress: What gave the ballad its existence as a poetic species was a choral, dramatic presentation. Refrain of the throng, and improvisation by various singers, leant heavily, as all primitive poetry teaches us, on repetition. To advance the action this repetition became incremental. The rhythmic form into which the ballad verse naturally ran is that four-accent couplet known everywhere in popular song. With the refrain this couplet formed a quatrain; in later and longer ballads, as also in some of the short "situation" ballads, the refrain is replaced by a second and fourth line, constituents of the regular stanza, which may be an actual substitution for the refrain, or a carry-over of the three-accent portion of the old *septenarius* or "fourteener". This account of the ballad discusses it as a poetic species. A discussion of the matter dealt with in actual ballads is a different question, which must not be confused with the other. This, taking us into the realm of folk-lore, myth, superstition and traditional history, does not call for investigation in an outline of literary development.

Let us now briefly consider the ballads as a body. The quantity of material is so great that only a few examples can be cited. Familiar and charming pieces like *The Nut Brown Maid* and *The Children in the Wood* are individual poems in the ballad manner, but have not the marks of popular tradition upon them. The oldest ballad, by record, is *Judas*, from a manuscript of the thirteenth century. *St Stephen and Herod* may be dated about 1450, the time also of *Robyn Hood and the Monk* and *Robyn and Gandeleyn*, which are followed, half a century later, by *Robin Hood and the Potter*, and by the earliest printed copy of *The Gest of Robyn Hode*. In print of the early sixteenth century comes a long outlaw ballad *Adam Bell, Clim of the Cleugh and William of Cloudesley*; and, slightly later, there follow in manuscript *Cheviot* and *Otterburn*, *Captain Car* and a version of *Sir Andrew Barton*. Only eleven ballads, G. L. Kittredge noted, "are extant in manuscripts older than the seventeenth century". The most important of all ballad sources is the folio volume (written about 1650) discovered by Bishop Percy. This contains a strange medley of poems good and bad, with many of the finest ballads interspersed. From this Percy drew his *Reliques*, printed in 1765 and sophisticated to suit eighteenth-century taste. The whole folio has since been printed. It is the most important of all ballad sources. To this has been added material gathered by many collectors, notably by Sir Walter Scott in his *Border Minstrelsy* (1802–3). The cultural importance of the old songs, ballads and dances was summed up by the musician Cecil Sharp in his *English Folk-Song: Some Conclusions* (1907) and—after his visit to America in 1916–18—in his introduction to *English Folk-Songs from the Southern Appalachians*.

Regarded as material, the oldest ballads are the ballads of question and answer made at dances and games. Close to this form is the "flyting" or challenging ballad, with its alternate request for impossible things. The ballad of domestic complication, or tragedy of kin, with a dramatic "recognition", looms large in all European tradition. The stealing of a bride was an obvious subject of this ballad of situation. Among elopement stories, *Gil Brenton* is worthy of note; the type, however, easily passes into the rout of tales about runaways, fair or foul, mainly localized in Scotland. Very different is the tone of two good ballads, *Willie's Lyke-Wake* and *The Gay Goshawk*, where love finds out the way by stratagem and inspires robust verse of the old kind.

Tradition at its purest characterizes the great ballads of domestic tragedy. *Edward*, for example, is so inevitable, so concentrated, that some critics would refer it to art; but tradition can bring about these qualities in its own way. *Lord Randal*, with its bewildering number of versions, *Little Musgrave and Lady Barnard*, a favourite in Shakespeare's day, *Glasgerion*, a simple but powerful ballad on a theme which no poet could now handle without constraint, *Child Maurice*, *The Cruel Brother*, *The Twa Brothers*—all these offer tragedy of the false mistress, the false wife, the false servant, and tragedy of more complicated matter. Wives false and wives true are pictured in two Scottish ballads, *The Baron o' Brackley* and *Captain Car*, both founded on fact. *The Braes o' Yarrow* knew another faithful wife. The treacherous nurse in *Lamkin*—a satiric name for its bloody and revengeful villain—long frightened Scottish children. Finally, there is the true-love. The adjective is beautifully justified in *The Three Ravens*, less well known than its cynical counterpart, *The Twa Corbies*. True-love is false in *Young Hunting*; and fickle lovers come to grief in *Lord Lovel*, *Fair Margaret and Sweet William*, and *Lord Thomas and Fair Annet*. Fate, not fickleness, however, brings on the tragedy in *Fair Janet*, *Lady Maisey*, *Clerk Saunders*; *Child Waters*, which both F. J. Child and the Danish philologist Svend Grundtvig praise as the pearl of English ballads, belongs to the group of poems celebrating woman's constancy under direct provocation.

Ballads of the funeral, echoes of the old *coronach*, are scantily preserved in English; *Bonnie James Campbell* and *The Bonny Earl of Murray* may serve as types; but the noblest outcome of popular lament is *Sir Patrick Spens*, which should be read in the shorter version printed by Percy in the *Reliques*, and should not be teased into history. Superstition, the other world, ghost-lore, find limited scope in English balladry. Commerce with the other world occurs in *Thomas Rymer*, derived from a romance. In *Sweet William's Ghost*, a great favourite of old, and in the best of all supernatural ballads, *The Wife of Usher's Well*, English balladry competes, in kind, with the riches of Scandinavian tradition.

Epic material of every sort was run into the ballad mould, and possibly the romances of Europe spring, in their own turn, from ballads. History, often perverted, but true as tradition, forms the matter of such ballads as *Sir Andrew Barton*, *King James and Brown* and *Mary Hamilton*; but this kind is best studied in the familiar pieces which have been traditional along the Scottish border. Refusing classification, there stand out those two great ballads, probably on the same fight, *Cheviot* and *Otterburn*. The version of the former known as *Chevy Chace*, "written over for the broadside press", as Child remarks, was the object of Addison's well-known praise; what Sidney heard as "trumpet sound" is not certain, but one would prefer to think it was the old *Cheviot*. Last of all, the greenwood with *Johnie Cock*, a precious specimen of the unspoiled traditional ballad. But the great figure is Robin Hood. Absolutely a creation of the ballad muse, he is the hero of a sterling little epic, and of thirty-six extant individual ballads, good and bad.

The aesthetic values of the ballad call for no long comment. They are the values which attach to plain, strong verse, intent upon its object. Tropes, figures and sophisticated literary tricks are alien to the ballad style. The metrical freedoms of the ballads are daring and successful and offer a stimulating contrast to the jog-trot measures afterwards imposed in the name of smoothness. Signs of musical setting or accompaniment can be easily recognized, for there is more life and freedom in words sung or spoken than in words merely written and printed. In "accomplishment of verse" the ballads are as little primitive as *Beowulf* or *The Iliad*; but they give a primitive and unspoiled poetic sensation, for they speak not only in the language of tradition, but also with the voice of the multitude. From one vice of modern literature they are entirely free: they have no "thinking about thinking", no "feeling about feeling". They can tell a good tale. They are fresh with the open air; wind and sunshine play through them; and the distinction, old as criticism itself, which assigns them to nature rather than to art, though it was overworked by the romantic school, and will always be liable to abuse, is practical and sound.

XVIII. POLITICAL AND RELIGIOUS VERSE TO THE CLOSE OF THE FIFTEENTH CENTURY

The Anglo-Norman literature of the period hardly falls within the scope of this volume. Our main concern is now with literature in English. The troublesome reigns of the kings from Edward III to Richard III moved poets to many kinds of utterance. Of the greatest, *Piers Plowman*, we have already spoken; we must now consider the more fugitive verse. Many specimens can be found in *Political Poems and Songs*, ed. Thomas Wright, 2 vols., Rolls Series (1859–61). Both Latin and English poems against the Lollards and songs against the friars are common. In the Middle Ages, popular singers who followed their calling along the king's highway helped, often enough, to fan the flames of rebellion, political and religious; and thus, consciously or unconsciously, they contributed to political and religious emancipation. The victory of Agincourt and the later siege of Calais gave further employment to song writers. But there were verses also of constructive intention. In 1436–7 a poem called *The Libel* (i.e. little book) *of English Policy* begins by "exhortynge alle England to kepe the see environ". This remarkable piece is the first example of propaganda in favour of a strong navy, and its influence was considerable in later years. The author does not overlook the importance of Ireland and Wales in strategy and commerce alike, and it is difficult to resist his conclusion:

> The end of bataile is pease sikerlye,
> And power causeth pease finally.

The last political poem to which reference need be made is a mocking dirge called forth by the high-handed execution of Henry VI's favourite, the unpopular Duke of Suffolk, in 1450. This, like other fifteenth-century songs—for it was probably sung—is remarkable for its metrical resource.

In the preceding chapter something was said in praise of the early religious songs. The same tenderness of feeling combined with perfection of form can be found in such poems as that beginning "Somer is comen and winter gon", in Eve's lines in the *Ludus Coventriae* beginning "Alas that evyr that speche was spokyn", in the exquisite carol from the early fifteenth-century Sloane MS. beginning "I syng of a mayden that is makeles", and in the *Quia amore langueo*, a poem of the fourteenth century occurring in several fifteenth-century manuscripts. Many examples of the songs of the period are given in *Political, Religious and Love Poems* (E.E.T.S. 1866, rev. 1903) and in Carleton Brown's *Religious Lyrics of the XVth Century*. There are, of course, duller and more sophisticated utterances than these. Mysticism often defeats by excess, and didactic purpose usually ends in boredom. But that happy sense of familiarity with the company of Heaven, which is one of the characteristics of an age of simple faith, finds delightful expression in hymns, and, above all, in the religious plays. These, which were written to be understood by the common folk, clearly reflect the taste of the people in the fourteenth and fifteenth centuries. It was not gold and frankincense and myrrh that would appeal most to the imagination of the idler in the market place, but a ball, a bird, and a "bob of cherys" which the visiting shepherds give to the Christ-Child, as they address him with "Hayll, lytyll tynë mop!" These writers and actors "served God in their mirth", but they were not allowed to go on their way unmolested. There are poems against miracle plays as against friars.

Of the purely didactic literature intended for daily needs a typical example is John Mirk's *Instructions for Parish Priests* (early fifteenth century), a versified translation from Latin. To this we may add *The Babees Book* (c. 1475), *The Lytille Childrenes Lytil Boke* (c. 1480), *The Boke of Curtasye* (c. 1450), and other works of instruction, in which the wise man teaches his son and the good wife her daughter. The middle of the fifteenth century gives us the *Book of Quinte Essence*, an early treatise on "natural science", from which we may learn (among other things) how "to reduce an oold feble evangelik man to the firste strenkthe of yongthe". And in a fourteenth-century manuscript the curious will even learn how "to make a woman say the(e) what thu askes hir". Woman was ever a disturbing factor, and the songs of medieval satirists do not spare her.

It has been sometimes urged that the fifteenth century, in the matter of purely English literature, is dull and uninteresting. That it lacks a Chaucer or a Spenser is certain; but a century, the beginning of which saw the English Mandeville translators at work, and the end of which saw one of those versions printed; a century to which may be credited *The Flower and the Leaf*, *The Paston Letters*, Caxton's prefaces and translations, *Le Morte d'Arthur*, *The Nut Brown Maid*, the ballads, the lyrics and carols, sacred and profane, and many of the miracle plays in their present form, can hold its own with even the best.

CHAPTER III

RENASCENCE AND REFORMATION

I. ENGLISHMEN AND THE CLASSICAL RENASCENCE

The classical Renascence, or rediscovery of classical thought and literature, implied both a knowledge of the classical writers and ability to use the Greek and Latin languages. Italy gave it birth, and it gradually spread beyond the Alps into Germany, France and England. It created a kind of cosmopolitan republic in a Europe almost savage, supremely war-like and comparatively untaught. It spread widely and silently until the mark of a well-educated person of either sex was ability to read Greek and to speak and write in Latin. There was, of course, another side to the picture. The devotees of Greek and Latin became disdainful of their mother tongues and were inclined to believe that cultured thought could find fit expression only in the language of Cicero. But their use of the common speech of this literary republic gave them an audience in all parts of educated Europe, and, in the course of years, enriched the vernaculars both with new words and with new graces of style and expression.

The cosmopolitan character of the Renascence is especially illustrated by the career of Erasmus, who belongs almost as much as Linacre, Colet and More to the intellectual history of England. Gerrit Gerritszoon (1466?–1536) was born at Rotterdam and took as a public name "The One Desired" in Latin and Greek, "Desiderius Erasmus". He visited England for the first time in the summer of 1499, and during a six months' stay came to know the chief English scholars, especially Colet, Grocyn, Linacre and More, of whom he writes with enthusiasm. Their influence upon him was profound; for they were not only great scholars, but men of lofty spiritual aspiration. Erasmus the humanist became Erasmus the Christian humanist. Colet taught him to distrust Aquinas as much as he had distrusted Duns Scotus, and to see in the editing and translation of the Scriptures a task worthy of a scholar's powers.

The pioneers of classical learning in England were obscure persons, whose names need not detain us here. One of them kindled the flame of scholarship in his pupil Thomas Linacre (c. 1460–1524), who later at Oxford studied Greek under Cornelio Vitelli, the first to teach Greek publicly in England. Thereafter Linacre spent some years in Italy, where he met the great figures of the Renascence and pursued the study of medicine. On his return to England he became famous both as scholar and physician. It was from Linacre that More learned Greek at Oxford. William Grocyn (c. 1446–1519) followed Linacre to Italy and met the same scholars. His lectures at Oxford on the writings of the so-called Dionysius the Areopagite, long supposed to have been a convert of St Paul, had remarkable effect, notably on John Colet (c. 1467–1519), Dean of St Paul's, whose own influence as the chief Christian humanist of England worked powerfully upon the generation that made the Renascence the instrument of Reformation. Colet seems to have awakened to his special vocation in Italy, probably under the influence of Savonarola. His was a typically English mind, conservative, practical, careless about exact definitions in theology, the value of the classical learning for him being the use it could be put to in effecting spiritual reform. From the logical and almost legal theology of Aquinas he turned to the earlier fathers and especially to the pseudo-Dionysius, who supported his belief that God could not be imprisoned in formulas. In particular he revolted from the prevalent mode of Scriptural exegesis that, laying stress on the words "the letter killeth but the spirit giveth life", rejected the plain words of the gospels and sought elaborately after analogical, anagogical and (as Tindale called them) "chopological" interpretations. Colet declared that the aim of a true interpretation of Scripture was to discover the personal message which the individual writer meant to give; and this led him, in his lectures on the Epistle to the Romans, to seek for every trace of the personality of St Paul. Colet was, in fact, the first to introduce the historical method of interpreting Scripture, and, as such, was far in advance, not merely of his own time, but of many succeeding generations. Colet is now best remembered by his educational work, and specially as the founder of St Paul's School. The Latin grammar written by himself and William Lily, the first headmaster of the school, and afterwards revised by Erasmus, remained the standard text-book for two centuries, and its use was very nearly made compulsory by Parliament. In 1758, after further emendations, it became the *Eton Latin Grammar*. Colet's determination not to allow any ecclesiastical control over his school, his openly expressed disbelief in the efficacy of relics and pilgrimages, and his refusal to leave money to be expended in masses for the benefit of his soul, indicate the spirit of a convinced religious reformer.

John Fisher (1459–1535), Bishop of Rochester, deserves brief mention in this place, not because he took high rank himself as a humanist, but because he was the means of bringing Erasmus to lecture on Greek in Cambridge (1511–14) at the very time when the university was changing from an ancient to a modern seat of learning.

Sir Thomas More (1478–1535), the associate with Fisher in his tragic death —and canonized with him in 1935—was the pupil of Linacre and Grocyn, the disciple of Colet, the beloved friend of Erasmus, and was the one member of the band of English humanists who had a distinct gift of literary genius. At Oxford he became a good Latinist and a fair scholar in Greek. Even when he was a highly successful lawyer with a lucrative commercial practice he lectured on the philosophy and history of Augustine's *City of God*. As a member of Parliament he resisted the royal exactions, and was reluctantly drawn into the royal service, in which, however, he rose rapidly, becoming in the end Lord Chancellor in succession to Wolsey. He was the first layman to hold that office. More had no illusions about his royal master, and the end came almost as he had foreseen. Having refused to take any oath which denied the Pope's supremacy in matters of faith he was confined in the Tower amid circumstances of spiteful and gratuitous hardship. The humorous serenity characteristic of his life never forsook him, and displays itself in the moving letters to his daughter, Margaret Roper, scribbled on scraps of paper with a piece of charcoal because writing materials had been taken from him. He went to his death in July 1535, jesting with the executioner in the act of mounting the scaffold. English history can show few baser acts than the judicial murder of this great and good man. More's literary fame rests on his history of Richard III (see p. 133) and his book universally known as *Utopia* ("Nowhere"), though he gave it a lengthy Latin title that actually does not include that famous name. It discusses in its few pages many of the problems, interests and activities of its time—political speculation, voyages of discovery, the iniquitous wars and leagues of rulers scrambling for extensions of dominion in Europe, royal indifference to social injustice, the growth of crime caused by lack of employment, and the possibilities of a polity in which health and well-being for all are deliberately sought, in which national service is applied to construction instead of to destruction, and in which a liberal existence is made possible by good-will and toleration. It is interesting to detect anticipations of modern social development in More's imaginary island, but the longest and most valuable part of the book is that which describes, not Utopia, but England. The brief account of Utopia itself is little more than an appended parable. In other words the book (like all its later progeny from Swift's *Gulliver* to Butler's *Erewhon* and Orwell's *Nineteen Eighty-Four*) is mainly a picture of its own time—a criticism of the present rather than a construction of the future. The force of its appeal is attested by the fact that it has added an indispensable word to the world's vocabulary. The book itself illustrates the pleasing internationalism of scholarship, for it was written by the Englishman More in the universal Latin, it received additions from the Flemish Peter Giles, it was revised by the Dutch Erasmus, it was first printed (1516) at Louvain, then at Paris, and then later at Basle, where it was illustrated by two woodcuts from the hand of the German Holbein. No edition appeared in England or in English until after More's death. Ralph Robynson's translation (1551) has the flavour of the time, but is less exact than later ones made in the seventeenth (Burnet), the nineteenth (Cayley) and the twentieth centuries (Paget, Richards). *Utopia* is best read in its own Latin, with a modern English translation. More's other works can be briefly summarized. His verses, English and Latin, are, for the most part, mediocre, but contain some pieces of great merit. They are interesting as revelations of a character at once humorous and serious, prepared for the best and the worst that life could offer. His translation into English of the *Lyfe of Johan Picus, Erle of Myrandula, a greate Lorde of Italy* (1510) is a treasury of ideals if not of facts. His controversial tracts, often unpleasing in tone, include *A Dyaloge...touchynge the pestylent Sect of Luther and Tyndale, The Supplycacyon of Soulys,* two parts of *A Confutacyon of Tyndales Answere,* a long *Apology* and *A Letter* against Frith (all *c.* 1530). More's English writings, first collected by W. Rastell in 1557, with their vivid idiomatic words, their carefully constructed well-balanced sentences, and their modulated cadences exhibit the scholar and the imitator of the Latin classics. Though *Utopia* was written in Latin, its author was one of the makers of English prose. The sketches of More's life by William Roper and Nicholas Harpsfield set the man before us. The best modern biography is *Thomas More* (1935) by R. W. Chambers.

Among those who, following Erasmus in his highly popular *Adagia* and

Colloquia, strove to make use of the writings of antiquity for the instruction and edification of their contemporaries were Sir Thomas Elyot (1490?–1546) and Dr Thomas Wilson (1525–81). The former is best known by his treatise, *The Boke named the Governour* (1531), and the latter by his *Arte of Rhetorique* (1553). Elyot's book is a lengthy and exhaustive treatise on the education which those who are destined to govern ought to receive. It is full of classical reminiscences taken either directly from the authors of antiquity or borrowed from the humanists of Italy. Elyot's reputation among his contemporaries rested on more than his *Boke of the Governour*. He wrote *The Castel of Helth* (1539) containing prescriptions and remedies largely selected from Galen and other medical authorities of antiquity. His two tracts, *A swete and devoute sermon of Holy Saint Ciprian of Mortalitie of Man* and *The Rules of a Christian lyfe made by Picus, erle of Mirandula* (1534), gave food for the soul. His translations and adaptations were very popular, and were often reprinted. Henry VIII encouraged Elyot in the compilation of his Latin-English lexicon: *The Dictionary of Syr T. Elyot knyght* (1538), revised later as *Bibliotheca Eliotae* (1545). If Erasmus popularized the classical Renascence for scholars, Elyot rendered it accessible to the mass of the people who had no acquaintance with the languages of antiquity. Wilson's *Arte of Rhetorique* is almost exclusively drawn from such old masters as Aristotle, Cicero and Quintilian. There is little or no originality in the volume, save, perhaps, the author's condemnation of the use of French and Italian phrases and idioms, which, he complains, are "counterfeiting the kinges Englishe".

It remains to note briefly two other instances of the spread of classical knowledge. School and college plays began to draw as much as possible from classical sources, both in character and in expression, and the great men of antiquity became familiar figures to the commonalty. By Shakespeare's time, as J. A. K. Thomson writes in *Shakespeare and the Classics* (1952), "some knowledge of Greece and Rome was impressed upon the most illiterate Elizabethan. There was an almost continuous succession of masques, shows, revels, processions, royal progresses and the like, in each of which there was sure to be one or more characters drawn from ancient history or mythology". Thus, classical learning, at first the possession of the few, passed gradually into the general inheritance. Shakespeare is not far distant from Chaucer by measurement of time; but the now familiar classical allusions, intelligible to Shakespeare's audience, would have been almost meaningless to the readers of Chaucer.

II. REFORMATION LITERATURE IN ENGLAND

The Reformation left its mark upon the national literature. It gave us, most notably, the English Bible and *The Book of Common Prayer*; but it also produced a number of tracts, treatises, sermons and books of devotion, which seemed to the age itself of hardly less importance. The temptation is strong to regard this Reformation literature as the descendant of Lollard tracts and versions; but it is the successor rather than the descendant; and the two movements are best regarded as successive manifestations of the same tendency toward critical and constructive revolt in religion.

The revival of letters had already shown its power at Oxford, where, as we have seen, Colet, More and Erasmus had directed it into religious channels. A few words should be said about the impulse which Erasmus gave to religious thought and learning in Cambridge. Fisher welcomed him there, and he became Lady Margaret Reader (1511). Tindale and Coverdale both admired him. Cranmer was notably influenced by him, and many others, of lesser fame, were inspired from the same source, and urged the pre-eminent claim of the Bible upon theological students. The English Reformation began at Cambridge, and the Cambridge movement began with Erasmus. The new movement took many forms, and spread in many ways. It was not always revolutionary, and in one direction it turned to older forms of devotion. Religion in England had enriched the liturgical services of the church with the Sarum use and with uses less popular, like those of Hereford and York; it had inspired the *Primers*, books of private devotion, translated in the fourteenth century from Latin into English, and printed at early dates and in many forms. Attempts were made to fit these to popular needs, and the noble result was *The Book of Common Prayer*. But even more important was the coming of the English Bible, the greatest monument of the Reformation in England. Colet at Oxford and Erasmus at Cambridge had proclaimed the supremacy of the Bible over the teaching of the church as the rule of Christian life; but many years were to pass and many good men were to suffer before the Bible in English became a permitted possession.

With the greater sharpness of national divisions and the stronger coherence of national languages, the use of the vernacular in the services of the church was more and more demanded throughout Christendom. In England the first step towards uniformity of liturgical use was the re-issue of the Sarum breviary (1542) for authorized use throughout the province of Canterbury. A chapter of the Bible was ordered to be read in English on Sundays and holy days, and in 1544 the Litany was put forth in English. Under Edward VI, an English communion service for the people was added (Easter, 1548). Henry VIII's *Primer* (1545) was the last of a long series of these popular works of devotion, and was intended to check the diversity which the printing press had intensified. Henry had ordered Cranmer to turn certain prayers into English and to see that they were used in his province. This royal *Primer* embodied the English Litany, the beautiful prose of which is undoubtedly Cranmer's. The same literary genius was now to work upon a larger field.

Thomas Cranmer (1489–1556) went to Cambridge and followed the usual academic course before he turned to the study of Erasmus. He worked with high distinction as priest and lecturer at the university until the advice he gave to Henry VIII in the matter of his divorce brought him into royal favour and a larger world. In 1533 he succeeded Warham as Archbishop of Canterbury. We are not required to discuss here the character of Cranmer either as a man or as an ecclesiastical statesman. Judged by the standard of More, he shows pitiful weakness; but he transfigured all his past by the courage of his end. What is not fully appreciated is that Cranmer's apparent vacillations represent faithfully much of the uncertain mind of the English Reformation. To lovers of English literature, Cranmer is not the instrument of Henry VIII and the victim of Mary, but a man with large liturgical knowledge and an exquisite ear for the language of devotion. There is a world of difference between the crude bareness of the Litany as he found it and the majestic rhythm he gave it. His actual writings are unimportant. He is not inspired except as a liturgist, and so his greatest work is *The Book of Common Prayer*, which, though owing very much to the literary and religious instinct of the age, owed most of all to him. The matters of doctrine and ritual involved in Edward VI's Prayer Book of 1549 and the later revisions do not concern us. As an example of English prose the book remains as Cranmer left it. It is admirable, not only as an absolute achievement in the writing of English, but as a compilation exquisitely tuned to every need of worship.

One new feature of the Prayer Book had been its exhortations. Not only was much Scripture introduced, but short discourses or admonitions, Scriptural, pointed, majestic, were also added. The wish to instruct shown by these compositions found a larger field for itself in the *Homilies*, the first book of which (1547) was edited by Cranmer, who himself wrote the homilies of salvation, of faith and of good works. A "seconde tome" issued under Elizabeth (in 1563) was lengthier, less interesting and feebler in style than the first book. The increasing stress laid upon edification made itself felt through the pulpit literature of the day.

Among popular preachers, John Longland (1473–1547), Bishop of Lincoln and Chancellor of Oxford, had a great following; so, upon the other side, had John Hooper, afterwards Bishop of Gloucester. But the reputation of these preachers was overshadowed by the greater fame of Hugh Latimer. Latimer (1485?–1555) had at first opposed the new teaching, but the influence of Thomas Bilney brought him over to the "Germans", as the Cambridge band of new theologians were called. Latimer attacked specially those abuses which Erasmus had satirized—indulgences, pilgrimages and veneration of images; upon the positive side he laid stress on the life and example of Christ, and held up a high ideal of conduct. His sermons, with their homely anecdotes and commonplace allusions, are valuable for us historically. They are even more valuable as a revelation of character. Latimer preached because he must. He knew nothing of literary art, but he knew how to deliver a message to the people.

William Tindale (d. 1536) is to us, above all, the translator of the Scriptures; but to his own age he was at least as much the theological pamphleteer. Of his early life little is known. He went to Oxford, and spent some time afterwards in Cambridge. It was about 1520 that he formed his great design of translating the Bible into English. Finding it difficult to do this in England he crossed to Hamburg in 1524. It was possible to print books abroad and send them into England by an evasion of the existing regulations. In Germany, Tindale came into contact with others who had left England for religious reasons. Some of them were fanatics of the most extreme kind, and his own absorption in his task and his curious love of self-assertion tended to make him somewhat peevish in his dealings. The story of his adventures abroad is not pleasing. It is a relief to turn from the violence of Tindale's pamphleteering to his Biblical translation. His scholarship was adequate, and he was not dependent upon the Vulgate alone. *St Matthew* and *St Mark* were published separately, but in 1525–6 the whole New Testament was printed and sent to England. Measures were taken against it; but they proved a failure. In 1534 Tindale published a revised edition with certain changes. In 1535 he was treacherously seized at Antwerp, and in 1536 he was burned at Vilvorde. But his great work was done. In the very year of his martyrdom an edition of his New Testament was printed in England. He had made more than a beginning with the Old Testament; he had, moreover, fixed the character of the English translations for evermore. Instinctively, like many writers and preachers of his day, he had expressed himself in the popular style, not in the larger phrase affected by scholars, and in that style the Bible remained.

Miles Coverdale (1488–1568), afterwards Bishop of Exeter, although inferior to Tindale in scholarship, was an inspired translator. He had been an Augustinian friar at Cambridge and had early connections with Sir Thomas More and Thomas Cromwell. He left England and probably met Tindale abroad. Not only did he thus enter the circle of Biblical translators, but he was urged by Cromwell to print an edition of his own. His translation, issued at Zurich in 1535, was the first complete Bible to be printed in the English language. The second edition, published in 1537, was the first complete Bible to be printed in England itself. Coverdale did not claim any extensive scholarship—his versions are based on German and Latin texts—and his own description of his work is modest; but his pains, nevertheless, had been great, and the Prayer-book Psalter bears eloquent testimony to his literary genius. The publicity which Coverdale, even perhaps above Tindale, had aimed at, was gained more largely by another edition. Thomas Matthew, or rather John Rogers, to give him his real name, formed another Bible by a combination of Tindale's Old Testament, as far as it went, and Coverdale's—the Apocrypha being included. This was printed at Antwerp in 1537.

Coverdale began to prepare a new edition in 1538, and again availed himself of some new Continental versions. This edition, known as The Great Bible, was published in 1539 and was ordained for use in churches. A second edition of it (1540), with a preface by Cranmer, is usually known as Cranmer's Bible. At last, an English Bible was set up in churches (May 1540) and was in general use, both public and private. One more edition of the New Testament, significant from the place of its appearance, and destined from its doctrinal bias to be widely popular, was the Genevan New Testament of William Whittingham (1557). The whole Bible (The Geneva Bible) appeared at Geneva (1560) with a dedication to Queen Elizabeth and with more apparatus than had hitherto been added, the text being due to Whittingham, helped by Anthony Gilby and Thomas Sampson. These versions, being respectively the first Testament and first Bible to be printed with verse divisions and in Roman type, mark a distinct stage. Under Elizabeth, and upon the initiative of Archbishop Parker, The Bishops' Bible was issued (1568); but in the end it was superseded by the Authorized Version (1611), prepared after the Hampton Court Conference. It should be noted that these Bibles varied in their treatment of the Apocrypha: Coverdale's, Matthew's and the Genevan Bible, following Continental Protestant usage, differentiated it from the Old Testament, and after 1629, when we have the first example, editions of Bibles without the Apocrypha became common. Apart from any critical or theological views supposed to be involved, this omission was a serious literary loss, which is now being more understood.

Very little use appears to have been made in Scotland of the earliest English translations. The Scots New Testament of Murdoch Nisbet (*c.* 1510) was, however, based upon Purvey's version of the earlier Wyclifite translation. The importation of Tindale's translation into Scotland checked the use of this, and perhaps deprived us of a whole Bible that would have been of great linguistic and literary interest. See further pp. 59 and 78.

One result of the growing use of the vulgar tongue in worship calls for mention. The hymns in the daily offices had always been popular, and some kind of substitute became necessary. An obvious source was the Book of Psalms. Thomas Sternhold, a Hampshire gentleman, and governor of the robes to Henry VIII, attempted to turn the minds of the nobles to higher things by circulating some of the Psalms in verse (1548). After Sternhold's death, John Hopkins, a Suffolk clergyman, published Sternhold's versions with some of his own (1549). In later editions he increased the number, and in 1562 *The Whole Booke of Psalmes*, by Sternhold, Hopkins, Thos. Norton and others, appeared in verse and was added to the Prayer Book. Not only was this done, but melodies, some of which are still in popular use, were also printed. A rival appeared in the Genevan Psalter, prepared by certain of the English exiles, and from this Calvinistic version descended the Scots Psalter of 1564.

One fact about Reformation literature may be noted. It began in the medieval fashion of composite or anonymous authorship. But presently the weight of well-known names began to tell, and the printing press, fixing once for all the very words of a writer, put an end to processes which had often hidden authorship. The Reformation began with medieval theses upon medieval controversies; it ended, in England, with the English Bible and the English Prayer Book, which are, in the best sense, popular, and as modern as any other great literature.

III. DISSOLUTION OF THE RELIGIOUS HOUSES

The dissolution of the religious houses in the sixteenth century affected learning as well as religion. The destruction of books was great. Libraries that had been collected through centuries vanished in a moment. A second kind of destruction was that of the homes of study which the religious houses, especially those of the Benedictines, provided for all who leaned that way. Intellectual unity with the Continent was broken, and there were no longer wealthy corporations able to send students abroad to acquire special knowledge. The education of children was affected by the dislocation of the usual channels of instruction; but many of the monastic schools continued to exist under different control. The Benedictine nuns kept schools attended by girls of gentle birth, and were, in fact, the only available women teachers of even the simplest elements of learning. The Edwardian (and later) grammar schools sought to replace the vanished monastic schools.

At both Oxford and Cambridge were large establishments to which monks and friars came to finish their education. The dissolution of the religious houses affected, it is said, the numbers of students at both universities; but general assertions about the losses or gains to learning through the dissolution should be made with caution. In one respect there was clearly a gain. The monasteries were the last strongholds of the medieval scholasticism which had long outlived its usefulness. Thinking had been a highly specialized professional activity of theologians. The medieval layman did not, in the modern sense, think at all. He left abstractions to the churchman, and when he meditated upon immaterial things gave to his speculations the forms of allegory. With the monasteries there passed away a vested interest in an exhausted system of thought. Thus, although more than three hundred years had to pass before the state began to recognize its responsibility for education, the removal of education from monastic control was a step in advance. Another gain that compensated for the loss of the old kind of intercourse with the monastic seats of learning abroad was to be found in the new connections of England with the vigorous life of northern Europe. Further, there gradually came a sense of intellectual release. It is hard to believe that the glories of Elizabeth's reign would have been just as refulgent in a land of monasteries.

That many books and manuscripts were destroyed is lamentable; that many others were dispersed is much less lamentable. Some found a home in the royal collections. Some were privately acquired, and, being made accessible, gave to a new school of antiquaries, led by John Leland (1506–52), the long buried and virtually unknown materials for research. Others followed Leland in his care for antiquities of literature and history. Matthew Parker (1504–75) diligently sought out the monuments and chronicles of old times, and Sir Robert Cotton (1571–1631) amassed the great collection of Saxon charters and other manuscripts (since 1753 in the British Museum) which is almost the prime fount of English history and literature. Thus, though the losses through the dissolution were serious, yet, through the general diffusion of knowledge and the widening of the limits of learning, we have become the inheritors of a treasure that could hardly have been ours without the payment of a heavy price.

IV. BARCLAY AND SKELTON: EARLY GERMAN INFLUENCES ON ENGLISH LITERATURE

Alexander Barclay (1475–1552), monk, and afterwards parish priest, is famous as the author of *The Shyp of Folys of the Worlde* (1509)—"The Ship of Fools" —translated and adapted from Sebastian Brant's *Narrenschiff* (1494). The idea of Brant's book was not new. The collection of various human types on a voyaging ship was just another medieval device, like the familiar pilgrimage. What was new was the manning of the ship with many different kinds of fools. Brant's notion of folly was very wide, and the book became a comprehensive satirical picture of the manners of the age. It attained large popularity and was at once translated, at first into Latin, in which form, probably, Barclay first knew it. According to his prologue, Barclay desired to "redres the errours and vyces of this our royalme of Englande, as the foresayde composer and translatours hath done in theyr contrees". Therefore, he followed his author "in sentence" rather than in word; that is to say, he used all the delightful freedom of the Tudor translators, making additions and omissions as well. His version (over fourteen thousand lines long) is more than twice as long as the Latin, and nearly three times as long as the original German. He uses the rhyme royal or Troilus stanza, but his language is plain and simple, as meant for ordinary readers and not only for the learned. Barclay deliberately tried to make Brant's book applicable to English circumstances. He vigorously condemns the misdeeds of officials, denounces unscrupulous prelates and bad priests, and like Piers Plowman takes the side of the poor against their oppressors. But he was a soundly orthodox churchman, unsympathetic to the reformers. The influence of *The Ship of Fools* in England is discernible in *Cocke Lorelles Bote* (c. 1510) with her crew of London craftsmen. R. Copland's *Hye Way to the Spyttel Hous*, published about 1536, was certainly suggested by Barclay's chapter on beggars and vagabonds. In later Elizabethan times the woodcuts of *The Ship of Fools* had some influence on the development of emblem books, and even when the purely literary influence of the poem had faded, it was still liked as a collection of satirical types, more real than the stock allegorical figures of medieval literature. There are frequent allusions to it in Elizabethan drama, which learned something from its character-drawing.

Barclay's *Egloges* (1515 and 1521) have an odd personal history which need not here detain us. They are five in number, and were not published together. As the first specimens of English pastoral poetry they would possess some historical importance, even if there were nothing else to recommend them. The matter for the fourth and fifth was taken from Mantuan, the rest from Aeneas Sylvius. Johannes Baptista Spagnuoli, called Mantuanus, was, next to Petrarch, the most famous Renascence Italian writer of Latin eclogues. In England, where, at that time, the Greek idyllic poet Theocritus was still quite unknown, Mantuan was valued even more than Virgil and was read in grammar schools to Shakespeare's time. In spite of their interest of matter and style, Barclay's *Eclogues* were soon forgotten. Spenser ignores them as he ignores other earlier attempts at pastoral poetry, and Spenser's contemporaries seem not to have heard of them. But it is Barclay, not Spenser, who is father of the English eclogue. His other works do not call for notice. Barclay never wrote without a moral, didactic or satirical purpose, and his conception of literature was medieval. But in his practice he anticipates later efforts, especially in the "character" and the pastoral.

John Skelton (1460?–1529) has left few biographical traces. He is mentioned by Caxton as a translator from the Latin and his own Latin verses are smooth; but his acquaintance with the Italian poets of the Renascence seems to have been small. It was the university of Cambridge, not the court of Henry VII, that made him *poeta laureatus*. He was well acquainted with English literature, and knew the difference in value between Chaucer and Gower; but, like others of the time, he overestimated Lydgate. Skelton was a "medieval", not a "modern". As a poet he is extremely versatile. Unfortunately many of his writings are lost, and even his extant works offer several difficulties of date. First editions are usually missing and probably some of his satires enjoyed manuscript circulation. His few known religious poems show him as ardent a champion of the old faith as Barclay. In *Colyn Clout* he speaks contemptuously of the reformers, and his vigorous *Replycacion agaynst certayne yong scolers adjured of late* (?1526) is severe upon heretics. Skelton was a priest, narrowly orthodox, and an ardent lover of his own country. Flodden Field gave him an opportunity for a hearty attack called *Skelton Laureate Against the Scottes*. But he knew also how to glorify noble ladies. Some poems in this vein appear in *A Goodly Garlande or Chapelet of Laurell* (1523), an allegorical poem in a variety of metres, full of grotesque self-glorification and built up with motives from Chaucer's *House of Fame* and the prologue to *The Legend of Good Women*. Skelton's originality is more evident in *Phyllyp Sparowe*, a poem addressed to a young lady whose pet sparrow had been killed by a cat. All the birds of the air are summoned to the burial, and among the mourners we find our old friend Chaunteclere and his wife Pertelote from *The Nun's Priest's Tale*. The short and lively metre is very effective and keeps up the attention throughout. That Skelton had an amazingly large stock of abusive terms is seen in *The Tunnyng of Elynour Rummyng*, a fantastical description of an old ale-wife and her guests. The metre is the same "Skeltonic" short verse as in *Phyllyp Sparowe*. His unfavourable view of court life is set forth in *The Bowge of Court* (i.e. rewards, or allowances, or board allowed to inferior court officials), an allegorical poem, written in Chaucer's seven-lined stanza. It is both an example of a dream poem with allegorical personifications, and a specimen of the "ship" allegory; for the scene of the vision is a vessel called "The Bowge of Court". The satire is severe, and must have annoyed the courtiers. In *Colyn Clout* (c. 1519), we are told by Colyn, the roaming vagabond, that everything is wrong in England and that the clergy are to blame for it. The most dangerous fact is that one man (i.e. Wolsey) has all the power. The lively metre adds considerably to the vivacity of the whole and is much more developed and refined than in *Phyllyp Sparowe*. After *Colyn Clout* came *Speke, Parrot*, imperfectly preserved and printed; but clear through all its incoherence is the attack on Wolsey. Still another attack is *Why come ye nat to courte*, a pungent and daring satire. Skelton's poems against Wolsey are grossly one-sided. Wolsey's statesmanship, his learning and the services he rendered to his country are unacknowledged; but Skelton was undoubtedly speaking with the voice of his times. In any case we must admire the poet's courage. The morality *Magnyfycence*, written about 1516, is the only specimen of the poet's dramatic production that has come down to us. It is entirely allegorical and contains little but tedious moralizing.

Skelton's poetic production shows an extraordinary variety. He moves with ease, sometimes with mastery, in all the traditional forms of poetry. In his longer poems he is very original, particularly where he uses his characteristic style, the short staccato rhymed lines that we have learned to call Skeltonic. The opening of *Colyn Clout* is a typical specimen:

> What can it avayle
> To dryve forth a snayle,
> Or to make a sayle
> Of an herynges tayle.

The immense vivacity and originality of Skelton and the freshness of his
utterance after the stock allegorizing of preceding poets must be heartily
acknowledged, but must not mislead the reader into supposing that he is to be
included among the greater English poets.

Compared with *The Ship of Fools*, most of the other contributions of German
to English literature in the beginning of the sixteenth century are insignificant.
Of German popular poetry next to nothing became known in England.
Coverdale tried to introduce the hymns, and his *Goostly Psalmes and Spiritual
Songes* (1539?) represent the first period of Protestant hymnology (1527–31).
From Germany, the English reformers learned to use effectively the dialogue
as a weapon in the religious struggle. One of the first, *Rede me and be nott wrothe*,
composed by two converted Greenwich friars, William Roy and Jerome
Barlow, at Strasburg in 1528, is a violent attack on the English clergy and
specially on Cardinal Wolsey. Purely English in spirit is the *Proper Dyalogue
betwene a Gentillman and a Husbandman* (1530), complaining of the oppression
of the lay folk by the clergy. Under Edward VI, dialogue against the Mass
flourished with the official sanction of the government. *Robin Conscience* (see
p. 110) is a good English example of the well-known "son against father" type,
showing strong influence of the morality play. The more elaborate form of
the "trial", used largely in Germany, was adopted in England, particularly by
William Turner (d. 1568), Dean of Wells, whose *Huntyng of the Romishe Fox*
(1543) was followed by the much better *Huntyng of the Romyshe Wolfe* (1554).
Under Mary, very few Protestant dialogues were written; and under Elizabeth,
German influence was dead. Towards the end of the century, translations of
sensational German news sheets occur sporadically in the Stationers' Register.
We hear (in a "ballad") of Bishop Hatto and of the Piper of Hamelin. Exposing
the coarseness of his time, Brant, in *Das Narrenschiff*, created a new saint,
Grobianus, who soon became the typical representative of rude and boorish
behaviour. The character became popular and was exploited by Friedrich
Dedekind, whose *Grobianus* was translated into English as *The Schoole of
Slovenrie* (1605). Traces of grobianism can be found in Dekker's *Guls Horne-
booke* (1609); and the figure of Grobianus appears utterly transformed in the
interlude *Grobiana's Nuptials* (Bodleian MS. 30), where it has become the type
of the Oxford man of Jacobean time with his affectation of simplicity.

V. SOCIAL LITERATURE IN TUDOR TIMES

The middle classes entered on the sixteenth century with the characteristic
tastes of their forefathers—a love of romance, of simple allegory, of vigorous
satire and of coarse humour, all of which had found expression in a literature
quite separate from monastic culture and the civilization of the court. They
viewed themselves and each other with the curiosity always evident when
communities become large and diverse—the kind of interest found in Chaucer's
Prologue and not found in *Beowulf*, because that interest is, literally, a civilized
interest. The pieces named in this section are evidence of the growth of popular
literature—they are not "literature" in the lofty sense; but our view of the time

would be imperfect without a little knowledge of them. Some cannot be dated exactly. *The Cambridge Bibliography of English Literature* should be consulted for detailed information.

As we have seen from the preceding pages, a ship with its passengers provided a simple formula for the presentation of character-sketches. *Cock Lorelles Bote* (1510) is a popular example of a ship of fools or knaves. The captain of the "bote" is the notorious Cock Lorell, a tinker, probably a real person, who was a by-word as late as Jacobean times, and the crew is an interesting collection of low-class characters. Another favourite formula was the burlesque will or testament, in which the ribald humorist could collect the objects of his satire as supposed legatees. The device is old, and, in the hands of Villon, had produced a great poem. An early English example is Copland's *Gyl of Braintfords Testament* (1560?). The hero of Dunbar's *The Testament of Mr Andro Kennedy* (1508) leaves his soul to his lord's wine-cellar. The most elaborate of bibulous wills is *Colin Blowbol's Testament*. An interesting later testament is *The Wyll of the Devyll* by Humphrey Powell (c. 1550), re-issued by R. Johnes (1577); it is a savage invective against the Roman Catholic Church, to which the devil, on his deathbed, bequeaths his vices and superstitions. Popular broadsides continued the literature of delineation, without reference to religious and political affairs. Among these may be mentioned some in which the formula is an order or fraternity, such as the *XX Orders of Fooles*, registered in 1569–70, and *A New Ballad against Unthrifts*. The universal subjection of mankind to death without respect of person or rank offers still another device for presenting a series of characters. The French *Danses Macabres* of the fifteenth century had already made notable use of this formula, which, in pictorial art, was presently to give us the *Dance of Death* by Holbein. Among English broadsides of this kind are *The Shaking of the Sheets* and *The Daunce and Song of Death*.

Satires on women abound, as in *The Boke of Mayd Emlyn* and *The Widow Edith*. *The Schole-howse of Women* expatiates at length on the vices of the sex, and uses both dialogue and disquisition—forerunners, we may say, of comedy and essay. The attack provoked replies such as Edward Gosynhyll's *The Prayse of All Women* (1542) and Edward More's *The Defence of Women* (c. 1558). Another satire on women, which combined the dialogue with the street ballad, is *The Proude Wyves Paternoster* (1560). The old theme of strife for supremacy in the house is illustrated in a *Merry Jest of a Shrewde and Curste Wyf lapped in a Morelles Skin* (1580?).

But the sixteenth century also desired something more than brutal satire and horse-play. The melancholy which Burton was to anatomize and Jacques to epitomize was always present and demanded curative relaxation. Once the minstrel and the jester were the chief purveyors of mirth, but now, in a world of printing, the "pills to purge melancholy" took the form of jest-books. Among famous foreign books of anecdotes belonging to this period, two may be specially mentioned, the Latin *Facetiae* (1470) of the Italian Poggio and the French *Cent Nouvelles Nouvelles* by an unknown compiler. The earliest English jest-book, *A C. Mery Talys*, referred to in *Much Ado*, was in print by 1526. So popular was it that it has almost disappeared. Nearly as popular was the *Tales and Quicke Answeres, very Mery* (1535), slightly less crude than its predecessor.

Anecdotes and jests always gain in point if they are associated with a known personality. English compilers soon found it advantageous to put a familiar name to their jests, and we have the *Merie Tales of Master Skelton*, a collection entered 1565–6 surviving as *Scoggin, his jestes* (1613) fathered on a perhaps mythical jester, and the jests attributed to Will Summers. To gratify the demand for coarse humour, German jest-books were put on the market in English translations. *Eulenspiegel* was translated from an abridged Antwerp edition by William Copland under the title *Howleglass* (1528), and the same printer produced an English version of the old Danish tale of Rausch as *Friar Rush*. Places, as well as persons, have a reputation, and to this day the mere names of certain towns will always raise a laugh. The best known example of place-humour is the *Merie Tales of the Mad Men of Gotam*. Jest books did not efface a kindred form of miscellany—books of riddles. Wynkyn de Worde printed *Demaundes joyous* (1511); and the *Booke of Merry Riddles* probably appeared before the earliest known edition of 1600. A further indication that the Englishman of those days was "merry" as well as melancholy, can be found in the almost universal habit of making music. Everybody sang. For the most primitive classes there were popular ballads, so-called, but to be sharply distinguished from the genuine ballads described earlier. The literary poverty of these products and their tendency to voice popular discontents drew upon them the condemnation of the scholars and the ban of the rulers. "Ballads" are frequently mentioned in proclamations as things to be suppressed. Very few survive, and they have no literary interest.

Most of the popular literature so far described is medieval in spirit and untouched by the Renascence. The growth of trade and the dislocation of industries gave rise to many tracts dealing with the vices that arise when the "new rich" have money to spend. Charles Bansley's *The Pryde and Abuse of Women* (c. 1550) belongs to a different world of satire from that of *The Schole-howse of Women*, or *The Proude Wyves Paternoster*. It is an indictment of female ostentation. *The Booke in Meeter of Robin Conscience* (1560), already noted as an example of dialogue, gives us a son reproaching his father with love of money, his mother with love of luxury, and his sister with love of artificial aids to beauty. *A Treatise of a Gallant* (1510?) attacks the vices of the new courtiers. The spread of gambling in fashionable circles produced the gentleman-thief, who is exposed as a menace in *A Manifest detection of the most vyle and detestable use of dice play and other practices etc.* (1552). The literature of social complaint is vigorous and is pointed by the sharp regrets of those who had expected a new world to come from the Reformation and the breach with Rome. This feeling found vigorous expression in Henry Brinkelow's *Complaynt of Roderyck Mors...unto the Parliament Howse of England* (1548). The growth of vagabondage caused by the evictions of husbandmen in the interest of sheep-farming had been one notable theme in More's *Utopia*. Robert Crowley, printer, puritan and preacher, turned from religious controversy to deal with the social abuses of the time in a set of tracts, the most interesting of which is *An Informacion and Peticion agaynst the oppressours of the pore commons of this realme* (1548). In this address to the parliament of Edward VI, the preacher fulminates against the rich in the language of the Psalms and Isaiah. As early as 1528, Simon Fish had made his powerful *Supplicacyon for the Beggars,* answered by Thomas More. Robert Copland's *Hye Way to the Spyttel Hous,* mentioned earlier, is a ghastly picture of destitution. The real beggar, as usual, created the impostor. John Awdeley's *Fraternitye of Vacabones* (1561) describes all the shams of professional beggary and shows how destitution is exploited commercially by a "boss", as we should now call him, who takes a large share of the spoils. Awdeley wrote to give information, not to contribute to the literature of types. Thomas Harman, who had tried to do good by keeping open house for the distressed, was naturally imposed upon by the professional pauper, and put forth *A Caveat or Warening for Commen Corsetors, Vulgarely called Vagabones* (first edition of unknown date; second, 1567). The book is meant as an "alarum" to forewarn honest citizens; but, in fact, it contains the researches of a sociologist.

While social miseries were inspiring a whole literature of narrative and exposure, the sixteenth-century spirit of cosmopolitanism was also finding popular expression. As early as *The Nature of the Four Elements* (1520) we have a conception of cosmography serving as a basis for a morality play. *The Fyrst Boke of the Introduction of Knowledge* (1547) is a collection of essays on the chief nationalities and kingdoms of Europe by the traveller and physician Andrew Boorde (1490?–1549), who also wrote *A Compendyous Regyment or a Dyetary of Helth* (1542), one of the earliest things of its kind in English. But no writer has embodied so much sentiment, learning, eloquence and dramatic power in his scientific treatises as William Bullein (d. 1576). His first book, *The Gouvernement of Healthe* (1558–9), contains Shakespearean reflections on the uneasy sleep of those who wear crowns. In 1562 he produced *Bullein's Bulwarke of Defence againste all Sicknes, Sornes, and Woundes,* modelling his title on Elyot's successful *Castel of Helth.* The most important of Bullein's works, from a literary point of view, is *A Dialogue both pleasaunte and pietifull wherein is a goodly regiment against the fever Pestilence with a Consolacion and Comfort against Death,* of which the earliest extant copy is dated 1564.

But though the popular printing presses were thus exposing fraud and enlightening ignorance, the superstitions of an earlier age were reappearing in an aggravated form. Belief in charms, magic, alchemy and astrology was as powerful as ever, and Robert Waldegrave (1554?–1604) published in 1580 an attack on prognostications in the *Foure Great Lyers, Striving who shall win the Silver Whetstone.* The general sense of corruption and wickedness led to an expectation of some unimaginable and awful calamity. Flyleaves appeared describing the birth of prodigies, many of them relating to the year 1562, which Holinshed and Stow record as specially fertile in monsters. But the superstitious excitability of the people exhibited its most dreadful phase in the revival of witch persecutions. In 1531 Henry VIII passed the first act against sorcery and magic; in 1562 the law was revived; and in 1575 and 1576 persecutions were renewed. It was an age of wild hallucinations. Yet there were enough sane readers to call for three editions of a burlesque by William Baldwin (1570?) which ridiculed sorcery, spells and transformations into cats, etc., under the title *Beware the Cat.* Belief in witchcraft was not confined to the vulgar and uneducated. The theology and science of Germany helped to encourage more informed fanatics. *The Discoverie of Witchcraft* (1584) by Reginald Scot (1538?–

1599) is the first great English contribution to this European controversy. It was primarily intended as a humanitarian protest, and it is essentially a work of investigation and exposition. Scot boldly criticized the legal methods of procedure with accused witches, and attacked all forms of credulity. But his treatise produced no effect on the beliefs of his time. Superstition was too deeply rooted in religion to be disturbed by medieval science.

The middle classes played an important part in forming the literature of the sixteenth century. While accepting the stories, satire and learning of the Middle Ages, they created a demand for English books that should reflect the tendencies of the present, and embody the humour and wisdom of the past. This popular literature continued to develop; but its tone begins to change. The note of Puritanism is heard. The production of popular tracts becomes more and more the business of professional writers, deliberately literary, and living in close association in London. In fact, with the first Elizabethan tracts we leave the last of the medievalists and come to writers who resemble modern journalists.

VI. SIR DAVID LYNDSAY

The year 1528 is marked by three events of importance in the history of Scotland. James V, after a long tutelage, became master of his kingdom; Patrick Hamilton, the protomartyr of the Scottish reformation, was burnt; and Sir David Lyndsay published his first work, *The Dreme*. A new Scotland was about to be born; and of this new Scotland the first clear voice is that of Sir David Lyndsay. Lyndsay (1490–1555) was the last of the Scottish Chaucerians, and owed something both to Dunbar and Douglas; but he is also the first of the modern Scottish poets. He did not write satire "at large", like Dunbar; he took a particular view of the troubles of his age, and marks the advent of the time when literature in Scotland was to be caught up in a fierce blaze of religious and national strife.

The Dreme was written after the escape of the young king from the control of the Douglases. Lyndsay had been the king's personal attendant, and had told him tales in his solitary hours; but now that the king was to assume the responsibilities of manhood, Lyndsay resolved to tell him a new and graver story; and to tell it without offence he adopted the medieval conventions of allegory. After a preliminary journey to hell, purgatory, the seven planets and paradise, we encounter a figure called John the Commoun Weill, who, typifying the honest virtuous man, sets forth the miseries of Scotland and the need for "ane gude and prudent Kyng". The poem, which is long and uses the Troilus (rhyme royal) stanza with fair success, is admonition rather than literature, but it has good passages. Lyndsay was made Lyon King of Arms in 1530. His reformatory zeal was, however, not silenced, and in *The Testament and Complaynt of our Soverane Lordis Papyngo* (popinjay or parrot) he exposed more particularly the corruptions and worldliness of the spirituality. After a glowing tribute to his poetic predecessors, from Chaucer onwards, he declares that, all the "polleit terms" having been used, he is reduced to record the complaint of a wounded papyngo. But Lyndsay makes little attempt to keep up the pretence of fable. The voice is the undisguised voice of the poet. The fable form is more strictly preserved in the latter part, and we get a satirical "testament" when the dying bird communes with its "holy executors", a pyot (representing a canon regular), a raven (a black monk), and a ged or hawk (a holy friar). A piece meant as a satire on the king's courtiers is *Ane Publict Confessioun of the Kingis auld Hound callit Bagsche*, in which an old dog tells the story of its life to the new pets of the king. In *Kitteis Confessioun* the satirist records unedifying particulars of a lady's interview with a priest at confession.

But by far the most searching of Lyndsay's satires is the long and elaborate drama entitled *Ane Satyre of the Thre Estaitis in commendatioun of Vertew and Vituperation of Vyce* (c. 1540–50). Our information on the early history of the drama in Scotland is scanty; but lack of information does not imply a lack of plays. We hear of one performance at Aberdeen as early as 1445, and there are other references; but Lyndsay's *Thre Estaitis* and the anonymous *Philotus* (c. 1600) are the only complete survivals. *Ane Satyre* is the work of a born dramatist; and in construction, variety, and command of stage "business" it is superior to any contemporary English piece. The nearest approach to it in dramatic development is Bale's *King Johan*, which is of later date. Lyndsay's play was certainly performed in 1540, and perhaps earlier. As a mirror of Scotland when Catholicism was tottering to its fall it has unique interest. The immensely large scale enables the playwright to present a comprehensive epitome of contemporary abuses, manners and morals, and we therefore encounter all the characters of early drama—figures allegorical and actual, sacred and profane. Our old friend John the Commoun Weill reappears, and rough justice is dealt out at the end. The most vivid parts of the play are the interludes, racily and broadly written. Though rather careless in technique, Lyndsay shows an easy command of the many kinds of metre with which he varies the matter of his long drama. The whole play is the most successful thing of its kind and time, and it can be read with admiration and enjoyment.

The Tragical Death of D. Beaton, written shortly after the murder of the Cardinal (1546), and the long *Dialog betuix Experience and ane Courteour*, sometimes called *Monarchie*, need no more than bare mention. The first is lugubrious; the second is diffuse, though it has some passages of sincere eloquence in its survey of fallen monarchies and its anticipation of the final judgment. Two other of Lyndsay's pieces may be named, *The Deploratioun of the Death of Queen Magdalene* and *The Historie of the Squyer Meldrum*. Neither is didactic in purpose. The former, in rhyme royal, is modelled on the aureate method adopted by Dunbar in his more ceremonial pieces; the latter, in couplets, which Lyndsay always used well, relates with friendly merriment, devoid of satirical purpose, the varied and surprising adventures of Squire William Meldrum, laird of Cleish and Binns. Lyndsay wrote too much, and the best of him has to be searched for. But he was a genuine poet, with his own honest character of utterance. No common mind could have carried to success the large adventures of the *Thre Estaitis*.

A social satirist of a much milder type than Lyndsay was Sir Richard Maitland (1496–1586). He has more in common with Dunbar than with Lyndsay, and he stands aloof from all parties. Neither as poet nor as satirist does he rank high.

Alexander Scott (1525–84) was even less concerned than Maitland with the activities of the reformers. Most of his pieces are amatory, and seem to have been influenced in style and spirit by the love lyrics in *Tottel's Miscellany*, 1557. Scott might have led a lyrical movement in his native land had not poetry been withered up by the ardours of religious zeal. Alexander Montgomerie (1556?–1610?), a disciple of Scott, was still more influenced by the English lyrists; yet even in the sonnet, of which he left no fewer than seventy examples, he has a certain individuality. He translated several of Ronsard's sonnets in the Ronsard form. *The Cherrie and the Slae*, an allegorical poem in a fourteen-line stanza, was long popular. A "flyting" between Montgomerie and Polwarth (i.e., Patrick Hume) shows the native vigour of the days of Dunbar. With Montgomerie, the school of the old "makaris" properly ends. While James VI, who published *Essayes of a Prentise* (1584) and *Poeticall Exercises* (1591), still remained in Scotland, poetry was practised by a few writers under his immediate patronage; but the end of such vanities was near. Poetry came under the ban of the reformers. Henceforth Scotsmen might snuffle, but they must not sing of joy or love. The Scottish Renascence was dead.

VII. REFORMATION AND RENASCENCE
IN SCOTLAND

From James I to Gavin Douglas, Scottish literature had been generally imitative, borrowing its spirit, its models, and its themes mainly from Chaucer, and seeking to please or amuse even when instructing; but from Lyndsay's *Dreme* of 1528 to the union of the crowns in 1603, we find a literature expressing the passions and convictions of men determined to direct a nation's spirit. It was the Reformation rather than the Renascence that affected Scotland, though the Scottish mind has always associated religion with learning. John Knox dated the beginning of the Reformation in Scotland from the preaching of Patrick Hamilton in 1527 and his martyrdom in 1528; and it is a production of Hamilton, *Patrikes Places*, that Knox adduces as the first specimen of Scottish Reformation literature. Literature in the ordinary sense it is not.

About the year 1546 there appeared a little volume which, after the Bible itself, did more for the spread of Reformation doctrines than any other book published in Scotland. No copy of the earliest edition is known and later prints call it *Ane Compendious Buik of Godlie Psalms and Spirituall Sangis, collectit furthe of sundrie partes of the Scripture*. It is always known in Scotland as *The Gude and Godlie Ballatis*, and it is, next to Knox's *Historie of the Reformatioun*, the most memorable literary monument of the period in vernacular Scots. It was probably compiled by three brothers, James, John and Robert Wedderburn, all ardent reformers. Besides metrical versions of some of the Psalms, the book contains "diveris other ballatis changeit out of prophane sangis, in godlie sangis"—pious "transversions" of old popular songs designed to glorify the Reformation and to vilify Rome. It succeeded only too well. For many years Scotland was without normal wholesome song.

To the year 1548 belongs the first production of John Knox (1505–72), who was to be at once the chief leader of the Scottish Reformation and its chief literary exponent. The work is called (title modernised) *An Epistle to the Congregation of the Castle of St Andrews: with a Brief Summary of Balnaves on Justification by Faith*. The greater part of Knox's writing has no more than historical interest, and there is no need to burden the memory with the names of extinct theological pamphlets. One piece, which had the greatest fame in his own day, is the best known by name in this. Knox, self-exiled for safety in Geneva, passionately desired to preach his gospel in England and Scotland, but this desire he saw thwarted by the two Marys who governed those countries. Out of his indignation came *The First Blast of the Trumpet against the Monstruous Regiment of Women* (1558). From the weightiest of authorities he proves that "regiment", i.e., government, by women is repugnant alike to nature and to God. The best answer to *The Blast* was the accession of Elizabeth in the very year of its publication. In 1559 the triumph of the reforming party in Scotland restored Knox to his country. As an immediate result of the victory of Protestantism, appeared the *First Book of Discipline*, not solely the work of Knox, but the expression of his spirit. It proposed, among other things, a system of national education, which, though long in coming, was an honour to Scotland when England was feebly fumbling with the problem. The parish schools of Scotland were the nurseries of her vigorous intellectual life. The most important of Knox's works is the *Historie of the Reformatioun of Religioun within the Realm of Scotland*, in five books, not printed till 1586. In vigour and vividness of writing, some of its scenes suggest Carlyle himself. It is, moreover, the first original work in standard prose that Scotland had produced. Knox's anglicized Scots was made a reproach to him by his Catholic adversaries.

To the same period belong other works, more or less historical, which show that prose had now become as successful a vehicle of expression as verse. Nearest in literary quality to the work of Knox is *The Historie and Cronicles of Scotland* by Robert Lindesay of Pitscottie (1500?–1565?), one of the few productions of the time which can be read with delight at the present day. Scott loved him as the nearest approach to a Scottish Froissart. The *Memoirs* of Sir James Melville (1535–1617) are history rather than literature and less attractive than the *Memorials of Transactions in Scotland* (1567–73) by Richard Bannatyne, Knox's secretary. Another example of the general interest in contemporary events is the delightful *Diary of Mr James Melville, Minister of Kilrenny in Fife* (1566–1601). With few exceptions the verse written during the Reformation struggle was prompted by the occasion of the hour. Printed in black letter on one side of a sheet, ballads of this character issued in a constant stream from the press of Robert Lekprevik, the Edinburgh printer. One of the principal authors was Robert Sempill (1530?–1595), of whom little is known beyond his zeal for the new cause. His two best pieces are the *Sege of the Castel of Edinburgh* and *The Legend of a Lymaris Lyfe*, the coarse vigour of which sufficiently explains his temporary popularity. Sir John Maitland, Sir William Kirkcaldy of Grange and the Rev. John Davidson also used verse for the expression of their opinions. But all the literature was not produced on the Protestant side. One of the Catholic writers, John Mair or Major (1479–1550), mentioned by Rabelais, has been called "the last of the schoolmen". His one book which is not a scholastic treatise, the *Historia Majoris Britanniae tam Angliae quam Scotiae*, boldly counsels political union as the solution of Anglo-Scottish difficulties. A notable specimen of vernacular prose is the curious production entitled *The Complaynt of Scotland* (1549?), the anonymous author of which was an adherent of the ancient church, and an ardent opponent of the English alliance. The *Complaynt* was formerly regarded as an original work, but it is now known to be a mosaic of verbatim translations from Alain Chartier and others, with digressions in Scots. Regarded merely as a specimen of early Scottish prose, however, the book has a special interest of its own. Archbishop John Hamilton's *Catechism* (1552) presents in the purest Scots of the time the fundamental Catholic doctrines in the simplest and most attractive form. Ninian Winzet (1518–92), author of *Certane Tractatis for Reformatioun of Doctryne and Maneris*, illustrates the anti-English feeling of the Catholic controversialists, an antagonism that extended to language as well as people. The highest place among Catholic writers of the period belongs to John Leslie (1527–96), Bishop of Ross, who chose the history of his country as his theme, and wrote with seriousness and moderation. His chief work, *De Origine Moribus et Rebus Scotorum* (1578), which narrates the national history from its origins, was afterwards translated into Scots by a Scottish monk at Ratisbon.

The revival of learning did not leave Scotland untouched, and its influence is specially manifested in Hector Boece (1465?–1536?) friend and fellow student of Erasmus, and first principal of the university of Aberdeen. His *Historia Gentis Scotorum* (1527) took Livy for its model, and told the best stories about Scotland that its author could find or invent, regardless of veracity or even probability. From him Holinshed (and therefore Shakespeare) derived the story of Macbeth. At the instance of James V, the *Historia* was translated into Scottish prose (1540) by John Bellenden, Archdeacon of Moray, one of the many versifiers who haunted the court, and his version is the first known vernacular prose book. Bellenden also translated five books of Livy, and the versified prologues to his translations earned him commendation as a poet from Sir David Lyndsay.

The pre-eminent Scottish humanist, however, is George Buchanan (1506–82). Buchanan held a lifelong conviction that Latin must eventually become the literary language of Christendom, and nearly all his works are in that language. We need neither discuss nor name most of them. At Bordeaux, where he was professor, he wrote two plays, *Jephthes* and *Baptistes*, original compositions modelled on classical examples. Some years later, at Coimbra, he translated (as an imposed penance) the Psalms into Latin verse, and thereby gained a most eminent place among modern Latin poets. Neither England nor Scotland seemed to offer a quiet home to a scholar, and Buchanan next took refuge in France, where he wrote *De Sphaera*, an exposition of the Ptolemaic cosmogony, in opposition to the system which had recently been promulgated by Copernicus. This remains, in matter and language, a curious instance of the scholarly infatuation that blindly mistook the course of the world's progress. After long exile Buchanan returned to his native country in 1560, and was closely attached to Mary, till the murder of Darnley turned him against her. In the service of his new friends he produced the only two pieces which he wrote in vernacular Scots, *The Chamaeleon; or the Crafty Statesman* (1570), a satire on Maitland of Lethington, and *Ane Admonitioun direct to the trew Lordis* (1571). In both,

Buchanan shows that he could write in Scots as nobly as in Latin. The greatest literary achievement of his later life is *Rerum Scoticarum Historia*, published in 1582, the year of his death. In it he enunciates those principles of political and religious liberty of which he had been the consistent champion throughout his career. His dialogue *De Jure Regni apud Scotos* (1579) long remained the classic defence of the Scottish Reformation and its claim to control kings. Buchanan's European fame as a scholar added to the glory of his country, and his spacious learning brought the gleam of humanism into the dusk of religious controversy.

VIII. THE NEW ENGLISH POETRY

The last feudal king of England fell at Bosworth in 1485. The reign of the bourgeois Henry VII shows us an England becoming national in religion and politics, and lifting up its head as a power to be reckoned with in Europe. With the cessation of the Wars of the Roses and the growth of a peaceful court, noble and aristocratic Englishmen had leisure for the literary pursuits which civilized the French and Italian courtiers. The English "moderns" of the sixteenth century were quite unlike the "medievals" of the fifteenth. Their poems had three marks of true lyric: they were brief, intense and personal. They forsook allegory and didacticism. They were modelled upon courtly European examples, and they had circulated shyly in manuscript. They were now to be made public in print. In 1557, a year before the accession of Elizabeth, appeared the famous volume, *Songes and Sonettes, written by the ryght honorable Lorde Henry Haward late Earle of Surrey, and other*, commonly known, from the name of its publisher, as *Tottel's Miscellany*. The names of two men are specially connected with this work: Sir Thomas Wyatt (1503–42) and Henry Howard (1517?–47) known as Earl of Surrey. Wyatt was employed on various diplomatic missions to the French and Italian courts, and it was from Italy that he derived his poetic education. Through various causes, some of which we do not fully understand, there had been a slackening of metrical strictness, and the fifteenth century, which produced some examples of beautiful rhythm, also produced many examples of mere approximation to rhythm. Wyatt and Surrey, strengthened by Italian technique, brought back to metre a recognizable order. Wyatt's chief instrument was the sonnet, a form which he was the first English writer to use. Of all forms the sonnet is the most compact and precise, and no better corrective could have been found for vague thought, loose expression, and irregular metre. Wyatt's model was the Italian poet Petrarch, whom, however, he did not closely follow. A correct Petrarcan sonnet contains fourteen lines, falling into groups of eight (the octave) and six (the sestet), the octave rhyming *abba, abba*, and the sestet having strictly two alternate rhymes, *cdcdcd*. Variations occur, especially in the number and order of the rhymes in the sestet. But the essentials of a Petrarcan sonnet are: (i) the division into octave and sestet, making something like two linked poems expressing different aspects of the same idea, and (ii) the absence of any strong final emphasis, such as a concluding couplet would give—such emphasis tending to make the sonnet fall into three parts instead of two. However, Wyatt, though generally using

Petrarcan rhymes for the octave, accidentally or deliberately chose to end most of his sonnets with a couplet, and thus helped to give a special character to the Elizabethan sonnet, which, as used by Surrey, settled down into three quatrains with alternate rhymes, and a final couplet. Any sonnet by Shakespeare will exhibit the fully developed Elizabethan form; and, from his mastery of all its possibilities, this non-Petrarcan sonnet is generally called Shakespearean. Milton was the first great English poet to use the strict Petrarcan form. The introduction of the sonnet form is Wyatt's first important service to English poetry; his second is the use of that form as the vehicle of personal emotion; and from the time of *Tottel's Miscellany* English poets who desired to make a brief emphatic declaration of personal feeling chose, almost by instinct, the sonnet form. Wyatt's poems fall into four groups: songs, epigrams, satires, and devotional pieces, each strongly personal. The songs are lyrics of great emotional appeal, particularly the justly famous *Forget not yet* and *They flee from me that sometime did me seek*. The epigrams are epigrams in the older, smoother sense; they are, in fact, like half-sonnets. His three satires are written in Dante's *terza rima—aba, bcb, cdc*, etc. This scheme of rhyme he uses also in *Certayne Psalmes...commonly called the vii penytentiall Psalmes* (1549). Wyatt's poetry conveys the charm of a brave and strong spirit. His technical faults are those of a pioneer. His chief claim to remembrance lies in his deliberate effort to raise the native tongue to dignity by making it, as Petrarch had made it, the vehicle of polite and courtly poetry. Both Wyatt and Surrey use the ordinary diction of their day, free alike from archaic affectation and from colloquial vulgarity. It seems difficult to believe that these modern poets died less than twenty years after the medieval Skelton.

The first thirty-two pages of *Tottel's Miscellany* are occupied by the poems of Henry Howard, Earl of Surrey, who takes precedence by rank, not by age, for Wyatt was a dozen years his senior. Surrey's work adheres in spirit to the code of the chivalric courts of love. He is far less original than Wyatt, but is a more accomplished versifier, especially in the Shakespearean form of sonnet, which he may be considered to have established. A favourite metre of Surrey, one that grew increasingly popular and degenerate, is the "poulter's measure" of alternate twelves and fourteens, deriving its nickname from the number of eggs that might go to the dozen:

> When sommer toke in hand the winter to assail,
> With force of might, and vertue gret, his stormy blasts to quail, etc.

In these and similar attempts Surrey shows himself a born poet with a good ear, knowing how to relate line to line and cadence to cadence. Surrey's clearest title to fame, however, rests upon his translations from the *Aeneid* into blank verse. The earliest known edition (undated, *c.* 1554) survives in a single copy. It is called *The fourth Boke of Virgill, intreating of the love between Aeneas and Dido translated into English and drawne with a strange meter by Henrye Howard Earl of Surrey worthy to be embrased.* The edition formerly taken as the first, *Certain Bokes of Virgiles Aeneis turned into English metre, by Henry Earle of Surrey* (1557) contains the second and fourth books. The movement against rhyme as a medieval barbarity, a movement of which, later, Milton was the explicit defender, had already begun. From whom (if from any) Surrey derived his inspiration is not important; to him alone belongs the honour of first using freely and continuously in English the great metre of Marlowe, Shakespeare, Milton and Wordsworth. The occurrence of occasional blank verse lines earlier is quite fortuitous. Surrey is a little stiff and too much inclined to make a break at the end of each line, but his use of the new metre is both skilful and pleasing. The life of Surrey was brief and tumultuous. Upon a ridiculous charge of high treason he was sent to the Tower, and there beheaded at the age of thirty. He was the last victim of Henry VIII.

Of the other contributors to *Tottel's Miscellany* only four are known by name: Nicholas Grimald with forty pieces, Thomas Lord Vaux with two, John Heywood the dramatist with one, and Edward Somerset with one. A hundred and thirty poems are by "Uncertain Auctours". Lord Vaux (1510–56) was a courtier trained in the spirit of chivalry. The bulk of his surviving poetry is found in *The Paradyse of Daynty Devises*, an anthology resembling Tottel's. A brave, simple, and musical writer, Vaux is among the best of the poets of his day. One of his poems in *Tottel* beginning, "I lothe that I did love", has achieved a strange immortality, for two of its stanzas (imperfectly remembered) are sung by the sexton who digs Ophelia's grave. Nicholas Grimald (1519–62) was no courtier, but a professed man of letters, chaplain to Bishop Ridley, and a translator of learned works from the Latin. It has been suggested that he was Tottel's editor. Grimald is particularly fond of "poulter's measure" and other long lines which, mainly by good use of his learning, he succeeds in keeping above the level of doggerel.

The historical importance of *Tottel's Miscellany* cannot be over-rated. It is the first surviving printed communication of polite poetry to the great variety of readers. The printing-press had definitely displaced the minstrel. Oral tradition lingered only among the unlettered, and printers now worked for a larger reading public. Courtly poets were still a little bashful, and sought anonymity for their utterances; but this reluctance was not enduring. We may note that the range of subjects among the uncertain authors in *Tottel* is limited, and a little old-fashioned. One of the poems included is a version of Chaucer's *Flee from the prese*. But in some a steady growth of allusion to classical stories is observable. The occasional use of alliteration may have been stimulated by the first printing of *Piers Plowman* in 1550; but alliteration was, and is, a rooted habit of English poets. *Tottel's Miscellany* clearly shows that there was no breach in continuity. Among Tottel's "uncertain auctours", according to his own account, was Thomas Churchyard (1520?–1604), page to Surrey, soldier of fortune, and a persistent minor poet. Early in his career he is found in controversy, and employing a weapon which he always found useful, the broadside. In 1563 came his best work, the long historical narrative of *Shore's Wife* in *A Mirror for Magistrates*. In 1575 he published the first of the books with the alliterative titles or sub-titles which he liked—*Churchyardes Chippes*. *A Praise of Poetrie* (1595) attempts to do in verse what Sidney's *Apologie* had done in prose. Grumbling and quarrelling, Churchyard wrote on, as Spenser says, "untill quite hoarse he grew". He is not important, but he is interesting.

Another aspect of the English character in poetry is notably shown by

Thomas Tusser (1524–80), who felt none of the French or Italian influence. Tusser is immortalized agriculturally for his introduction of barley crops, and poetically for the verses in which he expressed the wisdom of his eminently practical life. *A Hundredth good pointes of husbandrie*, etc. (including "huswifry") was published by Tottel in 1557, enlarged in 1571, and became successively in 1573, 1577, and 1580 *Five hundredth pointes of good husbandry*, the descriptive title itself being about a page long. Without extensive quotation it is impossible to do justice to Tusser's ripe and shrewd wisdom, and his astonishing metrical and verbal ingenuity. In *The Ladder to Thrift*, nearly eighty lines express the wisdom of Polonius in rhymes of the *-ie* or *-y* sound, and elsewhere, in the simple anapaests that come easily to his pen, he warns the reader neither to borrow nor to lend. Taking measures and feet that were English and familiar, Tusser polished and combined them with no contemptible skill, uniting an ease in movement with a terseness and exactness of expression that were new. Lying outside the main stream of English verse, Tusser has been too much neglected, and deserves re-discovery.

With Barnabe Googe (1540–94) we return to that main stream, for his eight eclogues derive more or less directly from classical sources. To trace the genealogy of a literary form is always interesting, but sometimes misleading. Does it matter who wrote the first pastoral, idealizing and beautifying the supposed conversations of shepherds? There is a fairly clear line of descent, and certainly some deliberate imitation. We have Theocritus and Virgil, and then fifteen centuries later some imitative Italians and Spaniards. Then we have the Englishmen, Barclay, Googe and Spenser. It would be overhardy to say that Spenser would not have written pastorals if Googe had not written his, but it is safe to assert that an existing model is useful even to the greatest of creative artists. The pastorals of Googe contained in his *Eglogs, Epytaphes and Sonettes* (1563) have the traditional form, but not quite the original content. His piping has a troubled sound. He is a strong Protestant, and may even be called an early Puritan. To him love is an evil that can be driven out by hard work and exercise. Two of the eclogues are said to be derived from the *Diana* of Montemayor, and to be thus among the first traces of Spanish influence in English poetry. The so-called "sonettes" are merely short poems. Googe survives historically rather than intrinsically.

George Turberville (1540?–1610), author of *Epitaphes, Epigrams, Songes and Sonets* (1567) and of *Tragical Tales translated by Turberville* (1587) stands upon the level of his friend Googe in poetic quality, but he survives more genuinely in one or two poems to be found in the anthologies. Of Humfrey Gifford, whose *Posie of Gilloflowers* was published in 1580, and of Matthew Grove, whose *Historie of Pelops and Hippodamia* with the *Epigrams, Songes and Sonnettes* that follow it was published in 1587, little need be said save that they carried the poetic tradition of Henry VIII's reign up to the eve of the Armada.

The other volumes calling for notice at this point are not books of original verse but collections more or less like Tottel's. The earliest to follow that famous *Miscellany* was *The Paradyse of Daynty Devises* (1576) by Richard Edwards (1523?–1566), a poet of no small merit, one of whose pieces ("The falling out of faithful friends renewing is of love") deservedly survives. Among the contributors are William Hunnis, Jasper Heywood, Lord Vaux, Francis Kinwelmersh, Thomas Churchyard, Edward Vere Earl of Oxford, Lodowick Lloyd, and George Whetstone. The collection has little resemblance to Tottel's. It contains some good poems, but the tone is monotonous. The pleasant woes of the lover and the sense of knightly obligation have given place to musings on the brevity of life and apprehensions of death and judgment. To *The Paradyse* succeeded in 1578 *A Gorgious Gallery of Gallant Inventions* by a certain Thomas Proctor. It is a minor production with many signs of exhausted inspiration. The forcible feebleness of the very title tells its story. *A Handefull of pleasant delites* (1584) by Clement Robinson and others (perhaps first printed in 1566) is a song-book with indications of the tunes to which the songs may be sung. The opening poem anticipates Ophelia's interpretation of the flowers, and another anticipates the style of Peter Quince's tragedy of *Pyramus and Thisbe*. The volume is slight, but it is the most worthy successor of *Tottel*.

IX. *A MIRROR FOR MAGISTRATES*

One very famous collection of poems, *A Myrroure for Magistrates* (1559, etc.)— the full title is almost an essay in length—forms a link between medieval and modern literature. It is a collection of "cautionary stories" of an early type, more extensive in scale than those which point a moral in *The Monk's Tale* of Chaucer. In a way, the book derives ultimately from Chaucer's own master, Boccaccio, whose work *De Casibus Virorum Illustrium* appeared here in a folio volume printed by John Wayland as *The Tragedies gathered by John Bochas, of all such Princes as fell from theyr estate throughe the mutability of Fortune, etc. Translated into Englysh by John Lidgate, Monke of Burye* (1555). It was intended that this exemplary work should be extended to include famous and unfortunate Englishmen. Accordingly, at the end of Lydgate's version of Boccaccio appears the title-page of a second part or volume: *A memorial of suche Princes, as since the tyme of King Richard the seconde, have been unfortunate in the Realme of England*; but nothing follows—it is a title-page without a volume. Apparently the authorities disliked "sad stories of the deaths of kings", and forbade publication.

Four years later publication was allowed, and we meet as editor a prolific minor writer, William Baldwin, who explains everything: the aim of the work being moral, here is a mirror in which we can behold the fatal mistakes of the fallen great ones; and so on. The story of the various editions of *A Mirror for Magistrates* belongs to bibliography rather than to literature, and needs no discussion here. The poems are written as if told in person to Baldwin, and they are introduced, ended, or connected, by prose remarks. Baldwin's first compilation (1559) included the tragic narratives of nineteen historical figures from Chief Justice Tresilian to Edward IV. The next edition (1563) gives eight more examples including the Duke of Buckingham and Jane Shore. In 1574, a new editor, John Higgins, thinking Baldwin's selection limited in period, decided to begin at the very beginning; and so we get Albanacte the son of Brutus, Locrinus, Sabrine, Cordila, Ferrex and Porrex, and others. Eleanor Cobham and Humphrey Duke of Gloucester were added in 1578. The work was very popular and continued to be issued with additions (the number of narratives finally amounting to ninety-eight) during a full half-century; but the book as a whole belongs to the curiosities of literature rather than to literature itself. Most of the poems are sheer doggerel written by unknown or unimportant authors. But there are exceptions, for instance, Churchyard's *Complaint of Shores Wife*, and *A lamentacion upon the death of Kinge Edwarde the 4*, attributed to Skelton. Two facts make *A Mirror for Magistrates* important to readers of today, first its influence, and next its revelation of one particular poet. It created a public for the chronicle-poem; and such works as Daniel's *Civil Wars*, and Drayton's *Barons' Wars* are in the direct line of descent. With the chronicle-poem came the chronicle-play; and there is something more than coincidence in the fact that over thirty historical plays exist on subjects in which the *Mirror* had first interested the public.

The participation of one poet is explained at length in the *Mirror* itself. One of Baldwin's contributors, Thomas Sackville (1536–1608), Lord Buckhurst and Earl of Dorset, had intended to write a connected series of stories himself, and naturally began with an *Induction*. Actually, he wrote but one story. Sackville's two contributions, then, are first an *Induction* to a collection that was never written (it is to be distinguished from the trivial *Induction* to the *Mirror* itself), and next *The Complaint of Henry Duke of Buckingham*, the one story he completed. Their high quality suggests that in Sackville we gained a statesman and lost a poet. Only the small extent of Sackville's work has prevented his inclusion among the masters of the grand style. His success is the more remarkable because the occasion of which he took advantage and the material he used were not specially favourable. Feeling that Baldwin and the collaborators had fallen far below the level of the design, Sackville turned for inspiration to Virgil and to Dante, and he maintains himself, though briefly, at their level. Although he has to vivify the usual shadowy medieval abstractions, he conceives and transmits his creations with astonishing power of conviction. Sackville's use of the Troilus stanza is beyond praise, and whatever he may have derived is marked by his own strong individuality. The *Induction* is a great poem, the last late flower of medievalism.

X. GEORGE GASCOIGNE

George Gascoigne (1542?–1577) affected a disdain of the pen, and describes himself as "George Gascoigne Esquire, professing armes in the defence of God's truth", though he abandoned this pose in later years. The early date, 1525, usually assigned to his birth cannot be accepted. The first volume associated with his name is *A Hundredth Sundrie Flowers bounde up in one small Poesie* (1573) ostensibly of composite authorship. Most of it reappeared in an altered form as *The Posies of George Gascoigne Esquire* (1575). The volume is a miscellany, and its contents include *A devise of a Maske*; a verse tale, *Dan Bartholomew of Bathe*; a military poem, *The Fruites of Warre* (or *Dulce Bellum Inexpertis*); *The Supposes*, a comedy translated from Ariosto; *Jocasta*, a tragedy adapted from Euripides; *The Pleasant Fable of Ferdinando Jeronimi and Leonora de Valasco*, a prose tale; and *Certayne notes of Instruction concerning the making of verse or ryme in English*, a short but detailed essay. Later works are *The Glasse of Government*, *a tragicall Comedie* in prose (1575), *The Princely Pleasures at Kenelworth Castle*, a kind of masque (1576), *The Steele Glas, A Satyre* (1576), *The Complaynt of Philomene, An Elegy* (1576), and various prose treatises of edification including a short pamphlet, *A delicate Diet, for daintie-mouthde Droonkardes* (1576), the alliterative title of which carries on an old tradition.

Gascoigne had no great measure of the creative spirit, and Gabriel Harvey rightly accuses him of dissipating his energies. His verse is pleasant and easy, though monotonous in its longer flights, and his prose is fairly free from the antithesis and alliteration which afterwards came to be the special qualities of Euphuism. Gascoigne is really notable because, in many departments of literature, he wrote the first things of their kind in English that we know—the first prose tale of modern life, the first prose comedy, the first tragedy translated from the Italian, the first masque, the first regular satire, and the first considered treatise on poetry. Gascoigne is seen at his best in short poems that forbid his fatal fluency. The higher mood of such pieces as *Gascoignes De Profundis* fits him less convincingly.

XI. THE POETRY OF SPENSER

After a lapse of almost two centuries we reach the first English major poet since Chaucer. Edmund Spenser (1552–99) was born in London, and was related to the great family of his name. At Cambridge he not only wrote his earliest sonnets, but came under three profound influences. The first was his friendship with Gabriel Harvey, a powerful and controversial scholar, to whom justice has yet to be done. The second was the refined and cultured "Puritanism", which, like that of Milton, was a revolt from coarseness and materialism in life and in religion. The third was the study of Platonic philosophy—not the Christianized neo-Platonism of the first Reformers, but the pure Platonism of the *Timaeus* and the *Symposium*. To the imagination of Spenser this proved exceedingly congenial, and confirmed him in his allegorical habit of conception and expression. His early *Hymns*, the first *in honour of Love*, the second *in honour of Beautie*, though not published till 1596 (*Foure Hymnes made by Edm. Spenser*), were inspired by his first experience of love, and written in the spirit of Plato.

He was brought by Harvey into the service of the Earl of Leicester, and met Philip Sidney, whose ardent imagination and lofty spirit greatly stimulated him. After toying, under Harvey's influence, with the possibilities of using in English a system of quantitative prosody (that *ignis fatuus* of English poets) he began to consider the forms in which he could express himself most naturally, and he turned instinctively to the pastoral and the romance, with their stock figures, the shepherd and the knight. The pastoral, as we have seen, was a popular form, offering an abundance of models. The extent of Spenser's debt to any of these is not really important. All that matters in a poem is what it is, not what it may have come from. Upon the "XII Aeglogues proportioned to…the XII monethes" forming *The Shepheards Calendar* (1579) the impress of a creative, originating poetic genius is clearly discernible. The book was dedicated to Sidney, who praised it highly, but objected, rather pedantically, to one of its greatest charms, namely "the olde rusticke language". Sidney, a typical figure of the Renascence, disliked Spenser's archaism, not in itself, but because it was unwarranted by classical originals. This kind of criticism was to have a long run. A more serious objection would have been that the pastoral, as Spenser wrote it, was a literary exercise with little hold on life. Spenser uses all varieties of the form, amatory, moral, religious, courtly, rustic, lyric, elegiac, and shows himself at once master of an old convention and herald of a new spirit in poetry. His language was deliberately archaic. Ben Jonson said that Spenser, in affecting the obsolete, "writ no language". The answer is that Spenser used the language in which Spenser could write. Every true poet creates his own idiom. What *The Shepheards Calendar* clearly reveals is the arrival of a great poet-musician, who excelled all his predecessors in a sense of the capacity of the English language for harmonious combinations of sound. To turn from the flatness of *The Steele Glas* to *The Shepheards Calendar* is to pass from honest and well-meant effort into a new world of absolute mastery.

From the pastoral Spenser proceeded naturally to romance. In 1580 he went to Ireland as secretary to the Lord Deputy, and there at Kilcolman Castle he continued his *Faerie Queene*, the first three books of which were published in 1590 on his return to England. As, in any creative sense, the poem shows no progress, but is at the end what it was in the beginning, some consideration of it may be given at once. The poem, as planned in twelve books, was never completed. Spenser himself has clearly stated his own intentions in the prefatory letter addressed to Ralegh, and to this the reader is referred. Like other great poets he felt himself called to teach; and desiring to set forth a picture of a perfect knight, he chose King Arthur as hero, rather than any person of his own time. Further, he desired to glorify his own dear country and its "most royal Queen". In much of his intention he was successful, but he was not completely successful. Spenser failed because he refused to follow his natural instinct for allegory and romance, the forms that most readily released his creative powers—in *The Allegory of Love* (1936) C. S. Lewis traced their history from *Le Roman de la Rose*—but turned aside to be instructive, and, in seeking to make the allegory edifying, forgot to tell the story. But if an allegory does not survive as a story, it does not survive as an allegory. *The Pilgrim's Progress* is, first of all, an excellent story; *The Faerie Queene* is not. Like every great poem, *The Faerie Queene* is entitled to its own imaginative life; but it must continue to be true to that life. Spenser, to use a common phrase, lets us down, when we are left wondering whether the false Duessa is a poetical character, or Theological Falsehood, or Mary Queen of Scots. He tried to do too many things at once; and, in elaborating intellectually the allegorical plot he has confused the imaginative substance of the poetic narrative. Homer, says Aristotle, tells lies as he ought; that is, he makes us believe his stories. Spenser tried to tell his lies while clinging to a disabling kind of truth; and so he does not convince his readers. Thus it is neither as an allegorist nor as a narrator that the author of *The Faerie Queene* holds his place. He lives as an exquisite word-painter of widely differing scenes, and as supreme poet-musician using with unrivalled skill a noble stanza of his own invention, unparalleled in any other language.

As the years advanced, Spenser seems to have felt that his conception of chivalry had little correspondence with the facts of life. Sidney was dead, and his own hopes of preferment were frustrated. In 1591 a volume of his collected poems was published with the significant title *Complaints*, including such works as *The Ruines of Time*, *The Teares of the Muses* and *Prosopopoia or Mother Hubberd's Tale*, in which the Ape and the Fox serve to satirize the customs of the court. In 1591 he returned to his exile in Ireland, and there, in the form of an allegorical pastoral, called *Colin Clouts Come Home Againe* (1595), he gave expression to his views about the general state of manners and poetry. In his *Prothalamion*, and still more, in his *Epithalamion*, he carries the lyrical style, first attempted in *The Shepheards Calendar*, to an unequalled height of harmony, splendour and enthusiasm. In 1595, he again came over to England, bringing with him the second part of *The Faerie Queene*, which was licensed for publication in January 1595–6. Finding still no place at court, he returned to Ireland in 1597; but, in a rising, Kilcolman Castle was taken and burned, and Spenser barely escaped with his life. His spirit was broken, and after suffering the afflictions of poverty, he died in January 1599. His posthumous prose dialogue, *A Veue of the Present State of Ireland*, written in 1596, is discussed in a later chapter. Spenser is the poets' poet, and his greatness cannot be diminished by the jeers of the tough-minded who find his poetic music and his poetic virtue too delicate for their manly taste.

XII. THE ELIZABETHAN SONNET

The sonnet, which was the invention of thirteenth-century Italy, was slow in winning the favour of English poets. Neither the word nor the thing reached England till the sixteenth century, when, as we have seen, the first English sonnets were written, in imitation of the Italian, by Wyatt and Surrey. But these primary efforts set no fashion. The Elizabethan sequences came long after the gentle effusions of Tottel's poets, and were not influenced by them. But when the writing of sonnets began in earnest it soon became a fashionable literary habit, and no poetic aspirant between 1590 and 1600 failed to try his skill in this form. The results are not inspiring. Sidney, Spenser and Shakespeare alone achieved substantial success; and their sonnets, with some rare and isolated triumphs by Drayton, Daniel, Constable and others, are the sole enduring survivals. *Tottel's Miscellany* contained sixty sonnets, for the most part primitive copies of Petrarch; but though the name "sonnet" is commonly used for poems in the succeeding anthologies, the actual sonnet form is rare. Gascoigne's *Certayne notes of instruction* not only described the Elizabethan sonnet accurately, but noted the general misuse of the term. It was contemporary French rather than older Italian influence that moved the Elizabethan mind to sonnet-writing. The first inspiration came from Marot (1495–1544); though the sonnet was not naturalized in France until Ronsard (1524–85) and Du Bellay (1525–60), who, with five others, formed the constellation of poets called *La Pléiade*, deliberately resolved to adapt to the French language the finest fruit of foreign literature. Philippe Desportes (1546–1606), a less important poet, was specially admired and imitated by the Elizabethans.

Spenser is the true father of the Elizabethan sonnet. He first appeared as a poet with the twenty-six youthful sonnets of 1569. His indebtedness to Du Bellay is declared in the title of one group of sonnets, *The Visions of Bellay*, and of another, *The Ruines of Rome by Bellay*. Another set, *The Visions of Petrarch*, he translates from Marot. These and the other sonnets of Spenser in *Amoretti* (1595) have his characteristic sweetness of versification. Spenser, it should be noted, uses the English and not the Italian form of the sonnet. Two of the sonnets in the *Amoretti* refer to the Platonic "Idea" of beauty which outshines any mortal embodiment. The "Idea", found also in numerous French writers, became a theme of later English sonnets, especially those of Drayton, who borrowed his very title from a sonnet-sequence by a minor French poet, Claude de Pontoux. The first Elizabethan sonneteer to make a popular reputation, however, was not Spenser, but Thomas Watson (1557–92), who was hailed as the successor of Petrarch and the English Ronsard after the appearance in 1582 of *The Hekatompathia or Passionate Centurie of Love*. But nearly all the hundred "Passions" are in a pleasing metre of eighteen lines (three sixes). Watson uses the normal Elizabethan form in the sixty sonnets of *The Teares of Fancie, or, Love Disdained* (1593). Neither these nor the "Passions" have much poetic value.

Sir Philip Sidney (1554–86), who follows Watson, is a prince among Elizabethan lyric writers and sonneteers, and, Shakespeare apart, is easily the best. The collection known as *Astrophel and Stella* was written between 1580–4 and though widely circulated in manuscript was not published till 1591 (piratically) and 1598 (regularly). With Sidney we come to the first real English "sonnet sequence", a collection of sonnets telling a story of love, like that of Petrarch for his Laura. The "hopeless love" of the sonnets must not be taken literally. Readers sometimes fail to distinguish between the truth of a poem and the truth of an affidavit, and are too often encouraged by critics who ought to know better. The sonnets of Shakespeare and of Sidney are as "true" as *Hamlet* or *Arcadia*; they are not required to have a different kind of truth. Sidney was indebted to foreign models, though he was much more original than his contemporaries. His sonnets are real contributions to English poetry. They have grace, ease and sincerity, and a genuine character reflecting the admirable spirit of the writer.

Of the numerous sonneteers who followed Sidney few need be mentioned. Shakespeare will be considered in his own place. Henry Constable's *Diana* (1592), Samuel Daniel's *Delia* (1592) and Thomas Lodge's *Phillis* (1593), all of which borrowed extensively from abroad, have each contributed something to the English anthologies. Michael Drayton's *Ideas Mirrour*, first printed in 1594 and steadily revised in several editions till 1619, gives us, in its final form, the one sonnet of its time worthy to be set by Shakespeare's, "Since there's no help, come let us kiss and part". Richard Barnfield's "If music and sweet poetry agree" deservedly survives. Barnabe Barnes, in *Parthenophil and Parthenope* (1593), is voluminous, but says little. Later, came two Scottish writers, Sir William Alexander, Earl of Stirling (1567–1640) who reaches a respectable level, and William Drummond of Hawthornden (1585–1649) whose "For the Baptist" is the one religious sonnet which has survived as a poem. With them may be mentioned Sidney's friend, that strange genius, Fulke Greville, Lord Brooke (1554–1628), whose *Caelica* sequence (not all sonnets) may be held to close the story. Sonneteering fell into disrepute and perished of its own insincerity. When Milton revived the true sonnet form it took a note which cannot be heard in any of the Elizabethan collections.

XIII. PROSODY FROM CHAUCER TO SPENSER

The contemporary existence of Chaucer, Gower and *Piers Plowman* enables us to observe with ease the three main tendencies or principles of English prosody. The foreign (chiefly French) tendency to strict syllabic uniformity is specially clear in Gower. The native tendency to irregular groups of syllables marked by strong accents with the emphasis of alliteration, and without the aid of rhyme or formal metre, finds its greatest exposition in *Piers Plowman*. The middle way, the shaping of normal English prosody out of English habit by the potency of French example, is shown triumphantly by Chaucer, who was a fine prosodist as well as a great poet. *Piers Plowman* is the last word in its own way of writing; no further advance in that direction was possible, and no further advance has ever been achieved. Strict syllabic uniformity never made a home in England, in spite of the example of Gower. On the other hand Chaucer not only accomplished many things, but opened the way for more.

The lyrists before Chaucer, many of them anonymous, had contributed much to the making of our verse forms. Octosyllabic couplets and stanza forms simple and elaborate abound, not as attempts, but as complete successes. Of course there are (as at all times) bad examples as well as good. What Chaucer did was to ensure, by his great example, that the successes became the staple of English poetry. His own greatest contributions to poetic form were the decasyllabic line in couplets and the seven-line decasyllabic stanza rhyming *ababbcc*—the famous "rhyme royal", or Troilus stanza. That he was the actual inventor of the decasyllabic line cannot be claimed, for it is the kind of thing that "grows"; but he was certainly the first to use it greatly and extensively, and he, and no other, gave it the place it holds in English poetry. Every stanza of *Troilus*, it should be remembered, ends with a decasyllabic couplet. The rhyme royal appears first in *The Compleynte unto Pite*; but it is more notably the stanza of *Troilus and Criseyde*. It is the stanza most affected by the authors of *A Mirror for Magistrates*, where it is touched by Sackville into a strain of the highest music.

The beauty of Chaucer's versification was obscured by the changes in pronunciation that followed quickly after his death. Even his admirers and imitators in the next generation failed to imitate his measures—or rather they imitated them out of measure; and later writers, like Dryden, failed to discover any measure at all. Thus, during the fifteenth century there seems to be a curious failing of the ear for verse, with a tendency to drop consistently into a kind of semi-rhythmic patter or mere jog-trot. The tendency was always present in the romances caricatured by *Sir Thopas*; but what we find, in particular, is the development of a special kind of doggerel combining the worst features of bad *Piers Plowman* lines and bad fourteeners. Even the *King Johan* of John Bale (mid-sixteenth century) produces lines like these:

> Releace not Englande of the generall interdictyon
> Tyll the Kynge hath graunted the dowrye and the pencyon
> Of Julyane the wyfe of Kynge Richard Cour de Lyon.

In Skelton we get a great variety of metres; but most of them cannot be used for really serious poetry—patter is never far away. The multitudinous pages of *A Mirror for Magistrates* exhibit many metres but painfully inadequate versification.

So far in condemnation. But the fifteenth century was also the century of the miracle plays, the ballads and the carols. The popular muse never fails. What did fail were the inadequate and formless imitations of Chaucer. The attempt, led by Harvey, to set English verse firmly on a basis of classical quantity is both a symptom of dissatisfaction and a demonstration of what was not the way of progress. Wyatt and Surrey were the exemplars of the true law and order. Gascoigne's *Certayne notes of Instruction concerning the making of verse or ryme in English* is a most interesting document, both in its condemnations and in its recommendations. It denounces the prevalent carelessness. It rebukes the misuse of the term "sonnet". It commends Chaucer's "riding-rhyme", i.e. the decasyllabic couplet. It warns poets against "rhyme without reason". It regrets the apparent loss of the tri-syllabic foot—rather oddly, as Tusser offers many good examples. Gascoigne himself, though a flat poet, was a good metrician.

Anarchy prevailed longest in the drama. The pure medieval drama had been remarkable for prosodic elaboration and correctness; but doggerel had broken in with the moralities and interludes, and by the end of the fifteenth century the drama was simply overrun by it. Bale's *King Johan* (*c.* 1538) and Preston's *Cambises* (*c.* 1569, the date of Spenser's first sonnets) show us doggerel in the sixteenth century trying hard to return to decency and order, with an eye on the "fourteeners". At last sceptred tragedy comes sweeping by in the blank verse of *Gorboduc* (1562), which, inflexibly stiff as it is, set the pattern for serious drama and developed into the marvellous instrument of Shakespeare himself.

The coming of *The Shepheards Calendar* is a landmark, not merely in poetry but in prosody. But it will be well if the reader makes very clear to himself the danger of studying something called "prosody" apart from the poetry of which it is the vehicle. The real charge against the fifteenth century is not the absence of good prosodists but the absence of good poets. What offends us in a well-intentioned writer like Stephen Hawes is not simply the low standard of prosody, but the low standard of poetry. Actually the fifteenth century had plenty of poetry. What it lacked was a compelling poet. Spenser, in the sixteenth century took up the work of Chaucer. In him, English poetry gained at last what it had lacked for two hundred years, a master of tone, time and tune. Moreover, his language is ours. Modernize Chaucer, and his verse falls to pieces; modernize Spenser, and though some pleasure of the eye is lost, the verse stands as firm and fast as ever.

XIV. ELIZABETHAN CRITICISM

In Middle English literature there is no literary criticism. That Chaucer had the critical spirit is clear from many passages in the poems. Further, the remarkable admiration for Chaucer himself expressed by other poets from his own time up to Gascoigne's notes on prosody indicates the presence of a critical understanding. But these utterances are casual. The first approach to a series of critical observations in English can be found in the shrewd and endearing prologues and epilogues of William Caxton, simple-minded though most of them are. But at least they were printed and circulated. Opinions about books and authors had begun to receive publicity.

In the middle of the sixteenth century there was a Cambridge "school" of criticism, represented by Roger Ascham, Sir John Cheke and Thomas Wilson, who set themselves deliberately against over-elaboration of style. They opposed "inkhorn" terms and the "aureate" phraseology of the fifteenth century, and were anxious that English should be written "pure". Ascham's book *The Scholemaster* (1570), the most readily accessible volume representing this school, contains some pungent criticism. He denounces *Le Morte d'Arthur*, "the whole pleasure of which booke standeth in two speciall poyntes, in open mans slaughter, and bold bawdrye". He deplores the lapse of English poets into rude beggarly rhyming, and demands the discipline of the classics in writing. It is very odd that Ascham, who had begun with the sturdy determination to write English matters in the English manner for Englishmen, should have been fanatically false to the English genius in poetry, by trying to establish classical "versing" in a language that refuses it. Spenser and Harvey, in correspondence, toyed with the idea of basing English verse upon classical models; but Spenser, fortunately, made this a matter of theory not of practice.

The first piece of pure literary criticism known in our literature is Gascoigne's *Certayne notes of Instruction*. This brief and excellent essay has already been noticed and need not again be quoted. A more considerable critical work, Sir Philip Sidney's *Apologie for Poetrie* or *Defence of Poesie*, not published till 1595, though written before 1583, arises out of a literary quarrel, the first debate of its kind in English literature. Stephen Gosson, himself a playwright, seems to have become convinced of the sinfulness of poetry in general, and in his *School of Abuse* (1579), dedicated to Sidney, indulges in severe moral strictures on the art. Spenser suggests that Sidney "scorned" both the book and its dedicator. Sidney did not "scorn" Gosson; but, leaving him unnamed, gave a polite reply in a little treatise that is both a "defence" of the poetic art and an "apology" for it. As a personal revelation the essay is entirely delightful. Its formal survey of poetry and its particular examples are alike engaging. Everyone knows the allusion to the old ballad of "Percy and Duglas". Sidney admires Chaucer, but of course with misunderstanding. He praises Surrey's lyrics, and likes *The Shepheards Calendar*, though he "dare not alowe" the "framing of his style to an olde rusticke language". He defends rhyme, and finds the drama faulty for not observing rules "neither of honest civility, nor skilfull Poetrie (excepting *Gorboducke*)". His slighting remarks about the popular drama almost suggest a personal incapacity to surrender to the essential "make-believe" of every play that ever was. Time quickly took its revenge upon Sidney by establishing the next fifty years as a golden age of the very kind of poetry he held in small esteem. His book, indeed, is like a great deal of criticism since his time, a theory unsupported by facts; for actually there was not a sufficient supply of good English poetry to afford a foundation for his doctrine. Nevertheless in its general texture and character it is an engaging little book.

The *Discourse of English Poetrie* (1586) by William Webbe is far below Sidney's in learning, in literary skill and in sympathy with the poetic spirit. But Webbe is enthusiastic for poetry according to his lights, and he has the advantage of writing later. His knowledge of the older English poets is the vaguest conceivable. However, he admires *The Shepheards Calendar*; though he is so bitten with the craze for classical "versing", that he tries to "verse" some of Spenser's lines to show how they ought to have been written. Had Sidney's gospel prevailed there would have been no Shakespeare; had Webbe's, there would have been no Spenser.

The Arte of English Poesie, anonymous, but full of personal allusions, has been attributed to Puttenham, George or Richard. It was published in 1589, but clearly belongs to an earlier date. It is the most systematic treatise of its times, and from it the reader could learn, not only about classical feet and the figures of speech, but how to arrange verses in the form of "lozanges", "tricquets", "pillasters", etc. The first part is a discussion of poetry in general, mainly classical; but the title of the second chapter is significant: "That there may be an Art of our English Poesie, as well as there is of the Latine and Greeke". However, Puttenham, like Sidney and Webbe, was writing a generation too soon—there was hardly any poetry to criticise. Puttenham gets no further than Sidney and "that other Gentleman who wrote the late shepheardes Callender". There are fragmentary critical notes by Sir John Harington in his translation of Ariosto, in the first instalment of Chapman's *Iliads* (1595), in Drayton, in Richard Carew's *The Excellency of the English Tongue* (1595–6?) first printed in Camden's *Remains*, and in the celebrated *Palladis Tamia* (1598) by Frances Meres, which, however, has no interest other than its detailed and invaluable references to Shakespeare.

The last of all strictly Elizabethan discussion of matters literary is the notable duel between Thomas Campion and Samuel Daniel on the question of rhyme. The two tracts, Campion's *Observations in the Art of English Poesie* (1602) and Daniel's *A Defence of Ryme* (1603) appeared just as the new century had turned, and both show a great advance in understanding. Campion (that exquisite rhymer) despises rhyme and endeavours to construct a rhymeless prosody, partly classical, but respecting the peculiarities of English. The *Defence of Ryme* with which Daniel replied is one of the best things of its kind in English. With true critical sense he presses home the main argument: Why object to rhyme on the ground that there is no rhyme in Greek and Latin poetry? and he lays down, for the first time in English, the great principle that "the Dorians may speak Doric", that each language and each literature is entitled to its own ways and its own fashions. If there could have been a combination of Puttenham's *Art of English Poesie* with Daniel's *Defence of Ryme*, we should have had an almost ideal tractate on English prosody.

Elizabethan criticism may be quoted as an example of the English habit of "muddling through", and arriving at sensible practice after some less sensible theorizing. The critics could not understand Chaucer; they recognized the tendency of English metre to lapse into doggerel; they tried to apply the only standards they knew, the standards of classical practice, both in the making of verse and in the writing of plays. Fortunately the poet-critics refused to practise what they preached. Spenser dallied with classical "versing", but wrote *The Faerie Queene*. And the English drama rose up and walked by itself without first aid from criticism. It should not be forgotten that there is such work as Richard Mulcaster's, which, though not strictly literary criticism, is linguistic and scholastic criticism of no unliterary kind. Mulcaster, as an apostle of the study of English by the English, is discussed in a later section.

XV. CHRONICLERS AND ANTIQUARIES

The chroniclers and antiquaries of the Tudor period, various as they were in style and talent, shared the same sentiment, the same ambition. They desired to glorify England. "Our English tongue", said Camden, "is as fluent as the Latin, as courteous as the Spanish, as Court-like as the French, and as amorous as the Italian"; but unfortunately he wrote his own works in Latin. The other chroniclers, writing in English itself, paid the land and the language a finer tribute. They were not always equal to the task they set themselves. Their works are largely the anecdotage of history, but the anecdote has usually a soul of truth. They hold a place somewhere between the historians and the journalists, for they have a keener eye for oddities and monstrosities than for policy or government. They have, too, the common weakness for beginning at a supposed beginning, and like to set out from the mythical Brutus—if not from some earlier hero. Thus Robert Fabyan (d. 1513), sheriff of London, who expanded his diary into a chronicle printed in 1516, felt bound to begin with Brutus.

The first Tudor chronicler, Edward Hall (d. 1547), had knowledge as well as enthusiasm. The earliest edition of his Chronicle (1542), called *The Union of the two noble and illustrate famelies of Lancastre & Yorke, etc.*, was effectively burnt by the order of Queen Mary; but when reprinted by Grafton in 1548 and 1550 it won deserved esteem. Up to the death of Henry VII Hall is a chronicler, translating the common authorities into his own ornate language. With the reign of Henry VIII he began a fresh and original work, writing of what he saw and thought. He was supremely patriotic, holding Henry to be the greatest of English monarchs, "the undubitate flower and very heire of both the sayd linages". Further he was a Londoner of the Londoners, exulting when the citizens scored a victory over the proud Cardinal. Ascham specially disliked what most appeals to a modern reader of Hall, namely his use of "strange and inkhorne tearmes" at one extreme and his racy simplicity at the other.

Raphael Holinshed's *Chronicles of England, Scotland, and Ireland* (1577, enlarged 1586) is wider in scope and more ambitious in design than the work of Hall. It begins with Noah and comes down to its own times. The book is a compilation fashioned by several hands. William Harrison contributed the *Description of England* and the *Description of Scotland* (derived from Boece and Major); the *Description of Ireland* was the work of Richard Stanyhurst and Edmund Campion; and Richard Hooker provided the translation of Giraldus Cambrensis. Holinshed's own contributions have better scholarship than we expect of his time. The one virtue that all the collaborators lacked is one that we can spare in this case, namely, an unadorned simple style. They write aureate English and are curious in the selection of "decking words". The popularity of Holinshed's *Chronicles* was deserved. Englishmen found in it a stimulating panegyric of their own country, and poets drew both matter and inspiration from its pages. The text of 1586 was severely "cut" by order of the Council; the "castrations" were separately printed in 1723. Harrison's *Description of England* gives a special distinction to Holinshed's *Chronicles*. His theme is whatever was done or thought in the England of his day, and nothing comes amiss to him. He is English of the English, dislikes foreigners, and still more the foreignized Englishman. A scholar and a man of letters, he was master of a style from which the wind of heaven has blown the last grain of pedantry. He has painted the truest picture we have of the England that Shakespeare knew.

John Stow (1525–1605) and John Speed (1552–1629) were chroniclers of a like fashion and a like ambition. They were good citizens as well as sound antiquaries, and, by a strange chance, they were both tailors. Stow was the more industrious writer of the two. In 1561 he issued an edition of Chaucer's works; later came his *Summarie of Englysh Chronicles*, and then, in 1580, he dedicated to Leicester a far better book, *The Chronicles of England from Brute until this present yeare of Christ*. Stow loved his books; nevertheless, his prose is the plainest and most straightforward of his time. Speed, on the other hand, in his *History of Great Britaine* (1611), was a born rhetorician; yet he supports his narrative more often than the others from unpublished documents. Like all the chroniclers he hymns the glory of England, "the Court of Queene Ceres, the Granary of the Western world, the fortunate island, the Paradise of Pleasure and Garden of God".

With William Camden (1551–1623) the chronicle reached its zenith. His *Rerum Anglicarum et Hibernicarum Annales, regnante Elizabetha* is by far the best example of its kind. Old-fashioned in design alone, the work is a genuine piece of modern history, in which events are set in proper perspective and proportion. Camden would stand far higher in general esteem if he had not mistakenly chosen to write his book in Latin. The *Annales* actually reached English by the roundabout way of a translation from the French. The first part of the original Latin (down to 1588) was published in 1615, the second part (from 1589 to the Queen's death) posthumously in 1627. The English version of the first part, with a fine flourishing title, appeared in 1625; a different translator turned the second part into English in 1629. On almost every page can be discerned the patriotic author's purpose and motive—to applaud the virtues of the Queen and to uphold the Protestant faith. In 1582 he took his famous journey through England, the result of which was his *Britannia* (1586). *Remaines Concerning Britaine* appeared in 1605. Camden's life was full and varied—he was a headmaster as well as a herald—and his character, as all his biographers testify, was candid and amiable. To our age, he is best known as the historian of Elizabeth. To his own age, he was eminent as an antiquary, and it was his *Britannia*, first published in 1586, and rescued from Latin by the incomparable Philemon Holland in 1610, which gave him his greatest glory.

Camden, like many other topographers, made use of the notes collected by John Leland (1506–52), a silent scholar, who, given a commission to travel in search of England's antiquities and records, spent six years in diligent tramping, and produced in 1546 *The laboryouse Journey and Serche of Johan Laylande, for Englandes Antiquitees, geven of hym as a newe yeares gyfte to kynge Henry the VIII in the XXXVII yeare of his raigne.* This was merely an instalment of what he intended. Like some other celebrated persons, Leland could collect materials but could not use them. He became a superstition. He lived on the reputation of the great book he was going to write; but, in the end, "upon a foresight that he was not able to perform his promise", he went mad and died. Leland's *Itinerary* was first published in 1710–12, and was re-edited two centuries later. It is a failure; it is unreadable.

As a topographer, it is Stow who takes his place by Camden's side. The *Survey of the Cities of London and Westminster* (1598 and 1603), as it was afterwards known, is a diligent and valuable piece of work, at once faithful and enthusiastic. To Richard Carew (1535–1620) we owe a *Survey of Cornwall* (1602). John Norden (1548–1625) has left merely a fragment of his *Speculum Britanniae* (1596). His *Surveyors Dialogue* (1607) may still be read with pleasure. What the travellers did for their country, Sir Thomas Smith (1513–77), in his *De Republica Anglorum; the Maner of Governement or Policie of the Realme of England* (written in 1565, printed in 1583), did for its law and government. No treatise ever owed less to ornament. It is, as the author declares, a map of government and policy. In style and substance the book is as concise as a classic, but it gives no hint of the varied accomplishments of its learned and sagacious author.

A different kind of chronicler is John Foxe (1516–87), whose *Actes and Monuments of these latter and perilous days…wherein are comprehended and described the great persecutions that have been wrought and practised by the Romishe Prelates…* (1563) became one of the most popular of books under the name of "Foxe's Book of Martyrs". The first form of it had appeared in Latin four years earlier. Foxe was a fanatic whose fixed purpose in life was to expose the wickedness of "the persecutors of God's truth, commonly called Papists". It is idle, therefore, to expect moderation or fairness from Foxe. As a mere performance, the *Actes and Monuments* is extraordinary. The fervid historian's energy never flags, and his homely yet dramatic style never fails to hold the attention. But one may be permitted to doubt whether the desire, either of writer or of reader, to delight in descriptions of physical torture can be considered wholly religious.

Most of the writers hitherto discussed were, so to speak, authors by instinct, who lacked discipline and were sometimes mastered by their own eloquence. But there are three writers, Sir Thomas More, George Cavendish (1500–61?), and Sir John Hayward (1564?–1627), who are scholars and historians rather than mere chroniclers. *The History of King Richard the thirde* (first printed in Hardyng's *Chronicle*, 1543) is properly attributed to More, who no doubt derived his information from the first-hand knowledge of his early patron

Cardinal Morton. Its high quality is attested by the fact that the dark and sinister portrait of Richard III drawn in its pages has endured ever since, in spite of vigorous challenge. George Cavendish's *Life and Death of Thomas Woolsey* has had a curious fate. It was circulated furtively in manuscript. Shakespeare read it, and Stow leaned upon its authority. It was not fully and faithfully published till 1667. Then the authorship was questioned. However, all doubt has been removed, and to George Cavendish, a simple gentleman of the cardinal's household, belongs the glory of having given to English literature the first specimen of artistic biography. Sir John Hayward devoted himself to the composition of history after classical models. His *First Part of the Life and Raigne of King Henrie the IIII* (1559), *The Lives of the III Normans, Kings of England* (1613), *The Life and Raigne of King Edward the sixt* (1630) and *The Annales of the First Four Years of the Raigne of Queene Elizabeth*, included in a later edition (1636) of the preceding work, are all good history and good reading. Bacon accused Hayward, humorously, of theft from Tacitus. At least it may be said of him that he sought sententiousness and found it. So we pass from annalist to artist. The chronicles are a mass of treasure. With the last three writers named begins in England the art of history.

XVI. ELIZABETHAN PROSE FICTION

Medieval fiction had normally assumed the form of verse, mainly because tales in verse could be more easily remembered and redelivered by the minstrels. Prose tales are a natural result of the printing press; and *Le Morte d'Arthur* was a striking example of the new possibilities. Prose fiction, regularly produced, is one of the numerous gifts of the Elizabethans to our literature. It was not a special creation, but the result of many attempts made in many ways—by imitation, by translation, by invention. The first appeal was naturally to courtiers, who were offered instruction as well as amusement. Spenser's *The Faerie Queene*, avowedly designed to present an ideal, is the last great poetical fiction. In the new age, when the knight had turned courtier, and castles had become houses, prose was the natural form for a story, though the polite pastoral still offered a model of machinery. But courtiers alone did not form the new reading public. The bourgeois mind was catered for in more realistic stories, in books of anecdotic jests, and in studies of roguery. There has always been a public for crime in fiction.

A great impulse to the composition of stories was given by the translators. William Painter (1540?–1594), in his *Palace of Pleasure* (1566–7), supplies versions of a hundred and one tales, many from Boccaccio and Bandello; Sir Geoffrey Fenton (1539?–1608), in his *Tragicall Discourses* (1567), reproduces thirteen tales of Bandello; and both, for the most part, are content with simple, faithful translation. In the stories which constitute *The Petite Pallace of Pettie his Pleasure* (1576), by George Pettie (1548–89), there is a "stylish" prose that is more than mere translation. George Whetstone's *Rock of Regard* (1576), mostly in verse, contains perhaps one original story, and of the eight stories which make up *Riche his Farewell to the Militarie Profession* (1581), by Barnabe Riche (1540?–1617), five are frankly "forged onely for delight". Translation led naturally to invention. In most of these tales the style is fantasticated; plain prose (as always) is a later development. Gascoigne's *The Pleasant Fable of Ferdinando Jeronimi and Leonora di Velasco*, already mentioned, is both our first modern short story in prose and a good example of the Italianate "stylized" tale with intercalated verses.

The first outstanding composer of courtly fiction devised for edification is John Lyly (1554–1606), dramatist and poet, whose most famous work has given the English language a word and perhaps a habit. *Euphues, the Anatomy of Wit* was out by 1578; *Euphues and his England*, the second part, appeared in 1580. Together they form an extensive moral treatise, and incidentally the first English prose novel. The whole hangs together by the thinnest of plots, for each incident and situation is merely an opportunity for instruction. The book owes much to North's *Diall of Princes* (1557), taken from Guevara, and to the *Colloquies* of Erasmus. In projecting a moral treatise Lyly stumbled on the novel. *Euphues*, with its famous style, has been much condemned by people who have never read it. Actually, in proportion and economy it is a great advance on the sprawling wordiness of much Tudor prose writing. Lyly's carefully shaped and balanced sentences represent in prose that movement towards design in verse which was the protest against doggerel. The success of *Euphues* led to a multitude of imitations—*Euphues* this, *Euphues* that, and so on. We need concern ourselves with none of them, except to note among the authors the name of Thomas Lodge. But edification was not a permanent element of romance, and pure, if fantastic, fiction began to appear—or rather to re-appear, for the old romances of chivalry were not forgotten. A pastoral setting, the adventures of the nobly born in simple life, the separation and reunion of royal kindred—these are motives that we can find alike in Sidney and in Shakespeare.

Sir Philip Sidney was eminently qualified by nature and circumstance to deal with such themes. *The Countess of Pembroke's Arcadia*—so called because it was written for, and revised by, his sister Mary Herbert, Countess of Pembroke—was begun in 1580 at Wilton and was posthumously published in 1590. Dissatisfied with the materialism of the court, Sidney indulged his fancy with ideal scenes and sentiments, and so we get pastoral idealism, the golden age, and similar agreeable fictions. To Sannazaro's *Arcadia* (1504) and Montemayor's *Diana* (1552), Sidney probably owed his main idea. But Sidney, the convinced member of Harvey's classical Areopagus, added not only such a song as "My true love hath my heart", but limping hexameters and elegiacs and experiments in *terza rima* and *ottava rima*. The style of the *Arcadia* shows a deliberate attempt at a picturesque prose, and therefore it is extravagant, with nothing of Lyly's balanced concision; but its best moments are very good indeed. Those who find the book too long and tedious will do well to remember that it was not written for the general public and a diffused circulation. In a sense, it is a mass of florid correspondence that passed between Sidney and his sister.

Robert Greene (1560?–1592), the second great romancer of the Elizabethan period, compared with the knightly Sidney, appears as a picturesque but pathetic Bohemian with "wit lent from Heaven but vices sent from Hell". His chief romances are *Pandosto* (1588), *Perimedes the Blacksmith* (1588), and *Mena-*

phon (1589). The first suggested the plot of *A Winter's Tale*. Pleasing features of Greene's less embittered stories are the attractive female characters and the charming verses.

Rosalynde, Euphues Golden Legacie (1590) by Thomas Lodge (1558?–1625) is deservedly celebrated, both as a source of *As You Like It*, and as an example of narrative art. It is itself based upon the pseudo-Chaucerian *Tale of Gamelyn* and tells its story with charm and skill. Emanuel Ford's *Parismus* (1598) and its sequel, *Parismenos* (1599), are obvious imitations of the works of Greene. Nicholas Breton is another of Greene's successors, his chief romantic work being *The Strange Fortune of two excellent princes* (1600). The Spanish romances, popularized by Anthony Munday in his English translations (1580–96), include versions of the Amadis and Palmerin cycles, far-off descendants of the Arthurian romance. See further, p. 241.

Before the last decade of the century was well advanced, the scene moved from Arcadia and Bohemia to London and Alsatia. Idealism gave way to realism. The chief writers in this kind were Greene, Nashe and Deloney. Greene's main strength lay in a relation of his own experiences. His auto-biographical work begins in *Greenes Mourning Garment* (1590) and *Greenes Never too late* (1590), and ends in 1592 with the death-bed utterances, *Greenes Groatsworth of Wit, bought with a Million of Repentance* and *The Repentance of Robert Greene*. Descriptions of London life appear in his *Notable Discovery of Coosnage* (1591), *The Defence of Conny-Catching* (1592) and *A Disputation between a Hee Conny-Catcher and a Shee Conny-Catcher* (1592)—a "conny" or "cony", being a simpleton, a "rabbit", easily "skinned" by rascals. These are all vigorous exposures of roguery. Greene also gave attention to the more respectable side of London life in his *Quip for an Upstart Courtier or a Quaint Dispute between Velvet-Breeches and Cloth-Breeches* (1592)—the eternal debate between court life and private simplicity. In these works of Greene we meet many varieties of rascaldom and Bohemianism, and among the characters of the theatre we are invited, bitterly, to observe a young "Shake-scene" patching up old plays.

The next great realist, Thomas Nashe (1567–1601), was, like Greene, a university wit who lived hard, wrote fiercely, and died young. In *Pierce Pennilesse his Supplication to the Divell* (1592) Nashe gives a fair taste of his quality, but his pamphleteering work is less interesting to us than his short picaresque novel, *The Unfortunate Traveller, or the Life of Jacke Wilton* (1594), the first of our historical tales and a remarkable anticipation of the manner of Defoe. To picaresque fiction Lodge also made one contribution, namely, *The Life and Death of William Longbeard* (1593), and in 1595 appeared Henry Chettle's *Piers Plainnes Seaven Yeres Prentiship* in which the *picaro* Piers relates his life-story to Arcadian shepherds in Tempe.

More than ordinary interest attaches to the work of Thomas Deloney (1543?–1607?), last of the Elizabethan "realists". Before 1596 he had written some fifty-six "ballads"; but after that date he turned to prose, and between 1596 and 1600 produced three narratives: *Thomas of Reading*, which honours the clothiers, *Jack of Newbury*, which celebrates a wealthy weaver, and *The Gentle Craft*, containing stories dedicated to shoemakers. The first two of these are uneasy efforts at Euphuistic fiction, but the third comes down to fact and gives us the career of Simon Eyre who, from a shoemaker's apprentice, rose to be Lord Mayor. In the hands of Dekker this became the delightful comedy we know as *The Shoemaker's Holiday*.

Elizabethan fiction, interesting as a series of attempts, achieved little more than a beginning, and, when compared with Elizabethan drama, can hardly be said to exist. The greatest problems of life are never propounded in the Elizabethan novel as they are in the Elizabethan play; and so the one survives as a curiosity of literature while the other remains a most extraordinary manifestation of the creative imagination. Historically, the novel is a later form of art than the play, and develops more tardily. People can listen before they can read. A form like the novel cannot come to its full strength till an alert reading public has been created. The earlier public read for edification or for controversy; when it wished for literary enjoyment it listened.

XVII. THE MARPRELATE CONTROVERSY

The Martin Marprelate controversy, theological in primary interest and bibliographical in secondary interest, touches literature at two points. It illustrates the development of the prose pamphlet and shows how a religious party, eager to proclaim its principles, successfully defied the official restraints upon liberty of printing.

The Tudor chroniclers agree in expressing the national satisfaction at the breach with Rome. The accession of Elizabeth seemed to promise a final purging of the church from all taint of Romanism. But episcopacy, priesthood and vestments remained, and the fanatics determined that these should be cast out. Under the feeble rule of Archbishop Grindal, it seemed that in church government England was going the way of Scotland. That prospect was displeasing to the Queen. James I uttered the significant phrase, "No bishop, no king"; but the sentiment was Elizabeth's, and she resolved to make the church do something to set its house in order. The sturdy John Whitgift (1530–1604), as strongly anti-Puritan as he was anti-Roman, was made archbishop in 1583; and the reply of the reformers (1584) was an anonymous tract from the press of Robert Waldegrave, lengthily styled *A Briefe and Plaine Declaration concerning the Desires of all those faithfull Ministers, that have and do seeke for the Discipline and Reformation of the Church of Englande*, but generally called from its running title, *A Learned Discourse*. So effective was its attack upon the established order that John Bridges, Dean of Salisbury, endeavoured to crush it with a quarto of fourteen hundred pages. In 1586 Whitgift had procured from the Star Chamber an extension of the existing censorship of books, which gave to him and the Bishop of London power to control the printing presses and to forbid the publication of seditious works; and when in 1587 there appeared *The Aequity of an Humble Supplication* by John Penry (1559–93), and in 1588 the anonymous dialogue briefly called *Diotrephes* by John Udall, Whitgift replied by imprisoning Penry, and disdaining to penetrate Udall's anonymity, fell upon Waldegrave the printer and silenced him by seizing his press and type. However, in some way Waldegrave preserved the means of printing, and, secreted at East Molesey, he became the chief engine in a famous controversy.

In October 1588 appeared a tract with the usual long descriptive title, part of which is worth quoting as a specimen of its time and kind. Referring to the Dean of Salisbury's treatise, it begins: *Oh read over D. John Bridges, for it is a worthy worke: Or an Epitome of the fyrste Booke of that right worshipfull volume, written against the Puritanes, in the defence of The noble cleargie, by as worshipfull a prieste, John Bridges, Presbyter, Priest or elder, doctor of Divillitie and Deane of Sarum...Compiled...by the reverend and worthie Martin Marprelate gentleman... The Epitome is not yet published....In the mean time let them* (i.e. the Bishops) *be content with this learned Epistle. Printed oversea, in Europe, within two furlongs of a Bounsing Priest, at the cost and charges of M. Marprelate, gentleman.* The bold, ribald gusto of this attack upon the bishops took the taste of the town and Martin's *Epistle* was the success of the day. But the hunt was up. Waldegrave fled to Northampton, to which Penry's wife belonged, and near which lived two friends of the cause, Job Throckmorton of Hasely and Sir Richard Knightley of Fawsley.

From Fawsley in November came the second of Martin's missiles, the promised *Epitome*, with a title as long as the first. In January 1589, Penry's house was raided; but the flying press was again on its travels. It came to rest at Coventry, in the house of John Hales, a relative of Knightley; and in March 1589 was issued Martin's third attack, a broadside, of which the title begins: *Certaine Minerall and Metaphisicall Schoolpoints to be defended by the reverende Bishops.* This was commonly known as *The Mineralls*. In January 1589 had appeared an official attempt to answer Martin's *Epistle*. It was called *An admonition to the people of England*, etc. The author was T. C., i.e., Thomas Cooper, Bishop of Winchester. Martin replied in March with his fourth tract, having the usual lengthy title, but beginning wittily with a London street cry *Hay any Worke for Cooper*.

At this point Martin suffered a check. The graver Puritans disliked their ribald champion, and Waldegrave abandoned his part in the enterprise. Another printer, John Hodgkins, was found, and from Wigston House at Wolston, near Coventry, came in July 1589 Martin's fifth tract, *Theses Martinianae*. A week later appeared the sixth tract, *The just censure and reproofe of Martin Junior*. Hodgkins had still another tract to print, *More Worke for the Cooper*; but he decided to move his quarters to Manchester. Here, however, he and his assistants were captured and sent to London, where Whitgift put them on the rack to extort confessions. But Martin was not utterly silenced; and from Wigston House came the defiant and hastily printed seventh and last tract, *The Protestatyon of Martin Marprelat*. Martin died with defiance on his lips, and *The Protestatyon*, recognizing that this was the end of Martinism, defiantly prophesied the death of "Lambethism". This was longer in dying than Martin supposed; but it fell with the head of Laud in 1645.

The flood of tracts, Martinist and anti-Martinist, belongs to the stream of religious controversy. Richard Bancroft (1544–1610), who succeeded Whitgift in the primacy, was responsible, not only for the measures which led to the arrest of Martin's printer, but for the prosecution of the anti-Martinist campaign by Martin's own methods of ribaldry. Richard Harvey, Lyly and Nashe are supposed to have been engaged in the controversy; and there appeared 1589–90 various tracts of which the titles are more amusing than the matter: *A Whip for an Ape* (Lyly?), *A Countercuffe given to Martin Junior* (Nashe?), *Martins Months Minde* (Nashe?—the cleverest of these tracts), *Pappe with a Hatchet* (Lyly?), *The Returne of the renoued Cavaliero Pasquill* (Nashe?), *Plaine Percevall* (Richard Harvey?), and *An Almond for a Parrat* (Nashe?). These are a few, and they are inferior to Martin's "flyting"—replies are rarely as bright as impudent attacks. The controversy ultimately sank into an unedifying squabble among the anti-Martinist pamphleteers, and the tracts produced have no concern with literature. The identity of Martin Marprelate, like the identity of Junius, is a matter for unending controversy. Evidence points most clearly to John Penry, hanged in 1593. But nothing known to be by Penry has the wild high-spirits of the Marprelate tracts.

Martin's audacious personality and large liberty of satire were something new and not easily forgotten, and he may be considered as a forerunner of the greater satirist whose *Tale of a Tub* was a brilliant attack upon all forms of religious controversy. Martin was ill-supported by the Puritan divines, who disliked his ribald humour and demanded sober seriousness. The preference was not wholly fortunate. From seriousness it is easy to pass to sourness. The Puritans banished the Comic Muse from England; she returned in 1660 as the handmaid of Silenus.

XVIII. *OF THE LAWS OF ECCLESIASTICAL POLITY*

The reigns of Henry VIII, Edward VI, and Mary had left the political and religious life of the country in ruins; to Elizabeth fell the task of reconstruction. Calvin at Geneva showed that he possessed in an eminent degree the power of ruling men; and English exiles sheltering there looked for the establishment at home of a similar government, not, indeed, because they loved religious freedom, but because they loved discipline, and preferred Puritan infallibility, founded upon the Scriptures, to Papal infallibility founded upon tradition. Pope and Puritan alike regarded the civil power merely as an instrument for use by religious dictatorship. But the daughter of the king who had torn England from Rome was not disposed to surrender it to Geneva. The Acts of Supremacy and Uniformity (1559) with the restored and revised second Prayer Book of Edward VI sought to find a plain way between the fanatics of both parties; but the returned Puritan exiles were vehement in demanding their spiritual Geneva. We think today of Calvinism chiefly as a creed; to the English Puritans of 1560 Calvinism was a polity in which the state was the church, and the church the people; and such a polity they sought to establish through Parliament.

In 1572 was published a celebrated brief address entitled *An Admonition to the Parliament* in which certain Puritan authors, probably John Field and Thomas Wilcox, set forth "a true platforme of a church reformed". Their ideals were the abolition of episcopacy and priesthood and a return to "purity of the word, simplicity of the sacraments, and severity of discipline". The *Admonition* is an excellent specimen both of contemporary prose controversy and of the perpetual delusion that Acts of Parliament can establish here and now an ideal common-wealth. It may be taken as representative of many similar demands. The great work of Richard Hooker was, immediately, a reply to the Puritan case (he refers to the *Admonition*), and, ultimately, an examination of the Christian institutes by one who combined on the loftiest plane of thought the qualities of a devout churchman, a great humanist and a lover of intellectual freedom. Richard Hooker (1553–1600) lived and died a simple parish priest, and all that the reader need know of him—his unfortunate marriage and his dispute with the aggressive Puritan Walter Travers—can be found in Izaak Walton's ever delightful *Lives*. The first four books of the treatise named *Of the Laws of Ecclesiastical Polity* appeared in 1594, the fifth in 1597. The sixth and eighth books did not appear till 1648 and 1651, and the seventh was printed in 1662. The posthumous books lack full authenticity. Hooker exposes the weakness of the Puritan case, its dogmatic assumption of its own infallibility. Throughout the book he argues quietly for a scheme of law, evolved by human needs, according to time and place, and not taken over from some vanished age and forcibly imposed upon another. The Old Testament theocracy is a guide, but not a fixed constitution, and the tyranny of texts must be resisted. In reading Hooker's treatise we must remind ourselves that its title is not *The Laws of* but *Of the Laws of Ecclesiastical Polity*, it being no design of his to lay down definite laws of church government but, rather, to discuss the principles whereon they are based. Hooker was pleading for tolerance and moderation, to which Puritan dictatorship was hostile. That Puritanism, in later days, came to be identified with what we call political progress must not obscure the fact that Elizabethan Puritanism was fighting for a completely reactionary religious tyranny. Hooker's fifth book takes us into the realm of great religious principles. It was the last to be published in his lifetime, and it is the most important. The whole treatise had great influence and contributed nobly to the subsequent development of the Anglican ideal; but Hooker's position was not that of the Laudian, much less that of the Tractarian, school of clergy. He was too liberal for both. He was neither pragmatic nor primitive.

Of Hooker's writing perhaps the most remarkable feature is the singular calmness and dignity with which he discusses the raging questions of his time. It can be best appreciated in its moments of grave eloquence. No previous writer had so combined controversy with consummate literary power. The voice of railing and of loud harangue is nowhere to be heard in his pages. But Hooker is more than a great prose artist. He is the voice of the true religion that, under whatever system of regulation, leaves the thoughts and aspirations of mankind free.

XIX. ENGLISH UNIVERSITIES, SCHOOLS AND SCHOLARSHIP IN THE SIXTEENTH CENTURY

During the political and religious troubles of the sixteenth century, Oxford and Cambridge naturally became objects of high policy because they had become part of English life and thought. From the time of Henry VIII they were therefore subject to successive "purgings" of all those teachers who were obnoxious to successive varieties of theological opinion. More tranquil times came with Elizabeth, who was herself a lover of learning, with a bias to national continuity and an aversion to the foreigner, whether Pope or Calvin. Her policy was wisely guided by William Cecil, and during her reign we find the universities restored to their normal function. By the Act of Incorporation (1571) each university attained the status of a corporation under the style of "The Chancellor, Masters and Scholars". It is not the least title to their place in the history of literature, that Oxford and Cambridge bred the men to whom we owe the Tudor Bibles, the Prayer Book and the Authorized Version. In general, it may be said that Oxford was hospitable to the Church doctrines of Hooker and that Cambridge cultivated an enlightened Puritanism.

The lines of classical study were nominally determined by requirements for degrees. Rhetoric in the wider humanist sense, philosophy, both ethical and natural, and logic were the accepted subjects. Greek, as a university study, steadily declined from the standard set up by Cheke. Whitgift, the strongest force at Cambridge, knew no Greek. Nothing in classical scholarship at either university at this period can be remotely compared with the work of Joseph Scaliger (1540–1609), nor can English learning show a scholar to rank with George Buchanan. The translators of Greek (like North) worked through French versions. Latin remained not merely a subject for study, but the language of scholars.

It is significant that in both universities the art of printing ceased at some date between 1520–30, to be restored at Cambridge in 1582, when Thomas Thomas was recognized as printer to the university, and at Oxford in 1585, when Joseph Barnes set up a press. But the centre of English printing and publishing was London. From 1586 licence to publish was granted by the Archbishop of Canterbury and the Bishop of London (see p. 137), and the only two presses authorized outside the London area were those of Oxford and Cambridge.

In the provision of schools, Elizabeth's counsellors took up the task where Edward VI's death had left it. To restore the local grammar school became a fashion. A new type of scholar, sometimes, like Thomas Ashton of Shrewsbury, a man of standing at court, or, like William Camden, a travelled historian, became headmaster. Sir Henry Savile and Sir Henry Wotton dignified the office of Provost of Eton. Education ceased to be mainly clerical, but great importance was attached to exercises in Latin prose and verse. To lay the foundations of prose style was the object of every master. English writing was probably more cared for than appears; for the discipline in Latin developed taste in words and a sense of the logical texture of speech.

The universities produced a few notable scholars. Sir John Cheke (1514–57), first Regius Professor of Greek at Cambridge, named in Milton's "Tetrachordon" sonnet, was eminent at home and abroad. Thomas Wilson, friend and disciple of Cheke, produced his famous *Arte of Rhetorique* in 1553. Wilson's treatise should be read side by side with Guazzo's *Civile Conversation*, translated by Pettie thirty years later (1586), with a preface in which he refers to Wilson and urges the need for a liberal expansion of English vocabulary. Other popular works were Richard Rainolde's *Foundacion of Rhetorike* (1563), Henry Peacham's *Garden of Eloquence* (1577), and *The Arcadian Rhetorike* (1588) of Abraham Fraunce, who quotes current examples of poetry and prose.

Roger Ascham (1515–68), perhaps the ablest Greek scholar in England, belonged to the circle in which Cheke, Thomas Smith, and Wilson were the chief figures. His *Toxophilus* (1545), a treatise on the art of shooting with the long bow, discusses, in the accepted dialogue form, the function of bodily training in education, and prescribes practice with the bow as a necessary national exercise. *The Scholemaster* (1570) is essentially the work of a scholar who has no illusions on the subject of Erasmian cosmopolitanism. Ascham demands English matter, in English speech, for Englishmen. He pleads for style, and urges that the way to gain it is to read both widely and exactly. Only in poetry did Ascham lapse into pedantry. He would recognize no English metres.

In passing from Ascham to Richard Mulcaster (1530?–1611) we step into a different world, for Mulcaster spent a busy life as a master of the two great day schools of the City of London—Merchant Taylors' and St Paul's. The fruit of his experience is embodied in two books, *Positions* (1581) and *The First Part of the Elementarie* (1582). His views of education are large, practical, and modern in the best sense. He wants education for all, and the best education for the best. More clearly than any writer on education Mulcaster saw the possibilities of exact training and enrichment of the mind in and through English. His lesson is even now imperfectly learned.

Il Cortegiano of Castiglione, translated by Sir Thomas Hoby as *The Courtier* (1561), is much more than a treatise on the upbringing of youth; however, its picture of the "perfect man" of the Renascence had a marked effect on higher education in England. There were many similar works, the enumeration of which is unnecessary. In spite of Ascham, men of the world sent their boys to complete their education abroad; and the finer minds returned with a deeper and more intelligent patriotism.

XX. THE LANGUAGE FROM CHAUCER TO SHAKESPEARE

During the period between the *Old English Chronicle* and *The Canterbury Tales* the organic character of the language vitally changed through the gradual loss of its inflections. The changes in vocabulary were much less radical. After 1400 this order was reversed. The modifications in grammar were slight; the developments in vocabulary were very great. The period 1400–1600 divides naturally into two centuries, the dividing point being, roughly, the date of Caxton's death (1491). The fifteenth century saw a steady increase in the importance of the vernacular and its ultimate triumph as the national language. The English of London, like the Greek of Athens and the French of Paris, became the standard of educated communication. The most striking fact about the vocabulary of the fifteenth century is the rapid supersession of native words by others mainly of French origin. The percentage of foreign words in Lydgate is higher than in Chaucer. This general increase is due not only to the literary impulse of translation and imitation but to the growth of commercial relations with France, Italy and the Low Countries. With the passing of inflections came an increased use of prepositional forms. Metrically, the most important change, as we have already noted, was the loss of the final syllabic *e*. Even in Lydgate there are signs that it had become mute, and later poets could not find four syllables in Chaucer's "grene yeres" or read with the right rhythm a line like "Tales of best sentence and moost solaas". Other changes in pronunciation occurred. The medial *gh* ceased to be pronounced. Lydgate rhymes "fought" with "about", as Chaucer never did.

In the sixteenth century we come to a time when scholars are concerned for the welfare of the language and seek to improve its powers of expression. Twenty-five years of printing had fixed in the rough the character of modern English. But Latin was still the main language of scholars, who chose it as their medium simply because it was permanent, whereas English "had not continued in one form of understanding for 200 years". Ascham's *Toxophilus* (1545) struck a shrewd blow for English, and Elyot, in his *Castel of Helth* (1534), deliberately used English for his science. The growing use of the native tongue coincided with the growing sense of national patriotism, and the revolt from Rome naturally tended to make English the language of religion. Two tendencies are to be observed, the one, that of the Cambridge scholars Cheke, Ascham and Wilson, who desired to keep the English tongue "pure"; the other, that of the poets, the true "makers", who desired to enrich their medium. The "enrichers" looked both ways; they revived words from the older vocabulary and they took in new words from foreign languages. Spenser borrowed from the Lancashire peasants for *The Shepheards Calendar*; the scholars borrowed from the classics and from French and Italian.

Some writers in using a learned word added a native word in explanation, a device to which we owe the pleasing doublets familiar in the Prayer Book, "we have erred and strayed", "when we assemble and meet together". From the classical importations the language gained capacity for nobler rhythms, and further enriched itself when the apparent synonyms began to assume distinct shades of meaning. Literary artists tried new compounds, and gave us "home keeping" youths, and "cloud-capt" towers. The language of the ordinary man in Britain and America was for centuries full of lovely words and phrases first made current by the translators of the Bible—"peace-makers", "heavy-laden", "high-minded", "help-meet", "the fat of the land", "a soft answer", "a labour of love", "the eleventh hour" and "the shadow of death".

Fragments of the older grammar lived on. "Can" and "may" could still keep their old meaning— "For they can well on horseback"; old imperatives, like "Break we our watch up" remained. The loss of inflections, and the attempt to keep the conciseness possible only in a synthetic language led to new constructions. Intransitive verbs were used as transitive, ordinary verbs as causal —"this aspect hath feared (i.e. caused fear to) the valiant"—and the infinitive was used with the utmost freedom. With the loss of the old grammatical gender came the new metaphorical or poetic gender which gave personality to phenomena and abstractions.

Elizabethan pronunciation is too technical to be discussed in a brief notice. Readers of Spenser and Shakespeare will have observed some differences evident in the rhymes. "One", pronounced as in "atone" was still current in the sixteenth century, and accounts for such forms as "th'one" and "such an one"— now an absurdity.

Elizabethan English was pre-eminently the language of feeling. Comparatively poor in abstract and learned words, though these were being rapidly acquired, it abounded in words which had a physical signification, and which conveyed their meaning with splendid strength and simplicity. This accounts in part for the felicitous diction of the Bible translations. Further, the Elizabethan had at his command all the distinctions, now lost, between "thou" and "you", the curious vividness of the ethical dative ("villain, knock me this gate"), and the emphasis of double negatives ("nor no further in sport neither") and double comparatives ("more elder"). Thanks to the English Bible, the Prayer Book and Shakespeare, Elizabethan English has never become really obsolete. Its diction and its idioms are still familiar, endeared and hallowed by literary tradition or sacred association.

CHAPTER IV

PROSE AND POETRY: SIR THOMAS NORTH
TO MICHAEL DRAYTON

I. TRANSLATORS

The translators of Elizabeth's age pursued their craft in the spirit of bold
adventure which animated Drake and Hawkins. Philemon Holland justly
described his enterprise as a conquest, and he hoped it would benefit his native
land. When North and Holland asked the Queen's protection for their masterpieces, they believed that Plutarch and Livy would prove sagacious guides to
her and to her counsellors. In giving to England wellnigh the whole wisdom
of the ancients, the translators provided not merely grave instruction for kings
and statesmen, but plots for the dramatists and entertainment for leisured
readers. They were impeded by no theories about translation. They would
not have understood the scientific care with which Dryden presently distinguished metaphrase and paraphrase. What they seized upon they transmitted
with its magnificence and momentum increased rather than diminished. Few of
them were scholars, and, when it suited them, they cheerfully translated
translations of translations.

Their range of discovery was wide. But it is odd that the classical drama
escaped them, and that the golden age of our drama should have seen the
translation of but one Greek play, and that one a mere paraphrase from an
Italian version of the *Phoenissae* of Euripides—the *Jocasta* of Gascoigne. From
Latin there was more. William Warner's *Menaechmi* of Plautus (1595) may
have given Shakespeare a hint for *The Comedy of Errors*. Seneca and Terence
were very popular, Seneca especially. As far as the Elizabethan drama was
classical it was Senecan. Seneca was translated by various hands between 1559
and 1567, and *Tenne Tragedies* were collected by Thomas Newton in 1581.
(T. S. Eliot's introduction to the 1927 edition in the Tudor Translations series
is reprinted in his *Selected Essays*.) The *Andria* of Terence was translated as early
as 1520 and was called, simply, *Terens in Englysh*. Richard Bernard's excellent
translation of all the plays appeared in 1598.

The historians fared better. Thomas Nicolls gave us a complete Thucydides
in 1550, and an unknown B.R. (Barnabe Rich?) two books of Herodotus in
1584. To the incomparable Philemon Holland we owe Livy (1600), Ammianus
(1609) and Xenophon's *Cyropaedia* (1632). Sallust appeared in several versions.
What Sir Henry Savile did for the *Histories* and the *Agricola* of Tacitus (1591),
Richard Greenwey did for the *Annals* and the *Germania* (1598). Xenophon
found other translators besides Holland, and Plutarch's *Lives* fell happily into
the hands of Sir Thomas North, whose genius gave them a second and larger
immortality.

The philosophers and moralists of the ancient world chimed with the humour of Tudor England, and the translators supplied those ignorant of the dead languages with a mighty armoury of intellectual weapons. Of Plato there seems to be nothing. Aristotle fared better, for the *Ethics* was translated by John Wilkinson in 1547 and the *Politics* by "I. D." in 1598, neither from the Greek. Far more popular were Cicero and Seneca, the chief instructors of the age. Caxton admired "the noble philosopher and prynce of Eloquence Tullius Consul Romayn" and printed in 1481 versions from the French of *De Senectute* and *De Amicitia*, the latter translated by John Tiptoft, Earl of Worcester. A long series of Tudor translations of Cicero begins in 1534 with *Three Bookes of Tullyes Offyces* by Robert Whytinton. Lodge's monumental version of Seneca's prose (1614) is undiminished even by comparison with Holland's translation of Plutarch's *Morals*. A special place in our affection has been taken by *The Golden Asse* (1566) of Apuleius translated by an unknown William Adlington.

The modern world yielded as rich a spoil as the ancient. From Italy came the stories that made Ascham exclaim "ten *Morte Arthures* do not the tenth part as much harme as one of those bookes, made in Italie and translated in England". He had in mind William Painter's *Palace of Pleasure* (1566–7) and Sir Geoffrey Fenton's *Certaine Tragicall Discourses written oute of Frenche and Latin* (1567). Few books of the time had a more immediate or profound influence than these. They entertained the court and were an inspiration to the poets and dramatists. Painter's oldest stories are taken from Herodotus, Livy and Aulus Gellius; and presently he seeks his originals in the works of Queen Margaret and Boccaccio, Bandello and Straparola. Whatever the origin and substance of his tales, he reduced them all to a certain plainness. His work was quickly intelligible to simple folk and the dramatists had no difficulty in clothing his dry bones with their romantic imagery. Fenton's *Tragicall Discourses* were drawn from Belleforest's French translation of Bandello. An odd fact is that no one translated Boccaccio's *Decameron*, save in fragments, till 1620, though the *Amorous Fiammetta* was done in 1587 by Bartholomew Young and *Philocopo* in 1566 by Henry Grantham. Sir Thomas Hoby's version (1561) of Castiglione's *Il Cortegiano* won the approval of Ascham, who declared that a year's study of it in England would do a young man more good than three years' travel in Italy.

Even stranger than the neglect of Boccaccio is the misunderstanding of Machiavelli, whose *Arte of Warre* was translated by Peter Whitehorne in 1560–2 and whose *Florentine Historie* was translated by Thomas Beddingfield in 1595, but whose *Prince* had to wait till the version of Edward Dacres, published in 1640. And thus we are confronted by what seems to be a literary puzzle. *The Prince* had a profound influence upon the thought and policy of Tudor England. It was a textbook to Thomas Cromwell; its precepts were obediently followed by Cecil and Leicester. The mingled fear and respect in which its author was held converted him into a monstrous legend. He is constantly cited, almost always with detestation, and the indignant references are invariably to *The Prince*, which was not translated, and not to *The Art of War* and the *Florentine History*, which were. A German scholar has counted more than three hundred references to *The Prince* in the dramatists alone. The explanation is simple. Those who did not read *Il Principe* in Italian derived their knowledge from a hostile treatise in French, a *Contre-Machiavel* as it was called, namely the *Discours sur les moyens de bien gouverner et maintenir en bonne paix un Royaume ou autre Principauté...Contre Nicholas Machiavel Florentin* (1576), written by Innocent Gentillet, a French Huguenot, fresh from the horrors of the Machiavellian massacre of St Bartholomew; and this was translated by Simon Patericke as early as 1602. So, thanks to Gentillet, the author of an unsensational recommendation of realism in government was regarded as a master of devilish cunning. He was known through the distorted picture drawn by an enemy. The legend persists to this day.

French was naturally better known than Italian, and it was from French versions of the classics that some of our best translators worked. The first important revelation of French thought to become popular in England was Florio's version of Montaigne's *Essayes* (1603), after which may be placed Thomas Danett's *Historie of Commines* (1596), a finished portrait of a politician. And France, also, like Italy, has her paradox. As we have no *Prince* before Dacres (1640), so we have no Rabelais before Sir Thomas Urquhart (1653). Earlier Rabelaisian allusions must therefore have been drawn from the original or from some version of which no trace remains.

Thomas Shelton's fine *Don Quixote* (1612–20) and James Mabbe's *Exemplarie Novells* (1640) as well as his *Spanish Bawd* (1631)—the *Celestina* of Fernando de Rojas—belong to the seventeenth century; but the sixteenth century took to its heart *The Diall of Princes* translated from Guevara by Sir Thomas North (1557). The earliest example of the picaresque novel, *Lazarillo de Tormes*, was "drawn out of Spanish" by David Rowland (1586).

The most famous, and perhaps the best, of Elizabethan translations is *The Lives of the Noble Grecians and Romanes* (1579), by Sir Thomas North (1535?–1601?). That Shakespeare used it, borrowing its very words as well as its stories, must be counted a unique distinction. It is not Plutarch. It is a new masterpiece on Plutarch's theme; and it came into English, not from the Greek, but from the French of Jacques Amyot. North's Plutarch is as far from Amyot's as Amyot's is from its original. Not merely the words, but the very spirit is transformed. Change the names, and you might be reading in North's page of Philip Sidney and Richard Grenville, of Leicester and the great Lord Burghley. For North, though he knew little of the classics, was a master of noble English. His prose escaped both frigidity and eccentricity, and so he holds a central place in the history of our speech.

Philemon Holland (1552–1637) was a translator of another kind. His legendary pen was apt for any enterprise. He was a finished master of both Greek and Latin, and so great was his industry that he is the hero, not of one, but of half a dozen books. He sought no aid from French or Italian. He went straight to the ancient texts. He was a scholar, and was felicitously called "the Translatour Generall in his age". Holland had a natural feeling for old words and proverbs, and he loved ornament with the ardour of an ornamental age. His industry was universally applauded. Livy's *Romane Historie* appeared in 1600, *Plinie's Natural Historie of the Worlde* in 1601, *The Philosophie, commonly called, the Morals* of Plutarch in 1603, and *The Historie of the Twelve Caesars* by Suetonius in 1606. It was said that he wrote the whole of Plutarch's *Morals* with one pen.

Holland has left us, not mere translations, but a set of variations upon ancient motives, to which we may listen with an independent and unalloyed pleasure.

John Florio's translation of Montaigne holds a place apart. Florio (1553?–1625) had neither the sentiment of North nor the scholarship of Holland. He brought to his task something that neither of these masters possessed—a curious fantasy which was all his own. He loved words for their own sakes with a love which Montaigne might not have appreciated, but which will be understood by any who know Florio's own famous dictionary, *A Worlde of Wordes* (1598).

The Elizabethan translations into verse are inferior to the translations into prose. For this there are many reasons, and the chief of all is that to translate a poet we need a poet of the same magnitude. Unfortunately some of the translators were pedants, not poets. The members of Harvey's Areopagus were on the wrong road. As Virgil and Ovid composed their poems in hexameters measured by quantity, it seemed proper to some translators to follow their example. Ascham began the controversy both by practice and precept. Gabriel Harvey, with massive learning, carried the doctrine further and drew Spenser after him— fortunately only in theory. The most amazing of all translators is Richard Stanyhurst (1547–1618), whose *Thee First Foure Bookes of Virgil his Aeneis translated intoo English Heroical Verse* was printed at Leyden in 1582, with two prefaces expounding the author's theory of verse and quantity. Like other poets, earlier and later, Stanyhurst adapts his spelling to suit his metre, and he uses the wildest words, new and old. Nothing but extensive quotation can convey the quality of this strange curiosity of literature, which, nevertheless, has more merits than those who have laughed at it seem willing to allow. Fortunately a reprint is available. Thomas Phaer's *Virgil*, which began to appear in 1558 and was completed in 1583, is composed in fourteeners; but though admired in its day its merits are small. The best beloved of all the ancient poets was Ovid, whose popularity is attested by many translations, among which may be named *The Fable...treting of Narcissus* by Thomas Howell (1560), *The Heroycall Epistles* by George Turberville (1567), *The thre first Bookes of Ovid de Tristibus* by Thomas Churchyard (1572) and *The Pleasant Fable of Hermaphroditus and Salmacis* by Thomas Peend (1565) and by Francis Beaumont (1602). To these we may add the *Elegies* of Marlowe. But of all the translations by far the most popular was Arthur Golding's *The XV Bookes of P. Ovidius Naso entytuled Metamorphosis* (1567). Using the popular "fourteeners", Golding produced a good level version of his master. His work has a special interest; for when we read such lines as

> Ye Ayres and windes: ye Elves of Hills, of Brookes, of Woods alone,
>   Of standing Lakes, and of the Night, approache ye everychone,

we know we are reading something that Shakespeare had probably read. Golding was also the translator of our best version of Caesar's *Gallic War* (1565), besides other works.

Another reign saw the completion of Chapman's vigorous and famous Homer; but as he published a translation of seven books of the *Iliad* in 1598, a word must be said here of his splendid achievement. To do full justice to Chapman's work a continuous reading is necessary. It shines less brightly in isolated passages than in its whole surface. The long swinging line of fourteen syllables chosen for the *Iliad* is so well suited to its purpose that we may fairly regret Chapman's abandonment of it for the heroic couplet in his rendering of the *Odyssey*. If Chapman the scholar sometimes nodded, Chapman the poet was ever awake, and his version of Homer takes its place among the masterpieces of his age.

Of modern poets there is not so long a tale to tell. Dante was unknown, and Petrarch was revealed, for the most part surreptitiously, by those who carefully copied him. The most widely read of contemporary foreign poets was Guillaume de Saluste, Seigneur Du Bartas (1544–90), whose *La Semaine*, a story of the Creation, with *La Seconde Semaine*, or the Infancy of the World, attained European popularity. This was translated into rhymed decasyllabic verse as *Du Bartas His Divine Weekes and Workes* (1592–9) by Joshua Sylvester (1563–1618). The immense celebrity of this work is not now very easily intelligible, nor can the possibility that Milton may have looked into it be offered as a convincing inducement to similar curiosity. Tasso's *Gerusalemme Liberata* found two translators in Richard Carew (1594) and Edward Fairfax (1600), and Sir John Harington, at the command of Queen Elizabeth, made a version of Ariosto's *Orlando Furioso* (1591) in eight-lined stanzas. As we have seen, the majority of Elizabethan sonnets may be said to represent translation or adaptation. Only the best of them have the stamp of original genius. Free and unlimited borrowing from ancient or foreign authors was an accepted tradition of the time and must not be regarded censoriously. All that the age demanded was success; how the success was obtained concerned nobody. Dryden's defence of Ben Jonson puts the case clearly: "He invades Authors like a Monarch; and what would be theft in other Poets, is only Victory in him."

II. THE AUTHORIZED VERSION AND ITS INFLUENCE

The greatest of all translations is the English Bible. It is even more than that: it is the greatest of English books, the first of English classics, the source of the greatest influence upon English character and speech. Apart from any questions of dogma and theology, the Bible has all the marks of a classic. Its themes are those of perpetual concern in great literature: God, Man and the Universe. It has, in spite of its vast diversity, a supreme unity. It is, in a singular degree, the voice of a people. It expresses the Hebraic temper and the achievements of the Hebraic genius; and its purely Hebraic portions, the Old Testament, have, as literature, a greatness and intensity beyond anything in the New. The Hebrew Psalms and the Hebrew prophecies clearly stand on a literary plane above the Greek epistles of St Paul.

In the Old Testament, as arranged, three species of literature are successively presented, narrative, poetry and prophecy. These are the obvious kinds, but further distinctions are clear. The narrative books are sometimes epical in their directness of story and vividness of character. The poetry is mainly lyrical, uttering in the voice of one person a universal cry. The prophetical books are, for the most part, poetry of the highest kind, rehearsing the relations between man and God. Both Old and New Testaments are rich in wisdom or proverbial literature. Nor should it be forgotten that the Gospels of the New Testament contain in little space an almost miraculous diversity of matter and unite in presenting with overwhelming simplicity a supreme tragedy. And though book differs from book in character, in aim, and in mere chronology, there is among them all a vital unity, which the least lettered reader instinctively feels.

The passions of the Hebrew authors were few and fierce and uttered themselves energetically. The writers had at their command a language whose very limitations compelled them to greatness of utterance. Hebrew has no philosophical or scientific vocabulary. Nearly every word presents a concrete meaning clearly visible through a figurative use. Such a language is the very medium of poetry. Further, the Hebrew writers were close to nature. There was no cloud or hubbub of words between themselves and things. Not only were their words simple and concrete, the structure of their sentences was simple. Their chief connective was "and". Their poetry was measured, not by feet, as in ancient Latin and Greek, but by word-accents, as in the most ancient poetry of many nations, including that of our English ancestors. Moreover, Hebrew poetry was dominated by the principle of "parallelism" of members—the enforcing a statement by repetition, by supplement or by antithesis, as in such familiar passages as these: "Wash me throughly from my iniquity: and cleanse me from my sin"; "Who is this king of glory: the Lord strong and mighty, the Lord mighty in battle"; "A wise son maketh a glad father: but a foolish son is the heaviness of his mother". The qualities, then, that fitted the Bible, beyond any other book in the world, for translation, are among others these: (i) universality of interest; (ii) the concreteness and picturesqueness of its language; (iii) the simplicity of its structure; (iv) a rhythm largely independent of the features, prosodical or other, of any individual language. To give English form to all these qualities the Tudor translators were richly equipped.

The first great translator whom we know by name is St Jerome (d. 420), the author, though he called himself the reviser, of the Latin Vulgate, which remained for long the standard version universally used by learned men. Old English showed itself singularly fitted for the expression of Scriptural ideas, as we know from the *Christ* of Cynewulf and the early paraphrases. Chaucer, in a couplet of *The Second Nun's Tale*, catches the note:

> Cast alle away the workës of derknésse
> And armeth yow in armure of brightnésse.

Of the first English versions we have already given some account. The Bible of 1611 came into existence as an incidental result of the Hampton Court Conference called by James I to consider the demands of the more aggressive Puritans. The lack of a uniform or agreed English version of the Bible was soon felt, and the King ordered the making of a new one. The Conference was held in 1604 and the work was published in 1611. The title page, so very explicit, should be quoted in full: *The Holy Bible, Conteyning the Old Testament, and the New; Newly Translated out of the Originall tongues & with the former Translations diligently compared and revised by his Majesties speciall Commandment. Appointed to*

be read in Churches. Imprinted at London by Robert Barker, Printer to the Kings most
Excellent Majestie. Anno Dom. 1611.

The Authorized Version was never formally "authorized". It won its way
by native worth. In matter it had profited by all the controversy regarding
previous translations. Practically every word that could be challenged had been
challenged. The fate of a doctrine, even the fate of a party, had, at times, seemed
to depend upon a phrase. The predominant version is Tindale's.

The influence of the Authorized Version cannot easily be distinguished from
the influence of the Bible in some earlier form. The Latin of the Vulgate is used
in most Elizabethan quotations. Spenser and Shakespeare knew, of course,
some older English versions; but later writers on both sides of the Atlantic, and
as diverse as Swinburne and Kipling, as Emerson and Melville, have clearly felt
the influence of the Authorized Version. Many of its phrases have become part
of the common speech and are scarcely recognized as Biblical. For instance
"highways and hedges"; "clear as crystal"; "still small voice"; "hip and
thigh"; "arose as one man"; "lick the dust"; "a thorn in the flesh"; "broken
reed"; "root of all evil"; "a law unto themselves"; "moth and rust";
"weighed in the balance and found wanting"; and many more. Selden complained that "Hebraisms are kept", especially certain Hebraic phrases. A typical
Hebraism is the use of *of* in such phrases as "the oil of gladness", "the man
of sin", "King of Kings"; but they are now as much English as they are
Hebrew.

When we think of the high repute in which the Authorized Version is held
by men of learning and renown, we must remember, too, that in a special sense
it has been the great book of the poor and unlettered. The one book that every
household in Britain and America was sure to possess was the Bible; and it was
read, sometimes ignorantly, sometimes unwisely, but always memorably. To
many a poor man the English Bible has been a university, the kindly mother
from whom he has drawn history, philosophy and a way of great speech.

III. SIR WALTER RALEGH

Sir Walter Ralegh (1552?–1618)—the name was thus usually spelt by himself
and was evidently pronounced Rawley—gained renown in his own time both
as man of action and as man of letters. He was haughty, daring, uncompromising, ambitious and arrogant, with an intellectual activity as abundant as his
physical energy—the kind of man that Elizabeth would at first have loved and
that James would always have hated. He was too much a monarch, too little of a
subject. He read and observed widely, and his ornate and decisive manner of
speech soon drew attention to his extraordinary gifts of mind and person.
That he was early known as a writer of verse is shown by his introductory
contribution to Gascoigne's *Steele Glas* in 1576; but very few of Ralegh's poems
were printed as his during his lifetime, and identification is now very difficult.
Modern criticism allows him no more than forty-three poems and fragments,
and even this estimate is inclusive rather than exclusive. The recovered fragment
of his lost *Cynthia*, a long poem addressed to the Queen, adds little to his fame.

Yet he was known and praised as a poet by many from Puttenham onwards. Spenser was his friend, and the mutual admiration of the two men appears in the prefatory prose and verse of *The Faerie Queene*. Some of his surviving pieces have the smoothness and even the superficiality of Elizabethan lyric; others have the daring of phrase and frankness of feeling that we associate with Donne. The "Milkmaid's song" beginning "If all the world and love were young" in answer to Marlowe's *Passionate Shepherd* shows his characteristic lyrical style; the scraps of verse (usually translations) in *The History of the World* show his oracular and almost prophetic strain. But there is so very little. In poetry as in life Ralegh was a king without a kingdom.

Ralegh's prose works are almost as elusive as his poems. Scarcely anything except *The History of the World* was published during his lifetime. Like other men of rank he was content with a manuscript circulation. Ralegh is said to have suggested the gatherings at the Mermaid Tavern, in Bread Street, where Shakespeare, Ben Jonson, and other play-writers met the more formal literary men of the day. Ben Jonson became travelling tutor to his son. Ralegh cultivated as well rather more dangerous friends, and was associated with Marlowe, Hariot and other daring free-thinkers. He was at all times a generous patron of learning, and assisted Richard Hakluyt materially in the collection of his *Voyages*.

The first work published by Ralegh was a tract called *Report of the Truth of the Fight about the Iles of the Açores this last Sommer* (1591). It appeared anonymously, but was republished by Hakluyt as Sir Walter Ralegh's. Here we have an account of the famous fight and death of his kinsman Sir Richard Grenville on the "Revenge". His love of adventure and his desire to regain favour at court, where Essex was no friend of his, led Ralegh to undertake his first expedition to Guiana, in 1595. When he returned, his enemies tried to discredit him by asserting that he had never been to Guiana at all. To defend himself, he at once wrote his *Discoverie of the large, rich and bewtiful Empyre of Guiana, with a relation of the Great and Golden Citie of Manoa* (1596); and this story of his adventures, excellently told, won immediate popularity, and was translated into German, Dutch and Latin. Besides these two tracts, nothing is known to have been published by Ralegh during the reign of Elizabeth. For a bibliography of Ralegh's works the reader should consult the original *Cambridge History of English Literature* or *The Cambridge Bibliography of English Literature;* his connection with the so-called "School of Night" can be studied in M. C. Bradbrook's book of that title (1936) or in E. Strathmann's *Sir Walter Ralegh: a Study in Elizabethan Skepticism* (1951).

Ralegh's life of adventure came to an end with the accession of James I. Accused of treason, he escaped the block, but was imprisoned in the Tower. A long captivity was intense cruelty to such a man, and to find alleviation he occupied himself with writing. It is entirely like Ralegh that, though more than fifty years of age, he began to compose a *History of the World*. As we have seen, history, as a branch of literature, had no existence in England. There were the works of the chroniclers and the antiquaries, but there was no survey. Ralegh desired to bring together all that was known of the history of the past and to use it as an introduction to the history of his own country; moreover his great book was to be for the people, not only for the learned. It was written in the pure strong English of which he had such easy command. Naturally he did not complete his immense task. The large folio which was actually published (1614) begins with the Creation and reaches 130 B.C. when Macedonia became a Roman province. More was planned but never written, and Ralegh's last voyage and shameful execution ended the great project. That he took his work as a historian seriously is shown by the fact that over six hundred authors are cited in the published volume. Its temper is shown in the famous and familiar passage on death. The book seems to have been instantly popular. Ten separate folio editions of it appeared within about fifty years. For the first time English readers could enjoy an account of the Persian, Greek and Punic wars written in the finest prose. The place of Ralegh's *The History of the World* in the development of English historical writing hardly concerns us. To the student of English literature it is a revelation of a great though faulty character and a monument of noble utterance.

IV. THE LITERATURE OF THE SEA: FROM THE ORIGINS TO HAKLUYT

The movement in the minds of men at the time of the Renascence received a new impulse from the new physical discoveries. Copernicus had seemed to enlarge the heavens; Columbus had enlarged the earth itself. Moreover, for the wide diffusion of the new knowledge there were now new instruments, the printing presses. More's *Utopia* (1516) gives early evidence of this stir in the minds of men; for its small compass includes the thrill of maritime adventure, of social speculation and of classical inspiration. Poetic imaginings were exceeded in wonder by the marvels discovered and revealed by storm-tossed mariners, in their reports to the merchant-adventurers of the Muscovy and Levant trades.

There were early adventures and early records of a kind, though voyages and explorations lay outside the experience of the monastic chroniclers. Nevertheless, Hakluyt includes stories from Bede, Geoffrey of Monmouth, Roger of Hovenden and others, and there were chronicles of the eastern expeditions made by Crusaders. The Asiatic journeys of Marco Polo between 1271 and 1295 aroused great interest in England, and the fictions of Mandeville clearly satisfied a need. But the literature of travel by sea was still unwritten.

The impulse to the recording of voyages inevitably came from the Continent, for Portuguese and Spaniards had been the pioneers in distant exploration. Records of the Spanish conquests in the New World were specially stimulating to the English mind. *De Orbe Novo* by Peter Martyr Anglerius began to appear about 1511; the great collection of voyages gathered by Giovanni Battista Ramusio came later, from 1550 onwards. The first English publications are not of great intrinsic interest. The real pioneer of English sea literature is Richard Eden (1521?–1576), who was not an original narrator, but a diligent interpreter of the work of others. His object was to make known to his countrymen what the Portuguese and Spaniards had done, and with that object he translated and published, from the Latin of Sebastian Münster, *A Treatyse of the newe India, with other newe founde Landes and Ilands, as well eastwarde as westwarde, as they are knowen and founde in these our Dayes* (1553). This was followed by a translation from Peter Martyr: *The Decades of the Newe Worlde or West India* (1555). Eden's object was to stir up our own seamen and merchants into emulation of the Spanish and Portuguese adventurers; and that he was practical as well as enthusiastic is shown by his *Arte of Navigation* (1561).

In 1553 Sir Hugh Willoughby had sailed for Cathay by the North-East, and had perished; but a narrative of his voyage was made in Latin and is translated in Hakluyt. The great Sir John Hawkins (1532–95) made his voyages to the West in 1562, 1564 and 1567 and published an account of the third as *A True Declaration of the Troublesome voyadge of M. John Haukins to the Partes of Guynea and the West Indies, in the yeares of Our Lord 1567 and 1568*. It is a vigorous and direct narrative of experiences, full of shrewd observations, and with a notable reflective quality. The North-West Passage had long inspired Sir Humphrey Gilbert (1539–83), and in 1576 he wrote his tract, *A Discourse of a Discoverie for a New Passage to Cataia*. None of the early navigators had any illusions about the dangers and the miseries of these long expeditions. Hakluyt has preserved a memorable account of Gilbert's last voyage; and there are few more striking pictures in English narrative literature than that of the intrepid seaman, on the September afternoon upon which his vessel the "Squirrel" was overwhelmed. "We are as near to heaven by sea as by land", he exclaimed, before he went down. Martin Frobisher's attempts on the North-West in 1576 and 1577 were described by his friend George Best in *A True Discourse of the Late Voyages of Discoverie for the finding of a Passage to Cathaya by the North-Weast under the Conduct of Martin Frobisher, Generall* (1578). An enlarged edition of Eden's *Decades* appeared in 1577 under the title *The History of Travayle in the West and East Indies*, edited by Richard Willes, who discusses the practicability of the North-West Passage to the East. Sir John Davys (1550?–1605) made his three great Arctic voyages, which were described by himself and others, and he wrote, besides, *The Seamans Secrets* (1594), a practical treatise on navigation, and *The Worldes Hydrographical Discription* (1595), in which the arguments against a North-West passage are vigorously attacked. Another fine sagacious contribution to the literature of discovery is *The Observations of Sir Richard Hawkins Knight, in his Voiage into the South Sea; anno Domini, 1593*. The author, son of Sir John, significantly remarks that want of experience is more tolerable in a general on land than in a governor by sea. Reports and narratives of adventures by sea were now current, and Shakespeare, for instance, makes several notable allusions to incidents of travel and to the published augmentation of knowledge.

For most of what we know about the great adventurers into strange seas we are indebted to Richard Hakluyt (1552?–1616). Hakluyt is a striking example of a man with a single purpose. Having heard, when chaplain to the English ambassador at the French court, that in the matter of voyages and adventures the English were everywhere despised for their "sluggish security", he resolved to take away the reproach and to collect such narratives as would prove to the world that Englishmen were as ready for risk as any others. His first published work was *Divers Voyages Touching the Discoverie of America & the Islands adjacent unto the same*, issued in 1582 and dedicated to Sir Philip Sidney. He published an account of French travels into Florida and made a revised edition of Peter Martyr's *De Orbe Novo* designed to further the study of scientific navigation. But Hakluyt's immortality rests upon his great collection, *The Principall Navigations, Voiages and Discoveries of the English Nation, made by Sea or Over Land to the most remote and farthest distant quarters of the earth at any time within the compasse of these 1500 yeares* (1589). The second edition in three volumes (1598, 1599 and 1600) enlarges the "compasse" to "1600 yeares". Hakluyt ransacked the chroniclers for such records of voyages as he could find. He investigated the papers of the merchant companies and, as he tells us, he journeyed far in order to interview travellers and examine records of exploration. It is characteristic of Hakluyt's spirit that he included *The Libel of English Policy* (see p. 95). Hakluyt's great compilation preserves for us a noble and valiant body of narrative literature of the highest worth, both for its own sake and for its interpretation of the Elizabethan age. The Hakluyt Society was founded in 1846 and undertook in 1965, with the Peabody Museum of Salem, Mass., an edition of the original work of 1589.

V. SEAFARING AND TRAVEL:
THE GROWTH OF PROFESSIONAL TEXT BOOKS AND GEOGRAPHICAL LITERATURE

Most of our writers of sea-literature were men who could fight a tempest or an enemy, but knew little of the craft of writing. Nevertheless, some of them were able to set down their experiences with moving simplicity. But we now pass to writers of another order. A literature of travel as distinguished from a literature of discovery began to grow.

The English seamen were confronted from the beginning by the monopolies of Portugal and Spain. Portugal laid claim to all that accrued from the exploration of Vasco da Gama; Spain to whatever accrued from the voyages of Columbus; and disputes between the two countries were settled by Pope Alexander VI, who assigned the west to Spain and the south to Portugal. Magellan had sailed south-west, and had been followed by Drake; but Spain was still supreme on the Pacific coast of South America; and if Englishmen were to find a monopoly of approach it must be by the north. Hence the tragic assaults on the icy terrors of the North-West Passage. A hundred projects for penetrating the great Pacific were in the air. The Dutch were grasping at the spoil of the Portuguese, and in England men of commerce became men of war, merchant and mariner being resolute to snatch the sceptre of the sea from the weakening grasp of Spain. Home-keeping Englishmen sought a wider knowledge of the world; and their needs were gratified by numerous volumes. The *Generall Historie of the Turkes* (1603) by Richard Knolles not only gave information but was written in a style admired by such later judges as Johnson and Byron. *The Travellers Breviat* (1601) by Robert Johnson and *Microcosmus* (1621) by Peter Heylyn (later enlarged in 1652 as *Cosmographie*) disclosed the countries of the known world to general readers. More considerable and original is *A Relation of a Journey begun An. Dom.* 1610 by George Sandys (1578–1644) descriptive of Turkey and the nearer East (1615).

To another class belongs the volume entitled *Coryats Crudities, Hastilie gobled up in five moneths travells in France, Savoy, Italy, Rhetia, commonly called the Grisons country, Helvetia alias Switzerland, some parts of high Germany and the Netherlands; newly digested in the hungrie aire of Odcombe in the County of Somerset*, 1611. Thomas Coryate (1577?–1617) was an oddity, and his book is a curiosity. Its title depicts the man. He was interested in himself as much as in his subject, and wrote in an amusingly extravagant manner. After his continental journey, Coryate visited Odcombe to hang up, in the parish church there, the shoes in which he had walked from Venice. In the next year he set out on his remarkable journey overland to India, and he died at Surat. Coryate visited Constantinople, Aleppo and Jerusalem, crossed the Euphrates into Mesopotamia, waded the Tigris, joined a caravan and, ultimately, reached Lahore, Agra and the Mogul's court at Ajmere. This exploit entitled him to address a letter to his friends at the Mermaid as "Right Generous, Joviall, and Mercuriall Sirenaickes" and to subscribe himself as "the Hierosolymitan-Syrian-Mesopotamian-Armenian-Median-Parthian-Indian Legge-stretcher of Odcombe in Somerset, Thomas Coryate". His letters and the curious compilation entitled *Thomas Coryate Traveller for the English Wits: Greeting. From the Court of the Great Mogul* (1616) display acute observation and a lively understanding of what he saw.

The mantle of Hakluyt fell upon the shoulders of Samuel Purchas (1575?–1626), a great editor of narratives and a man of many words, but of less modesty than his predecessor. *Hakluytus Posthumus, or Purchas His Pilgrimes, contayning a History of the World, in Sea Voyages and Lande Travells, by Englishmen and others*, was published in 1625. For ten years Purchas was vicar of an Essex parish near the mouth of the Thames, and doubtless began his own collections at this time, and took down narratives from the lips of those who had travelled far. Prior to the publication of his *Pilgrimes*, he had written *Purchas His Pilgrimage, or Relations of the World and the Religions observed in all ages and places discovered from the Creation unto this Present* (1613), and *Purchas his Pilgrim; Microcosmus, or the Historie of Man* (1619). Purchas, who had never travelled more than two hundred miles from his Essex birth-place, was inferior to Hakluyt, but he was his worthy successor, his later collaborator, and the depository of some of his collections. The great series of narratives he edited will preserve his name with that of his master and inspirer.

Several interesting publications of the time relate to Virginia. Hakluyt had a proprietary right in the colony; its exploration occupies a large place in his *Navigations*; and his last work was *Virginia Richly Valued* (1609), a translation from the Portuguese of de Soto's narrative. Thomas Hariot's *A Briefe and True Report of the new found Land of Virginia* appeared in 1588. With Virginia the names of Ralegh and Captain John Smith (1580–1631) are specially associated. Smith's famous book, *The Generall Historie of Virginia* (1624; p. 778 below) is not only a fine, forcible piece of narrative, but a call to England to maintain a powerful navy.

Sir Francis Drake Reviv'd (1626), published by Sir Francis Drake the younger, is the source of most of our knowledge of Drake's exploits in Central America.

But in spite of gallant adventures, England failed to establish a monopoly in any of the new regions. The Spanish Main remained Spanish. The Portuguese held to the East Indies till dispossessed by the Dutch, who fought strenuously to keep out the English. Nevertheless, it is the East rather than the West that begins to be the centre of interest. A rise in the price of pepper owing to Dutch troubles led to a meeting of London merchants in 1599; and from this small beginning came the foundation of the East India Company in 1600. Many of the narratives in Purchas relate the adventures of Englishmen in India, China and Japan—the story of William Adams in the last named country being specially attractive. Two other works are of special interest: a translation (1617) of a Spanish letter under the title *Terra Australis incognita, or A new Southerne Discoverie, containing a fifth part of the World lately found out by Ferdinand de Quir* (Pedro Fernandez de Quiros) *a Spanish captaine; never before published*: and *A Briefe Discovery, or Description, of the most famous Island of Madagascar* (1646) by Richard Boothby. It is doubtful whether De Quiros explored the mainland of Australia; the Dutch certainly did. England does not come into the story till the time of Captain Cook.

Towards the end of the seventeenth century serious writers began to concern themselves with the provision of men for the ships and with the health and treatment of the seamen. A distinction was made between war ship and merchant vessel, and between practical commanders and gentlemen captains. Drake had already encountered the latter difference and had settled it by saying "I must have the gentleman to haul and draw with the mariner and the mariner with the gentleman". Sir William Monson (1569–1643), author of the *Naval Tracts*, not printed till the eighteenth century, links the age of Drake with the days of the Civil War. He had been flag-captain with Essex at Cadiz, and part of his writing deals with the duties of officers and men. His opinions have weight as embodying the views of a vigilant and sagacious officer. *An Accidence or the Path-way to Experience, necessary for all young Sea-men, or those that are desirous to goe to Sea* (1626), reprinted as *The Sea-man's Grammar* (1653), by the famous Captain John Smith, unites the scientific and practical parts of seamanship. Inevitably there grew up (as in the later days of sail and steam) a kind of conflict between the "painfull seaman" who knows the real working of a ship, and the "mathematicall seaman" who would fail in contest with the "ruffe and boisterous ocean". Luke Fox who wrote the quaintly named *North-West Fox, or Fox from the North-West Passage* (1635) represented the hard-bitten practical man, and he wrote with excellent vigour; Thomas James, author of *The Strange and Dangerous Voyage of Captain Thomas James in his Intended Discovery of the North-West Passage into the South Sea* (1633), was an equally sound scientific commander. These are probably the two earliest separately published narratives in "North-West" literature. Sir Henry Manwayring, captain of the "Unicorn" in the Ship Money fleet of 1636, tried to revive interest in naval efficiency during the demoralized days of Charles I with *The Sea-Man's Dictionary* (1644); and Captain Nathaniel Boteler in his *Six Dialogues about Sea Services* (1685) properly exalts the great office of captain at sea. His book is one of the best of its kind and time. Besides these tracts and treatises there were many broad-sheets of songs and numerous allusions in the works of the poets. The English literature of piracy had to wait till the time of Defoe. Finally let us notice the appearance in 1689 of *Gloria Britannica, or The Boast of the British Seas*, containing a statistical account of "the Royal Navy of England". It is the first approach to a Navy List.

VI. THE SONG BOOKS AND MISCELLANIES

The poetic accomplishment which had belonged to a few courtiers like Wyatt and Surrey in the days of Henry VIII had spread, in the days of Elizabeth, to almost every man of education. Some of the sweetest lyrics in Elizabethan poetry were written by persons whose names are unknown to this day. The poems were passed round in manuscript, were read, or sung, and have survived in written song books or in printed miscellanies. As there was no notion of copyright, in the present legal sense, popular poems could be gathered into anthologies and might appear in more than one collection; other attractive pieces could be borrowed from the acknowledged works of popular poets.

As we pass from the earlier to the later anthologies we observe two main differences: a great rise in the level of accomplishment, and a more joyous note in song. The immediate successors of *Tottel's Miscellany* contain verse that is feeble in performance and medievally lugubrious in substance. The true Elizabethan anthologies catch the moment of joy or of sorrow as it flies, and embody it in sweet, fresh, felicitous utterance. Even the graver, reflective pieces have lost the sense of eternal wrath to come. The voice is not so much English as universal. There is little reference to events or tendencies of the time. The language of pastoral survives in a few conventional references to shepherds, pipes and flocks, but there is no exact significance in the words, and the machinery of the eclogue has vanished.

As we should know if we had merely the evidence that Shakespeare affords, music was a natural activity of Elizabethan man. Everybody sang, lords and lackeys alike. Song took two main forms, which we can roughly call the solo and the concerted piece. The "air" was a setting of stanzas to a tune with an instrumental accompaniment. The "madrigal" was an unaccompanied piece for three, four, five or even more voices, with the parts polyphonically woven. English music of Tudor and early Stuart times is a very noble national possession, and William Byrd is among the greatest composers of any time or place. The secular airs and madrigals provide a very considerable body of verse, some of it of high quality, and nearly all of it anonymous.

Another fruitful source of lyric is the drama. Every playwright of importance has contributed something to the great procession of English song, John Lyly nobly leading the way, followed by Greene, Peele, Shakespeare, and Ben Jonson. Lyrics from the song books and the plays are therefore an important part of the poetry of the time.

In addition there are the miscellanies, the collections of poems by various hands, of which *Tottel* is the great exemplar. The first to show the influence of the new life and vigour is *The Phoenix Nest...Set foorth by R. S.* (1593). This tends to follow the older manner of *Tottel*; and one of its contributors is "N. B. Gent", i.e. Nicholas Breton, who belongs to that school and uses its popular fourteener and poulter's measures: but another contributor, "T. L. Gent", i.e. Thomas Lodge, definitely strikes the fresh Elizabethan note.

The next anthology, *Englands Helicon* (1600), is not only the best of its time, but nearly the most engaging of all poetical collections. *The Phoenix Nest* was largely anonymous; *Englands Helicon* is starred with shining names. Scarcely a poet of the day is without a place in it. Some of the pieces signed "Ignoto" are attributed to Ralegh; but almost the only certain fact about that great man's verses is the uncertainty of their authorship. Nicholas Breton still maintains here the old tradition, his long line (internally rhymed) really flowing and not merely jogging along. The "Shepheard Tonie" who signs some delightful lyrics is possibly Anthony Munday, translator and playwright. Another contributor is Richard Barnfield (1574–1627), whose verses here and in other volumes entitle him to esteem for the moments when, forgetting intellectual foppery and affectation, he sings naturally and sweetly about the country. The better-known contributors from Sidney and Spenser to Drayton and Browne do not need notice. The title page of the book is anonymous. The dedication is signed "A. B." and what may be called the anthologist's apology is signed "L. N."; but the compiler of *Englands Helicon*, whoever he may have been, was clearly a man of taste, the only lapse being the amount of space given to Bartholomew Young, whose artificial and elaborate pastorals (mainly derived from Montemayor) fall below the level of the rest. Very engaging are the poems described as taken from the songs of famous musicians—Morley, Byrd, Dowland and others. Music and sweet poetry were in full accord in those spacious days. The contrast between the *Helicon* poets and those of the *Tottel* school is very great. In place of the few, repeated measures, the cramped movement and the halting progress of the early poetry, we find ease, grace, swiftness and freedom in metres of all kinds. The combination of technical subtlety and ingenuity with artistic sincerity and simplicity is the specially remarkable quality of the Elizabethan lyric.

Englands Parnassus (1600) edited by "R. A." (probably Robert Allot) is a book of "elegant extracts", a selection of quotations from all the poets of the day, grouped under appropriate heads. Though badly edited, it is an interesting curiosity of literature. The last of the Elizabethan anthologies, and a most charming example, is *A Poetical Rapsody* issued by two brothers, Francis and Walter Davison, in 1602. The one striking new name is that of Thomas Campion; but most of the poems are anonymous, many by an unidentified "A. W." There are sonnets, and some poems are called "Phaleuciacks"—imitations of the hendecasyllabics of Catullus:

> Muse not, Lady, to read so strange a metre,
> Strange grief, strange remedy for ease requireth.

The "classical" will o' the wisp was still being fitfully pursued. The heyday of Elizabethan song passed with Gloriana herself. The closing decade of her reign was a time of deep disturbance and even of apprehension; and we now come to poets in whom a graver note is heard.

VII. ROBERT SOUTHWELL, JOHN DAVIES,
WILLIAM WARNER, SAMUEL DANIEL

Of the graver themes in verse two writers are specially representative, Robert Southwell of religious poetry, Samuel Daniel of humanistic and historical. In purely religious poetry the age was not rich. Few poets failed to write religious verse of some kind; but only one poet of the age is in essence a religious poet, Robert Southwell (1561–95), who lived and died for his faith. Born a Catholic, he became a Jesuit, and with Garnett took part in the work of the English mission inaugurated by Robert Parsons and Edmund Campion. For six years he carried on his perilous task, but was seized in 1592. After thirteen applications of the torture, and more than two years of imprisonment, he was hanged and quartered at Tyburn in 1595. Most of his poems were written in prison. He knew quite well what was before him, and he wrote as a dedicated person. He was anxious that the poetic art should be lifted above such vain and amatorious themes as that of Shakespeare's *Venus and Adonis*, published in 1593, and almost certainly read by him, for his *Saint Peters Complaint* (1595) is written in the same metre and adopts the same adorned and excessive manner. This attempt to express the eternal through the imagery of the temporal was not repugnant to the practice of his Church, which has always sanctioned material representations of the immaterial. Some of his shorter poems were collected under the title *Maeoniae* (1595). Southwell's religious ecstasy took a lyric, not a didactic, form of utterance; and his peculiar spiritual fervour and physical intensity are singularly manifest in the one poem of his universally known, *The Burning Babe*.

A good way of learning to appreciate Southwell's poetry is to compare it with that of another religious poet, John Davies of Hereford (1565–1618). The model of his uninspired verse was Sylvester's *Du Bartas*, upon which he founded his long poem, *Microcosmos* (1603); but he owed something also to his namesake, Sir John Davies, whose *Nosce Teipsum* formed the basis of *Mirum in Modum* (1602) and *Summa Totalis* (1607). The antithesis and paradox prominent in Southwell may be found also in Davies, but wearing the air rather of scholastic pedantry than of living and convincing truth.

In Samuel Daniel (1562–1619) we reach the leading example of the graver reflective poetry of the last Elizabethan years. There is no dialectic in his poems and no system advanced; but in his "vast philosophic gravity and stateliness of sentiment", to use Hazlitt's words, he resembles Wordsworth, who was attracted by him and quoted him memorably on two occasions. Daniel began his literary career with the *Delia* sonnets (1592). *The Complaint of Rosamund* (1592) in rhyme royal stanzas is a tragic plaint of Henry II's mistress and was probably suggested by Churchyard's tale of *Shore's Wife* in *A Mirror for Magistrates*; but it is much more modern in tone and technique. A comparison of the two poems is instructive. *Musophilus; containing a Generall Defence of Learning* (1599) shows another side of Daniel's mind. Here he is the apostle of culture, urging the importance of literature as a refining and enlarging element of life. The poem presents a sound case for the discipline of letters. Daniel's interest in history and his general gravity of mind moved him to the composition of his long poem, *The*

Civile Wares betweene the Howses of Lancaster and Yorke (1595, 1609). This contains nearly nine hundred eight-lined stanzas, and though not free from the monotony of a chronicle, it includes much wise and dignified poetry. Ben Jonson criticized Daniel adversely, but Spenser admired him, and one of the writers in the *Poetical Rapsody* hails him as "Prince of English poets" for his success in the three kinds of verse, Lyrical, Tragical and Heroical. The *Civil Wars* will never be as generally admired as the *Epistle to the Lady Margaret, Countess of Cumberland, Ulisses and the Syren,* and some of the sonnets, but it should not be ignored. Daniel's *Defence of Ryme* against those who tried to force the stream of English poetry into classical channels clearly shows him as a master of language, with no taste either for the archaism of Spenser or for the classicism of Gabriel Harvey. Better than any argument was his own accomplished use of English, to which he gave a classical gravity and feeling.

Daniel's *Civil Wars* had learned something from Lucan's *Pharsalia* and something, probably, from William Warner (1558?-1609), whose long historical poem *Albions England* (1586)—the full title is almost an essay—begins with the Flood and, in successive editions, reaches his own times. It is written in the old rhymed fourteeners and, though often clumsy and dull, tells some good stories. Like Drayton's *Poly-Olbion* it delights in legend; but it lacks the haunting regret which inspires Drayton's protest against the inroads of time, and lacks also, in its superficial sturdy patriotism, the philosophic and humane intention of Daniel's *Civil Wars*.

VIII. THOMAS CAMPION

Thomas Campion (1576–1620) is in a special sense a lyric poet; for his best verses were written by himself for his own music. His Latin *Poemata* (1595) does not greatly interest the student of English literature, except as an indication of the determined classicism which inspired his *Observations in the Art of English Poesie* (1602) written "against the vulgar and unartificial custom of riming", and answered by Daniel's *Defence of Ryme*. Campion was not only a poet and musician, he is an early example of the union between poetry and medicine. In his capacity as physician he had some slight connection with the celebrated Overbury poisoning case; and in music his *New Way of Making Fowre Parts in Counter-point* was for a long time an accepted text-book. Campion's place in English literature depends, however, not on these *parerga* but on *A Booke of Ayres, Set foorth to be sung to the Lute, Orpherian and Base Violl* (1601), *Two Bookes of Ayres* (c. 1613), and *The Third and Fourth Booke of Ayres* (c. 1617). His masques are less interesting save in their purely lyrical portions. Campion's lyrics are remarkable for their exquisite quality and their metrical resource. He is a link between the Elizabethans and the Carolines. Possibly there are times when the musician impeded the poet; but in the best of Campion's lyrics an apparently artless ease conceals a subtle mastery of syllabic tones and values. A reference to the poems contained in all anthologies of English verse will show not merely the intensity but the variety of Campion's poetic gift.

IX. THE SUCCESSORS OF SPENSER

Sidney's famous apology for poetry and the English language worked upon his admirers so greatly that they one and all wished themselves poets. Inspired by his precepts and by Spenser's example, they took to their pens. No subject was considered unfit for poetry. Fulke Greville, Lord Brooke, was moved by state-craft; George Wither by the Puritan spirit; Browne celebrated the joys of country life: Sir John Davies and Drummond of Hawthornden explored the realms of the spirit; Phineas Fletcher took for his subject the whole construction of man; his brother Giles, the Christian faith.

William Drummond of Hawthornden (1585–1649) came of an ancient Scottish family. Two other poets memorably entered his life, Michael Drayton in correspondence, and Ben Jonson in person. Rough notes of Jonson's talk exist in a transcript by another hand, and this was first printed in 1842. Its authenticity has been doubted. Like many other poets of his day Drummond was moved to verse by the untimely death of Prince Henry, eldest son of James I, and his pastoral elegy *Teares on the Death of Moeliades* appeared in 1613. Death was again the occasion of his song; for when in 1616 the elegy was reprinted, it was accompanied by a set of sonnets, songs and madrigals expressing his grief at the death of the lady whom he was to have married. *Flowres of Sion* appeared in 1623 with a prose essay on death, called *The Cypresse Grove*, in which Drummond reaches his highest sustained level. The longest of the "Flowers", *An Hymn on the Fairest Fair*, is an admirable composition in which the poet is stirred (like Dante) by

> That essence which, not mov'd, makes each thing move,
> Uncreate beauty, all-creating love.

Drummond is not an important poet, but he is curiously attractive, for his spiritual conception of love and beauty makes him a kind of link between Spenser and Shelley. His sonnets are excellent examples of their kind, and, in general, he uses many verse forms with easy mastery. One of the *Flowers of Sion* anticipates the stanza of Milton's *Nativity Ode* almost exactly. Oddly enough, after the publication of *Flowers of Sion*, Drummond seemed to wake from con-templation to activity, and was thereafter a busy man. But he had ceased to be a poet.

George Wither (1588–1677) is known to most readers as the subject of a short essay by Lamb. He had a stormy life. His harmless verses frequently gave offence and the author became well acquainted with the inside of the Marshalsea or Newgate. During the Civil War he took arms for the Parliament and became successively captain, major and major-general. The Royalists caught him and were about to hang him, when Sir John Denham pleaded for his life on the ground that while Wither lived he (Denham) could not be called the worst poet in England. Wither was a voluminous writer—indeed he wrote too much. His principal works are *Abuses Stript and Whipt: or Satyricall Essays* (1613), mild attacks on the vices of human nature; *The Shepherds Hunting* (1615), a set of eclogues; *Fidelia* (1615), "an elegiacal epistle"; *Faire-Virtue, the Mistress of*

Phil'arete (1622), a collection of verse, much of it in the octosyllabic couplet which Wither used largely and well; *The Hymnes and Songs of the Church* (1624); *Britains Remembrancer* (1628); and *Haleluiah or Britains Second Remembrancer* (1641). Wither does not rise high as a religious poet; but his pastorals are attractive. They are not in the urban convention; the figures may be formal, but the freshness of the country air is always present. Wither had the true sincerity characteristic of the finest Puritan spirit. It is a piece of irony that a poet of such serious intention should be best known by the gay lines, "Shall I, wasting in despair".

William Browne of Tavistock (1591–1643) began like Wither, Drummond and others with the inevitable elegy on Prince Henry. The first book of *Britannias Pastorals*, his longest and most famous work, appeared in 1613, the second in 1616; but the third remained in manuscript till 1852. His poems show a capacity for friendship, and he was intimate with many poets of the day. Spenser was his master, and after Spenser, Sidney. In the second song of the second book of the *Pastorals* he passes in review the English poets, and praises them with sound discernment. Upon "well-languag'd Daniel" he fixed the now inevitable epithet. Browne was a scholar. He was interested in old manuscripts and printed a poem of Occleve with *The Shepheards Pipe* (1614), offering to publish more if it should please. Apparently it did not please. His own poems, however, with their fresh simplicity, continue to please; and Browne is immortal as the author of "Underneath this sable hearse", formerly attributed to Ben Jonson.

Fulke Greville, Lord Brooke (1554–1628) was an exact contemporary of Sir Philip Sidney, whose life he wrote. He belonged to the older school of men, who, like Castiglione's ideal courtier, cultivated the art of poesy as part of a gentleman's equipment; and therefore, although he was a grave and austere statesman who held high office, he felt it a duty to write in verse. But, excepting the tragedy of *Mustapha* (1609) and a few poems in *The Phoenix Nest* and *Englands Helicon*, nothing was formally published during his life-time. In 1633, five years after his death, appeared *Certaine learned and elegant Workes...written in his Youth*; in 1652 appeared his excellent life of Sidney, and in 1670 *The Remains of Sir Fulk Greville, Lord Brooke, being Poems of Monarchy and Religion, never before printed*. In these for the first time was printed *Caelica*, the set of poems called "sonnets". Greville's prose *Letter* to a lady is a noble and too little known utterance. Charles Lamb's quotations from the tragedies *Alaham* and *Mustapha* with his critical comments are still the best introduction to the work of this strange, high-thinking and deep-feeling nobleman, remarkable for his exalted ideas of the state and his exalted devotion to the Queen. Poetry seemed to be natural with him and yet to come from him unnaturally stiffened with a devoted statesman's sense of duty. His epitaph, written by himself, is the best epitome of his life: "Fulke Grevil—Servant to Queene Elizabeth—Councellor to King James—and Frend to Sir Philip Sydney. *Trophaeum Peccati*."

Sir John Davies (1569–1626)—not to be confused with John Davies of Hereford—was a man of Lord Brooke's pattern, though without his memory of "the spacious days" and without his deep austerity. But he, too, was a man of affairs and rose to high position in the state. His greatest poem *Nosce Teipsum* appeared in 1599, and the earlier *Orchestra, or a Poeme of Dauncing* in 1596. The latter, a delightful dialogue in 131 seven-lined stanzas, flows with appropriate ease. The title of the greater work explains its scope: *Nosce teipsum! This oracle expounded in two elegies.* (1) *Of Humane Knowledge,* (2) *Of the Soule of man and the Immortalitie thereof.* Its elegiac stanzas are gravely written and have occasionally a note of modern questioning. Davies does not take a prose theme and embroider it with verse, he uses verse and its beauties to embody his feeling about ultimate things. With the engaging ingenuity of his time, that loved to turn verse into patterns, Sir John Davies wrote *Hymnes of Astrea in Acrosticke Verse* (1618)—twenty-six poems, some quite charming, each making an acrostic with the name Elizabetha Regina.

Sir Henry Wotton (1568–1639) owes his fame to one poem of exquisite grace, "You meaner beauties of the night", to another of memorable quality, "How happy is he born and taught", and to a *Life*, written with all the charm and humour of Izaak Walton, prefaced to *Reliquiae Wottonianae* (1651) which contains his collected writings. Like Greville and Sir John Davies, Wotton was a man of great affairs, and ended by becoming Provost of Eton. Logan Pearsall Smith's *Life and Letters* (1907) supplements Walton with greater attention to the varied aspects of Wotton's career.

With the two brothers Giles (1588–1623) and Phineas Fletcher (1582–1650) the muse of poetry passes from state to church. Both brothers were in holy orders. Giles's *Christs Victorie, and Triumph in Heaven, and Earth* (1610) is written in 265 eight-lined stanzas, containing many passages of individual beauty and dramatic power. The vigour of his phrase and the loftiness of his aim combine to make him a worthy link in the chain which connects his great master Spenser and his great successor Milton. Phineas wrote much more, and, though just as serious, had a lighter touch. *Brittains Ida, or Venus and Anchises* (1628) is a pretty poem in the style of Shakespeare's *Venus and Adonis*. His immense poem *The Purple Island: or the Isle of Man* (1633) in seven-lined stanzas is colossal in scope, for it proposes to explore the secrets of man's nature. His enthusiasm for the delicate mechanism of the body is occasionally expressed in a way that causes amusement. *The Locusts or Appollyonists* (1627) and *Elissa an Elegie* (1633) are more attractive as poems. The first is in a nine-lined, the second in a seven-lined stanza, both interesting variants from Spenser. The Fletchers were steeped in Spenser's poetry, and carried on the Spenserian tradition. Milton clearly knew the work of the Fletchers. But there is a vital difference. In *The Locusts* the fall of Lucifer is merely a prelude to an onslaught on the Jesuits. Milton humanized the devil; Fletcher diabolized the priest. Some of the lines have a familiar note:

> To be in heaven the second he disdaines:
> So now the first in hell and flames he raignes,
> Crown'd once with joy and light: crowned now with fire and paines.

Milton had certainly read that.

X. MICHAEL DRAYTON

Michael Drayton (1563–1631) was a major poet of his age; but neither the present nor any future age will believe that a complete knowledge of his very extensive poetry is a necessity of intellectual life. Born a year before Shakespeare and dying when Milton's earliest poems were already written, Drayton kept in touch with the poetical progress of a crowded and swiftly-moving period and embodied its changes and varieties in his own practice. He has thus a special interest for the student of poetry, apart from his peculiar merits as a poet. Drayton's earliest work, *The Harmonie of the Church* (1591), a versification of various passages of the Bible, mainly in the old "fourteener" and poulter's measure, suggests *Tottel*, or one of its old-fashioned successors. The next, *Idea, The Shepheards Garland, Fashioned in nine Eglogs* (1593), passes from *Tottel* to Spenser, for whom Drayton had a high and continuing admiration. Drayton's eclogues avoid the Spenserian archaisms, and abandon the tradition that the pastoral should moralize the spectacle of the time, lamenting a nobler past and deploring the present. That strain was to be heard once more in *Lycidas*. The identity of the lady (or the ladies) who may (or may not) have been Drayton's "Idea" is a matter for over-curious biographers, not for the student of literature. We have already pointed out (p. 126) that the theoretical "Idea" comes from Plato, and the poetical "Idea", as a theme for sonnets, from the French. In his next poems Drayton passes from Spenser to Daniel, whose *Complaynt of Rosamund* stimulated his outburst into historical legend, and we have in succession, *Peirs Gaveston, Earle of Cornwall* (1593), *Matilda. The faire and chaste Daughter of the Lord Robert Fitzwater* (1594), *The Tragicall Legend of Robert Duke of Normandy* (1596), and *The Legend of Great Cromwel* (1607). These all suffer from the jog-trot which seems inevitable in versified history and which *A Mirror for Magistrates* had established as a kind of precedent. Nevertheless there are good passages of description and feeling; and certain utterances in *Great Cromwel* foreshadow Dryden in the use of poetry for argument. Daniel again appears in the story, for his *Delia* sonnets are the inspiration of Drayton's *Ideas Mirrour* (1594), though subsequent revisions tended to give the sonnets the tone of Sidney rather than of Daniel. Popular opinion acknowledges only one masterpiece among all Drayton's sonnets ("Since there's no help"); but the final edition of 1619 includes few that have not something masterly in them. *Endimion and Phoebe: Ideas Latmus* (1595), in rhymed decasyllabic couplets, is a pleasing treatment of classic story, perhaps influenced by Shakespeare's *Venus and Adonis*.

For the next few years Drayton devoted himself to historical poetry. *The Mortimeriados* of 1596 in seven-lined stanzas was rewritten as *The Barrons Wars* (1603) in eight-lined stanzas, with an interesting prose preface defending the change of form. In 1597 he published *Englands Heroicall Epistles*, enlarged later, in which pairs of historical characters exchange letters expressed in smooth and firm decasyllabic couplets. In 1603 came "the quiet end of that long-living Queene" whom he had praised in one of his sweetest songs. She had done nothing for him, and her successor did no more, though hailed by a gratulatory poem. Perhaps to this cause can be attributed Drayton's outbreak into satire with *The Owle* (1604) followed in 1606 by *The Man in the Moone*, both in couplets. Neither can be called successful. The year 1604 also saw a return to his first scriptural manner in poems about Moses, interesting as a survival of the belief that poets should make commonly known the Biblical stories. Much more important is the volume of *Poemes Lyrick and Pastorall* (1606), which contains the memorable "Fair stood the wind for France". The pieces are varied and arresting. We get suggestions of Milton's *Nativity Ode; To the Virginian Voyage* is Marvell with a difference; *The Heart* begins to approach Donne. Drayton's *Poemes* should be part of any comprehensive reading of poetry.

Drayton must long have been engaged on his lengthiest and greatest work, the first part of which was issued in 1613 *as Poly-Olbion or A Chorographicall Description of Tracts, Rivers, Mountaines, Forests, etc.* It contained the first eighteen songs. Nine years later came a new issue with "twelve Songs, never before Imprinted". The thirty books or songs of *Poly-Olbion* with the prose "illustration" full of varied learning make probably the longest single poem of any English writer; and, had there been encouragement, Drayton would have added more. But the *magnum opus* fell flat. Nevertheless, it exhibits immense variety and it has genuine poetic interest, though naturally it does not stay always at the height of poetic argument. While *Poly-Olbion* was being completed, Drayton did little else. In 1627, however, came a volume beginning inauspiciously with the Agincourt song magnified into a long and dullish piece, but containing as well *Nimphidia*, a perfect mock-heroic poem. Drayton was not a poet of supreme imagination, and if he lacked the finer virtues of omission, he atoned by noble displays of variety. Everything he wrote has its loftier moments; he is often "golden-mouthed", indeed, in his felicity of diction, whether in the brave style of his youth or in the more delicate manner of his age. He is a kind of poetical epitome. There is something of almost every kind of poetry in him. Drayton may not be read, but he is delightful to read in.

XI. DONNE

From the time of Wyatt and Surrey, English lyrical and amatory poetry had been inspired by Italian writers of whom Petrarch was the chief; and when that immediate influence had waned, it was revived by the example of the French Petrarchians, Ronsard, Du Bellay and Desportes. The poet who broke the Petrarchian tradition was John Donne (1571?–1631). With him begins a new era in the history of English lyric poetry, of English satire, and of English elegiac and religious verse. He was at once the chief inspirer of his younger contemporaries and the first herald of the poetry of eloquence and argument. His mother was a daughter of John Heywood, the Marian dramatist, and of Elizabeth Rastell, who was herself the daughter of Elizabeth, sister of Sir Thomas More. John Donne (the name is sometimes written Dun or Dunne, and was so pronounced) came therefore, on his mother's side at least, of a line professing the old faith, and was himself bred in it. Although he became an Anglican divine, he was never quite an Anglican poet. Something was retained from the faith of his childhood. The representation of the metaphysical by the physical was a natural instinct with Donne, but that kind of representation is frequently present in Catholic devotions and would deeply influence an impressionable child. He entered Lincoln's Inn in 1592, and, apparently, studied and played with the singular intensity which was essential in his nature. Through Sir Henry Wotton, with whom he had been intimate at Oxford, Donne was brought into contact with Essex, and took part in the expedition to Cadiz (1596) and the Azores (1597). In the second of these adventures he was associated with young Thomas Egerton, son of Sir Thomas, Lord Keeper of the Great Seal, and on his return became secretary to that statesman; but his hopes of preferment were ruined by a secret marriage in 1601 with Anne More, a relative of Egerton. He was imprisoned and dismissed from his post. During his early years he had visited Italy and Spain and received some general influence from the tone of Italian and Spanish literature, but not discernibly from any particular authors. Of all Elizabethan poets he is the most independent.

From 1601 to 1615 Donne's life was one of humiliating dependence on patrons; and it is remarkable that his two greatest funeral elegies, *An Anatomy of the World* (*The First Anniversary*) and *Of the Progress of the Soul* (*The Second Anniversary*), were written on the occasion of the death of a young girl whom he had never seen—Elizabeth, daughter of Sir Robert Drury. He wrote extensively for other patrons, and assisted Thomas Morton in his controversies with the Roman Catholics. Like other poets, he wrote an *Elegie on the Untimely Death of the Incomparable Prince, Henry*. To this period belong, too, his prose *Biathanatos*, a casuistical discussion of the question *that Selfe-Homicide is not so Naturally Sinne that it may never be otherwise*, the *Essayes in Divinity*, containing his own reasons for accepting Anglicanism, and *Pseudo-Martyr*, showing that *those which are of the Romane Religion in this Kingdome, may and ought to take the Oath of Allegiance.* The last was published in 1610, the other two appeared posthumously.

Such were Donne's "steps to the altar". As early as 1607 his friend Morton had urged him to take Orders; but he had refused, perhaps for religious reasons, perhaps because the irregularities of his life disturbed his conscience. However, finding, like George Herbert, that the world had no use for him, Donne entered the Church and was ordained in 1615. The time of privation and suitorship was over. His advancement was rapid. He became divinity reader at Lincoln's Inn, where many of his sermons were preached; and in 1621 King James made him Dean of St Paul's. He would certainly have gone further; but his fiery soul had burnt his body to decay. He rose from a sickbed in 1631 to preach what people called his own funeral sermon, *Death's Duell*, and died soon after.

Only four of Donne's poems were published in his lifetime, and two of these were in the publications of others. *An Anatomy of the World* (*The First Anniversary*) appeared in 1611, a second edition in 1612 containing *Of the Progress of the Soul* (*The Second Anniversary*). One poem is included among the panegyrics in *Coryats Crudities* (1611), and the elegy on Prince Henry finds a place in Sylvester's *Lachrimae Lachrimarum* (1613). Of his prose, a few separate sermons, some controversial works and the *Devotions upon Emergent Occasions* (1624) were published. His collected sermons were issued by his son in three successive volumes some years after his death. His poems, however, had a wide circulation in manuscript; and, as always happens in such cases, the textual integrity of his work is hard to establish. The first collection appeared in 1633, and a fuller one in 1635, with the poems disposed in the groups now usually adopted: *Songs and Sonets, Epigrams, Elegies, Epithalamions, Satyres, Letters to Severall Personages, Funerall Elegies, The Progress of the Soule, Divine Poems*. Donne's *Satires* are abrupt and harsh in style; nevertheless they attain in their couplets something of the freedom and suppleness of later dramatic blank verse. They are not only wittier than those of his contemporaries, but weightier in their criticism of life. The *Elegies* are the fullest record of Donne's more cynical frame of mind and the conflicting moods which it generated. A strain of impassioned paradox runs through them. The verse, though harsh at times, has more of the couplet cadence than the satires, and there are not wanting passages of pure and beautiful poetry. But there is no echo of Petrarch's formal woes in Donne's passionate and insolent, rapturous and angry, *Songs* and so-called *Sonets*. If Donne's sincere and intense, though sometimes perverse and petulant, moods are a protest against the languid conventionality of Petrarchian sentiment, his celebrated "wit" is no less a corrective of the lazy thinking of the sonneteers, their fashioning and refashioning of the same outworn conceits. In spite of harsh lines, the lyrics contain his most felicitous effects. He made the stanza, long or short, simple or elaborate, the harmonious echo of that union between passion and argument which is the essential quality of the "metaphysical" lyric.

One remarkable poem, bearing the same title as *The Second Anniversary* is *The Progress of the Soule. Infinitati Sacrum. 16 Augusti 1601. Metempsycosis. Poema Satyricon*. A prose epistle extends the Pythagorean doctrine of metempsychosis from animals to vegetables, and proposes that the poem shall relate all the passages of the apple eaten by Eve; but it goes no further than Temech, "sister and wife to Cain, Cain that first did plough"; and the poem closes abruptly with a stanza of Byronic scepticism and scorn. It was not intended for publication. Very different from this is the other *Progress of the Soul—The Second Anniversary*, which is the finest of Donne's funeral elegies. It is not merely rich in jewels of utterance, it is also a true *meditatio mortis*, developed with the serried eloquence, the intense, dull glow of feeling and the sonorous cadences which we find again in the prose of the sermons. The same intense spirit burns in the best of his *Divine Poems*. Donne is not only the first of the "metaphysical" love poets, he is, likewise, the first of the introspective, religious poets of the seventeenth century.

Donne's fame as a prose writer rests on his sermons. In them all the qualities of his poems are present in a different medium—the swift and subtle reasoning, the powerful yet often quaint imagery, the intense feeling, and, lastly, the wonderful music of the style, which is inseparable from the music of the thought. The early essays in prose, called *Paradoxes and Problems*, not fully collected till 1652, give us glimpses of the daring young poet who wrote the satires. *Ignatius his Conclave* (1611) is a bold and witty flight of satirical prose which has not received the praise it deserves. *Biathanatos, Pseudo-Martyr* and *Essays in Divinity* are much less profitable and exhibit few of the qualities that make the sermons almost unique in our prose.

Donne, whether as poet or as prose-writer, is the worst of models for imitation. His very faults are dangerously attractive. Few poets are so disconcerting.

If we had less of him we should think more of him. Certain lines and passages read alone have a supremacy of achievement that seems to place him with the greatest of writers. But that supremacy is fitful and unmaintained. Too often the poet is seduced into the maze of intellectual ideas, and, with conscious audacity, resorts to twists and turns of cerebral activity and dissonant ejaculation. Nevertheless, his astringency acted beneficially in counteracting the tendency of Elizabethan poetry towards fluency and facility. In his hands, English poetry became less florid and more condensed in thought and speech. There are subtle qualities of vision, rare intensities of feeling, surprising felicities of expression, in the poetry of Donne that one would not sacrifice for the smoothness of more untroubled art. His life can be read in Izaac Walton (1640) or in Gosse's *Life and Letters* (1899); the best edition of his poetry is Sir Herbert Grierson's Oxford edition of 1912.

XII. THE ENGLISH PULPIT FROM FISHER TO DONNE

The Reformation did not originate popular preaching, nor did popular preaching originate the Reformation. It was always the duty of a parish priest to instruct his flock, and from instruction to exhortation, discussion and argument is but a short way. Nevertheless, the Reformation gave an impetus to preaching. It ensured the preacher an expectant congregation; and the more controversial he was the better they liked him. If it is remembered that, in the days when readers were few and newspapers had no existence, the preacher had the opportunities of the journalist, the length of sermons and the popular passion for them cease to be surprising. Authority, therefore, whether ecclesiastical or civil, could not afford to ignore the power of the pulpit, and sought to control it by a rigorous system of licensing. At dangerous moments general preaching was silenced and the few privileged pulpits were strictly supervised. The result was that in the country at large preachers were reduced to silence and the congregations to the harmless fare of the Homilies. In considering even the spoken language of religious controversy, the reader must remember that the idiom of theology was Latin, just as the idiom of law was French. This was not the effect of mere tradition or clerical conservatism. The technique and the terms of theology were firmly established in Latin and in no other language. English in the sixteenth century had attained to many felicities, but it had not yet become the language of abstract science. For many years English theologians had to wrestle with the difficulty of making Latin terms clear in English before they won the two great triumphs, liturgical and theological, marked by Cranmer's *Prayer Book* of 1549 and Hooker's *Ecclesiastical Polity* of 1594.

From Fisher to Donne almost all great preachers preached without book. Donne speaks of spending eight hours in writing out a sermon already delivered. John Fisher (1459?–1535), the saintly and martyred Bishop of Rochester, was urged to print some of his sermons, and, in 1508, there came from the press of Wynkyn de Worde *This treatyse concernynge the fruytful sayinges of Davyd the kynge & prophete in the seven penytencyall psalmes. Devyded in seven sermons.*

Others followed later. Fisher's literary skill is visible in his many comparisons and images, some homely and humorous, others far-fetched and over-elaborate. The actual technique of sentence-structure in English obviously causes him difficulty, and certain long sentences do not work out exactly. Nevertheless, the two funeral sermons on Henry VII (1509) and the Lady Margaret (1509) display a noble and sonorous rhetoric with all the charms of rhythm and cadence. Colet is more modern in style. He is the expositor rather than the allegorist; and in his denunciation of abuses he has the courage of Latimer.

Hugh Latimer (1490–1555), bishop and martyr, achieved the kind of success that came to no other English preacher before Whitefield and Wesley. So absorbed was Latimer in his preaching that he did not trouble about publication. His free and easy discourses, good talking rather than set speeches, were written down by other hands, probably without revision by their author. No word or illustration is too homely for him to use. He avoids theological subtleties, and he is fearless in denouncing sin. No one today holds Latimer's views about Papists and Anabaptists; but bribery is still bribery. The old man's last words to Ridley, his fellow-sufferer at the stake, are known to all and enshrine at once his courage and his humour.

The Edwardian and Marian preachers did not argue deeply. Their sermons aimed, like election addresses, at hitting the popular fancy. With the Elizabethan settlement, the style of preaching changed. A generation had grown up habituated to theological controversy. The sermons of John Jewel (1522–71), Bishop of Salisbury, have therefore less appeal to readers than to the disputants who hail him as the "father of English Protestantism". Nevertheless, it is a pleasure to read anything which says what it means so exactly and so easily as Jewel's famous "challenge" sermon against Romish practices preached at Paul's Cross in 1559 and published in 1560.

There is no need to discuss Hooker's sermons, as they have the great qualities of his master-work. But we should notice one service he rendered to the contemporary pulpit: he set an example of moderation. Reverencing truth wherever he found it, he disdained the popular anti-Roman scurrility of his day and had the courage to declare that "the Church of Rome is a true Church of Christ, and a sanctified Church".

The strict enforcement of the penal laws, and the limited and furtive nature of their opportunities of worship, prevented Roman Catholics in England from contributing to the general store of printed sermons. Controversial and devotional writings exist in sufficient quantity to show that there were men who might have made good use of happier times. Edmund Campion's letters are attractive, Robert Parsons's *Christian Directory* (1585) received the compliment of many Protestant editions, and the rich fancy of Robert Southwell's tracts, such as *Mary Magdalens Teares* (1591) and *The Triumphs over Death* (1595), won the praise of Francis Bacon.

The Puritan tendency to exalt the sermon affected its quality. Once, Hooker remarks, religious men chiefly wearied their knees and their hands; now they exercise merely their ears and their tongues. Lancelot Andrewes (1555–1626) also speaks out against the habit of listening to sermons as a kind of gratification. In his own preaching Andrewes had the homely mannerisms of the day, but the holiness of his life and the sincerity of his aims were not doubted by the most frivolous. His learning was fitly employed in the translation of the Pentateuch for the Authorized Version; it was less happily used in his sermons, which are learned, not in style, but in the severe ordering of his thought. They are therefore less generally known than his *Private Devotions—Preces Privatae—* written for his own use, in one or more of the learned languages, and translated into English by other hands; but their appeal, if not wide, is deep.

Of the sermons of Donne we have already spoken. They were in all respects more "sensational" than the severely argued discourses of Andrewes and they were, and still are, more generally popular. But there is no need to doubt Donne's sincerity, even though his "literary" devices are rather obvious. Plainly he rejoiced in his own power; but he impressed his own age, as he impresses the reader of today, with his tremendous earnestness. Death, the preacher's great commonplace, is with him a reality.

XIII. ROBERT BURTON, JOHN BARCLAY, JOHN OWEN

The first half of the seventeenth century was eminently an age of learning, and three authors carry specially this mark of their period. Two of them, Owen and Barclay, delivered themselves in Latin, one producing the best known body of Latin epigram since Martial, the other the most famous work in Latin prose fiction since Apuleius. Burton would have written in Latin if a printer could have been found. As it is, Latin is never absent from his pages. For width of reading, rather than precise scholarship, Burton may count among the most learned of English writers. The study of man was the purpose of all three; and this aim they pursued with an engaging eagerness for detail that is sometimes hard to distinguish from pedantry.

Remarkable as *The Anatomy* seems, there was nothing remarkable in the author or his life. Robert Burton (1577–1640) was a permanent resident at Oxford, using the resources of his own Christ Church library and the newly-founded Bodleian with a scholar's appetite. He was "by profession a divine, by inclination a physician". He held minor ecclesiastical preferments and would have liked promotion to something higher. The first edition of his famous work appeared in 1621 as *The Anatomy of Melancholy, What it is. With all the Kindes, Causes, Symptomes, Prognostickes, and Severall Cures of it. In Three Maine Partitions with their severall Sections, Members and Subsections. Philosophically, Medicinally, Historically, Opened and Cut up. By Democritus Junior.* If the lengthy title is carefully read the student will avoid the not unusual mistake of supposing that the work is the disorderly commonplace book of a vast and curious reader. The book is as seriously intended as a modern psychologist's treatise on repressions, and it differs from such a work only in its literary excellence, its elaborate precision, its rich humour and its perfect honesty. The first "partition" deals with the definition, causes, symptoms and properties of melancholy; the second (and shortest) with the cure; the third (in its final form by far the longest), with the definition, symptoms and cure of the two distinct species, love melancholy

and religious melancholy. Burton's humour is pervasive and inseparably intertwined with his irony and the kindly commonsense of his attitude to life. He
has touches of Montaigne, yet remains as English as Chaucer or Fielding. Neither
in daring of thought nor in harmony of words can he rival Sir Thomas Browne,
to whom he has been compared and with whom he certainly has this in common, that the same readers seem drawn to both. Burton possessed an inordinate
appetite for reading; but it is absurd to suppose that he was pedantically devoted
to obsolete books. What is obsolete for us was not obsolete for the seventeenth
century. Burton quoted from standard works of his time and quoted their
quotations. Though his prose does not attain the altitude at which Sir Thomas
Browne moves with ease, Burton was consciously concerned about his vocabulary and the rhythm of his English. The changes made in each new edition are
evidence of his efforts to ease the running of his sentences. There is no need to
dwell upon the influence of Burton. Johnson admired him. Sterne pillaged him.
Lamb parodied him. Coleridge annotated him. Southey transcribed him. Keats
versified him. Byron praised him. The present age has sumptuously reprinted
him. His academic play *Philosophaster* and his Latin verses do not need notice.

John Barclay (1582–1621) is a pleasing example of the cosmopolitan Scot.
He was born in France; he married a Frenchwoman; he lived successively in
England and Italy; he was obscurely connected with the court of James I; and
if he failed to obtain high state preferment it was not through lack of endeavour.
Intellectually, Barclay was a compound of the student, the man of letters and
the curious observer of affairs. Most of his works have no interest for us. His
main importance for the history of literature rests on his two adventures in
fiction, both in Latin, *Euphormionis Satyricon* and *Argenis*, the one a contribution
to the development of the picaresque novel, the other a finished example of
ideal romance. In plot, Barclay's satirical novel is merely a string of adventures.
The narrative does not end, it just breaks off. *Argenis* (1621) is a more mature
work than *Euphormio* (1603); there is a clearer intention, there is a carefully-
constructed plot, and there is a perceptible advance in style. We need not describe the story. According to one view, *Argenis* is a political treatise cast in the
form of a novel. According to another, it is an elaborate historical allegory.
According to another, it is simply a romance. That there is really a fusion of
romantic, political and historical motives is proved by the author's own words.
Before the close of the seventeenth century, the Latin text of *Argenis* was
reprinted between forty and fifty times. Its popularity is proved by translations
into ten languages and more than one continuation. There are several English
versions, the last by Clara Reeve, the "Gothick" novelist (1772); it is called
The Phoenix.

The *Epigrammatum Ioannis Owen Cambro-Britanni Libri Tres* (1607) with
three succeeding volumes made the name of the witty Welshman John Owen
(1563?–1622) long famous in Europe. He is the British Martial, with the wit
and snap of his model. Of the favourable impression which he made upon his
contemporaries, there can be no doubt. Five English translations of the whole or
part of his epigrams appeared before 1678, the earliest by John Vicars in 1619.
The strangest phenomenon about Owen's influence is to be found in the German
literature of the seventeenth century. A whole school of writers arose who

devoted themselves to epigram, after the manner of Owen. In the eighteenth century his work was still alive. Lessing criticized him with severity, but paid him the sincerest form of flattery. Cowper translated some of his epigrams. In the second year of the French Republic, one of the very first books issued from the press of Didot was the epigrams of Owen. Owen will never again be as highly valued as in the past, but the present neglect of his work is quite undeserved.

XIV. THE BEGINNINGS OF ENGLISH PHILOSOPHY

Parts of the present section recapitulate some of the matter contained in earlier pages and to these the reader should refer. With Francis Bacon's *Advancement of Learning* (1605) the English language becomes for the first time the vehicle of an important treatise in philosophy. Hooker's *Ecclesiastical Polity*, which preceded it by eleven years, belongs to theology rather than to philosophy. Bacon's predecessors had used the common language of learned men; he was a pioneer in daring to employ English for a work of speculation, even though he proposed to write his *magnum opus* in Latin. The place of birth or residence of a medieval philosopher had no influence on the ideas or style of his work. Philosophy was international and universal. Bacon's use of the English language has therefore caused him to be regarded, not very soundly, both as the beginner of English philosophy and as the type of English philosophical genius.

From the end of the eighth century, when Alcuin of York was summoned to the court of Charles the Great, down to the middle of the fourteenth century, when the work of Ockham was finished, there was a long succession of British scholars among the writers who contributed to the development of philosophy in Europe. The most important names in the succession are Johannes Scotus Erigena, John of Salisbury, Alexander of Hales, Robert Grosseteste, Roger Bacon, Johannes Duns Scotus, William of Ockham and Thomas Bradwardine. The philosophy they represented was, mainly, an attempt at the systemization of knowledge; and the instrument for this synthesis was found in the logical conceptions and method of Aristotle. Philosophy was regarded as the handmaid of theology; and theology was based upon ecclesiastical authority. But in the laborious erudition and dialectical subtleties of the schoolmen there is seldom wanting a strain of deeper thought, which attains its full development in medieval mysticism.

To Erigena may be traced both medieval mysticism and the scholastic method. He seems to have been born in Ireland about 810, and to have proceeded to France some thirty years later. He was the predecessor of scholasticism, but was not himself one of the schoolmen. His anticipation of them consists not only in his dialectical method but also in his recognition of the authority of the Bible and of the Fathers of the Church as final. On the development of mystical thought he exercised a very great influence by his translation of the pseudo-Dionysian writings, which, first distinctly known in the early part of the sixth century, came to be received as the genuine work of Dionysius the Areopagite, converted by St Paul (Acts xvii, 34). Erigena could hardly have had much acquaintance with the work of Aristotle, whose writings did not become known till the beginning of the thirteenth century, and then in Latin translations from the Arabic versions and commentaries made by Avicenna of Persia (980–1037) and Averroes of Cordoba (1126–1198), who themselves probably used other Eastern versions.

Aristotle's writings, at first viewed with suspicion by the Church, were afterwards definitely adopted, and his authority in philosophy became an article of scholastic orthodoxy. The great systems of the thirteenth century—especially the most enduring monument of scholastic thought, the *Summa* of St Thomas Aquinas—are founded on his teaching. But uniformity of opinion was not maintained completely or for long, and three schoolmen of British birth are to be reckoned among the most (if not the most) important opponents of St Thomas. These are Roger Bacon (1214?–1294), Duns Scotus (1265?–1308?), and William of Ockham (1280?–1349?). "Scotism" became the rival of "Thomism" in the schools. The effect of Duns Scotus's work was to break up the harmony of faith and reason which had been asserted by St Thomas.

Duns Scotus denied the validity of natural theology, believing that there could be small connection between reason and revelation. With Ockham, who was a pupil of Duns Scotus, the separation between theology and philosophy, faith and reason, was made complete. In his view, whatever transcends experience belongs to faith, not to argument. He opposed "Realism"—the belief that "universals" or general ideas had somehow and somewhere a real existence, and became the greatest exponent of "Nominalism"—the belief that general ideas were abstractions to which names had been given. "Occam's razor", *Entia non sunt multiplicanda* (entities are not to be postulated without necessity shown) was the axiom by which William dissected every question. Incidentally, he was advanced in his political views, defending the power of the temporal sovereign against the claims of the Pope. The *Doctor Singularis et Invincibilis* is the last of the great schoolmen, for his work struck at the root of the whole scholastic system.

Of Roger Bacon's life, works and misfortunes we have already spoken. He is a most striking example of genius thwarted by time and circumstances. His originality could have no scope in a world of thought narrowly limited by theological orthodoxy, and he suffered persecution and long imprisonments. Roger Bacon's learning seems to have been unique in his time; he read Aristotle in Greek, and expressed unmeasured contempt for the Latin translations. He was acquainted with the writings of the Arab men of science, whose views were far in advance of all other contemporary knowledge. His doctrine of scientific method has been compared with that of his more famous namesake. No less decisively than Francis, Roger rejected the claims of permanent authority in matters of science; like him, he took a comprehensive view of knowledge and attempted a classification of the sciences. But Roger, unlike Francis, was also a mathematician, and looked upon mathematical proof as the type of sound demonstration. Further, he saw the importance in scientific method of two steps inadequately recognized by Francis Bacon—the deductive application of elementary laws to the facts observed, followed by the experimental verification of the results.

Between Roger and Francis Bacon there are no outstanding names in English philosophical literature. Wyclif's philosophical beginning is lost in the greater glory of his religious activities; and after Wyclif we have to wait till the sixteenth century before we encounter even minor writers like Everard Digby and William Temple. The controversy between Digby and Temple at Cambridge, Digby asserting the old Aristotelianism and Temple maintaining the new *Dialectica* of Ramus, a Calvinist who ended as a victim of St Bartholomew's Eve, has interest for us, because Francis Bacon may have been acquainted with their views. Temple shows at least a glimmer of understanding that scientific reasoning must proceed, not from universals to particulars, but from particulars to universals.

While these controversies occupied the schools, William Gilbert (1540–1603), a royal physician, was engaged in the researches and experiments which resulted in the publication of the first great English work of physical science, *De Magnete magneticisque corporibus* (1600). Gilbert expressed himself as decisively as did Bacon afterwards on the futility of expecting to arrive at knowledge of nature by mere speculation or by a few vague experiments. He had, indeed, no theory of induction; but he knew that he was introducing a "new style of philosophizing". Gilbert has been called "the first real physicist and the first trustworthy methodical experimenter". He was the founder of the theory of magnetism and electricity; and he gave the latter its name, *vis electrica*. He explained the inclination of the magnetic needle by his conception of the earth as a magnet with two poles; he defended the Copernican theory; and in his discussion of the attraction of bodies there is a suggestion of the doctrine of universal gravitation. Gilbert also reached a correct view of the atmosphere as extending only a few miles from the surface of the earth.

The greatest philosopher of the time, Francis Bacon (1561–1626), led an important public life as statesman and jurist. He was the younger of the two sons of Sir Nicholas Bacon, Lord Keeper of the Great Seal. But the sudden death of his father in 1579 left him with small means and he had to begin making his own way in life. He turned to the bar for an income, and to his mother's relations, the Cecils, for promotion. He entered Parliament in 1584; but office was long in coming. Neither the Queen nor the Cecils would help him. The places he sought were never unworthy nor beyond his merits; but he sought them in ways not always dignified. He became Solicitor-General in 1607, Attorney-General in 1613, Privy Councillor in 1616, Lord Keeper in 1617, and Lord Chancellor in 1618. He was knighted in 1603, created Baron Verulam in 1618, and Viscount St Albans in 1621. A few weeks later, charges of having received bribes from suitors in his court were brought against him. Bacon was convicted on his own confession, and sentenced to deprivation of all his offices, to imprisonment in the Tower during the King's pleasure, to a fine of £40,000, and to permanent exclusion from Parliament. The imprisonment lasted a few days only; the fine was made over to trustees for Bacon's benefit; but, in spite of many entreaties, he was never allowed to sit in Parliament again. The amount of attention given to Bacon's downfall is a tribute to his greatness. People seem to expect from him a standard of conduct that would have been scarcely intelligible to his age. The politicians who procured his disgrace were not ministers of virtue. They were moved by dislike, not of bribery, but of the man; for it is a singular and significant fact that while everybody admires Bacon nobody loves him. He is the least liked of all great English writers. But excesses of blame and defence are both to be deprecated as out of the picture, whether of the man or of his time. Having at last attained great place Bacon took, as many other famous persons took, before and after him, what seemed the normal fruits of office. We bow with admiration before the sublime integrity of another Lord Chancellor, St Thomas More; but we must recognize that few are born to wear the ascetic's hair-shirt and the martyr's crown. Bacon was certainly not numbered with the saints. There was no trace in him of the English romantic or sentimental strain; instead, he had full measure of the passionless realism that we may call, as we will, scientific, judicial or Machiavellian. He could present implacably the case for the prosecution against his friend and benefactor, the rash and romantic Essex, inevitably doomed, whoever appeared for or against him. We may shudder at what seems the black ingratitude of Bacon, but we must not suppose that the age felt our repugnance. Men lived dangerously then, and took what came to them. Bacon was not the man to throw away his life for a lost cause; yet, oddly enough, he was a martyr to science, for he died of a chill contracted while experimenting with the preservative properties of snow. Pope's too famous line, "The wisest, brightest, meanest of mankind" can be dismissed as merely sentimental—or even journalistic. Bacon was such a man as could have done the work he did; and there the matter should rest. We are not to expect incompatibles of anyone.

In the midst of legal and political labours Bacon never lost sight of his larger ambitions. He published the first edition of his *Essays* in 1597, the second (enlarged) edition appearing in 1612, and the third (completed) edition in 1625. *The Twoo Bookes of Francis Bacon of the Proficience and Advancement of Learning Divine and Humane* appeared in 1605, *De Sapientia Veterum* in 1609, *Instauratio Magna* (*Novum Organum*) in 1620. After his disgrace, Bacon lived at Gorhambury, the paternal estate, and there he devoted himself to writing. *The Historie of the Raigne of King Henry the Seventh* appeared in 1622, and *De Augmentis Scientiarum* in 1623; the *New Atlantis* was written in 1624 and published in 1627; at his death he was at work on *Sylva Sylvarum; or A Natural History* (1627), and he left behind him many sketches and detached portions of his great but incomplete design.

Bacon considered himself devoted to three objects: the discovery of truth, the welfare of his country, and the reform of religion; and of these three objects, the first always held the highest place in his thoughts. "I confess", he wrote to Burghley about 1592, "that I have as vast contemplative ends as I have moderate civil ends: for I have taken all knowledge to be my province." The last familiar sentence is usually taken to mean that Bacon proposed absurdly to possess the totality of information, when his design, simply, was to investigate the means and method of all knowledge. As Macaulay says, "The knowledge in which Bacon excelled all men was a knowledge of the mutual relations of all parts of knowledge".

Bacon intended that his Great Instauration or Renewal of the Sciences should be set forth in six parts. Of these, the first three are represented by considerable works, although in none is the original design carried out with completeness; the last three are represented only by prefatory matter. Latin was to be the language of all. *The Advancement of Learning*, which, in great part, covers the ground of the first division, was not written as part of the plan; but *De Augmentis*, which takes its place in the scheme, is little more than an extended Latin version of the *Advancement*. Bacon begins by reviewing the existing state of knowledge, dwelling on its defects and pointing out remedies for them. This is the burden of the first book of the *Advancement* and of *De Augmentis*. In the second book, he proceeds to expound his division of the sciences:

The parts of human learning have reference to the three parts of man's understanding, which is the seat of learning: history to his memory, poesy to his imagination, and philosophy to his reason.

It is with the last of these divisions that Bacon is chiefly concerned, and he sub-divides that into Divine philosophy, Natural philosophy, and Human philosophy, for all things are "stamped with this triple character, of the power of God, the difference of nature, and the use of man". Bacon's most important thoughts concern natural philosophy, which he discusses with careful distinctions, into which we cannot here follow him.

Both for its style and for the importance of the ideas which it conveys, *Novum Organum*, the second part of the *Instauratio*, ranks as Bacon's greatest work. To its composition he devoted the most minute care, and its stately diction is a fit vehicle for the prophetic message it contains. Bacon's object was to establish or restore the empire of man over nature. This empire depends upon knowledge; but in the mind of man there are certain obstacles to knowledge which predispose it to ignorance and error. The tendencies to error he called "idols"—images or phantoms by which the mind is misled. The name "idol" is taken from Plato and is used as the opposite of "idea". In the *Novum Organum* four classes of idols are distinguished: idols of the tribe, of the cave, of the market-place, and of the theatre. With these graphic titles as his text, Bacon works out a doctrine which shows both originality and insight. Underlying all this part of his teaching is the importance of an objective attitude to nature and of the need for investigation. From particular facts men must pass to general truths by gradual and unbroken ascent.

Bacon is almost as contemptuous of the old induction, which proceeded from a few instances to general laws, as he is of the syllogism. His new induction is to advance by gradual stages of increasing generality, and it is to be based on an exhaustive collection of instances. Bacon was right in principle, but he expected more of the inductive method than it can give. A method cannot exist perfectly in a vacuum. It is worked by human instruments, which are liable to error. Nature does not stand still while investigators collect instances. Further, Bacon misunderstood the nature and function of hypothesis, upon which all scientific advances depend, and he under-valued the deductive method, which is an essential instrument, not indeed of discovery, but of verification. Moreover, his knowledge of the exact sciences was deficient; and so his great scientific contemporary, Harvey, was wittily just when he said that Bacon wrote science like a Lord Chancellor. Darwin, however, declared that he worked "on true

Baconian principles, and, without any theory, collected facts on a wholesale scale". But Darwin, like Bacon himself, was richly endowed with the scientific imagination, which Bacon seems to take for granted. The "great instauration" was not completed. Bacon was working on *Sylva Sylvarum*, a collection of material (in English) for the third part of the *Instauratio*, when he died.

Bacon's observations on private and public affairs, familiarly expressed in the celebrated *Essays*, are full of practical wisdom of the kind commonly called "worldly". He was under no illusions about the ordinary motives of men, and he thought that "we are much beholden to Machiavel and others, that write what men do and not what they ought to do". Bacon's contributions to human philosophy do not rank in importance with his reforming work in natural philosophy. He drew a distinction between public and private good; but that was a matter of general debate. His influence upon the thought of his own time was singularly slight. A later period recognized his greatness, without fully comprehending it. Bacon made no discoveries in natural science and propounded no scheme of philosophy. What he gave to the modern world was something that it lacked, a science of science, a philosophy of philosophy. He dispelled the last obscuring mists of medieval "authoritarianism" in thought and made straight the highway of investigation; and this great achievement he effected not only by his vast and various learning, but by his unrivalled lucidity of mind and his unrivalled lucidity of expression. He did more than anyone else to free the intellect from preconceived notions and to direct it to the unbiased study of facts, whether of nature, of mind, or of society; he vindicated an independent position for the positive sciences; and to this, in the main, he owes his position in the history of modern thought.

A younger contemporary of Bacon was Edward Herbert (1583–1648), elder brother of the poet. He had varied and distinguished military and diplomatic adventures and was created Lord Herbert of Cherbury in 1629. After some half-hearted support of the King's cause, he ultimately sided with the Parliament. His works were historical, literary, and philosophical. The historical works can be dismissed as unimportant. His literary works, his poems and especially his autobiography (not printed till 1764), are of much higher merit. His philosophical works give him a distinct and interesting place in the history of thought. His greatest work *De Veritate* (1624) was enlarged by various dissertations in 1645. In 1663 appeared his *De Religione Gentilium*, a treatise on what would now be called comparative religion. Underlying all experience and belonging to the nature of intelligence itself are certain "common notions". "What is in all men's ears we accept as true." Herbert set forth five "common notions" of religion, representing the whole of "primitive religion" before it had been corrupted by priests. This is a creed of pure Deism, and Herbert has been justly called the father of English Deism. He had no idea of the historical development of belief, and honestly regarded anything beyond his deistical "common notions" as sacerdotal adulterations of primitive rational religion. Nevertheless, he deserves remembrance as the first Englishman to make religion, as a universal human phenomenon, the subject of thoughtful speculation.

XV. EARLY WRITINGS ON POLITICS
AND ECONOMICS

The English constitutional monarchy and Parliamentary government have been deliberately imitated by many nations of the world, even though both have been modified or abandoned later. Elizabethan and Jacobean times are specially interesting as marking the development of both, as now understood; but it is characteristic of the English people that there is no standard body of political literature corresponding to that growth. The written references are casual rather than systematic. As always in England, practice took precedence of theory.

Three phases of conscious political life are discernible in the sixteenth and seventeenth centuries: an intense national and patriotic sentiment; a desire for an acceptable but unoppressive central authority; and a determination to maintain national independence and to extend national influence. The strongest literary evidence for this threefold spirit is to be found in the chroniclers and in the poets. Camden and Shakespeare both write of England with extraordinary fervour; Harrison's *Description of England* and Drayton's *Poly-Olbion* are documents of patriotism; the younger Drake's *The World Encompassed by Sir Francis Drake* (1628) extols the expansion of England almost as a duty to God.

Later theorists who have discerned in the polity of other nations lessons or models for ourselves would have found no support from English writers, who, as early as Sir John Fortescue (1394–1476) in his *De Laudibus Legum Angliae*, concentrated their attention on England as if it were the only type of polity worthy of consideration. Sir Thomas Smith, in his *De Republica Anglorum* (1583) does allude to other states, ancient and modern, but he feels that the superiority of England lies in the fact that it is a commonwealth, in which crown, nobility, burgesses and yeomen have each a part to play. It is specially interesting to note that Sir Thomas Smith classes England, not among the monarchies, but among the democracies. John Selden (1584–1664), in his *Titles of Honour* (1614), does not exalt the kingly office unduly, but recognizes it as the necessary source of honours and grades in society. A point to notice is that the well-ordered community, with a monarch at the head, was habitually spoken of as the *respublica* or "commonwealth", the latter term being regularly applied to the English realm long before it was officially adopted under the Long Parliament. The personality of Queen Elizabeth was a powerful stimulus to the exalted devotion of great men in her age. English enthusiasm for a royal ruler may be said to begin with her. We have already noted the rise, during the Middle Ages, of a *cultus* of reverence for women, expressed most profoundly in devotion to Mary, Maiden and Mother, Queen of Heaven. The convulsions of religious revolution during the reigns of Henry VIII, Edward VI and Mary had perplexed the faithful and tinged with doubt the special forms of devotion, even devotion to the Mother of Sorrows. But devotion to a womanly ideal seems to be a necessity of civilized nature; and with the accession of the bold, fascinating, incalculable daughter of Henry VIII, dazzling in accomplishment and infinite in variety, came a thrilling embodiment of the ideal. The cult of the Virgin Queen became a national variation of the cult of the Virgin Mother. None recognized this more acutely than the Elizabethan Puritans, and their detestation of "the monstruous regiment of women" was deepened. But they were only a menace, not yet a danger. They could not succeed against triumphant woman. From the panegyrics of Camden to the acrostics of Davies, chronicler and poet united in devotion to the fair Vestal thronëd by the West. The bull of Pius V (1570) which excommunicated Elizabeth and released her Roman Catholic subjects from allegiance had no other effect than to strengthen her appeal to the devout enthusiasm of her people.

But devotion to the Queen did not solve the problem of monarchy. Royalty might be the source of honours; but what was the source of royalty? Was it derived from papal authority? Was it inherent in a certain line or stock? Was it conferred by public assent? Robert Parsons the Jesuit, in his *Conference about the Next Succession to the Crowne of England* (1594), contents himself with denying inherency, and Sir John Hayward, in his *Answer to...a certaine Conference* (1603), affirms the hereditary principle. But we have to remember that Great Britain at this time contained two separate kingdoms, and that on this very question of royalty they had taken two different courses. Scotland had become thoroughly Calvinistic, and the inherent authority of a hereditary monarchy was not consistent with the doctrines of Calvin. In Geneva there was no one to contest the Calvinist claims; but as soon as Calvinism crossed the Channel its pretensions came into conflict with the claims of monarchy. The most powerful note of defiance came from John Knox (1505?–1572) in *The first Blast of the Trumpet against the Monstruous Regiment of Women* (1558), and he was followed by George Buchanan (1506–82) whose *De Jure Regni* (1579) boldly declared that kings hold their power from the people and may be judged by the people. In Scotland the triumph of the Presbyterian polity in 1580 created throughout the country a series of representative assemblies which took complete possession of the national ecclesiastical system; and this polity treated the monarch as subject to the ecclesiastical democracy. *The True Lawe of Free Monarchies* (1598), attributed to King James, attacked this position and intimated the Stuart doctrine of divine right, a doctrine now usually misunderstood, and not intelligible without reference to other contemporary views of kingship. In England, the attempt of the Puritans to capture the political machinery was frustrated by Elizabeth at the beginning of her reign; but the example of Scottish success was continually before them. The English view, as far as there was a view, seems to have been that a monarchy which succeeded was a rightful monarchy, and need be no further discussed. The monarchy of Elizabeth was successful and accepted; the monarchy of James I was much less successful and was accepted with misgivings; the monarchy of Charles I was unsuccessful and was terminated. The question of divine right, therefore, seemed rather academic, and did not greatly interest the people. On the other hand, they were not very willing to accept a dethroning Presbyterian autocracy in place of a dethroning Papal autocracy. Then, as now, the English idea of successful government cannot be associated with formal theory. A successful government is one that can keep in office.

The theory of government was, therefore, not the theme of any memorable treatise. As we have already pointed out, Machiavelli was not known in English.

He came into Elizabethan literature, not as an influence on polity, but as a villain of the popular stage. Much more important to the general mind than theories of governance was the practical question, how far private interests and public welfare were compatible. The conflict of "ideologies", so far from being a peculiar symptom of modern life, was acute throughout the Middle Ages, when the Church denounced private enterprise as inimical to the common weal. Indications of this feeling can be found in such lay works as Caxton's *The Game and Playe of the Chesse* (1475), Starkey's *Dialogue between Cardinal Pole and Thomas Lupset* (sixteenth century), and More's *Utopia* (1516). John Hales's *A Discourse of the Common Weal of this Realm of England* (written 1549, published 1581) takes a new line, and argues that the pursuit of private interests need not be injurious, but may be profitable, to the state. With the development of trade came the need for capital; but the feeling against usury was still strong. Thomas Wilson's *Discourse uppon usurye* (1572) condemned interest as leading to extortion, and an ecclesiastical canon of 1604 declared it wrong to demand a fixed rate of interest for loans; but Gerard de Malynes (fl. 1586–1641), who applied common sense to economic questions in such works as *A Treatise of the Canker of Englands Commonwealth* (1601), *The Maintenance of Free Trade* (1622), and *The Center of the Circle of Commerce* (1623), some of them replies to another economist, Edward Misselden, one of the Merchant Adventurers, insisted that moderate interest, which gave free play to capital, was for the public good, and that harm arose only when excessive rates were charged. This was the view adopted by Parliament in 1624. The new commercial morality was accepted by the state, and the efforts of churchmen like Laud to maintain the medieval view of usury failed. The name of "usurer" was applied only to the extortioners who sought to charge excessive rates. *The Merchant of Venice* is an interesting side-light on history.

Trade in the larger sense led to the formation of the great commercial companies of the seventeenth century. The Merchant Adventurers and the Eastland Companies gave rise to some printed debate, which we need not notice. They were associations of independent traders; but the East India Company was a joint stock venture, and the question of taking capital out of the country naturally arose. The classic defence of such enterprises is found in Thomas Mun's *A Discourse of Trade from England unto the East Indies* (1621) and *England's Treasure by forraign trade* (1664).

The Irish question was also with us in those days, and, strangely enough, the two best known contributions to the matter were made by poets. Edmund Spenser's *A Veue of the Present State of Ireland*, written 1596, though not printed till 1633, and Sir John Davies's *A discoverie of the true causes why Ireland was never entirely subdued etc.* (1612) both discussed ways of bringing Ireland into line with the English ideal of well-ordered society. Settlements from England and Scotland were made, the most interesting being that carried out by the London companies which turned Derry into Londonderry.

Some interesting writing which we have no space to discuss arose out of the draining of the Fens and the development of the fishing industry, two different activities in both of which the English were urged to learn from the Dutch. The literature of mendicancy, vagabondage and imposture mentioned in an earlier chapter presents a picture of social degradation which deprives the sixteenth century of any claim to be part of a fabulously merry England and explains the necessity for the Elizabethan Poor Law measures of 1601.

XVI. LONDON AND THE DEVELOPMENT OF POPULAR LITERATURE

When the last feudal king of England fell at Bosworth Field in 1485 the reign of politics began. With the Tudor sovereigns came government instead of rule. The nobles, no longer petty war-lords of armed retainers in their own demesnes, forsook the field for the Court, where alone, now, preferment was to be won. There were other important movements. The sack of Antwerp in the "Spanish fury" of 1576 diverted Flemish trade to London, which soon became a capital of European commerce. London, therefore, offered attractions of many kinds, and the young men who flocked thither to seek their fortunes at Court, or in the royal service, or at the Inns of Court, or in commercial adventures, formed a new element in society and fell an easy prey to hosts of ingenious tricksters and unscrupulous tradesmen. The centre of government and commerce is also the centre of extravagance and dissipation and of those who minister thereto. London had grown in size. Oxford and Cambridge were in closer touch with the capital. The Renascence had made learning fashionable, and the new "moderns" exhibited their superiority by patronizing literature and employing a decorated and affected form of speech. Courtiers, graduates, divines, soldiers, lawyers, merchants, tradesmen, women and even 'prentices, made a great variety of readers, and there arose a generation of brilliant and often impecunious young men who became authors from ambition or necessity, and gratified the public desire for literary airs and graces flavoured with the realism of London life.

Thomas Lodge led the way with *An Alarum against Usurers* (1584), describing in elaborate euphuistic style the dangers to which thriftless young men were exposed. He was followed by Thomas Nashe in *The Anatomie of Absurditie* (1589), which, though affected in manner, foreshadows the literature of counsel and reflection expressed in the essays of Bacon. Four years later Robert Greene struck a new note by discarding the elaborations of euphuism and adopting the directness of realism in the "conny-catching" pamphlets and autobiographical warnings already described (p. 136). Greene's combination of realistic invention and personal moralizing proved very popular and set a fashion that fiction was to follow for several centuries. The death of Greene in 1592 left Nashe the chief exponent of realism. Something has already been said of his contributions to fiction and to the Marprelate controversy; a brief summary must now be given of his later activities. Nashe's experience as a disputant had given point to his style and cogency to his argument. He had learned that a quasi-religious appeal is always popular, especially when heightened by a note of ribaldry; and so *Pierce Penilesse his Supplication to the Divell* (1592) represents the lackpenny author as addressing his complaint to the devil, since appeals to the Church are useless. The Seven Deadly Sins had been banished by the Reformation from popular religious mythology as papistical; but they had returned by way of literature, and we find them, for instance, as a comic interlude in Marlowe's *Faustus* and as a vehicle for invective and imagery in Spenser's *Faerie Queene*. Nashe uses them in his *Supplication* as convenient categories under which he could present types of character, English and foreign. The age echoed with controversy, and Nashe aspired to be an English Aretino. To make sure of a resounding antagonist he took up a quarrel that had arisen between Robert Greene (now dead) and Gabriel Harvey, and a "flyting" at once began. Literary duels had long been an accepted tradition, and "flytings" were as much a part of literary convention as "violent attacks" are still a part of political convention. Nashe's *Strange Newes of the intercepting certaine Letters etc.* (1592), also known as *The Apologie of Pierce Penilesse*, is in the vein of Martin Marprelate, and poured out wild vituperation upon Gabriel Harvey, who retaliated with *Pierces Supererogation* (1593). The reply to this was not at once forthcoming, for Nashe chose to appear as a religious reformer in *Christs Teares over Jerusalem* (1593), to which he prefixed a declaration of peace and goodwill to all men. There was evidently a Puritan public to which Nashe thought it profitable to appeal. The style of *Christs Teares* is still vigorous, but the vituperation is modified, and something like a pulpit manner is evident. Nevertheless, there are touches of satire and an outspoken exposure of the London stews. Europe at this time was agitated by a literal belief in the Scriptural warning that "the devil is come down unto you, having great wrath", and evidence of his power was being discovered everywhere. The literature of witchcraft, already mentioned, was considerable. Nashe seized this opportunity to compose *The Terrors of the Night* (1594), in which some of his remarks on dreams and moral fears are quite intelligent. The same year saw the appearance of his novel *The Unfortunate Traveller*. Skirmishing between Nashe and Harvey broke out again in 1594, and in 1596 Nashe produced *Have with you to Saffron Walden, or, Gabriell Harveys Hunt is up*, a triumph of invective and scurrilous portraiture. Nashe passed through two years of adversity, and reappeared in 1599 with *Nashes Lenten Stuffe*. Having received hospitality in Yarmouth, he repaid it by this mock panegyric on the herring—the "lenten stuff" of the title. The piece is excellently written; but young men in London did not want to read about herrings in Yarmouth. No more pamphlets came from Nashe. What he may have contributed to drama will be considered later. Nashe is an important figure in the development of English prose. He took the language of Tudor euphuism, cleared it of its conceits, and turned it into an instrument of natural, vivid and varied speech. He wrote nothing of the highest order; but he may be credited with many of the virtues as well as a few of the vices of vigorous and lively journalism.

Verse satire flourished throughout the sixteenth century. Joseph Hall (1574–1656), a young clergyman, claimed the honour of being the first English satirist with his *Virgidemiarum* (1597). Perhaps Hall was unacquainted with the work of Wyatt, Gascoigne, and certain others; but his claim to originality is partly justified, as he was the first to take Juvenal as a model. Like subsequent imitators of Juvenal such as Dr Johnson, Hall turned the Roman form into effective criticism of his own time, ridiculing, for instance, the antique affectations of Spenser and the extravagances of "Turkish Tamberlaine". The first three books (1597) of *Virgidemiarum* are termed "toothlesse satyrs", because they aim at institutions, customs, or conventionalities; the last three (1598) are styled "byting satyrs", because they attack individuals under pseudonyms which were probably no disguise to contemporaries. Other writers found Juvenalian invective attractive. Edward Guilpin, in *Skialetheia* (1598), protested against the feeble poetry of the age and claimed that satire and epigram were the only antidote. John Marston, the dramatist, added *Certaine Satyres* to his *Metamorphosis of Pigmalions Image* (1598), and, in 1599, produced another volume of satires called *The Scourge of Villanie*, both containing much ridicule of his literary contemporaries. "Flytings" threatened to become a craze; but Whitgift and Bancroft, acting on their new authority, issued an order in 1599 that "noe Satyres or Epigrams be printed hereafter".

As the physicians had explained temperament to be dependent on the predominance of one of the four "humours" or moistures—phlegm, blood, choler and melancholy—it became fashionable to dignify any eccentricity or pose with the name of "humour", and to deem the most miserable affectations worthy of literary comment. We need not enumerate the Juvenalian satires that dealt with the "humours" of unpleasing persons. The "comedy of humours" will receive consideration later.

The brief epigram had contended with the satire for popularity, and we have Thomas Bastard's *Christoleros: Seven bookes of Epigrammes* (1598), John Weever's *Epigrammes in the oldest Cut and Newest Fashion* (1598), and *The Scourge of Folly* (1611) by Davies of Hereford. But at the beginning of the seventeenth century writers discovered that the Theophrastian "Character" gave more scope for literary quality. Theophrastus (373–284 B.C.) in his *Characteres* had sketched the peculiarities of Athenian citizens and produced a distinct literary creation. Joseph Hall, the satirist, presently to become Bishop of Exeter and of Norwich, and to be expelled by the Puritans, turned from Juvenal to Theophrastus and published his *Characters of Virtues and Vices* (1608), depicting such moral types as "The Happy Man", "The Humble Man", "The Ambitious Man", and so forth. *The Man in the Moone* (1609) by W. M. is another book of "types", with ingenious machinery. Sir Thomas Overbury, victim of a famous poisoning case, had written a poetical "character", *A Wife*, and this was published (1614) after his death with the addition of other characters, not all by him. A young lawyer, John Stephens, produced in 1615 *Satyrical essayes, characters and others* in prose and verse. But the most famous book of its kind appeared anonymously at Oxford in 1628 under the title *Micro-cosmographie: or, A Peece of the World Discovered, in Essayes and Characters*. The principal author was John Earle (1601?–1655), afterwards Bishop of Salisbury, a man of gravity and learning, and so his characters are composed with deeper insight and surer command of style than those of Overbury or Stephens. In the form of character sketches Earle presents the moral importance of "the trivial round, the common task", of the day's unrecorded words and deeds, and *Microcosmographie*, with its quiet wisdom and its avoidance of oddity, is therefore the best example of its kind in English.

The character sketch is well on the way to the essay. Montaigne's first essays had appeared in 1580; and he is the father of that form as a modern literary creation, whatever ancient anticipations may be found. English imitations began to appear, but nothing calls for attention till we reach the little pamphlet entitled *Essayes. Religious Meditations. Places of persuasion and disswasion*, published in 1597— ten short pieces, the first called *Of Studies*. The title-page bears no name; but there is a dedicatory letter to "M. Anthony Bacon his dear Brother" signed "Your entire loving brother. Fran. Bacon". Thus appeared one of the most famous of English books. It was followed in 1600 by *Essayes by Sir William Cornewalyes* and in 1601 by Robert Johnson's *Essaies, or Rather Imperfect Offers*, the latter definitely instructive. Florio's translation of Montaigne appeared in 1603. Later writers tended to blend the essay and the character—for instance, Geffray Mynshul in *Characters and Essayes of a Prison and Prisoners* (1618) and Nicholas Breton in *Characters upon Essaies morall and divine* (1615); and the form might have degenerated had not Bacon taken it up again. As the inventor of that kind of writing in English, he felt called to exhibit its best qualities; and so in 1612 he carefully revised the first little collection and added twenty-eight new essays in a smoother, less desiccated style. By 1625 his final edition was complete. This collection contains fifty-eight essays, written with a perfect mastery of language in a spirit of lofty confidence. The excellence of these famous compositions lies mainly in the fact that in them Bacon is "table-talking", and not writing in the manner befitting grave philosophy. Those who find the *Essays* unexalted and curtly undeveloped forget that they are oracular utterances, thrown out, as in conversation, for the reader to expand in his own mind. The full-voiced Bacon is to be sought in the *Great Instauration*. Owen Felltham's *Resolves* (1623) established the essay's right to add sacred topics to the moral topics discussed by Bacon. A high level of prose reflection was reached in the desultory notes which Ben Jonson was making out of his vast reading. In 1640 these were published posthumously as *Timber, or Discoveries made upon men and matter*. Although most of the substance has its origin in the books of other writers, *Timber* is not a mere work of paraphrase and transcription. A sense of manly integrity can be clearly discerned in this selection of the world's wisdom, and the style has a colloquial simplicity more humanly appealing than the oracular judgments of Bacon. We need not pay attention to the literature in prose and verse evoked by the new habit of smoking or "drinking" tobacco, except to remark that King James himself joined in the fray with his *A Counterblaste to Tobacco* (1604); nor need we discuss the numerous rogue-books of the period. We can pass at once to the most important pamphleteer of Jacobean London, Thomas Dekker the playwright.

Dekker (1570?–1637?) is the first literary artist of London street life. *The Wonderfull Yeare* 1603 is remarkable for its vivid and harrowing description of London in the grip of the plague. *The Seven Deadly Sinnes of London* (1606) uses the old medieval machinery for an indictment of the city's modern vices. *Newes from Hell; brought by the Divell's Carrier* (1606) is another medieval device adapted to modern use—the visit to hell and purgatory. A pamphleteer with Dekker's curiosity about life and his gift of realistic description would be certain to publish tracts on roguery, and, in 1608, he produced *The Belman of London*, using the same kind of material as his sixteenth-century predecessors. A sequel is *Lanthorne and Candle-light or the Bell-mans second Nights-Walke* (1609), in which, after a number of picturesque episodes, the devil decides to make a visit to London. Dekker's most famous tract, however, is *The Guls Horne-booke* (1609), ironically instructing the "modern" young man of the day how to become completely odious. It is the most vivid picture we possess of Jacobean London. *A Strange Horse Race*, which followed in 1613, is an odd production in which knowledge is presented under the form of "races"— astronomy, for instance, being a race of the heavenly bodies. Dekker wrote clear and attractive prose of distinctive character. Other tracts are mentioned on p. 256.

A contemporary of Dekker was Samuel Rowlands, whose *Tis Merrie when Gossips meete* (1602) and *Greenes Ghost haunting Conie-catchers* (1602) revert to the older style. But in *Looke to it; for Ile Stabbe ye* (1604), a verse piece, he combines the old "Dance of Death" with the new "type" satire. In similar vein is his dialogue *A terrible Battell betweene the two consumers of the whole world: Time and Death* (1606). The beginning of the poem has an almost Miltonic grandeur. Romance of the old style came in for ridicule, and we may mention as an example of its kind *The Melancholie Knight* (1615) by Rowlands, the verse monologue of a character disgusted with his own age and infatuated with the enchantments of older times. The anonymous compiler of the *Merrie Conceited Jests of George Peele* (1607) found a framework for his detached anecdotes in the attractive personality of literary Bohemians. So great was the interest in personalities that there was a keen public for *Kemps nine daies wonder* (1600), in which the actor vivaciously describes the episodes of his morris dance from London to Norwich. Richard Brathwaite, adopting the name of a proverbial drunkard, describes a pilgrimage through the towns and villages of England in *Barnabae Itinerarium or Barnabee's Journal* (1638). The booklet is a triumph of easy rhythmic verse. On a lower level are anonymous "bacchic" pieces like *Pimlyco or Runne Red Cap* (1609) in which the poet describes a crowd of people seeking drink. Another form of popular literature is found in the broadsides and ballads which represented at a lower level the old Tudor love of music. Songs were sold and sung at the street corners, and continued to be thus sold and sung as late as the time when Silas Wegg at his little stall won the heart of Mr Boffin by dropping into a ballad. The ballad-mongers anticipated the lower forms of modern journalism in giving the public what the public is always alleged to want, "amazing" news, "startling" revelations, and vivid accounts of monstrosities, portents, prodigies, disasters, crimes, executions, confessions and repentances. Only the absence of "sensational" divorces assures us that we are not moving among the familiar features of the modern popular newspapers.

XVII. WRITERS ON COUNTRY PURSUITS AND PASTIMES

While the great Elizabethans were creating their masterpieces of universal literature and the lesser Elizabethans were pouring out their prose and verse pamphlets of London life, others were producing books which, designed as guides and instructors in the rural pursuits of men for whom polite literature scarcely existed, sometimes themselves became literature. Before the Elizabethan period there had been few books on country life—*The Book of St Albans* (1486), Walter of Henley's *Book of Husbandry* (thirteenth century, printed about 1510) and John Fitzherbert's *New tract or treatyse...for all husbande men* (1523), were the most important. Elizabethan books are numerous, and many are the work of one person, Gervase Markham (1568?–1637), poet, dramatist, soldier, linguist, agriculturist, horticulturist, horseman, cattleman, dog-lover, rural encyclopedist, and last, but not least, the bold continuator of Sir Philip Sidney's *Arcadia*. The materials used by him and other writers are drawn from two main sources, first the stock of native lore, and next, an abundant foreign literature in certain branches of rural pursuits. Markham's interests were many; but the subject nearest and dearest to him was horses. His *Discource on Horsemanshippe* appeared in 1593. In 1607 came his chief work, *Cavelarice, or the English Horseman*, with a delicious descriptive title a paragraph long, in which he asserts that he can teach horses "to doe tricks like Bankes his Curtall"—an allusion to the famous performing horse Marocco, which achieved not merely a European reputation in life, but an eternity of fame after death, for it is the arithmetical "dancing horse" of *Love's Labour's Lost*, Act 1, Sc. 2. To complete *Cavelarice* with veterinary information he brought out in 1610 *Markhams Maister-peece*. In fact, Markham was so prolific that the stationers grew alarmed, and in 1617 he was induced to sign a promise to produce no more books about "the Deseases or cures of any Cattle, as Horse, Oxe, Cowe, Sheepe, Swine and Goates &c." Nevertheless, *Markhams Faithfull Farriar* appeared in 1630. Apart from his books about horses, Markham produced an encyclopedia of rural occupations under the alluring title, *A Way to get Wealth* (1631, etc.), together with numerous other works that cannot even be named here.

Leonard Mascall (d. 1589), quoted by Markham as an authority, wrote upon grafting and poultry, and produced *The government of cattell* in 1587, and *A Booke of fishing with hooke and line* in 1590. Barnabe Googe, whom we have already met as a poet, translated the *Foure bookes of Husbandry collected by M. Conradus Heresbachius* (1577). Sir Hugh Platt, an interesting person whose activity extended to other matters besides agriculture, was known as the author of many curious inventions, a number of which are described in his *Jewell House of Art and Nature* (1594). *The Grete Herball* (1526), founded on the French *Grand Herbier*, was the earliest of its numerous kind in English. William Turner, the reforming Dean of Wells, who had a garden at Kew, diversified his Protestant polemics with botanical pursuits; and his *New herball* (1551–62) is considered a starting point in the scientific study of botany in England. The *Niewe herball* (1578) of Rembert Dodoens, turned into English by Henry Lyte from the French version of L'Écluse (Clusius), was very popular. It was from Dodoens that John Gerard derived and adapted a great part of his celebrated *Herball or generall historie of Plantes* (1597). In 1629 John Parkinson, an ardent botanist and lover of flowers, brought out his delightful *Paradisi in sole Paradisus terrestris, or a garden of all sorts of pleasant flowers which our English ayre will permitt to be noursed up: with a kitchen garden...and an orchard*, the woodcuts for which were specially done in England. This was followed in 1640 by his great herbal, *Theatrum botanicum*, with its description of nearly 3800 plants and its 2600 illustrations. Parkinson deserves to live for the excellent pun the title page of his earlier book makes upon his name: "Paradisus-in-Sole" being "Park-in-sun". The prolific and inevitable Markham contributed as largely to the literature of vegetables as to the literature of animals. His least important works are the contributions to poetry and drama with which he endeavoured to enter literature by the front door.

XVIII. THE BOOK TRADE, 1557-1625

The outstanding fact in the history of English printing and bookselling during the period under consideration is the incorporation of the Stationers' Company in 1557. This official recognition served a double purpose: the control of publication by the state and the control of the trade by its own reputable members. The old Guild or Fraternity of Scriveners developed into the craft of Stationers, of which all persons connected with the book trade in the City of London were required to become members. After the incorporation in 1557 came the admission of the Company in 1560 as one of the Liveried Companies of the City. The "trade" was now fully established as a recognized commercial corporation.

Under the rules of the Company, every member was required to enter in the Register the name of any book or copy which he claimed as his property and desired to print. The registers were merely commercial in intention, but, in spite of manifest defects, mainly of omission, they form a marvellous storehouse of bibliographical information. The Marian authorities who gave the Stationers their charter were not moved by literary enthusiasm. On the contrary, their aim was to establish efficient machinery for the suppression of seditious and heretical publications. This purpose was clearly evident after Mary's death; for, in the first year of Elizabeth's reign, the Stationers' charter was confirmed and the regulation of printing made even more stringent in the *Injunctions geven by the Queenes Majestie*, one of which provided that nothing should be printed till it had been seen and licensed by the Archbishops, the Bishop of London, or some other specified dignitaries. The censorship thus established was to have a long life. That the authorities meant the *Injunctions* and later orders to be taken seriously is proved by the fate of William Carter, who had published "naughtye papysticall" books, and who, for printing *A treatise of schisme*, held to be seditious, met the sanguinary death of a traitor at Tyburn in 1584. Nevertheless desperate men took risks, and "Martin Marprelate" successfully defied the authorities in several bold attacks on the bishops before his activities were suppressed. That interesting story, already told, need not be repeated here. The attentions of the Company were not confined to illegal productions; the brethren themselves were well looked after, and the accounts of fines imposed for irregularities show that a rigorous supervision was at least attempted.

A cause of much dissatisfaction among the printers was the number of printing monopolies granted during the reign of Elizabeth. The exclusive right of printing law-books, school-books, almanacs and dictionaries was given at various times to certain printers, and the other members of the trade were naturally dissatisfied. On the one side were the possessors of profitable privileges or valuable copyrights; on the other side were ranged the unprivileged men who were driven to speculative business, and picked up anything—poems, plays or ballads—that the sounder men disdained. To the unprivileged printers, therefore, we owe the preservation in print of the greater part of the poetical, dramatic and popular literature of the time. There were, in fact, many piratical publishers who infringed the monopolies of the privileged persons. Such a one was bold John Wolfe who declared that he would print anything and everything. It is sad to observe the fate of this Luther of printing—he himself made the audacious comparison: the rebel prospered, became respectable, and helped to put down other rebels.

In 1582 there were twenty-two printing houses in London. In 1586 there were twenty-five. By 1640 the number had risen to sixty. There were more journeymen printers than could find work, and in 1587–8 the Company limited the number of copies of one impression of a book to 1250 or 1500. This gave more work, as the type had to be re-set for each new impression. Several bibliographical puzzles have arisen as a result of this re-setting of successive impressions. It was easier to become a bookseller and publisher than to become a printer. Anyone could acquire a stock of books by purchase and offer them for sale in one of the stalls or booths round St Paul's, the most popular centre of the book trade. To acquire property in a new publication the would-be publisher had to procure a manuscript, enter it in the Register and get someone to print it for him. This done, he could distribute copies by exchange for copies of new works from other publishers, and so acquire both profit and new stock. Distribution by exchange seems to have been common. Stationers sometimes engaged authors to produce works for them; and correcting and editing for the press afforded occupation for scholars in the more important printing houses. Translation was a stock kind of hack work, especially after 1622, when news-sheets began to be issued, with extracts from foreign "Corantos". Dearth of news was easily made good by imaginative hacks, and the debased "ballad" gave employment both to writers and printers.

So far, we have heard nothing of the author. How did authors get profit from their work? To the professional writer a patron was almost as essential as a publisher. A famous name in the dedication gave a book a greater chance of success; moreover the accepted dedication of a work often meant a substantial gift from a princely patron; hence the prevalence of fulsome dedications. There was no "copyright" as we understand it. Any stationer with a manuscript could enter it and publish it as his copy—how he came by the manuscript being nobody's business; and as popular poems (for example) had sometimes a large manuscript circulation, an unscrupulous printer could usually obtain a copy. The author had no redress. It was in this way that Sidney's *Sonnets* in 1591 and Shakespeare's *Sonnets* in 1609 first attained the dignity of print, if that description may be applied to such mean typographical productions. Ingenious persons, like John Minsheu the linguist and John Taylor the water-man, tried "printing at their own charge", but found, as other authors have found ever since, that the real problem is not publication but distribution. Dramatists were the special prey of piratical printers. The companies of players did not want their popular successes to be staled by print, and did not readily offer them for publication; but plays could be taken down in shorthand or reproduced from memory by an actor. There were complaints, but there was no redress. The printers and publishers of the early Shakespeare quartos belonged almost entirely to the class of unprivileged men. Details of their names and deeds will be found in the larger *History* and in A. W. Pollard's *Shakespeare Folios and Quartos* (1909) and *Shakespeare's Fight with the Pirates* (1920). The story is a fascinating piece of literary detective-work. *Venus and Adonis* (1593) and *Lucrece* (1594) were properly authorized publications. The posthumous Shakespeare Folio of 1623, being a large venture, was the joint undertaking of several stationers.

English printing during the period under review was devoid of typographical merit in style, beauty and accuracy. Some of the early "black letter" books maintained the older tradition of good craft; but no one in England learned either to cut or to use good roman type. The illustrations in English books of the period were greatly inferior to contemporary Continental work, of which they were often bad imitations. Woodcuts were generally used, but illustrations of a better class appeared after the introduction of copper plate engraving in 1540. Much interest attaches to the early editions of the English Bible, several of which were actually printed on the Continent, even some that bear an English imprint. The great international book fair was held in Frankfort, and business-like English booksellers attended. One of them, John Bill, began in 1617 to issue versions of the Frankfort catalogue, to which from 1622 to 1626 he added a supplement of books printed in English. The first actual *Catalogue of English Printed Bookes* was that of Andrew Maunsell (1595).

Books were not very cheap. Here are some seventeenth-century prices: the Cambridge quarto Bible, with Psalms, 7s., the London quarto Bible, with notes and concordance, also 7s., and Bibles in octavo, 3s. 4d. Testaments in octavo cost 10d., and in duodecimo, 7d. Quarto plays and similar productions were issued at sixpence, and ephemeral pamphlets were sold at twopence, threepence, or fourpence. To obtain a modern equivalent, these prices must be multiplied by ten or more.

The provinces were supplied by fairs or by travelling chapmen. In the first half of the sixteenth century printing had been carried on in several provincial towns, but the products were mainly theological, and by 1557 the activity of local presses had ceased. No actual printing was done in Cambridge from the cessation of John Siberch's press in 1522 until the appointment of Thomas Thomas as university printer in 1582. The Stationers' Company tried hard but unsuccessfully to prevent the restoration of a university press at Cambridge, but accepted meekly the revival of printing at Oxford in 1584 and the official recognition of the press there in 1586. The Cambridge story is told in *The Cambridge University Press 1521–1921* (1921) by Sir Sydney Roberts and *The First Cambridge Press* (1955) by E. P. Goldschmidt.

Chepman and Myllar began printing in Scotland in 1508, and the work of the Scottish press at once assumed a strongly national character; but the close association of Scotland with the Continent resulted in the printing of the more scholarly works abroad. There was in Scotland no association like the London Stationers' Company. The beginning of printing in Ireland is represented by the *Book of Common Prayer*, printed in 1551 at Dublin by a London printer. The first use of Irish characters in print is found in 1571. But early Irish printing produced nothing of importance.

XIX. THE FOUNDATION OF LIBRARIES

Libraries grew naturally out of the accumulation of manuscripts and printed books in the monasteries, cathedrals and universities. The dissolution of the religious houses and the burning zeal of later reformers destroyed or dispersed many priceless treasures; but something was saved from the ruins. At Corpus Christi, Cambridge, when Archbishop Parker bequeathed his noble collection, the original library had almost disappeared. When he became Master in 1544 he took strict measures against further losses. Parker stands at the head of modern book collectors. As Elizabeth's first Archbishop he was able to choose from the salvage of the destroyed religious houses, and he used his privilege wisely. At Oxford, college libraries had been unscrupulously plundered by the Edwardian commissioners and little of value or importance remained at the beginning of the seventeenth century. Although a regard for learning was supposed to be a characteristic of James I, the royal pedant cared little about books. It was owing to Prince Henry that the royal library was saved from spoliation and to Sir Thomas Bodley (1545–1613) that the "Old Library" in the university of Oxford was re-established. Bodley, who was English resident at The Hague from 1588 to 1596, resolved to make the restoration of the library at Oxford the life-work of his retirement from public affairs. In 1602 the library was formally opened with about 2500 volumes. Among later benefactors of the Bodleian was Archbishop Laud who gave some 1300 manuscripts in eighteen different languages and also his fine collection of coins. Robert Burton bequeathed many books, and Oliver Cromwell presented some Greek and Russian manuscripts.

The public library of the university of Cambridge dates, apparently, from the first decades of the fifteenth century. The earliest catalogue contains 122 titles. The catalogue of 1473 contains 330, classified and arranged. Parker is among the later benefactors of the Cambridge library.

The Chetham library in Manchester was founded by Humphrey Chetham (1580–1653), a wealthy tradesman. In 1630, Sion College was founded as a corporation of all ministers and curates in London and the suburbs. During the Commonwealth it received many, and retained some, of the books from old St Paul's. Those that went back were destroyed in the Great Fire.

In singular contrast to the numerous collections which have been dispersed by war, the library of Trinity College, Dublin, originated in a victory won by an English army. In 1601, after the rebellion in Munster had been crushed, the conquerors at Kinsale subscribed the sum of £700 for the purchase of books to be presented to the college; and in 1603 James Ussher and Luke Challoner were sent to London to expend the money. While thus employed, they fell in with Thomas Bodley, engaged in a like errand on behalf of the Bodleian. By 1610, the original forty volumes in the library of Trinity College had been increased to 4000. Ussher's own library, after many adventures, including a veto by Cromwell on its sale abroad, and its ultimate purchase by the Parliamentary army in Ireland, also found its way to Trinity.

The library of the university of Edinburgh was enriched by a valuable gift from the poet, William Drummond of Hawthornden, who nobly observed in his preface to the catalogue, that, as good husbandmen plant trees for the future, so we, who have profited by antiquity, should do something to provide for posterity.

CHAPTER V

THE DRAMA TO 1642. PART I

I. THE ORIGINS OF ENGLISH DRAMA:
INTRODUCTORY

In the first pages of the present chapter we go back many years to consider the beginnings of English drama. Readers who have not ready access to original texts will find helpful illustrative matter in A. W. Pollard's *English Miracle Plays*, J. Q. Adams's *Chief Pre-Shakespearean Dramas* or A. C. Cawley's Everyman volume *Everyman and Medieval Miracle Plays*.

English drama is a growth entirely of its own kind. Attic drama was the choicest product of an age which was as brief as it was wonderful. Spanish drama, nearest to English in the exuberance of its productivity, is associated with the decay of the nation's vigour. French classical drama was bound by its relations to a royal court, and debarred from an intimate union with the national life. English drama grew with the development of the whole nation and attained its full stature when England had become decisively a power in the world. Nothing resembling drama, as ordinarily understood, can be shown to have existed as a form of Old English literature. Dialogue there may have been; but dialogue is not drama. Dialogue is the interchange of speeches. Drama means spiritual conflict (tragedy) or social complication (comedy). Stories in Old English are narrative, not dramatic. Whether plays were acted in Britain during the Roman occupation we do not know. The Teutonic invaders who came when the Romans left may have met some wandering mimes on the Continent, but otherwise their ignorance of the Roman theatre must have been complete. The Roman drama during the Empire had perished of realism. Instead of murder in jest, there was the ghastly reality of slaughter in the arena. The gladiator displaced the actor, who took to the roads and became a vagrant entertainer; but little real drama remained for any wandering histrion to carry about. Roscius, the great actor, flourished a century before the building of the Coliseum. The drama had to be born again; and, very strangely, it was born of the church—strangely, because from the time of Tertullian the church had been vigorous in denunciation of theatrical ways and deeds. There are few traces in England or elsewhere of such medieval classical imitations as the feeble and over-rated plays written in the tenth century by Hrotswitha or Roswitha, the Benedictine abbess of Gandersheim in Eastphalian Saxony, with Terence as the dramatic model and with fanatical exaltation of virginity as the morbid and monotonous subject. Monastic drama was not necessarily performed solely for the instruction of monks and nuns. Medieval monasteries were the centres of busy general life. After the Conquest we hear of dramatic performances by pupils—one at Dunstable about 1110; but the native drama did not find its beginning in such literary and scholastic exercises. For the main lines of development we must look to the histrionic efforts of the popular entertainers of crowds, to the communal festivals with their ancient ritual of dance and song, and to the liturgy of the church.

The medieval church was the church of the people in a sense hardly comprehensible by the modern world. The large unseated space of a cathedral was a centre of public life as well as of edification. Religion that penetrates the whole being can tolerate the kind of jesting that now seems irreverent. So the medieval church could permit the Feast of Fools, with its ass and mock-king, and the Feast of Boys, with its Boy Bishop, during the winter revels that stretched from the feast of St Nicholas (6 December), the saint of the boys, to the Holy Innocents and the Epiphany. How far these outbreaks of licence, with their burlesques of the sacred ritual, were dim memories of heathen winter ceremonies need not concern us. Their importance lies in this: that they involved impersonation and public performance, even though they were burlesques; that some features of the comic ritual (e.g. the riding of the ass) could be diverted, by the church's remarkable gift of adaptation, to more solemn uses; that, for the central ceremonies, the stage was the church fabric; and that for the processions the scene was enlarged to the church precincts, the adjacent market-place and the neighbouring streets. But, apart from such seasonal outbreaks, the sense of drama is felt in the whole liturgy. The Mass, being the daily re-enactment of a sacrifice, is in essence dramatic, especially at the Passion season, when the Gospel for the day on Palm Sunday and Good Friday becomes a kind of Passion Play. As far back as the tenth century, Aethelwold, Bishop of Winchester, in *Regularis Concordia...Monachorum*, the explanation or adaptation of the Benedictine Rule (p. 13), describes with minute "stage directions" how the intercalated trope of the Resurrection in one of the Easter morning services shall be performed. Four brethren, duly habited, were to dispose themselves, one as the Angel of the Sepulchre, the others as the Three Marys. The Angel was to say, *Quem quaeritis in sepulchro, O Christicolae?* (Whom seek ye in the sepulchre, O Christians?); the Marys were to reply, *Ihesum Nazarenum crucifixum, O caelicola* (Jesus of Nazareth the Crucified, O Heavenly one); and the Angel was to answer, *Non est hic; surrexit sicut praedixerat* (He is not here; He is risen as He foretold); and so on. Tropes were interpolations meant to supplement and enrich the plain order of service, and we first hear of *Quem quaeritis* at the great Benedictine Abbey of St Gallen in Switzerland as early as the ninth century. The tropes were chanted, not spoken. There were other tropes—of the Ascension and the Nativity, the latter feast lending itself readily to dramatic questions and answers at the *praesepe* or Crib, the institution of which, as a feature of the Christmas season, long antedates St Francis, to whom its invention is popularly attributed. *Quem quaeritis* was gradually expanded to include events before and after the visit to the Sepulchre; more characters were introduced, more space was needed, and the scene was extended from the Easter sepulchre at one altar to the whole church, then to the churchyard, and then to the adjacent market-place. Liturgical drama, acted by ecclesiastics, moved from the church into the streets and became sacred drama acted by the laity. The original chanted Latin was modified by the introduction of spoken passages in the vernacular and presently gave place to the native tongue interspersed with fragments of Latin.

The Shrewsbury School fragments show a combination of liturgical Latin with vernacular drama for performance in church (MS. 15th cent.). To the twelfth century (probably) belongs the famous Norman-French—perhaps Anglo-Norman—play of *Adam*, which survives incompletely, but which, as it now exists, contains several episodes with elaborate stage-directions for performance, and uses Latin for the semi-liturgical passages and French for the general action. Of course there were zealots who reprobated the dramatic method of appealing to the populace, and one oft-quoted passage declaring that it is forbidden "myraclis for to make or se" is found in *Handlyng Synne* (early fourteenth century) by Robert Mannyng. We may here remark that "miracles" became a general name for plays based on scriptural or sacred story; the somewhat later and more sophisticated "moralities" were didactic religious allegories of the kind beloved, as we have already noted, by the medieval mind. The term "mysteries", often used, is open to several objections: it was never applied in England to the miracle plays or morality plays in their own time; it was first used by later historians of English drama; it is a French, not an English term; and no one is quite sure what it meant exactly, even in French. The "morality", when extended to secular abstractions, became the "interlude".

The austerer clergy might deplore the dissemination of sacred story dramatically as a source of abuse and an opportunity for sin; but the development of the drama as a public institution received unexpected encouragement from the very Head of the Church. In 1264, the year of his death, Pope Urban IV instituted the festival of Corpus Christi in honour of the Blessed Sacrament, and the decree was made operative by Clement V in 1311. The new festival was to be celebrated by processions on the Thursday after Trinity Sunday. Now processions or "ridings", especially when enriched by "disguisings", i.e. the use of decorative or symbolical costume, appealed strongly to the medieval mind. Most happily had the date of the new festival been chosen. The Feast of Fools, the Feast of Boys, and all celebrations of the Nativity, sacred or profane, belonged to the inclement winter season. Even the Easter rejoicings fell in the fickle and often chilly spring. But Corpus Christi was assigned to the long days of summer; and from its processional pageantry developed the cycles of plays that give us our first native drama and remain among the happiest survivals of medieval literature in England.

The English plays were written to please as well as to edify. Those who find irreverence in their homely incidents and rough humours do not understand medieval religion or medieval art. The sincerity of deep feeling in the grief of Mary, shown in one of the *Ludus Coventriae* plays, is as unimpeachable as the touching simplicity of the Towneley shepherds' salutation to the infant Jesus, beginning "Haylle comly and clene". The linguistic problems raised by the various groups of plays are too technical for brief discussion, but any intelligent reader can appreciate the keen sketches of character and the great variety of the verse, which ranges from elaborate stanza forms to doggerel alexandrines, and includes some delightful examples of lyrical utterance. In short, these plays exhibit a combined looseness and ingenuity of versification in complete harmony with their freedom of treatment and sincerity of purpose.

A word of warning should be added. We have naturally given first place to religious drama, because something is known about it. But primitive secular drama may have existed, and the performance of liturgical tropes may have been imitated from popular dramatic activities of some kind. The church has always been ready to divert even heathen rites to its own purposes. All we are entitled to say is that there is clear surviving evidence for the existence of primitive religious drama and no surviving evidence for the existence of primitive secular drama. The line of development is not clear.

II. SECULAR INFLUENCES ON THE EARLY ENGLISH DRAMA: MINSTRELS, VILLAGE FESTIVALS, FOLK PLAYS

Nothing survives to show what secular entertainments resembling drama existed in Roman Britain or in Anglo-Saxon England. The literature of medieval Germany and France, however, can produce fragments that seem to imply the existence of primitive farces; and by the fourteenth century in England we have the *Interludium de Clerico et Puella*, a very elementary dramatization of the tale better told in *Dame Siriz*. The word "interludium" or interlude is ambiguous. It may mean something "played between" the parts of something else, like a musical intermezzo, and it may mean a piece "played between" performers, i.e. distributed dialogue instead of solo recitation. The term was applied to pieces which, unlike the moralities, employed secular characters for secular instruction or diversion; but no definition can be strictly applied, for the miracles themselves were sometimes spoken of as interludes. The name, indeed, was given to almost any kind of play. Thus the tragedy of *Pyramus and Thisbe* presented by Peter Quince and his Athenian amateurs in a hall of the Duke's palace was an interlude, and is expressly thus described.

The minstrels, the successors of the Northern bards or "scops", were the ordinary medieval entertainers. In France there grew up a distinction between the Norman *trouvères* who sang of war, and the Provençal *troubadours* who sang in the softer south their songs of love. The Norman Conquest brought into England not only reputable minstrels like Taillefer and Rahere, but entertainers of many kinds. Under this foreign invasion the English singer lost his repute and was forced to appeal to his despised fellow-countrymen. Thus a higher and lower class of entertainer existed side by side, the Norman *trouvère* and the English minstrel, the former maintaining the tradition of the artificial *estrifs* or *débats*—compositions in which two characters represent different points of view —and the latter appealing by various means to the general crowd. Naturally the common minstrels' patter was never written down. But in some obscure way they helped to keep alive the elementary notion of dramatic entertainment. By the fifteenth century—we do not know how or why—religious drama had passed from the church to the amateur performers of town or guild and the minstrels stood apart as professional actors or entertainers. As a means of self-preservation they formed a guild of their own. Further, they challenged the amateurs by becoming "interlude players" themselves; and while towns encouraged the amateurs, wealthy patrons found it easier to hire the professionals. The development of such troupes of "interlude players" into the regular dramatic companies, such as "my lord chamberlayne's menne" in the reign of Elizabeth, is a natural process.

A much more obscure influence on the drama is found in the "folk-play". From primitive rites of spring and winter, imploring or celebrating fertility in land and beast, developed symbolical performances showing the death and arising of some victim, animal or human. The maypole still recalls the dance round the sacred tree. Sword-dances are another remnant of old rites, with killing and restoring to life as a main incident, and with a tendency to develop into mummers' plays, of which St George (who, in Hanoverian times, becomes "King George") is the hero. But about all these matters there is more conjecture than certainty. Another instance of folk-festivals turned into plays and modified by the introduction of characters of later date is the development of the May game into the Robin Hood play. Perdita in *The Winter's Tale* refers to the "Whitsun pastorals". The "Whitsun pastoral" or "May game" was denounced by the clergy as early as the thirteenth century. In France, Robin and Marion were type names of the shepherd lover and his lass, and it has been suggested that the names passed into England and became appropriated to Robin-à-Wood or Robin Hood and Maid Marion. A fragment of a "play" of *Robin Hood and the Sheriff of Nottingham* dating from the sixteenth century is extant and has often been reprinted; but it is little more than a ballad in which different characters speak. A later play is specifically headed *Here beginnethe the play of Robyn Hoode, verye proper to be played in Maye games.* "Robin Hood", whoever he was—the question is discussed in Sir Edmund Chambers, *The Medieval Stage* (1903)—became a popular national hero of ballad as well as of elementary drama.

III. THE EARLY RELIGIOUS DRAMA: MIRACLE PLAYS
AND MORALITIES

The growth of the medieval religious drama pursued the same course in England as in the other Catholic countries of Europe. We have already mentioned the *Quem quaeritis*. Priests (we are told) had very laudably introduced this dramatic appeal "in order to fortify the unlearned in their faith". These words reveal to us the original purpose of Christian drama: it was to be a sort of living picture-book for those to whom the Latin of the liturgy was unintelligible.

The first Anglo-French dramatist known to us by name is Hilarius (fl. 1125) a pupil of Abelard, and probably an Englishman. Among his songs of worldly merriment and "goliardic" libertinism characteristic of the wandering scholars, we find three short religious dramas, one on the raising of Lazarus, one on the story of Daniel and one on a miracle of St Nicholas. The last contains some French interspersed among the Latin. Intrinsically the plays are of no great value. The important fact is that they exist at this date. William FitzStephen in his *Life of Thomas Becket* (c. 1180) mentions that London, instead of the *spectacula theatralia* acted in Rome, possesses other, holier, plays of saintly life. These plays, written no doubt by Norman ecclesiastics, were not likely to have been in English. But they have not survived and we therefore know nothing about them. The play of *Adam* and the play of the *Resurrection*, the oldest dramatic poems in the French language, have no connection with England beyond the conjectured fact of their composition here in the twelfth century. English makes its appearance in drama as inserted verses or as paraphrases of the Latin texts. It is sometimes claimed that the earliest pure English plays known to us are the *Isaac* (incomplete) and the *Jacob* now preserved as part of the Towneley Plays; but of this claim to priority there is no proof, though the pieces are certainly primitive in versification and general style. A poem on Christ's descent into hell (*The Harrowing of Hell*, dating from the thirteenth century), has often been called the earliest English play, but it is a dramatic poem or debate which the reciter could deliver with changes of voice for the characters. The growing development of the drama is attested by the inevitable clerical disapprobation. But in spite of warnings from orthodox preachers and denunciations by fanatical Wyclifites, the religious plays as a means of edification and amusement flourished with the development of town life. Resemblances between English and foreign plays indicate, not any mutual indebtedness, but a common source of inspiration. The community of religious thought and ideas in the whole of European society during the Middle Ages is something the reader must never forget. There was a "matter of Christendom" irrespective of national boundaries. In no country did the religious drama reach the greatest heights of poetical beauty; but in England it certainly achieved the charm of ingenuousness and the attraction of metrical variety. The authors sought, simply and sincerely, to touch the hearts of unlettered hearers; and it is quite in character that none of the writers are certainly known by name and that not a single miracle play was printed till later times. Naturally, the comic scenes show most originality, for in these there is nothing borrowed from any theological authors, and there is much that indicates the free movement of the popular mind within the large limits of accepted doctrine.

As already noted, the institution of the feast of Corpus Christi stimulated the development of popular religious drama. It became customary for the Corpus Christi processions to be composed of groups typifying the ecclesiastical conception of universal history from the day of creation to the day of judgment. The groups were composed by the different crafts, who competed in making their show as fine as possible. These group-shows passed easily from tableau to drama, and plays appropriate to the crafts were performed—the boat-builders (in the York series) undertaking the building of the Ark, and the goldsmiths the gifts of the Magi. In the Chester plays the temptation of Eve is naturally entrusted to the drapers. The actors stood on a stage ("pageant") which moved about on wheels, and stopped at certain stations. Every drama was divided into a series of little plays. As one pageant rolled away and another approached, the spectators were called to order by some vociferous person—Herod, for instance, armed with the great sword which slew the Innocents. The word "pageant" was sometimes applied to the pieces as well as to the structures. Corpus Christi plays are recorded at Beverley in 1377 and at York in 1378.

Of such processional plays, three almost complete cycles have been handed down to us, those of York, Wakefield and Chester. Besides these, we possess individual plays from the cycles of Coventry, Newcastle upon Tyne and Norwich, and another set alleged to belong to Coventry. Two fifteenth-century plays of Abraham and Isaac are also, probably, part of a cycle. Each cycle has distinguishing qualities and a pronounced character of its own. The York series, written in the fifteenth century, contains forty-eight complete single plays, and shows many original features in the representation of the Passion.

The Towneley Plays, so called because the unique manuscript came from Towneley Hall in Lancashire, evidently belong to the crafts of Wakefield, and they were performed, not on movable "pageants', but on fixed stages erected along the route of the procession. The thirty-two plays in this series are not of one style or of one period. Some represent earlier forms of plays in the present York cycle; some are undistinguished didactic pieces; some are plainly the work of one poet with marked individuality and strong humour, who, in writing the plays of Noah, of the First Shepherds, of the Second Shepherds, and of the Magi, has given us the most delightful examples of their kind.

The twenty-four plays in the Chester cycle were perhaps derived from French originals, and were Whitsuntide, not Corpus Christi, plays. Some of the scenes are religious in the more sober sense, though the traditionally humorous figures of Noah's wife and the Christmas shepherds are retained. Unlike the Towneley plays, the Chester cycle is entirely homogeneous and was probably the work of a single author, who may have been Ranulf Higden the chronicler.

With the *Ludus Coventriae* and Coventry Plays we meet a difficulty of nomenclature. A manuscript of 1468, which became the property of Sir Robert Cotton in 1630, is described in a later hand as *Ludus Coventriae sive Ludus Corporis Christi*; but the forty-two plays therein contained do not certainly belong either to Coventry or to Corpus Christi; and the confusion is increased by the fact that we possess two actual Corpus Christi plays of the Coventry crafts, the play of the Shearmen and Tailors and the play of the Weavers. The difficulty can be avoided by reserving the name "Coventry Plays" for the latter two and calling the larger set by the Latin title. The *Ludus Coventriae* is clearly later than the other cycles, and in its use of allegorical abstractions approximates to the morality plays. There is less humour, and more tendency to deal with later developments of doctrine and worship. The pageant of the Shearmen and Tailors in the pair of true Coventry plays shows an elaborate treatment of the Nativity, in skilful and varied verse, beginning with the Annunciation and ending with the flight to Egypt. It should be noted that the *Ludus Coventriae* plays are sometimes referred to as the "Hegge Plays", from the name of a former owner of the manuscript.

A Digby MS. (15th cent.) at Oxford contains three plays and a fragment, the subjects of the three being the Conversion of St Paul, St Mary Magdalene and the Massacre of the Innocents. They are quite separate compositions which have been copied into one manuscript and do not form a set. The verse is elaborate, and the style is that of the later moralities. Other individual plays, such as the Croxton play of the Sacrament and the Brome play of Abraham and Isaac must be left undiscussed. The first is crude, the second excellent. Some very interesting plays in Cornish (fourteenth to sixteenth century), performed on "rounds" in the peninsula, belong to England, but hardly to English literature. The curious may read them in translations.

In the later Middle Ages there grew up another kind of dramatic poetry in which the characters were personified types of virtue or vice or worldliness. This kind of play is partly an independent growth and partly a development of the didactic side of the miracle plays. They are usually termed morality plays—the name "morality", so applied, is at least as old as the beginning of the sixteenth century. From about the middle of the fifteenth century date three famous moral plays known as the Macro Plays from a former owner of the manuscript. In one of these, *Mankynde* (*c.* 1473), the typical man is assailed by Nought, New-gyse and Now-a-days with their minstrels, and is saved by Mercy. The second, called by some *Wisdom* and by others *Mind, Will and Understanding* (*c.* 1460), shows us Anima and her Five Wyttes, with the three "Christian powers" of the title betrayed by Lucyfer and saved by Wysdome. In the third, *The Castle of Perseverance* (*c.* 1425), the earliest surviving example of its kind, it is "Humanum Genus" who is fought for by his Good Angel with attendant Virtues, and his Bad Angel with attendant Vices. *The Pride of Life* (MS. imperfect) may be earlier still. Each play has its own elaborate stanza form. The most famous of all the moralities is the now well-known *Everyman* belonging to the end of the fifteenth century. One significant fact may be observed. In following the progress of religious folk-drama, with its happy air of improvization, towards the drama of moral contest, with its more formal argument, we gradually pass from anonymity to known authorship, and, the time being fortunate, from manuscript to print.

The moralities tended to become less allegorical and more realistic and historical. In the interlude *Nature* (printed 1530–4), by Henry Medwall (fl. 1486), Sensuality drives away Reason from Man, to whom however he is reconciled by Age. In the anonymous *propre newe Interlude of the worlde and the chylde, otherwyse called Mundus and Infans* (printed 1522) Man leads a dissolute life and does not come to himself until, old and broken, he is released from Newgate, where he "laye under lockes". Similar in character are *Youth* (printed 1530–5) and *Hycke Scorner* (printed 1515–16), in the latter of which Hycke Scorner and Imagynacyon (who had been shackled together in Newgate) come to repentance through Pytie and Contemplacyon. All these are written in stanza form. *Magnyfycence, A goodly interlude and a mery, Devysed and made by Mayster Skelton, Poet Laureate* (printed 1530?) is in rhymed couplets. Skelton and Medwall are the earliest writers of English plays whose names have been preserved. Appealing as are some passages of the miracle plays, their general inferiority to the newer morality plays, with their more significant art and their greater freedom of invention, can hardly be denied. But miracles fell, in the end, before the spirit of the age. Religion became a matter of high politics. With the triumph of anti-Romanism and the growth of militant Puritanism the days of the popular religious drama were done. England had ceased to be merry. Cant, which had no place in medieval religion, became one of the new "notes of the Church". The pious chansons of Geneva drowned the wood-notes wild of "Haylle, comly and clene", and these were never heard on the stage again.

The miracles went under; the moralities survived, and dealt with their old subject, man as an object of contention between the good and the bad qualities of the soul. Such was the theme of *Like wil to like quod the Devel to the Colier* by the schoolmaster Ulpian Fulwell (printed 1568). But the most remarkable of such plays is *A new interlude and a mery of the nature of the iiij elements* (printed 1526?) by John Rastell (d. 1536), printer, and husband of Sir Thomas More's sister. This finds new dramatic themes in astronomy and geography. Similarly in the "comedie" *All for Money* by Thomas Lupton (printed 1578) the value of scientific adventure is dwelt upon, and the unjust distribution of wealth and the poverty of scholars are symbolized in some of the strangest of allegorical creations. One personage from the miracle plays still lingered on the stage, a combination of clown and devil, called Tutivill (the name has several forms), who came to be known as the "Vice"; and he with his dagger of lath made all the mischief he could. It is curious that nearly all plays which introduce a devil make him a semi-comic person.

Two other early dramatists known to us by name are John Bale and Sir David Lyndsay. Bale (1495–1563) was a zealous Protestant theologian who wrote many plays of which few have survived. His *Comedy concernynge thre laws, of nature, Moses and Christ* (1548) is in the vein of the old moralities. A far more lively moral picture is unrolled by the Scottish statesman and author David Lyndsay in *Ane Pleasant Satyre of the Thre Estaitis*, already discussed. But interludes opposed to church teaching as fixed by the sovereign were now forbidden. Bale fled from England, declaring that plays which told the truth were no longer allowed. Under Edward VI, R. Wever's *Lusty Juventus* (printed 1565) makes the virtues quote St Paul while the devil swears "by the Mass" and "by the Virgin". Under Mary, *a merye enterlude entitled Respublica* (acted 1553) denounces those who have enriched themselves with church property. But the Elizabethans were to have the last word.

Criticism and history of the early drama must of course be based upon the material we possess. There is no clear line of descent. That the existing plays represent the whole dramatic efforts of two centuries cannot be supposed; but in the miracles, moralities and interludes that have happened to survive we clearly discern a vigour, a humour, a beauty of feeling, a deep sincerity and a stubborn national personality all promising well for the drama to come.

IV. EARLY ENGLISH TRAGEDY

Three stages may be marked in the history of Renascence tragedy: (1) imitations of Seneca; (2) translations; and (3) imitations of Greek and Latin plays. Three further subdivisions may be noted: (1) the treatment of secular subjects in the style of the familiar sacred plays; (2) the close imitation of classical models; and (3) the blending of those two modes into a form of tragedy at once artistic and popular.

The extraordinary influence of Seneca, who was a "closet" dramatist, not a theatre dramatist, is a fact which we must accept and need not discuss. Italy was naturally the home of Senecan drama, and its development there is most interesting, though to us, at the moment, irrelevant. Early French tragedy developed features of the Senecan model which were alien to English taste and tradition, especially the elaboration and extension of the choral lyrics. Our own earliest tragedies are both Senecan and English. Richard Edwards's *Damon and Pithias* (probably acted 1564), John Pickeryng's *Horestes* (printed 1567), R. B.'s *Apius and Virginia* (printed 1575) and Thomas Preston's *Cambises* (licensed 1569–70) approximate to the Senecan model, but have nothing classical about them except the names. The first makes an attempt to copy Seneca's *stichomythia* (i.e. dialogue of alternating lines), and the last mentions Seneca in the prologue; but in their action they are as realistic as later melodramas, and endeavour to present visibly hangings and stabbings and flayings. Our early playwrights accepted the bloody traditions of the miracle plays and handed on to the theatres a physical realism which was evidently in accord with popular taste. *Horestes* combines history with morals, the prompter of evil being the "Vice". In Bale's *King Johan* (c. 1538) the morality draws its themes from history, Sedition becoming Stephen Langton and Usurped Power becoming the Pope. There are other allegorical abstractions to remind us that we are still in the realm of the morality play. This historical-morality is the kind of development that we should expect.

The reader must appreciate the crude effects, the abstract morality and the skimble-skamble verse of these early efforts at tragedy before he can begin to understand the apparently excessive praise bestowed by Sidney and others upon *Gorboduc*, written by Thomas Norton (1532–84) and Thomas Sackville, and acted before Queen Elizabeth at the Inner Temple in 1562. To us it seems lifeless; to its time it seemed a revelation. Its imitation of Seneca's form and style is obvious; yet it shows independence, not only in the choice of a native theme, but in the strong individuality of treatment. The old miracles and moralities were democratic plays; *Gorboduc* is aristocratic. There is almost no action or agitation. It is noble, austere, remote and high-spoken. The blank verse may sound mechanical, but it is dignity itself after the doggerel of its contemporaries. The story comes from Geoffrey of Monmouth and the *Mirror for Magistrates* (see p. 121), and the play was published as *Ferrex and Porrex*, the two brothers whose strife is the theme of the tragedy. The latter part of the play shows the hand of Sackville and there touches its greatest height. Nothing finer had appeared on the English stage. In Italy it had been the practice to enliven stage performances with spectacles between the acts. Our authors follow the Italian custom, but use their allegorical dumb-shows with marked originality. Further, they disregarded the precepts and practice of the Italian followers of Aristotle which insisted on the unities of time and place, and so gave to English tragedy from the beginning that liberty of action which was to be one of its greatest glories.

When the members of Gray's Inn presented a comedy and a tragedy in 1566 they took *Gorboduc* as their model for the latter. *Jocasta* is written in blank verse, which *Gorboduc* had introduced to the English stage, and its composition was divided between George Gascoigne and Francis Kinwelmersh, the former contributing the major part. The full title reads: *Jocasta: A Tragedie written in Greeke by Euripides, translated and digested into Acte by George Gascoygne and*

Francis Kinwelmershe of Grayes Inne, and there by them presented, 1566. The translation was not made from Euripides, but from an Italian adaptation. *Jocasta* can hardly have encouraged the development of English tragedy, as it was the translation of an imitation, and in no sense an original work.

Neither *Gorboduc* nor *Jocasta* had shown genuine romantic passion, and it seemed, therefore, as if there were a real opportunity for development when *Gismond of Salerne* was presented in 1567–8 by "the worshipful company of the Inner Temple Gentlemen". In the printed form it is called *Tancred and Gismund*. The story is dramatized directly from Boccaccio; but the several authors, the chief Robert Wilmot, were either too timid or too incompetent to handle the terrible theme, and almost any story would have been ruined by the persistent Senecan *stichomythia* emphasized by the alternately rhyming lines; for the blank verse of *Gorboduc* and *Jocasta* had been unwisely abandoned. However, in spite of all its faults, *Gismond of Salerne* boldly attempts a new theme, and does, in some measure, set human passion on the stage.

In 1588 a very full entertainment of "devises and shewes" was set before Queen Elizabeth at Greenwich "by the Gentlemen of Grayes Inne". After an elaborately allegorical introduction, with lengthy speeches, came the play itself, called *The misfortunes of Arthur (Uther Pendragons Sonne) reduced into Tragicall notes by Thomas Hughes one of the societie of Grayes Inn*. There are five acts, each with its preliminary dumb show, and the whole concludes with an Epilogue, which at least proves that the great verse instrument of English drama was being shaped and polished. The matter of the play is drawn from Geoffrey of Monmouth, the manner from Seneca's *Thyestes*.

These academic plays acted by gentlemen of the Inns of Court did something for the drama. They set a standard of lofty effort and they established blank verse as the medium. Let us now consider the players of "common Interludes in the Englishe tongue" who were continually harried by the London civic authorities, and alternately repressed and encouraged by the Queen. The organization of strolling players and noblemen's servants into regular companies, together with the building of the first theatres, gave the drama the standing of a profession, and attracted to it the "university wits", who were soon to raise it to the dignity of an art. Seneca was still the standard, and two dates are therefore important, 1581 when separately translated plays of Seneca were collected and published as his *Tenne Tragedies*, and 1589 when Greene's novel *Menaphon* appeared with a slashing preface by Thomas Nashe, from which we gather two facts, first that the university "gentlemen" were contemptuous of meaner playwrights who relied upon Seneca in English, and next that by 1589 there appeared to exist a *Hamlet* with tragical speeches in the Senecan style. It seems probable that the person specially attacked by Nashe is Kyd. Kyd, Marlowe and Marston, though not wanting in Latin, certainly borrowed from Seneca without acknowledgment. Elizabethan tragedy adopted not only Seneca's five acts, and occasionally his choruses, his stock characters and his philosophical commonplaces, but his exaggerated passions, his crude horrors and his exuberant rhetoric.

Fortunately the wave of patriotic feeling culminating in the triumph over the Armada inspired some of the chroniclers, and these, in their turn, gave our playwrights a store of national themes to draw upon. Thomas Legge's *Richardus Tertius* (between 1570–80) is a Senecan treatment of comparatively recent English history; but *The Famous Victories of Henry the fifth* (acted before 1588) departs from the Senecan manner; and *The Troublesome Raigne of John* (printed 1591), perhaps the best example of plain chronicle-history in drama, has nothing classical about it. Both are "popular" plays; and the latter, which gave Shakespeare not merely a plot and a character (Fawkonbridge) but a national note, directly exhorts Englishmen to listen to an English theme—they having heard "Scythian Tamburlaine".

The True Chronicle History of King Leir, and his three daughters, Gonorill, Ragan and Cordella (probably acted 1594) has an interest of its own apart from Shakespeare's use of it. It is well contrived and free from the tedious "sentiments" of "English Seneca" and the extravagant rhetoric brought into vogue by *Tamburlaine. The Lamentable Tragedie of Locrine...Newly set foorth, overseene and corrected, By W. S.* (1595) and *The First part of the Tragicall raigne of Selimus* (1594) have aroused much discussion of authorship, which we need not here augment. There appears to be some connection between the plays, as a few passages, slightly varied, are common to both. Both show the characteristic signs of Senecan-Italian influence.

After the establishment of public theatres, writers of tragedies and chronicles tended to appeal to popular audiences and to disregard the classical authorities dear to the gentlemen of the universities and the Inns of Court. English tragedy moved away from the frozen dignity of *Gorboduc* towards the warm humanity of the best old miracle plays. Nevertheless, from the Senecan models it derived not only its persistent defects of sensational horror and insistent declamation, but some recognition of the necessity for dignity of person, loftiness of utterance, and real, though not mechanical, unity and coherence.

V. EARLY ENGLISH COMEDY

One feature of medieval literature is its anonymity. The passing of the medieval spirit is marked by the disappearance of impersonality and the appearance of declared authorship. Plays began to be printed with the writers' names, and among the earliest of these are some of John Heywood's interludes. John Heywood (1497?–1587) was in the service of Henry VIII as a musician. He belonged by marriage to the circle of Sir Thomas More, and his own daughter became the mother of John Donne. In his combination of steadfast orthodoxy with exuberant gaiety and zeal for reform Heywood resembled the author of *Utopia*. The new era following the death of Queen Mary drove him from England, and he died abroad. Thus, although Heywood lived to the eve of the Armada, his extant plays date from the reign of Henry VIII, and three of these were printed as early as 1533. He belongs in spirit to the period of the morality plays; nevertheless his distinctive achievement is that he dispenses with vague allegory and gives a realistic representation of contemporary citizen types. His "new and very mery enterludes" therefore bring us far on the road towards fully developed comedy. Of the pieces definitely attributed to him, three form an allied group: *A Dialogue concerning Witty and Witless* (first printed 1846), *The Play of the wether* (1533) and *A play of love* (1534). They are dialogues or debates discussing a set theme, and their method is forensic rather than dramatic. In the first, characters dispute whether it is better to be witty or witless; in the last, two pairs of characters debate about love. In the second, the personages number ten; but they still discuss an abstract theme, namely, weather-control. *The Playe called the foure P P* is later and was printed probably in 1544. A dispute between Palmer, Pardoner, and Potycary about the value of their respective occupations is referred to an Autolycus-like Pedler, and a contest of mendacity ensues, the winning lie being that of the Palmer who declares:

> I never sawe nor knewe in my consyens
> Any one woman out of paciens.

Two other pieces attributed to Heywood show a definite dramatic advance: *A mery Play betwene the pardoner and the frere, the curate and neybour Pratte* (1533) and *A mery play betwene Johan Johan the husbande, Tyb his wyfe, and syr Jhann the preest* (1533). In the first a dispute between the pardoner and the frere reaches the extreme of physical violence, and the curate and neybour Pratte intervene. We are in the atmosphere of Chaucer, but drama has replaced narrative. Much the same may be said of the second play (probably from the French) in which a duped husband, a lickerish priest and a complaisant wife provide the situations. Both are successful farces, which have left mere dialogue far behind. It can justly be claimed that a stronger hand is to be found in the three plays last named than in the earlier dialogues; More himself may have collaborated in them. That More had a natural gift for drama is thought worthy of notice by his first biographer, William Roper.

A still nearer approach to true comedy was made by *A new commodye in englysh in maner of an enterlude etc.* generally known from its chief characters as *Calisto and Melebea* (printed c. 1530) and sometimes called *Beauty of Women*. It was adapted from *Celestina*, the celebrated Spanish work which took Spain and Europe by storm in spite of its prolixity. The unknown English author has definite dramatic power, and narrowly missed giving English drama its first romantic love-tragedy. But the medieval passion for pointing a moral overcame him and ruined the end of his piece.

But the most interesting of all early plays in the "mixed" manner is one which, in a sense, is both the earliest and the latest, namely *a godely interlude of Fulgens Cenatoure of Rome and Lucres his doughter* by Henry Medwall, chaplain to Cardinal Morton and author of *Nature*, for it was probably acted in 1497, printed 1512–16, and was lost (save in a fragment) until 1919. It is clear that More, Rastell, Heywood and Medwall were in close association, and the dramatic works of the last three were probably influenced by the first. *Fulgens and Lucrece* achieves the success which *Calisto and Melebea* missed. The story has human interest and the characters are credible figures, not mere abstractions. Its greatest success is achieved in the "comic relief", which shows genuine invention. *Fulgens and Lucrece* is the first secular comedy known in our literature. All the comedies so far named use rhymed verse of sorts, the famous old rhyme royal stanza being ingeniously adapted to dialogue in *Fulgens* and in *Calisto*. Heywood rhymes with greater variety. The blank verse which makes a noble appearance in *Gorboduc* is unknown to the early comedies.

The classical revival on the Continent began to influence the English stage early in the sixteenth century. Naturally, the first performances of classical plays and adaptations took place in schools and other seats of learning. Special interest attaches to the appearance of the boys of "the Gramarskolle of West-minster" in 1569 before Queen Elizabeth in plays of Terence, for the Latin play at Westminster was to become a permanent institution. There were still earlier school performances at Eton and St Paul's—at the latter in 1527. But it was at Oxford and Cambridge that the humanist drama attained its full develop-ment, and in some colleges "compulsory drama" was enjoined by the statutes.

The earliest extant memorial in English of the revived study of Roman comedy is a translation of the *Andria*, entitled *Terens in Englysh*, printed by John Rastell about 1520; but the bold step of writing an entirely English comedy on classical models was taken by Nicholas Udall (1505–56). Udall was a Win-chester and Oxford man who became an exponent of Lutheran views, but found himself able to conform under Queen Mary. In 1533 he published *Floures for Latine spekynge selected and gathered out of Terence*—phrases from the plays with their equivalents in English. He was headmaster of Eton from 1534 to 1541, but lost his post for misconduct. A letter of 1554 shows that he exhibited "Dialogues and Enterludes" before the Queen, perhaps performed by West-minster boys, for he was headmaster there from 1554 to 1556. Udall was evidently a man of versatile powers, but unfortunately he survives mainly in mere records and allusions. The sole work which remains to illustrate his dramatic gift is *Ralph Roister Doister*, perhaps performed in 1553 or 1554 by Westminster boys. In imitation of Plautus and Terence, Udall substituted for the loosely knit structure of the English morality or debate an organic plot divided into acts and scenes. Within this framework, he adjusted figures borrowed from Roman comedy, but transformed to suit English conditions, and mingled with others of purely native origin. *Ralph Roister Doister* has genuine life as an English comedy, and does not live merely historically. *Gammer Gurton's Needle*, another academic comedy, by an unknown writer, is discussed later.

Yet another adaptation from Plautus is *A new Enterlued for Chyldren to playe, named Jacke Jugeler*, entered for printing in 1562–3, but written, very probably, during the reign of Mary. Jack Juggler, the "Vice", assumes the identity of Jenkin Careaway and makes that hapless lackey believe in the loss of his own personality. In spite of its classical origin, *Jack Juggler* is little more than a briskly written farcical episode. It appears to embody an attack on the doctrine of transubstantiation, and must be the only case of the "confusion of identity" common in farce translated into the service of controversial theology.

But Tudor writers found inspiration in the work of contemporary Conti-nental humanists as well as in works of the classical period. The *Thersites* in Latin hexameters by the Frenchman whose name is Latinized as Ravisius Textor was adapted into a very free English version acted in 1537. The medley of English metres and the comic allusions to English traditional heroes, including "Robin John and Little Hode", helped to give the adaptation a convincing native air. With another of Textor's Latin dialogues, *Juvenis, Pater, Uxor*, we reach a theme which had a considerable run of popularity—the Prodigal Son. One fragmentary version has been called *The Prodigal Son* (1530); another, by Thomas Ingelend, is called *The Disobedient Child* (c. 1570). A writer who cannot be identified with certainty wrote, probably about 1560, a play, *Misogonus*, which enables us to claim for England the credit of having produced one of the most elaborate and original comedies on this theme. *The Historie of Jacob and Esau*, licensed for printing in 1557, but extant only in an edition of 1568, may be grouped with the "prodigal son" plays, though it varies from the standard type in its use of song and the by-play of servants. With Gascoigne's *The Glasse of Government* (1575), we return to the more orthodox type of prodigal son play. But the author adds a complication by doubling the principal characters. Two fathers are introduced, each with a pair of sons—the younger a model of virtue and the elder a scapegrace. The harshly Calvinistic spirit of *The Glass of Government* makes it a Puritan tract in the disguise of a humanist play. Gascoigne had already made a new contribution to English drama by giving us the first native form of an Italian comedy of intrigue. His *Supposes*, acted at Gray's Inn in 1566, is a version of Ariosto's *Gli Suppositi*, which, written first in prose and afterwards rewritten in verse, was first performed in 1509. It is one of the earliest regular comedies in a European vernacular. Gascoigne appears to have utilized both the prose and the verse editions; but his translation is entirely in prose, the use of which for dramatic purposes makes *Supposes*, translation though it be, a landmark in the history of English comedy. The dialogue has a polish and lucidity which anticipate the kindred qualities of Lyly's dramatic prose. Its enduring reputation is attested by its adaptation about 1590, with considerable changes, and in verse form, as the underplot of the anonymous *Taming of a Shrew* (not to be confused with Shakespeare's). Another English version of an Italian comedy is *The Bugbears* (ptd. 1897), an adaptation of *La Spiritata* by the Florentine A. F. Grazzini; but this is in verse. Other Italianate plays are recorded, but have not survived. The early Elizabethan *Tom Tyler and his Wife* (date unknown) is a good example of farcical comedy in verse; but a comparison between it and *The Taming of a Shrew* will show how much English comedy had gained from foreign models, both in structure and in diction.

The fusion of classical with native elements appears very clearly in Richard Edwards's *Damon and Pithias*, a "tragical comedy", already referred to (see p. 202). Though originating in Latin drama this is a thoroughly English play. George Whetstone's *Promos and Cassandra*, printed in 1578, is another tragicomedy belonging to the line of *Damon and Pithias*. It is based on one of the tales in Cinthio's *Hecatommithi*, though the names of the leading figures are changed, as they were to be changed yet again by Shakespeare, when, in his *Measure for Measure*, founded on Whetstone's play, he gave to the story its final form. With its sustained level of workmanlike though uninspired alexandrines and decasyllabic lines, including some passages of blank verse, *Promos and Cassandra* is a good example of romantic drama as written before the period of Shakespeare's immediate predecessors. Both Edwards and Whetstone wrote prefaces expounding their theory of the function of comedy, insisting that comedy must be true to its own life. The principle is vital. What the writers of comedy had yet to learn was the artistic use of prose as a form of expression —that comedy without style loses half its charm. John Lyly first clearly divined that secret and taught comedy to speak in its proper language. To him we now pass.

VI. THE PLAYS OF THE UNIVERSITY WITS

During the sixteenth century, the drama, now settled into a regular entertainment, seemed at first to be developing along two divergent lines, which we may loosely describe as courtly drama acted by young gallants and choir children in halls and noble houses, and popular drama acted by common players of interludes in the yards of inns and later at The Theater, the first London playhouse, erected in 1576. The literary men from Oxford and Cambridge took the drama as their special province. They drew a sharp distinction between the civilized theatre of the Court and the common playhouse of the vulgar; and, claiming the first for themselves, denounced "the alcumists of eloquence, who (mounted on the stage of arrogance) think to outbrave better pens with the swelling bumbast of a bragging blanke verse", and commit "the digestion of their cholerick incumbrances to the spacious volubilitie of a drumming decasillabon". It is Marlowe, university man though he was, who may be meant, for had not the drumming decasillabons of *Tamburlaine* caught the ears of the playhouse groundlings? These quotations from the arrogant essay of Thomas Nashe prefacing Robert Greene's *Menaphon* have a curiously familiar ring. Nashe does not actually use the modern phrase about reading this or that "in the original", but he expresses contempt for the meaner sort "that never ware gowne in the Universitie", and leaves "to the mercie of their mother tongue (those) that feed on nought but the crummes that fal from the translators trencher". Kyd is perhaps the man here intended. Antagonism was fiercer then than now because the world of letters was smaller and the competition keener.

The leader of the university group was John Lyly (1544–1606), of Oxford and Cambridge, whose receptive mind was hospitable to the more delicate graces of literature. That his material was usually some slight theme suggested by stories of the classical deities may be gathered from the titles of his plays— *A most excellent comedie of Alexander, Campaspe and Diogenes* (1584), *Sapho and Phao* (1584), *Endimion the Man in the Moone* (1591), *Gallathea* (1592), *Midas* (1592), *Mother Bombie* (1594), *The Woman in the Moone* (1597), and *Loves Metamorphosis* (1601). Most of these are described as being "played before the Queenes Majestie" by the "Children". The dates given are dates of printing. Lyly found models for style and matter in Sir Thomas North's *The Diall of ~~nces~~* (1557) and in George Pettie's *The Petite Pallace of Pettie his Pleasure* (1576). ~~theless~~ his sentences, elaborately, artificially framed, are his own, and ~~ark~~ of a genuine literary personality. Lyly's immaterial view of love ~~d~~ his interest in "behaviour" shows the influence of *Il Cortegiano* ~~ascence~~ discussions of courtly conduct. His supposed allegorizing ~~litics~~ is not original, for that was the method of the later moralities. ~~urse~~, is he original in his free use of the lyric as an incident in drama.

The boy actors were also singers; and there is always the possibility that the songs in any play are insertions and not original poems. What, then, was Lyly's personal contribution to English drama? The first is the establishment of prose as the right medium of expression for comedy. To pass from the doggerel of the early popular comedies to the conversation between Apelles and Campaspe is to pass into a new world of expression. Lyly's next contribution is the establishment of high comedy as a form of drama tolerable to people of breeding and cultivation. In true comedy the main substance is neither the intensity of consuming passion nor the laxity of unrestrained coarseness, but a social complication that may be serious or amusing. High comedy demands a nice sense of phrase; and Lyly was the first master of prose style in English comedy. He was essentially a court dramatist, and added to drama the feminine qualities of delicacy, grace, charm and subtlety. The English drama was masculine already to the point of swaggering. Lyly refined it and took it out of the alehouse into the presence-chamber.

George Peele (1558–97) was at Oxford for several years. His plays, with dates of first publication, are *The Araygnement of Paris: A Pastorall* (1584), *The Famous Chronicle of king Edward the first* (1593), *The Battell of Alcazar* (1594), *The Old Wives Tale* (1595), and *The Love of King David and Faire Bethsabe* (1599). His hand is probably to be found in other works, and he has been credited with a share in such Shakespeareana as *Locrine* and *Henry VI*; but these attributions are not established. Though Peele's dramatic career was very short, his work shows great variety. Whether he wrote by chance upon any subject or whether he was deliberately experimenting must remain a matter for speculation. The obvious facts are that *The Arraignment of Paris* is a pastoral-masque, *Edward I* a chronicle-history flavoured with romance, *King David and Fair Bethsabe* a modernized miracle play, and *The Old Wives Tale* a satirical drama with romance not far away. The last named is the best known of Peele's plays. The title is really *The Old Wife's Tale*, for the play is a story by an "old wife" to three wanderers in the forest. The incidents of the tale enact themselves visibly, and prove to be a foretaste of *Comus*. The absurdities and impossibilities of romantic drama are pleasingly parodied, and the play is thus a predecessor of *The Knight of the Burning Pestle*. There is also a "privye nippe" at the English-hexameter fanatics like Stanyhurst, in such lines as:

> Phylyda phylerydos, Pamphylyda florida flortos,
> Dub dub a dub, bounce quoth the guns, with a sulpherous huffe snuffe.

The Old Wife's Tale is the first English play to embody literary criticism in its jests. Though much of Peele's work is untidily disposed and carelessly executed, he had a clear vision of literature as an art: *primus verborum artifex*, Thomas Nashe called him. His feeling for the musical value of words can hardly be missed by the careful reader.

Robert Greene (1558–92) was a member of both universities. He seems to have travelled widely and he probably knew at first hand the Italian authors to whom his work is most indebted. He was one of those not uncommon Englishmen who fly between the extremes of Bohemian licence and Puritan idealism. That his life offers several problems, attractive to investigators, shoul be clear from the discussion of his pamphlets in an earlier chapter (see p. 136). It is generally agreed that the order of his surviving plays is this: *The Comicall Historie of Alphonsus King of Aragon* (printed 1599), *A Looking Glasse for London and England* (with Thomas Lodge, printed 1594), *The Historie of Orlando Furioso* (printed 1594), *The Honorable Historie of frier Bacon and frier Bongay* (printed 1594), and *The Scottish Historie of James the fourth* (printed 1598). *Alphonsus* is merely imitation of Marlowe, especially of *Tamburlaine*. *James IV* is not, as its title suggests, a chronicle play, but the dramatization of a tale from Cinthio's *Hecatommithi* and introduces Oberon, King of the Fairies, whom another was to borrow. In *Friar Bacon* Greene develops the mere hint of an old romance into the idyllic incidents of Margaret of Fressingfield, Lacy and the King. *Orlando Furioso* comes from Ariosto, but is far away from its original. Probably only a portion of Greene's dramatic work survives. To him has been attributed some share in such famous plays as *Selimus*, *The Troublesome Raigne of John*, *The First Part of the Contention betwixt the Houses of Yorke and Lancaster*, and *The True Tragedie of Richard Duke of Yorke* (i.e. *Henry VI*, Parts II and III); but these attributions cannot be proved; on the other hand there are reasons for believing that he wrote *George a Greene, the Pinner of Wakefield* (ptd. 1599) and that it is one of his latest plays. Unlike Peele, Greene was no haphazard dramatic story-teller. Lyly prepared the way for high comedy by his dialogue, his artificial characters and his feeling for style; Greene carried the path further into the region of complicated plot, verisimilitude and simple human feeling.

Thomas Lodge (1558–1625) was educated at Oxford. He began his playwriting as early as 1582, and his novel-writing as early as 1584 with *The Delectable Historie of Forbonius and Prisceria*. *Rosalynde, Euphues golden legacie*, appeared in 1590, and *Scillaes Metamorphosis*, a book of verse in 1589. Lodge was a facile writer; and in quick succession came his two plays, *The Wounds of Civill War* (1594) and *A Looking Glasse for London and Englande* (1594), his book of verse, *A Fig for Momus* (1595), and his romantic story, *A Margarite of America* (1596). Apparently he wrote no more, though he lived for another thirty years. He became a Catholic, and settled down to the life of a physician. Of his plays only two survive. *The Wounds of Civil War*, which is a *Titus Andronicus* with all the thrills and horrors left out, is evidently the work of a man neither by instinct nor by practice a dramatist. It affords no clue as to his share in *A Looking Glass for London* which he wrote with Greene. Lodge added nothing to the development of the English drama.

Thomas Nashe (1567–1601) has already been mentioned in preceding pages as pamphleteer and story writer. Apparently he went into drama as one determined to leave no form untried. He contributed some unassignable part to —ve's *Dido Queene of Carthage*, and to a lost play called *The Isle of Dogs* which got him into trouble. *Summers Last Will and Testament*, acted in —le opportunity to judge Nashe's real dramatic quality. The title —eason, but to the celebrated jester, Will Summers or Sommers. —at his best one must read his pamphlets and *The Unfortunate*

—ur five "university wits" certainly helped the development of the drama; but not a single play by any of them has genuine life for the stage of to-day. Like others of the same kind they were more successful in proclaiming their superiority than in proving it. The apparently diverging streams of literary drama and popular drama were to be drawn together in one mighty flood by the genius of writers whom we are next to consider, Marlowe, a daring scholar from Cambridge, who did not disdain the public, and Shakespeare, a new poet from the provinces, who took the popular drama as he found it, and gave it back to the world transfigured.

VII. MARLOWE AND KYD

Whether *The Spanish Tragedy* is earlier than *Tamburlaine*, as some suppose, does not greatly matter; for, historically, Kyd and Marlowe are not easily separable; they both attained great popularity at the same time and both fell together.

The sentimentalists can no longer make a pathetic story out of Christopher Marlowe's life (1564–93). Additions to our knowledge have left us few illusions. Marlowe, son of a Canterbury shoemaker, passed from the King's School in his native city to Cambridge, where he absorbed the music and the legends of Latin poetry and indulged in some unusual reading and speculation. Though he lived as wildly as Greene and Nashe, he was never one of their fellowship. He was, in fact, a "university wit" who had made himself common, and appears to be pointed at with Nashe's finger of scorn. The facts about his life and works are as obscure as the circumstances of his death. He had become notorious for "atheism", and he was fatally stabbed in a Deptford tavern at the end of a long day spent with three men of very dubious repute. Some time before, Kyd had been arrested for "mutinous sedition", but was released after Marlowe's death, having shown that heretical papers found in his room belonged to Marlowe, whom he accused of blasphemy. There is no profit in speculating on what was behind Marlowe's death. He had lived dangerously and was such a man as could have written his plays. (The most reliable biography is *The Tragicall History of Christopher Marlowe*, 1942, by the American scholar John Bakeless). His literary life begins with an undated translation of Ovid's *Amores*, called *Elegies* by the publishers. This has more merits than it is usually allowed. Like Shakespeare, Marlowe set forth on his way as a poet of classical amorism, but, unlike Shakespeare, he did not immediately find his natural magic and music. Marlowe's first original work was *Tamburlaine the Great*, in two parts, played in 1587 or 1588 and printed anonymously in 1590. The grandeur of the style, the powerful acting of Alleyn and the superiority of the piece to the plays which had so far held the popular stage gave *Tamburlaine* great popularity. Yet, save in one obscure and hostile allusion by Greene, the author is nowhere named. Even Heywood, who mentions both Marlowe and *Tamburlaine* in his *Apology for Actors*, does not clearly associate them. The dramatic excesses of the play were disliked by some, but, of course, the real offence was that Marlowe succeeded. Like Swinburne he carried the young men away by the irresistible force of style. *The Tragicall History of D. Faustus*, of which the first known edition is quarto of 1604, is assumed to be his next play and is dated *c.* 1588; but there is good reason for refusing it a date earlier than 1592. *Faustus*, however, is not so complete a thing as *Tamburlaine*. The comic scenes are almost abjectly bad, and prove either that Marlowe's excesses of humour are worse than his excesses of tragedy, or that his play has suffered from foolish theatrical additions. Nevertheless the greatest parts of *Faustus* show him at the height of his poetic and dramatic magnificence. The same difficulty is presented in another play, *The Jew of Malta*. It is mentioned as early as 1592; but as there is no evidence that it was printed before 1633, we have a reasonable excuse for disclaiming the poorer passages as playhouse alterations. In *The Troublesome Raigne and Lamentable Death of Edward the Second* (printed 1593–4), Marlowe gave us the first historical play of the type which Shakespeare followed in *Richard II. The Massacre at Paris* and *The Tragedie of Dido Queene of Carthage* complete the list of Marlowe's accepted dramas. The first known edition of the former is undated; it was acted in 1593; the earliest text of the latter belongs to the year 1594. *The Massacre*, badly transmitted, has fitful power. *Dido*, usually dismissed with undeserved contempt, bears the name of Nashe on its title as co-author; but of Nashe's hand there is little trace.

The supposed association of Marlowe with works attributed to Shakespeare or used by Shakespeare must be barely mentioned in a survey such as this. Assertions about composite authorship are easy to make and hard to establish or refute. Still, composite authorship and revision by several hands are known facts of the time. Readers should trust their own convictions and not accept attributions too readily. In *Titus Andronicus* and in *Henry VI* there is some show of argument for Marlowe's hand. The full-bodied verse of *Titus* and the soaring, defiant character of Aaron might be the work of the author of *Tamburlaine*, but might equally well be the work of a young admirer. Marlowe may have had a share in *Henry VI*, but the nature and extent of that share (if any) cannot be discussed briefly. At this time of day it is impossible to distinguish between the verse of Marlowe and the verse of a young poet writing with Marlowe's infectious tune in his head. *Arden of Feversham* is one of the pseudo-Shakespearean plays in which some students have detected Marlowe's hand. The whole question is discussed in F. P. Wilson's *Marlowe and the Early Shakespeare* (1953).

Two other works, non-dramatic, remain for mention: *Hero and Leander* and *Lucan's First Booke Translated Line for Line*, both entered for printing in 1593. The first, unfinished, was published in 1598, afterwards with a completion by Chapman; the second appeared in 1600. The famous short poem "Come live with me and be my love" appeared first in *The Passionate Pilgrim* (1599) and in a fuller form, in *Englands Helicon* (1600). The nearly simultaneous appearance of these pieces appears to indicate an effort by friends to leave little of the poet's work unprinted. We gather, from various allusions, that he had friends and admirers in spite of his ill-repute.

If a historian is to dwell, not upon Marlowe's faults, but upon his power, and the fact to be recorded is that Marlowe is a prime creative force in our literature, and a creative force of a new kind. Till Marlowe's genius made possible and credible such daemonic figures as Tamburlaine, Faustus and Barabas, whose tragic doom is compelled by forces within themselves and not by mischances from without. Marlowe's heroes confront the fates; they are not the sport of destiny. Marlowe himself has the self-possession of the strong man, and could use his sources creatively. His violence is native, and the inequalities in his art are the effect of his strength, not the signs of undeveloped power. His work was finished at an age at which few poets have really begun. *Edward II* stands by itself among his plays. There is a temptation to overpraise it. Because it is the first complete historical play of the stricter type without lapses into foolery, it is singled out as Marlowe's best dramatic effort. But it merely seems the best because it never sinks to the worst depths of *Tamburlaine* and *Faustus*. Just as certainly it never touches their greatest heights. In passion and word-music the play is inferior to the greater pieces; it lacks, too, the touch of caricature that gives them convincing vitality. Still, it is the first successful attempt we have at the interpretation of history on the stage; for a successful history-play must interpret history, it must not merely label figures with historical names. The earlier historical plays were only another form of the cautionary historical poems in *A Mirror for Magistrates*. After Marlowe's *Edward II*, Shakespeare's *Richard II* and its great successors became possible; but Marlowe could never have attained the all-embracing versatility of Shakespeare. *Edward II* shows his limitations as clearly as his powers. No one remembers its characters and scenes as one remembers the characters and scenes of *Richard II*.

Marlowe gave his age true tragedy. He also gave it tragedy's true instrument, great verse. *Gorboduc* had taught blank verse how to speak on the stage; *Tamburlaine* taught it how to sing. Indeed, it might be said that Marlowe's genius is operatic, and he obviously learned something of his music from Spenser. His famous passages are like great solos, superbly lyrical and appropriate, but not integrally woven into the texture of the drama. His dramatic blank verse unites the formal dignity of *Gorboduc* with the musical fluency of *The Faerie Queene*; and so it is rhythmically free and inventive, capable alike of magic and of majesty, always the master and never the slave of its metrical pattern. And though his daemonic figures may seem excessive in deed or aspiration, their poetic speech, however "mighty", is spontaneous, natural, and even simple.

Thomas Kyd (1558–94) appears to be the person held up to contempt by Nashe in his preface to *Menaphon* as an example of those who "could scarcelie latinize their necke-verse if they should have need". Kyd's great offence was that he had made an immense theatrical success with *The Spanish Tragedy*. The extent of Kyd's Latinity may not have been great; but though he "never ware gowne in the Universitie" he was a fellow pupil with Spenser at Merchant Taylors'. His translations from the Italian and French, which seem to have annoyed Nashe specially, are quite unimportant. The Italian work is a pamphlet, and the French a version of Robert Garnier's *Cornélie* under the title *Pompey the Great, his fair Corneliaes Tragedie* (printed 1594—there is no record of its being acted). Other works attributed to him raise too many bibliographical problems to be accepted readily. *The First Part of Jeronimo*, extant in a quarto of 1605 possibly a "first part" to *The Spanish Tragedie*, but not very probably written by Kyd himself. *The Tragedye of Solyman and Perseda* (published 1592) perhaps be his, for that is the subject of the play within the play in *The Spanish Tragedie*; but it is quite definitely inferior to that piece. Even the *Tragedie* itself is a problem. Its date is unknown. It may have been written just before 1588. By 1592 it was enjoying great popularity. Its first known quarto is dateless; but even that is described as "Newly corrected and amended of such grosse faults as passed in the first impression", so it may not be the first; the second known quarto appeared in 1594, and the third in 1599. None of them gives the least clue to the author's name; and it is not till 1612 that "M. Kid" is named casually by Heywood, as the author, in his *Apology for Actors*. The play out-Senecas Seneca in its wild horrors and in the excesses of its style. But there can be observed a faint resemblance to *Hamlet*, not merely in details of the story, but in the halting, suffering, distracted, self-communing character of Hieronimo, who was an entirely new kind of tragic hero. *The Spanish Tragedy* is the first example we possess of the Hamlet type of play.

Kyd can be easily underrated. His contribution to drama is intrinsically as well as historically important. He was the first English dramatist to discover the bearing of episode and of dramatic "movement" upon character, and the first to give the audience a hint of the development that follows from this interaction. In other words, he is the first English dramatist who writes dramatically. We have parted company with the older declamatory tragedy of the English Senecans, with the "operatic" tragedy of Marlowe, and we are nearer the manner of Shakespeare. That the young Shakespeare knew *The Spanish Tragedy* is evident. Was there a closer association? What are the "whole Hamlets" of "tragicall speaches" referred to by Nashe in 1589 and apparently associated with Kyd? Did Kyd write a play upon the well-known story of Hamlet? Did Shakespeare make that play the basis of his own? Does the First Quarto of *Hamlet* (1603) carry over some sections of an older, non-Shakespearean play? There is no certain answer to any of these questions. Perhaps in some obscure library there lies unrecognized the lost *Hamlet* of Kyd, or another, as the lost *Fulgens and Lucres* lay unrecognized till 1919. Perhaps, on the other hand, there never was such a play.

VIII. SHAKESPEARE: LIFE AND PLAYS

...am Shakespeare (1564–1616), in the biographical sense, we know both ...nd too little. The diligence of investigators has amassed a quantity ...n, most of which is utterly useless and irrelevant. We do not want ...Shakespeare's lawsuits. We do not need any personal conjectures ...but we urgently need much bibliographical and textual informa-...orks. Of this we possess far too little; and the more frankly we ...ce the less likely we are to be deceived, first by the sentimental ...e piety fills the blanks in Shakespeare's life with pleasing ...ents, and next by the incorrigible cranks and less illiterate ...ferent piety assigns all the work called Shakespeare's to ...of the peerage. But two great unassailable facts we do know ...et: first, that a man named William Shakespeare lived and wrote, was seen by many, was admired for his works, and was liked for his qualities; second, that a great mass of work was known by friends and by rivals to be his, and was published as his by people who had been, so to speak, in the making of it. We have as much vital information about Shakespeare as we have about most artists of any early period. If we know rather more about Ben Jonson, it is because Ben was the kind of writer, found in all ages, who can never resist talking about himself. And, actually, what we know of Ben Jonson's life is of singularly little aid to the understanding of Ben Jonson's works.

There is abundant contemporary testimony to the work of Shakespeare. Our most precise and almost disconcertingly exact piece of early information is the summary of works given in a little volume called *Palladis Tamia; Wits Treasury* (1598) by Francis Meres (1565–1647), a Cambridge divine and schoolmaster. The book is a series of choice passages from famous authors, followed by *A Comparative Discourse of our English Poets with the Greeke, Latine and Italian Poets.* Meres includes Shakespeare's works among those which have built lasting monuments to their authors. He includes Shakespeare among the "Lyrick poets". He includes Shakespeare among the "Tragicke poets". He includes Shakespeare with "the best for Comedy amongst us". He includes Shakespeare with those who "are the most passionate among us to bewaile and bemoane the perplexities of love". But the most extensive allusion is the following paragraph, which must be quoted in full:

As *Plautus* and *Seneca* are accounted the best for Comedy and Tragedy among the Latines: so *Shakespeare* among ye English is the most excellent in both kinds for the stage; for Comedy, witnes his *Gentlemen of Verona,* his *Errors,* his *Love labors lost,* his *Love labours wonne,* his *Midsummers night dreame,* & his *Merchant of Venice*: for Tragedy his *Richard the 2. Richard the 3. Henry the 4. King Iohn, Titus Andronicus* and his *Romeo and Iuliet.*

No play called *Love labours wonne* exists, and identification is nothing but an exercise in ingenuity. For practical purposes, then, the Meres list contains eleven and not twelve plays. Meres proceeds by numbers in all his judgments—making balanced ones and twos and threes, and here he balances six comedies and six tragedies. His list of Shakespeare's plays is therefore selective and not exhaustive, and Shakespeare is the only writer whose works are named so extensively. The *Discourse* cites over eighty English writers; and if any person totally unacquainted with English literature were asked to read through the list and to say which of them all seems to be the greatest, the most various, and the most highly praised, he would, without any hesitation, name Shakespeare. This fact is worth reams of speculation. Shakespeare, with his greatest works still unwritten, takes first rank in the estimate of a stiff contemporary critic.

Upon one matter of controversy we must touch very briefly. The propositions alleged by Baconians and others can be summarized baldly as follows: (1) We know little about Shakespeare's life and upbringing; (2) therefore he must have been an ignorant boor; (3) and therefore his plays, which show multiscience, if not omniscience, must have been written by a member of the peerage. We need not discuss these propositions. They refute themselves. As we know little about Shakespeare's life and upbringing we do not know what he knew. The plays exhibit nothing resembling omniscience or even multi-science. There is not the slightest correlation between great learning and great creative power. The symptoms interpreted as evidence of omniscience are exhibited daily by journalists and barristers. The belief that special capacity for scholarship, creative art and public affairs can be found only in the "upper classes" is a curious and almost pathetic superstition of the servile or genteel mind. The cranks who have declared that the plays of Shakespeare are too good for an actor to have written have never noticed that they are too bad for a Lord Chancellor to have written. They contain elementary mistakes of fact. They are unoriginal in substance. They are haphazard in form. They are full of loose ends. They are thoroughly untidy. They contain singularly few literary allusions. They bear every mark of hasty improvization. They smell of the theatre, never of the study. They are not, in any respect, considered works. A man with Shakespeare's unrivalled power of registering peculiarities of human character could easily acquire and assimilate the kind of knowledge shown in the plays. What we know definitely about Shakespeare's education is that he studied in two great seats of learning, the theatre and the world. As an actor and dramatist Shakespeare inherited three centuries of tradition. He heard the thunders of *Tamburlaine* and *The Spanish Tragedy* rolled forth by Edward Alleyn, an inspiring person on the stage, and off the stage so solidly minded that he is remembered today, not as an actor, but as a benefactor to education. As a poet, Shakespeare met very early the differently inspiring Earl of Southampton, his first patron, a dazzling young nobleman through whom he got to know the great world and grew familiar with the courtier's, scholar's, soldier's eye, tongue, sword. There must have been similar stimulating influences that we can only guess at. The kind of knowledge eminently possessed by Shakespeare is something beyond mere acquisition—the kind of knowledge that comes only to "an experiencing nature"; and the experiencing nature, like creative genius, is a gift, not an acquirement. People have made a "Shakespeare mystery" by trying to find reasons for what is beyond reason. All creative genius is a mystery, and utterly inexplicable.

Another kind of difficulty made about Shakespeare will have small power to alarm those who have traced in these pages the development of the drama from church services to the anonymous and unprinted miracle plays of the guilds, from them to the anonymous and occasionally printed morality plays, from them to plays prepared for performance in schools or universities or inns of court, and from them to plays written for the general public. Why did Shakespeare not publish his plays? The answer is that a play was meant to be published in speech, not to be published in print. It was a theatrical property, not a work of literature. Even poems of a personal kind were kept in manuscript. Meres bestows praise upon Shakespeare's "sugred Sonnets among his private friends"; and they remained among his private friends for ten years after Meres had mentioned them; further, when they were printed in 1609 there is no evidence that they were published with the author's consent. Shakespeare was willing to publish his carefully composed *Venus and Adonis* and *The Rape of Lucrece*; but his improvizations and adaptations for the stage he viewed with the practical eye of a man of the theatre, and they stayed with the players for whom they were written and to whom they belonged. What is remarkable about the publication of Shakespeare's plays is not that the author took no interest in preserving them for posterity, but that, seven years after his death, the two surviving members of the original Chamberlain's company should have made a great volume of them. That was an unprecedented tribute of contemporaries and colleagues to his memory and to his greatness.

The real problems in the study of Shakespeare arise from the fact that we have in print a mass of theatrical literature never prepared for the press. Some of it is ill-printed; some of it is misprinted. The plays in the First Folio are roughly grouped, but they are not arranged. We do not know the chronological order of their composition. In any one play there may be strata of several different periods. Theatrical literature beyond any other is liable to addition, subtraction, modification and revision; and the attempt to date any play from internal evidence is hazardous. A specific allusion in a passage dates that passage: it does not necessarily date the whole play. Still, though no confidence can be placed in any list of the plays chronologically arranged even by the most solid of critics, we are fairly sure of the plays belonging to the early, middle and late periods of Shakespeare's working life; and our consideration of them can begin from the Meres list. Possible dates of composition are given.

Not one of the plays in that list, *Titus* excepted, was published till the year before Meres wrote, and three were not printed till the issue of the Folio of 1623. Greene's allusion in *A Groatsworth of Wit* cites a line of *Henry VI*, a play not mentioned by Meres. The special value of the Meres list and its date is that the eleven plays named form a compact block of early work, and so give us a definite standard of reference—we know that certain works are early and from them we learn the characteristics of "earliness". But we know very little else, and it is precisely here that we desire to know more. The alleged escapades of Shakespeare's youth do not interest us. We want to know how he began as a poet. What first moved him to write? How did he discover his gift for adapting and composing plays in verse? What, actually, is the very earliest example of his writing that has survived? Was *Venus and Adonis* literally the first heir of his invention, as he called it? What share had he in the three parts of *Henry VI*, which Meres did not mention, but which Heming and Condell included in the Folio? *Tamburlaine* and *The Spanish Tragedy* might have inspired him to early adventures in the heroic style; but how did he reach the wit, the humour and the assured mastery of verse exhibited in a delightful early comedy like *Love's Labour's Lost*? These are some of the questions to which we desire an answer; but answer there is none.

Unquestionably two of the earliest plays are *The Comedy of Errors* (c. 1592) and *Titus Andronicus* (c. 1593). *The Comedy*, derived somehow from the *Menaechmi* of Plautus (with twins doubled), is an ambitious farce containing here and there touches in the serious style of the early Shakespeare. *Titus Andronicus* must receive more notice than it deserves. Because it is crudely horrible it has been thought unworthy of Shakespeare and has been denied to him. This is sentimentalism, not criticism. A play, *Titus Andronicus*, was acted, apparently, as early as 1593 and printed in 1594; Meres, who was not a sentimentalist, but a prim and formal student of literature, names it without a qualm next door to *Romeo and Juliet* as one of Shakespeare's tragedies; further, Shakespeare's own intimates and dramatic associates printed it as his in the Folio of 1623. If we reject this evidence, what evidence can we accept? *Titus* is a "Tragedy of Horrors", which an observer of Marlowe's successful bloodiness could confidently offer to an audience that remembered the fires of Smithfield and received as a public spectacle the abominations of Tyburn. There is no sound literary reason for refusing to accept *Titus* as a first adventure in the tragedy of horror by the future author of *King Lear*. At the other extreme is *Love's Labour's Lost* (c. 1594), an exquisite artificial comedy to which less than its due admiration is given. It is the finest comedy that the English stage had produced at that date, and it is the finest example, at that date, of the successful application of charm, humanity and style to the drama, not even excepting the more obvious Titanism of *Tamburlaine* and *Faustus*. The author of *Titus Andronicus* might have written *Tamburlaine*; the author of *Tamburlaine* could never have written *Love's Labour's Lost*. Shakespeare's youthful comedy foreshadows things that he was to do better afterwards; Marlowe's tragedies foreshadow no kind of development. They could not be developed, they could only be repeated.

These three "earliest" plays are succeeded by three "earlier", *The Two Gentlemen of Verona*, *All's Well that Ends Well* (supposing, for the moment, a first version of that to be *Love's Labour's Won*) and *The Taming of the Shrew*. *The Two Gentlemen* (c. 1594) is the insecure handling of a romantic story; but it shows a grasp of character far from insecure, and it shows the verse-medium steadily settling into blank verse that is both beautiful and practicable. *All's Well* (c. 1602) is an oddly unsatisfactory play, crude enough to be early, yet mature enough to be late. Its chief failure is the heroine, Helena, who does not really let us know what manner of woman she is; its greatest success is the old Countess, about whom there is no doubt of any kind. An early date for *All's Well*, as it stands, cannot be accepted. *The Taming of the Shrew* (c. 1594) seems, at first sight, to be adapted from *The Taming of a Shrew* (printed 1594); but the latter may be nothing but an attempt at a reported version of Shakespeare's play, eked out with quotations from Marlowe. No one would claim that the play is a great addition to the Shakespeare canon, successful as it is after its own fashion.

Of the other seven plays in the Meres list, we can be content to say that they are all "early". *Romeo and Juliet* (c. 1595) is Shakespeare's greatest triumph up to this date. It is a pure tragedy of youth told in verse that is both youthful and intense. No such loveliness of music had been heard before on the English stage. Some of the characters are mere diagrams; but Romeo, Juliet, Mercutio and the Nurse are now part of the world's mythology. *A Midsummer Night's Dream* (c. 1596) is a triumph of a different kind. There is the stuff of half a dozen poetical comedies in it, yet not in the least confusedly disposed. *The Merchant of Venice* (c. 1596) is not so completely successful. The parts do not flow into each other as in *A Midsummer Night's Dream*. Some seem less mature than others; and it is possible to believe that the different strata are of different dates.

The chronicle plays mentioned by Meres introduce a new division of Shakespeare's work. As we have seen, the first chronicle plays hovered between history and morality and did not attain full artistic success till Marlowe wrote *Edward II*. In no kind of drama did the genius of Shakespeare find a fuller field for expatiation. His three greatest gifts, his power of poetic expression, his power of character-creation, and his power of weaving both into a story, were exactly what was needed to turn these formless agglomerations into real organisms, possessing life and beauty. The three parts of *Henry VI* (c. 1590–1), ignored by Meres, were included by the editors of the First Folio in the canon of Shakespeare's works. Parts II and III of *Henry VI* were published as *The First part of the Contention between the two famous Houses of Yorke and Lancaster* (printed 1594) and *The true Tragedie of Richard Duke of Yorke and the death of good King Henrie the Sixt* (printed 1595). These plays have been themselves the subject of much contention between famous critical houses; but readers should not be seduced by these contentions into early partizanship and should in particular beware of the confident exponents of the higher criticism who will distribute definite portions of a play called Shakespeare's among five or six different authors. No one is required to believe in the literal inspiration of the First Folio. That no word of Shakespeare's is to be found out of it or that no word but Shakespeare's is to be found in it are two extreme propositions, which, like all extremes, are the concern only of fanatics. Sensible persons will believe that the vast space between those extremes is Shakespeare's own. After all, the evidence of the Folio is contemporary evidence, which critics centuries later cannot lightly set aside. Those who fail to catch the voice of Shakespeare in some passages of *Henry VI* must be without ears; and if other passages sound much less like him, the reason is that his first attempts to speak out loud and bold in the prevalent style of chronicle-history would naturally be as unlike his later achievements as *The Comedy of Errors* is unlike *Twelfth Night*.

Richard II (c. 1596) has no traceable original, but it had a model in Marlowe's *Edward II*; Shakespeare's Richard, however, is a finer achievement than Marlowe's Edward, though the part is not strongly or even variously supported. In fact, *Richard II* is more of a lyrical monologue than any other play by Shakespeare, with the monologue very exquisitely written.

King John and *Richard III* are both examples of the adaptation and working up of existing materials. In *King John* (c. 1596) Shakespeare took much of *The Troublesome Raigne of John King of England*, but heightened the presentation considerably. *Richard III* (c. 1593) bears much less resemblance to *The True Tragedie of Richard III*, and derives something indirectly from the life of Richard by Sir Thomas More, included in Holinshed's *Chronicles*. It has some famous scenes, but its chief triumph is the character of Richard, which has attracted every great actor from Burbage to Irving and from Irving to Olivier. The puzzling problems of the text and its transmission do not concern us here.

Last in the Meres list comes *Henry IV* (c. 1597) worked up from an older piece, *The Famous Victories of Henry the fifth*, but more remarkable than any of the earlier chronicles for complete transformation of the merest brute material into magnificent art. The two parts of this play are continuous and together form one of Shakespeare's very greatest achievements. In particular, the blending of history with invention is a triumph of accomplishment. The curious and universal humanity of Shakespeare's portraiture, so utterly different from the shrill striving of so-called realism, is scarcely anywhere shown more finely than in Nell and Doll, a pair of trulls who become almost endearing figures. It is a detail worth noticing how prodigal Shakespeare has been of Warwickshire and Gloucestershire reminiscences in this play.

Early in the Folio of 1623 comes *The Merry Wives of Windsor* (c. 1600). No attempt was made to fit this Falstaff story into the historical series; and so it is lost labour and idle sentimentality to lament the decadence and defeat of a triumphant figure. There are many compensations. The *vis comica* of the piece is perfect; its invention and variety are abundant; and the actual construction is more careful than usual. So admirable are the characters, especially the two "wives", with their sterling honesty carried into the region of charm, that the half-patronizing, half-apologetic, tone sometimes adopted towards *The Merry Wives*, as a "farce", is singularly amusing to a liberally catholic student of literature.

Measure for Measure (c. 1604), which follows in the Folio, some have found an unsatisfactory play with great things in it, with the problem evaded, not solved, and the "happy ending" unhappily contrived. But others have seen it as one of Shakespeare's maturest comedies, a wholesome affirmation which does not juggle with values, but says plainly that vice is vicious and forgiveness a supreme virtue.

After *Measure for Measure* in the Folio comes the *Errors*, and then *Much Ado about Nothing* (c. 1599). The Hero-Claudio story is as old as story-telling. Beatrice and Benedick, the duellists of sex who capitulate to each other, are Shakespeare's own, and, with the constabulary of Messina, are the making of the play. The piece is "good theatre" and carries itself successfully by sheer dramatic speed over some very shaky passages of plot; but it is not a play that a reader returns to with affection. A point sometimes overlooked is that the play is almost entirely in prose—and very good prose, too.

As You Like It (c. 1600) borrows some of its story from Thomas Lodge's *Rosalynde, Euphues golden legacie* (1590) and a little from the pseudo-Chaucerian *Tale of Gamelyn*; but the positive charm of Rosalind, the marrowy moralizing of Jaques, and the unfailing fool-wisdom of Touchstone are Shakespeare's own. The defects of the story—even the unconvincing final "revolution" communicated by a messenger—are swept away in the freshness of the forest breezes.

To follow one boy-girl romance with another was to take a great risk; but Shakespeare took it and triumphed; for *Twelfth Night* (c. 1600) bears no resemblance to *As You Like It*. This play is the perfection of romantic comedy. There is not a failure in it; though the stage sometimes puts a few of the parts out of drawing. Orsino is not a marrowless fop, but a romantic Renascence lover. Malvolio is neither hidalgo nor clown. He is a humourless, over-anxious custodian of other people's morals, with conscientiousness developed to the point at which it is transformed into the luxury of boundless self-approval. The world knows many such, in places high and low.

The Winter's Tale comes next in the Folio, but this, being manifestly late, may be postponed, and consideration given to the remaining histories. The first of them is *Henry V* (c. 1599), which owes something to *The Famous Victories* already mentioned in connection with *Henry IV*. That the play is fervently patriotic has displeased certain critics. But Henry V is not a figure out of a "historical treatise"; he is the hero of a heroic poem. The fresh presentment of Pistol and the addition of Fluellen demonstrate the inexhaustibleness of the poet's comic invention.

The last remaining, and probably the last written, of the English history group is *Henry VIII* (c. 1613), which presents remarkable peculiarities, and which has been divided up among several possible authors. It is a loose and patchy composition; and though there are points of great and truly Shakespearean interest of character, it cannot be said that the characters unify the play in the Shakespearean manner. Those who knew best thought there was enough Shakespeare in it to justify its inclusion in the Folio.

With the classical plays we come to a new and very interesting group. *Troilus and Cressida* (c. 1601) was issued twice in 1609, the second time with the unusual addition of a preface. The editors of the Folio included it among the tragedies and omitted its name from the list of contents. In senses more than one it is a "problem" play; but the matters for debate cannot be set forth here. We may, if we are disposed, call *Troilus and Cressida* a history without dignity, a comedy without laughter and tragedy without tears, but we are bound to admit that it is a masterpiece of its kind. Equally puzzling, though not in the same way, is *Timon of Athens* (c. 1607), which, though manifestly late, bears many marks of immaturity, one being its meagreness. There is nothing in *Timon* that Shakespeare, at one time or another, may not have written; there are some things which hardly anyone but Shakespeare can have written; but the play as a whole is both undelightful and unedifying. Readers should not be too readily seduced into accepting dangerous and unwarranted personal interpretations of *Troilus* and *Timon*. There are some unpleasant things to be said about human nature, and Shakespeare chose to say them in unpleasant plays; but he said them as one steadfastly affirming the good and refusing to think of evil otherwise than as evil.

The two plays which may be called Greek stand in the sharpest contrast to the great Roman trio, based, in Shakespeare's most easy-going fashion, on North's *Plutarch*, but made his own absolutely and for ever. None of the three was printed till the Folio appeared. *Julius Caesar* (c. 1600) has its magnificent scenes and memorable characters. The use of the crowd as part of the drama is a great touch. *Coriolanus* (c. 1607), a much austerer play, has an odd power of provoking outbreaks of strong political feeling. The mob, the democracy, is cruelly exposed, but hardly more cruelly than aristocracy in the person of the hero himself. With *Antony and Cleopatra* (c. 1607) we pass into a different world. *Julius Caesar* is fine; *Coriolanus* is admirable; *Antony and Cleopatra* is superb. It is among Shakespeare's highest achievements. The beauties of its versification and diction are almost unparalleled in number, diversity and intensity; and the two great poetic motives, love and death, are transcendently employed. In addition it is a masterly chronicle play dramatizing whole years of history and keeping them dramatically one. Nowhere has even Shakespeare surpassed his hero and heroine, who go down magnificently to destruction with their imperfections as crowns upon their heads; and we feel that for them the world was well lost. The last scenes attain the absolute of beauty in human speech.

Somewhere near the last Roman plays in time of composition is the perplexing *Pericles* (c. 1607), which was printed as Shakespeare's twice in 1609, again in 1611 and again in 1619; but it was not included in the First or Second Folio, and made its first "collected" appearance in the Third Folio (1664). Some of it is altogether below Shakespeare at his worst; but the end, with its note of infinite pity and understanding, is lifted to the level that is Shakespeare's own.

In the years between *Julius Caesar* and *Antony and Cleopatra* Shakespeare produced what may be called the four wings of his spirit, *Hamlet, Othello, King Lear* and *Macbeth. Hamlet* (c. 1602) is the most voluminously discussed play ever written; and we may say at once that if people were to read the play itself more often than books about it their minds would be less confused. Many difficulties disappear if we remember that Shakespeare dramatized an old and well-known story, and assumed that his audience would fill up any gaps. Shakespeare's *Hamlet* is the fair surface of a story with many strata, and here and there the primitive material shows through. The only surviving English version of the old story, called *The Hystorie of Hamblet*, is dated 1608, but this was obviously not the first appearance of the legend in English, as Nashe had referred to "whole Hamlets of tragicall speaches" as long before as 1589. *The Hystorie of Hamblet* is one of the few contemporary parallels or preliminaries to Shakespeare worth reading; for it shows, first, what was the current version of the story, and next, what parts of that story had, and what had not, any interest for Shakespeare. Thus, the feigned madness of the primitive Hamlet did not interest Shakespeare at all: he mentions it, he does not exploit it. Put briefly, the play of Shakespeare is the story of a sensitive and cultured man's revolt from the carnality and grossness of human life. To interpret Hamlet's revolt from carnality as a personal tragedy of Shakespeare himself after some humiliating and disillusioning experience is very tempting; but as we do not know a single fact to support the interpretation we should refuse to listen to those who make it. The first puzzle about Shakespeare's *Hamlet* is provided by the "bad" quarto of 1603. This is probably a rough version "potted" from memory by actors who could remember only parts of the true text and added bits from other sources. The full text appeared in 1604. The Folio of 1623 abbreviates the 1604 quarto, probably for stage use, but does not add to our knowledge. Sensible persons, therefore, will dismiss theories and forget the crude pamphlet called the First Quarto, and be content with the *Hamlet* that two centuries of careful criticism has handed on as the true text. The story, as there told, is simple to those who read simply, and it is worked out dramatically by the largest and richest gallery of characters to be found in any single play. Perhaps the most extraordinary fact about the characters in *Hamlet* is that they are not extraordinary; and that, perhaps, joined with the imperial speech of which so many phrases have become current coin of quotation, is the secret of its fascination. For once, we see ourselves as the greatest of seers saw us, and the spectacle reaches into our very souls.

This is true also of *Othello* (c. 1605). The characters are not super-human or the sport of implacable destinies. They fail and fall through the faults and follies that are common to the least extraordinary of mankind. Iago, far from being the super-subtle Italianate fiend that fanciful criticism has made him, is an almost commonplace bad man of the kind that instinctively tries to pull down whatever it feels to be above itself, but not quite beyond itself. In a modern village community Iago would be a writer of anonymous letters. The simple-hearted, elementary Othello might see in Iago a demi-devil; Emilia knew better. The textual independence of the first two Quarto versions and the first two Folio versions offers a curious problem of bibliography beyond our present range of discussion. We may briefly note that the verse of *Othello* has a magnificent operatic style totally unlike the meditative elegiac note of *Hamlet*.

Macbeth (c. 1606) is so much shorter than the other great plays of its period that it seems to be a cut-down version. We have nothing but the Folio text to help us. Further, even the text we have shows evidence of different strata of composition. The interest is concentrated almost entirely on the two chief characters, who demand a super-humanity of performance to which few players have been able to rise. Almost anybody succeeds as Hamlet; almost everybody fails as Macbeth; and so the play is regarded as a "Jonah" of the theatre. Macbeth himself is a marvellous variant sketch of Hamlet, with this difference, that Hamlet expatiates melodiously upon what he cannot begin to do, and Macbeth expatiates even more melodiously upon what he cannot cease from doing. Lady Macbeth is peerless alike in triumph and in defeat. Few of Shakespeare's plays are lovelier in language. The fresh handling of the supernatural—and of different strata of the supernatural—is not the least wonderful part of the play; indeed, Shakespeare's handling of agencies more than earthly is one of his greatest triumphs.

The power of *King Lear* (c. 1606) is so stupendous that we are astonished to remember that it makes no use of the supernatural. *King Lear*, like its companions in the great *quatuor*, has special virtues, but it resembles them and *Antony and Cleopatra* in a certain regality of tone which hardly appears elsewhere. The beginning, which has been objected to, is a true beginning, for it begets all the evil that follows. Gloucester, who jocosely sows the wind, bitterly reaps the whirlwind, and in the tempest guilty and innocent perish together. That the blinding of Gloucester is found shocking testifies to the exaltation of tragedy by Shakespeare to heights far beyond the level of *The Spanish Tragedy*, in which such an incident would be almost unremarked. The catastrophe is properly complete. Those who feel the need for some kind of "happy ending" are incapable of tragedy and should recline at ease upon sentimental novels. Cordelia, often feebly represented, is a piece of stubbornness—her own father's daughter, and they fall, as they should, together. In its unsparing purgation of the spirit *Lear* is the greatest of Shakespeare's tragedies.

Last come the famous three: *Cymbeline*, *The Winter's Tale* and *The Tempest*, where no idle fancy has seen "the calmed and calming *mens adepta*" of which Fulke Greville speaks in his great passage of prose, *A Letter to an Honourable Lady*. *Cymbeline* is one of those plays which seem in reading to be afflicted with the wildest extravagances of time and place, and which in stage performance show an unsuspected unity of organization. It is unequal, but it is full of fresh and lovely invention. *The Winter's Tale* is as loosely built as *Cymbeline* and like that play is great in episodes. The poignant domestic tragedy, the pastoral scenes and the rogueries of Autolycus made the play. Here, as in *Pericles*, the unity of time is defied to the extent of making a child grow into womanhood before our eyes. Yet it is important to remember that Shakespeare always respects the unity of time in spirit. Years may seem to pass, but the old grow no older. Hermione is the same fair woman at the end as she was at the beginning. There are no "time schemes" in Shakespeare. "For ever wilt thou love and she be fair" is the only law of time in Shakespeare.

Shakespeare's magical swan-song *The Tempest* is, in construction, sharply different from *Cymbeline* and *The Winter's Tale*, for it is the most compact of plays, and it is almost "regular" in time, place and action. One detail relating to time deserves mention. Stage tradition makes of Prospero an elaborately upholstered piece of senility, when the play clearly makes him a vigorous man, father of a barely adolescent child, and instantly ready to re-assume the governance of his lost dukedom. Gonzalo's quotation from Montaigne is an invaluable autobiographical touch giving us a clue to one of the creative influences on Shakespeare's own development. The magical loveliness of the story and the tender melancholy of the subtly suggested farewell to a life of creative art sometimes obscure the fact that the play contains not a little of the old Shakespearean violence and villainy. To refuse to see a leave-taking in this perfect creation, with the symbolical breaking of the staff and burial of the book is surely an idle scepticism. Shakespeare is not the only artist who knew that his days of creation were numbered; and in this play with its title of storm and its story of charity almost divine we reach the sunset hour and music at the close.

Shakespeare, by reason of his supremacy, has suffered much, both from the orthodox and the heretical. The former have made him a national and semi-sacred bard beyond criticism, the latter have made him the target of obtuseness and dubiety. What the historian has to record is that from the date of the tribute of Francis Meres in 1598 to the present time, he has remained the unchallenged chief of English letters and the English theatre. As long as there was a stage to put them on, the plays of Shakespeare have, in some form or other, kept their place on it. The theatre itself has changed beyond recognition during the centuries, but the plays of Shakespeare have fitted all varieties of building or no building, all methods of presentation, whether in the theatre or in the film, radio or television studio, all styles of acting and all tastes in drama. It has been possible for a diligent theatregoer to see every one of the thirty-seven plays produced; and of at least a dozen of them it can be said that they hold the stage by sheer popular appeal, when not a single play by any of his contemporaries genuinely survives. In some countries Shakespeare is more popular than any native dramatist, and his appeal to children is extraordinary.

A sensible person will begin his reading of Shakespeare with Shakespeare himself and not with his critics and commentators. Problems and difficulties cannot be considered by those to whom they have never really become problems and difficulties. The important thing is to get the Shakespearean atmosphere, to feel the breath of the Shakespearean spirit. Shakespeare has never been surpassed in the power to unfold a story on the stage, in the power to create the characters who unfold the story, and in the power to combine story, character and utterance in a texture so perfectly implicated that, though the parts are clearly discerned in the whole, the whole is greater than its parts; and this mastery of triple counterpoint, displayed with an ease of execution that makes the elementary, uncombined association of story, character and utterance in any play by Marlowe or Webster seem, in comparison, the patchwork of gifted amateurs, is shown as plainly in an early composition like *Love's Labour's Lost* as in a late composition like *Antony and Cleopatra*. And so the stories and the characters of Shakespeare have become part of the world's mythology. That neither may have been his own invention is unimportant; it is Shakespeare's shaping genius that makes them live. The prodigality of his creation in character is equalled only by its almost divine impartiality. He never weights the scales against any person, but draws hero and hangman with the same kind of mastery. He never presents a case or pleads a cause. His characters really live. They are not the "type" characters of a different kind of drama: Shylock is not The Usurer, he is a human being who lends money. Shakespeare is not squeamish, but, equally, he is not grossly coarse for coarseness' sake. He is so thoroughly wholesome that the appropriate remarks of his less cleanly characters seem natural and need no defence. That there are occasional horrors, even in the best plays, must be accepted as a tradition of the stage of his day; but here again the excesses are as few in Shakespeare as they are many in his predecessors and successors. Shakespeare has no mannerisms in his style. The rhetoric is occasionally overcharged—again the tradition and very formation of his stage must be pleaded in defence—and there is sometimes a superfluity of word-play, which cannot be excused, save as the exuberance of a genius for words. Shakespeare coins freely and royally and uses a larger vocabulary than any other writer. He is not easy to read, because every word contributes something to his effect; yet the flexibility of the Shakespearean style is as wonderful as its exquisite texture.

Shakespeare's versification is one of the guides to the order of his works. The earliest plays cited by Meres exhibit the "single-moulded" lines of Marlowe's fashion; the less early plays, while still keeping mainly to the single-moulded line, show more flexibility and a tendency towards rhyme and even to stanza forms. Plays of his great maturity—the *Hamlet* period—show perfect fluency, the blank verse keeping up its great tune, but moving with complete ease in every kind of utterance, from crisp dialogue to symphonic soliloquy. In plays of the later period the rhythms become subtler and more difficult, the "feminine ending" (i.e. an unaccented eleventh syllable) and the variation of the pauses giving a special kind of undulation to the verse-paragraphs. We can merely note, without comment, the grace and ease with which varied kinds of verse are used on special occasions, for choruses, insets, masques, interludes, and so forth.

It must be added, for the fact is often forgotten, that Shakespeare's prose is copious in quantity and high in quality, and ranges at ease from magnificent eloquence, through the polished exchanges of high comedy, to the crisp and racy patter of minor characters. Shakespeare's prose dialogue is definitely better than that of anyone of his age, both in itself and as the medium of drama. Moreover, Shakespeare's prose is real prose and not the mere relapse of a poet's verse. Indeed, there is no respect in which Shakespeare fails to be the master of all who have ever worked in words. He is complete and supreme, in conception and in execution, in character and in story—not an unnatural, full-blown marvel, but an instance of genius working itself up, on precedent and by experiment, from promise to performance and from the part to the whole.

William Shakespeare: A Study of Facts and Problems (1930) by Sir Edmund Chambers is the most reliable biography. It was abridged by Charles Williams in 1933 under the title *A Short Life of Shakespeare with the Sources*. The sources of the plays were considered by Geoffrey Bullough in *Narrative and Dramatic Sources of Shakespeare* (1957–69). An Oxford symposium *Shakespeare's England* (edited by Walter Raleigh, 1916) set the poet in his time. A Cambridge symposium *A Companion to Shakespeare Studies* (edited by Harley Granville-Barker and G. B. Harrison, 1934) set him for the twentieth century. *Shakespeare and His Stage* (1948) was the first volume of an annual *Shakespeare Survey*, edited by Allardyce Nicoll, who was succeeded by Kenneth Muir. Other books and editions are mentioned on pp. 231, 234-6, 239-40, etc., as well as under the names of Shakespeare's critics from Ben Jonson to Dr Johnson, from Coleridge to Wilson Knight.

IX. SHAKESPEARE: POEMS

Shakespeare's poems have suffered even more than the plays from the misguided zeal of those who wish to find in them either the details of personal biography or proofs that Shakespeare is not himself but several Elizabethan or Jacobean peers. Nevertheless the main facts are simple. *Venus and Adonis* was licensed on 18 April 1593, and appeared shortly afterwards with a fully signed dedication by the author to the Earl of Southampton, in which he describes the poem as "the first heire of my invention". It was followed a year later by *Lucrece*, again dedicated to Southampton. Both poems were very popular, and were praised by contemporaries. In 1598 the invaluable Meres referred to Shakespeare's "sugred Sonnets among his private friends" as well as to *Venus* and *Lucrece*; and in 1599 William Jaggard, an impudent and unscrupulous printer, included two of these sonnets (138 and 144) in a small miscellany of poems which he called *The Passionate Pilgrime. By W. Shakespeare*. The whole collection of sonnets was published ten years later (1609) by Thomas Thorpe, with Shakespeare's name, but without any sign of recognition from him. We do not know whether he authorized or approved the publication; but we know that he did not repudiate it by any surviving protest or by issuing a better edition. Thorpe subjoined to the *Sonnets* a poem in rhyme royal stanzas called *A Lover's Complaint*, about which we know nothing more. In *The Passionate Pilgrim*, the enterprising Jaggard had not merely included the two sonnets referred to, but had assigned the whole of the poems, of which three others were taken from *Love's Labour's Lost*, to "W. Shakespeare", although some had already appeared with the names of their writers. Nine are unidentified. It appears that, in this instance, Shakespeare did protest; at any rate, the dramatist Thomas Heywood, from whom Jaggard, in a later edition, "lifted" two more poems to add to the original twenty, says that Shakespeare was "much offended"—a little personal fact, the value of which has been insufficiently appreciated. One gathers, at least negatively, that Shakespeare was not "offended" by the publication of the sonnets. Lastly, there exists a rather obscure, very curious and, in parts, extremely beautiful short poem called *The Phoenix and the Turtle*, which, in 1601, was added to Robert Chester's *Love's Martyr*, as a contribution by Shakespeare:

Jonson, Chapman, "Ignoto" and others contributing likewise. This was reprinted ten years later, and we hear of no protests from any of the supposed contributors. Thus, *Venus* and *Lucrece* are genuine, acknowledged publications. The *Sonnets* came dubiously into print, but were never repudiated, and their genuineness has not been seriously challenged. *A Lover's Complaint* may be Shakespeare's, though it is so unimportant as to be hardly worth discussion, and this can be said, too, of *The Phoenix and the Turtle*. Some of the unidentified pieces in *The Passionate Pilgrim* are pleasant enough to make us hope they are rightly assigned to Shakespeare. *Sonnets to Sundry Notes of Music*, often separately entered in the contents of editions, is not a separate work, but a division, with sub-title, of *The Passionate Pilgrim*.

There is nothing, therefore, in the bibliographical history of the poems to justify any special diversion from the study of them as literature. But, beyond all question, there is perilous stuff of temptation away from such study in the matter of the *Sonnets*. And, unfortunately, Thomas Thorpe stuck a burning fuse in the live shell of this matter by prefixing some couple of dozen words of dedication in capitals: "*TO . THE . ONLIE . BEGETTER . OF . THESE . INSUING . SONNETS . MR . W . H . ALL . HAPPINESSE . AND . THAT . ETERNITIE . PROMISED . BY . OUR . EVER-LIVING . POET . WISHETH . THE . WELL-WISHING . ADVENTURER . IN . SETTING . FORTH . T . T.*" It would be rash to guess, and impossible to calculate, how many million words of commentary these simple nouns, adjectives and verbs have called forth. And neither dedication nor commentary has any real importance for the lover of poetry. They appeal to the wrong kind of curiosity, and have a special fascination for persons to whom all poetry is nothing but a vast acrostic and to whom nothing not acrostic is ever poetry. The exact identification of "Mr. W. H." could tell us nothing vitally important about our supreme poet and dramatist; and so the sensible course is to dismiss that embarrassing phantom and his delusive dedication from our minds, and to think of the sonnets as poems, and not as puzzles. But we must return briefly to the earlier pieces.

The poet happily called *Venus and Adonis* "the first heire of my invention". It is exactly what a child of poetical youth should be. The story is but the excuse for a series of beautiful and voluptuous pictures in mellifluous, if slightly "conceited", verse. It is all sheer poetry for poetry's sake, with abundance of exquisite lines that musicians have naturally seized upon for songs. The poem comes three years after *The Faerie Queene*, and, like that great invention, proves that mastery of English poetic rhythm has passed from experiment to certainty. It has been usual to recognize a certain advance in *Lucrece*—so called on the title-page, though called *The Rape of Lucrece* in the headlines. The story is serious and is seriously told, without any wantoning in the pleasure of poesy. But it is difficult to put the poem as evidence of genius and as a source of delight even on a level with *Venus and Adonis*, much more to set it above that poem. What is specially remarkable, in the work of one who was to be the greatest master of character, is that Lucrece herself is so very little of a person. From the author of *Venus and Adonis* we might expect almost anything in poetry; from the author of *Lucrece* we should expect nothing beyond the more sober work of a Drayton or a Daniel.

As we have seen, sequences of sonnets about love, real or assumed, became an irresistible poetical fashion during the decade from 1590 to 1600. To this period and to this species belong the sonnets of Shakespeare, which differ from the others only in being much better poems singly and collectively. Some of them, as we know from Meres, were in circulation by 1598, and, as we have said, they were published as a body in 1609, without visible sign of the author's approval and therefore without guarantee that the poems were arranged as he wished. Still, that volume is our sole authority. Modern literary detectives have ransacked the little book for "clues", and, as a result, some have produced elaborate new arrangements of the poems, some have identified all the persons in the drama—the identifications being far from identical—and some have made a confident distribution of the poems among at least five authors. The disconcerting and contradictory conclusions of the detectives should confirm the reader in a resolution to take the volume of 1609 as it stands, and to read it as a collection of poems and not as an assortment of conundrums. A dim kind of story can be discerned in the collection. Sonnets 1–126 are addressed to a handsome youth; a break is marked by the incomplete form of 126; sonnets 127–152 are addressed to a "black" woman, wanton, perverse and alluring; sonnets 153 and 154 are conventional exercises. The handsome boy has betrayed his friend the poet, and there is allusion to a rival poet who seeks the young man's favours. Very little else can be got from the story. We may take the view that the whole thing is a mere literary exercise, a continuation, sometimes in matter and often in manner, of *Venus and Adonis* and *Love's Labour's Lost;* or we may take the view that the sonnets contain a complete, precise, unadorned and undistorted account of certain passages in the life of the poet. If the first view is thought unlikely, what can be thought of the second? Would any man set down in poems for circulation the exact story of his intimate relations with identifiable persons? Even Pepys resorted to the privacy of shorthand. Yet it is the extreme "exhibitionist" view of Shakespeare that is accepted by those who take the poems as veritable documents in the poet's life story. That Shakespeare (like other men) had disturbing emotional experiences which he projected into poems and plays may be taken as possible; that the sonnets describe details of these experiences can be dismissed as impossible. And, upon any interpretation, the story comes to very little and tells us next to nothing. We may note, if we will, as curious facts, that the story and characters of the sonnets resemble nothing in the plays, but that, in certain early works, the poet calls attention to women of "black" favour—Rosaline in *Love's Labour's Lost*, the unseen Rosaline in *Romeo and Juliet*, and Hermia in *A Midsummer Night's Dream*. There let the matter rest. The sonnets of Shakespeare, we repeat, should be read as a collection of poems, not as an imperfect and improbable detective story. We must not fail to remember that the author of the sonnets was also a dramatist.

The sonnets are of the "English" form (now generally called "Shakespearean"), i.e. they are each built up of three quatrains with a final "clench" in the shape of a rhyming couplet; Shakespeare does not use the "Italian" octave and sextet form. Nevertheless many of the sonnets have the real "two-poem" character of the Italian form—i.e. there is a break in thought at the end of the octave. Others are more continuously wrought. Regarded as poems, the sonnets are at the height of their kind. The poems other than the sonnets are either tentative essays or occasional "graciousnesses" for a special purpose; the sonnets themselves have an intensity of central fire that makes most of the sonnets of the other Elizabethan sonneteers seem tepid exercises.

X. PLAYS OF UNCERTAIN AUTHORSHIP ATTRIBUTED TO SHAKESPEARE

The foundations of the Shakespearean apocrypha were laid in Shakespeare's own lifetime. Such was his popularity that plays in which he had no hand were entered upon the Stationers' Register as his, or were published with his name or initials on the title-pages. After his death publishers continued to attribute plays to him, and the theories of scholars in the course of centuries have augmented the attributions. The convenient collection called *The Shakespeare Apocrypha* (ed. C. F. Tucker Brooke) names forty-two of such plays and prints fourteen, including one, *Sir John Oldcastle*, which the decisive evidence of Henslowe's diary proves to be by four other writers. We are thus left with an actual thirteen. Disregarding six plays which were claimed by their publishers as Shakespeare's but which have not survived, we may classify the doubtful pieces in this way:

(1) Plays published in Shakespeare's lifetime and bearing his name or initials: *Locrine* (1595); *The first part of the...life of Sir John Oldcastle* (1600); *The...life and death of Thomas Lord Cromwell* (1602); *The London Prodigall* (1605); *The Puritaine* (1607); *A Yorkshire Tragedy* (1608); *Pericles* (1609). Two of these may be dismissed: *Pericles*, which has been added to the canon, and *Sir John Oldcastle*, which is not Shakespeare's, though his name appears in a quarto of 1600, dated fraudulently by Thomas Pavier, a printer of proved dishonesty.

(2) Plays published after Shakespeare's death and bearing his name as sole or joint author: *The Troublesome Raigne of John King of England* (published anonymously in 1591, initialled in 1611, and re-issued as Shakespeare's in 1622); *The Two Noble Kinsmen* (by Fletcher and Shakespeare, published in 1634); *The Birth of Merlin* (published as the work of William Shakespeare and William Rowley in 1662).

(3) Plays attributed to Shakespeare merely because they were bound together in a volume labelled "Shakespeare Vol. I" from Charles II's library: *Mucedorus* (1598); *The Merry Devill of Edmonton* (1608); *Faire Em* (1631—a quarto, c. 1593, exists).

(4) Plays attributed to Shakespeare by later critics. These are numerous; but only three need be mentioned: *Arden of Feversham* (1592), *Edward III* (1596) and *Sir Thomas More* (not printed till 1844).

The second issue of the Third Folio (1664) adds to the thirty-six plays of the First Folio seven of those named above: *Pericles, The London Prodigal, The History of Thomas Lord Cromwell, Sir John Oldcastle, The Puritan Widow, A Yorkshire Tragedy*, and *Locrine*.

There is no external evidence of value about these uncanonical plays. The fact that a publisher declared a work to be Shakespeare's tells us something about his popularity but nothing about his authorship. The true canon rests upon the Folio of 1623; and the exclusion of a play from that volume must be taken as strong, but not necessarily irrefutable, evidence against it. Plays in which Shakespeare had a major or a minor share may not have been available for use by the editors and publishers of that volume. Nevertheless it is unlikely that much was allowed to escape from an enterprise of such magnitude. There remains, therefore, the evidence furnished by the plays themselves—the internal evidence of style, diction, metre, etc., evidence which is indubitable and even decisive, but which is extraordinarily "subjective", for to people with strongly fixed views the same piece of evidence tells different stories and yields different conclusions.

The question of Shakespearean authorship is not the only point of interest presented by the doubtful plays. So varied are they in character that they furnish us with an epitome of the Elizabethan drama during the period of its greatest achievement. Almost every class of play is here represented, and one class—that of domestic tragedy—finds, in *Arden of Feversham* and in *A Yorkshire Tragedy*, two of its best examples. The Senecan tragedy of vengeance is exemplified by *Locrine*; the history, chronicle or biographical play by *Edward III*, *Sir Thomas More* and *Cromwell*, and, less precisely, by *The Birth of Merlin* and *Fair Em*. The romantic comedy of the period is illustrated by *Mucedorus*, *The Merry Devil* and *The Two Noble Kinsmen*; and *The London Prodigal* and *The Puritan* are types of that realistic bourgeois comedy which, in Stuart days, won a firm hold upon the affections of the play-going community.

Of the apocryphal tragedies the earliest was probably *Locrine*, which, in its main outline, is a Senecan revenge tragedy, the direct successor of *Gorboduc*. It contains passages of good rhetoric and some vigorous clown scenes; but nowhere can be found the faintest trace of the Shakespearean hand. There are, indeed, some liberal borrowings from Spenser. *Arden of Feversham* was first claimed as Shakespeare's by a Faversham antiquary in 1770. The author may justly be called the first English dramatic realist, for he refused to "tragedize" his matter in the Marlowe-Kyd fashion, and triumphed in his own way. *A Yorkshire Tragedy* is a less successful domestic drama than *Arden of Feversham* in the same style of realism. The story was used by George Wilkins in *The Miseries of Inforst Mariage* (1607), but Wilkins provided a happy ending. It has been suggested that Wilkins wrote both plays, and that his hand can also be found in *Pericles* and *Timon*.

Edward III was first claimed for Shakespeare by Capell in 1760. That Shakespeare added some finer, romantic touches to an old chronicle play is quite possible, and certain good judges allow him part of it. *The Troublesome Raigne of John* is merely the two-volume play of 1591 which Shakespeare used as material for *King John*. The...*life and death of Thomas Lord Cromwell* and *Sir Thomas More* are biographical rather than historical. The theme in both is a life, not a reign, and in neither does Henry VIII appear. *Cromwell* bears on its title-page the words "Written by W. S."; but it contains no trace of Shakespearean authorship. In every respect *Sir Thomas More* is superior to *Cromwell*. There is no probability that this play was ever published or performed in Elizabethan times— the sympathetic portrait of Henry VIII's noblest victim would hardly have been tolerated by Henry VIII's daughter. The play has an extraordinary interest because of the theory that a portion of it is not only composed by Shakespeare but is actually written in his hand. The view was first put forward in 1871 by Richard Simpson, a notable student of Shakespeare, and was argued at length by A. W. Pollard and other scholars in *Shakespeare's Hand in "Sir Thomas More"* (1923). In the manuscript of the play there are additions by several hands, and the fourth of these is considered to be Shakespeare's own, both in composition and in handwriting. The evidence is not, and cannot be, conclusive; but the evidence in favour is much stronger than the evidence against, and scholars of unimpeachable competence and integrity have accepted it. As a dramatic utterance, the scene is good enough to be Shakespeare's, some of the lines having an almost irresistibly persuasive power. Other "hands" in this remarkable piece of collaboration have been identified as Munday's, Chettle's and Dekker's.

The Birth of Merlin: Or, The Childe hath found his Father is a lively medley in which legendary history, love romance, necromancy and all kinds of *diablerie* jostle each other; but it shows no trace of Shakespeare's workmanship. *Faire Em* is a mingling of fictitious English history with love romance—brief, not tedious, and certainly not Shakespeare. *The Merry Devill of Edmonton* recalls *Frier Bacon and Frier Bongay* in its highly popular blending of scenes of magic and the black art with a romantic love comedy standing out against a pleasant background of English rural life; but it is not Shakespeare's. Even more popular than *The Merry Devil* was the court piece, *A Most pleasant Comedie of Mucedorus, the kings sonne of Valentia and Amadine the kings daughter of Arragon, with the merie conceites of Mouse.* It is a very primitive piece with which Shakespeare can have had no connection.

The London Prodigall is full of bustling life, but is wholly wanting in the finer qualities of dramatic art and poetic speech. There is some resemblance to the Charles Surface story of Sheridan's *School for Scandal*; there is no resemblance to anything of Shakespeare's. *The Puritane Or The Widdow of Watling-streete* (also called *The Puritaine Widdow*) is a realistic comedy of intrigue, bordering, at times, upon farce, and its main object is ridicule of the Puritan party and of London citizens. Shakespeare, plainly, had nothing to do with it.

The Two Noble Kinsmen is described on the title-page of the first known edition (1634) as "Written by the memorable Worthies of their Time; Mr. *John Fletcher*, and Mr. *William Shakspere. Gent.*" Most of the plot comes from *The Knight's Tale* of Chaucer, and to this the dramatists have added the story of the gaoler's daughter. The play has some imaginative power, energy of thought and colour of romance, and, in its lighter scenes, may be said to approach the manner of Shakespeare; but it exhibits none of Shakespeare's skill in the telling of a story; indeed, on the stage it is lifeless and bookish. The play has been claimed for Fletcher with possible aid from Massinger; but the Shakespearean authorship of some part of it is still firmly accepted by a few critics. We should notice that it was not among the seven plays added to the Third Folio.

XI. THE TEXT OF SHAKESPEARE

From time to time people are heard demanding a "standard text" or "plain text" of Shakespeare, unsullied by the ingenuities of editors. Such a demand arises from ignorance or confusion. It presupposes the existence of exact contemporary copy prepared for the press and purified from the errors of printing. No such body of matter exists or ever has existed. The major sources of misunderstanding about the text of Shakespeare are, first, an assumption that conditions of publication were the same in the sixteenth century as in the twentieth, and next an assumption that plays were written for printing. Publishing in the days of Shakespeare was more piratical than it has been since. All publishers were not pirates. Indeed, most of them were entirely respectable persons; but some were more adventurous than scrupulous and published surreptitiously procured copy without regard for the author's views. It is useful to remember that even today, when new means of transmission and multiplication have come into existence (e.g. films, broadcasting and television), there is some difficulty in adjusting the "rights" of all concerned. Textual difficulties are further complicated by the fact, already mentioned, that plays were written for performance, not for printing. We have seen that the "university wits" tried to draw a distinction between plays for court or college performance and plays for the common theatres. That distinction held good in the press to this extent, that common plays were considered inferior matter hardly worth the dignity of print. Plays were, so to speak, mere scenarios to be translated into performance by stars like Edward Alleyn and Richard Burbage; and they were worth as little in themselves as the scenarios which are now translated into performance by stars of the film world. Philip Henslowe, theatre manager, knew the prices of plays and of playwrights, as he knew the prices of bricks and timber, and noted them with business-like detail in a diary which survives among the papers at Dulwich College. He paid fivepence for a copy of Shakespeare's *Sonnets*. It was Shakespeare himself, as much as any man, who gave to plays a publication value, and his first plays came early into print.

Who sold a play to a publisher? (1) A play might be honestly sold by the company which owned it, when they thought its drawing-power had ceased; and they would probably hand over the much used theatre-copy; or (2) it might be sold less honestly by one or two hard-up members of a company, who would vamp up as much of the play as they could recollect, their own parts, naturally, being best remembered; or (3) it might be taken down in shorthand by someone anxious to procure copy for publication, or someone hired by an amateur of letters, desirous of possessing the words that had pleased him. There are refinements on these processes, but these instances are enough for present purposes.

Here is a list of Shakespeare's plays separately published before his death. Reprints and duplicates are not recorded. They appeared as small quarto pamphlets, and in this form are conveniently referred to as "the Quartos". The plays marked * are "bad quartos", i.e. maimed and unauthorized editions which probably came into print by methods (2) or (3) described in the preceding paragraph.

1594 Titus Andronicus

*1594 The First Part of the Contention betwixt the Two Famous Houses of York and Lancaster (i.e. Henry VI, Pt. 2)

*1594 The Taming of a Shrew (a version of The Taming of the Shrew)

*1595 The True Tragedy of Richard, Duke of York (i.e. Henry VI, Pt. 3)

*1597 Romeo and Juliet

1597 Richard II

1597 Richard III

1598 Henry IV (Pt. 1)

1598 Love's Labour's Lost. "Newly corrected and augmented." (These words seem to imply that there was another printed edition, which has not survived.)

1599 Romeo and Juliet. "Newly corrected, augmented and amended."

1600 Henry IV (Pt. 2)

1600 A Midsummer Night's Dream

1600 The Merchant of Venice

1600 Much Ado about Nothing

*1600 The Chronicle History of Henry the Fifth

*1602 Sir John Falstaff and the Merry Wives of Windsor

*1603 Hamlet. (This mysterious bad quarto is immediately followed by a better edition.)

1604 Hamlet. "Newly imprinted and enlarged to almost as much again as it was, according to the true and perfect Copy."

1608 King Lear

1609 Pericles, Prince of Tyre

1609 Troilus and Cressida

After Shakespeare's death and just before the First Folio was published appeared a quarto version of *Othello* (1622). The following plays were never printed, as far as we know, till the publication of the First Folio (1623): *Henry VI* (Part I), *The Two Gentlemen of Verona*, *The Comedy of Errors*, *The Taming of the Shrew* (Shakespeare's revised version), *King John*, *As You Like It*, *Julius Caesar*, *Twelfth Night*, *Measure for Measure*, *All's Well that Ends Well*, *Macbeth*, *Timon of Athens*, *Antony and Cleopatra*, *Coriolanus*, *Cymbeline*, *The Winter's Tale*, *The Tempest*, *Henry VIII*. The Folio contained the first "true texts" of *Henry V* and *The Merry Wives*.

In 1619 W. Jaggard and T. Pavier attempted to make an unauthorized collection of Shakespeare by binding up a few real and spurious plays: *The Whole Contention* (two parts), *Pericles*, *The Merry Wives*, *The Merchant of Venice*, *A Midsummer Night's Dream*, *Henry V*, *King Lear*, *A Yorkshire Tragedy* and *Sir John Oldcastle*, some with false dates, but all printed in 1619. This fraud was first fully discovered by A. W. Pollard and discussed in works mentioned on p. 190. The immediate effect of "the false folio" of Pavier and Jaggard was to cause Shakespeare's old friends and fellow actors John Heming and Henry Condell to work at a full and worthy collected edition; and this came into being as a large folio volume in 1623—the famous "First Folio", which forms, with the Bible of 1611, the major glory of English literature. A great debt of gratitude is due to Heming and Condell, who worked hard and honestly according to their lights—they were men of the theatre, not men of letters—for without them we should probably have lost twenty famous plays. Their date, 1623, is already perilously far away from Shakeseare's retirement and death, and every succeeding year would have hastened the inevitable attrition of theatrical documents. The strong remarks in the prefatory address about "stolne and surreptitious copies, maimed and deformed by the frauds and stealthes of injurious impostors that expos'd them" perhaps refer not so much to the bad early quartos as to the more recent piratical enterprise of Jaggard and Pavier. The Second (1632), Third (1663 and 1664) and Fourth (1685) Folios are testimonies of the most solid kind to the enduring admiration for Shakespeare, but they added nothing of authority to the text, though, as we have seen, the Third Folio included seven new plays, of which one only, *Pericles*, has been taken into the canon. The Fourth Folio modernizes the spelling, but it takes over most of the errors committed by the Second and Third. The period of printers and copyists lasts, therefore, to the end of the seventeenth century. With the eighteenth century comes the period of scholars and editors. The whole process is similar to that undergone by any classical text.

It is fitting that a poet laureate and dramatist should be the first editor of Shakespeare. Nicholas Rowe's edition (1709) was pioneer work and deserves high praise. If it is remembered that Rowe had no tradition of scholarship to draw upon and very small actual means of making a text (he worked on the Fourth, not the First, Folio), the wonder is that he did so well. It was Rowe who attempted the first systematic division and location of scenes, the lists of *dramatis personae*, the clear entrances and exits, and other additions designed to make a difficult body of old literature intelligible to readers and actors of a much later age. Rowe modestly called no special attention to his editorial work. His labours were depreciated by those who profited most by them. His emendations were silently introduced into his text and silently appropriated by his successors. Rowe also attempted the first life of Shakespeare, and, in seeking for materials, found and adopted certain legends and probabilities which long remained part of biographical tradition.

The next editor, Alexander Pope (1725), brought to his task a poet's instinct and an exquisite metrical sense. But for the drudgery of editorial labour he was totally unfitted, and, though he added passages from the quartos and identified as verse various lines printed as prose, his failures were many. These were severely exposed in *Shakespeare Restored* (1726) by Lewis Theobald (1688–1744), the first important critic and reviser of the old texts. Theobald's most brilliant emendation was made in the story of Falstaff's death, where he turned the meaningless "and a Table of greene fields" into "and a' babld of green fields" —an emendation generally accepted by later editors but criticized by the American scholar Leslie Hotson in the *Times Literary Supplement* (6 April 1956). Pope had no talent for editorial workmanship, but he replied to Theobald's criticism by making him the hero of *The Dunciad*. Theobald's own edition of Shakespeare appeared in 1733. He was followed by Sir Thomas Hanmer (1744), who produced an edition for gentlemen by a gentleman, with everything handsome about it, except the text. The next editor, William Warburton (1698–1779), Bishop of Gloucester, was one of those bullies of literature whose success is incredible to later ages. His edition (1747) is remarkable alike for its insolence and its ignorance. His conjectures would furnish a curiosity shop of impossible words. Almost the sole value of Warburton's edition is that it drew from

Thomas Edwards in 1748 an ironical supplement, which, reissued as *The Canons of Criticism*, takes high place among critical studies of Shakespeare. The long-announced and long-delayed edition of Dr Johnson appeared in 1765 and atoned for its technical defects by the great preface, which is one of the landmarks in English literary criticism. With the next editor, Edward Capell (1713–81), begins the scientific study of the text, for he was the first to make complete and exact collations of all the old copies and thus to put textual criticism on the right path. His arrangement of the lines is that now usually followed. Capell's edition began to appear in 1768. George Steevens (1736–1800), who, in 1766, had done good service by printing twenty old quartos, took over Johnson's edition, made good its defects, and published the whole in 1773. Steevens was a learned and impish scholar—the Puck of commentators. He profited, with marked ingratitude, by Capell's researches. The next important name is that of Edmund Malone (1741–1812), the greatest Shakespearean scholar of his age. After contributing various supplements to other editions he produced his own in 1790. The publishers began to "pool" their Shakespearean collections in editions combining all the most useful features. What is known as the Third Variorum Edition (1821), edited by Malone and Boswell (son of Johnson's biographer), belongs in date to the nineteenth century, but is an encyclopaedia of eighteenth-century studies in Shakespeare. Its twenty-one volumes are still indispensable to any comprehensive Shakespearean library.

Among those who contributed to the general explication of Shakespeare by work other than editorial may be named Thomas Tyrwhitt with his *Observations and Conjectures upon some Passages of Shakespeare* (1766), in which occurs the first reference to the *Palladis Tamia* of Meres, Richard Farmer with his *Essay on the Learning of Shakespeare* (1767), and Francis Douce with his *Illustrations of Shakespeare* (1807). Among the first nineteenth-century editors were S. W. Singer and J. P. Collier, the latter of whom did valuable work with the Shakespeare Society, which was formed in 1840, and was the source of many important studies. Unfortunately Collier lapsed into dishonesty, and produced emendations, not as his own, but as contemporary manuscript corrections in his copy of the Second Folio. The Shakespeare Society did not survive the exposure of Collier's forgeries, and everything touched by Collier now unhappily lies under suspicion. James Orchard Halliwell (afterwards Halliwell-Phillipps), a youthful member of the old Shakespeare Society, produced a magnificent folio edition (between 1853 and 1865) which is still of value. Nikolaus Delius in 1854–61 produced a sound text based on first-hand study; and in 1857 Alexander Dyce published his scrupulously careful and honest edition, the best of its time. The work of Dyce prepared the way for what was long the standard text, *The Cambridge Shakespeare*, edited (1863–6) by W. G. Clark and J. Glover, re-edited (1891–3) by W. Aldis Wright. This text was used in the popular one-volume *Globe* edition and in Sir Israel Gollancz's *Temple Shakespeare* (1894–6, succeeded by M. R. Ridley's *New Temple Shakespeare*, 1935–49). Later work includes the excellent *Arden Shakespeare* (edited 1899–1924 by W. J. Craig and R. H. Case, revised 1951–66 by Una Ellis-Fermor and H. F. Brooks), many great volumes from Philadelphia of a *New Variorum Shakespeare* prepared by Howard Furness and Howard Furness Jr, the publication of facsimile reprints of all the quartos and folios, and the issue of the *New Cambridge Shakespeare* (1921–66), edited by Sir Arthur Quiller-Couch, John Dover Wilson and other scholars, with their fresh approach to the textual and bibliographical problems. G. B. Harrison's *Penguin Shakespeare* (1937–66) prints a text as near as possible to that used in the Globe Playhouse. R. B. McKerrow's *Oxford Shakespeare* began in 1965.

XII. SHAKESPEARE IN EUROPE AND AMERICA

It is a tribute to the power of the Elizabethan drama that it found an audience on the Continent at a time when literary taste was under the spell of the revived classic traditions, and was intolerant of irregularity, wildness and excess. There was, of course, no formal triumph of Shakespearean freedom over classical regularity. The Elizabethan plays conquered, not as works of literature, but as theatrical "thrillers" of a new and fascinating kind. Towards the end of the sixteenth century and throughout the seventeenth, English actors from time to time crossed to the Continent and travelled through much of northern and central Europe, giving roughly garbled and intensified versions of their outstanding successes, and aiming at the "sensational" rather than at the quieter effects. Passion, not poetry, was their purpose. The English comedians proved very popular, and left many traces of their passage, not the least remarkable being German plays written in imitation of the English pieces. Some of these are anonymous theatrical products, but Jacob Ayrer, Andreas Gryphius and Christian Weisse wrote acknowledged pieces in the English, and even in the Shakespearean manner. There is not the least evidence that Shakespeare himself travelled with any of these troupes; but versions of his most effective plays were given; and one curious relic remains in the German *Fratricide Punished*, a crude caricature of *Hamlet*, which existed in a manuscript of *c.* 1710, and which some critics have rashly assumed to be the transcript of an early—perhaps the very original—*Hamlet*; but obviously, and especially to those who saw it acted in 1924, the piece is nothing but a German version or adaptation of Shakespeare's play, as vamped up, garbled and "potted", probably from memory, by resourceful players without "parts". Thus some of Shakespeare's work became known, after a fashion; but there is no evidence that his name or the name of any English author was attached to the matter served up by these strollers. The performances were actors' shows, not literary exhibitions.

The name of Shakespeare was barely mentioned abroad before the end of the seventeenth century. Foreign readers got their first real information from the remarks in Temple's *Essay of Poetry*, which had been translated into French in 1693, and from Addison's criticism in *The Spectator*, which had been published at Amsterdam in French in 1714. The revocation of the Edict of Nantes had led to a wide dispersion of the intelligent French Huguenots and a consequent demand for French versions of attractive current literature. But the great discoverer of Shakespeare for Europe was Voltaire, who, beginning with curiosity and ending with antagonism, was interested enough to keep writing about him. French drama of the seventeenth century, and especially French tragedy as written by Corneille and Racine, had developed in obedience to supposed classical laws and strictly respected the unities of time, place, action and kind— all very good things, for their other names are continuity, stability, simplicity and congruity. There was perfect decorum on the French stage. Phaedra, in Racine's play, kills herself unseen, and the terrible death of Hippolytus is reported in a long narrative declamation. The story of their conflict has no complication, and the action proceeds without pause and in one place. Such was French tragedy, and it was accepted everywhere but in England as the model; and even in England Sidney had long before demanded classical congruity and decorum. Shakespearean tragedy developed, not from examples of classical restraint, but from the realism of the "miracles" and the horrors of Seneca; and so a play like *Julius Caesar*, with the hero openly slain by the conspirators, with Brutus and Cassius perishing violently on the stage, and with the visible, audible ghost of Caesar himself intervening in an action that ranges in place from Rome to Philippi and includes comic interludes by the crowd, had for Voltaire the fascination of complete impropriety. To him Shakespeare was a natural, uncouth genius, full of the wayward errors of raw invention. Voltaire, who came to England in 1726, embodied his interest in Shakespeare not only in his *Lettres sur les Anglais* (1733), but in *La Mort de César* (1735) and other plays; and a Shakespeare vogue began to develop in France. But Voltaire grew less tolerant of Shakespeare's wayward genius when enthusiasm for it showed signs of spreading, and especially when Germany stole a march on France and produced in 1741 a full translation of *Julius Caesar* by Caspar Wilhelm von Borck, the first translation of a Shakespearean play into any foreign language. Voltaire was not the man to endure rivals, either in creation or in criticism. Borck's *Julius Caesar* gave young German enthusiasts like Lessing their first glimpse of a new poetic drama, and marks the beginning of German romanticism. French interest in Shakespeare was further stimulated when, in 1745, Pierre Antoine de La Place published synopses, with illustrative passages, of certain Shakespeare plays; and Voltaire saw with resentment that his fascinating barbarian was not only being stolen from him by others, but was being offered seriously to cultivated people as a legitimate artist in drama.

Knowledge and appreciation of Shakespeare in France developed rapidly, and even reached the point of constraining one anonymous essayist to contribute a *Parallèle entre Shakespear et Corneille* to *Le Journal Encyclopédique* in 1760. Voltaire, incensed by this challenge to French supremacy, issued his *Appel à toutes les Nations de l'Europe*; but this did not prevent Diderot from admiring the "Gothic colossus", or Le Tourneur from embarking upon a new and much more ambitious translation in 1776. Voltaire carried his appeal by letter to the highest court, and on 25 August 1776 his denunciation was solemnly read by d'Alembert to the French Academy. A second letter from Voltaire followed on 7 October, and was published as the preface to his tragedy *Irène*, the performance of which had been his last triumph in Paris. "Shakespeare is a savage with sparks of genius which shine in a horrible night." This was Voltaire's final verdict. As Jusserand remarks, he who, all his life, had been the champion of every kind of liberty refused it to tragedy alone. But an avenging irony pursued him; for Jean François Ducis, who succeeded to Voltaire's seat in the Academy.

produced versions that put Shakespeare effectively on the French stage and enabled Talma, in *Othello*, to gain one of his greatest triumphs. The versions of Ducis were little more than perversions, but they were not greatly worse than the distortions which satisfied English playgoers from the days of Davenant's *Macbeth* and Dryden's *Tempest* to the days of Colley Cibber's *Richard III* and Nahum Tate's *King Lear*.

Though French literature was fashionable in the Germany of Frederick the Great, Shakespeare steadily grew in favour. Lessing, who resented French dictatorship of the drama, saw in Shakespeare, first, a kinship to the German *Volksdrama*, which his influence might rekindle, and next, a greater affinity with Greek drama than could be found even in Corneille. Between 1762 and 1766 appeared Wieland's prose translation. Its faults are obvious enough, but its consequences filled Wieland and Lessing with something like dismay; for the young men who read Wieland's translation were not interested in "Shakespeare the brother of Sophocles"; they went wild over "Shakespeare the voice of Nature". They did not criticize, they worshipped; and Shakespeare became the ultimate voice of romanticism, whose utterances were as much beyond question as the phenomena of nature. The new enthusiasm reached Goethe, twenty years the junior of Lessing. Better translations were made, and Germany's greatest actor, Friedrich Ludwig Schröder, electrified audiences from Hamburg to Vienna with his Shakespearean interpretations. The performance of *King Lear* in Vienna on 13 April 1780 was a landmark in the history of the theatre. So complete was the conquest that Shakespeare has never since lost his commanding position on the German stage. Unfortunately, German enthusiasm led to a falsely romantic interpretation of Shakespeare, the outstanding effort in this kind being the egregious discussion of *Hamlet* in the first part of *Wilhelm Meister*, published in 1795–6, though begun twenty years before. Much of the "gushing" criticism to which Shakespeare was subjected during the nineteenth century originates in German romanticism of the *Sturm und Drang* period. But, fortunately, there was more than mere empty enthusiasm. August Wilhelm Schlegel was stimulated by Goethe to pursue the task of a new translation and the nine volumes appeared between 1797 and 1801. With this marvellous translation German labours to naturalize the English poet reach their culmination. The extent of Shakespeare's influence in Germany can hardly be exaggerated. He not only set German dramatic literature free from the restraint of French "rules", he led it into a romantic world of which the French classic stage knew nothing.

In France the influence was naturally not so deep or so lasting; but the precursors and leaders of the new romantic movement found inspiration in Shakespeare. Stendhal (Henri Beyle) in his *Racine et Shakespeare* (1823) took Shakespeare's side emphatically against the classics, and Guizot not only revised Le Tourneur but lauded Shakespeare as a dramatic poet. In 1822 an attempt of English actors to produce Shakespeare in Paris had failed; but in 1827 a renewed attempt, with the co-operation of Charles Kemble, Macready and Edmund Kean, awakened the enthusiasm of all literary Paris; and, under the influence of this excitement, Victor Hugo wrote his famous manifesto of the new romantic movement, the preface to *Cromwell* (1827). Alfred de Musset's whole dramatic work is permeated and coloured by Shakespearean influence. That influence is equally discernible in the paintings of Delacroix and in the compositions of Berlioz. From this time, the supremacy of Shakespeare in modern literature has not been seriously questioned in France. Better translations were made, the most notable being that of François Victor Hugo, son of the great poet (1859–66), and there have been later individual translations of high merit. But Shakespeare was never naturalized in France as he was in Germany. Performances of his plays, though sometimes dramatically electrical and politically disturbing, are matters for special occasions and for a special public.

Throughout the nineteenth century, Germany, like France, continued to produce translations of Shakespeare. The assertion, sometimes made, that Germany "discovered" Shakespeare will need no refutation for those who have read the preceding pages. But we must readily admit that Germany has paid a noble tribute to Shakespeare by devoting to the study of his works all the resources of scholarship and by devoting to the presentation of his works all the resources of the stage. August Schlegel's *Lectures on Dramatic Art and Literature* (1809–11) may be said to have revealed Coleridge to himself; and Coleridge brought his own kind of transcendentalism to the interpretation of Shakespeare. After German romance came German philosophy, with the result that, during part of the nineteenth century, the influence of Hegel was strongly felt in German criticism. This led to an excessive preoccupation with metaphysical theories of tragic guilt and tragic purpose, to a misleading confusion of moral and aesthetic standards and to a too confident reliance on *a priori* theories of literary genius. The Hegelian influence, it should be noted, has strongly affected some eminent English critics of Shakespearean tragedy. However, the works of numerous German writers, whether scholars, critics or philosophers, have in one way or another contributed something to the elucidation of Shakespeare; and since 1865 the *Shakespeare Jahrbuch* has been the valuable repository of patient and laborious research. To record the history of Shakespearean performances on the German stage is beyond the scope of this work; but we may note briefly that, on the occasion of the Shakespeare tercentenary in 1864 (when the *Shakespeare-Gesellschaft* was founded) a complete cycle of the chronicle plays was performed at Weimar, and that from 1874 onwards at Saxe-Meiningen Duke George II attracted the attention not only of all Germany but of other lands to stage representations of rare pictorial beauty and historical accuracy.

Of other parts of Europe it may be said generally that the north followed Germany and the south followed France. Italy first learned of Shakespeare through Voltaire. The work of translation was begun by Leoni early in the nineteenth century, continued by Rusconi and completed by Carcani. But Italy's most memorable tributes of honour to Shakespeare have been the tragic impersonations of Salvini and Ristori, and the operatic versions of many composers, culminating in the *Macbeth*, *Otello* and *Falstaff* of Verdi. Considering the kinship between Shakespeare and the masters of the Spanish drama, it is strange that Spain had no translation till modern times. In the north of Europe Shakespeare was long in establishing himself; but Scandinavia and Denmark have both made contributions to Shakespearean study, the works of Georg Brandes, for instance, achieving popularity far beyond his native Denmark. Holland, which learned very early something about Shakespeare, did not get satisfactory full translations till late in the nineteenth century. In Russia, Poland and Hungary, Shakespeare has long been popular.

Some tribute ought to be paid to the independence and originality of American contributions to Shakespearean criticism and research. By borrowing the best elements in English critical methods and combining them with German thoroughness and patience—and with the practical assistance of richly-endowed fellowships and foundations—American scholars have thrown much light on dark places and contributed very materially to our understanding of Shakespeare's work and times. In the biographical field, for example, there have been the researches of C. W. Wallace and Leslie Hotson. The *Life* (1923) by Joseph Quincy Adams is a biography comparable to Sir Sidney Lee's or to Sir Edmund Chambers's, to name the two chief modern biographies by British scholars, while *The Globe Playhouse* (1942) by John Cranford Adams is the best account we have of the theatre where Shakespeare worked. Among many other notable books by twentieth-century American scholars, mostly published by the presses of various American universities, may be mentioned *Middle-class Culture in Elizabethan England* (1935) by Louis B. Wright and *William Shakspere's Small Latine and Lesse Greeke* (1944) by T. W. Baldwin, both works of considerable scope and learning. If the tide of fortune has cast onto American university beaches many books and manuscripts that might otherwise have remained in British hands, American scholars have not been slow to return the compliment and publish their researches for the benefit of us all.

XIII. LESSER ELIZABETHAN DRAMATISTS

Philip Henslowe, shrewd man of business, included theatrical management among his activities, and kept a rough diary from which we learn something about the lesser dramatists of the last Elizabethan years. We have no such record as Henslowe's for the company in which Shakespeare played and wrote. The Chamberlain's men managed their own business co-operatively and sought to secure plays of good quality that would be sure of a run. Henslowe, on the contrary, seems to have gone in for popularity at any price, and he believed that success was to be found in collaboration. The virtue of a dramatic piece lay in its suitability for performance, not in its suitability for publication; and several authors would be more likely than a single writer to provide actable sensations quickly. Works thus produced are not likely to survive. We can be reasonably sure that no important play of Shakespeare's has been lost; the bulk of Chettle's and Munday's work has perished. The lesser dramatist does not stamp his individuality upon his adaptations or collaborations or modernizations, and his work is not easily identifiable. Nevertheless, in the writings of the popular playwrights who were a little too early to be deeply affected by the powerful influence of Shakespeare or Jonson there is a curiously attractive quality. Munday's anticipations of Shakespeare are more intrinsically interesting than Brome's patient imitations of Jonson.

Henslowe's diary begins to record payments made to dramatists at the close of 1597. The entries come to an end, for the most part, in 1603. During this time, twenty-seven authors are named as composers of plays or parts of plays. The work of ten can be dismissed as unimportant. Of the remaining seventeen, six are writers of force and distinction, not to be reckoned as "lesser": they are Chapman, Dekker, Heywood, Jonson, Middleton and Webster. We may note that, of these six, only Chapman refuses to collaborate with inferior men; that Jonson, when collecting his plays in 1616, included nothing belonging to this period; and that Middleton and Webster are not named in the diary till 1602. Rowley and Smith began writing in 1601; Rankins is mentioned only in 1599 and 1601. Eight writers are left who constitute the main group of lesser men writing for the Elizabethan stage between the end of 1597 and the beginning of 1603. These, in alphabetical order, are Henry Chettle, John Day, Michael Drayton, Richard Hathwaye, William Haughton, Anthony Munday, Henry Porter, and Robert Wilson. The comments of Francis Meres in 1598 upon English contemporary writers enable us to check this result. Of Henslowe's men Meres names, among "our best for tragedy", Drayton, Chapman, Dekker, Jonson; among "the best for comedy", Heywood, Munday, Chapman, Porter, Wilson, Hathwaye, Chettle.

Of the lesser men, Anthony Munday, oddly called by Meres "our best plotter", is the most considerable and interesting. His long life, moreover, of eighty years (1553–1633) covers the whole of the Elizabethan and Jacobean era of dramatic activity. He had a varied experience. He was apprenticed to a stationer; he took up anti-Roman controversy; he tried (and dismally failed) to be an extempore actor in the manner of Tarlton and Kemp; he took to letters and made translations of romances such as *Amadis of Gaul*, *Palmerin of England* and *Palladine of England*; he wrote "ballads" which put him into contact with old stories, and he worked hard as a dramatist for Henslowe between 1594 and 1602; further, he was a "city poet" for twenty-six years and helped to devise the pageants for the annual "riding" of the Lord Mayor. Munday's numerous occupations made him a mark for satire during "the war of the theatres". Ben Jonson in *The Case is Altered* introduces him as "Antonio Balladino", a pageant poet, "when a worse cannot be had"; and the anonymous *Histrio-Mastix* (c. 1589, revised by Marston) calls him Posthaste. Munday's chief surviving "original" plays are: *John a Kent and John a Cumber* (c. 1594); *The Downfall of Robert, Earle of Huntington, Afterward called Robin Hood of merrie Sherwodde* (1601); and *The Death of Robert, Earle of Huntington* (1601) in collaboration with Henry Chettle. Munday further collaborated with Drayton, Hathwaye and Wilson in the pseudo-Shakespearean *Sir John Oldcastle*. *John a Kent and John a Cumber* was very popular. On lines laid down by Greene in *Friar Bacon and Friar Bungay*, it describes the "tug for maistree" between the two wizards John a Kent and John a Cumber. The comic scenes faintly suggest Bottom and his mates; and Shrimp, John a Kent's "familiar", with his "invisible music", less faintly suggests Ariel. Munday, the writer of ballads, was familiar with the stories of Robin Hood. In his *Downfall of Robert* he tries, not very successfully, to blend the ballad element with sober history. The play is better on the romantic side, and the rhyming lines run more happily than the blank verse. Possibly

the poet of the Forest of Arden may have learned something from it. That the
poet of *Macbeth* remembered such phrases as "made the green sea red" and
"the multitudes of seas dyed red with blood" seems hardly deniable. The
second Robin Hood play, from which the last quotation is taken, and to which
Chettle added an Induction and some scenes, contains, in the "lamentable
tragedy of chaste Matilda", strains of a higher mood than anything we know
Munday to have written. His lost plays hardly concern us; but we may note
that a continuation of *Sir John Oldcastle*, in which he had a share, is among them.
Munday is one of the minor Elizabethans eminently worthy of sympathetic
study. To Munday has been attributed *Fedele and Fortunio, The...fine conceited
Comoedie of two Italian Gentlemen* (1585). No perfect copy of this was known
till 1919. The chief character, Captain Crackstone, is the prototype of Jonson's
Bobadill and the other braggarts of the Elizabethan stage. The attribution of the
play to Munday is questioned. Yet another play attributed to him is *The
Weakest goeth to the Wall* (1600), which, unlike *The Two Italian Gentlemen*,
contains a good deal of blank verse. Barnabe Bunch speaks some Falstaffian
prose; but Jacob van Smelt is a character that indicates Dekker as a possible
author or adapter. A play in the same general style as Munday's is the anonymous *Looke about you* (1600). We are in the region of mingled chapbook and
history. There are reminiscences of *The Comedy of Errors* and, still more clearly,
of the Falstaff scenes in *Henry IV*. The play has also been assigned to Dekker
and to a certain Anthony Wadeson. The dates are those of first publication;
but *John a Kent* was not printed till 1851.

If Munday deserves mention for the length of his days, Henry Chettle
(d. 1607?) should be named for the extent of his output. Henslowe associates
him with some fifty plays. Chettle, like Munday, was apprenticed to book-
production; but what is most generally remembered about him is that he
edited *Greenes Groatsworth of Wit* and apologized in his own *Kind Harts
Dreame* (1593) to the two anonymous dramatists (most probably Marlowe and
Shakespeare) who had been the special objects of Greene's malignity. Meres
names Chettle as among our "best for comedy"; but no comedies have survived.
The one extant play of Chettle's is a gloomy piece called *The Tragedy of Hoff-
man or A Revenge for a Father* written about 1602 and published in 1631. It is a
series of horrors, and may be described as Kyd coarsened and unredeemed. His
Englands Mourning Garment (1603), written to commemorate Queen Elizabeth's
death, is excellent prose, and contains good descriptions of contemporary poets
in verse. With Chettle has been associated another gloomy play, *Two Lamentable Tragedies*, printed in 1601, but assigned on the title-page to an unknown
"Rob. Yarington" who has been conjectured to be the "Wm. Haughton" of
other entries in Henslowe's diary. The play deals with two murders; the first
is the murder of Robert Beech by Thomas Merry in 1594, the second is the
murder of the babes in the wood, placed in an Italian setting. As the play
possesses, intrinsically, very small value, we need not discuss the problems of its
composition. It shows how incredibly bad the Marlowe type of villain can
become when presented without the saving grace of poetic imagination. The
one surviving play definitely given to William Haughton is *Englishmen For my
Money: or A pleasant Comedy, called, A Woman will have her Will*, written about

1598 and printed in 1616. Its picture of the lanes of the old City of London, in which, for a night, the characters play hide and seek, and its homely and lively sketches of citizen life, give the play an attractiveness of its own. It may be called an anticipation of Ben Jonson. Another extant play which Henslowe's diary assigns to Haughton but which the title-page gives to an unidentified "I. T." is *Grim the Collier of Croyden; Or, The Devil and his Dame: With the Devil and Saint Dunston* (written about 1600, published 1662). This combines a comic plot with a perversion of history. The comic scenes are clearly a development of the improvisations in which Tarlton and Kemp succeeded and Munday failed.

Henry Porter is described by Meres as one of "the best for Comedy amongst us". He wrote, wholly or in part, several plays for Henslowe; but of these the only survivor is *The Pleasant Historie of the two angrie women of Abington*, twice printed in 1599. The play is a strong and sturdy picture of rural life; it smacks of the soil, and has in it something of the vigour and virility which stamp Jonson's best work. Ben was not so isolated as he supposed. Just as we can perceive a background to Shakespeare's genius in the work of Munday and Chettle, so the comedies of such men as Haughton and Porter prove that Jonson's art was in the air when he began to write.

Of Richard Hathwaye (an interesting name!), numbered among "the best for Comedy", nothing survives but his unidentified share in *Sir John Oldcastle*. Robert Wilson also contributed to that piece; and he (or another of that name) published *A right excellent and famous Comoedy called The three Ladies of London* (1584), *The Pleasant and Stately Morall of the three Lordes and three Ladies of London* (1590) and *The Coblers Prophesie* (1594), all attractive works that reach back to the tradition of the moralities. Wentworth Smith may be the W. Smith who wrote *The Hector of Germaine*, acted about 1613 and printed in 1615; his connection with other "Smith" productions cannot be ascertained.

Michael Drayton, like Shakespeare, is a writer who took care of his poems and no care of his plays. Meres puts him among the best for tragedy, and Henslowe records payments to him for over twenty plays, mainly in collaboration; but his share in the first part of *Sir John Oldcastle* alone survives. The poems show that Drayton's genius was essentially undramatic.

John Day received payment from Henslowe once as sole author, and he collaborated in twenty-one plays. The only survivor of these compositions is *The Blind-Beggar of Bednal-Green* written about 1600 and printed in 1659. It is a confused, hastily-written "ballad-play", not so pleasant and sweet as Munday would have made it. Day's better work belongs to the Jacobean period and will be considered later.

Samuel Rowley did little for Henslowe. With W. Bird he made additions to Marlowe's *Faustus*. His one surviving play is *When you see me, You know me. Or the famous Chronicle Historie of King Henry the eight* (printed 1605). This leaves the region of popular legend, and attempts to dramatize actual history. Rowley's play is of great interest as the forerunner of *Henry VIII*, but has its own merits. The scenes in which Will Summers appears carry us back to the days when the leading clown could hold up the progress of the play by his irrelevant jesting. There is extant also *The Noble Souldier*, printed in 1634 as "written by S. R.". It is an interesting play, containing work by Day and probably by Dekker. If any substantial part of the work is Rowley's, the favourable impression of his talent produced by *When you see me, You know me* is deepened.

Besides the popular Elizabethan drama, there was an unpopular Elizabethan drama, which failed because it aimed too high and remained tied to classical methods and traditions. In France, a Senecan style of drama dominated the stage, and, through the French poet Robert Garnier (1534–90), exercised a strong influence upon a coterie of distinguished literary people in England. Mary Sidney, Countess of Pembroke, translated Garnier's *Marc-Antoine* into scholarly English blank verse as *Antonius* (1592), using lyrical measures for the choruses, and reaching, in this part of her work, a high level of excellence. Daniel's *Cleopatra*, printed in 1594, was a kind of sequel to Lady Pembroke's play, and his *Philotas* (1605) was a second study in the same style. Both plays are meritorious and may be read with pleasure. Kyd's translation of Garnier's *Cornélie* is mentioned earlier. In touch with this circle of poets was a genius of very singular and rare quality, Fulke Greville, Lord Brooke, who produced two plays which were probably written in the main before the end of the century—*Mustapha*, printed 1609, and *Alaham*, printed posthumously. Though Greville imitated the Senecan model he produced a kind of drama that is Greek in its intensity and severity, but peculiar to itself in its selection of dramatic types and character from the world of politics and statesmanship. He tells us, significantly, that he writes for "those only that are weather-beaten in the sea of this world". The verse of his choruses, strange, stiff, oracular, have an almost disquieting note of unnatural calm. The originality of Greville's work becomes clear when we compare it with the dull though able *Monarchicke Tragedies* (1604–7), i.e. *Croesus, Darius, The Alexandraean, Julius Caesar*, by Sir William Alexander, afterwards Earl of Stirling (1567–1640). Greville is the seer or Hebrew prophet of the Elizabethan dramatists, and altogether a fascinating, solitary figure.

XIV. SOME POLITICAL AND SOCIAL ASPECTS OF THE LATER ELIZABETHAN AND EARLIER STUART PERIOD

The later years of Elizabeth and the earlier years of her successor were a period of turbulence and unrest, an age of bold spirits, fearless alike of life and death. During that period of great events we shall not find perfect correspondence between the course of literature and national affairs; nevertheless the drama pursued its own natural way and reflected the intense life of its time. In the earlier half of Elizabeth's reign the drama, still moving onwards in tentative forms, was only gradually finding its way into English literature at all. Sir Philip Sidney, president of his little classical Areopagus, had small praise for English poetry and still less for English drama. *Gorboduc*, indeed, was honoured with compliment and criticism; but for the "naughtie Play-makers and Stage-keepers" there was nothing but censure. Yet by the time of his death in 1586 the foundations had been well and truly laid of the magnificent dramatic creation that we rightly call Elizabethan.

The peculiarity of Elizabethan monarchy was that it was Elizabethan. Only the cranks bothered about theories. Elizabeth herself was better than any theory of government. So the dramatists are all ardent monarchists and loyalists. That the Queen neither brought into England a foreign prince to share her throne nor raised any proud Leicester to her level gave a curious intensity to the devotion of her people. She was completely English, too, in her attitude towards the great religious controversies of her time, leaning neither towards Rome nor towards Geneva; and it is significant that a year after her death command was given for the great new version of the Bible, which in spirit, though not in date, is Elizabethan. So the dramatists are generally as anti-papal as they are anti-puritan—even Ben Jonson's conversion having no perceptible influence on him as a writer. It must not be forgotten that distrust of Catholics was due, not to dislike of their faith, but to suspicion of their loyalty. To the popular mind every Jesuit was an emissary of the enemy. The strife with Spain, which included the marauding adventures of the great seamen and the protection of the Netherlands, culminated in the defeat of the Armada; yet there is no contemporary play which mentions Drake and there is scarcely an allusion to the great victory. We forget that the defeat of the Armada ended nothing but the Armada. To contemporaries it was only an incident. The Spanish danger still remained a menace; and it was rearing its head at England's very doors in Ireland. On the other hand the fate of Essex, a prominent figure in the long war, could not escape notice from the dramatists; for Essex, like Southampton, like Mountjoy, like "the incomparable paire of brethren" William and Philip Herbert, Sidney's nephews, to whom the First Folio was dedicated, was a patron of poets and a friend of letters; and to him there are numerous references which audiences of the time could not fail to identify.

The court of Elizabeth exhibited an openness to intellectual interests such as only her unfailing regard for learning and letters could have long maintained. No similar intellectual exertion was made by James I, whose literary tastes, like most of his thoughts and impulses, were mean. The sovereign and the greater nobles were girded round with elaborate etiquette and ceremonial. Neither Elizabeth nor her royal father was so accessible to messengers and strangers as are some of Shakespeare's monarchs. The courtiers were typified in life by Sidney and in art by Hamlet; but we are not to suppose that the population of England was composed of Sidneys and Hamlets. Part of the attraction of Sidney was that he was a brilliant exception. But the important fact is that the type was admired and accepted. The "low brow" in mind and morals had not then attained to the glory of general adulation and emulation.

The repute of trade was steadily rising. Shakespeare depicts the bourgeois Fords and Pages with sympathy; but like other dramatists he is severe with usurers. The modern passion for wealth merely for wealth's sake would have met, too, with small mercy at the satiric hand that drew Sir Epicure Mammon.

The greatest charm of an English house, its garden, might almost be described as an Elizabethan addition to English domestic life; before this period, private horticulture had chiefly directed itself to the production of kitchen vegetables and medicinal herbs. Flowers were now coming to be much prized, and the love of them displayed by several Elizabethan dramatists, pre-eminently by Shakespeare, was fostered by a desire to gratify popular taste.

That there was gluttony and intemperance is evident from the protests of Hamlet against the drunkenness for which the change from light French wines to the heavier "Sherris sack" beloved by Falstaff was probably responsible. The "new vice" of taking tobacco is not mentioned by Shakespeare; but Ben Jonson gives us "Signior WHIFFE", who had "come to spit private, in *Paules*".

In the Elizabethan and early Stuart ages, an excessive love of dress was as marked a national characteristic as a fondness for the pleasures of the table. Actors delighted to display gorgeous costumes on the stage. Shakespeare alludes very definitely to articles of dress and personal adornment; but whether the characters are Greek, Roman or Danish, whether the times are Homeric or Renascence, the details are English and contemporary.

The naval and military professions as such played very small part in the social history of the country. No standing army was kept up for warfare. The local authorities could always form a militia on paper and fill it with recruits of the kind that Falstaff collected from Mr Justice Shallow. In London and elsewhere order was kept by watchmen with their brown bills—familiar figures of Elizabethan comedy. The general security of the country, no doubt, was greater than of old; and though highway robberies were not uncommon, a hue and cry could follow highwaymen successfully from Gad's Hill to Eastcheap.

The clergy held no very high standing, as far as the drama gives evidence, but they were generally intelligent and even learned men. The dramatists never ridicule the doctrines of Puritans, but are legitimately concerned with their moral pretensions and "humours". The feeling against Jews was merely the persistence of ancient prejudice, for Jews in London throughout the whole of the period were few in number and little known. Shylock and Barabas are not portraits from life.

Among the professions, the law took a high place, and many of our dramatists, with Shakespeare at their head, show familiarity with legal terms and processes. The Inns of Court were great social institutions and to them the drama and the masque are heavily indebted.

The physician's profession, about this time, was being disentangled, on the one hand, from that of the clergyman, and, on the other, from the trade of the apothecary and of the barber, who united to his main functions those of dentist and yet others. Medical treatment was old-fashioned in no flattering sense of the term. To new diseases it was savage, to mental trouble, barbarous.

Booksellers were beginning to flourish, and even playwrights could acquire a competence. It is curious that in this period of intense dramatic activity only about nine persons seem to have combined, like Shakespeare, the functions of actor and author; actually, writers of popular plays sometimes express the general contempt for actors. Exceptionally, poets (Munday and Jonson are examples) might hold municipal or official situations.

The cultivation of music was one of the most attractive features of Shakespeare's age and was common to all ranks and both sexes. There is no English poet so clearly at home in music as Shakespeare. The external conditions of the drama proper were such that it could owe little or nothing to architect, sculptor or painter; the achievements of Inigo Jones belong to the history of the masque.

That the yeomen and labouring classes are sympathetically depicted will hardly be denied by any unprejudiced student of the drama. It is not just to illustrate the contempt of the Elizabethan drama for the masses either by satirical pictures of mobs and popular rebellions, or by particular phrases of particular characters. Shakespeare depicts his mechanicals with a Dickensian understanding.

Though life seemed cheap and was lightly forfeited, violent crime was held in abhorrence. The public punishments, sometimes very horrible, must be remembered when we encounter scenes of physical horror in the plays; but how few these are must have been noticed by every reader. Shakespeare is remarkably free from them. That there was strong feeling and high spirit can be seen in martyrdom as well as in ruthlessness. But the final cause of this high spirit was the belief in things worth living for and worth dying for—a belief which lies at the root of noble endeavour, and without which no nation will continue to be great.

The position of women—a sure clue to the character of any age—is exhibited pleasingly by all the dramatists. The legal rights of women may have been few; but their social freedom was large. The lot of women in the Victorian age was, by comparison, barbarous and primitive. Shakespeare's own female characters compose a wonderful Legend of Good Women. The noblest of all feminine types will not be sought for in vain in the Elizabethan and Jacobean drama; and he would err who should look for them only on the Shakespearean heights.

It is fitting that a chapter discussing the earlier dramatists should conclude with a tribute to Lamb's *Specimens of English Dramatic Poets who lived about the time of Shakespeare* (1808), a delightful work, which, in spite of textual defects, long served to give general readers their first acquaintance with the Elizabethan and Jacobean dramatists—an acquaintance further stimulated by Hazlitt's lectures. During the nineteenth century useful editions of the major writers were produced, and the fervid essays of Swinburne and the modernized texts of Havelock Ellis's popular *Mermaid Series* (1887–1909)—since supplemented by a more scholarly *New Mermaid Series*—helped to make the contemporaries and successors of Shakespeare better known. In 1907, almost exactly a century after the publication of Lamb's *Specimens*, the Malone Society began its issue of exact reprints of old plays under the general editorship of Sir Walter Greg, and a new and higher standard of textual accuracy was established. Greg's edition of Henslowe's diary and papers (1904–8) and his *Bibliography of the English Printed Drama to the Restoration* (1939–59) are important contributions to the history of the drama.

CHAPTER VI

THE DRAMA TO 1642. PART II

I. BEN JONSON

Benjamin Johnson (1572?–1637) or Jonson (he finally preferred the latter spelling) is better known to us than any of his literary contemporaries. He liked talking about himself and he liked others to talk about him. No dramatist is less impersonal. Huge of body, bibulous and brawling, he loved Latin as heartily as canary, and could write the tenderest epitaph as well as the grossest epigram. He rode his hobbies hard, confusing his scholarship with pedantry and his verse with theory; but few have ever served learning and poetry with so wholehearted a devotion.

A false charge of his ill-feeling towards Shakespeare has been maintained. There are no facts to support it. In conversation with Drummond he said that Shakespeare "wanted art"; and if he meant that Shakespeare was careless in construction or had little time for Renascence theories of dramatic correctness, he was right. When the actors boasted that Shakespeare never blotted a line, he replied: "Would he had blotted a thousand"; and he rightly objected to this being thought malevolent; for if he meant that there was danger in the Shakespearean fluency, he was right. He girded a little at Shakespeare in one or two passages; but even in later and presumably more enlightened times the most successful playwright of the day has sometimes been told by his friends that he is fallible. Ben declared that he loved and honoured the man "on this side Idolatry"; and if all lovers of Shakespeare had remained "on this side Idolatry" we should have been spared much foolish verbiage. The ten words of the famous line in his First Folio tribute, "He was not of an age, but for all time", contain more essential truth about Shakespeare than ten dozen fulsome biographies. No other of Shakespeare's contemporaries has left so splendid and so enthusiastic a eulogy of the master.

Ben Jonson was sent, in spite of his poverty, to Westminster School, where Camden, his lifelong friend, was master. He was not educated at either university, although, later, he received honorary degrees from both. He served as a soldier in Flanders, and in 1597 is found employed as both actor and playwright by Henslowe, none of his plays for whom, however, survive. Meres, in *Palladis Tamia*, mentions him as one of the six most excellent in tragedy. No tragedy of this period exists. On 22 September 1598, he killed a fellow actor, Gabriel Spencer, in a duel and narrowly escaped hanging. While in prison, he became a Roman Catholic; but, twelve years later, he returned to the Church of England. We know many facts about Ben Jonson's life, though few are of real value to criticism. He had periods of prosperity and poverty, living now in the sunshine and now in the shadow of court favour. Literary indiscretions brought him more than once into trouble. A specially interesting episode in his life was a visit to Drummond of Hawthornden in Scotland during 1619 (see p. 162). Drummond, evidently, made rough notes of Ben's remarks, but the sole existing manuscript is not contemporary. Whether entirely genuine or not, the observations are in character. At the Mermaid Tavern Jonson is alleged to have had many wit-combats with Shakespeare, and seems to have established himself as a literary dictator, in anticipation of his namesake. Ben Jonson the poet and dramatist shared an uneasy bed with Ben Jonson the scholar and critic. What the artist would have done excellently by instinct the critic required to be done less excellently by rule; so Ben Jonson has engaged the attention of persons and periods that are disconcerted by sheer creative fecundity and prefer writers with theories that can be discussed. Jonson disapproved of the course that the drama had taken since *Tamburlaine* and *The Spanish Tragedy*. He disliked fantastic comedy, wide-ranging chronicle-history and stupendous tragedy. The stage, he thought, should not "Fight over Yorke and Lancasters long warres", carry its characters far "ore the seas", spread itself over excessive periods of time and exhibit violent revolutions in character and condition. The stage's main concern should be none of these things,

> But deeds, and language, such as men doe use;
> And persons, such as Comoedie would chuse,
> When she would shew an Image of the times,
> And sport with humane follies, not with crimes.
>
> (Prologue, *Every Man in his Humour*.)

Jonson believed that the remedy for the excesses of the contemporary stage was to be found first, in imitation of classical examples of restraint (that perpetual panacea!) and next, in a greater infusion of realism. Both appeared to be present in the comedies of Terence and Plautus; and an immediate satirical touch could be given by a use of the "humours" (see p. 184), the mingling of which determined men's dispositions. The term "comedy of humours" is best represented in modern language as the "comedy of types". There were dangers in the method. The new comedy might escape monsters only to fall into diagrams. Jonson had too much creative exuberance to narrow himself into diagrams, but he gives us his characters in the flat, not in the round. And the curious irony of his reform is that his "type" satirical figures appear to belong to the same order as the "type" tragical figures of Marlowe. In general he approximates more to Molière than to Shakespeare, and anticipates the artificially patterned figures of Restoration comedy. Further, Jonson, like other artists who have announced a programme of reform, did both less and more than he proposed—the author-critic proposes and the author-artist disposes, whether his name is Wordsworth or Wagner; but the generality of readers, always anxious for thought-saving labels, have taken Jonson at his word, and he goes down to posterity neatly ticketed in all the text-books as the inventor of the comedy of humours. Actually the greatest asset in any play by Jonson is Jonson. The exuberant personality is always there, with its appetites, its enmities and its self-esteem: indeed, in some plays there is too much Jonson, and we thank heaven for Shakespeare's superb impersonality. With years Jonson seemed to grow more resentful of humanity's foibles and to display a searing indignation that fed upon itself. One of his last plays (or revisions) was *A Tale of a Tub*; and we are reminded of another satirist who wrote *A Tale of a Tub* and fell into the depths of misanthropy. Although Jonson was more careful than Shakespeare about publication, his works raise several unsolved problems of bibliography. These we shall not discuss. In 1616 appeared a folio edition of *The Workes of Beniamin Jonson* containing nine plays, four entertainments, eleven masques and two collections of poems; and so, for the first time, playhouse products (with more reputable additions) came into literature as "Works". Perhaps the appearance of this volume suggested the "false folio" of Shakespeare which Jaggard and Pavier attempted in 1619. In the end, Ben Jonson fell on evil days, and died when he had passed out of fashion. He was buried in Westminster Abbey without any monument; but a chance admirer's inscription on his gravestone has proved unforgettable, however read: "O rare Ben Jonson". The folio of 1616 was reprinted in 1640, with a second volume containing matter uncollected or unprinted. A collection of memorial eulogies by many famous men of the time appeared in 1638 with the title *Jonsonus Virbius*. Ben Jonson, unlike most dramatic authors of his time, proclaimed certain critical views, and the present account of them is a necessary preface to notes upon his individual works. To these we can now pass.

Jonson's prose includes notes for an *English Grammar*, of small importance, and *Timber: or Discoveries; Made upon Men and Matter; As they have flow'd out of his daily Readings; or had their Refluxe to his peculiar Notion of the Times*. Both appeared in the posthumous volume of 1640. Perhaps the name *Timber* carried on the "notion" of *The Forest* and *Underwoods*. This slight but very attractive work (oddly dated 1641) has already been mentioned (p. 185).

Jonson's poems are contained in the collections called *Epigrams*, *The Forest* and *Underwoods*, the first two included in the folio of 1616, the third in the posthumous second volume of 1640. In the main, they are strong, manly, intelligent utterances, less read than they should be. But there is an almost wilful hardness and stiffness of articulation. The exquisite "Queen and Huntress" and the popular "Drink to me, only, with thine eyes" are exceptional in their felicity; and two supposed poems, often quoted, "It is not growing like a tree" and "Have you seen but a bright lily grow", are merely single stanzas cut out of less happy longer poems. "Underneath this sable hearse" is now usually assigned to William Browne. In general, Jonson seems to have refused the grace and melody of verse for ingenuities of idea and expression. Ben might say of his contemporary Donne that "for not keeping of accent he deserved hanging", but he did not himself escape a certain grittiness of style and substance. His poetical cerebrations, however, aroused the enthusiasm of imitators like the one who asked to be "sealed of the tribe of Ben". There are in Jonson's poems numerous admirable pieces, like *To Penshurst* and *To Sir Robert Wroth* that, leaving Spenser behind, reach forward to Dryden.

Jonson's plays fall into well-defined classes: masques, comedies, tragedies and one charming pastoral, unfinished, *The Sad Shepherd*. The masques suffer inevitably from being the *libretti* for music, dancing and spectacle, but their inventive art is full of resource, though they rarely touch the heights of poetry. They are discussed later (see p. 283). But Jonson's place in literature is determined by his dramatic work for the popular theatres. Some of it is lost. His additions to an enlarged revision of *The Spanish Tragedy* (1602) are not convincingly identified. He begins for us as a dramatist with *The Case is Alterd* (*c.* 1597), which he did not include in his collected works. The caricature of Anthony Munday as Antonio Balladino had more point for its time than for ours. The play is not a "comedy of humours", and indeed is not important. Jonson's real beginning was with *Every Man in his Humour* (acted 1598, printed 1601, revised 1616) which begins a new chapter in the history of English drama. It is, and it was intended to be, a revolt from the Shakespearean comedy, in matter as well as in style—though it was first acted by the Chamberlain's Company, with Shakespeare himself among the "principal comedians". Like Wordsworth, Jonson wanted normal facts expressed in normal speech—nothing "tempestuous". The lines already quoted from the Prologue to the 1616 edition state the author's general thesis; but the play itself is free from the laboriousness that often results from devotion to a theory. The general inspiration is derived from Plautus; but the piece is highly individual in matter and in character. Bobadill, indeed, is the greatest of Jonson's early creations. It is worth noting that Dickens knew and acted this character. The play is written mainly in terse and pointed prose, only the two old men and the ladies using blank verse. The revision of 1616, which changed the scene and characters from Italy to London, was a happy inspiration, for Jonson is at his best in the life of his own city. The next plays unfortunately show no advance. *Every Man out of his Humour* (acted 1599, printed 1601) is long-winded, didactic, and over-charged with satirical criticism of his contemporaries. *The Fountaine of selfe-love. Or Cynthias Revells* (printed 1601) resembles *Every Man out of his Humour* in its censure of follies and in its lack of interest. Only the lively Induction and the "Queen and Huntress" song save it from utter dullness. Jonson's arrogance as censor of his contemporaries had drawn upon him the resentment of his fellow-dramatists, and a "war of the theatres" began. In *Poetaster, or The Arraignment* (printed 1602) Jonson gave a countercuff to his antagonists by ridiculing Marston as Crispinus and Dekker as Demetrius, and presenting himself as Horace. The play has its good moments, but Jonson's passion for censure was making him tedious.

Jonson now turned to Roman tragedy, and in *Sejanus his Fall* (printed 1603) and *Catiline his Conspiracy* (printed 1611) he attempted a reform similar to that which he had striven for in comedy. He sought to treat Roman history with scholarly accuracy and to exemplify upon the public stage what he regarded as the essential rules of tragic art. But Jonson's theory proved hampering; and he possessed little of Shakespeare's power to transpose incidents and events into terms of a spiritual conflict. There is less essential unity in *Sejanus* and *Catiline* than in *Coriolanus* and *Antony and Cleopatra* with all their expatiation. Jonson's tragedies are not saved by some magnificent scenes and moments, and on the whole they represent another failure (if only a partial failure in the case of *Sejanus*) to turn English drama back into the classical channel.

The four comedies which followed *Sejanus* take first rank as Jonson's masterpieces. In *Volpone or The Foxe* (1606, printed 1607) the chief character, a miser and sensualist, works on the greed of his acquaintances, and exposes their hypocrisy. Plot, characters and blank verse unusually vigorous and flowing all show Jonson at his best. *Epicœne or The Silent Woman* (1609, date of first printing uncertain) is less intent on moral castigation, and, perhaps on that account, is the most agreeable, even if it is not the best, of Jonson's comedies. In *The Alchemist* (1610, printed 1612), Jonson essays another large canvas of tricksters and gulls. The entire play is in blank verse, which is most skilfully adapted, as required, to rapid dialogue or to orations. The characters, especially Sir Epicure Mammon and the two canting Puritans, are masterly. The satire on alchemy flavours the fun without destroying it; and the picture of Elizabethan London is without an equal, unless it be in *Bartholomew Fayre* (acted 1614, printed in posthumous folio). In the presentation of manners and character, *Bartholomew Fayre* may, indeed, be held to outrank even *The Alchemist*. It has "all the fun of the fair", and something of its rankness, bustle and disorder. But the principal characters are drawn with painstaking exactness and with unflagging animation. The Induction appears to gird at Shakespeare for introducing a "servant-monster", masques and "the concupiscence of jigs and dances" into serious plays, for it was part of Jonson's plan to keep the "kinds" in drama separate. Moreover, the fantasy of such a play as *The Tempest* was outside Jonson's range of appreciation or ability; and so his own *Bartholomew Fair*, as a comedy of manners, is written wholly in prose—prose remarkable for its clearness and flexibility. The kind of comedy which it presents has endured in prose fiction—in Fielding, Smollett and Dickens; but, with the coming of Puritanism, it was driven from the stage, though some of it crept back by way of the Victorian music-hall.

The Divell is an Asse (acted 1616) despite some brilliant social satire betrays on the whole a flagging invention; and there is nothing much more to be said for the remaining plays, *The Staple of Newes, The Newe Inne, The Magnetick Lady: Or Humours Reconcil'd* and *A Tale of a Tub*. Dryden curtly called the last three "mere dotages", but L. C. Knights in *Drama and Society in the Age of Jonson* has pointed out the merits in topical satire of the best scenes in *The Staple of Newes*.

The great excellence of Jonson's plays is their exuberance of invention, especially in character. His main technical fault is sheer garrulity, or it might be more politely called sheer thoroughness, which refuses to let person, speech or situation pass till everything possible has been said. Yet, in spite of all limitations, Jonson's comic characterization and the "wholeness" of his dramatic invention remain among the greatest achievements of the English theatre. He never puts us off with half the truth and never betrays our trust in his artistic sincerity. What most discourages the reader of Jonson is the absence of charity. In play after play we find him declaring "Now step I forth to whip hypocrisy". Comedy, of all forms of literature, has its duties in the street or tavern as well as in Arden or on the sea-coast of Bohemia; but Jonson, unlike Dekker, found neither charm nor heroism in London streets, just as he found neither the truth and passion that lay at the heart of Puritanism, nor the joy and fancy that stirred the light-hearted moods of Fletcher, Shirley, or Herrick. But he mirrored what he saw of men and manners with an untiring fidelity, and both heightened and coloured his picture with a hearty and virile humour, and interpreted it with a sound and honest morality. For imaginative idealism we must turn to another and greater master.

II. CHAPMAN, MARSTON, DEKKER

In Elizabethan and Jacobean times the drama was the most popular form of expression; and just as writers without any noticeable gift for fiction now write novels, so writers without any noticeable gift for drama then wrote plays. Of these latter, George Chapman (*c.* 1559–1634) was an example. He was by nature a poet; he was not by nature a dramatist. He never learnt to think in any character but his own; and his plays seem to be written, not by natural instinct, but by main strength. We know nothing of his early years. Apparently his first work was a volume of sacred verse, *The Shadow of Night*, published in 1594, followed by the ecstatic *Ovid's Banquet of Sence* in 1595. After this he was busy as poet and dramatist till 1614 and gained friends and repute. Meres in 1598 praised Chapman as one by whom our language had been mightily enriched, and included him among the poets celebrated for tragedy and for comedy, as well as among translators. Essex was one of his patrons, and after him Prince Henry; but with the prince's death in 1612 all patronage ceased—"Homer no patron found nor Chapman friend." He ceased to write twenty years before his death. By assertive disintegrators and reconstructors the name of Chapman has been unhappily entangled with Shakespeare's. There are those who find traces of Chapman's work in many plays of Shakespeare, who confidently identify Chapman with the "rival poet" of the *Sonnets*, who believe that Holofernes in *Love's Labour's Lost* is a satirical portrait of Chapman, and who are sure that *Troilus and Cressida* is a burlesque of Chapman's zeal for Homer and the Homeric heroes. The reader is urged to avoid the barren seductions of any and all of these theories, and to take Chapman as he is known and declared, marking, as he reads, an extraordinary unlikeness in every particular to the poet with whom he has been uncritically paired. After the poems already named Chapman did better things. In his continuation of Marlowe's *Hero and Leander* (1598), he not unworthily completed an incomparable fragment, and in *Euthymiae Raptus*; *or the Teares of Peace* (1609), dedicated to Prince Henry, he reached his happiest mood as an original poet. Distinction of mind and intellectual vigour are apparent in all Chapman's work; but his finest verses possess gnomic and didactic, rather than lyric, quality.

Though Chapman was known as a dramatist in 1598, only two plays by his hand are extant which were produced before that date—*The Blinde begger of Alexandria* (printed 1598) and *An Humerous dayes Myrth* (printed 1599). Both are comedies, and neither deserves particular notice. *Al Fooles* (printed 1605), another comedy, apparently first produced under the title *The World runs on Wheels*, displays a surprising advance in dramatic technique. *The Gentleman Usher* (printed 1606) and *Monsieur d'Olive* (printed 1606) are comedies of small importance, a judgment that applies even more strongly to *The Widdowes Teares* (printed 1612). Chapman's fame as dramatist rests upon his tragedies founded on French history, of which *Bussy D'Ambois* (printed 1607) and *The Revenge of Bussy D'Ambois* (printed 1613) have always and rightly received most attention. These plays owed their success to the flavour of recent history, to the character and career of the chief figure, formed by nature for an invincible hero of romance, and to the glowing rhetoric which rises in places to pure and impassioned poetry. The second play is inferior in dramatic interest but, with its ghost demanding revenge, it is suffused with memories of *Hamlet,* to which it is clearly indebted. If intellectual interest and noble eloquence sufficed to constitute a dramatic masterpiece, *The Conspiracie, And Tragedie of Charles Duke of Byron, Marshall of France* (printed 1608) would give Chapman rank among great playwrights. But it is an epic rather than a drama. In his next tragedy, *Caesar and Pompey* (printed 1631), Chapman turned from contemporary to classical history; but the play is feebly handled and the characters fail to communicate themselves. *Chabot Admirall of France* (printed 1639), *Revenge for Honour* (printed 1654) and *Alphonsus Emperour of Germany* (printed 1654) are also attributed, at least in part, to Chapman. His fame would not be increased by the certainty that he had written any of them. Jonson observed that, next himself, only Fletcher and Chapman could make a masque. If Chapman made many, they have vanished, for only one remains. It is mentioned on p. 284.

By "a fallacy of duration" Chapman lives in the tribute of a later poet; and, indeed, "Chapman's Homer" is his chief title to fame. Something has been said of this in an earlier chapter (see p. 148). The first instalment, *Seaven Bookes of the Iliades of Homere,* was published in 1598. In 1609 the first twelve books appeared, and the complete *Iliad* about 1611. The first twelve books of the *Odyssey* in the heroic couplet appeared in 1614, and the second twelve within another year. *The Georgicks of Hesiod* was his next translation and it appeared in 1618. In 1616, both the *Iliad* and the *Odyssey* were issued in a folio entitled *The Whole Workes of Homer, Prince of Poets,* and with *Batrachomyomachia,* the *Hymns* and the *Epigrams* in 1624, the first complete translation of Homer into English was made, and the author could say, "The work that I was born to do is done".

John Marston (1575?–1634) is one of the most attractive of the lesser dramatists. He began his literary career as a satirist, entered the dramatic field at the end of the sixteenth century, but left the theatre for the church a few years later. A collected but incomplete edition of his plays was published in 1633. Few writers have asked less of posterity or have taken a more modest view of their value. Nevertheless Marston's literary life was not free from strife. In 1598 he published *The Metamorphosis of Pigmalions Image. And Certain Satires,* and in 1599 *The Scourge of Villanie,* thereby provoking a controversy with Hall, who had claimed to be the father of English satire (see p. 183). In the "war of the theatres" (see p. 251), Marston's name is prominent. He aimed an occasional shaft at Shakespeare, but his chief attack was directed against Jonson, who, in his early comedies, drew unflattering portraits of his contemporaries and presented himself as the honest exposer of pretences. We need not wonder that he was facetiously saluted by Dekker in his "three or four suites of names, Asper, Criticus, Quintus, Horatius, Flaccus". About 1599 *Histrio-Mastix* was performed, in which Jonson thought he was ridiculed. The play, an early work of uncertain authorship, was revised for this occasion by Marston. Jonson retorted upon Marston and others in *Every Man out of his Humour. Jacke Drums Entertainment* (acted 1600, printed 1601), an anonymous play in which Marston was thought to have had a hand, returned to the attack. *Cynthia's Revels* contained counter-attacks by Jonson, and *Poetaster* was still more vigorous. The next assault on Jonson came in *Satiro-Mastix, Or the untrussing of the Humorous Poet* (acted 1601, printed 1602), written by Dekker, perhaps with Marston's help. In this some of Jonson's own characters were cleverly introduced. Though the play falls short of *Poetaster* in construction, its mockery is more genial and its humour more sparkling. In yet another play Jonson was the target of satirical jest, Marston's *What You Will*, probably written (1601) before *Poetaster* and revised later; and with this play the war of the poets came to an end. In 1605 we find Marston collaborating with Chapman and Jonson in *Eastward Hoe*. Audiences of the day were able to take and enjoy the points of the quarrel in a way denied to us. Shakespeare, though alluded to in several plays, appears to have taken no part in the "war", perhaps because, as an actor as well as a dramatist, he had to be professionally neutral.

Marston's own dramatic activity was confined to about eight years. His first play, *Antonio and Mellida* (printed 1602), with its sequel *Antonio's Revenge* (1602), may be said to take us back to the world of *The Spanish Tragedy*. Marston is closer to Seneca than to Shakespeare. The satirical comedy *What You Will* (printed 1607) has already been mentioned. A marked advance is apparent in *The Malcontent* (printed 1604), which, with a Hamlet-like character, Malevole, is more of a close-knit work of art. *The Dutch Courtezan*, published in 1605, shows still further advance in the handling of plot and character, but it is surpassed by *Eastward Hoe* (printed 1605), written by Marston, Chapman and Jonson, a brilliant and enjoyable piece. This satire on the needy Scottish adventurers who came south with the new king gave great offence, and the collaborators found themselves in prison with their ears and noses in jeopardy. As a picture of city life *Eastward Hoe* has great merits. 'Comedies are writ to be spoken, not read; remember the life of these things consists in action", remarks the author in the preface to his play entitled *Parasitaster, Or the Fawne* (printed in two editions 1606), and certainly, though no doubt fairly successful on the stage, this play offers small excitement to the reader. Marston had promised "to present a tragedy which should boldly abide the most curious perusal". This was *The Wonder of Women or the Tragedie of Sophonisba* (printed 1606). It is not fully satisfying as a tragedy, but it certainly deserves curious perusal, for it contains some excellent passages of writing. *The Insatiate Countesse* (printed 1613), the last play published as Marston's, is, in a later edition, given to William Barkstead. It was probably left incomplete by Marston. After a dramatic beginning which is more than merely promising, Marston turned his back on letters and quietly took up the work of a parish priest. In his art there is nothing that can be called completely successful. But he has an arresting quality. When we are about to condemn, he suddenly flashes into unexpected splendour, and his best characters refuse to be forgotten.

Thomas Dekker (1570–1641) was a man of many parts, and endearing in all of them. He wrote for Henslowe many plays which have not survived, and he poured himself out in a stream of miscellaneous writing. To the mental energy and literary facility of Defoe, he added the genial kindliness of Goldsmith. Two plays printed in 1600, *The Shomakers Holiday. Or the Gentle Craft* and *The Pleasant Comedie of Old Fortunatus*, are enough to give Dekker a place in the history of drama. The first is full of vigorous, jovial life, and brings all London before the eyes—the London of honest tradesmen and apprentices and rather less honest courtiers. Sim Eyre the shoemaker who becomes Lord Mayor is an immortal character. The second play has less life, but it has definite quality. *Satiro-Mastix*, Dekker's reply to Jonson's *Poetaster*, has already been referred to. In the first part of *The Honest Whore* (printed 1604), Middleton had a share; the second and much superior part is mainly, perhaps entirely, Dekker's (printed 1630). Four less important pieces, *The Whore of Babylon* (printed 1607), strongly Protestant and patriotic, *If It be Not Good, the Divel is in it* (printed 1612), *Match Mee in London* (printed 1631) and *The Wonder of a Kingdome* (printed 1636), complete the list of plays which can with any confidence be assigned to Dekker's unassisted pen. The last-named was probably worked over again by John Day. There are several other plays in which Dekker was a collaborator. We know that Middleton had a share in the first part of *The Honest Whore*, and a share, perhaps the largest, in *The Roaring Girle* (printed 1611), whose heroine, Moll Cutpurse, masquerades as a London gallant; we know that Webster took part in the composition of *West-Ward Hoe* and *North-Ward Hoe*, comedies of intrigue, the first preceding and the second following the Jonson-Chapman-Marston *Eastward Ho*, and in *The Famous History of Sir Thomas Wyat* (all printed 1607). The name of Massinger is associated with Dekker's in *The Virgin Martir* (printed 1622), and Chettle and Haughton assisted in writing *Patient Grissill* (printed 1603) from which come Dekker's well-known and delightful lyrics "Art thou poor..." and "Golden slumbers kiss your eyes". *The Witch of Edmonton* (acted about 1621) was written with John Ford and William Rowley, and Ford assisted with *The Sun's Darling* (acted 1624).

Dekker has nothing resembling the intellectual power of Jonson, but he has something which has sweetened him for posterity, namely charm. He was not clever, yet he succeeded where more richly endowed men failed. For the student of Elizabethan social life, Dekker's prose is even more important than his plays. Some account of his pamphlets has already been given (see p. 185). Both in *The Wonderfull Yeare* (1603) and in *A Rod for Runawayes* (1625), Dekker anticipates Defoe in the realism and force of his descriptions. *Worke for Armorours, or the Peace is broken* (1609), with its motto, "God help the Poor, the rich can shift", allegorizes the eternal conflict of classes in the war of the rival queens, Money and Poverty. His indignant account of the whipping of a blind bear for the amusement of "creatures that had the shapes of men and faces of Christians" must endear him to all. No reader of Dekker (not to mention Shakespeare) can doubt that what Arnold called "the victory of the prose style, clear, plain and short" was already won by our dramatists before the advent of Dryden, the virtues of whose prose were partly derived from his studies in their school. *Dekker his Dreame* (1620) is a mixture of prose and verse, which opens with an apocalyptic vision of the end of all things; it is much less attractive than an earlier religious work, *Fowre Birds of Noahs Arke* (1609), a remarkable collection of prayers, distinguished by a deep spirit of devotion, exquisite feeling and sensitive phrasing.

III. MIDDLETON AND ROWLEY

Like his contemporaries, Thomas Middleton (*c.* 1570–1627) wrote for Henslowe several plays of which only the names survive; but a large body of work, his own, or written in collaboration, still remains. Middleton, a strangely elusive personal figure, is specially associated with William Rowley, of whom, also, little is known. It is possible that *The Mayor of Quinborough*, which was printed with Middleton's name in 1661, is the earliest play of his that we have; and possible that we have it only in a revised state. *Blurt Master-Constable*, the first published of his plays (1602), shows Middleton setting off spiritedly on the comedies of intrigue which were to form the first division of his work. The prose has become swift of foot, and slips easily into verse and back again. *The Old Law*, written *c.* 1599, printed 1656, is ascribed to Middleton, Massinger and Rowley; but in 1599 the two latter were in their middle 'teens and hardly capable of authorship. The play is very unequal, and the probable revision has not pulled it together. *The Phoenix*, acted in 1604, appears to be an attempted imitation of Jonson. The two plays which followed, *A Trick to Catch the Old-one* and *A Mad World, My Masters* (both printed 1608), are among the best of Middleton's comedies, with easy dialogue, and with characters that definitely transmit themselves. Middleton's figures seldom fail to have genuine life. There is true and good human feeling even in some of the most shameless scenes of *Your five Gallants* (printed 1608). We remember Middleton's comedies less for their separate characters than for a kind of "criticism of life" of which the characters are the unexpected exponents. The strongest scenes of *The Roaring Girle* give us this sense of character acting beyond itself. We remember, also, passages of a marvellous and sometimes cruelly comic reality, such as the death scene in *A Chast Mayd in Cheape-side* (acted 1611) where an old sinner makes his exit in grotesque and frightened repentance. The prose of Middleton, as we see it in the comedies, is a pungent, fluent, very natural and speakable prose. Only at times, as in *The Famelie of Love* (printed 1608), does it become pedantic. Verse, to Middleton, is a native idiom; he speaks in it easily, bending it as he pleases to any shade of meaning, filling it with stuff alien to poetry and yet keeping its good metre. He has a few fine passages where imagination has fastened upon him, and dictated his words. Apparently he found no difficulty in collaboration. *The Widdowe*, not printed till 1652, was perhaps revised by Fletcher; and *No Wit, no Help, like a Womans*, printed 1657, was revised by Shirley. We find Rowley's name beside Middleton's on the title-pages of *The Old Law*, *A Faire Quarrell*, *The World tost at Tennis*, *The Spanish Gipsie*, and *The Changeling*: most, that is, of Middleton's best later work. The manner and measure of this collaboration is not easy to discover.

The plays published under Rowley's name or initials are: *A new Wonder, A Woman never vext* (1632); *Alls Lost by Lust* (1633); *A Match at Midnight* (1633); and *A Shoo-maker a Gentleman* (1638). The dates are dates of publication. In *The Witch of Edmonton*, published in 1658 as "a Tragi-Comedy By divers well-esteemed Poets; William Rowley, Thomas Dekker, John Ford, etc.", the share of Rowley is difficult to make out. In the plays which he wrote in collaboration with Middleton, his hand has been most generally traced in the comic underplots. In the two chief plays which he wrote by himself, he wove comic prose not ineffectively into more serious substance. In *Alls Lost by Lust* Rowley proves himself a poet by his comprehension of great passions. In *A new Wonder* he shows us the strange vehement feelings, both petty and ardent, of businessmen, their small prides and large resolutions.

That Middleton learnt from Rowley, or did, with his help, more than either of them could do by himself, is evident for the first time clearly in *A Faire Quarrell* (printed 1617). Soon after, they collaborated in the entertaining masque *The World tost at Tennis* (printed 1620). For the most part, Middleton's masques are tame and tedious, without originality in the invention or lyrical quality in the songs. No detailed account need by given of them. To the time of his masques (*c.* 1614) may be assigned *The Witch* (first printed 1778), written alone, and perhaps his first attempt at a purely romantic play. It is through the interpolation, as it obviously was, of certain lines of his witches' songs in the text of *Macbeth*, that a play in which the main action is almost a grotesque parody of the romantic drama has come to be looked upon as one of Middleton's chief works. To the same time must be assigned the tragedy called *The Changeling* (printed 1653), in which Rowley had some share. This remarkable play is one of the best non-Shakespearean tragedies of the period. The villainous De Flores has real individuality, and Beatrice, his employer and then his victim, exhibits a gradual development of character, moving inevitably deeper and deeper into sin, for which there is hardly a parallel outside *Macbeth*. *The Spanish Gipsie* (*c.* 1621), a tragi-comedy with light relief, is another play of joint (and even doubtful) authorship which has genuine romantic value.

Anything for a Quiet Life, printed in 1662, is a return to the earlier manner of the farcical comedies of city life. But in two plays published together in 1657 we see the last mood of Middleton, after his collaboration with Rowley was at an end. *More dissemblers besides Women* is a tangle of virtues and hypocrisies, of serious meanings and humorous disguises. *Women beware of Women* contains some of his most assured work. It is based on the history of Bianca Cappello, and it depicts with great power scenes and characters almost wholly vile. With one more experiment, and this a masterpiece of a wholly new kind, "the only work of English poetry", says Swinburne, "which may properly be called Aristophanic", the career of Middleton closes. *A Game at Chesse* (printed 1625) is a satire, taking the popular side against Spain. But it is more than a satire; it is a critical indictment, not of city manners or personal vices, but of the nation's policy. Politics and literature are here for the first time made one in an English play. Middleton's genius was varied and copious, and he showed capacity to do almost every kind of dramatic work with great vigour. Though none of his plays is satisfactory throughout, there is, in almost all of them, a quality or character that rises beyond the dramatic conventions of the time, and appeals to the deepest convictions of every age. The social implications of Middleton's plays may have importance but cannot be studied in a brief sketch.

IV. THOMAS HEYWOOD

Thomas Heywood (1572?–1650?), though a writer of the second rank, has, for the student, interest of the first order. In his long literary life he attempted almost every kind of play, except the comedy of cruel "humours" from which his simple heart shrank; and he succeeded in writing the first genuinely moving domestic tragedy in which all the action lies on the plane of ordinary existence. In addition he is pleasantly communicative about himself and the theatre of his time. By 1596, Heywood is mentioned in Henslowe's diary as writing, or having written, a play; and in 1598 he became an actor.

Heywood's industry was enormous. He declared that he had "either an entire hand, or at the least a main finger" in two hundred and twenty plays, a tremendous total even for thirty-seven years' connection with the theatre; and we may reasonably suppose that the main finger of adaptation did more than the entire hand of composition. He gave little or no thought to the destiny of his plays as "literature". To have finished his play and brought it on the stage was enough for him. But his remarks about the printing of plays are too instructive to be overlooked. He objected to the appearance of one corrupt copy, which had been taken down by some enterprising expert in stenography, who "put it in print (scarce one word trew)"; though he did not produce a correct edition. He made no attempt to collect his plays as *Works*. "One reason is, that many of them by shifting and change of Companies have been negligently lost; Others of them are still retained in the hands of some Actors, who thinke it against their peculiar profit to have them come in Print, and a third, That it never was any great ambition in me, to bee in this kind Voluminously read."

The surviving plays are numerous; and other works, compiled in the intervals of play-writing, are as bulky as they are unimportant. There is a translation of Sallust (1608); there is *Troia Britanica or Great Britaines Troy* (1609); there is *The Life and Death of Hector* (1614) adapted from Lydgate's Troy Book; and there is *The Hierarchie of the Blessed Angells. Their Names, Orders and Offices* (1635), from which Lamb extracted an amusing disquisition on the meagre baptismal names of our poets, as for instance:

> Mellifluous *Shakespeare*, whose inchanting Quill
> Commanded Mirth or Passion, was but *Will*;

concluding with himself, "I hold he loves me best that calles me Tom". The *Nine Bookes of Various History, concerning Women, inscribed by the names of the Nine Muses* (1624), was followed in 1640 by *Exemplary Lives and Memorable Acts of Nine the Most Worthy Women of the World. Three Jewes. Three Gentiles. Three Christians*. More important are *Englands Elizabeth* (1631), an expression of his patriotism, and *An Apology for Actors* (1612), the simple and modest defence of his own assailed profession, as well as a valuable document. Interest of another kind attaches to *Pleasant Dialogues and Drammas* (1637) containing translations from Lucian together with prologues, epilogues, epigrams, etc., as it shows the ageing author collecting his scattered compositions. Most of these books, however, would be cheerfully sacrificed for Heywood's *Lives of All the Poets*, begun about 1614, but never finished, and now lost.

The first of Heywood's plays calling for notice is *The Foure Prentises of London. With the Conquest of Jerusalem* (published 1615, acted some years earlier). In this piece chronicle-history and popular romance are combined in a singularly ingenious fashion. That the play was popular is proved by the allusion made to it in *The Knight of the Burning Pestle*, in which Beaumont and Fletcher ridiculed those very civic tastes which Heywood's play had sought to gratify. A chronicle play, *King Edward IV* in two parts (printed 1599), is attributed to Heywood, though there is no definite evidence of authorship. Its sentiment, humour, and one might even say its "commonness" are all in character. Of Heywood's other chronicle play, *If you know not me, You know no bodie: Or The troubles of Queene Elizabeth*, the first part was surreptitiously printed in 1605 from copy made by a piratical stenographer, and is little better than a jumble of misprinted fragments. As we have remarked, Heywood published his indignation, but not a better version. *Part II* (1606), which is better preserved, was not better worth preserving. To the period 1611–13 belongs a series of plays, *The Golden Age* (1611), *The Silver Age* (1613), *The Brazen Age* (1613) and *The Iron Age* (in two parts, *c.* 1632), in which he dramatized classical myths from Saturn to Ulysses. The characters are very numerous; but even the indefatigable exertions of "old Homer" as presenter and chorus, aided by occasional dumb-shows, hardly succeed in bridging the gaps and presenting the invisible. The dates are dates of printing.

The earliest play in which Heywood attained real eminence is *A Woman Kilde with Kindnesse* (published 1607), which is both his best play and the best play of its kind. *Arden of Feversham* and *A Yorkshire Tragedy* had been striking attempts to use for serious purposes on the stage certain calamities of domestic life; but these two tragedies rely more upon horror than upon infelicity. In *A Woman Killed with Kindness* there is no physical horror, no deed of blood; the stage is filled by the moving spectacle of life and happiness irrevocably lost by the lapse of a woman who is sinful without being wicked. It is a play true to its own level of life and justifies the inspired observation of Lamb that Heywood was "a sort of *prose* Shakespeare". Heywood's tragedy is in quite good verse; but it is verse that remains for the most part on the pedestrian level.

The Wise-Woman of Hogsdon (*c.* 1604, printed 1638), a lively comedy, has a complicated plot and many grotesque characters. *The Fayre Mayde of the Exchange*, published anonymously in 1607 and attributed to Heywood by some scholars, offers a lively picture of city life. *The Royall King, and the Loyall Subject* (acted about 1602) is almost certainly Heywood's, though on this occasion he essayed a flight into purely romantic drama. *The Rape of Lucrece*, printed in 1608, is in a different style, if style of any sort can be ascribed to this odd medley of tragedy and vaudeville. It contains the one lyric known to have come from his pen—"Packe cloudes away, and welcome day". *The Fair Maid of the West*, printed in 1631, is another romantic comedy in which we have the note of patriotism and a breath of the sea. *The English Traveller*, printed in 1633, was probably acted in or about 1627. The main plot turns on the idea which lies at the root of Heywood's finest dramatic designs—that, if to err is human, to forgive is what raises humanity beyond the earth. Nothing need be said about *The Captives* (not printed till 1883), or *A Mayden-Head well lost* (printed in 1634), or *A Challenge for Beautie* (printed in 1636), or *Loves Maistresse: Or, the Queens Masque*, performed in 1633.

Passing by Heywood's seven pageants (1631–9) written for city festivals, we come in conclusion to two plays in which he collaborated with other writers. Of these, *Fortune by Land and Sea* (acted *c.* 1607, printed 1655) was the joint production of Heywood and William Rowley. In substance it is a domestic drama in Heywood's most characteristic manner, and it bears witness once more to his love of the sea. *The late Lancashire Witches* was printed in 1634 as the joint work of Thomas Heywood and Richard Brome. The story of the play was based on an account of the doings of certain Lancashire women, of whom twelve had suffered death as witches.

Heywood achieved success in the chronicle history, the romantic drama and the comedy of manners. In addition, he wrote at least one masterpiece in domestic drama, the kind of work in which his candid sincerity and simple charity found their most congenial expression. He was not strong in the art of construction, and his plays are almost invariably weakened by their secondary plots. He was devoid of any lyric vein, though his strong national and civic patriotism should have moved him to song. His unaffected simplicity has led to his being underrated by critics who like dramatists of larger pretensions.

V. BEAUMONT AND FLETCHER

The names of Beaumont and Fletcher having been jointly attached by the unfounded claims of early publishers to over fifty plays, some preliminary account of the two authors must be given before the plays are discussed. Francis Beaumont was born about 1584 and died in 1616. John Fletcher (cousin of the poets Giles and Phineas) was born in 1579 and died in 1625. An examination of these dates will show that the amount of collaboration between two authors, one of whom died at thirty-two, can hardly have been extensive. Their joint work began about 1608 and covers therefore no more than eight years. Only four of the plays, two anonymous and two attributed to Fletcher, were published in the lifetime of Beaumont; five more, two anonymous and three attributed to Beaumont and Fletcher, were published in the lifetime of Fletcher; and there is no evidence that any one of these issues was authorized by the two writers, separately or jointly: the books were nothing but publishers' ventures. Trade enterprise went even further; for in 1647, twenty-two years after the death of Fletcher and thirty-one years after the death of Beaumont, a publisher produced a folio volume professing to contain the works of Beaumont and Fletcher "never printed before", with one omission, the copy for which had been mislaid. The contents numbered thirty-four plays and one masque. This publication produced at least one important protest, the main points of which are these: (1) that Beaumont had very little part in the plays, (2) that Massinger, not mentioned, contributed to several, and (3) that Fletcher was the principal author. The protest had so little effect that in 1679, a century after Fletcher's birth, appeared *Fifty Comedies and Tragedies. Written by Francis Beaumont and John Fletcher, Gentlemen*, containing all the contents of the 1647 volume together with eighteen other plays which in the course of years had been printed separately. These facts should lend emphasis to what has already been said in these pages about the publication of plays, namely that the authors had little to do with the matter and that publishers were ready to put on their title-pages any names likely to attract buyers. The Shakespeare Folio of 1623 is unique in being compiled and warranted, not by publishers, but by two editors, both friends of the author and fellow-actors with him. The publishers of the 1647 and 1679 volumes, with their false assertion of joint authorship, bequeathed to subsequent criticism a legacy of disputed assignment which is never likely to be settled with universal acceptance. E. K. Chambers in *The Elizabethan Stage* cautiously assigns two plays wholly or substantially to Beaumont: *The Woman Hater*, and *The Knight of the Burning Pestle*; six plays wholly or substantially to Fletcher: *The Woman's Prize*, *The Faithful Shepherdess*, *Monsieur Thomas*, *Valentinian*, *Bonduca* and *Wit without Money*; seven plays to the Beaumont-Fletcher collaboration: *Philaster*, *The Maid's Tragedy*, *A King and no King*, *Four Plays in One*, *Cupid's Revenge*, *The Coxcomb* and *The Scornful Lady*; the rest he describes as "of doubtful authorship, and, in some cases, period", most of these doubtful works being the joint composition of Fletcher and various collaborators, mainly Massinger.

An examination of the works named above will show two hardly disputable conclusions: first that Beaumont had greater dramatic and poetic genius than Fletcher—such works as *The Knight of the Burning Pestle*, *Philaster* and *The Maid's Tragedy* showing finer construction and a firmer hand than any of Fletcher's later work; and next that Fletcher had a keener sense of popular stage effect and an easier fluency in writing than Beaumont. Beaumont leaned back a little towards the Elizabethan tradition; Fletcher was more "modern", more ready to give a new public what it wanted. Fletcher's liveliness of manner was due in part to a metrical style of easily recognizable idiosyncrasy. Its most obvious characteristic is the use of redundant syllables in all parts of the line, but especially at the end. Extrametrical syllables—one, two, or even three—abound. Fletcher's aim, apparently, was to give the blank verse line something of a conversational fluency. He was, in fact, trying to make the best of both worlds, to write verse and to produce the effect of colloquial prose.

In the altered Jacobean times the manner of Fletcher grew increasingly popular. Even Shakespeare was moved to abandon tragedy for romantic tragi-comedy in his last years. *Cymbeline* and *The Winter's Tale*, though in their best parts far beyond the scope of Beaumont and Fletcher, are nevertheless in the Beaumont and Fletcher manner. The new age demanded shows and entertainments which did not make any serious appeal to the intellect; hence, on the one hand, the increasing passion for court masques of extravagant splendour and, on the other, the eager appetite for plays with plots that provided thrilling excitement and surprises. Further, there was a lowering of moral standards and a setting up of affected notions of "honour"—"honour" being merely a mode of self-consciousness; and in the new comedies the new public found a new style of conversation which amused it without fatiguing it. "Shakespeare to thee was dull", exclaimed the dramatist Cartwright, addressing Fletcher; and Dryden, comparing Beaumont and Fletcher with Shakespeare, said that "they understood and imitated the conversation of gentlemen much better".

Beaumont had invention; Fletcher drew his stories from the usual sources, and most happily from Cervantes and other Spanish writers; but although this was the golden age of Spanish drama, no play of Fletcher's appears to have been founded on any known Spanish play. He wrote with great ease and seems to have found collaboration congenial to his nature. That the general substance of his work is thin cannot be denied. The most memorable parts of his plays are not any particular scenes, but the lyrics, of which there are over seventy, the best known being the invocation to Melancholy, "Hence all you vain delights" in *The Nice Valour*.

The so-called "Beaumont and Fletcher" plays are traditionally classified as tragedies, tragi-comedies and comedies. Twelve rank as tragedies and twenty as tragi-comedies; but there is no advantage in this distinction, as the serious plays belong essentially to the same class. We will take a rapid survey of the more serious plays first, giving approximate dates of production. *The Faithfull Shepheardesse* (acted *c.* 1608), Fletcher's pastoral drama, did not succeed on the stage; nevertheless it is an excellent specimen of its class, with true poetic beauty; and Milton paid it the compliment of imitation in *Comus. Philaster* (*c.* 1610), the first play that brought Beaumont and Fletcher into notice, has poetic and dramatic merits, though the story falters. The leading place among the dramas of Beaumont and Fletcher has always been assigned to *The Maides Tragedy* (*c.* 1611); and the justice of this popular judgment cannot be questioned. *A King and no King* (*c.* 1611), written by both, was hardly less celebrated than *The Maides Tragedy*; but its imitation Falstaff and its dallying with incest do not recommend it to later times. *Cupids Revenge* (*c.* 1612), written by both, is mythological, and rather diffuse. *Four Plays in One*, of uncertain date, consists of an Induction and four "*Triumphs*"—"*of Honour*", "*of Love*", "*of Death*" and "*of Time*"—the former two, the better, by Beaumont and the latter two by Fletcher. *The Captaine* (*c.* 1612), by Fletcher with an uncertain collaborator, perhaps Massinger, is unimportant. *The Honest Mans Fortune* (1613) is mere patchwork by several authors, of whom Fletcher was one. *Bonduca* (*c.* 1614), mainly by Fletcher, is founded, like *Cymbeline*, upon ancient British history. *Valentinian* (*c.* 1614), by Fletcher alone, is a typical example of his work in tragedy. The situation is admirably prepared; but the restless introduction of "surprises" is disconcerting and fatiguing. The play is exceptionally rich in lyrics. *The Bloody Brother, or Rollo, Duke of Normandy* (*c.* 1616) is an effective play by several collaborators. Fletcher, Massinger and a third author took part in the tragedy of *Thierrey and Theodoret*, which probably belongs to the year 1617. *The Queene of Corinth* (*c.* 1617), by Fletcher, Massinger, and probably some third hand, is a poor play, and *The Loyal Subject* (1618), by Fletcher with unidentified collaboration, is merely dramatized romance, with no complication or resolution. *The Knight of Malta* (*c.* 1618), by Fletcher, Massinger and a third collaborator, has many of the elements of a fine drama. The plot of *The Mad Lover* (*c.* 1619), by Fletcher with some assistance, is completely absurd. Fletcher's attempt at a Shakespearean Fool in this play is a pitiful failure. *Women pleas'd* (c. 1619), by Fletcher with assistance, is still more faulty in construction.

The tragedy of *Sir John van Olden Barnavelt* (1619), by Fletcher and Massinger, has special interest as a dramatization of contemporary history. *The Custome of the Countrey* (c. 1619), by Fletcher and Massinger, founded on the *Persiles y Sigismunda* of Cervantes, is a drama of considerable merit. It is doubtful whether Fletcher had any hand in *The Lawes of Candy* (c. 1620); Massinger probably was the principal author. *The Double Marriage* (c. 1620), by Fletcher and Massinger, is a poor play, with a confused plot and no sufficient reason for the catastrophe. On the other hand, *The False One* (c. 1620), by the same authors, is a drama of considerable rhetorical brilliance. *The Pilgrim* (c. 1621), by Fletcher with assistance, contains a madhouse scene, evidently to the taste of the time. *The Prophetesse* (c. 1622), by Fletcher and Massinger, *The Island Princesse* (c. 1621), perhaps Fletcher's, and *The Sea Voyage* (c. 1622), of mingled and doubtful authorship, have no interest other than the remoteness from ordinary experience of the circumstances and localities represented. *The Beggars Bush* (c. 1622), by Fletcher and Massinger, contains a realistic representation of vagabond life which gave it exceptional popularity. *The Lovers Progress* (c. 1623) is originally by Fletcher, but extensively revised by Massinger. The ghost scene at the inn, admired by Scott, has some comic humour, but serves chiefly to show how incapable Fletcher was of dealing with the supernatural. *The Maid in the Mill* (c. 1623), by Fletcher and William Rowley, is an ill-constructed play, with some poetry, and some fairly good comic business. *A Wife for a Month* (1624), perhaps by Fletcher alone, is far superior in construction to most of the author's dramatic romances. *Loves Pilgrimage* (date uncertain) is a romance from Cervantes, apparently rewritten by Shirley with insertions from Jonson's *The New Inn*. *The Faire Maide of the Inne* (1626) was produced after Fletcher's death, and it is doubtful whether he had any hand in it. Another example of a drama wrongly ascribed to Beaumont and Fletcher in the folio of 1679 is *The Coronation*, which is known to be by Shirley. On the other hand, *A Very Woman*, ascribed to Massinger, is in part by Fletcher. *The Faithful Friends*, first printed in Weber's edition of 1812, has no claim to be included among the Beaumont and Fletcher works. Two celebrated plays associated with the name of Fletcher have already been mentioned in another connection—*Henry VIII* and *The Two Noble Kinsmen*. Of the first we may say (borrowing Heywood's phrase) that Fletcher may have had a hand in it; of the second that Shakespeare may have had a finger in it.

  We pass next to the comedies. *The Woman Hater* (c. 1606), generally attributed to Beaumont alone, turns upon the humorous eccentricity of the principal character, a feature also discernible in *The Scornful Ladie* (c. 1609), by Beaumont and Fletcher, an excellent comedy of its kind. The mock heroic style, in which Beaumont excelled, is exhibited in these two comedies, but attains its triumph in *The Knight of the Burning Pestle* (1607), a comic masterpiece with a 'prentice elevated to the role of a Don Quixote. In *The Coxcombe* (c. 1610) we have a romantic comedy with two distinct plots, Beaumont probably contributing the romance and Fletcher the comedy. In the other comedies Beaumont had probably no hand. Fletcher is the predominant partner, though other writers worked with him. Several of the plays may be classed together as exhibiting the Jonsonian concern with "humours", though not the Jonsonian manner. These are *The Little French Lawyer* (c. 1619) by Fletcher and Massinger, *The Nice Valour*, an apparent revision of Fletcher (c. 1624), and *The Humorous Lieutenant* (c. 1619) by Fletcher, probably with assistance. A combination of romance and comedy is found in *The Spanish Curate* (c. 1622) by Fletcher and Massinger. *Wit At severall Weapons* is a poor play of unknown date and its authorship is very uncertain. *Wit Without Money* (c. 1614), by Fletcher alone, is much better, having at least a tolerably well connected plot and lively dialogue. *The Womans Prize: or, The Tamer Tamed* (date unknown), by Fletcher, is a supposed continuation of the marriage experiences of Petruchio, the tamer of the Shrew. *The Night-Walker, or the Little Theife* (of uncertain date) has more of London local colour than any of the rest, but this is probably due to Shirley, who worked upon the play after Fletcher's death. *Monsieur Thomas* (date uncertain), by Fletcher alone, can hardly be called a good play though it has a good story. On the other hand, *The Chances* (date uncertain) and *The Wild-Goose Chase* (acted 1621), perhaps by Fletcher alone, stand in the first rank among his comedies; in them we see the lively style of dialogue which gained him the reputation of "understanding the conversation of gentlemen". *The Wild-Goose Chase* is the original of Farquhar's *The Inconstant*. Of all Fletcher's comedies *Rule a Wife And have a Wife* (c. 1624) was the most popular and kept the stage longest, and it is certainly a good specimen of its kind. *Loves Cure* (c. 1622) contains little that can be ascribed to Fletcher. *The Noble Gentleman* and *The Elder Brother* were both produced upon the stage after Fletcher's death. The former is a rather poor play, and has no apparent traces of his hand; the latter, one of the best comedies of the collection, is by Fletcher and Massinger. The construction is good and the characterization excellent.

It was said by Dryden in his essay *Of Dramatick Poesy* that in Beaumont and Fletcher's plays the English language perhaps arrived at its highest perfection. What Dryden meant was that the language of the plays had escaped the perils of Elizabethan metaphor and "conceit" and had attained to something like directness and lucidity of statement. To this achievement Fletcher contributed most; but we must not overlook the share of Massinger, whose poetical eloquence contributes much to the grace of style in the later plays. The popularity of the Beaumont and Fletcher plays throughout the seventeenth century had definite influence upon the development of the classical, Augustan style in the eighteenth. But, in the end, we are forced to admit that this large mass of work has left us little that is permanently memorable. Even if we assent to the supposition that Shakespeare "imitated" Beaumont and Fletcher in his last romantic comedies, we shall do well to remember that everybody knows Caliban and Miranda, Autolycus and Perdita, Imogen and the royal outlaws, and that nobody, except a few special readers, can recall any character from Beaumont and Fletcher. To have crowded the stage with figures from over fifty plays and yet to have bequeathed nothing to the stock of national mythology is an artistic failure that the baroque flourishes of the Beaumont and Fletcher drama cannot conceal.

VI. PHILIP MASSINGER

The life of Philip Massinger (1583–1640) was, by his own account, not very
prosperous; but his works show no sign of defeat and indicate a courageous
spirit. He did not hesitate to make political references; and though, unlike the
authors of *Eastward Ho*, he suffered no imprisonment, he was compelled to
make drastic alterations in his plays. In the "Prologue at Court" to *The
Emperour Of The East* (1632) he complains of the harsh treatment of his play,
written carefully and harmlessly:

> And yet this poor work suffer'd by the rage
> And envy of some Catos of the stage.

His intellectual courage was shown in a very striking way. In an age when
Jesuit priest was synonymous with detested spy and traitor, when Dekker in
The Whore of Babylon, Barnes in *The Devil's Charter*, and Middleton in *A Game
at Chess* held up to public execration Rome and all its ways and works, Massinger in *The Renegado* makes Francisco, a Jesuit priest, the "true religious
friend" of all the characters for whom the sympathy of the audience is engaged.

As we have seen, Massinger began as a collaborator with Fletcher, though he
made no public claim to any share in their joint production. His name first
appears in 1622 on the title-page of *The Virgin Martir*, which is described as
"Written by Philip Messenger and Thomas Dekker". Massinger began his
work when the inevitable "younger generation" thought Shakespeare fair
game for their wit and hailed with enthusiasm the superficial excitements of
Fletcher. That Massinger was influenced by Fletcher is clear, but his constructive
art is more severe and economical. He had literary skill but he had no true
literary personality; and when he borrows images from Shakespeare he uses
them with no profit to himself. A comparative survey of the women of Shakespeare and of Massinger shows how rapidly the moral character of the English
stage had changed. The younger generation demanded sexual stimulation, and
this Fletcher and Massinger provided. The seduction of a youth by an experienced
woman is a device he used more than once. As a stimulant of another kind
Massinger gives scenes of prolonged and repeated physical torture. The virtues
of Massinger's characters are conventional and their vices monstrous; but he
contrives to fit them with appropriate language. There are some passages of
fine eloquence in Massinger, genuinely part of the dramatic texture, and not
tacked on, like his most famous purple patch, the Roman actor's defence of his
calling.

The names and the dates of production of Massinger's plays can be simply
stated together. *The Duke of Millaine. A Tragaedie* (before 1623); *The Unnaturall
Combat. A Tragedie* (before 1623); *The Bond-Man: An Antient Storie* (1623);
The Renegado, A Tragaecomedie (1624); *The Parliament of Love, A Comedy*
(1624, not printed till 1805); *A New Way to Pay Old Debts. A Comoedie* (before
1626); *The Roman Actor. A Tragaedie* (1626); *The Maid of Honour* (1626);
The Great Duke of Florence. A Comicall Historie (1627); *The Picture. A Trage-
comedie* (1629); *The Emperour Of The East. A Tragae-Comedie* (1631); *Believe as*

you list. A Comedy (1631, not printed till 1849); *The City Madam, A Comedie* (1632); *The Guardian, A Comical History* (1633); *A Very Woman. A Tragi-Comedy* (1634); *The Bashful Lover. A Tragi-Comedy* (1636). To these must be added the collaborations with Fletcher and Dekker, and *The Fatall Dowry: A Tragedy* (published 1632), written with Nathan Field. The general character of these plays has already been indicated. Brief notes on a few typical examples will suffice. *The Unnatural Combat* is a tragedy of the exaggerated type, with a tremendous villain Malefort, who slaughters his son and burns like Shelley's Count Cenci with incestuous passion for his daughter. *The Duke of Milan* is another excessive tragedy, with another great villain, Francisco, who forces a fatal conclusion by painting the lips of dead Marcelia with poison, that Sforza, kissing them, may die. *The Bond-Man* retells the story, as old as Herodotus, of the revolt and subjugation of the slaves. *The Renegado*, with its scene in Tunis, gives us a clash of East and West with a happy ending for Christianity—an ending about as honest as the despoiling of Shylock. *The Parliament of Love* is founded on the southern Courts of Love. *The Roman Actor*, which has Domitian for villain, is a tragedy of imperial lust and cruelty, with a highly dramatic use of play within play. *The Great Duke of Florence* is a courtly comedy of no great value with Cosimo dei Medici as a benevolent tyrant. *The Maid of Honour*, a much stronger play, contains stirring scenes of love and war, with a truly heroic heroine, Camiola, and the inevitable woman wooing a man, this time not lecherously. *The Picture*, an excellent comedy, is based on the old story of a portrait which changes as the subject begins to prove unfaithful. *The Emperor of the East*, with Theodosius the younger, Pulcheria and Eudocia as chief characters, comes to a rather impotent conclusion. Massinger is at his best, not in his unnatural tragedies, but in two comedies. *A New Way to Pay Old Debts* held the stage down to the close of the nineteenth century and is still occasionally revived. Hazlitt's account of Edmund Kean's performance as Sir Giles Overreach is a kind of monument to Massinger as well. *The City Madam* is an excellent comedy with another Doll Tearsheet among its characters, and Luke Frugal as a very complete villain. *The Fatal Dowry*, a gloomy piece, held the stage under another name, for it was adapted by Nicholas Rowe as *The Fair Penitent* and was more successful than any play of his own. That Massinger has genuine constructive power as a playwright and some power as a dramatic poet is evident in all his works. Dorothea the Virgin Martyr may owe some of her success to Dekker; Sir Giles Overreach and Luke Frugal are Massinger's own creations and hold the memory when the characters of Beaumont and Fletcher are forgotten.

VII. TOURNEUR AND WEBSTER

Tourneur and Webster form a pair of dramatists remarkable for their sombre and macabre genius. Neither is much known to us personally. Cyril Tourneur (1575?–1626) published poems, *The Transformed Metamorphosis* in 1600, *A Funerall Poeme* on Sir Francis Vere in 1609, and *A Griefe on the Death of Prince Henrie* in 1613. But he interests us mainly as the reputed author of two plays: *The Revengers Tragaedie* (anon. 1607) and *The Atheist's Tragedie . . . Written by*

Cyril Tourneur (1611). The earlier, anonymous play (one of the supreme masterpieces of Jacobean drama) was regularly attributed to Tourneur during the seventeenth century. These two works raise several problems with which we must here deal summarily. Were they both anonymous, should we attribute them to the same author? Scholars differ in their answers to this question, and mention, rather timidly, some possible authors (including Middleton) for the earlier play. But their arguments for separate authorship are, in the main, insecurely based on the superiority of the earlier play to the later. We assume, of course, that dates of publication represent dates of composition. Lateness does not always imply superiority to earliness. A writer may attempt to repeat an early success and produce nothing but an inferior imitation. A more particular question about Tourneur's work is this: Are the two works sufficiently alike in matter, style and tone to be attributed to the same author? The answer must be that they are more like each other than either is like anything else of the time, and the balance of probability is that the same hand wrote both. Another question is this: if both plays were anonymous, could they be clearly assigned, separately or jointly, to any known authors? The answer must be that though both plays are "revenge" tragedies, of which we have numerous examples, no dramatists of the time have the singular touch of poetic style common, in varying degrees, to both these plays. We may note that though no single character emerges with any conviction of verisimilitude, the two plays are as homogeneous as, say, Verdi's "revenge" opera, *Il Trovatore*; but what is more profitable to remark is that the author is a poet whose imagination is poisoned by the sense of universal vanity and corruption, but who lights up his festering material with flashes of genius, and who is capable of rising to visions of grace, beauty and truth.

We know nothing certain about the life of John Webster (1580?–1625?). His literary activity falls into three periods: the first, that of collaboration and apprenticeship (1602–7); the second, that of the two great tragedies (1610–14); the third, that of the tragi–comedies beginning about 1620. Of these the first is unimportant. He contributed to *The Famous History of Sir Thomas Wyatt* (printed 1607); he made some additions to Marston's *The Malcontent*; with Dekker he collaborated in the pleasant citizen comedies, *Westward Ho* and *Northward Ho*, already mentioned. The real Webster begins at the period of his two great tragedies. The first of these, printed in 1612, is called in full *The White Divel: Or the Tragedy of Paulo Giordano Ursini, Duke of Brachiano, With the Life and Death of Vittoria Corombona the famous Venetian Curtizan*. The second, printed in 1623, but written probably ten years before, is *The Tragedy of the Dutchesse of Malfy*. Among people of his own day Webster had not the vogue of Beaumont and Fletcher; but later criticism has pronounced his genius to be of a higher and rarer kind. His debt to Shakespeare has often been pointed out. It appears in many turns of thought, phrase and character. But more important than any resemblance is the originality of his contribution to the development of the Elizabethan drama; and, in particular, his place among the dramatists of revenge. Here, he falls into line with the long succession of writers, beginning with Kyd, who took up the tale of Seneca's *Thyestes* and *Agamemnon* and, during more than twenty years, rang all the changes upon the theme of vengeance. The development of the revenge motive in drama is an interesting subject for study. The "ghost", which survives as late as Shakespeare's *Hamlet*, disappears, and the avenging "hero" tends to become a villain, with revenge as his excuse. As a last refinement there may be forgiveness and atonement. In a sense *The Tempest* is the noblest of revenge plays. There is no ghost in *The Revenger's Tragedy* and, at the very moment of victory, the cup of triumph is dashed from the lips of the "revenger". In *The Atheist's Tragedy* vengeance is thrust down from the rank of duties, and forgiveness is exalted in its stead. *The White Devil* shows a further variation. Revenge for innocent blood is once more the main theme of the dramatist; but it appears, not as a duty, but as a passion, the vindictive rancour of wounded pride; and our sympathies are no longer with the avengers, but with their victim. This change is even clearer in *The Duchess of Malfi*, for the victim of the avengers now appears as the heroine; and, as if to mark the change most unmistakably, the whole of the last act is devoted to the nemesis which falls upon the avengers. The old motive of revenge as a sacred duty—the motive of *The Spanish Tragedy* and *Hamlet*— is thus weakened almost to extinction.

Three more plays of doubtful authorship have been assigned to Webster— *The Devils Law-Case* (printed 1623), *A Cure for a Cuckold* perhaps with W. Rowley (not printed till 1661) and *Appius and Virginia* (not printed till 1654), which is now plausibly assigned to Heywood. Nothing but bare reference need be made to *Monuments of Honor*, a City pageant, and *A Monumental Columne*, an elegy on the death of Prince Henry (1613). The latter contains a few turns of thought and phrase that suggest the author's spiritual affinity with Donne.

Webster lives as the author of two tragedies which are great even though they tend to lapse into a chaos of melodramatic horror. Vittoria and the Duchess are among the great creations of the Elizabethan-Jacobean drama, surpassed by none outside Shakespeare. Further, Webster is a poet of sombre genius. His imagination loves to linger round thoughts and symbols of mortality, to take shape in "strange images of death". Yet nothing is more remarkable than the thrift with which Webster uses this perilous material. His reserve presents the strongest contrast with the wild waste of the other dramatists of blood. His work has noticeable pictorial quality and suggests kinship with the art of the painter. The general manner of Webster's utterance is imaginative and coloured with a love of curious learning. His verse, which can exhibit both grace and severity, is capable of sudden flashes and of a singular musical cadence, as in Cornelia's dirge from *The White Devil*, beginning, "Call for the Robin Red-breast and the Wren".

VIII. FORD AND SHIRLEY

The publication of the First Folio of Shakespeare in 1623 had a two-fold influence. Dramatists now possessed numerous printed examples for study and had precedent for producing dramas to be read as well as seen. Ford and Shirley are notable examples of this literary stage of development.

John Ford (1586–1639?) was a man of independent mind and capable of espousing unpopular causes. Thus, his first publication, *Fames Memoriall* (1606), is an elegy on Charles Blount, Earl of Devonshire, who had lived under a cloud and died out of favour. Ford's romantic tendencies were further displayed in his *Honor Triumphant; or the Peeres Challenge, by Armes Defensible etc.* (1606). In this there is nothing important beyond the fact that at the age of twenty he is writing prose and verse romantic in spirit, and showing a tolerant attitude towards unconventional conduct. *The Monarches Meeting*, appended to this pamphlet, is an early instance of the stanza of Gray's *Elegy*. Ford's non-dramatic work closes with *A Line of Life* (1620), a didactic tract on conduct, apparently influenced by Bacon's *Essays*.

Ford's earliest attempts at dramatic writing were made in collaboration with Dekker. The masque called *The Sun's Darling* can be dismissed as unimportant. His share in *The Witch of Edmonton*, written with Dekker and Rowley, is difficult to identify. The first printed drama of his own was *The Lovers Melancholy*, acted in 1628 and published in the following year. This slow-moving romance of a melancholy prince was clearly influenced by Burton's *Anatomy of Melancholy* and by the "reunion" or "recognition" plays of Shakespeare's latter days, *The Winter's Tale*, *Cymbeline* and *Pericles*. Its good qualities revealed a poet who only needed discipline in stagecraft to achieve distinction. Ford acquired this technical skill with wonderful rapidity, if we are correct in supposing *The Broken Heart* (printed in 1633) to have been his next play. The plot shows much originality, though Lamb has over-praised both the conduct of the drama and the heroism of Calantha, its heroine. We do not, really, believe in any of it. In Ford's next tragedy, *Loves Sacrifice* (printed 1633), illicit passion is the main subject. *Tis Pitty Shees a Whore* (printed 1633) is the tragedy most frequently cited as evidence of Ford's "decadent" tendencies. Actually the play gives no such evidence. Incest between brother and sister is toyed with as a theatrical titillation in Beaumont and Fletcher's *A King and no King*, and is there disgusting; in *Tis Pitty She's a Whore* the theme is used tragically, and is not disgusting, but is something almost as disconcerting: it is unconvincing. Ford has not the power to make us believe in the overmastering urgency of a passion that must inevitably be fatal to both lovers. To Ford, as to other contemporary dramatists, incest was a theme for a play; we are not to suppose that there was any intended challenge to accepted morality.

The air clears in *Perkin Warbeck* (printed 1634), a successful return to the chronicle-history, which had scarcely been touched for a generation. Obviously inspired by Shakespeare, the play really succeeds with a singularly difficult subject. The comedy of *The Fancies, Chast and Noble* (printed 1638) is much less important, and deals (like Wycherley's *Country Wife*) with supposed male impotence. The list of Ford's extant plays closes with the romantic and unimportant comedy, *The Ladies Triall* (acted 1638).

Some have seen Ford as a special case of "decadence" in the Elizabethan drama. But there is plenty of "decadence" (to use no stronger word) in Ford's contemporaries, especially in Fletcher and Massinger. The difference between Ford and the rest is that he writes with sympathy for the tempted soul and the others write with a desire to exploit the temptation. Ford's sympathy is given to persons, not to transgressions. He cannot justly be charged with decadence. In his attempts at comedy Ford sinks to a lower level than any dramatist of his class. But his understanding of the human heart torn by conflicting passions and his mastery of an expressive diction and of a gravely cadenced blank verse give him a distinguished position among dramatists of his time.

James Shirley (1596–1666) was schoolmaster, cleric and convert to Rome. Henrietta Maria was one of his patrons and he was chosen to write the masque, *The Triumph of Peace*, which the four Inns of Court presented to the king and queen in 1634. Between 1635 and 1640 he engaged in dramatic work in Ireland. He was still writing plays when the closing of the theatres in 1642 put an end to his dramatic activities and drove him to educational publications which we need not discuss. He perished, with his wife, of misery and privation during the Great Fire of 1666.

In 1646 Shirley collected and published a number of his non-dramatic poems. Many of them appeared originally as songs in the dramas, or as prologues and epilogues; others are conventional pieces, conventionally written. One song rises above the rest, and is among the great lyrics of English literature. "The glories of our blood and state", the funeral chant of Calchas over the dead body of Ajax which closes *The Contention of Ajax and Ulisses for the Armor of Achilles* would preserve the memory of Shirley if all his dramas had been lost. The closing of the theatres forced Shirley into print, and so nearly forty plays by him are extant. If we had less we might think more of him. Of the plays that are tragic or semi-tragic, the earliest is *The Maides Revenge* (1626). *The Traytor*, one of his strongest, appeared in 1631, which was also the year of *Loves Crueltie*. *The Dukes Mistris* (1636) and *The Polititian* (printed 1655) are tragi-comedies of no great importance; but *The Cardinall* (1641) ranks with *The Traitor* as one of Shirley's best plays. With it the long line of Elizabethan tragedy comes to an end not entirely unworthy.

The comedy of Shirley falls into two main classes, the comedy of manners and romantic comedy. The scenes of the comedies of manners are, for the most part, laid in London or its immediate neighbourhood and give a lively picture of City life in the time of Charles I. These comedies of manners, ten in all, begin with Shirley's first dramatic attempt, *Love Tricks: or, the Schoole of Complement* (1625). This was followed by *The Wedding* (1626), *The Wittie Faire One* (1628), which is bright in dialogue and ingenious in construction, *Changes: Or, Love in a Maze* (1632), *Hide Park* (1632), which presents a realistic picture of fashionable life, *The Ball* (1632), written with Chapman, *The Gamester* (1633), *The Example* (1634) and *The Lady of Pleasure* (1635), which is usually regarded as Shirley's best example in its kind. *The Constant Maid* belongs to the Irish period and is not remarkable. Unless otherwise described, the dates are dates of production.

Fourteen plays can be included in the class of romantic comedy. The scenes are laid in Mediterranean countries and the action usually takes place at court. *The Brothers* (1626), with a scene in Madrid, is, however, not a court comedy. In *The Gratefull Servant* (1629) the type of romantic comedy is thoroughly established. *The Bird in a Cage* (printed 1633) contains a sarcastic attack on the Puritan fanatic William Prynne, then in prison. *The Young Admirall* (1633) was admired as being in the "beneficial and cleanly way of poetry". *The Opportunitie* (1640) and *The Coronation* (1635) call for no comment—except that the latter was absurdly included in the 1679 folio of "Beaumont and Fletcher".

The Royall Master (1638), *The Doubtfull Heir* (1640) and *The Gentleman of Venice* (1639) belong to the Dublin period. *The Arcadia* (1640) boldly attempts to dramatize Sidney's romance. *The Humorous Courtier* (printed 1640) is not remarkable, but *The Imposture* (1640) is a cleverly manipulated piece of complicated invention. *The Sisters* (1642) was the last play by Shirley performed before the theatres were closed. *The Court Secret*, the latest of Shirley's regular dramas, was not acted till after the Restoration.

Other miscellaneous pieces remain to be mentioned. The most curious of these is an extraordinary medley, something between a chronicle play and a miracle play, written for the Dublin theatre, and called *St. Patrick for Ireland* (printed 1640). Interesting in a different way is the allegorical drama, *Honoria and Mammon* (pub. 1659), an elaboration of a morality, *A Contention for Honour and Riches*, which Shirley had printed in 1633. *The Tragedie of Chabot Admirall of France* (printed 1639) is ascribed on the title-page of the quarto to Chapman and Shirley. Besides the masques introduced into nine or ten of his plays, Shirley has left three separate productions of this class: *The Triumph of Peace* (printed 1633), *The Triumph of Beauty* (printed 1646) and *Cupid and Death* (performed 1653). *The Contention of Ajax and Ulisses for the Armor of Achilles* (printed 1659), often described as a masque, is a short dramatic piece, intended for private production.

Shirley was not a great dramatist, and he suffers by comparison with his predecessors. But he has merits. He is sometimes tedious, but he is not often gratuitously immoral or sensational. Shirley, unlike Ford, displays genuine comic invention, both in character and in situation. His verse is sound but undistinguished, the one immortal lyric being exceptional.

IX. LESSER JACOBEAN AND CAROLINE DRAMATISTS

The numerous minor playwrights of the period, beginning with John Day, almost the last of the Elizabethans, and ending with Sir William D'Avenant, almost the first of the Restoration dramatists, can receive but short notice.

John Day (c. 1574–c. 1640), mentioned on p. 243, was one of Henslowe's men. His comedy *The Ile of Guls* (printed 1606), has a plot taken from Sidney's *Arcadia*. *Law-Trickes*, or *Who would have Thought it* and *Humour out of Breath* (both printed 1608), exhibit the neatness and compactness of his dialogue. *The Parliament of Bees*—this being but the beginning of an extensive title—is a set of twelve short dialogues in verse or a series of pastoral eclogues. It was not published till 1641. The music of Day's verse is sweet and unostentatious. One who seems a wanderer into the realm of Jacobean drama is the Elizabethan sonneteer Barnabe Barnes, whose fine historical tragedy *The Divils Charter* (1607) has Pope Alexander VI as a very villainous villain. Another belated Elizabethan is Robert Armin (c. 1580–1612), who succeeded Kemp as the chief actor of comic parts in the Chamberlain's Company about 1600. His single play, printed 1609, is entitled *The History of the two Maids of More-clacke; With the life and simple manner of John in the Hospitall*. He may have done no more than provide his own fool's part, and had the rest written by other hands. The play has genuine dramatic power, forcible eloquence and fine poetry. His other compositions, not plays, are *Foole upon Foole, or, Six Sortes of Sottes* (1605), a prose tract, amplified, in 1608, into *A Nest of Ninnies*, and *The Italian Taylor and his Boy* (1609), a verse translation from the Italian, written with considerable dexterity.

Middleton's influence on comedy is apparent in the two surviving plays of the lawyer Edward Sharpham—*The Fleire*, acted probably early in 1606, and *Cupids Whirligig*, produced about a year later. Both plays were frequently reprinted, and were evidently popular farces. Much better than these is the single play *Ram-Alley or Merrie Trickes*, acted perhaps as early as 1609 and extant in several quartos. The author is Lording Barry, whose odd first name has been wrongly interpreted as "Lodowich" and as a title "Lord". Ram Alley was a peculiarly disreputable region and the play abounds in coarseness. Many echoes from Shakespeare's plays are introduced, by way of parody and of imitation. *Greenes Tu Quoque or The Citie Gallant*, a successful farcical comedy, was printed in 1614 as by "Jo. Cooke, Gent." of whom nothing whatever is known. The "Greene" of the title is Thomas Greene the actor who made it popular. *The Hogge hath lost his Pearle* (printed 1614) is another single play, by an unknown Robert Tailor. It is less good than *Greenes Tu Quoque*, though, like that, full of interest for the student of Jacobean London.

With Nathan Field (1587?–1633?) we reach, not a belated Elizabethan, but a true Jacobean, a follower of Ben Jonson, and an actor in his plays. Like Armin he is immortalized among the actors named in the First Folio of Shakespeare. Jonson called Field "his scholar". His first play, *A Woman is a Weather-cocke*, was produced in 1610. His second play, *Amends for Ladies*, followed soon after, and was intended to atone for the anti-feminism of its predecessor. Field's wit is considerable and is not a mere copy of Jonson. Besides writing these two comedies, Field collaborated with Fletcher in *The Fatal Dowry*. Richard Brome (pronounced Broom), like Field, was a literary son of Ben Jonson, and was traditionally supposed to have been educated by him. Fifteen of Brome's plays have come down to us. Four of these were published in quarto in Brome's lifetime; five were printed together in 1653, shortly after his death (1652); five in 1659; and one other, in quarto, in 1657. The plays can be conveniently classed as comedies of manners, romantic comedies and romantic dramas of intrigue. These divisions exhibit Brome's debt to Jonson, for the first class is much the largest, and includes nine plays, *The Northern Lasse*, *The Antipodes*, *The Sparagus Garden*, *Covent Garden Weeded*, *The New Academy, or The New Exchange*, *The Damoiselle*, *The Court Beggar*, *The Madd Couple well matcht*, *The City Witt*. The brightest and best of Brome's comedies of manners is *The City Witt, or The Woman wears the Breeches*, and it is the best because it most successfully keeps in one key. Brome's masterpiece, *A Joviall Crew, or the Merry Beggars*, was his latest play. It was produced in 1641 and kept the stage till it came to be the very last play acted before Parliament closed the theatres in 1642. *A Jovial Crew*, with three others, *The Love-sick Court*, *The Novella* and *The English Moor*, form Brome's plays of romantic intrigue. *The Queen and Concubine* and *The Queenes Exchange* are typical of Brome's pure romantic manner. The first is better than the second and shows capacity in its kind. Brome's art is simple and fresh, and his work reveals a genuine courageous character.

Among Jonson's most eager admirers was Thomas Randolph (1605–1635), a Fellow of Trinity College, Cambridge. By the time he made Jonson's acquaintance he had written his two earliest "shews"—*Aristippus* and *The Conceited Pedler*, which were printed in 1630. The marvellous agility of the rhyming in *Aristippus* recalls Browning's feats in that kind. In March 1632, King Charles visited Cambridge, and the Trinity men acted before him *The Jealous Lovers*, written for the occasion. It is Randolph's only failure. After the king's visit, Randolph left Cambridge for London. His best play *The Muses Looking-Glasse* was presented about 1632. His fine pastoral *Amyntas* (c. 1633) has merits, but it challenges comparison with finer work by Jonson and Fletcher, whereas *The Muses Looking-Glasse* is unique of its kind. Randolph died at the age of twenty-nine; and his achievement, considerable as it is, is an earnest only of what his matured powers might have given us.

The lesser dramatists who occupied the stage from the later years of James to the closing of the theatres exhibit either featureless mediocrity or pretentious extravagance. Thomas May (1595–1650), the historian of the Long Parliament, whose character Clarendon and Marvell unite in decrying, began his literary career with two comedies, *The Heir* and *The Old Couple*, written about 1620. *The Heir* is a Fletcherian tragi-comedy, *The Old Couple* a play of Jonsonian intrigue and manners. After producing these plays, May turned to the work by which he is best known—his translations of the *Georgics* and of Lucan's *Pharsalia*. Jonson's influence and that of the classics turned May to classical drama, and he produced three tragedies, *Antigone*, *The Theban Princess* (c. 1626), *Cleopatra* (1626) and *Julia Agrippina* (1628). It has been suggested that he is the author of the anonymous *Nero* (ptd. 1624). May's tragedies are a pale reflection of *Sejanus* and *Catiline*. The meritorious activity of Robert Davenport begins in 1623. Three of his plays survive, two comedies and a tragedy. The tragedy, *King John and Matilda*, is a careful re-writing of Munday and Chettle's *Death of Robert, Earl of Huntingdon*; but *The City-Night-Cap* and *A New Tricke to Cheat the Divell* are both of them interesting and able comedies. They all belong to the period before or after 1630. Thomas Nabbes produced his *Hannibal and Scipio* in 1635 by revising an older play. His *Microcosmus* (printed 1637) is called a "morall masque". His best work is to be found in his three comedies, *Covent-Garden*, *Totenham-Court* and *The Bride*, acted 1632, 1633 and 1638. Nabbes breaks away from the prevailing coarse type of comedy intended to hit the taste of the man about town. Two writers who were among the "sons of Ben" and of great repute in their day need not detain us long. William Cartwright (1611–43) rose to be the most noted man in his university of Oxford as a strenuous scholar, an admired dramatist and a "seraphical" preacher. His first play, probably, was his comedy *The Ordinary*, produced about 1635. This was followed by three tragi-comedies, *The Lady Errant*, *The Royall Slave* and *The Siedge or Love's Convert*. After taking holy orders in 1638, he did not write any more plays. Jasper Mayne (1604–72), dramatist, translator and archdeacon, was, like his friend Cartwright, an admired preacher. He produced a tragi-comedy, *The*

Amorous Warre, and a comedy, *The Citye Match*, acted at Whitehall by the king's command in 1639. Mayne's most useful contribution to the literature of his country was his *Part of Lucian made English* (1644).

One striking figure stands out among the mediocrities. In 1642, the year of the closing of the theatres, Sir John Suckling (b. 1609) poisoned himself in Paris. All his plays are not worth his handful of incomparable lyrics; but they have some salt of genius in them. *Aglaura* (1638), a tragedy of court intrigue, contains the famous, "Why so pale and wan, fond lover?" *The Goblins* was probably written next; it was acted in 1638, and is Suckling's best play. Sheridan knew this and used it. "Here's to the maiden" (in *The School for Scandal*) was suggested by a catch in *The Goblins*. The tragedy *Brennoralt* is a work of higher level. It did not appear till 1646; but it had been printed in a shorter form in 1640 as *The Discontented Colonell*. Suckling's style perceptibly strengthens in the play. It has a general note of Byronic melancholy which Suckling's own suicide makes more significant. A friend and companion in arms of Suckling, who died before him, was Shackerley Marmion (1603–39), author of the considerable poem *Cupid and Psyche*. He produced three comedies before his poem, not, as we should expect, in the romantic vein, but all of them rather thin imitations of Jonson. They are *Hollands Leaguer* (1632), *A Fine Companion* (1633), and *The Antiquary* (1634), the last being the best.

Some of the later Jacobean dramatists initiated the type of play which, in its full development at the Restoration, came to be known as the "heroic drama". In this connection the tragi-comedies of Lodowick Carlell have importance. Carlell (said to be of the stock which produced Carlyle) was a Scot. His plays are *The Deserving Favourite* (1629), *Arvirargus and Philicia* (1639), *The Passionate Lovers* (1655), and *Two New Playes, Viz* 1. *The Fool would be a Favourit.* (2) *Osmond, the Great Turk* (1657). The degeneration of the great blank verse instrument of drama is specially to be remarked. Dryden's use of rhyme was certainly needed to bring back some form into this chaos. The plays of Henry Glapthorne are examples of decay in style. His comedies, *The Hollander* (1640) and *Wit in a Constable* (1640), at their worst sink as low as Cartwright and, at their best, touch the level of Mayne or Nabbes; but his more serious works, *The Ladies Priviledge* (1640), *Argalus and Parthenia* (1639) and *Albertus Wallenstein* (1639), are at least no worse than the parallel efforts of Carlell, Mayne, Cartwright, or Thomas Killigrew, the last of whom wrote a folio of unimportant plays. But it is William D'Avenant whose work best enables us to observe the transition to the heroic drama of Dryden. His first two plays were tragedies in Fletcher's grimmest style, and these were followed by two able comedies which enjoyed considerable popularity. After 1630, illness incapacitated him for several years. When he resumed work his style had altered, and four plays, *Love and Honour*, *The Platonick Lovers*, *The Fair Favourite*, and *The Unfortunate Lovers*, acted 1634–8, show him in the "heroic" vein, and as the leading exponent of the cult of platonic love, of which Henrietta Maria herself was the patron. D'Avenant lived to revive the theatre shortly before the Restoration and to contribute to its literature after that date. He will, therefore, receive some further notice in a later chapter.

X. THE ELIZABETHAN THEATRE

When Elizabeth came to the throne, she found attached to the court not only musicians and minstrels, but eight players of interludes. Companies of such players had long been attached to the households of men of rank, whose "livery" or badge they wore on their sleeves. A few months after her accession, Elizabeth issued a proclamation ordering that no interlude should be played without being announced beforehand and licensed by appropriate authorities; and in 1572 the status of unattached companies was finally settled by a law providing that common players of interludes not belonging to a baron or honourable personage of greater degree, or not having a licence from two justices of the peace, should be deemed rogues and vagabonds. The early part of Elizabeth's reign saw not only the triumph of the professional actor over the amateur, but the supplanting of the old players of interludes by the better equipped companies then newly formed by nobles anxious to please their sovereign. A full account of the Elizabethan theatre and actors is outside the scope of this volume. In earlier chapters we have seen the development of drama from the church services into the popular miracle plays. But besides these public and popular performances there were of course the private interludes played in the halls of great houses. Our early drama was the domain of healthy amateurism. Professionalism came in later, and was very properly suspected. The earliest professional performers, descendants of the fallen minstrels, were literally mountebanks. They stood up in the market-place with the jugglers and the vendors of medicines. Between itinerant entertainers and the reputable persons who performed in privileged places there was a great gulf; and the history of the theatre is the history of the closing of that gulf. The tradition of the single entertainer survived in the improvisations of comedians like Tarlton and Kemp, who held up a play for their personal shows.

When performers became a troupe, the market-place was less suitable than the kind of inn-yard which survived as late as the celebrated morning on which Mr Pickwick, Mr Perker and Mr Wardle entered the White Hart Inn near the Borough Market and found Mr Samuel Weller engaged in burnishing a pair of painted tops. Round the yard were the buildings of the inn, with galleries off which the rooms opened. Mr Weller had already been conversing from his ground level with a chambermaid leaning over one of the galleries. The essential difference between such an inn-yard and a theatre is small. All that is lacking is a stage, which a platform could soon provide; the sheds and pent-houses were available as retiring and attiring rooms, and it was easy to arrange that characters could, when necessary for the action, be seen "above", or be "discovered". The "Bell", the "Bull", the "Cross Keys" and the "Bell Savage", all within the City of London, were the scenes of theatrical performances in Elizabethan times; and that fact brings us to another point of importance. The authorities of the City of London were unsympathetic to theatrical performances. There were good reasons in Elizabethan times. Theatrical performances attracted crowds of undesirables. They tempted people from their proper work, especially apprentices, who were as turbulent as the "students" in those parts of Europe where political revolutions used to be habitual. Moreover the close pack of groundlings communicated all the infectious diseases. And so we have the curious spectacle of the royal court desiring theatrical performances and the municipality determined to have neither play-houses nor play-going. The opposition of the City to the theatre was countered by the erection of a theatre just outside the City's jurisdiction. So in 1576 Elizabethan London got its first theatre, called The Theater, in Shoreditch, outside the Bishopsgate entrance to the City. It is associated with the Burbage family, James, and his sons Richard and Cuthbert. The Theater, like most of its immediate successors, was a round open building—the inn-yard, in fact, rounded for the convenience of the spectators. The next theatre, The Curtain, was a kind of chapel-of-ease to The Theater, near which it was built, but on the Moorfields side. It was built about 1577 and was used till 1592. Apparently it was reconditioned in 1596. For London's next theatre we have to cross the river at London Bridge and go through Southwark to Newington Butts. The Newington Theatre is first mentioned in 1580; but it did not last long; it was too far away from London. The fourth London theatre (1587–92) was one of the most celebrated, The Rose, belonging to Philip Henslowe, an acute man of business, whose various undertakings would have earned him in later days the title of captain of industry. The Rose Theatre was, for Henslowe, not an artistic hobby but a business speculation. Here appeared Edward Alleyn, greatest actor of his time, as Tamburlaine and Faustus; and here Henslowe kept his account book or diary of expenses which, tangled and almost incomprehensible as it is, is a document of the highest importance in the history of Elizabethan drama. The Swan, another Bankside theatre, was probably ready for use in 1595. Dramatically its history is unimportant; but the house has acquired celebrity from the fact that a drawing of its interior is in existence. The description accompanying the drawing states that the building would hold three thousand persons in the *sedilia* or galleries. The number is not so surprising as appears at first sight; it represents about $1\frac{1}{2}$ per cent of the total population of London and Westminster —a population greatly addicted to public amusements, from bear-baiting to executions.

The most famous of all Elizabethan play-houses, The Globe in Bankside, Southwark, literally rose out of The Theater, for when that building was taken down in 1598 the materials were used for the new play-house. Bankside, just across London Bridge, was a regular pleasure resort. At The Globe played the Lord Chamberlain's men with Shakespeare as one of the company; and here were produced the greatest glories of our literature. It was a syndicate business, and evidently profitable to the shareholders. Shakespeare apparently made a small competence from it. It was probably first used in 1599; it was certainly used for *Every Man out of his Humour* in 1600; and it continued to be the most famous house in London till it was burnt down in 1613. It rose from its ashes and remained in use till 1642. The Globe, like the other major theatres, was large. An audience of 3000 is mentioned by a foreign visitor. The general site of The Globe Theatre is known; but the precise spot is still a matter of controversy. The success of The Globe led Henslowe and Alleyn to think about a successor to the decaying Rose. Henslowe decided to go north, and chose a site just outside Cripplegate. Here was built The Fortune play-house—square, instead of round. It was opened in 1600 and burned down in 1621, and with it perished many unprinted manuscript plays. Another venture of Henslowe's was The Hope, in Bankside, newly built as a theatre in 1613. It had no important history. Across the river, however, at Blackfriars, was the old Dominican monastery building, part of which had been used by the Master of the Revels, and was leased in 1576 to Richard Farrant, Master of the Windsor Chapel Children, ostensibly for practice, but actually for public performances. This theatrical occupation by various companies of boy actors lasted from 1576 to 1590 and forms the first period of The Blackfriars Theatre. A new chapter begins in 1596 when James Burbage acquired more of the Blackfriars property and converted it into a "private" theatre—what would now be journalistically called a "luxury theatre", covered in and well appointed. James was succeeded in the enterprise by his famous son Richard. It will be seen that The Blackfriars Theatre was almost contemporary with The Globe. The Corporation of the City of London, not approving of a theatre within its borders, tried to close it in 1619; but the Privy Council interfered, and The Blackfriars Theatre continued in use till 1642. The office of *The Times* newspaper now stands on its site.

The Red Bull in Clerkenwell is almost entirely post-Elizabethan, so is The Cockpit, a private theatre in Drury Lane, used from 1615 to 1642. Near Blackfriars was the old priory of the Carmelites or Whitefriars, the hall of which was used from about 1608 to 1609 for dramatic performances. Later on (1629) a play-house was built close by known as The Salisbury Court. Salisbury Square, in "Newspaper land" off Fleet Street, indicates its position.

The theatres were closed by order when London had its regular visitation of "the plague", and sometimes a theatre was closed for a period for disciplinary reasons, when a play had given offence to the court. During long closures the actors went on tour, usually in a company below the London strength, and gave adaptations of their London successes. Thus, Leicester's company played at Stratford-on-Avon in 1587. There was little difficulty in fitting an Elizabethan play to any building, because the Elizabethan theatre had no stage in the modern sense. The Elizabethan theatre had a platform-stage projecting into the auditorium; the modern theatre has a picture-stage framed by the proscenium. The difference is vital. On the picture-stage the characters converse; on the platform-stage the characters declaim. On the picture-stage there is visual illusion, and the illusion makes possible dramatic pauses in the action; on the platform-stage there is no visual illusion, and there can be no pauses—the action must be incessant, and there must be an ever-flowing stream of words. A stream of speech was as imperative in an Elizabethan play as a stream of song in a Rossini opera. There was good and bad speech as there was good and bad singing. That declamation sometimes became ranting we know from *Hamlet*; and the clowns often upset the balance of a play. There were no unities of time or place on the Elizabethan stage, because there was no need for them. Anything can be supposed to happen on a vast empty platform. But it must not be supposed that the Elizabethan stage had any theories of austerity. It loved trappings and costumes and effects and would have had scenery had scenery been possible. But speech—speech swift, unbroken, rhythmical, musical—that was the life of an Elizabethan play.

The dramatic companies developed naturally from the entertainers who formed part of royal and noble households. Court pageants and revels need performers. Philostrate, in *A Midsummer Night's Dream*, managed the dramatic entertainments at the court of Theseus, Duke of Athens, as Goethe managed the dramatic entertainments at the court of the Grand Duke of Weimar. The history of the Elizabethan dramatic companies does not concern us. In the most flourishing days the two main companies were "the Admiral's men" and "the Chamberlain's men". Alleyn was the greatest actor among the Admiral's men, Richard Burbage was the greatest actor among the Chamberlain's men. There were no women in the companies, female parts being taken by attractive boys before their voices broke. The Elizabethan boys may not have produced a Siddons or a Terry, but they can scarcely have been worse than many actresses. Actors were, of course, not fixed members of a company, but could be transferred as readily as Association footballers. Plays were bought by the company, and the manuscripts formed part of the company's stock. The company might sell a play to another company, but disliked printing it, because another company could then play it without payment. For the same reason, the author was not encouraged to print his play; the company purchased the script, and it was considered sharp practice for the author to sell it also to a bookseller. As we have already pointed out, many plays crept into print in a mangled form through various crooked ways. Theatrical finance was mainly conducted on the share system. One share or more might be purchased, or might be allotted instead of salary.

The accession of James I brought the old Elizabethan theatre to its end. Private companies ceased to exist. The position of the favoured companies was assured by the issue of licences which brought them directly under royal patronage, and by the statute of March 1604 the Chamberlain's, the Admiral's and Worcester's men became respectively the King's, Prince Henry's and the Queen's. All public theatricals remained directly under royal patronage during the reigns of James I and Charles I, until the ordinance of the Lords and Commons of September 1642 closed the theatres and terminated all performances.

XI. THE CHILDREN OF THE CHAPEL ROYAL AND THEIR MASTERS

An important part in Elizabethan drama was played by boy actors from the royal chapels and the public schools. Children, as we know, can be trained to do almost anything, and their manner in performance is engaging. The chief duty of the boys engaged for the Elizabethan royal chapels in London and Windsor was, of course, to sing at divine service; but they also sang at secular court entertainments, and played in masques and pageants, and then played in more important pieces, until at last, as we know from a famous passage in *Hamlet*, they became a craze, and drew public patronage away from the adult companies. Into the early history of the Children of the Chapel we need not enter, nor need we discuss performances of Latin plays at schools. We may conveniently begin at 1561, when Richard Edwards, master of the royal choristers in London, was empowered to "take up" children for the chapel. Edwards was succeeded by William Hunnis, who in his turn was succeeded by Nathaniel Giles in 1597. The most famous master of the children of the Windsor Chapel was Richard Farrant, who ruled from 1564 to 1580, and, as we have already seen, arranged dramatic performances at Blackfriars. Distinct from the royal chapel children were boys from the choir school at St Paul's. Under various masters the "Children of Paules" distinguished themselves in dramatic entertainments, first at the school itself and then at the Blackfriars, where they seem to have combined temporarily with the Children of the Chapel. The Children of Paul's were served as dramatist and director by the famous John Lyly; but he began with the Children of the Chapel, and he had no official connection with the school. The combination did not endure, and the Children of Paul's and the Children of the Chapel resumed an independent existence. Soon after the accession of James I the Children of the Revels were dissociated from the Chapel choristers, and in time the craze for boy actors died down. The one boy actor whose name endures is Salomon Pavy, whose untimely death was mourned by Ben Jonson in a beautiful little epigram.

Almost every dramatist of importance had his work played by the children. All the plays of Lyly were acted before the Queen by the "Children of Paules" either alone or with the "Children of her Maiesties Chappel". The children of one or other company produced important plays by Peele, Marlowe, Beaumont and Fletcher, Chapman, Day, Dekker, Ben Jonson, Marston and Middleton. Shakespeare's hostile allusion in *Hamlet*—almost his only direct discussion of contemporary affairs—is specially interesting, as no play of his was given to the public by the children, some of whom, however, grew up to join the Globe company.

XII. UNIVERSITY PLAYS: TUDOR AND EARLY STUART PERIODS

An interesting factor in the development of English drama is found in the plays written and performed by members of the two universities on certain occasions. These activities were at first purely educational, but amusement would keep breaking in. Seneca, not Sophocles, was the pattern of the English humanist when he endeavoured to write tragedy, and the earliest extant university plays are Biblical tragedies framed on the Senecan model. Their author was the Nicholas Grimald, whom we have already met as a poet. The first of these, *Christus Redivivus*, printed at Cologne in 1543, combines a Senecan treatment of the Gospel story of the Resurrection, with a comic underplot centring in the four Roman soldiers who guard the sepulchre. Grimald's second tragedy, *Archipropheta*, printed at Cologne in 1548, dealt with the career of John the Baptist. A leading spirit at Cambridge was William Stevenson, who is perhaps the author of *Gammer Gurtons Nedle*, though Martin Marprelate persists (perhaps jocularly) in attributing it to Doctor John Bridges. This celebrated piece was written some time after 1550 and was not published till 1575. It is of enduring interest as the earliest university play in English which has come down to us. It shows little trace of scholarly influence, for it is written in rugged "fourteeners" and uses the south-western dialect which became the conventional form of rustic speech on the Elizabethan stage.

The golden period of academic drama dates from the visit of Queen Elizabeth to Cambridge in 1564. Here she was entertained with certain plays in Latin, not now extant. In 1566 the Queen visited Oxford where she saw *Palamon and Arcyte* by Richard Edwards. The loss of this play is specially regrettable, for it treated the same story as that of *The Two Noble Kinsmen* half a century before the pseudo-Shakespearean piece was written. What is remarkable about these entertainments offered to Royalty is their seriousness and the variety of their intellectual appeal. Into the academic society which could produce such pieces presently entered Marlowe, Peele, Greene, and Nashe, and from it they carried lessons destined to exercise a momentous influence on the native drama.

To 1580, but to no special occasion, belongs a famous play acted at St John's College, Cambridge, *Richardus Tertius*, by Thomas Legge (1535–1607), Master of Caius, a writer praised by Meres. It departs from the Senecan model in its disregard of the unities, but it is Senecan in metre, in language, and in excess of declamation. Greene was at Cambridge when the play was produced and Marlowe entered in the following year. Legge's play must have been known to both. A fact worthy of notice is that the two wooing scenes in Shakespeare's *Richard III* have no source in Holinshed, but are anticipated in Legge's tragedy. The most important Senecan dramatist of the universities is William Gager (*c.* 1560–1621) of Christ Church, Oxford. The first of his Latin tragedies, *Meleager* (1581), was revived in 1584 in the presence of Sidney, who no doubt rejoiced in its correctness. In his *Dido* George Peele took part. *Oedipus*, of uncertain date, is only partly extant in manuscript; but *Ulysses Redux*, a vigorous dramatization of the end of *The Odyssey*, was printed (1592) soon after its production, and provoked a controversy with John Rainolds of Queen's, a Puritan antagonist of the drama. The modern Italian writers provided other models. *Victoria* by Abraham Fraunce of St John's College, Cambridge, drew upon Pasqualigo's prose comedy *Il Fedele*, also the source of Anthony Munday's (?) *Fedele and Fortunio, or the Two Italian Gentlemen*. Of numerous other Cambridge adaptations from the Italian the only one that need be mentioned is the anonymous *Laelia*, founded upon *Gl' Ingannati*, so near in plot to *Twelfth Night* that some critics have claimed it as the direct source.

The plays so far considered are academic in character. We have now to pass to plays that present studies and incidents of university life. One diverting example is the anti-Harvey *Pedantius*, written *c.* 1581. For attacks on the Harveys, Latin was the suitable instrument; but when the college playwrights took a hand in the eternal antagonism of "town and gown", they naturally used English. The most famous of such plays is the anonymous *Club Law*, acted about 1599 at Clare, and re-discovered in the early twentieth century in the library of St John's. Broadly contemporary with *Club Law* is the *Parnassus* trilogy, which takes first rank among the productions of the university stage. Only one part was published at the time (1606); the others remained in manuscript till 1886. Whoever he was, this playwright of St John's, Cambridge, was a writer of great gifts. In *The Pilgrimage to Parnassus* and the two parts of *The Return* the author describes the difficulties, the temptations and the hardships of a scholar's life. There are many references to contemporary writers. The several allusions to Shakespeare, obviously meant as sarcastic jests directed at the most popular writer of the day, have been taken solemnly and seriously by some later critics as tributes to the master. The three parts of *Parnassus* (edited by J. B. Leishman in 1949) should be known to all students of the drama. Another successful Cambridge drama is *Lingua, or The Combat of the Tongue and the five Senses for Superiority* (1607), by Thomas Tomkis. The plot is concerned with the attempt of *Lingua*, the tongue, to vindicate her claim to be a sixth sense. Tomkis also wrote *Albumazar* (1615), revived by Garrick.

Oxford was less fruitful in plays than Cambridge and seems to have required the stimulus of royal visits. King James I and his son Prince Henry visited Oxford in 1605 and special preparations were made to entertain them. But the royal pedant, unlike his predecessor, was not amused. He was inclined to leave half-way through one play and fell asleep at another. But a play produced on the fourth evening made amends. It was *The Queenes Arcadia* by Samuel Daniel, memorable as the first English pastoral drama written for the academic stage— Cambridge having broken the ground first with *Pastor Fidus*, a Latin version of Guarini's *Il Pastor Fido*. A curious point in Daniel's charmingly written play is an allusion to the prophecy made by the witches to Banquo, when, as far as we know, *Macbeth* was not yet written. In 1615 King James and Prince Charles went to Cambridge and saw an unsuccessful Latin play, *Aemila*, by Edward Cecil; but ample amends were made on the following evening when, in the hall of Trinity, *Ignoramus*, by George Ruggle, was launched on its triumphant career. James liked *Ignoramus* so much that he returned to Cambridge to see it again.

When Charles I and Henrietta Maria visited Cambridge in 1632 they saw *The Rival Friends* by Peter Hausted, and *The Jealous Lovers* by Thomas Randolph. The same royal pair visited Oxford in 1636 when they saw *The Floating Island* by William Strode, with music by Henry Lawes. Equally successful were *Loves Hospitall* by George Wilde and *The Royall Slave* by William Cartwright. The scenic effects by Inigo Jones and the music of Lawes gave great satisfaction. The academic stage was to number yet one more illustrious recruit in Cowley, whose *Naufragium Joculare*, based on classical sources, was acted at Trinity College, Cambridge, in 1638, and was followed in 1642 by his satirical comedy *The Guardian*, remodelled, after the Restoration, into *Cutter of Coleman Street*. But the royal visit to Oxford in 1636 marks the close of these elaborate university displays which had begun with Elizabeth's coming to Cambridge in 1564. When Oxford, some seven years later, again opened its gates to Charles, it was not to entertain him with "masques and triumphs", but to afford him shelter against the forces of the Parliament.

The lesser Elizabethan dramatists were not rediscovered till the nineteenth century: the university dramatists have scarcely been discovered at all, and much of their work remains unprinted. Yet to the academic stage we owe a great variety of compositions, very few of which we have been able to mention. Royal patronage of university drama lent it a special glory and linked the culture of the two universities with the throne in a way that later times lamentably missed.

XIII. MASQUE AND PASTORAL

That the period of the Renascence was a period of appeal to the eye the history of pictorial art sufficiently shows. In Elizabethan England costume was splendid and entertainments magnificent. The theatre did not lend itself to lavish spectacle, but atoned for this deficiency by words that abounded in glowing imagery. It was the court, not the theatre, that was the abode of spectacle. From the time of Henry VIII to the closing of the theatres in 1642, masque and pageantry held their place as the most important and magnificent of the arts. The leading dramatists were called in to devise spectacles; but their words, however splendid, were not the masque. The masque in its glory was an appeal to the eye as well as to the ear, a blaze of colour and light, a succession of rapidly changing scenes and tableaux, crowded with wonderful and beautiful figures. The practical imagination of Inigo Jones (1573–1652) was as important to the masque as the imaginative invention of Ben Jonson. The words alone are merely the libretto with the setting left out.

We have already dwelt upon the function and importance of medieval processions. The great spectacle in Westminster Hall in the year 1502 when Prince Arthur was married to Princess Katherine of Aragon was a procession that had become very like an elaborate ballet. Edward Hall the chronicler describes with enthusiasm the pageantry of Henry VIII's reign; and it is Hall who uses the word "mask" in a description of a court festival at the Epiphany in 1512, but the word obviously implies no more than some covering of the faces during the pageant.

A masque in its matter is general rather than particular. It is not intense or individual. It gives us not Hamlet, but Melancholy, not Othello, but Jealousy, not Shylock, but Avarice: and so, in presenting qualities, it can moralize an occasion allegorically instead of exploiting a situation realistically. A masque, therefore, is capable of insertion as an interlude in a play, and we find in Shakespeare, for instance, masques as widely different as the "ostentation, show, pageant or antick" of the Nine Worthies in *Love's Labour's Lost* and the significant "revels" in *The Tempest*. The English poet whose genius is most akin to that of the masque is Spenser. *The Faerie Queene* is an immense undramatic masque. "Entertainments" given by noble persons to a visiting sovereign usually took the form of a masque. One, by Sir Philip Sidney, of considerable merit, has survived, *The May Lady*, presented in 1578, when the Queen visited his uncle, the Earl of Leicester, at Wanstead. Some of Lyly's plays have affinities with the masque. The influence of Lyly upon Jonson is clearly seen in *Cynthia's Revels*, wherein we can discern how a great realist came to succeed as a writer of masques. One famous piece which is neither masque, nor pastoral, nor drama, but something of all three is Peele's *Arraignment of Paris*.

The first court masque after King James's accession was Daniel's *The Vision of the Twelve Goddesses* (1604); but the greatest of all masques were those of Ben Jonson, who found in that form a release for the poetic activities of his multifarious genius. He approached the masque by way of "entertainments". Among these are *The Satyr*, or *Althorp Entertainment* (1603), *The Coronation*

Entertainment (1604) and *The Penates, or Highgate Entertainment* (1604). Jonson's first court masques were *The Masque of Blackness* (1605) and *The Masque of Beauty* (1608). Between these came *Hymenaei* (1606) to celebrate the marriage of the Earl of Essex and Lady Frances Howard. *Lord Haddington's Masque*, usually called *The Hue and Cry after Cupid*, was produced at court in 1608. Jonson's next royal masque, *The Masque of Queens* (1609), is notable for its use of an "anti-masque", in which forms of ugliness, in this case hags or witches, acted as foils to beauty. *Prince Henry's Barriers* (1610), a tilting entertainment, is remarkable for its Arthurian setting. *Oberon, The Faery Prince* and *Love Freed from Ignorance and Folly* were played in 1611. *Love Restored* (1612) contains scenes that moved the masque towards Aristophanic comedy. Next came *The Irish Masque* (1613), *A Challenge at Tilt* (1614), *Mercury Vindicated from the Alchemists* (1615), *Christmas his Masque* (1616), *The Golden Age Restored* (1616), *The Vision of Delight* (1617) and *Lovers Made Men, or The Masque of Lethe* (1617). *Pleasure Reconciled to Virtue* is remarkable because it introduces "Comus the god of cheer or the Belly". An interval follows. Then came *News from the New World Discovered in the Moon* (1621), *A Masque of the Metamorphosed Gipsies* (1621), *The Masque of Augurs* (1622), *Time Vindicated* (1623), *Pan's Anniversary* (1624), *Neptune's Triumph* (1623), *The Fortunate Isles* (1625), *The Masque of Owls* (1626), *Love's Triumph through Callipolis* (1630) and *Chloridia* (1630), the last revived in 1935. To discuss these numerous compositions severally is not possible here; but we may say generally that a knowledge of them is necessary to an adequate estimate of Jonson's genius. His poetical invention runs more freely in the masques than in some of the plays.

The marriage of James I's daughter Elizabeth to the Elector Palatine in 1613 was the occasion of magnificent festivity. The first great show was *The Lords Masque* by Thomas Campion; the second, *The Masque of the Middle Temple and Lyncolnes Inn* by George Chapman, and the third, *The Masque of Grayes-Inne and the Inner Temple* by Francis Beaumont. Chapman makes an "ante-masque" of the "anti-masque" and calls his prose dialogue "a low induction". Campion's masque is pure poetry of which his songs are not the least good part. Beaumont's masque is remarkable for the high quality of its blank verse. His innovations in the anti-masque, however, tended to break up the masque into a kind of variety entertainment. As a masque-writer Jonson had no successor. Of Shirley's *Triumph of Peace* (1633) and Carew's *Coelum Britannicum* (1633) it has been said that the first is chaos active and the second chaos inert. D'Avenant's *Salmacida Spolia*, in which the King and Queen took part in 1640, has so large a number of successive "entries" in the anti-masque as to make it very like modern pantomime.

Akin to the masque in its generalizations and its remoteness from reality is the pastoral play, of which the two most famous examples both belong to Italy, Tasso's *Aminta* (1581) and Guarini's *Il Pastor Fido* (1590). Abraham Fraunce translated *Aminta* in 1587; and, as we have seen, a Latin version of *Il Pastor Fido* was acted at Cambridge before 1605. Daniel's *The Queenes Arcadia* of 1605, partly derived from *Aminta*, was the first English "Pastorall Trage-comedie". In 1614 was performed his second, *Hymens Triumph*. The Elizabethan and Jacobean period has left us three other masterpieces of the kind, *The Faithful*

Shepherdess of Fletcher, *The Sad Shepherd* of Jonson, and the *Amyntas* of Thomas Randolph. Fletcher's pastoral is little more than a lyric poem in semi-dramatic shape; but it is an exquisite composition. Jonson's *The Sad Shepherd*, left unfinished at his death, is another example of the poet's versatility. Randolph's *Amyntas or the Impossible Dowry* (printed 1638) follows the conventions of Tasso and Guarini, and its plot is deliberately artificial, removed from any contact with life's realities.

XIV. THE PURITAN ATTACK UPON THE STAGE

The theatre has always offended the purists. Even when the miracle plays were accepted as a proper means of making known sacred story there were zealots who denounced them. The Reformation, as such, was not hostile to the stage. Indeed, the more enlightened reformers, themselves influenced by a renewed interest in classical drama, saw in the religious play a weapon of controversy. But the English stage was destined to become secular. The religious changes in England were eminently affairs of state, and stage criticism of public affairs was not permitted. Elizabeth's proclamation of 1559 expressly forbade the stage to meddle with such matters.

When Geneva replaced Wittenberg as the capital city of the Reformation and Protestants became Puritans, it was discovered that the drama had no authority in Holy Writ and could not be allowed in a Christian commonwealth. In England, the Elizabethan drama was the heir of the miracle play, and as this was partly liturgical and partly traditional it was doubly damned, since, like the maypole, it was heathen, and, like the mass, popish. A growing spirit of Sabbatarianism found special offence in the acting of plays on Sundays; moreover, the dressing of boys as women was an abomination. Further, play-houses were the means of disseminating disease and their general ungodliness invited particular disasters, such as falling galleries and even earthquakes.

In 1559 an early voice was heard in defence, namely *A woorke of Joannes Ferrarius Montanus, touchynge the good orderynge of a common weale....Englished by William Bavande*, wherein it was declared that the drama "doth minister unto us good ensamples"; but Sir Geoffrey Fenton, famous translator of *Certain tragicall discourses*, anticipates, in *A forme of Christian pollicie* (1574), nearly all the later Puritan arguments against the stage. Roger Ascham was no Puritan in the narrow religious sense, yet no Puritan denounced plays more drastically than Ascham denounced popular romances, especially *Le Morte d'Arthur*. We must distinguish between the humanists who hated pleasure of an unworthy kind and the inhumanists who hated pleasure of any kind. It was the latter kind of Puritan who was the real menace, and who triumphed in the end not only over drama, but over art, consigning to equal destruction a cathedral or a playhouse, a statue or a picture, a rose-window or a treasury of music. William Alley, Bishop of Exeter, in *Ptochomuseion, The Poore Mans Librarie* (1565), denounces plays, and is the first printed Elizabethan antagonist of the drama on moral grounds. Many violent sermons followed—one by William Crashaw, father of the poet.

A frontal attack by treatise was begun in 1577 by John Northbrooke, a

Puritan divine, whose volume bears a lengthy title which is the best account of its tendency: *Spiritus est vicarius Christi in terra. A Treatise wherein Dicing, Dancing, Vaine playes or Enterluds with other idle pastimes &c commonly used on the Sabboth day, are reproved by the Authority of the word of God, and auntient writers. Made Dialoguewise.* The book seemed to have attracted small notice; but a second edition appeared in 1579, the date of the most celebrated attack of its time, the pamphlet called *The Schoole of Abuse, Conteining a pleasaunt invective against Poets, Pipers, Plaiers, Jesters, and such like caterpillers of a Commonwelth; setting up the Flagge of Defiance to their mischievous exercise....By Stephen Gosson Stud. Oxon.* Now Gosson had been a player and had written plays, without much success; and it has been doubted whether his very lively attack is anything more than a piece of cleverness. However, *The Schoole of Abuse* was successful with the public. It drew a reply called *Honest Excuses* (1579) written by Thomas Lodge—probably his first publication—almost immediately suppressed by the licensers; but the players retorted more effectively by reviving Gosson's plays. To a volume called *The Ephimeredes of Phialo* (1579) Gosson next added *A short Apologie of the Schoole of Abuse.* Late in 1580 appeared a book which devoted itself exclusively to the subject of stage plays. It was entitled *A second and third blast of retrait from plaies and Theaters,* and, lest there should be any mistake as to the source of its inspiration, it bore the arms of the Corporation of London upon the reverse of its title-page. The inference is that the civic authorities had called in an auxiliary force; and it has been suggested that the writer was Anthony Munday. In 1582 the actors retorted by producing at The Theater *The Playe of Playes and Pastimes,* a new piece in the manner of the old moralities, exhibiting the foolishness of Puritans. The play is not extant; but we know of it from Gosson himself, who in 1582 published *Playes confuted in five Actions,* directed against Lodge and *The Playe of Playes.* Gosson soon disappeared from theatrical controversy, took orders and became rector of St Botolph, Bishopsgate. A fatal accident during a bearbaiting at Paris Garden produced one notable pamphlet, *A godly exhortation, by occasion of the late judgement of God shewed at Parris-garden,* by John Field, a famous Puritan. It appeared in 1583, the year in which was published a much more famous work, *The Anatomie of Abuses* (the full title forms a long descriptive paragraph) by Philip Stubbes, whose special line of activity was the collection of admonitory horrors. It was quickly followed by a second part, both "made dialogue-wise". Stubbes intended denunciation and destruction, but, by the singular fate that attends books, his work survives as an invaluable account of Elizabethan popular amusements. In 1588 the attention of the Puritans was diverted by Martin Marprelate; the attacks ceased, and defences of the stage appeared in Greene's *Francescoes Fortunes* (*Greenes Never too late,* 1590) and in Nashe's *The Anatomie of Absurditie* (1589) and *Pierce Penilesse* (1592).

With the accession of James, the great acting companies were, as we have seen, placed under the direct patronage of the crown. This was not entirely to the advantage of the theatre. In the eyes of the militant Puritans crown and stage now formed an unholy alliance. Moved no doubt by some special attack, Thomas Heywood the dramatist published in 1612 *An Apology for Actors,* a modest and pleasing prose work, with useful contemporary allusions.

In 1625, the year of King Charles's accession, a more sinister attack was made in the anonymous *A Short Treatise against Stage Playes*, which is addressed to Parliament, round which the hopes of the Puritan reformers were beginning to gather. And then in 1633 appeared the most violent of all the accusers, the indomitable, intolerant, moral fanatic William Prynne (1600–69), whose *Histriomastix* contains eleven hundred pages with a title longer than most prefaces. He gave no quarter to his opponents, and he received none; for being accused of applying an opprobrious epithet to Queen Henrietta Maria he was sentenced to lose his ears, to stand in the pillory, to pay a fine of £5000 and to be perpetually imprisoned. The life sentence was cancelled at the Puritan triumph, and Prynne had no £5000 to pay; but the rest of his sentence was carried out. The Puritans triumphed; but for political rather than for moral reasons. Players were minions of royalty. Disquiet had fallen upon the theatre, as we learn from *The Stage Players Complaint*, a little tract printed in 1641. Few contemporary documents give a better picture of the gloom and sense of impending catastrophe that had come over the nation. On the 2nd of September 1642, the Long Parliament, which had released Prynne, imprisoned Laud and executed Strafford, passed an ordinance abolishing all play-houses, and further ordinances were made in 1647 and 1648 ordering players to be whipped and hearers to be fined. The curtain had fallen for ever upon the English drama of Shakespeare, his predecessors and his immediate successors. A long dramatic tradition was broken. When the theatres reopened, they found a teased and acrimonious world from which the great universal spirit of Shakespeare was gone, never to return. If sometimes we regret that Shakespeare is so far away, his words difficult and his texts a puzzle, let us be glad that he lived and died before the frozen hands of Zeal-of-the-Land Busy had been laid upon his natural warmth and immeasurable charity.

The Puritan Attack on the Stage 307

In 1633, the year of King Charles's accession, a more sinister attack was made in the anonymous *A Short Treatise against Stage Playes*, which is addressed to Parliament round which the Puritan reformers were beginning to gather. And then in 1632 appeared the most violent of all the accusers, the indomitable, intolerable Prynne (1600-69), whose *Histriomastix* contains eleven hundred pages with a title longer than most prefaces. He gave no quarter to his opponents and he received none; for being accused of applying an offensive passage to Queen Henrietta Maria he was sentenced to lose his ears, to stand in the pillory, to pay a fine of £5000 and to

CHAPTER VII

CAVALIER AND PURITAN

I. CAVALIER LYRISTS

The reign of Charles I was made illustrious by an outburst of gallant and devoted song. Lyric poetry was indeed no new thing in English literature. But though the Caroline lyric continued in form the national habit of song which had long been practised and which had passed from privacy to publicity in *Tottel's Miscellany*, the note of Cavalier poetry is new. The fantastic idealism of Petrarch vanishes, and there is a return to the franker emotions of Anacreon, Catullus and Horace. The sonnet, in particular, disappears. Elizabethan conventionalism had killed it, and it had to be born again in a new age with a new inspiration. Donne fashioned a kind of song for himself; Jonson sought inspiration in classical models— going to the heart of classical poetry, and not bothering, as some of his misguided predecessors had done, about the quantitative skeleton and the sin of rhyming. The influence of Jonson on the younger generation of poets was powerful.

First and greatest of the Caroline poets is Robert Herrick (1591-1674). Little is known of his life until 1627, when he took orders. Two years later, he received from the King the living of Dean Prior, Dartmoor, and exchanged the Jonsonian gatherings in City taverns and the revels of Whitehall for the sober duties of a parish priest. This revolution in his career inspired one of his best poems, his *Farewell unto Poetry*. Having refused to subscribe to the Solemn League and Covenant, he was ejected in 1647 by the Long Parliament. We know little about his life for the next dozen years. Soon after the Restoration he went back to his living at Dean Prior, where he died a bachelor, in spite of the Julias, Antheas and Corinnas of his famous lyrics, whose "silv'ry feet" and "tempestuous petticoats" he had celebrated. His poems were circulated in manuscript and a few came separately into print in various publications; but the main collection did not appear till 1648. With a reference to his home in the West it was beautifully called *Hesperides: or, the Works, both Humane and Divine of Robert Herrick, Esq.* Herrick is often spoken of as a Cavalier lyrist; but he is much more than this: he can write the old, simple songs which the typical Cavalier lyrists—Carew and Suckling—would have found rustic, but which the contemporaries of Spenser and Shakespeare would have loved. He never lost the spirit of the Elizabethan miscellanies and he never forgot the folk-song of the cornfield and the chimney corner. Herrick refused to bow the knee to metaphysic wit and remained faithful to Jonson, and, through him, to the great lyrists of classical antiquity. Every lyric he wrote reveals his inspired command of metre and rhyme. Scarcely any poet has used short lines so exquisitely. Herrick's sacred verses, or *Noble Numbers* (with a title-page dated 1647, but contained in *Hesperides*, 1648) enlarge our view of his unique personality, but scarcely add to his fame as a poet. He followed the example of Donne in dedicating his powers to religion, when he entered the church; but he could not change the temper of his mind. Strangely enough, Herrick's poems achieved no great contemporary fame, and he had to wait till the end of the eighteenth century before he took his rightful place as one of the greatest of English lyric poets.

Thomas Carew (1598?–1638) also belonged to "the tribe of Ben", and numbered Suckling, D'Avenant and George Sandys among his friends. He provided the court masque *Coelum Britannicum* and wrote other poems. None had been collected before his death, and the volume, *Poems. By Thomas Carew, Esquire*, issued in 1640, was incomplete. Carew is usually ranked second to Herrick as a lyric poet; but Herrick's country life gave him themes and feelings of which Carew remained wholly ignorant. But he has a fine sense of structure in poetry. His lyrics of two stanzas have a mutual balance and relation that suggest the Petrarchian sonnet. Probably his best poem is the finely and frankly sensuous *The Rapture*. Carew's spiritual home is the city and the court, not the country and the parsonage.

"Easy, natural Suckling" has won for himself, since the days of the Restoration, an assured place in the line of English poets as the typical Cavalier lyrist, the arch-representative of Pope's "mob of gentlemen who write with ease". Yet his literary work, fairly considerable in bulk, was the product of such leisure as he could find in a life of town pleasures or in the activities of a soldier's career. John Suckling (1609–42) abandoned the law for the camp. In 1637 appeared the string of witty, but carelessly written, verses, entitled *A Session of the Poets*. Of his plays we have already spoken. Suckling sat in the Long Parliament; but his efforts for the King failed, and he fled to France and died by his own hand in 1642. His works appeared as *Fragmenta Aurea. A Collection of all the Incomparable Pieces, written by Sir John Suckling. And published by a Friend to perpetuate his memory* (1646). Though he wrote a few serious pieces, Suckling's fame depends upon his lyrics, some of which first found a place in his dramas. Unlike Herrick and Carew he owed little to Ben Jonson, whose restraint, classical colour and fastidious workmanship made no appeal to him. He was in spirit a poet of improvisation. He would not, and could not, take pains. An audacious wit and an impetuous ease of movement give Suckling his special charm. One of his best sustained efforts can be found in the twenty-two stanzas of his mock epithalamium *A Ballad upon a Wedding*.

Richard Lovelace (1618–58) took part in the Scottish campaigns of 1639 and 1640. He was in the Long Parliament, but his Royalist sympathies sent him to the Gatehouse, Westminster, where he wrote his most famous lyric, *To Althea from Prison*. He was freed and went to France. On his return in 1648 he was again committed to prison, where he prepared his *Lucasta: Epodes, Odes, Sonnets, Songs, etc. to which is added Amarantha, a Pastorall, by Richard Lovelace, Esq.* (1649). Set at liberty after the execution of the King, he seems to have lived a poor and wretched life, and in 1658 the once gay and handsome Richard Lovelace died in poverty. A year later appeared *Lucasta: Posthume Poems of Richard Lovlace, Esq.* The place of Lovelace in English poetry is curious. He would have been more famous had he written less. His two or three perfect lyrics are buried in a mass of frigid, extravagant and artificial versification which is best forgotten. But *Althea* and the *Lucasta* songs are immortal.

II. THE SACRED POETS

The religious poets of the seventeenth century hold a unique place in the history of English sacred verse. They were not in any sense a school—their very individuality testifies to a general intensity of personal religious emotion not confined in that age, as some suppose, to the Puritans. First of these writers in general appeal is George Herbert (1593–1633). The fascination of George Herbert is due as much to his character as to his writings. Walton's *Life* made him almost one of the saints of the Anglican church; but nine editions of *The Temple* had appeared before Walton wrote. George Herbert came of the famous and noble family of his name, and he was born, let us note, on the Welsh border, at Montgomery. One of his brothers was the celebrated Lord Herbert of Cherbury; another was Sir Henry Herbert, Master of the Revels. George Herbert caught very early the infection of verse from his mother's friend, Donne, whom he resembled in cherishing hopes of worldly advancement. He sought with unabashed eagerness the office of Public Orator at Cambridge and used his opportunities in that post almost shamelessly. But for some cause unexplained he failed to gain any high place in the world, and the death of James I in 1625 put an end to his hopes. He then turned his mind to the church. By 1626 he was so far on his way as to be installed as a prebendary of Lincoln. His ills of mind and body are traceable in poems of the period. In 1630, through the solicitation of his kinsman the Earl of Pembroke, he was instituted to the rectory of Fulston St Peter's with Bemerton, Wiltshire; on 19 September he was ordained priest. Three years later (1633) he was dead, and lies buried under the altar. It is difficult to believe that Herbert's priesthood was of less than three years' duration; but that period, short though it was, gained him a reputation of unusual sanctity. His collection of verses *The Temple, Sacred Poems and Private Ejaculations*, sent to his friend Nicholas Ferrar from his death bed, was published later in the same year. It was, as he described it in his last message, a picture of his many spiritual conflicts and his final peace. *The Temple* is a unique collection of Anglican poetry, and is so accepted. It is less often read as the story of a spiritual conflict. That Herbert was a most conscientious artist, carefully polishing and re-setting his poems is clear from the manuscript versions. At times, his ingenuity misleads him into what can only be called tricks, like the representation of the echo in *Heaven*. The verses shaped like an altar and the "Easter wings" came under Addison's condemnation of "false wit"; but many of Herbert's fellow poets took pleasure in such devices. The boldness of his faith is matched with bold images of expression which rarely fail. He is never thin or facile, and his intensity, attained by daring omission and abrupt suggestion, is wonderful. *Love* is one of the most deeply moving religious lyrics in the language. Herbert's other works do not call for notice here. The Latin orations and poems have small intrinsic value, and the posthumous prose work, *A Priest to the Temple, or, The Countrey Parson, his Character, and Rule of Holy Life* (1652), does not belong to his poetry, and will be noticed later.

It is hardly possible for two religious poets to be more unlike than George Herbert and Richard Crashaw (1612–49). Herbert suggests the quiet devotion of the Collects in the English Prayer Book; Crashaw suggests the ecstasy of a devotee before the relics of a saint. Yet Crashaw was the son of an anti-Papal preacher whose fulminations from the pulpit led the Puritan attack on the stage. Richard began to write verses at Cambridge and gained the repute of being "a very bird of paradice" for unworldliness. His skill in "drawing, limning, graving" is exemplified in the designs which he prepared for *Carmen Deo Nostro*. His ardent religious temperament was specially attracted by St Teresa, who had been canonized in 1622. That he would have gone naturally to Rome is hardly to be doubted; but when the whole Anglican system crashed with the downfall of the King and the triumphant Puritans deprived him of his Peterhouse fellowship in 1644, there was but one way for him; and we next hear of him in 1646, in Paris, and already a Roman Catholic. He was in sore straits, and was helped to Rome. He died soon after. Although Crashaw was at Cambridge when *The Temple* was published there, it was in Spanish and Italian models that he found his chief inspiration, and a curiously high proportion of his work, both early and late, consists of translations, many of which have compelling interest. His most famous secular lyric, *Wishes: to his (supposed) Mistress*, is memorable because it is altogether his own. Crashaw's special place in literature has been won by such religious outpourings as *To the Name above every Name*, *Hymn to the Name and Honour of the Admirable Saint Teresa*, and *The Flaming Heart, upon the Book and Picture of the Seraphical Saint Teresa*. Crashaw has little of Herbert's sedulous art. He is very unequal and sometimes excessive, but he is never tepid, and his best is superb. His two chief volumes are *Steps to the Temple. Sacred Poems with other Delights of the Muses* (1646) and the posthumous *Carmen Deo Nostro, Te Decet Hymnus, Sacred Poems collected, corrected, augmented*, published in Paris, 1652.

Within a few months of Crashaw's death appeared *Silex Scintillans: or Sacred Poems and Private Ejaculations. By Henry Vaughan Silurist* (1650). The author Henry Vaughan (1622–95), elder of twin-brothers, was born, like Herbert, on the border of Wales and his chosen name, "Silurist", expresses his intimate love of the land with which his life was associated. He was one of the tribe of Ben, and would have us believe that he sought inspiration for his verses in churchwarden pipes and "royal witty sack, the poet's soul". The record of these London days is the small volume of *Poems, with the tenth Satyr of Juvenal Englished* (1646) in which there is little that is memorable. Some vital experience of which we know nothing changed the current of his life, and of that change the enduring memorial is *Silex Scintillans*, containing his most remarkable poems. He ascribes his conversion to "the blessed man, Mr George Herbert". Vaughan found himself in *Silex Scintillans*. Another volume, *Olor Iscanus* (named from his native river, the Usk), begun earlier than *Silex Scintillans*, but not published till 1651, does not add anything of importance either in its prose or its verse to his greater achievement. Unlike Herbert, Vaughan rarely knows when to stop. His enduring contributions to literature are those poems in which, with words of complete simplicity, he seems to establish immediate communion with realms beyond the normal life of man. Such poems as *The World, They are all gone into the world of light, Corruption, Childhood*, and *The Retreat* are like nothing else in English poetry, though Wordsworth found the germ of his great *Ode* in the last. From the author of such poems one expects more than he actually gives us. A later volume, *Thalia Rediviva* (1678), contains also poems by his twin brother Thomas; but it is not important. Vaughan is a man of one book—or rather a man of a few poems and a few lines that have an unexampled power of making us conscious of eternity.

The religious and mystical literature of the seventeenth century was suddenly enriched in the twentieth through the discovery by the bookseller and man of letters Bertram Dobell of Thomas Traherne (*c.* 1620–74), whose chief work till then had been unprinted. Like Herbert and Vaughan, he came from the Welsh borders, and like Herbert he became a priest. His *Roman Forgeries* (1673) and *Christian Ethicks* (1675) are unimportant. *A serious and patheticall Contemplation of the Mercies of God* published posthumously and anonymously in 1699 brings us nearer to the real man, who was, however, not fully disclosed till the publication of his *Poems* in 1903, his prose *Centuries of Meditations* in 1908, and *Poems of Felicity* in 1910. These reveal an original mind, dominated by certain characteristic thoughts, which are commended to the reader by a glowing rhetoric and a fervent conviction. Traherne's prose, though not resembling the deeper tones of Sir Thomas Browne, has the same searching and consoling music. As a poet, Traherne never mastered his technique. His poems are often diffuse and full of repetitions. When his poetry informs his prose we seem to be listening to an inspired anticipation of Blake.

To the right and left of Herbert stand William Habington and Francis Quarles. William Habington (1605–54), after being educated at St Omer and Paris with a view to his becoming a priest, returned to England and married Lucy Herbert, whom he celebrated in *Castara*, published anonymously in 1634. Successive editions enlarged it and revealed the author's name. His own modest estimate of his verses will not be challenged, that they are "not so high as to be wondred at, nor so low as to be contemned".

Francis Quarles (1592–1644), like Habington, was uninfluenced by Donne. His chief literary idol was Phineas Fletcher, "the Spenser of this age". His literary career began in 1620 with *A Feast for Wormes*, a facile paraphrase of the book of Jonah; *Divine Fancies* (1632) gave a better taste of his quality, and anticipated, in *The World's a Theater*, some of the success which attended *Emblemes* (1635), the most famous English example of a class of writing which began with the Milanese doctor, Alciati, a century earlier. Herbert felt the appeal. Crashaw designed the emblems for his own last volume; and Vaughan's *Silex Scintillans* took its name from the frontispiece of a flinty heart struck with a thunderbolt, and began with a poem, *Authoris de se Emblema*. Quarles, a more sedulous and less original emblemist, had something of his own to say. His liveliness and good sense, his homely words and rough humour are enough to account for, and to justify, his popularity.

Of all these writers it may be said that they and the secular lyrists trod the same paths. They never walked the smooth and facile way of later hymn-writing. They were sacred poets, not from fashion or interest, but from choice and conviction. "The very outgoings of the soul" are to be found alike in Herbert's searching of the heart, in Crashaw's ecstasy, in Vaughan's mystical rapture, and in Traherne's penetrating simplicity.

III. WRITERS OF THE COUPLET

To Edmund Waller Dryden assigned the credit of bringing about that revolution in the writing of English verse which gave it "smoothness" and "numbers", that is, the power of expressing itself tersely in self-contained rhyming distichs requiring no prolonged effort from the reader. Yet the decasyllabic couplet had been employed with complete success by Chaucer and by Elizabethan writers. Drayton, especially, had given an example of couplet-writing in which there is as little overrunning of the sense from couplet to couplet as in any of Waller's most admired poems. But verse had relapsed into untidiness. The go-as-you-please lines of the later dramatists and the "not keeping of accent" for which Ben Jonson declared that Donne should be hanged both indicated a need for the re-imposition of regularity. Sir John Beaumont (1583–1627), brother of Francis, had remarked of contemporary poetry, first, that

> On halting feet the ragged poem goes
> With accents, neither fitting verse nor prose;

and next "that in every language now in Europe spoke",

> The relish of the Muse consists in rime,
> One verse must meet another like a chime.
> (*To His Late Majesty, Concerning the True Form of English Poetry*)

Already we have the couplet style in being.

Beaumont doubtless learned much from Drayton; so did Sandys, another practitioner in the same form. George Sandys (1578–1644) travelled much in the East and in America and wrote a *Relation* of his oriental journeys. He began working at a translation of the *Metamorphoses* of Ovid in couplets and published the whole in 1626. To a later edition (1632) he added a translation of the first book of the *Aeneid* in the same form. His command of the couplet is adequate, and he expresses the Ovidian matter with point and terseness. But that this was not his only measure is proved in *A Paraphrase upon the Psalms of David* (1636), and similar transcriptions. Sandys has little importance as a poet; but his verse achieves regularity, if not perfect smoothness; and therefore to the younger generation he seemed a model of clear compact form. His influence was great.

But the new age really dawned with Edmund Waller (1606–87). His earliest known attempt in verse appears to be the poem *Of the Danger His Majesty (Being Prince) Escaped in the Road at St Andero*, in which he shows very considerable mastery of the self-contained couplet, though he runs it on in certain places; but in such later works as the miniature epic called *The Battle of the Summer-Islands* and in a translation from the fourth book of the *Aeneid* he proves that he has mastered the form. But of course it is absurd and unjust to think of Waller merely as a writer of couplets. His verses are as varied as his life. The actual quantity of his poetical composition is not great and much of it is love poetry almost of the Elizabethan type, with Sacharissa (Dorothy Sidney) as the cruel fair one, together with other nymphs bearing names as charming. It is by such songs as *Go, lovely Rose*, *The Self-Banished*, *On a Girdle*, *Behold the brand of beauty tost* that Waller holds his place in the affection of readers. He showed no special care in the collection of his poems, and his work has to be sought in various volumes issued between 1645 and 1685. His virtues appear to be mainly negative. He found a want of "smoothness" in English verse, and tried to supply it. Actually, he had little else to give. His achievement in English verse was to make his contemporaries familiar with a rhymed couplet in which each line was marked by regular beats and each couplet by the finality of easy rhyme. The generation that hailed him as an innovator and inventor liked him for his deficiencies more than for his positive virtues.

The couplet was successfully extended to descriptive poetry by Sir John Denham (1615–69), whose one celebrated piece *Cooper's Hill* was published in 1642, though its most famous lines beginning "O could I flow like thee" did not appear in that first form. Denham made classical translations or adaptations from Virgil and Homer, wrote a tragedy, *The Sophy*, and attempted occasional verse in various metres; but nothing genuinely survives except the one pleasing piece which is the first of its rather artificial kind in English poetry. Denham makes no consistent use of the stopped or self-contained couplet, and in *Cooper's Hill* there is ample proof that its occurrence in the poetry of this age is the result, not of a fixed metrical design, but of an effort to be direct and intelligible in expression. Denham did not invent the habit of looking on scenery as composed of certain conventional elements, with conventional equivalents in poetic diction; but *Cooper's Hill* strongly encouraged that habit. Various satires ascribed to Denham are almost certainly not his.

Abraham Cowley (1618–67), the greatest poet of his day, saluted by Denham as combining all the gifts of all his predecessors, is now, by an odd turn of fate, remembered chiefly for his delightful little prose *Essays* (with verse interwoven) once buried in a great volume of his works. He began writing while still at school, and at Cambridge, as we have seen (p. 282), contributed to university drama. Cowley's career during the Rebellion was considered a little dubious; but not everyone is called upon for a life of heroic sacrifice to a lost cause. His poems, certainly, are lacking in character. *The Mistress: or Several Copies of Love Verses* first appeared in 1647, and was reprinted in 1656 as part of a fourfold collection of poems, I, *Miscellanies*, II, *The Mistress*, III, *Pindarique Odes* and IV, *Davideis*. The *Miscellanies* and *The Mistress* are composed of lyrics written in a variety of irregular metres. Of the *Miscellanies*, Cowley thought little; yet this collection contains most of the poems by which the anthologists would now represent him. One, *The Chronicle*, a great contrast to the tortuous fancies of his love-poems, is among the best English examples of gay trifling in verse. From Donne Cowley took a trick of exasperating cleverness and caught his master's mannerisms rather than his inspiration. When Cowley chose to be natural he was far more tolerable than when he aspired to the cloudy magnificence of Donne. His *Pindarique Odes* may be odes, but they are not Pindaric. Their voluble licence of metre bears no resemblance to the elaborately ordered measures of Pindar. Cowley, either ignorant or oblivious of Pindar's metrical design, sought to reproduce the "Enthusiastical manner" of Pindar with its digressions and bold similes. What he actually accomplished was to make himself unreadable. The four books of *The Davideis, a Sacred Poem of the Troubles of*

David, are written in decasyllabic couplets. As the name implies, the *Aeneid* was its model. Cowley has some narrative art and the poem is not dull; but it is almost worse than dull, it is clever and superfluous. The couplet is entirely without character and lacks the style even of a minor poem like *Cooper's Hill*. Cowley failed in metre as he failed in style through his weakness for too much of everything. After 1656 his poetical work is small in quantity. The *Ode upon the Blessed Restoration* (1660) greeted the return of Charles II and *A Discourse by way of Vision concerning the government of Oliver Cromwell* (1661), in prose and verse, loyally vilified the departed Protector. The volume of *Verses lately written upon several occasions* (1663) contains an ode to the Royal Society, and this may serve to remind us that in 1661 Cowley published a brief prose *Proposition for the Advancement of Experimental Philosophy*. The folio edition of his works issued in 1668 contained, in addition to the poems of 1656 and 1663, the *Several Discourses by way of Essays, in Verse and Prose*, a delightful little collection, almost the only part of Cowley's work now readable. His reputation, great in his own day, rapidly declined. Johnson said what he could for Cowley; but later readers find it difficult to share even the modified enthusiasm of the great man.

Sir William D'Avenant (1606–68) endeavoured to exhibit the right restraint of poetic fluency, not in the couplet, but in a four-lined decasyllabic stanza rhyming alternately—the stanza of *Annus Mirabilis* and Gray's *Elegy*. This is the form used for his incomplete "epic" poem *Gondibert*, of which the first two books were published in 1650 with a long preface addressed "To his most honour'd friend Mr Hobs", together with "The Answer of Mr Hobbes to Sr Will. D'Avenant's Preface before *Gondibert*". The interest of these prose essays exceeds that of the poem, which has no real life or charm, and does little more than prove that it is possible to be diffuse in the most compact of stanzas. D'Avenant's other poems do not call for notice; his dramatic works are considered on p. 347.

IV. LESSER CAROLINE POETS

The writers whom we may group as the lesser Caroline poets have been subjected more to disparagement than to criticism. But without some knowledge of their work we do not clearly see the passing of the Elizabethan into the Augustan age. The spirit which at its fullest inspiration produces Spenser and Shakespeare produces at its lowest Chamberlayne and Kynaston. Revulsion from the extravagances of Benlowes and Cleveland shapes and confirms the orderly theory and practice of Dryden and Pope. It happens, also, that the group of lesser Caroline poets includes authors of almost every type of the English romance in verse, that they contribute to the story of the heroic couplet, and that one of them gave hints to Keats in his revival of their own form. Some of them possess individual interest, but they can be more profitably discussed according to poetic kind; and we can begin at once with the heroic or romantic narrative.

The heroic romance is adequately represented by the *Pharonnida* (1659) of William Chamberlayne (1619–89), whose other works call for no discussion here. *Pharonnida* may be described as an attempt at an unhistorical novel in verse. It is a blend of Ariosto, Tasso, and the kind of romances beloved by Don Quixote. Its fourteen thousand lines unfortunately fail to tell a coherent story, and probably there was never one to tell. The form is the decasyllabic couplet, but the couplet run on in a fashion which Sir John Beaumont disliked and which the *Quarterly* reviewer of Keats (who knew *Pharonnida*) was to dislike still more.

Thealma and Clearchus, attributed to "John Chalkhill" by Izaak Walton, and published by him in 1683, is exactly on the same lines as *Pharonnida*—heroic, with a touch of the pastoral, and couched in the same sort of verse. After line 3170 appear the words "Thealma lives" with the added note *And here the author died, and I hope the reader will be sorry*.

A very curious example of the heroic poem is the *Leoline and Sydanis* (1642) of Sir Francis Kynaston (1587–1642), who founded a kind of literary academy called *Museum Minervae*, and who made known his enthusiasm for Chaucer by translating *Troilus and Criseyde* into Latin rhyme royal, the measure he also adopted for his original English romance. The story is laid in Wales and Ireland but has no connection with any known romance of either region. In mere poetical value *Leoline and Sydanis* is the inferior of *Thealma and Clearchus*, and very far the inferior of *Pharonnida*; but as a story it is infinitely superior to both, and it sometimes ventures to be not merely heroic, but heroi-comic.

Other romance writers of the period must be accorded no more than bare mention—Patrick Hannay (d. 1629), author of *Sheretine and Mariana* (Jacobean not Caroline), Shackerley Marmion, author of *Cupid and Psyche* (1637), William Bosworth or Boxworth, author of *The Chaste and Lost Lovers* or *Arcadius and Sepha* (1651), Nathaniel Whiting, author of *Albino and Bellama* (1637), and Leonard Lawrence, author of *Arnalte and Lucenda* (1639). The point to notice about all the Caroline writers of poetic romance is that they are really groping after romantic fiction. If Chaucer had written *Troilus and Criseyde* in prose as good as its verse he would have given us our first romantic novel. The Caroline romance writers all try to tell a story, and they insist on telling it in verse, because the "notions" of romance and poetry appeared to be inseparable. We may notice further how the Chaucer-Spenser tradition persists even in the age of "correctness" supposed to have been inaugurated by Waller and his forerunners.

Some of the romance-writers produced lyrics after the fashion of Jonson and Donne. Among them is Kynaston, whose *Cynthiades or Amorous Sonnets* (1642) contains verses combining quaintness of thought and expression with mellifluous variety of accompanying sound. Of lyrists proper the best known is Henry King, Bishop of Chichester (1592–1669), whose poems, *The Legacy*, *The Exequy*, *The Dirge* and other elegiac pieces have caught something of the spirit of Donne without his fierce intensity. The lines in *The Exequy* to his dead wife,

> Stay for me there; I will not fail
> To meet thee in that hollow vale,

are unforgettable. King's secular lyrics have often an appealing, exquisite quality. One piece, persistently attributed to King, and claimed for Francis Beaumont and several others, is the familiar *Sic Vita*, "Like to the falling of a star". Poems passed about in manuscript were frequently transcribed by admirers, sometimes with wrong or fanciful attributions. Hence the confusion. With King should be mentioned another bishop, Richard Corbet (1582–1635) of Oxford and Norwich, whose *Certain Elegant Poems* (1647) includes the delightful *Farewell Rewards and Fairies*.

Another remarkable lyrist is Thomas Stanley (1625–78), who holds a respectable place in the history of English literature as editor of Aeschylus, as author of the first serious English *History of Philosophy* (1655–87), and as a poet both original and in translation, as well as a copious translator in prose. The mere list of Stanley's works may suggest an industrious pedant, curiously combined with a butterfly poet. But his work actually possesses very considerable charm. His poems, collected in 1650, deserve rediscovery.

John Hall (1627–56) was both poet and pamphleteer. *Horae Vacivae* (1646), a book of essays, was followed by *Poems* (1647). Hall, too, was an ardent translator. He is also a "divine" poet, and yet does not disdain light and trivial pieces. Hall has a definite lyric gift, and his poems, sacred and profane, have a life of their own.

Well known by her coterie name as "the matchless Orinda", is Katherine Fowler (1631–64), married to a Welshman named James Philips. She translated Corneille's *Pompée*, and part of his *Horace*; but she is more interesting as the writer of miscellaneous poems (1664), the best of which are addressed to her women friends. There is no great power in any of them, but there are touches of magic, here and there, that entitle her to consideration as a poet.

Among the numerous poets of the period two acquired notoriety if not renown, Richard Flecknoe (d. 1678?), in whose work it is easy to discover some justification for Dryden's posthumous maltreatment of him, and the poet-painter Thomas Flatman (1637–88), whose unlucky name earned him the contempt he by no means deserved. The rest, and they are many, must pass unnamed in a brief summary; but the curious who seek them out can be assured of finding something profitable. Even the *Mel Heliconium* (1642) of the industrious schoolmaster Alexander Ross will yield both sweetness and light in the shape of an unforgettable stanza like this:

> We're all in Atalanta's case,
>   We run apace,
> Untill our wandring eyes behold
>   The glitt'ring gold:
> And then we lose in vanity
> Our race, and our virginity.

But there are two writers who must have more particular treatment—Edward Benlowes and John Cleveland. Benlowes (*c.* 1605–76) was a strong Royalist, and was for a time a Roman Catholic. Samuel Butler, Pope and Warburton all ridicule him as a figure of fun, his chief offence being a long and singular composition entitled *Theophila or Love's Sacrifice, A Divine Poem* (1652). The name suggests a romance, but "Theophila" is merely a name for the soul; and the titles of the several cantos—"Praelibation", "Inamoration", "Disincantation", and so on, will at once suggest the note of theological mysticism which runs through it. Unfortunately Benlowes chose, first, to use an extraordinary form—

successive triplets of ten, eight and twelve syllables; next, to pour out his difficult matter without plan or order; and, lastly, to use extraordinary coinages of word and phrase. Some of it sounds like an elaborately unsuccessful parody of Browning, especially as Benlowes "loves to dock the smaller parts-o'-speech":

> Does Troy-bane Helen (friend) with angels share?
> All lawless passions idols are:
> Frequent are fuco'd cheeks; the virtuosa's rare:
> A truth authentic. Let not skin-deep white
> And red, perplex the nobler light
> O' th' intellect; nor mask the soul's clear piercing sight.

And when he begins one of his three-lined stanzas with

> War hath our lukewarm claret broach'd with spears

he is surely the very first to anticipate the "fancy" use of "tapping the claret" so familiar in boxing circles in Regency and Victorian times. Yet Benlowes is not a madman or a mountebank. He seems, at times, almost to attain the devotional ideal for which he strove; he seems, also, to have a dim and confused notion of that mixture of passion and humour and grotesqueness later characteristic of Carlyle and Browning; but he never quite succeeds, mainly because he was not self-critical enough to know where to stop. Benlowes is a curiosity of literature; but he is a poetical curiosity.

John Cleveland or Cleiveland (1613–58) was a Royalist who suffered imprisonment. He was at Christ's College, Cambridge, when Milton was still in residence. He was quite a celebrated poet, and had published as early as 1640. A volume, *Several Select Poems*, appeared in 1647. His appeal was strong and wide, and endured long after his death. A large proportion of his work was "straight-from-the-shoulder" political satire, couched in the very extravagance of the metaphysical fashion, yet managing to achieve clearness, and employing not only the stopped antithetic couplet, but trisyllabic measures that had frightened most of the Elizabethans and Jacobeans. He has no long and no specially noteworthy poems. The best are political pieces, like *The Rebel Scot*, *The King's Disguise*, *The Mixed Assembly* and *Rupertismus*. Some of the earlier romances mentioned in preceding pages were anticipations of the popular novel; some of Cleveland's poems were anticipations of the popular newspaper, and would now require a wealth of elucidation which they will never receive and which they do not deserve.

The unimportant writers here presented have a kind of importance, for they are the voice of a period. Their merits and their faults arose from a striving after that daring and headstrong vein which had made the fortune of the great Elizabethans. They had no help from criticism, for criticism there was none, even if they had desired it. They fell between two ages. They were past Spenser and had not reached Dryden. There was, as yet, no tradition of prose romance, and there was, as yet, no critical voice to proclaim that stories, even in verse, should be told in language devised to convey meaning, not to conceal it. They were not to blame for adopting the "metaphysical" style; they were to blame for neglecting to observe that when this style is not sublime it tends to be ridiculous.

V. MILTON

The life and the works of Milton are interrelated with a closeness that makes some biographical detail a necessary prelude to an account of his writings. He lived his books and wrote himself into them. His own life was not eventful, but the times were; and of those times Milton made himself intensely a part. His parentage is interesting. John Milton (1608–74) was born in London, the son of John Milton who had taken to law business after being disinherited by his father for abandoning Roman Catholicism and conforming to the Church of England. The poet's younger brother Christopher reversed the process, and as a Catholic became a knight and judge under James II. An elder sister Anne married and became the mother of John and Edward Phillips, both of whom are our prime sources of information about their uncle. The elder John Milton was a man of broad culture and a musician whose compositions entitle him to respectful mention in musical history. The boy John was unusually studious and passed from St Paul's School to Christ's College, Cambridge. It soon became evident that "the lady of Christ's", so called from his personal beauty and his refusal to be a "man" (in the wilder undergraduate sense), possessed a character of adamant. He was soon at war with the authorities, though he lived down the hostility; but the young Milton at Cambridge is the essential Milton, studious, unique and unsubmissive to arbitrary authority, expecting more from humanity than common humanity could ever give, yet ardent, emotional, impressionable. After leaving Cambridge he lived at Horton, near Windsor, whither the elder John had retired with a moderate fortune. He had at least twelve years, counting the Cambridge and Horton periods together, of dedicated study and literary concentration, and in this he was both fortunate and unfortunate. He had much contact with men's minds in books; he had no contact with men's minds in the world; and to the end of his days Milton tended to think of man as spirit and never of man as mere clay. To the period of solitary study and preparation for life-work at Horton succeeded the tour which took him to Italy in the spring of 1638 and plunged him literally and figuratively into the vivid life and sunshine of an Italian summer. A projected extension of his tour to Sicily and Greece was abandoned when the state of public affairs made him feel the impropriety of dalliance abroad when his countrymen were striking for freedom at home. He turned northwards, and in Florence met the almost legendary Galileo, blind and aged. He reached England in August 1639, being then in his thirty-first year.

Whatever else Milton may have brought from Italy, he certainly brought with him a resolve to resist any approximation of church government in England to church government in Italy. And so the next twenty years were to be devoted to work which his soul considered necessary, but which for posterity has but casual and accidental profit. He became what we call a publicist; and his written work was journalism of a kind—an attempt to give the largest number of persons certain convictions about public affairs. But journalism is literally matter for a day; and the journalism of Milton is not exempt from that objection. Inevitably a man of Milton's temper was anti-Royalist and anti-Episcopalian.

A phrase from *The Doctrine and Discipline of Divorce* sums up all that Milton fought against throughout his life: "The restraint of some lawful liberty which ought to be given to men, and is denied them." Liberty to think and to speak on matters of the deepest concern to the spirit of man seemed to Milton denied by King and Bishop. The Parliament side appeared to stand for liberty of the spirit, and Milton gave himself fully to that cause. He was presently to learn that liberty, as some of the Puritans understood it, meant no more than liberty to restrain the liberty of their opponents.

Immediately, however, Milton, home from his tour, had to face the ordinary duties of life. He set up house in London and took pupils, first his nephews and then others. Two important events followed: in 1641 he fired his first shot in the great conflict of his time, *Of Reformation touching Church Discipline in England*; and some time in or before 1643 he married Mary Powell, a girl of seventeen, half his own age, belonging to a family of Oxford Royalists. We know little about this marriage and must beware of taking too seriously biographical novels like Anne Manning's *Mary Powell* (1855) which is favourable to Milton, or Robert Graves's *Wife to Mr Milton* (1943) which is not. Like other great men before and since, Milton appears to have made an unsuitable choice and, with his tendency to expect from human beings more than human frailty could give, probably did not make the best of a bad business. Mary very soon returned to her family in Oxford and did not come back. That Milton, feeling strongly about the marital relation, was deeply moved is certain; it is also certain that he recovered his calmness and that he bore no resentment; for after two years (during which his tracts on divorce were written) he not only took back his wife, but, the year being 1645, fatal to the royal cause, received her family as well. Mary bore him three daughters and died in 1652 at the birth of a fourth. This long period of reconciliation and re-establishment is usually forgotten or ignored. Milton's publications on the subject of divorce had one important effect not commonly remembered in that connection. The abolition of the Star Chamber in 1641 left the press free, and there was an immediate outpouring of vehemently controversial literature. The Long Parliament, as hostile as any king or church to liberty of opinion, re-imposed in 1643 the restraints upon printing. Milton published both the first (1643) and the second (1644) editions of *The Doctrine and Discipline of Divorce* without licence, and the Stationers' Company petitioned Parliament to deal with him. Then it was that Milton issued the noblest of his tracts, the written oration called *Areopagitica; A Speech of Mr John Milton For the Liberty of Unlicenc'd Printing, To the Parliament of England* (1644); but he pleaded in vain. For another half-century printing was to remain under the rigorous restraint of whatsoever person or persons ruled the country. Not till 1695 did the state relinquish its hold on the press.

Before the death of Mary in 1652 much had happened. The King was executed in 1649 and Milton was engaged in the war of pamphlets that ensued. He abandoned teaching, and in 1649 was made Latin secretary to the newly-formed Council of State. Prolonged strain upon eyes congenitally disordered produced complete blindness in 1652; but he continued his secretarial work with assistants, and held his post till the Restoration. In 1656 he married a second wife, Catherine Woodcock, who died in childbirth in 1658 and is the "late espoused saint" of a beautiful sonnet. With unshakeable tenacity Milton continued his controversial writing up to the eve of the Restoration, though every cause he had worked for was lost. When the King came into his own, and discreditable vengeance was taken on the regicides, dead and alive, Milton underwent some ill-treatment, but not much—he was spared, not in the least because he was a great man, but because he was unimportant; but he lost a large part of his property, and his circumstances became straitened, though never really narrow. In 1662 he married a third wife, Elizabeth Minshull, who survived him for half-a-century. The Great Fire destroyed the old family house in Bread Street and the Plague drove Milton to Chalfont St Giles; but he returned to London, and the last years of his life were serene. These are the years of the Milton legend; for sentimental legends grew as naturally round the blind Milton as about the deaf Beethoven. They should be ignored. Milton was, in his own way, a simple and sociable person. He had his books, tobacco, and wine—for though habitually temperate he was never ascetic—and he had numerous friends and visitors, English and foreign, not the least important being Andrew Marvell and John Dryden. Legends about his harshness to his daughters (who were not his amanuenses) should be disregarded. Milton lived on amicable terms with his wife's Royalist relations, with his own Royalist nephews, and with his Catholic brother and family. He suffered in his later years from gout and died of it. He lies buried in an unidentified spot in St Giles's, Cripplegate.

Such was the life of this celebrated man. Milton's inflexible personal righteousness and his singular majesty of utterance have made him the least popular of the great English poets. Indeed it is still possible to feel for passages in Milton's writings as well as in his life the aversion which made the incurably romantic Royalist Samuel Johnson disparage him in the *Lives of the Poets*. What the serious reader of English literature must avoid, here as elsewhere, however, is not the natural inclination of feeling, but tame submission to the dictates of any coterie of the moment which demands that a famous poet shall be dethroned in favour of some current and transient fashion in verse. The prose and verse of Milton have "the might, majesty, dominion and power" of the prose and verse of Dante, though readers may feel, for different reasons, uncomfortable with both.

As the writings of Milton are arranged in most collected editions in a way that gives little help to the reader, we shall find it useful to consider them in strict chronological order. In such a consideration the first fact that appears is that Milton is a bilingual writer, quite a large part of his *omnia opera* being written in Latin, which to him was almost a second native language. The common separation of his foreign from his English writings is convenient, but misleading, as it leaves puzzling gaps at certain periods of great activity. The apparent contrast between the precocity of Cowley and the comparatively slow development of Milton is less strong than it seems. Milton's paraphrases of Psalms 114 and 136 were "don by the Author at fifteen yeers old". *On the Death of a fair Infant dying of a Cough* is marked *Anno aetatis* 17. To the period between sixteen and twenty-one belong numerous Latin poems of great personal interest and naïve poetical charm—*Elegia Prima*, to his friend Charles Diodati, *Elegia Secunda*, on the death of Richard Redding, University Bedel at Cambridge,

Elegia Tertia, on the death of Lancelot Andrewes, Bishop of Winchester, *In Obitum Procancellarii Medici* (on the death of the vice-chancellor, Dr Goslyn, Professor of Medicine), *In Obitum Praesulis Elienses* (on the death of Nicholas Felton, Bishop of Ely), *In Quintum Novembris* (on the Fifth of November), *Elegia Quarta*, to Thomas Young, *Elegia Quinta*, on the coming of spring, a poem with urgent youthful passion in it, *Elegia Sexta*, to Charles Diodati, with a reference to the *Nativity Ode*, *Elegia Septima*, describing his first falling in love, the poem *Naturam non pati Senium* declaring the vigour of the world against those who protested its decay, and *De Idea Platonica*. All these, which may be read in the excellent English versions of William Cowper, form no mean achievement for a young man.

But in addition to these poems there are the *Prolusiones Quaedam Oratoriae* of his Cambridge undergraduate days, not published till 1674. These prose academic exercises were first translated in 1932 by Phyllis Tillyard, with a commentary by E. M. W. Tillyard, author of *Milton* (1930) and *The Miltonic Setting* (1938). They contain interesting autobiographical touches, and they show Milton, still in his youth, as rebel and controversialist. The first, *Utrum Dies an Nox praestantior sit?* mentions the hostility his audience probably feel towards him; the second, *De Sphaerum Concentu*, contains his first reference to the Platonic doctrine of the music of the spheres; the third, *Contra Philosophiam Scholasticam*, boldly attacks the arid Cambridge educational discipline to which he was being subjected and contains a reference to his eyesight; the fourth and fifth are scientific. The sixth, of special interest, is *In Feriis aestivis Collegii, sed concurrente, ut solet, tota fere academiae juventute*—the famous *Vacation Exercise* of which only the short passage in English verse is usually printed. It shows that Milton was now a scholar of importance at the university, as he was chosen to deliver this discourse; it exhibits him in a gay and jocular vacation mood; it refers to the pleasing change in opinion about him since he delivered his first oration; and it contains a defensive allusion to his nickname "the lady". Having delivered the *Oratio* and the *Prolusio* he passes to the third part and begins "Hail native Language", and continues with the significant lines that show him already contemplating some grave theme for poetry. The seventh Prolusion, later than its predecessors, *Beatiores reddit Homines Ars quam Ignorantia*—"Art makes men happier than Ignorance"—is an eloquent effusion in praise of "the higher truth and the higher seriousness" as prime necessities in the life of man. These numerous early works in prose and verse are important, first because they dispel a suspicion of youthful sterility and next because they show the mature Milton already implicit in the young. Those who wish to know Milton from the beginning must begin by knowing these, the least known of his works.

But contemporary with the sixth Latin elegy is the ode *On the Morning of Christ's Nativity*, as full of youthful "conceits" and far-sought beauties, as an early Italian picture of the Nativity is full of loving, engaging detail, and as full, too, of the same moving appeal. Its command of metrical and verbal music is wonderful. It is unique in English poetry and unique in Milton; for when he essayed a companion poem of the same kind, *The Passion*, he failed; and, being the most self-critical of poets, knew he had failed, and said so. To this period belongs also an important group of early poems, the little *Song: On May Morning* with its "warm desire", the sonnet *O Nightingale*, and five sonnets and a "canzone" in Italian, all translated by the invaluable Cowper. These were long assumed to be related to the Italian tour (Cowper's translation of one introduces the phrase "on foreign ground"); they actually predate it by many years, and they prove first, that Milton at twenty-one was eagerly studying the Italian poets, and next, that his ardent nature, always responsive to female beauty, had been fired by an Italian lady in England whose name was that of the Italian province, Emilia. Milton's imposed chastity and his youthful inflammability are evidence of a strong creative urgency, and refute the legend of the poet as a bloodless, marrowless, sexless, remote and emaciated Puritan. On the purely literary side these poems are important as marking the return to English literature of the sonnet—but the sonnet of a kind vastly different from the Elizabethan, the sonnet reinspired from the Italian original, the sonnet into which Milton was to pack more matter than any sonnets before contained. Dated 1630 are the lines to Shakespeare printed in the Second Folio (1632). They are excellent, and their contrast between Shakespeare's "easie numbers" and another's "slow-endeavouring art" is significant. Very little later were written the two Hobson poems, half-humorous, half-pathetic, and successful of their kind. *An Epitaph on the Marchioness of Winchester* is both a good example of seventeenth-century funerary art and a notable study for the verse of *L'Allegro*. The familiar sonnet on attaining the age of three-and-twenty reveals Milton's high expectation from himself, but seems to non-Miltons unnecessarily accusatory. All he had failed to do was to shape definitely his course in life.

The beautiful miniature masque *Arcades*, called precisely by Milton "part of an entertainment presented to the Countess Dowager of *Darby* at *Harefield*, by som Noble persons of her Family", is oddly misunderstood to be a fragment of Milton, when it is simply the whole of Milton's "part of an entertainment". The songs, especially "O're the smooth enameld green", are perfection; and the decasyllabic couplets of the Genius's speech have deep interest as being Milton's most considerable serious attempt in this form. *Arcades* shows us the Milton of *Comus* already arrived; but between those two inventions lie other pieces of great interest. Three, belonging to Milton's twenty-fourth or twenty-fifth year, are similar in tone and in workmanship—*On Time*, *Upon the Circumcision*, and *At a Solemn Musick*. They show that Milton had abandoned the unhappy manner of *The Passion* and that he had found his own "Solemn Musick". All three, short as they are, exhibit two aspects of the great Miltonic style, power of lofty and sustained flight and skill in building rhythmical verse paragraphs. The last of the three, the most sublime short poem in English, has naturally attracted musicians from Handel to Parry.

Closely following these three come the ever lovely pair *L'Allegro* and *Il Penseroso*, pure poetical essays in autobiography, showing us the studious Milton at Horton first in his lighter and next in his graver mood. Though poets before and since have used the octosyllabic couplet, these two poems stand as the type of perfection in that form. We called them "essays", and they are indeed diversions; for Milton returned almost at once to his graver course with the poem which we call *Comus* and which he, knowing that its theme is chastity, not lubricity, does not call by that name. It is, simply, *A Maske presented at Ludlow Castle 1634: on Michaelmasse night etc.* For this Henry Lawes, friend of the Milton family, wrote the music and played in it the Attendant Spirit. The story probably owes something to the "old wife's tale" in Peele's play (see p. 209). The actual dramatic effect of the piece is not great; but it was meant to be a family entertainment, not a drama. Nor need we follow Johnson and other critics in discussing whether it is truly a "masque" or not. Considerations of that kind are quite irrelevant. The only real question is whether it is a good poem; and to that question successive generations have given an emphatic answer. One special point of interest is that Milton here discards for his dialogue the couplet which he had used in *Arcades*, and adopts blank verse, the rest of the piece being in octosyllabic couplets or lyrical measures. It would be difficult to find a poem in which "profit and delight" are more perfectly blended. The *Maske*, issued anonymously in 1637, is the very first of Milton's published volumes.

To that year belongs his next great poem; and perhaps in the interval there may have been paternal solicitude for his future, as the important Latin poem *Ad Patrem*, though full of pleasing gratitude, is a little defensive. Two Latin letters of the same year to Charles Diodati declare expressly that he is meditating a great flight and letting his wings grow. Then, as a specimen of what he hoped to do, we have *Lycidas* printed in 1638 among other tributes to Edward King, his friend and contemporary, drowned in the Irish Sea off the Welsh coast in the preceding year. The criticism of this perfect poem offers us another example of the singular indisposition of people to let Milton write his own poems in his own way. Johnson's onslaught upon it is one of the major ineptitudes of literature. The poem has been condemned as "artificial"—a strange charge to bring against any work of art. For the use of the pastoral convention in an elegy Milton had ample precedent. What is most generally forgotten, however, is that the poem was exactly of the kind, tone, and literary ancestry that would have appealed to the dead subject of it. The general scheme is that of a classical pastoral elegy, and the verse form is a very singular and rewarding arrangement of free and strict composition. That the poem tells us more about Milton than King is clearly our gain. In one of its passages we hear for the first time a note "prophesying war". St Peter, coming among other symbolical figures to bewail the dead, is made to deliver a tremendous denunciation of the corrupt clergy of the time. The year of *Lycidas* is the year of the attempt to force the Laudian prayer-book on Scotland. The strict propriety of this digression has been questioned; but a test is simple: who would wish that strain of the higher mood away? Certainly not the least affecting part of the poem is the "return" to the pastoral note.

In 1638 Milton left England for Italy, and there was necessarily some slackening of written production. Nevertheless to the Italian period belongs one excellent composition, the epistle to Giovanni Battista Manso, the aged and noble Marquis of Villa who had been the friend and biographer of Tasso. The verses to Salzilli and to Leonora, the Roman singer whose voice touched his heart, need only the barest mention. On his way home, however, Milton heard of the death of his friend Charles Diodati, and at Horton in 1639 wrote his elegiac tribute, *Epitaphium Damonis*, which is a Latin and lesser *Lycidas*. It was the last long poem he wrote for many years. The Arthurian epic he proposed to write did not perish, for it could not come to birth.

We now pass to what most people consider Milton's lost years, the twenty years given to prose controversy, broken all too rarely by the few sonnets—themselves sometimes notes in controversy. Milton settled in London in 1640, the year of the Short Parliament, the year of the first meeting of the Long Parliament, the year of the impeachment of Strafford and Laud. A man of Milton's character could not keep out of the conflict; and it is characteristic of his entire lack of self-seeking that almost every one of his controversial works was issued anonymously. In 1641 appeared *Of Reformation touching Church Discipline in England. Of Prelatical Episcopacy* followed in the same year. It has less interest. The dismaying title of *Animadversions upon the Remonstrant's defence against Smectymnuus* needs explanation. The "Remonstrant" was Bishop Joseph Hall and "Smectymnuus" was a "portmanteau" name composed of the initials of five militant Puritan divines: S M (arshall) E C (alamy) T Y (oung) M N (ewcomen) U U (i.e. W) S (purstow), who had vigorously attacked episcopacy. Cleveland has some good lines on "Smectymnuus". *The Reason of Church Government urged against Prelaty*, and *An Apology against a Pamphlet call'd a Modest Confutation of the Animadversions of the Remonstrant against Smectymnuus* (1642), incredible as it may seem, contain, as does the first *Animadversions*, passages of fascinating autobiographical interest. As a pleasing *intermezzo* between this pamphlet war and the next, we have the delightful sonnet "Captain or Colonel".

In 1642 or 1643 came the provocation of his wife's disloyalty; and there followed in quick succession *The Doctrine and Discipline of Divorce* (1643), *The Judgement of Martin Bucer concerning Divorce* (1644), *Tetrachordon* (1644) dealing, as the name implies, with four relevant passages on marriage in Scripture, and *Colasterion* (1645), a reply to a critic of the first. Of these only the first and third are important. The *Doctrine and Discipline* states a personal view, *Tetrachordon* a social view, of the marriage relation. As footnotes to these publications, which were a little shocking to Milton's co-religionists, we have the two sonnets: "A Book was writ of late" and "I did but prompt the age". Even finer interludes are the tractate *On Education* (1644) and *Areopagitica* (1644).

The divorce controversy died away in 1645, the important year that saw the publication of his earlier poetical work as *Poems of Mr John Milton, both English and Latin, Compos'd at several times...* (1645). And so, after the storms of prose controversy came the lovely peace of his early poetry. An odd and pleasing addendum to the volume is the Latin Ode *Ad Joannem Rousium* sent with a second copy of the *Poems* to John Rouse, Bodley's librarian, when the first failed to reach him. There is an interlude of quiet. The triumph of religious intolerance in Parliament drew from Milton nothing more than the sonnet called *On the new forcers of Conscience under the Long Parliament*—a sonnet, however, with a "tail" and with the sting in the tail: "New *Presbyter* is but old *Priest* writ large". He proceeded with his own work, sketching a History of Britain and continuing the collection of notes on his religious opinions which were to take shape as *De Doctrina Christiana*. The noble sonnet to Fairfax belongs to 1648.

The interval of peace was short. In 1649 Charles was executed, and immediately afterwards appeared *The Tenure of Kings and Magistrates* written while the trial was being arranged. The fatal blunder of the execution turned public opinion in the King's favour, and the publication of *Eikon Basilike*, supposed to have been written by him in prison, deepened the popular feeling. *Eikonoklastes*, written by order of Parliament, endeavoured to undo the effect of the royal volume. It is an unpleasing work. Vilification of the dead is not a good man's task. The killing of the King was a nasty business, and not even Milton could make it otherwise. An attack from abroad was delivered against the regicide government. Salmasius, the great French scholar, successor of Joseph Scaliger at Leyden, was engaged by Charles II to indict the regicides, and he appealed to Europe with his *Defensio Regia pro Carolo I*. To this Milton replied with the fierce *Pro Populo Anglicano Defensio* in 1651, followed by *Defensio Secunda* in 1654, and *Authoris pro se Defensio* in 1655. They were almost tragically useless. It was the genius of Cromwell, not the genius of Milton, that made the Commonwealth respected in Europe. The *Defensio* and the *Defensio Secunda* are translated in the usual collection of prose works; the *Pro se Defensio* is not. All three contain the coarser scurrilities of controversy; all three contain personal passages of deep interest. In the end, nothing could save the government. The meaner side of Puritanism continued to flourish. Cromwell, the hope of England, died in 1658. Nevertheless, Milton wrote on as if in desperation, and we have in quick succession *A Treatise on Civil Power in Ecclesiastical Causes* (1659), *Considerations touching the likeliest means to remove hirelings out of the Church* (1659), *A Letter to a Friend concerning the Ruptures of the Commonwealth* (1659), and finally, with Charles II almost at the gates, *The Ready and Easy Way to Establish a Free Commonwealth* (1660), addressed to General Monck, who was already preparing to bring the King back. The great struggle was over. Milton had lost everything but his creative spirit and his faith in God.

The prose writings of Milton are overshadowed by his verse and are usually misjudged. They are thought to be improper employment for a poet. They are considered to be extremist or fanatical documents. They are held to be of no practical value, as they deal with causes long since lost or won. They are said to have failed of their purpose because *The Doctrine and Discipline of Divorce* did not give us the divorce laws, because *Areopagitica* did not give us a free press, and because *The Tenure of Kings and Magistrates* did not give us a constitutional monarchy. Not one of these judgments has any critical validity. Milton must be taken as the man he was, patriot and publicist as well as poet. It is within no critic's competence to say that a Langland, a Milton, or a Shelley must stick to poetry and not meddle with the social order. Poets are entitled to the liberty of ordinary men; but no poet is the better or the worse poet for political reasons. The test is not the currency of opinions, but the literary result. Milton was fully entitled to write in prose upon any subject that appealed to him; but his prose must abide the question we ask of his verse, Does it succeed? To argue that *Areopagitica* is a failure because it did not give us a free press shows an extraordinary confusion of ideas. *Areopagitica* did not turn votes, but it remains the noblest tract in English. Its theme is of perpetual interest and it could not, even today, be published in some countries. The other pamphlets may be grouped into three classes: (1) The episcopacy controversy, (2) the divorce controversy, and (3) the monarchy controversy. Of (3) we can say at once that the literary results are not very profitable, first, because much of the matter is in Latin, and next, because some of it, in any language, is mere journalistic violence. But there is a valuable *residuum* of general doctrine and autobiography. The chief English work, *The Tenure of Kings and Magistrates*, is an entirely successful pamphlet. What we may call the post-Cromwell pamphlets are remarkable as an exposition of unpractical politics. Of (1) we can say that though the question of episcopacy no longer fires the emotions of most modern readers of English, it was a burning question in Elizabethan and Stuart times. Milton makes a strong case for his views, and in the course of his argument achieves great eloquence. Of (2) we can say that Milton's handling of the difficult subject of divorce is very reasonable. We must remember that a semi-sacramental view of marriage still prevailed in the minds of non-Catholics, even though they denied it the name of a sacrament. Milton's arguments are therefore almost entirely religious, or ecclesiastical. But he makes out his case; he is never excessive; and he touches, incidentally, on vital matters. The first of the divorce pamphlets is successful both as prose argument and as prose eloquence. Two general considerations should not be overlooked. The first is that very little of any pamphlet literature genuinely survives, and that Milton's pamphlets can hardly be less read than the tracts of Swift or the speeches of Burke. The next is that the prose of Milton is difficult because much of it is deliberately forensic in the classical manner. Milton was in spirit a Renascence scholar. His mere vocatives, as in the opening of *Areopagitica*, have genuinely puzzled some adventurers. No fit reader can open *Of Reformation* without feeling the presence of a master of prose, though of prose clinging so tenaciously to an ancient mode of expression that an effort of mind must be made to adjust it to the present. Some of Milton's difficult oratorical flights are simpler when spoken aloud than when read rapidly by the eye. Finally let us say that from the prose of Milton, whatever the subject or occasion, can be drawn a collection of great utterances forming an incomparable testament of noble ideals nobly expressed. We may properly regret his outbursts of violence. But controversy then was not squeamish, and he felt great provocation. As dear as life to him was liberty: liberty of the conscience to believe and liberty of the mind to think, without restraint by authority; and to oppose restraint upon liberty he did not disdain to fling away his singing robe and step down into the very mire of conflict.

We now return to the poet. At what period Milton decided to abandon the Arthurian or some similar national theme for a poem to match the *Aeneid* or the *Iliad* we do not know, but the times being what they were, it is not difficult to understand why the Fall of Man should seem an appropriate subject for a great tragedy or a great epic. We do not know when *Paradise Lost* was begun; but we know that it was printed and ready for sale in August 1667. It appeared as a small quarto, with the poem in ten books, price three shillings. A revised and augmented edition with the ten books divided into twelve appeared in 1674. The usual amount of sentiment has been shed upon the smallness of the financial reward it brought—£18 is the total. It is difficult to make people understand that commercial authorship is a late invention. The really surprising fact about

Paradise Lost, when the unparadisal times are considered, is its success. Indeed, it never failed to sell. The superstition that Addison's essays first gave it popularity is absurd. The plain facts are that 1300 copies were sold in eighteen months; that at least 3000 were sold in ten years; that six editions appeared before the close of the century, and nine before Addison wrote. Dryden, the greatest of the younger generation of men of letters, did it justice from the first. Roscommon, who died in 1685, had praised and imitated it. Before Addison took up the matter at all there was a style in verse recognized as "the manner of Milton". Equally ridiculous are the suggestions that Milton "took" his poem from the Hebrew or the Italian or the Dutch or the Anglo-Saxon or some other tongue. A great writer may have a source, as a great painter or a great sculptor may have a model. All Shakespeare's sources are open to any writers; but there has been no general outpouring of *Hamlets* and *Lears*.

A detailed criticism of Milton's greatest poem is not possible here. A few general remarks may be offered. Some readers, including those who should have known better, have troubled themselves variously about the subject, the hero and the theology of the poem. A poem does not become unreadable when its theology is no longer accepted. The theology of *Paradise Lost* is machinery, as the mythology of the *Iliad* is machinery. The "hero" of the poem is Man; the "villain" of the poem is Satan. The subject of the poem is the Fall of Man and the promise of his redemption. Those who maintain that Satan the rebel is the real hero fail to understand that the adversary of God and Man must be presented in majesty and magnitude if he is to be worthy of his place in the story—that he must have, in fact, all the fascination of evil. In the story, Milton's Satan is a failure; and Milton draws him as a failure, treats him, indeed, with the contempt due to colossal folly. And though few of us may believe in a material Hell and a personal Devil, the essential doctrine of the poem is eternal. The temptations of man, his conflicts with evil, his aspirations, his failures, and his repentances—these abide, whatever the current fashion in theology or philosophy may be. The life of every man (Milton implies) is the story of Paradise lost and sought: reasonable existence is only possible as long as man aspires beyond himself and believes in the validity of the great ideals we call justice, goodness and mercy.

Paradise Regained was alleged by the Quaker Ellwood to have been written at his suggestion in order to show "Paradise Found". It tells a different kind of story in a different kind of blank verse. It shows us a perceptibly older Milton even more unorthodox than before. The main objection to the story, that the conclusion is inevitable and foreseen, loses part of its force when we remember that Milton, always unorthodox, had become almost an Arian, and that the Temptation of Christ (the Second Adam) was a second conflict between Man and the temptations of the world, the flesh and the devil. There is nothing in *Paradise Regained* that can touch the first two books of *Paradise Lost* for magnificence; but there are many passages that may fairly be set beside almost anything in the last ten.

With *Paradise Regained* in 1671 was published Milton's last work *Samson Agonistes*, which combines poetical and personal appeal with an intensity unequalled except in Dante. The parallel of Samson and Milton himself is extraordinary, and the poet, with his strong autobiographical tendency, has brought it out still further. The blindness, the triumph of political enemies, the failing strength and closing life, the unbroken and undaunted resolution—all are in both. And there are less certain, but most suggestive, added touches. In the Dalila passages of *Samson*, we see that combination of susceptibility to female charms and distrustful revolt against them which is thoroughly Miltonic. And surely we see, in the altercation with Harapha, what Milton would have liked to say—and perhaps did say—to some "overcrowing malignant". But quite independently of this, *Samson Agonistes*, from the purely literary point of view, is a poem of the highest interest and of the greatest beauty.

For a moment we must return to prose in order to mention the oddly attractive *History of Britain* (1670) and *History of Moscovia* (1682), but specially to call attention to the lengthy *De Doctrina Christiana*, lost and not discovered till the nineteenth century. For readers of Milton the importance of this work (suggested, no doubt, by the book of an earlier Christ's man, William Ames), lies not merely in its assembly of unorthodox doctrine, but in its clear demonstration, first, that Milton had not reached a Christian creed that fully satisfied him, and next, that (as every reader has observed) the theology of *Paradise Lost* is fluid and not consistent, and shows a later variation in *Paradise Regained*.

In prosody Milton is an important figure. He sought to elaborate, for non-dramatic poetry, a medium which would permit all the order found in classical verse and all the freedom possible in English verse. In *Paradise Lost* he disparaged rhyme; but in *Samson* he returned to rhyme in choruses, though not universally or regularly, but rather with an extension of the occasional use which he had tried in *Lycidas*. The literary idiom of Milton is entirely his own, and it failed when used by his eighteenth-century imitators.

The Miltonic vastness of suggestion as contrasted with Dantean exactness of precision has been a theme for comment since Macaulay's famous essay. It is part of his peculiar majesty. Great variety he has not: neither has he the Shakespearean intimacy and insight. Although he is never unnatural, nature is never the first thing that suggests itself in him; and, though he is never ungraceful, yet grace is too delicate a thing to be attributed to his work, at least after *Comus*. His subjects may attract or repel; his temper may be repellent and can hardly be very attractive, though it may have its admirers; but in sublimity of thought and majesty of expression, both sustained at almost superhuman pitch, he has no superior in English.

VI. CAROLINE DIVINES

The earlier years of Charles I show the English Church in a warmly attractive light. A happy middle way between Pope and Puritan seemed to have been found. The thoughts and style of the great poets and prose writers of the preceding generation still enriched the utterance of the Caroline preachers. The Church of England was in settled possession, with a king who was her devoted son. Roman Catholic divines did not seriously affect the national literature. They had to remain obscure to escape persecution. When the Catholic writers had influence at all it was indirect. Crashaw drew inspiration from Spanish, not from

English Catholic mystics. But apart though this influence stands, it has not a little interest and charm, as may be seen in *Sancta Sophia, or Holy Wisdom...* *extracted out of more than forty Treatises written by the Venerable Father Augustin Baker* by Father Hugh Paulin Cressy, first published in 1657. Though Baker's treatises are cumbrous in style, there are felicities of thought which give *Sancta Sophia* a definite place in the literature of devotion. The nearest parallel, in the English literature of the time, to the *Sancta Sophia* of Baker is the *Centuries of Meditations* of Thomas Traherne; yet Traherne, above all things, is an Anglican. His style is that of a poet who is also a master of prose; and there is in him, as we noted on p. 292, something of the richness of Sir Thomas Browne and something of the inspired simplicity of Blake.

It is impossible to give a brief summary of the impressive mass of writing produced by Richard Baxter (1615–91), nor is it necessary; for *Reliquiae Baxterianae* (1696), his own "narrative of the most memorable passages of his life and times", posthumously published, bears witness to his energetic and masterful mind, and his one enduring treatise, *The Saints Everlasting Rest* (1649–50), shows a fine Puritan spirit shaping his utterance into classic simplicity. Baxter disapproved of much in church doctrine and practice, and found his right sphere of work as chaplain in the Parliamentary forces. But he came to deplore the growth of sectarianism, and spent much time in retirement, writing the book which made him famous.

There was a scholarly side to Caroline divinity. Henry Hammond (1605–60) has been called "the father of English Biblical criticism"; and certainly his *Paraphrase and Annotations on the New Testament* (1653) was an achievement in theological scholarship. But the most valuable of all his extensive works are his sermons, models of the best Caroline prose in restraint, clarity and distinction, and eloquent for a virtue then almost unknown, Christian toleration.

Robert Sanderson (1587–1663), who lived to become a bishop at the Restoration, and is embalmed in the exquisite prose of Izaak Walton, was another of the Caroline Anglicans who made the Church of England notable for its preaching power. He was at his best in the revision of *The Book of Common Prayer*, for which he wrote the admirable preface which begins "It hath been the wisdom of the Church".

William Chillingworth (1602–44), the most conspicuous controversialist of the age of Charles I, began by attacking Roman Catholicism, then became a Catholic himself in 1630, and in 1634 abjured that faith and returned to the Church of England. Out of these changes and controversies emerged his most famous book, *The Religion of Protestants a safe way to Salvation* (1638). The "safe way" is to be found in free inquiry; and Romanists and Puritans agreed in denouncing Chillingworth's demand for liberty of thinking as blasphemous.

In a famous passage Clarendon has described the wits and theologians who were intimate with the fascinating Lucius Cary, Viscount Falkland, who was killed at Newbury in 1643. At his Oxfordshire house, Great Tew, he loved to consort with scholars. Lettice, his wife, was a typical devotee of the Church in Charles I's days, and her *Life*, called *The Returns of Spiritual Comfort, etc.* (1648), written by her chaplain John Duncon, is a most fascinating biography. Chillingworth was one of the Great Tew "academy". Another was John Earle, author of *Microcosmographie*. Yet another was "the ever-memorable" John Hales of Eton (1584–1656), Canon of Windsor and chaplain to Laud, who was for his time the "broadest" of churchmen and cherished the hope of unity among all English Christians. His *Golden Remains* were issued posthumously in 1659; *Sermons preached at Eton* appeared in 1660, and a collection of tracts in 1677.

There were others besides Hales who sought for peace. The name of Nicholas Ferrar (1592–1637) of Little Gidding calls up at once a picture of an English household that was also a house of religion. For twenty-one years, his "Protestant Nunnery", composed of the family of his brother and his brother-in-law, carried on its life there, respected by all, and visited with affectionate regard by Charles I. The Little Gidding establishment was made familiar to many readers by Shorthouse's novel *John Inglesant* and later by Eliot's poem. Ferrar translated or adapted *The Hundred and Ten Divine Considerations* (1638) from Juan de Valdes, with notes by George Herbert. Herbert's own prose work, *A Priest to the Temple, or, The Countrey Parson, his Character, and Rule of Holy Life*, seems to have been finished in 1632, but did not appear in print till 1652. It is not without verbal reminiscences of the writer's poetry; yet the prose is good prose, not poetry spoilt.

The dominating figure in the Caroline church was William Laud (1573–1645), who had been the disciple of Andrewes, had preached Donne's funeral sermon, had ordained Nicholas Ferrar and was the patron of Sanderson, Hales and Chillingworth. The tragedy of a devout and sincere life may be found in his attempt to do in the seventeenth century what was hardly possible in the sixteenth, namely to make one national, loyal church with one liturgy, in the whole realm of Great Britain. His failure in England was serious; his failure in Scotland was disastrous. It was inevitable that Laud came to represent spiritual dictatorship as Charles came to represent political dictatorship. In an account of the Caroline divines it is impossible to avoid the inclusion of Laud; but nothing that he wrote genuinely survives as literature.

The more sober side of controversy is well represented by Joseph Hall (1574–1656), bishop, satirist, poet, preacher, as well as controversialist. In 1640 he issued, with Laud's approbation and assistance, his *Episcopacy by Divine Right, Asserted by J. H.*, and thus made himself the target for Milton's attack. Hall's *Meditations and Vows* (1605) in three books, each containing a "Century" of meditations (like the *Centuries* of Traherne), has passed into the canon of Anglican devotional literature.

One oddly notable Caroline divine is John Gauden (1605–62), Bishop of Worcester, whose chief title to fame is that he either wrote *Eikon Basilike: the Portraicture of His Sacred Majestie in His Solitudes and Sufferings* or compiled it from notes or memoranda of meditations and prayers actually made by Charles himself. It is a masterpiece of its kind, and created the tradition of Charles I as an Anglican martyr. Forty-seven editions were produced with surprising rapidity; those who tried to answer it—Milton among them—failed utterly to obliterate the impression it had created. The other works of Gauden have no place in the history of literature.

Jeremy Taylor (1613–67), Bishop of Down and Connor, may be said to survive more truly as a man of letters than as a theologian. His gift of elaborate eloquence has made him popular with people to whom his theological convictions mean little. He wrote voluminously; and few men who have written so much have left more books that still retain their value: the sermons, ingenious, fertile, convincing; *A Discourse of the Liberty of Prophesying* (1647), a noble plea for toleration; *Ductor Dubitantium* (1660), still the only English treatise of any importance on casuistry; *The Golden Grove* (1655), with its piety; the *Discourse of the Nature, Offices and Measures of Friendship* (1657), with its charm; *The Rule and Exercises of Holy Living* (1650), *The Rule and Exercises of Holy Dying* (1651), *The Worthy Communicant* (1660), with their sagacious, corrective, kindling instruction—all these have continued to hold a place in the affections of a great variety of readers. It is possible to dislike intensely Jeremy Taylor's manner of writing; it is hardly possible to deny that he succeeds in his own way. Though he was the contemporary of Milton, his prose is popular and modern: it can be read easily, when Milton's must be studied.

The divines of the Caroline period are conspicuously English, even if some influence from foreign mystics be allowed. They are the voice, not of a vague church, but of a definite Church of England. Anglicanism was never so attractively and attachingly itself as in the golden days of Nicholas Ferrar and George Herbert.

VII. JOHN BUNYAN, ANDREW MARVELL

The Civil War made a breach in the historical continuity of English literature. The period of conflict and controversy between the reigns of Charles I and Charles II forms a kind of hiatus between Elizabethan and Restoration literature. Milton, the greatest writer of that period, belongs in spirit to the earlier age, when books were written to be read by scholars, and when classical learning gave form and pressure to English style. Marvell, too, is a writer who says in one age what belongs in spirit to another. We are conscious of a kind of "hold-up" of natural growth during that hiatus. Would Milton have been the same Milton had there been no ecclesiastical upheaval, no Civil War, no execution, no Commonwealth? What would he have done between 1640 and 1660? The question cannot be answered, but to ask it is not entirely useless.

In the period following the gap, we come upon writers who seem born into a new country of literature, writers who have no literary ancestry. The most striking example is John Bunyan (1628–88). He had the barest rudiments of learning, and at the age of sixteen he was drafted into the Parliamentary army, where he served under Sir Samuel Luke, the Puritan knight whom Butler lampooned as Sir Hudibras. It is one of the curiosities of literature that John Bunyan the Puritan enthusiast and Samuel Butler the satirist of Puritan enthusiasts were both in the service of this worthy knight, the one as a soldier and the other as secretary. After his release from army service in 1647 Bunyan began to study the Bible closely, and upon the Bible the whole of his literary life, as well as his religious life, was founded. He joined the fellowship of a sectarian body and in 1653 was asked to preach in Bedford and the villages around. Here he was attacked in open congregation (after the rough fashion of the times) by the disciples of George Fox, especially by a Quaker sister. The most interesting result of the encounter was that Bunyan endeavoured to express his views in a book, *Some Gospel Truths Opened* (1656), and when the Quaker replied, rapidly produced a second. A third piece of controversy, *A Few Sighs from Hell*, was published in 1658. With the Restoration came both persecution and the really vital part of Bunyan's history. In 1660 he was committed to Bedford gaol for the crime of preaching, and there he remained for twelve years, that is, until the Declaration of Indulgence in 1672. During the first six years of his confinement he published no fewer than nine books, the last of which, *Grace Abounding to the Chief of Sinners* (1666), first of the four outstanding creations of his genius, has long been recognized as one of the great books of religious experience.

On his release in 1672 Bunyan was elected pastor of the congregation in Bedford of which he had been a private member; but when the Declaration of Indulgence was revoked in 1675, he was again imprisoned, this time in the small town gaol on Bedford bridge. Here and then it was that he wrote the first part of *The Pilgrim's Progress from this World to That which is to Come*. It appeared early in 1678, but received characteristic additions in a later edition of the same year, and, again, in the third edition (1679). The diligence of those who explore sources and prolong parallels would persuade us that a poor tinker who spent twelve years of his prime in prison had contrived to possess and to peruse the whole literature of allegory in order to imitate it or to borrow from it. But the idea that the life of man is a toilsome pilgrimage is not really recondite and is as likely to occur independently to a devout Puritan in the seventeenth century as to any poet, preacher or mystic in any of the centuries preceding. The true source of *The Pilgrim's Progress* is obvious; and to find it we need look no further than the strait gate and the broad and the narrow ways of the Gospel. The superabundance of scriptural references in *The Pilgrim's Progress* should surely satisfy those who hunger and thirst after sources. There is no need to say anything about the book by way of criticism; for its characters, its scenes and its phrases have become a common possession. Creeds may change and faiths may be wrecked; but the life of man is still a pilgrimage, and in its painful course he must encounter the friends and the foes, the dangers and the despairs that Bunyan's inspired simplicity has drawn so faithfully that even children know them at once for truth.

Between 1656, the date of his first book, to 1688, the date of his last, Bunyan wrote no fewer than sixty different works. There are, however, but four which genuinely survive, *Grace Abounding*, *The Pilgrim's Progress*, *The Life and Death of Mr Badman* (1680) and *The Holy War made by Shaddai upon Diabolus* (1682). Macaulay declared that, if *The Pilgrim's Progress* had not been written, *The Holy War* would have been our greatest English allegory. *Mr Badman* looks forward to Defoe and the English novel of the eighteenth century.

In passing from Bunyan to Marvell we pass from the Puritan homely and rough-hewn to the Puritan cultured and polished. Andrew Marvell (1621–78) was the son of a Yorkshire parson. He travelled extensively in Europe, and became an accomplished linguist. From 1650 to 1652 he resided at Nun Appleton, the delightful house of Lord Fairfax in Yorkshire, as tutor to Mary Fairfax, and here wrote some of his best poems. He became Milton's assistant as Latin secretary, and in 1659 entered Parliament, where he was a vigorous and uncompromising defender of local and national interests. From 1663 to 1665 he was abroad again as secretary to Lord Carlisle, and afterwards resumed his parliamentary work. The first collected volume of his poems was badly censored. Marvell had much of the upright and incorruptible character of his great exemplar, Milton, of whom he was the outspoken defender; but he had something that Milton was the poorer for not possessing, the "buxomness" (in the old sense) that enabled him to adjust himself to the facts of life and yet to maintain his principles unimpaired. And so, in his greatest poem, the *Horatian Ode upon Cromwell's Return from Ireland*, he could pay his homage to the Protector and yet include an imperishable tribute to the royal dignity of Charles I. There is no finer poem of its kind in English literature. Horatian, too, in another sense, is Marvell's delight in gardens, fields and woods, so that, in a special sense, he is the poet of the open air. Marvell's power to mingle beauty with seriousness is exemplified very notably in the *Bermudas*, the song of the Laudian exiles. Indeed, one has only to name his most familiar poems to recall some of the best of our lyrics—pieces that combine English charm and Latin gravity. Few English poets excel Marvell in sheer success of style. He has scarcely a failure. *The Nymph, To His Coy Mistress, The Picture of T. C., The Garden*, all the "Mower" pieces and the pastoral dialogues, are worthy of a place in any anthology of the best. The deeply-felt patriotism of Marvell is to be heard in his satires, which, circulated clandestinely, remained unpublished till 1689 when they appeared in *A Collection of Poems on Affairs of State*. *A Dialogue between two Horses* is a scathingly successful comment on affairs of the day. The longest of his satires, probably issued in 1667 as a broadsheet, and dealing with the Dutch wars, is called *Instructions to a Painter*, in imitation of Waller's panegyric with the same title, which had set a fashion in such "Instructions" and "Advices". Marvell's poem is a bitter indictment of the lax and lazy court which had brought upon England a painful humiliation by the Dutch. Marvell made no collection of his works. The incomplete *Miscellaneous Poems by Andrew Marvel* appeared in 1681.

Marvell's surviving prose works include private correspondence, a long series of letters which he wrote to the civic authorities of Hull, his constituency, on the doings of Parliament, and certain controversial works. The longest of all is *The Rehearsal Transpros'd* (1672–3), an elaborate and successful essay in satirical controversy. In Buckingham's farce, *The Rehearsal*, Bayes (i.e. Dryden) is made to speak of the rule of "transversion" by which he turns prose into verse and verse into prose, and is told that the latter process should be called "transprosing". Marvell caught up this word, using it as part of the title of his book, in which he held up to ridicule the writings of Samuel Parker (whom he calls "Mr Bayes"), one of the worst specimens of the ecclesiastics of Charles II's reign. Though over-long for readers who are not at home in the times, it is a crushingly successful satire which really subdued its victim. *Mr Smirke; or, the Divine in Mode* (1676) is in the same vein. Marvell gives us not only wit and banter, but, also, powerful advocacy of great truths and defence of public rights wantonly violated. There was a Miltonic strain in him, a spirit which resented and resisted unrighteousness. The eighteenth century took little account of Marvell. He may be said to have been rediscovered by Wordsworth and Lamb and appreciation has been steadily growing. His power as a prose writer is insufficiently acknowledged. His lyrics have their place in all the anthologies; but he should be seen in his true magnitude as one of the finest characters and noblest writers of his age. His life can be read in *André Marvell: Poète, Puritain, Patriote* (1928; trans. 1965) by Pierre Legouis; his *Poems and Letters* were edited by H. M. Margoliouth in 1927.

VIII. HISTORICAL AND POLITICAL WRITINGS

1. *State Papers and Letters*

We need not seek to define the limits within which history becomes literature, because no definition is possible. The miracle sometimes happens, and we do not know why. All we need do at the moment is to give a brief account of certain historical works relating to our period. For full information the reader must consult the extensive bibliography in Vol. VII of the original *History*.

The first great collection of English state-papers is that of John Rushworth, who was appointed clerk-assistant to the House of Commons in 1640, and secretary to the Council of War in 1645. His *Historical Collections of Private Passages of State, Weighty Matters in Law, and Remarkable Proceedings in Five Parliaments* appeared in eight volumes from 1659 to 1680 and covers events from 1618 to the trial of Strafford in 1641. Rushworth was the first to offer a presentation of cause and effect, with strict regard for historical truth, in an age of strong passions and distorted evidence.

The most important body of authentic materials for the history of both the domestic and the foreign policy of Oliver Cromwell is the *Collection of the State Papers of Secretary John Thurloe* (1616–68), which extends from the year 1649 to the Restoration, with the addition of some papers belonging to the last eleven years of Charles I. The volumes were published in 1742. Against Thurloe an "antidote" was posthumously supplied in the important collection known as the *Clarendon State Papers* preserved in the Bodleian and calendared in four volumes, published at various dates between 1872 and 1932.

The early Stuart age had inherited from the Elizabethan a prose diction intent upon the display of two qualities not always mutually reconcilable— amplitude and point. Queen Henrietta Maria, as the daughter of Henri IV, was a kind of French Elizabeth. Her letters have a style of their own, which, in the earlier among them, is accentuated by her pretty broken English. As the toils close round the King and she is perpetually urging him to burst through them, the letters to her "dear heart" gain in intensity what they lose in charm. The collection was published in 1857.

Cromwell's letters, which, when necessity obliged, were matter-of-fact and business-like, are full of those touches of intimacy and those suggestions of individual conviction which give to a letter its true charm and its real force. Cromwell was a born letter-writer. His speeches are, in the main, reported and do not exist in any text of his own. Carlyle's edition of the *Letters and Speeches* (1845) has given popularity to Cromwell's utterances.

The value of ambassadorial despatches as materials of history was recognized at an early date. Few publications of this kind had greater importance than a posthumous work by Sir Dudley Digges, Master of the Rolls (1583–1639), entitled *The Compleat Ambassador: or Two Treaties of the Intended Marriage of Qu. Elizabeth of Glorious Memory* (1654), containing a history of the negotiations as to the Anjou and Alençon matches.

Sir Henry Wotton (1568–1639) was one of the most accomplished, as he was one of the most voluminous, letter-writers of his age. Many of his letters are printed in successive editions of *Reliquiae Wottonianae*; but others have been published in recent times. Wotton was a master of table-talk as well as of high politics. His two famous poems, *The Character of a Happy Life* and *On his Mistress, the Queen of Bohemia*, have achieved a permanence that would probably have astonished him.

Another kind of correspondent was the "intelligencer", the ancestor of the journalistic "special correspondent", employed by an ambassador abroad or a family at home to furnish budgets of news. Of such "intelligence" is composed *The Court and Times of James I* (1848) transcribed by Thomas Birch. The most prolific "intelligencer" in this collection is John Chamberlain. Chamberlain's letters possess all the freedom of later journalism, without its "sensationalism".

The letters of Francis Bacon are of prime importance. Bacon himself was in so many respects greater than his age that the chief significance of his own priceless letters lies in their biographical value. But the many-sidedness of his great mind is shown in them as clearly as his personal character.

Among collections representing persons or families who played a part in affairs of the day may be named *The Fairfax Correspondence* and the *Memorials of the Civil War*, not published till the nineteenth century. Of unfailing interest and importance are the *Letters and Papers of the Verney Family* and the *Memorials of the Verney Family* (published during the nineteenth century) presenting the story of an English gentleman's family of the higher class from the reign of King John to the fall of King James. The *Correspondence of the Family of Hatton* (1601–1704), though it cannot compare in breadth of interest with the Verney papers, is one of the most amusing of the collections dating from this period. The volumes appeared in 1878.

But the most widely representative of all correspondents and intelligencers of the period is James Howell (1594?–1666), historiographer-royal of England, whose literary fame rests on his *Familiar Letters* or *Epistolae Ho-Elianae*, a book with a place of its own in the literature of essays and table-talk, clothed in the mainly fictitious form of personal letters. Howell's adventures ranged from Parliament to prison and provided abundant material for the volumes of *Letters* which appeared between 1645 and 1655. They mingle fact and fiction as agreeably as obviously, and their range of interest is astonishing. Howell was an indefatigable writer. *Dendrologia, Dodona's Grove, or the Vocall Forest* (1640) is a political-botanical allegory of much ingenuity. Bare mention only can be accorded to his roughly humorous and satirical *A Brief Character of the Low Countries under the States* (1660) and *A Perfect Description of the Country of Scotland* (1649). His *Instructions for Forreine Travell* (1642) anticipates the elaborate prefatory matter to which Baedeker has accustomed travellers of later date.

But he was a traveller at home, too, for *Londinopolis; An Historical Discourse or Perlustration of the City of London* (1657), is a careful guide book, with a survey of the City's several wards, and special mention of its law-courts.

Of Coryate and his *Crudities* (1610), as well as of other English travellers, something has been said on p. 156. Midway between Coryate and Howell come the selections published of Fynes Moryson's *Itinerary* (1617, completed nineteenth century). The whole work is written in Latin; the English version is also by Fynes Moryson (1566–1617). Though by no means infallible in his statements of fact, Moryson is not habitually inaccurate. The fourth part of the *Itinerary* was printed in 1903 as *Shakespeare's Europe*. Some typical extracts are included in John Dover Wilson's anthology *Life in Shakespeare's England* (1911).

IX. HISTORICAL AND POLITICAL WRITINGS

2. Histories and Memoirs

We pass now to a consideration of works in which the writers sought not only to present an account of past events, but to interest the political thinker.

Bacon's *History of the Reign of King Henry the Seventh* (1622), which is both one of the best and one of the earliest of our historical monographs, was composed in 1621. Though in substance a compilation, it embodies Bacon's own conception of the character of the King. The style of this work possesses the characteristic attraction of Bacon's writings.

Lord Herbert of Cherbury's *Life and Reign of King Henry the Eighth* (1649) marks an advance in historical composition. His celebrated *Autobiography* has the interest of a personal revelation but its historical value is slight. *The Life of Henry the Eighth* is a later work, and exhibits dignified ease of style and power to use original sources effectively.

Thomas May (1595–1650), secretary to the Long Parliament, and already noticed (p. 274) as a dramatist, contributed notably to national history by the publication in 1647 of his *History of the Parliament in England: which began November the Third, 1640, with a short and necessary view of some precedent yeares.* The work holds the balance very fairly and contains important speeches and documents.

A curious place is occupied by the *Secret Observations on the Life and Death of Charles King of England* by William Lilly (1602–81), which is the second part of a larger tract, *Monarchy, or no Monarchy, in England* (1651). In the first part various prophecies are treated as fulfilled; in the second there is an account, very fair, though rather anti-episcopalian and anti-royalist, of Charles I from childhood to death. Lilly's occult works call for no notice here.

Peter Heylyn (1600–62), joining to the instincts of a historian the eagerness of a publicist, suffered under the Parliament as a Laudian and the antagonist of Prynne. In 1659 he published *Examen Historicum*, somewhat critical of Fuller's *Church History*, and later entered into controversy with Baxter. After the Restoration he brought out his chief work *Ecclesia Restaurata*, or *The History of the Reformation of the Church of England* (1661). *Cyprianus Anglicus, or The History of the Life and Death of Archbishop Laud* (1668), which defended Laud against Prynne's invective, and *Aerius Redivivus, or The History of Presbyterianism* (1670), which traces back to Calvin the origin of England's troubles, were published posthumously. This remarkable man was no bigot, but controversy was irresistible to him.

In Scotland, religious history was more eagerly written than national history. The earliest record of the Scottish reformed church is *The Booke of the Universal Kirk of Scotland*. This was partly destroyed by fire in 1834. What remains is an invaluable document for much of the national history. Archbishop John Spottiswoode's *History of the Church of Scotland*, first printed in 1665, is prelatical, but singularly free from bitterness. On the other hand, David Calderwood's *Historie of the Kirk of Scotland, beginning at Patrik Hamilton and ending at the death of James the Sixt* (printed 1842–9), is the work of an indefatigable adversary of prelacy.

In the history of Elizabethan Ireland a special place is taken by Edmund Spenser's *Veue of the Present State of Ireland* (written 1596). Spenser had not the temper of a historian, and his tract hardly survives examination. He represents the policy which was fatal to both countries, namely a conviction that Ireland must be colonized into a lesser kind of England under English government. The style of Spenser's essay is business-like, and the dialogue form is used with ease. The important historical narrative *Pacata Hibernia* (1633) was written by someone associated with Sir George Carew, president of Munster. Carew himself translated from the French Morice Regan's twelfth-century *History of Ireland*. Sir John Davies the poet, author of *Nosce Teipsum*, who became Speaker in the Irish House of Commons in 1613 and later Chief Justice of Ireland, was concerned in the great plantation of Ulster. His *Discoverie of the True Causes why Ireland was never entirely subdued...until the beginning of his Majestie's happie Raigne* (1612, reprinted 1613) marks out the lines on which the system of government consistently pursued by him was conducted. The authorship of the *History of the Irish Rebellion and Civil Wars in Ireland, with the true State and Condition of that Kingdom before the Year 1640* has been disputed; but there seems to be no doubt that it was the work of Clarendon, with whose name it was brought out in 1720, and in whose *History* it was afterwards incorporated.

We are thus brought to the great name of Edward Hyde, first Earl of Clarendon (1609–74), whose literary powers laid the foundation of his political greatness and remain his foremost title to enduring fame. He abhorred the unconstitutional title of Prime Minister, but he would not have rejected the title of first great English historian. His political career is not our concern; but it may be briefly summed up in the statement that he was a constitutional supporter of royalty when his convictions cost him the favour of the Long Parliament, and a constitutional critic of royalty when his convictions cost him the favour of Charles II. Clarendon had no gift of popularity; but it was his virtues rather than his faults that gave offence. That he was allowed to die in exile and disgrace is a measure of the worth of the king for whom he had done almost everything. He began his historical work during the period 1646–8 when the royal fortunes were darkest. About twenty years later, when in exile, he began writing his own *Life*, which naturally told much the same story as the unfinished *History*. Soon after 1671 he made up his mind to a process of "contamination" or amalgamation for which a parallel cannot easily be found. He fitted portions of the *Life* and the *History* together carefully and left the manuscript in the condition in which it was posthumously published as *The History of the Rebellion and Civil Wars in England* (1702–4). It has been called patchwork; but it gains by its defects, and has some of the qualities that belong to a reasoned history, and some of those that belong to a personal memoir. It presents a gallery of portraits which neither Thucydides nor Macaulay has surpassed. Clarendon was influenced by classical models and later by his compulsory habituation to the French language and literature; but he was original enough to form his own style; and the first great historical writer in our literature is, at the same time, a great writer of English prose. His minor works, including *Contemplations and Reflections upon the Psalms of David* and various *Essays Divine and Moral*, were first published in *The Miscellaneous Works...a Collection of Several Valuable Tracts* (1727).

The memoir literature of the period is so extensive that only a few typical productions can be mentioned. *The Memoirs of Robert Carey* written by himself (printed 1759) gives an account of Elizabeth's last days. It is short, and is sometimes appended to the very interesting *Fragmenta Regalia, or Observations on the late Queen Elizabeth her Times and Favourites* (1641) by Sir Robert Naunton (1563–1634), of whom Bacon said that he forgot nothing. Edmund Ludlow's *Memoirs* (1698), written in exile after the Restoration, presents the view of a famous republican general who was, as well, a persistent adversary of Cromwell's dictatorship.

The most famous of all biographical stories of a Parliamentary soldier is *The Memoirs of the Life of Colonel Hutchinson* written by his widow Lucy, together with a fragment of her own autobiography, first published in 1806 and ever since recognized as a classic of its kind. The inseparable companion and contrast to this book is *The Life of William Cavendish, Duke of Newcastle* (1667), by Margaret, his wife, presenting an equally fascinating portrait of a Cavalier. Pepys ridiculed it, Lamb eulogized it. Were it less extravagant it would be less convincing; for the Duchess wrote as she must. She also wrote other works; but this is her one real achievement.

Bulstrode Whitelocke (1605–75), republican statesman, tells the story of his own times in *Memorials of the English Affairs* (1682), and occasionally deviates into subjects of less severity. His *Journal of the Swedish Embassy...of 1633 and 1654* gives us a picture at first hand of Queen Christina.

X. ANTIQUARIES: SIR THOMAS BROWNE, THOMAS FULLER, IZAAK WALTON, SIR THOMAS URQUHART

To the writers named above, the term "antiquary" can be applied more as a tribute of affection than as a strict definition. They all had a strong sense of the past, and they possessed an extraordinary gift of prose writing which, alike in large eloquence and in mere quaintness, suggests the backward rather than the forward glance.

Thomas Browne (1605–82), born in London, established himself at Norwich, the city with which his life is peculiarly associated. The Civil War disturbed the years of his maturity, but Browne, though Royalist and anti-Puritan by instinct and conviction, was so much a man of science as to feel that the struggle was no active concern of his. He pursued his quiet beneficent life of study and healing and waited for better times. Charles II knighted him in 1671. An ideally happy and useful life ended on his birthday, 19 October, and he lies buried in the church of St Peter Mancroft, Norwich. With one exception Sir Thomas Browne's works are small tracts. The first of them, *Religio Medici*, was written about 1635. With a glance at a later religious confession we might call it an *Apologia pro Vita Sua*. It is an attempt to make his religious opinions clear to his own mind and to defend himself and his profession against the ancient charge of impiety. Men of all kinds in all ages are impelled to some effort at religious stock-taking. Almost at the time when Browne was considering his fundamental beliefs, Milton was beginning to make the collection of religious opinions which formed the basis of his unfinished and unpublished *De Doctrina Christiana*. *Religio Medici* was evidently shown to people, and it began, like other famous books, to have a manuscript circulation; and one copy, getting into the hands of a printer, was published in 1642. The egregious Sir Kenelm Digby, author of vainglorious personal *Memoirs*, secured a copy and, in the space of twenty-four hours, read it, and made *Observations* which he sent (characteristically) not to Browne, but to a publisher. Browne protested mildly, and took the only revenge possible for an aggrieved author—he produced a better edition of his own (1643). And so, by an odd chance, many subsequent editions quote, by way of annotation, from Digby's self-satisfying observations. A curiously personal blend of major reverence and minor scepticism has helped to give *Religio Medici* great popularity with generations of readers. There is generally comfort in another's certitude.

Browne's next and largest work (1646) is of a much less esoteric character. Its Greek and English titles *Pseudodoxia Epidemica* and *Vulgar Errors* are not translations of each other. "Pseudodoxy" is opposed, in the abstract, to "orthodoxy"; but the treatise, after a few chapters on the general subject, divagates, with obvious gusto, into an enormous collection of particular "tenets" which Browne subjects to treatment with the mild but potent acid of his peculiar scepticism. To the careful reader, its curious pages will suggest reflections upon the relation of evidence to truth. Browne is perpetually fascinating because the question of that relation inspires some of his gravest eloquence.

During the troubled years from 1646 to 1658 Browne seems to have published nothing; but in the latter year appeared one small volume containing two wonderful tracts which distil the quintessence of his thought and expression, *Hydriotaphia, Urne-buriall... Together with the Garden of Cyrus, or the Quincunciall, Lozenge, or Network Plantation of the Ancients, Artificially, Naturally, Mystically Considered with Sundry Observations*. Both were occasions for the outpouring of their author's remarkable learning, of his strange quietist reflections on the mysteries of the universe, of his profound though unobtrusive melancholy, and of the intensely poetical feeling which denied itself poetical expression and took the form of marvellous prose. They were the last things that he himself published. In 1684 appeared *Certain Miscellany Tracts*; in 1690 *A Letter to a Friend*,

Upon occasion of the Death of his Intimate Friend; and long after, in 1716, *Christian Morals*. There were other posthumous notes and some letters. *Urn Burial* is the rich deliverance of a mind that had long kept watch o'er man's mortality. The last chapter, beginning "Now since these dead bones", is one of the most triumphant and sustained pieces of sublime rhetoric to be found in prose literature. The posthumous pieces have not been taken so lovingly to the hearts of readers; but they must not be overlooked. *A Letter to a Friend* is slight, and has paragraphs used again in the more profitable *Christian Morals*. Browne wrote consistently the kind of prose that Milton wrote fitfully. Both, by the way, are almost the only writers of their time to show acquaintance with Dante. In his letters, Browne is easy and pleasingly familiar. His much praised "style" is, of course, inseparable from his matter. His unique gift is that he was able to give rich expression to deep convictions, and perhaps even deeper doubts.

Compared with Browne, Thomas Fuller (1608–61), a curious contemporary complement and contrast, is merely quaint. He began his career with verse that is entirely negligible. His first important book, *The Historie of the Holy Warre* (1639–40), tells the story of the Crusades. *Good Thoughts in Bad Times* (1645), *Good Thoughts in Worse Times* (1647) and *The Cause and Cure of a Wounded Conscience* (1647) are, as the dates imply, "tracts for the times". *The Holy State and The Profane State* (1642) is, on the whole, his most popular work. This curious book is a sort of blend of the abstract "character" popular at the time, and of examples which are practically short stories with real heroes and heroines. *A Pisgah-sight of Palestine* (1650) gives us in its very title one of Fuller's characteristic phrases. *The Church History of Britain; from the Birth of Christ till 1648* (1655) was attacked by Heylyn for its merits of wit and impartiality rather than for its defects as connected history. *The History of the Worthies of England*, a delightful compilation never finished, was published posthumously in 1662. The so-called "wit" of Fuller has been liked by the witty and disliked by the dull. He has many shrewd and homely touches, and likes to "grow to a point". To expect many readers to read all Fuller's books would be unreasonable; but nobody should think that he understands Fuller or Fuller's age until he has read at least one of them completely.

Izaak Walton (1593–1683) comes down to posterity more lightly laden than any man in the history of English literature. Two small books form his *omnia opera*. To include him among the antiquaries needs no great effort, for everything he wrote is touched with a love of old, but not unhappy, far-off things. We tend to think of Walton as a London tradesman who made a hobby of fishing, as Surtees's character Jorrocks, another London tradesman, made a hobby of hunting. Actually, Walton was a Stafford man by birth and twice "married into the clergy", one wife being related to Cranmer, the other to Bishop Ken. It is not surprising that with him biography became a kind of hagiography. Like Browne, he was temperamentally incapable of being anything but a Royalist and an Anglican. That side of him appears most clearly in the *Lives*. The other side, exhibiting the Englishman's love of the countryside, the hills and dales and streams, is shown delightfully in *The Compleat Angler, or The Contemplative Man's Recreation* which took its first form in 1653. The sub-title is significant. The *Angler* is a "piscatorial classic", but it has been read and loved by countless people who have never encountered fish except at table. It is an exquisite book. There is no dullness and no stagnation; the characters walk briskly, talk vigorously, angle, eat and drink like cheerful men of the world. The passage of time has given the book a further importance, for it is a pretty "compleat" picture of a way of life that has gone.

The *Lives* have a curious history. They are all casual and occasional. Sir Henry Wotton having died without writing a promised biographical preface for Donne's sermons, the task devolved upon Walton, who knew both Donne and Wotton. *The Life of Donne* first appeared in the 1640 edition of Donne's sermons. It followed naturally that Walton should also write the biographical preface to *Reliquiae Wottonianae* (1651). Another failure was the cause of his writing *The Life of Mr Rich. Hooker* (1665), whom of course Walton was too young to know, and whom he perhaps misrepresented, through partial and prejudiced information. *The Life of Mr George Herbert*, for Walton the type of saintly Anglicanism, followed in 1670. *The Life of Dr Sanderson* (1678) was another prefatory memoir. Walton's *Lives* are more varied in biographical technique than the casual reader supposes. But that he tells all the truth about all of his characters cannot be maintained. His Donne is the author of the Sermons; his Herbert is the Country Parson. There is more realism in the account of Hooker whom he did not know than in the account of Donne whom he did. The quality that never fails in Walton's portraits is charm. He makes the reader in love with his characters, and (a point of importance) in love with the best qualities of his characters, and (a point of even greater importance) in love with the religion of his characters. It is by their convictions that characters live.

Thomas Urquhart or Urchard of Cromarty (1611?–1660?) was as aggressively Scottish as Browne, Fuller and Walton were quietly English. After a wildly adventurous career at home and abroad, he returned to Scotland and, in 1653, published his great translation of the earlier part of Rabelais. The Third Book (1693) was the last he attempted. Urquhart was a strange compound of swaggerer and pedant—a Pistol-Holofernes. He called himself *Christianus Presbyteromastix*, a bold title for a Scot. His elaborately Greek-named treatises are mere curiosities of literature. *The Trissotetras...or, A Most Exquisite Table for Resolving all manner of Triangles* (1645) is for those who are "Mathematically affected". *Pantochronocanon* (1652) with nearly a page of title deduces the pedigree of all the Urquharts from Adam. From this, and from its successors, *Ekskubalauron* (1652) and *Logopandecteision or an Introduction to the Universal language* (1653), it will be seen that Urquhart had an inspired gift of jargon which made him the foreordained translator of Rabelais. His glaring faults and foibles served him as well as his gifts and graces in this task, but they have produced a fixed impression in England that Rabelais is as wild as his translator. Motteux, Urquhart's successor, did his work very well, but something has gone out of it; and Sir Thomas Urquhart remains the last of the great translators with the Elizabethan spirit of adventure.

XI. JACOBEAN AND CAROLINE CRITICISM

On the very threshold of the seventeenth century we are confronted by the great figure of Bacon, who first defined the relation of poetry to the imagination, and attempted a classification of the arts and sciences based on the divisions of the mind. Further, he envisaged literature as having certain external relations with the age in which it is produced, not as a thing *in vacuo*, but something expressive of the "Time Spirit", of which he was the first to have a fairly adequate conception. In addition to his general doctrine, Bacon has given us a few memorable concrete judgments. His statement that art becomes more delightful when "strangeness is added to beauty" foreshadows Pater's definition of romanticism, and his assertion that art works "by felicity not by rule" places him in opposition to the whole tendency of criticism in the century that was to follow.

The great apostle of "rule" was his contemporary Ben Jonson. "Laws" and "principles which could not err" first entered English criticism through the agency of Jonson. It is true that Sidney, in his *Defence of Poesie*, had espoused the "three unities", and it was perhaps from Sidney that Jonson derived his original impetus toward the acceptance of the classical tradition; but Jonson not only transmitted the doctrine successfully to the public, he exemplified it in his own practice. Plays, prefaces, prologues, epilogues and poems all expound the message of order in literature, of the tempered spirit as opposed to boisterous energy and emphasis. The prose collection, *Timber*, bears witness to the sincerity of his convictions. Jonson's doctrines had a profound influence on the younger men about him.

But despite changes of taste, a number of Elizabethan survivals may be found in the very heart of this period. The chapter on poetry in Peacham's *Compleat Gentleman* (1622) forms a kind of text book borrowed from Puttenham. To 1637 belongs Suckling's *Session of the Poets*, with its casual and ironical judgments of some of his contemporaries.

In the next decade or two the influence of France is paramount both in the theory of translation and in the critical trend towards simplicity in style. Translation was not to be slavish imitation, but a new creation on the basis of the original. Cowley apparently believed that he was improving on Pindar in his *Pindarique Odes*. Denham was another advocate of the "new" translation, which however was as old as the Elizabethans.

The critical fight for simplicity in style found justification in *Mythomystes* (1632) by Henry Reynolds, which did in criticism what the most involved of metaphysical poets did in verse: it plunged into mysteries and applied the darkest of speculations to the elucidation of the obvious. The necessity for the brilliant common sense of Dryden becomes clearer after a reference to *Mythomystes*.

The critical position of Milton is defined by himself. In the *Tractate of Education* (1644) he commits himself expressly to the tradition of Aristotle, Horace and their Renascence followers; and to that tradition he remained faithful throughout his life. His almost unforgivable attack on rhyme in the preface to

Paradise Lost is not an inheritance of the old Spenser-Harvey classicism, but a formulation of his own opinions. Fortunately his theory is finally refuted by his practice. In prose and in verse alike Milton is "old-fashioned".

Bacon gave poetry a definite place in his scheme of the arts and sciences; but he did not analyse the process by which imagination transforms the materials of life into creative art. This was the peculiar work of Thomas Hobbes. Hobbes left an impress on critical terminology, and his psychology became the groundwork of Restoration criticism. His theory of poetry is a logical result of his philosophy of mind. "Time and Education", he tells us, in his answer to D'Avenant's Preface, "begets Experience: Experience begets Memory; Memory begets Judgement and Fancy; Judgement begets the strength and structure, and Fancy begets the ornaments of a Poem." His distinction between "Judgement and Fancy" became a commonplace of criticism in the period of classicism: "Fancy" or "Wit" sees resemblances between disparate objects; "Judgement" or "Reason" finds difference in objects apparently similar; and so "wit" and "judgement" were placed in a sort of conventional opposition and became critical catchwords. Further, Hobbes, finding a parallel to the philosophical division of the universe into three regions, celestial, aerial and terrestrial in the poetical division of mankind into three regions, court, city and country, appropriates to the latter three sorts of poetry, "heroique, scommatique (i.e. scoffing) and pastoral". The "heroique poem narrative is epique, the heroique poem dramatique is tragedy"; the "scommatique narrative is satyre, dramatique is comedy"; the pastoral is simply pastoral narrative or pastoral comedy. As, apparently, he could not fit lyric poetry into his scheme of correspondences, he dismissed it as trifling.

D'Avenant's long preface to *Gondibert* (1650) is a dilution of the aesthetic theory of Hobbes. From France he derived support for his antipathy to the metaphysical "conceits", and his attack on that manner of writing was pioneer work in English criticism. He distinguished clearly between what was "unusual" and what was "affected". Cowley, the junior of D'Avenant by a dozen years, occupies a similar position; but he influenced his time more by his practice in poetry than by formal criticism. Occasionally in his essays we meet a striking observation, as when he remarks of a "warlike, various and a tragical age" that it is "best to write of, but the worst to write in". Cowley does not accept the moralistic theory of verse; he seeks to communicate delight. The progress of seventeenth-century criticism can be roughly indicated by saying that Hobbes deeply influenced D'Avenant and Cowley, and that Dryden began where they left off.

Most of the critics concern themselves with literary principles and refrain from critical judgments. When they face the individual poet or individual poem their method is that of the "roll-call", a catalogue of poets, in which one name follows another, each with its tag of critical comment. The first extended critique in English seems to be that which Sidney, in his *Defence of Poesie*, devotes to the tragedy of *Gorboduc*. Puttenham's "censure" of the English poets is typical roll-call criticism. Critical judgment begins most notably with Jonson. His famous lines to Shakespeare form the first real critical tribute to a great English poet. Verse rather than prose was the first vehicle of the literary critical portrait, and commendatory poems such as those in *Jonsonus Virbius* (see p. 250) and those prefixed to the 1647 folio of Beaumont and Fletcher and to other collections contain some of the most acute criticism of the first half of the seventeenth century. One famous criticism in verse is Drayton's *To My Dearly Loved Friend, Henry Reynolds, Esq., of Poets and Poesy* (1627), which contains, among other excellent things, the justly celebrated lines on Marlowe. But Drayton's note is that of the "roll-call".

Criticism in the first part of the seventeenth century failed in the application of the principles it elaborated. It notably failed to explain or appraise the works of the great poets and playwrights of the Elizabethan age. Not till the age of Dryden was the "roll-call" really displaced by the critical study of a poet and his work. The great essay *Of Dramatick Poesie* (1668), with its appraisal of *The Silent Woman* and its sketches of Shakespeare, Jonson and Fletcher, marks the beginning of a new era in English criticism.

XII. HOBBES AND CONTEMPORARY PHILOSOPHY

The philosophical writings which belong to the period following Bacon's death show but slight traces of that great man's influence. His genius was recognized, and he was quoted on special points; but his leading doctrines were generally ignored. Logic remained medieval, though books had already begun to appear in English. Of these we need take no account here, beyond mentioning the first, Thomas Wilson's *The Rule of Reason*, published as early as 1552. Religion rather than science was the chief stimulus to philosophical thought. Nathanael Culverwel tells us in his work *Of the Light of Nature*, published posthumously in 1652, that, as Aquinas holds, the law of nature is a copy of the eternal law, and "this eternal law is not really distinguished from God himself". We are reminded of Hooker. The doctrine of "the law of nature" was the main strength of the philosophical writers who dwelt upon moral obligations. It can be found in William Ames who wrote *Conscience* (1639) and *Medulla Theologica* (probably printed 1628), the latter of which influenced Milton's ideas of Christian doctrine, and in the indefatigable Joseph Hall who wrote *Characters of Virtues and Vices* (1608) and *Decisions of Diverse Practical Cases of Conscience* (1649). But the greatest work of the kind in English, and perhaps the greatest treatise on casuistry ever written by a Protestant theologian, is the *Ductor Dubitantium* of Jeremy Taylor (1660), a comprehensive study of Christian ethics. The interesting John Selden (1584–1654), historian, jurist and "table-talker", barely touches the fringe of our subject. He, characteristically, identified the law of nature with international law.

But the great name in seventeenth-century philosophy is that of Thomas Hobbes of Malmesbury (1588–1679), who was the centre of controversy in his time and is still regarded by some people with resentment and disapproval. In 1628 he translated Thucydides. Shortly afterwards he fell in love with geometry, being attracted specially by the fascination of Euclid I, 47, and throughout his long life regarded philosophy as something with demonstrable certainty, like mathematics.

During his travels between 1634 and 1637 he met various philosophers in Paris, including Descartes and Gassendi; and in Florence he talked with Galileo, as did Milton a year later. Through the influence of Galileo Hobbes arrived at the view that motion is the fundamental conception for explaining not only the physical world, but the reactions of man and society. His *Elements of Law, Natural and Politic*, not published in one volume till the nineteenth century, reduces the doctrine of justice and policy to "the rules and infallibility of reason" after the fashion of mathematics. Part of the book was issued in 1650 as *Human Nature: or the Fundamental Elements of Policy*. The rest of it appeared later the same year as *De Corpore Politico: or the Elements of Law, Moral and Politick*. Hobbes's political philosophy being definitely monarchical, he went to France in 1640 to escape the Long Parliament, and remained there eleven years among the royalist *émigrés*. While in Paris he planned a great philosophical work in three parts dealing respectively with matter, human nature and society. But as society and its governance appeared to be the special question of the day, he dealt at once with that in a treatise first called *Elementorum Philosophiae Sectio tertia De Cive*, in 1642. This came to be known briefly as *De Cive*, and it appeared in English (1651) with the title *Philosophical Rudiments Concerning Government and Society*. The much more famous *Leviathan Or the Matter, Form, and Power of A Commonwealth Ecclesiastical and Civil* was published in the same year (1651) when Hobbes returned to England. As he maintained, without qualification, the complete subordination of church government to the civil power, he had all the religious parties united against him. He published the first part of his system as *Elementorum Philosophiae Sectio prima De Corpore* in 1655 and the second as *Elementorum Philosophiae Sectio secunda De Homine* in 1658.

It is an ironical fact that the philosopher who formed himself upon mathematics because it was "free from controversies and dispute" should have been the most hated writer of his time. Indeed, the author of *Leviathan* could hardly have expected to escape controversy, and he did nothing to avoid it. His political absolutism offended the politicians. His reduction of the church to something like a spiritual police force infuriated the clergy. His *Questions concerning Liberty, Necessity and Chance* (1656) drew upon him a fire of episcopal pamphlets. His denunciation of the universities as the home of "Aristotelity" and the bulwark of papal power armed the dons against him. His mathematical disquisitions on the squaring of the circle and the quadrating of the sphere were pulverized by two Savilian professors at Oxford, John Wallis and Seth Ward, and his scientific speculations engaged the keen mind of Robert Boyle. He was publicly denounced as a heretic, and *Leviathan* was mentioned in Parliament as a blasphemous book; but Hobbes could not or would not refrain from writing. *Behemoth: The History of the Civil Wars of England* (1679, better edition 1681) and *A Dialogue between a Philosopher and a Student of the Common Laws of England* (1681) belong to this time though published posthumously. In his old age—if such a man can ever be called old—he began translating Homer and published *The Iliads and Odysses of Homer* in 1675. His *Historia Ecclesiastica* in elegiac verse dates from his eightieth year, and when he was eighty-four he wrote his autobiography in Latin verse. At ninety he returned characteristically to controversy with *Decamerum Physiologicum; or Ten Dialogues of Natural Philosophy* (1678). He died at ninety-one.

Hobbes is one of the most remarkable of English philosophers both for his matter and his style. His prose, never seeking for richness of utterance, has that virtue of virtues in a philosopher, perspicuity. His strong, clear, serviceable writing makes it difficult for a reader to believe that he was born in the year of the Armada, twenty years before Milton, whose prose seems in comparison archaic. His fame as a writer rests mainly upon three books: *Elements of Law, Natural and Politic, Philosophical Rudiments concerning Government and Society* and *Leviathan*. The religious teachings of Hobbes were as repugnant to Churchman as to Dissenter. Neither was likely to accept the view that religious truth is what the civil government directs us to believe, and both Catholic and Puritan united in detestation of his calmly destructive opposition to the claim of any organized spiritual power to political dominion. He sums this matter up in a famous sentence: "The papacy is no other than the ghost of the deceased Roman Empire, sitting crowned upon the grave thereof." The reader who encounters modern denunciations of Hobbes will do well to ascertain the religious and political views of the writers: the *odium theologicum* still pursues him as the author of *Leviathan*. To the idealists Hobbes's moral notions were specially repugnant. Good and evil have no absolute existence. Good is what gives pleasure, evil is what gives pain. Hobbes may be said to have influenced negatively the course of speculation in England for many years. The main pre-occupation of philosophical and religious writers was to refute Hobbes. It is significant of the temper of seventeenth-century England that Giordano Bruno, author of *Spaccio della Bestia Trionfante*, was burnt alive in Rome in 1600, and that the author of *Leviathan* was allowed to publish, unmolested, his root-and-branch treatises against accepted theology. His doctrine of political absolutism was almost equally unpalatable, yet he was never in danger. The figure of the Leviathan dominates his most famous book, and he argues over and over again that there is no alternative between absolute rule and social anarchy. But *Leviathan* is more than a tract for its troubled times. It is a work of great and enduring importance just because it is not a mere political pamphlet. It states an extreme case; but it is a case that needs to be stated even if its precepts are rejected.

The most powerful criticism of Hobbes's political theory which appeared in his lifetime was contained in the *Oceana* of James Harrington, published in 1656. *Oceana* is an account of an imaginary commonwealth, but it has none of the social charm of More's *Utopia* and none of the scientific interest of Bacon's *New Atlantis*. Much of it reads like a state paper or the schedules of a budget, united to a *roman à clef* with everything easily identifiable. Harrington advocates artificial equality and the limitation of private possessions. Nevertheless he recognizes the importance of the outstanding man. Like so many "paper constitutions", *Oceana* loses sight of the ordinary world of ordinary people. The final objection is that it is rather dull reading.

Some criticism of the political philosophy of Hobbes is contained in Sir Robert Filmer's *Original of Government* (1652) and *Patriarcha* (1680), though, like Hobbes, Filmer has no belief in the equality of man and inclines to absolutism of a kind. Bishop John Bramhall and Archbishop Thomas Tenison also published refutations of Hobbes. More fundamental criticism was forthcoming from

certain of the Cambridge Platonists, especially Cudworth and More, to whom
further reference is made in later pages.

Associated with some members of the Cambridge school was Joseph Glanvill,
an Oxford man. His first and most famous book was *The Vanity of Dogmatizing*
(1661), an anecdote in which inspired Matthew Arnold's *Scholar-Gipsy*. Glanvill
taught that the right direction of inquiry is to seek truth in the great book of
nature, and not to keep poring upon the writings and opinions of philosophers.
And so he found promise and hope in the activities of the Royal Society.
Investigation into natural phenomena was no longer regarded, as it had been
in the days of Roger Bacon, as a kind of black magic or Satanism. Francis Bacon
had pointed out the way along which the study of science must move. He had
set science free from the dominion of medieval theology, and taught men to
study the book of nature with the solicitude and exactness of contemplation due
to a divine revelation. The Royal Society, praised in verse by Cowley and in
prose by Glanvill, was a manifest sign of intellectual freedom at last secured.

XIII. SCHOLARS AND SCHOLARSHIP, 1600–60

In the seventeenth century English humanism concerned itself as much with
theology as with letters. Rome, as we sometimes forget, was regarded as a
national as well as a religious enemy; and against Rome the great defence was
the Bible. William Chillingworth's *Religion of Protestants* (see p. 310) not only
declared that the Bible contained the religion of Protestants but claimed the
right of the private conscience to interpret it. The Puritans, founding everything
on the Bible, might have confined English scholarship to the narrowest of
limits. But there were other influences at work. Exploration and discovery
had intellectual results. Eastern languages were learned and transmitted, and
oriental MSS. were triumphantly brought home to eager scholars. Nor must
we forget the close connection between English and foreign scholars. Many of
the Elizabethan bishops had lived in Germany or Switzerland during the
Marian persecutions. The chief glories of scholarship in the seventeenth century
were clustered together in Holland, and with the Protestant countries on the
Continent English divines and scholars were in the closest touch. Latinized
names like Budaeus, Turnebus, Salmasius, Grotius, Heinsius, Scioppius, Vossius,
Baronius and Scaliger concealed Frenchmen, Dutchmen, Germans and Italians
and made scholars international. From the elder Heinsius Ben Jonson borrowed
most of the matter for *Timber*. Francis Dujon, a Dutch scholar of German birth,
Latinized his name to Franciscus Junius, lived in England for thirty years,
produced an edition of Caedmon in 1655 and lends his name to the important
Junian manuscript at Oxford, given to him by Archbishop Ussher, another
great scholar, who engaged Thomas Davies, resident at Aleppo, to secure
oriental manuscripts for him. The adventures of Antonio de Dominis, who
came from a Dalmatian archbishopric to be Dean of Windsor, read like a piece
of fiction.

The influence of Roman Catholic scholarship perhaps constituted the most
potent stimulus to the efforts of Protestant erudition at this time. In the latter

half of the sixteenth century the Company of Jesus had regained France and southern Germany for Rome. Jesuit colleges were the admiration of every scholar. The greatest of Roman Catholic researchers, Cardinal Baronius, produced between 1588 and 1609 his twelve folios of *Annales Ecclesiastici*, which gave back to the Catholics pre-eminence in theological learning. Protestant scholarship devoted itself to refutation of Baronius, the greatest effort coming from England, though not from an Englishman—*De rebus sacris et ecclesiasticis exercitationes XVI ad Baronii annales* (1614) by the great Genevan scholar Isaac Casaubon (1559–1614), who died a prebendary of Canterbury. The influence of Casaubon stimulated specially the Anglican divines who, in the seventeenth century, began to challenge the Puritan dominance. Patristic learning and knowledge of church history became an essential part of scholarship. Sir Henry Savile (1549–1622), Provost of Eton and the founder of famous chairs at Oxford, was not only a scholar in history but the chief labourer in the production of a great edition of St Chrysostom (1610–13). Familiarity with the Fathers became the aim of serious theologians. Writers like Robert Burton and Sir Thomas Browne refer familiarly to the ancient divines, and the Puritan William Prynne, in *Histriomastix*, quotes from seventy-one Fathers and refers to fifty-five Synods.

The seventeenth century entered into a noble heritage of accumulated knowledge of the classics. Latin was, naturally, what people are always trying to devise artificially, a universal language. It was the most practical of acquirements, and until French became the patois of diplomacy Latin was used in speech as well as in writing as a medium of international discussion.

The seventeenth century saw a great advance in the study of Greek, which was a prime necessity for any student of the Bible. The aim of school and university, in their Greek studies, was mainly theological. Serious theological study required, in addition to Latin and Greek, a knowledge of Hebrew. The scholars who prepared the Authorized Version included some who had "Hebrew at their fingers' ends" and to whom Syriac, Chaldee and Arabic were familiar tongues. John Selden (1584–1654) was not only renowned as a jurist, but was famous as the scholar who collected oriental manuscripts and wrote *De Dis Syris* (1617), a history of the idol deities of the Old Testament. An odd combination is found in Abraham Wheelock (1593–1653) who was an authority on Persian, Arabic and Anglo-Saxon. He produced an edition of Bede and began the compilation of an Anglo-Saxon dictionary. Meric Casaubon (1599–1671), learned son of a more learned father, published classical commentaries on Marcus Aurelius and on Epictetus, and wrote on the Hebrew and Anglo-Saxon languages. The combination of Anglo-Saxon with oriental languages is not so odd as it seems. Theological literature, as students have sometimes noticed, is plentiful in Anglo-Saxon. Immense scriptural commentaries like the five folio volumes of Matthew Poole's *Synopsis Criticorum...S. Scripturae* (1669–76) were produced, together with epitomes—"marrows", "sums" and "bodies" of divinity representing every shade of belief. On the subject of church government numerous treatises were written, and in doctrinal interpretation Bishop John Pearson's *Exposition of the Creed* (1659) took rank as a masterpiece of the period.

The medieval conception of the authority of Aristotle and scholasticism was transferred in all its strength and its narrowness to the Bible. The Puritan vision of a theocracy on earth made the Bible a universal text book, and every word of it was intensely studied by learned and unlearned alike, with a conviction of its literal inspiration. That Puritan belief in the infallibility of the Bible had dangerous, disagreeable and even grotesque consequences will hardly be questioned; but that it helped to give British and American life its sobriety, its sincerity and its fixed trust in character rather than in cleverness should, on the whole, be gratefully admitted.

XIV. ENGLISH GRAMMAR SCHOOLS

The foundation of famous English schools is a fascinating subject which must be studied in the larger *History*. We have here space for but a few facts. The transition from the medieval scholastic view of education to the humanistic view was not rapid. William of Wykeham founded Winchester and New Colleges as definitely limited vocational places of instruction. He had no theories about the "public school spirit" or the "grand old fortifying classical curriculum". He aimed at creating a supply of learned clerks for service in church and state. Schools of any kind that remotely resembled monastic institutions were menaced by the Act of 1547 which gave the property of chantries and religious guilds to the crown. It has been harshly said that "King Edward VI's Grammar Schools" were those fortunate enough to escape the destructive zeal of the royal commissioners.

Upwards of one hundred and thirty free grammar schools trace their beginning to the reign of Queen Elizabeth. Generally speaking, the "free school" was open to the sons of all "freemen" within the specified limits. A "public school", on the other hand, was open to the whole kingdom, and thus, almost necessarily, involved payment, at least for maintenance or board. Of the gradual change of one into the other, the foundation of John Lyon at Harrow offers a remarkable illustration. Beginning as a free grammar school in 1571 it developed during the seventeenth century into a school attracting the sons of well-to-do parents. It may be mentioned that a Southwark man, John Harvard (1607–38), after graduating at Cambridge left England for Massachusetts and bequeathed half of his estate for a college to be devoted to "the education of the English and Indian youth of this country in knowledge and godlynes". Thus began the Cambridge of the New World.

The education given in the schools was traditionally classical and rigid. The expulsion of Anglicans from offices of all kinds during the Puritan domination naturally led to many changes in school and university alike. Change of some kind was necessary. Oxford and Cambridge still lingered in the medieval past. Milton resented the dead scholasticism of Cambridge and Hobbes sneered at the "Aristotelity" of Oxford. Wealthy parents preferred private tutors to public schools, and the sons of noble families went on a grand tour abroad under the care of learned tutors—such as Hobbes himself. The maintenance of discipline at the larger public schools, where pupils remained till nineteen or twenty, was a matter of difficulty; nevertheless, as we have already seen, the schools in the seventeenth century produced scholars of great if limited learning. The languages and the literature of theology and of classical antiquity were their main concern. In the pursuit of learning, the endurance of pupils was only equalled by the ferocity of the teachers. It is a curious fact that the celebrated beaters of children—such as Dr Busby of Westminster with his "little birch", whose pupils included Dryden—are affectionately remembered when those who sought to introduce a softer discipline are forgotten.

XV. THE BEGINNINGS OF JOURNALISM

The circulation of news in some form is a necessary accompaniment of civilized life. The development of printing naturally assisted the development of newspapers; but newspapers owe their existence, not to the press, but to the circulation of letters. In Elizabethan and Jacobean times journalists were private, not public institutions. Thus, Essex had his staff of "intelligencers", and Sir Dudley Carleton, James I's ambassador, had in John Chamberlain a valuable purveyor of news. It was long before journalism could call a vexed, controlled, censored and licensed press to its aid. Royal eyes looked upon printing as upon coining, that is, as a privilege to be granted, not as a right to be exercised. Printed journalism crept into existence in the form of broadside ballads about startling events, and gradually expanded into occasional pamphlets, usually termed *Relations*. English periodical pamphlets, like English books, were first printed abroad—the place Amsterdam, the date 1620. The first Englishman to publish them was Thomas Archer in 1621. He was soon imprisoned and was succeeded in the same year by Nicholas Bourne. Other stationers, of whom Nathaniel Butter was chief, joined Archer and Bourne as publishers; but in 1625 Archer appears to have published a periodical in competition with Butter and Bourne. News of foreign wars formed the matter to be distributed. Like early books, these pamphlets had no definite short title or "catchword"; the first titles were those of the journalists: *Mercurius Britannicus* was Archer, not a newspaper. The general term used for sheets conveying news was *Coranto*, i.e. a current relation of events; and by that name Ben Jonson ridiculed them in *The Staple of Newes* (1626). In 1632 the Star Chamber prohibited the printing of news from foreign parts. However in 1638 Butter and Bourne were granted the monopoly of printing foreign news and No. 1 of the new "newsbook" was dated 20 December 1638 with the title *An abstract of some speciall forreigne occurrences brought down to the weekly newes of the 20 of December*. But the way of the journalist was still hard. The Long Parliament, which abolished the Star Chamber in 1641, had not the least intention of abolishing control of the press, and in 1643 a good Presbyterian, Henry Walley, clerk to the Stationers' Company, was made licenser. This ensured active commercial control over the disseminators of news, and from that time journalists may be said to have attained at least toleration. The "newsbooks" of the period usually contained two quarto sheets, i.e., sixteen pages, sold at a penny. It is to be noted that they were called "books". The terms "news-sheet" and "newspaper" were not used.

To follow in any detail the course of journalism from Samuel Pecke's *Diurnall Occurrences* of 1641 to the Restoration would end in a long catalogue of unimportant names. The Parliamentary side has to its discredit a mass of illiterate, dishonest, scurrilous, fanatical and acrimonious periodical publications. Except for brief periods between 1643 and 1648 there was scarcely any Royalist press, and what there was appears to be comparatively respectable. Cromwell's journalistic record is as bad as any modern dictator's. His "jackal", or chief propagandist, Henry Walker, who used the anagrammatic name "Luke Harruney", put out between 1647 and 1660 a succession of newsbooks, pamphlets and other means of controversy exceeding the sum of any other writer. George Fox, in calling him "Oliver's priest", a "liar" and a "forger of lies" understated the truth. When Cromwell attained to power, Walker was held in great honour. He had early gained the notoriety of the pillory for flinging a pamphlet *To Your Tents O Israel* into the carriage of Charles I after the attempt to arrest the five members; and he ended by giving a mendacious account of Cromwell's last moments and by writing a religious eulogy of Charles II in 1660. The most notorious of early journalists was one of the worst of men. Another of Cromwell's pressmen was the almost equally voluminous Marchamont Nedham, who was far better educated than Walker, but equally unprincipled. In 1650 he was allowed to start the first permanent official journal of the regicide government, *Mercurius Politicus*. Cleveland the poet, who did good work for the Royalist side, attacked Nedham in a merciless exposure called *Character of Mercurius Politicus* (1650). "Mercurius", with some added qualification —"Aulicus", "Civicus", "Rusticus", and so forth, was a favourite name for the news pamphlets, or rather for their writers. In 1655 Nedham began another official periodical, *The Publick Intelligencer*. One curious fact about the rebellion pamphlets is that though some of the writers were scarcely literate, the writing is usually good. There was doubtless much careful revision by correctors of the press, among whom were some of the ejected Anglican clergy, glad to earn a living.

When the Rump resumed its sittings for the second time in 1659, its Council of State allowed two journalists, Nedham and Oliver Williams, to publish news twice a week. The brother-in-law of General Monck got permission for a third paper to appear and selected as his writer a young schoolmaster named Henry Muddiman, who had never written for the press before. On Monday 26 December 1659, the new journalist issued his first newsbook, *The Parliamentary Intelligencer* (afterwards *The Kingdom's Intelligencer*); and some days later the first number of his other weekly book, *Mercurius Publicus*, appeared. Thus began the career of the most famous of all the seventeenth-century journalists, one whose principal paper, *The London Gazette*, first issued in 1665, was still appearing three hundred years later. Muddiman was granted the important privilege of free postage. Anyone was at liberty to send him, without charge, news and information from all parts of the country—a matter of importance to the government—and he, having collected his matter, sent out closely written "news-letters" to subscribers, post free, for £5 a year. In this odd fashion government and public were both served and a general desire for a regular transmission of news was created. By the end of the reign of Charles II the journalistic struggle for existence had scored two notable victories, first an official recognition of the public need for news, and next the toleration of written news-letters, amplifying the meagreness of licensed print.

XVI. THE ADVENT OF MODERN THOUGHT IN POPULAR LITERATURE. THE WITCH CONTROVERSY

Every age, however enlightened it thinks itself, has its superstitions. The chief superstition of the seventeenth century was a firm belief in witchcraft, and a belief, rather less firm, in the demons who had been incorporated into medieval theology from the dethroned heathen deities. The brief and menacing text in Exodus "Thou shalt not suffer a witch to live" clearly proved the existence of witches and the duty of destroying them. It is characteristic of Hobbes that he asserted the necessity of punishment, not because witchcraft was a reality, but because belief in it was a reality. In 1603 King James caused his treatise *Daemon-ologie* (Edinburgh, 1597) to be published in England, and though this dialogue has the jejuneness and insipidity which characterize the literary efforts of that royal pedant, Parliament dutifully followed his lead with an act condemning all witches to death. Then came an outburst of arguments proving both the existence of relations between human beings and the devil and the urgency of destroying all who trafficked in that unholy alliance. Impostors and perjurers abounded, and witch-finders found as profitable a public as modern psychical experts.

It was inevitable that the stars should be considered to have a special and predictable influence over events on earth, and so "Judicial Astrology" came to be recognized as one of the seven liberal arts. Though theologically banned as heresy against the doctrine of free-will, men clung to it, as men will always cling to some hope of gifts from chance. Here again we have an extensive literature, the main argument of which is that, if astrologers predict rightly, their knowledge must come from commerce with the devil.

Human love of mysticism together with a desire to create the precious metals and to cure all diseases united enthusiasts into a secret society under the symbol of the Rosy Cross. Rosicrucianism reached England from Germany in the seventeenth century. Robert Fludd and Thomas Vaughan (brother of the poet) sought in occultism a cure for the ills of the world. Their doctrines helped to disseminate a purer conception of God and man; but the attempted substitution of vague allegorical aspiration for practical Christianity led nowhere.

It may be claimed that the popular and ribald literature of the Cavalier times helped to clear the air overcharged with menacing heaviness. This was certainly true of politics. The writings of Cleveland were of great service. While *Corantos*, *Mercuries* and *Diurnalls* were developing into newspapers, the popular verses and penny broadsides were serving the purpose of leading articles of a kind intelli-gible to the man in the street. With all its errors and excesses, the Great Rebel-lion was, for many men, a crusade against the vices of feudalism. Pamphleteers turned their attention to abuses in the administration of justice. The system of imprisonment for debt had been attacked as early as 1618, and the unnecessary sufferings of all prisoners engaged the attention of thoughtful minds.

At the end of the Civil War people began to frequent coffee-houses, because a cup of the newly-imported Turkish beverage cost only one penny and was supposed to cure minor ailments. Coffee-houses became places of discussion. A "coffee-house literature" began to grow up, and writers of dialogues chose the coffee-house as an attractive background for their discussions. Letters were another expression of the new civility, and the new generation looked for their model to the French court, where a period of peace and concentrated government had developed a more refined and intellectual ideal of social life. The taste for novels of chivalry had never quite died out and now became again fashionable. Translations of the interminable romances of La Calprenède and Madeleine de Scudéry began to appear; and with the translations came imitations. More practical civilizers collected anecdotes and apophthegms likely to teach exact thought and good manners. Selden's *Table Talk* (1689), was welcomed because of its tolerance, moderation and breadth of view. The Baconian essay, with its large generalities, began to lose ground, and writers of miscellanies passed from the general to the particular. The way was being prepared for Steele and Addison.

Even the belief in astrology and witchcraft was at last assailed in a civilized spirit. The best work against superstition was done by John Webster (1610–82) —not, of course, the dramatist, but a Puritan minister and doctor. His book *The Displaying of Supposed Witchcraft* (1677) did more good than all its predecessors by bringing the controversy into an atmosphere in which the superstition could not live: the atmosphere of confidence in nature and reverence for an immaterial God. At a time when Harvey, Newton and Locke were teaching men to investigate and not fear the mysteries of life, Webster insisted that all evidence in support of sorcery should be subjected to the same scientific scrutiny. The period of witch persecutions is one of the darkest blots on English civilization —and on the Puritan civilization of New England (p. 781 below)—and it produced a literature no less dreary. Before we pass too heavy a judgment on that evil time, we should remind ourselves that the desire to inflict suffering belongs to the lower minds of all ages, and that modern persecutors justify their passion for the spectacle of torture by alleging the intensity of their religious, moral, social, or racial convictions.

CHAPTER VIII

THE AGE OF DRYDEN

I. DRYDEN

In the forty years of English literary production between the Restoration and the beginning of the eighteenth century, Dryden is the most conspicuous personality and the leader of almost every movement; yet of all great English poets he is the most restrained, the least enkindling. John Dryden (1631–1700) passed from Westminster to Cambridge, which, apparently, did not do much for him; but there is no need to take too seriously the familiar compliment to Oxford. The fact is that Dryden was not in any sense an academic person. About 1657 he settled in London to which he remained faithful for the rest of his life. He emerged as a public writer with *A Poem upon the Death of His Late Highness, Oliver, Lord Protector of England, Scotland and Ireland*, first published separately early in 1659, and revised later as *Heroick Stanzas consecrated to the Memory of His Highness Oliver, etc.* Few poets seem to have been less moved by spontaneous lyric impulse. Nearly everything Dryden wrote was almost automatically suggested by events in contemporary public life. His next productions were, first, *Astraea Redux. A Poem on the Happy Restoration and Return of his Sacred Majesty Charles the Second* (1660) and next, *To His Sacred Majesty, A Panegyrick on his Coronation* (1661). With these may be mentioned the lines *To My Lord Chancellor*, offered to Clarendon on New Year's Day 1662. All three are in the decasyllabic couplet which Dryden writes at once with firmness, smoothness and precision. The first group of Dryden's poems was brought to a close by *Annus Mirabilis, the Year of Wonders, 1666. An Historical Poem: containing The Progress and various Successes of our Naval War with Holland, under the Conduct of His Highness Prince Rupert, and His Grace the Duke of Albemarl. And describing The Fire of London* (1667)—the full title is worth quoting as it is a compact summary of the poem, which is a masterpiece of its own kind. In writing it Dryden returned to the "Gray's Elegy" quatrains of the *Heroick Stanzas* and used them with complete mastery. Preceding it is *An Account of the Ensuing Poem in a Letter, etc.*, one of Dryden's early critical essays. A sentence in the letter refers to a play, and may serviceably remind us that Dryden did not progress simply from poem to poem. He wrote many plays of different kinds; but before we discuss them something should be said about the drama of his day.

How far the law against play-acting was evaded during the eighteen years that followed the closing of the theatres in 1642 is a matter for later discussion. At the moment we should remember two facts, first that plays continued to be read in England, and next that the exiled Charles and his court were accustomed to plays abroad. In spite of the zealots there was still a public for printed drama. The second edition of the Shakespeare Folio (1632) was current. The second edition of Ben Jonson's *Works* had appeared in 1640. The first collected folio of the Beaumont and Fletcher plays was published in 1647. Other collections as well as numerous individual publications appeared. Thus the English drama, though under public condemnation, continued to live.

Foreign influences, or rather, foreign fashions, were in vogue, first because Henrietta Maria was a Frenchwoman, and next because, after the failure of the royal cause, many Englishmen of the better class lived abroad until the Restoration; and just as, in a former age, the type of serious drama had been set by the intrinsically unimportant Seneca, so in the present period the type of serious drama had been set by the intrinsically unimportant Alexandre Hardy, whose most celebrated play, *Mariamne*, dates from 1610, and whose vogue endured beyond his death in 1630. Hardy represented in France the kind of drama represented in England by the Beaumont-Fletcher collection. The great austere works of Corneille and Racine came much later and had little influence on the English dramatists. The "near-tragedy" of Hardy was much more to the English taste. The beginnings of Molière may, for our present purpose, be placed in 1658, when, both as actor and writer, he first appeared before Louis XIV and his court. Him the later writers of comedy pillaged without compunction. Another foreign influence upon the drama was that of the French and Spanish romances. With the *Astrée* (1610-12) of Honoré d'Urfé began the movement towards elaborately sentimental romance culminating in the works of La Calprenède, Madeleine de Scudéry, and the Comtesse de La Fayette. The main theme of these romances was heroic love in large dimensions, but comporting itself with elaborate conventionality; and either in translations or in the original tongue they were the favourite fare of the English reading-public of the middle and later sixteen-hundreds.

It was in this period of foreign fashion that Dryden betook himself to the writing of plays, which, in their printed form, were accompanied by excellent prose essays or dedications written with consummate mastery. *The Wild Gallant* (acted 1663), his first play, was not very successful, and hardly deserved to be. Dryden acknowledged that he was not fitted to write comedy, and consoled himself by observing that it was an inferior sort of composition. A brief summary may be made here of all his comedies. *The Wild Gallant* was written in prose, as was *Sir Martin Mar-All, or the Feigned Innocence* (1667, printed 1668), based on Molière's *L'Étourdi*. This was successful. In prose also is the main portion of *The Assignation, or Love in a Nunnery* (1672, printed 1673), a piece of small interest. *Marriage-à-la-Mode* (produced at the same date) greatly pleased the town, with its mingled blank verse and prose. *Limberham, or The Kind Keeper* (acted in 1678), is entirely in prose and has dramatic merits. Dryden's last comedy, *Amphitryon*, produced as late as 1690, is again a mixture of prose and blank verse. It is both brilliant and loose.

Dryden's second acted play, *The Rival Ladies* (acted 1664), shows him passing from comedy into tragi-comedy, where his genius was more at home. The play is specially remarkable for its use of rhyme as a feature of dramatic verse, a practice defended by Dryden in a dedication to Lord Orrery, the earliest of his critical excursions. To this subject he afterwards returned at greater length, both in his *Of Dramatick Poesie, An Essay* and in his *Essay of Heroick Plays;* but he did not claim the innovation as his own. D'Avenant in the semi-operatic *The*

Siege of Rhodes (enlarged 1656) and Etherege in *The Comical Revenge, or Love in a Tub* (1664) had extensively used the heroic couplet, and Lord Orrery had written the whole of his *Henry V* (*c.* 1664) in that measure. The question of priority is not really important. It seems to be forgotten sometimes that much early English drama is written in rhymed verse (though not decasyllabic) and that, in his early plays, Shakespeare uses rhymed decasyllabic verse extensively.

The success of *The Rival Ladies* led Dryden to consider carefully a form of tragi-comedy, in which the serious part, executed in verse, should be accompanied by a less serious underplot, carried out in prose. The formula was not new; the novelty lay in the treatment. Three of Dryden's plays belong to this class. *Secret Love, or The Maiden Queen* (acted 1667) is founded mainly on *Le Grand Cyrus* of Madeleine de Scudéry. In *The Spanish Fryar, or The Double Discovery* (acted 1680) the comic effect predominates. The Friar is a specimen of the unctuous type which, from Chaucer to Dickens, has given unfailing delight. His last tragi-comedy, *Love Triumphant, or Nature will Prevail* (acted 1694), is mainly a repetition of *Marriage-à-la-Mode*, and did not succeed.

This summary has ranged widely through Dryden's life. Let us return. After the success of *The Rival Ladies* in 1664, he assisted his brother-in-law Sir Robert Howard in the production of almost the first "heroic" play, *The Indian Queen* (1664, printed 1665). This proved popular, and Dryden was encouraged to write a "sequel" called *The Indian Emperor, or The Conquest of Mexico by the Spaniards* (acted 1665), by which the success of the new species was established and his own reputation as a playwright assured. His other plays which in form and treatment belong to the same "heroic" order are *Tyrannick Love, or The Royal Martyr* (acted in 1668 or 1669), the two parts of *Almanzor and Almahide, or the Conquest of Granada* (acted 1669 and 1670) and *Aureng-Zebe* (acted 1676). Thus the number of "heroic" plays by Dryden is small. But the other writers in that kind are insignificant. Dryden is the one master of the English "heroic" play, that is, the romantic, magniloquent, far-fetched play, which is parallel to the high-flown foreign romances. Themes and characters are all "out-size". Every man is a super-man and every passion is a super-passion. For this exaggeration the only possible vehicle is the heroic couplet, which is "cothurnated" or elaborately "stilted" speech. A succession of such plays soon began to pall upon the spectator. There is nothing so soon exhausted as excess, and the species was doomed to self-destruction as Dryden himself recognized.

Dryden's apologetic *Essay of Heroick Plays* appeared in 1672 with *The Conquest of Granada*. The more important *Of Dramatick Poesie, An Essay* appeared in 1668, the immediate occasion being an essay by Sir Robert Howard, doubting the appropriateness of the rhymed heroic couplet to dramatic verse. Dryden's famous conversation-essay is written with great spirit and fine critical understanding. He claimed that the French principle of the unities could be combined with English freedom of treatment, and that Jonson's humour might be coupled with Corneille's rhyme. Howard replied to Dryden's *Essay* a little authoritatively, and Dryden answered in *A Defence of an Essay of Dramatick Poesie* (1668) prefixed to the second edition of *The Indian Emperor*. The essay is an admirable example of raillery in debate, and it contains, among other asides of wisdom, the excellent remark that "poesy only instructs as it delights". The truth of this is indisputable and is constantly forgotten by the theorists. *The Conquest of Granada* (printed 1672) may be described as the heroic play *par excellence*. It is, in every sense, splendid. Dryden had now reached the height of his popularity. A self-commendatory tone in the *Epilogue* to *The Second Part of the Conquest of Granada* (1672) drew upon him some attacks, to which he replied in *A Defence of the Epilogue, or An Essay on the Dramatick Poetry of the Last Age*, one of his poorest pieces.

But punishment for the overweening poet was at hand in *The Rehearsal* (acted 1671), a burlesque dramatic concoction by several wits, including the Duke of Buckingham, Thomas Sprat, and (it is alleged) Samuel Butler. One or two of the "heroick" dramatists had been considered for the role of victim; the success of *The Conquest of Granada* and his appointment to the laureateship made inevitable both the selection of Dryden and the name of "Bayes". Like Sheridan's *The Critic*, *The Rehearsal* is both an amusing *revue* of forgotten ineptitudes and a successful exhibition of the spirit of burlesque. As a criticism of Dryden it is itself inept.

Between *The Conquest of Granada* and *Aureng-Zebe*, Dryden had produced, besides the comedies *The Assignation* and *Marriage-à-la-Mode*, a tragic "piece of occasion" *Amboyna, or The Cruelties of the Dutch to the English Merchants* (1672), and an "opera", *The State of Innocence and Fall of Man* (1674), which merits no more than the remark that its dramatization of *Paradise Lost* was intended as an act of homage to Milton, as the accompanying essay, *The Author's Apology for Heroick Poetry, and Poetick Licence*, makes clear. Better known than Dryden's adaptation of Milton are his adaptations of Shakespeare. We have to remember that Shakespeare was already "old-fashioned" in form and language, and that there could be no offence in following Shakespeare's own example in telling a dramatic story over again in a way appropriate to the demands of a new age. The first of these adaptations was *The Tempest, or The Enchanted Island* (acted 1667, printed 1670), in which however the main hand is that of D'Avenant, who provided a male counterpart for Miranda, a sister for Caliban and a female Ariel. Dryden's *All for Love, or The World Well Lost* (acted 1677, printed 1678) is not an adaptation of *Antony and Cleopatra*, but a free treatment of the same subject on his own lines. The agreeable preface takes a bold line and declares rather than defends the author's dramatic intentions. The play should be judged on its own merits, and not as a rival to Shakespeare's superb invention. There is, actually, much in the play that calls for sincere praise. Dryden was almost unconsciously reverting from French to Elizabethan models. Once again, in *Troilus and Cressida, or Truth Found too Late* (printed 1679), Dryden concerned himself with a Shakespearean play. *Troilus and Cressida* is not Shakespeare's most agreeably successful play; but Dryden's is definitely a failure. With it was printed the remarkable *Preface concerning the Grounds of Criticism in Tragedy*, offering a reasonable application of Aristotelian theory to English practice.

Brief mention may be made of Dryden's collaboration with Lee in *Oedipus* (acted 1678) and in *The Duke of Guise* (acted 1682)—the latter begun by Dryden many years before. *Albion and Albanius* (played 1685) was a poor libretto for a feeble musician; but *King Arthur or The British Worthy*, a "dramatick opera" produced in 1691 with Purcell's music, was better. One number, the tenor solo "Come if you dare", is known to many who do not know its source. The "opera" when revived proved a pleasing example of successful collaboration. After the close of King James II's reign Dryden produced two more plays which may be regarded as a worthy consummation of his dramatic development. *Don Sebastian* (acted 1690) is a romantic play in blank verse and prose. In the preface, Dryden, as usual, claims the dramatist's right to tell the story in his own way. He shows no knowledge of *The Battle of Alcazar*, a century older, attributed to Peele. The tragedy which followed, *Cleomenes, the Spartan Hero* (acted 1692), is finely conceived and finely carried through on the lines of French classical tragedy, though with unrhymed verse. With it Dryden's career as a dramatist closes. *The Secular Masque*, written for his own benefit, and played only a short time before his death in 1700, has no enduring value. Dryden attempted many kinds of dramatic composition and attained a very notable degree of success in all; but it was only in the heroic play that he surpassed all his rivals and followers. Though he did not enjoy writing plays, he enjoyed writing about the drama, and it is to the close and honest scrutiny of his own reactions to the theatre that we owe the magnificent body of prose criticism which alone would ensure him a memorable place in English literature. Incidental to his plays are the numerous prologues and epilogues. There is no species of composition in which he so happily mingles wit and wisdom, and in which those who came after him so clearly failed to reach his eminence.

To make this survey of Dryden's contributions to dramatic art and literature, we had to leave the general story of his career in the year of *Annus Mirabilis*, 1667. In 1670 he was made Poet Laureate and Historiographer Royal. Gradually he became the most famous writer of his day; but though he was much observed as he sat in his accustomed seat in Will's Coffee-house, everything seems to show that he was a quiet and retiring man, unconcerned by the broils which disgraced the republic of letters. He seems never to have been popular. Few English poets have been more violently and extensively attacked, and few have remained so unperturbed. Compared with the calm reserve of Dryden, the personalities of Pope seem vulgar. We have already remarked that Dryden's genius responded instantly to movements of his time; he therefore found in the aims and methods of the Whig intriguers a subject made to his hand. Who should succeed Charles II? His Catholic brother, James? The anti-Catholics led by the brilliant and unprincipled Shaftesbury tried to set aside that succession. The infamous Popish Plot of Titus Oates and the tragi-comic attempt to place Monmouth on the throne were incidents in the conspiracy. But before the final collapse Shaftesbury was arrested and sent to the Tower. The Middlesex Grand Jury threw out the bill against him and a medal was struck in his honour. These were the circumstances in which Part I of *Absalom and Achitophel* appeared in 1681. Part II, of which only a little is Dryden's (much is Nahum Tate's), appeared in 1682. Both were anonymous. By giving his satire a Biblical setting and presenting Monmouth and Shaftesbury as the rebellious Absalom encouraged by the wily counsellor Achitophel (2 Sam. xv–xviii), Dryden caught the ears of the Whig and Puritan citizens of London who had been Shaftesbury's strongest supporters. *Absalom and Achitophel* remains the greatest political satire in our literature. The incomparable brilliancy of its diction and versification can hardly be over-praised; but its supreme excellence lies in its sketches of character. The shrunken counterparts of Dryden's great inventions can always be found in any Government or Opposition of any age. In 1682, Shaftesbury, who recognized that the game was up, fled to Holland. Monmouth was arrested and the Duke of York was not afraid to show himself in England. *The Medall. A Satyre against Sedition. By the Author of Absalom and Achitophel* appeared in that year. It pursues Shaftesbury, the medallist of the Whigs, with unrelenting vigour. There were immediate replies, among them *The Medall of John Bayes*, attributed to Shadwell, his former associate. Dryden replied with *MacFlecknoe, or A Satyr upon the True-Blew-Protestant Poet, T. S.* (1682). Those who know the incomparable lines on Shadwell need scarcely be reminded of them; those who do not must seek them in the first of great English mock-heroic poems. From it Pope derived his idea of *The Dunciad*. This cycle of Dryden's writings is completed by his share in the *Second Part of Absalom and Achitophel*, published a few weeks after *MacFlecknoe*. Dryden's characters of Doeg and Og (Settle and Shadwell) are triumphs of haughty satirical contempt.

With *Religio Laici, or a Laymans Faith* (1682), we come to Dryden's most personal and spontaneous composition; but even here we cannot forget that religion was partly a political question. In Browne's *Religio Medici* the important word is the first; in Dryden's *Religio Laici* the second. The prose work is an exultation in the mysteries of religion; the poem is the common-sense of a layman weary of the warring theologians. *Religio Laici* represents a halfway house on the road which Dryden was following and which led him, like the writer of a later *Apologia*, to Rome. It is a poem that deserves more attention than it usually receives.

Charles II died in 1685, and was succeeded by James II. To the peacefulness and even to the possibility of that succession, the poems of Dryden contributed not a little; but his services were ignored or minimized. His laureate odes *Threnodia Augustalis* (1685) on the death of Charles and the *Britannia Rediviva* (1688) on the birth of the prince afterwards to be famous as the Old Pretender are of small importance. The personal effect on Dryden of the succession of a Catholic king was to lead him into the Church where authority was supreme. The easy charge that Dryden obsequiously followed the victorious side cannot be maintained. The author of *Religio Laici* was clearly seeking for the guidance of some kindly light; the author of the poem *To The Pious Memory of the Accomplisht Young Lady, Mrs Anne Killigrew* (the best of his lyrics) was plainly moved, as feeling men of his years are often moved, by a sense of too long surrender to a "lubrique and adult'rate age", and by the need for a spiritual discipline with its healing obligations. When the political cause for which he had fought was utterly lost, Dryden refused to accept the new régime, was deprived of places and pensions, and saw his lost laurels crowning the head of MacFlecknoe himself. But before the fall and flight of James, Dryden produced several works of importance. He took a hand in a new translation of Plutarch (afterwards revised by Clough), and he embarked upon verse translations of Ovid, Virgil, Horace and Theocritus. The hope long cherished of writing an epic poem receded more and more into the background. A great poem of a different kind was still to come. Stillingfleet had made unfavourable religious comment on Dryden, and Dryden's reply took the form of a long allegorical fable *The Hind and the Panther. A Poem. In Three Parts* (1687). The poem is the longest of Dryden's original productions in verse; but it is carried with unmistakable vigour to its abrupt close. There is no sign of failing power. Its perfect sincerity brought him into favour with neither religious party. William and Mary came in, and Dryden was dismissed and disgraced.

From the time of the Revolution he became a hard-working man of letters in the modern sense. With the assistance of his two elder sons he brought out in 1693 a complete translation of Juvenal and Persius, prefaced by one of the most delightful of his essays, *A Discourse concerning the Original and Progress of Satire*. In 1697 appeared his translation of Virgil. Dryden's Virgil is literally Dryden's Virgil, and was expected to be. Its readers were already familiar with Virgil's Virgil, and wanted to know how a great English poet would treat that familiar story. Its successes and its failures are equally plain. The freedom which Dryden had assumed as a translator of the Roman poets he carried a step further in the reproductions of Chaucer and of Chaucer's frequent source, Boccaccio. The whole volume, with a preface dated 1699, has the curious title *Fables, Ancient and Modern*. Dryden, like other eminent persons of a date still later, did not know how to read Chaucer and charges that admirable metrist with "writing thousands of... Verses, which are lame for want of half a foot, and sometimes a whole one, and which no pronunciation can make otherwise". Nevertheless he recognized both the quality and the magnitude of Chaucer, and his Chaucerian poems, like his Shakespearean plays, are acts of homage, and recommended the old poet to readers of another generation. The prose *Preface* to the *Fables* is one of the most delightful and one of the most unconstrained of all Dryden's prose pieces. The last period of Dryden's literary labours also witnessed his final endeavours in lyrical verse—a species of poetry in which he achieved a more varied excellence than is always placed to his credit. The *Song for St Cecilia's Day* (1687) and *Alexander's Feast; or The Power of Musique* (1697) have been over-praised and are now under-valued. They are, if one may say so, more amusing than pieces of such solemnity should be, and the attempts to make "the sound an echo to the sense" appeal just a little to the sense of fun. But English poetry would be the poorer without them. Thus, in labours manifold, and not without a disquietude of spirit from which the decline of life is rarely exempt, Dryden's days drew to their close. He was still vigorous, but if he trounced Blackmore with almost savage energy, he hailed with generous praise the work of younger writers like Congreve. He died in the last year of the century which he had adorned and was buried in Westminster Abbey, in the grave of Chaucer.

Dryden's great literary achievements were not ignored by his own age and have never ceased to receive admiration. More than any of his contemporaries, he is entitled to be called the father of modern English prose; and though in verse the next generation claimed to improve upon his model, the model, nevertheless, was his. In blank verse he is almost as strong as in his chosen instrument, the couplet. His prose combines with ease of flow and forcible directness a lucidity of arrangement suggestive of French example. The debt of later English prose to Dryden is inestimable. His plays are the most abundant contribution to the dramatic literature of the Restoration period. In his non-dramatic verse he left scarcely any kind of poetry unattempted except the epic proper, in which, had his heart's desire been fulfilled, he would have followed the example of the great poet to whom no political or religious differences ever prevented him from paying an unstinted tribute of admiration. His satirical and didactic poems are among the most successful attempts ever made to conduct arguments and deliver attacks in polished metrical form. He is one of the most English of poets in his chief defect as well as in his excellence: he could not wear his heart upon his sleeve and he seemed ashamed to allow himself a visible excess of emotion. What he was not he at no time made any pretence of being. What he did he did with the whole strength of one of the most vigorous intellects given to any poet, ancient or modern, with constant generosity of effort, and, at the same time, with masculine directness and clear simplicity of purpose.

II. SAMUEL BUTLER

By a singular piece of literary good luck Samuel Butler (1613–80) became secretary to Sir Samuel Luke, the Puritan colonel (Bunyan's commander), and found in that fanatic the model for Sir Hudibras, and in the motley crew of zealots who surrounded him the inspiration for a comic epic. At Luke's house, no doubt, he composed many of his prose *Characters*, though some were written after the Restoration. One hundred and twenty of these *Characters* appeared (but not till 1759) in *The Genuine Remains in Verse and Prose of Mr Samuel Butler*, and sixty-eight more, together with a number of miscellaneous *Observations and Reflexions*, were edited in 1905–8 by A. R. Waller. The *Characters* are good examples of that once popular form of composition. *Hudibras* itself appeared in three parts, the first in 1663, the second in 1664, and the third much later in 1678. It was at once received with great enthusiasm, especially by Charles II, who rewarded the poet with a gratuity of £300. But most of Butler's life was unfortunate and he died in abject penury.

Hudibras is a mock-heroic poem dealing with the pretensions and hypocrisies of the Presbyterians, Independents and the rest of the "caterwauling brethren", who, styling themselves saints, helped to overthrow the monarchy and hoped to establish a sectarian tyranny of which they should be the leaders. Butler wrote it with conviction and enjoyment. The general machinery and the actual name come from *The Faerie Queene*; but clearly the strongest influences are those of Cervantes and Rabelais. Cervantes supplies the plot and the setting, Don Quixote and Sancho serving as models for Sir Hudibras and Ralpho; Rabelais supplies the general comic extravagance of parody. To mention predecessors whom a writer has known and liked is merely to intimate a community of enjoyment in which the reader may like to share. There is no suggestion of any lack of originality in this or in similar instances. Butler was clearly an original satirical genius with a skill in comic rhyming which has been, in its turn, the inspiration of many successors.

Hudibras is the most remarkable document of the reaction against Puritanism at the Restoration. Its turns of wit, racy metaphors and quaint rhymes have secured its continuance as an English classic, even though much of its matter and many of its allusions are now scarcely intelligible without profusion of comment. Sparkling wit and humour enliven the discussions which make up much of the book and many memorable couplets are excellent as general criticism and have become almost household words. The three parts each contain three cantos. Whether Butler meant to bring his poem up to the Virgilian twelve by adding another three we cannot say. The third part is the least satisfactory in form and one almost expects another instalment to restore proportion.

Hudibras may be taken as the seamy side of *The Pilgrim's Progress*. Bunyan's Christian, and indeed Bunyan himself, eagerly accepted the Bible as the final and complete guide to life; but there were many of the zealots whose balance was destroyed by the most inflammatory and the least intelligible parts of Holy Writ. It is not against righteousness, but against the deluded victims of self-righteousness that Butler turns the sharp and merciless edge of his satire. He did not confine himself to the eight-syllabled (often nine-syllabled) couplet. Of the two volumes of *The Genuine Remains* the second is mainly in verse, beginning with *The Elephant in the Moon*, directed against Sir Paul Neale, a member of the Royal Society. The subject is treated metrically twice over—in octosyllabic verse, Butler's special metre, and then in the rhymed decasyllables of Dryden. It seems as though Butler had experimented to find the most suitable vehicle for his satire. This poem is followed by nine satires, one or two of which are written in the longer metre. The collection concludes with a number of *Miscellaneous Thoughts* in epigrammatic form, many of them containing bitter reflections on the poet's ill-fortune in life. But his lesser works are not of great importance. Butler survives as the author of *Hudibras*, a unique poem, racily English, and acutely critical, not only of its own age, but of hypocrisy in all the ages.

III. POLITICAL AND ECCLESIASTICAL SATIRE

The accounts just given of Dryden and Butler should have shown, first, that the Restoration established political and religious satire among the kinds of English poetry, and, next, that "political" and "religious" are, in this period, two terms for the same thing. The Civil War created parties, the Restoration established them. The ignoble squabbles over the Exclusion Bill created a new kind of conflict, the violent interchange of hostile words. Butler gave the "caterwauling crew" no quarter. "The True-Blew Protestants" discharged their foulest artillery upon Dryden. Pamphlets in prose and squibs in verse were the common missiles on both sides. The first great critic of the disgusting court and government of Charles II was Andrew Marvell, whose knowledge of affairs and statesmanlike insight gave added power to the poetic force of his satires. But Marvell was not a party man. The real party struggle began with the Exclusion Bill, and the true father of party strife in England is Titus Oates. "Petitioners" for the passing of the Exclusion Bill and "Abhorrers" of Achitophel's invasion of royal prerogative soon acquired the nicknames "Whig" and "Tory";

and under these conditions of popular passion violence established itself as a method of political controversy.

The laureate of Titus Oates and the Popish Plot was John Oldham (1653–83), whose life, character and circumstances combined to make him an ardent revolutionary. He was by nature and inclination a satirist; but unfortunately he digressed from his "only province" into Cowleyan "Pindarique" odes. His vice of turgidity and his method of heaping effect on effect to reach one great towering climax were encouraged by Cowley's influence. The ode *Upon the Works of Ben Jonson* contains just criticism, but falls far short of the sublime it essays to reach. The *Satyr against Vertue* enlists, for the first time, the "Pindarique" hyperbole in the service of irony. Oldham's real power was clearly exhibited in *A Satyr upon a Woman, who by her Falsehood and Scorn was the Death of my Friend* (1678). Here he makes use of the heroic couplet, which was his most effective medium. But this poem was soon surpassed by his chief work, the four *Satyrs upon the Jesuits*, published as a whole in 1681. They owe much to Juvenal. The harshness of the versification and the air of violence differentiate sharply the satires of Oldham from those of his great contemporary Dryden. His Jesuits are rejoicing and self-conscious villains, and they fail as indictments because they are incredible. Oldham is not really a great satirist. He did not care enough for truth for its own sake. He is merely violent in an age when violence was in fashion. Oldham's other works call for no comment. It is tempting, but useless, to speculate upon the poet he might have become had his life not been cut short by the excesses of his violent spirit. Dryden, though of the other party in politics and religion, generously saluted the early ripeness of Oldham, even while indicating his characteristic defect—"the harsh Cadence of a rugged line".

The succeeding swarms of satirical effusions by known and unknown writers settled round two main points, the Exclusion Bill and the Revolution. But the earlier failures of Charles II's reign were not forgotten. Waller's well-meant but unfortunate *Instructions to a Painter, for the Drawing of the Posture and Progress of His Majesty's Forces at Sea*, designed to celebrate "the Victory obtained over the Dutch, June 3, 1665", invited satirical reprisals when the Dutch not only began to obtain victories over His Majesty's Forces at sea but sailed up the river Thames and threatened His Majesty's own capital city. We mentioned (p. 314) Marvell's deadly imitation of Waller. There were other *Advices* or *Instructions* on various themes. To Denham, Marvell, Dryden, Oldham and Butler were attributed many pieces which they did not write; and when the most popular productions were reprinted in such collections as the volumes entitled *Poems on Affairs of State* issued between 1697 and 1716 the false attributions were still maintained. *Absalom and Achitophel* and its sequel *The Medal* produced their own crop of replies, and the Popish Plot was naturally the inspiration of a whole tribe of scurrilous penmen, whose productions it would be tedious to mention. There were of course many "ballads"—imitations of popular songs to well-known tunes. Tom D'Urfey (1653–1723) was the most popular ballad-composer under the Restoration. But all political ditties are unimportant compared with *Lillibúrlero*, the tune of which, absurdly claimed for Purcell, conferred an instant and extraordinary success on Thomas

Lord Wharton's doggerel. It is unnecessary to cite other examples. "We don't want to fight, but by Jingo if we do" is a music-hall song that sharply summed up popular political feelings in 1877 and gave a word to the language; but we do not quote it among the masterpieces of Victorian literature. So, although *Lilliburlero* sang a monarch out of three kingdoms and was whistled on significant occasions by Sterne's Uncle Toby, it remains a piece of scarcely comprehensible and entirely worthless doggerel. The greatest prose satire of the period was Marvell's *The Rehearsal Transpros'd*, mentioned on p. 314.

IV. THE EARLY QUAKERS

The rise of the Quaker movement in England, which began with the public preaching of George Fox (1624–90), was marked by a surprising outburst of literary activity. The new conception of religion was propagated with extraordinary zeal. It is not our business to discuss religious differences; but we may say briefly that whereas the churchman reposed upon tradition and the Puritan upon the Bible, the Quaker found certitude in a direct experience of God in the soul. It was the fate of these sincere and exalted enthusiasts to be persecuted more rancorously by the Puritan sects than by the church itself. The "Inward Light" of the Quakers shone in many loathsome prisons of the Lord Protector's England.

George Fox, founder of the Society of Friends (first called "Quakers" by Justice Bennett at Derby, because, said Fox, "we bid them tremble at the word of the Lord"), was, like Bunyan, an unlearned man inspired by the Bible. It is not Bunyan, however, whom Fox seems most to resemble. His true brother in spiritual genius is St Francis of Assisi. What Fox took from the Bible was practice rather than doctrine. His associates were "Friends", and men and women stood on equal terms. He had one of the sure marks of genius: he was a great organizer; and the Society rose like an exhalation under his inspiration, covered England with its influence, and circulated quantities of printed matter in defiance of all authority. So completely practical was Quaker Christianity that even blasphemers preferred to deal with Quaker tradesmen because of their honesty.

The mystic is commonly impelled to make known to others his experience of God in the soul, and early Quaker literature, therefore, is the record of a spiritual conflict rather than the assertion of a creed. George Fox's *Journal* is by far the most noteworthy of all these records. It has hardly a rival in religious literature of its kind. Yet it has no literary form and was, for the most part, dictated. It was first put into grammatical English by Thomas Ellwood and other Friends, but the original has now been published *verbatim* and there is a useful abbreviation. It has a penetrating fervent simplicity which goes straight to the heart of the reader. Whether his story be gentle or horrible, George never lifts his voice to shrillness of protestation or complaint. Some of the vignettes, as we may call them, that illustrate his narrative make unforgettable pictures. Indeed the whole book is deeply moving.

Thomas Ellwood (1639–1713), a man of liberal education, was constrained by conviction to throw in his lot with the despised "people of God". He was an intimate friend of William Penn and Isaac Penington, and was for some years engaged as reader to Milton in his blindness. It was Ellwood, according to himself, who suggested to Milton the theme afterwards worked out in *Paradise Regained. The History of the Life of Thomas Ellwood, written by his own hand* (1714) gives a very lively picture of his inward struggles, of his passive resistance to the monstrous tyranny of his father, and of his share in the persecutions to which all his people were subjected. His description of prisons and prison life in the seventeenth century has high historical value. The *Journal* of John Gratton (1641–1712), another Quaker of good education, is of great interest to the student of religious psychology. Equally attractive is *An Account of the Convincement, etc.* (1710) by Richard Davies of Welshpool, who tells the story of his own sufferings, and of the first propagation of the "truth" in Wales. *The Memoir of John Roberts* of Cirencester (1623–83) was written by his son Daniel in 1725. For its brightness and unfailing humour, it well deserves an honourable place in English religious literature. In his preface to the first complete edition, entitled *A Quaker of the Olden Time* (1898), Oliver Wendell Holmes called it a book of gold.

William Penn (1644–1718), son of the Admiral Penn frequently mentioned by Pepys, is the most widely known of the early Quakers—chiefly as the founder and first governor of the colony of Pennsylvania. His character has been assailed by Macaulay and others; but there seems no reason to doubt that he remained absolutely sincere and worthy of the respect in which he was always held by his people. The best known of his early works, *No Cross No Crown* (1669), was written at the age of twenty-four, while he was in the Tower for the "blasphemy" of a pamphlet, *The Sandy Foundation Shaken* (1668), in which he had assailed what were regarded as the strongholds of the Christian faith. He wrote *No Cross No Crown* "to show…that the denial of self…is the alone way to the Rest and Kingdom of God". More of a mystic than Penn was his friend Isaac Penington (1616–79), son of one of the regicide judges. The love story of Penington and his wife is a record of noble heroism. Penington is voluminous and diffuse, and attains to real expression only in short passages. The testimony of Mary Penington to his goodness is an exquisite and moving passage of prose. There is no more pathetic figure in the history of early Quakerism than that of the unhappy James Nayler (1617–60) whose wild preaching led some of his followers to hail him as the Messiah. His "last Testimony", taken down about two hours before the end of his wild and tortured life, reads like the words of a man whose life had known nothing but the ecstasy of contemplation. Another beautiful tribute to the spirit that animated the early Quakers is given by William Dewsbury (1621–88) in *The Faithful Testimony, etc.* shortly before his death during a long and terrible imprisonment in Warwick Castle. Lamb's famous essay *A Quakers' Meeting* recommends "above all church-narratives" the *History of the Rise, Increase, and Progress of the Christian People called Quakers* (1717) by the Anglo-Dutch Quaker William Sewel (1654–1720) and calls attention to the *Journal* and other writings of the American Quaker John Woolman (1720–72).

The Quakers were attacked by Bunyan and by Baxter, as well as by innumerable forgotten sectaries; and both attacks and defences are now scarcely readable. The prodigious *apologia* of Samuel Fisher (1605–65) entitled *Rusticus ad Academicos* contains nearly 800 pages of interminable sentences; nevertheless it has rewarding and even amusing moments. One book, out of all the welter of controversy, can be read today with interest and profit, *An Apology for the True Christian Divinity*, by Robert Barclay (1648–90), first of the very few theologians whom the Society of Friends has produced.

Among the purely literary efforts of the Quakers, mention should be made of William Penn's *Some Fruits of Solitude* (1693), which has been a consolation to many readers besides R. L. Stevenson, who wrote of the comfort he had gained from it while sick and lonely in San Francisco in 1879. It is a collection of aphorisms, "fruits", as Penn calls them, "that may serve the reader for texts to preach to himself upon". The exalted mysticism of the Quakers found no memorable expression in verse—there is no Quaker Herbert or Crashaw. The only contemporary approach to poetry in the movement is to be found in a little volume of letters and poems entitled *Fruits of Retirement*, by Mary Mollineux (born Southworth), published shortly after her death in 1695.

The Quaker movement gradually settled into a sect, but a sect quiet, distinguished and unaggressive. With the eighteenth century, the glow of the first experience faded, and the third generation of Quakers, while retaining much of the purity, unworldliness and spirituality of their predecessors, became, for the most part, the children of a tradition. That tradition inspired the work of Elizabeth Fry and her fellow reformers and such later literature as Caroline Fox's *Memories of Old Friends* (1882) and the *Poverty and Progress* (1941) and other industrial investigations of Seebohm Rowntree.

V. THE RESTORATION DRAMA

1. D'Avenant, Etherege, etc.

Like all fanatical large-scale prohibitions, the closing of the theatres in 1642 could not be strictly enforced. There were surreptitious performances, in and out of London, either at the houses of noblemen or in actual play-houses like The Cockpit and The Red Bull. If plays were forbidden, "entertainments" were not. So we hear of "drolls" or "droll-humours", as they were called—farces or humorous scenes adapted from popular plays and staged on extemporized platforms. Thus, a "droll" entitled *Merry Conceits of Bottom the Weaver* was printed as early as 1646. "Drolls" derived from *Hamlet*, *The Merry Wives* and other plays were acted in spite of the penalties.

Towards the close of Cromwell's rule, the laws against dramatic entertainments appear to have been somewhat relaxed, and Sir William D'Avenant, who had been governor of the royal company of players, and had held a patent, dated 1639, empowering him to erect a new play-house, was obviously the man to provide for a returning interest in plays. He obtained authority for the production of a kind of semi-dramatic entertainment, which, though given at private houses, was public to those who paid for admission. D'Avenant's earliest venture of this sort was entitled *The First Day's Entertainment at Rutland House*, "by declamation and music, after the manner of the ancients", staged in 1656. This venture has been called "an opera", though it is little more than two pairs of speeches diversified by music. After this came a more ambitious entertainment. This was the celebrated "opera" *The Siege of Rhodes* (1656), which included "perspective in scenes" and "the story sung in recitative music". It may be worth while to remember that opera, i.e., sung drama, appeared in Italy at the very end of the sixteenth century, as an attempt to revive the peculiarities of Greek drama. *The Siege of Rhodes* is claimed as the first English opera; and though its musical texture is slight there is no greater gap, operatically speaking, between *The Siege of Rhodes* and *Rinaldo* than between *Rinaldo* and *Don Giovanni*. *The Siege of Rhodes* has been also described as the first English play to employ scenery and the first in which an actress appeared on the English stage. Neither of these statements is entirely correct. Ladies of the court had appeared in the Jacobean masques and French actresses appeared in London as early as 1629. In 1658 D'Avenant opened The Cockpit Theatre in Drury Lane, producing there two similar operas, *The Cruelty of the Spaniards in Peru* (1658) and *The History of Sir Francis Drake* (1659).

On the very eve of the Restoration, John Rhodes obtained a licence from the existing authorities for the formation of a dramatic company. A second company gathered at The Red Bull, a third at Salisbury Court in Whitefriars. At the Restoration, Charles II issued a patent to Thomas Killigrew and Sir William D'Avenant, empowering them to "erect" two companies of players. Killigrew's company soon became known as the King's, and D'Avenant's as the Duke of York's. In 1661, the latter moved to a new play-house in Portugal Row, Lincoln's Inn, and later, after D'Avenant's death, to the sumptuous theatre in Salisbury Court. D'Avenant's house was commonly called "the opera" from the performance of musical plays there. The King's Company (Killigrew's), variously housed before 1663, removed in that year to the Theatre Royal in Drury Lane.

Thomas Killigrew (1612–83) had been reared as a page in the court of Charles I, and continued a favourite companion of Charles II. Among his earlier plays are *The Prisoners*, *Claracilla* and *The Princess*. *The Parson's Wedding*, which appeared in the collected edition of 1664, is, like the others, a pre-Restoration play, and, being very loose, was very popular. Two brothers of Thomas, Sir William and Henry, also wrote plays, which have no value as literature.

The works of Sir William D'Avenant (see p. 275) were posthumously collected in 1673. Several of his rewritten plays, such as *Love and Honour*, *The Wits* and *The Platonick Lovers*, long remained popular favourites; but most of his work after the Restoration was mere adaptation—*Macbeth*, with "alterations, amendments, additions and new songs" and *The Tempest or the Enchanted Island* written with Dryden. Shakespearean adaptations were common at the Restoration—*Measure for Measure* with Beatrice and Benedick introduced and the concoction named *The Law against Lovers*, and *Romeo and Juliet* transformed into a comedy. Pepys saw many Shakespearean performances and is loud in praise of Betterton as Hamlet. However mangled by alterations, Shakespeare continued to hold the stage.

The dramatists and actors were naturally loyalists, and after the Restoration we find an outburst of anti-Puritanism. General Monck was still in the north when John Tatham produced his piece of dramatic journalism, *The Rump, or the Mirrour of the Late Times* (1660), which boldly lampoons the notabilities of the Commonwealth. Another comedy of the type is Sir Robert Howard's *The Committee*, produced in 1665 and long popular. A better written comedy, though it was less successful, is Cowley's *Cutter of Coleman Street* (1664). Comedies satirizing the Puritans were popular throughout the reign of Charles II, as may be seen in such productions as Lacy's *The Old Troop* (before 1665), Crowne's *City Politics* (1673), and Mrs Behn's *The Roundheads* (1682), borrowed from Tatham's *The Rump*.

A few individual playwrights of the Restoration maintained the old traditions of English drama. Foremost among them was John Wilson (1627?–96), whose two comedies *The Cheats* (1662) and *The Projectors* (1664) are Jonsonian. Besides these excellent comedies, Wilson is the author of an excellent tragedy, *Andronicus Comnenius* (1664), in blank verse. His fourth play, *Belphegor, or the Marriage of the Devil* (1691), repeats the familiar story told by Machiavelli and used by Jonson in *The Devil is an Ass*, as well as by others. Brief mention only can be accorded to Sir Robert Stapylton's comedy *The Slighted Maid* (1663) and his tragi-comedy *The Stepmother* (1663). Whether the trivial but witty comedy, *Mr Anthony*, printed in 1690, be the work of Roger Boyle, Earl of Orrery, or not, it calls for favourable notice here. The Duke of Newcastle, too, and his clever Duchess both wrote plays. Two comedies by the Duke—*The Humorous Lovers* and *The Triumphant Widow*—were printed in 1673; and twenty-one plays by the Duchess were published in a folio volume of 1662. But comedy, on the revival of the stage, was not to be confined to satire on recent events or to imitations of Jonson. New wares were imported from abroad, and especially from Spain.

The effect of Spanish literature upon English, especially in drama, has been unduly minimized by historians and critics who have not possessed the material upon which a judgment can be based. There had long been regular intercourse with Spain since the time of James I, and visitors to the Peninsula saw many plays that have not survived or attained to print. Thus Lope de Vega, almost an exact contemporary of Shakespeare, is said to have written over two thousand plays, most of which are entirely lost. About five hundred survive, and not even all of these have been printed. The reports of those who saw these plays were current in literary circles; and though we cannot adduce printed Spanish "originals", we can adduce a very large number of plays with Spanish characters, Spanish themes and Spanish attitudes, as well as a large number of plays based, either directly or through adaptations, upon Spanish stories. The most popular pre-Shakespearean play was *The Spanish Tragedy*. Cervantes offered to our dramatists material which they were not backward in using. There is nothing specially Spanish in Shakespeare, except the fine caricature of Armado; but characters with unmistakably Spanish names appear in plays that have nothing to do with Spain—Iago being the most striking example. Fletcher, Middleton, Rowley, Massinger and Shirley all clearly drew directly or indirectly from Spanish sources. With Samuel Tuke's *Adventures of Five Hours* (written in 1662) so much admired by Pepys, and George Digby's *Elvira, or The Worst Not always True* (printed in 1667), we reach unquestionable examples of the immediate adaptation of Spanish dramas to the English stage. Both these comedies are favourable specimens of the popular "cape and sword" drama invented by Lope de Vega. George Digby, Earl of Bristol, had been ambassador of James I at Madrid, where he translated other comedies of Calderon besides the original of his *Elvira*. Sir Thomas St Serfe's *Taruzo's Wiles, or the Coffee House*, Orrery's *Guzman* and Mrs Behn's *Dutch Lover* and *The Rover* are other popular plays that came, in some way, from Spain. Crowne's *Sir Courtly Nice* and part at least of Wycherley's comedy *The Gentleman Dancing-Master* can be assigned to Spanish originals. Very often, Spanish stories filtered into England through the drama of France. Steele's *Lying Lover*, *The Perplexed Lover* of Mrs Centlivre and Colley Cibber's *She Would and She Would Not* are later plays derived from Spanish sources. The matter may be summed up thus: the pro-Spanish fashion instituted by James I coincided with the most extraordinary period of fertility in Spanish drama. There was considerable friendly intercourse, and there were many plays identifiably adapted from Spanish sources. To refuse to acknowledge any further Spanish borrowings because printed originals cannot be cited is to take a merely legal view of evidence.

Spanish adaptations were gradually superseded by borrowings from the writers who made brilliant the reign of Louis XIV. Many of the expatriated Royalists had lived in France and were familiar with the current plays and novels. As we have pointed out, it was the less important writers who were most popular. The greatest, Corneille and Racine, did not affect English plays, though people talked about their observance of the "unities" or the "rules". The one French writer of the first rank who directly affected English dramatists was Molière, whose earlier work corresponds, in point of time, with the latest years of royal exile. No one foreign author has been so plundered by English playwrights as Molière; and his humane spirit fortunately recalled them from the intricacies of Spanish intrigue and the wearisome repetition at second hand of the "humours" of Ben Jonson. That the finer qualities of Molière escaped his English imitators is obvious and even natural. It is always easier to imitate manner than genius. Molière supplied scenes, personages or suggestions to D'Avenant's *Playhouse to be Let*, Dryden's *An Evening Love*, *Amphitryon* and *Sir Martin Mar-all*, to Sedley's *Mulberry Garden*, Wycherley's *Country Wife* and *The Plain Dealer*, Shadwell's *Sullen Lovers* and *The Miser*, and Crowne's *The Country Wit* and *The English Friar*.

Before French adaptations became generally popular in Restoration times, a new dramatist, schooled in France, gave expression to the spirit of the age in the kind of plays that came to be called "the comedy of manners"—exhibitions of artificial social life with occasional glimpses of real feeling. Little is known of Sir George Etherege (1634?–91). His first play, *The Comical Revenge, or Love in a Tub* (1664), was partly serious, and is written in prose and rhymed couplets; but his next, *She wou'd if She Cou'd* (1668), is a prose comedy and a better work. The indolent author waited till 1676 before producing his last and best comedy, *The Man of Mode, or Sir Fopling Flutter*. Etherege held diplomatic posts in various parts of Europe. His correspondence, which included letters to and from Dryden, is full of life and gay gossip. Whether he was the first of his contemporaries to use rhymed couplets in a play is one of those useless questions that need no discussion. He was one of the first. Either by natural inclination or by the example of Molière, Etherege was moved to give his hearers the "comedy of manners" instead of the "comedy of humours" associated with Jonson and his imitators, and his plays have the air of light improvisations which must have given the sixteen-sixties the kind of unexpected pleasure that Oscar Wilde gave the eighteen-nineties. The dialogue of Etherege is almost uniformly witty and is seldom overdone and unsuited to his personages. He is not too brilliant for life.

The closest immediate follower of Etherege in comedy is Sir Charles Sedley (c. 1639–1701), whose earliest comedy *The Mulberry Garden* (1668) is written in Etherege's mixture of prose and heroic couplets. Sedley gained a deserved reputation alike for the clearness and ease of his prose and for a light lyrical gift, seen at its best in the famous "Not, Celia, that I juster am" and in the hardly less excellent "Ah, Chloris! that I now could sit". *The Mulberry Garden* is bettered in *Bellamira, or the Mistress* (1687), founded on the *Eunuchus* of Terence, and presenting a lively, if coarsely realistic, picture of contemporary pleasure-seeking. *The Grumbler* (1702) is a mere adaptation from the French. Sedley's tragedies call for no comment. John Lacy's *The Old Troop* (c. 1665), *Sawny the Scot* (c. 1667), *The Dumb Lady* (c. 1669), butchered from Molière, and *Sir Hercules Buffoon* (1684) are merely an actor's plays. Edward Ravenscroft pillaged Molière and other writers for his numerous pieces, one of which, *London Cuckolds* (1682), was acted annually on Lord Mayor's day for a century.

It is curious that the first woman to write professionally for the English stage began her career when the morality of English drama was at its lowest. Aphra or Aphara Johnson (1640–89) married a Dutch merchant named Behn. Mrs Behn's novels do not concern us here. Between 1671 and 1689 she wrote fifteen plays. Like her contemporaries she borrowed much, but she is genuinely inventive, and keeps both action and dialogue in easy motion. Her most popular play was *The Rover, or The Banished Cavaliers* (1677, second part 1681). *The Dutch Lover* (1673) is a favourable specimen of cloak and sword comedy. Other plays deal with contemporary town life, most of them lifted bodily from earlier English plays. For example, *The Debauchee* (1677) is based on *A Mad Couple well matched* by Richard Brome, *The Town Fop*, of the same date, on George Wilkins's *Miseries of Enforced Marriage*, and *The City Heiress* (1682) on Middleton's *A Mad World, My Masters*. In *The Roundheads* (1682) she simply took over the plot of Tatham's *The Rump*. It is idle to pretend that Aphra Behn's plays have great merit. What they have is the kind of movement that succeeds in the theatre.

William Wycherley (1640–1716) got his early dramatic experience in France, where he was educated. Though he lived long enough to be friendly with Pope, nearly fifty years his junior, his literary activity covers a very short period, for his first play, *Love in a Wood, or St James's Park*, appeared in 1671, and his last, *The Plain Dealer*, in 1676. Between these come *The Gentleman Dancing-Master* (1672) and *The Country Wife* (1675). *The Gentleman Dancing-Master* apparently did not succeed, although it is a diverting comedy, with a story borrowed from Spain. *The Country Wife* was misjudged in Victorian times because of its dramatic device of supposed male impotence. In Wycherley's hands it produces no frivolous entertainment, but something more resembling a savage exposure of folly and shams. But not until we reach *The Plain Dealer*, Wycherley's last and best comedy, borrowed from *Le Misanthrope*, do we recognize that this blasphemer in the halls of beauty is, after all, at heart a moralist, indignantly flagellating vice as well as laughing cynically at its excesses.

VI. THE RESTORATION DRAMA

2. *Congreve, Vanbrugh, Farquhar, etc.*

William Congreve (1670–1729) was born near Leeds, but, owing to a change in his father's military command, was educated with Swift at Kilkenny School and at Trinity College, Dublin. He deserted law for literature, composed a story called *Incognita, or Love and Duty Reconciled* (interesting solely because it is his), and then, in 1693, came upon the town with *The Old Bachelor*. Dryden, now in the plenitude of his power, generously hailed the rising star. The play is bright and easy, but confused in action. At no time of his life did Congreve learn how to tell a story on the stage.

In the same year (1693), *The Double Dealer* was played at Drury Lane. In character, style and construction it is above its predecessor; but the machinery of the play is still conventional. Maskwell is the familiar villain of melodrama, and a kind of ancestor of Sheridan's Joseph Surface. *Love for Love* (1695) was performed at the new theatre in Lincoln's Inn Fields. Its plot is the most intelligible that Congreve devised, the dialogue has brilliance, and the characters convince. Judged by the highest standard of comedy, *Love for Love* fails because it does not remain true to its own life throughout; but it certainly has a kind of life. In 1697 Congreve gave his players, not another comedy, but *The Mourning Bride*, a rash experiment in the later Elizabethan drama. To a modern ear *The Mourning Bride* is fustian; but the taste of the time hailed it as a masterpiece, and it held the stage for many years. We may note that it opens with the familiar line: "Music hath charms to soothe a savage breast", and that its third act concludes on a famous tag, the sense of which is borrowed from Cibber:

> Heaven has no rage, like love to hatred turned,
> Nor hell a fury, like a woman scorned.

Three years later, in 1700, Congreve's masterpiece, *The Way of the World*, was played at the theatre in Lincoln's Inn Fields. That it was a failure on the stage is not remarkable, for it is still a failure on the stage. That Millamant sails triumphantly into our hearts and that the dialogue is written with dazzling brilliance cannot hide the harsh facts that the story (if it can be called a story) is unintelligible and that the action (if there can be said to be any action) is feeble. But, failure though it is, *The Way of the World* touches a height that Congreve nowhere else attained. Some of it is comedy perfectly brilliant; some of it is near to tragedy almost poignant. It shows possibilities of dramatic excellence that Congreve, with his indolence, failed properly to exploit.

It would be difficult to find a more obvious contrast to Congreve than Sir John Vanbrugh (1664–1726). In the sense that Congreve was a man of letters Vanbrugh was not a man of letters at all. He was a man of a bluff temper and vigorous understanding, who easily communicated to his works the energy and humour of his mind. His grandfather came from Ghent and, like others of foreign descent, Vanbrugh became more English than the English. In 1697 he produced *The Relapse, or Virtue in Danger*, and instantly established his reputation. This broad and lively farce owed its inspiration to Cibber's *Love's Last Shift*, and it exists for the display of Lord Foppington, Sir Tunbelly Clumsey and Miss Hoyden, three caricatures of the kind that delighted the author. *The Provok'd Wife*, produced in 1697, is in all respects a better play. Sir John Brute is Vanbrugh's masterpiece. He stands out in relief by the side of Lady Brute and Belinda, who are far nearer to common life than are the fine ladies of Congreve. Sir John Brute was long a commonplace of fiction, and made a last notable appearance as Sir Pitt Crawley in *Vanity Fair*. Still more vivid as a painting of life is the fragment, *A Journey to London*, left unfinished at Vanbrugh's death. Like many of his contemporaries, Vanbrugh did a great deal of adaptation from obvious foreign sources. None of his versions is memorable, save *The Confederacy* (1705). Among its characters, Dick Amlet and Brass are of the true breed. The last years of Vanbrugh's life were devoted to architecture: he designed Blenheim Palace and his own Haymarket Theatre and jointly with Nicholas Hawksmoor—author of a *Short Historical Account of London Bridge* (1736)—the Clarendon Building at Oxford.

Three years after *Love for Love*, and one year after *The Relapse* and *The Provok'd Wife*, an attack was delivered on the theatre in *A Short View of the Immorality and Profaneness of the English Stage* (1698) by Jeremy Collier, a non-juring clergyman, who specially arraigned both Congreve and Vanbrugh. That Collier had a case is quite undeniable, but it is just as certain that he ruined it through sheer excess. The radical fallacy of all such attacks is that the censor arraigns a whole activity upon the evidence of a few chosen instances. To assert that *The Country Wife* is not nice does not prove that *Twelfth Night* is nasty. Further, Collier was incapable of distinguishing between fact and representation. He assumed that the poet who successfully depicted rascals was the advocate of rascality. There can be no doubt, however, that Collier's attack aroused much public sympathy. Everybody knew that the stage was immoral and profane, whatever else it may have been. After a time the stage-authors began to write in their own defence. More wisely guided, they would have held their tongues. Neither Congreve nor Vanbrugh emerged with credit from the encounter. They evaded the main issue and were as confused as Collier himself. D'Urfey rushed into the field with a preface to *The Campaigners* (1698) and skirmished like a light horseman. With far greater solemnity did John Dennis, who himself was not attacked by Collier, defend the *Usefulness of the Stage, to the Happiness of Mankind, to Government, and to Religion* (1698). Collier replied with superfluous violence, and the war of pamphlet and prologue lasted a long time. We need not follow its course here. The stage was in need of reformation, and it was reformed. Vice was less often presented as a virtue, and infidelity for infidelity's sake ceased to be dramatically proclaimed as the chief end of man. Collier's real object was to abolish the stage, not to reform it, and he should have begun, not ended, with his *Dissuasive from the Play-House* (1703). To be deluded by dislike for Collier's fanaticism into asserting that when reformation gradually came it owed nothing to Collier, but arose from a change in the manners of the people, is to be the victim of mere text-book criticism. Collier was one of the causes as well as one of the symptoms of that change.

George Farquhar (1678–1707) who, being an Irishman, had naturally joined in the fight, appeared too late to feel the parson's whip. He began his career as Congreve was closing his, and put life, as he knew it, into his comedies without pretence of restraint. Ireland, the recruiting officer, the disbanded soldier, love, the bottle, and the road—these he handled with the freedom and joyousness of one who knew them well. Farquhar borrowed with impunity; he used the most exhausted devices; he left his dialogue unpolished; and he dismissed criticism with the remark that "the rules of English comedy don't lie in the compass of Aristotle or his followers, but in the Pit, Box, and Galleries". Farquhar was right; and in his own practice he showed that the one thing needful is genuine vivacity. He came to London in 1698, with *Love and a Bottle* in his pocket, and made an instant conquest of the theatre. A year later followed *The Constant Couple, or a Trip to the Jubilee*, which showed a clear advance in workmanship. Thereafter came two failures, and then, in 1705, a piece of good fortune sent Farquhar on military duty to Shrewsbury; and he brought back with him a comedy, *The Recruiting Officer*, which he dedicated "to all friends round the Wrekin". In this he takes the comedy of manners perceptibly nearer the novel. A year later was played *The Beaux Stratagem*, the masterpiece of its author. Full of the gaiety and bustle of the road, it depicts the life of taverns and the highway and moves in an atmosphere of boisterous merriment. A sense of undefeated spirit is communicated by all Farquhar's plays and accounts for their lasting interest.

The lesser lights of the Restoration stage need the barest indication. Thomas Shadwell (1642?–1692), Poet Laureate, popular in his own day, now lives in the immortal couplets of *MacFlecknoe*. But he was not so completely foolish as those couplets imply. He was a distant disciple of Ben Jonson and he had sense enough to borrow from Molière, who is the source of *The Sullen Lovers* (1668), *The Miser* (1672) and *Bury Fair* (1689). Shadwell offers quite early examples of the comedy of manners in *The Humorists* (1670) and *Epsom Wells* (1672). He had the wit to make Don Juan the hero of *The Libertine* (1676), and with *The Squire of Alsatia* (1688) he caught the taste of the town. Shadwell gives a faithful picture of his age, roughly rather than finely drawn, and, to that extent, more veracious. His work kept the stage for many years.

Thomas D'Urfey (1653–1723), a French Huguenot by descent and a denizen of Grub Street by profession, who turned his hand to any form of composition, left a vast number of boisterous farces and bombastic melodramas. His more serious plays, mere burlesques of tragedy, are in "Ercles' vein". *The Siege of Memphis* (1676) and *The Famous History of the Rise and Fall of Massaniello* (1700) can scarcely be matched, for sheer fustian, in English literature. The plays which he dignifies by the name of comedy are mere farces. There is no trick of the time which he does not employ. *Madam Fickle* (1676) his first play and *The Fool Turn'd Critic* which followed in the same year are nothing but collections of situations from earlier plays. Many years later, in 1709, "sing-song D'Urfey" astonished the town with a play of a wholly new pattern. It was called *The*

Modern Prophets, and was described by Steele as "a most unanswerable satire against the late spirit of enthusiasm" (i.e. fanaticism). Save in the writing of songs, D'Urfey was a man of very slender talent; but his later works mark the beginnings of the sentimental comedy which was to displace the artificial comedy.

Colley Cibber (1671–1757) was a born man of the theatre. His plays were no more than scenarios for the display of his company's talents. His best-known piece, *Love's Last Shift* (1696) is, as far as we know, the first. He adapted as freely as he wrote, and improved Shakespeare as cheerfully as he improved Mrs Centlivre. His version of *Richard III* lasted well into the nineteenth century. But Colley Cibber has one claim upon our regard, which all his journey-work would not merit. He left us in *An Apology for the Life of Mr Colley Cibber, Comedian* (1740) a record that shows no trace of envy, malice or any uncharitableness. It is delightful, simple and sincere, and the finest and most appealing portrait he has drawn is his own. Cibber's laureate odes, sunk in the waters of oblivion, no longer trouble us. We may even forget the manufacturer of mechanical plays. The kindly and shrewd historian of the theatre will still be entitled to our gratitude, though the bays sit oddly on his brow.

VII. THE RESTORATION DRAMA

3. The Tragic Poets

Compared with Dryden, the contemporary writers of heroic and tragic plays are scarcely worth consideration. The relaxed morals of the post-Puritan period found comedy more agreeable than tragedy. People wanted to be "amused", and took their amusements lightly. Repetitions of stock themes could not distress those who had forgotten today what they had seen yesterday. Such tragedy as the Restoration stage produced has no qualities of permanence. In the time of D'Avenant tragedy tended to become operatic, without the advantage of dramatic music; in the time of Dryden tragedy tended to become heroic, without the advantage of French restraint. The influence of the French stage upon the English has always been very slight. Shakespeare, in spite of all mis-understanding and opposition, has been far more popular in France than Racine has ever been in England. Of the major French dramatists the first to be known in England was Pierre Corneille, for a version of *Le Cid* by Joseph Rutter was played before King Charles and Henrietta Maria as early as 1637. Shortly after the Restoration, Corneille found a worthy translator in Katherine Philips, "the Matchless Orinda", whose version of *Pompée*, in rhymed verse, was produced in London in 1663. *Heraclius* translated by Lodowick Carlell was played in 1664. In 1671 John Dancer's translation of *Nicomède* was acted at the Theatre Royal in Dublin. Other translations were published but, apparently, not acted. While Corneille thus became known and appreciated, his great contemporary Racine had to wait for recognition till the next century. The industrious Crowne put forth, in 1675, an utterly inadequate version of *Andromaque*, and Otway came out with *Titus and Berenice* (1677), which had almost no success. A similar fate befell two other versions of plays by Racine—*Achilles, or Iphigenia in Aulis*

(1700) by Abel Boyer the historian, and *Phaedra and Hippolitus* (1706) by Edmund Smith the poet. Public taste, no doubt, was being educated, for in 1712 *The Distrest Mother*, Ambrose Philips's skilful adaptation of *Andromaque*, met with immediate and lasting popularity. But English writing was very little influenced by the French style, though there were many defenders of its "rules". French plays were plundered, not imitated.

After Dryden, the foremost place among the tragic writers of the Restoration age is held by Thomas Otway (1652–85). His first play, *Alcibiades* (1675), a tragedy in rhymed verse, is a dreary and stilted piece. In his next play, *Don Carlos* (1676), Otway was more happy. The scenes are handled with vigour, and the play was effective and popular. The largely fictitious romance *Don Carlos* by the Abbé de Saint-Réal was the source both of Otway's and of Schiller's play, but there is no evidence that one suggested the other. Two capable versions of French plays followed (1677)—*Titus and Berenice* from Racine's *Bérénice* and *The Cheats of Scapin* from Molière's *Fourberies de Scapin*. Otway's loose comedy *Friendship in Fashion* (1678) showed no aptitude for that form of composition. In 1680, however, appeared *The Orphan*, a tragedy in blank verse, one of the two plays upon which the fame of Otway rests. The other, *Venice Preserv'd, or a Plot Discover'd*, a tragedy in blank verse, was first acted in 1682. Though the story of the play is taken from another semi-historical narrative by the Abbé de Saint-Réal, the finest character, Belvidera, is a creation of Otway himself. *The Orphan* is lachrymose rather than tragic; *Venice Preserv'd* is in the grand manner of tragedy and its major characters held their place in the repertory of great players well into the nineteenth century. In magnitude of emotion and eloquence of speech *Venice Preserv'd* is worthy to rank with all but a few of the masterpieces of the Jacobean age.

Nathaniel Lee (1653?–92) produced between 1675 and 1681 eight tragedies and a tragi-comedy, all with quasi-historical settings. His first plays, which hardly call for mention, are mostly in rhymed verse; but in 1677 Lee produced the blank-verse play entitled *The Rival Queens, or The Death of Alexander the Great*, which proved an immediate and lasting success. From it comes the oft-misquoted line "When Greeks joined Greeks, then was the tug of war". *Mithridates, King of Pontus*, another blank-verse play, followed in 1678; and in 1679 Dryden and Lee co-operated in the composition of *Oedipus, King of Thebes*. *Theodosius, or the Force of Love*, one of Lee's most successful plays, was produced in 1680. In 1682 Dryden and Lee again joined hands in *The Duke of Guise*. Lee ended as a drunkard and madman. None of the finer qualities are to be found in him; but his plays were not meant to be read; they were plays for the kind of theatre that preserved the old rhetorical tradition.

Of John Crowne (fl. 1680) very little is known, or need be known. Merely to recite the names of his dull tragedies would consume more space than he deserves. His first comedy *The Country Wit* (1675) is an outline of his later and better plays. After making versions of Shakespeare's *Henry VI* he returned to comedy in *City Politics* (1683), and *Sir Courtly Nice, or It cannot be* (1685). The latter is by far the best of Crowne's plays, and has in it something of the true spirit of comedy. His last two comedies are *The English Friar* (1690) and *The Married Beau* (1694), both borrowed from foreign sources. Crowne's tragedies have all Lee's turgidity, with none of that author's redeeming picturesqueness.

Thomas Southerne or Southern (1660–1746) wrote numerous unimportant comedies which need not be named. It was not until 1694 that, in *The Fatal Marriage, or the Innocent Adultery*, he achieved a play of any value. Southerne's other great success, *Oroonoko, or the Royal Slave* (1696), is, like its predecessor, a mixture of blank verse and prose: it was based upon the novel of the same title (*c.* 1678) by Aphra Behn. His later plays are not important. Only in *The Fatal Marriage* and *Oroonoko* does Southerne attain to any power; and his success was of the kind that makes those plays the first steps towards popular melodrama.

Elkanah Settle (1648–1724), like Shadwell, lives in the superb couplets of Dryden, who depicted the pair as Doeg and Og in *Absalom and Achitophel*. And just as a single couplet of *MacFlecknoe* has immortalized Shadwell, so a single couplet of *The Dunciad* has consigned to eternal damnation the activity of Settle as City poet and laureate of the Lord Mayor's Show. Settle began his career as a dramatist with the dull and foolish tragedy *Cambyses, King of Persia* (1666). This was followed by *The Empress of Morocco* (1673), which was almost as bad, but which was so successful that Settle felt himself at least the equal of Dryden and behaved accordingly. He had his reward. From that time until 1718 he produced numerous bombastic tragedies of the poorest sort. At the time of the Popish Plot he became notorious for his rapid changes of opinion. To this period belongs his disgraceful play *The Female Prelate* (1680), on the subject of Pope Joan. But pliability could not save him, and he sank to writing and acting "drolls" for Bartholomew Fair. His opera *The Fairy Queen*, adapted from *A Midsummer Night's Dream*, deserves mention solely because the music was provided by Purcell.

A few other dramatists of the time must be briefly named. John Dennis (1657–1734), author of *Three Letters on the Genius and Writings of Shakespeare* (1711), was a critic of some power, but justified Pope's ridicule of him by his plays, which were uniformly unsuccessful. John Hughes (1677–1720) belongs, in point of time, to the next period, but his manner is emphatically that of the Restoration. Besides the operas *Calypso and Telemachus* (1712) and *Apollo and Daphne* (1716), he wrote *The Siege of Damascus* (1720). Hughes exhibits some power. George Granville, Lord Lansdowne (1667–1735) wrote an adaptation, *The Merchant of Venice* (1696), a comedy, *The She Gallants* (1696), a tragedy, *Heroick Love* (1698), and an opera, *The British Enchantress* (1706). None has any value. Mrs Aphra Behn, whose comedies have already been mentioned, wrote several uninteresting tragedies; and Mrs Mary Manley, who achieved an unenviable reputation as a novelist, likewise produced several lurid tragedies, of which the first, *The Royal Mischief*, appeared in 1696. Thomas Rymer (1641–1713), whose criticism of Shakespeare in *The Tragedies of the Last Age* (1678) achieves the depths of ineptitude, published in 1678 one of the last specimens of rhymed tragedy, *Edgar, or the English Monarch*, which, strictly observing the classic rules the want of which he denounced in Shakespeare, is both unreadable and unactable.

One notable and indeed honourable name closes the story of Restoration drama. Nicholas Rowe (1674–1718) holds a unique position as a link between the late Restoration dramatists and those of the Augustan age. His first play, *The Ambitious Step-Mother* (1700) and his second, *Tamerlane* (1702) are ineffective; but his next piece, *The Fair Penitent* (1703), proved one of the most popular plays of its time. It takes its plot from Massinger and Field's *The Fatal Dowry* (1632), and its "haughty, gallant, gay Lothario" has become a familiar synonym for a heartless libertine, and was the model for Lovelace in Richardson's *Clarissa Harlowe*. *The Tragedy of Jane Shore* "in imitation of Shakespeare's style" was produced in 1714 and gave Mrs Siddons later one of her great parts. *The Tragedy of the Lady Jane Grey* (1715) may be taken as evidence of the beneficent change that had come over the English stage since the Revolution of 1688 and the publication of Jeremy Collier's *Short View*. Rowe, who appealed for the tears of his audience, made a special line in distressful heroines: women, rather than men, are at the heart of his tragedies. Only *The Fair Penitent* can be said to survive. But Rowe has a greater claim on our respect. He was the first editor of Shakespeare (see p. 234); and though his work was inevitably faulty, it was honourably done, and it set the pattern which all succeeding editors have followed.

VIII. THE COURT POETS

The court poets of the Restoration concern the historian of manners as well as the historian of literature, for they were the voice of a revolt against Puritanism. Charles himself was intelligent and liked people who amused him. His courtiers flourished therefore both by their wits and by their wit. They were the foes of everything serious, though some of them, like Sir Charles Sedley (p. 351), wrote tender love lyrics that remind us of Wyatt and the Elizabethans.

John Wilmot, Earl of Rochester (1647–80), the one man of genius among them, gained an easy ascendancy over the Court and assumed all the freedoms of a chartered libertine. He quarrelled with Mulgrave, but extricated himself from the inevitable duel in a way that brought him much discredit. At first friendly with Dryden, he was piqued by the greater man's complacency in success, and set up Crowne as a rival dramatist. Mulgrave's anonymous *Essay on Satire* (1679), which Rochester believed, or pretended to believe was Dryden's, gave him an occasion of offence which he hastened to use; and Dryden, then a sickly and elderly man, was waylaid and cudgelled one night by a pack of ruffians hired by the Earl. Rochester died at thirty-three, as complete an example of ill-used talent as the history of literature affords. He was a born poet, with a slender gift for lyric and a stronger gift for satire, shown specially in *A Satyr against Mankind* (1679). But some of Rochester's pieces are only second-rate. His lines *To Sir Car Scrope*, who had charged him with cowardice, are very fierce, but their subject cruelly told him in reply that his pen was as harmless as his sword. His *Trial of the Poets for the Bays* and his *Epistolary Letter to Lord Mulgrave* do not live in the same world as the satires of Dryden, or Pope, or Marvell. His tragedy *Valentinian* was adapted from Fletcher. Rochester's works were not completely collected till John Hayward's edition of 1926; his Life was written in 1934 by Vivian de Sola Pinto, author also of a notable study of Sedley.

The reputation of Charles Sackville, Lord Buckhurst and then Earl of Dorset (1638–1706), is a puzzle of literary history. An age lavish of panegyric exhausted in his praise all its powers of flattery. Yet when we turn from the encomiasts to the poet's own works, we find them to be no more than what Johnson called them, "the effusions of a man of wit". No poem of his really survives except the celebrated song *To all you Ladies now on Land*, and his authorship of even that is disputed. There is nothing more to say about a poetical reputation as lightly earned as any we know.

John Sheffield (1684–1721), Earl of Mulgrave, later Marquis of Normanby and Duke of Buckingham, was neither an amiable person nor a tolerable poet. Those who wish to study the "art of sinking" in couplets can be recommended to his most important poem, *An Essay on Poetry*, for that purpose, but for no other. His *Essay on Satire*, which cost Dryden an encounter with Rochester's hirelings, has the accent of the scold in every line. Sheffield's poetical flight and political career were equally low.

Wentworth Dillon, Earl of Roscommon (1633–85), nephew of the great Strafford, meddled in the affairs of court as little as he practised its vices. He was an honest man and perhaps something of a prig. A friend of Dryden, he engaged that great man's sympathy for his favourite project, the founding of a British Academy which should "refine and fix the standard of our language". His *Essay on Translated Verse* is just such a poetic exercise as might have been read before such a body. Nevertheless, a reading of that poem will disclose the unexpected source of many familiar quotations. Horace was Roscommon's master, and the disciple's version of the *Art of Poetry* is attractively personal. Roscommon was among the first of his time to discover the greatness of Milton, and one of many who have tried to reproduce in English the plangent harmonies of *Dies Irae*.

We must beware of supposing that the fashionable court poets represent the whole spirit of Restoration England. Sound and serious work in art and science, as well as in literature, was done during a period too often dismissed as trivial. Purcell, Wren and Newton are as much a part of their age as Rochester, Mulgrave and Dorset. The legend of the Wicked Restoration Courtier should itself be modified in the light of such books as Pinto's and *The Court Wits of the Restoration* (1948) by J. H. Wilson.

IX. THE PROSODY OF THE SEVENTEENTH CENTURY

The first Elizabethan poets, disliking the popular doggerel of the early Tudor dramatists, sought to bring back order into verse by two curiously different methods. One was a training of their own lines to move in a steady iambic tramp "from short to long"; the other was an attempt to fix upon English syllables the measures of classical prosody. Harvey, Sidney and Spenser pursued the classical ideal in theory; Stanyhurst proved it impossible in practice. But the ancient hope dies hard; and quantitative English hexameters have been attempted even in the twentieth century, although the fact is obvious that the English ear, metrically keen, does not recognize "short and long", as such, in English, even when assisted by orthography. The English ear has a different kind of habituation. So the classical method of restoring order to verse failed; and modern English poetry began its march to glory with the tramping "left, right" of poulter's measure in *Tottel's Miscellany*. What is very odd is that while Tudor poetry seemed to have fettered itself with a two-foot movement, Tudor music had attained the chainless liberty of what we now call "free verse". Music, whether ecclesiastical or secular, was so plastic in movement that well-meaning editors ruined its flexibility by tying it up in the regular bars of the classical period. The later Elizabethan poets and their successors caught the lilt of music, and when musician and poet were combined in one person, as in Thomas Campion, the lyric was set at liberty.

Another great factor in the liberation of English verse was blank verse, especially the blank verse of drama. Alike in Surrey's *Aeneid* and in our first blank-verse tragedy, *Gorboduc*, the lines are undeviating in their tramp from short to long. But the authors of *Gorboduc* were not really dramatists. Real dramatic verse is a kind of music, not a kind of metrical prose. Not many more than thirty years lie between *Gorboduc* and *Romeo and Juliet*; yet it is already clear that such lines as Romeo's speech in the tomb cannot be forced into the unvarying pattern of *Gorboduc*; and the impossibility is clearer still when we come a little later to *Hamlet*. Nevertheless behind all the apparent freedom of the Shakespeare lines we discern the ghostly pattern of archetype, warning them not to venture too far. Some of Shakespeare's successors did venture too far, especially in their addition of redundant syllables, until their alleged blank verse became a kind of slovenly prose.

Lyrical poetry shows a steady advance because there was a steady advance in lyrical poets. Place side by side any blameless effusion from *Tottel's Miscellany* and such a song as *Take, O take those lips away*, or *Queen and Huntress, chaste and fair*, and the superiority of the later verse as verse is as clear as the superiority of the later poem as poem—so far as the two qualities can ever be separated. The Jacobean and Caroline lyrists kept their inventions at the height, whether they were as craggy as Donne or as easy as Suckling. Most of their Restoration successors were not simply inferior as technicians, they were inferior as poets.

The outstanding name in the prosody of the seventeenth century is that of Milton, who ranks in this respect with Chaucer, Spenser and Shakespeare. With one important development during his time, however, Milton had little to do, though the experiments of *Samson* show that he may have thought of it latterly. This was the employment of the anapaest—not in occasional substitution for the iamb, but as the principal base-foot of metre. Between the age of doggerel and the mid-seventeenth century it is rare in regular literature; but folk-song kept it; and in such pieces as *Mary Ambree*, which, perhaps, is as early as 1584, there is no mistake about it. Dryden, however, brought his great metrical skill to the support of trisyllabic measures in various songs and in portions of his odes. Prior, too, makes effective use of the anapaest.

The octosyllabic couplet magnificently used by Milton was humorously used by Butler in *Hudibras*, which naturally inspired other satirists to make it their vehicle. Butler's excellent versification usually receives less praise than it deserves, merely because its purpose is comic.

But the chief prosodical event of the seventeenth century was the resurgence and development of the decasyllabic couplet, as a fact, together with the inculcation of "smoothness and numbers" in verse, as a doctrine. The couplet in itself was no new thing. It had been practised magnificently by Chaucer, exquisitely by Spenser, charmingly by Marlowe and efficiently by Drayton. Now, like blank verse, the couplet can be used in two ways: it can be "stopped" or it can be "run on". The most familiar example of the free or run-on couplet is the opening of Keats's *Endymion*, in which the rhymes do not tie down the sentence-endings. The end-stopped couplet can be illustrated from any lines in Pope—say, the conclusion of *The Dunciad*. Metrically the two forms are identical; psychologically they are quite dissimilar. It is impossible to write the same kind of poem in either form. The crucial point, of course, is the rhyme. Rhyme is a natural end-stop; if the sentence passes over the rhyme (it is argued), why rhyme at all? As late as the first foolish reviews of Keats that objection was urged. The reader who has been puzzled to know why a minor poet like Edmund Waller, coming after Spenser and Shakespeare, and contemporary with Milton, was hailed as the "reformer of our numbers" will now perhaps see a gleam of light. Blank verse, run on, or sagging with redundant syllables, and couplets, run on, and disregarding the recurrent snap of rhyme, began to wear a slovenly look. Waller, tightening and tidying up verse into neat, trim, lucid couplets, with syllables that could be numbered off, appeared to give our poetry "sweetness, numbers and smoothness", although, actually, his later and better verse tended to "run on", and none of it is remarkable for easy movement.

It was a greater poet than Waller who used the couplet with such emphatic mastery that it dominated English verse up to the date of Wordsworth's first published poems. Dryden exploited all its forms and possibilities in compositions of all kinds from his worst plays to his best poems. His couplet is not, like Pope's, "bred in and in" and severely trained and exercised; it is full-blooded, exuberant, multiform, showing, sometimes, almost the rush of the anapaest, and sometimes almost the mass of the blank verse paragraph. But you can never mistake the five-spaced distribution of the line.

Another region of verse in which Dryden exhibited his mastery was the irregular ode. More or less irregular strophes had been successfully achieved by Spenser; and Ben Jonson (at the other extreme) had attempted pieces which exhibited the strictly regular correspondence in the lines of strophe and antistrophe, and the regular division of strophe, antistrophe and epode. But poets like Cowley had fastened the austerely regular name of "Pindaric" upon so-called "odes" which were without form and void. In later times the irregular ode produced some magnificent poetry, but most of those who practised it between 1650 and 1750 produced nothing but formless bombast.

X. MEMOIR AND LETTER WRITERS

1. Evelyn and Pepys

Diaries as a form of expression suited to certain natures have been common in many ages, and they have been used normally as the material for reminiscences, autobiographies and biographies. Few have been printed in full; and of these few the greatest are the diaries of John Evelyn and Samuel Pepys, the first a personal record of events and the second a personal self-revelation of the frankest kind. It is one of the curiosities of literature that neither of these famous works came into general knowledge until the nineteenth century. The Evelyn discovery was almost accidental. William Upcott (1779–1845), the literary antiquary, employed by Lady Evelyn to inspect the manuscripts at Wotton House near Dorking, was particularly attracted by the two volumes of a diary, found, it is said, in a basket of clothes. He advised publication, and secured the help of William Bray (1736–1832) as editor. The work was published in 1818 and received by the public with great satisfaction. It has continued to be reprinted as a standard work in a large number of different forms. One diary led to the other. The volumes of Evelyn contained several references to Samuel Pepys, and these drew attention to the six mysterious manuscript volumes, written in shorthand, preserved in the Pepysian Library at Magdalene College, Cambridge. An undergraduate, John Smith, undertook to decipher them, although the celebrated stenographer W. B. Gurney told him they were indecipherable. Smith worked for nearly three years, usually for twelve or fourteen hours a day, and completed his task. John Smith is one of the unrecognized heroes of English literature, for the first edition is always called by the name of Lord Braybrooke, the editor of the two volumes of selections published in 1815.

Evelyn and Pepys were lifelong friends, and they had many business relations in connection with the Navy which were carried on in a spirit of mutual esteem. Evelyn belonged to the class of "men of quality", and was a frequenter of courts, while Pepys, who was very much the "poor relation", had to make his own way in the world by his tenacity of purpose and great abilities. The two diaries differ widely both in character and extent. Evelyn's work covers a very great part of his life; Pepys's, though of greater length, occupies little more than nine years of a busy career.

John Evelyn (1620–1706) was an English gentleman of the best kind. He was a whole-hearted Royalist, but greatly disliked the idea of Civil War. He travelled abroad and tells us just the things we want to know. His first book, *Liberty and Servitude*, translated from the French, was published in 1649, and later in that fatal year he again left England and did not return till 1652, when the Royalist cause seemed lost and the Commonwealth firmly established. He was in regular correspondence with Charles II. In 1660 (the year in which the diary of Pepys begins) Evelyn became a Fellow of the newly founded Royal Society, to which Pepys was elected in 1664. He was distressed by the smoke of London and wrote *Fumifugium* (1661) proposing remedies, in which (as usual) the government was deeply interested without actually arriving at the point of doing anything. Also in 1661 he wrote *Tyrannus, or the Mode* urging the use of an English dress instead of foreign fashions. Pepys and Evelyn again join hands in an odd fashion about the Navy. "Heart of oak are our ships", says the song; but if there are no trees, there can be no ships. The Navy Office referred the matter to the Royal Society, and the Royal Society referred it to Evelyn. Thus originated that noble book *Sylva* (1664), which revived the spirit of planting in England. Like Pepys, Evelyn stuck to his duties during the Plague year. At the time of the Great Fire of London, he was ready with help; and, like

Christopher Wren and Robert Hooke, he prepared a plan of considerable merit for the improved building of London. To the two great diaries we owe many vivid pictures of this great calamity. Evelyn's *Life of Mrs Godolphin*, the young and beautiful friend whose death was a great blow to him, is one of the little gems of English biography. The tribute of his wife to his own excellence a is moving utterance.

Far different was the life of Samuel Pepys (1633–1703). Evelyn was a public figure more fully revealed by his diary. Pepys, save to the few who recalled a dim and forgotten donor of old books to his college library, was a completely unknown person. Strange paradox, that the most intimately known Englishman of the past should have lain unnoticed for over two centuries in the dust of an obscure grave in a remote City church! After the resurrection of the man came the rediscovery of the official, and the ingenuous, childish, fretful, and frivolous lover of wine, women and song proved to have been a conscientious administrator in an age of conscienceless venality, an inspired worker for the Navy, a stout patriot, and as wise a critic of men and affairs as of plays and music. (The third volume of Sir Arthur Bryant's *Samuel Pepys*, 1933–8, is aptly entitled *The Saviour of the Navy*.) In 1658 he became clerk (at a salary of £50) to George Downing (who gave his name to Downing Street). The diary opens on 1 January 1660. Through the influence of his kinsman, Sir Edward Montagu, Earl of Sandwich, Pepys obtained a minor secretaryship and was later appointed Clerk of the Privy Seal as well as Clerk of the Acts. He remained courageously at his post during the Plague and the Fire. He reformed the victualling and financial administration of the Navy, and, indeed, lacked nothing but high rank to make him a great figure in public life. Being merely a commoner of great administrative genius he was naturally relegated to obscurity. In January 1664, he suffered his first great calamity. Like another inconspicuous commoner, John Milton, he developed symptoms of blindness. He was compelled to abandon his beloved reading and writing, and bade farewell to his private world in May 1669, when he made the last affecting entry in his diary and closed the mysterious volumes which were not to be read again till the world of Clarendon and the Cabal had changed to the world of George IV and George Stephenson's first railway.

Pepys lived for thirty-two years after the closing of the diary, in which he never made another entry. He became Secretary to the Admiralty in 1673, and Master of Trinity House in 1676; but in 1678 he was one of the victims of the Popish Plot. The triumph of scoundrelism could not overlook so true a servant of the country. He was sent to the Tower; but the failure of carefully manu-factured evidence against him led to his release in 1680. He had lost his office and his living. He was, however, sent to Tangier in 1683, and wrote a diary which gives an interesting picture of the condition of the place and a vivid account of its maladministration. In 1684 he was reappointed to his Secretaryship and embarked again on a campaign of naval reform; but at the Revolution of 1689, the man who had spared no pains in his endeavour to place the country in a proper condition of national defence was sent by the new government to the Gatehouse in Westminster as an enemy to the State. He was released, and entered into a period of honourable retirement, during which he was considered and treated as "the Nestor of the Navy". He had already served in the House of Commons. He wrote his *Memoires of the Navy* (1690) and kept up his many activities, including experimental science. In 1700 he removed from London to what Evelyn calls his "Paradisian Clapham". Here he lived with his old clerk and friend, William Hewer, and died in the presence of the learned George Hickes, the non-juring Dean of Worcester. The last two Stuart kings were precisely £28,007. 2s. 1¼d. in his debt, but the new government of William and Mary did not feel that they were called to discharge a debt of honour incurred in the national service.

The popular "mystery" of Pepys's diary is not very mysterious—or at least it is no more mysterious than any other product of creative literary genius. For Pepys, without knowing it, was a creative artist. Any person can put himself into a book, and many writers do little else than expose in print their self-pity and self-admiration. What the true creative artist does is to "objectify" or "externalize" his experience, so that it becomes one (and probably the most important) of the phenomena that interest him as artist. He neither applauds nor condemns: he simply re-creates. Pepys the artist contemplated with interest the external creature called by his own name and set down his failings and his aspirations with Defoe-like veracity of detail. Pepys is the only writer of his kind known to history. There are many diarists, there is only one Pepys. For whom did Pepys write his diary? people fondly ask. The question is best answered by another: For whom did Rembrandt paint his self-portraits? For whom (taking a different instance) did Sir Thomas Browne write *Religio Medici*? The creative instinct compels creation; and a genuine artistic creation, though it has a personal origin, has a continued interest for others. But as Pepys told the truth about living people as well as about himself, he naturally wrote in a language that he believed nobody else could read. He himself is his own triumphant creation. So perfect is the picture that his very faults appeal to our affection.

2. Other Writers of Memoirs and Letters

The anonymous *Memoires de la Vie du Comte de Gramont*, published for the first time at Cologne in 1713, is universally acknowledged to be a masterpiece of French literature. Yet this book was written by an Englishman, and it deals chiefly with the English court of Charles II. The author was Anthony Hamilton (1646–1720), grandson of the Earl of Abercorn. Some of the earlier matter may have come from Gramont himself; but the later portion is quite different in treatment and bears definite signs of Hamilton's own authorship. Gramont died in 1707 and apparently had made no attempt to claim or to publish the book. There is no need to discuss its value as history; its value as literature is unquestionable, and it may be said to have created the prevailing view of Charles II's court. Its brief and vivid descriptions confirm the impressions left by Pepys. *The Memoirs of Sir John Reresby* (first published 1734) is the work of an accomplished man who united in himself the qualities of a courtier and those of a country squire. He tells us much about the villainies of the Popish Plot. Sir Richard Bulstrode (1630–1711) in his *Original Letters* (1712) and *Memoirs* (1721) is a first-hand authority for the long period covered by his life. Reresby and Bulstrode hover on the boundaries of literature, and occasionally cross the frontier.

Let us turn to some women of the time. Though the *Memoirs of Lady Fanshawe* remained unpublished in full till 1829–30, they challenge comparison with any memoirs of the age to which they belong. Anne Fanshawe's life covers the period between 1625 and 1680 and her story is fresh and fascinating. The *Letters of Rachel Lady Russell* (1683), the devoted widow, as she had been the faithful wife, of William Lord Russell, a noble victim of Charles II, virtually begin with the death of her husband on the scaffold in 1683. Her chief correspondents were divines, to whom she writes with serene and devout self-possession. Although small in bulk, the *Memoirs of Queen Mary II*, published in 1886, should not be overlooked, as she is a sovereign who has had less than her due from posterity. Her letters are unusually attractive.

The diaries of Pepys and Evelyn and the Gramont memoirs are established classics. The other works here named, though less generally known, deserve to be read for their own sake as well as for their historical interest.

XI. PLATONISTS AND LATITUDINARIANS

The interest of Anglican literature does not cease with the Caroline divines. Bishop Burnet declared, in effect, that the Church of England was saved, during the perilous times of the seventeenth century, by a "new set of men" who appeared in Cambridge. They are commonly called "the Cambridge Platonists", and they deserve more notice than we can here afford to give them.

Benjamin Whichcote (1606–83) gained through many years of preaching the esteem of widely differing believers, including Cromwell himself. He sought to counteract the fanatic canting of the Puritan extremists, especially the "enthusiasm" of that constant by-product of English liberty, the rabid sectary convinced of a call to promulgate some eccentricity of doctrine or conduct. Anthony Tuckney, a Puritan divine, charged Whichcote with the abominable crime of studying books other than the Scriptures—even the works of "PLATO and his schollars". Whichcote good-humouredly suggested that spiritual understanding might be advanced by the kind of reasoning that inspired the discoveries of Galileo and Harvey. It is characteristic of a modest and broad-minded thinker that he published nothing himself. His principal writings are to be found in *Select Sermons* (1698), *Several Discourses* (1701), and *Moral and Religious Aphorisms* (1703), containing in the enlarged edition of 1753 the correspondence with Tuckney.

Whichcote perhaps derived some of his "Platonic" doctrines from the *Commonplaces* (1641) of John Sherman (d. 1671), who quotes Plato's rule, "Not who, but what"—"Let us not so much consider who saith, but what is said." The title of his book *A Greek in the Temple* (1641) indicates that his appeal is from the Latin church to the Greek philosophers. It is possible to regard Sherman as the first inspirer of the Platonist group in Cambridge.

But the outstanding and most memorable name among the Platonists is that of Henry More (1614–87), who imbibed mysticism in youth from *The Faerie*

Queene. He entered Christ's College, Cambridge, almost as Milton left it, and there remained till his death, profoundly influencing numerous pupils. Unlike Whichcote and Cudworth, More wrote and published voluminously. In his *Psychozoia Platonica* (1642), reprinted (enlarged) in *Philosophical Poems* (1647) as *A Platonick Song of the Soul*, he confessed himself the disciple of Plato and Plotinus. This remarkable and often singularly beautiful poem, with its prose discussions, had an equally remarkable but inferior contemporary of the same order in *Psyche, or Love's Mystery* (1648) by Joseph Beaumont (1616–99), alleged to have been praised by Pope, in spite of its thirty thousand lines. Henry More wrote rapidly, producing numerous works of which only a few can be named here. In 1652 appeared *An Antidote against Atheism* and in 1656 *Enthusiasmus Triumphatus*, a searching exposure of Puritan "enthusiasm". *The Immortality of the Soul* (1659) takes over some of the prose-matter of the *Song of the Soul*. In 1660 came *An Explanation of the Grand Mystery of Godliness*, containing an attack on judicial astrology. *The Mystery of Iniquity* (1664) and *Divine Dialogues* (1668) aroused much interest by their gloomy prophetic tone. More's keen sense of the "something afar", which it was the duty of Christians to seek with the purity of spirit and the single-minded devotion of the great men of science, was a powerful "antidote to atheism" in the age of Hobbes. He gave to Anglican theology a mystical armour that enabled it to withstand the assaults of the Hobbesian materialists and the Puritan fanatics.

Contemporary with More at Christ's was the Master, Ralph Cudworth (1617–88), who was as laborious as More was facile. His profound *Treatise concerning Eternal and Immutable Morality* remained in manuscript, and was not published till 1731. *The True Intellectual System of the Universe* appeared in a faulty edition in 1678 and in a better form in 1743. But by that time the fashionable, sceptical Church-and-State world of Hanoverianism had no use for the ancient and abstruse speculations of the admirable Cudworth.

Almost at the time when More had passed from his Platonic poems to his first treatises and Cudworth was still wrestling with his unpublished manuscripts, two remarkable disciples of theirs rose and vanished with equal suddenness—Nathanael Culverwel (d. 1651) and John Smith (1618–52). Culverwel's *An Elegant and Learned Discourse of the Light of Nature* appeared in 1652, and Smith's *Select Discourses* in 1660. Smith, like More, was concerned to prove the immortality of the soul, but directed his argument mainly against classical sceptics like Lucretius, not against modern materialists like Hobbes. More is sometimes vague and even sometimes ridiculous; Smith is neither, and his work, though not large in bulk, is a striking contribution to the mystical thought of the day. Culverwel is, in some respects, the best of the Cambridge Platonists, for he strikes out memorable sentences that are still valid as essential truth. He defines his own purpose as "giving to reason the things that are reason's and unto faith the things that are faith's". "Revealed truths are never against reason, they will always be above reason." More and Cudworth do not seem to have welcomed warmly the latitudinarian views of Smith and Culverwel, tending as they did to exalt abstract truth at the expense of definite dogma.

The spirit of compromise between breadth and dogma is exemplified in Joseph Glanvill (see p. 328). In the main, he was in agreement with Cudworth and More, *Lux Orientalis* (1661) being chiefly a defence of the theory held by the latter as to the prior existence of souls. In *Sadducismus Triumphatus* (1681) Glanvill defends the belief in witchcraft; yet he admired the researches of the Royal Society, of which he was a Fellow.

Other eminent divines either held, or inclined to, the latitudinarian view, strongly presented by the Platonists, that there was spiritual truth beyond the limits imposed by sectarians of any kind. While "breadth" or latitudinarianism may promote a large and peaceable communion, it may (and some say it did) produce the flatness and apathy which were charged against the English Church in the next century. Dogma may lack breadth; it does not lack direction, and it gets somewhere.

XII. DIVINES OF THE CHURCH OF ENGLAND

For a time the loyalist pulpit at the Restoration matched in extravagance of utterance some of the Puritan "enthusiasm". It gradually lowered its tone and tamed its style, but it showed no signs of creative genius. Herbert Thorndike (1598–1672), for example, is interesting as a complete Catholic Anglican, advocating confession, reservation, and prayers for the dead; but his importance is not literary. John Cosin (1594–1627) was, like Thorndike, a liturgiologist, but is best known by *A Collection of Private Devotions* (1627).

A greater writer than any of these, Isaac Barrow (1630–77), died at forty-seven, but left a mark of originality upon the theology of his age. He knew the Europe of his time and he was the first theologian to use the prose manner that we call Addisonian. His posthumous treatise *On the Pope's Supremacy* was remarkable for its breadth of view. Barrow's influence upon theology and the-ological prose was entirely beneficent. He can be profitably studied in *Sermons preached upon several occasions* (1678). Barrow's *Exposition of the Creed, Decalogue and Sacraments* did not displace the work, on different lines, of his older contem-porary, Bishop John Pearson (1613–86), a notable preacher and an accurate patristic scholar. Pearson's *Exposition of the Creed* (1659) long remained the standard treatise on its subject.

Two eminent Scotsmen next attract our attention. Robert Leighton (1611–84), who became Archbishop of Glasgow, is honourably distinguished as an advocate of toleration. His prose is simple and dignified, and his writing abounds in aphorisms. To Coleridge, Leighton had the true note of inspiration—of "something more than human". None of his work was published in his life-time. A collection of sermons appeared in 1692. With Leighton may be coupled his countryman Gilbert Burnet (1643–1715), more famous as historian than as theologian. He was intimately conversant with ecclesiastical matters during something like half a century. Born in the land of presbytery and Calvinism, he became an episcopalian and an Anglican. But his interest lay in personal religion more than in theology. He was a glorified "man in the street", always aware of, and intensely impressed by, what partisan laymen were saying. His *Exposition of the Thirty-Nine Articles* (1699) was, for more than a century, as famous as Pearson's *Exposition of the Creed*. His ministration to the dissolute

Rochester, who died a believer and a penitent, was one of the strongest memories of his life, and he has preserved it with real charm in *Some passages in the Life and Death of the right honourable John Earl of Rochester* (1680). *The Pastoral Care* (1692) is straightforward and sensible in manner and opinion. Had Burnet never written a word of history, he would still deserve a permanent place among English writers. As a contrast we may mention Edward Stillingfleet, Bishop of Worcester (1635–99), who was the antithesis of Burnet in character. His personal attractiveness gave him wide popularity; men called him "the beauty of holiness". His *Irenicum* (1659), which regards the system of church government as unimportant, gave him a place among "latitude men".

The most popular of all the preachers of the Revolution period was John Tillotson (1630–94), a "latitudinarian" who rose as much through the pulpit as through politics to be Archbishop of Canterbury. A large collection of his sermons appeared in 1717. Tillotson had the extempore manner. His style is simple and easy, and it earned high praise from Dryden. But the most striking example of the new pulpit manner was Robert South (1634–1716). South, before all things, was original. He rejected the flowers of Taylor and outdid the simplicity of Tillotson. His *Animadversion on Mr Sherlock's Book entitled a Vindication of the Holy and ever-blessed Trinity* is the liveliest essay in theological criticism of the time. William Sherlock's *Practical Discourse concerning a Future Judgment* (1691) is a piece of sound and sober prose; but he will be remembered less as a voluminous author than as the theme of South's racy criticism. Specially remarkable is the solitary and dignified figure of George Bull (1634–1710), Bishop of St David's, the one English ecclesiastic of the period who, preaching in English but writing in Latin, attained to European fame. Bossuet praised his *Judicia Ecclesiae Catholicae*, and his *Harmonia Apostolica* gained great renown. His works were translated in the Oxford *Library of Anglo-Catholic Theology* (1842–55).

But we must leave the successful churchmen and turn to a sacrificed band who came into existence at a crisis in the national history. When William and Mary were called to the throne there were many divines who felt that, having taken the oath of allegiance to one king, they could not take it to another, while the Lord's anointed was still alive, though dispossessed by secular law. From their refusal of the second oath they were called "non-jurors", and they went into voluntary spiritual exile. The leader was Archbishop Sancroft (1617–93), one of the seven bishops who had withstood James II. In his day, he had wielded his pen adroitly. His *Fur Praedestinatus*, a delightful satire on Calvinism, was an early work; but archbishops cannot afford to be satirical in print; and when he became a non-juror, Sancroft refrained from all written works. Of greater literary importance are such engaging figures as Ken and Hickes. Thomas Ken (1637–1711) is one of those religious writers whose words reveal a beautiful soul. He wrote only when he felt deeply. *Ichabod* (1663) tells of his disappointment with the church after the Restoration. His poetry (including the famous evening hymn "Glory to Thee, my God, this night", adapted from Sir Thomas Browne) came readily from his pen; his prose is still an excellent example of what educated men wrote naturally in his day. George Hickes (1642–1715) was a scholar as well as a man of piety. He learnt Hebrew that he might discuss

Rabbinical learning with Charles II's favourite minister, the Scottish secretary Lauderdale, and "Anglo-Saxon and Meso-Gothic" for his own pleasure. His enormous *Linguarum veterum septentrionalium thesaurus grammatico-criticus et archaeologicus* is a marvel of erudition, and immortal as containing the first mention of *Beowulf*. Another attractive writer among the non-jurors is Robert Nelson (1665–1715), who in his *Companion for the Festivals and Fasts* (1704) produced one of the most popular of religious books. Nelson did for the Church of England in prose what Keble, more than a century later, did in poetry. He showed the romance of its past, the nobility of its ideal, the purity of its forms of prayer.

XIII. LEGAL LITERATURE

In a brief summary like the present a full account of our legal literature can find no place. Interested readers are therefore referred to the corresponding chapter and bibliography of the original *History*. The first period of English legal literature is that in which the Saxon, Anglian and Mercian kings, beginning with Ethelbert, *c.* 600, began a record of the "dooms" of their folk. The second period is that in which, from Alfred to Canute, kings began to issue royal ordinances. The third period is that in which the Norman rulers endeavoured to discover and record what had been the "law of Edward the Confessor", to which the English seemed attached.

From the reign of Henry II we get legal writings of a new type, exemplified by *Tractatus de Legibus et Consuetudinibus Regni Angliae* by Ranulf de Glanvil or perhaps by Hubert Walter, and Henry de Bracton's *De Legibus et Consuetudinibus Angliae* (*c.* 1256). From 1292 we have an almost complete series of *Year Books* recording cases adjudged. The fifteenth century saw two notable additions to legal literature, Sir John Fortescue's *De Laudibus Legum Angliae* and Sir Thomas Littleton's *Tenures*. To the sixteenth century belongs William Lambarde's *Eirenarcha*, a manual for justices of the peace.

When James I came to the throne, the great unsettled constitutional question was whether the country should be governed by *rex* or by *lex*. Foremost among those on the side of *rex* was Francis Bacon, the lifelong rival and personal enemy of the formidable Sir Edward Coke (1552–1634), who was the embodiment of *lex* and the zealous political enemy of absolute monarchy. Coke produced many legal books; but his fame, as a writer, rests fundamentally upon two, namely, his *Reports* and his *Institutes*. To him was largely due the legend of Magna Carta and many imaginary rules of law. Contemporary with these party men, however, were some devoted purely to research, rightly called the fathers of the scientific study of legal history. Foremost among them was John Selden (1584–1654), the most erudite Englishman of his day. To a wide classical scholarship he added a remarkable knowledge of archaeology, history, philology and legal antiquities. He was endowed, moreover, with a mind free from prejudice, a well balanced judgment, a calm judicial temperament. In 1618 he wrote his treatise, *Mare Clausum* (not published till 1636), an attempt to vindicate England's claim to sovereignty over the narrow seas against the attack which Grotius had made upon it in his *Mare Liberum*.

In 1649 the Commonwealth was established, and in 1650 a committee was appointed to consider the matter of legal reform. Parliament resolved that one thing, at any rate, should be done: English should be made the language of the law. But when discussion turned from this principle to questions of substantial reform, the Puritan leaders were more "enthusiastic" than helpful. Hugh Peters wanted to take over the laws of Protestant Holland; John Rogers wanted simply the law of Moses. Before long Cromwell settled the matter by the establishment of a military despotism and martial law. The main literary products were Matthew Hale's *London's Liberties* (1650), Thomas Hobbes's *Elements of Law* (1640), and William Prynne's *Collection of Fundamental Liberties and Laws* (1654–5). The Restoration brought back the common law, and the old French and Latin jargon. At this period we again meet the name of Sir Matthew Hale (1609–76), whose most notable work was his fragmentary *History of the Common Law of England* (printed 1713). A thorough survey of the field of early law and the institutions connected with it was made by Sir William Dugdale in his *Origines Juridicales* (1666). In 1679 a collected edition of the *Year Books* appeared. But the old law did not lack its critics. Prominent among these was the irreconcilable William Prynne. In 1669 he published his *Animadversions on the Fourth Part of Coke's Institutes*. A much more formidable critic, however, both of Coke and of the laws of England, was Thomas Hobbes. In his *Dialogue between a Philosopher and a Student of the Common Laws* (published posthumously in 1681) he assails the legal and political principles of Coke and the other opponents of the Stuart autocracy. As a writer on law Hobbes has not even yet been fully appreciated.

It is right that the written words of these great jurists should be mentioned in a history of literature in its broad sense. Actually, however, there is but one of the company who has found his way into the intenser literature which is part of every man's reading. We mean Selden; for Bacon belongs to philosophy rather than to law. *Table-Talk: being the Discourses of John Selden Esq. Being His Sense of various Matters of Weight and High Consequence; relating especially to Religion and State* was first published in 1689, thirty-five years after Selden's death, and nine years after that of his sometime amanuensis, Richard Milward. Selden's *Table-Talk*, like Ben Jonson's *Conversations*, is one of those annoying posthumous works which lack the formal certitude of authenticity. The strong voice of authority is almost certainly Selden's; but the rather confusing alphabetical sequence of the utterances may be Milward's. "Table-Talk" is hardly the best name for a collection of autocratic deliverances, some, like *Preaching*, several pages long, and some, like *Councils* and *Trinity*, condensing a treatise into a few trenchant lines. But, however titled, it is an inexhaustible little book, characteristically pronounced by Dr Johnson to be superior to any of its French rivals.

XIV. JOHN LOCKE AND SOME ECONOMISTS

John Locke (1632–1704) is the most important figure in English philosophy, though others have excelled him in genius. His active interests included medicine, and his writings on economics, on politics and on religion expressed the best ideas of the time. His great work, *An Essay concerning Human Understanding*, may have seemed only to show the grounds in the human mind for honesty, liberty and toleration; but actually, by its "historical plain method", it gave a new direction to European philosophy. Locke did not graduate as a bachelor of medicine at Oxford till 1674. His medical knowledge made him acquainted with the Earl of Shaftesbury, Dryden's Achitophel. He became a member of Shaftesbury's household and saved the statesman's life by a skilful operation. He directed the education of the boy who became third earl and author of *Characteristics*. He shared the mutations of Shaftesbury's fortunes and, after the statesman's flight and death, the philosopher withdrew to Holland. Here he continued his literary work, and before he returned to England in 1689 the *Essay concerning Human Understanding* seems to have reached its final form. Locke could have taken high place under the new government; but he was content with minor offices that enabled him to absent himself a good deal from London. From 1691 to his death he lived in the Essex household of Sir Francis Masham, whose wife Damaris, his old pupil, was a daughter of Ralph Cudworth, the Cambridge Platonist. With Cudworth's type of liberal theology he became more and more in sympathy.

He had not published anything before his return to England in 1689; and by this time he was in his fifty-seventh year. In 1689 his Latin *Epistola de Tolerantia* was published in Holland, a corrected English translation being issued in 1690. The controversy which followed this work led to the publication of *A Second Letter concerning Toleration* (1690) and *A Third Letter for Toleration* (1692). In 1690 the book entitled *Two Treatises of Government* was published, and a month later appeared the long expected *Essay concerning Human Understanding*, on which he had been at work intermittently since 1671. It met with immediate success, and led to a voluminous literature of attack and reply. Its most vigorous critic was Stillingfleet. Among Locke's correspondents and visitors were Sir Isaac Newton and Anthony Collins, the future Deist (see p. 407). The extent and variety of Locke's interests are attested by later works—*Some Considerations of the Consequences of the Lowering of Interest, and Raising the Value of Money* (1691), and *Further Considerations* (1695); *Some Thoughts concerning Education* (1693); *The Reasonableness of Christianity* (1695), and, later, *A Vindication* of the same against certain objections. Among writings which were published after his death are commentaries on the Pauline epistles, a *Discourse on Miracles* and, most important of all, the small treatise on *The Conduct of the Understanding*, originally designed as a chapter of the *Essay*.

Locke opened a new way for English philosophy. He undertook a systematic investigation of the human understanding with a view to determining the truth and certainty of knowledge and the grounds of belief, on all matters about which men are in the habit of making assertions. In this way he introduced a new department, or a new method, of philosophical inquiry, which has come to be known as the theory of knowledge, or epistemology; and, in this respect, he was the precursor of Kant and anticipated what Kant called the critical method. Like other great books, the *Essay* had a simple beginning. A discussion with friends on some unimportant matters led to no conclusion; and Locke saw that before inquiries could be profitable, it was necessary to settle "what objects our understandings were, or were not, fitted to deal with". Locke proposed to expound this on a single sheet of paper next day; but the "single sheet" became the *Essay*, and the "next day" arrived twenty years after. Locke's interest centres in the traditional problems. He refuses to "meddle with the physical consideration of the mind", though he has no doubt that the understanding can be studied like anything else. All the objects of the understanding are described as *ideas*, and ideas are spoken of as being in the mind. The term "idea" implied no contrast with "reality". Locke avoids any presupposition about matter, or mind, or their relation. He begins neither with mind nor with matter, but with ideas. His first inquiry is "how they come into the mind"; his next business is to show that they constitute the whole material of our knowledge. His treatment of "the association of ideas" is an afterthought, and did not appear in the earlier editions of the *Essay*. It is out of place in a history of literature to expound or criticize the doctrines of a particular philosopher. We must be content to state briefly his main conclusion. The real existences to which knowledge extends are self, God, and the world of nature. Of the first we have, says Locke, an intuitive knowledge, of the second a demonstrative knowledge, of the third a sensitive knowledge. "God has set some things in broad daylight"; but of others we have only "the twilight of probability". With that we must be content.

Locke's practical interests find ample scope in his other works. In *Two Treatises of Government* he refutes Sir Robert Filmer's doctrine of absolute power and propounds a theory which reconciles individual liberty with collective order. His economic writings are particular rather than general, and, when considered, should be related to the economic arguments produced at the time by Sir Josiah Child, Sir Dudley North and, especially, Sir William Petty, who devoted himself to what his most famous book indicates in its title, *Political Arithmetic* (1690). Petty distrusted vague generalities and required exact statements. Thus, he defined interest as "a reward for forbearing the use of your own money for a term of time agreed upon"—a definition that carries us far beyond the old notion of "usury".

Locke's plea for toleration in matters of belief has become classical. His exclusion of Papists and atheists must not be blamed as inconsistency. To Locke a Roman Catholic was not a person who professed a particular kind of religion, but a person who professed allegiance to a foreign and hostile potentate; and an atheist was a person who, in repudiating the accepted contract between man and God, repudiated the basis of social contracts. His *Thoughts concerning Education* and his *Conduct of the Understanding* must always be considered in any discussion of their subject. That a man of Locke's quality of mind propounded a theory of education at all was a great gain: at least there was something to discuss. Locke had the gift of making philosophy speak the language of ordinary life. No one can fail to admire the lucid, dignified and unostentatious prose in which he conveyed his philosophy and made it universally intelligible.

Of writers opposed to Locke we need only mention John Norris of Bemerton (1657–1711), a voluminous author of discourses, letters, and poems, as well as of the longer and more systematic work on which his fame depends, *An Essay towards the Theory of the Ideal or Intelligible World*, the first part of which was published in 1701, and the second in 1704. In temper of mind, Norris may be regarded as the antithesis of Locke. He represents mysticism as against the latter's critical empiricism, and he has been praised by those mystically inclined perhaps rather more than he deserves.

XV. THE PROGRESS OF SCIENCE

With the exception of anatomy and astronomy, the sciences lagged a century and more behind the arts. The first and greatest advance was made in anatomy, when the great Belgian Vesalius dared to turn away from Galen and search into the human body. His *De corporis humani fabrica* (1543) is one of the landmarks of human knowledge. Contemporary with Vesalius, though older in years, is Copernicus of Poland, whose *De Revolutionibus*, completed in 1530 and published in 1543, the year of his death, definitely reassembled for succeeding generations the machinery of the universe. Man lost the starry spheres and gained the solar system. In the seventeenth century new methods and new appliances appeared. John Napier of Merchiston made known his discovery of logarithms in 1614 and the first tables were published in 1617. Seven years later, the slide rule was invented by Edmund Gunter. Decimals were coming into use and, at the close of the sixteenth century, algebra was being written in the notation we still employ. William Gilbert, physician to Queen Elizabeth, had published his experiments on electricity and magnetism in the last year of the sixteenth century. Galileo was using his newly constructed telescope; and, for the first time, Jupiter's satellites, the mountains in the moon, and Saturn's rings were seen by human eyes. The barometer, the thermometer and the air pump, and, later, the compound microscope, all came into being at the earlier part of our period, and by the middle of the century were in the hands of whoever cared to use them.

In his *Tractate on Education* Milton advocates the teaching of medicine, agriculture and fortification—the last being an exceedingly practical kind of applied mathematics. By the time of *Paradise Lost* the learned accepted the Copernican system, though the world at large remained Ptolemaic. The two systems, as Mark Pattison pointed out, "confront each other in the poem, in much the same relative position which they occupied in the mind of the public". The evidence of diaries and memoirs tells us much about the place of science in the life of an educated man. Lord Herbert of Cherbury, John Evelyn and Samuel Pepys are all examples of busy men whose wide range of knowledge included science.

The Marquis of Worcester, popularly credited with premature discovery of the steam-engine, was little more than an ingenious dabbler in mechanical crafts; but Sir Kenelm Digby, if we can believe his *Memoirs* (1628), was a more serious student of science, particularly of chemistry. In mathematics John Wallis of Cambridge was a forerunner of Newton and had the wide education of his age. His *Arithmetica Infinitorum* contained the germs of the calculus, suggested the binomial theorem to Newton, evaluated π and first used the current symbol for infinity. Another mathematical ecclesiastic was Seth Ward, Bishop of

Exeter and afterwards of Salisbury. Ward and Wallis refuted Hobbes's attempted proof of the squaring of the circle.

Like the distinguished mathematicians just mentioned, Isaac Newton (1642–1727) took a keen interest in certain forms of theology current in his day; but in his intellectual powers he surpassed them all. He was the founder of the modern science of optics. His discovery of the law of gravitation, and his application of it to Kepler's laws of planetary motion made him the founder of the science of gravitational astronomy. His discovery of the method of fluxions entitles him to rank with Leibniz as one of the founders of mathematical analysis. His chief work, *Philosophiae Naturalis Principia Mathematica* (1687), has been described as the greatest triumph of the human mind. Though Newton belongs to the history of learning rather than to the history of letters, his name adorns either chronicle. His fame as a man of science was European; but his dabbling with interpretations of Biblical prophecies must be consigned to the history of aberrations.

The second man of outstanding genius in British science in the seventeenth century was William Harvey (1578–1657). Harvey, "the little choleric man", was in his thirty-eighth year when, in his lectures on anatomy, he expounded his new doctrine of the circulation of the blood to the College of Physicians, although his *Exercitatio Anatomica de motu cordis et sanguinis* did not appear till 1628. In the convincing demonstration of his discovery only one link of evidence was missing, and this was supplied shortly after Harvey's death by Malpighi, whose use of the compound microscope, not available to Harvey, enabled him to reveal the capillaries.

Great as were the seventeenth century philosophers in the biological and medical sciences, they were equalled by workers on the physical side. Robert Boyle (1627–91), son of the Earl of Cork, was, even as a boy of eighteen, one of the leaders in the comparatively new pursuit of experimental science. His first love was chemistry. He settled at Oxford, where he arranged a laboratory and had as assistant the famous physicist Robert Hooke. He invented something like the modern air-pump. He confirmed Harvey's great discovery. He busied himself with the weight, with the pressure and with the elasticity of air, and with the part it played in respiration and in acoustics. He was the first to distinguish a mixture from a compound, to define an element, to prepare hydrogen. Like Newton, he wrote on religion as well as science and he founded the Boyle Lectures in defence of Christianity.

It was men such as these that re-established the Royal Society in 1660. This great institution has not only had the longest existence among the scientific societies of the world, but anticipated its own birth in 1645, when the Philosophical College came into being. During the Civil War this body divided itself between Oxford and London. At the Restoration, the London meetings were resumed, and in 1662 the Society received the royal charter. Among its early presidents were Wren, Pepys and Newton—Newton for twenty-five years from 1703 till his death.

XVI. THE ESSAY AND THE BEGINNING OF MODERN ENGLISH PROSE

The period we have been considering is noteworthy for the general emergence of a prose style very little different from the English of today. This was not a new creation. Its main virtues, lucidity, precision and sobriety can be found in the works of Hobbes, who was born in the year of the Armada. Before we pass to examples of the "new prose" we should observe a fact too frequently overlooked, namely, that writing in prose has two main purposes, which may be distinct, or which may combine, especially when the writer is a man of genius. Prose may be used to convey facts or to convey feelings. In other words, there is a prose which reports and a prose which creates. The purpose of Milton and Jeremy Taylor in their great symphonic passages of prose-music was not to instruct but to move. Such writing as theirs can convey great truths, but it cannot easily convey minor truths. What happened in the seventeenth century was not that there grew up a public which demanded plainer prose, but that there accumulated a mass of information which demanded plainer prose. There may be poetry in the art of healing; there must be plain prose in a treatise on anatomy. Men of science like Newton and Boyle, when they did not write in clear Latin, felt they must write in clear English; in fact, the Royal Society did demand plain and unadorned English from its members, as Thomas Sprat, the first historian of the Society, records. In 1664 his colleagues gave effect to their views by appointing a committee for the improvement of the English language, which included, besides himself, Waller, Dryden, and Evelyn. One other fact must be remembered. The seventeenth century had a much larger reading public than the sixteenth. In the sixteenth century learned men wrote to instruct or to annihilate each other. In the seventeenth century men wrote for "the Town". They did not try to annihilate, they tried to argue. The admirable John Wilkins (1614–72), afterwards Bishop of Chester, one of the founders of the Royal Society and its first secretary, had recommended in his popular *Ecclesiastes or the Gift of Preaching* that the style of the pulpit should be plain and without rhetorical flourishes. Tillotson's sermon, *The Wisdom of being religious* (1664), is, in its perfect plainness and absence of rhetoric, an instructive contrast to the imaginative discourse which Jeremy Taylor delivered, only eight months earlier, at the funeral of Archbishop Bramhall. Stillingfleet preached in plain English, and South not only preached in plain English, but mocked at those who did not.

The influence of France upon England in the seventeenth century has already been mentioned. Though the Civil War checked for a time the French studies of Englishmen, it ultimately contributed to their diffusion; for it sent many English men of letters to Paris. In 1646 Hobbes, "the first of all that fled", Waller, D'Avenant, Denham, Cowley and Evelyn were gathered together in the French capital. There were many others. The heroic romances were not the only examples of French literature read and translated in England when the Restoration came. Versions, good and bad, appeared of works by Pascal, Descartes, Boileau, Bossuet, Malebranche, La Rochefoucauld, La Bruyère, Le

Bossu and Rapin. Saint-Évremond was long in England, and one of his friends was Cowley, who gave a lighter touch to the essay. Prose became more urbane.

One delightful example of personal prose can be found in the letters written by Dorothy Osborne to her future husband, Sir William Temple, between 1652 and 1654. Temple himself (1628–99), once a great figure, has fallen out of notice, but he is still important. His *Letters*, first collected by Swift (1700–3), are interesting in historical matter and simple and unaffected in manner. The same clear and agreeable prose appears in his *Memoirs*. His essays, or, as they were called, *Miscellanea*, appeared in three parts; the first in 1680, the second in 1692 and the third in 1701. The most widely read of these essays, *Upon Ancient and Modern Learning* (1692), was inspired by a stupid literary quarrel which had raged in Paris. The essay has no importance, but it produced two notable works, Swift's *Battle of the Books* and Bentley's annihilation of the supposed letters of Phalaris. The most agreeable of the essays are *Of Poetry*, *Upon the Gardens of Epicurus or Of Gardening* and *Upon Health and Long Life*. Temple writes like a fine gentleman at his ease, without any affectation, but with considerable negligence.

Like Cowley, Temple came under the spell of Montaigne. In 1685 Montaigne was popular enough in England to warrant the publication of a new translation of his essays from the pen of Charles Cotton (1630–87). Cotton sometimes misses his author's meaning, but he does not write sheer nonsense, as Florio sometimes does. Cotton's work is dedicated to George Savile, Marquis of Halifax (1633–95), whose own *Miscellanies*, first collected in 1700, carry the stamp of a most attractive character. His finest piece of writing is the praise of truth in *The Character of a Trimmer* (1688)—a passage worthy of Montaigne. His admirable *Character of King Charles the Second* was not published till 1750. *A Letter to a Dissenter Upon the Occasion of His Majesties late Gracious Declaration of Indulgence* (1687) and *The Anatomy of an Equivalent* (1688) have both point and style. More in the nature of an essay is *The Ladies New Years Gift, or Advice to a Daughter* (1688), addressed to his own daughter, mother of Lord Chesterfield, author of the celebrated *Letters*. It is entirely delightful. Indeed, Halifax has hardly yet received his due, either as a public figure of high integrity or as a writer of what may be called, in the best sense, "gentleman's prose". His *Maxims* (1693) are the finest things of their kind in English.

The greatest creative force in prose was Dryden, and probably his greatest prose achievement was the *Preface* to the *Fables*. When, nine years later, Steele wrote the first number of *The Tatler*, he found both a model and an instrument ready to his hand.

CHAPTER IX

FROM STEELE AND ADDISON TO
POPE AND SWIFT

I. DEFOE: THE NEWSPAPER AND THE NOVEL

Daniel Defoe (1659–1731) is known to most readers as a pioneer novelist of adventure and low life. Students know him further as a prolific pamphleteer of questionable character and many disguises. His early biographers regarded him not only as a great novelist but as a martyr to liberal principles and homely piety. Some of his own contemporaries saw in him a political traitor, a social outcast, and a venal scribbler whose effrontery was equalled only by his energy. Something of the truth can be found in all these views. The novelist we know grew out of the journalist and political hack we have almost forgotten. Defoe is specially interesting for his date. He was born thirty-one years after Bunyan, on the very eve of the Restoration. The acute manifestations of religious eccentricity, shown at their height during the Commonwealth, and all comprehensively labelled "Puritanism", did not survive the Restoration, which re-established the Church of England and buttressed its supremacy with many Acts of Parliament. The wilder Puritans, with their hope of some new theocracy, ceased to exist; the next generation of religious liberals were not Puritans; they bore no resemblance to Sir Hudibras and Ralpho; they had no trace of the cant and snuffle of the "caterwauling crew"; they maintained the old tradition of the Presbyterians and Independents; and as they refused to conform to the re-established Episcopalian Church, they were Nonconformists or Dissenters. Bunyan was the last of the Puritans; Defoe is the first typical Nonconformist or Dissenter in our literature.

When Defoe established his periodical *The Review* in February 1704, the English newspaper was less than fifty years old. Among Defoe's predecessors in journalism (see p. 332) two figures of special importance stand out: Henry Muddiman, the best news disseminator of his day, and Roger L'Estrange, who was beaten by Muddiman as an editor of "newsbooks", but who, as journalist, pamphleteer and man of letters, was Defoe's true prototype. Sir Roger L'Estrange (1616–1704) was a zealous royalist of good family and suffered in the great struggle. In 1659 he wrote many pamphlets and broadsides advocating the restoration of Charles II, and after that happy event he was made one of the licensers of the press. His political newspaper, *The Observator*, curiously cast in dialogue form, ran from 1681–7. He supported James II and lost any hope of advancement at the Revolution. There is no need to cite his forgotten productions; but mention should be made of his *Fables of Aesop* (1692) and its successor, *Fables and Stories Moralized* (1699). His translations are noticed later.

Between the suppression of *The Observator* in 1687 and the founding of *The Review* in 1704 various papers appeared. James Dunton brought out his *Athenian*

Gazette, afterwards *The Athenian Mercury* (1690–6), as an organ for those curious in philosophical and recondite matters. Defoe was one of the curious. In 1695 the Licensing Act was allowed to lapse and several new journals were at once begun—*The Flying Post*, a tri-weekly Whig organ, the Tory *Post Bag*, and *The Post Man*. These were primarily disseminators of news. They were supplemented, in 1702, by the first of the dailies, *The Daily Courant*. In 1704 Defoe began *The Review* as an organ of moderation, ecclesiastical and political, and of broad commercial interests. Defoe's journalistic originality appears in his abandonment of the dialogue form and of violent partisanship. He cultivated moderation, and sought to gain acquiescence rather than to embitter animosities.

Defoe's life and work defy summary. A few general considerations will help us to understand him. Like Dickens (whom in some ways he resembles) he was highly endowed with the "experiencing nature". Nothing was too small to escape his notice, nothing was too large to fit into his comprehension. His curiosity was insatiable, and he knew how to turn the smallest detail to literary account. To write was as natural to him as to breathe. He made fiction seem like truth and truth seem like fiction. Neither his mind nor his character can be called lofty; yet his gifts were many and various. He was the perfect journalist. He could write on anything or nothing. If it be charged against him that he was venal and dishonest, the charge lies more heavily against the statesmen who made crooked use of him.

Defoe was born in London and sent to a dissenting school at Stoke Newington. Details of his early commercial career are somewhat obscure, and do not concern us here. During his first phase we may call him a tradesman-publicist. We hear of a verse satire in 1691; but his first real book was the *Essay upon Projects* (1697), a surprising display of versatility and modern ideas. To name all the publications known to be Defoe's would need several pages. Here we must be content with a notice of some typical pieces, and we can therefore pass at once to his most famous early publication, his lively verse-satire against those who jeered at the foreign birth of William III. It was called *The True-Born Englishman* (1701) and it had the popularity it deserved. As rhymed journalism it has never been equalled. "The Author of *The True-Born Englishman*", as Defoe called himself, having made a true beginning, had no intention of stopping. His most important publication of 1702 was the tract *The Shortest Way with the Dissenters*. In this Defoe assumed the character of a "high-flying Tory" and argued ironically that the shortest way of dealing with the Dissenters was to extirpate them. But the age had no taste for irony. The Whigs and Tories were waging a bitter war over the succession to the childless Queen Anne. Defoe's pamphlet angered both parties. The Whigs, having taken it seriously, were suspicious of a man who could dissemble so well; and the Tories, finding they had been hoaxed by a Whig, were furious. Defoe was arrested, sentenced to imprisonment during the Queen's pleasure and to public exposure in the pillory. He met his fate with courage. He wrote a spirited *Hymn to the Pillory* and, when exposed, though not "earless" as Pope has it, he was "unabash'd", and the mob gave him a popular triumph. The Tories had overreached themselves. Defoe was liberated at the end of 1703, probably through the influence of Robert Harley, Earl of Oxford, half Whig, half Tory, first the friend and then the rival of the brilliant Henry St John, Viscount Bolingbroke, both of whom were important factors in Defoe's career.

Not even imprisonment or his employment as a busy agent for Harley could check the stream of Defoe's pamphlets and poems. In 1703 and 1705 he produced two volumes of his collected writings—the only collection ever made by himself. Defoe's real achievement at this time was his establishment of *The Review*, a model of sound, straightforward journalism. It first appeared in February 1704 and was suppressed in June 1713. *The Review* is creditable not only to Defoe, but to Harley, his patron, who first perceived the political importance of the press. We leave without mention many political writings of 1704 and 1705 and come at once to a first glimpse of Defoe passing from journalism to fiction; for a year later (1706) appeared *A True Relation of the Apparition of one Mrs Veal, the next Day after her Death, to one Mrs Bargrave at Canterbury, the 8th of September,* 1705. This, at one time thought to be a hoax written to sell the pious sermon to which it was added, is actually a clever journalistic working up of a ghost story current at the time.

From the autumn of 1706 to the spring of 1710, Defoe was at work in Scotland, and did some of the underground labour that made the Union of 1707 a practicable affair. But he was unrewarded; for when he returned to England in penury, Harley himself was out and the Whigs were in. Defoe was allowed to transfer his services, and was sent back to Scotland. His main production of 1708–9 is the huge and methodically accurate *History of the Union*. In 1710 the Whig government made the foolish mistake of impeaching a political divine named Sacheverell for a Tory sermon, and there was a sudden outburst of enthusiasm in favour of the victim. Defoe did what pamphlets can do against mob excitement, but the Whigs went out and the Tories came in. That Defoe was trying to serve two sides can hardly be doubted; but the statesmen, especially St John, were models of duplicity. Defoe himself never wavered in his support of the Hanoverian Succession or his opposition to the Jacobites. For the second time Defoe ventured on irony, attacking the Jacobites in 1712 with his *Reasons against the Succession of the House of Hanover*. But the literal Whigs prosecuted him for issuing a treasonable publication, and once more he was imprisoned. *The Review* ceased to appear; but he began at once to edit a new trade journal, *Mercator*, in the interest of Bolingbroke's treaty of commerce. By the end of 1713 he had secured a pardon under the Great Seal for all past offences. A year later he produced the pamphlets called *A General History of Trade* which have led some to call him the father of Free Trade.

Queen Anne died in 1714. The Tory intriguers were routed. The Hanoverians came in and the Jacobites came out. But the Whigs triumphed and kept their hold upon English politics till George III became king nearly fifty years later. At this point begins Defoe's most dubious period. It seems clear that between 1716 and 1720 he was employed as a "secret agent", working with the Jacobite publisher Nathaniel Mist, and contributing information to the Whig ministers. Whether his preliminary apologia, *An Appeal to Honour and Justice, tho' it be of his worst enemies* (1715), is genuine or a clever piece of impersonation can hardly be determined; but it has been taken quite seriously by biographers. In the same year he produced a *History of the Wars of Charles XII*, and the first instalments of *The Family Instructor*, besides numerous pamphlets. The year 1717 saw the end of his career as a political controversialist.

A new Defoe now appears. It was in April 1719 that the first part of *Robinson Crusoe* was published. Defoe was nearly sixty years old, but he had hitherto written nothing that would have preserved his name for posterity. During the next few years he was to become the most extraordinarily prolific old man in the history of English literature. He had lived actively. He had read whatever fiction was current in his time, and literary impersonation was almost a second nature in him. *Mrs Veal*, written in 1705, shows his ability to make a story vivid and credible by a skilful use of circumstantial detail. He had, moreover, the true creative writer's gift of looking at his experience objectively. Having read some account of Alexander Selkirk, he found no difficulty in impersonating a castaway sailor. The immediate and permanent popularity of *Robinson Crusoe* is a commonplace of literary history. Defoe, who always had a keen eye for his market, produced, in about four months, *The Farther Adventures* of his hero, and, a year later, *Serious Reflections during the Life and Surprizing Adventures of Robinson Crusoe*. But it is only the original that lives. True to his age and nature, Defoe wrote for edification; but the book suddenly assumed its own life. Defoe did not write the first English novel, but he wrote the first English novel of genius.

Numerous journalistic publications belong to the *Robinson Crusoe* year, but Defoe's next work of importance was *The History of the Life and Adventures of Mr Duncan Campbell* (1720), the deaf and dumb conjurer. Immediately after came *The Memoirs of a Cavalier*, an absorbing story of the wars in Germany and England. A month later appeared a fine example of the fiction of adventure, *The Life, Adventures and Piracies of the Famous Captain Singleton*. In this and in his next great book, *The Fortunes and Misfortunes of the Famous Moll Flanders* (January 1722), we find Defoe beginning to display remarkable powers of characterization. *Moll Flanders* is supreme as a realistic picture of low life, just as the book of the next month, *Religious Courtship*, is an unapproachable classic of middle class smugness and piety. To the wonderful year 1722 belong *Due Preparations for the Plague* and *A Journal of the Plague Year*, besides *The Impartial History of Peter Alexowitz the Present Czar of Muscovy* and *The History and Remarkable Life of the truly Honourable Colonel Jacque*. After the almost unmatched fertility of 1722, the next year was barren; but in 1724 we have our prolific and masterly writer once more, for that is the date of *The Fortunate Mistress*, better known as *Roxana*, the story in which Defoe makes his greatest advance toward the construction of a well-ordered plot. This, also, is the year of one of the best of his sociological works, his treatise on the servant question, *The Great Law of Subordination Considered*, as well as of the first volume of *A Tour Thro' the whole Island of Great Britain*. Before the year closed, he had written the last of his generally accepted works of fiction, *A New Voyage round the World*. *The Political History of the Devil* (1726) and *The Friendly Daemon* (1726) with numerous other works belonging to the same year hardly call for notice; but 1725–7 produced *The Complete English Tradesman*, that bourgeois classic, and 1728 saw *A Plan of the English Commerce*, the remarkable *Augusta Triumphans*, a piece of Utopian reconstruction for London, and the interesting *Memoirs of an English Officer....By Capt. George Carleton*.

Nothing but death could end Defoe's enormous productiveness. His final years are a little mysterious, and his last book, *The Compleat English Gentleman*, was not published till late in the nineteenth century. His death was hardly noticed, and his reputation sank in the aristocratic Augustan period. His labours for the Union and the Protestant Succession caused some well-meaning people in later years to discover in him the lineaments of a British Patriot and Christian Hero. But there is no need to praise Defoe for imaginary virtues. He was the most prolific writing machine known to us. He wrote masses of party-journalism, yet he was free from rancour. He was never brilliant; but he employed dullness almost magically. There are no flashes of revelation in his work; instead, there is a quiet accumulation of commonplace that gives an almost unbearable illusion of truth. As a writer and as a figure in public affairs, Defoe is second only to Swift; he has something of Dickens in him, as we remarked, but perhaps even more something of Henry Mayhew in his mixture of curiosity and compassion. No man has been injured more by the sheer quantity of his work; no man will be injured more by attempts to claim for him impossible virtues. It should be enough that Defoe was not only the author of *Robinson Crusoe* and *Moll Flanders*, but that he had in him something of the uncalculating love of liberty which is the real mark of a tribune of the people.

II. STEELE AND ADDISON

Steele and Addison are writers of talent who rose almost to genius because they instinctively collaborated with the spirit of their age. Public decency was returning. After the fireworks of the Restoration and the nocturnal rowdiness of its lecherous "gentlemen" a calmer morning dawned. The steady, quiet, middle-class began to make themselves heard. Of this cleaner urbanity Addison and Steele were the voices. Richard Steele (1672–1729) led the way, and he is curiously attractive because in his own person he combined Restoration impulses and Augustan restraint. He was an Irishman and a soldier, both rake and moralist, finding in himself the sins he was most ready to condemn. His reading sat in judgment on his conduct; and his first publication, therefore, was *The Christian Hero: an Argument proving that no Principles but those of Religion are sufficient to make a great man* (1701). This book was long popular as a guide to conduct, but actually it was his own cry of spiritual distress.

Steele turned next to the stage. He tried to make money by amusing his audience and to do good by instructing them. He covered the usual ground of Restoration drama, but he sought to paint virtue and vice in their true colours. Vice never triumphs, though virtue may suffer. In *The Funeral, or Grief-à-la-mode* (1701), his first and best constructed comedy, a highly improbable plot brings virtue a delayed reward. In *The Lying Lover* (1703) young Bookwit suffers a number of painful experiences and ends by marrying the sweetheart whom he had courted with a fidelity rare even on the stage. *The Tender Husband* (1705) sacrifices dramatic probability to an unconvincing picture of conjugal fidelity.

Steele had not yet found either himself or his public. His public he presently found in the coffee-houses, where men got together, as in the later clubs, and

conversed, and practised the social amenities. The coffee-house assemblies were
not coteries or studio-cliques. They were parties of ordinary persons, who did
not talk like books. Steele, having lost his place at court and being in need of
money, thought there might be profit in a periodical appealing to the coffee-
house public; and so on 12 April 1709 appeared the first number of *The Tatler*.
The paper came out three times a week, and each issue (unlike *The Spectator*)
contained several essays, dated, according to their subjects, from different
coffee-houses. Thus *The Tatler*, at its beginning, was hardly more than an
improved imitation of Defoe's *Review* or Dunton's *Athenian Mercury*. Having
found his public, Steele next found himself, and, as sometimes happens, he
discovered himself in an impersonation. From Swift he borrowed Isaac Bickerstaff, and soon Bickerstaff, with his familiar, Pacolet, developed from Swift's
astrological humbug into a general commentator on civilized life. In this thin
disguise, Steele touched on questions of breeding, good taste, courtesy and
chivalry. He set forth a reasonable ideal of a gentleman and taught a new respect
for women. To heighten and illustrate his discussions of family life he invented
a lady editor, Jenny Distaff. Had it occurred to him to weave the familiar
incidents of the essays into the history of Jenny Distaff, he would have been well
on the way towards the domestic novel. But Steele could not develop his own
ideas, whether of criticism or of character. He needed a collaborator. *The Tatler*
continued to appear three times a week until 2 January 1711, and then ceased
abruptly: we do not know why. The most probable reason is that Steele's
invention had given out and the task of going on had become laborious. The
least probable, though most pleasing, explanation is that he recognized the
superiority of another writer, who had contributed some essays to the paper.

That other was Joseph Addison (1672–1719), who had been at Charterhouse
with Steele. Addison's political career does not concern us; but it may be
mentioned that he held many important public offices and became a privy
councillor. The least satisfactory part of his political career is that which brought
him, at last, into a pamphlet-quarrel with his old friend Steele. But we are
concerned with their collaboration, not with their conflicts. Steele was impulsive, communicative, adventurous; Addison was reserved, taciturn, careful. He
had produced the expected Latin poems and dissertations, and the chief fruits
of his four years' travel after leaving Oxford were his *Dialogues upon the Usefulness of Ancient Medals* (posthumously published in 1721) and his *Remarks upon
Several Parts of Italy* (1705). His first contribution to what may be called public
literature was *The Campaign, A Poem, to His Grace the Duke of Marlborough*
(1705), containing the celebrated lines about the whirlwind and the storm, and,
more important to the author, containing sentiments about British freedom
and valour which were pleasing to the Whig politicians. Addison began to
prosper, and to be pointed out in the coffee-houses. He became urbane as well
as academic and official, and instead of using ancient literature to illustrate
medals, he discovered how to make it illustrate the weaknesses and peculiarities
of his contemporaries. *The Tatler* gave him his opportunity. His natural restraint
teaching him to avoid the natural volubility of Steele, he found the perfect
style for "occasional literature"—lucid, colloquial, full of individuality and yet
chastened by classic examples in the choice of words. Steele discontinued *The*

Tatler in January 1711. In 1710 the Whig ministry had fallen. Addison felt a financial as well as a literary call to continue his essay writing; and so, on 1 March 1711, *The Spectator* was born.

The Spectator was not *The Tatler* revived. The old paper was a medley; its successor was a series of literary pamphlets, each confined to a single theme, grave or gay. It appeared daily and so grew into the life of its readers like a trusted friend. "Isaac Bickerstaff," the astrologer, perished with *The Tatler*; the new author was "Mr Spectator", who not only gave his name to the paper but typified the spirit in which it was written. Naturally he had to be a member of a club. Steele invented the Spectator's club as he had invented the Trumpet Club for *The Tatler*. There were six typical members: Sir Roger de Coverly, once a town-gallant, and now a county-gentleman; Captain Sentry, a retired soldier of quiet tastes; a lawyer (anonymous) who resides at the Inner Temple; Will Honeycomb, a fop and wit; a gentle clergyman; and Sir Andrew Freeport, a merchant, specially notable, for he marks the first appearance of the bourgeois as a serious figure in modern English literature. The moneyed gull of Jacobean and Restoration comedy had gone. The middle-class had become the hero of the new literature. The last number (555) of *The Spectator* appeared on the 6 December 1712. Apparently Addison and Steele felt that they had exhausted that vein of writing. Addison now began to work again on his tragedy, *Cato*, which was produced in 1713 at a time of great political excitement. The success it had then it can never have again. To say it is dead is too much, for it was never alive. Addison's prose comedy *The Drummer; Or, the Haunted House* was produced at Drury Lane in 1715, but did not succeed.

In 1713 Steele returned to literature and started several periodicals, of which *The Guardian* is the most important. To this Addison contributed fifty-one papers. In 1722 came Steele's last complete comedy, *The Conscious Lovers*, remarkable because it resumes in brief all Steele's best ideas on life and character. Steele and Addison produced other work separately. But when they ceased to collaborate in *The Spectator*, which was revived for a few months in 1714 by one of their circle, they became authors of secondary importance. Their work was done. They were complementary writers. Steele was more original, Addison was more effective. Together, they succeeded because they were the voice of a new and civilized urban life.

III. POPE

The work of Pope was long a battlefield of criticism. Everyone agreed that he was a polished literary artist, the type of the restraint considered classical. What was urged against him was that he left the free air of heaven for the atmosphere of the coffee-house, and that he mechanized verse to suit an age of prose. Actually, Pope represents a reaction against artificiality and a return to nature. He descends directly from Waller and Dryden; he revolts indirectly from Donne. He could not breathe in the heavy air of the metaphysical poets; and so the paradox of Pope is that he is the chief figure in a romantic revolt. Let us abandon, he says in effect, the perverse, obscure, tormenting of words and emotions; let us go back to health and Horace.

Alexander Pope (1688–1744) began life with several disadvantages. He was the child of elderly parents, he was physically weak and deformed, and he was a Roman Catholic. His feeble health denied him a school, his faith denied him a university; and so the most instinctively classical of our poets missed the intensely classical education of his day. But there were advantages. He grew up in an indulgent home on the verge of Windsor Forest, and his intellectual isolation gave him intellectual freedom. While still a child, he "lisped in numbers". He read and wrote incessantly, and, as he grew, cultivated the acquaintance of older men to whom he submitted his juvenile efforts for criticism and correction. Thus his *Pastorals* went from hand to hand before their publication in 1709. That they are bookish is not surprising, for the writer was young, and the pastoral was at this date a literary exercise; but his mastery of metre is at once evident. *Windsor Forest* (1712) belongs to the period of the *Pastorals*, though it attempts to apply observation and reading to a larger theme. Less fortunate is the Virgilian eclogue *Messiah* (1712), which fails to make the Biblical prose of Isaiah impressive in the couplets of the eighteenth century.

The real Pope is first encountered in *An Essay on Criticism* published in 1711. A poet so careful of form was likely to discuss the principles of his art, and Pope naturally turned for inspiration to the *Ars Poetica* of Horace and the writings of those who had imitated it. Though most of the statements are commonplaces, they have taken permanent form through the writer's genius for poetic aphorism. With the *Essay on Criticism* Pope became famous. His next work established him. Based on an actual incident, *The Rape of the Lock* (1712) became at his hands a blend of the mock-heroic, the satirical and the fanciful, unmatched in English poetry. It is what Hazlitt called it, an exquisite specimen of filigree work. An enlarged edition appeared in 1714. Two poems, of uncertain date, appear in his collected works of 1717, *Eloisa to Abelard* and the fine *Elegy to the Memory of an Unfortunate Lady*. In these Pope made a sustained attempt to present pathos and passion. His friendship and affection are expressed with singular charm in three *Epistles*, (1) *To Mr Jervas with Dryden's Translation of Fresnoy's Art of Painting*, (2) *To a Young Lady with the Works of Voiture*, (3) *To the Same on her leaving the town after the Coronation*. The last two *Epistles* were written, in the first instance, for his friend Teresa Blount, and transferred afterwards to her younger sister Martha. His affection for Martha Blount endured for thirty years and helped him through what he himself grimly called "this long disease, my Life".

Pope's literary activity in the first period of his career was both intense and varied. Drama he left alone, though he contributed to Gay and Arbuthnot's *Three Hours after Marriage*. His *Ode for Music on Saint Cecilia's Day* is inferior to Dryden's. There is not much lyric quality in the poetry of Pope; but the aphoristic quality is highly developed. He was not prosaic. On the contrary, he was satisfied with nothing less than poetic perfection. What may be called the Pope formula may be stated thus: the lines are strictly iambic—there are no tri-syllabic feet and very few inversions; the rhymes fall preferably on monosyllabic words, which thus receive the full terminal stress; one of the rhyming words is, where possible, a verb. In that apparently narrow form Pope achieved as much variety as other poets have achieved with a variety of measures.

By the date of his *Works* of 1717, Pope had already published the first instalment of his most laborious enterprise, the translation of the *Iliad*. Pope's Homer, like Dryden's Virgil, was not intended to make known an unknown author. His readers were familiar with Homer in Greek; what they wanted was to hear Homer speak in the accents of their time. The first four volumes appeared in 1715, 1716, 1717, 1718, and the last two in 1720. The harvest-home was sung by Gay in *Mr Pope's Welcome from Greece*. Tickell's version of the first *Iliad* was published on the same day as Pope's first volume and was alleged to be inspired by Addison. With all its faults Pope's translation is a great success. As Bentley admitted, it is not Homer, but it is a poem, which few translations are. The reader who cannot find beauty in Pope is not likely to find much in Homer. Shortly after the long labour of the *Iliad* was over, Pope was engaged in two fresh enterprises. The translation of the *Odyssey* was shared with Elijah Fenton and William Broome, to whom half the books were allotted, Fenton taking I, IV, XIX and XX, and his colleague II, VI, VIII, XI, XII, XVI, XVIII and XXIII, while Pope translated the rest and assumed, in addition, the task of revision. The first three volumes were published in 1725, and the remaining two in the next year. But the homely, domestic, romantic *Odyssey* is less successful than the heroic, oratorical *Iliad*. The other task, which he undertook at the invitation of Jacob Tonson the bookseller, was a new edition of Shakespeare, published in 1725. Pope's scholarly disqualifications for such a work were great, and the mistakes he made were carefully pointed out by Lewis Theobald, who therefore unjustly gained the bad eminence of being the first hero of *The Dunciad*. Among the shorter pieces of this period is the *Epistle to Robert Earl of Oxford*, almost unsurpassed for variety of music and dignity of style.

Thanks to Homer, Pope had thriven; but he was apt to brood over injuries, real or imaginary, and employ to the full his "proper power to hurt". Pope, Swift, Gay, Parnell and others had been in the habit of meeting at Arbuthnot's rooms in St James's Palace. From this informal club came later the idea of satire on various forms of pedantry, in the person of an imaginary Martinus Scriblerus. In 1727 appeared the first two volumes of *Miscellanies*; the last volume (1728) contained the severe character of Addison which had already made a first appearance; but the piece that created most stir was Pope's *Martinus Scriblerus peri Bathous: or the Art of Sinking in Poetry*, a prose essay in which the "Bathos or Profund" is discussed and illustrated by devastating quotations from Pope's detested contemporaries, Ambrose Philips, Theobald and Dennis. *The Dunciad* had no immediate connection with Martinus Scriblerus. Its real origin was Theobald's *Shakespeare Restored* and Pope's painful recognition that the strictures of that acute critic had struck home. *The Dunciad* (Books I–III) appeared anonymously in 1728. Its success was immediate. Pope was emboldened to bring out a more elaborate form in 1729; but the authorship was not openly acknowledged till 1735. The main idea of *The Dunciad* was taken from *Mac-Flecknoe*, and in emulating his master's great satire, Pope must have felt that he was put upon his mettle. But Pope, unlike Dryden, was fundamentally wrong. It was not Theobald's failure as a dramatist that moved him, but Theobald's unquestionable success as a critic.

Pope's poetical energy during the next few years was deeply influenced by

Bolingbroke, who attracted his admiration and who drew his attention to philosophical or ethical questions as matter for verse. The first result was the *Epistle to the Earl of Burlington, Of Taste* (1731), afterwards altered to *Of False Taste*, and ultimately called *Of the Use of Riches*. It is a finished specimen of Pope's art and attitude. The next *Epistle* was that *To Lord Bathurst* also entitled *Of the Use of Riches* (1732). The *Epistle* called *Of the Knowledge and Characters of Men* came out in the next year. The *Epistle* entitled *Of the Characters of Women* was kept back till 1735. During this period Pope had been busy with his *Essay on Man*, Epistle I of which appeared in February 1733, II and III following in the course of the year. These were anonymous, as he was diffident of their reception. The fourth appeared under his name in January 1734. Pope was incapable of producing a sustained philosophical poem of any value, but we must not overlook the exquisite workmanship of separate passages or the interest of the whole as an attractive, if shallow, expression of contemporary thought.

The year 1733 marks the beginning of a singularly successful form of Pope's literary activity. Bolingbroke suggested an imitation of the First Satire of Horace's second book, and the result was one of Pope's greatest successes. Lord Hervey and Lady Mary Wortley Montagu, both contemptuously mentioned, published a counter-attack. Pope replied in his *Epistle to Dr Arbuthnot* (1735). This magnificent outburst of autobiography, self-laudation, satire and invective contains some of Pope's most finished and brilliant work. Two of its celebrated full-length attacks are those on Lord Hervey and Addison. Other versions of certain Satires and Epistles of Horace appeared between 1734 and 1737. They have been called perfect translations, "the persons and things being transferred as well as the words". The series was closed by the ponderously entitled *One Thousand Seven Hundred and Thirty-eight; a Dialogue something like Horace*, a second dialogue following later in the same year. The *Imitations* of Epistle I, vii and the latter part of *Satire* II, v in octosyllabic verse (1738) are of a totally different character, being attempts to copy Swift's manner. The *Satires* (II and IV) *of Dr Donne Versified* were included in the *Works*, Vol. II, 1735. It may be remarked that the one year, 1738, saw the publication of the Horatian *Dialogues* of the elderly Alexander Pope and the Juvenalian *London* by the young Samuel Johnson. Pope himself made no complete collection of his works, and his text is almost as difficult to establish as that of Shakespeare. His first editor, the admiring Bishop Warburton, took various liberties, and collected the poems named in this paragraph as *Satires*, using the *Epistle to Arbuthnot* as *Prologue* and the *Dialogues* of 1738 as *Epilogue*. Not till John Butt's ten-volume Twickenham edition of 1939–67 was a worthy effort made to produce a sound text. Five volumes of the *Correspondence* followed in 1956.

The New Dunciad appeared in 1742. While gratifying many personal grudges, as in the notorious (but very amusing) lines on the aged Bentley, the satire was, to a large extent, general. Pope had descried a new hero. The amiable and harmless Colley Cibber had not hesitated to make fun of *Three Hours after Marriage*, the play to which Pope had contributed. In a new edition of the whole poem, incorporating this fourth book, Pope therefore dethroned Theobald and elevated Colley Cibber to the vacant seat. Though some hold that Pope injured the original design of the poem by his alterations, they will scarcely deny that the conclusion of the fourth book is one of the high lights of his verse.

During the nineteenth century Pope was often denied the name of poet and was made to suffer for the faults of his worst imitators. By some people, and especially by scholars, he has been liked in every age, and his admirers now tend to increase rather than to diminish. In spite of the Windsor home and the retreat at Twickenham, Pope's spiritual home was the parish of St James. He was essentially urban; and the romantic period, which sought the beauty which has strangeness in it, would have none of him, even though Byron was his last great champion and Lamb on a celebrated occasion sprang to his defence. In literature there is a voice of the city and the senate as well as of the mountains and the waters. Poetic truth may be spoken in a polished as well as in a rustic or a prophetic manner. If to have written the most polished verse we know, to have charged words with a vivid and exciting energy, to have penned couplets or lines that remain perpetually memorable, to have presented a view, however narrow, of man and human life—if to have done these things is to be a poet, then only the utmost hardihood of folly or perversion can deny that name to Pope. On the other hand, we have but to turn to the lyrics of Blake or Words-worth to find a world of poetry almost completely different from Pope's and which appeals to other readers or to other moods of the same mind.

IV. SWIFT

Jonathan Swift (1667–1754) was the reputed son of a Jonathan Swift who had followed a more prosperous older brother, Godwin, from Yorkshire to Ireland. Jonathan's career was brief. He obtained a small legal post in Dublin and died. Several months later, a son, Jonathan, was born. There is a possibility that his real father was Sir John Temple, Master of the Rolls in Ireland, and father of Sir William Temple, who was therefore Swift's older half-brother. A nurse took the child to Whitehaven and kept him there three years; and, not long after his return to Dublin, the mother returned to her relatives in England, leaving the boy in his uncle's care. Thus, in a curious sense, Jonathan Swift was both fatherless and motherless; and we need feel no surprise at the growth of strange legends about his birth. He was sent to Kilkenny School, where he met Congreve, and, at fourteen, was entered as a pensioner at Trinity College, Dublin. When he accused his uncle of giving him the "education of a dog", he really meant that Oxford or Cambridge would have been more to his heart's desire than an Irish university. Swift, born in Ireland almost by accident, and afterwards identified with Ireland against his hopes and wishes, had no tender-ness for the land of his birth.

In 1688 Godwin, who had lost his fortune, died, and Swift was left without resources. He joined his mother at Leicester, and sought for other connections. The most obvious was the celebrated diplomatist Sir William Temple (see p. 376) then living in retirement at Moor Park in Surrey, about forty miles from London. Temple's father had been a friend of Godwin Swift; Temple himself had known the Swifts in Ireland; and Lady Temple (Dorothy Osborne) was said to be a connection of Swift's mother. Swift therefore entered the service of Temple, and became a kind of secretary. The arrangement was not happy for anybody. The ladies of the house ignored or patronized the proud and sensitive young man. That Temple meant to be friendly is certain; it is also certain that he never apprehended the real measure of Swift's capacity and that his efforts to find for him a place in the world of affairs were not very energetic. Nevertheless, life at Moor Park was of immense value to Swift. He grew familiar with public affairs and with the rich experiences of his patron, and he formed the lasting affection of his life. Dependant found sympathy with dependant. The companion of Temple's sister, Lady Giffard, was a widow, Mrs Johnson; and Mrs Johnson had two daughters, one of whom, Esther, was eight years old, and a great favourite with the family, when Swift was charged, among other duties, with her tuition. She was possibly Temple's daughter and therefore—Swift may have thought—his own niece. He made one effort to escape from servitude. In 1694, disappointed that Temple had found no place for him, he took the only course that seemed to promise advancement, and was ordained. Temple obtained for him the prebend of Kilroot, and the fated connection with Ireland was resumed. In 1696 he left Ireland and returned to Moor Park where he remained till Temple's death in 1699.

During one of the foolish periodical controversies about the merits of ancient and of modern literature, Temple felt called upon to defend the classics, but unfortunately cited the spurious "Epistles of Phalaris" as an example of ancient excellence. He was answered by William Wotton, and, in 1697, Swift wrote his contribution to the controversy, *The Battle of the Books*, which, however, was not published till 1704. The death of Temple left him without a place. He was given the living of Laracor, and found himself once more in Ireland, and alone. It was therefore arranged that Esther Johnson should live in Dublin, with a Mrs Dingley, related to the Temples, as chaperon. Swift was thirty-four, and Esther, henceforth his "Stella", was an attractive girl of twenty. The proprieties were strictly observed, and Swift and Stella never met except in the presence of a third person. But Swift was soon back in England, and on familiar terms with wits and ministers.

His pamphlets of 1708–9 on ecclesiastical questions show his conviction that the Whigs were unfriendly to the Church; and when the Whigs triumphed in 1708, he knew his hopes of preferment were vain, and retreated to Ireland. The prosecution of Sacheverell brought the Tories back in 1710. Swift returned to London, and the events of the three following years, with all his thoughts and hopes, are set out before us in his letters to Esther Johnson and Mrs Dingley afterwards to be known as the *Journal to Stella*. The efforts of the Tories were now devoted to bringing the war with France to an end. Swift composed, in November and December 1711, two formidable pamphlets in favour of peace. By this time he had attained a position of great importance, and the authority he possessed and the respect he received gave him much pleasure. Recognition of his services was made difficult, however, by doubts about his orthodoxy, Queen Anne being immovably hostile. At last, in 1713, he was made Dean of St Patrick's, a promotion fatal to his ambitions, for it banished him once more to Ireland. His health was bad, and his reception in Dublin was anything but friendly. In October he returned to London. But the aspect of affairs threatened disaster. The Queen was dying. The succession was unsettled. Harley and St John had quarrelled, and there was some Jacobite plotting. Swift was in a difficulty; but the death of the Queen in 1714 settled the matter. With the triumph of the Whigs and the defeat of his friends, all Swift's hopes finally disappeared and he returned to his vast and empty deanery in Dublin.

Here he found trouble of another kind. His long, peaceful association with Stella was disturbed by a strange complication. On his visits to London he had become intimate with Hester Vanhomrigh, supposed to be twenty, but probably older. Swift was forty-three; but the disparity of age mattered little to Hester. In their friendly intercourse she was "Vanessa" and he "Cadenus", an anagram of *decanus*, i.e. "dean"; and to her he wrote (*c.* 1713) a poem *Cadenus and Vanessa*, not meant for publication, indicating that his feelings were friendly and abstract. But abstract friendship had no meaning for Vanessa. She was passionately in love; and, on the death of her mother, she and her sister retired to Ireland, a step very embarrassing to Swift. About 1723 a crisis occurred. The usual story is that Vanessa provoked Swift's wrath by demanding to know what were the relations between him and Stella. What is certain is that when Vanessa died in 1723 she made no mention of Swift in her will, which names many other friends, including the philosopher George Berkeley, to whom she left half her property. The truth of the matter is that we know almost nothing about the relations between Swift and the two women who figure in his life, and should not take too seriously the interpretations, romantic, psychological or pathological, which have been made by some twentieth-century critics. Not the least ironical fact in the extraordinary life of Swift is that in the end he became an Irish patriot, and attained national popularity. But life was clouded for him by his own increasing infirmities and by Stella's illness. She died in January 1728, after making a will which describes her as "spinster". For Swift life soon became an acute torture, and in a sense he was dead before he died. A tumour on the brain maddened him with deafness, blindness and giddiness. In 1742 he fell into a condition of dementia. Three years later he was dead. Dublin was hushed into silence at the passing of the strangest character that ever emerged from that remarkable city. It may be added, as a last satiric touch, that not till Sir Harold Williams's edition of the *Poems* (1937) and H. J. Davis's of the *Prose Works* (1939–59) was any serious attempt made to produce full, true and accurate editions of his writings.

The earliest and the most characteristic of Swift's books is *A Tale of a Tub written for the Universal Improvement of Mankind*, composed about 1696 and published in 1704. Like all but one of his books it is anonymous. In form it is a pungent allegorical satire upon the contending religious parties of the day; but the essayistic digressions are an important part of it. Few more entirely characteristic first books have ever been written. It contains almost every quality Swift possessed—his intellectual power, his polished irony, his savage mockery, his terrifying humour and his immense vitality. Some of the chapters or essays are unequalled as examples of plain prose. The nearest parallel to the prose of Swift is the verse of Pope. With this short work was printed another. The origin of Swift's *Full and True Account of the Battel Fought last Friday between the Ancient and the Modern Books in St James's Library*, generally known as *The Battle of the Books*, has already been mentioned. The fact that Swift was backing his patron in a lost cause does not lessen the interest of the book, for Swift cared little about the matter as long as he could make the pedants ridiculous. It is an excellent piece of satirical humour.

Swift's most famous and most popular book belongs to the years of his maturity and disillusionment. *Travels into Several Remote Nations of the World, by Lemuel Gulliver, first a Surgeon, and then a Captain of Several Ships*, was published anonymously at the end of October 1726. It took the town by storm. Three famous controversialists, all born in the same century, have furnished the juvenile libraries of the western world with three perpetual volumes, *The Pilgrim's Progress, Gulliver's Travels* and *Robinson Crusoe*. The success of Swift in scoring a hit on the wrong—or the lesser—target is almost ludicrous, though we should remember that from the first the book was successful with children as well as their elders, "from the cabinet council to the nursery", as Pope and Gay wrote to Swift. Young readers are usually content with the voyages to Lilliput and to Brobdingnag, duly modified. The latter and more terrible parts of the book they wisely let alone. Any discussion of the "sources" of *Gulliver's Travels* is totally vain. What matters in a book is not whence it might have come but what it is. Everything that makes *Gulliver* immortal has its source in Swift, and in Swift alone.

In 1708 Swift began a brilliant series of pamphlets on Church questions. The first piece—a masterpiece of irony—was *An Argument against abolishing Christianity*, in which he banters very wittily writers who had attacked religion. Another pamphlet, *The Sentiments of a Church of England Man with respect to Religion and Government*, was written in a more serious strain. A third, *A Project for the Advancement of Religion and the Reformation of Manners* (1709), highly praised by Steele in *The Tatler*, is curious as a proposal for "auto-suggestion" in religion. Other tracts, able as they are, belong to the history of controversy rather than to the history of literature. *A Letter to a Young Gentleman, lately entered into Holy Orders* (1721) is specially attractive for its revelation of Swift's interest in the study of the English language. The finest and most successful of Swift's political pamphlets is *The Conduct of the Allies and of the late Ministry in beginning and carrying on the present war* (1711), a masterpiece of argument written in the perfection of plain prose. *Some Remarks on the Barrier Treaty* (1712) is a supplement to it. Swift's other political pamphlets, too numerous to name, show the same kind of power; but their matter has now an interest that is mainly historical.

The pamphlets relating to Ireland form a very important part of Swift's works. His indignation at the ill-treatment of the country in which he was compelled to live grew from year to year. The series began with *A Proposal for the Universal Use of Irish Manufacture, in Cloaths, etc.* (1720), advocating a scheme for boycotting English fabrics. It was followed by the tracts in which he attacked the grant of a patent to an English merchant, William Wood, to supply Ireland with coinage of the lower denominations. In 1724 appeared the first of the pamphlets known collectively as *The Drapier's Letters*. It was called *A Letter to* the Tradesmen, Shopkeepers, Farmers and Common People of Ireland *concerning the Brass Half-pence coined by Mr Woods*, and purported to be by "M. B. Drapier". It was written in the simplest language, and could be understood by all. In *A Letter to Mr Harding the printer*, he urged that the people should refuse to take the coins. The third letter, *Some Observations...relating to Wood's Half-pence*, intensified the controversy; and the *Letter to the Whole People of Ireland*, declaring that the Irish should be as free as their brothers in England, practically ended the scheme, though other publications followed. Wood's patent was cancelled, and he received a pension instead. The "Drapier" triumphed; and Ireland lost its needed small change. In *A Short View of the State of Ireland* (1728) Swift gives a touching account of the condition of the country. The series of pamphlets reached its climax in *A Modest Proposal for preventing the Children of Poor People from being a Burthen to their Parents, or the Country, and for making them Beneficial to the Publick* (1729), in which, with searching irony and bitterness, Swift suggested that the poverty of the people should be relieved by the sale of their children as food for the rich. The pamphlet is both a terrible indictment of Irish helplessness and a terrible parody of political argument.

On literary subjects, Swift wrote little. In 1712, he published his *Proposal for correcting, improving and ascertaining the English Tongue*, in the form of a letter to Harley. In this tract, to which he allowed his name to be affixed, he urged the formation of an academy, which was to fix a standard for the language. Nine years later, Swift published in Dublin an amusing satire, *A Letter of Advice to a young Poet: together with a Proposal for the Encouragement of Poetry in this Kingdom* (1721). In the rather patronising *Letter to a Very Young Lady on her Marriage* (1727), Swift advises his friend to listen to the talk of men of learning, as few gentlemen's daughters can read or understand their own native tongue, or even be brought to spell correctly.

Swift's poetry has the merits of his prose, but not many other merits. To trace and identify all his writings in verse is a heroic task. He began by writing frigid "Pindaric" odes, after the fashion of Cowley. But Dryden's good-humoured criticism turned him to lighter verse, modelled on Butler in style, and generally satirical in matter. One of the earliest and best of his playful pieces is the graceful *Baucis and Philemon*. The famous *Cadenus and Vanessa* (1726) gives, in a mock classical setting, Swift's account of his acquaintance with Hester Vanhomrigh. Much more pleasing are the pieces which Swift wrote year by year on Stella's birthday. He is here at his best in verse. At the other extreme are his satires on women, which are some of the most horrible verses ever written. Savagery has full play in his political ballads and skits. *On Poetry: a Rapsody* (1733) was thought by Swift to be his best satire. At least it contains his most frequently quoted lines. His greatest poem, *On the Death of Dr Swift* (1731), with its mixture of humour, egotism and pathos, is a moving piece, the last lines being strangely applicable to his actual end.

Of Swift's correspondence, by far the most interesting is that with Esther Johnson, afterwards known as the *Journal to Stella*. His style, always simple and straightforward, is here at its best. Both in this and in his general correspondence, the ease and vivacity of the writing can hardly be matched in epistolary literature. Much has been written in defence of Swift since the unsympathetic studies of Macaulay, Jeffrey and Thackeray appeared, but he still remains something of a mystery. (Perhaps the best of more recent critical-biographical interpretations is that by John Middleton Murry, published in 1954). It is not easy to reconcile his contempt for mankind with his affection for his friends and their affection for him; or his bitterness against women with the love he inspired. It is, again, difficult, in view of the decorum of his own life, and his real, if formal, religion, to explain the offensiveness of some of his writings. The normal physiological circumstances of life seem to have filled him with inexplicable horror. The early years of poverty and dependence left an indelible mark on him, and he became a proud, embittered man. Had he been born to rank and wealth he might have taken a leading, perhaps a decisive place in the tangled politics of the time.

Swift wrote the perfection of plain prose, with easy rhythm and exquisite cadence. He has no idiosyncrasy, yet the sheer force of personality is overwhelming. Earnestness, satire, cynicism, invective, all proceed with the same decorum of outward gravity. Swift wrote many small works, the effect of which is cumulative. In a brief sketch like the present, which cannot discuss or even name the greater part of them, he must inevitably appear with his magnitude lessened. But a reading of the works recorded in the preceding paragraphs will show that in intellectual energy and penetrating force of style he was the greatest writer of his age.

V. ARBUTHNOT AND LESSER PROSE WRITERS

The name of Dr John Arbuthnot (1667–1735) is familiar to all readers of Pope, Swift and their associates; but his actual writings are known to few, mainly because he took no pains to preserve his work or to separate his contributions from various joint enterprises. He was born in Scotland, and, after settling in London to practise medicine, became the Queen's physician in 1709. He defended the Union between England and Scotland in a pamphlet, *A Sermon...* *on the subject of the Union* (1706) and was soon in close touch with the anti-Marlborough party at Court. In September 1710 Swift came to London from Ireland, and undertook the management of the Tory periodical, *The Examiner*; and the acquaintance between the Irish and the Scottish wits soon ripened into affectionate intimacy. Arbuthnot was responsible for a series of pamphlets published in 1712, to create a feeling in favour of ending the war with France. The first was called *Law is a Bottomless Pit, exemplified in the case of the Lord Strutt, John Bull, Nicholas Frog, and Lewis Baboon, who spent all they had in a Law Suit*. Other "John Bull" pamphlets followed in quick succession and they were all rearranged later and published in 1727 as *The History of John Bull*. These pamphlets carried on, in their own way, the work done by Swift in *The Conduct of the Allies* and *The Examiner*. Later in 1712 Arbuthnot published an amusing pamphlet entitled *The Art of Political Lying*. He was one of the club of Tory statesmen and writers who called each other "Brother" and had weekly meetings. Soon we hear of the Scriblerus Club, and of a proposal to publish the *Memoirs of Scriblerus*. The *Memoirs* were not published until 1741, but the influence of the Club can be felt in other pieces, such as *The Dunciad* and *Gulliver*. The death of the Queen put an end to Arbuthnot's public importance. His remaining works are to be identified with difficulty, and of those known to be his some are scientific. His one surviving poem of interest is *Know Yourself* (1734). *The History of John Bull* is the most attractive of Arbuthnot's works. Though it is far below the level of *A Tale of a Tub* it deserves credit for the clearness of its satirical allegory and its skill in political characterization.

Contemporary with Arbuthnot and friendly with Swift and other High Church Tories was William King (1663–1712)—not to be confused with two other contemporaries of the same name, one of whom was the Archbishop of Dublin, the other the Jacobite principal of an Oxford college who wrote the mock-heroic poem *The Toast* (1732). King's first noticeable piece was an amusing *Dialogue showing the way to Modern Preferment* (1690), and later he joined Charles Boyle in the campaign against Bentley in the very clever *Dialogues of the Dead* (1699). His *Miscellanies in Prose and Verse* (1705) embodied some of his best work. King is an interesting writer who deserves to be better known.

Literary criticism at the end of the seventeenth century owed much to Boileau and Rapin, who pleaded for "good sense" and urged the wisdom of following classical models. Thomas Rymer (1641–1713), already mentioned (p. 357), published in 1674 *Reflections on Aristotle's Treatise of Poesie*, a translation from Rapin. But his principal literary work was *The Tragedies of the Last Age consider'd, etc.* (1678) in which he defended the classical as against the Shakespearean manner. He returned to the attack in *A Short View of Tragedy, etc.* (1693). Both essays have historical interest as attempts to criticize Shakespeare by standards inapplicable to his work. Gerald Langbaine is known chiefly by his *Account of the English Dramatic Poets* (1691), a new edition of which was brought out by Charles Gildon in 1699 under the title *The Lives and Characters of the English Dramatic Poets*. It is a most useful compilation. John Dennis, already mentioned, author of *Three Letters on the Genius and Writings of Shakespeare* (1711), was another of the critics who found Shakespeare wanting in "art", though gifted with some "natural" qualities. John Hughes (1677–1720), another critic-dramatist (see p. 357), produced *The Works of Mr Edmund Spenser...with a glossary explaining the old and obscure words* (1715), the first attempt at a critical edition of Spenser.

VI. LESSER VERSE WRITERS

Matthew Prior (1664–1721), obscurely born, had the fortunate gift of attracting profitable friends. He got to Westminster School and passed to Cambridge. In 1687 he joined with Charles Montagu, one of his early friends, in writing *The Hind and the Panther Transvers'd to the Story of the Country and the City Mouse*. People began to take notice of him, and during the winter of 1690–1 he obtained an appointment in the English Embassy at The Hague, the meeting place of the coalition against Louis XIV organized by William of Orange. The illness of his immediate principal gave the young attaché many opportunities of personal converse with William, and, inevitably, his first poems assume a laureate form and have little genuine value. We need not name them. It is in *The Secretary*

(1696) that we get the first real touch of Prior's quality. The lilting anapaests, which he used so well, describe the jocund progress of the English secretary to a week-end holiday. His diplomatic work succeeded, and honours accumulated upon the poetic official; but, like Swift, he moved towards the opposite political party and began to act with the Tory chiefs, Harley and St John. He was now cultivating his gift for lighter verse, and producing witty and kindly epigrams as well as humorous poetic anecdotes. The delightful stanzas *Written in the Beginning of Mezeray's History of France* were loved by Sir Walter Scott. *An Ode Inscribed to the Memory of the Honourable Colonel George Villiers* contains some of his finest lines and shows increasing mastery of the couplet. Like Defoe and Swift, Prior was involved in the political conflicts of Queen Anne's reign, and on the death of the Queen the Whigs imprisoned him, hoping to extort from him something incriminating against Harley and St John. They failed; and after two years of confinement he was released. Prior was greatly liked, especially by children, one of whom, Harley's grand-daughter, said that he made himself loved by every living thing in the house—master, child, servant, and animal.

Prior had great versatility. In addition to the lyrical verse by which he is best known, he wrote three longer poems which deserve mention. *Henry and Emma, a Poem, Upon the Model of The Nut-brown Maid* is an elegant and misguided attempt to apply the classic eighteenth-century manner to simple romance. Few people who misquote the line "Fine by degrees, and beautifully less" know that it is intended as a compliment to Emma's bodily shape. *Alma, or The Progress of the Mind*, discusses the vanity of the world. In its theme as well as in its form, it approaches *Hudibras*; but its superior urbanity cannot conceal its lack of force. Prior returned to the theme more seriously in *Solomon on the Vanity of the World*, a lengthy piece in couplets, which is not now likely to be read. Of satires in verse no complete examples are to be found among his poems, though the two delightful *Epistles to Fleetwood Shephard, Esq.* are in that vein; but Prior was fertile in a wide variety of light satirical narrative in verse, from the familiar *fabliau* to the humorous ballad or character-sketch and epigrammatic sallies of all sorts. The best instances of Prior's success in the *fabliau* are *An English Padlock* and *Hans Carvel*. In *Down-Hall, a Ballad*, he achieves a humorous character-sketch of the landlady of the Bull at Hendon; but the best example of his playful insight into character is the poem recovered by A. R. Waller for his edition of *The Writings of Matthew Prior* (1905–7) and named *Jinny the Just*. His poems to children are among the best of their kind, and his various "Cloe" songs, though not of the highest excellence, have a delightful kind of prettiness. Prior's shorter poems mark him as the earliest and most successful among masters of English familiar verse. He wrote well in many forms. His imitation of Spenser is poor, but it was at least attempted. His imitation of Chaucer failed simply because (like Dryden) he did not understand Chaucer's versification. Such attempts must be remembered as evidence that there was still a hunger for poetry in a form more free than the Wallerian couplet. Prior succeeded best with the octosyllabic couplet and various forms of the anapaestic line, the latter of which he uses very skilfully. As a prose writer he shows considerable skill, but the existing pieces are unimportant and need not be discussed. Never great, Prior is always good, and engages the affection of those who unbend to his easy charm.

The spoiled child of the Queen Anne fraternity of poets was the pliant fabulist John Gay (1685–1732). His first experiment was a blank verse piece called *Wine* (1708), an imitation of John Philips's *Cyder*. *The Fan* in three books (1713) imitates the Pope of *The Rape*. More important is *The Shepherd's Week* (1714) in six cantos, written in successful ridicule of the urban pastorals of "Namby-Pamby Philips", for Gay was a born parodist. At the end of 1715 he composed what is probably his best remembered poem, *Trivia, or The Art of Walking the Streets of London*, in three books, imitated from Swift. The idea is good, the versification neat, and the mock heroic style admirable. In 1727 he brought out his *Fables* (a second part followed posthumously in 1738) and won with them a poetical success that kept his name alive for a century and more. They are ambling, slipshod, and far indeed from the perfection of La Fontaine, but they have not been excelled in English. To a chance remark by Swift, that a Newgate pastoral might make "an odd pretty sort of thing", we owe Gay's most enduring invention, *The Beggar's Opera* (1728) which not only had a successful revival in London in 1920–3 in Arnold Bennett's adaptation but in 1928 was modernized by the German dramatist Bertolt Brecht in *The Threepenny Opera*. Rich, the manager, produced *The Beggar's Opera*, and it made Gay rich and Rich gay. Its prohibited sequel *Polly* (1729), though less good, proved even more successful in print. Gay's later years were uneventfully spent in the house of his faithful patrons the Duke and Duchess of Queensberry. Though not strikingly gifted he had the art of succeeding. He died, in Pope's phrase, "unpension'd, with a hundred friends". Gay's longer poems, with the exception of *The Shepherd's Week* and *Trivia*, hardly survive. Of the shorter, the best is *Mr Pope's Welcome from Greece*, the *ottava rima* of which has a spontaneous flash and felicity. Everybody knows *Black-Eyed Susan*. Mention should be made of one piece by Gay immortalized by another hand, the *Acis and Galatea* which Handel set to music.

Ambrose Philips (1674–1749) occupies a larger place in the literary disputes of the day than his works deserve. He became a target for missiles of all kinds because he was a Whig when all the wits were Tories. His *Pastorals* appeared (1709) in Tonson's *Miscellany*, his being the first, and Pope's the last, in the same volume. Pope of course put him in *The Dunciad*, and Carey or perhaps Swift fixed upon him that perversion of his Christian name by which he survives. Philips had the qualities of his defects and responded naturally to the older music of English poetry. In 1723 he brought out *A Collection of Old Ballads*, including *Robin Hood*, *Johnny Armstrong* and the famous *Children in the Wood*. The ballads are, in the main, bad versions, but the collection was one of the earliest of its kind. *The Distrest Mother* (1712), his version of Racine's *Andromaque*, has already been mentioned (p. 356).

Thomas Parnell (1679–1718) was born in Dublin. From his younger brother the famous Irish patriot was directly descended. A minor poet in the Augustan reflective tradition, Parnell had perceptible influence on the work of Goldsmith, Collins and Blair. *A Nightpiece on Death* is an early example of a convention which reached its acme with Gray's *Elegy*. The one poem of Parnell's that really survives is *The Hermit*, which tells the eastern tale familiar in the Latin of *Gesta Romanorum* and still more familiar in the French of Voltaire (*Zadig*, Chap. xx).

His longest effort, *The Gift of Poetry*, can now hardly be taken seriously. Like others of his time Parnell was a sedulous translator.

Anne Countess of Winchilsea (1661–1721) had an eye for the simple beauties of nature, and having attracted the uncritical attention of Wordsworth, her blameless efforts were overpraised by later Wordsworthians. The short *Nocturnal Reverie* (cited by Wordsworth) is slight and pleasing, without entirely escaping the contemporary note of elegance. *The Spleen, a Pindarik Poem*, full of italicized abstractions, must not be confused with Matthew Green's better poem of the same name.

John Pomfret (1667–1702), like Lady Winchilsea, was over praised for his rustic note by the natural reaction to the eighteenth century of critics in the Wordsworthian age. His anonymous poem *The Choice: A Poem written by a Person of Quality* (1700) became famous because, in the usual fashion, people speculated about the authorship instead of appraising the verses.

Thomas Tickell (1688–1740) was an ardent Whig, who found preferment through his enthusiasm for Addison. As Addison rose, his admirer rose with him. Addison incurred Pope's enmity mainly in his *protégé's* behalf, and Tickell now lives solely as satellite, executor and panegyrist of Addison. His elegy (characterized by Johnson as "sublime and elegant") *To the Earl of Warwick on the Death of Mr Addison* furnishes his chief claim to poetic honours.

The great collections of the poets, especially that for which Dr Johnson wrote his celebrated "Lives", have preserved the writings of some eighteenth-century figures who, without offence, may be called versifiers rather than poets. Their names figure in the allusive writings of Dryden and Pope, and we can therefore hardly ignore them. Brief notice, however, must be their portion in these pages.

George Granville (1667–1735), first Baron Lansdowne, has already been mentioned (p. 357) as a dramatist. Neither his "Myra" lyrics nor such longer pieces as *Beauty and Law* and *The Progress of Beauty* deserve much attention. William Walsh (1663–1708), a gentleman of fashion and place, won the approval of Dryden and of Pope as a critic. Like Lansdowne, he rarely fails to illustrate "the art of sinking" in poetry. He is better in some of his lyrics. *The Despairing Lover* and *The Antidote* may be mentioned as typical pieces. William King (1663–1712) has already been noticed as a prose-writer (see p. 393). His most celebrated work in verse is *The Art of Cookery in Imitation of Horace's Art of Poetry* (1708). A sequel is *The Art of Love in Imitation of Ovid de Arte Amandi* (1709). With them may be mentioned *The Furmetary, a very Innocent and Harmless Poem* (glancing at Garth's *Dispensary*), *Mully of Mountown* (Mully is a cow) and *Orpheus and Eurydice*, all in a robustly humorous vein. William King is the most readable minor writer of his time. The most unreadable, Sir Richard Blackmore (d. 1729), is one of those unfortunate writers who live in the satire they have invited. Blackmore's invitation is large and hearty. Having (says Johnson) in two years produced ten books of *Prince Arthur*, in two years more (1697) he sent into the world *King Arthur* in twelve. His ardour was unabated by the ferocity of criticism, and in 1700 he published *A Paraphrase on the Book of Job. Eliza, an epic poem in ten books* (1705), *Alfred, an epic poem in twelve books* (1723) and, above all, *Creation, a Philosophical Poem* (1712), demonstrating the providence of God, are in the grandest possible manner. Blackmore was a physician. Another was Sir Samuel Garth (1661–1719), whose one famous production (1699) is *The Dispensary, A Poem in Six Cantos*, an early example of "high burlesque". It ridicules a medical squabble of the day, and is a successful essay in the mock-heroic.

Isaac Watts (1674–1748) is one of those formerly "immortal" authors of whom everybody still knows something, even though they may misquote it, in Watts's case, from the affectionate parodies in *Alice in Wonderland*. Watts was an amiable and attractive Nonconformist minister who compelled the admiration even of so staunch a churchman as Johnson. His most famous pieces are contained in *Horae Lyricae* (1706), *Hymns* (1707), *Divine Songs for Children* (1715) (enlarged later as *Divine and Moral Songs for Children*) and *Psalms of David* (1719). Besides ambitious and unsuccessful pieces which we need not name, these contain every Victorian child's friends, the dogs who bark and bite, the busy bee, and the sluggard, as well as the famous hymns *When I survey the wondrous Cross*, and *O God, our help in ages past*, which still grip at the heart, even of the least godly. When the simplicity of Watts really succeeds it has the highest kind of success.

John Philips (1676–1709), Oxford and Tory, not to be confused with Ambrose, Cambridge and Whig, wrote, in *The Splendid Shilling* (1701), an amusing burlesque of Milton and a piece of real blank verse in the age of the couplet. *Blenheim* (1705), another blank verse piece, is a failure. *Cyder, a Poem in Two Books* (1708) is a successful essay in blank verse—indeed, the first blank verse poem of importance since Milton, whom Philips studied with profit. Elijah Fenton (1683–1730) and William Broome (1689–1745) were both translators "in Milton's style", and assisted Pope in the translation of *The Odyssey*, but not in Milton's style. Their original verse is unimportant. Neither Edmund Smith, already mentioned as translator of Racine, nor Joseph Trapp (1679–1747), first Professor of Poetry at Oxford, calls for detailed notice. Henry Brooke (1703–83), the gifted and eccentric author of *The Fool of Quality*, was a poet and dramatist long before he published that remarkable work. *Universal Beauty* (1735) is an attempt at a philosophical poem. A very curious piece called *Conrade*, purporting to be an ancient Irish legend, can hardly be without obligations to Macpherson—unless, indeed, the obligation lies the other way. David Malloch (1705–65), who for prudential reasons changed his name to Mallet, just as his father, a Macgregor, had already changed his to Malloch during the outlawry of the clan, had some disreputable transactions in his life, and was rewarded with the editorship of Bolingbroke's works. His first publication, *William and Margaret* (1723), is based on an old ballad fragment. It is in the eighteenth-century manner; but it helped to set that century on the road of true romantic poetry. His larger poems do not deserve mention. In collaboration with Thomson he wrote the masque called *Alfred* (1740) in which *Rule, Britannia* appears. It is not certain which poet wrote that number, nor is it important; for it is the tune, not the poem, that makes the song. *Edwin and Emma* (1760), another poem in the ballad stanza, suggests Goldsmith, and is less successful than *William and Margaret*.

Richard Savage (d. 1743) owes his fame to an unsubstantiated romance of noble birth and to his friendship with Johnson, who wrote his life. *The Wanderer*

(1729) is one of the worst of long and didactic verse-tractates. *The Bastard*
(1728), much shorter, has a false air of pathos and indignation. It contains one
memorable line: "No tenth transmitter of a foolish face". Stephen Duck
(1705–56) was a more truly tragic figure. A Wiltshire farm-labourer with a
gift for verse, he was taken up by the "best people"; but, feeling unable to fulfil
the absurd expectations of his backers, committed suicide. His *Caesar's Camp on
St George's Hill* (1755) is imitated from Denham's *Cooper's Hill*. Aaron Hill
(1685–1750), a busy poetaster, playwright and inventor, managed to be both
the literary foe and personal friend of Pope. In sprightliness, which he essayed,
Hill nowhere approaches the justly famed *Pipe of Tobacco* of Isaac Hawkins
Browne, a series of parodies which is one of the pleasantest items in Dodsley's
collection.

Two other writers deserve mention, less as poets than as the servants of poetry.
Leonard Welsted (1688–1747) wrote a good deal of verse which gained him a
place in *The Dunciad*; but his translation of Longinus is good and the attached
comments show that, if he could not exactly produce poetry, he could appreciate
it in Spenser and Shakespeare to a degree not common in his day. Christopher
Pitt (1699–1748) made a translation of Virgil (1740) which displaced Dryden's
in the favour of the eighteenth century, and wrote miscellaneous poems,
including many minor translations, which need no comment. His really
important translation, that of Vida's *Art of Poetry* (1527), is one of those things
which are good of their kind whether the kind be good or not. No student of
the history and criticism of poetry should fail to read Vida, and will lose very
little of him in the version of Pitt.

Not least in this procession of minor poets is the elusive and engaging figure
of Henry Carey (d. 1743), creator, in the farce-burlesque of *Chrononhotonthologos*, of many quaint names and some actual lines of verse which stick in the
memory; probably inventor of Ambrose Philips's nickname, "Namby-Pamby",
and of the set of skittish verses attached to it; musician, playwright, and, it is
said, suicide; who, in the end, lives in our hearts as author of the delightful
words, and the almost more delightful music, of *Sally in Our Alley*. Many of
the poets named in these paragraphs owed either their first publication or their
wider popularity to Robert Dodsley (1703–64), footman, verse-writer, playwright and publisher. Nearly all testimonies to "the good natured author of
The Muse in Livery "(1732) are favourable. The publisher of *Old Plays* (1744)
and of *Poems by Several Hands* (1748–58) must, necessarily, have been a man of
enterprise and intelligence, and students of literature are perpetually in his debt.

VII. HISTORICAL AND POLITICAL WRITERS

1. *Burnet and Others*

The historical and political writers of the period now under review may be
grouped round the striking figures of Burnet and Bolingbroke, who represent
two opposite views of politics and history. Gilbert Burnet (1643–1715) was
born and educated in Scotland. When he became a minister at the time of the
Restoration, he naturally added politics to religion, for the two regions of

activity were in fact scarcely separable. Burnet was not less fallible and faulty than most political prelates, but his defects have been magnified by the zealots, who hated his good qualities more than his faults. His impatience with Episcopalian and Presbyterian extremists diverted him from theology to history, and in 1673 he completed his earliest historical work, *The Memoires of the Lives and Actions of James and William Dukes of Hamilton and Castleherald* (1677) composed from documents linked by a thread of narrative in the French manner. In writing it Burnet had found the real direction of his gifts. He came to London, and was at first well-received by Charles II, who had liked *The Memoires of the Hamiltons*. But though he did not retain official favour, he was made preacher at the Rolls Chapel, and came into friendly contact with Tillotson, Stillingfleet, Tenison and other representatives of latitudinarianism. The most important of his productions in these London years, which were the years of the "Popish Plot" and the Protestant reign of terror, was *The History of the Reformation of the Church of England* (1679–81). This, though it appealed to the spirit of the time, was a moderating influence. It is both sincere and readable, and has value as a record.

Between Burnet's greater works come several attractive interludes. The best of these is the account of the last phase in the life of Rochester, already mentioned (p. 368). To a slightly later date (1682) belongs the publication of *The Life and Death of Sir Matthew Hale*, an admirable little biography. Soon afterwards, as if one great lawyer had led him to another, he published (1684) a translation of More's *Utopia*, which, for general readers, is a much better version than the Tudor translation of Robinson. In the last years of Charles II's reign, Burnet declined to throw in his lot with the violent Protestants. He was deprived of his appointments and went into exile. While abroad he became known to the Prince of Orange, and when the Revolution of 1688 established William and Mary on the throne Burnet was made Bishop of Salisbury. For Mary he had sincere esteem, and published (1695) an *Essay* in her memory. Anne liked him less, and the Tories mocked him, but he worked conscientiously for the Protestant Succession.

We now come to the work which Burnet knew was the real labour of his life. The two folio volumes of Burnet's *History of My Own Time* appeared posthumously in 1723 and 1734 respectively. No doubt Clarendon's *History of the Rebellion* gave Burnet his first impulse; but his model (and title) should rather be sought in the *Historiae sui Temporis* of the seventeenth-century French historian Jacques de Thou. The sincerity of his work was, from the first, disputed by irreconcilable censors, and his style as a writer has been as harshly criticized as his matter. Comparisons with Clarendon lead nowhere. There is no fixed style for the writing of history. Burnet has not the rolling periods of Clarendon, but his conversational manner is precisely that suited to his own purpose. He is excellent as a teller of stories, less excellent as a portrayer of the full-length character. Burnet may be charged with time-serving and lack of courage, even as a historian; he cannot be charged with enmity to moderation and the right to think freely under the law.

Contemporary with Burnet is John Strype (1643–1737) who amassed a great collection of historical documents, and did not commit himself to print till he was fifty. His *Memorials of Thomas Cranmer, Archbishop of Canterbury* (1694) was succeeded (1698) by *The Life of the Learned Sir Thomas Smith*, which does equal justice to that scholar's work for the state and his work for the teaching of Greek. Then followed the lives of Bishop Aylmer (1701); "the learned Sir John Cheke" (1705); Archbishop Grindal (1710); Archbishop Parker (1711) and Archbishop Whitgift (1718). Meanwhile, he had also been at work upon his *magnum opus, Annals of the Reformation and Establishment of Religion* (1709–31). The last of Strype's important publications is his *Ecclesiastical Memorials, Relating chiefly to Religion and the Reformation of it* (1721). Strype is a laborious artizan of history, not an artist; but he is one of the first pioneers of historical research.

Jeremy Collier (1650–1726) the non-juror has already been noticed (p. 353) as author of a celebrated attack on the stage. He was one of those fearless, conscientious, fanatical heroes who assert their convictions at any cost. His principal occupation in retirement was the preparation of *The Great Historical ...Dictionary,* based on *Le Grand Dictionnaire historique* of Louis Moreri. Collier's *Dictionary* appeared in successive volumes during 1701–5. It was followed by his chief work, *The Ecclesiastical History of Great Britain* (Vol. I, 1708; Vol. II, 1714), which is naturally "anti-Burnet" and a manifestation of zeal. Fanatical to the last, Collier was a schismatic even among the non-jurors.

Andrew Fletcher of Saltoun (1655–1716), a learned and patriotic Scot, takes his own place as an original political writer. His *Discourse of Government with relation to Militias* (1698) opposes a standing army, and points to the sea as Britain's real defence. In the same year Fletcher wrote *Two Discourses on the affairs of Scotland,* one of which prescribes the drastic remedy of domestic slavery, especially for the Highlanders. He completed at the end of 1703 a short piece called *An Account of a Conversation concerning a Right Regulation of Government for the Common Good of Mankind.* Here is to be found "the famous saying", attributed to "a very wise man", that, "if a man were permitted to make all the ballads, he need not care who should make the laws of a nation".

VIII. HISTORICAL AND POLITICAL WRITERS

2. *Bolingbroke and Others*

The historical and political writings of Henry St John, Viscount Bolingbroke (1678–1751), were nearly all written in the latter half of his life, after the collapse of the Tory party at the death of Queen Anne. During his prosperity he was the friend and patron of the "wits", founded the "Brothers" club, made use of Defoe, and delighted in the society of Pope, Swift, Prior, Arbuthnot and other brilliant figures in the world of letters. In 1710 Bolingbroke inspired the production of a journal to support the Tories in a vigorous campaign against the Whigs. This was *The Examiner* (to be distinguished from other periodicals of that name), of which between thirty and forty numbers appear to have been published up to the spring of 1712. Swift and Prior had a part in it. During the first part of his exile he wrote his celebrated *Letter to Sir William Wyndham,* a masterpiece of lighter controversial prose, not published in his lifetime. The more stilted and formal *Reflections on Exile* belong to 1716.

When he was allowed to return to England, Bolingbroke opened the attack upon the entrenched Whig ministry of Walpole and Townshend with another periodical, *The Craftsman*, which began to appear at the end of 1726 and lasted for several years. It was edited first by Nicholas Amhurst, who called himself "Caleb D'Anvers", and then by Thomas Cooke, who was called "Hesiod Cooke" from his translation of that poet (1728). Contributions are difficult to identify; but Bolingbroke certainly wrote the *Remarks upon the History of England* which appeared between 5 September 1730 and 22 May 1731. His famous attack on Walpole, called *A Dissertation upon Parties*, appeared in *The Craftsman* in the autumn of 1733; but it failed in its purpose; Walpole was not overthrown, and Bolingbroke retreated across the Channel again. Once more settled in France he returned to an old purpose of writing a history of his times. Immediately, however, he propounded his views on the philosophical treatment of history in the *Letters on the Study and Use of History*, addressed in 1735 to Lord Cornbury, Clarendon's great-grandson. In these letters, which influenced Voltaire as well as English writers, Bolingbroke propounds the familiar thesis that history is philosophy teaching by examples. In tone they anticipate the sceptical irony of Gibbon. About the same time he also composed *A Letter on the True Use of Retirement and Study* (1736). Of greater importance is *A Letter on the Spirit of Patriotism*, written in 1736. The theme is one which was to occupy Bolingbroke's mind during the remainder of his life. He looked to the younger generation as the hope of a national party inspired by ideals of patriotism. Readers of Disraeli (who was influenced by Bolingbroke) will find in this doctrine the germ of the "Young England" ideal engagingly set forth in some of the novels. In 1738 Bolingbroke composed the last and most brilliant of his contributions to political literature, *The Idea of a Patriot King*. It was not printed till 1749, when the public situation had greatly changed. It became the political bible of the party which set its hopes on Frederick Prince of Wales, and then on his son, afterwards George III. Burke called Bolingbroke a presumptuous and superficial writer, and the charge is not entirely untrue. He wrote well, but he had little to say. He dabbled in philosophy, and the superficial optimism of Pope's *Essay on Man* was derived from him.

Few of the other historical writers deserve notice here. The best history of England in the earlier half of the century was not an English book at all, but the French *Histoire d'Angleterre* of Paul de Rapin, published at The Hague in eight volumes in 1724. It was translated by Nicholas Tindal in 15 volumes (1725–31), was added to by Thomas Lediard (author of *The Naval History of England* and *The Life of John Duke of Marlborough*) in his *The History of the Reigns of William III and Mary, and Anne*, was still further continued by Tindal, and was later taken over by Smollett. English historical writing owes a great debt to Tindal; for, like Rapin himself, he was not a party man and sought to record ascertained truth. Another Frenchman, Abel Boyer (1667–1729), a Huguenot settled in England, produced *The History of King William III* in 1702 and *The History of the Reigns of Queen Anne, King George I and King George III* in twenty-seven parts between 1703–29.

John Oldmixon (1673–1742) was the kind of writer who inevitably found his way into *The Dunciad*. His earliest historical work, *The British Empire in*

America (2 vols. 1708), was at least designed to meet a real need, and *The Secret History of Europe* (4 parts, 1712–15) was a frank and fierce attack upon the Tory government and its subservience to France. But he incurred the special enmity of the Tory wits by the *Essay on Criticism* prefixed to the third edition (1727) of *The Critical History of England, Ecclesiastical and Civil* (2 vols. 1724–6). *The History of England during the Reigns of the Royal House of Stuart* (1730–9) states at length the charge against the Oxford editors of Clarendon of having altered his text for party ends. Undaunted by infirmity, Oldmixon wrote his interesting *Memoirs of the Press, Historical and Political, for Thirty Years Past, from 1710 to 1740*, but did not live to see the book, which appeared in 1742.

An enduring position in English historical literature is held by the biographies of his kinsmen written by Roger North (1653–1734), who early took to the "loyal side" and consistently referred to the Whigs as "the faction". The whole series of personal sketches, now generally known as *North's Lives of the Norths*, can be justly described as one of the delights of English personal literature.

IX. MEMOIR WRITERS, 1715–60

Under the first two Georges, English society became consolidated into what Disraeli, with his accustomed iridescence, described as the "Venetian oligarchy". The King was not King, so to speak, by grace of God, but by grace of the Whig nobles. He was a "Doge", a figure-head, maintained by the ruling classes, whose great estates included pocket boroughs sending subservient members to Parliament. The Whig aristocracy ruled the country, with a few protesting growls from the regions of finance and few more penetrating noises from Tory rectories and country-houses. Public life was unashamedly corrupt. A patriot was a man who had no place, or had lost a place. If the tide turned, patriots became placemen, and placemen patriots. It was a brilliant and unprincipled period, and it has not escaped record.

Chief among the chroniclers is Lady Mary Wortley Montagu (1689–1762), whose work, however, takes us far from England to the Levant. Lady Mary was a keen observer with the frankness characteristic of an aristocratic age. At twenty-three she eloped with Edward Wortley Montagu, who afterwards became ambassador to the Porte. She expressed herself to her friends in letters and to herself in a diary. Besides assuming Turkish attire, she studied the Turkish language, and did something to make the Near East really known. After her return to England in 1718, she introduced inoculation against smallpox. She was at first the friend and afterwards the foe of Pope, who is alleged to have made love to her and to have been laughed at. After her daughter had eloped with Lord Bute, Lady Mary went abroad again in 1739, and wrote numerous letters, mainly to Lady Bute; and it is through her correspondence, not through her essays or her *Town Eclogues* (preserved in Dodsley's collection) that she acquires a place in the history of English literature. The *Complete Letters* were edited in 1966–7 by Robert Halsband, who wrote in 1956 an excellent biography of Lady Mary.

Precursor in chief of Horace Walpole as court gossip, scandalmonger and memoir-writer was John, Lord Hervey (1696–1743). Early in 1720 he married the reigning beauty, Molly Lepell, the toast of all the wits. A close association between Hervey and Lady Mary Wortley Montagu offended both Pope and Horace Walpole. Hervey attempted to reply to Pope in Pope's own manner, but the poet had the last word in the *Epistle to Arbuthnot*. During the last fifteen years of his life Hervey composed his *Memoirs*, which remained in manuscript for a century and appeared as *Memoirs of the Reign of George the Second* (1848). The book gives a wonderfully vivid picture of the court of the second George. The *dramatis personae* are the King, the Prince, Walpole, Bolingbroke, Chesterfield—and the writer hates them all, sees all their characters at their worst and depicts them with merciless satire. The complete work, edited by R. Sidgwick in three volumes, was not published till 1931.

X. BURLESQUES AND TRANSLATIONS

The underworld of letters had as vigorous an existence in the age of Dryden and Pope as in the age of Marlowe and Shakespeare. But the later, sceptical age was less serious than the earlier, religious age. The difference is clearly shown in a pair of "guides" to London life: *The Gull's Hornbook* of Dekker makes London seem like an ante-chamber to hell; *The London Spy* of Ned Ward makes London seem like Tom Tiddler's Ground. All periods possessing no deep convictions desire to "take down" the great figures of the periods possessing deep convictions; and so the minor writers of the Dryden-Pope period rejoiced in dethronement. In burlesque their acknowledged master was Paul Scarron (1610–60), and their model his *Virgile Travesti*. The fashion was already overpast in France when Charles Cotton made his first experiment in English burlesque. In 1664 he published under the title *Scarronides, or Virgil Travestie*, a mock poem on the first book of the Aeneid; he added the fourth book later, and in 1675 put some of Lucian's dialogues into "English fustian", with the title *Burlesque upon Burlesque: or the Scoffer Scoff'd*. Cotton's method was simple; he took his originals, degraded the stories, and re-told them in coarse Hudibrastic octosyllabics.

Butler's verse, which seemed very easy to write, was imitated by other mockers. The boldest of them all was Edward Ward (1667–1731) always called Ned, who combined the crafts of publican and poet. He was a journalist in verse. His *Hudibras Redivivus* (1705) is a gazette in rhyme. He had prodigious industry, and to cite merely the names of his works would give him more space than he deserves. His one masterpiece is *The London Spy*, "compleat in eighteen parts" (1698, collected 1703). The plan is simple. An exile from London revisits the city and is taken "round the town" by an old school-fellow.

Contemporary with Ned Ward was the famous "Tom Brown of Shifnal" or "Tom Brown of facetious memory" (1663–1704), whose *Amusements Serious and Comical Calculated for the Meridian of London* (1700) pictured the metropolis with less truth than Ward, but with greater wit. Brown was something of a scholar. He translated Persius and mimicked Horace. The best of his work is journalism, illuminated always by the light of scholarship. He was one of the team which translated Scarron's *Le Roman Comique*, and his works, collected into four volumes (1707–11), contain a diversity of matter that will always find him readers of a kind. Everybody knows a few lines by Tom Brown, for, to retaliate on the Dean who had threatened him with expulsion from Christ Church, he turned Martial's lines to Sabidius into—"I do not love you Dr Fell".

Translation into the current speech of the day was a flourishing activity. Brown collaborated with others in a version of Petronius, and with John Phillips (not to be confused with John Philips) and others in a version of Lucian. John Phillips (1631–1706) was bred in classical learning by his uncle John Milton, whose influence he early shook off. In the laborious extent of his translations he was a near rival to Philemon Holland, and gave the readers of his day versions of numerous forgotten foreign romances, histories and voyages. His most celebrated work was *The History of the Most Renowned Don Quixote...made English according to the Humour of our Modern Language* (1687), in which, wrote Charles Whibley, "with untiring energy he illustrates Cervantes from the life of the taverns which he frequented".

Peter Motteux (1660–1718) was of the same kind but of different breeding. He turned his hand to anything. He wrote plays without the smallest distinction and he furnished the plays of others with doggerel prologues. He edited *The Gentleman's Journal* (1692–3), for which *Le Mercure Galant* served as a model. His translation of Rabelais (1693) gives him a sure place in history. His style is as far from the Gallic gravity of the original as from the humorous eloquence of Sir Thomas Urquhart. Nevertheless the version of Motteux has the attraction of representing vividly the "cant" of his day.

For Roger L'Estrange, the work of translation was but a profitable interlude in a busy, active life. We have already mentioned his activity as pamphleteer and journalist (see p. 377). His work as translator was done with the utmost thoroughness. He was the master of many tongues, but his chief qualification for the task was a mastery of his own language. His *Aesop's Fables* (1692) is the best of his performances, and his *Select Colloquies out of Erasmus* (1680) comes near it. He ranged from Terence and Cicero to Quevedo and Josephus. He is at his best with the less grave originals.

Charles Cotton (1630–87)—"the hearty, cheerful Mr Cotton" of Lamb— was another inveterate translator who tried to make his versions true originals. Much that he translated has now no importance or interest; but his version of Montaigne abides, and his continuation (1676) of *The Compleat Angler* assures him of immortality. Cotton's *Poems on Several Occasions* (1689) won the approval of Coleridge, Lamb and Wordsworth.

The most industrious and by no means the least distinguished of the translators of his time was Captain John Stevens or Stephens (d. 1726). It was through his skill and learning that much of Spanish and Portuguese history and literature became widely known to his countrymen. He revised Shelton's *Don Quixote*; but though we owe to him *Pablo de Segovia, the Spanish Sharper*, and a collection of novels with the title *The Spanish Libertines*, his preference was for history and travel, such as *The History of Charles V*, *The Portuguese Asia* and *The Spanish Rule of Trade to the West Indies*.

XI. BERKELEY AND CONTEMPORARY PHILOSOPHY

The half-century of English thought which followed Locke's death was rich in serious speculation. Discussion was directed mainly to three problems—the problem of knowledge, the problem of religion and the problem of morality; and Locke's influence affected thinkers of all kinds. In the present section this division of the problems will be followed, and the writers will be considered as metaphysicians, deists or moralists, even though their works may fall under more than one head.

1. *Metaphysicians*

George Berkeley (1685–1753) was educated at Trinity College, Dublin, and remained there as fellow and tutor till 1713. These are the most remarkable years of his life. His important books were all written during this period; for the later and more charming works added nothing to the original views he had formed before he was twenty-eight. His *Essay towards a New Theory of Vision* appeared in 1709, his *Principles of Human Knowledge, Part I* in 1710; and when, in 1713, he got leave of absence from his college and set out for London, it was to print his new book, *Three Dialogues between Hylas and Philonous*. These three books reveal the new thought which inspired his life. He travelled abroad, and returned to find England in the depth of depression after the collapse of the South Sea Bubble. Berkeley believed that the disaster was caused by the decay of religion and public spirit, and said so eloquently and earnestly in the anonymous *Essay towards Preventing the Ruin of Great Britain* (1721). His appointment to the valuable deanery of Derry gave him resources which he at once began to use in promoting a noble and fantastic scheme, the foundation of an educational Utopia in Bermuda, to reform the English colonists and civilize the American savages. This plan he recommended in his *Proposal for the better supplying of Churches in our foreign Plantations* (1725), and chanted his hopes in the only surviving verses he wrote, with the memorable line, "Westward the course of empire takes its way"—on account of which the town of Berkeley in California (and therefore, fittingly enough, Berkeley University) was called after him. Berkeley sailed for the west in 1729, landed at Newport, Rhode Island, and waited for the promised grant from Walpole. It never came. Berkeley did not even see the still vexed Bermoothes; but though he built no college, he builded better than he knew. He left his impress upon New England theology, and he stimulated the provision of American university education. On his return Berkeley joined in the religious controversies of the age. In the delightful dialogues of *Alciphron, or the Minute Philosopher* (1732), written in the seclusion of his home in Rhode Island, he applied his general principles in defence of religion against the free-thinkers. In 1733 appeared his *Theory of Vision, or Visual Language Vindicated and Explained*; and in 1734 he published *The Analyst*, a bold "relativist" criticism of Newtonian mathematics. Berkeley was made Bishop of Cloyne, but his heart was still given to social reform and religious speculation. Reform is represented by *The Querist* (1735), composed entirely of penetrating interrogations; speculation is represented by *Siris: a*

Chain of Philosophical Reflexions (1744), which begins by expounding the medicinal virtues of tar-water, and ends in an exposition of idealism.

Berkeley's "immaterial hypothesis" was very early conceived, but was not fully declared to the world at once. *An Essay towards a New Theory of Vision* deals with one point only—the relation between the objects of sight and the objects of touch. The essence of his doctrine consists in two propositions—that the objects (or ideas) of sight have nothing in common with the objects (or ideas) of touch, and that the connection of sight and touch is arbitrary, and learned by experience only. Sight and touch have no separable "abstract" common element in which they both consist. The argument is brief; but whatever the defects of its conclusion, the *Essay* is one of the most brilliant and lucid pieces of psychological analysis in the English language. The little *Treatise concerning the Principles of Human Knowledge* carries the war against philosophical abstractions a stage further. It is one of the works which have had a critical influence upon the course of European thought. The fresh step which Berkeley took was short and simple; when taken, it shows us the whole world from a new point of view. Philosophers, such as Locke and Descartes, had found difficulty in defending the reality of the things which they supposed to be represented by the ideas. Berkeley solves the difficulty by denying the distinction. The ideas *are* the things. It is mind, not matter, which creates. Into the spiritual or religious application of his doctrine—the need for an omnipresent eternal Mind—we need not enter. The later works, *Hylas* and *Alciphron*, both show him using the dialogue form in argument with a skill never excelled in English philosophical literature. But he did not work out his spiritual interpretation of reality into a system. His mind, like that of Sir Thomas Browne, was essentially religious; and in *Siris*, the last of his philosophical works, religious thought emerges from the midst of reflections on empirical medicine and old-fashioned physiology. Its prose is a perfect example of philosophical composition.

Arthur Collier (1680–1732), a Wiltshire clergyman, published in 1713 *Clavis Universalis: or a New Inquiry after Truth. Being a Demonstration of the Non-Existence, or Impossibility, of an External World.* In this book he reached independently, and by a different procedure, the same conclusions as Berkeley.

2. Deists

The first half of the eighteenth century was the period of the deistical controversy in English theology. The chief writers commonly classed together as deists are Charles Blount, John Toland, Anthony Collins and Matthew Tindal. Bolingbroke and the third Earl of Shaftesbury are usually included among the deists; but neither paid much attention to theological controversy. Deism was a natural result of the fierce religious controversies. It was both a symptom of exhaustion and a search for a solution. In its best aspect, deism was an attempt to find a natural or rational religion—a religion which admitted a God, but not a creed, a reason, but not a mystery, an understanding, but not a revelation. It was one of several attempts to find an abstract religion of religions, valid for all times and all places—a "world-religion"; and like later attempts at universalism it failed, because it assumed that men are fortified, consoled and sustained by reason. Deism never became popular. It suffered a worse fate. It became fashionable. Deism, too, suffered much from its prophets. Few of them could write. Power and persuasion were on the side of those who, from Berkeley to Butler, defended, not any religion, but the Christian religion.

The father of English deism was Lord Herbert of Cherbury, who has been discussed earlier (see p. 178). Charles Blount (1654–93), first of the later deists, accepted Lord Herbert's views. In his *Anima Mundi* (1679) he defended a system of natural religion, and emphasized the merits of the heathen religions. *Great is Diana of the Ephesians* (1680) is an attack on priestcraft. His translation of *The Two First Books of Philostratus, concerning the Life of Apollonius Tyaneus* (1680) contains comments that further attack the fundamentals of Christianity.

A more important writer was John Toland (1670–1722), an Irish Catholic educated at Scottish universities. In a sense, he moved with the times, for his spiritual progress, not clearly traceable in his books, was from Catholicism to something like Pantheism; and he deserves more respect than he has received. Locke, in *The Reasonableness of Christianity*, sought to show that Christianity was reasonable. Toland, in *Christianity not Mysterious* (1696), went a step further, and sought to show that nothing contrary to reason, and nothing above reason, can be part of Christian doctrine. There are no mysteries in it. Faith is knowledge. Toland's book became more than famous, it became infamous, much to his astonishment. But his mind travelled on. He had left Catholicism far behind, and showed few symptoms of any kind of churchmanship in his later works. In *Amyntor* (1699), a defence of his *Life of Milton* (1698), and in *Nazarenus; or Jewish, Gentile, and Mahometan Christianity* (1718), he shows considerable knowledge of early apocryphal Christian literature. That Toland was ever a deist in the usual sense may be doubted. He was rather a free-thinker in search of a faith.

Free-thinking was the declared position of Locke's friend and disciple Anthony Collins (1676–1729), whose best-known work is *A Discourse of Free-thinking, occasioned by the Rise and Growth of a Sect call'd Free-thinkers* (1713). What may be called the two main motives in the faith of Collins, belief in reason and hatred of priestcraft, are indicated by the titles of his earliest works—*Essay concerning the use of Reason* (1707) and *Priestcraft in Perfection* (1709). Collins held firmly to a belief in God as established by reason; but he was a hostile critic of the Christian creed. A small book called *A Philosophical Inquiry concerning Human Liberty and Necessity* (1715) is an acute and clearly-written argument in favour of the necessitarian solution of the problem.

The most significant work of the whole deistical movement, often known as "the Deist's Bible", was the book by Matthew Tindal (1656–1733) called *Christianity as Old as the Creation: or, the Gospel, a Republication of the Religion of Nature* (1730). Its argument is fundamental. God gave man reason; reason establishes the clear truth of natural religion; therefore Christianity is superfluous. Tindal's other works, much earlier in date, do not call for much notice, though one of them, *The Rights of the Christian Church asserted* (1706), shared the fate of Henry Sacheverell's sermons, being burnt with them in 1710 by order of the House of Commons.

The line between deists and churchmen was not always drawn very clearly. There was much common ground and some of the discussions were not closely relevant to either view. One controversialist, William Whiston (1667–1752), the Cambridge mathematician and theologian, in opposing rationalism was led back to Arianism, and published a work, *Primitive Christianity Revived* (1711–12), which cost him his Cambridge professorship. His translation of Josephus (1737) has proved of more lasting value than his theology. Conyers Middleton (1683–1750) showed how near a clergyman might come to the deistical position. He denied verbal inspiration and rejected the evidence for ecclesiastical miracles in *A Free Inquiry into the Miraculous Powers which are supposed to have existed in the Christian Church through several successive Ages* (1748).

Among the opponents of the deists, the two greatest were Samuel Clarke and Joseph Butler, who will be noticed later; but the loudest was William Warburton, Bishop of Gloucester, who was always ready to write upon anything and against anybody. He has already been mentioned (p. 234) as probably the worst of Shakespeare's many editors. To the deistical controversy, he contributed a typically lawyer-like production, *The Divine Legation of Moses demonstrated on the Principles of a Religious Deist* (1737–41), a vast work, never completed, intended to refute a deistical charge that the books of Moses contain no reference to the doctrine of a future life. Nothing more need be said of it.

3. Moralists

Samuel Clarke (1675–1729) was not a man of original genius; but, by sheer intellectual power, he came to occupy a leading position in English philosophy and theology. In 1704 and 1705 he delivered two courses of Boyle lectures, entitled respectively, *A Demonstration of the Being and Attributes of God*, and *A Discourse concerning the Unchangeable Obligations of Natural Religion, and the Truth and Certainty of the Christian Revelation*. His other works hardly need mention. Clarke's ethical doctrine shows some traces of originality. The view that morality is not arbitrary, but belongs to the order of the universe, had found frequent expression in theories of "the law of nature". Clarke goes one step further in holding that goodness is a certain "congruity" of one thing with another.

A more fruitful line of ethical thought was followed by Clarke's contemporary, the third Earl of Shaftesbury (1671–1713), grandson of Dryden's Achitophel. His writings were published in three volumes, entitled *Characteristics of Men, Manners, Opinions, Times*, in 1711; a second edition, carefully revised and enlarged, was ready at the time of his death in 1713. The unfinished complementary *Second Characters* was published in 1914. The prose of Shaftesbury is always clear, and free from the traditional technicalities. He is usually reckoned among the deists, but he disliked theological controversy of any kind. He opposed persecution, and though he did not actually say that ridicule is the test of truth he certainly regarded ridicule as a specific against superstition. He believed that man has both personal and social (or natural) affections. Further, in man there is a "sense of right and wrong", to which Shaftesbury gives the name "the moral sense"—a phrase that has helped to keep his name in memory.

As thinker, humanitarian and writer, Shaftesbury had many fine qualities to which justice has not yet been done.

The doctrine of the moral sense was developed by Francis Hutcheson (1694–1746), first of modern Scottish philosophers, and author of *An Inquiry into the Original of our Ideas of Beauty and Virtue* (1725), and *An Essay on the Nature and Conduct of the Passions and Affections, with Illustrations on the Moral Sense* (1728). His *System of Moral Philosophy* (1755) was published after his death. The ideas of Shaftesbury reappear in these works in a somewhat more systematic form. Hutcheson was, historically, the forerunner of the Utilitarians. In his first work he even used the formula—"the greatest happiness for the greatest numbers"—afterwards, with a slight verbal change, made famous by Bentham.

Hutcheson's first work was described on the title-page as a defence of Shaftesbury against the author of *The Fable of the Bees*. In 1705 Bernard Mandeville (1670?–1733), a Dutch physician resident in London, had published a pamphlet of some four hundred lines of doggerel verse entitled *The Grumbling Hive, or Knaves Turn'd Honest*. This was republished (1714, 1723), with elaborate discussions, as *The Fable of the Bees; or, Private Vices, Public Benefits*. Mandeville marks a reaction both against the optimism to which Shaftesbury and the deists gave philosophical expression, and against the conventions associated with popular morality. He was clever enough to observe that luxury and vice accompany large prosperity and shallow enough to mistake them for its foundation. Mandeville was in no sense a philosopher; but his paradoxes have not been completely answered, nor, in an imperfect world, can they ever be without some foundation.

Joseph Butler (1692–1752), Bishop of Durham, was the greatest theological writer of his own time, and one of the greatest of any time. He published two books only—*Fifteen Sermons* (1726) and *The Analogy of Religion, Natural and Revealed, to the Constitution and Course of Nature* (1736). His writings have no charm or magic of style; but they have a grave dignity and close-knit texture that will always appeal to the educated mind. Butler's condensed and weighty argument hardly admits of summary; indeed, he was distrustful of any attempt at a system of philosophy, and was content to accept probability as the guide of life. Grant, as the deists granted, that God is the author of nature, then religion follows naturally. Nature and morality are so connected as to form a single scheme. There are no difficulties in the doctrines of religion not paralleled by difficulties in the course of nature. This is the "analogy" to the establishment of which Butler's reasonings are directed. They are so exhaustive, so thorough and so candid, that critics of all schools are agreed in regarding his as the final word in a long controversy.

XII. WILLIAM LAW AND THE MYSTICS

To discuss the mystical thought of the free-thinking period may seem to require little space or labour. As the preceding pages have shown, this was an age of religion without mystery, of a theoretical God and a mechanical universe, of Christianity, not as something to be lived, but as something to be proved.

Never before in England had men written so much about religion and practised it so little. Such appears to be the judgment we must pass on the age of the deists. But, like all easy summaries, this is only part of the truth. Besides the scepticism of Bolingbroke there was the immaterialism of Berkeley. Besides the corrupt place-hunting of politicians, there was the conscientious self-sacrifice of the non-jurors. Self-sacrifice and spiritual exaltation were very notably combined in the inspiring life of William Law (1686–1761), author of one of the great English classics of religion. The early Quakers had the mystical conviction of union with God. Some of them were probably influenced by the teachings of Jacob Boehme, whose works had been put into English between the years 1644 and 1692. Almost as persuasive with others were the writings of Madame Guyon and Archbishop Fénelon. The influence of the mystics may be traced in many manifestations, even in Newton's great discovery; for it is almost certain that the idea of the three laws of motion first reached Newton through his eager study of Boehme; but it touches English literature specially in the writings of Law. Law had a curiously paradoxical career. After being ordained and becoming a fellow of his college at Cambridge, he refused to take the oaths of allegiance to George I, and thus lost his fellowship and voca-tion. Though an ardent High Churchman, he was the father of Methodism. Though deprived of employment in his church, he wrote the book which most deeply influenced the religious life of a century and more. Though a sincere Christian, he was the classic exponent of Boehme, a thinker abhorred and mistrusted alike by orthodox divines and by Wesleyan leaders. One of the oddest connections in English literature is that between Law and Gibbon. Law was tutor to the father of the historian, and lived for several years at Putney as "the much honoured friend and spiritual director of the whole family". Gibbon's autobiography criticises Law with great respect and qualified praise; but even qualified praise for a mystic is high testimony from such a man as Gibbon. The publication of *A Serious Call* brought him renown, and he was revered and consulted by an admiring band of disciples. He settled near Stam-ford with Hester Gibbon, the historian's aunt, and another lady, and lived a life of personal piety and public good works in charity and education till his death twenty years later.

Law's writings fall into three divisions, controversial, practical and mystical. His controversial works are directed against a curious assortment of opponents: Hoadly, latitudinarian Bishop of Bangor, Mandeville, a sceptical pessimist, and Tindal, a deistical optimist. These writers represent three main sections of the religious opinion of the day, and Law cheerfully confronts them all. What is generally called the Bangorian controversy arose at the accession of George I. The Church, always on the side of "the Lord's anointed" in Stuart times, found itself in difficulties, first when James II was declared to have forfeited the throne, and next when a parliamentary king from Hanover ascended the throne as George I. For devout churchmen to accept William was difficult; to accept George was impossible. The posthumous papers of George Hickes, the non-juror, charged the Church with schism, and Benjamin Hoadly, Bishop of Bangor, came forward as champion of Crown and Church. Hoadly was an able thinker and writer, and in his *Preservative against the Principles and Practices of the Non-Jurors* (1716) he attempts to justify the civil power by reducing to a minimum the idea of church authority and even that of creeds. Law's *Three Letters to the Bishop of Bangor* (1717–19) argued unanswerably that if Hoadly's contentions are accepted, the episcopalian constitution disappears, the church becomes a lay body of teachers, and the free-thinkers triumph in a creedless organization. Hoadly did not attempt to answer. Law's next work, *Remarks on the Fable of the Bees* (1723), replies to Mandeville's paradoxes in a style at once buoyant, witty and caustic. *The Case of Reason* (1731) is Law's answer to the deists, and especially to Tindal's *Christianity as Old as the Creation* (1730). The deists professed to find a rational God and a rational universe, with no mystery about either. Law replied, in effect, that man himself is a mystery, that his universe is a mystery, and that to take reason as the one sufficient guide to truth is to fall into the deepest error.

Two of Law's books, *A Practical Treatise upon Christian Perfection* (1726) and *A Serious Call to a Devout and Holy Life. Adapted to the State and Condition of All Orders of Christians* (1728), have been more read than any other of his writings. They are not controversial. They show that the way to Christian life is not through doctrine or ceremony, but through a change in temper and principle. *Christian Perfection* has much charm and beauty, but it is quite over-shadowed by the wider popularity of *A Serious Call*, a book of extraordinary power, persuasive style, racy wit, and unanswerable logic. Few books in English have exerted such a wide influence. It sowed the seed of Methodism, and, undoubtedly, next to the Bible, it contributed more than any other book to the spread of Evangelicalism.

It was in the latter part of his life that Law became a definite mystic, though mystical writings had long attracted him. When he was about forty-six, he came across the work of the seer who set his whole nature aglow with mystical fervour. Jacob Boehme (1575–1624) or Behmen, as he has usually been called, was a poor peasant shoemaker of Görlitz, who, like Blake (whom he influenced) lived in a glory of inner illumination. He was interested in all mystical specula-tion, eastern and western. He did not distinguish between physical and spiritual knowledge. For him they were two aspects of the same ultimate unity. The central point of his philosophy is the fundamental postulate that all manifesta-tion necessitates opposition. The cosmic opposition is the will which says "yes" and the will which says "no". "Without contraries is no progression" is the way Blake puts it in *The Marriage of Heaven and Hell*. Any full account of Boehme's doctrine would be out of place in such a volume as this. We must accept him as important because he helps to explain the spirit of two great English writers, Law and Blake. Blake saw visions and spoke a tongue like that of the illuminated cobbler; and Law recognized at once the hunger of the soul that is the mark of the true religious mystic.

The two most important of Law's mystical treatises are *An Appeal to all that Doubt* (1740) and *The Way to Divine Knowledge* (1752). To discuss their teaching would take us far from our immediate purpose. We must therefore say no more than this, that Law's simplicity and sincerity were combined with an unusual gift of literary expression which gave his teaching a wide and instant appeal. Few men have more endearingly shown the beauty of holiness.

The two most famous disciples of Law were John and Charles Wesley—until John discovered that Law seemed to attach no importance to the doctrine of the Atonement; and thereafter described mystics as those who slighted the means of grace. Perhaps the most charming and most lovable of Law's followers was John Byrom (1692–1723), who might be called Law's Boswell if he did not more resemble Goldsmith. The collection called *The Private Journal and Literary Remains of John Byrom* (1854–7; re-edited 1950 by Henri Talon) is a delightful and far too little known work. Byrom's religious verse is not likely to be much read; but everyone knows the hymn "Christians awake" and most people know the "Handel" and the "Pretender" epigrams attributed to him.

Henry Brooke, already noticed (p. 397) as a poet, was another writer deeply imbued with Boehme's thought, and his expression of it, imbedded in that curious medley of stories, adventures and arguments, *The Fool of Quality* (1766), reached, probably, a larger public than did Law's own treatises. The book is a most extraordinary mixture of gaiety and gravity, of genius and foolishness. It found favour with John Wesley, who reprinted it in 1781, shortened and modified, as *The History of Henry Earl of Moreland*. In this form it was read by generations of devout Wesleyans.

XIII. SCHOLARS AND ANTIQUARIES

1. *Bentley and Classical Scholarship*

At the end of the seventeenth century, the history of scholarship is illuminated by the great name of Richard Bentley (1662–1742), a born scholar with an unrivalled sense of words in their time and place. In 1692 he was chosen as first Boyle lecturer—Robert Boyle, the natural philosopher, having founded (as we have mentioned) a lectureship in defence of the Christian religion. Two years later Bentley was appointed keeper of the royal libraries, with official lodgings in St James's Palace. Shortly afterwards he became involved in the famous and foolish controversy which later involved Swift (pp. 376, 388, 390). Sir William Temple had written an essay in which he praised ancient literature at the expense of modern, and had cited the so-called "Letters of Phalaris" as an example of the superiority. Charles Boyle, a relative of Robert, published an edition of the Letters (1695) and took a chance of making an insulting reference to Bentley. In 1694 William Wotton entered the lists against Sir William Temple in defence of modern learning; and in 1697 a second edition of this book included an appendix in which Bentley not only declared the letters of Phalaris to be spurious, but blamed Boyle's tutors for allowing him to display his ignorance. The "wits" of Christ Church thereupon took up the quarrel and tried to crush Bentley by personal ridicule. At this point another great man took a share in the conflict, young Jonathan Swift, Temple's *protégé*, in the amusing *Battle of the Books*. Bentley settled the controversy finally in his *Dissertation upon the Epistles of Phalaris* (1699), which not only disposed of Phalaris and his defenders, but made readers aware of the "higher criticism" by which a competent scholar can distinguish between ancient authors of different dates as readily as an ordinary reader can distinguish between Chaucer and Masefield. In 1699 Bentley became Master of Trinity, and at once was involved in a conflict with the Fellows which lasted for nearly forty years. The nature and causes of that quarrel do not concern us, but we may note that Bentley did much to reform studies and discipline, that he was friendly to science, and that he was hospitable to foreign scholars. Most of his work belongs to the history of classical learning. Two books, however, call for mention, his *Remarks upon a Late Discourse of Freethinking* (1713), in which he ridiculed the scholarly pretensions of Anthony Collins, and his edition of *Paradise Lost* (1732), in which he amended Milton's text as if it were a corrupt ancient manuscript. The book is a curiosity of literature and is almost a parody of the "higher criticism".

2. Antiquaries

The opening of Bodley's library at Oxford in 1602 stimulated the researches of scholars among local and historical records, and encouraged the formation of collections of antiquities.

One of the first to use the new materials was Sir William Dugdale (1605–86), whose book *The Antiquities of Warwickshire* (1656) set a new standard in works of its kind. But Dugdale's greatest achievement is *Monasticon Anglicanum*, an account, enriched by original documents, of the English monastic houses. It appeared in three volumes, 1655, 1661, 1673. In 1722–3 Captain John Stevens (see p. 404), to whom is attributed the English abridgement, brought out two supplementary volumes. In 1658 Dugdale produced his *History of St Paul's Cathedral* and thus preserved a record of the building and monuments that were destroyed in the Great Fire of 1666. *The History of Imbanking and Drayning of divers Fenns and Marshes* (1662) gave him an opportunity for telling the whole story of Hereward's stand against the Conqueror. *Origines Juridicales* (1666) and *The Baronage of England* (1675–6) are further monuments to his zeal for research. His "church and king" principles found expression in *A Short View of the Late Troubles in England* (1681). Dugdale was both an excellent scholar and an excellent writer.

The most characteristic figure in the Oxford group is Anthony Wood (1632–95), or Anthony à Wood as, in later years, he pedantically styled himself. Dugdale's *Warwickshire* inspired his *Historia et Antiquitates Universitatis Oxoniensis* (1674), and this he later enlarged and transcribed into English. Being asked to append biographical notices of Oxford writers to the accounts of the colleges, he produced the *Athenae Oxonienses* (1691–2), the monumental work upon which his fame rests. His autobiography and journal notes, published in 1891–1900 under the title of *The Life and Times of Anthony Wood...as Described by Himself*, show that the asperity of some of his biographical comments was a natural part of an unpleasing character.

Thomas Hearne (1678–1735) was a scholar of different temper. He became assistant keeper in the Bodleian Library, and one of his first productions fitly commemorates the founder: *Reliquiae Bodleianae, or Some Genuine Remains of Sir Thomas Bodley* (1703). *Ductor Historicus, or A short System of Universal History and an Introduction to the Study of it* (1704–5) indicates the direction of his interests. He published John Leland's *Itinerary* (1710–12) and *Collectanea* (1715);

but his most important service to historical study was the production of an admirable collection of early English chronicle histories, issued from 1716 to the year of his death. An autobiographical sketch and some extracts from the diaries, with the title *Reliquiae Hearnianae*, were not published till 1857.

One of the chief contributors to Wood's *Athenae* was John Aubrey (1626–97), whose *Brief Lives* gathered the floating traditions about Shakespeare, Ben Jonson, Ralegh, and Bacon. It is a delightful collection. One of the modern editions was edited by the novelist and biographer Anthony Powell, author of *John Aubrey and His Friends* (1948). The only book which Aubrey himself published, *Miscellanies* (1696), reveals the credulous side of his character which made Wood call him "magotieheaded".

Among the more ancient monuments of antiquity, Stonehenge was the most fruitful cause of speculation. Aubrey assigns to it a Druidical origin. Inigo Jones sought to trace a Roman original. Walter Charleton, in *Chorea Gigantum* (1663), endeavoured to "restore" it to the Danes, and William Stukeley, in 1740, produced his *Stonehenge, a Temple Restor'd to the British Druids*. Druidism or neo-Celticism was a curious revival, specially interesting because it affected Blake and other poets. "In yonder grave a Druid lies" wrote Collins in his *Ode on the Death of Thomson*. Unfortunately the movement did not attract the serious historians of the time.

The efforts of Archbishop Parker in the sixteenth century to further Old English studies produced many votaries, among whom are to be counted William Somner, whose *Dictionarium Saxonico-Latino-Anglicum* was issued in 1659, Francis Junius, George Hickes, Bishop Edmund Gibson, editor of the *Old English Chronicle*, William Elstob, and his learned sister Elizabeth, who published an Old English grammar in 1715. The *Typographical Antiquities* of Joseph Ames (1749) gives the first real history of printing.

It would be improper to conclude this section without reference to two great private collections of books and manuscripts which are now among the treasures of the British Museum. The library of Sir Robert Cotton was immensely rich in spoils from the dispossessed monasteries and was generously open to scholars. The Harleian library, no less remarkable in its way, was collected by Robert Harley, first Earl of Oxford, and his son. On the death of the second earl, the printed books (upwards of 20,000 volumes) were purchased by Thomas Osborne, remembered as the publisher of *The Harleian Miscellany* (1744–6). This reprint of a selection of tracts from the Harleian library was edited by William Oldys and Johnson, who also worked together for some time upon a catalogue of the whole collection. Oldys, who deserved a better fate, spent a large part of his life in hack-work for booksellers. To an edition of Ralegh's *History of the World* (1736) he prefixed an elaborate life of the author, perhaps his most important work.

Though some of the voluminous publications of the antiquaries here named may not survive as contributions to English literature, they deserve record as treasuries of ancient traditions which are the material of literature.

XIV. SCOTTISH POPULAR POETRY
BEFORE BURNS

During a large portion of the sixteenth and nearly the whole of the seventeenth century, a blight had fallen on secular verse in Scotland. It is difficult to tell what was the actual effect of the kirk's repressive rule on the manners, morals, habits and ancient predilections of the people; but there is evidence that the old songs, though superseded by *The Gude and Godly Ballatis*, were not extinguished. After the accession of James VI to the English throne, the better classes were less submissive to the kirk's authority, and to them we owe some of the songs preserved by Ramsay, songs which are Scottish in character, though English in metre and style.

Some of Ramsay's songs have known authors—Lady Grizel Baillie, Lady Wardlaw, and William Hamilton of Gilbertfield. The old poetic methods of the "makaris" were preserved or revived by Robert Sempill (1595?–1665?) in his famous elegy on *The Life and Death of Habbie Simson, Piper of Kilbarchan*, the chief merit of which is the stave, which existed long before Sempill (see p. 35), but which he revived and gave back to Scottish vernacular poetry. It will be instantly recognized as a form peculiarly associated with later Scottish verse:

> And when he play'd, the lasses leugh
> To see him teethless, auld, and teugh.
> He wan his pipes beside Barcleugh,
> Withouten dread;
> Which after wan him gear eneugh;
> But now he's dead.

The outstanding figure of the vernacular revival was Allan Ramsay (1686–1758), who was an unknown journeyman wig-maker when James Watson published his famous *Choice Collection of Comic and Serious Scots Poems both Ancient and Modern* (1706–9–11). Ramsay, in his early publications, showed command of a satirical manner and of a light gift for humour. But his crowning poetical achievement is the pastoral drama entitled *The Gentle Shepherd* (1725), which depicts the humours of rustic life without its grossness. He instituted a circulating library, not for the dissemination of theology, but for the general diffusion of light, ameliorating literature. Indeed, he did more than any other man to further the intellectual revival of which Edinburgh became the centre. Apart from this, by the publication of his own verse, of *The Tea-Table Miscellany* (1724–32), and of *The Ever Green, being a Collection of Scots Poems, wrote by the Ingenious before* 1600 (1724), containing verse of the old "makaris", obtained chiefly from the Bannatyne MS., he disseminated a love of song and verse among the people. Ramsay is entitled to the gratitude of his countrymen. His pioneer work as editor, publisher and librarian gives him more genuine importance than some Scotsmen of superior genius can claim.

Other figures worthy of notice are Alexander Pennecuick (d. 1730), with a gift for broad humour and satirical portraiture, and William Hamilton of Bangour (1704–54), whose one notable composition is the melodious *Braes of Yarrow*. Alexander Ross acquired much fame in the northern counties by his pastoral *Helenore or the Fortunate Shepherdess* (1768), which is specially interesting as a specimen of the Aberdeenshire dialect. Quite the equal of Ross as a song-writer was John Skinner, an episcopalian minister, whose *Tullochgorum* so captivated Burns by its cheerfulness that he pronounced it to be "the best Scots song Scotland ever saw". Mrs Cockburn, a relative of Sir Walter Scott, wrote, besides other songs which have not attained to popularity, a version of *The Flowers of the Forest*. A more vernacular version, "I've heard them Lilting at the Ewe Milking" by Jane Elliot, was used by Herd, but an authentic copy was obtained by Scott for *The Border Minstrelsy*. Of a considerable number of songs of the eighteenth century the authorship is either doubtful or quite unknown. Some were preserved by David Herd, and are included in his *Ancient and Modern Scottish Poems* (1769—enlarged 1776). Neither Peter Buchan's *Gleanings of Scotch, English and Irish Ballads* (1825) nor Robert Hartley Cromek's *Remains of Nithsdale and Galloway Song* (1810) can be regarded as trustworthy.

For Jacobite songs the main published authority is still James Hogg's *Jacobite Relics of Scotland* (1819–21). The texts are untrustworthy, though the notes are useful. In fact, Hogg edited the *Jacobite Relics* very much after the fashion in which Scott edited *The Border Minstrelsy*.

The succession of the Scottish bards at this period closes, as it began, with a remarkable personality. The ill-fated Robert Fergusson (1750–74) died in a madhouse at the age of twenty-four. His feeling for rustic life is revealed in his odes *To the Bee* and *The Gowdspink*, delicately descriptive, humorous and faintly didactic, and in *The Farmer's Ingle*, a perfect picture of a winter evening in a farmhouse kitchen. But it was as the poet of his native Edinburgh that he was to make his mark—the "Auld Reekie" of tavern jollifications and street scenes. The verse of Fergusson (collected 1773, 1779) is small in bulk, and of course it has the faults of youth; but the genuineness of his inspiration is beyond question.

XV. EDUCATION

The history of education from the Commonwealth to the death of George II is a dismal story. The main points to notice are these: that the Restoration gave to the now triumphant Church of England a monopoly of teaching as well as of preaching; that the two great universities remained medieval in studies and methods, and closed their doors against all but members of the Church of England; that the Dissenters set up academies of their own, which began to succeed, and which were therefore attacked by the Schism Act of 1714 for-bidding anyone not a member of the Church of England to keep a school; that there was no provision of education for girls; that some attempts were made to mitigate the dreadful ignorance and degradation of the very poor by means of charity schools aided by religious societies, of which the Society for Promoting Christian Knowledge (1699) is the best known; and that even these feeble attempts were attacked as socially and politically subversive. For another two centuries and more the spirit of religious faction, engendered at the Restoration, was to impede the establishment of a system of national education in England. But a period is not wholly dark that saw the publication of Locke's *Some*

Thoughts Concerning Education (1693) and Defoe's *Essay upon Projects* (1697) and his *Compleat English Gentleman* (c. 1730). This, too, was the age of the great Moravian, John Amos Comenius, who familiarized Europe with the idea of national education and who was invited to England by the Long Parliament in 1641. The Civil War terminated any peaceful activities. The Commonwealth, however narrow some of its Puritan ideals, did have its educational proposals; the Restoration ensured the triumph of orthodoxy and ignorance.

CHAPTER X

THE AGE OF JOHNSON

I. RICHARDSON

In the eighteenth century the English novel grew quietly to its full stature. The Elizabethans had toyed with romance and with realism; Bunyan had made a story out of his religious convictions; Addison and Steele had expressed common beliefs and sentiments in essays with a touch of fiction; Defoe had given to homely fact an imaginative appeal. The way for the modern novel was thus fully prepared. A clearer day of probity and fervour among the general public had followed the rake-hell noctambulism of the Restoration. A new public for a new fiction was ready, and almost expectant. Richardson, a contemporary of John Wesley, is the typical figure of a changed order.

Samuel Richardson (1689–1751), a master-printer, appeared to be the complete English tradesman, and nothing more. And yet, by one of the inexplicable whims of nature, this diligent, prosperous "bourgeois" was endowed with a creative gift, narrow but intense, and wrote a masterpiece of fiction which plunged England and the Continent into the pleasing excitement of tears. The literary history of Richardson is simple. It begins with his first novel, written when he was fifty, and composed almost by accident. He had been asked by two friends, printers like himself, to prepare for them "a little volume of letters, in a common style, on such subjects as might be of use to those country readers who were unable to indite for themselves". The book came out in 1741, and is best described by its own lengthy title: *Letters written to and for particular Friends, on the most important Occasions. Directing not only the requisite Style and Forms to be observed in writing Familiar Letters; but how to think and act justly and prudently, in the common Concerns of Human Life.* One of the subjects treated in this collection is the special danger attending an attractive girl employed as a domestic servant. Out of this grew *Pamela; or Virtue Rewarded*, published in two volumes (1740) and followed a year later by two further volumes, describing the heroine's life after her marriage. The epistolary form adopted by Richardson now seems clumsy and even irritating; but the letter was clearly Richardson's natural form of expression. The objection, seriously made, that Pamela could hardly have written so much in the intervals of her working-day is ludicrously irrelevant. The epistolary form of story is a convention, which, like every other artistic convention, must be judged by its success, not by its adherence to facts. Time-schemes are important only when they are a necessary part of the plot.

The success of *Pamela* in kitchen and boudoir alike proved that Richardson had given his public what the novel-reading public has demanded in some form ever since, namely, realism and romance nicely blended. As a work of art, the book is a crude first attempt, redeemed by unmistakable genius.

Pamela herself is the least sympathetic of Richardson's heroines, and might even be called immoral, in the sense that she puts a price on her virtue. That the price is marriage scarcely alters the fact. But the age drew no fine distinctions, and the book swept the country with a wave of collective emotion. Though Richardson intended Pamela herself to point a moral, the artist in him got the better of the moralist, and the character, as genuine creations must, began to live her own life. With all its faults, Richardson's first novel belongs to an order of artistic achievement and psychological truth which English literature had scarcely known since the decay of Elizabethan drama.

The success of *Pamela* called out many burlesques, but only one deserves mention, *An Apology for the Life of Mrs Shamela Andrews, etc.*, by *Conny Keyber* (1741). This was obviously written by someone (probably Fielding) who wished to annoy both Richardson and Cibber. The skit has little merit. Fielding's real "anti-*Pamela*" was *Joseph Andrews*.

Richardson's next book, *Clarissa*, might almost be considered to be his own answer to *Pamela*. The "hero" of *Pamela* was a rake reformed by marriage, and the moral author saw some danger in that example. His next rake should be the complete thing, and so *Clarissa, or, the History of a young Lady*, was designed to be a painful demonstration of the perfidy of man. The first edition consisted of seven volumes, two of which were issued in 1747 and the rest in 1748. That *Clarissa* is eminently Richardson's best work cannot be questioned. It has great breadth and great depth, and the moral purpose is subdued to the human tragedy. It is, in a singular degree, both exquisite and powerful. Clarissa herself is a genuine creation, winning, warm and natural, and therefore liable to her own disaster. The growth of her feeling for Lovelace is depicted without a false touch. Lovelace himself is convincingly drawn and the Harlowe family and others among the subordinate figures are depicted with a wealth and vigour of characterization hitherto unknown in English fiction. Unfortunately the book goes on too long, and the end is deliberately extenuated. But what now offends its later readers did not offend its immediate audience. Readers begged that Clarissa should be spared; but Richardson resolutely if tardily slew her, and when the end came, England burst into a wail of lament; nor was it long before the contagion of sorrow spread to the Continent.

As *Clarissa* had grown out of *Pamela*, so *Sir Charles Grandison* grew out of *Clarissa*. Richardson's female friends would not rest satisfied with his portrait of a good woman; they desired him to give them a good man. He addressed himself to the task with eagerness and yet with difficulty. Richardson could depict women; he could not depict men. But the success of Fielding's *Tom Jones* (1749), with its "low" morals, seemed a kind of challenge; so the artist took up the moralist's burden, and *The History of Sir Charles Grandison: in a Series of Letters published from the Originals by the Editor of Pamela and Clarissa* came out between November 1753 and March 1754. His contemporaries enjoyed it, Jane Austen loved it, but posterity has rightly refused to read it, for here the moralist triumphs over the artist. Nevertheless, the book is richer in characters than either of its predecessors, Charlotte Grandison, in particular, being a triumph of a new kind.

Richardson's minor productions do not call for notice except as examples of the eternal delusion that the moralist is more important than the creative artist. He lives as author of *Clarissa*; but though this has abundant life and not mere historical importance, the novels of Richardson will never recapture their former popularity. It is not his length or his form, but the nature of his mind that repels. D. H. Lawrence in *Pornography and Obscenity* went so far as to say, with some justification, that "Boccaccio at his hottest seems to me less pornographical than *Pamela* or *Clarissa Harlowe*". Finer shades have been added to our notions of conduct, and Richardson's "values" seem lopsided. Sexual respectability, however important, is not the whole and final concern of human life. Richardson's prose, considering his lack of personal culture, bears witness to a remarkable natural gift. Though occasionally "genteel", it displays the strength of racy idioms and the charm of native English simplicity. Richardson's influence upon the course of English and European literature cannot be overestimated. He produced the first novels of sentimental analysis and made everyday manners and ordinary persons acceptable in fiction. The French found in him a herald of the revolt which enthroned natural feeling in the place of romantic rhodomontade. All three novels were translated by the eminent Abbé Prévost, author of *Manon Lescaut*; *Clarissa* itself was closely imitated by Rousseau in *La Nouvelle Héloïse* and Diderot's *Éloge de Richardson* (1761) presented him as a great creative spirit. It is odd to think that the prim, priggish little English printer became one of the literary forces in the moral and social unrest which culminated in the Revolution. Hardly less profound or extensive was his influence in Germany. Goethe felt it and became indirectly Richardsonian in *The Sorrows of Werther*. Even in Italy, two plays adapted from *Pamela*, by no less a man than Goldoni, made a great sensation.

II. FIELDING AND SMOLLETT

The English novel, firmly established by Richardson, was further developed by Fielding and Smollett, who, though not exact contemporaries, depicted different aspects of the same kind of life. In a magnificent allusion to Fielding's supposed illustrious ancestry, Gibbon predicted that *Tom Jones* would outlive the palace of Escorial and the imperial eagle of the house of Austria. It has outlived both. The monastery is a museum and the empire a memory. *Tom Jones* not only continues to be read, but was made into a successful light opera by Sir Edward German in 1907 and into a successful film in 1963.

Henry Fielding (1707–54), though not related to the Habsburgs, came of good family and was educated at Eton and Leyden University. He began as a playwright with *Love in Several Masques* (1728), a comedy in the Restoration manner, but soon found a real talent for burlesque. *The Author's Farce And the Pleasures of the Town* (1730) satirized the new craze for opera and pantomime; but much more important is *Tom Thumb* (1730) enlarged as *The Tragedy of Tragedies; or The Life and Death of Tom Thumb the Great* (1731), a parody of Young's tumid tragedy *Busiris*. This deserves to rank with *The Critic* as a piece both humorous in itself and apt in its apprehension of dramatic absurdity. Good, too, is *The Covent Garden Tragedy* (1732), a burlesque of Ambrose Philips's

The Distrest Mother. In 1732 Fielding adapted Molière's *Le Médecin Malgré Lui*
as *The Mock Doctor* and in 1733 *L'Avare* as *The Miser.* This was followed (1734)
by *The Intriguing Chambermaid* and *Don Quixote in England.* Early in 1736 he
took the Little Theatre in the Haymarket, formed a company of actors, and in
this and the following year produced *Pasquin* and *The Historical Register for
the year 1736.* But Fielding's outspoken political criticism called into existence
a Licensing Act (1737) which ended his career as a dramatist. This important
matter will be mentioned again in a later page. Having dismissed his company,
Fielding forsook the theatre and turned to law and journalism. In 1739 appeared
the first number of *The Champion,* published thrice a week. Fielding, like his
great successor Dickens, was a natural crusader, and his social indignation finds
an attractive expression in the *Champion* papers.

To speculate upon the part played by chance in the making of a great man
is an agreeable diversion. Would Dickens have become the Dickens we know
if he had not been engaged to write humorous letterpress to pictures of Cockney
sportsmen? Would Richardson have become the Richardson we know if he
had not been asked to write model letters? Would Fielding have become the
Fielding we know if Richardson's narrowly virtuous *Pamela* had not offended
his broader charity? These are engaging questions; but the immediate fact is
that Fielding, already skilled in dramatic parody, was tempted to parody
Pamela, and set to work. Whether *Shamela* was a trial effort we are not sure. If it
was, Fielding was immediately drawn to something on a larger scale; and the
parody, like *Pamela* itself, grew beyond the author's first intention till it became
his first published novel, *The History of the Adventures of Joseph Andrews, and of
his Friend Mr Abraham Adams. Written in Imitation of the Manner of Cervantes,
Author of Don Quixote* (1742). As Pamela was tempted by her master, so her
brother, Joseph Andrews, is tempted by his mistress. And then, as happened in
Pickwick, the book came alive and insisted on going its own way. Lady Booby
the mistress practically disappears; Joseph slips into the second place, and the
chief character in the story is the poor clergyman, Parson Adams, an immortal
creation. The reference to Cervantes on the title page is a clear indication that
Fielding found the easy narrative form of *Don Quixote* as natural to him as
Richardson had found the descriptive and analytic epistle.

In 1743 Fielding issued three volumes of *Miscellanies.* The first contains some
verses which are negligible. The second contains the long fragment in the manner of Lucian, *A Journey from this World to the Next,* one of Fielding's happiest
satirical inventions. The third contains the most brilliant piece of work that he
had yet achieved, *The Life of Mr Jonathan Wild the Great.* Hitherto his irony had
but flashed. In *Jonathan Wild* it burns with a fierce flame. Few more universally
apposite satires on "greatness" have been written. The Jacobite rebellion of
1745 inspired him to composition of a different kind, and in *The True Patriot*
and *The Jacobite's Journal* (1748–9) he sought to arouse a better national feeling.
The sincerity of his public spirit was proved when he became a magistrate in
1748, and—together with his blind half-brother Sir John Fielding (d. 1780)—
endeavoured to remedy at the root the evils due to ignorance, poverty, and
drink.

The History of Tom Jones, A Foundling appeared early in 1749. Fielding had called *Joseph Andrews* a comic epic poem in prose; the title is better deserved by *Tom Jones.* The general plan of the story is steadily coherent and follows a clear epic course. That some parts of it, as fiction, are less good than others may be allowed; but, in spite of all its imperfections, *Tom Jones* is the first long English novel conceived and carried out on a plan that secured artistic unity for the whole. That Tom himself is sometimes despicable will hardly be denied; but Fielding made his hero fallible that he might make him human. Like every other writer, Fielding has his defects. He could draw the warm and lovable Sophia; he could not have drawn the exquisite and tragic Clarissa. A spiritual conflict would have been unintelligible to him. His concern was with such a being as man in such a world as the present. Fielding had not a great soul; but he had a great heart.

Fielding's last novel, *Amelia* (1751), is by universal consent inferior to its predecessor, partly because the essayist, sharply separated from the novelist in *Tom Jones,* intrudes upon the story. However, the book, as a whole, is the work of a mellower, soberer Fielding than the author of *Tom Jones*—a Fielding touched with tears.

In 1752 Fielding returned to his old love, the occasional newspaper, and issued *The Covent Garden Journal,* which contains the best of his essays. Later publications related to his professional interests, such as his influential *Proposal for Making an Effectual Provision for the Poor* (1753). His health was now entirely broken down, and in the summer of 1754 he was ordered south. On the way he wrote *A Journal of a Voyage to Lisbon* (1755), which is full of his peculiar charm. He died in that city and is buried there. In Fielding's greater work we are intensely aware of a magnanimous character, charitable and sympathetic to human weakness, tolerant of lapses and honest follies, contemptuous of smugness, meanness and hypocrisy. But there is no idiosyncrasy in the perfect good-breeding of Fielding's prose, which he used with unostentatious art in a form and pattern of narrative that the English novel was to follow for more than a century afterwards.

Several years younger than Fielding was Tobias George Smollett (1721–71), who was born in Scotland and apprenticed to a surgeon in Glasgow, and came to London, at the age of eighteen, to make his fortune, not by the practice of his profession, but by the production of a tragedy, *The Regicide.* The refusal of any manager to produce this play seems to have left him with a permanent grievance. Having obtained an appointment as surgeon in the navy, he sailed in 1740 to the West Indies, and learned much of the rough life at sea and of those who lived it. Having left the service he set up as a surgeon in London and published various poems of no value or interest. He then turned to work of a much more ambitious kind, and in 1748 published his novel *The Adventures of Roderick Random.* Fielding had named *Don Quixote* as the model for *Joseph Andrews;* Smollett acknowledged Le Sage's *Gil Blas* as the literary parent of *Roderick Random.* The "picaresque novel"—the realistic novel of rascaldom, travel and adventure—was not a new thing to the countrymen of Daniel Defoe; but Smollett gave to the old form a new life and enriched it with freshly invented characters energetically acting in circumstances as yet unexploited. He is the first novelist of the navy and the literary father of the "British tar".

Smollett's taste for farce, horseplay and violence enabled him to depict faithfully a crude and violent kind of life. He writes with the frank brutality of the old naval surgeon, and modern readers find his physical insensitiveness disconcerting.

Roderick Random made Smollett famous, and he at once proceeded to publish his unfortunate tragedy *The Regicide*, with a preface full of railing at those who would not see its merits. He made—or revised and corrected—an English translation of *Gil Blas*, which was published in 1749. Two years later appeared *The Adventures of Peregrine Pickle* (1751), the most vigorous and vivacious of his works and the most successful in comic characterization. Hawser Trunnion, Lieutenant Hatchway and Tom Pipes are genuine creations. Smollett disfigured his first edition with an attack on those whom he considered his enemies, including Fielding, and disgraced himself by a further literary assault on Fielding, though the first attack was withdrawn from later editions of the novel. The "go-as-you-please" form of the picaresque novel permitted the inclusion in *Peregrine Pickle* of the once-admired but now utterly tedious *Memoirs of a Lady of Quality*.

Smollett attempted to set up a medical practice in Bath, and, having failed, reviled the celebrated waters of that city, and returned to London, where he established a literary factory at Chelsea, employing several hacks whom he regaled at the Sunday dinners described in *Humphrey Clinker*. His next novel was *The Adventures of Ferdinand Count Fathom* (1752), which owes something to *Jonathan Wild*, but lacks the clear perception which Fielding had of the difference between greatness and goodness. The products of the factory included a translation of *Don Quixote* (1755), a *History of England* (1757, etc.), a *Compendium of Voyages* (1756) and a translation of Voltaire's works (1761, etc.). Smollett was also engaged in work for various magazines, in one of which appeared *The Adventures of Sir Launcelot Greaves* (1762), a wretched imitation of *Don Quixote*.

Like Fielding, Smollett was driven abroad in search of health, and his experiences produced the *Travels through France and Italy* (1766), an entertaining book, which lacks, however, the fine spirit of Fielding's *Voyage to Lisbon*. It is in epistolary form. Sterne, who met Smollett on the Continent, describes him with pungent truth as "Smelfungus" in *A Sentimental Journey*. Once more at home, Smollett displayed his most rancorous and Rabelaisian mood in *The History and Adventures of an Atom* (1769), a brutal satire on British public affairs.

Bad health drove him again from England, and at Leghorn he wrote his last and most agreeable novel, *The Expedition of Humphrey Clinker* (1771). The tone and temper of the book are much sweeter, and almost for the first time Smollett appears as a genial humorist. Matthew Bramble, the testy old bachelor, and Lismahago, the needy Scottish soldier, are additions to the gallery of national characters. For this novel Smollett uses the epistolary form and manages it deftly. *Humphrey Clinker* was his last effort, and, like Fielding, Smollett died in exile.

Both Fielding and Smollett tried their hands at the drama before finding their true medium. But life had forsaken the stage of that day, and these two men mark the point at which the criticism of life, formerly expressing itself in the play, now expressed itself in the novel. Fielding was the essayist novelist of character, Smollett the exuberant novelist of incident. Thackeray and Dickens are their direct descendants. It is a curious fact that all four of these vigorous inventors died at ages which we should now call young. Only Thackeray and Dickens passed—and that by very little—the age at which Richardson began his first novel.

III. STERNE AND THE NOVEL OF HIS TIMES

During the twenty years that followed the death of Richardson new elements were added to the novel, and of these the chief is "sentiment" or "sensibility", the master in that kind being Sterne. Apart from him the writers of the time fall into three groups, (1) the novelists of sentiment and reflection, typified by Henry Mackenzie, (2) the novelists of home life, typified by Fanny Burney, and (3) the novelists of "Gothick" romance, typified by Horace Walpole and Clara Reeve.

Laurence Sterne (1713–68) was born at Clonmel, Tipperary, the son of Ensign Roger Sterne and great-grandson of the Richard Sterne who was Archbishop of York 1664–83. He was educated at Cambridge, took holy orders and was made perpetual curate of Coxwold in Yorkshire in 1760. He was not the kind of priest in whom the Anglican Church can feel any pride. Little is known about his life, and even that little is not very reputable. Our concern, however, is with the writer. The publication of *Tristram Shandy* was begun in 1760 (Vols. I and II), and continued at intervals until the year before the author's death. In 1762 Sterne's health, always frail, broke down, and he began the travels of which *A Sentimental Journey through France and Italy by Mr Yorick* (1768) is the delightful literary product. Save that Sterne died in London and not abroad, it will be noticed that his life roughly follows the Fielding-Smollett pattern. The author of *Tristram Shandy*, cool copyist of other men as he was, must be accepted as an original and originating power in literature. He showed that there were untried possibilities in the novel. He opened new fields of humour. He created a style more subtle and a form more flexible than any found before him. The novel, as left by Fielding and Smollett, might have settled into a chronicle of contemporary life and manners. Richardson had struck memorably into tragedy, but his one great story stood alone. Sterne invented for English literature the fantasia-novel, which could be a channel for the out-pouring of the author's own personality, idiosyncrasy, humours and opinions. Instead of form, there was apparently formlessness; but only apparently, for Sterne was the master of his own improvisations. Sterne may therefore be called a liberator—even the first of the "expressionists". His success left the novel the most flexible of all literary forms.

Sterne's odd humour appears in the very title of his book, *The Life and Opinions of Tristram Shandy, Gentleman*; for it has been truly remarked that the "life" is that of the gentleman's uncle and the "opinions" those of the gentleman's father. Tristram, titular hero and narrator, remains unborn during much of the story and plays no part in the rest. The undying trio, Walter Shandy, My Uncle Toby and Corporal Trim are humorous both in the narrow or Jonsonian sense, and in the larger or Shakespearean sense. My Uncle Toby and

Corporal Trim are variations of genius upon Don Quixote and Sancho Panza. They are on a lower plane, but the relation between them is full of beauty, as well as of humour.

Of Sterne's indecency too much can be made. That he has not the broad humour of his other master, Rabelais—that his fun in this kind provokes the snigger rather than the hearty laugh, can be at once admitted. What is unfortunate about Sterne is that much of his own personal life seems to give unpleasant point to the least pleasant parts of his writing. We should like a priest to be more priestly. But actually the most offensive quality in Sterne is the new "sensibility" or "sentimentalism". When the "spot-lights" are manipulated with design so palpable as in the death of Le Fever or the story of the dead ass, the author goes far to defeat his own purpose; for he at once calls in question his own artistic sincerity. The pathos of Dickens is naturally poured out; the pathos of Sterne is unnaturally put on. But his artistic sins can be forgiven for the sake of an insinuating, irresistible humour in which no English writer has excelled him. His *Sermons of Mr Yorick* (1760–9) and *Letters from Yorick to Eliza* (1775) have a biographical rather than a literary importance.

Henry Mackenzie (1745–1831) carried the eighteenth century well into the nineteenth. After the publication of *The Man of Feeling* in 1771, the year of Scott's birth, he was recognized as the literary leader of Edinburgh society. That novel, intrinsically unremarkable, is noteworthy as a reversion to the Coverly type invented by Addison. The story is purely episodic. It is completely without humour, and owes nothing in form or in spirit to Fielding or Smollett. Mackenzie was, as Scott called him, "the northern Addison", though he comes near to Sterne in his working of the "sentimental "vein. In his next book, *The Man of the World* (1773), Mackenzie achieved both a plot and a villain, though neither can be called important. His last and best book, *Julia de Roubigné* (1777), strikes a wholly different note and places him in the straight line of descent from Richardson. It owes much to *Clarissa*, and is one of the few tragedies to be found in the early stages of the English novel.

More genuinely important is Henry Brooke (1703–83), an Irishman, whose best known book *The Fool of Quality* (1766) has already been mentioned (pp. 397, 412). Brooke was a man of many activities, and deserves serious study. In *The Fool of Quality* the "free fantasia" form of discussion, diversion and sentiment indicates a debt to Sterne; the substance of the social discourses shows clear understanding of Rousseau; and the strain of exaltation comes from Law and the mystics. It is a remarkable compound. Brooke's other novel, *Juliet Grenville* (1774), does not call for notice.

From the novel of sentiment to the tale that sought to give both a sense of terror and a sense of the past is a startling transition. It began with *The Castle of Otranto* (1765) struck off at fever heat by Horace Walpole (1717–97). Though slight and more than a little absurd, it has the importance of being the first thing of its kind in English. It was written in conscious reaction against the domesticities of Richardson, and sought both to substitute for the interest of the present the appeal of the past, and to extend the world of experience by the addition of the mysterious and the supernatural. The performance is bungling; but the design is original and effective. Walpole gave us the first "Gothick" romance.

He was followed by Clara Reeve (1729–1807) who wrote several stories of which only one is remembered, *The Champion of Virtue, A Gothic Story* (1777), the foolish title of which was happily changed to *The Old English Baron* in the second edition (1778). When it is remembered that another of her productions is called *Memoirs of Sir Roger de Clarendon, a Natural Son of Edward the Black Prince* (1793), it will be seen that Clara Reeve thought she had her feet firmly in the past, though, in fact, her fifteenth century conducts itself singularly like the eighteenth. Still, the attempt to recapture romance was made. If Horace Walpole and Clara Reeve had done no more than claim that the boundaries of the novel might be extended to include the glamour of the past and the thrill of the supernatural, they would deserve remembrance; but their actual performances are not entirely contemptible.

With the novels of Frances (Fanny) Burney (1752–1840) we pass into another world. Fanny was the daughter of Dr Burney, the amiable historian of music. During her youth, and until some years after the publication of her second novel, she lived in the most brilliant literary society of her day. In 1786 she was appointed second Keeper of the Robes to Queen Charlotte, a post which she held for four years, to her own great discomfort, but to the delight of those who read her fascinating *Diary*. After her release, she married (1793) General d'Arblay, an emigrant of the Revolution, and from 1802 to 1812 she lived in France, returning only to publish her last novel, *The Wanderer* (1814). In *Evelina* Fanny Burney wrote the first English novel of home life. The motherless Evelina goes out into the world, and her adventures are related in a series of letters with a vivacity and swift succession of incident entirely original. Her way is beset with comic characters who are new creations in English fiction and foreshadow the far-off Dickens. Johnson aptly called Fanny Burney his "little character-monger". She was the first to give flesh and blood to sheer vulgarity. Her best qualities are seen in *Evelina* (1778). *Cecilia* (1782) and *Camilla* (1796) have stiffened into something unnatural, and *The Wanderer* (1814) scared even Macaulay, who was not easily frightened by anything in the shape of a book. Spontaneity is among the best gifts of the novelist; and few books are more spontaneous than Fanny's first novel. The same gift appears in her *Diary* with its brilliant and easy succession of characters and incidents. Fanny Burney was the first writer to see that the ordinary embarrassments of a girl's life would bear to be taken for the main theme of a novel. Macaulay justly saluted her as the first English novelist of her sex; he forgot that she was the first English novelist of her kind, without respect of sex.

IV. THE DRAMA AND THE STAGE

We have noted in former chapters various signs of change in the drama— Collier's attack on Restoration indecency, the battle of the "rules" between those who demanded the correctness of the French classics and those who defended the freedom of Shakespeare, the coming of sentimental comedy in D'Urfey, Cibber and Steele, the coming of sentimental melodrama in Southerne, and the coming of sentimental tragedy in Rowe. During the eighteenth century there were further movements in the directions indicated. Collier was succeeded by Law, who published in 1726 *The Absolute Unlawfulness of the Stage Entertainment fully demonstrated*. The battle of the plays continued with apparent, if not actual, vigour, though the author of *Cato* and the translator of Voltaire put out remarkable defences of Shakespeare, and the age of classical restraint and regularity produced the first great editions of the natural and irregular dramatist. Italian opera, typified by Handel's *Rinaldo* (1711), came upon the town, and its charms and absurdities provoked satire, epigram and essay. The masque and the dumb-show subsided together into the pantomime, i.e., action accompanied by music. Ballad opera, typified by Gay's wildly successful *Beggar's Opera* (1728), foreshadowed the Victorian comic operas of Gilbert and Sullivan. There was much movement, but there was no advance. The theatre was steadily losing its power as a serious criticism of life, and lost it entirely when the Licensing Act of 1737 established a censorship of plays. Fielding the suppressed playwright became Fielding the unsuppressed novelist—though the fiction in *Miscellanies* (1743) may have been written, or begun, before the Act was passed. The supremacy in creative entertainment passed from the acted drama to prose fiction.

Something of the Restoration spirit can be found in the comedies of Susannah Centlivre (1667–1723), which show skill in comic intrigue, in fluency of prose dialogue, and in the provision of mechanical characters that provided good parts for the comedians. *The Wonder! A Woman keeps a Secret* (1714) gave Garrick one of his best parts, and *A Bold Stroke for a Wife* (1718), with its "false" and its "true Simon Pure", long held the stage. Mrs Centlivre's effort at blank verse tragedy shows her incapable of either verse or tragedy.

The early Georgian tragedies of Edward Young, the poet of *Night Thoughts*, recall the violent action of Elizabethan drama, and Fielding had therefore an easy task in turning the heroics of *Busiris* (1719) to mockery in his burlesque tragedy, *Tom Thumb*. *The Revenge* (1721) recalls the heroic drama of the Restoration. But a new note was presently heard; for in *The London Merchant, or The History of George Barnwell* (1731), George Lillo (1693–1739) gave the English stage its first domestic tragedy in prose. Domestic tragedy was no novelty on the English stage; *Arden of Feversham* and *A Woman Killed with Kindness* are both tragic and domestic; but they are noble; *George Barnwell* sinks to the level of the booth. For his old story of the apprentice ruined by a courtesan, Lillo not only forsakes verse but uses prose that is a travesty of human speech. In *Fatal Curiosity: A True Tragedy of Three Acts* (1736), he essays domestic drama in blank verse. His other works do not call for mention. Ridiculous as he appears today, Lillo was preparing the way for serious prose drama; and his "bourgeois" tragedy had influence upon Diderot in France and upon Lessing in Germany. *George Barnwell* could beget something better; Addison's *Cato* could beget nothing. In England the chief follower of Lillo was Edward Moore (1712–57). His early comedy, *The Foundling* (1748), has some suggestion of Steele's last sentimental comedy; but Moore's tragic and moral bent unite most forcibly in *The Gamester* (1753), which is prose domestic tragedy with a definite advance towards naturalness of diction. Henry Brooke disdained the domestic story and took northern history as his province in *Gustavus Vasa* (1739), a theme handled with a great gesture, though the verse is mere theatrical diction.

While Moore and Lillo were experimenting with naturalistic tragedy, Voltaire was endeavouring to re-assert the classical standards. We have already discussed (p. 237) his attitude to Shakespeare. What is usually unnoticed is that Voltaire borrowed far more from Shakespeare than he was ever willing to acknowledge. In 1726 he began a long residence in England, and between 1734 and 1776 about a dozen of his plays were acted here in adaptations, three by Aaron Hill, who denounced his attacks on Shakespeare. Hill's *Merope* (1749) and Arthur Murphy's *The Orphan of China* (1759) were the most successful. Voltaire exerted some influence on a few unimportant playwrights, and he and his doctrines were cried up, mainly by the ultra-literary, who, as usual, found artistic salvation in something foreign. To them, Shakespeare was rather like what Dickens was to the literary exquisites of a later age; nevertheless Shakespeare, in editions and productions however faulty, was the most popular and most powerful figure in eighteenth-century drama. Interest in the earlier French classics, which had languished since Ambrose Philips's *The Distrest Mother*, was momentarily revived by William Whitehead's *The Roman Father* (1750), a version of Corneille's *Horace*; but we hear of little else in that kind. The French classical drama was never anything but a transient, embarrassed phantom on the English stage. English drama has always been English.

The vein of dramatic burlesque struck by Gay in *The Beggar's Opera* was developed by Fielding and Carey. The spirit of Fielding's *Tom Thumb* is maintained in Henry Carey's *Chrononhotonthologos, the Most Tragical Tragedy that ever was Tragediz'd by any Company of Tragedians* (1737), and, less effectively, in *The Dragon of Wantley* (1734), a slighter piece, which displays, in the words of its dedication, "the beauty of nonsense, so prevailing in Italian opera". Fielding did not disdain the composition of short works. The eighteenth century liked an "after-piece", usually a farce or a pantomime, to follow the major entertainment. As we have already seen (p. 421), Fielding helped to make theatrical history by his bold satire on Walpole in such pieces as *Pasquin* (1736) and *The Historical Register for 1736* (1737); for the result was the Licensing Act of 1737, which reduced the theatres to two (Drury Lane and Covent Garden) and brought plays, prologues and epilogues under the censorship of the court. State control of the drama, originally a political device, later pretended to be moral and in 1894, for example, banned Shaw's *Mrs Warren's Profession* as "immoral and otherwise improper for the stage".

The greatest name in the dramatic history of the eighteenth century is not that of a playwright, but that of a player, David Garrick (1717–79), born, like Johnson, at Lichfield. His "natural" method of acting not merely gave special interest to his Shakespearean revivals, but stimulated the writing of less "stagey" plays. Garrick (like many later producers of Shakespeare) felt at liberty to "modernize" the old author whom he presented to "modern" audiences; but his masterly acting outweighed the infelicities of his acting versions. Moreover, a fact often forgotten, Garrick's versions were purity itself compared with the seventeenth-century perversions which they displaced.

In contrast to many conventional dramas of the period, John Home's *Douglas* (first acted at Edinburgh in 1756 and in London in 1757) strikes a romantic note. It was so successful that patriotic Scots like David Hume believed they had discovered a northern dramatist who combined "the true theatric genius of Shakespeare and Otway, refined from the unhappy barbarism of the one and the licentiousness of the other". Age has withered *Douglas*, and custom staled the declamation of Young Norval. Yet the play had a fresh quality in its native background and romantic atmosphere, and it held the stage for many years.

The growing poverty of English drama is evident in comedy as well as in tragedy. Formal comedy was displaced by farce, a form of drama exploited by Samuel Foote (1722–77), an Oxford man turned comic actor, who evaded the Licensing Act by establishing himself in 1747 at the Little Theatre in the Haymarket and inviting people to come to a "Concert of Musick" or an "Auction of Pictures". In the end he was given a patent, which, though limiting his activities, really created a third patent theatre. Almost the only remembered piece of "the English Aristophanes" is *The Mayor of Garret* (1764). Garrick himself wrote a number of lively farces, such as *The Lying Valet* (1741), *Miss in her Teens* (1747), *The Irish Widow* (1772) and *Bon Ton* (1775). James Townley's *High Life below Stairs* (1759) is another farce that long maintained its popularity.

Among the playwrights of the Garrick era, Arthur Murphy (1727–1805) may serve as a type of prolific industry. His dramatic efforts include farces, comedies, adaptations from Voltaire, adaptations from Molière and tragedies such as *Zenobia* (1768) and *The Grecian Daughter* (1772). He was in no sense original, but he fashioned pieces that could be acted well. Murphy was the first editor of Fielding and wrote an essay on Johnson. Another popular compiler of entertainments was Isaac Bickerstaff (*c.* 1735–*c.* 1812) whose *Love in a Village* (1762), *The Maid of the Mill* (1765) and *Lionel and Clarissa* (1768) departed from the ballad opera (set to old tunes) and travelled towards the comic opera (set to new). Charles Dibdin, later a prolific playwright, supplied some of the music.

More important is George Colman the elder (1732–94), who shows some feeling for genuine comedy. *The Jealous Wife* (1761) is an early example of a dramatized novel, for it is based on *Tom Jones*. With the collaboration of Garrick, Colman produced a genuine comedy in *The Clandestine Marriage* (1776). The "source-mongers" have tried to find an original of Mrs Malaprop in the Mrs Heidelberg of this play; but Mrs Heidelberg is merely illiterate, and has nothing of Mrs Malaprop's pure but unrequited passion for polysyllables. Colman's activities were numerous and creditable.

Sentimental drama retained its popularity. Six days before Goldsmith's *Good-Natur'd Man* finally achieved its belated production at Covent Garden, Garrick triumphantly produced at Drury Lane Hugh Kelly's *False Delicacy* (1768). In contrast with the moderate favour accorded to Goldsmith's piece, *False Delicacy* won a theatrical triumph. Kelly's only other play deserving mention is *A School for Wives* (1773). The period was barren of great or even of good plays.

V. THOMSON AND NATURAL DESCRIPTION
IN POETRY

If it is remembered that James Thomson was born in 1700 and died in 1748, and that Pope was born in 1688 and died in 1744, it will be seen that they were almost exact contemporaries, and that the picture, sometimes drawn, of Thomson leading a revolt or reaction against Pope is quite as remote from fact as a picture of Hardy leading a revolt against Meredith. Pope and Thomson were interested in different poetical "matters", but they spoke the same poetical language. In reverting to older models like Spenser and Milton, Thomson was not innovating, he was obeying a natural impulse felt by numerous other contemporary poets.

Thomson belonged by birth to the Scott country, and came to London in 1725 to seek his fortune as a writer. His first "Season", *Winter*, appeared in 1726. *Summer* appeared in 1727, and *Spring* in 1728. *Autumn* completed the collected volume published as *The Seasons* in 1730. His connection with various patrons involved him in politics, and his *Britannia* (1729) eulogized the Prince of Wales and condemned Walpole's policy, although the *Poem sacred to the Memory of Sir Isaac Newton* (1727) had been inscribed to Walpole himself. In 1730 he went abroad as travelling tutor. He complained that the Muse did not cross the Channel with him, and his ambitious poem *Liberty* (1734-6) confirms the accuracy of his judgment. He fell in and out of place, always lightly, and his later days were not without reverses of fortune. His tragedy *Coriolanus* was produced during the year after his death. The story of the emotion shown by Quin in the delivery of the prologue is a testimony to the affection which Thomson inspired in his friends.

Of Thomson's poetical work *The Seasons* and *The Castle of Indolence* alone have any importance. That he chose blank verse for *The Seasons* may have been due to the influence of Milton, but is much more probably due to his own feeling. Even minor poets have natural and underived inclinations; and, as a matter of fact, Thomson never used the couplet in any lengthy poem. The urban poetry of Thomson's time was more concerned with man than with nature. It is Thomson's peculiarity that the description of natural phenomena, in an age which overlooked their artistic value, was his chief concern. His observation was keen and intelligent; he had a genuine and not merely a literary feeling for nature; and though he exhibits no sublime intensity of spiritual feeling, he constantly acknowledges the Divine force which

pervades,
Adjusts, sustains and agitates the whole.

But Thomson, a dweller in the Castle of Indolence, and "more fat than bard beseems", is not a spiritual poet. The most popular passages of *The Seasons* are those episodes which take the form of sentimental and artificial anecdotes appropriate to the season under discussion.

Thomson's patriotic and political poems have already been named and need no discussion. Much more important and intrinsically pleasing is *The Castle of Indolence* (1748), written in the manner and stanza of Spenser; but it has none of Spenser's poetic gravity and virtue. Thomson was incapable of suffering, and could not, like Spenser, teach in song. As a tribute from a lesser poet to a greater, it deserves sincere esteem.

Thomson's dramatic work includes five tragedies and the masque of *Alfred* written with Mallet. This has already been noticed (p. 397). He had no special talent for the stage—certainly no power of characterization. *Sophonisba* (1730), *Agamemnon* (1738), *Edward and Eleonora* (1739), and the posthumous *Coriolanus* (1749), need no more than bare mention. *Tancred and Sigismunda* (1745) can be excepted, for it held the stage for many years during "the palmy days" of heroic, rhetorical acting. It may be added that Thomson's interest in Milton is attested by his edition of *Areopagitica* "With a Preface by another hand" (1738)—the other hand being his own.

The influence of Thomson was strongly felt by the younger generation of poets—by Collins, who dedicated a beautiful *Ode* to his memory, and by Gray, in whose work reminiscences of the elder poet can be traced. One writer, older in years, who took Thomson's blank verse as a model, is William Somervile —this form is more correct than Somerville—(1675–1742). His poem, *The Chace*, not written till 1735, discusses hunting in its various forms, with due poetical divagations, and leaves a pleasing picture of an English country gentle-man with rural convictions, bookish enthusiasm and a tendency to composition in verse. *Field Sports* (1742) is a short poem in the same vein. *Hobbinol, or the Rural Games* (1740), dedicated to Hogarth, is a blank verse burlesque inspired by "the Cider Poem and Splendid Shilling" of John Philips. The prose preface strikes a social note of some interest, for it is "anti-bourgeois" and "pro-farmer" in true John Bull fashion.

In the *Edge-Hill* of Richard Jago (1715–81), a strong taste for moralizing was combined with appreciation of "Britannia's rural charms, and tranquil scenes". Warwickshire, a fertile nurse of poets, was his native county and provided him with his subject. The poem illustrates the influence of Milton upon a reader of slight poetic habit.

A constantly recurring name in the literature of the time is that of George Lyttelton (1709–73), first baron of the name, the friend of Thomson, Pope and Shenstone, and a power in politics. The most pleasing of his poems is the *Monody* of 1747, a long elegy to his wife, which suffers by its frequent reminiscen-ces of *Lycidas*, with which it cannot endure comparison. The influence of French literature is felt in Lyttelton's imaginative prose works: the very titles of the satiric *Persian Letters* (1735) and *Dialogues of the Dead* (1760) are copied from Montesquieu and Fénelon. He was Thomson's editor, and, in that capacity, reduced the lengthy *Liberty* from five books to three, without making it any less unreadable.

VI. GRAY

Thomas Gray (1716–71) was born in London, son of a selfish, despotic and violent man of business in the City. His mother had two brothers, Robert and William, the first a fellow of Peterhouse, the second a master at Eton. It followed naturally that Gray went first to Eton and then to Cambridge. At Eton his two chief friends were Horace Walpole, son of the Prime Minister, and Richard West, grandson of Bishop Burnet. These three, with a fourth, Thomas Ashton, formed "the quadruple alliance". West was a scholar with a thin vein of poetry and a tendency to melancholy (like Gray himself), and his premature death in 1742 was a deep sorrow to his friend. The quadruple alliance was broken up in

1734. West went to Oxford, Gray to Cambridge, and an attractive correspondence was begun. Gray professed himself out of sympathy with Cambridge; but as he lived in the university for most of his life, the profession was not without some youthful affectation. No form of learning came amiss to him. His uncle Robert had given him not only a knowledge of the classics but a life-long passion for scientific observation in almost every department of vegetable and animal life. In his later years he regretted his early neglect of mathematics, and dreamt even then of repairing the loss. His curiosity about foreign literature, especially French, was very keen, and he became interested later in northern studies.

In 1739 Gray set out for a European tour with Horace Walpole. We know nothing of the relations or arrangements between them. In Paris they met the author of *Manon Lescaut* and saw Racine's *Britannicus*, which Gray began to imitate in a blank verse tragedy, *Agrippina*, of which two hundred lines survive. During the passage to Italy over the Mont Cenis, Gray received his first deep impressions of mountain grandeur. After reaching Italy, Gray and Walpole quarrelled and parted. We do not know the cause of their difference, but it must have been serious. Gray was a man of strong, sincere and independent character, and when reconciliation took place some years later, he told Walpole with complete frankness that the old relations would not be restored. On his journey home Gray visited the Grande Chartreuse for a second time. It was probably on this occasion that he left in the album of the fathers the beautiful alcaic ode *O tu severi Religio loci*. In 1741 the death of his father narrowed the family resources, and Gray lived for a time with his mother at Stoke Poges, where she made her home. West, with whom he had continued his correspondence and to whom he had sent the *Ode to Spring*, died in 1742, and at Stoke Poges Gray wrote his *Sonnet on the Death of Richard West*, the *Hymn to Adversity*, *Ode on a Distant Prospect of Eton College* and a splenetic *Hymn to Ignorance* (a fragment). The death of West deeply affected him. In Florence Gray had amused himself with writing for West a Latin version of Locke's famous *Essay*. To this production he gave the sounding name *De Principiis Cogitandi*, but referred to it humorously as "Tommy Lucretius". Having written over two hundred lines (it is the longest piece of verse by Gray we have) he gave it up; but the death of the friend to whom it had been addressed moved him to add in 1742 what he calls *Liber Quartus*, an affecting fragment of thirty lines worthy of being set beside Milton's *Epitaphium Damonis*.

Gray returned to Cambridge, where he found it comfortable to live on a small income. He sent Walpole the amusing *Ode on the Death of a Favourite Cat* (Walpole's), and interested himself in various friends, including William Mason, his first (and worst) editor, and the wild and reckless Christopher Smart. Gray had a great gift for friendship; but apart from his deeply loved mother we hear of no women in his life. It is a little curious that Horace Walpole, too, though his female friends were many, remained the complete bachelor. In June 1750, Gray sent from Stoke to Walpole a thing with an end to it (we paraphrase his words), a merit that most of his writings have wanted, and one whose beginning Walpole had seen long ago. This was the famous *Elegy*, and Walpole appears to have circulated it freely in manuscript, with the result that the magazines got hold of it: and Gray, to protect himself, made Walpole send it to Dodsley for immediate printing. The elegiac quatrain had been used before, e.g. in D'Avenant's *Gondibert* and Dryden's *Annus Mirabilis*; but in Gray's hands, it acquired a new beauty and a music of its own. After the *Elegy* came the humorous *A Long Story*, which had a personal cogency now difficult to discern. Of the *Stanzas to Richard Bentley* (1752), with one specially fine passage, only a mutilated copy survives. Bentley (son of the scholar) was the artist responsible for *Designs by Mr R. Bentley for Six Poems by Mr T. Gray* (1753), the first approach to any collection of Gray's poems.

On 26 December 1754 Gray completed the ode entitled *The Progress of Poesy*; it had been nearly finished two before. It was not published until 1759, when Walpole secured it for the Strawberry Hill Press, together with *The Bard*. Between *The Progress of Poesy* and *The Bard* comes, chronologically, the semi-Wordsworthian fragment called (probably by Mason) *Ode on the Pleasure arising from Vicissitude*; but it should not be allowed to separate the two long poems, which Gray had printed together as Ode I and Ode II with a motto from Pindar. They form an original literary experiment in which historic or legendary fact is presented romantically. *The Bard* bears traces of the northern studies which found expression in *The Fatal Sisters* and *The Descent of Odin*. A curious evidence of the influence of *The Bard* can be detected in the Ossianic impostures, which in certain places definitely imitate that poem.

In 1757 Gray was offered the laureateship in succession to Colley Cibber, and refusing the honour that had previously graced the brows of Shadwell, Tate, Rowe and Laurence Eusden, saw it more fittingly accepted by William Whitehead. During 1759–61 he spent some time in London studying the Old English manuscripts of the newly opened British Museum, and recording observations probably intended for the history of English poetry which was never executed. From 1762 till his death in 1771 he made several tours through the more romantic scenes of England and Scotland, and wrote delightfully about them to his friends. In 1768 he was given the professorship of modern history at Cambridge and in 1769 wrote the *Installation Ode* when the Duke of Grafton was made chancellor of the university. He died suddenly and was buried by the side of his beloved mother at Stoke Poges.

Some poets survive by a few grains of precious metal extracted from the mass of their work; Gray has the metal without the mass. The total bulk of his poetical work, including that in languages other than English, is very small, and of that small amount very little was printed in his lifetime. He made no attempt to collect his writings, or to prepare them for publication, or to make them generally known. His prose is enormously larger in quantity than his verse, and includes familiar letters that are among the most delightful in the language. His poems aroused the critical hostility of Johnson, who suspected him of Whiggism, and found his verse "licentious" but who, in regard to the *Elegy*, "rejoiced to concur with the common reader". An example of the "licence" that displeased Johnson is the use of "honied" as an adjective formed from the noun "honey". Both Shakespeare and Milton had used it. But Johnson's life of Gray, like his life of Milton, is one of his major blunders. Later, Gray encountered the hostility of Wordsworth and Coleridge. Gray would have thought the former's ponderous analysis of his early sonnet to West amusing; and he would have set down Coleridge's complaint that nouns like "Confusion" and "Conquest" (printed with the eighteenth century capitals) were faulty personifications as little better than ignorance. The most remarkable and least remarked fact about Gray's few poems is their strong idiosyncrasy. They are not only the best of their kind, but they have no rivals. The *Elegy* and the two great *Odes* are unique.

Almost everything that Gray wrote remained in manuscript at his death, and he suffered the misfortune of having for an editor William Mason, who conceived it his duty to publish, not what Gray wrote, but what he thought Gray ought to have written. It has taken a long time to clear the text of Gray, especially his letters, from the adulterations of Mason. Gray's projected history of English poetry was never written. The loss is ours, for his sympathy with the early poets was intense. In his love for the old and his adventures into the new, he anticipates an age that was to develop both his romantic instincts and his classical restraint.

VII. YOUNG, COLLINS AND LESSER POETS OF THE AGE OF JOHNSON

Various collections from *Dodsley* to *Chalmers* gave the lesser poets of the eighteenth century favourable opportunities of establishing themselves in the affection of the public. Only one, Collins, can be said to have succeeded. Young enjoyed for long an almost European celebrity; Shenstone, Dyer, Green, Blair, Armstrong, Akenside, Beattie and Smart had their numerous admirers; but of these Dyer and Smart survive only in a few poems, and the others survive hardly at all, save as names on disregarded volumes or as lives in the Johnson collection. But they have all something to say about the literary fashions of their time.

Edward Young (1683–1765) spent a long life in a vain quest for advancement. He sought popularity as a dramatist, tried to enter Parliament, and generally attempted to attain the public success of Addison. Even the Church, to which he finally looked, did not give him any spectacular place. Addison's administrative, and Prior's diplomatic, honours were not unmixed blessings to their possessors; but they made Grub Street intolerable to the younger generation of writers, who now assiduously looked for sinecures. Young began with poetical solicitations and compliments to those in power, produced his play *Busiris*, and wrote a needless *Paraphrase on Part of the Book of Job* in couplets. In 1721 appeared his one famous play *The Revenge*, and, a little later (1725–8), the seven satires forming the *Love of Fame, the Universal Passion*. During the years 1728 to 1730 were published the amazingly ridiculous pieces called *Ocean* and *Imperium Pelagi*. *The Complaint, or Night Thoughts on Life, Death and Immortality* in blank verse began to appear in 1742, other parts following in 1743, 1744 and 1745. A third play, *The Brothers*, appeared in 1753, and his last work of importance, *Resignation*, in feeble ballad stanzas, in 1762. The immense and long-enduring popularity of *Night Thoughts* will not return. It is hard reading, nowadays, even for the most energetic lover of poetry; and the rest of Young, except the seven satires, which occasionally strike fire, is harder. That Young had poetic feeling is evident; that he had no poetic artistry is equally evident. Yet some of his lines—like "Procrastination is the thief of time"—have become household words. If Young were judged by his best short passages he would seem to be a real poet; in the mass he achieves no more than verbiage. But it should be remembered that the seven satires of Young preceded those of Pope, and that some of the lesser poet's lines are good enough to be attributed to the greater.

William Collins (1721–79) was a most unhappy man, for he was the prey of intermittent imbecility, and was for long denied even the relief of complete lunacy. He has suffered, too, the misfortune of becoming a cudgel in the hands of critics like Swinburne, who, believing him "to reannounce with the passion of a lyric and heroic rapture the divine right and god-like duty of tyrannicide", used him to beat the poets, especially Gray, who had shown no public inclination for the murder of kings. The bulk of Collins's poetry is small, and the circumstances of his life made an authoritative collection impossible. When Collins is at his best, as in the exquisite *Ode to Evening*, the *Dirge in Cymbeline* and *How sleep the brave*, he is a poet, not a minor poet; but in the *Persian Eclogues* (1742)—later called *Oriental Eclogues* (1757)—he is little more than a poetaster of the eighteenth century. Even in some of the odes the poetaster appears and obscures the poet. The splendid outburst of the *Ode to Liberty* sinks at the end into bathos; the *Ode to Peace* and the *Ode to Pity* have the stock epithets and the stock images of the poetaster. *The Passions, an Ode for Music* maintains a wild coherence among its dim personifications, and the posthumous *Ode on the Popular Superstitions of the Highlands of Scotland*, faulty in text, lacks neither spirit nor poetic quality. At his best Collins is a true lyric poet of exquisite quality.

John Dyer (1699–1757), though his claim to memory rests mainly upon one short piece, must be recognized as a true poet. *The Fleece* and *The Ruins of Rome* are interesting in themselves, but are now more perilously interesting as examples of high-flown verse applied to subjects not calling for Miltonic eloquence. *Grongar Hill* (1725), however, is one of those poems which occupy a place of their own. It is really a little wonder in subject and in form alike. It uses exquisitely the octosyllabic couplet of Milton's famous pair of poems and it expresses the genuine feeling for nature which was to be the special greatness of Wordsworth. It is slight, but it is irresistible.

Of Matthew Green (1696–1737) the best account is that given in *Dodsley*, which contains his one enduring poem, *The Spleen, an Epistle to Mr Cuthbert Jackson* (1727)—not to be confused with the "Pindarik Poem" of that name by Lady Winchilsea. Green was a "quaker-freethinker" and discharged his duties at the Custom House, we are told, with the utmost diligence and ability. His octosyllabic couplets move with ease and his matter is expressed with humour and acuteness. Epicureanism of the lighter kind has seldom been better illustrated in verse.

Robert Blair (1699–1746), contemporary with hearty, cheerful Matthew Green, was neither hearty nor cheerful. He, too, was the poet of one poem, *The Grave* (1743), which was instantly popular and still survives. The blank verse has a certain rugged massiveness, and occasionally flings itself down with real momentum. It would be hard to find two poets of more different schools than Blair and Blake. Yet it was not a mere association of contradictories when Blake illustrated Blair. The close coincidence of *The Grave* and *Night Thoughts* need occasion no dispute about indebtedness. The two poems are quite independent. Mortuary reflections were in the air.

John Armstrong (1709–79), a Scottish doctor, wrote one notable poem, *The Art of Preserving Health* (1744). It was very popular, but is now one of the curiosities of literature, interesting as a triumph of Miltonic form over intractable matter.

Richard Glover (1712–85), like Armstrong, wrote "tumid and gorgeous" blank verse; but, unlike him, he offers not the slightest provocation to direct or indirect amusement. His celebrated ballad, *Admiral Hosier's Ghost*, may be called an accidental success in the broadside manner. Glover did nothing else like it. His "great" Miltonic performances, *Leonidas* and *The Athenaid*, once highly praised, will never be read again, save by the hardier students of poetry.

William Shenstone (1714–63) had genuine poetic gifts. He was a gentleman-farmer, born in the Somervile-Jago country, on the Leasowes estate which he adorned in the most lavish fashion of artificial landscape. His *Moral Pieces* include lengthy poems in a variety of metres—blank verse, couplets and octo-syllabics. The one outstanding success is *The Schoolmistress*, "in imitation of Spenser". It parodies the Spenserian manner in kindly fashion; it has real poetic feeling and catches very happily the difficult note of rustic simplicity. His *Inscriptions* begin with one poem known to everybody: "Here, in cool grot and mossy cell"; the others fail to reach that standard. *The Levities; or Pieces of Humour* contain a few good things; the twenty-four *Elegies* contain scarcely any. The four parts of *A Pastoral Ballad* are notable because they attempt the three-foot anapaestic metre illustrated by the familiar opening of the second, "My banks they are furnished with bees". Best known of his short poems is one in the *Levities* entitled *Written at an Inn at Henley*, with its excellent last stanza.

Mark Akenside (1721–70), unlike Shenstone, who might have written better in the seventeenth or the nineteenth century, belongs emphatically to the eighteenth, although his one long poem *The Pleasures of Imagination* (1744)—rewritten as *The Pleasures of the Imagination* in 1757—contains a few passages which anticipate Wordsworth, both in manner and in sentiment. Akenside's *Hymn to the Naiads* can be cited as a good example of eighteenth-century blank verse. *An Epistle to Curio* is an example of the satiric couplet.

Christopher Smart (1722–71) found poetry in a madhouse and wrote his best two poems there. *A Song to David*, first completely recovered in the nine-teenth century, has received its full reward—perhaps (the common fate of rediscoveries) more than its full reward. Much of it is taken at secondhand from the Bible and it abounds in repetition and verbiage; but the tide of poetry carries the poem right through, and the reader with it; the old romance-six or *rime couée* once more acquires soar and rush, so that the whole crowd of emotional thought and picturesque image sweeps through the page with irresistible force. Smart's other serious poems, including such efforts as *The Hilliad*, a frag-mentary satire with notes, the *Ode for Music on St Cecilias Day*, the *Hymn to the Supreme Being* (in stanzas) and the Seatonian Prize poems (in blank verse) on various attributes of the Supreme Being, have no genuine poetical life. His *Fables* and lighter pieces in a Hudibrastic or Swiftian vein are sometimes very amusing. The second madhouse piece, *Rejoice in the Lamb* or *Jubilate Agno*, not published till 1939, has some deeply moving lines, extraordinarily suggestive of Blake.

William Falconer (1732–69) was a man of the sea who wrote one poem famous in its time, *The Shipwreck*. It will not recapture its fame. Much of it is "stock", and the few personal touches are of the faintest. The sailor found in the end a sailor's grave.

James Beattie (1735–1803) was a much larger figure. He retains historic interest as a pioneer of romanticism and the most considerable of the numerous imitators of Spenser. His one important poem is *The Minstrel, or the Progress of Genius* (Book I, 1771; Book II, 1774), which presents the usual "stuff" of romanticism—hills and vales, knights and witches—but without the Spenserian virtue or the Spenserian music. His minor poems have no importance. He tried the manner of Gray in ode and in elegy, and he failed in both. Beattie was professor of moral philosophy at Aberdeen, and wrote prose works that once were famous.

The eighteenth century expressed itself, not in one kind of poetry, but in many kinds. The faded romances of these half-forgotten poets are some of the kinds.

VIII. JOHNSON AND BOSWELL

The Johnson whom everybody knows is the Johnson of the Reynolds portrait and the Boswell life. But the first was painted when he was already "the great moralist", and the second conceived when he was the most famous figure in the world of contemporary letters. The very greatness of his personality has unjustly obscured his greatness as a writer. He has become dissociated from his works. People who pretend to read the essays of Addison do not attempt to read the essays of Johnson. The loss is theirs. Johnson's contributions to miscellaneous literature offer many examples of excellence, but they are so numerous that they cannot be cited here. Those who desire details should consult *The Cambridge Bibliography of English Literature*.

Samuel Johnson (1709–84) was born at Lichfield, the son of a bookseller. As a schoolboy he exhibited his characteristic ease of acquisition, tenacity of memory, and lack of application. In his father's shop he learned how to tear the heart out of a book without laborious reading, and what he once possessed he never lost. He was intended to follow his father's business, but after two years at home he contrived to proceed to Oxford. His residence was irregular and he left without taking a degree. Of his early manhood there are few records. He did some schoolmastering, but his instincts led him early to writing. The first of his books was the translation of *A Voyage to Abyssinia by Father Jerome Lobo* (1735). The main interest of the volume now lies in the short preface, for the matter and the style are already Johnson's own.

Two years after his marriage to a widow in 1735, he forsook the Midlands for London, which was thereafter his home. Having no profession, he became by necessity an author. He looked to find employment on *The Gentleman's Magazine*, which had been founded by Edward Cave in 1731, and which had steadily grown in public favour. Johnson's first contribution appeared in March

1738. From that time he was regularly employed. He at once asserted some sort of literary control, and helped to guide the fortunes of the publication through a grave crisis. Reports of the proceedings in Parliament had been given in the *Magazine* since 1732; but in 1738 the House of Commons declared such reports to be a breach of privilege. The *Magazine* retorted by producing "debates in the Senate of Magna Lilliputia". Johnson at first assisted in editing these, and was sole author of those which appeared from July 1741 to March 1744. What he did was to write up the reports from notes supplied to him. When they were taken as actual reports he ceased to write them. To the *Magazine* he also contributed several biographies. In 1744 Johnson published his life of the unfortunate poet Richard Savage, a work important for the glimpses it gives of Johnson's own early life in London. Savage was not an attractive character, but Johnson is both impartial and generous. His *Life of Savage* is a model of how to tell the truth in biography. With a few alterations it was included later in *The Lives of the Poets*. After bibliographical work with William Oldys on the Harleian library—the occasion of two very interesting essays (1742–4)—Johnson proposed a new edition of Shakespeare (1745); but Warburton's edition (1747) spoiled his plan, and he turned to another even more laborious, a dictionary. The *Plan of a Dictionary of the English Language* was issued in 1747, and, at the desire of Dodsley, was addressed to the Earl of Chesterfield. Johnson did not confine himself to the labours of the *Dictionary*. During the eight years of its preparation he wrote his greatest poem, and gave new life to the periodical essay.

Johnson's early verses have very slight interest. Indeed, apart from the touching lines on Levett, he wrote only two considerable poems, *London* and *The Vanity of Human Wishes*. The first of these, *London: a Poem, in Imitation of the Third Satire of Juvenal*, was published anonymously in May 1738, on the same day as Pope's *One Thousand Seven Hundred and Thirty-Eight, a Dialogue something like Horace*, and thus, accidentally, invited a comparison which appears to have gone in Johnson's favour. *London* is good, but is easily surpassed by *The Vanity of Human Wishes*, written in imitation of Juvenal's tenth satire, and published, with Johnson's name, in 1749. The poem is completely satisfying as a statement of its theme. It is not less valuable as a personal document. Johnson was not a pessimist, but he believed that there was more to be endured than enjoyed in the general condition of human life, and he said so, with his habitual sincerity. Of his early tragedy *Irene*, not produced by Garrick till 1748, it is enough to say that its moral dialogues, its correctness of plan and its smoothness of verse do not suffice to give it any rank as a drama.

Johnson's next great undertaking was *The Rambler*, which appeared every Tuesday and Saturday between 20 March 1750 and 14 March 1752 (208 numbers). The least satisfactory part of this periodical is the title. *The Rambler* never rambles. It pursues its way in a steady, unswerving march. Times had changed. Between the appearance of *The Tatler* in 1709 and the appearance of *The Rambler* in 1750 there had been an almost unparalleled development of journalistic enterprise. The periodical essay no longer offered the attractions of novelty. That *The Rambler* succeeded is a tribute to Johnson's force of literary character. Its only rival is still *The Spectator*, from which, however, it differs essentially. Steele and Addison gave their essays a semi-novelistic interest. Johnson is purely essayistic. The prose of *The Spectator* is light and easy; the prose of *The Rambler* is majestic and sonorous. No one is required to affirm the exclusive superiority of either for all occasions and all themes.

In writing *The Rambler* Johnson had specifically sought to establish a correct and worthy literary language. That aim he pursued more directly in compiling his great dictionary. Most of the earlier dictionaries had been mere vocabularies, giving explanations of difficult words. Nathan Bailey's *Universal Etymological English Dictionary* (1721) had attempted to record all words used in English. Johnson purposely omitted technical terms, and thought not so much of the reader as of the writer and the purity of the language. The inclusion of quotations was Johnson's most notable innovation in English lexicography. He wanted to make clear the actual literary use of words, and he was able to employ a supreme talent for definition. He was not merely a scholar of immense reading, he was a born man of letters with an instinct for the finest shades of meaning. The respect accorded to him by his successors can be taken as the highest tribute to the value of his great linguistic survey. The famous letter to Lord Chesterfield, which disclaimed that nobleman's patronage, and perhaps gave the death-blow to literary patronage altogether, was first made public by Boswell. The *Dictionary* appeared honourably without any dedication. Johnson often reproached himself for idleness, and, indeed, he was slow in beginning any task, but to the labours of the eight years between the inception of the *Dictionary* in 1747 and its publication as *A Dictionary of the English Language* in 1755 it would be hard to find a parallel.

In June 1756 he issued new *Proposals* for an edition of Shakespeare, and he hoped to have the work completed by the end of the following year. But even Johnson's gigantic powers now felt the strain of his long labours. He began to suffer from mental depression, and he sought relief, not in medicine, but in company. Talk was his best tonic. Only the need for money impelled him to write. We leave unmentioned certain journalistic adventures and pass to his second series of essays, *The Idler*, which appeared every Saturday from 15 April 1758 to 5 April 1760 in *The Universal Chronicle, or Weekly Gazette*. In one respect *The Idler* is better than *The Rambler*. It is lighter in touch; moreover, the character of Dick Minim the critic achieves the kind of personal success the weightier essays had lacked. While *The Idler* was in progress Johnson's mother died, and her death was the occasion of his grave story, *The Prince of Abissinia, A Tale* (1759). The name *Rasselas* did not appear on a title-page till the posthumous edition of 1787. It is a parable rather than a tale, and it stands apart from the general course of the English novel; but it is a consistently beautiful and moving little book, written in prose of a singular dignity. *Rasselas* may be called the prose *Vanity of Human Wishes*. Wise readers will frequently refresh themselves with its ripe wisdom and its noble rhythms.

The promised Shakespeare was not forthcoming, and subscribers began to be discontented. A pension of £300 a year awarded to him in 1762 set him free from hack-work and the Shakespeare appeared at last in 1765. This has already been mentioned (p. 235) and need not be discussed again; but we may repeat that the great *Preface*, which settled for ever the battle of the "rules", is a permanent addition to the literature of criticism. A generation later, the French "romantics" found their case stated in Johnson's *Preface*, and they did not better what they borrowed.

Hereafter, Johnson did not, on his own initiative, undertake any other large work. He was employed in what we may term creative conversation. In 1763 he met Boswell; in 1764 he founded with Reynolds "The Club"; in 1765 he gained the friendship of the Thrales. A tour in Scotland with Boswell from August to November 1773 produced the ever delightful *A Journey to the Western Islands of Scotland* (1775). In July and August 1774 he made a tour in North Wales with the Thrales, but did not publish a companion book, though his *Diary* was printed posthumously in 1816. He was happily resigned to leisure and friendship, when on Easter Eve 1777 a deputation of booksellers asked him to undertake, at the age of sixty-seven, what was to prove his masterpiece. *The Lives of the Poets* arose out of a business venture. The London booksellers wished to produce an edition of the poets which should have the attraction of biographical prefaces by a writer of authority. Johnson was invited to do this work and he accepted. He had nothing whatever to do with the text or the authors selected, and always resented hearing of "Johnson's Poets". His *Lives*, perhaps the greatest body of critical opinion in the English language, were written for use by those undertaking the publication. Their independent publication (1781) was an afterthought. The most obvious feature of *The Lives of the Poets* is the equipoise of biography and criticism. Johnson was always interested in human life, and so his poets are never mere authors. This completeness of interest is the explanation of his few notorious failures. A romantic "Church and King" Tory could not feel at home with a regicide republican like Milton, nor could an old struggler have much admiration for the fugitive and cloistered virtue of Gray. Moreover, the fashion of Johnson's mind made him incapable of appreciating the elaborated art of *Lycidas* and *The Bard*. We have to accept the honest defects of strong integrity. Of Dryden and Pope Johnson wrote in friendship, but abated nothing of his severity in criticism. With the revision of *The Lives of the Poets*, Johnson's career as an author closed. He became an honoured public character, and when he died, the Abbey was inevitably his last home. That his reputation was strongly founded is attested by many records of admiration. Collections of stories about him had begun to appear in his lifetime, and now his friends competed in serious biography. Mrs Piozzi's (i.e. Mrs Thrale's) *Anecdotes of the late Samuel Johnson* (1786), fervently if oddly written, gives a clear picture of his strength and weakness. In marked contrast is the *Life* (1787) by Sir John Hawkins, the solid book of an "unclubable" magistrate and antiquary, with great knowledge and little intuition. He had known Johnson for over forty years and, on many points, he is our chief authority. The merits of Mrs Piozzi and Hawkins were united and augmented by Boswell. He had been collecting material since his first interview in 1763. After Johnson's death he set to work in earnest and spared himself no trouble.

It is often thought, and nearly as often said, that Johnson owes his immortality to Boswell. The certain and obvious fact is that Boswell owes his immortality to Johnson. Boswell's life is the story of a failure turned to success by a strong devotion. James Boswell (1740–95) was the son of a Scottish judge, and was destined for a legal career, in which he might have succeeded; but what he really desired was a sudden and splendid success in literature or politics. He wrote minor verse and published in 1763 the *Letters between the Hon. Andrew Erskine and James Boswell, Esq.* in which his characteristic vanity is redeemed by his disarming frankness. He returned to Edinburgh in 1766 from his Continental travels, during which he had met Voltaire, Rousseau, and General Paoli of Corsica. In 1768 he published his *Account of Corsica*, which won what he called "amazing celebrity" and which might have kept his name in the memory of a few dauntless readers. He edited a collection of twenty letters by himself and others, and published them under the title *British Essays in favour of the Brave Corsicans* (January 1796). He had made Johnson's acquaintance in 1763, and cultivated the great man's friendship during visits to London. He was called to the English Bar, but had no success. His admiration for Johnson inspired him to the one great achievement of his life. Boswell was unsatisfactory as a son, as a husband and as a father. His faults were numerous and almost shockingly unconcealed; but it is absurd to suppose that he had neither character nor intelligence. He was liked; he was the frankest of diarists, and in biography he was a great artist. Boswell's *Johnson* is incontestably the greatest biography in the English language; it is almost incontestably the greatest biography in any language; moreover, it is elaborately planned and elaborately built. A fool would have magnified his own importance in the story, and this Boswell never does.

The rediscovery of Boswell has been both gradual and dramatic. The first find was that of his letters to William Johnson Temple, published in 1857. Seventy years later a mass of letters and manuscripts, including that of the *Tour to the Hebrides* 1785, the companion piece to Johnson's *Journey*, was discovered at Malahide Castle, and in 1930 a further hoard was found at Fettercairn House. The material thus recovered clearly demonstrates the sedulous artistry of a great biographer. The *Life of Samuel Johnson LL.D.* appeared in 1791, and was revised and augmented by Edmund Malone in the third edition (1799). The classic nineteenth-century edition was, appropriately enough, published at Oxford in 1887, being edited by George Birkbeck Hill of Johnson's own college of Pembroke. This was revised 1934–66 by the eminent Johnsonian scholar Lawrence Fitzroy Powell, who was the first to have the opportunity of consulting Boswell's original draft and the other Boswell Papers discovered at Malahide. He was able to work in collaboration with the American scholar Frederick A. Pottle of Yale University, author of *The Literary Career of James Boswell* (1929) and himself the collaborator and successor of Geoffrey Scott in the eighteen-volume edition of *The Private Papers of James Boswell from Malahide Castle* (1928–34). The Yale editions of the *Private Papers*, edited by Pottle, began in 1950 with *Boswell's London Journal*, which out-Pepys Pepys in frankness. *Samuel Johnson* (1944), by another American scholar Joseph Wood Krutch, is the best modern biography, giving more attention to the early years than Boswell was able to do. Johnson's *Letters* were edited by Robert William Chapman in 1952.

IX. GOLDSMITH

Oliver Goldsmith (1728–74), born somewhere in Ireland, expressed his character abundantly in his writings, but gave us little information about his life. In all that happened to him, early or late, he appears to have been a helpless, engaging, ingenuous simpleton, the born prey of even the least accomplished rascals. He went to Trinity College, Dublin, as a sizar, and bitterly resented the humiliation. He was refused ordination. He acquired, no one knows how or where, the degree of M.B., which he proudly appended to his name. That he ever had any patients can hardly be known for they could not have survived. He wandered on foot about the Continent, yet recorded no details of his passage. We would gladly surrender most of the compilations he did write for one book he did not write, an account of the way in which "he disputed his way through Europe". In 1756 he arrived in London, quite destitute. He tried many vocations, though apparently not authorship; but this at last he reached. He did some writing for *The Monthly Review* (1757) and published his first book, *The Memoirs of a Protestant condemned to the Galleys, etc.* (1758), translated from the French. To get funds for some possible medical employment he issued by subscription *An Enquiry into the Present State of Polite Learning in Europe* (1759), which, despite its portentous title, is racy and readable in passages where Goldsmith is writing from personal experience.

In a little periodical called *The Bee* (6 October–24 November 1759) Goldsmith first revealed his powers as critic and essayist. He made the acquaintance of Percy, and later, of Johnson. John Newbery the publisher enlisted him for *The Public Ledger*, in which during 1761 his *Chinese Letters*, afterwards collected as *The Citizen of the World* (1762), first appeared. There are few better volumes of essays in English. The easy, natural style, the simple wisdom, the good humour and the shrewd sense of proportion in life, give *The Citizen of the World* a high place in our prose literature. It seems impossible that writings so sagacious should be the work of a man so ineffectual. Various compilations of no importance occupied him from 1761 to 1764. But in 1761–2 he was writing *The Vicar of Wakefield*, and in 1764 he published *The Traveller; or a Prospect of Society*, his first important poem. The didactic purpose of the poem has lost its importance; what remains is the charm, the perfect simplicity and sweetness of the expression and the exquisite finish of the verse. The author of *The Traveller* was a genuine poet, and not an eighteenth-century poetaster.

The success of *The Traveller* made readers inquire for other works by the "Oliver Goldsmith, M.B." whose name appeared on the title page. A volume called *Essays. By Mr Goldsmith* was issued in 1765 containing some of his best papers from *The Bee, The Public Ledger* and other magazines, together with some fresh specimens of verse. It then occurred to the joint proprietors that this might be a fitting opportunity to bring out *The Vicar of Wakefield*, the manuscript of which had been bought by them in 1762. The book was accordingly published in two small volumes in March 1766. Why it was not issued before is not clearly known; but evidently the publishers thought little of their bargain, and were justified in their doubts by its lack of immediate success. But its sale, if slow, was steady, and has never ceased. *The Vicar of Wakefield* is a perfect example of the permanently self-reproductive book. It has never had to be re-discovered or written up, and its success has been international. The apparent artless simplicity of its manner can deceive only those who think that to be easy and natural in writing is open to any novice with a pen. What is often unnoticed in *The Vicar* is its power of invention—its unforced range from the world of idyllic simplicity to the world of complete rascaldom. Not merely in the character of Dr Primrose does *The Vicar* anticipate *Pickwick*.

Goldsmith went on working at the compilations which paid better than masterpieces; but towards the end of 1766 his ambitions began to move in the direction of the stage, with its prospects of ready cash. He had already essayed a Voltairean tragedy, now happily lost. The success of Garrick and Colman's *The Clandestine Marriage* as a counterblast to the craze for sentimental drama encouraged him, and in 1767 he completed *The Good Natur'd Man*. All that remained was to get it acted. Garrick maltreated both play and author, who withdrew his piece and gave it to Colman at Covent Garden. After many delays it was produced by a desponding manager and with a depressed cast; nevertheless it had very fair success. But it is not a play that endures. We hear next of other compilations—Roman and English Histories for Davies and *A History of Animated Nature* for Griffin.

In 1768 Goldsmith lost his brother, and the flood of memories aroused carried into being a new poem, *The Deserted Village* (1770), his finest work in verse. It is unnecessary to inquire curiously whether the village is Irish or English, or, indeed, any definite spot. The way of poetry is to transfigure particulars and recreate them into abiding truths. The essential Goldsmith is in this poem—the Goldsmith of the character sketch and the Goldsmith of sweet and persuasive writing. Again he returned to desk work with a life of Boling-broke and an abridgement of his Roman History. It was about this time that he threw off the delightful medley of literary recollection and personal experience known as *The Haunch of Venison*, in which the ease and lightness of Prior are wedded to the best measure of Swift.

But his last triumph was at hand. Once more he essayed a "comic" comedy as a counterblast to Cumberland's sentimental *West Indian*, just produced, and once more he endured the stage's delays; but the play, first called *The Old House: a New Inn*, was at last produced at Covent Garden in 1773 as *She Stoops to Conquer; or, the Mistakes of a Night*, and scored a success. It remains one of the best of English comedies; for, with all its farcical circumstance, the root of the matter is sound. Many a man rendered mute by respectable company becomes a swaggering blade when at ease in his inn; the repressed self expands and blossoms into vivacity. Goldsmith's great comedy has never failed to hold the stage.

Goldsmith's last metrical effort was the shrewd and delightful *Retaliation*, a series of epitaph-epigrams, left unfinished at his death, and prompted by Garrick's jest against him as "Poor Poll". "Poor Poll", who, no doubt, was lacking in the reverence that successful men expect, could talk very much to the point when he wished. His objection to Johnson that in any attempt at fable he would make the little fishes talk like whales may be said to compress whole volumes of criticism in its few words. We should beware of accepting as a true estimate of Goldsmith the reports of prejudiced observers like Garrick and Boswell. The actor received little flattery from the critic; the Scotsman was jealous of the Irishman. The fact is pretty plain—and was recognized by Washington Irving in his *Goldsmith* (1849) and John Forster in his *Life and Times of Oliver Goldsmith* (1854)—that Goldsmith's poems, essays, novel and comedies could not have been written by the pitiful Tom-fool he is sometimes made out to be. His most striking characteristic is the individuality of his genius. He resembled no one, he belonged to no school, and he founded none. He was but forty-six when he died; and he was maturing to the last.

X. THE LITERARY INFLUENCE OF THE MIDDLE AGES: MACPHERSON'S OSSIAN, CHATTERTON, PERCY AND THE WARTONS

The Middle Ages, as we call them, have influenced English writers more profoundly through architecture than through literature. The "Gothick" romances of Walpole and Clara Reeve sought to produce, not stories in tune with medieval thought and feeling, but stories appropriate to a setting of ruined abbeys and crumbling arches. Even Scott, who made the Middle Ages popular, is less concerned with the fashion of men's minds than with the fashion of men's costume and dwellings. Medieval verse has seldom been revived, save as conscious imitation or parody, the one exception being the ballad measures, which thrive so naturally through the nineteenth century that people forget how much their revival owes to the eighteenth, with *The Ancient Mariner*, greatest of modern ballads, coming at its very end. The eighteenth century, eager for romance, found it in the "vaulted aisle" of Congreve's *Mourning Bride*, in "the long-drawn aisle and fretted vault" of Gray's *Elegy*, and in the "ruin" of the first, and the "time-hallowed pile" of the second, version of Collins's *Ode to Evening*. What the eighteenth century found in medieval literature was not wild romance, but classic simplicity. Dryden and Pope found this in Chaucer; Gray found it in other old English poets; Addison found it in *Chevy Chace*, and used it as a stick to beat the followers of Donne. Addison does not call the old ballads "Gothick"; he calls the elaborate imitators of Cowley "Gothick".

The seventeenth and eighteenth century scholars who broke into medieval antiquities and discovered much poetry by the way were chiefly concerned with chronicles and state-papers. What appealed to the reader of Tennyson or Rossetti or Morris as peculiarly medieval was not apparent to Hickes or Hearne or Rymer. They were not in search of "glamour". The first great find was the old northern heroic poetry—"Islandic" as Percy spells it. When Gray wrote *The Descent of Odin* and *The Fatal Sisters*, he drew from sources which the antiquaries had made known in the seventeenth century; and his poems are the first example of the literary influence of the Middle Ages.

Of course, in one sense, literature was full of the Middle Ages. Ariosto, type of the Renascence, drew his matter from the old romances. Through Chaucer and Spenser, through Sidney's *Arcadia*, through many chapbooks and through the unprinted living folklore of England, the Middle Ages formed the minds of Dryden and Pope and their contemporaries. But for a distinct and deliberate revival of the past one must go to Sir William Temple's remarks about the Death Song of Ragnar Lodbrok in his essay *Of Heroic Virtue*. With this begins the vogue of "old unhappy far-off things, And battles long ago" as the theme of romantic literature. The honourable, courageous viking was launched to try his fortune in romance; and he started with the great advantage of having really lived, as the fabulous heroes of Ariosto had not. When Temple again took up "runic" literature in his essay *Of Poetry*, he was consciously pursuing the real progress of poetry from its early life among historical barbarians.

Temple derived his knowledge, not from English scholars, but from northern scholars whom he met at Nimeguen; but northern studies were already flourishing in England, especially at Oxford, where the German-born philologist Francis Junius (or François Du Jon) the younger (1589–1677) had left not merely the great Junian Codex, but the founts of type from which were printed his Gothic and Old English Gospels, as well as the grammar of George Hickes (1689) afterwards included in the magnificent *Thesaurus* (1703–5) of that astonishing scholar. Hickes's *Thesaurus* is a great miscellaneous work on the antiquities of all the Teutonic languages. One page in it (Vol. 1, 192) has the authority of an original Old English document, for there he printed the heroic lay of *Finnsburh* from a manuscript at Lambeth which was afterwards lost. On the opposite page and immediately following is an Icelandic poem: Hervor at her father Angantyr's grave. This poem is translated into English prose, and it had considerable effect on modern literature. It is repeated, under the title *The Incantation of Hervor*, by Percy, as the first of his anonymous *Five Runic Pieces* (1763); and, after this, it became a favourite subject for paraphrase. Percy's second piece is *The Dying Ode of Ragnar Lodbrok*, which had also caught the attention of the elder Thomas Warton. It will be seen that Old English had none of this success. Perhaps if Hickes had translated *The Fight at Finnsburh* as well the story might have been different; but he did not. However, it must be admitted that the Icelandic poems succeeded by their heroic and passionate qualities. The merits of Old English were less obvious.

Gray's two translations from the Icelandic are the finest result of these antiquarian studies. To Gray himself the Icelandic poems specially appealed, because they exactly correspond to his own ideals of poetic style—concise, alert, unmuffled, never drawling or clumsy. But Gray felt there was nothing more to be done with them. He was not a Macpherson. He did not "improve" them or even imitate them; but he sought to recapture something of their spirit in *The Bard*—a British, not a Scandinavian poem.

The interest in the ballads was not specially medieval. Their long popularity is attested by the praise of Sidney and Addison and by imitations that pre-date Percy's re-discovery. Between ballads and "runic" pieces it seemed as if English poems earlier than Chaucer were neglected; but we know from Pope's scheme of a history of English poetry that they were not forgotten. Pope's liberality of judgment may be surprising to those who take their opinions ready made. He never repudiated his debt to Spenser; and when he compares Shakespeare to "an ancient and majestick piece of Gothick architecture" he intended high praise. But before the medieval poetry of England could be explored, there came the triumph of Ossian, which overwhelmed the scrupulous experiments of "runic" translators, and carried off the greatest men in a common enthusiasm.

James Macpherson (1736–96) did well at the university of Aberdeen. His literary tastes and ambitions were keen. In 1758 he published a poem, *The Highlander*. In 1759 he met John Home, the author of *Douglas*, who was full of the romantic interest in the Highlands, which he passed on to Collins, and which was shared by Thomson. Macpherson really knew something about Gaelic poetry, but his literary taste was very decided, and he honestly thought that the traditional Gaelic poems were not very good. He saw the chance for original exercises on Gaelic themes. Home wanted stories with the true Gaelic spirit, and Macpherson supplied them. In 1760 appeared *Fragments of Ancient Poetry collected in the Highlands of Scotland, and translated from the Gaelic or Erse language*. Then Macpherson went travelling in the Highlands and Western Isles, and the result was *Fingal: An Ancient Epic Poem in Six Books* (1762). In this volume was also published, among shorter pieces, *Temora, An Epic Poem*. In 1763 this poem, too, was completed in eight books. Macpherson promised to publish the originals; but it is clear he intended to take from Gaelic verse no more than suited his own literary purposes. He spoke slightingly of the Irish tales of Finn, and called his hero Fingal. In fact, he meant his poems to be not merely romantic, but patriotic, like the *Iliad* and the *Aeneid*. His fabrications are intended to glorify the history of his native country, and Fingal and Oscar (like King Arthur in *The Brut*) are victorious foes of the invaders. Moreover, Fingal is made to appear a better man than Cuchullin. Macpherson thus provoked Irish scholars and English sceptics equally. Among the latter the stoutest was Dr Johnson, whose letter to Macpherson is one of his most characteristic utterances. Macpherson declined to produce his originals. He had found a public and he gave the public what it happened to want—romantic love and romantic scenes of a large, vague and misty kind, together with patriotic feeling and a respect for the standard epic ideal. "Sensibility" had come in a new and attractive form. Macpherson was not a deliberate fabricator, like Chatterton. He based his productions upon actual matter. He began with apparently harmless imitations and then found himself compelled by circumstances to go on. The real point, often overlooked, is that people liked Ossian for its own sake, not for its supposed faithfulness to barbarous originals—neither Goethe nor Napoleon, for instance, had the faintest interest in the language of Highland savages. They wanted poetry, not philology. Ossian offered an eager age "huge cloudy symbols of a high romance"; and the Biblical language, with its parallelisms drawn from the major prophets, gave the needed air of familiarity to the remote matter. Macpherson was original enough, in a peculiar way, to touch and thrill the whole of Europe, and he takes his place in the history of literature as well as in the history of imposture.

The contribution of Thomas Percy (1729–1811) to the medieval revival was much more genuine and durable. Percy was an Oxford man and became Bishop of Dromore in 1782. He had begun with volumes of Chinese pieces. His interest in old literature, stimulated by the success of Ossian, produced the

Five Pieces of Runic Poetry (1763); his fortunate discovery and rescue of an old folio manuscript volume at the house of Humphrey Pitt of Shifnal produced the famous *Reliques of Ancient English Poetry* (1765). This manuscript, like the older and finer Thornton MS. at Lincoln, was a family collection of poems new and old. Percy merely made a selection, and, seeking to interest readers rather than to instruct scholars, gave his choice amended to the needs of the time. There was no deliberate falsification, and the virulent attack made on him by Joseph Ritson in *Ancient Engleish Metrical Romancees* (1802) was totally gratuitous. It was through Percy's *Reliques* that the Middle Ages really came to have an influence in modern poetry, and this was an effect far greater than that of Ossian (which was not medieval) or that of *The Castle of Otranto* (which was not poetical).

It is strange that there should be so little of the *Reliques* in the work of Thomas Chatterton (1752–70), most famous of all literary deceivers. His grandfather and great-grandfather had been sextons at the church of St Mary Redcliffe, Bristol, and documents from Canynge's coffer in the muniment room had fascinated him. From them he made a dream-world of his own. The childhood of Sordello in Browning's poem resembles Chatterton's. He was a real poet, and, as he grew up, employed his old phantom company to utter his new poetry, the chief figure being that of a priest, Thomas Rowley. There are two Chattertons, the one who wrote his own poems and the one who invented the Rowley poems. But they are essentially one. The Rowley poems are not an imitation of fifteenth-century English verse; they are really new poetry of the eighteenth century, with one remarkable experiment in the rhythm of *Christabel*. All that is old about them is the spelling, freely imitated from the worst fifteenth-century practice, and the vocabulary, taken from available dictionaries. Chatterton does not seem to have cared for Chaucer, except as a source of words. He studied the glossary, not the text. His poetry and his medieval tastes are distinct. The irregular verse of the old ballads has no place in the Rowley poems. The real master of Chatterton is Spenser, and he wrote the final alexandrine of the famous stanza with more complete understanding than any of the mature eighteenth-century imitators had shown. In Chatterton's medieval imitations there is nothing essentially wicked. But later he attempted to impose his frauds as genuine—he tried to take in Horace Walpole with *The Ryse of Peyncteynge in Englande writen by T. Rowleie 1469 for Mastre Canynge*, a fraud very properly refused by Walpole. In April 1770 he had come to London to try his fortune as an author and journalist. With time and better luck he would have succeeded; but he reached the last depth of destitution, and, rather than beg or sponge, he poisoned himself in his room off Holborn. Chatterton was slightly influenced by Macpherson; but Macpherson was merely a capable writer, and Chatterton was a poet, with a true shaping mind. His impersonality is amazing; he does not make poetry out of his pains or sorrows, and when he is composing verse he seems to have escaped from himself. The intrinsic value of his work is not great; but no history of English literature can omit the name of this "marvellous Boy" who "perished in his pride" before he was eighteen.

The Wartons were devoted to the Middle Ages through their appreciation of Gothic architecture. It began with Thomas Warton the elder (1688–1745), who let his two sons Joseph (1722–1800) and Thomas (1728–90) understand what he himself admired in Windsor and Winchester. The elder Thomas was made Professor of Poetry at Oxford in 1718, and deserved the post for his praise of the neglected early poems of Milton. His medieval interest is shown by his Ragnar Lodbrok paraphrase. The younger Thomas had his father's tastes, and proved this in his work on Spenser and Milton, in his projected history of Gothic architecture, as well as in his history of English poetry, for which the *Thesaurus* of Hickes had prepared the way. He represents the easy-going university life embodied in the famous miscellany which he edited, *The Oxford Sausage*. He was Professor of Poetry from 1757 to 1767, Camden Professor of History from 1785 and Poet Laureate in the same year. His *History of English Poetry* (in three volumes, 1774, 1778, 1781) was severely criticized not only for inaccuracy but for incoherence. But it was (and is) a mistake to expect from a history of poetry the same kind of coherence as from the history of a country. In a history of literature, desultory reading and writing are far from useless; and Warton's *History* outlived the writings of critics more thoroughly disciplined. Thomas Warton was the first to expose the Rowley poems. Joseph Warton did not care for the Middle Ages as his brother did, but he saw more clearly than Thomas how great a poet Dante was, and he had that appreciation of Spenser and Milton which was the chief sign and accompaniment of medieval studies in England. His judgment of Pope and of poetry agreed with the opinions expressed by Richard Hurd, Bishop of Worcester (1720–1808), whose volume called *Letters on Chivalry and Romance* (1762) praised the "fine fabling" of Ariosto, Tasso and Spenser for giving to the "charmed spirit" something more grateful than the polished poetry of good sense could offer.

At the same time as Thomas Warton, another Oxford man, Thomas Tyrwhitt (1730–86), with vast and varied learning, was working at Old English poetry. His *Essay on the Language and Versification of Chaucer* and his *Introductory Discourse to the Canterbury Tales* are the complement of Warton's *History*. Warton is not very careful about prosody; Tyrwhitt, like Gray, was interested in the history of verse, and, by a remarkable effort of grammatical detective work, he made out the rule of Chaucer's heroic verse which had escaped notice for nearly 400 years. Tyrwhitt is the true restorer of Chaucer. Though the genius of Dryden had discovered the classical spirit of Chaucer's imagination, the form of his poetry remained obscure and defaced till Tyrwhitt explained it. The art of the grammarian has seldom been better justified than in Tyrwhitt's great contribution to medieval scholarship.

Mention should be made of some other revealing volumes, the *Specimens of the Early English Poets* (1790) and the *Specimens of the Early English Metrical Romances* (1805) compiled by George Ellis (1753–1815), friend of Canning and Scott, and joint founder of *The Anti-Jacobin*. The romance volume is still valuable for the general reader unlikely to read ancient texts "in the original".

That the eighteenth century was not an "age of prose" darkly interposed between two "ages of poetry"; that it sought and found in romance the beauty which has strangeness in it; and that there was no subsequent sudden "romantic revolt" with a consequent re-discovery of nature, or wonder, or feeling, should be clear from the facts here noted.

XI. LETTER WRITERS

Horace Walpole (1717–97)—christened Horatio—is the prince of letter writers. There is no need to compare him with Gray or Cowper or Lamb. In sheer quantity and variety Horace Walpole takes first place. His letters number about four thousand and his correspondents nearly two hundred. His larger works are almost valueless and nearly forgotten; his letters survive triumphantly as a real contribution to literature. His circumstances were fortunate. As the son of Sir Robert Walpole he was born with a right, which no one then disputed, to the ease of sinecures. He became a Member of Parliament in 1741, and was in the House till 1768. He was a regular attendant at the sittings, his descriptions of which have great interest. It should be recorded that he tried hard to save the life of the unfortunate Admiral Byng. The most important event in Walpole's life was the acquisition of Strawberry Hill, near Twickenham, which he made into an imitation Gothic castle, and filled with artistic treasures and curiosities. Unfortunately he had little genuine artistic feeling, and collected the wrong things. Most of his first knowledge of the arts he owed to the purer sense of Gray; left alone he became "Gothick" in the worst sense. The one really important part of the "Castle" was the printing press, the *Officina Arbuteana*, which he installed in 1757, and upon which he printed the *Elegy* and the two *Odes* of Gray. Walpole was a dabbler in literature from his early life. His first substantive work was *A Catalogue of the Royal and Noble Authors of England* printed at the Strawberry Hill press in 1758. His next book, *Anecdotes of Painting in England*, printed at the Strawberry Hill press in 1762, still maintains a kind of life. But neither is important and both are full of errors. His next works were *The Castle of Otranto* (1764–5), a romance, and *The Mysterious Mother* (1768), a tragedy. Byron affirmed that Walpole was "the father of the first romance and the last tragedy in our language", and praised both highly. *The Castle of Otranto* has been mentioned on p. 425. *The Mysterious Mother* may be dismissed at once as intolerably dull and pretentious. *Historic Doubts on the Life and Reign of Richard III*, written about the same time as *The Mysterious Mother*, offers a fair example of Walpole's literary work. He had a good subject, but was too languid to undertake proper research.

Horace Walpole's real works are his letters, which he took seriously, because, being an admirer of Mme de Sévigné, he thought good letters worth the trouble of writing. They have almost every good quality but one, and that is charm. The very sincerity of his letters—and sincerity must be allowed him without question—reveals the fundamental lack of character which prevented his undoubted talents and unrivalled opportunities from having any creative effect on the world. There is no need to follow Macaulay in denouncing him as a kind of monster. A man may be an affected, frivolous, fantastical and over-fastidious placeman without being wicked. Rich though Walpole's letters are in anecdote, their vital interest is autobiographical, and what may be called his general thesis is found in a letter of 1772 to Horace Mann, his chief correspondent: "this world is a comedy to those who think, a tragedy to those who feel".

The next famous letter writer of the age, Philip Dormer Stanhope, fourth

Earl of Chesterfield (1694–1773), was one of the foremost English statesmen of his age. He is unfortunate in being remembered first as the object of Johnson's tremendous rebuke and next as the original of Sir John Chester in *Barnaby Rudge*. But there is much to be said in his favour. He was a highly cultivated man and a capable minister. His oratory, though as studied as his wit, was much admired. He was generous and enlightened, and accepted Johnson's denunciation without malice. His general correspondence is natural, kindly and witty. Chesterfield's fame as a letter writer rests mainly on his *Letters to his Son* (1774) and those *to his Godson* (1890). His devotion to these two young men is an indication of his fundamental sincerity. It ought never to be forgotten that Chesterfield's letters were in the strictest sense private. They were the frank advice of an undeluded experienced elder to young men about to enter the fashionable world in which manners counted more than morals. Chesterfield has borne the public scrutiny of his private communications (augmented in Bonamy Dobrée's edition of 1932) without loss of dignity, and deserves the unsought fame they have brought him.

Fanny Burney's diaries and letters give her a high place among the distinguished chroniclers of eighteenth-century life. In the *Early Diary* (1768–78), edited by Mrs Ellis (1889), the doings of her family are fully displayed, and the professional world of Dr Burney is brightly sketched. In the later *Diary and Letters* (1778–1840), edited by Mrs Charlotte Barrett and Austin Dobson in 1904, we hear much of the larger life she encountered as second Keeper of the Robes to Queen Charlotte for five laborious years. The characters of the diaries are more firmly drawn than the characters of the novels.

Mrs Elizabeth Montagu (1720–1800), chief of the "Blue-Stockings" (see p. 510) and the lion-hunters, had a natural brightness which grew into an assurance of wit. Her fame has diminished and her letters are not now widely read. Her *Essay on the Writings and Genius of Shakespear...with some Remarks upon the Misrepresentation of Mons. De Voltaire* (1769) was a good defence, which has had its day.

David Garrick was a brilliant and agreeable letter writer. The two quarto volumes of his correspondence, published in 1831–2, have strong personal interest. With Garrick may be mentioned his friend Sir Joshua Reynolds (1723–92), whose *Discourses* (1769, etc.) addressed to Academy students, are, in a sense, public letters upon the art he honoured and adorned.

Hannah More (1745–1833) has lost her fame as a formal author, but still retains her importance as a writer of letters. She came to London from Bristol and gained at once the cordial esteem of the Johnson and Montagu circles. Her vividly characterized correspondence can be ranked with that of Fanny Burney.

Gilbert White (1720–93) is an interesting example of a man who became an English classic writer without intention or desire. His *Natural History and Antiquities of Selborne* (1789) is, in fact, not a book at all. For some twenty years or more (1767–87), White wrote a series of letters to Thomas Pennant and Daines Barrington containing his observations on natural phenomena and the habits of animals. In 1770 Barrington suggested publication; but White was indifferent, and waited for eighteen years before preparing anything for the press. Not till 1789 did the book actually appear. The life of Gilbert White was

as limited as a life can be, for he was born and died at Selborne; but the charm
of his book is unfading and Selborne is remembered still as his home. Another
country parson, not in Hampshire but in Somerset and Norfolk, was James
Woodforde (1740–1803), whose *Diary* (1758–1802) was edited by John Beresford
in 1924.

Special interest attaches to a group of letter writers who may be called the
Warwickshire coterie, as they lived in or about that county. The two chief
ladies in the case are, first, the half-sister of Bolingbroke, Henrietta Knight,
afterwards Lady Luxborough, and next, Frances, Duchess of Somerset. Barrels,
the home of Lady Luxborough, became the centre of a literary society which
included Shenstone, Somervile, Jago and Richard Graves. The correspondence
of these friends and others of note has unusual interest. Shenstone himself wrote
letters which some think better worth reading than his poems. But he wrote
too much and too often. He is not free from affectation.

Richard Graves (1715–1804) was a poet, a translator, a diligent correspondent
and a model country parson. *The Spiritual Quixote* (1772), his most famous
story, is a picture of early Methodism and of the road-life of its time. *Columella,
or the Distressed Anchoret* (1776) has much the same kind of interest. More
delicate than *Columella* are the two charming little volumes entitled *Eugenius or
Anecdotes of the Golden Vale* (1785), which not only suggest the beauties of the
Wye valley but indicate a knowledge of the sufferings of the poor almost as
intimate as Crabbe's. Graves has sincere and unaffected charm.

XII. HISTORIANS

1. Hume and Robertson

When Voltaire, writing acidly in 1724, said of the English: "As for good
historians, I know of none as yet; a Frenchman (Rapin) has had to write their
history", he was but repeating what Addison and Bolingbroke had said before
him and anticipating what Johnson and Gibbon said after him. Yet actually the
interest in historical works was very great. Political disputants could appeal to
Clarendon and Burnet for judgment on particular periods, and to useful, if
unliterary, compilations for general historical narrative. The publication, at the
expense of the State, of *Foedera et Conventiones* (1704–35), edited by Thomas
Rymer and Robert Sanderson, laid a new foundation for historical study by
presenting actual public documents. Rapin knew the value of this collection and
made much use of it.

A change in the character of British historical writing began in the middle of
the century. That Hume and Robertson, two of the three great historians, were
Scottish, is capable of some ingenious explanations, but is probably no more
than a coincidence. The important fact is that all three were influenced by
French literature, two of them, Gibbon and Hume, having spent some years
abroad. David Hume (1711–76) regarded history with the eye of a philosopher.
He believed in something called "man", which reacted in the same way to the
same conditions, and he therefore held that a study of the past would reveal
principles of action valid in all ages. History is thus a record of experiments in

living. His appointment as librarian to the Faculty of Advocates at Edinburgh in 1752 gave him command of a large library, and he at once began work on his *History of England*. As a philosopher he was attracted to the constitutional side of history and he therefore chose the reign of James I as his starting point, because it was then that the House of Commons first constructively attacked royal prerogative. The first volume of his *History of Great Britain*, containing the reigns of James I and Charles I, appeared in 1754. It failed to attract a public; but the second volume (1756), which ended with the Revolution of 1688, appealed to Whig sentiment, and not only sold well, but stimulated a demand for its predecessor. Hume worked backwards, and published in 1759 two volumes on the Tudor reigns, completing the work in 1761 with two on the whole period from Julius Caesar to the accession of Henry VII. The book made him, he said, "not merely independent but opulent"; and it long kept its place as a standard work. The earlier parts are the least successful, first because the historian had no deep knowledge of the authorities, and next because the philosopher was out of sympathy with "ages of barbarism". The work was very well written, and, as always, historians who could not write declared it unsound. Modern research has invalidated much of Hume's matter; but his work still retains importance as the first large-scale History of England to attain high rank as a literary composition.

William Robertson (1721–93), a Presbyterian Minister of Edinburgh, published in 1759 his *History of Scotland during the Reigns of Queen Mary and James VI until his Accession to the Crown of England*. The *History of Charles V* followed in 1769 and the *History of America* in 1771. Much later came the *Disquisition concerning the Knowledge which the Ancients had of India* (1791). Robertson's style, in its lucidity and ease, bears a strong likeness to that of Hume. His narrative power is well shown in his description of the voyage and landing of Columbus; and, generally, his *America*, though lacking in modern authority, is a delightful book to read. Robertson deserves his fame as the first British historian to attempt a wide general view of history. The success of Hume and Robertson had shown that there was money in history; and there followed numerous compositions which need not be named here. We pass therefore to the greatest of all English historians.

XIII. HISTORIANS

2. Gibbon

The supremacy of Gibbon among English historians is beyond dispute. He was long in discovering what he wanted to write, but he had no doubt about the kind of knowledge he wanted to acquire, and this he sought with unfaltering determination. He was fortunate enough to achieve the great work which proved the sum of his life's labours and to identify himself and his fame with one great book. Macaulay, the only English historian whose literary genius can be compared with Gibbon's, left but a noble fragment of his great design. Gibbon, as he tells us in a passage which can never be read without emotion, laid down his pen on a beautiful summer night in 1787, conscious that his life's work was done and that his life itself was nearing the end. His sense of having accomplished something great was perfectly just. *The Decline and Fall of the Roman Empire* is an enduring monument of research, an imperishable literary possession and one of the highest encouragements to intellectual endeavour to be found in the history of letters. But it is an odd fact that the historian of the Roman Empire did not succeed in completing a short sketch of his own life. He made six or seven attempts, from which his friend John Baker Holroyd, first Earl of Sheffield, assisted no doubt by his lively and observant daughter Maria Josepha, extracted the delightful *Memoirs of My Life and Writings*. Gibbon's own sketches have since been reprinted (1896); his *Letters* (1896) and his *Journal* (1929) extend our knowledge materially.

Edward Gibbon (1737–94) was born at Putney, his grandfather being a city man who became wealthy during the South Sea "boom", was impoverished when the "Bubble" collapsed, and acquired and again lost a respectable fortune. With a liberality of mind rare in company-promoters, he engaged the saintly William Law as spiritual director of his household. Gibbon's father was taught by Law; Gibbon's aunt Hester became one of Law's devotees. Another aunt, Catherine Porten, was more to the child Gibbon than either of his parents. Gibbon spoke of Law with respect and of his Aunt Porten with deep affection. These facts are not irrelevant: they refute the charge that Gibbon was a chilly sceptic with anaemic feelings. Actually, he was an affectionate child and an almost passionate friend. He had little education save that which he gave himself by incessant reading. At Westminster School he was unhappy; and before his boyhood was really over, he was entered as a gentleman-commoner at Magdalen College, Oxford (1752). Few passages of his *Memoirs* are better known than that in which he indicts the Oxford of his day. The monks of Magdalen, dissolved in port and prejudice, ignored him. Lonely and friendless, Gibbon, like other anxious, eager youths, sought the consolation of religion; but the Church, as represented at Oxford, gave him none. Bewildered by his reading of Conyers Middleton's *Free Enquiry*, which seemed to end in unbelief, he fled, as many have done, to the other extreme, and was received into the Church of Rome, which not only gave him certitude but appealed to him as the historic Church of Europe. He fell by a noble hand; for it was the reading of Bossuet that finally determined him. An Oxford man going over to Rome in 1853 might seem to be following the course of nature; an Oxford man going over to Rome in 1753 was flying headlong on the road to social perdition. The gates of Oxford were closed against Gibbon for ever. His distracted father, feeling that scepticism was at least more fashionable than Catholicism, first consigned him to David Mallet, poetaster, deist and editor of Bolingbroke, but in a few weeks sent him off to Lausanne into the household of a Calvinist minister named Pavillard, who was astonished to meet a thin little youth with a large head propounding the best arguments ever used in favour of Catholicism. The escape from Oxford was the salvation of Gibbon. Oxford could have done him little but harm. At Lausanne he became a European. He had to learn French as a new daily language, and it was French literature, especially the writings of Voltaire, and not, as the good Pavillard fondly supposed, the Protestant argument, that drew Gibbon away from Rome. But his misadventures were not yet over. Escaped from Rome, he fell captive to the bright eyes of Suzanne Curchod, daughter of a

Protestant pastor. Having no means, they naturally contemplated marriage; but the proposal, being referred to Gibbon's father, was peremptorily vetoed. He "sighed as a lover, but obeyed as a son"; and though not yet a historian, helped by his great refusal, to make history; for Suzanne married the future statesman Necker, whose dismissal precipitated the outbreak of the French Revolution. It remains to be added that their daughter was the celebrated Mme de Stael. Gibbon's abdication may be considered justified.

He returned from Lausanne in April 1758, now a mature man, an exact Latin scholar, a widely read student, and an actual author; for he had written an *Essai sur l'Étude de la Littérature*, published in its original French in 1761. But before it appeared he had yet another surprising adventure, for he joined the Hampshire militia, in which, for two years, he held in succession the rank of captain, major and colonel. The Hampshire colonel proved useful to the historian of the Roman Empire. It may be observed, not without astonishment, that Gibbon, whose many historical authorities were to be Greek, did not begin a systematic study of that language till he was twenty-four. That his purpose was to write history he knew; but what history he could not decide. He made and abandoned several projects. The dedicated historian still awaited his call. It came clearly to him on a definite day, the 15th October 1764. After the disbanding of the militia, Gibbon set out on a continental tour. He crossed the Italian frontier in April 1764, and reached Rome in October. Then it was, as he relates in a memorable and thrilling passage, that the call came; and he knew that he had found his theme.

In the present sketch we need not mention Gibbon's minor writings, which are interesting solely because they are his. The death of his father left him with lessened means (the grandfather's second fortune having vanished), but he was able to establish himself in London in 1772 and give himself up to work and to duty; for in 1774 (the year in which he became a member of Johnson's "Club") he entered Parliament, supported Lord North with silent votes, and was rewarded in 1779 by a Commissionership of Trade and Plantations, which he held till its abolition in 1782. The salary of the office was of much importance to him; and, disappointed in his hopes of other official employment, he felt he could no longer afford to live in England.

But though his political career ended in failure, the first instalment of his great historical work, of which Vol. 1 was published in 1776, took the town by storm. Three editions were rapidly exhausted. He was already famous. But he had infuriated the orthodox. What positive views on religion Gibbon held it would be difficult to define; but he was certainly not an orthodox Christian, and in his history he took a detached and historical view of the rise and growth of Christianity in the Empire. Distrusting "enthusiasts" of any kind, he felt no natural sympathy with those who in any period wrote and acted in the belief of a special divine possession. His famous fifteenth and sixteenth chapters therefore gave great offence; but though the gravely ironic note is intentional, Gibbon, writing for the "enlightened" of his age, certainly did not mean to displease quite so deeply and extensively as, in fact, he did. Most of the furious attacks made upon him by the orthodox have now no value of any kind, and we need not discuss them. Gibbon himself was unperturbed.

His indifference to criticism is shown by the fact that, though the popular welcome extended to his second and third volumes (1781) was, at first, fainter, it was only then that he finally resolved to carry on the work from the fall of the Western to that of the Eastern Empire. About this time, too, he resolved to abandon the distractions of social existence in London for a literary life abroad, and in the autumn of 1783 he settled at Lausanne. Here, in a retirement which was anything but cloistered, he brought to a close (1787) the main work of his life, of which the three concluding volumes (IV-VI) were carried by him to England and published in April 1788. The golden passage in which he describes the conclusion of the work has already been mentioned. He returned to Lausanne in 1788, and made up his mind—once more setting an example which but few men of letters have found themselves able to follow—to undertake no other great work. In 1791 the bereavement of Lord Sheffield brought Gibbon back to England, which, in the disturbed condition of Europe, he did not attempt to leave again. He was characteristically careless of his health, and died in London three years later. He was buried in the Holroyd tomb in the quiet little church of Fletching, in Sussex, close to the gates of Sheffield Park, the hospitable home of his friend—almost his brother by adoption. Gibbon, who had a genius for friendship, never married. We are curiously reminded of Hobbes and Locke, Gray and Walpole.

The Decline and Fall is not only the greatest historical work in the English language, it is perhaps the greatest piece of literary architecture in any language. It is faultless in design and in detail, and its symphonic narrative power is superb. That something in it remains to be corrected simply means that historical research has not halted; but in the main Gibbon is still the master, above and beyond date. He followed truth, as he understood it, wherever truth was to be found, and his honour as a historian cannot be impugned. Further, he is one of the great masters of English prose. His power of narrative is equalled by his gift of argumentative statement, and, in all parts of his work, his style is one which holds the reader spellbound by its stately dignity, relieved by a subtle personal character. The best edition is J. B. Bury's (1896–1900); G. M. Young (1932), Christopher Dawson (1934) and C. V. Wedgwood (1955) are among the distinguished historians who have written on Gibbon; his *Life* was written by D. M. Low in 1937; a complete edition of his *Letters* was edited by J. E. Norton in 1955.

There were numerous other writers who attempted works in ancient history; but we need mention only one, William Mitford (1744–1827), whose *History of Greece*, suggested to him by Gibbon, appeared in ten volumes (1784–1810). This held the field until it was superseded by the works of Thirlwall and Grote.

XIV. PHILOSOPHERS

Hume, Adam Smith and Others

Two friends, David Hume and Adam Smith, have had a powerful influence upon human thought. David Hume (1711–76), whom we have already met (p. 451) as a historian, combined a passion for literature with a desire to seek in human nature itself for an explanation of the means whereby truth is established. He believed that philosophers had concerned themselves too much with abstractions like "virtue" and "happiness". In 1734 he retired to study in France, and returned in 1737. The first two volumes of *A Treatise on Human Nature* appeared in 1739, though they were written after the third, published in 1740. A series of *Essays, Moral and Political* came out at intervals between 1741 and 1748. *Philosophical Essays concerning Human Understanding* (1748) was republished as *An Enquiry concerning Human Understanding* (1758). *An Enquiry concerning the Principles of Morals* (1751) was thought by Hume to be the best of his writings. Later works included *Political Discourses* (1752), *Essays and Treatises on Various Subjects* (1753–4) and *Four Dissertations* (1757). Besides his extensive work as a philosophical writer, Hume did much service as an official abroad and at home. He was received with great favour in social and literary circles in France; and in England he befriended Rousseau, who repaid his kindness with violent suspicion and ingratitude. His character bears the signs of true greatness.

Hume's philosophical writings (edited 1874–5 by Thomas Hill Green and T. H. Grose) are numerous and important, but he was not the constructor of a philosophical system, he was rather the sceptical critic of philosophical systems. For him the explanation of the problem of knowledge is the human way of knowing and feeling. In other words, his approach to understanding is psychological. According to Locke, the material of knowledge comes from two different sources, sensation and reflection. Hume's primary data are all of one kind, "impressions" and "ideas", the latter being a weaker state of the former. The law of gravitation has a parallel in the law of association of ideas. The commonest example of association is cause and effect, and this association is a mental habit, not an ultimate necessity. Belief is simply a lively idea associated with a present effect. Hume's political speculations are of less importance; but he is the philosophical father of the Utilitarians, and he anticipates something in Adam Smith. His essay *Of Miracles* (contained in an *Enquiry concerning Human Understanding*) and *Dialogues concerning Natural Religion* (1779) aroused most discussion in his time because of their sceptical tendency. His general philosophical criticism had great influence at home and abroad, Kant being one famous thinker stimulated by him. Hume's writings are remarkable for their perspicuity and ease of style. Philosophy, in his pages, bears herself with grace as well as gravity. His *Life* was written in 1931 by J. Y. T. Greig, who also edited his *Letters* (1932).

Adam Smith (1723–90) of Kirkcaldy went first to the university of Glasgow, and then to the university of Oxford, which, though he condemned it as comprehensively as Gibbon, he made his home for six years. Smith became professor of logic (1751) and of moral philosophy (1752) at Glasgow, and in 1759 he published his *Theory of Moral Sentiments*, which brought him immediate fame. Like Hobbes, he travelled abroad as a tutor. In Paris he was received into the remarkable society of economists commonly known as the "Physiocrats", whose leaders were Quesnay and Turgot; but Smith was not seriously indebted to the Physiocrats. The views he had in common with them he had formed before he knew them. After his return from France in 1766, Smith settled down quietly at Kirkcaldy and devoted himself to the composition of his great work,

An Inquiry into the Nature and Causes of the Wealth of Nations, which was published in 1776. In 1778 he removed to Edinburgh as Commissioner of Customs.

Adam Smith survives as the writer of two unequal works, the first produced by a scholarly professor, the second produced by a man who had seen something of the world. Books of ethical theory usually have no long life, and *The Theory of Moral Sentiments* cannot now be regarded as important. Adam Smith is frequently spoken of as the founder of political economy. But in the attempt to isolate economic facts he was anticipated by Sir James Steuart's *Inquiry into the Principles of Political Economy* (1767), though the book has no merit either as literature or as science. Still, it existed. *The Wealth of Nations* is a great advance upon the *Moral Sentiments* in literary art and construction. Adam Smith wastes no time on preliminaries, but plunges at once into his subject, and considers the nature of Wealth. Wealth consists not in the precious metals, but in the goods which men use or consume; and its source or cause is labour. The philosopher thus isolates the fact of wealth and makes it the subject of a science. But he sees this fact in its connections with life as a whole. Further, in the division of labour he sees the first step taken by man in industrial progress. His treatment of this subject has become classical. Like other philosophers of the time, he assumed that there was a natural identity of public and private interests. It is a comfortable belief that society would be served best if everybody looked after his own interests. But the belief itself is incapable of verification, and subsequent industrial history on the whole refutes it.

Up to Adam Smith's time, the regulation of industry had been almost universally admitted to be part of any government's functions. Smith made a comprehensive survey of these attempts at regulation or restriction, and he maintained that they were uniformly pernicious. He was, in fact, the real apostle of free trade; but he was not a "doctrinaire", for he held that natural liberty must sometimes be restrained. Many of Adam Smith's principles seem so obvious that we forget how new they were when he propounded them. Some of them are already forgotten; and a time may come when they will have to be reaffirmed. Even though, as a text book, *The Wealth of Nations* must be called out of date, it remains a genuine contribution to literature in its vivid pictures of the life and commerce of its day, and in its power of stating difficult abstractions in a way convincing even to mercantile minds. The oddest fact is that this practical treatise was the work of an engagingly absent-minded man unable to spend or to save a shilling profitably.

A few notes may be appended on other philosophical writers of the time. Among the psychologists, the most important place belongs to David Hartley (1705–57), a physician, whose *Observations on Man: his Frame, his Duty, and his Expectations* appeared in 1749. The rapid march of philosophical thought in the previous forty years was apparently unknown to him. The theological part of his book was antiquated even when it first appeared; but the first or psychological part of the book has two striking features: it is a systematic attempt at a physiological psychology, and it develops the theory of the association of ideas in a way which influenced, far more than Hume did, the views of the later associational school of James Mill and his successors. Hartley, as we know, attracted Coleridge, who gave the philosopher's name to his eldest son.

Abraham Tucker (1705–74) was a psychologist of a different temper. He was a critic of Hartley's physiological doctrines, and he excelled in that introspective analysis which has been practised by many English writers. Tucker was a country gentleman whose chief employment was a study of the things of the mind. The first fruit of his reflection was a fragment *Freewill, Foreknowledge and Fate* (1763), published under the pseudonym "Edward Search"; certain criticisms of this piece produced, also in 1763, *Man in quest of Himself: or a Defence of the Individuality of the Human Mind*, "by Cuthbert Comment". Thereafter he did not turn aside from his larger task, *The Light of Nature Pursued* (1765–74). Though Tucker cannot be taken seriously as a philosopher, his great work is full of interest. Most people know something of Tucker from Hazlitt's excellent preface to an abridgment of the seven volumes of *The Light of Nature Pursued*.

Richard Price (1723–91), a Welsh Unitarian minister, was a much more considerable man than Burke's contemptuous denunciation of him in the *Reflections on the French Revolution* would cause a reader to suppose. His *Observations on Reversionary Payments* (1771) made a distinct advance in the theory of life assurance. His *Appeal to the Public on the Subject of the National Debt* (1772) is said to have contributed to the re-establishment of the sinking fund. He was drawn into the current of revolutionary politics and became a leading exponent of "new" ideas. His *Observations on the Nature of Civil Liberty, the Principles of Government, and the Justice and Policy of the War with America* (1776) made him famous in two continents. The Revolution in France was the occasion for *A Discourse on the Love of our Country* (1789), which provoked Burke's *Reflections*. Price cannot now be considered important, but he influenced the thought of his time.

Joseph Priestley (1733–1804) had many points of sympathy with Price. His work in science is mentioned in a subsequent chapter (see p. 709). His philosophical views were expressed and defended in *Disquisitions relating to Matter and Spirit* (1777), in *The Doctrine of Philosophical Necessity* (1777) and in *A Free Discussion* (1778). Of greater interest than these, however, is the short *Essay on the First Principles of Government* (1768). Priestley anticipated Bentham in taking utilitarian considerations as the basis of a philosophical radicalism, instead of the prevalent dogmas about "the natural rights of man".

William Paley (1743–1805), the once famous author of *A View of the Evidences of Christianity* (1794), was a Senior Wrangler as well as a theologian. Nearly all his books owe something to others; his *Horae Paulinae*, more original, was notoriously less successful. Paley's power of marshalling his arguments gave his works a longer life as academic text-books than they deserved as original compositions. He is now almost forgotten.

The most powerful reply to Hume came from a group of scholars in Aberdeen. Of this group, Thomas Reid (1710–96) was the most notable member, and he was the founder of the school of Scottish philosophy known as the "Common Sense School". With him were associated George Campbell and James Beattie, as well as other men of mark in their day. The earliest contribution to the controversy—Campbell's *Dissertation on Miracles* (1763)—dealt with a side issue; but it is of interest for its examination of the place of testimony in knowledge. Campbell's later work, *The Philosophy of Rhetoric* (1776), contains much excellent matter. Beattie's *An Essay on the Nature and Immutability of Truth* (1770) is not a work of originality or of distinction, but it is vigorously written, and it brought him as much fame as did his poems. Reid's *An Inquiry into the Human Mind on the Principles of Common Sense* was published in 1764. His later and more elaborate works—*Essays on the Intellectual Powers of Man* and *Essays on the Active Powers of Man*—appeared in 1785 and 1788 respectively. Reid was a clear thinker and a serious critic of Hume. To discuss the part he ascribed to "natural suggestion" or "common sense" in the interpretation of experience is beyond the purpose of this volume.

XV. DIVINES

The orthodox theological literature of this period has no very remarkable qualities and calls for little discussion here. Self-satisfied pronouncements by comfortable Church-and-State bishops have no relation either to literature or to religion. Mystics like William Law were strange exceptions to the prevalent complacency. Not till Count Zinzendorf and the Moravians completed the impression which *A Serious Call* had made on the heart of John Wesley did the literature of religion receive a new impetus and inspiration. Butler, of course, the one exception, lives in an intellectual world of his own. A few outstanding works may be briefly named.

Among the orthodox scholars, William Wake (1657–1737), Archbishop of Canterbury, left one valuable contribution to theological literature in his translation of the Apostolic Fathers (1693). The touching story of a young non-juror's life, told by his father, is related in *A Pattern for Students in the University, set forth in the Life of Mr Ambrose Bonwicke, Sometime scholar of St John's College in Cambridge* (1729). Joseph Bingham (1668–1723), the greatest ecclesiastical antiquary of his time, published his *Origines Ecclesiasticae, or The Antiquities of the Christian Church* in successive volumes from 1708 to 1722. Daniel Waterland (1683–1740) produced, in *A Review of the Doctrine of the Eucharist* (1737), a treatise that long remained a classic of Anglican theology. Thomas Wilson (1663–1755), who refused preferment and was made Bishop of Sodor and Man against his will, lived for nearly sixty years in his see the life of a primitive saint. His *Maxims* and *Parochialia* (1791) show a knowledge of human nature not very common among saints or clergymen, and his *Sacra Privata* (1786), which indicates how this knowledge was obtained, places him with Andrewes among the masters of English devotional literature. He is the oft-quoted Bishop Wilson of Matthew Arnold's *Culture and Anarchy*.

The Methodist movement, like the "romantic revolt" in poetry, was a protest against formalism. Fervour had gone out of the English Church. In its formularies there was life, but the formularies were a dead letter, and the life needed awakening. The young Oxford students who founded Methodism sought to revive the old devotion. There was no idea of separation. The move- ment was distinctly a Church movement, and Wesley's own spiritual inspiration came from Jeremy Taylor. John Wesley (1703–91) and his brother Charles (1707–88) both went to Oxford, where Charles founded a group or society of young men who desired to follow the Church's rules of fasting, almsgiving and prayer, and to receive the Holy Communion weekly. The Oxford divines were amused, amazed, annoyed. One of the earlier members was George Whitefield (1714–70), perhaps the greatest orator of the eighteenth century. John Wesley went to America in 1735, Charles in 1736, Whitefield in 1738. The freedom of missionary work rendered each of them disposed to new religious influences. Wesley and Whitefield gradually drifted apart. Wesley was greatly influenced by the Moravians, Whitefield by the Calvinism which seemed to be dying a natural death in the Church of England till his influence revived it. In 1740 Wesley severed his connection with the Moravians and in 1743 the followers of Whitefield became distinguished as Calvinistic Methodists. Wesley began to ordain ministers in 1784, at which date he must be regarded as severed from the Church of his baptism and ordination. Whitefield became the founder of what was called Lady Huntingdon's Connection. He hardly belongs to literature. One of those deeply influenced by the Methodist movement at Oxford was James Hervey (1714–58), whose *Meditations Among the Tombs* and *Contemplations on the Night*, which met with extraordinary success in their day, illustrate most effectively what may be called the debased Jeremy Taylor style of literary architecture. The fiercely controversial Augustus Montague Toplady (1740–78), who attacked Wesley in the now forgotten *Historic Proof of the Doctrinal Calvinism of the Church of England*, is remembered as the writer of the hymn "Rock of Ages".

Of John Wesley himself as a writer it need only be said that he was, with the pen as with the tongue, a master of strong, simple, direct English. His *Journal* has something of the charm of Pepys. No abridgment does it justice. Everywhere in it one meets the straightforward, clear-eyed observer, enthralled by the Divine vision which he saw and tried to make known among men, yet endowed with shrewd humour, and (unlike the pious Hervey) tolerant of such "profane" literature as Prior, Home, Thomson, Lord Chesterfield and Sterne. He delighted to quote the classics; but he had not the sense of style which was born in his brother Charles. John was no poet; but Charles wrote more than six thousand hymns, among them *Jesu, lover of my soul* and *Love divine, all loves excelling*. These two remarkable brothers give Methodism an honoured place in the history of English literature.

XVI. THE GROWTH OF DISSENT

The Independent and Presbyterian opponents of Anglican episcopalianism in the reign of Charles I seem to be political parties rather than religious bodies; and their descendants of the next generation were forced by the persecutions of the Restoration to assert themselves with political vigour. Dissent long remained true to its beginnings. If the Church of England was lethargic, Dissent was aggressive. The Free Churches claim to have asserted the principle of religious toleration. Historically, the claim is untenable, for, during its transient triumph under the Commonwealth, Dissent was intolerant and repressive. There are few uglier stories in the history of religion than the persecution of the Quakers. Dissent cried aloud for toleration when it was not tolerated; when it found that toleration was to include Romanism it refused toleration even for itself. Toleration is not a religious virtue. Toleration comes with social strength and individualism in a state. It is a lay, not a clerical attitude of mind. There may be toleration where there is an alliance between church and state; there is no toleration when the church is the state, or when the state is the church.

The history of English Nonconformity between the Restoration and the Oxford Movement is much more interesting than the history of the Church of England during that period. The subject is beyond our scope, but we can briefly remark the tendency to division and sub-division. The "religion of the Bible" became many religions. After a brief period of concord Presbyterians and Independents drew apart. From the Independents came the Congregationalists. The Baptists divided among themselves. Anti-Trinitarian views had been current among Protestants during the sixteenth century, but were not tolerated. Calvin burnt Servetus in 1553, nevertheless Socinus, i.e. Sozzini (1539–1604), boldly affirmed ultra-rational views about the divinity of Jesus and the doctrine of the Atonement. Milton, Locke, Newton and Watts were all unorthodox. Liberal views about the Trinity and the nature of Jesus began to appear in the Church in the seventeenth century and affected the Nonconformist bodies, from which there drew apart a separate band calling themselves Unitarians. Unitarianism represented a full revolt against the Calvinism still strongly held by many of the Dissenting bodies of the time. Among the Unitarians appeared some remarkable men, from Price and Priestley in the eighteenth century to Martineau and the New Englander Channing in the nineteenth.

The eighteenth century owes a great debt to Dissent for its wholesome educational zeal. The attitude of the Anglican Church towards the dissenting academies was hostile. They were held to be nurseries of schism and rival institutions to Oxford and Cambridge themselves. The bent towards Unitarianism shown by the more enlightened tutors tended to frighten away first lay pupils and next pupils preparing for the ministry. The Anglican public schools and universities continued their ancient routine; the modernist dissenting academies gradually dwindled into decay. They had no root of authority, civil or religious.

XVII. POLITICAL LITERATURE, 1755–75

The political literature of the period between the death of Henry Pelham in 1754 and the accession of George III in 1760 is not of general interest. The accession of George entirely changed the situation. That sovereign, determined not to be a "Doge", but to be a king in fact as well as in title, hastened to rid himself of the great Pitt and to install his Scottish friend Lord Bute as head of the government. To Englishmen of the eighteenth century a Scotsman was the "undesirable alien"; and Bute's obvious incapacity increased the odium aroused by his nationality. Bute felt the need of a journalistic ally, and naturally chose a brother Scot, Smollett, who in 1762 began to issue a weekly pro-Bute paper called *The Briton*.

The Briton was a pitiful failure, and would not be worth mentioning if its title had not given a sting to the title of an anti-Bute paper *The North Briton*, edited by John Wilkes (1727–97). That demagogue, like some later specimens of his kind, was a complete rascal, but he was an able rascal, and he was a born journalist. In 1755 he obtained a seat in the Commons as member for Aylesbury. No profits accrued, so he naturally became a patriot, turned to journalism, and attacked the Government. He began with articles against "foreign" favourites; and when *The Briton* appeared in May 1762 he retorted in June 1762 with *The North Briton*, an obvious gibe at Bute's nationality. Week by week the new periodical continued its attacks on the Government, printing the ministers' names in full, without the usual subterfuge of dashes and stars. Bute could find nothing actionable in the paper until No. 45 impugned the truthfulness of the speech from the throne regarding the Peace of Paris. The long Government persecution of Wilkes which followed the publication of No. 45 and the later contest with King and Parliament over the Middlesex election belong to history and not to literature. Wilkes was a bad man and a good journalist who had the knack of suffering for a right cause, and he knew how to tune public opinion. The eighteenth century scarcely gave scope enough for his peculiar abilities; it made him Lord Mayor. The twentieth would have made him a peer.

Wilkes had for coadjutor a more eminent man of letters, the poet and satirist Charles Churchill (1731–64). Churchill was the son of a clergyman. Although in orders he devoted himself to the pleasures of the town and was soon in financial difficulties. He attracted attention by his verses, most of which do not now deserve attention. His most famous and still his most important poem is *The Rosciad* (1761), a satire on popular dramatic figures. Its success was immediate and extraordinary. For the rest of his life Churchill was involved in acrid literary warfare. His reputation made him known to Wilkes, and in the orgies at Medmenham Abbey the last remnants of his clericalism vanished. Quite half of *The North Briton* was written by him. Judged by the ordinary standards he was a thoroughly bad man; but his devotion to Wilkes was whole-hearted, and no mean action is anywhere recorded of him. Churchill's verse is truculent and loud, but it has spirit and strength. His *Apology* (1761) was a savage reply to reviewers of *The Rosciad*—one of whom he supposed was Smollett. The main object of his best satire, *The Prophecy of Famine* (1763), was to decry and ridicule Bute and the Scots, though there is also an undercurrent of deserved mockery at the reigning fashion of pastoral poetry. Mere mention is all that need be accorded to *An Epistle to William Hogarth* (1763), *The Conference* (1763), *The Duellist* (1763), *Gotham* (1764), and *The Times* (1764), the last having the kind of interest that booksellers in their catalogues style "curious". A poet praised by Cowper may seem worthy of esteem; but Cowper was his schoolfellow at Westminster. In actual value the satires of Churchill are far below those of Dryden and Pope, simply because his originating creative power is of an inferior order. In spite of much slashing and violent writing he has left only one phrase that remains current, the casual allusion to "apt Alliteration's artful aid". Churchill is interesting and easy to write about, and so he has been over-praised.

Prose was more effective than verse in the political controversies that followed Bute's resignation. The flood of pamphlets continued, and we should note the appearance of attacks in the form of letters, signed with semi-classical names. Henry Sampson Woodfall, editor of *The Public Advertiser* since 1758, had made a feature of political correspondence signed by such names as "Anti-Sejanus", "Cato Redivivus" and so forth, none of which was exclusively applied to any one writer. It was in October 1768 that "Junius", the most celebrated of all the political correspondents of *The Public Advertiser*, made his first appearance, though, by his own account, he had already written under various names. He was an old-fashioned Whig, and a warm, almost an impassioned, adherent of the former Prime Minister, George Grenville, and for some reason the violent enemy of the Duke of Grafton. The series of letters of Junius proper began in January 1769. Under his signature (or its alternative "Philo-Junius") he assailed the ministers and judges responsible for the prosecution of Wilkes. Actually Junius effected nothing. He states sound Whig principles with remarkable lucidity; yet the letters when read in collected form disclose a personality fundamentally evil. That, perhaps, is the strongest evidence for the major complicity of Sir Philip Francis in the business; for Philip Francis was a very bitter antagonist. It is possible to overrate the actual value of the letters as the prose of invective; but they are certainly well written; the sentences, brief, pithy and pungent, exhibit a delicate equilibrium in their structure. The anonymity which he marvellously preserved enabled Junius to maintain that affectation of superiority which distinguished him; but we should not forget that this lofty gentleman was engaged in the lowest methods of controversy. The wildest guesses as to his identity were made in his own day and after. The only judgment the historian of literature is entitled to make is that there is more evidence for the authorship of Sir Philip Francis than there is against it. One person need not have written all the letters or invented all the matter. At the present day, when popular journalism keeps itself at screaming point, the letters of Junius may seem tame. But they were new things and bold things of their kind. Full appreciation of their quality is less likely to come from a steady perusal of them in a volume, than from a more occasional reading, as if they were letters appearing in a serious newspaper of today attacking the reigning sovereign or the most prominent members of the current government. The letters ceased with a searching attack on Lord Mansfield in January 1772. Later in that year appeared the first authorized collected edition. No clue was given to the identity of the writer or writers.

Sir Philip Francis (1740–1818), the reputed author of the letters of Junius, was born in Dublin. In 1773 he was appointed a member of the Governor-General's Council in India. His long feud there with Hastings brought him into public notice, and after his return to England in 1781 he became the relentless engineer of the campaign against the great man. His attitude to Hastings exhibits an almost fanatical kind of hatred, and his political failure accounts for his bitterness. The strongest argument urged against his identity with Junius is the failure of his other correspondence to attain the Junian level. But too much can be made of this. It is well known, both in journalism and in psychology, that some people can write better under assumed names than under their own. A personality inhibited by the uneasy publicity attaching to confessed authorship is released by the comfortable security of anonymity. But the case is certainly remarkable. The identity of Junius is the best-kept secret in the history of journalism. *Stat nominis umbra.*

CHAPTER XI

THE PERIOD OF THE FRENCH REVOLUTION

I. BURKE

Edmund Burke (1729–97), the writer who used most completely the oratorical style in English prose, was a Dublin Irishman, born of a Protestant father and a Catholic mother, and educated as a Protestant at Trinity College. He came to London and entered the Middle Temple in 1750, but was never called to the Bar. His first tentative excursions into literature were an ironical answer to Boling-broke in *A Vindication of Natural Society* (1756) and an essay in aesthetics after Addison in *A Philosophical Enquiry into the Origin of our Ideas of the Sublime and Beautiful* (1756). They are not important, though we get from them intimations of Burke's personal convictions. Throughout his life, feeling, and not reason, was the power that moved him.

Burke's public career began in 1759 when he became editor of *The Annual Register* and secretary to William Gerard Hamilton— "Single Speech Hamilton"—Chief Secretary for Ireland. In 1765 he entered the House of Commons and became Secretary to Lord Rockingham, then in power. During the short life of Rockingham's first ministry and the sixteen years of opposition that followed, Burke was the animating spirit of the Rockingham Whigs. He fought for the freedom of the House of Commons against the subsidized interests of the "King's friends", and the freedom of the American colonies against the claims of the King's friends to tax them directly. The writings in which his views are most fully preserved are *Observations on a late publication entitled "The Present State of the Nation"* (1769), *Thoughts on the Cause of the Present Discontents* (1770), the speech *On American Taxation* (1774), that *On moving his Resolutions for Conciliation with the Colonies* (1775) and *A Letter...to...[the] Sheriffs of...Bristol* (1777). As the American war drew to an end, Ireland and India became Burke's chief concern. By his support of Irish trade, he lost in 1780 the representation of Bristol, which his opposition to the American war had gained for him in 1774; and *Two Letters...to Gentlemen in the City of Bristol* (1778), with the *Speech at the Guildhall, in Bristol, previous to the late Election* (1780), are the noble record of his courage, independence and wisdom in the hour of defeat. Burke had given much time to a study of Indian affairs, and in 1785 he entered upon the campaign against Hastings which was to occupy him for ten years. To 1785 also belongs the famous *Speech on the...Nabob of Arcot's Private Debts*. His last crusade was that against the new government in France. A crescendo of indignation swells through a rapid succession of publications: *Reflections on the Revolution in France* (1790), *A Letter...to a Member of the National Assembly* (1791), *An Appeal from the New to the Old Whigs* (1791), *Thoughts on French Affairs* (1791), *Remarks on the Policy of the Allies* (1793), and *Letters...on the Proposals for Peace with the Regicide Directory of France* (1795–7).

Burke died in 1797 with his last hopes for justice to Irish Catholics shattered, and believing that England was about to make dishonorable peace with the enemy across the Channel.

Of the tracts named above, the first in which Burke's principles are stated with an eloquence that gives him a place in literature is that known as *Thoughts on the Cause of the Present Discontents*. The policy of the King and the "King's friends" towards the Middlesex election and towards the American colonies seemed to Burke highly dangerous. There was, he felt, no safer method of government than the openly debated "pro" and "con" of party. The attempted reassertion of royal prerogative took us back to the fatal days of Charles I. No modern student of history bases any convictions about the American struggle on the mere taxation question. The great point at issue was the right way of securing the loyalty of any overseas dominion to the home government. In Burke's view, acts of state should be guided by three main principles which can be indicated in three questions: Is this expedient or worth while? Is this good for the persons most affected? Is this justified by experience? He alone seems to have understood the problem of governing and maintaining the empire which Chatham's successful wars had called into existence. Of his American speeches, the greatest, as it is the most elaborate, is the second, *On Conciliation*; but the first, *On American Taxation*, combines in a wonderful manner simplicity and directness of reasoning with ardour and splendour of eloquence.

The obstinate stupidity which Burke deplored in the policy of George III and his ministers towards America he found undiminished in their policy towards Ireland. His Irish tracts are among the least read of his pieces, but they deserve attention, both for the excellence of their matter and for the temperateness of their utterance. In the letters *To a Peer of Ireland on the Penal Laws* (1782), *To Sir Hercules Langrishe* (1792) and the earlier *Speech at the Guildhall, in Bristol* (1780) the theme is simply this: stupidity has lost us America, stupidity will lose us Ireland. Events have justified the indictment.

Burke felt strongly that India should be governed for the good of its inhabitants, and not for the profit of the East India Company and its servants. Warren Hastings was to him the type of misrule, and against that unhappy man he directed all his power of invective. But Hastings, whatever his faults may have been, was a great ruler, and we cannot help feeling, when we read the ferocious denunciations, that Burke was engaged, not in prosecution, but in persecution.

Burke's violent opposition to the French Revolution of 1789 seems unnatural, but is not inexplicable. The eloquent champion of the American farmer and the Indian ryot appeared to have nothing to say for the French peasant. All his eloquence was reserved for the oppressors. The cause of his antagonism was twofold and was deeply inherent in his nature. He could no more believe in "the rights of man" than he could believe in the rights of kings; further, he was sure that any assertion of such rights savoured of atheism. Burke's instinct was true. The Revolution was a challenge, not only to kingship, but to all establishments. A change was coming in the way of human thought. He felt it, he feared it, he opposed it. With the *Reflections* should be read *An Appeal from the New to the Old Whigs* (1791), published anonymously and written in the third person. These two pamphlets form the most complete statement of

Burke's anti-revolutionary philosophy. Unsound as he seems in his veneration of mere prescription, Burke was thoroughly sound in his suspicion of "Reason" enthroned as the sovereign power. Burke's revolt against the Revolution is almost exactly parallel to Wordsworth's revolt against Godwinism. From "political justice" Wordsworth turned to the emotions and the prejudices of the peasant, and found himself a poet again. It is easy to dislike Burke on the Revolution; but it is not difficult to be warned by him against the perpetual menace of the doctrinaire. He died before any final issue was even in sight, and there is no evidence that he foresaw the shape and course of events.

Two productions of Burke stand apart from his great crusades; they are the speech on Economical Reform (1780) and the *Letter to a Noble Lord* (1796). The first is the most quietly persuasive and genial of his writings; the second is a formidable piece of controversy. Burke had been granted a pension, and none had better deserved it. The grant was bitterly attacked, especially by the Duke of Bedford, who appeared to consider that any grants, pensions or places should be reserved for those who did not need them, did not deserve them, and did not come from obscure families. Burke's *Letter* is not merely a great example of invective, it is a great example of a very rare thing, invective that is creative.

Burke's eloquence belonged to a past age. The splendour of his imagery and the sonorousness of his periods link his prose with that of the great sixteenth and seventeenth century writers. He brought into politics the faults as well as the genius of a major prophet. He is at times unrestrained, unjust, unwise; nevertheless the greatness of his mind outweighs his faults, and he remains the only orator whose speeches have secured a permanent place in English literature.

II. POLITICAL WRITERS AND SPEAKERS

In 1784 the King once more triumphed over the Whigs, and young Pitt became master of Parliament. The devotees of Fox formed the *Esto Perpetua* Club and began to harry the enemy. Someone hit on the happy idea of a mock review of a mock epic, and in *The Morning Herald* appeared a series of "Criticisms of *The Rolliad*". *The Rolliad* was a mythical epic named from John Rolle, M.P., a stolid Tory who had tried to cough down Burke. He was provided with an ancestor, the Norman Duke Rollo, whose imaginary adventures supplied matter for a burlesque of the *Aeneid*. The new style of skit proved very popular, and the authors did not carry it on too long. It was succeeded by another kind of burlesque, *Political Eclogues*, in which Pitt and his friends appeared as Virgilian shepherds. This, in its turn, was followed by a series of *Probationary Odes* for the laureateship, then vacant by the death of Whitehead in 1785. The poetical level of all these pieces was not very high, but at least they were more civilized than the political satires of Churchill. The only one of the authors worth mention is George Ellis, the scholar.

One outstanding figure among the verse satirists on the Whig side is "Peter Pindar", the pseudonym adopted by John Wolcot (1738–1819) at first a doctor and afterwards a clergyman. He discovered the genius of Opie the painter, ran him as a speculation, and quarrelled with him. He imitated *The Rolliad* in *The*

Lousiad (1785) and in 1787 produced another skit, *Ode upon Ode*, which attained great popularity. The absurdities of the yearly official odes to the King invited reprisals; and Wolcot, hampered by few convictions and fewer scruples, found a ready market among indignant Whigs for his small scandal. He is, perhaps, the best of English caricaturists in verse. *Bozzy and Piozzi* (1786), the title of which explains itself, is another excellent piece of caricature.

When Pitt boldly faced the aggressiveness of French republicanism abroad and of its partisans at home, he found a lively and trenchant ally in *The Anti-Jacobin* (1797–8), founded by George Canning. It remains the best thing of its kind. The deadly conviction of its attack was made more effective by its witty manner. Among the writers were the many-sided, brilliant Canning, George Ellis, by this time a fervent Tory and repentant of *The Rolliad*, and John Hookham Frere, country gentleman, diplomatist, traveller, translator of Aristophanes, and the first to imitate in English the satiric Italian epic. The editor was William Gifford (1756–1826), whose literary brutalities have blackened a character admirable in many ways. He was one of those luckless persons born with the instincts of scholarship in penurious circumstances that denied him a scholar's education. After a miserable boyhood he was sent to Oxford, and was able to make something of a name by his satires, *The Baviad* (1794) and *The Maeviad* (1795), directed against the ridiculous "Della Cruscan" school of poets and the small dramatic fry of the day. When *The Anti-Jacobin* was set on foot, his sledge-hammer style and industry made him a suitable editor; but he was mainly concerned with its prose. He did his task well, and in 1809 became first editor of *The Quarterly Review* and held his post for fifteen years. He seemed to find relief for the bitterness engendered by his menial years in savage attacks upon all suspected of Liberalism. The shameful onslaught in the *Quarterly* upon Keats can be neither forgotten nor forgiven. The verse of *The Anti-Jacobin* "guys" very gaily the early revolutionary bleatings of Southey and his friends. The "Knife-Grinder" sapphics in imitation of Southey are immortal.

One of the butts of *The Anti-Jacobin* was "Mr. Higgins of St. Mary Axe" —in real life William Godwin (1756–1836), a political philosopher and novelist, to whom harsh justice was measured out in life, and to whom true justice will never now be done, because he is not quite important enough to pay for resuscitation. He is remembered as the husband of Mary Wollstonecraft (1759–97) and the father-in-law of Shelley; he ought to be remembered as a sincere thinker in whose character there was not a trace of self-seeking or self-display. Much conscientious, ephemeral work was done by him in history and literature; but he was brought into sudden prominence by a book of startling opinions, *Political Justice*, published in 1793. The influence of this book was great among the younger generation. Godwin was a born system-maker; philosophy and politics were, for him, indistinguishable, and of his views on both he was an eager advocate in public and private. So we find him writing proselytizing novels, *Caleb Williams* and *St Leon*, which he hoped would insinuate his views in the general mind. During these years, he met and married another writer of innovating beliefs. Mary Wollstonecraft, to use her maiden name, is a far more attractive person than her placid husband. After beginning as a teacher she passed several years as a publishers' hack, till her *Vindication of the Rights of*

Woman made her name known in 1792. It was the first blast of the trumpet in the battle for women's freedom. Unfortunately, Mary Wollstonecraft was too consistent. She entered upon a conscientious "no-marriage" with a far from conscientious American, Gilbert Imlay, who left her with a daughter, known as Fanny Imlay, to support. Mary failed in an attempt at suicide. Soon after, she and Godwin formed an attachment, which, in accordance with their principles, was free; but they married in 1797 in order to safeguard the interests of their children. Before the end of that year, the birth of a child, the future wife of Shelley, was fatal to the mother. She had been a generous, impulsive woman, always affectionate and kind. Godwin's second choice of a wife was less fortunate and conduced to the unhappy experiences of his latter days. Always in difficulties of one kind or another, he lived out a courageous philosophical life of eighty years. William Godwin and Mary Wollstonecraft were gallant rebels of immense courage; but they were unfortunate advertisements of a new social order. They committed the crime of failure. Tragedy was bound up in the texture of their lives. Mary died just as hope and happiness seemed dawning for her. Shelley's passion for her daughter, Mary, led to the suicide of his first wife. Poor Fanny Imlay committed suicide at twenty-two because she refused to be a burden upon Godwin. Claire Clairmont, daughter of the second Mrs Godwin and step-sister of the second Mary, played a dubious part in the lives of Shelley and of Byron, the latter being the father of her daughter, Allegra. To exclaim with Matthew Arnold "What a set!" is tempting, but unjust. Godwin and Mary Wollstonecraft rank high, and deserve to rank high, among those who have tried to solve the eternal problem "How ought man to live?" That their way was not Matthew Arnold's way does not prove they were wrong. And it was a thorny path they trod.

In one respect Mary's way was quite wrong. Whether marriage is, or is not, a kind of servitude is a debating-society topic; but whether a girl is, or is not, a kind of boy is a practical question. Mary was a complete educational rebel. She wrote *Thoughts on the Education of Daughters* (1787), and the whole point of her argument is that a woman should be educated on equal terms with a man. This was taken to mean that a woman should have a man's education. A century and a half later, people were beginning to re-discover that a woman ought to have a woman's education, and that a good girls' school was not necessarily an exact imitation of a good boys' school. Her most famous book, *A Vindication of the Rights of Woman*, is a brave piece of pioneer work, and its influence upon later reformers was powerful and creative. *A Vindication of the Rights of Men* (1790) is a footnote to Burke's *Reflections on the French Revolution* and should be read with that work. Mary Wollstonecraft's letters are attractive and moving.

Godwin's *An Enquiry Concerning Political Justice* was a Bible to young revolutionaries like Wordsworth in the days when he could write:

> Bliss was it in that dawn to be alive,
> But to be young was very heaven.

Some of the blissful youths of that dawn, in Hazlitt's ironical sentence, lost their way in Utopia and found it in Old Sarum. But with massive placidity Godwin continued to believe in man. His weakness (and it is the fatal weakness of all the "planners") is that he believed mankind had only to be given good reasons for a better life and Utopia would follow. His faith was boundless. All that was necessary for the success of his system was a perfect world inhabited by perfect beings. Godwin's *Political Justice* must not be judged by the criticisms of those who found it profitable to apostatize. Even Coleridge repented of the harshness he had dealt out to a book he once had loved. Hazlitt remained faithful, and his sketch of Godwin is still excellent. Godwin's style deserved some success. He was always clear and forcible; his sentences convey his exact meaning without effort, and display a kind of composed oratorical effect. He gained a larger audience for his novels, but the only one that can be said to survive is *The Adventures of Caleb Williams, or Things as They Are*, published in 1794. Another, *St Leon*, is memorable for its portrait of Mary Wollstonecraft. H. L. Brailsford's *Shelley, Godwin and their Circle* (1913) is the best introduction to their work.

From Godwin, who, in his worst days, kept round him a tattered cloak of magnanimity, it is an abrupt change to his fellow-revolutionary, the coarse-grained, shrewd Thomas Paine (1737–1809). Yet Paine's public spirit led him to disregard all profit from his widely sold political works. He was a born pamphleteer, never happy unless he was divulging his opinions for the welfare of the human race as he conceived it. He spent all his earlier years in the struggle to make a decent livelihood, and at last emigrated to Philadelphia. In 1776 he became famous by his pamphlet, *Common-Sense*, which consolidated American opinion in favour of war. Peace brought him moderate rewards and a retirement which he could not endure. He returned to England and soon became involved again in politics. The French Revolution proved a new turning-point in his career. In 1791–2 he attacked Burke in the two parts of *The Rights of Man*. To escape arrest he fled to France, where he became a member of the Convention, and, barely escaping the guillotine because of his opposition to the execution of Louis XVI, founded the new sect of Theophilanthropists. In 1802 he went once more to America, only to find that his *Age of Reason*, published in 1794–5, had lost him nearly all his friends. Paine was a prince of pamphleteers, and his work rarely rises above the pamphleteering level. He was shallow, but he was shrewd; his style was always clear, and though it had no charm, it had sincerity. He was not, like Godwin, a social philosopher: nevertheless he expounded a radical constructive policy, including parliamentary reform, old age pensions and a progressive income tax.

The heir to the pamphleteering eminence of Paine was a much more original and memorable person. The father of William Cobbett (1762–1835) was a small farmer and innkeeper in Hampshire, and William educated himself with indomitable pluck while serving as a soldier. He went to France, learnt the language, emigrated (like Paine) to Philadelphia, and took up the pamphlet-writing trade. Under the apt pseudonym of Peter Porcupine he conducted a pro-British and anti-French campaign, until he was ruined by libel cases and obliged to return to England in 1800. He was welcomed in Government circles, and started work as a Tory free-lance. His first venture, *The Porcupine*, failed; but his second, *Cobbett's Political Register*, a weekly newspaper which he began in 1802, gained the public ear. At first Tory, then Independent, at last strongly Radical, he maintained till his death an influence of which no persecution and no folly could deprive him. Besides other publishing ventures, including *Parliamentary Debates*, later undertaken by Hansard, and *State Trials*, he combined business and pleasure as a model farmer. All went well until, in 1810, he received a sentence of two years' imprisonment on account of an invective against military flogging. Throughout the reign of George IV he was a leader of political opinion. He knew the marketable value of books combining instruction and exhortation with a strong flavour of personality, and his *Advice to Young Men* (1829) and even his *English Grammar* (1817) are still thoroughly readable. By 1830 his fortunes were re-established; the Reform Act opened the doors of Parliament to him, and he sat in the Commons till his death in 1835.

Cobbett's enormous personal vanity must not lessen the esteem due to his outspoken criticism of public life. He was essentially a farmer and hated large towns, especially the "Great Wen" (London) and the stock-jobbing and paper-money upon which the towns throve. He not only loved the country, he knew it, and he was master of a style in which to express his knowledge. The *Rural Rides* (1830), which depict the England of his day, have an assured permanence. Others might paint rural scenery; Cobbett scans the looks and manners of the labourers and considers whether they have enough to make life bearable. The autobiography he intended to write under the title *The Progress of a Ploughboy to a Seat in Parliament* was compiled from his writings by William Reitzel, published under that title in 1933, and reissued as *The Autobiography of William Cobbett* in 1947. His *Register* was the model and inspiration of later Radical popular journals such as Richard Carlile's *Republican*, Henry Hetherington's *Poor Man's Guardian* and John Cleave's *Gazette*. Paine and Cobbett together were the main inspiration behind the lives recorded in such autobiographies as Samuel Bamford's *Passages in the Life of a Radical* (1844), *The Autobiography of a Working Man* (1848) by Alexander Somerville of the Scots Greys, the *Autobiography* (1872) by the Chartist poet Thomas Cooper, *The Life and Struggles of William Lovett* (1876) by the cabinetmaker who assisted Francis Place—"the Radical tailor of Charing Cross"—to draft the People's Charter in 1838, and *Sixty Years of an Agitator's Life* (1892) by George Jacob Holyoake who was largely responsible for the abolition of the newspaper tax in 1855. The struggles of Cobbett and his successors against this and other government measures are recorded in Collet Dobson Collet's *History of the Taxes on Knowledge* (1899).

The great tradition of parliamentary oratory was maintained by Pitt, Fox, Sheridan, Canning and Grattan; but their speeches are not now read either for enjoyment or enlightenment. Like the great actor, the great orator survives as a memory. Burke stands apart, for he did not succeed as an orator; he spoke his written compositions, and his auditors hurried out to dine.

III. BENTHAM AND THE EARLY UTILITARIANS

Jeremy Bentham (1748–1832) is famous as the leader of a school of thought and practice which is known sometimes as Utilitarianism, sometimes as Philosophical Radicalism. He was a prodigy from his childhood. His first publication, *A*

Fragment on Government, published anonymously in 1776, attracted much attention. Between 1785–88 he travelled in the east of Europe and spent some time in Russia, where his brother held an important industrial post. There he wrote his *Defence of Usury* (published 1787); there also, from his brother's method of inspecting his work-people, Jeremy derived the plan of his "Panopticon"—a scheme for prison management, which was to dispense with Botany Bay and transportation; but the government failed in the end to adopt it.

In 1789 Bentham published the work (already privately printed) which gives him a place among philosophers, *An Introduction to the Principles of Morals and Legislation*. In this he uses for the first time the now hard-worked term "international". Bentham's methods of writing were unusual. He wrote what he had to say and left his editors or collaborators to fit the matter into his scheme. His most considerable helper was Étienne Dumont, who gave literary form to many of the principles which the master propounded in notes and conversation. But the most famous associate of Bentham was James Mill (1773–1836), whose mind was almost as spacious as his master's and whose genius was more practical. Bentham knew man; Mill knew men. Although full of projects for reform, Mill was a successful man of affairs, and rose to high office in the East India Company's service, where one of his colleagues was Thomas Love Peacock, the novelist. Mill helped to give the new philosophy a party, a programme and an organ. The party came to be known as Philosophical Radicals. Their organ was *The Westminster Review*, founded by Bentham in 1824. Their programme was a demand for constitutional reform as a preliminary to legislative and administrative improvements. Mill gave much literary assistance to Bentham; he edited *A Table of the Springs of Action* (1817); he prepared, from the author's manuscripts, an *Introductory view of the Rationale of Evidence*; and his brilliant son, John Stuart Mill (1806–73), edited *The Rationale of Evidence* in five volumes (1827).

Bentham's *Fragment on Government* is the first attempt to apply the principle of utility in a systematic and methodical manner to the theory of government. It is a brief commentary on Blackstone's own *Commentaries*. Sir William Blackstone (1723–80), first Vinerian Professor of Law at Oxford and afterwards a judge, owes his fame to his *Commentaries on the Laws of England* (1765–9), a work distinguished for its clear, eloquent and dignified style. But Bentham found Blackstone's theory of government not only false but meaningless, and in the course of his criticism constantly appeals to fact against constitutional fiction and employs as his standard the principle of utility. He derided the notion of any "social contract". Hume had taught him that "the foundations of all *virtue* are laid in *utility*". Hume thus asserted a qualitative utility; but quantitative utility was Bentham's point—"It is the greatest happiness of the greatest number that is the measure of right and wrong." Like all famous "sayings", this is credited with numerous "origins". What is usually overlooked is that the true originator is not the man who makes, but the man who circulates. Bentham gave general currency to the phrase, and for him "the greatest happiness of the greatest number" was the criterion of utility in legislation and administration. *An Introduction to the Principles of Morals and Legislation* contains the fullest and clearest account of Bentham's main ideas.

Bentham's power was derived from the combination in his mind of two qualities, the firm grasp of a single principle, and a truly astonishing mastery of details. His "utility" principle and his relentless application of it made him the founder of a new and powerful school, the rise of which is specially remarkable in an age that believed in "natural rights" of which man had been robbed by "governments". Rousseau had made this doctrine popular, and in the American Declaration of Independence of 1776 it became the foundation of a democratic reconstruction of government. Bentham's view was emphatic: rights are created by law; "*natural rights* is simple nonsense: natural and imprescriptible rights, rhetorical nonsense—nonsense upon stilts". The numerous works collected as Bentham's need not here be named or discussed. He ranged beyond politics, but his genius was comprehensive rather than profound. He could discuss the forces or values that can be measured in terms of pleasure or pain; but into history, art and religion he had no insight, and, unconscious of his limitations, believed himself equally able to deal with these immeasurable things. Like other "planners" he sometimes failed to distinguish between a reason and a cause, and he constantly assumed that men are nearly all alike and that they are controlled by intellectual interests. But he inspired modern administrative efficiency and may be called the father of bureaucracy.

Certain of Bentham's occasional papers appeared in *Annals of Agriculture*, which, begun in 1784, extended to forty-five volumes. Its editor, Arthur Young (1741–1820), is the most celebrated of English writers on agriculture. His remarkable talent is best shown in *Political Arithmetic* (1774), *Tour in Ireland* (1780) and the famous *Travels in France* (1792). Young had the good fortune to visit France shortly before the Revolution, as well as after it had broken out, and his observations are invaluable. His writing is of excellent quality, exhibiting both ease of manner and epigrammatic power.

Thomas Robert Malthus (1766–1834) was counted among the Utilitarians, but he questioned the over-estimate of the intellectual factor in conduct, and doubted the fashionable doctrine of perfectibility. He saw that even if perfection were attained, it could not be stable. Population would expand beyond the means of subsistence, and the result would be inequality and misery. He expressed his views in *An Essay on the Principle of Population* (1798). A storm of controversy followed its publication; but its teaching made notable converts like Pitt and Paley as well as notable enemies like Shelley, Peacock and Cobbett. Malthus studied the matter further, and five years later (1803) replied to his critics in a new edition, which is, in fact, almost a new book. The first edition shattered the ideal of a future golden age; the second shattered the ideal of any past golden age. Even though the theory of an arithmetical progression for food and a geometrical progression for population may be inexact, the warning was needed. Malthus was not blind to considerations of a more favourable kind. He saw that the "struggle for existence" (the phrase is his) was a great stimulus to labour and a cause of human improvement. At a later date, Darwin and A. R. Wallace, working independently, found in his book a statement of the principle which, in their view, explained biological development. Malthus was the first to make a clear demonstration of the fact that human existence depends upon a working balance between population and food. An age of wild and windy beliefs in the perfectibility of human existence if only certain forms of government replaced other forms of government eminently needed the stern corrective arithmetic of Malthus.

During the period of Bentham's supremacy, the tradition of a different type of philosophy was carried on by Dugald Stewart (1753–1828). For twenty-five years (1785–1810), he was Professor of Moral Philosophy at Edinburgh. The first volume of his *Elements of the Philosophy of the Human Mind* appeared in 1792, the second in 1814, the third in 1827. His *Outlines of Moral Philosophy* was published in 1794 and *The Philosophy of the Active and Moral Powers* in 1828. Stewart was a pupil and a disciple of Reid, though he avoided the use of the term "common sense", which, as employed by Reid, had produced the impression that questions of philosophy could be decided by an appeal to popular judgment.

IV. COWPER

William Cowper (1731–1800) was a sweet, simple, instinctive poet, whom we should refuse to accept, at anybody's bidding, as the leader, or forerunner, or anticipator of something called "the romantic revolt". Only bad poets deliberately strive for dissidence and difference. What matters in poetry is, simply, poetry, not theories of poetry, even when promulgated by poets. Cowper, certainly, was not a revolutionary of any kind. His inclinations were towards the past, not towards some undiscerned "poetry of the future". He was not a "modern"; his admired master was Milton, whose poems in foreign languages he has most excellently and usefully translated for less learned generations. Cowper wrote just the sort of poetry that it was natural for him to write, as Pope wrote just the sort of poetry that it was natural for him to write. Pope and Cowper did not write the same kind of poetry, because they were not interested in the same kind of things; but that difference does not require us to set one poet against the other. What matters only is the absolute worth of what they wrote. Cowper, indeed, exclaimed, "God made the country and man made the town"; but Cowper's charge against Pope was not that he was an artificial poet of the town, but that by his very excellence in verse he

> Made poetry a mere mechanic art,
> And every warbler has his tune by heart.

The events in the life of Cowper were few but remarkable. He was born of a good family and was sent to Westminster School, where, like Gibbon, he was unhappy. One of his masters was Vincent Bourne, whose Latin poems he translated, and one of his friends was Charles Churchill, whose satirical poems he praised. From Westminster he passed in 1750 to a study of law, and led a normal and apparently happy life. He flirted with his cousins Harriet and Theodora, the latter of whom he wanted to marry; the former was to come into his life years after. The proposed marriage was forbidden by Theodora's father, first because of the consanguinity and next because of William's disquieting tendency to morbidity. The cousins were forbidden to meet or even to correspond, and when to this disappointment in love was added the death of

Cowper's father and the accidental drowning of his best friend, his mind became deranged and he attempted suicide.

When the doors of a private asylum closed upon William Cowper at the age of thirty-two, his life in the busy world of men appeared to have come to an end; but two years later he was well enough to pass into the care of Morley Unwin, a retired clergyman, and his wife Mary. When Unwin was accidentally killed, Mary devoted herself to the delicate poet, and their long association is one of the famous friendships in literary history. Unfortunately they moved from Huntingdon to the less pleasant Olney, in order to receive the religious ministrations of the celebrated John Newton, once in the slave trade, but now a convinced Evangelical. One happy result came from the new association, namely, Cowper's collaboration with Newton in *Olney Hymns* (1779), a collection which included Newton's *How sweet the name of Jesus sounds* and Cowper's *God moves in a mysterious way*. When Newton left in the next year for a London living, Cowper found himself without occupation—the poet in him lacked a stimulus to expression. But Mary encouraged him to write. His first long poem *Anti-Thelyphthora* (1781) has only temporary interest. Mrs Unwin next proposed as a subject the progress of error; and going eagerly to work, Cowper wrote eight satires: *Table Talk, The Progress of Error, Truth, Expostulation, Hope, Charity, Conversation* and *Retirement*. But the gentle recluse who had never lived in the world could not write bitterly, even with the unseen spirit of Newton prompting him. However, the clear, neat verses were achieved and were published in the volume called *Poems by William Cowper, of the Inner Temple, Esq.* (1782), which contained as well some of the short poems by which he is generally remembered.

A new friend, Lady Austen, came into Cowper's life in 1781 and touched his spirits and his poetry to finer issues. She was a woman of the world, and knew that Cowper needed diversion, not preoccupation with moral problems; and the subject she lightly suggested for a poem was the sofa in his room—perhaps she had been reading Crébillon. Cowper gaily accepted the challenge, and the result was one of the happiest and friendliest of English poems, *The Task*, in six books, *The Sofa, The Time-piece, The Garden, The Winter Evening, The Winter Morning Walk* and *The Winter Walk at Noon*, with their exquisite vignettes of landscape. Cowper's love of nature was the love that asks no questions and poses no problems. His poems are the simple artistic record of simple, genuine experience. The tendency to didacticism, natural to a man of Cowper's experience, is present in *The Task*, but we cheerfully accept his teaching, if only because it has been his own support in trouble. The love of man for man, the love of man for animals, for the meanest thing that lives—this is the principal moral message of *The Task*. Rousseau, no doubt, had said something like it before, and Rousseau was in the air. But in Cowper it is the natural underived expression of his own tender, affectionate nature, and no English poet has given it such perfect utterance. When published in 1785, *The Task* was followed in the same volume by *Tirocinium* and *The Diverting History of John Gilpin*. In *Tirocinium* the attack on the brutality and immorality of public schools may have been just and is certainly vigorous; but this is not the kind of poetical composition in which Cowper excelled. Of *John Gilpin* there is no need to speak.

Everyone knows that immortal story. Later editions of his poems included the exquisitely tender lines *On the Receipt of my Mother's Picture out of Norfolk*. She had died when he was six years old.

In 1786 Cowper and Mrs Unwin moved from dreary Olney to a cheerful house and neighbourhood at Weston, and enlarged their circle of acquaintances, thanks, partly, to his cousin Harriet, now Lady Hesketh. Cowper's life continued to be happy; and during these pleasant years he wrote a number of his best short poems, which were not published till after his death. His translation of Homer (1791) is a kind of protest against Pope's, which he rejected as too artificial. But Cowper, in trying to make Homer dignified made him dull. The greatest merit of his version is that it kept him for a time from the despair which was to destroy him in the end. Mrs Unwin sickened in 1791 and her life of heroic devotion drew to its close in 1796. After that Cowper was past help, past cure. Popularity, success, affection could do nothing to lighten the darkness within. His last original work is the powerful and ghastly poem called *The Castaway*.

Cowper is a minor poet, but he is a poet who must be read. Not to know him is to miss a creative "character", an engaging combination of lovableness, simplicity and charm. There is no more companionable poet than Cowper. The egregious William Hayley wrote his life and first made known to English readers the treasure of Cowper's letters—Southey's later edition is much better. Like everything else about him, they are unique. They are so simple that anybody could have written them; but the fact is that nobody has written anything like them. Like a charming companion on a day's ramble he talks delightfully about anything—or nothing. His letters had a modern edition in five volumes (1904–25) by Thomas Wright of Olney; the best modern biography is David Cecil's *The Stricken Deer* (1929); Gilbert Thomas's *William Cowper and the Eighteenth Century* (1935) relates the poet to his time.

V. WORDSWORTH

Readers will begin a study of Wordsworth most profitably if they dismiss from their minds the usual ideas of him as the leader of a "Romantic Revolt" and as the apostate from his early liberal ideas, and think of him as a great English poet, tenacious, indomitable and unsubmissive, carving his own way slowly to understanding of himself, and winning, in the end, the love and admiration of readers, not by any moral message or theory of art, but solely by the penetrating beauty of his poems. Wordsworth has the divine "quantity", the "maximum" of inspiration that makes a great profound poet like Shakespeare or Milton, and not the lesser visitation of the spirit that makes a minor poet like Thomson or Cowper. With a clear conviction of Wordsworth's absolute value as a poet of any time, readers may then usefully consider his particular relation to the movements of his own time.

Few poets have told us more of their early lives. *The Prelude* is not only the greatest of poetical autobiographies, it is also a source of positive information. William Wordsworth (1770–1850) was born at Cockermouth in Cumberland.

His mother died when he was eight, his father when he was thirteen. Like Coleridge, Wordsworth was denied the blessing of a happy home. He was sent to school at Hawkshead and lived in poverty at the cottage of a village dame. He had no intellectual company and found creative solace in his precious books, and in personal freedom from restraint. Hawkshead was his home, except at holiday periods, from his ninth to his eighteenth year. He went in 1787 to St John's College, Cambridge, where he found little to interest him. He became very solitary and appeared to be uncompanionable and morose. The truth, unrecognized even by himself, is that he was suffering from the "growing pains" of a poet. The young Wordsworth never "lisped in numbers"; he had to fight for expression. In 1790 he made a tour through France to the Alps with a fellow student, travelling on foot like a pedlar. His *Descriptive Sketches* is a poetical record of the tour. After leaving Cambridge he settled in London for a time. His patrimony had been spent on his education, and he was without a profession or any qualifications for a profession. Before the end of 1791 he was back in France again, and there remained till the end of 1792, on the eve of the Terror.

It is often forgotten, when the revolutionary sympathies of Wordsworth, Coleridge and Southey are discussed, that Wordsworth actually lived in France during some of the most stirring scenes of the new order. He became a convinced revolutionist, and was eager to join the Girondists. Had he done so his head might have fallen with those of Condorcet and Madame Roland. Genius did not save his fellow-poet André Chénier from the guillotine. Wordsworth was removed from danger almost by luck. He had fallen in love with Marie-Anne Vallon, daughter of a family still Royalist and Catholic; but there could be no recognized marriage between her and an irreligious, revolutionary foreigner without rank, position, present means or future prospects. Nevertheless a daughter was born to them in December 1792. At the end of 1792 or early in 1793 Wordsworth came to England to publish his poems and find some means of living. Return was suddenly barred, for in February 1793 began the war which lasted till the short-lived peace of 1802. Wordsworth was cut off from personal communication with France for nine years. The later story of Annette and the "Dear child, dear girl" of the sonnet "It is a beauteous evening, calm and free", composed on Calais Beach in 1802, belongs to biography, not to literature. What is important for the reader to notice is the extraordinary implication of Wordsworth's early life with French affairs, and the powerful disturbance of his feelings during a critical period. The story of his early passion and the later business relations with Annette, fully known to several persons, nevertheless remained one of the best kept secrets of literary history and was not revealed till George McLean Harper's *William Wordsworth: His Life, Works and Influence* (1916) and Emile Legouis's supplement to his *Early Life of Words-worth* (1896), *William Wordsworth and Annette Vallon* (1922). The disclosure of Wordsworth's strength of feeling was disturbing to those who had piously accepted him as a Victorian pastoralist; it can hardly have surprised any careful reader of *The Prelude*, even in the revised version. *Vaudracour and Julia*, which has the special interest of telling something like the story of Wordsworth and Annette, with the ranks of the lovers changed, was at first a natural part of *The*

Prelude. It was afterwards dissociated from the poet's personal story and published as a narrative in the collection of 1820.

Wordsworth's activities in France were not confined to attempts to make himself a French citizen. He began to feel sure that poetry was his destiny and that nothing else in life was important to him. Very little exists from his pen that is really juvenile. Most noteworthy is the sonnet *Written in Very Early Youth*, with its characteristic first line; but there is nothing else till we reach *An Evening Walk* completed in 1789, and the *Descriptive Sketches* written by the Loire. These furnish abundant evidence of his power to "see into the life of things", though they are written in the poetic dialect of the eighteenth century. They should be read in the first and not in the revised versions. They were published in 1793 after his flight from France. Wordsworth had come back to England a revolutionist at heart and out of sympathy with the rising national feeling. When war began he did not conceal his hatred of King, Regent and Ministry. His prose *Letter to the Bishop of Llandaff*, his poem *Guilt and Sorrow* (or *Incidents on Salisbury Plain*) and the first text of *The Prelude* are clear evidence of his feelings. When the French Revolution passed into the Terror, Wordsworth lost his trust in immediate social reform. He turned to abstract meditation on man and society, and Godwin's *Political Justice* became a kind of Bible that comforted his distress. But the abstract anarchistic doctrine of Godwin was utterly useless to a creative poet; and the pessimism it produced bore fruit in his one dramatic work, *The Borderers*, written in 1795 though not published till 1842. *The Borderers* cannot claim intrinsic poetic or dramatic merit; but it enabled Wordsworth to write himself free from any perfectionist illusions.

Wordsworth had much to endure in life; but it is curious how frequently certain pieces of good luck befell him at critical moments. The war between England and France saved him from an unsuitable alliance. His return to England at the end of 1792 perhaps saved him from the guillotine in 1793. In 1795, when all his resources seemed exhausted and the life of a poet unattainable, salvation dropped from the clouds in the form of a legacy of £900, left him by a young friend who believed that immediate relief might help him to live for poetry. To the frugal Wordsworth £900 was a fortune. It enabled him to acquire at once two immensely valuable companions, his sister Dorothy and his friend Coleridge. Dorothy Wordsworth (1771–1855) is one of those engaging, selfless, and devoted women about whom it is difficult to speak without excess of enthusiasm. Probably she was, of all persons known to us, the nearest to being a poet without ever writing a poem. Her Grasmere and Scottish Journals are full of the raw stuff of poetry. Since 1788 she had been living with an uncle in Norfolk. The newly enriched William bore her off to Racedown in Dorsetshire, where they set up house together. Brother and sister were passionately attached to each other. Dorothy's letters make their mutual love known to us and show us depths of Wordsworth's nature scarcely revealed by his poems. The delight of brother and sister in each other and their daily rambles together were the first agents in his spiritual recovery. But that the poet's mind remained gloomy for a time is shown by his pastoral *The Ruined Cottage* (or *The Story of Margaret*), which afterwards found a place in the first book of *The Excursion*. It is a heart-

rending narrative, without any sign of the poetic message with which Wordsworth was soon to think himself entrusted.

The consciousness of a message came to him after he had removed from
Racedown to Alfoxden in 1797 in order to be near Coleridge, who was then
living at Nether Stowey. It is impossible to define exactly the share of each in
the elaboration of those opinions which they seemed, for a time, to hold in
common. Wordsworth was more intensively creative; Coleridge was more
widely discursive. An omnivorous reader and a tireless talker, Coleridge opened
a new world to one who had hardly gone beyond the rationalism of the
eighteenth century. But Wordsworth was not an intellectual dilettante; nothing was of any use to him that he could not make part of his experience. He
firmly believed in the restorative power of nature and in the validity of natural
emotions; and so he planned *The Recluse*, as early as March 1798, "the first
great philosophical poem in existence", as Coleridge anticipated, which was to
employ his highest energies for seventeen years. Though never completed, the
monument exists in fragments of imposing magnitude—the first book of *The
Recluse*, properly so called, written in 1800; *The Prelude*, written between 1798
and 1805; and *The Excursion*, which, though it includes passages composed as
early as 1797, was not finished until 1814. The intercourse with Coleridge gave
birth to less ambitious and more immediate verse, to the famous *Lyrical Ballads*
of 1798, a second edition with a second volume following in 1800. After some
fruitless attempts at collaboration, the two friends agreed to divide the field of
poetry. To the share of Coleridge fell such subjects as were supernatural, or, at
any rate, romantic; Wordsworth's part was to be events of everyday life, by
preference in its humblest form. So Coleridge wrote *The Ancient Mariner*, while
Wordsworth told the tales *Goody Blake* and *Simon Lee*. The latter are poems of
literary revolt, intended to show that the Muse could stoop to conquer. What
can be easily forgotten, however, is that such a supreme outpouring as the *Tintern
Abbey* lines belongs to the same period and is part of the same programme. Indeed,
to Wordsworth, *Tintern Abbey* and *Goody Blake* were the same kind of poem.

The certainty that he had found his true purpose in life sustained and exalted
Wordsworth through the years from 1798 to 1805. This was a period of plain
living and high thinking, a period, too, of careful reading intensely devoted to
the older English poets; and to it belongs nearly all that is supremely great in his
work. After a visit to Germany (1798–9) he settled in his native Lake district, and
before the close of 1805 he had written the one book of *The Recluse*, much of
The Excursion, the whole of *The Prelude* and the best of his shorter poems and
sonnets. The great *Immortality* ode was nearly completed. Had he died then,
having lived as long as Byron and longer than Shelley or Keats, the work he
left would have entitled him to renown almost as great as that which afterwards
came to him. He was thirty-five—"nel mezzo del cammin di nostra vita". In
1802 he had married Mary Hutchinson in whom he found an inestimable
blessing. But trouble began to press upon his spirits. Coleridge, once the quickener
of his life and brother of his soul, Coleridge, to whom the great outpouring of
The Prelude was addressed, was already sunk in opium and had forsaken his high
calling. The world was going wrong. Wordsworth was not a recluse. He was
keenly sensitive to public affairs; and across the water in the land where new

hope for mankind had seemed to dawn, an upstart Emperor was crowned by a captive Pope in 1805. At the beginning of that year Wordsworth had suffered a grievous and unforgettable loss when his noble brother John had gone down with his ship in the waters of the Channel. A glory had passed away from the world; a power was gone which nothing could restore; and the poet turned, as we all must, to Duty. Wordsworth's *Ode to Duty* (1805) is not the preaching of a moralist; it is the utterance of a poet's resignation. He is no longer the exuberant son of joy; he is resigned to the burden of living. That note is heard most poignantly in the *Elegiac Stanzas* (1805) mourning the death of his brother. After that year Wordsworth was an altered man. He began to age, to look fearfully at the course of the world, and to cling to what had been from of old. Formal religion came to have a meaning for him. The changes in the man are discernible in the alterations he made in *The Prelude*. But he worked on. The wonderful *Poems* in two volumes (1807) may have seemed a poor harvest after seven years; but much of what he had written still remained unpublished, especially *The Prelude*, not known in its first form till Ernest de Selincourt's edition of 1926, and not known in any form till after the poet's death in 1850. Of *The Excursion*, published in 1814, we must admit that it is a noble poem ruined by its own excess. Though different speakers are introduced, their speeches are mere ventriloquism. Wordsworth himself plays all the parts and does not play them well. And so, in spite of many golden moments, *The Excursion* is a disappointing termination of *The Prelude*, which, either in its early or its late form, is the greatest blank verse poem written since *Paradise Lost*. Everybody must read *The Excursion* once; the sagacious among readers will then know which parts of it need not be read again. But there are no parts of *The Prelude* that can be safely omitted.

The romantic and beautiful *The White Doe of Rylstone* (1807) shows the saddened Wordsworth tranquilizing a tragedy into something not too painful to endure; the stoical *Laodamia* (1814) shows him striving for an almost Olympian serenity. The long remaining years of his career (1814–1850) added little to his best verse. The days of full, spontaneous creation were over. His public views grew less progressive. There was no apostasy, but only gradual change. The bare literal truth is that his long age sought security after much early adventure. His fame grew slowly but steadily and was attested by his appointment as Poet Laureate in 1843. Before the close of his life in 1850, Wordsworth could feel assured that he had become one of the great poetical influences of the time.

Three general remarks in conclusion are all that can be made here. The first is this, that empty repetitions of the stock objection, that nothing published after the volumes of 1807 matters very much, should be regarded as uncritical. The absolute value of many later volumes is very great. If they did not raise the rank of Wordsworth it was because his rank was hardly capable of further exaltation; but such volumes as *The White Doe* (1815), *The Waggoner* (1819), *Peter Bell* (1819), *The River Duddon* (1820), *Ecclesiastical Sketches* (1822), *Memorials of a Tour on the Continent* (1822), and *Yarrow Revisited* (1835), to say nothing of *The Excursion* with its magnificent passages and *The Prelude* with its triumphant revisions, would have given something near the first rank to any poet who had not written the earlier volumes. Indeed, it would be interesting to hear which poets would have stood higher. The second general remark is this, that we should beware of ascribing the "two voices" wittily discriminated in J. K. Stephen's sonnet to a weakness of Wordsworth's special creed about poetic diction. A poet's creed usually amounts to no more than this, that the kind of poetry he feels most able to write is the kind of poetry that ought to be written. After all, Wordsworth's creed, such as it was, justified his best poems and his best passages. The special defect of Wordsworth is not that he professed certain beliefs, but that, like many other creative artists, he had no power of self-criticism. He was so fully conscious of the feeling behind his utterance, that he was unable to know when he had transmitted the feeling and when he had failed to transmit it. No one could have convinced Wordsworth that *The Sailor's Mother* was a worse poem than *Lucy Gray*. The third general remark is that we must not be misled by enthusiastic assertions that Wordsworth is valuable as the "teacher" of this or that doctrine. Thus, the actual doctrine implied in the *Ode on the Intimations of Immortality* has not the slightest value, even if it were true. What is valuable is the exquisite poetic rendering of the poet's feeling about the change from youth to age. Those who are most deeply moved by that poem are not those who believe literally that every human infant arrives trailing clouds of celestial glory. The value of any creative writer's work depends upon his power of giving artistic expression to what is true for him. We are not required to accept his beliefs as true for us before we can participate in the beauty of his revelation.

Wordsworth's peculiar originality is to be sought in his expression of what nature meant to him. He has no special beauty of minute particulars. Two poets as unlike as Crabbe and Tennyson surpass him in accuracy of observation. But no one has ever surpassed him in the power of giving utterance to some of the most elementary, and, at the same time, obscure, sensations of man confronted by the eternal spectacle of nature. These sensations, old as man himself, come to us as new, because Wordsworth was the first to find words for them. He is unique, too, when he puts man in a natural setting and makes him part of it, rather than the observer of it, as in the unsurpassable *Michael* and *Leech-Gatherer*. In verbal felicity scarcely any English poet has surpassed him at his best; and in verbal flatness no English poet of his rank has sunk so low. All creative artists must be taken for their best; their worst is the price they have to pay for their success. It should be added that Wordsworth's prose writings, of which his *Convention of Cintra* pamphlet (1809) and the celebrated prefaces and essays on the nature of poetic expression are the best examples, have great dignity of manner and strong, if fitful, critical power. That Wordsworth ever succeeded in giving convincing form to his view of poetic diction may be doubted; but that is a matter about which readers should be left to form their own conclusions, for a first-hand study of Wordsworth's essays in criticism and the relevant chapters of Coleridge's *Biographia Literaria* must be regarded as a necessary part of the discipline of letters. The famous Preface by Matthew Arnold to the Golden Treasury edition of the *Poems* (1879)—reprinted in his *Essays in Criticism*—remains the best introduction and the finest tribute. The most scholarly edition of the *Poetical Works* is that edited 1940–9 by Ernest de Selincourt and

Helen Darbishire, the former of whom edited 1935–9 *The Letters of William and Dorothy Wordsworth*. The best modern biography is probably the one in two volumes (1957–65) by Mary Moorman, daughter of the historian G. M. Trevelyan and (most appropriately) Matthew Arnold's great-great-niece.

VI. COLERIDGE

Coleridge survives as a poet unique in inspiration and unique, though uncertain, in achievement. But he was also philosopher, critic, theologian, moralist and talker. With the strongest will in the world, a man so variously endowed would have found it hard not to dissipate his genius; with a will exceptionally infirm, the wonder is that he should have left so much, rather than so little. Excepting a few poems of his earlier years, he completed nothing he began, and began little of what he proposed. Few men have paid so disastrously in moral bankruptcy for wealth of mental patrimony.

Samuel Taylor Coleridge (1772–1834) was born at Ottery St Mary, the son of a country clergyman, curiously pedantic, dreamy and unworldly, who died in 1781. Poor Coleridge, at the age of nine, was sent off to the rough life of Christ's Hospital, and was never to know again, as child or man, the meaning of domestic solicitude and creative love. Books were his chief solace, and in a short time he became the amazingly erudite "inspired charity boy" of Charles Lamb's famous essay *Christ's Hospital Five-and-Thirty Years Ago*. He was moved to the writing of English verse by the tepid and blameless sonnets of the Wiltshire parson-poet William Bowles; but no explanation of this outburst should be looked for in Bowles. When the moment for incandescence has come, any book, any poem, any line of any poem will kindle the fire. But there were other excitements. He fell in love, as youths will, with the sister of a schoolfellow, just at the time when he should have been living the studious life of a penniless youth in search of a clerical career. He entered Jesus College, Cambridge, in 1791, and in 1793, under the spur of debt or ill-starred love, or both, he suddenly bolted from the university and enlisted in a regiment of light dragoons. His friends procured his discharge and he was readmitted, with due penalties, to his college. Some two months later (June 1794) began that acquaintance with Southey, then an Oxford undergraduate, which was deeply to colour the next few years of his life. He took no degree; and his chance of preferment in the church utterly vanished. Under the stronger will of Southey, he became a fiery revolutionist. A "Pantisocracy" to be founded on the banks of the Susquehanna as a perfect community was enthusiastically discussed between the two friends, but it was not a movement in tune with the universal fraternity of the age—it was to be an aristocratic, not a democratic, Utopia. One might call it a reading-party combined with a back-to-the-land ideal. "What does Your Worship know of farming?" asked Lamb of Coleridge; but no doubt Coleridge had an "idea" of farming, as he had an "idea" of most things. Southey dealt out to him one of three young women named Fricker as the appropriate wife for a Pantisocrat—Southey himself taking the second, and their associate Robert Lovell the third. Of course the luckless Coleridge got the wrong one; but almost any woman would have been the wrong one. Sara Fricker, who became Mrs Coleridge in 1795, had many deficiencies, but she is entitled to our pity, for Coleridge was probably the most disastrous husband (except Shelley) who ever lived. From the beginning to the end of his life Coleridge was incapable of understanding the duty of fulfilling an obligation, though his sense of an obligation as an "idea" would inspire him to torrents of eloquence. One of the unwritten tragedies in the history of English literature is the affection he inspired in Dorothy Wordsworth, whose tense and responsive mind was later to snap under the strain of repressed emotion.

The poetry of Coleridge's early manhood (1794–8) is a mirror of himself, eloquent, loose-girt, strongly inclined to preach. Most of it lacks individuality. His earliest poetical volumes are *Poems on Various Subjects* (1796), *Ode on the Departing Year* (1796), *Fears in Solitude*, with *France, An Ode*, and *Frost at Midnight* (1798). There were earlier prose tracts. It is sometimes urged that Wordsworth's period of full inspiration was short; but Coleridge's was shorter still. For a year or two Coleridge spoke in poetry as mortal man had seldom spoken before; and then having wandered into his metaphysical Venusberg he could never get out. William and Dorothy Wordsworth first revealed him to himself. In daily intercourse with them, first at Stowey (1797–8), then more fitfully in the Lake Country (1800–3), all his enduring poetry was composed. After his fatal visit to Germany he became hypnotized by what seemed his power of explaining the inexplicable; and in the frothy sea of German metaphysics, with opium as the beckoning siren, Coleridge the poet was engulfed.

Though the poet was dead, the philosopher might have accomplished a giant's work in criticism, had it not been for his moral debility; for Coleridge, oddly enough, had a journalist's ability to write when he had to. His attempt to revert in 1796 to an eighteenth-century type of periodical called *The Watchman* failed at the tenth number, but he was a contributor to *The Morning Post* between 1798 and 1802, and later produced *The Friend* which ran to twenty-eight numbers from 1809 to 1810, and was afterwards republished, much revised, in later years. He worked, too, for Dan Stuart on *The Courier*. His powers of spoken monologue were exhibited in various Unitarian pulpits (one appearance being immortalized in Hazlitt's essay *My First Acquaintance with Poets*) and afterwards in various courses of lectures on Shakespeare and other poets between 1810 and 1818, a venture which ought to have succeeded, but which failed through the incapacity of the lecturer to keep to time, to place or to subject. His moral debility was increased by the opium habit, the beginnings of which go back as far as 1797. Two things alone saved him from total shipwreck: first, the unwearied tenderness of friends, old and new, and, next, some remnants of the religious impulse which continued to exert itself against reiterated defeat. After ten years of debasement, he sought refuge with James Gillman, a physician of Highgate (1816), and remained an "inmate" till his death in 1834. This period of obligation finally evaded was the happiest of his life. He had an illusion of success. His talk, his lectures and his occasional writings attracted a new generation; and in the admiration of the young he could forget the humiliations of the past. His wife and family he scarcely ever saw after 1804. He left to Southey the labour of supporting them.

Coleridge's later volumes of verse were *Christabel*; *Kubla Khan*; *The Pains of Sleep* (1816) and the collection called *Sibylline Leaves* (1817). All that endures of his poetry could be contained in a few score pages; and, with some exceptions, it was written during the six years when he was in constant intercourse with Wordsworth (1797–1803). The influence of the two men upon each other is most remarkable. Neither wrote anything of permanent value till they had met. The immediate effect of Wordsworth on Coleridge was *The Ancient Mariner*, his one perfect finished poem, which should be sometimes read in its simpler original form as it appeared in *Lyrical Ballads* of 1798. The elaborate prose gloss did not appear till *Sibylline Leaves* of 1817. Before 1797 Coleridge had given no promise of what he was to be as a poet. "I cannot write without a body of thought", he laments in a letter to Southey (11 December 1794); and a "body of thought" stiffens such early efforts as *Religious Musings* and the *Ode on the Departing Year*. After the meeting with Wordsworth the need for "a body of thought" disappears. Of all poems in the English language, the best parts of *The Ancient Mariner*, and the whole of *Kubla Khan* and *Christabel* are most free from "a body of thought". The prose rigmarole in which Coleridge tells the story of the coming and going of the vision called *Kubla Khan* may be partly self-deception. So far from being purely an opium dream, *Kubla Khan* may be the product of one unexpected lucid interval before the fumes closed up once more the expression of the spirit.

The Ancient Mariner is peculiar in possessing, as *Kubla Khan* does not, a story that could be told in prose. The astonishing fact in Coleridge's three miraculous poems is that every incident, every sentence, almost every epithet, can be traced to something in his reading—as was proved by the American scholar John Livingston Lowes in his study of Coleridge's sources *The Road to Xanadu* (1927). In one sense they are the least original of poems; in another sense they are the most striking example of what the creative imagination can do with mere matter of fact. Except Lamb, contemporary critics, friendly or hostile, missed the magic of the *Mariner* and found fault with it. Coleridge, too sensitive to the verdict of friends, felt they were right; and this feeling was in part responsible for his failure to contribute *Christabel*, finished or unfinished, to the enlarged edition of *Lyrical Ballads*, and for his subsequent attempts to give his *Mariner* fantasy some logical coherence. The first part of *Christabel* was written almost immediately after *The Ancient Mariner*, and shortly before the little band at Stowey was broken up, never again to meet under such "indulgent skies". Though the famous metrical scheme is not so new as Coleridge supposed, it is new as Coleridge used it, and in his use of it there is a magic that no former or subsequent writer ever captured.

Part of the ill-luck that pursued Coleridge is the interpretation of his friendship and short partnership with Wordsworth into an identity of poetic aims and methods. The obvious fact is that they were poets of different essence. Wordsworth was as incapable of writing *The Ancient Mariner* as Coleridge was of writing *The Leech-Gatherer*. From William and Dorothy he learned to look at nature both largely and minutely; but in his poetry he presents natural details with a magic entirely his own. Wordsworth, by comparison, is realistic. Of his place in the poetic movement of his time there is no need to speak at length.

It was the hour of romance; and of pure, ethereal romance, the poetry of Coleridge is the supreme embodiment. He was indifferent to the medieval properties dear to Scott. It was in the subtler, more spiritual, regions of romance that Coleridge found his home. Even the poetically moral conclusion of *The Ancient Mariner* is a sign of the spiritual presence which, in his faith, bound "man and bird and beast" in one mystical body and fellowship. Oddly enough he showed some talent for the drama. *Remorse* (1813—an expansion of the earlier *Osorio*), in the style of Schiller's *The Robbers*, lacked the full courage of its theme and inclined to current stage sentiment, but it had a fair run. *Zapoyla*, "in humble imitation of *The Winter's Tale*", is less static, but less successful. More important are his translations (1799–1800) from Schiller's *Wallenstein* trilogy. *The Fall of Robespierre* by Coleridge and Southey can be dismissed as an efflorescence of revolutionary youth.

Of Coleridge's prose works the most important is *Biographia Literaria* (1817), and even of this only the beginning and ending are valuable. The middle part, containing philosophical matter foolishly taken without acknowledgment from Schelling, has no importance. The earlier part of the book has autobiographical value; the latter part, which gains immensely in interest if read with Wordsworth's collected poems and preface of 1815, which, together with *The Excursion* (1814), partly inspired it, contains some of the finest philosophical poetic criticism in the English language. In his critical judgment Coleridge was far more magnanimous to Wordsworth than Wordsworth was to him. The just enthusiasm of his praise is equalled only by the respectful delicacy of his difference; and against Wordsworth's detractors he spoke fearlessly. As a critical appreciation of a new, contemporary and unpopular poet, *Biographia Literaria* has not been equalled.

The *Lectures* on Shakespeare and other poets are the next valuable part of Coleridge's prose. Unfortunately only fragmentary reports exist. That he borrowed from Schlegel is hardly deniable; still, he made available to English readers of Shakespeare a view that was both new and precious, even though its romantic tendencies developed later in the nineteenth century into the sentimental "Bardolatry" from which the eighteenth century was free and from which the twentieth had to escape.

Of Coleridge's contributions to philosophy the most valuable was his introduction of German writers to English readers. His own addition to the thought of his time was an attempt to replace the mechanical Benthamite interpretation of life and nature by one consistently spiritual, indeed religious; and he deeply influenced those who gave new life to Anglican theology. He did not convince all his hearers or readers. Carlyle observed bluntly that Coleridge had discovered "the sublime secret of believing by the reason what the understanding had been obliged to fling out as incredible". Few think of Coleridge in connection with political philosophy. Yet there is no subject to which, throughout life, he gave more time and thought, from the days of *Conciones ad Populum* and *The Watchman* (1795–6) to those of *The Friend* (1814) and *The Constitution of Church and State* (1830). Coleridge habitually spoke of himself as the heir of Burke; but like his great exemplar he had no constructive ideal.

The four volumes of Coleridge's *Literary Remains* (1838–9) contained some excellent matter since distributed in various collections of lectures and miscellanies. But apart from *Biographia Literaria* and briefer utterances that may be called notes or table-talk the prose of Coleridge is not very profitable. Some of it is as clumsy as it is cloudy. Seductive titles like *Aids to Reflection* (1825) and *Confessions of an Inquiring Spirit* (1840) have beguiled many into beginning hopefully books they have never succeeded in finishing. *Anima Poetae* (1895), containing unpublished matter gathered from S. T. C.'s notebooks, proved a delightful discovery, because it presented the "table-talker" and aphorist once again. Coleridge's letters are indispensable to a true understanding of him, even though their excess of self-accusation and self-pity is somewhat hard to tolerate, and their expansiveness too often reminiscent of another famous master of the epistolary style, Wilkins Micawber. When criticism has said its worst, however, Coleridge remains not only the great poet of *The Ancient Mariner* but what John Stuart Mill truly called him: one of the "seminal minds" of his age.

VII. CRABBE

George Crabbe (1754–1832) was born at Aldeburgh, on the Suffolk coast. He began as a medical apprentice, but entered the world of letters in 1775 by publishing a poem called *Inebriety*, rawly and roughly imitated from Pope in versification, and frankly drawn from life in substance. Drunkenness was nasty and Crabbe bluntly said it was. His own father was an example of the vice and the young poet's life was very unhappy. To the years 1775–9 belong several religious poems and a blank verse composition entitled *Midnight*. In 1779 Crabbe took the bold step of abandoning his provincial medical work and seeking a literary livelihood in London. Few poets have more courageously endured privation and disappointment. His attempts at public verse attracted not the least notice. Having reached almost the last stage of destitution he wrote early in 1781 to Burke, who gave him personal and material aid and encouraged him to enter the church. He was ordained at the end of 1781.

Among the poems shown by Crabbe to Burke was *The Library*, published in 1781, an interesting and original, though not a very individual composition. His next poem was an attempt to contrast village life, as the writer knew it, with the Arcadian life described by authors of pastorals. When completed, the poem was published as *The Village* (1783), and it introduced a new poet of pronounced character to the English public. The work was needed. The pastoral, beginning in beauty, had become a piece of literary humbug. Gay's *Shepherd's Week*, with its parody of Ambrose Philips, had helped to kill it; and Crabbe owed something to the form and tone of this excellent poem. Disdaining literary idealism, he told the plain truth about the English village. "Nature's sternest painter, yet the best", Byron said of him, in a well-known line. For over twenty years he was poetically silent. Then, in 1807, at the age of nearly fifty-three, Crabbe published another volume, which contained, besides reprints of the earlier pieces, some important new poems, *The Parish Register*, *The Hall of Justice* and *Sir Eustace Grey*. In these, and especially in the first, we find Crabbe the realistic verse-novelist of country life. His next publication was

The Borough, a poem in twenty-four parts or "letters", published in 1810, and familiar to modern audiences as the origin of Benjamin Britten's opera *Peter Grimes* (1945), followed by *Tales* in 1812. After a lapse of seven years came the last volume published in his lifetime, *Tales of the Hall* (1819), containing some of his finest work. Though most of the stories are sad, they show delicate apprehension of the finer shades of thought and temper. Crabbe left much manuscript verse, some of which was published in the *Collected Works* of 1834, which also included the *Life* by his son George, a classic biography since published separately.

Crabbe's time and place in literature should be observed. He began to write in a barren age, when the power of Pope was waning. Almost contemporaneously with his first characteristic poem, *The Village*, appeared the first volume of Cowper. By the time of his death, Coleridge, Wordsworth, Byron, Shelley and Keats had done their main work. Nevertheless, he held his own for a long time, and has numbered very great men among his admirers. Crabbe enlarged the scope of poetry and also of fiction: he was Jane Austen's favourite poet. He refused to draw delusively pleasing pictures of the life he knew well on its seamy side, but he never sought the unpleasant for its own sake. He may be called the first of modern realists, even though his medium was the elegant couplet of the eighteenth century. He had nothing of Wordsworth's vision, nor, in fact, did he ever seek to make audible the mighty harmonies of nature. He was a loving and an exact observer of natural beauty and he told his plain tales with a strong sense of character, a moral earnestness and an artistic restraint that have justly earned him a definite place of his own in the history of English poetry.

VIII. SOUTHEY AND LESSER POETS OF THE LATER EIGHTEENTH CENTURY

It is easy to be unjust to Robert Southey (1774–1843), who, after beginning as a revolutionist, lived to abandon all his old principles and to become, as a leading spirit of *The Quarterly Review*, the anonymous executioner of all who retained or subsequently acquired any liberal ideas. On the other side, it must be said that every man has the right to recant juvenile beliefs and to write even sternly in defence of different beliefs acquired by adult experience. The events in Southey's life are not remarkable. He was sent to Westminster School, from which he was expelled for an outspoken composition against flogging. He went later to Balliol. Of his early association with Coleridge and the great ideal of a Pantisocracy we have already spoken. But the immediate destination of Southey was not the Susquehanna, but Spain and Portugal, where he was required to help his uncle, who was chaplain at Lisbon. In the Peninsula he gained a knowledge of the languages and found subjects that were used later in his compositions; his translation of the *Chronicle of the Cid* (1808) deserves favourable mention. After various occupations he found that writing was the real work of his life, and he settled at Keswick. He was made Poet Laureate in 1813. We may feel that, compared with Coleridge, Southey is an unsympathetic figure; we may feel that he deserved the castigations he received from Byron and Hazlitt and even from Lamb; but we must not forget that Southey lived an honourable life, that while Coleridge talked, Southey worked—worked himself literally to death on the treadmill of "miscellaneous authorship"—and that he supported not only his own household, but the widow of Lovell and the wife and family of Coleridge, who, without him, would have been homeless and unhappy.

To discuss Southey's large-scale poetical works is hardly necessary, for they are not read, they never will be read, they do not deserve to be read. Presenting outwardly an imposing frontage, they are within entirely null and void. They are the product of literary industry, not of literary creation. Probably no man who wrote so much has contributed so little. Everyone knows the few popular short pieces, such as *After Blenheim* and the lines beginning "My days among the dead are passed"—unquestionably his finest poem; and they are all we need to know. For record we note the principal volumes: *Poems* (1794) by Southey and Lovell; *The Fall of Robespierre* (1794), a juvenile drama by Southey and Coleridge; *Joan of Arc* (1796), an epic; *Poems* (1797); *Thalaba the Destroyer* (1801); *Madoc* (1805); *The Curse of Kehama* (1810); *Roderick, the last of the Goths* (1814), and *A Vision of Judgment* (1831), famous as the laureate exercise in bathos which provoked Byron's retaliatory comic masterpiece with the same title. There is nothing to say about any of them. Excepting the last, they are not even bad, for then they might be amusing. Not one indicates so much as a transitory visitation of the creative spirit.

Upon most of Southey's prose compilations a similar judgment must be passed; though here the exceptions are more numerous. No one will ever read *The History of Brazil* (1810–19), or *The Book of the Church* (1824). But *Sir Thomas More: or Colloquies on the Progress and Prospects of Society* (1829) and *Essays Moral and Political* (1832) are precursors of the social criticism of Ruskin and Morris, written when Southey had become associated with Lord Ashley (afterwards Earl of Shaftesbury) in his campaign for factory legislation. There is also the excellent *Life of Nelson* (1813) and the less excellent *Life of Wesley* (1820). *Lives of the British Admirals* (1833, etc.) can be read in, rather than read. *The Doctor* (1837–47) contains the immortal story of the three bears. The posthumous *Commonplace Books* (1849–51) will set up any miscellaneous journalist with matter for the whole of his working life. The edition of Cowper and the selections from the poets are admirable. When Southey's prose is good, as in the story of Nelson's death, it is very good indeed. Hardly anything he wrote is so rewarding as his own correspondence, which, if he had refrained from writing his poems, would have convinced us that he was a poet.

In many respects Southey was a happy man. He obtained the two great desires of his heart, a cheerful family life and a busy life of letters, and for their sake he endured heavy burdens. He never wrote below himself, and even after nearly fifty years of almost daily production, he never became slipshod. To his good qualities even bitter political enemies like Byron and Hazlitt bore testimony; and he had enthusiastic friends like Landor.

Among the minor poets of the century few only can be noticed here. Two belong to the pre-Southey period, Christopher Anstey (1724–1805) and John Hall-Stevenson (1718–85). Anstey, who had scholarship, produced the famous

New Bath Guide (1766), a series of verse-letters, mainly in light anapaests of the Prior type, which at once became popular. Hall-Stevenson takes us back to Sterne, for he was "Eugenius", master of "Crazy Castle", and author of *Crazy Tales* (1782), *Makarony Fables* (1767), *Fables for Grown Gentlemen* (1770), together with some political skits.

Erasmus Darwin (1731–1802) was poet, physician, and grandfather of the great Charles. His celebrated composition *The Botanic Garden*, of which *The Loves of the Plants* (1789) and *The Economy of Vegetation* (1792) are the constituent parts, is historically important as the work in which elaborate "poetic diction" is even more incongruously applied to crude facts of science than in the poems in Gilbert White's *Selborne*. The absurdities of *The Loves of the Triangles*—the witty *Anti-Jacobin* parody—are hardly greater than those of the serious original. In the controversy about Charles Darwin's theory of "natural selection", the simple evolutionary views of Erasmus Darwin, as expressed in his *Zoonomia* (1794–6) and *Phytologia* (1799), were re-affirmed, not altogether without malice, by Samuel Butler.

The egregious William Hayley (1745–1820) would be forgotten had he not made celebrated contacts with Cowper and Blake. *The Triumphs of Temper* (1781) and numerous other works in prose and verse are now utterly vacuous. Hayley was a kindly but oppressive and possessive man. He did really help some more gifted men, and that is the best we can say of him.

For the very nadir of the poetic art one must go beyond even Hayley, to Robert Merry (1755–98) and those about him—the school commonly called "the Della Cruscans" from the Accademia della Crusca of Florence, of which Merry was an actual member. The English Della Cruscan school had been preceded in certain characteristics by some earlier work, such as that of Helen Maria Williams (1762–1827), who narrowly escaped execution as a Girondin. But, in itself, it combined German romanticism, French sentimentality and Italian trifling into almost imbecile English balderdash and was inadequately rather than excessively chastized in the satires of Gifford and Mathias. One of the band, "Anna Matilda", i.e. Mrs Cowley (see p. 502), the author of *The Belle's Stratagem* (1782), was certainly not devoid of sense.

It is pleasant to turn to William Lisle Bowles (1762–1850), famous first because his *Fourteen Sonnets written...during a Journey* (1789) inspired two poets, Coleridge and Southey, and next because his edition of Pope (1807) inflamed a third poet, Byron. Feeble as they seem, his sonnets had a note of poetic truth indiscernible in Darwin, Hayley, and the Della Cruscans, and must have appealed strongly to those weary of mere diction. But it was Milton, not Bowles, who inspired Wordsworth's supreme compositions in the sonnet form. Bowles was courageous in faith as well as in practice; he chastized Pope for want of vision, and when Campbell and Byron stood out to defend Pope's craftsmanship, they found the Wiltshire parson no mean fighter. Perhaps both sides forgot that, in the best poetry, whether by Pope or by Wordsworth, inspiration and expression unite into one creation.

IX. BLAKE

William Blake (1757–1827) has been so often re-discovered and so regularly identified with the fancies of the re-discoverers that the reader should be clear, at the outset, about certain facts. The first is that Blake was born when Johnson was at the zenith of his power, twelve years before Wordsworth and fifteen years before Coleridge came into the world. *Poetical Sketches* appeared a year before Johnson's death. These points of time may serve to remind us that Blake was not an ill-used and unrecognized contemporary of Swinburne. A second fact is that Blake received nothing resembling an ordinary education; and, being brought up in a Swedenborgian family inclined to the cloudier parts of religion, he had little acquaintance with the ordinary Englishman's religious ideas. A third fact is that his own reading, apart from the poets, included imaginative treatises on Gnosticism and Druidism. From discussions of Gnosticism he learned that the Supreme Creative God and the Just and Jealous God of the Mosaic law were different beings—that the God of Vengeance and the Devil were identified as evil spirits. A definite Oriental dualism of good and evil is an essential feature of Gnosticism. From Gnosticism, too, Blake derived his doctrine of the "Emanations" or cosmic female forms which are pursued by the corresponding "Spectres" or male forms. Another source of Blake's cosmogony is the curious "Celtic" or "Druidical" revival of the eighteenth century, as exhibited in such works as William Stukeley's *Stonehenge* (1740), Edward Williams's *Poems, Lyric and Pastoral* (1794), Edward Davies's *Celtic Researches in the Origin, Traditions and Languages of the Ancient Britons* (1804), Jacob Bryant's *A New System of Ancient Mythology* (1774), which provided some of Blake's names, and Edward Jones's *Musical and Poetical Relicks of the Welsh Bards* (1794), from all or any of which he would learn that the ancient inhabitants of Britain were descended directly from Noah, who taught them the purest traditions of primitive faith and language reaching back to Adam and to God Himself. The Druids taught Pythagoras, who taught the Greeks. So Blake tells us that Adam was a Druid and that the Greeks were Druids. When Blake makes Jesus walk upon England's pleasant pastures, he speaks literally, not figuratively. A fourth fact is that Blake regarded himself not as a simple singer but as a seer. When, however, he left the region of pure song in which the poets had been the directors of his natural instincts, he wandered precariously into a new world of expression without the guidance either of formal education or of good models. Education may not do much for a poet, but it can teach him what to leave out. Blake, like others of his time, accepted the language of Ossian as the language of sublimity, and in that cloudy idiom he endeavoured to transmit a personal mythology as alien to English mental habit as that of a Hindu. He failed because there was no common ground of matter or of manner on which writer and reader could meet. A fifth fact is that Blake's works were never published, in the ordinary sense of the term. *Poetical Sketches*, his first precious booklet, was a printer's job; the succeeding books were charming or elaborate artistic productions appealing to collectors, and incapable of wide diffusion among ordinary readers. Very few copies were produced. Sometimes the pictorial designs say something not clearly expressed in the text. Still, it is upon cold print and not upon glowing design that Blake must depend for his place in English literature. The circumstances of production prevented any wide knowledge of his work and not till the end of the nineteenth century and the beginning of the twentieth could readers be sure that the texts presented what Blake had actually written. The facts here enumerated may prevent readers from following too readily those who have given esoteric interpretations of defects, deficiencies and difficulties in Blake arising from the circumstances of his life. Blake is sometimes obscure simply because he did not know how to make himself clear, not because he was unusually profound. But, with all deductions made, he remains one of the most astonishing of men, a true mystic to whom the eternal was the natural and the human indistinguishable from the divine.

Blake was born in Soho, and apprenticed to an engraver. Being sent to make drawings in ancient churches, especially Westminster Abbey, he fell under the influence of Gothic art, which became to him the supreme expression of truth, while classicism was the embodiment of error. Gothic art was but one of the influences upon the growing boy. Another was the compelling power of the poets he read and tried to imitate—as all true artists imitate. The imitations were not more than experiments to Blake himself; but in the eyes of friends they were performances; and so, in 1783, they were printed as *Poetical Sketches* —a shabby, mean little book, but one of the most astonishing first volumes ever produced. Very few of the lyrics date after 1778, and one is as early as 1769. There are, of course, several failures; but some of the pure lyrics are not only original in substance and daring in form, but exquisite in quality. To this juvenile production belong such perfect poems as *To the Evening Star, How sweet I rom'd from field to field* (written at fourteen), *My silks and fine array* and *To the Muses*, with its memorable last stanza. It is doubtful whether so precious a collection of *juvenilia* ever came from any poet.

Blake's mundane world began to widen. He studied drawing at the Royal Academy, where he never felt at home; he was a natural rebel, and an Academy is quite properly the guardian of tradition. The good Sir Joshua ventured to give Blake some very innocuous and even helpful advice about his drawing; and from that moment Reynolds was consigned for ever to the lowest circle of Blake's Hell. But Blake found new friends in Stothard, Barry, Fuseli, and Flaxman. In those days all illustrations to books were produced by hand-engraving, and Blake had no difficulty in earning a living. By this time he had a wife to support; for with characteristic intuition he picked out an almost illiterate girl and married her. She proved an excellent wife. She knew her husband was a genius, and accepted him without troubling her mind with attempts at under-standing. Blake's friendship with Flaxman brought him into cultured society, in which he felt so out of place that he expressed his feelings in a curious work called *An Island in the Moon*. When *An Island* does not anticipate the conversa-tions of *Crotchet Castle* it anticipates the conversations of *Alice in Wonderland*. The book belongs to *c.* 1783–4, and it was unknown till the twentieth century. It is the largest example of Blake's humour; but he was not educated enough to write literary absurdities with the firm touch of Peacock or Lewis Carroll.

Inspiration could not help him there. The next publication of Blake was the enchanting little coloured volume called *Songs of Innocence* (1789), in which he revised some songs from the *Island*, wrote others of the same nature, and in 1794 added as an example of "Contrary States" the collection called *Songs of Experience*. No separate edition of *Songs of Experience* is known. The full title of the complete work is *Songs of Innocence and of Experience shewing the Two Contrary States of the Human Soul*. The two sets of songs should be read together. They are nearly all as intimately connected as *The Lamb* in the *Innocence* series and *The Tiger* in the *Experience*. In the one "the little girl lost" is found; in the other she is lost because she has learned. The contrast between the pair of "Chimney-Sweepers" is almost unbearable. In the first *Holy Thursday* we have the sweetness of charity; in the second the bitter crime of poverty. The poems are genuine evocations of the spirit of childhood, and they are real songs. The day was coming when to Blake the symbol was to be more than the song.

The first of the symbolical rhythmical chants, *Tiriel*, written in 1789, was not actually printed till 1874. The second, *The Book of Thel*, the next book to be issued in Blake's method of engraved and coloured reproduction, also belongs to 1789. The idyllic gentleness of its imagery and the not unpleasant blending of simplicity and formalism in the Ossianic diction, proclaim the mood of *Songs of Innocence*. Blake now began to meet persons, including Thomas Paine, favourable to the French Revolution. To this period belong the curious little sets of prose aphorisms, two called *There is no Natural Religion* and one called *All Religions are One*, as well as a work entitled *The French Revolution, A Poem in Seven Books*, alleged to have been "printed in 1791"; but only one book survives, in ordinary typography, and this was probably a proof. It was not really published till 1923. No more has ever been found. Whether more was written and destroyed as dangerous we do not know. The year 1790 is probably the date of the greatest of Blake's early productions, *The Marriage of Heaven and Hell*, though some put it as late as 1793. This opens with an unrhymed lyric, and then proceeds in prose aphorisms long and short, rich in iconoclastic paradox. Here we have the first fruits of Blake's Gnostic reading, in which he found the dualism of Good and Evil, with Evil as the work of the Just God of the Law and Good as the work of the liberal Creative Spirit. The "Memorable Fancies" are written in mockery of Swedenborg's "Memorable Relations". *The Marriage of Heaven and Hell* fully introduces Blake as a revolutionary mystic assailing the false dualism of accepted religion. When religion has become a punitive code of laws for the obsequiously submissive, then active Evil is better than passive Good. Love joined to Energy is the "marriage of Heaven and Hell".

In 1793 Blake moved to Hercules Buildings, Lambeth, and there spent the happiest and most crowded years of his life. Many of his works belong to the history of painting and engraving, like his famous illustrations to the *Book of Job, The Grave* and *Night Thoughts*. One of his patrons at this time, Thomas Butts, bought regularly, and these transactions touch literature because of the valuable letters sent by Blake to his patron. *Visions of the Daughters of Albion* (1793) is the first of the lesser works among the "Lambeth Books". In it we meet Urizen, his God of the restrictive Law. Blake's belief in physical freedom was part of his doctrine of enlightened liberty. One recalls with interest that during these years he knew Mary Wollstonecraft. Parallel with *The Visions*, and probably composed at the same time, is *America: a Prophecy*, dated 1793. It is a short, beautiful and beautifully engraved poem. The combat of America with England is taken as a symbol in the developing life of man, with Urizen as the source of all repressive codes.

Up to this point Blake's writings preserve the spontaneity and confident strength that mark *The Marriage of Heaven and Hell*. But now a more sombre note is heard. The exquisite, heart-taking poetry of the early songs gives place to the troubled utterance of prophecy. The *Songs of Experience* themselves mark a change of spirit; and in his true Lambeth books Blake is less the affirmer of faith and more the denouncer of errors—a woeful change in a poet. With that change came a change in his power of expression. The period of pure poetic inspiration had passed. What we demand of any kind of poem is that it shall succeed in its own kind. Blake does not succeed in the kind he now chose to write. His early poems came straight from his heart with perfect natural simplicity. In his later confusion of Gnosticism and Druidism, with additions from Swedenborg, Boehme and Law, and complications induced by the French Revolution, Blake was lost when he came to expression. The fault is not that his poetry became implicated with ideas, but that it became implicated with ideas imperfectly apprehended. To see visions is not enough; the poet must be able to say what he saw. An accomplished writer would have said what he fancied he saw; but Blake was not an accomplished writer, and he was fiercely honest. He tried hard to find truth for himself in the forms of his own myth-ology and he tried to transmit his convictions in the only dialect of sublimity he knew. But that semi-Scriptural, semi-Ossianic dialect is not the medium for an artist. It conceals rather than reveals "minute particulars"; it avoids the sharp demands of quality by resorting to clouds of quantity; and so, as Blake wrote on, the major poet is heard but intermittently in the long soliloquies of the minor prophet. Other poets have become bewildered "in the midway of this our mortal being", but few so stupendously as Blake, who, as engraver, could give almost monstrous energy to figures that, as poet, he could not make intelligible. He could not say all he wanted to say, and he was therefore driven to invent the mythology contained in *The Book of Urizen* (1794), with its complements *The Book of Ahania* (1795) and *The Book of Los* (1795). *Europe* (1794) and *The Song of Los* (1795), though they have the same mythological basis, approach rather nearer in tone to *America*. Milton now comes perceptibly into the story. Believing that the poet was of "God's party" and justified the evil that He did, Blake denounced him; but feeling drawn, as he could not help being drawn, to the poetic beauty of Milton, he discovered that Milton re-pented, and, because he was a poet, "was of the Devil's party without knowing it". Hence *The Book of Urizen* contains obvious inversions of Miltonic episodes. In *The Book of Ahania* Blake further identifies Urizen, as the author of the Mosaic code, with Jehovah. In the remaining member of this trilogy, *The Book of Los*, the strangeness of the symbolism makes interpretation a matter of conjecture. In *Europe* and *The Song of Los* Blake turns from universal history to consider the portents of immediate emancipation through the French Revolution. This change is reflected in the greater prominence given to Los and Enitharmon, who, as Regents of this world, act as the ministers of Urizen to transmit to men his systems of religion and philosophy. Here Blake utters his plainest criticism of Christianity. Probably about 1795, he began *Vala or The Death and Judgement of the Ancient Man, A Dream of Nine Nights*. Later on he altered this to *The Four Zoas, The Torments of Love and Jealousy in The Death and Judgement of Albion the Ancient Man. Vala* remained in manuscript and was never properly printed till the twentieth century. The four Zoas are Urizen (Reason), Urthona (Spirit), Luvah (Passion) and Tharmas (the Body). To describe the nine nights of the poem, or to elucidate the huge cloudy symbols of his vision is beyond us here. Judged as literature, the poem suffers by reason of its formlessness and incoherence; yet there are scattered passages of much imaginative power.

The prosperity of the Lambeth period drew to a close, and through the influence of Flaxman Blake was offered engraving work by William Haley. In 1800 Blake and his wife went to live with that self-satisfied dabbler in the arts at Felpham, near Bognor. Hayley was well-meaning, but possessive, patronizing and philanthropical. Blake's growing resentment expressed itself in biting epigrams, and at last he escaped and returned to London in 1803. He had endured much, and was now to know poverty immediate and prospective. At Felpham he had revised *Vala* into *The Four Zoas* and had almost certainly begun the next great poem, *Milton. Milton, A Poem in Two Books, To Justify the Ways of God to Men*, was written and engraved between 1803–8. From the preface has been taken the beautiful lyric beginning "And did those feet in ancient time", wrongly called "Jerusalem", which, in Parry's setting, has become so familiar. Almost everything in it is misunderstood. The "dark Satanic Mills", for instance, do not refer to the wrongs of industrial operatives, about which Blake knew nothing. There is, however, in *Jerusalem* itself the song beginning "England! awake!" of the same character and almost as attractive. In *Milton* the spirit of the dead poet descends from his place in eternity and inhabits the living poet in order to annihilate the spiritual error to which *Paradise Lost* has given currency. Similar to *Milton* is *Jerusalem: The Emanation of the Giant Albion* produced between 1804–20. Here Man, or Albion, is the battle-ground wherein the forces of imagination contend against the forces of natural religion. Of the two *Milton* is preferable. Whether as poem or as design it is a great piece of work. *Jerusalem* is less easily comprehended.

The next period of Blake's life is sad. He laboured hard, and was not merely neglected, but openly derided. He was grossly cheated by the publisher Cromek over his picture of the Canterbury Pilgrims, but he endeavoured to place himself in public notice by an exhibition of his works held in 1809, the *Descriptive Catalogue* of which is an invaluable addition to his writings. The most violent criticism of Blake with definite assertion of his madness came from Southey. Charles Lamb, as usual, was on the side of the angels. A few other pieces demand mention. The theme and dramatic form of *The Ghost of Abel* (1822) were suggested by Byron's *Cain. Auguries of Innocence* (*c.* 1801–3) may be regarded as a fragmentary poetic form of *The Marriage of Heaven and Hell*. Many other fragments of great value were recovered from manuscripts, especially from that known as the Rossetti MS. The reserve of poetic power in Blake is most clearly revealed in *The Everlasting Gospel* (*c.* 1810). Blake's prose has the directness and simplicity that distinguish his best poetry. Most of it is scattered as scribbled notes and *marginalia*. It is vigorous, epigrammatic, and at times peculiarly eloquent. His letters (edited by Sir Geoffrey Keynes in 1956) have intense interest and should be carefully read. His life was admirably written by Alexander Gilchrist in 1863.

We sometimes forget, when we blame those who neglected Blake and left him to die in poverty, that his literary works were concealed rather than published. Wordsworth and Coleridge scarcely knew of his existence. While Wordsworth was still a schoolboy, Blake had found, and was using with consummate art, a diction almost perfect in its simplicity, aptness and beauty. His passion for freedom was akin to that which moved Wordsworth, Coleridge and Southey in their earlier years, though, in its later form, it came nearer to Shelley's revolt against convention. The final note of Blake's career is not one of tragedy. His own works and the record of others show that he had subdued the world to his own unconquerable spirit. Both literally and metaphorically, he died singing.

X. BURNS: LESSER SCOTTISH VERSE

Robert Burns (1759–96) and William Blake were almost exact contemporaries, Blake being two years older. There is some resemblance in the circumstances of their early life. Both were born into religious homes, one concerned with the remote mysteries of doctrine and the other narrowly pious in the Scottish way. Blake was for ever in search of a valid religion; Burns soon forsook the faith that meant for him little more than hypocrisy and repression. Had Blake known anything of the life of Burns, he could hardly have helped citing him as a victim of Urizen. Both were poor, yet escaped the worst evil of poverty—illiteracy. Blake received the elements of education at home, and thereafter made the great "seer-poets" and mystics his text books. Burns, better educated formally, thanks to the determination of a strong-minded father, found his natural reading in the Scottish verse of *The Tea-Table Miscellany* and *The Ever Green* of Allan Ramsay, in *The Lark*, in Watson's *Choice Collection*, in Lord Hailes's *Ancient Scottish Poems*, and in Herd's *Ancient and Modern Songs*; in addition he knew something of the accepted, and especially the recent, English writers.

Matthew Arnold, in a famous essay on poetry, dismisses the claim of Burns to the first rank because of his constant preoccupation with "Scotch drink, Scotch religion and Scotch manners". The reason is not valid. Arnold's objection lies less against Burns than against the countrymen of Burns, who seem determined to admire him, not because he is a great poet, but because he is a Scottish poet. Burns is great enough to be admired as a poet. The German song writers who set his lyrics to music were attracted by poems that could be sung, not by oddities of local dialect. Actually the divergence of Burns from normal English vocabulary is not very great and not disabling to the southern or to the American reader. The true importance of the language in which Burns wrote his best poetry is not its importance to local patriotism, but its importance to Burns himself. He carefully studied English verse and English prose; but he wrote more freely when he could use the kind of tongue spoken by those for whom he first began to write. When he wrote in normal English he was "behaving"; when he wrote in the speech of his natural associations he was spontaneous.

Robert Burns, born at Alloway, was the elder of two sons of a pious Ayrshire farmer. The story of their hard struggle with the unremunerative soil of Scotland belongs to biography. Robert had to make long journeys to pursue his education. He was far from robust, and often enough his growing body suffered because he rarely had enough proper food. Quite early he began to show a rheumatic tendency. As he grew, he was impelled to write by his first affections. We cannot follow him in the moves he made in search of some useful agricultural acquirements—surveying, flax-dressing, and so forth. Everywhere he found companions of his own sex with whom he joined in clubs for debating, as well as friends of the other sex about whom he wrote verses. He saw more of life, some of it with sailors, who taught him to drink deep, and encountered books, such as those of Sterne, Richardson and Mackenzie, which taught him something of the larger social world. Better still, he discovered a modernized volume of Blind Harry's *William Wallace*, and was kindled to write of his native land. The projects for his advancement all failed, and the father died in 1784 full of dismal apprehensions about the future of his elder son.

On the advice of Gavin Hamilton, a genial lawyer, the two brothers took a farm at Mossgiel near Mauchline, and at Mauchline Burns was publicly condemned in open church for his transgressions. An old friend, John Rankine, having heard of Robert's ordeal, wrote to ask the truth. Instead of sending the usual prose reply, Robert replied in the *Epistle to John Rankine*. This was the true release of Burns the poet after his formal labours in the art of writing. The real Burns had arrived; that is, the Burns who wrote what he alone could write. *The Twa Herds* followed a falling out of two local pastors. The public reprimand of Gavin Hamilton for lax church attendance by an "Auld Licht" named William Fisher gave Burns an opportunity which he splendidly took in *Holy Willie's Prayer*. This and other poems enjoyed an immense manuscript circulation. But Burns was soon in desperate personal and domestic trouble and resolved to escape by emigrating to the West Indies. He naturally desired to leave behind some literary relic of himself, and, after taking the advice of friends, issued what is now one of the most celebrated "first books" in the history of English literature, *Poems, chiefly in the Scottish Dialect*, Kilmarnock, 1786. His hopes revived. Books might produce money even though farming had failed.

Edinburgh became interested in the new poet, and to Edinburgh he went in 1786. Almost his first act was to visit the grave of Fergusson. But there was no grave. The poor poet had been huddled into Scottish earth as a pauper; and Burns might have read in that unidentified grave an omen of his own ill-success. Edinburgh patronized the "manly peasant", but did nothing for him. He had hoped to get some modest post under the government; but no offer was made. He returned to Mossgiel. A second visit to Edinburgh and a tour through part of the Highlands kindled him to his Jacobite verses, and a second edition of his volume was beginning to sell. To this period belongs his correspondence with Margaret Chalmers ("Peggy") and Mrs Agnes McLehose ("Clarinda").

Solicitation at last (about 1789) brought him an exciseman's place at £40 a year; and he settled at Ellisland near Dumfries. The next short period contains some of his noblest work. He was deeply moved by the dying songs of his country—old Highland melodies and feeble words lingering in frail human memory. Two publications, James Johnson's *The Scots Musical Museum*, 5 vols. (1787–1803) and *A Select Collection of Original Scottish Airs for the Voice* by George Thomson, 6 vols. (1793–1811) made efforts to preserve the dying lyrics. The first was a sincere and humble effort, the second more pretentious. To these publications Burns contributed about three hundred songs and adaptations. Unlike Thomas Moore, Burns was entirely destitute of an ear for music; yet by some inexplicable instinct he could fit new words to old tunes without a failure. In 1790 he wrote perhaps his greatest poem, *Tam o' Shanter*, at a sitting—the "perhaps" being merely a hesitation as to whether the best of all is not *The Jolly Beggars* or *Death and Doctor Hornbook* or the *Address to the Unco Guid*...

Ellisland farm failed like all the others. At the end of December 1791 Burns left the land and went into Dumfries as an exciseman at a salary of £70 a year. That is the most that Scotland ever did for its greatest poet. The end came in a few years. Burns drank deep with the squireens of Dumfries, professed revolutionary sympathies, quarrelled with the local gentry, and steadily lost his power of work. Returning late one night after a carouse, he fell into the snow and slept. Then returned upon him in full all the rheumatic tortures that had so far but played with him, and after long and excruciating torment of mind and body he died in 1796. Whether Dumfries is the place in Scotland in which Burns suffered most is perhaps disputable; but Dumfries proudly exhibits his house and tomb and monument to its numerous visitors.

Burns was in the full sense an "original". He had no clear poetic ancestry. Of the old vernacular poets he knew only the examples in the versions of Ramsay and others. *The Lark*, a collection of Scottish and English songs, was, he says, his *vade mecum* and he was also a voluminous reader of "those Excellent New Songs that are hawked about the country in baskets, or exposed in stalls in the streets". Much of his pure technique he derived from a study of the greater English writers as represented in various collections. Thus, *The Cotter's Saturday Night* in the Kilmarnock volume of 1786 is a fine piece, but a curious hybrid; for its stanza is the Spenserian, borrowed, not from the great original, but from Beattie, and, being almost free from dialect, the poem even suggests Goldsmith of *The Deserted Village*. Burns, like Brueghel, is strongest in rustic themes. He attains to the highest triumphs of his art in depicting the manners and circumstances of his fellow peasants, and in dealing with rustic beliefs, superstitions, customs, scenes and occasions. His themes did not always afford scope for the nobler possibilities of poetry, and to that extent Matthew Arnold was justified in his denial of the highest rank to Burns. But his mastery of the serio-comic, semi-supernatural, and macabre manner in verse is complete, and he uses all the old stanza forms superbly. No more withering, scornful, serio-comic piece than *Holy Willie's Prayer* exists. *Tam o' Shanter* and *The Jolly Beggars* are masterpieces of the wild kind. Just as he used the "Habbie" stanza perfectly in *Poor Mailie's Elegy*, so he showed equal mastery of the *Christis Kirk* stave in *The Holy Fair* and *Halloween*. He used the stave of *The Cherrie and the Slae* in the

Epistle to Davie; but in the opening and final recitativos of the boisterous *Jolly Beggars* he employed it for humorous descriptive purposes with a picturesque felicity not surpassed in verse. Indeed, the forms of *The Jolly Beggars* are evidence of an immense technical mastery. Burns thought of the drama, but did not actually write a play. The last years of his life were fruitful in the songs that give him not merely a national, but a universal reputation. To name any fifty of them would be but to name fifty of the world's best songs. A true song, whether by Heine, or Goethe, or Shakespeare, or some obscure and distant singer whose very name has perished, transcends all difficulties of language and oddities of dialect and comes home to the hearts of all men everywhere; and so in spite of their association with "Scotch drink, Scotch religion and Scotch manners" the poems of Burns entitle him to a place among the great poets of the world. Arnold's "English" estimate can fittingly be supplemented by the opinions of modern Scottish critics like Hugh MacDiarmid, Edwin Muir, Catherine Carswell, John Speirs, and David Daiches.

Many writers, who must be briefly dealt with, belong to the category in which fervent patriots would include Burns, namely, Scottish poets, rather than great poets. Some have already been named in an earlier chapter (see p. 415). First comes a notable group of women. Joanna Baillie (1762–1851) belongs chiefly to the theatre by right of her nine *Plays on the Passions* (1798–1836) and her successful tragedy *De Montfort* (1800) in which Kemble and Siddons appeared. *Fugitive Pieces* (1790) and *Metrical Legends* (1823) contain most of her Scottish verses. Lady Anne Lindsay—afterwards Barnard—(1750–1825) is known by one popular song *Auld Robin Gray*. Susanna Blamire (1747–94), of English birth and descent, is remembered for *And Ye shall walk in Silk Attire*. Mrs John Hunter, wife of the famous anatomist, has achieved immortality in *My Mother bids me bind my Hair*, which was set to music by Haydn. Caroline Oliphant, Lady Nairne (1766–1845) is specially remembered for one song, *The Land of the Leal*—a woman's song, the frequent substitution of "Jean" for "John" being mere sentimentalism; but Lady Nairne also wrote *The Lass of Gowrie*, *Hunting Tower*, *The Auld Hoose*, *The Rowan Tree*, *Caller Herrin'*, the immortal *Hundred Pipers* and *The Laird of Cockpen*. Her Jacobite songs include *Wha'll be King but Charlie*, *Will Ye no come back again* and a version of *Charlie is my Darling*. Lady Nairne is the greatest of Scottish women poets.

The lesser male poets include Sir Alexander Boswell (1775–1822) of Auchinleck, the eldest son of Johnson's biographer, who contributed to various collections and in 1803 published anonymously *Songs Chiefly in the Scottish Dialect*. Robert Tannahill (1774–1810) the Paisley weaver published in 1817 a volume of *Poems and Songs* which are monotonously amorous. His most famous poems are *Jessie the Flower of Dunblane* and *The Braes of Balquither*. William Motherwell (1797–1835), also of Paisley, was a journalist and a collector of poems which appeared in *The Harp of Renfrewshire* (1817), and *Minstrelsy Ancient and Modern* (1827). His *Poems Narrative and Lyrical* appeared in 1832; and, together with James Hogg, he brought out in 1834–5 an edition of Burns.

Next to Burns, by far the most considerable poet of humble birth was James Hogg, the Ettrick Shepherd (1770–1835). Till he was nearly thirty he had never learned to read or write; but when he heard *Tam o'Shanter* recited, he was so moved that he vowed to become Burns's successor. Hogg could not succeed Burns, who was in intellectual power as well as in mastery of song, far above him. However, he had a pleasing fluency, and his eccentricity of manner made him rather a butt among the wits of Edinburgh. He lives vividly as the irrepressible "Shepherd" of the *Noctes Ambrosianae* in *Blackwood's Magazine*. Unlike Burns, he resolved to conquer Edinburgh as a man of letters; and he actually succeeded. The reputation of Hogg now rests mainly on *The Queen's Wake* (1813), which contains his most familiar lines, *Bonny Kilmeny*. Though Hogg had vowed to succeed Burns, his poetry is more akin to that of Scott. It is in his one novel, *The Private Memoirs and Confessions of a Justified Sinner* (1824), rather than in his verse, that Hogg truly succeeds the Burns of the anti-Calvinist satires.

John Leyden (1775–1811), like Hogg, the son of a shepherd, was associated with him in supplying Scott with ballad versions for *The Minstrelsy of the Scottish Border*; he later had a distinguished career in India. Allan Cunningham (1784–1842), a Dumfriesshire man of oddly assorted employments, supplied Robert Hartley Cromek with most of the pieces and information contained in his *Remains of Nithsdale and Galloway Song* (1810), its poetic contents being mainly fabricated by him, though, in some cases, he merely modified traditional versions of old songs. His *Songs of Scotland Ancient and Modern* (four volumes, 1825) include some of his own compositions; but it is by his non-Scottish *A wet sheet and a flowing sea* that he is best known. Lady John Scott (Alicia Anne Spottiswoode, 1811–1900), a late survival, was the author of one of the best known of Scottish songs, *Annie Laurie*, based on an original belonging to the seventeenth century.

With the purely secular verse flourished a school of sacred verse, of which Blair's *The Grave* is an example. Two young men, Michael Bruce and John Logan, studied together at Edinburgh University. Bruce died in 1767, at the age of twenty-one; and, in 1770, Logan published, from papers supplied by the family, *Poems on Several Occasions by Michael Bruce*, with poems by other authors. In 1781 Logan, now a minister, published a volume of poems containing an improved version of *The Cuckoo*, which had appeared in Bruce's volume, together with certain metrical paraphrases of Scripture. *The Cuckoo* and the paraphrases have been claimed for Bruce; but Logan's *Braes of Yarrow* and other poems in the volume show as great poetic aptitude as any pieces by Bruce. The question of authorship remains unsettled.

XI. THE PROSODY OF THE EIGHTEENTH CENTURY

In an earlier section (see p. 359) it was shown that there was a changing practice in prosody with hardly any contemporary theory to accompany it. We shall now find that, during the period covered, there was no great revolution in poetic practice, but a body of poetic theory so considerable as to be almost the foundation of that study in English literature. The one main prosodical principle of the period (Ossian and Blake are of course exceptional) is that which directs the restriction of every line to a fixed number of syllables with a fixed fall of stresses. Of this principle the greatest example was Pope. But though the couplet of Pope is invulnerable and imperishable, it is unfortunately not inimitable. The dangers of monotony and of convention were fatally illustrated in the glittering frigidity of Erasmus Darwin. However, the heroic couplet did not suppress other metrical forms. The octosyllabic couplet and the Spenserian stanza both achieved success, and blank verse, inspired by Milton, reproduces sometimes that great poet's manner and sometimes only his mannerisms. The limiting effect of the prevailing regularity is shown most oppressively in the lyric. The wild and formless "Pindaricks" of the seventeenth century continued among poets with more manner than matter, but gradually tamed their wildness when real poets like Collins and Gray began to write Odes. In smaller and lighter work, the adoption of the anapaest by Prior was almost as fortunate as his patronage of the octosyllables. The influence of the ballad was strong, and Gray in his *Elegy* showed once for all what could be done with the elegiac stanza. There was also a return to the old "romance six" or *rime couée* of which Smart's *Song to David* is a noble example. But all these forms, with the exception of the woollier Pindarics, are as regular as the couplet.

Prosodic theory is much more adventurous than prosodic practice, and becomes, in the eighteenth century, important almost for the first time—for no one could take seriously the recommendations of Gabriel Harvey and his friends about classical versing. In 1702 there appeared, written or compiled by an obscure person named Edward Bysshe, an *Art of Poetry*, often reprinted, though almost worthless. But its brief introduction, "Rules for Making English Verses", is an important statement of a clear case. Bysshe formulates the principles underlying the poetic practice of his time. He is strictly syllabic. There are no feet in English, merely a certain number of syllables, preferably ten. Upon certain of these syllables stresses may fall; and between certain of these syllables pauses may be made. He never mentions dactylic or anapaestic verse, but admits that accents may fall oddly in low and disagreeable kinds of verse. Elisions, to reduce redundant syllables, he allows; but as for stanzas of intermixed rhyme (e.g. the Spenserian), "they are now wholly laid aside" in longer poems. This gives us a miserably restricted prosody; but it is the official prosody of the fashionable poets of the day. The "regular" poets were content to follow Bysshe till Coleridge and Southey routed him in the next century. Other prosodists were not so placable. Pope, in his almost single prosodic reference, a letter of 1710 to Henry Cromwell, is the complete follower of Bysshe; but Charles Gildon in his *Complete Art of Poetry* (1718) and *Laws of Poetry* (1721) revolted against Bysshe's syllables and accents, and introduced a system of applying musical terms and notes to prosody. John Brightland in his *English Grammar* (1711) started another hare—the question of accent *versus* quantity—which has been coursed ever since, and which, also, will probably never be run down; for it is an obvious fact that in English poetry a syllable which is unquestionably "long" may be used as "short", and *vice versa*. Edward Mainwaring took the musical view, and initiated the practice of regarding the normal decasyllabic line as beginning with an anacrusis or "up-beat". The catalogue of eighteenth-century prosodists, thenceforward, is a long one, but only a few writers can be noticed here.

Joshua Steele in *Prosodia Rationalis* (1779) declared prosody to be essentially a matter of musical rhythm. Tyrwhitt, in his justly famous edition of Chaucer (1775–8), showed himself a real prosodist and, by grammatical detective work, rediscovered the right way of reading that poet. Gray was the first to recognize the presence and the continuity of the trisyllabic foot in generally disyllabic metres from Middle English downward; and he exhibits in his fragmentary *Metrum* many other signs of historical knowledge and metrical vision. Johnson, in his prosodic remarks on Milton, Spenser and a few others, is, professedly, at least, of the straitest sect of believers in fixed syllabism; yet he makes so many concessions that he almost reaches the extreme of admitting that any verse is successful if it succeeds. John Mason in his *Power of Numbers* (1714) is somewhat inclined to musical views of prosody and he settles the dispute of accent *versus* quantity by saying sensibly that what principally determines quantity in English is emphasis or stress. Mitford's chief claim to praise is that he gives in his *Inquiry into the Principles of the Harmony of Language* (1804) what is not to be found in any other prosodist of the eighteenth century except Gray, a regular survey of actual English poetry from the time that its elements came together. Last we have Cowper, who discusses prosody in a few letters and whose utterances are therefore fragmentary. He laid down the salutary rule that "without attention to quantity good verse cannot possibly be written", by which he meant (as Mason taught) that the syllable intended to bear emphasis should be big enough to be able to bear it.

The period, though not of great importance, was of great interest. Writers were taking regular notice of prosody. Few of them, except Gray and Mitford, actually studied the practice of poets over a long period; most of them proceeded preposterously by formulating abstract principles and requiring the poets to conform.

XII. THE GEORGIAN DRAMA

Though the last forty years of the eighteenth century produced few English plays of any importance, the period is interesting historically, as showing how variable are the conditions of dramatic success. The decay of the drama was partly due to the advance of the actor, for the theatre of the later eighteenth century, like the cinema of the twentieth, relied upon the "star", not upon the piece. When Burbage and Betterton played, the actor was an intermediary, and made the necessary contact between the author's words and the auditor's sensibilities. When the actor became a thing-in-himself, the playwright merely provided material for the "star" to glitter in. People no longer went to the play, they went to see Garrick or Mrs Abington, Foote or Mrs Clive. This was true right to the end of the nineteenth century. People did not go to the Lyceum to see *The Merchant of Venice*, they went to see Irving as Shylock and Ellen Terry as Portia. Indeed it might almost be said that nineteenth-century drama began in the eighteenth. The developing taste for spectacular pieces and the demands of the actors for better opportunities of display had changed the very form of the theatre itself. The old platform-stage had become the modern picture-stage framed in the proscenium. Visible illusion became possible, and pantomime, i.e. action without speech, engaged the attention of Garrick himself. New forms of lighting enabled performers to play visibly with looks instead of audibly with words. But there was no national drama. At Hamburg in Lessing's time (1767) and at Weimar later in Goethe's time (1791), dramatic art could still exist. In England, the pious followers of the great evangelical preachers abhorred an institution which encouraged looseness, exalted a fictitious code of honour and drew people from the meeting-house. The respectable were suspicious of the theatre, but the fashionable made it their public resort and went, not to see or hear, but to be seen and heard. Readers of *Evelina* will learn much about the theatre of the day.

The plays themselves became more affected, sentimental, and theatrical. They ceased to have any true relation to life. Richard Cumberland (1732–1811) devised theatrical tangles and undid them by drastic and sometimes almost tragic action. *The Brothers* (1769) contains pirates, a storm and a shipwreck as well as tearfully sympathetic characters. *The West Indian* (1771) presents the imagined freedom and sincerity of the plantations in contrast with city life. But early in the seventies there was a curious reversion of public taste. Adaptations from Voltaire and Molière came back, and William Mason composed *Elfrida* (1772) with a Greek chorus. Colman the elder borrowed from Plautus and Terence to produce *The Man of Business* (1774), and Cumberland drew inspiration from the *Adelphi* to write *The Choleric Man* (1774). Burgoyne's brief comedy *The Maid of the Oaks* belongs to the same year. But the two authors most conspicuously associated with the revolt against affectation and sentiment were Goldsmith and Sheridan. Of Goldsmith we have already spoken (p. 443). *The Good Natur'd Man* (1767) had failed, not through its weakness, but through its strength. The genteel could not endure what we should call the realism of the bailiffs' scene. *She Stoops to Conquer* (1773), no matter what originals there may be for its plot, is a complete creation. It is spirited, humorous and veracious.

With Goldsmith as a writer for the stage it is natural to couple Richard Brinsley Sheridan (1751–1816), in all senses a more complete dramatist. His grandfather was a friend of Swift, and his father was a friend (if also the butt) of Johnson. His mother Frances Chamberlaine was a novelist. His tumultuous and varied life was shot through with genius and romance. His marriage with the beautiful Elizabeth Linley, daughter of the composer, forced him to turn to the stage as a means of providing for his extravagant household. He produced successful plays and became lessee of Drury Lane Theatre, passed from the stage to politics, and became a great orator, the rival of Burke, and a member of the Government. He was one of the leaders in the impeachment of Hastings, and he was the friend and mouthpiece of the Prince Regent. With the loss of his seat in Parliament Sheridan's career in the state ended; and when to the steady failure of the old theatre was added a conflagration that destroyed the new, his career went up in smoke. He was completely ruined and almost destitute. The last satirical event in a tumultuous life was a magnificent funeral in Westminster Abbey. Sheridan's first play *The Rivals* (1775) shows the hand of the born dramatist. The substance comes from stage "stock"—probably every detail had appeared in some other play. But *The Rivals* is an original creation by a writer with a genius for the stage. It is an "artificial" comedy, i.e., it deals mainly with surfaces, and with surfaces elegantly polished. It belongs to the world of the stage and remains perfectly true to that world. It is, too, a comedy of the times, appealing to a polished society composed of better elements than the disreputable ladies and gentlemen of Restoration comedy. The main characters of *The Rivals* still live and have their counterparts. *St Patrick's Day* and *The Duenna* can be dismissed without remark, and we need say no more of *A Trip to Scarborough* than that it is an adaptation of Vanbrugh's *The Relapse*. But *The School for Scandal*, which appeared in May 1777, is the last great English comedy in the old manner and exhibits the excellence and the limitations of the Georgian theatre. Once more Sheridan was as content with stock characters as Shakespeare was with stock stories, but the play, "artificial" in form, is a serious comedy in its revelation of the feeling that the elegant surface may cover, and the stock characters have a genuine life of their own. The brilliance of the dialogue matches the brilliance of invention. In this respect Sheridan's comedy has only one equal, Congreve's *The Way of the World*. Sheridan's last play, *The Critic* (1779)—for we may dismiss the dismal *Pizarro* (1799) adapted from Kotzebue —does not attempt to touch the heights. It descends comfortably and amusingly to the little wars of the theatres, and pillories the poetasters and intriguing critics who ranged themselves on the side of sentimental drama. It meant more to its own audience than it means to us, who cannot instantly recognize Sir Fretful Plagiary as a caricature of Richard Cumberland; but its criticism has general validity and its delightful dialogue still carries it through triumphantly. The second act, instead of developing a plot, changes into a parody. Puff's tragedy, *The Spanish Armada*, is a pseudo-historical drama, and the spectators are entertained with brilliant and memorable inanities that are the best kind of parody— the parody of style, tendencies, characters, pretensions and devices. When *The Critic* was played as an afterpiece to *Hamlet*, the madness of Tilburina in white satin must have had a point it has never since achieved. So ended the comedies of Sheridan. The best of them have held the stage ever since they were written.

The kind of drama ridiculed in *The Critic* was then popular. Hannah More's *Percy* packed Covent Garden at a time when *The School for Scandal* was the attraction of Drury Lane. Hannah More was a woman of strong character, masculine intellect and passions, which, thwarted in life, were almost bound to find expression in literature. She had already composed *The Inflexible Captive*, a classical drama in which the hero, Regulus, steadily declaims his way through five long acts. *Percy* shows what havoc a virtuous man may work, if he is passion's slave. *The Fatal Falsehood* (1779) proves how love, in an unscrupulous heart, may lead to even more appalling crimes. After this effort, Hannah abandoned the theatre and devoted her pen to the propagation of religion.

Among writers of another sort we find Mrs Hannah Cowley (1743–1809), once a Della Cruscan (see p. 488), who, having put forth a sentimental effusion, *The Runaway* (1776), went over to real comedy and produced *The Belle's Stratagem* (1780), in which the heroine adopts the ancient device of pretending to be a hoyden to test her lover, and conquers by unsuspected charm. *A Bold Stroke for a Husband* (1783) maintains the traditions of sound comedy. The most remarkable playwright of this decade is General John Burgoyne (1723–92). The author of *The Maid of the Oaks*, on returning from America, had resumed his literary employment, and after writing an opera in 1780, produced in 1786 *The Heiress*, which won a fortune and was preferred by some critics to *The School for Scandal*. It is almost the last production of the eighteenth century to retain the spirit of comedy. It shows genuine invention, and has style in its excellent prose.

Place was found for the drama of social criticism. Thomas Holcroft (1745–1809), whose life was written by Hazlitt, was a dauntless fellow worker with Godwin and Paine. He had begun as early as 1778 with *The Crisis*; but it was not till 1792 that he produced *The Road to Ruin*, his most durable play, though *The Deserted Daughter* is a more striking indication of the tendency of the theatre. This manages to convey in melodramatic form the doctrines of the Godwin circle. The Godwinian theme was further elaborated by Mrs Inchbald and Colman the younger. Elizabeth Inchbald (1753–1821), born Sampson, began as an actress, but found her true vocation in writing for the stage. Her first play, *The Mogul Tale*, a farce (1784), showed promise; her next, *I'll tell you What* (1785), showed performance; and her next, *Such Things Are* (1787), showed achievement. *Wives as they Were* (1797) and *Every One has his Fault* (1793) showed that she understood some of the problems of marriage; but problems of any kind in her numerous plays had to be resolved into the sort of happy ending that brought tears to the eyes of a sentimental generation. Among her services to the theatre must be counted her collections of plays, *The British Theatre* (1806–9), 25 vols. and *The Modern Theatre* (1809), 10 vols. It may here be observed that though there were Godwinian plays, Godwin's chief theatrical success was *The Iron Chest* adapted from *Caleb Williams*; but this is not Godwinian; it is a "thriller", suiting the macabre qualities in the art of Edmund Kean and Henry Irving. George Colman the younger (1762–1836), son of the dramatist George Colman the elder, displayed ingenuity in giving a romantic atmosphere to his conventional ideas. His first real success was gained with *Inkle and Yarico* (1787), in which the West Indies form the setting of a strong sentimental drama. *The Heir at Law* (1797) is a pleasant, good-hearted piece with a genuinely comic character in Dr Pangloss. Thomas Morton (1764–1838), father of a later dramatist, John Maddison Morton, wrote comedies acceptable to his time, but added some touches of personal whimsicality. *The Way to get Married* (1796) has amusing characters. *A Cure for the Heartache* (1797) presents the eternally comic theme of the tradesman attempting to play the gentleman. *Speed the Plough* (1798), with its frequent allusions to the censures of "Mrs Grundy" (as invisible as Mrs Harris), has added a character to the national mythology.

To name all the minor dramatists and the adapters of Kotzebue who flourished at this time is unnecessary. John O'Keefe (1747–1833) was an actor till overtaken by blindness. He wrote numerous stage pieces, of which only two need be named, the opera *Merry Sherwood*, containing the famous song, "I am a Friar of Orders Grey", and *Wild Oats* (1791) containing a character, Rover, which remained a favourite part with comedians down to the time of Charles Wyndham. Richard Cumberland continued unceasingly to supply the theatre; but his later industry produced nothing more noteworthy than *The Jew* (1794). It is characteristic of this period that one of its dramatic sensations was the success of "the Infant Roscius", William Henry West Betty (1791–1864), who from eleven to sixteen played the "heavy leads" with such success that the House of Commons adjourned one day in 1805 in order to see his Hamlet. In short, the actor was everything, the play nothing. When Sheridan laid down his pen, the English stage had to wait for nearly a hundred years before *Arms and the Man* and *The Importance of Being Earnest* arrived to offer intelligent persons comedy worth reading as well as worth seeing. The novel, not the play, was to absorb a century's creative activity.

XIII. THE GROWTH OF THE LATER NOVEL

It may seem an arbitrary extension of literary chronology to include in one chapter a novelist who was born when Dryden was still writing and another novelist who died when H. G. Wells was born. But we can at once abridge that monstrous hiatus of nearly two centuries to a bare fifty years. Thomas Amory may have been born in 1691, but *John Buncle* did not get completed till 1766; and though Peacock's *Gryll Grange* appeared in 1861, it is a tale of precisely the same kind as *Headlong Hall*, which appeared in 1816. Thomas Amory (1691–1788) is better known from Hazlitt's enthusiasm than from his own writings. Few facts have been ascertained about his life, though something can be assumed from his books. Readers desirous of exploring Amory should not begin with his first publication, *Memoirs of Several Ladies of Great Britain* (1755), for it has less of the true Amorian flavour than the second, *John Buncle*, published in two volumes (1756, 1766). The *Memoirs* entirely disregards its own title and dissipates itself into miscellaneous writing of astonishing variety. In *John Buncle* Amory shows himself able to talk a little more like a man of this world, even if the world seems consistently unusual. There are ladies, arts, sciences, wanderings, mansions, scenes, arguments, and so forth. Though *John Buncle* was published when the author was seventy, it is as fresh, spontaneous and strong as the utterance of a full-blooded and unusually intelligent young man. The book is certainly long; but it is the pace, not the length that is difficult. Thus, almost at the beginning of the novel as a form of art, appears the eccentric, idiosyncratic English variety of the species.

From the extraordinary Amory and his one extraordinary book we can naturally pass to the extraordinary Beckford and his one extraordinary book *Vathek*. William Beckford (1760–1844) was born at Fonthill, Wiltshire, and lived in many countries. In his youth he was master of what seemed an immense fortune; but he was by nature or pose a misanthrope, and his wealth certainly seemed unable to buy him natural happiness. All he wrote gives evidence of some abnormality. He was such a man as could have written his books. His first, *Dreams, Waking Thoughts and Incidents* (1783), displayed many of the affectations natural in a much-travelled, rich and clever young man. Beckford castigated it severely when he reprinted it fifty years later as *Italy, with Sketches of Spain and Portugal* (1834), a fascinating work. His *Modern Novel Writing; or the Elegant Enthusiast* (1796) and *Azemia* (1797) were no more than rather clever burlesques. His last work, *Recollections of the Monasteries of Alcobaça and Batalha*

(1835) has great interest. One other production that deserves mention is the satire upon fanciful writing about art called *Biographical Memoirs of Extraordinary Painters* (1824). Had Beckford not written *Vathek* these books would hardly have attained mention in a history of literature; but they have certainly been unjustly overshadowed by that immortal story. Not even the *Episodes of Vathek*, first discovered and printed early in the twentieth century, has taken its place beside the original work. *The History of the Caliph Vathek* was originally written in French and published in 1787 in Paris and in Lausanne, the two versions differing slightly. But actually it was first published in England in 1786. The explanation is simple. Beckford asked (or did not ask) a clergyman named Samuel Henley to translate it; and for some reason Henley published the book in 1786 as if translated by himself from the Arabic. Beckford retorted by publishing the two French originals in 1787. He wisely refrained from including the *Episodes*. A little Orientalism goes far with modern readers; and it so happened that the tolerable length for an Oriental tale had been fixed by the intuitive genius of Voltaire. Beckford, who was something of an ironist (as befitted the purchaser of Gibbon's library), set out in his youth to produce a Voltairean tale of the East. The subject grew in his mind and became at last the gloomily splendid and terrible invention it is. There is nothing else like *Vathek* in our literature; and Beckford, with all his wasted wealth, lives as the man of one small book.

From the great eccentrics we pass to certain "novelists with a purpose". Most important of the group is William Godwin, who has been discussed on p. 467. *Caleb Williams* (1794) and *St Leon* (1799) are certainly powerful. Their successors, *Fleetwood* (1805), *Mandeville* (1817) and *Cloudesly* (1830) have far less distinction; but they prove that Godwin had many qualities of a good novelist. He was, however, not "quite" a novelist, as he was not "quite" anything. Success always eluded him. With Godwin we naturally associate Thomas Holcroft, whose first novel, *Alwyn* (1780), is picaresque rather than purposeful; but *Anna St Ives* (1792) and *Hugh Trevor* (1794) are similar in general temper to *Caleb Williams*, and, indeed, to *Political Justice* itself. Mrs Inchbald was also an intimate friend of Godwin and was in fact sought in marriage by that hapless man before he was punished with Mrs Clairmont. Mrs Inchbald's stage experience helped her with her novels, which borrowed from her plays. *A Simple Story* (1791) and *Nature and Art* (1796) long held their place as minor classics of fiction. Robert Bage (1728–1801), the last of the group, was a Quaker who became a Freethinker, an active man of business, and a novelist in the evening of his life. He was influenced by Rousseau, Diderot and Voltaire, deriving from them his revolutionary principles and his freedom of thought and expression. He had genuine talent and bears reading again. His most typical book is the last, *Hermsprong, or Man as he is not* (1796). It was preceded by *Man as he is* (1792).

The celebrated and admirable Maria Edgeworth (1767–1849) just touches the fringe of the revolutionary group. Her father, Richard Edgeworth—himself worthy of a place in any novel of eccentric character—affected his daughter's work very much for the worse, by the admixture of purpose and preachment which he either induced her to make or intruded on his own account. His influence was derived from the earlier French thinkers, chiefly Marmontel, whose very title, *Contes Moraux*, suggests *Moral Tales*. Fortunately Maria's own genius was too strong to be vitally diverted either by her father or by any Frenchman, and it worked in three main directions. Her first line of production was the regular novel, ranging from *Belinda* (1801) to *Helen* (1834), and including *Tales from Fashionable Life* (two series, 1809, 1812), *Patronage* (1814) and *Harrington* (1817). *Belinda* is nearly a great novel. Her second and best line of production is the group of Irish stories, which influenced the nationalistic bent of writers as diverse as Scott and Turgenev, and which Macaulay cited as evidence in his *History*. The group begins early in 1800 with *Castle Rackrent*, and is filled out with the later and better *Absentee* (1809) and *Ormond* (1817), which are masterpieces of their kind. Smollett had used national characteristics farcically in his novels; Maria Edgeworth is the first novelist to make national character the whole matter of her narrative. She is neither farcical nor tragical; she is firmly, quietly natural. Her third line of production is, in another way, her very own—the books for or about children. *The Parent's Assistant* (1796–1801), *Early Lessons* (1801), *Moral Tales* (1801), *Popular Tales* (1804), *Frank* (1822), and *Harry and Lucy* (1825) are truly remarkable, for in them, almost for the first time in post-Shakespearean literature, real children appear. Maria Edgeworth was devoted to her father, who ruthlessly used her, as if she had no right to a life of her own.

Readers of Jane Austen will remember the list of "horrid mystery" novels given by Isabella Thorpe to Catherine Morland. The "tale of terror" had a great run of popularity (with all classes) at the end of the eighteenth century and the beginning of the nineteenth. Some of them were trash of the most abject kind. If such a man, or even such a boy, as Shelley could perpetrate such utter rubbish as *Zastrozzi* and *St Irvyne*, the gutter scribbler was not likely to do much better. And just as three or four real story-tellers have emerged from the modern horde of semi-literate murder-merchants, so three fairly considerable figures may be discussed among the producers of the tales that thrilled Catherine Morland. These are Ann Radcliffe, Matthew Gregory Lewis, and Charles Robert Maturin. Ann Radcliffe (1764–1823), born Ward, was an original writer, in that she first fully exploited the romance of the past, the distant, the unfamiliar, the picturesque, and the supernatural. Her rank is low; but she gave Scott his method and Byron his hero, and so, through them, may be said to have moved all Europe. Of her first novel *The Castles of Athlin and Dunbayne* (1789) and of her posthumous *Gaston de Blondeville* (1826) it is enough to say that the first is tentative and the last a failure. *A Sicilian Romance* (1790) is a little better, though not much; but it gives at once the Radcliffe formula—a wildly persecuted heroine flying through, or immured within, castles, dungeons, forests, caves, and so forth, arriving at last at a perfectly happy ending. Her three most important novels, *The Romance of the Forest* (1791), *The Mysteries of Udolpho* (1794) and *The Italian* (1797) are variations on this theme. The chief fault of the Radcliffe novels is not that they are too wild, but that they are too tame. The reader not only knows that all will be well, which may be desirable, but also that everything will be explained away, which is not desirable. Sir Walter Scott, whose account of Mrs Radcliffe is still the best, rightly indicates her real trick in a single word—suspense. But it must be added that the suspended reader is badly let down at the end.

Matthew Gregory Lewis (1775–1818) was clever enough to note that a foreseen happy ending robbed a "thriller" of its thrill. But he went to the other extreme and made *The Monk* (1796) such a mess of murder, outrage, *diablerie* and indecency that it did not please people even so little squeamish as Byron, and has seldom been reprinted in its original form. Ordinary reprints give the author's much revised version. Lewis, before his early death, wrote or translated other novels; but none of them attained the vogue of *The Monk* or of his plays and verses. *The Castle Spectre* was played at Drury Lane in 1797, *The East Indian* in 1799 and *Timour the Tartar* in 1811. With Scott and Southey he compiled *Tales of Wonder* (1801).

The kind of novel represented by Mrs Radcliffe and "Monk" Lewis flourished at the end of the eighteenth century and reached up into the nineteenth, where it perceptibly influenced the work of Bulwer Lytton; but it engaged only one other writer worth mention, Charles Robert Maturin (1782–1824), novelist, dramatist and clergyman of Dublin. His first book *The Fatal Vengeance* (1807) is unimportant; but *The Wild Irish Boy* (1808) and *The Milesian Chief* (1811) are additions to the Irish literature represented by Miss Edgeworth. His tragedy *Bertram*, produced by Kean at Drury Lane (1816), was a great success, and is the subject of a rather sour criticism by Coleridge reprinted in *Biographia Literaria*. *Women* followed in 1818; and then in 1820 he produced his masterpiece *Melmoth the Wanderer*. Its central theme—the old bargain with Satan, refreshed and individualized by the notion of that bargain being transferable—is more than promising; and it has been praised by writers as little alike as Balzac and Rossetti.

The two sisters Porter, Anne Maria (1780–1832), who commenced author at twelve, and Jane (1776–1850), who postponed her debut till a later age, had a great following. Anne is now forgotten, though her output of novels, feebly romantic, was prodigious. Jane is remembered by her *Thaddeus of Warsaw* (1803) and *The Scottish Chiefs* (1810), which once were read by everybody and acquired European fame. Her other works need not be named.

Another celebrated book of its time is *Anastasius, or Memoirs of a Modern Greek* (1819) written by Thomas Hope (1770–1831), who, like Beckford, was very wealthy, and collected sculptures on a magnificent scale. *Anastasius* contains the materials of a good romantic novel, and had it been written by (say) Dumas it would still be read; but its author was mastered by his own considerable acquirements and tells us too much instead of letting his tale tell itself.

This chapter of remarkable novelists must end with one of the most remarkable of all, Thomas Love Peacock (1785–1866), a writer too little appreciated by the great variety of readers. His works include poems, plays and essays, all with a marked idiosyncrasy. Peacock is a most odd combination of sincerity, satire, cynicism and romance; indeed, he was an oddity in every way. He was like an autocratic old "don" of the fruity period, yet he was never at any public school or university, and expressed complete contempt for those institutions. His classical scholarship was immense, though not of the "examination" kind, for he read all the most ancient authors as he read the most modern, for sheer personal enjoyment. Much of his life was spent at the East India House, where an official colleague was James Mill. At the other extreme he was a close friend of Shelley, whose *Defence of Poetry* was a reply to Peacock's *The Four Ages of Poetry*. His novels (the main concern of this chapter) are seven in number, and fall into two groups, with an odd one in the middle. *Headlong Hall* (1816) is a delightful diagram of its successors, *Nightmare Abbey* (1818), the most amusing of all, *Crotchet Castle* (1831), the most idiosyncratic of all, and *Gryll Grange* (1860), the ripest of all. The next group contains two novels, *Maid Marian* (1822) and *The Misfortunes of Elphin* (1829), the first a Robin Hood story and the second a tale of ancient Wales, both intensely romantic and yet delightful satires upon romance. The odd novel is *Melincourt* (1817), which is much longer than the others, and contains, as they do not, some dull passages, and carries its joke too far. Through his most cynical and prejudiced pages Peacock scattered some of the most singable songs ever written. Almost every political and social craze of his time is pilloried in his fables, and much that he denounced still eminently deserves denunciation. His prose is the most Voltairean achieved by any English writer; but when the right place comes he slips imperceptibly into passages of real beauty. There was a curious linking of ages, styles and manners when the author of *Crotchet Castle* became the father-in-law of the author of *The Egoist*.

XIV. BOOK PRODUCTION AND DISTRIBUTION,
1625–1800

A history of printing and publishing during the period named above is beyond the scope of this work and must be studied in the appropriate chapter and bibliography of the larger *History*. All we can give here is a brief record of the main facts and dates. A Star Chamber decree in 1637 re-enacted the Elizabethan ordinance of 1586 (see p. 137). When the Long Parliament abolished the Star Chamber in 1641 the press was thus, almost by accident, released from restriction. The censorship was hastily re-established in 1643 (see p. 300) and was re-enforced by Cromwell in 1649. At the Restoration the royal prerogative in the printing of books and pamphlets was strongly asserted by the Licensing Act of 1662 and Roger L'Estrange, a fanatical Royalist (see p. 377), was made surveyor of the press. The Act was renewed at the accession of James II. State control of the press was abandoned in 1695, and the "Liberty of Unlicenc'd Printing" for which Milton had contended half a century before was conceded. Of different restraints upon printing we shall speak later.

The year 1709 saw the passing of the first Copyright Act, which established authors and disestablished publishers, to the great astonishment of both parties. As we have seen, books were the property of the stationers who entered their copy in the Company's registers and received authority to print. Authors had no status. The freedom of the press granted in 1695 encouraged numerous pirates, and the aggrieved publishers, not content with legal redress, agitated for statutory recognition of property right in their works—*their* works, observe, for they cared nothing about the authors, though to make the Bill seem respectable, they were willing to throw the poor hacks a few crumbs. The Act of

1709 duly recognized property in books, and gave authors copyright for fourteen years, with an additional fourteen if they were still living. All seemed well. The gratified publishers fondly believed that when the authors' meagre rights had been satisfied, the books would then be the publishers' property in perpetuity. But they found they had gained a statute and lost their estate; for the Courts construed the Act to mean that when the term of copyright had expired, books were (as they should be) anybody's. Later Acts extended the periods of copyright, and the position of authors slowly but steadily improved.

Famous among early publishers was Henry Herringman who issued Dryden's first important poems; but greatest of all was Jacob Tonson (1656–1736) who was concerned in most of the major enterprises of his time. He was succeeded by two relatives of the same name. Bernard Lintot was openly, and the rascally Edmund Curll was obscurely, associated with Pope. Another great name is that of Robert Dodsley (see p. 398) who issued the still important *Collection of Old Plays* (1744–5) and the *Collection of Poems by Several Hands* (1748–58). Dodsley entrusted to Burke the editorship of a new venture, *The Annual Register* (1759), which still regularly appears. An interesting feature of eighteenth-century publishing was the co-operation of several houses in the production of such large scale works as Johnson's *Dictionary* and the collected poets for which Johnson wrote the *Lives*. Works in weekly parts ("Paternoster Row Numbers") were also issued, and "Cooke's Pocket Library" in sixpenny numbers became popular. John Murray and Longmans were well established during the eighteenth century. Among provincial printers and publishers the most renowned were John Baskerville of Birmingham, Joseph Cottle of Bristol, whose *Early Recollections* and *Reminiscences* tell us much about the youth of Coleridge and Southey, the Foulis brothers of Glasgow, and Archibald Constable and James Ballantyne of Edinburgh, who were to be memorably associated with Scott. The Strawberry Hill press of Horace Walpole should not be forgotten. There were, too, famous vendors of books, such as Robert Scot, Christopher Bateman and James Lackington, whose "Temple of the Muses" in Finsbury Square was one of the sights of London and whose *Confessions* and *Memoirs* are full of interest. It was in the shop of Thomas Davies that Boswell first met Johnson—whose own father was a Lichfield bookseller. Some publishers and booksellers (as we have seen) were also authors. Thus, to John Nichols, one of a family in the "trade", we are indebted for the valuable *Literary Anecdotes of the Eighteenth Century* in nine volumes (1812–15). But possibly the most remarkable of all was Alexander Cruden (1701–70), who, in the course of a varied career, became a bookseller and compiled his famous *Complete Concordance to the Holy Scriptures* (1737) in the intervals of business. By the end of the century the publishing and selling of books had become a flourishing and important activity, whose subsequent fortunes can be read in such books as *Archibald Constable and his Literary Correspondents* (1873) by his son Thomas Constable, *A Publisher and his Friends* (1891) by Samuel Smiles (about the firm of Murray) and *The House of Macmillan 1843–1943* (1943) by the novelist Charles Morgan.

XV. THE BLUE-STOCKINGS

During the first half of the eighteenth century, Englishwomen had little education and even less intellectual status. The first attempt to create a circle in which intelligent conversation should take the place of cards or scandalous chatter was made by Mrs Elizabeth Vesey (1715–91), in whose literary gatherings the term "blue stocking" gained currency. Benjamin Stillingfleet, grandson of the Bishop, cultivated botany and Bohemia, and though gifted and brilliant, was not, in appearance at least, respectable. Being invited by Mrs Vesey to one of her "conversations", he excused himself as sartorially unfit. Upon which the lady exclaimed: "Don't mind dress; come in your blue stockings"—i.e. in blue or grey worsted, the everyday wear, instead of black silk, the correct wear for assemblies. "Blue-stocking" or "undress" parties became a kind of catchword, and gradually, in the ironic course of time, the phrase applied to a man became applied to the women he met at these assemblies.

Mrs Vesey originated blue-stocking circles, but the "Queen of the Blues" was Mrs Elizabeth Montagu, of whom something has already been said (see p. 450). Mrs Montagu had her failings, but she was a warm-hearted and generous woman, who used her wealth to support failing friends and her interest to encourage rising talent.

Of the blue-stocking circle none was more "darkly, deeply, beautifully blue" than Mrs Elizabeth Carter (1717–1806)—unmarried, but called "Mrs" in accordance with contemporary custom. By undaunted courage and industry she won for herself a large, though inexact, acquaintance with many languages, ancient and modern. She had her first volume of poems published at twenty-one, translated works from the French and the Italian, and courageously turned Epictetus into the polite idiom of her times. The translation was published in 1758 and gained for the modest author a small fortune and a European reputation.

The blue-stocking, however, whose fame reached to the furthest ends of the earth—though as a philanthropist rather than as a blue—is Hannah More (1745–1833), whom we also met on p. 450. Her connection with the blues represents the "gay and worldly" side of her serious life—she had not yet become "the eminent divine". She was a scribbler from her earliest years, and at twenty-two fell in love with a wealthy man who, however, twice shirked the actual fact of marriage; and when Hannah resolutely refused to be considered a third time, he gratefully settled £200 a year on her and left her to pursue the less dangerous path of letters. She came to London in 1774, and got into contact with Garrick, who introduced her to Mrs Montagu. Everyone recognized in her a woman of character, and she found no difficulty in winning success as a writer. The death of Garrick affected her so deeply that she abandoned the writing of plays and took to philanthropy. She even attempted, said Cowper, "to reform the unreformable Great" and her *Thoughts on the Importance of the Manners of the Great* (1788) went into many large editions. The tracts with which she tried to reform the poor, *Village Politics* (1793) and many of the *Repository Tracts* (1795–8), had an amazing success, and were found so well-suited to the purpose that the Religious Tract Society was formed to continue the work. Her poem

Bas Bleu, or Conversation, which owed its name, as she explained, to the mistake of a Frenchman who translated the English term literally, is an interesting comment on the whole movement. Her most popular book, *Coelebs in Search of a Wife*, appeared in 1809.

Mrs Chapone, born Hester Mulso (1727–1801), occasionally gave blue-stocking receptions that were "rational, instructive and social", and also, unfortunately, somewhat spiritless and dull. Her *Letters on the Improvement of the Mind* (1777), in its day considered an educational work of the first import-ance, is now only interesting as presenting an obsolete ideal of female propriety.

The blue-stockings were sometimes ridiculous, but they must not be dis-missed as unimportant. They did much to diffuse a general interest in literature and they helped to make society more decent.

XVI. CHILDREN'S BOOKS

Books for children can be divided into two classes, books that convey information and books that offer, or seem to offer, entertainment. The general defect of all early books for children may be put thus, that in lauding truth they denounce fiction as falsehood. "Keep them", says Hugh Rhodes's *Boke of Nurture* (c. 1545) "from reading of feigned fables, vain fantasies, and wanton stories, and songs of love, which bring much mischief to youth". A terrible fact in the history of controversy, whether political or religious, is that the minds of children are the favourite battleground of ruthless adults. The religious fanatics of the sixteenth and succeeding centuries tormented the minds of children with fears of speedy death and the almost unescapable certainty of hell-fire. Thomas White, Minister of the Gospel, in *A Little Book for Little Children* (1702)—there were two books of this name—urges the young not to read Ballads and foolish Books, and offers them instead horrible stories of martyrdoms drawn from Foxe. The anonymous *Young Man's Calling etc.* (1685) outdoes White in examples of martyrdom. The most widely read of these oppressive compilations was James Janeway's *Token for Children: being an Exact Account of the Conversion, Holy and Exemplary Lives, and Joyful Deaths of Several Young Children* (?1720) a supreme example of morbid and gloating piety.

It was the "chapbook", i.e. the books vended by "chapmen" or pedlars, that whispered the last enchantments of the middle ages into the ears of children during the eighteenth century and part of the nineteenth. Boys and girls were compelled to read the guides to goodness; but they loved to read the old stories. In these penny and twopenny booklets surviving fragments of the old romances were enshrined. Who wrote the versions is not known. They may have been abbreviations of old texts, or they may have been oral versions committed to print independently in some obscure way. They were issued all over the king-dom. Apparently they were not meant for children, for some have the kind of coarseness which it is the privilege of adults to enjoy; but children seized upon them as they seized upon *The Pilgrim's Progress* and *Gulliver's Travels* and *Robin-son Crusoe*. The indigenous heroes of Britain—Tom Thumb, the several Jacks, Tom Hickathrift, Friar Bacon and others—were here preserved in a vernacular epic cycle. Wordsworth in *The Prelude* refers with affection to these old romantic stories. After 1800 the chapbooks ceased to be issued. James Catnach of the Seven Dials printed them to death and better things took their places.

The chief additions made in the eighteenth century to books in forms suitable for children were *Crusoe, Gulliver, Philip Quarll* (a pseudo-Crusoe), collections of nursery rhymes, various versions of Perrault, and later the Arabian tales. *The Arabian Nights* reached England early in the eighteenth century from Galland's French version. In 1697 Charles Perrault published his *Histoires ou Contes du Tems Passé* supposed to have been related by his own little son—who might have heard them from his nurse. An English translation appeared about 1729, and English children possessed for ever the stories of Red Riding Hood, Bluebeard and Cinderella. The deep significance of nursery rhymes may be left to the anthropologist and the psycho-analyst; but the important literary fact is that when *Tommy Thumb's Pretty Song Book* (1744) was published in two volumes some unknown hand established a classic. Other collections followed without adding much new matter. The various *Mother Goose* volumes probably derived their name from Perrault's frontispiece, which bore the legend *Contes de ma mère l'Oye*; but who the aboriginal Mother Goose may have been is unknown.

The production of children's books had been a matter of chance. John Newbery first made a great business of it. Before the mid-century he settled at the address in St Paul's Churchyard so long associated with his name. Most famous of his publications was *Goody Two Shoes*, said to have been written by Goldsmith. The great characteristic of Newbery's books is that they were attractively produced. Of his successors and imitators we need say nothing, except that William Godwin the philosopher, among his many luckless activities, set up as a publisher of children's books and gave the world the Lambs' *Tales from Shakespeare*.

The period which ended in 1825 may be described as one of strife between the moral tale and the fairy tale. The moral tales of Hannah More and Mrs Chapone were certainly well written, and even the redoubtable Mrs Sarah Trimmer, so eminently "good", wrote one really notable child's book apart from tracts and educational works, though probably it would not be recognized by its original title: *Fabulous Histories: Designed for the Instruction of Children, respecting their Treatment of Animals* (1786). Here are to be met those excellent little robins, Pecksy, Flapsy, Robin and Dick; here, too, the learned pig is gravely discussed. But Mrs Trimmer was so much afraid of "French principles" that she supported a denunciation of *Cinderella* as a compendium of vice. Mrs Mary Martha Sherwood was another antagonist of the fairies. Her most famous work, *The Fairchild Family* (1813-8), is still read, though not seriously. Her other sedulously righteous books need not be named. Maria Edgeworth, who echoed her father's devotion to Rousseau, has already been mentioned (p. 505). The most famous disciple of Rousseau, however, was the eccentric Thomas Day. It has been said that in France Rousseau produced a Revolution, but that in England he produced *Sandford and Merton*. Day's famous work (1783-9) now survives as a joke, but the reader who can see past the egregious Mr Barlow will find much excellent matter in it.

After *Divine Songs* by Isaac Watts, the most celebrated book of verses for children is *Original Poems* (1804) by Ann and Jane Taylor, members of a numerous family, all of whom wrote industriously. Here we have several established favourites, of which the best known, perhaps, is *Twinkle, Twinkle, Little Star*. An anonymous contributor to the volume was Adelaide O'Keeffe (daughter of the dramatist) who also wrote books of her own. Two of her lines have not only fine rhythm but embody close observation:

> The dog will come when it is called;
> The cat will walk away.

Best of the imitators of the Taylors is Elizabeth Turner, whose *Cautionary Stories* are contained in the volumes prettily named *The Daisy* (1807) and *The Cowslip* (1811). *Poetry for Children* (1808) by Charles and Mary Lamb is less successful.

Eminent among the less pronounced philanthropists were Dr Aikin and his sister Mrs Barbauld, whose *Evenings at Home* (1792–6) is a companionable and homely miscellany. Charles and Mary Lamb's *Mrs Leicester's School* (1807) was certainly a moral book, and rather a dull one; but their greatest triumph was the *Tales from Shakespeare* (1807), mostly Mary's, Charles contributing only four tragedies. By all the rules this book should have failed. It mangles the plays, and the language is Shakespeare paraphrased without being made simple; nevertheless the book has had an enormous circulation.

Despite the moralists, the fairy or fanciful tale continued to flourish. William Roscoe's *The Butterfly's Ball and the Grasshopper's Feast* (1807), written for his son, is still remembered. The modern era can be dated almost by one book— George Cruikshank's edition of the *German Popular Stories* of the brothers Grimm (1824–6). Once again, English childhood re-entered fairyland by foreign aid. *Dame Wiggins of Lee* (1823) attracted the attention and eulogy of Ruskin. *The History of Sixteen Wonderful Old Women* (1820) contains the first instance of the metrical form commonly called the limerick, usually ascribed to Edward Lear. A further step forward was made by Sir Henry Cole ("Felix Summerly") and his publisher in the volumes of *The Home Treasury* (1843, etc.); and Catherine Sinclair's delightful *Holiday House* (1893) showed that not only was amusement harmless, but naughtiness itself might be venial and even pleasant. William and Mary Howitt wrote many attractive books, and Mary has the honour of first introducing Hans Christian Andersen in 1846. "Peter Parley", a name that covered several writers, not all definitely identified, was popular in many forms, and Harriet Martineau's *The Playfellow* (1841) in four parts contained stories (like *Feats on the Fiord*) which, when published separately, had a long run.

So we find ourselves passing into the vast juvenile and nonsense literature of the Victorian period. This is not our immediate concern; but we can say at once that there is no better proof of the greatness of a household, a country, or a period than its readiness to laugh at itself and to concede to the young complete liberty of reading.

CHAPTER XII

THE NINETEENTH CENTURY. PART I

I. SCOTT

Walter Scott (1771–1832) was born in Edinburgh, then almost a foreign city to Englishmen, the son of a lawyer and the descendant of stout Border ancestors. A mischance of infancy left him lame for life but did not abate his extraordinary physical vigour. Debarred from youthful sports he grew up with books, and, even better, with a tenaciously remembered store of Border ballads and tales. He received the usual education at the Edinburgh High School and University, but was not "bookish" in the schoolmaster's sense. In 1785 he entered his father's office and was admitted advocate in 1792. Legal duties first carried him into the Highlands at a time when the '45 was less than "sixty years since". He had in a high degree the happy gift of being at home with people of every kind and of making them at home with him. Thus he grew naturally into a keen understanding of human character. In 1792 he made the first of his seven annual "raids" into the wild and primitive district of Liddesdale, to explore the remains of old castles and peels, to pick up such samples as were obtainable of "the ancient riding ballads", to collect other relics of antiquity and to enjoy "the queerness and the fun" associated with the rough hospitality of those unsophisticated regions. All these circumstances combined to give Scott, from childhood to manhood, a full education in and through the "matter of Scotland" —and especially in the "matter" of pre-Reformation Scotland. The blighting hand of the Kirk had been laid not merely upon human instincts and their humane expression, but upon the heroic national past. All that had happened in the Catholic period was regarded as the violence of idolatrous dark ages out of which the "Holy Willies" had led a repentant people. Burns never quite escaped the clutches of the Kirk; but Scott was free; and to a revival of interest in the past Scott contributed more than anyone. It was something to make the romance of Scotland known to the English; it was even more to make the romance of Scotland known to the Scottish.

The romantic ardour kindled in Scott by the traditional songs and stories moved him to make his first venture into print. Soon after he left school his enthusiasm for ballad poetry had been intensified by a reading of Percy's *Reliques*. He then began to seek for romantic stories in French and Italian; and when he acquired German he found a new balladry current in that tongue. Bürger's *Leonore* specially attracted him, and his first publication (anonymous) was *The Chase and William and Helen: two ballads from the German of Gottfried A. Bürger* (1796). This was followed in 1799 by a version of Goethe's *Goetz von Berlichingen*. The German romantic ballad, splendidly exemplified by Goethe's *Erlkönig*, which he translated rather feebly, appealed to Scott as a successful form of the "tale of terror", then popular. Having gained confidence by translation, he proceeded to imitation, and Monk Lewis accepted some of his ballads for the projected *Tales of Wonder*, which, however, did not appear till 1801. A slight pamphlet, *Apology for Tales of Terror* (1799), which included his ballad translations and imitations, was sent for private printing to an old schoolfellow, James Ballantyne of Kelso, and in this small way began a momentous association with that printer. But Scott now went on to consider a more ambitious work, a collection of all the Border songs that he knew. In 1799 he was made Sheriff of Selkirkshire. This appointment multiplied his opportunities for the acquisition of material and for augmenting his topographical knowledge. An acquaintance-ship with Richard Heber, the great book collector, greatly assisted his literary researches, and he received valuable suggestions from the remarkable young Borderer, John Leyden, from William Laidlaw his future steward, and from James Hogg. The book was published as *Minstrelsy of the Scottish Border* (1802) in two volumes, a third, which included ballad imitations by himself, Lewis and others being added in 1803. It was a very faulty collection, and it was much improved later. Scott mingled some of his texts to get a "best" version and took other liberties which are now regarded as editorially unsound. Nevertheless, with all its faults, the *Minstrelsy* was a splendid achievement. It made familiar a wealth of matter totally unknown outside the Border communities; it pre-served fragments of fast vanishing tradition; and it led to the more exact study which has produced the great ballad collections of modern times.

Scott was now ready for original composition. Three incidents combined in setting him to work. He received from the Countess of Dalkeith the Border legend of Gilpin Horner, "the goblin page"; he had finished editing the old metrical romance, *Sir Tristrem*; and he had heard recited the still unpublished *Christabel* of Coleridge, with its fascinating metrical scheme. He proposed there-fore to tell a Border story which should have the character both of a ballad and a metrical romance, expressed in something like the cadence of *Christabel*; but when he began to work at his poem, it insisted, as true creations ever will, on living its own life, and became a poetic romance supposed to be recited by an aged minstrel to the Duchess of Buccleugh and her ladies at Newark Castle. So came into existence Scott's first large original work, *The Lay of the Last Minstrel* (1805). The sequence of old Border scenes and incidents is elaborated with an admirable combination of antique lore, clan enthusiasm and vividly picturesque art. By nature Scott was a great improvisator; he created his impression more by the ardour and vividness of his presentation than by the charm of a subtle and finished art. His next poetical story, *Marmion* (1808), is so full of heroic matter on a large scale that its form seems almost unimportant. The culmination of the story is Flodden, and the fortunes of the faulty hero, Lord Marmion, are simply the means of approaching the great theme. In *The Lay*, said Scott, the force is laid on style; in *Marmion* on description. The opening picture of Norham Castle in the setting sun gives the keynote, and scene after scene follows culminating in the dramatic picture of the stress and tumult of the Flodden conflict. Some of its details are among the best known passages of Scott's poetry; but the story does not flow quite so freely as the happy improvisation of *The Lay*. In *The Lady of the Lake* (1810) the force is laid on incident. The poem sets before us an almost continuous succession of exciting occurrences.

Yet it lives chiefly by its enchanting descriptions of scenery. It made Loch Katrine part of every man's romantic geography. In construction it is simple. Introductory stanzas of Spenserian form lead to cantos in octosyllabics, with interspersed songs that are among the most familiar of lyrics. In *Rokeby* (1813) the force is laid on character. But the poem has never been really popular, we want Scott to write about the Border or Loch Katrine, not about Marston Moor; but at least we must admit that he has included in it two of his most delightful songs. In *The Lord of the Isles* (1818), again, the historic interest is powerful—almost too powerful; but the pageantry of the poem is admirably managed. Of the less important romances—*The Vision of Don Roderick* (1811), *The Bridal of Triermain* (1813) and *Harold the Dauntless* (1817)—little need be said; nor need we do more than chronicle Scott's well-meant dramatic efforts—*Halidon Hill* (1822), *Macduff's Cross* (1822), *The Doom of Devorgoil* (1830) and *The Tragedy of Auchindrane* (1830). The genius of Scott was too Homeric for the drama, but his power as a writer of pure lyric is underestimated. In the novels, as well as in the poetic romances, there are lyrical strains of exquisite quality. Even Burns could never have achieved the haunting suggestion of *Proud Maisie*.

Scott had come to the end of his resources as a writer of tales in verse. Moreover, his instrument had proved to be limited in range. His poems kindle a physical ardour, but they do not reach the profounder emotions. When Byron, borrowing some of his methods, applied them to more passionate uses, Scott frankly acknowledged his defeat and declined a contest in which he could not succeed. It was a happy decision. His poetic romances represented a mere fraction of his endowments. His novels were to allow fuller scope for his natural gifts and acquirements, and for his wholesome humour as well as his comprehensive sympathies. Before he began his career as novelist he had reached his forty-third year, and he had served an arduous apprenticeship in literary and historical study. Merely to name his miscellaneous works, which included labours so diverse as editions of Swift and Dryden and numerous critical essays, would consume too much space. One general remark, however, should be made. Scott, full of antiquarian ardour, was never a mere antiquary. Like Dickens he populated every region he described, and his memorable characters are in number second only to those of the later master. What is most astonishing is that his life as a novelist covered only eighteen years.

For reference it may be useful to have a bare list of the novels as published. They are as follows: *Waverley, or 'Tis Sixty Years Since* (1814); *Guy Mannering, or The Astrologer* (1815); *The Antiquary* (1816); *Tales of My Landlord* (*The Black Dwarf* and *Old Mortality*, 1816); *Tales of My Landlord*, Second Series (*The Heart of Midlothian*, 1818); *Rob Roy* (1818); *Tales of My Landlord*, Third Series (*The Bride of Lammermoor* and *The Legend of Montrose*, 1819); *Ivanhoe, A Romance* (1820); *The Monastery, A Romance* (1820); *The Abbot* (1820); *Kenilworth, A Romance* (1821); *The Pirate* (1822); *The Fortunes of Nigel* (1822); *Peveril of the Peak* (1822); *Quentin Durward* (1823); *St Ronan's Well* (1824); *Redgauntlet* (1824); *Tales of the Crusades* (*The Betrothed* and *The Talisman*, 1825); *Woodstock; or the Cavalier* (1826); *Chronicles of the Canongate* (*The Highland Widow, The Two Drovers, The Surgeon's Daughter*, 1827); *Chronicles of the Canongate*, Second Series (*St Valentine's Day; or The Fair Maid of Perth*, 1828); *Anne of Geierstein*;

or *The Maiden of the Mist* (1829); *Tales of My Landlord*, Fourth Series (*Count Robert of Paris* and *Castle Dangerous*, 1832). All the novels except the *Tales of My Landlord* and the *Chronicles of the Canongate* were described as "By the Author of Waverley". Their success was, as people now say, "sensational". Indeed, as far as any creative work can be called new, *Waverley* was an entirely new phenomenon in the world of novels—new in setting, in incident, in character, in historical interest, and, what can easily be overlooked, new in the authoritative touch of a master's hand. It made an immense success and set people speculating eagerly about the author. Oddly enough the next two novels, *Guy Mannering* and *The Antiquary* were not historical, but were tales of contemporary life. Both are among the very best in sheer interest of story and in richness of characterization. Many good judges like *The Antiquary* best of all, and never tire of reading it. With *Old Mortality* (another triumph) Scott plunged back into the past, and there remained for some time, passing with ease from century to century. His variety is immense. *The Heart of Midlothian* succeeds as tragedy of the domestic kind. *The Bride of Lammermoor* succeeds as tragedy of the loftier kind. *Ivanhoe, Kenilworth* and *Quentin Durward* are triumphant historical romances. *Rob Roy* carries us excitedly into wild Highland adventure. *The Legend of Montrose* and *Wandering Willie's Tale* in *Redgauntlet* are masterpieces in the lesser dimensions.

To dwell upon each novel in turn is hardly necessary. A few general questions naturally arise. How was it that Scott did not discover his true strength till he was well past middle age? The answer is that his true strength was already displayed in his verse-romances. All his poems were, in fact, short novels, written in verse. He did not cease to be a poet when he wrote his prose tales. The next question, whether he would have passed to prose stories without the stimulus of Byron's greater popularity in verse can be partly answered by saying that *Waverley*, published in 1814, had been begun, in a fashion, several years earlier—in fact, before Byron had published anything. Another natural question is why Scott concealed his authorship for so many years. Scott was over forty when *Waverley* was published. He had a great reputation to lose if his new venture proved a failure. So he decided to run no risks and to publish his novel (as many predecessors, including Jane Austen, had published theirs) anonymously. Further, there is both excitement and freedom in writing unobserved and unknown. *Waverley* having proved a success, he would not risk a tame anti-climax by putting his name to the next. In other words, Scott saw material advantage in maintaining the mystery; and to material advantage Scott was never insensible. He was an imperial spender. His great ambition—an ignoble ambition, some may think it —was to found a new house of Scott. A great house, a great estate and a great name—these were the infirmity of his noble mind; and to achieve them he plunged into dubiously honest speculations with printing and publishing and fell to ruin. The tragedy was complete; for by the time his obligations were discharged and a new fortune might, after his death, have come from the copyrights, his sons were dead, and there were no "Scotts of Abbotsford" left.

Scott has Homeric qualities. He has, beyond any question, the note of greatness. Like Shakespeare, he does not judge, he records. His set and unrelated descriptive passages, new and fascinating to his own contemporaries, have become tedious; but when he brings nature into his story he is superb. The special quality of Scott is the peculiar combination in him of the humorist with the romance writer, of the man of the world with the devoted lover of nature and ardent worshipper of the past. With him, romance was not primarily the romance of love, but the general romance of human life, of the world and its activities, and, more especially, of the warring, adventurous past. Unlike Jane Austen, Scott was unnatural with the conventional and at ease with the eccentric. His almost mechanical rapidity of production forbade any kind of revision. How immensely he might have bettered the literary quality of his novels by careful revision there is sufficient proof in that splendid masterpiece *Wandering Willie's Tale*, the manuscript of which shows many important amendments. His tremendous efforts to meet the liabilities of his financial imprudence cost him his life. There are few more affecting stories in literary biography than his long Odyssey in search of health and his return home to die.

The vogue of Scott extended to Europe and greatly influenced the course of romantic story. Of modern English writers Scott and Byron had the largest following on the Continent, and in France, especially, coloured and stimulated the great romantic movement at the beginning of the nineteenth century. Scott was intensely curious about larger areas of life and time than any novelist before him, and he enlarged the sympathies, the emotions, the experience, of his readers. Clara Reeve and Ann Radcliffe had written about the past and the remote as if they were unreal and unsubstantial; Scott made the past and the remote a credible extension of normal life. And so, after Scott, could come Alexandre Dumas and Victor Hugo.

II. BYRON

George Gordon (1788–1824), sixth Lord Byron, was the only son of "Mad Jack" Byron by his second marriage with the Scottish heiress, Catherine Gordon. The father had formerly married and greatly ill-used the Marchioness of Carmarthen, who bore him a daughter, Augusta, with whom, later, Byron's name was scandalously connected. The poet was born in London, but, owing to his father's withdrawal to France to escape from his creditors, he was brought very soon by his mother to Aberdeen. Here his early years were spent, and the impressions which he received of Deeside, Lochnagar and the Grampians remained with him throughout his life and left their mark upon his poetry. He was only three when his father died, and he was brought up by his mother, who was almost the worst conceivable of parents. Harassed by poverty, and alternating hatred and passion for the beautiful lame child, she stung him by mocking at his deformity and maddened him by her furies of rage. He ran as wild as a colt on the Scottish mountain side. Suddenly all was changed. By the death of his great-uncle in 1798, the boy succeeded to the title and the Byron estates of Newstead Priory and Rochdale. People who have professed inability to understand what they call Byron's pose of misanthropy have forgotten many things, but specially they have forgotten the fiercely proud, acutely sensitive child tormented throughout his most impressionable years by the indignities of poverty and the furious passions of a half-distracted mother. Few young poets have had a more lamentable childhood.

But he was happy at Harrow. Byron had the gift of attracting friends, and he read widely and promiscuously in history and biography, but never became an exact scholar. To these schoolboy years belongs the story of his romantic, unrequited love for Mary Ann Chaworth. From Harrow Byron proceeded to Trinity College, Cambridge; but the University, though it widened his circle of friends, never quite won his affections. While at Harrow, he had written a number of short poems, and in January 1807 he printed for private circulation a slender volume of verse, *Fugitive Pieces*, the favourable reception of which led to the publication, in the following March, of *Hours of Idleness*. This was avowedly the work of a boy, and though it contains some of the worst pieces ever written by a great poet, it also contains some promising matter, and deserved something better than the elaborate horseplay to which Brougham subjected it in *The Edinburgh Review*. Being one of those wicked men who defend themselves when attacked, Byron replied in 1809 with the famous *English Bards and Scotch Reviewers*, as fine a satire as any young man of his age ever produced. His sudden maturity is remarkable. When he came of age he took his seat in the House of Lords, and though, like Disraeli, he did not instantly succeed, there is no reason to suppose that in happier circumstances he would have failed in politics.

In 1809 Byron set out with his friend John Cam Hobhouse for a tour in the East. He was away for more than a year, and the impressions he received of the life and scenery of Spain, Portugal and the Balkan peninsula profoundly affected his mind and influenced his subsequent work. His letters form a singularly vivid record of the gay life of Spanish cities, the oriental feudalism of Ali Pasha's Albanian court, and, above all, of the aspirations and memories that clustered round Athens. The Near East, now familiar to every tourist, was in those days as remote and legendary as the deserts of Asia. The earliest fruits of his travels were the first two cantos of *Childe Harold* (1812), which not only made him instantly famous but remain among his most characteristic works. The romantic Childe was, rightly or wrongly, identified with the poet himself and increased the glamour that surrounded his person. For three years he was the idol of English society, and was pursued by adoring ladies, one of whom, the novelist Lady Caroline Lamb, wife of Lord Melbourne, created a public scandal by her infatuation.

In 1815 came the great tragedy of Byron's life, his marriage to Miss Anne Milbanke. There is no reason to suppose that he desired anything but a quiet settlement in life with a person who offered not merely grace and beauty, but the promise of peace. Byron was unspoiled by adulation and was an affectionate man, as his numerous friendships prove. But there came a sudden fatal breach, and early in 1816, shortly after the birth of his daughter Ada, Lady Byron left his house, and the most brilliant and most fascinating Englishman of the day was driven by slanderous tongues into exile, and never saw child, wife or England again. Lady Byron herself accused him of nothing but "insanity"; and though there was a formal separation, no dissolution of the marriage was ever proposed. It is probable that the main truth is very simple: Byron, like other men of genius, married the wrong person. Lady Byron was a narrowly righteous woman who devoted herself to charitable works. She was good in the kind of way utterly disastrous to a man of genius with his moods and impulses, his ardours and exaltations. But speculation is not our affair. What concerns us is that Byron was both bewildered in mind and lacerated in feeling. But he was not the man to beg for explanations or to endure a second insult. Macaulay well observed in the *Edinburgh Review* fifteen years later that there is "no spectacle so ridiculous as the British public in one of its periodical fits of morality". Byron knew well enough what Regency morality was like, and to be called black by very dirty vessels at once amused and disgusted him. In Venice, his new home, he prepared himself for the task of levelling against social hypocrisy the keenest weapons which a piercing wit and versatile genius had placed at his command.

The inevitable question whether we gained or lost by Byron's perpetual exile can be answered without difficulty. That the man who died for Greece might have done much for England during the agitation for Parliamentary Reform and Catholic Emancipation is pure surmise; what can be affirmed without hesitation is that we gained not only a superb writer of letters which are some of the gayest in our language, but a poet of European understanding. Byron was the first of English poets to write with that larger sympathy. His friends at home saved him from being cut off from native interests, and he found in a fellow exile, Shelley, a fruitful companion. Thus his poems, though written on foreign ground, were addressed to (and sometimes directed at) his own lost country. He assailed with scathing contempt the poets, like Southey, Coleridge and Wordsworth, who had reconciled themselves with what he considered political degeneration. Even in the early *English Bards and Scotch Reviewers* he had denounced the new romantics and lauded Dryden and Pope as the heroes of classical tradition. Nor was this mere perversity. A careful reading of his works will show that while much of Byron's poetry enlarges the horizon of romanticism, he never wholly broke away from the Augustan poetic diction. Pope he revered, and he defended him in *A Letter to John Murray, Esq. on the Rev. W. L. Bowles's Strictures on the Life and Writings of Pope* (1821).

Byron was not, like Macaulay's Jacobite, an exile pining for home. He had been as deeply affected by his early travels through southern Europe as Goethe had been by his Italian journey. Life under the wide-waving Crescent was the reality of romance. The stirring scenes that Scott recalled from the past were enacted every day under Byron's own eyes among the fastnesses of Albania. Southey and Moore got up their oriental poems from books; Byron drew upon his own experience. When *Childe Harold* was begun at Janina in 1809, the hero may have seemed to his creator an imaginary figure; but between the composition of the first two cantos and the third there had intervened for Byron a bitter and wounding experience. The third (1816) and fourth (1818) cantos show, in comparison with the first two, a far greater intensity of feeling and a deeper reading of life. Something of the early glitter remains; but it is no longer cold. The schoolmasters have done their worst with the Waterloo stanzas without diminishing their beauty; and as we move onwards through the Alps and Italy, the verse of Byron fits the scene with words that are instantly recalled by every lettered traveller.

There were Eastern pieces belonging to what we may call the pre-separation period. *The Giaour* (1813), *The Bride of Abydos* (1813), *The Corsair* (1814), *Lara*

(1814), *The Siege of Corinth* (1816), and *Parisina* (1816), were hastily written to please the public and to divert the poet himself. After making his home on the Continent, Byron attempted verse of another kind; but the appearance of *The Prisoner of Chillon* in 1816, *Mazeppa* in 1819, and *The Island* in 1823 shows that he never wholly relinquished his delight in the verse-tale. Upon some of the earlier stories the influence of Scott is discernible; *The Corsair* and *Lara* indicate that Byron had passed from Scott to Dryden. In *Parisina*, and still more in *The Prisoner of Chillon*, there is a welcome return to a simpler style. Love of political freedom, always the noblest of his passions, inspired *The Prisoner of Chillon*, which is both dignified and sincere. *The Island*, the last of Byron's verse-tales, written just before his fatal journey, shows that his powers were unimpaired.

To the years that succeeded his final departure from England belong his works in dramatic form. As in the poems, there is alternation between the romantic and the classical modes. *Manfred* (1817), *Cain* (1821), and *Heaven and Earth* (1824) are romantic alike in spirit and structure; *Marino Faliero* (1820), *The Two Foscari* (1821), and *Sardanapalus* (1821) represent a deliberate attempt on the part of the author to break loose from the domination of the Elizabethan masters and to fashion tragedy on the neo-classic principles of Racine and Alfieri. This has nothing to do with date. When his theme is romantic Byron is romantic; when his theme is historical he is classical. In *Manfred*, as in the third canto of *Childe Harold*, we recognize the spell which the Alps exercised on Byron's genius. Some influence from Goethe's *Faust* appears in the opening soliloquy; but the characteristic Byronic manner appears in the main story depicting an outcast from society, stained with crime, and proudly solitary. The play is as much and as little autobiographical as the other works. In *Cain* we witness the final stage in the evolution of the Byronic hero. The note of rebellion against social order and against authority is stronger than ever; but the conflict is one of the intellect rather than of the passions. In its day *Cain* was considered gross blasphemy; readers of the present time are more likely to admire its idyllic passages. *Heaven and Earth*, written in fourteen days, was taken as an act of repentance for the impiety of *Cain*; but as it is fragmentary, incoherent and even uninteresting, the supposed repentance seems incomplete. When we pass from Byron's romantic and supernatural dramas to his Venetian tragedies and *Sardanapalus*, we enter a very different world. Here, in the observance of the unities, the setting of the scenes and in all that goes to constitute the technique of drama, the principles of classicism are observed. *Sardanapalus* is, from every point of view, a greater success than either of the Venetian tragedies. In *Werner* and *The Deformed Transformed* there is a return to the romantic pattern, but neither carries conviction.

It is an easy transition from Byron's historical dramas to such poems as *The Lament of Tasso* and *The Prophecy of Dante*, which take the form of dramatic soliloquies. The mood of *The Lament* is one of unavailing sadness; *The Prophecy* is both more ambitious and more charged with personal emotion. The Dante who speaks is the apostle of that political liberty which had grown dear to Byron at a time when he was living in a country that lay under the Austrian yoke. To complain that Byron's *terza rima* fails to reproduce Dante's effect is uncritical. No English *terza rima* can reproduce the Italian, which is full of the feminine rhymes unnatural in the English language.

The most important group of Byron's poems still remains for consideration. His discovery of the Italian medley-poem, written in the *ottava rima*, was for him a revelation. His wavering between the classical and romantic principles ended in a reconciliation of both in a new medium of satirical burlesque, unconstrained and whimsical, and delighting in the sudden anticlimaxes and grotesque incongruities which find a spacious hiding-place in the *ottava rima*. It was Frere's *The Monks and the Giants* (1817) which first disclosed to him, as he gratefully acknowledges, the fitness of the metre for effects of this sort. But his true masters are the Italians themselves—Pulci in the fifteenth century, Berni in the sixteenth and Casti in the eighteenth. Had he not been an exile, he would never have written his great comic masterpieces, for they are Italian through and through. *Beppo* might be a tale from the *Decameron*. In *The Vision of Judgment* the verse remains the same but embodies a different spirit. Southey's fulsome panegyric of George III with this title becomes the text for delightful mockery and pungent satire. In *Don Juan*, the work upon which his powers were chiefly expended during the last years in Italy (1818–23), Byron attains to the full disclosure of his personality and the final expression of his genius. The variety both of matter and style is infinite, and the metrical invention unflagging. From any point of view *Don Juan* is unique.

The last and greatest chapter in Byron's life begins in 1821 with the Greek struggle for liberation from Turkey. The movement found many enthusiastic supporters among the English, especially those who had been inspired by the second canto of *Childe Harold*, and Byron decided to devote himself actively to the cause. Just before setting sail in 1824 he received a highly courteous greeting in verse from Goethe. On his arrival he found affairs grossly mismanaged, chiefly through ridiculous factions among the Greeks themselves. In his labours to secure effective unity Byron showed himself a practical statesman and a born leader of men. But the end was near. In April 1824 he was seized with rheumatic fever after sailing wet to the skin in an open boat; and on the nineteenth he died. His death was a severe blow to Greece, and plunged the nation into profound grief; when the news reached England, Tennyson, then a boy of fourteen, carved the words "Byron is dead" upon a rock at Somersby and exclaimed "the whole world seemed darkened to me". Had he lived he might have been king of liberated Greece. His body was brought to England, and, Westminster refusing him, he was buried in the village church of Hucknall Torkard, outside the gates of Newstead Abbey, once his home. Such was the end of this great and famous Englishman, better understood and appreciated abroad than by his own people. It is a superficial view that finds Byron monotonously Byronic. Like other great poets he is always himself. His variety is as remarkable as his vivacity. Only in the pure lyric is he below the best; and so the reader should not seek to know Byron in selections. *Childe Harold*, *The Vision of Judgment* and *Don Juan* alone will convince any responsive spirit that Byron at his best is not only a great poet, but the kind of poet the world always needs to mock its baser and inspire its loftier movements.

III. SHELLEY

The younger group of poets, Byron, Shelley and Keats, was separated from the elder, Wordsworth, Southey and Coleridge, by almost a generation. The latter responded eagerly to the great uprising of peoples that began in 1789; the former rebelled against the revival of traditional oppression that began after 1815. This difference is curiously marked by the fact that while the earlier group drew its inspiration from the motherland, the latter was almost foreign, two living in banishment and drawing their inspiration from the life of other lands and the third retreating still further into ancient mythology. Tory society, which received the older group into its bosom, laid a heavy hand on the younger. Byron, whom it feared, was driven into exile; Keats, whom it derided, was bludgeoned; Shelley, whom it loathed, was caught in the meshes of the law. The tragic and early deaths of all three seemed a judgment on manifest wickedness.

The most obnoxious of all to the compilers of the Six Acts was Percy Bysshe Shelley (1792–1822), grandson of a baronet and the descendant of Sussex squires. At his first school he became an eager reader and began to study chemistry. At Eton he was fascinated by the classics and science and studied the sceptical and scientific Lucretius, as well as the English eighteenth-century philosophers. Here, too, he wrote two wild and worthless romances, *Zastrozzi* (1808) and *St Irvyne, or the Rosicrucian* (1810), and collaborated with his sister Elizabeth in *Original Poetry by Victor and Cazire* (1810), the year in which he entered University College, Oxford. There, with his friend Thomas Jefferson Hogg, he produced in 1811 a pamphlet, *The Necessity of Atheism*, which caused the expulsion of both. This date begins a series of disasters. Shelley, lodging alone in London, was attracted by a pretty girl of sixteen named Harriet West-brook, daughter of a retired coffee-house keeper. He took Harriet to Edinburgh, where they went through an irregular marriage ceremony in August 1811, the husband being nineteen and the wife less than seventeen. He sought the acquaintance of Godwin, being attracted by his political individualism and his ethical determinism. The one appealed to Shelley's hatred of tyranny, the other to his passion for ideal unity. But things were not going well. Harriet could not live up to Shelley, and Shelley could not live down to Harriet. Their precocious ardour had cooled. Two characteristic adventures took place at this time, one a propagandist visit to Ireland, and the other a brief stay at Bracknell with some ardent vegetarians, where he met Peacock, who could never have been a vegetarian, ardent or tepid. The literary product of the latter adventure was *A Vindication of Natural Diet* (1813). In Ireland Shelley strangely hoped to begin his conversion of the world. He wrote several pamphlets, the chief being an *Address to the Irish People*, but he left that intractable island bitterly disillusioned.

All this time there had been another woman in the background, Elizabeth Hitchener, a Sussex schoolmistress, ten years his senior, who was madly enamoured of him and aspired to marry him, and with whom during 1811 and 1812 he maintained a correspondence which began with philosophy and ended with ardours. Harriet knew of the correspondence, joined in it, and did not object till moved by her sister. Shelley invited Miss Hitchener to visit them at Lynmouth in the summer of 1812 after the Irish fiasco. She made herself intolerable to everybody, especially to Shelley, who felt at last that he ought to do something about her and proposed his remedy for every ill, an annuity till she was settled. Few people escaped Shelley's well-meant monetary gifts.

At Lynmouth he had written *A Declaration of Rights* in order to produce in England the emancipation he had failed to produce in Ireland. He scattered copies in the air by balloons, and in the sea by bottles; but the only practical effect was the six months' imprisonment of his own servant, who had been caught posting advertisements of the seditious publication in Barnstaple. His *Letters to Lord Ellenborough* (1812) advocating the release of Thomas Paine's publisher had no other result than the retention of the unfortunate man in gaol. Shelley then settled in Wales at Tremadoc, where he took up with enthusiasm the building of a seawall. Meanwhile he was writing his first long poem, *Queen Mab*, which, when published surreptitiously in 1813, did him great damage. In that year his daughter Ianthe was born and in the next a son, Charles. Hearing that his Scottish marriage with Harriet was not legal, he married her again in England, although the estrangement between them was almost complete. A few months later they separated for ever.

Shelley then fell violently in love with Mary Wollstonecraft Godwin, daughter of the two philosophers. As he could not marry her, they went off together to Switzerland in 1814, with Clara ("Claire") Clairmont, daughter of the second Mrs Godwin, as companion. After a return to England Mary bore him a son early in 1816, but Shelley, now tired of the Godwins, set out again for Switzerland with Mary and the inevitable Claire, whose intrigue with Byron was unknown to them. The great event of this journey was the meeting with Byron at Geneva. Byron's interest in ghost stories prompted Mary to begin *Frankenstein*. But the restless pair were soon back in England, and there tragedy fell upon them. In October 1816 Fanny Imlay, Mary's half-sister, killed herself —it was alleged without foundation that a hopeless passion for Shelley had made her desperate; and then in December Harriet committed suicide. Shelley, now free, at once married Mary. Admirers of Shelley declare that Harriet's death had nothing whatever to do with Shelley; but it is not pleasant to find him writing to Mary, "everyone does me full justice, bears testimony to the upright spirit and liberality of my conduct to her". The critics who can see nothing but evil in Byron, and nothing but idealism in Shelley, should really ask themselves whether in the life of any poet there is such a trail of disasters as that which this "beautiful but ineffectual angel" left behind him from 1811 to 1816, in full conviction of his own righteousness and his importance in the regeneration of the world.

The suicide of Harriet led at once to Chancery proceedings, prompted by her implacable sister; and the case dragged through 1817, while Shelley and Mary were settled at Marlow, with Peacock as neighbour. Lord Eldon, the Tory Chancellor, having considered Shelley's life, and having had portions of *Queen Mab* explained to him, deprived Shelley of the custody of his two children. Ianthe married and lived to a good age; Charles died in childhood. They had no part in Shelley's life. In March 1818 he left England for ever, accompanied, as usual, by Claire Clairmont, with her tragic little daughter Allegra. In Italy he renewed his acquaintance with Byron, and visited Venice, Naples, Rome, Leghorn and settled at last in Pisa. His first children by Mary both died, but in 1819 another son, Percy Florence, was born, who succeeded to the baronetcy and lived to 1889. The final move was made to a lonely villa on the Bay of Spezzia. New and important friends had been made: Edward John Trelawny —who wrote *Adventures of a Younger Son* (1831) and *Recollections of the Last Days of Shelley and Byron* (1858)—Edward Williams and his "wife" Jane, and an appealingly romantic young woman, Emilia Viviani. Old friends like Medwin and Hogg reappeared. The beginning of a friendship with Keats was ended by the younger poet's death. In June Shelley left Spezzia to meet Leigh Hunt at Leghorn. The meeting was very happy. On 8 July 1822 Shelley and Williams left Leghorn for Spezzia in their boat and never arrived. No one knows what happened. The bodies were washed up some days later at Viareggio and were cremated on the shore in the presence of Byron, Leigh Hunt and Trelawny, the last of whom snatched Shelley's heart from the expiring flames, and this and the other remains were gathered into a casket and buried by the wall of the old Protestant cemetery in Rome, under the shadow of the Pyramid of Caius Cestius.

Shelley's last years were made happy by friends and comparative peace; but his life with Mary was not entirely successful. His interest in Jane "Williams", in Emilia Viviani, and in some other women, excited in Mary a resentment that almost amounted to jealousy. However, the shock of her loss and the new duty of editing her husband's scattered and unfinished verses gave a fullness to Mary's life, and she was left with two great memories from the past, Shelley's love and Shelley's death. The reader of Shelley must remember that the poet had no chance of revising or suppressing his early, ill-considered work, and that much of his later work was published by Mary and was never overseen by him.

It has been necessary to dwell at some length upon the life of Shelley in order to account for the abhorrence in which he was held. Disaster had left Byron free to pursue a course already begun; disaster had found Shelley with his true vocation undiscovered. In *Queen Mab* Shelley's Godwinian creed is proclaimed from the mouths of legendary personages. He was soon to leave *Queen Mab* far behind. In 1815 he wrote *Alastor*, his first authentic and unmistakable poem, modelled upon the austere music of Wordsworth's blank verse. Its final lines are some of his noblest. He endeavoured to set out in prose some of his philosophic convictions; but the unfinished essays *On Love*, *On Life*, *On a Future State*, *On Metaphysics*, *On Morals*, *On Christianity* are not remarkable as literature or as speculation, though they show that his mind was moving away from Godwin to some more spiritual philosophy. To his meeting and travels with Byron Shelley owed much. Their very difference was a stimulus. The *Mont Blanc* stanzas and *The Hymn to Intellectual Beauty*, belonging to this period, express the Shelleyan idealism with a new loftiness of assurance; but the state of England during the winter which followed (1816–17) offered little support to optimism, and Shelley expressed his feelings in a revolutionary epic. *Laon and Cythna* (later renamed *The Revolt of Islam*), written from 1817 to 1818, is a brilliant dream-fabric of poetry, with figures that wage the eternal war of love and truth against tyranny.

Kindred impulses inspired the fragment *Prince Athanase. Rosalind and Helen*, begun at Marlow and finished in Italy, is a Shelleyan attempt at the romantic tale to which Scott and Byron had lent a vogue. The spell of Italy first becomes fully apparent in the poems composed at Byron's villa near Este—especially in *Lines written among the Euganean Hills*. The cynicism of the disillusioned elder poet called out in protest all Shelley's faith and hope for men. *Julian and Maddalo* gives a fascinating account, undoubtedly true in substance, of their intimate talk. From Este Shelley turned south. Many vivid letters to Peacock and the *Stanzas written in dejection near Naples* (December 1818) make the journey live for us. Since his arrival in Italy he had brooded over the plan of a lyrical drama. Of many competing themes he chose Prometheus; but not the Aeschylean Prometheus with its impotent conclusion. The story had to be transformed to fit Shelley's Godwinian faith in the perfectibility of man. Pain, death and sin were transitory ills. Religion, too, man would necessarily outgrow, for the gods were phantoms devised by his brain. So the tyrant Jupiter is thrust down, and his fall is the signal for the regeneration of humanity; man's evil nature slips off like a slough; Prometheus is "unbound". But, in a sense, his tragedy has newly begun, for in a series of visions he is shown what evil man will do to man; yet still the hope of final regeneration remains. Under forms of thought derived from the atheist and materialist Godwin, Shelley has given, in *Prometheus Unbound*, magnificent expression to the faith of Plato and of Jesus.

Unlike Byron, Shelley had no historic imagination and he felt little interest in the metropolis of Papacy. The one figure of medieval Rome that attracted him was Beatrice Cenci, and he resolved to make her the central figure of a poetic drama. In writing it he had in mind the great tragic actress Eliza O'Neill, and he sent the play to Covent Garden for performance. Not unnaturally it was declined. *The Cenci* as a tragedy for the stage does not really succeed. Cenci himself is a monster; Beatrice cannot justify her parricide, simply because the dreadful incentive is incapable of dramatic representation. Only in her death does Beatrice become a moving figure. *The Cenci* is a play for the study, not for the theatre.

Shelley did not attempt any further work for the stage. He was otherwise moved. In 1819 social discontent in England had become acute. The Peterloo affair roused his fierce indignation, and in brief stinging quatrains (with a few variations) he lashed the man whom he chose to hold responsible for the threatened revolution. *The Masque of Anarchy* is much more, however, than a derisive arraignment of the "arch-anarch" Castlereagh—a statesman later almost canonized. In another satiric outburst, *Peter Bell the Third*, Shelley attacks at once the reactionary politician and the "dull" poet who in earlier days had hailed with rapture the dawn of the revolution. The two indictments, for Shelley, hung together. Wordsworth was dull because he had been false to his early ideals. Wordsworth's poem (written in 1798) had been parodied by J. H. Reynolds, the friend of Keats; hence the "Third" in the title of Shelley's piece. It is the most pointed of his satirical poems. In the quasi-Aristophanic drama *Swellfoot the Tyrant* (1820), on the scandal of George IV and the Queen, Shelley's attempt at humour is drearily unsuccessful.

The beginning of 1820 found the Shelleys at Pisa, their home for the next two years. Here were written some of his best known poems—*The Sensitive Plant*, almost impalpably beautiful, *The Witch of Atlas*, a more airily playful essay in poetic myth-making, and a few experiments in narrative, *A Vision of the Sea*, *Orpheus*, and the fragmentary *Fiordispina*, which, however, with all their glimpses of alluring beauty, confirm the impression that story, as such, was never part of Shelley's strength. A stronger tone appears in the great revolutionary odes *To Naples* and *To Liberty* written in the intricate Pindaric form which Shelley now chose to embody his revolutionary ardour. But politics interpenetrated the poetry. *The Ode to the West Wind*, on the other hand, originates directly in that impassioned intuition which is the first condition of poetry. Nowhere does Shelley's voice reach a more poignantly personal note or more perfect spontaneity. *The Cloud* and *The Skylark*, everybody's favourites, are as remarkable for their varied music as for their inspired interpretation of mood. The *Letter to Maria Gisborne* (1820) commemorates an intellectual friendship, and reveals the Shelley of sparkling and sprightly converse. *Epipsychidion* (1821) commemorates a friendship of another kind. Shelley had lately translated the *Symposium* of Plato. In Emilia Viviani he thought he saw realized the visionary beauty which, from "youth's dawn", had beckoned to him in all the wonder and romance of the world. But sublime Platonic free love can hardly be transferred from the universal to the particular without causing some earthly trouble. Emilia, more than any of Shelley's kindred spirits, aroused the jealousy of Mary. *Epipsychidion* enshrines a rare and strange mode of feeling, accessible only to the few; we pass, however, into a larger air when we turn from this Platonist bridal hymn to the great elegy lamenting the death of Keats, which was felt by Shelley as a calamity for poetry, and for everything in nature and humanity to which poetry gives enduring expression. The stately Spenserian stanza of *Adonais* (1821), to which Shelley communicates a new magnificence of his own, accords well with the grandeur of the theme. It was at this richly creative period that Shelley wrote (1821) his memorable *Defence of Poetry*. Peacock's essay, *The Four Ages of Poetry*, had stirred him to a "sacred rage", and his *Defence* ranges far beyond the scope of literature. Poetry is defended as revealing the order and beauty of the Universe. Here, too, may be mentioned his letters, all fascinating, those to Miss Hitchener and to Harriet having special biographical value. In the flights of lovely song that came from Shelley during the last months there is more of tender intimacy than of cosmic magnificence. Most of them are inspired by his feelings for the "magnetic" Jane. There is almost a foreshadowing of the end in their note of evanescence. *Hellas* (1822), drawn from him by the Greek war of liberation, is itself a prolonged lyric, with a sighing cadence in its final chorus. In their last home on the Spezzian bay Shelley was working at *The Triumph of Life*. But the poem was never finished. The sea engulfed the poet and his song was done.

That Shelley is among the greatest lyric poets is beyond dispute. What is in question is the value of his larger works with their prevailing theme of creative love. Matthew Arnold accused him of lack of matter, and in a famous sentence described him as "a beautiful and ineffectual angel, beating in the void his luminous wings in vain." That will not quite do. There was much in Shelley's life that was not beautiful, not ineffectual and not angelic; but in his song there is a breath of the eternal spirit. No one supposes that the static life of perfect love envisaged by Shelley can exist in the material world. But it is still a vital question whether man is at the end of his spiritual resources, or whether he can continue the re-creation of himself to something nearer to the Shelleyan ideal. Is evil always to triumph? Must hate and death return, must men kill and die? To all readers Shelley will remain the consummate inventor of lyric harmonies; but to a few he will be still more precious for the glimpses he has given of a life more worthy of the spirit of man than that which now afflicts us.

IV. KEATS

John Keats (1795–1821) was the eldest son of a livery-stable keeper in Finsbury Pavement, London. Sent as a child of eight to a school at Enfield, he attracted the interest and, before long, the devoted friendship, of the junior master, Charles Cowden Clarke, to whom he owed his first initiation into poetry. Keats was not destined to go to any public school or university, but entered St Thomas's Hospital as a student, and lived in lodgings in the Borough. It is a fact, curious but perhaps not important, that Keats never had a home of his own. The numerous deaths in his family forced him into a succession of lodgings, and it was in a Roman lodging that he died. His attachment to medicine was not strong or permanent. His inclinations were as simply and purely poetical as those of any poet who has ever lived, and his first friends were men of letters. About 1813 Clarke read to the young surgeon's apprentice Spenser's *Epithalamion*, and put into his hands *The Faerie Queene*. From that moment his destiny was sealed. His earliest extant poem (1813) was an *Imitation of Spenser*. Yet Spenser was to count for less in his poetry than other Elizabethans to whom Spenser led him; and it was the arresting experience of "first looking into Chapman's Homer" that prompted his earliest great sonnet. There were less favourable influences. He met Leigh Hunt, and later at Hunt's cottage met Haydon, Hazlitt and Shelley. In Haydon's devotion to art there was much that a young poet could admire; in the Shelley of that time there was, as yet, hardly anything to admire. The sincere prose of Hazlitt was a strengthening influence; but the facile verses of Leigh Hunt were to be his undoing. His first volume of poems (1817) owed all its weakness to Hunt and its strength to himself. Keats, a mere boy, was in the gushing drawing-room song stage, and from Hunt he got increase not decrease of his faults. But with the songs and imitations came a group of sonnets, some very good, one, the Chapman's Homer, excellent; and after that, the long *Sleep and Poetry*, which, for all its occasional sinkings, is a vision of beauty, steadily growing richer as well as purer and more intense. Few young poets have written with more promise and greater accomplishment.

Endymion, the work of the twelve months from April 1817 to April 1818, has the invertebrate structure, the insecure style, the weakness in narrative and the luxuriance of colour and music natural to one who still lived more in sensation than in thought, but also the enchanted atmosphere and scenery, and the sudden reaches of vision, possible only to one whose senses were irradiated by imagination. The brief, manly and moving Preface tells us of the young poet's aspirations, and the poem itself, whatever its faults, is a testament of beauty that bears constant reading, and grows in grace and strength with every renewal of knowledge.

Before *Endymion* was complete, he had planned with his friend John Hamilton Reynolds a volume of tales from Boccaccio. Keats chose the fifth story of the fourth day of the *Decameron*, that of Lisabetta and the pot of basil. The clear Italian setting was harder for him than the loosely imagined classical scenes of *Endymion*; and it is not till after Lorenzo's murder that the imaginative transformation of the story becomes complete. What Boccaccio evaded Keats worked upon in the spirit of the old ghostly ballads, and made *Isabella* a tale of horror that is full of beauty. Superficially and technically *Isabella* is a better piece of work than *Endymion*, though below it in greatness as a poem; but both are immature when compared with the wonderful creations of the following autumn and spring. Those six months were a time of immensely rapid growth, not merely in imaginative power and technical mastery, but in intellectual range and vigour, and in moral grip. The man, as well as the genius, is awake. His letters, which take rank with *The Prelude* as a revelation of the growth of a poet's mind, are specially illuminating for the year 1818. The experiencing mind was beginning to find experience, and, as usual, in the beginning was a woman. Keats responded ardently to the appeal he found in Fanny Brawne. His work ceased to be tentative and became assured. The extraordinary beauty of the 1820 volume (i.e. the 1818–19 poems) and the equally extraordinary richness of his letters of the same period show us Keats developing in mind and feeling under the influence of his passion, and developing in technique because of his new energy. He was, like Shakespeare, a strongly "physical" poet, rejoicing in sounds, colours, textures, odours, and his physical ardour gives to the poems of this time an extraordinary richness. *The Eve of St Agnes* is unique in its combination of remote romantic beauty and palpable physical loveliness.

Endymion was published, and was battered by the brutes of *Blackwood* and the *Quarterly* in attacks that are permanent blots in the history of our literature. The Tory hounds were after the blood of anyone associated with Leigh Hunt, who had endured his persecution and imprisonment with a nobility and courage that discredited his persecutors. Keats offered a promising target, and the gentlemen of the press made the most of it. It is now the fashion to say that the hostile reviews made no difference to Keats. They certainly made no difference to Keats's development; he was going to make himself a poet in his own way without any quailing before Regency ruffianism; but the attacks made a great difference to Keats's actual health. He was sick with the pangs of love and he was very sick in body, after the hardships of a foolishly protracted tour through the Highlands, from which he returned to nurse his dying brother; and these wanton assaults came as a cruel addition to his many ills. There is, there can be, no defence. *Blackwood* pursued him even after death.

Keats was already past *Endymion*, and knew it perfectly well, without information from any critics. The ill-fated Scottish tour had been undertaken in part as a clearing of his spirit and a strengthening of his powers. Six months after the completion of *Endymion*, *Hyperion* was begun. It was a giant step forward, which neither the intimate study of Milton nor his first experience, on the

Highland tour, of mountain glory and gloom and of the relics of ancient beliefs, makes less wonderful. Whether he could have finished it we do not know; but when he felt that he was being oppressed by the spirit of Milton, who seemed to dictate his very form of verse, he deliberately ceased, and the great fragment ends with an uncompleted sentence. He took it up again in 1819 and tried to remodel it as *The Fall of Hyperion*, in the form of a vision. Though this is no more successful than the original, and indeed shows signs of failing powers, it is of great interest as showing the workings of the poet's mind. During 1819 he had been renewing his study of Dante in Cary's fine version, and *The Fall of Hyperion* approaches Dante as closely as *Hyperion* approaches Milton. There is a sense of symbolical vision about it, and it follows the Dantean conception (already implicit in *Sleep and Poetry*) of an ascent from garden to temple and thence to shrine. Thus insistently did Keats, with symbol and image, press home the thought that beauty, the ideal, can only be won through pain, and that poetry is incomplete if it evades and leaves unexpressed "the agonies, the strife of human hearts". Though *The Fall* does not equal *Hyperion*, it contains some lines which the poet never surpassed. It is unfortunate that this version of *Hyperion* was not published till 1856-7, and then mistakenly as a "first version"; and this it was generally taken to be for many years, on the editor's authority.

In describing *The Fall of Hyperion* we have diverted from the contents of the great volume of 1820. First in that marvellous volume came *Lamia*, a reversion to the romantic tale in couplets, with Dryden as a model. It is romance with a difference. Here Keats shows his mastery of a new kind of beauty—the beauty that has evil in it, the beauty of destruction. Though the poem has one or two touches of Keats at his worst, it is stronger, terser and tenser than anything he had so far written. Following *Lamia* came *Isabella*, already discussed; and after that came *The Eve of St Agnes*. In this poem of pure loveliness, the menace of evil is kept distant, a barely audible muttered bass to the song of romance. The stanza, handled with perfect mastery, shows that Spenser was in the author's mind. And then to prove that *The Eve of St Agnes* itself could be equalled, and surpassed, came the group of odes and fragments—*To a Nightingale*, *On a Grecian Urn*, *To Psyche*, with *To Autumn* and *On Melancholy* following the intercalated joyous octosyllabics, *To Fancy*, *Bards of Passion*, *The Mermaid Tavern*, and *Robin Hood*. *Hyperion* closed the volume. With one exception, the *Autumn* ode is the last complete poem of Keats. The last of all, written a year later, is, with Milton's *Methought I saw*, among the most moving of English sonnets.

In the early winter months of 1820 Keats was attacked by consumption. He was invited by Shelley to Italy, but refused the invitation. Keats knew he was a dying man, and needed a nurse, not a new friend. He had many friends, truest of all being Charles Armitage Brown and Joseph Severn the artist, who solaced his last weeks of suffering. With the latter he travelled to Italy in the hope of some alleviation. On the vile and rough voyage a star shone out, and drew from him his last utterance, the sonnet *Bright Star*. The unhappy man knew that he would never see England again and never see the being "for ever loved and still to be enjoyed". He died in Rome, and was buried in the Protestant cemetery. Seventeen months later all that was left of Shelley was interred in the adjacent graveyard.

Knowledge of the greatness of Keats grew slowly, and it was not till 1848 that Richard Monckton Milnes (Lord Houghton) felt assured that he could issue a *Life, Letters and Literary Remains* in two volumes, thus giving to the public a collection of remarkable letters and a number of equally remarkable poems, including a group of splendid sonnets. Among the less good matter was a drama, *Otho the Great*, written with Brown, and an ineffective attempt at a Byronic political satire, called *The Cap and Bells*. On the other hand, *La Belle Dame sans Merci* exhibited a new side of his romanticism and the exquisite *Eve of St Mark* showed his capacity to depict what was cool, quiet, reserved and devout. The gradual accumulation of letters (to Maurice Buxton Forman's magnificent edition of 1947) has been the greatest service done to Keats since his death; and with the poems and the letters the student of Keats may be well content. The biographies have been largely unsuccessful. Keats is still the best authority on Keats. And he is like no other poet. Neither Wordsworth nor Shelley pursued beauty with such ardour. Abstractions distinguishable from beauty—nature, liberty, love—and truths with which imagination had little to do counted for much with both. The vision of Keats was never distorted by theories. He was a pure poet. No one is in less need of defence, but we should read him with special sympathy. The value of a poem is absolute. Whether it was written by an old man or a boy does not matter in the least. But Keats died at the age of twenty-five years and four months, an age at which the most celebrated poets have scarcely accomplished anything. Now a consideration of Keats's age, though it should not affect our estimation of his best poems, should certainly prevent us from being unjust to his worst. Everything we have from him might be called *Juvenilia*, and never have the *Juvenilia* of a poet been so cruelly scanned. He had not time to prune his own redundancies, he had scarcely time even to read what he had written. The tale of his creative life is barely five years. It is a miraculous and moving story.

V. LESSER POETS: ROGERS, CAMPBELL, MOORE AND OTHERS

In the ribald dedication to *Don Juan* Byron declared that "Scott, Rogers, Campbell, Moore and Crabbe" would try out with posterity the question of endurance against the "renegade" poets of the Lakes. Posterity has decided; and though it rejects Southey, it has put Wordsworth above them all. Rogers, Campbell and Moore are relegated to permanent minority.

Samuel Rogers (1763–1855) was the son of a banker and became head of the firm in 1793. Once known to all as author of *The Pleasures of Memory* (1792) he is now known to some for *The Table Talk of Samuel Rogers* edited by Dyce in 1856 and *Recollections* edited by William Sharpe in 1859. Almost the only passages of his poetry which endure are to be found in *Italy* (1822–8). He retired early from business, became celebrated for his breakfast-parties of very mixed guests, and talked well and caustically. An examination of the poetry of

Rogers proves it to be almost faultless—almost, but not quite; for its vital defect is that none of it is alive. The whole mass of it fails to communicate the thrill of conviction given by a single line of Keats or Wordsworth.

Thomas Campbell (1777–1814) is in a different case. He, too, wrote long poems, *The Pleasures of Hope* (1799) and *Gertrude of Wyoming* (1819), which were equally popular in Britain and America, but he is best remembered for his short pieces such as *Ye Mariners of England*, *The Battle of the Baltic* and *Hohenlinden*. Campbell did some useful work in prose; and his *Specimens of the British Poets* (1819) had a long life of usefulness.

Thomas Moore (1779–1852) wrote a great deal of verse in many kinds and attained great popularity; but in bulk he is not largely read. Personally he was an irresistible fellow, the friend of many from the gravest to the gayest. It was Moore whom Byron chose to represent him after death, a duty which Moore performed admirably in the seventeen volumes of Byron's poems, letters, journals, and life (1832–5) though he consented to the destruction of Byron's own *Memoirs*. Moore began his own works with a translation of Anacreon in 1800. He continued with *The Poetical Works of the late Thomas Little Esq.* (1801), not very reputable, and much altered afterwards. *Corruption* and *Intolerance* (1808), two satirical poems, show that Moore had not the nature of a satirist. *Lalla Rookh, An Oriental Romance* (1817) amply gratified the taste for eastern stories, and is still readable. *The Fudge Family in Paris* (1818) is the kind of light and kindly satire that Moore could write and that anyone can read. The Moore who genuinely survives is the poet who did for Irish song what Burns did for Scottish. *A Selection of Irish Melodies* published in ten parts between 1807 and 1834, *Irish Melodies* (1820) and *A Selection of Popular National Airs* (1815, etc.) contain not merely beautiful lyrics, but beautiful lyrics that let themselves be sung.

These three poets had their being in the Waterloo period. There are others who look forward to the Corn Laws, Reform, Chartism and even the Crimea. Nearly the eldest, the most famous by birth and promise, but, in a way, the most unfortunate, was Hartley Coleridge (1796–1849), first son of the great S. T. C., who had many of his father's weaknesses and none of his father's luck in falling soft. He attracted much affection, and asked little more of the world than to be left alone to pursue the studious life he loved. His larger works, *Biographia Borealis* (1833) and *Worthies of Yorkshire and Lancashire* (1836), are publishers' compilations. His poems were first printed in 1833, but were more fully collected in two volumes with a memoir by his brother Derwent (1851), who also published in the same year his *Essays and Marginalia*.

Thomas Hood (1799–1845) is another of the lovable, delightful writers whom unmerciful disaster pursued relentlessly through a life of sickness and drove to an early grave. Beginning as an illustrator, he soon found that literature was the true bent of his genius. A post on the staff of *The London Magazine* brought him into contact with many well-known writers of the day, especially John Hamilton Reynolds, whose sister he married, and whose own poetic gift was lost in the blaze of glory attending his friend Keats. The poems of Hood are arbitrarily divided into "Serious" and "Comic", an absurd arrangement, suggesting that his comic poems are not also serious, and that his serious poems are humourless. The "serious" poems known to everybody are *The Song of the Shirt*, *The Bridge of Sighs* and *The Dream of Eugene Aram*, all three unquestionable poetic successes, even though not of the higher kind. *Miss Kilmansegg and her Precious Leg* and the *Ode on a Distant Prospect of Clapham Academy* are perfect examples of the serio-comic. And then, with the various ballads rich with glorious puns, we must reckon the great comic odes, such as *To W. Kitchener M.D.*, and *To the Great Unknown*. The only difficulty offered by Hood in his "occasional" poems is that, like most others of their kind, they are filled with lost allusions. Hood was driven almost literally to write himself to death, and much that he produced need not be remembered. His variety is immense. The only strain he never attempted was the song of self-pity. He was a fellow of infinite jest, and kept death at bay with a smile. He might have stepped out of the pages of Shakespeare.

Winthrop Mackworth Praed (1802–39) is sometimes ranked with Hood, but the two have little in common except the gift of writing light verse. Praed was of aristocratic descent, founded *The Etonian*, and carried his gifts to Trinity College, Cambridge, and thence into Parliament and high place. As a serious poet Praed does not survive. He is remembered for such charming pieces as *A Letter of Advice* and *The Vicar* and for his serio-comic or macabre *The Red Fisherman*.

Sir Henry Taylor (1800–86) led a long and honourable life which linked the French Revolution to the very eve of Queen Victoria's Jubilee. His main contributions to literature are the four tragedies, *Isaac Comnenus* (1827), *Philip van Artevelde* (1834), *Edwin the Fair* (1842) and *St Clement's Eve* (1862). *Philip*, his best play, was long highly esteemed, and it gives us the familiar line "The world knows nothing of its greatest men"; but it is as finally dead as the other three. All contain numerous passages of something that looks like poetry, but does not keep on looking like it for long. One might call Taylor a belated Elizabethan who had wandered home through Germany. His *Autobiography* (1885) and his *Correspondence* (1888) are likely to outlast his poetry.

George Darley (1795–1846) survives strangely as the author of a song not considered his. The compiler of *The Golden Treasury* found what seemed an anonymous song of the Caroline period, *It is not beauty I demand*, and included it among the seventeenth-century group of his book. The author, it is true, was not alive; but he might have been. Darley's pastoral drama *Sylvia, or The May Queen* (1827) was edited in 1892, and his poem *Nepenthe* (1836) in 1897. The dates are significant. There was a fashion in the Nineties for the curious clotted utterance of which Darley was a master. His stanzas beginning *Listen to the Lyre* seem to be the source of the exquisite rhythm of Meredith's *Love in the Valley*.

Another favourite of the Nineties was Maria Edgeworth's nephew Thomas Lovell Beddoes (1803–49), whose chief work is a play entitled *Death's Jest Book or The Fool's Revenge*, ready for publication as early as 1829 but not published till 1850. Beddoes, too, was a belated Elizabethan, yet he is also modern. He was a physician and a physiologist and might himself have been a character by Ibsen. The blank verse of the *Jest Book* is likely to be less attractive now than some of its songs.

Another dramatist is Charles Jeremiah Wells (1800–79), whose *Stories after Nature* (1822) fell flat, as did his poetical drama *Joseph and his Brethren* (1824) until it was drastically re-written and issued in 1876 with a eulogy by Swinburne which few modern readers have found justified.

Richard Henry Horne (1803–84), who turned the "Henry" into "Hengist", endeavoured to live up to the more tempestuous name by adventures in many lands, including naval service in Mexico and gold-digging in Australia. His *New Spirit of the Age* (1844) was written with the help of his friend Mrs Browning (then Miss Barrett). His tragedies, from *Cosmo de' Medici* and *The Death of Marlowe* (both 1837) to *Laura Dibalzo* (1880), are inevitably, like those of Taylor, Wells and Beddoes, pseudo-Elizabethan, literary rather than dramatic. His jest of publishing his one poem of merit, the quasi-epic *Orion*, at the price of one farthing, may have had publicity value, but invited equally cheap epigram. *Orion* faintly suggests *Hyperion*, and *The Death of Marlowe* has at least one Marlovian line in the passage that begins "Last night a squadron charged me in a dream".

Charles Whitehead (1804–62) gave us *The Solitary* (1831) in respectable Spenserians, *The Cavalier* (1836) a play, and certain quasi-historical novels, together with some "crime" literature, including *The Autobiography of Jack Ketch* (1834). The last was so successful that he was invited to contribute prose sketches to humorous drawings by Robert Seymour. Whitehead made the great refusal, and recommended Dickens, who began to write *Pickwick Papers*. Thus Whitehead is, in a sense, immortalized by the work he did not write.

The achievements of Moore and Praed in light verse were anticipated by James and Horace Smith, whose *Rejected Addresses* (1812) were supposed to have been received by the managers of Drury Lane in competition for the honour of recitation at the reopening of the burned-down theatre. It is a series of pieces in the manner of the best (and the worst) writers of the day; and as a complete book of parodies has hardly been surpassed.

Among the most memorable books of serio-comic verse a high place must be given to the work of an elderly clergyman named Richard Harris Barham (1788–1845), who, after holding various ecclesiastical posts with dignity, became "Thomas Ingoldsby", author of *The Ingoldsby Legends*, which, first creeping shyly forth in magazines, appeared next in a collected volume in 1840, with a second and third series in 1847. Some high-principled and feeble-minded churchmen permitted themselves to believe that Ingoldsby was undermining the High Church movement by ribaldry; when the truth was that Ingoldsby was making the pomp and ceremony of the Church interesting to people who, without him, would have been flatly uninterested in ritual. The Church that cannot stand a joke or two is not well founded. Ingoldsby contrives his grotesques with a masterly hand and the best of his *Legends* remain justly admired.

This period saw the reappearance of the poetesses. They had not been wanting, indeed, since Lady Winchilsea took the torch from the Matchless Orinda and passed it on to others even less important. There had been, more recently, Anna Seward (1747–1809), that Swan of Lichfield, who sang so much and so long before her death that she has been entirely inaudible since, Hannah More, that "powerful versificatrix", and Anna Letitia Barbauld (1743–1825), who had uttered the one single memorable stanza beginning "Life! we've been long together", in a poem otherwise immemorable. But the first thirty years or so of the nineteenth century, even before the definite appearance of Mrs Browning, saw, in Joanna Baillie, Mrs Hemans and "L. E. L.", three persons who, for no short time and to no few persons, seemed to be poetesses; while there were one or two others, such as Caroline Bowles, Southey's second wife, and Sara Coleridge, daughter of S. T. C. and sister of Hartley, who deserve to be added to them. Joanna Baillie (see p. 497) wrote lyrics in Scots that have been praised by her compatriots. Felicia Dorothea Browne (1793–1835), the charming and beautiful Mrs Hemans, was praised by Wordsworth. She knew that her numerous volumes of verse were worth little, even though the public bought them, and she thought she might be remembered by half-a-dozen little pieces like *Casabianca*. She was exactly right. Felicia Dorothea Hemans gave a glimpse of poetry to many who were unable to detect it elsewhere. The blight which S. T. C. cast upon his son Hartley likewise fell upon his gifted daughter Sara (1802–52), whose fairy romance, *Phantasmion*, contains some attractive verses —verses which she would probably have bettered, had she not been doomed to spend her life in putting some order into her father's "remains", a task shared by her cousin Henry Nelson Coleridge, who married her. Caroline Bowles (1787–1854) was no relative of William Lisle Bowles. Her little verses are neither pretentious nor silly, but they are the mere cowslip wine of poetry. Letitia Elizabeth Landon (1802–38) published poems and novels that represent the "gush" of Mrs Hemans at its worst.

Some other poets deserve notice in history, if only for the extent of their performances or the celebrity they attained. Henry James Pye (1745–1813) was a member of Parliament and of the Militia (like Gibbon), and a London police magistrate (like Fielding). His poetry, including pindaric odes and an epic called *Alfred* (1801), is no worse than that of many other writers noticed here. Unfortunately he was chosen to succeed Warton as Poet Laureate in 1790 and was thus promoted to a perpetuity of ridicule. William Sotheby (1757–1833), a friend of Scott, translated well the *Georgics* of Virgil, and both the *Iliad* and *Odyssey*. His original poems are not important. Edwin Atherstone (1788–1872) needed all his years for *The Fall of Nineveh* in thirty books, together with *The Fall of Herculaneum* and *The Handwriting on the Wall*. His subjects, it will be seen, are marmoreal or granitic, but not so tremendous as the courage of any who would attempt to read him. John Abraham Heraud (1799–1887), a noted dramatic critic, wrote *The Descent into Hell*, *The Judgment of the Flood* and other poems. Robert Pollok (1798–1827) might have attained the immensity of these two poets had he lived as long; for besides *Tales of the Covenanters* he had written a lengthy poem called *The Course of Time* (1827), which some professed to find wonderful, but which more confessed to finding unreadable. Robert Montgomery—really Gomery (1807–55)—author of poetical effusions called *The Omnipresence of the Deity* (1828) and *Satan, or Intellect without God* (1830) is remembered by the article in the *Edinburgh Review* in which Macaulay attacked the persistent puffing of sham religious works as poetry and used Montgomery as an example. Among the twitterers who followed Moore must be named

Bryan Waller Procter (1787–1874), better known as "Barry Cornwall". His long life, his notable family, his friendships with great writers from Lamb to Dickens, and his own pleasant character, have tended to give his writings an importance which they do not deserve. Thomas Haynes Bayly (1797–1839) is remembered as the literary father of the "drawing-room song". One of his own most popular songs made, probably, its last appearance in Shaw's *Back to Methuselah.*

Community of circumstance, of misfortune and (in part) of subject has linked Robert Bloomfield (1768–1823) and John Clare (1793–1864) together. Both were agricultural labourers; both made themselves authors under difficulties; both were patronized; neither made the best use of the patronage; and both died mad, though, in Bloomfield's case, actual insanity has been questioned. Bloomfield's *The Farmer's Boy* appeared in 1800 and was followed by other volumes of pleasing rural quality. Clare published *Poems Descriptive of Rural Life and Scenery* (1820), *The Village Minstrel* (1821), *The Shepherd's Calendar* (1827) and *The Rural Muse* (1835). His collected *Poems* were published in 1935; his *Letters* in 1951. The pathos of the poet's life is deeply moving; but the value of poetry is absolute and does not depend upon whether the verses were written in or out of asylum or workhouse. Lamb thought that Bloomfield had "a poor mind", and put Clare higher. Posterity has confirmed his judgment. Bloomfield was a versifier, Clare is a poet.

Robert Stephen Hawker (1803–75), "the Vicar of Morwenstow", wrote one famous piece, *The Song of the Western Men*—an original poem with a traditional refrain. His numerous other poems are contained in *Records of the Western Shore* (1832–6) and *Cornish Ballads* (1869).

A more difficult case is provided by another clerical poet, William Barnes (1801–86), of Dorset. The question is whether his sweet, sincere and sometimes very moving poems would have had strength enough to survive without the support of the Dorsetshire dialect—in other words, whether it is not the unearned increment of dialectical quaintness that keeps some of them still alive. To discuss this would be to incur some danger. There is no doubt whatever that Barnes was fiercely sincere. He was such an ardent Anglicizer that he endeavoured to replace every scrap of grammatical terminology derived from Latin by a pure English term, however awkward. His poetical works are *Poems of Rural Life in the Dorset dialect* (1844); and *Hwomely Rhymes: a Second collection* (1859). Burns and Barnes must not be cited as parallel cases. Burns is a major poet concerned only to write poetry; Barnes is a minor poet concerned chiefly to exploit the dialect of his shire.

James Montgomery (1771–1854) was no connection of the inferior Robert, though he, too, wrote epics or quasi-epics, which, however, are less remembered than his many hymns which include such popular favourites as *Songs of praise the angels sang.*

Ebenezer Elliott (1781–1849), "the Corn Law Rhymer", hated Communism, Chartism and Socialism as much as he hated the Corn Laws. To him the Corn Laws not only taxed the People's Bread, but took money from enterprising manufacturers like himself and gave it to lazy, unenterprizing farmers. His main works are *The Village Patriarch* (1829), *Corn-Law Rhymes* (1831), *The Splendid*

Village etc. (1833–5). No one would find the poetry of Elliott more than fourth rate were it not for its subsidiary political interest.

Elliott was one of Southey's *protégés*. Another was Henry Kirke White (1785–1806), whose slight book of verses, published at eighteen, tells us little about him. One piece, much altered by others, has become the familiar hymn, *Oft in danger, oft in woe.*

Very different was the lot of Henry Francis Cary (1772–1844), who lived a bookish life and made himself justly famous by a piece of translation. In 1805 he published a blank verse translation of the *Inferno* and in 1814 *The Vision; or Hell, Purgatory and Paradise of Dante Alighieri*. Upon this his fame securely rests. Cary also made translations from Pindar and Aristophanes, and compiled prose successors to Johnson's *Lives*.

Probably no "single-speech" poet has attracted more attention than Charles Wolfe (1791–1823), the author of *The Burial of Sir John Moore*. No other poem among Wolfe's *Remains* has anything like its quality.

Reginald Heber (1783–1826), Bishop of Calcutta, who worked himself into an early grave by apostolical labours in an Oriental see, wrote numerous books in prose, as well as *Poems and Translations* (1812) and *Hymns* (1827). To have written *From Greenland's icy mountains* and *Holy, Holy, Holy* is to have gained, if not immortality, then its nearest substitute, an affectionate remembrance.

We have considered a large number of poets who range from pre-Waterloo to post-Crimean times. One curious fact is that most of them look forwards and not backwards—they are all post-Wordsworthian. They exhibit change, so to speak, in the very act; but there is no uniform kind of change. Another curious fact is that, despite individual tendencies to imitation, all these poets show a general air as of sheep without a shepherd. There is no master-spirit among them; but neither is there any definite emergence of novelty in outlook or in technique. No one is suppressed, but nevertheless no one emerges.

VI. REVIEWS AND MAGAZINES IN THE EARLY YEARS OF THE NINETEENTH CENTURY

During the eighteenth century the "Magazine" was well established. With the nineteenth century was born a new kind of periodical, the "Review". Between the Review and the Magazine there was a real distinction, though there was naturally something in common. The Magazine was a miscellany designed for rational entertainment. It might contain criticisms of books, but it did not confine itself to reviewing. To its pages essayists, correspondents and poets sent original contributions. The note of the Review, on the other hand, was advocacy, and more especially, political advocacy. It strove to instruct or persuade its readers by the presentation of definite views in the form of essays which purported to be discussions of books named at the head of the articles. Sometimes the books were the theme of the essay, sometimes they were merely its excuse, and were mentioned only to be dismissed. The greatest of reviewers, Macaulay, offers specimens of all kinds of procedure. His review of Croker's edition of Boswell not only tore Croker into fragments, but proceeded to give an original critical study of Dr Johnson. On the other hand, his essay on Warren Hastings merely alludes to the book of which it is supposed to be a review, and at once plunges into critical biography. The Reviews did not print either original poetry or fiction; but the Magazines, which did, also published certain reviews. Such was the main distinction between a Magazine and a Review. In the first quarter of the nineteenth century, the two great Reviews—*The Edinburgh* and *The Quarterly*—and two brilliant Magazines—*Blackwood's* and *The London*—sprang to life, and, on the whole, they conformed to the original distinctions of type. The strict anonymity of the articles in the Reviews gave them weight and power, but the power was sometimes grossly abused.

Of the four periodicals mentioned, *The Edinburgh Review* has the most interesting history. It was founded by three young men, then quite unknown to fame, Francis Jeffrey (1773–1850), a Scottish advocate, still almost briefless, Sydney Smith (1771–1845), a distinguished Wykehamist and Oxonian, who, while waiting for an English living, was in Edinburgh as a private tutor, and Henry Brougham (1778–1868), the future Lord Chancellor, who had only lately been called to the Scottish Bar. The first number (October, 1802) was a great success. From the beginning the *Edinburgh* was clearly on the side of Liberalism and held tranquil views about the French Revolution; but it refused to tolerate the slightest departure from ancient ways in the world of letters. Southey's *Thalaba* fell under Jeffrey's lash in the first number. Jeffrey remained anti–Wordsworthian all through; but he was earnest and merely obtuse—he was not a "killer" like certain writers in other periodicals. Scott contributed several literary articles, but his romantic Toryism was at variance with the spirit of the *Edinburgh*. Of the early contributors the best was Sydney Smith, famous throughout his life as a brilliant humorist and as the advocate of serious reforms. Not all who delighted in the clever jesting and high spirits which distinguished him, alike in social intercourse and in the written page, were able to recognize the thoroughness and sincerity of his character, and his genuine desire to leave the world a better place than he found it. The ungrateful Whigs did as little for him as the Tories had done for Swift. Henry Brougham, the youngest of the three founders, was to become, in a few years and for a time, one of the most powerful political leaders in England. Hardly any public man of the nineteenth century approached more nearly to the possession of genius. But Brougham's great gifts were impaired by very serious faults of character and temper which earned him the hatred of many and the distrust of all. In complete contrast was Francis Horner (1778–1817), who wrote on economical subjects and who, by mastery of knowledge and rectitude of character, gained such esteem that his early death was deplored by both sides in the House of Commons as a national disaster. The most interesting event in the history of the *Edinburgh* was the appearance of No. 85, dated August 1825, which, with many other varied and interesting articles, contained one called *Milton*. Its command of matter and compelling originality of style made it the talk of the town. Its author, Thomas Babington Macaulay, thereafter became one of the chief props of the *Edinburgh* and contributed to it a long series of essays.

The success of the *Edinburgh* naturally made the other side anxious to have its own review. Scott was willing to help a new review into existence, but he was unwilling to undertake the editorship. Murray, the publisher, appealed to Canning, but after some delay, the editorship was pressed on Gifford, Canning's old associate in *The Anti-Jacobin*. Thus the *Quarterly*, unlike the *Edinburgh*, was brought out by party politicians of high standing. The first number appeared in February 1809. That the *Quarterly* has unhappy passages in its history is not to be denied; but we should remember that its review of *Emma* (by Scott) gave Jane Austen her first public encouragement. Among the worst of all reviewers was the Right Honourable John Wilson Croker (1780–1857), Member of Parliament, and afterwards Secretary to the Admiralty, who wrote with unhappy regularity for *The Quarterly Review*. Croker was the kind of Tory who never learned anything, never forgot anything, and never forgave anything. The man who was in part responsible for the disgraceful attack on Keats, who furnished Disraeli with the model for the loathsome Rigby in *Coningsby*, and who went out in futile confidence to meet Macaulay with a fatally vulnerable edition of Boswell's *Johnson*, has earned at least a footnote in a history of English literature.

Blackwood's Magazine was more simply produced. The success of Constable with the *Edinburgh* and of Murray with the *Quarterly* set other enterprising publishers to work, and William Blackwood came out with a magazine designed first to be a Tory rival in Edinburgh to the *Edinburgh* itself, and next to promote the fame of his publishing house. But his first numbers were failures. He determined to make a sensation at any cost, and turned to three very differently gifted men for support—Lockhart, in later days to become famous as editor of the *Quarterly* and the biographer of Scott; Wilson, afterwards popular as a writer under the name of "Christopher North"; and Hogg, the Ettrick Shepherd. The result of their joint lucubrations was the famous "Chaldee MS.", which, in language parodied from Scripture, overwhelmed with scathing satire and personal ridicule the best known and most respected notabilities of the Scottish metropolis. Blackwood had calculated rightly. The sensation was made; and *Maga*, as it was popularly called, became famous in England and Scotland alike. *Blackwood* soon distinguished itself by the scandalous violence of its attacks. Coleridge, Hazlitt and Leigh Hunt were notable victims, and it pursued Keats virulently in life and after his death. It is difficult now to admire Wilson for anything; it is impossible to admire the rowdiness which he introduced into *Blackwood* and which was maintained with zest by a later contributor, the Irishman William Maginn. John Gibson Lockhart (1794–1854), a son of the manse, won distinction both at Glasgow and at Oxford, and made special studies in German and Spanish. He created a small sensation in Edinburgh with *Peter's Letters to his Kinsfolk* (1819), and gained a more reputable success with *Ancient Spanish Ballads* (1823). He married Scott's daughter Sophia. John Wilson (1785–1854), by a gross piece of political jobbery, was elected to the Chair of Moral Philosophy in the university of Edinburgh, the really great candidate, Sir William Hamilton, being passed over. Maginn, who joined to Irish effrontery a complete lack of scruple, did some good work later in founding *Fraser's Magazine* (1830) on the same lines as *Blackwood*. It is said that he first suggested the famous *Noctes Ambrosianae* in *Blackwood*. These "dialogues of the day", named from Ambrose's Tavern, began in 1822 and lasted to 1835. Most of the work was Wilson's.

The London Magazine (1820–9) had a short but distinguished career, during which it introduced to its readers the works of men who were to take a very high place in British literature. Among its contributors were De Quincey, Lamb, Hazlitt and Keats. But even the mild *London* has its tragic story. Its first editor was John Scott, who, having attacked Lockhart, was challenged to a duel. The combat was averted at the last moment; but Lockhart's second, Jonathan Christie, felt he had been insulted, and at another meeting the unhappy John Scott was mortally wounded.

Despite their evil deeds, the Reviews and Magazines did useful service. They helped to create and stimulate public opinion. The experience of the world shows that even bad criticism is better than none. Criticism destroys the fatal complacency that comes of a too undisputed life. Kings had their critical jesters; dictators require obsequious flatterers. In later times the great reviews lost their importance. The newspapers of the nineteenth century, with vastly greater and swifter means of disseminating views as well as news, took their place as organs of public opinion.

VII. HAZLITT

Like the poets, the essayists were affected by the great upheaval in France. Thus, two of the greatest, Lamb and Hazlitt, welcomed the change but responded in different ways. We can read Lamb without caring greatly what century he lived in ; we cannot understand Hazlitt without knowing something of his attitude towards public affairs. The measure he applied to all men was this: were they friends of the revolutionary spirit, or were they apostates who had gone over to the enemy? The foe, and especially the apostate, he attacks directly, indirectly, by inference, by allusion, by quotation. Hazlitt has been charged with soreness of feeling; but what hurt him was not the attacks of enemies, none of whom ever made him bow his head, but the apostasy of those who once exclaimed: "Bliss was it in that dawn to be alive", and then enlisted in the ranks of reaction. In his feeling about Napoleon Hazlitt was own brother to the heroes of Heine and Béranger. And yet, holding and proclaiming sentiments at complete variance with those held by the majority of his countrymen, he seemed genuinely surprised that he was unpopular. There is much to admire in the intrepid honesty that refused to compromise at a time when suppleness promised comfort and profit.

Dissent was in his blood. William Hazlitt (1778–1830) was born at Maidstone, the son of a Unitarian minister of simple, unworldly character and great powers of mind. The father's intractability of conscience (which he passed on to his son) led to certain differences with his congregation, and the Hazlitt family moved to Ireland in 1780, and thence to America in 1783, where they remained till 1787. Later in that year the father became Unitarian minister at Wem in Shropshire, and there young Hazlitt spent most of his youth. He was intended for the ministry and was sent to Hackney Theological College in 1793; but his elder brother had settled in London as a painter, and during visits to the studio William discovered an active interest in painting and philosophy and no interest whatever in theology. He was soon back at Wem, where he painted, read, walked and philosophized with the fierce intensity revealed in many later essays. Then came the great, unforgettable and decisive moment in his life. Early in 1798 the celebrated Mr Coleridge arrived at Shrewsbury as successor to Mr Rowe, the Unitarian minister there. To describe how Hazlitt met Coleridge and how Coleridge became for him a kind of god who taught him the gospel of revolution and gave him the thrill of poetry is happily unnecessary, for it is all written in Hazlitt's own *My First Acquaintance with Poets*, which many consider to be among the best of English essays and which a few consider to be the best of all. The intellectual tragedy of Hazlitt's life was the fall of Coleridge. He saw this God-gifted man slowly subside into the depths of opium and reactionary Toryism—the latter of which he probably thought the more poisonous. After the meeting with Coleridge, Hazlitt felt that he must strive to accomplish something. He took up again a cherished piece of youthful speculation, *An Essay on the Principles of Human Action*. He walked countless miles to visit the picture-galleries in great houses. He returned with ardour to painting. He crossed to Paris, and fell in love with Napoleon. He visited the Louvre, and fell in love with the spoils of Italy. He stayed several months in Paris, making copies of pictures and actually selling them. Then, returned to England, he went about painting portraits (the best-known being Lamb as a Venetian Senator), and suddenly discovered that the thing to do was to write. He came to London in search of a literary career, and soon found the friends he needed. He married, quite unsuitably, Sarah Stoddart, an acquaintance of Mary Lamb. Her chief contribution to his life was Winterslow, near Salisbury, where she had a cottage. To the Winterslow region Hazlitt often repaired to obtain the solitude that was one of his needs. After a short time William and Sarah went to Scotland and got a divorce. There was a second marriage, of dubious validity, to a Mrs Bridgewater, but the new husband and wife speedily parted and never saw each other again. Though he had two wives, both living, Hazlitt remained a solitary man.

His industry was amazing. In twenty-five years he gradually made his way to fame from absolute obscurity, without prestige of family, without formal education and without friends of influence. He won distinction as a lecturer; his criticisms on books, pictures and plays were widely read; he became known as a good talker; and he attracted the notice of the most brutal as well as the most gifted of reviewers. His collected works occupy about six thousand printed pages. Probably no English author who has written so voluminously has left so much that is first-rate. Very much more of Hazlitt survives than of De Quincey, and far more than of Lamb. Hazlitt's most notorious book is the worst he wrote: the *Liber Amoris* (1823, enlarged later), an account in dialogue, letters and narrative, of his infatuation with Sarah Walker, a girl of the house in which he was lodging.

An Essay on the Principles of Human Action (1805) got published at last, and if it tells us nothing new about Hartley or Helvetius, it tells us much about Hazlitt himself. A critic has complained that Hazlitt had a "common mind". That is precisely his great distinction. Hazlitt is the common, wholesome, sensible man raised to an uncommonly high degree of receptivity and expression. He was totally without eccentricity or affectation. He looked squarely at human activities and enjoyed intensely all that the common man enjoys casually. Strong as his opinions were, he never let politics impede his admiration. There was no more passionate lover of the ultra-Tory Scott than the ultra-Radical Hazlitt. He scarified Wordsworth as an apostate, yet declared him "the most original poet now living". He fell upon Coleridge the backslider and adored Coleridge the inspirer of his youthful ardours. He attacked great men because he thought them great, not because he thought them little, and about great men he tells us great things, not mean things.

Hazlitt's earliest publications are tentative efforts or workman-like compilations. In the intervals of labouring at them he was beginning to contribute to magazines and to discourse to audiences those general and critical essays by which he is remembered. He had no formal literary training, but in his goings to and fro he had laid hold of some of the great books of the world and had taken them to his bosom as if they were living beings. Perhaps his greatest service to his time was the attention he directed to Shakespeare. He had none of Coleridge's inspiration, but he gave the common reader sensible guidance in his first acquaintance with poets. The main collections of his lectures are *Characters of Shakspear's Plays* (1817, 1818), *Lectures on the English Poets* (1818, 1819), *Lectures on the English Comic Writers* (1819), and *Lectures on the Dramatic Literature of the Age of Elizabeth* (1820). The *Political Essays* (1819) belonging to this period is probably the most neglected of his first-rate books. Hazlitt's criticism of his contemporaries in *The Spirit of the Age* (1825) is in accord with his courageous position on all questions. He wrote of the living as frankly as he wrote of the dead. There are some displays of ill-temper; but there is so much fine appraisement that these essays are almost the last of Hazlitt's writings which the lover of English literature would surrender.

Besides being a critic of the printed drama Hazlitt is the first of our great dramatic critics. He wrote for several papers, and many of his articles are reprinted in *A View of the English Stage* (1818). Others appeared posthumously. Hazlitt is delightful as a dramatic critic precisely because he had a "common" mind. He did not go to the theatre to air his "views"; he went because he liked going to the play and seeing "the happy faces in the pit". In particular, he is the historian of Edmund Kean's tremendous effects on the boards. Hazlitt was a pioneer. Before his day, honest reviews of plays hardly existed. He was fearlessly outspoken, and declared that the critic had no obligations to theatre, manager, or actor. Yet another of Hazlitt's great interests was pictorial art. No essayist contemporary with him was his equal in natural aptitude or in knowledge of what the painter was trying to achieve. He disliked the current fashion for vacuous portraiture and stereotyped religious scenes, and before Ruskin was born he had hailed Turner as a master of atmospheric effects. He propounded no system or philosophy of art; he just liked pictures, and wrote about what he liked. Hazlitt's opinions will be found in *Sketches of the Principal Picture Galleries in England* (1824), *Notes of a Journey through France and Italy* (1826) and *Conversations of James Northcote Esq., R.A.* (1830), the last a rich and delightful book full of sage comments on art and life. Other essays on the fine arts were published posthumously.

The best known part of Hazlitt's work is the large mass of miscellaneous essays contributed to various magazines and contained in such familiar volumes as *The Round Table* (1817), *Table-Talk* (1821–2), and *The Plain Speaker* (1826)— the last two being his finest collections. Many essays were not reprinted in his life-time, and some were gathered in his *Literary Remains* (1836). Another volume of *Sketches and Essays* appeared in 1839. A delightful volume called *Winterslow: Essays and Characters written there* (1856) contains some already familiar essays, together with some magnificent pieces, like *My First Acquaintance with Poets*, never reprinted before. Hazlitt's prose resembles the best kind of talk. It is active, challenging, cheerfully dogmatic and personal, entirely free from pose—"I hate all idiosyncrasy", he said—and he adorns his utterance with scraps of quotation blended or distorted which are the despair of his editors. He has no message and no moral and will never be the angel of any coteries or the toast of any societies. To the end he was resolute and independent. His last labours were given to a *Life of Napoleon* in four volumes (1828–30); but through the dishonesty of the publisher he got nothing. It is not a good life of Napoleon, but it is quite a good life of Hazlitt. He died in solitude, save for the comforting presence of Charles Lamb, saying, when the end came, "Well, I've had a happy life". We need not doubt it.

VIII. LAMB

Some knowledge of the domestic life of Charles Lamb (1775–1834) is helpful to an understanding of his works. John Lamb, his father, was the personal servant of Samuel Salt, a bencher of the Inner Temple. He married Elizabeth Field, a Hertfordshire woman. They lived in Salt's house at 2 Crown Office Row, Mrs Lamb acting as housekeeper. Their eldest son, John, called by Lamb "James Elia", was born in June 1763. Mary Lamb ("Bridget") was the second surviving child, born in December 1764. Charles, the youngest, was born 10 February 1775. Salt's house in the Temple was Lamb's home for the first seventeen years of his life. Few boys were brought up in more delightful surroundings—on one side a collegiate peace and the River Thames; on the other the roaring voice of central London. To Lamb his London home was as great an inspiration as his mountain home to Wordsworth. His youth was passed in poverty; but fortunately a presentation to Christ's Hospital procured him the elements of a sound education. He was an odd little creature with a pronounced stammer, and so was barred from the higher flights of scholarship which swept his older contemporary Coleridge on to Cambridge and disaster. Coleridge was homeless. Lamb's home was near at hand, and in holiday times he and his sister visited grandmother Field, who was housekeeper at Blakesware, a country mansion. Blakesware is the *Blakesmoor in H———shire* of a celebrated essay, and united with the Temple buildings in giving the impressionable child recollections that he never forgot. There were excursions to the source of the New River, and tramps to the home of his relations at Mackery End. So, city-bred though he was, Lamb had early contact with nature.

Lamb left Christ's Hospital in 1789, and two years later obtained an appointment in the South-Sea House; but after a few months he entered (1792) a scene of greater activity, the East India House in Leadenhall Street, where, for thirty-three years, he performed his daily duties. Between 1792 and 1796 the friendship with Coleridge was continued in fervent talks and in the trickle of sonnets which Lamb showed to his gifted friend. Four were published in Coleridge's *Poems on Various Subjects* in 1796. At the end of 1795 came the first note of tragedy. Lamb had some kind of mental collapse and spent six weeks in a private asylum. Nothing is known about his breakdown and nothing like it occurred again. But there was insanity in the family and it declared itself with the horror of an Elizabethan tragedy. Poor Mary, overworked, overwrought, taxed beyond endurance by a helpless mother, a half-senile aunt and a querulous father, had a sudden fit of mania in which she stabbed her mother to death. The poor woman was removed to an asylum, and if the advice of John had been taken, she would have remained there for ever. But Charles undertook the permanent care of her, and thus in his twenty-third year found himself pledged to the support of a father in his second childhood, a dying aunt and a sister whose returning sanity was liable to fail again at any moment. The father, now in the bare half-light of reason, could be kept quiet only by cards; and Charles, as soon as he returned from his daily work, had to devote himself to playing the old man to sleep. His Sundays and holidays were spent with Mary in the private asylum. At last (1799) the father died. Charles was not only spared his nightly ordeal, but could take Mary to live with him, until the signs of recurring insanity warned them that she must go back for a time. So passed many years, the periods of Mary's insanity becoming longer and longer, until in later years, Charles being dead, she was permanently insane. It is the saddest of stories, lightened by the gleams of quiet day-to-day heroism and exquisite affection. People have ventured to pity and even to condemn Charles Lamb. Coleridge took the slightly superior "gentle-hearted-Charles" attitude, which Lamb properly resented, for he was made of stronger stuff than Coleridge and could face the facts of life from which Coleridge fled. Moreover, it was the small purse of a hard-working clerk that contributed, out of all proportion, to relieve the distresses of his friends. Lamb too, has been grossly and unwarrantably held up as a shocking example of the effects of intoxication—the man who did thirty-three years of daily exemplary service in a great corporation. Had he taken to drink as a means of relieving the pressure of his troubles he could have been forgiven. But he did no such thing. His occasional over-indulgence in the social glass was temperance itself compared with the sedulous, inveterate laudanum-drinking of Coleridge.

In 1796 began the association between Coleridge and Charles Lloyd, a young Birmingham Quaker. Lamb, suffering from a sense of loneliness, conceived a strong attachment for his friend's disciple. To the second edition of Coleridge's *Poems* (October 1797) were added poems by Lamb and Lloyd; and in 1798 appeared a small volume of *Blank Verse, by Charles Lloyd and Charles Lamb,* to which Lamb contributed seven poems. From Lloyd, Lamb got that liking for the Quakers which appears in several pieces of writing. But Charles Lloyd was a bad friend for Lamb. His sensitiveness bordered on mental distraction, and he died deranged. In *Edmund Oliver,* a novel published in 1798, Lloyd expressed some feeling against Coleridge, and managed to effect a breach between

Coleridge and Lamb. The friendship was soon renewed, but never upon the same level. Lamb's first independent work in prose, *A Tale of Rosamund Gray and Old Blind Margaret*, was published in the summer of 1798. Already he had had some share in James White's *Original Letters, etc., of Sir John Falstaff* in July 1796. *Rosamund Gray* is a sombre and tragic narrative; but it can hardly be said to survive, except for Lamb's sake. The same must be said of his tragedy, called at first *Pride's Cure*, but named in its revised form *John Woodvil* (1802). Although without original merit or dramatic interest, the play bears witness to Lamb's careful study of the sixteenth and seventeenth century dramatists. In these pursuits Lamb gradually shook off his melancholy, and his life with Mary at this time is tenderly recorded in *Old China*, one of his best essays. Towards the end of 1799 he made a new and valuable friend, Thomas Manning, a Cambridge mathematician, versatile and laughter-loving. Their correspondence produced a series of letters full of Lamb's finest humour. Cambridge also contained George Dyer of Emmanuel, who seoddity and simplicity were a perpetual delight to Lamb. Indeed, Dyer might almost be called Lamb's own literary creation. Casual writing for the papers occupied his leisure during the next few years. In 1802 the Lambs visited Coleridge at Greta Hall, without losing any of their attachment to London. The *Tales from Shakespeare* were begun in 1806, Mary doing most, Charles himself contributing only four tragedies. As Shakespeare whole and unmitigated for the young was at that time never thought of, the volume really gave many youthful readers their first acquaintance with a great poet. Before this classic appeared in January 1807, Lamb's silly farce *Mr H.* was given at Drury Lane without success. His true service to the drama was to be of a better kind. Another work for the young, *The Adventures of Ulysses*, based on Chapman, appeared in 1808. Although it is a finer book than the *Tales* it has had nothing like the same success. In *Mrs Leicester's School* (1809) Mary Lamb had the principal share, Charles himself contributing only three of the ten stories. The book has small interest and no importance. With *Mrs Leicester's School* and the artless rhymes of *Poetry for Children* (1809) the joint work of the brother and sister came to an end. *Prince Dorus* (1811), a fairy-tale in decasyllabic couplets, was Lamb's last work for children. The excellence of Mary's writing shows that, at normal times, her intelligence and judgment were very sound.

Lamb's next literary venture was the justly famous *Specimens of English Dramatic Poets who lived About the Time of Shakespeare* (1808). This work rediscovered for its age the Elizabethan dramatists. Many people cannot share Lamb's enthusiasm for these authors; some, on the other hand, have declared that Lamb ruined his authors by presenting as poetry what should be presented as drama. The objection is unreal and quite suppositious, as a glance through the book will show. The radical point is that the old dramatists were not known, and that Lamb sought to make them known in extracts chosen with sure dramatic instinct and enriched with brief notes that are little masterpieces of just criticism and eloquent prose. Now that the dramatists are known and accessible we need not go on reading extracts; but we must not be asked to revile the man who made them known and so helped to make them accessible. During the next years Lamb was steadily ripening by reading and reflection into a serious essay writer, and giving frequent and memorable examples of his power in letters to numerous friends. To Leigh Hunt's *Reflector* he contributed such excellent articles as *The Genius and Character of Hogarth* (1811) and *The Tragedies of Shakespeare* (1812). His serious and matter-of-fact *Recollections of Christ's Hospital* in *The Gentleman's* for June 1813 is a forerunner of the beautiful later essay. At this time, too, Lamb wrote for *The Philanthropist* those *Confessions of a Drunkard* which have been taken seriously as the repentant outpourings of a dipsomaniac. In 1818 appeared the *Works of Charles Lamb* (2 vols.) containing some of the work hitherto mentioned. Lamb continued to write for such magazines as *The Examiner* and *The Indicator*. But the great event in his life was the appearance in *The London Magazine* for August 1820 of an essay entitled *Recollections of the South-Sea House* signed "Elia". Its success was so outstanding that from October 1820 to the end of 1823, Elia was a regular contributor to this brilliant but short-lived periodical. Lamb was now forty-five, and he had happily discovered in his reminiscences the true material of his best writing. Few essayists have so tenderly and humorously combined poetry and truth in their evocations of the past. The volume called *Elia* appeared in 1823. The original "Elia" whose name Lamb borrowed (and pronounced "Ellia") was an Italian clerk known to him in business. The next important event in his life happened on 29 March 1825, when he left the India House for ever as a superannuated man, with a generous pension allowing an equally generous remainder to Mary, if she survived him. But Lamb was too far gone in bad health to enjoy his liberty long. The rest of his work is slight and unimportant. In 1827 he moved, rather mistakenly, to Enfield, then really in the country. He found delight in the neighbourhood of his favourite Hertfordshire and in correspondence with, and occasional visits from, his friends. In May 1833 he moved to Edmonton. That year saw the marriage of his adopted daughter Emma Isola to the publisher Edward Moxon and the publication by Moxon of *The Last Essays of Elia*; the July of 1834 saw the death of Coleridge; the December of that year saw his own. Mary lived on till 1847.

It is tempting to say that Lamb's are the best essays in English, because they are rich in the charm that is one of the rarest gifts of genius; it is just to say that Lamb's finest essays are the nearest of all to poetry, not only because they often touch the height where prose eloquence passes into poetry, but because, whether grave or gay, reminiscent or personal, they have in some degree the creative imagination which it is the privilege of poetry to possess in full. And in support of this claim we would adduce, not one of the most popular pieces, but such a passage as the meeting with Dodd in the essay *On Some of the Old Actors*. Could poetry itself do more? The *Letters* stand on equal terms with the essays and are a sufficient rebuke to the psychologists who try to explain "Elia" as a mask, as a piece of defence-mechanism put up by Lamb to hide his misery from himself. Elia is implicit in the earliest of Lamb's letters. Indeed, few writers are so consistent as Lamb, from his worst puns to his deepest reflections. The magic of his style is enhanced by its intensely literary quality. He belonged in spirit to the seventeenth century, and the language of his favourite authors, closely woven into the texture of his mind, found its way without an effort into his prose. His deeper harmonies recall Sir Thomas Browne, a spirit akin to his own in courage, in quietness and in grave curiosity. It is in prose that Lamb the poet is to be found. His verse is quite unimportant, even when pleasing. Through the *Essays of Elia* and the *Letters*, which seem almost to create the figures of their recipients, there shines the spirit of the man, alive to the absurdities of the world, tender to its sorrows, tolerant of its weaknesses.

IX. THE LANDORS, LEIGH HUNT, DE QUINCEY

Walter Savage Landor (1775–1864), John Henry Leigh Hunt (1784–1859) and Thomas De Quincey (1785–1859) resemble each other sufficiently to justify a joint discussion. They belong by birth to the eighteenth century, yet lived long into the nineteenth. Landor, the friend of Southey, lived to be the friend of Swinburne. Their contemporaries stretch in a long line from Sheridan to Shaw. All three were voluminous writers, all three were inclined to eccentricity, and two of them, Landor and Hunt, were caricatured by Dickens in *Bleak House*. This has been deplored; but the real cause for regret is that De Quincey did not join them in that excellent story. None of the three reached unchallengeably the first rank in literature, but each (Hunt excepted) has had champions who declared, even with passion, that he did. All present some textual difficulties. A reasonably complete edition of Landor did not exist till 1936. De Quincey left deposits of writing, published or unpublished, as he crept from one lodging to another, and made no attempt at collection till he was an old man. Of Leigh Hunt there never has been and never will be a complete edition—no one wants to read in a hundred volumes what they now scarcely read in seven.

Landor's prose and Landor's verse are so alike in character that the bare fact of metre is almost the sole distinction. Of the two, the prose is sometimes richer than the verse in diction and imagery. Landor shows a characteristic compound of styles. No one can ignore either his fondness for Greek subjects or the magical air of Hellenic quality which he casts around them, nevertheless in such works as the would-be epic *Gebir* and the drama *Count Julian* he moves in the world of romance. Landor's verse is very considerable in extent, and as he was specially skilled in framing epigrams, sometimes in the modern sense, but nearly always in the Greek sense of that term, his individual pieces are multitudinous. After a volume of *Poems* (1795) and *A Moral Epistle* (1795), he published in 1798—contemporaneous with *Lyrical Ballads*—his *Gebir*, which created in its age what *Sordello* was to create in the next, a legend (quite unfounded) of total incomprehensibility. It has numerous beautiful passages, still more numerous beautiful lines and phrases, but it is fatally lacking in character and interest. Landor produced many verse-pieces in dialogue form, and called them *Acts and Scenes*, expressly noting that "none of them were offered to the stage, being no better than *Imaginary Conversations* in metre". But *Count Julian* (1812) is a "closet" drama of the kind frequently put forth in Landor's time. Three other dramatic works in verse, *Andrea of Hungary*, *Giovanna of Naples* and *Fra Rupert* (1839–40) belong to later years of Landor's work, but not to a later manner, for one especially remarkable fact about Landor is the unchanging style of his work through a remarkably long life. His *Hellenics*, of which there are fifty, are idylls in the Greek fashion, and as such they use or disuse at pleasure the dialogue form. It is impossible even to name Landor's numerous other verse compositions in narrative or in dialogue form. He is seen at his best in shorter lyrical pieces, some of the most delightful coming from such late volumes as *The Last Fruit off an Old Tree* (1853), and *Dry Sticks, fagoted* (1858).

Landor is more generally known and liked as a writer of prose. *Imaginary Conversations* did not begin to be published till he was past the middle of his long life; but he was untiring in the production of them to the very last, and their sheer quantity is almost daunting. Range and treatment are wonderfully varied, yet a sense of monotony is inescapable, in spite of moments in which the prose mounts almost to the heights of poetry. The one department in which Landor definitely fails to succeed is humour. Critical opinion about Landor has taken the lead from his own declaration: "I shall dine late, but the room will be well-lighted, and the guests few but select." Many have invited themselves to this banquet of the superior. His contemporaries admired not only his writings, but his ebullient character. The unmeasured laudation of Swinburne followed; and others felt themselves almost socially promoted by their admiration for an aristocratic (though ultra-Liberal) writer. This is rather a pity; for Landor is a very fine, and even a unique writer, definitely not of the first rank, but rich in reward for those who are content to approach him on the normal terms. He has some great show pieces of prose, and a few perfect short poems; but his characters are never "human effluences", they are effluences of books and of a fantastic individual combination of scholarly taste and wilful temperament.

Leigh Hunt came into literature without any of the advantages possessed by the wealthy Landor. Like Lamb and Coleridge, he was at Christ's Hospital, and oddly enough, like Lamb, a stammerer. He quickly passed into journalism in 1808 to help his brother John in editing *The Examiner*, a weekly newspaper which in the face of danger continued to assert liberal opinions. The climax came in 1813 when Hunt was sentenced to two years' imprisonment and fined £500 for telling part of the truth about the Prince Regent. He further endured the vilest attacks from the reviewers, especially from *Blackwood*. Leigh Hunt's courage and insubmission must never be forgotten when we remember the more Skimpolish features of his character. To give even a list of Leigh Hunt's works is impossible. He began with poetry, and in the course of his long life wrote a fair quantity of it. His most considerable piece, *The Story of Rimini* (1816), tries to tell a tragic story beyond his range in rhymed couplets beyond his power. Leigh Hunt's real strength is to be found in prose, especially in those pieces with intercalated verse translations or illustrations. Of such are *Wit and Humour* (1846), an essay with well-chosen examples from the English poets; *Imagination and Fancy* (1844), the same kind of thing, and important enough to have been taken at one time as a major pronouncement on its theme; *A Jar of Honey from Mount Hybla* (1848), an essay on pastoral poetry with illustrations from many sources, and illustrations of another kind by Dicky Doyle, whose *Punch* cover suggests a Leigh Hunt idyll. Besides these there are collected essays in *Men, Women and Books* (1847), and discursive works like *The Town* (1848), of a type once manufactured annually by every publisher. Last and not least is the famous and indispensable *Autobiography* (1850). Hunt was invited by the impulsive Shelley to Italy in 1821, to help him and Byron in producing a new and important review called *The Liberal*. Hunt set out, accompanied by a wife and seven children. A week after the Hunt cavalcade arrived, Shelley was drowned. Byron and Hunt were never in sympathy, and after four excellent numbers *The Liberal* perished, and Hunt was back at Highgate. He lived on for many years, doing incessant journalistic and literary work and setting a model for other writers. *Sketches by Boz* were in the Hunt manner and *Household Words* followed the Hunt pattern. In criticism, Hunt has the merit, which Macaulay long ago assigned to him, of a most unusual and, at the time, almost unique catholicity.

De Quincey was the son of a wealthy linen-merchant. In 1802 while still at Manchester Grammar School he was seized with a desire to wander, and went off to the hills of Wales. He thereby forfeited most of his income; and when his wanderings brought him to London, where he starved in an empty house in Soho with the forlorn girl Ann, as frail as himself, he forfeited all. This very strange story is told in *The Confessions of an English Opium Eater*, written many years later. By 1803, he was decoyed back to civilization, and entered Oxford, where he indulged himself in a wide range of reading, including German philosophy; and being smitten, as one might say, by Coleridge, made him a gift of £300, anonymously, wishing, with needless delicacy, to spare the poet's feelings. It was at Oxford that he first took to opium. He affiliated himself to the great men of the Lakes by taking over Dove Cottage when Wordsworth left it, and stayed there for twenty years. He married Margaret Simpson, the daughter of a dalesman, and in some way, which it is not necessary to discuss here, offended the Wordsworths. When he left the Lakes he went to Edinburgh, and lived in its neighbourhood, creeping about like a delicate little ghost from lodging to lodging, writing incessantly, and dying in the city itself at the age of seventy-four. It may be added that he was born plain Quincey, and assumed the honorific prefix, thereby satisfying both his own pride and our sense of euphony.

The most curious fact about De Quincey as a writer is that, during a long life devoted to letters, he published only two books, *Klosterheim* (1832), and a *Logic of Political Economy* (1844). Everything else took the form of magazine or cyclopedia articles, and of these *The Confessions of an English Opium Eater* were alone collected after their appearance in *The London Magazine* and published in 1822. Perhaps even more curious is the fact that the demand for a collected De Quincey came first from the United States. The American activity stirred James Hogg, the Edinburgh publisher, to action; for in 1852 he asked De Quincey to undertake a collected edition of his writings. De Quincey was then over sixty-seven, the most wayward, dreamy and unearthly of creatures; and apparently his preferred method was to sit down and write all his articles over again. But with much stimulation and much restraint (for he was liable at any moment to propose new works on a large scale) a beginning was made and the first volume appeared in 1853. The American edition was completed in 1859, the British in 1860.

The reader of De Quincey is likely at first to be most conscious of his faults, and these may at once be admitted and dismissed. The first is a chronic long-windedness, a steady refusal to come to the heart of his matter; the next is a desire to magnify his learning; the next is a maddening sapience, perhaps caught from Coleridge; and the next is an elaborate and intolerable facetiousness. His articles on some of the Germans, for instance—Kant, Herder, Goethe, Schiller—are made up of mere "rigmarole", the kind of sapient and yet actually empty writing that could be used to pad out any kind of article on any subject. He is always about to begin, and then draws suddenly to a close without having said anything. And in the midst of a serious passage he will break off to indulge in infantile facetiousness. His fame depends ultimately upon the *Opium-Eater*, the *Reminiscences of the English Lake Poets* (contributed to *Tait's Edinburgh Magazine*), and the three "fantasias", *On Murder considered as one of the Fine Arts*, *The English Mail Coach* and *Suspiria de Profundis*. For some these contain the most moving examples of prose eloquence we possess; for others they are detestable examples of the sham sublime. De Quincey will always divide readers; but the truth appears to be between the extremes. Certainly nothing is more intolerable than the fine writing which has a palpable design on the reader; and in De Quincey there is plenty of that; but when eloquence grows and mounts in natural ascent the feelings of the reader are heightened in natural response; and in De Quincey there is plenty of that. In spite of his obvious faults, De Quincey is a very considerable writer, much less artificial and much more spontaneous than Landor, and the reader must take him in the mass, cherishing his best and ignoring his worst. One of his twentieth-century admirers was D. H. Lawrence.

As a postscript, there should be a brief notice of Landor's younger brother Robert Eyres Landor (1781–1869) who, withdrawn into a country parsonage and having no passion for controversy, allowed his early play *The Count of Arezzi* (1824) to be attributed to Byron and his later story *The Fawn of Sertorius* (1846) to be attributed to his brother, and destroyed, it is said, most of the copies of the three other plays which came in a single volume between them— *The Earl of Brecon*, *Faith's Fraud* and *The Ferryman* (1841). The few people who have read him acknowledge his complete individuality of style.

X. JANE AUSTEN

Jane Austen had in a high degree a gift that some more imposing authors have had in a low degree, or in no degree at all, namely, the gift of self-criticism. She wrote of the life she knew, and never tried to write of the life she did not know. No one understood better than the author of *Pride and Prejudice* the limits she must not pass. Jane Austen (1775–1817) was born at Steventon, in Hampshire, of which her father was rector. She had one sister, the heroically-named Cassandra, and five brothers, two of whom became distinguished admirals. She was taught by her father, and lived quietly at various homes in Hampshire and in Bath. She did not travel, went to London merely as a visitor, saw nothing of "high life", and, after a long period of bad health, died at Winchester in her forty-second year. She made no pretensions to be a literary lady, but wrote in the common sitting-room of her family, sharing some of her secrets with her beloved sister. She read the ordinary English classics of her time. She enjoyed

Fanny Burney, but shrewdly recognized the places where Fanny was writing beyond her means. She enjoyed Richardson even to the extent of bestowing upon *Sir Charles Grandison* what seems to modern readers an excess of admiration. And of course she read the current "Gothick" romances with amused contempt.

Her inborn sense of comedy was aroused very early by the absurdities of sentimental novels, and some juvenile literary efforts, not printed till 1922, take the form of burlesques in Richardsonian epistles, which reproduce with impish gravity and humorous restraint the ardours of passionate lovers. *Love and Freindship* (so spelt), dated 1790, was evidently written for domestic entertainment. It contains, potentially, nearly every quality the writer was to show in her mature works. The swoonings and sudden deaths are managed with immense comic effect. The transition from these *juvenilia* to her first published books can be found in the fragment of an epistolary novel called *Lady Susan*, first printed in 1871. It was written about 1794. A little later, *Elinor and Marianne*, a first sketch for *Sense and Sensibility*, was written in letters. The author did not offer it for publication, and never afterwards attempted the epistolary form of novel. Actually the first of her published novels to be written was *Pride and Prejudice*, which, under the title *First Impressions*, was composed during 1796-7. Her father offered it to Cadell, who refused it. *First Impressions* had been completed some three months when the young author began to re-write *Elinor and Marianne* as *Sense and Sensibility*; but this did not appear till 1811. It is thus her first published book, and its success was immediate. In 1798 she began to write *Susan*, the first draft of *Northanger Abbey*; and this she sold to a publisher, who, however, failed to issue it, and Jane did not recover her manuscript till 1816. It was posthumously published as *Northanger Abbey* in 1818, perhaps with some revision, and with apologies for "those parts of the work which thirteen years have made comparatively obsolete". In 1803 or 1804 she began a story which was never finished, and which was first published as *The Watsons* in 1871, with some other fragments, in the second edition of J. E. Austen-Leigh's *Memoir*.

After 1803 there came a gap of several years in Jane Austen's literary work. The rejected *First Impressions* was triumphantly revised, and appeared as *Pride and Prejudice* in 1813—her second publication. In 1812 she began *Mansfield Park*, which was published in 1814. *Emma* was begun in January 1814, finished in March 1815, and published in 1816. *Persuasion*, last of her regularly published stories, was begun in 1815 and finished in July 1816. The manuscript was still in her hands at her death, and it was published posthumously with *Northanger Abbey* in 1818. All her books appeared anonymously, but her name was given in the short biographical notice prefixed to the volumes of 1818. In January 1817 she had begun to write a new novel, but after the middle of March could work no more. No reason has been ascertained for the gap in her work from 1804 to 1811. The odd fact is that from 1811 to the end she worked steadily.

From this unavoidably tangled tale of Jane Austen's literary activities there emerge two main facts: first that the dates at which her books were published tell us little about the dates at which they were composed, and next that she was a careful craftsman, prepared to give long consideration to her tasks. The earliest stratum of her work, as we now have it, is represented by *Northanger*

Abbey, which, apparently, was allowed to retain most of its first form. Both theme and treatment support the supposition. A quietly humorous observant girl with a gift for writing would naturally want to ridicule the passion of women, old and young, for grotesque and exorbitant romances. Catherine, the simple heroine, has naive charm, and is in character, though not in years, much younger than the more critically studied Marianne Dashwood and Fanny Price. *Sense and Sensibility* represents the next stage. It was written from small experience, and is weaker in character and control than any of the other novels. *Pride and Prejudice* comes next in 1813. One would be glad to see the first draft which Cadell refused; for the work as published is one of Jane Austen's masterpieces. It has the Shakespearean (and Dickensian) quality of describing absurd and disagreeable people delightfully. Jane Austen's next novel, *Mansfield Park*, is less brilliant than *Pride and Prejudice*, but it is the widest in scope of the six. The development of Fanny Price, from the shy little girl into the woman who marries Edmund Bertram, is one of Jane Austen's finest achievements in the exposition of character. This book most clearly shows the influence of Richardson. *Emma* was written rapidly and confidently after the success of its predecessors. That Emma is loved for her faults as well as for her virtues is testimony to the fineness of Jane Austen's art. *Persuasion*, written when the author's physical powers were failing, is a quiet story, rich in character and sparing of incident. There is no sign of mental failure.

In Jane Austen's novels there are neither peasants nor noblemen. Her world is comfortably off, and no one seems to work for a living. She never describes great passions or seeks to point any moral. She is completely detached and impersonal. In a national literature a little inclined to excess she represents the triumph of understatement. With complete verisimilitude she gives us commonplace persons, not types, and they reveal themselves completely and consistently in narrative and conversation of almost extraordinary ordinariness. Jane Austen's poise and self-control, her perfect fitting of her quiet utterance to her quiet purpose, are as clearly marks of creative genius as the exuberance and expansiveness of the more heroic creators. The high praise given to her by Scott and Macaulay is explicable and deserved. They acknowledged the fine artistic sincerity that shone out from the mass of contemporary novelistic rubbish.

XI. LESSER NOVELISTS

With Scott and Jane Austen successfully representing the two extremes of novelistic manner at this time, it is surprising that there was no great outcrop of imitations. The novelists who might have produced imitation Scott or Austen followed their own individuality or derived hints from earlier exemplars.

Susan Edmonstone Ferrier (1782–1854) wrote novels which have something of the rough sarcasm of Smollett, mingled with a strong didactic flavour and with occasional displays of sentiment in the manner of Mackenzie. To her personal friend Scott (who was once supposed to be the author of her novels) she may have owed something in her studies of Scottish life, but Maria Edgeworth was her principal model. Her first novel, *Marriage*, written in 1810 but not published till 1818, is full of vigorous work. The studies of the Highland family into which an English lady of aristocratic birth and selfish temper marries by elopement are spirited and humorous. *The Inheritance*, published in 1824, has more unity. *Destiny*, published in 1831, is chiefly remarkable for the character of McDow, the minister. Susan Ferrier was a Scottish novelist of power, whose work is still fresh and interesting.

Frances Trollope (1780–1863), mother of Adolphus and Anthony, was the wife of a poor, embarrassed scholar. She resolved to save the domestic situation, and, having lived in the United States for several years, produced her *Domestic Manners of the Americans* (1832) which caused an explosion, to be followed later by another, when Dickens wrote *Martin Chuzzlewit*. Mrs Trollope was left a widow in 1835 and settled at Florence in 1843. Her chief novels are *The Vicar of Wrexhill* (1837), in which a wicked clergyman is the principal character; *The Widow Barnaby* (1838), in which the widow is the buxom, coarse kind of body who might have been drawn by Smollett; and *The Widow Married* (1840), a sequel. She was a most prolific writer, and rough and crude as much of her work is, her power and her directness are qualities of their own kind.

Catherine Grace Gore (1799–1861) was eminently "the novelist of fashionable life", and as such was caricatured by Thackeray. *Mrs Armytage, or Female Domination* (1836) is her nearest approach to a novel of the first rank. Recalling Jane Austen in its general tone, it is quite unlike her in its gravity, its didactic note and its use of incident.

Letitia Elizabeth Landon, the poet, scarcely survives as a novelist, although *Ethel Churchill* (1837), may take its place among the second-rate novels of the day. So, too, may the *Granby* (1826) of Thomas Henry Lister (1800–42), with its manly hero and its baseborn, reckless, but not unattractive villain. Lister's dialogue was considered brilliant.

Mary Wollstonecroft Shelley takes her place among the immortal "horrific" novelists, for her *Frankenstein, or the Modern Prometheus* (1818) has given a name, often misapplied, to popular mythology. (Frankenstein is the hero, not the monster). The tale was the product of a wet summer in Switzerland, when Byron suggested that each member of the party should write a ghost story. People naturally believed that Shelley had invented the theme; but this Mary expressly denied, and her denial may be accepted, for a later work, *The Last Man* (1826), shows the same kind of power—suggestive of H. G. Wells—of making the impossible seem rational, by basing it upon the logic of science. Shelley assisted by writing part of the *Frankenstein* preface.

Catherine Crowe (1800–76) not only delighted in ghosts and similar occasions of terror, in *The Night Side of Nature* (1848) she attempted to find a scientific explanation of such things; and the result is an engaging volume of mingled story and speculation. In her two novels, *Adventures of Susan Hopley; or Circumstantial Evidence* (1841) and *The Story of Lilly Dawson* (1847), the horrors are more substantial.

George Croly (1780–1860) deals little with the supernatural, but has a distinct affinity with the novel of terror. The principal aim of his chief novel, *Salathiel* (1829), is to overwhelm the reader with monstrous visions of horror and dismay. The theme of the story is the destruction of Jerusalem by the Romans under Titus; and here, as in *Marston* (1846), a romance of the French Revolution and the subsequent European warfare, Croly joins the ranks of historical novelists. His heroes are modelled on Byron's, and his prose on De Quincey's.

George Payne Rainsford James (1799–1860) professed to be a follower of Scott, but followed him at a long distance. There is more than a touch of the Radcliffe mysteries about some of his almost innumerable novels. His supposed favourite opening gambit of two cloaked horsemen (or a solitary horseman) wending their (or his) way through the precipitous pathways of the Apennines on an evening of threatening splendour made him an easy prey to such burlesque as Thackeray's *Barbazure*. But there was more than nonsense in James. *Richelieu* (1829), *Darnley* (1830), and their successors interested his contemporaries, and fascinated many small boys (with a talent for skipping) for a generation after. Like Scott and Ainsworth, he enlarged the world for young readers, and increased their knowledge of history in a way undreamed of by schools.

William Harrison Ainsworth (1805–82) was a man of strong and vigorous intelligence as well as an indefatigable writer. From *Rookwood* (1834) to *Stanley Brereton* (1881), a long list of historical novels (some of them with pleasingly horrible pictures) gratified several generations of readers—generally young. Among the best are *Jack Sheppard* (1839), *The Tower of London* (1840), *Guy Fawkes* (1841), *Old St Paul's* (1841), *Windsor Castle* (1843), and *The Lancashire Witches* (1848). These and others can still delight men as well as boys, thanks to their energetic movement and their vivid though rough style of narration.

Frederick Marryat (1792–1848) descends from Smollett rather than from Scott. He entered the Navy in 1806 and saw much active service. He became Post-Captain in 1826 and was awarded the C.B. in the same year. He was a thoroughly capable officer with strong modern views on humanity and efficiency in the Service. He was very far indeed from being merely a naval officer who wrote sea-books for boys. He falls only a little below the first rank. He is equally strong in incident and in character, particularly in such books as *Peter Simple* (1834), *Mr Midshipman Easy* (1836), *Japhet in search of a Father* (1836), *Jacob Faithful* (1834) and *Snarleyyow* (1837). The stories he really wrote for boys—*Masterman Ready* (1841), *The Settlers in Canada* (1844) and *The Children of the New Forest* (1847)—remain favourites on the junior shelf. The vitality of Marryat (who was one of the earliest influences on Joseph Conrad) will be better appreciated after a glance through the once popular sea-stories of his contemporary, Captain Frederick Chamier (1796–1870)—from *Ben Brace* (1836) to *Tom Bowling* (1841).

John Galt (1779–1839) led a varied life at home and abroad. He met Byron in the Levant and afterwards wrote a much criticized *Life* of the poet. His novels, *The Ayrshire Legatees* (1821), *The Entail* (1823) and *The Annals of the Parish* (1821), give admirably minute and real studies of rural life in Scotland, full of strong delineation of character and forcible detail. Galt was the true founder of what was later called the "Kailyard School" of fiction. He is an important figure in the history of the novel of nationality.

David Macbeth Moir (1798–1851), poet and humorist, wrote for his friend

Galt the concluding chapters of a novel, *The Last of the Lairds*, and was the author of *The Life of Mansie Wauch, Tailor in Dalkeith* (1828), a partly satirical and very amusing study of humble Scottish character.

XII. THE OXFORD MOVEMENT

The movement which is called from its battle-ground the Oxford Movement, or from its methods of controversy the Tractarian Movement, or from the name of one who had directly very little to do with it, the Puseyite Movement, stood apart from the thought and common feelings of the time. Men went on thinking and writing in other fields of activity as if there were no such persons as Newman and Keble and Pusey, or, like Carlyle, dismissed them contemptuously as insignificant. Viewed from afar the Oxford Movement appeared to be a theological dispute among the local clergy in a university city; in the course of a few years it was to shake the whole Church of England and change the very nature of its being.

During the eighteenth century the Church had sunk into stagnation. Its liturgy was in practice reduced to a minimum. The Wesleys at Oxford, seeking to take the Prayer Book as a guide to methodical religious life, found themselves regarded as eccentric fanatics. The earlier defection of the Non-jurors and the later defection of the Methodists left the Church little more than the formal voice of the State. Early in the nineteenth century a few fervent spirits began to feel the dissatisfaction that had been felt by the Wesleys, and they were aided by influences the Wesleys had never known. The disquisitions of Coleridge and his interest in the great English divines had given new life to Anglican theology; the romances of Scott had made pre-Reformation worship strangely attractive. To the power of Scott's influence the detestation of the ultra-Protestant Borrow is a testimony. Theologically, the immediate ancestors of the new reformers were the Caroline divines, who had, however, begotten another line —the high and dry Tory Churchmen, almost the last of whom was a remarkable person, Alexander Knox (1757–1831) of Dublin, whose writings and correspondence, published posthumously in nine volumes (1834–7), show him to have anticipated the views of the Oxford reformers. Knox had himself said as early as 1816, "The Old High Church race is worn out". But old Martin Routh, who had known Dr Johnson, lived on till 1854. The first blast of the trumpet came from John Keble (1792–1866), who, in the Assize Sermon at Oxford delivered in 1833, denounced the Erastian stagnation of the Church as national apostasy. Newman regarded Keble's sermon as the beginning of the Oxford Movement. Almost at the same time, there met at the rectory of Hadleigh in Suffolk a company of like-minded men, under the presidency of the rector, Hugh James Rose (1795–1838) a Cambridge scholar, to whom the Oxonians looked for light and leading. Indeed, it has been said with some truth that the Oxford Movement began at Cambridge. The "Hadleigh Conferences" and the Assize Sermon appealed mainly to the clerical and academic authorities. There was no dealing with the general public, as such. The most celebrated *Tracts for the Times* were addressed, not to the sheep, but to the shepherds.

It is no part of our concern to trace the history of the Oxford Movement. We have to consider simply what contributions to literature arose from it or inspired it. The earliest and most popular was Keble's *The Christian Year*, an anonymous book of verses in two volumes (1827), sub-titled "Thoughts in Verse for the Sundays and Holydays throughout the year". It has been called Wordsworth and water, and there is certainly some suggestion of the more placid Wordsworth in the quiet, sweet, reflective poems of the book. Far indeed from the piercing utterances of George Herbert, these gentle verses of Keble nevertheless embody something of the spirit of the English Book of Common Prayer.

Two brothers, Richard Hurrell Froude (1803–36) and James Anthony Froude (1818–94), were of varying importance in the Movement. The younger, James Anthony, was at first affected by Newman, and took orders, but rejected both, and lived to become the lay historian who made a hero of Henry VIII. The elder, a fiery spirit, was self-consumed with religious ardour. Had he lived, he might have made the Movement more violent and sudden. His burning spirit consumed his body, and he travelled with Newman to the Mediterranean in search of health. The main result of the voyage was the beginning of the poems called *Lyra Apostolica*, first published as a volume in 1836. With the return of Newman began the issue of *Tracts for the Times*. The first (1833) was a small and unexciting sheet; the last (No. 90), *Remarks on Certain Passages in the Thirty-Nine Articles* (1841), aroused a storm that drove Newman, its author, out of the Church. After the death of R. H. Froude appeared the two volumes of his *Remains* (1838, 1839) which assailed with unsuspected power the Reformation and all its ways and works. Froude's *Remains* acted as a purge. The timid were driven from the Movement, the vigorous were strengthened to proceed.

Among the contributors to the Tracts was Edward Bouverie Pusey (1800–82), who was well acquainted with rationalist German theology, and quite unaffected by it. He was not in any sense a leader of the Oxford Movement, though he gave it strength by his share in issuing *The Library of the Fathers of the Holy Catholic Church, anterior to the division of the East and West* (1836–85). After Newman's defeat and collapse, Pusey (with Keble quietly aiding) became the revered and sagacious leader of the "High Church" Anglicans.

One of the most charming writers in the Movement was Isaac Williams (1802–65), who, in a special sense, was a disciple of Keble. *The Cathedral* (1838) shows little of Keble's technical mastery, but it has genuine feeling: it persuades and quickens. Williams was the writer of Tracts 80 and 87, *On Reserve in communicating Religious Knowledge*, which created almost as much indignation as Newman's Tract 90.

The man who did most to make and to break the force of the Movement was the elusive and bewildering John Henry Newman (1801–90), who, following truth as he conceived it, read himself out of "Low" Church into "High", and out of "High" into the even greater altitude of Rome. Though in Oxford the eyes of all were upon the vicar of St Mary's as the most potent and alluring figure there, he was in perpetual perplexity about his own faith. He had no great learning; but he magnetized and attracted the young. Keble and Isaac Williams gave the Movement poetry; Newman gave it the almost more seductive music of prose. Very few of the books written during his Anglican period are important, because he was writing himself out of one perplexity into another. It was not until he had finally written himself into the Roman Church, as he did in the *Essay on the Development of Christian Doctrine* (1845), and solved his perplexities by finding rest in a Church which appears to have none, that he began to speak out firmly. The storm aroused by Tract 90 made Newman's position in the English Church untenable, and after painful delay he was received into the Roman Church in 1845. So ended the Oxford Movement, as such. Of Newman's many books not all belong to literature. First by right of personal interest comes *Apologia pro Vita Sua*, issued in parts during 1864, and published as a volume in 1865. Kingsley had charged him (as Thomas Arnold had before) with inculcating economy in the use of truth. Kingsley had a sense that something was wrong with Newman; but he made an untenable accusation, blundered in supporting it, and thus delivered himself into Newman's hands. Newman refused any further controversy with Kingsley and wrote, instead, an autobiographic history of his religious opinions, and asked, in effect, is this the portrait of a liar or of a seeker after truth? The *Apologia* is among the great autobiographies of the world, though no one lacking sympathy with Newman's religious troubles can read it with full enjoyment; and some may even read it as a curious case of self-deception. There is more general profit in Newman's sermons, the best of which are to be found in such volumes as *Sermons preached before the University of Oxford* (1843), *Sermons bearing upon Subjects of the Day* (1843), *Discourses Addressed to Mixed Congregations* (1849), and *Sermons Preached on Various Occasions* (1854). Of much wider appeal is *The Idea of a University*, containing two works previously published, *Discourses on the Scope and Nature of University Education* (1852), and *Lectures and Essays on University Subjects* (1858), both being delivered by him in his capacity as Rector of the ill-fated Catholic University in Dublin. This book shows Newman at his best, polished, urbane, persuasive, and delicately humorous. Despite its forbidding title, *The Present Position of Catholics in England* (1851) is a splendid piece of sustained and varied argument expressed in prose eloquence that is never merely rhetorical. *The Grammar of Assent* (1870) carries the argument of probability, the cornerstone of his master Butler, on to new ground. The collection called *Verses on Various Occasions* (1868) contains most of Newman's poems from *Lyra Apostolica*, with the remarkable *Dream of Gerontius* (1866) relating the passing of a man's soul from his body to the Divine presence. The musical setting of this by Elgar has made it the best known work of Newman after the *Apologia* and the famous hymn *Lead, kindly Light*.

Several of the younger followers of Newman attained to celebrity in literature. Richard William Church (1815–90), one of the many literary Deans of St Paul's, gained high esteem for his studies of St Anselm, Dante and Spenser, as well as for his brief and attractive history of the Oxford Movement. Richard Chenevix Trench (1807–86), though a Cambridge man, was in sympathy with the Oxford men through his master Hugh James Rose. Trench passed from the Deanery of Westminster to the Archbishopric of Dublin, and has left us his still useful volumes, *The Study of Words* (1851), and *English Past and Present* (1859), which remind us that language is "fossil poetry". His *Sacred Latin Poetry* (1849) first made known to readers of its day the glories of the medieval hymns. William Stubbs (1825–1901), most solid of historians and Bishop, first of Chester and next of Oxford, was a convinced Tractarian in belief, and reverenced Pusey, whom he called master. Another Cambridge man in sympathy with the Oxford Movement was John Mason Neale (1818–66), the vigorous foe of "liberalism", the writer of a *History of the Holy Eastern Church* (1847–51), and the adaptor from ancient sources of many well-known hymns including *Jerusalem the golden*, and *Good King Wenceslas*. All his hymns are contained in *Collected Hymns, Sequences and Carols* (1914). Frederick William Faber (1814–63), who followed Newman to Rome, is another famous hymnologist, best known for *Hark, hark, my soul*. His great-nephew, the publisher Sir Geoffrey Faber (1889–1965), wrote a study of the Oxford Movement called *Oxford Apostles*, published the same year, 1933, as Christopher Dawson's more orthodox study *The Spirit of the Oxford Movement*.

The glamour of the Oxford Movement touched many who were far from the time and place of conflict. It tuned the pulpits to a new dignity; and in the poetry of Digby Mackworth Dolben and of Christina Rossetti it kindled a new life exuberant and aflame. To Christina Rossetti the Catholic theology of the English Church was the very breath of life, and she accepted its sternness without dispute. Neo-Catholicism even spread to the novels, not always happily. J. M. Neale wrote stories. Newman himself put some very good polemical work into *Loss and Gain* and the historical *Callista*. Nicholas Wiseman, the Catholic Archbishop of Westminster and founder of the *Dublin Review* (later called the *Wiseman Review*), wrote *Fabiola*, an effort of the same kind. But most widely influential of all was the long line of stories written by Charlotte M. Yonge (1823–1901) in Keble's own parish of Hursley. *The Heir of Redclyffe* (1853) has not yet lost its appeal.

It may be said in conclusion that the chief aim of the Oxford Movement was to make plain to Englishmen the historical continuity of their national Church. It was not ritualistic. It sought to rekindle the English liturgy, not to decorate it. While the Tractarians were still in their cradles, the wonderful old scholar, theologian and Tory, Martin Joseph Routh (1755–1854) President of Magdalen, had shown the Church of England the rock upon which it was built, by the publication of the first part of his *Reliquiae Sacrae* (1814), in which he collected the fragments of early Christian writings up to the first Nicene Council and edited them with a remarkable combination of affection, erudition and sagacity. He set the tone for the Oxford writers. Theology and history were inseparable. Accuracy was all important. "I think (he said) you will find it a very good practice always to verify your references, sir." In a sense, this was the spirit of the Oxford Movement. The real teaching of the Church would be found if you went back to the right sources.

XIII. THE GROWTH OF LIBERAL THEOLOGY

That a Church whose ministers resembled the Mr Collins of Jane Austen needed some reformation was clear to many besides the leaders of the Oxford Movement. What was not clear was the direction and nature of the desired reformation. The Tractarians had sought it by proclaiming the living continuity of the English Church with the Church of the ante-Nicene Councils, and by rekindling the authentic fire of the English liturgy. At the other extreme were those to whom the literal words of the Bible were the sole and sufficient guide to life and the sole and sufficient source of revelation. Such were the Evangelicals; and what a man might suffer who dared to point out inconsistencies in the Gospel narratives may be read in *Phases of Faith* (1853), written by Francis William Newman, younger brother of the man who was later to write the *Apologia*. A singular spectacle is offered by the course of these two brothers, who, both starting in youth from Evangelicalism, gradually diverged, one ending a Cardinal of Rome, the other embracing a skeleton outline of religion compiled from all the creeds of all the nations. *Phases of Faith* is a lean, arid book, much less readable than the *Apologia*, although the author had led a life far more exciting and adventurous than his brother's. There was a third brother, Charles Robert Newman, who became an agnostic and contributed essays to Holyoake's *Reasoner*.

Evangelicalism did not run to literature. Its aim was the conversion, not the entertainment, of its followers. Hannah More's *Cheap Repository Tracts* had an enormous vogue, and a simple moral tale by Legh Richmond, *The Dairyman's Daughter*, reached two million copies. Charles Simeon (1759–1836), with his wider interests, published almost nothing except homiletic literature, "skeletons" of sermons, as he frankly called them. Even a professed work of learning like Joseph Milner's *History of the Church of Christ* (1794–7) aimed chiefly at edification. Neither Joseph nor his brother Isaac Milner, who brought the history down to Luther's reformation, thought it necessary to read anything in Luther's language. Evangelical theology concentrated itself upon a few favourite doctrines which formed the scheme of salvation. Biblical interpretation commanded but a narrow field of interest; the unfulfilled prophecies alone gave scope for speculation. The rigid theory of literal inspiration foreclosed inquiry, and the Evangelicals retained that theory longest of all. They were sometimes narrow and bigoted. Their merit lay in their pastoral zeal and in their philanthropy. Prominent among them were Lord Shaftesbury, Sir James Stephen, Dr Bowdler, editor of "the family Shakespeare" (1818), Zachary Macaulay, father of the historian, William Wilberforce, whose *Practical View of...the Religious System* (1797) found a vast number of readers, and Henry Thornton, great-grandfather of the novelist E. M. Forster, whose house on Clapham Common inspired Sydney Smith's description of the Evangelicals as "the Clapham Sect".

What Tractarians and Evangelicals alike feared was an invasion by the Germans, to whom nothing was sacred. When Wolf had exploded Homer as a myth and Niebuhr had exploded Livy as a mythologist, what might not others do to the books of the Bible? What, indeed, had they not already done? No patriotic general, foreseeing the effects of an invasion of the land by German infantry, could have been more vigilant than Pusey was against an invasion of the mind by German theology. And Pusey, unlike Newman, really knew German theology. On this point High and Low Church were united. But the watchmen availed not. What they feared was already within the gates, in the persons of their own countrymen, afterwards called (probably by A. H. Clough) the "Broad" Church, as something lying conveniently between "High" and "Low". One great man whose writings were an inspiration to "High" and "Broad" alike was the convenient and ever-helpful Coleridge. *Confessions of an Inquiring Spirit*, published posthumously in 1840, combats the contemporary view that the Bible was not to be "reasoned about in the way that other good books are".

There was movement, other than Tractarian, in Oxford itself. Edward Copleston (1776–1849), Provost of Oriel from 1814–28, encouraged free and unfettered criticism among the intellectuals. His *Advice to a Young Reviewer* is an excellent piece of irony. Oxford, generally, feared the Oriel fellows, and nicknamed them the Noetics. The ablest of the group was Richard Whately (1787–1863), afterwards Archbishop of Dublin, who, in a brief association with Newman, did his less assured junior some rough good. Whately was a logical and totally unromantic person, and had no patience with the Tractarians on the one hand, or the Evangelicals on the other. Another famous Oriel theologian was Thomas Arnold (1795–1842), afterwards headmaster of Rugby, who accepted the modern methods of critical research in Biblical study, feeling sure that his faith in God and his hope of eternal life did not depend upon the accuracy of a date.

There was a movement, too, outside Oxford. Julius Charles Hare (1795–1855), whose chief contributions to the literature of the Broad Church movement are his own sermons collected as *The Victory of Faith* (1840) and *The Mission of the Comforter* (1846), collaborated with Connop Thirlwall in a translation of Niebuhr, and with his brother Augustus William in the composition of *Guesses at Truth* (1827). Connop Thirlwall (1797–1875) passed from the bar to the church after translating Schleiermacher's *St Luke* in 1823.

One of the greatest of the Broad Churchmen was Frederick Denison Maurice (1805–72), who, under the influence of Coleridge, passed from dissent at Cambridge to Oxford and holy orders. But his outspoken *Theological Essays* (1853), repudiating the orthodox views of eternal punishment and the Atonement, lost him his professorship at King's College, London. With the same disregard of popularity and the same risk of misunderstanding, Maurice proclaimed himself a Christian Socialist. Of course both Christians and Socialists hastened to disown him. It is to Maurice, chiefly, that we owe the Working Men's College, and the Queen's College for Women. Charles Kingsley (1819–75) was, like Maurice, a Christian Socialist, and under the name of "Parson Lot" wrote many articles on social reform. Frederick Robertson (1816–53) entered the Anglican Ministry without any academic fame, and by the time of his early death had published only a few casual sermons. Yet, already, he was known as a unique preacher. Other sermons were published posthumously, and none, not even Newman's, found so wide a range of readers. They are the utterances of an entirely independent mind, criticizing obsolete modes of theological expression, and exalting spirit above form. Maurice, Kingsley and Robertson represented the "Liberalism" which Newman considered "the great apostasy".

Two other famous men in the Broad Church movement were Benjamin Jowett (1817–93), the almost legendary Master of Balliol, and Arthur Penrhyn Stanley (1815–81), Arnold's favourite pupil. Jowett's most considerable work was his commentary on the Epistles to the Thessalonians, Galatians and Romans, which appeared on the same day as Stanley's commentary on the Epistles to the Corinthians (1855). The freshness of Jowett's treatment is still unexhausted. Stanley was interesting, but, as always, too miscellaneous. Everything reminded him of something else, and his *Lectures on the Jewish Church* (1863–76) abounds in parallels, sometimes good and sometimes forced.

One historical event in the Broad Church movement was the publication in 1860 of a volume called *Essays and Reviews*, written by seven authors who were described by one of their more orthodox opponents as "the Seven against Christ". It was not in any sense a manifesto, or a collective pronouncement, but it created as great a sensation as Tract 90. There was, of course, no heresy in the volume. Mark Pattison surveyed the tendencies of religious thought from 1688 to 1750, Jowett urged that the Bible should be interpreted like any other book, and so on. The volume created a major sensation in its day, but its interest is now almost entirely historical.

There were similar movements for freedom in other churches. In Scotland, the biblical contributions of William Robertson Smith (1865–94) to the ninth edition of the *Encyclopaedia Britannica* excited a growing hostility from 1875 till 1881, when he was removed from his professorial chair at Aberdeen. But there was a larger public ready to form its own judgment when he published his popular lectures, *The Old Testament in the Jewish Church* (1881) and *The Prophets of Israel* (1882). Another victim of heresy-hunting was John William Colenso (1814–83), Bishop of Natal and author of popular mathematical text books, who published *The Pentateuch and Book of Joshua critically examined*, in seven parts (1862–79). Colenso had been a devoted worker among the Africans in the new diocese, and had come to reject the doctrine of eternal punishment. His biblical criticism, which was not very soundly based or expressed, drew upon him a storm of abuse and persecution. Colenso and his sisters lived on in Natal, ministering to the Africans.

More comforting to earnest readers disturbed by controversy was an anonymous book, *Ecce Homo*, published in 1865. Its author proved to be John Robert Seeley, afterwards Professor of Modern History at Cambridge. Seeley deplored the danger to true religion if Christian ethics disappeared in the civil war of theologians. He regarded Christianity as natural fellow-feeling or humanity raised to the point of enthusiasm. Huxley and Matthew Arnold, in their various ways, exposed the weakness of die-hard literalism in religion. But, apart from controversy, good constructive work was done in the creation of a sound school of theological scholarship by three Cambridge contemporaries and friends, Brooke Foss Westcott, Fenton John Anthony Hort, and Joseph Barber Lightfoot. Westcott and Hort's main work was the recension of the Greek text of the New Testament; Lightfoot was concerned with the Pauline epistles and the Apostolic Fathers.

At the same time there was a welcome escape from the determinist and utilitarian fashions in theology. James Martineau (1805–1900), the veteran Unitarian, had in earlier life adopted the determinist and utilitarian theories of morals, but he proved their effective critic in his *Types of Ethical Theory* (1885). Three years later, he vindicated theistic belief in *A Study of Religion*. Sharp divisions began to disappear. High Churchmen had travelled more than half way from the Tractarian to the Liberal position when, in 1889, a group of Oxford friends issued *Lux Mundi* as a re-statement of Christian faith. It aroused at first almost as much consternation as *Essays and Reviews*. Even that Church which rates highest the principle of authority had difficulties with some who sought to create a Catholic atmosphere in which the modern mind may breathe more freely. The most distinguished of English "modernist" Catholics were George Tyrrell (1861–1909), author of *Nova et Vetera* (1897), *Christianity at the Cross Roads* (1909), and a fascinating *Autobiography* (1912), and the Anglo-Austrian theologian Baron Friedrich von Hugel (1852–1925), who wrote *The Mystical Element of Religion* (1908).

XIV. HISTORIANS

Writers on Ancient and Early Ecclesiastical History

It is remarkable that the success of Hume, Robertson and Gibbon stimulated no fresh development of historical writing in Britain. For the main inspiration of nineteenth-century historical literature we must look to the Continent, and especially to the *History of Rome* (1811, etc.) of Niebuhr, which first gave to English students a clear perception of the critical method in the treatment of history. The English translation of Niebuhr by Connop Thirlwall and Julius Hare (1828, etc.) was at once denounced as the product of scepticism. Nevertheless Niebuhr kindled the enthusiasm of Thomas Arnold, whose *History of Rome* (1838–43), though now out-of-date as a text book, remains a most readable narrative. Few works of its kind conform more closely to the demand of Acton in later years, when he declared, "if we lower our standard in History we cannot uphold it in Church and State". What Arnold would have done further is mere matter for speculation; for a year after his appointment as Regius Professor of Modern History at Oxford in 1841 he died suddenly. Arnold's narrative was, in a sense, continued by Charles Merivale (1808–93). *The History of the Romans under the Empire*, issued in seven volumes between 1850 and 1864, bridges the gap between Arnold and Gibbon. Merivale epitomized the earlier part of his history under the title *The Fall of the Roman Republic* (1853). An authoritative position among English histories of ancient Rome was held by George Long's *Decline of the Roman Republic* (1864–74). Long wrote with lucidity and judgment and had in him a strain of high philosophic morality that fitted him to be the translator of Marcus Aurelius.

The influence of the new school of historical criticism is conspicuous in two

English historians of Greece who adorned this age of our literature. Thirlwall's *History of Greece* (1835–44) appeared in eight volumes; the *History of Greece* by George Grote (1794–1871) appeared in twelve volumes between 1845 and 1856. The pair were schoolfellows, but their lives diverged widely. Thirlwall became a bishop; Grote entered the family banking house. Thirlwall's *History* was worthy of a furnished mind and a self-controlled character. In general, however, it was superseded by Grote's. Thirlwall was the better writer, though not the better historian. Grote's later volume, *Plato and the other Companions of Sokrates* (1865), may be regarded as a supplement to the *History*. On Grote's work was largely founded *The History of Greece* by Sir George William Cox (1827–1902), who was associated with Freeman in *Poems Legendary and Historical* (1850).

The next most notable contribution to the history of Greece was made by George Finlay (1799–1875), whose work was oddly produced. Being (like Byron) an enthusiast for Greek independence, he began by writing a *History of Greece from its Conquest by the Crusaders to its Conquest by the Turks, 1204–1461* (1851). He then went back and wrote a *History of the Byzantine and Greek Empires, 716–1453* (1853–4). He continued the tale in a *History of Greece under Othoman and Venetian Domination, 1452–1821* (1856). To this he added a *History of the Greek Revolution to 1843* (1862). His work was then collected posthumously into seven volumes by H. F. Tozer as *A History of Greece from its Conquest by the Romans to the Present Time, 146 B.C. to A.D. 1864* (1877). Finlay's great work thus covers two thousand years. He led a varied and interesting life (partly related in an autobiography) and he is entitled to his fame as a pioneer among those who have essayed the continuous, as well as the exact, treatment of an all but incomparable theme.

The *History of Sicily* (1891–4), by Edward Augustus Freeman, had necessarily touched upon Phoenicia. The history of Phoenicia as a whole was included in the vast field of the labours of George Rawlinson (1812–1902). His first great production was *The History of Herodotus* (1858–60) in which a new English version was accompanied by a large apparatus of historical and ethnological notes. It was followed by a notable series of works embodying the results of recent discoveries in the East. *The Five Great Monarchies of the Eastern World: Chaldaea, Assyria, Babylonia, Medea and Persia* (1862–7) did not cover the whole of the great scheme, and Rawlinson added *The Sixth Great Oriental Monarchy* (Parthia) in 1873, and *The Seventh* (Sassanian) in 1876. *Egypt, Phoenicia* and *Universal History* were the subjects of later volumes.

Henry Hart Milman (1791–1868), poet and historian, was more immediately known for his verse dramas and his hymns. His first historical work was *The History of the Jews* (1829), remarkable as one of the earliest books to adopt in England the German approach to the Bible as a collection of historical documents. Milman gave further proof of his courage by preparing a new edition of Gibbon, which, when enlarged by contributions from other scholars, held the field till it was generally superseded by Bury's. *The History of Christianity from the Birth of Christ to the Abolition of Paganism in the Roman Empire* was not published till 1840, and it was followed in 1854–5 by his principal work, *The History of Latin Christianity, including that of the Popes to Nicholas V*. Milman did not possess the creative imagination of his great predecessor, Gibbon, but he had breadth and generosity of judgment, the qualities of which ecclesiastical history always stands in need.

Dean Stanley of Westminster has already been mentioned (p. 561). His one enduring work is the *Life of Arnold* (1844), which has the rare merit of being written from the heart. Stanley's various historical works can hardly be said to survive. The *Lectures on the History of the Eastern Church* (1861) and the *Lectures on the History of the Jewish Church* (1863–76) contain many well-drawn and vivid historical portraits. They show some freedom of critical inquiry and judgment, but the time had passed when, as in Milman's earlier days, worthy people were shocked at hearing Abraham called a sheikh. William Bright (1824–1901), author of several favourite hymns, will be remembered as well for the industry and lucidity that make his *History of the Church*, A.D. 315–451 (1860) still one of the standard works on its subject.

Thomas Hodgkin (1831–1913) undertook the task of supplementing the vast enterprise of Gibbon. Like Grote, he came to history from business, and steadily produced the eight volumes of his greatest work, *Italy and her Invaders*, between 1880 and 1899. Hodgkin was a chronicler rather than a great narrative historian. His translation of the letters of Cassiodorus (1886) introduced many readers to a fascinating personality. Mention should also be made of his memoir of George Fox (1896), the founder of the religious body of Friends to which he belonged (see p. 345) and with whose spirit of human kindness he was signally imbued.

Among historians of the ancient world on the heroic scale was John Bagnell Bury (1861–1927), whose *History of Greece*, *History of the Later Roman Empire*, and *History of the Eastern Roman Empire* are informed by first-hand knowledge of eastern sources. Bury's brief *History of Freedom of Thought* (1914) was a stimulating but rashly optimistic essay. His most notable contribution to general literature is an edition of Gibbon which has now superseded all others.

XV. SCHOLARS, ANTIQUARIES AND BIBLIOGRAPHERS

1. Classical and Oriental Scholars

The most notable scholar of the early nineteenth century was Richard Porson (1759–1808). Born in poor circumstances, he was helped by friends, and went to Eton and Trinity, Cambridge. He soon showed astonishing gifts of scholarship; but life was hard to Porson and he retaliated with the kind of dipsomania that impelled him to drink anything that had a sting in it. The first work that brought him fame was the *Letters to Travis* (1788–9)—George Travis being the incautious archdeacon who sought to maintain against Gibbon the genuineness of I St John v. 7. Porson demolished Travis and did not hesitate to utter some acute criticism of Gibbon himself. Porson owed his inspiration to Bentley. Like his master he belongs to classical rather than to English scholarship. He would have achieved far more if his sobriety had equalled his honesty. For Cambridge and for England he created the ideal of finished and exact verbal scholarship. Among Porson's older contemporaries was Samuel Parr (1747–1825), who has been called as good an imitation of Dr Johnson as the Whigs deserved to have. He accomplished little of permanent value, and for most people survives as the subject of one of De Quincey's best essays. Porson had a high opinion of John Horne Tooke (1736–1812), whose reputation rests on *Epea Pteroenta or The Diversions of Purley* (1786), which had the merit of insisting on the importance of the study of Gothic and Old English. The date of its appearance also marks the birth of the science of comparative philology, for in that year Sir William Jones declared the importance of Sanskrit and asserted that it had a common source with Greek and Latin.

A deflection from the Porsonian tradition towards broader scholarship is exemplified by Samuel Butler, headmaster of Shrewsbury from 1798 to 1836, and Bishop of Lichfield for the last three years of his life. An account of his work as headmaster and bishop was written by his grandson of the same name, the author of *Erewhon*. Among the ablest of Samuel Butler's pupils was Benjamin Hall Kennedy (1804–89), who succeeded Butler at Shrewsbury, held the Greek professorship at Cambridge for the last twenty-two years of his life and was the original of Dr Skinner in *The Way of All Flesh*. William Hepworth Thompson, Master of Trinity, produced admirable commentaries on the *Phaedrus* and *Gorgias* of Plato, and did much towards widening the range of classical studies in Cambridge. Among his contemporaries at Trinity was John William Donaldson, whose name is remembered for his comprehensive work *The Theatre of the Greeks* (1836). William George Clark (who founded the Clark Lectures at Cambridge) published in his *Peloponnesus* (1858) the results of a Greek tour taken in the company of Thompson. The standard critical edition of Shakespeare (the Cambridge Shakespeare) was produced by Clark and J. Glover, and was re-edited by William Aldis Wright (see p. 235). Hubert Ashton Holden edited many classical texts and produced in *Foliorum Silvula* a collection of passages for translation which gave to many their first real acquaintance with English poetry. Kennedy's successor as Regius Professor of Greek was Richard Claverhouse Jebb, famous as the accomplished editor of Sophocles and Bacchylides, and as the eloquent author of *The Attic Orators*. As Member of Parliament for the university of Cambridge, Sir Richard Jebb was succeeded by Samuel Henry Butcher, whose most famous works are the translation of the *Odyssey* (made with Andrew Lang) and his edition of Aristotle's *Poetics*. Contemporary with Butcher was Arthur Woolgar Verrall, celebrated for his unconventional editions of Euripides. Sir John Edwin Sandys nobly served the cause of learning with his great *History of Classical Scholarship* (1903–8) and Thomas Ethelbert Page crowned a lifetime of work in the classics by editing the *Loeb Library*, which made the ancient writers known to many who knew them imperfectly or not at all.

Greek scholarship was well represented at Oxford by Henry George Liddell, Dean of Christ Church, and Robert Scott, Master of Balliol, joint authors of the standard Greek and English lexicon, published in 1843, now re-edited. Scott was succeeded at Balliol in 1870 by Benjamin Jowett, who in 1855 had succeeded Thomas Gaisford as Professor of Greek. Jowett's complete translation of Plato was achieved in 1871, and was followed by his translations of Thucydides and of the *Politics* of Aristotle. Jowett's contemporary, Mark Pattison, Rector of Lincoln, is remembered by scholars as the author of *Isaac Casaubon*, and of essays, especially on Scaliger. As Regius Professor of Greek, Jowett was succeeded by Ingram Bywater, whose most memorable work was done on the *Poetics* of Aristotle. Bywater was succeeded as professor by the famous scholar and translator Gilbert Murray, who receives more extended notice in a later chapter.

John Conington (1825–69), editor and translator of Virgil and Horace, completed the Spenserian rendering of the *Iliad* by Philip Stanhope Worsley, translator of the *Odyssey*. A translation of the *Iliad* into blank verse was published in 1864 by the Earl of Derby. In 1858 William Ewart Gladstone produced *Studies on Homer and the Homeric Age*, and summed up his conclusions eleven years later in *Juventus Mundi*. The Homeric question was vigorously discussed by John Stuart Blackie, the famous Professor of Greek in Edinburgh. George Long (1800–79) produced translations of thirteen of Plutarch's *Roman Lives*, of the *Meditations* of Marcus Aurelius, and of the *Manual* of Epictetus. Long contributed to the indispensable series of classical dictionaries planned by Sir William Smith (1813–93), who deserves to be remembered as a great organizer of learned literary labour.

Among the Latinists of England a foremost place is taken by Hugh Andrew Johnstone Munro (1819–85) whose masterly text and translation of Lucretius (1864) remains a standard work. John Eyton Bickersteth Mayor (1825–1910) published his *Juvenal* in 1853, and left the stamp of profound learning upon all his works. Five years younger than Mayor was the Latin scholar, educational reformer and legal writer, Henry John Roby (1830–1915), with an honourable record of public work. Henry Nettleship (1839–93) completed Conington's Virgil and published *Contributions to Latin Lexicography*. Robinson Ellis (1834–1913) is best known as the learned editor of Catullus. Of later contributions to scholarship, perhaps the greatest is the edition of the letters of Erasmus by Percy Stafford Allen (1869–1933).

Among the scholars of Scotland, William Young Sellar (1825–90) produced in his *Roman Poets of the Republic* a masterpiece of literary criticism, which was followed by similar works on Virgil, and on Horace and the elegiac poets. In Ireland two resounding names are those of John Pentland Mahaffy (1839–1919), a versatile scholar, and Robert Yelverton Tyrrell (1844–1914), most famous for his edition of Cicero's *Correspondence*. Tyrrell's devotion to ancient and modern literature was combined with a keen wit and a felicitous style.

As long ago as 1733, the Society of Dilettanti began to produce a long series of great archaeological works. The tradition thus founded was well maintained. Among the discoverers of ancient civilizations in the nineteenth century appear the familiar names of Austen Henry Layard, Arthur Evans and W. M. Flinders Petrie—to be followed in the twentieth century by such archaeologists as Leonard Woolley, Mortimer Wheeler and (a "digger" in two senses) the Australian prehistorian Gordon Childe.

Christopher Wordsworth, Bishop of Lincoln, and Henry Alford, Dean of Canterbury, produced commentaries on the Greek Testament. The work of Westcott, Hort and Lightfoot has been mentioned on p. 562. English and American scholars joined in the revision of the Authorized Version of the New Testament from June 1870 to November 1880.

William Aldis Wright, besides editing a commentary on the Book of Job, was secretary of the Old Testament Revision Company from 1870 to 1885. At Oxford, the professorship of Hebrew was held for fifty-four years by Edward Bouverie Pusey (see p. 556), author of *A Commentary on the Minor Prophets* and of *Lectures on the Prophet Daniel*; and for thirty years by Samuel Rolles Driver, author of *An Introduction to the Literature of the Old Testament*.

Arabic was ably represented in the nineteenth century by Edward William Lane (1801–76), author of the great Arabic lexicon, and translator of *The Arabian Nights*. Edwin Henry Palmer (1840–82) showed the highest genius for the acquisition of Oriental languages, and died in Arabia in the service of his country. The cuneiform inscriptions of Persia, Assyria and Babylonia were deciphered between 1837 and 1851 by Sir Henry Creswicke Rawlinson. Among Chinese scholars, the most eminent in the nineteenth century were the three missionaries—Robert Morrison (1782–1834), author of the first Chinese-English dictionary (1815–23); Walter Henry Medhurst (1796–1857), author of an English-Japanese (1830), as well as a Chinese-English and English-Chinese (1842–3), dictionary; and James Legge (1815–97), translator of some Taoist classics, and of the whole of the Confucian canon. Their most famous successor in the twentieth century was Arthur Waley (1889–1966) who translated Chinese poems (1916–18), *The Nō Plays of Japan* (1921), *The Analects of Confucius* (1938) and the great Chinese prose classic *Monkey* (1942).

The first Englishman who worked at Sanskrit to any purpose was Sir Charles Wilkins (1749?–1836). In 1786 Sir William Jones had pointed out the affinity of Sanskrit with Greek, Latin, Gothic and Celtic. The study of the language was specially promoted by Horace Hayman Wilson (1786–1860) and by Sir Monier Monier-Williams (1819–99), who completed his Sanskrit-English dictionary in 1872. The great German scholar Friedrich Max Müller (1823–1900), who had settled at Oxford in 1848, published an edition of the *Rigveda* in 1849–73, and edited from 1875 the important series known as *The Sacred Books of the East*. Edward Byles Cowell (1826–1903) was the first holder of the professorship of Sanskrit at Cambridge. It was from Cowell that Edward FitzGerald learned the language of Omar.

2. English, Scottish and Irish Scholars and Antiquaries

The dictionary of Anglo-Saxon begun by Edward Lye was completed by Owen Manning in 1776. Benjamin Thorpe, who studied at Copenhagen under Rask, published Rask's *Anglo-Saxon Grammar* in English in 1830, translated *Caedmon* in 1832 and *Beowulf* in 1855, and edited *The Anglo-Saxon Chronicle* in 1861. John Mitchell Kemble, of Trinity College, Cambridge, a friend and pupil of Jacob Grimm, edited *Beowulf* in 1833. Richard Morris in his *Specimens of Early English* (1867) distinguished the chief characteristics of the three main dialects of Middle English, the Northern, Midland and Southern. Joseph Bosworth, after publishing his larger dictionary in 1838, filled the chair of Anglo-Saxon at Oxford from 1858 to 1876, and helped to establish the Elrington and Bosworth professorship at Cambridge. The chair was held from 1878 to 1912 by Walter William Skeat, the editor of Chaucer and Langland.

Among the numerous works of the archaeologists, mention should be made of *The Antiquities of the Common People*, first published by Henry Bourne in 1725, re-issued in an expanded form by John Brand in 1777, and greatly enlarged by Sir Henry Ellis, principal librarian of the British Museum. The many-sided antiquary Sir John Evans (1823–1908) is best remembered as the author of three important works, each of them a masterpiece in its special department of study: (1) *The Coins of the Ancient Britons* (1864); (2) *The Ancient Stone Implements, Weapons, and Ornaments of Great Britain* (1872); and (3) *The Ancient Bronze Implements, Weapons and Ornaments of Great Britain and Ireland* (1881). *A History of British Costumes*, the result of ten years' study, was published by a versatile writer, James Robinson Planché. Frederic Seebohm published *The English Village Community* (1833) and other fascinating works. *The Architectural History of the University and Colleges of Cambridge*, begun by Robert Willis, was continued and brought to a successful conclusion by John Willis Clark, who also deserves to be remembered for his fine volume on the history of libraries, entitled *The Care of Books*. The antiquities of Scotland, as well as those of England and Wales, were explored by Francis Grose, an accomplished scholar of Swiss origin, whose work, *The Antiquities of England and Wales*, begun in 1777, was completed ten years later. *The Antiquities of Scotland* followed in 1791. Grose was a friend of Burns who warned his fellow-countrymen: "A chield's amang you taking notes, And, faith, he'll prent it."

A high place among the literary and historical antiquaries of England is due to Thomas Wright (1810–77) who, in 1838, was associated with John Mason Neale and Thomas Crofton Croker in founding the Camden Society. Wright was further associated, in 1840, with Croker and with Alexander Dyce, J. O. Halliwell (-Phillipps) and John Payne Collier, in founding the Percy Society for publishing old ballads and lyrical pieces. In 1836 he published four volumes of *Early English Poetry*, and in 1842 issued his *Biographia Britannica Literaria*, a rich mass of materials, arranged with taste and judgment. The years from 1834 onwards saw the foundations of many societies for the publication of antiquarian literature. Frederick James Furnivall (1825–1910) founded the Early English Text, the Chaucer, the Ballad, the New Shakespere, the Wyclif and the Shelley Societies. In its first century of existence (1864–1964) the Early English Text Society published nearly four hundred texts. Israel Gollancz succeeded Furnivall as Director, being succeeded in turn by A. W. Pollard, R. W. Chambers, C. T. Onions and Norman Davis.

Sir Thomas Duffus Hardy began the publication of many ancient historical documents, and when Sir John Romilly became Master of the Rolls, the celebrated Rolls Series came into being. Among the many literary antiquaries who made their mark as editors of some of the volumes in this great series may be mentioned John Sherren Brewer, Henry Richards Luard and James Gairdner. The *Historia Minor* of Matthew Paris was edited for the Rolls Series in 1866–9 by Sir Frederic Madden, who also edited Layamon's *Brut* in 1847. A transcript of *The Register of the Company of Stationers of London*, from 1554 to 1640, was published in 1875 by Edward Arber, who also edited *The Term Catalogues*, the eight volumes entitled *An English Garner, The English Scholar's Library* and the series issued under the title *English Reprints*.

In Scotland the publication of *Popular Ballads and Songs from tradition, manuscripts and scarce editions* by Robert Jamieson in 1806 was greeted by Scott as a great discovery. Scott was the first President of the Bannatyne Club, founded in 1823 in memory of George Bannatyne, who wrote out in 1568 a vast collection of Scottish poems in a folio volume of 800 pages, now preserved in the National Library in Edinburgh. David Laing, a learned bookseller, edited a large number of works of Scottish poetry and prose. Scotland was specially prolific in clubs or societies for the publication of texts.

In Ireland Thomas Crofton Croker's *Researches in the South of Ireland* (1824) was followed by his *Fairy Legends and Traditions*, his *Legends of the Lakes*, and his *Popular Songs* (1839). John O'Donovan, who has been described as "probably the greatest native Irish scholar", produced a *Grammar of the Irish Language* and ably edited a series of important texts, culminating in his monumental edition of *The Annals of...the Four Masters* (1848–51). The work of George Petrie and Eugene O'Curry is referred to in a later chapter. Sir Samuel Ferguson not only re-organized the records department, but, as a poet, aimed at embodying in modern verse the old Irish legends. In Ireland, as in Scotland, there were some antiquarian societies. Patrick Weston Joyce manifested his love of Irish songs and of folk-music in *Ancient Irish Music* (1882), *Irish Music and Song* and *Irish Peasant Songs in the English Language* (1909). The historical antiquary Sir John Thomas Gilbert wrote *Celtic Records and Historic Literature of Ireland* (1861), and edited *Facsimiles of the National Manuscripts of Ireland* (1874–80). Whitley Stokes and Robert Atkinson were prolific in literary labours for Irish literature.

3. Bibliographers

Joseph Ames may be said to have led the way in bibliography by the publication of his *Typographical Antiquities* in 1749. William Beloe, a pupil of Samuel Parr, produced in 1806–12 six useful volumes entitled *Anecdotes of Literature and Scarce Books. Bibliographia Poetica*, a catalogue of English poets of the twelfth to the sixteenth centuries, was published by Joseph Ritson in 1802. It was severely handled by Sir Samuel Egerton Brydges in his *Censura Literaria*. Ritson was a laborious and accurate investigator, but there was an almost morbid bitterness in his criticism of other men's labours. Sir Samuel Egerton Brydges produced, in the ten volumes of his *Censura Literaria* (1805–15), "titles, abstracts, and opinions of OLD ENGLISH BOOKS". He also published *The British Bibliographer* (1810–14), and *Restituta; or Titles, Extracts, and Characters of OLD BOOKS in English Literature Revived* (1814–16). Brydges printed many rare Elizabethan texts at his son's private press at Lee Priory, near Canterbury. A literary interest of wide range is represented by the pleasing and discursive works of Isaac D'Israeli, entitled *Curiosities of Literature* (1791, 2nd series 1823), *Calamities of Authors* (1812–13) and *Quarrels of Authors* (1814).

Among famous collectors of books must be named the Duke of Roxburghe, the sale of whose library stimulated the formation of the Roxburghe Club which did excellent work under Sir Frederic Madden and Thomas Wright. Thomas Frognal Dibdin (1776–1847) produced in 1809 *The Bibliomania*; but his major work is the pleasant treatise entitled *The Bibliographical Decameron*,

*or Ten Days' Pleasant Discourse upon illuminated Manuscripts, and subjects connected
with Early Engraving, Typography and Bibliography* (1817). Two bibliographical
works of the highest importance were produced by a London bookseller,
William Thomas Lowndes: (1) the four volumes of *The Bibliographer's Manual
of English Literature* (1834), and (2) *The British Librarian,* or "book-collector's
guide to the formation of a library" (Parts i–xi, 1839). *The Bibliographer's
Manual* was enlarged by Henry George Bohn (1857–64), whose own *magnum
opus* was the *Guinea Catalogue* of old books (1841); "Bohn's Library"
of reprints was a first-rate collection which retained standard rank for many
years.

A bibliographical and critical account of the rarest books in the English
language was supplied in the *Notes on Rare English Books* published in 1865 by
John Payne Collier, who also printed *Extracts from the Registers of the Stationers'
Company for* 1555–70, and edited *The Roxburghe Ballads,* as well as several works
for the Camden, Percy and Shakespeare societies, and the two volumes entitled
Shakespeare's Library (1843). Collier's Shakespeare forgeries have been mentioned (p. 235). A catalogue of the manuscripts of the Chetham Library in
Manchester was produced in 1841–2 by Halliwell-Phillipps, who edited many
works for the Camden, Percy and Shakespeare Societies, and produced a
magnificent edition of Shakespeare in twenty folio volumes, and facsimiles of
the Shakespeare quartos. Richard Copley Christie left to Manchester a valuable
library. His colleague Walter Arthur Copinger founded in 1892 the London
Bibliographical Society, printed in the same year his *Incunabula Biblica* and
published in 1895–8 his supplement to Hain's *Repertorium Bibliographicum,* in
which 6832 works printed in the fifteenth century were added to the 16,311
registered by Hain. Three thousand *incunabula* (i.e. "cradle" or "infancy"
books, printed before 1500) in the Bodleian were catalogued in 1891–3 by
Robert Proctor, who included notes upon these in his *Index of Early Printed
Books in the British Museum* (1898). A useful *Register of National Bibliography*
was produced in two volumes in 1905 by William Prideaux Courtney. A
remarkable knowledge of bibliography was possessed by Henry Bradshaw,
librarian of the Cambridge University Library from 1867 to 1886. A society for
publishing rare liturgical texts was founded in his memory. *The Book Hunter,*
a discursive volume describing the delights of book-collecting, was written by
John Hill Burton. Andrew Lang's *The Library* (1881) is one of several delightful
bookish publications. *A Dictionary of Anonymous and Pseudonymous Literature of
Great Britain* was published in 1882–8 by Samuel Halkett and John Laing.

More modern times have seen great extensive and intensive development in
bibliographical research. The publications of The Bibliographical Society,
including *A Short-Title Catalogue of Books . . . 1475–1640* (1926) by A. W. Pollard
and G. R. Redgrave (extended to 1700 by Donald Wing, 1951, and later to the
eighteenth century) and *A Bibliography of the English Printed Drama to the
Restoration* (1939–59) by W. W. Greg, are of the highest value. Outstanding
contributions to individual bibliography are the Blake (1921), Browne (1924)
and Donne (1932) of Geoffrey L. Keynes, the Trollope (1928) of Michael
Sadleir and the Dryden (1939) of Hugh Macdonald. *An Enquiry into the Nature
of Certain Nineteenth Century Pamphlets* (1934) by John Carter and Graham

Pollard has the fascination of a detective story. A. W. Pollard's contributions to Shakespeare bibliography have been mentioned (p. 190). Earlier works in general bibliography were superseded by *The Cambridge Bibliography of English Literature* (1940) edited by F. W. Bateson, "paradoxically, of Oxford", as he remarked in his admirable *Guide to English Literature* (1965) which was partly based upon it. A Supplement was edited in 1957 by another Oxonian, the Australian-born scholar George Watson, who was also responsible for the *Concise* version (1958) and was general editor of the complete revision of the entire work (1969–).

CHAPTER XIII

THE NINETEENTH CENTURY. PART II

I. CARLYLE

Thomas Carlyle (1795–1881) was the strongest moral force in the literature of his time. In an age of triumphant commercial success and material self-satisfaction he affirmed without fear the claims of the spirit and the eternal need for righteousness in the dealings of man with man. It is one of the oddities of literary chronology that Keats and Carlyle were born in the same year. The younger outlived the elder by sixty years, and seemed never to belong to the same world. Carlyle came from the part of Scotland and from the kind of stock that had produced Burns. People sometimes assert that Carlyle's mind was formed in the metaphysical mists of Germany; the truth is that his mind was formed in the realities of a bare cottage in Scotland. His independence of spirit, his rocky, unpliant, unconceding nature, could have come from only one country in the world. In Scotland sheer poverty could then fight and starve its way to higher education. Carlyle strove and starved as a poor student at Edinburgh university, and though he got little from his classes or teachers, he won for himself, by hard reading, the freedom of literature. He left the university in 1814 without taking a degree. He had begun his studies with half-hearted aspirations towards the ministry; but these were soon abandoned. We do not usually consider Carlyle in a mathematical light; but it was as mathematical tutor that he first tried to make a living. At Kirkcaldy, where he was teaching, he encountered romance in the person of Margaret Gordon, a pupil of much higher social standing than his own. The intervention of her family ended the romance abruptly, and Carlyle smarted from the social as well as the personal blow. But in 1817 a more celebrated woman came decisively into his life, not as a person, but as a book. This was Madame de Staël, daughter of the lady whom Gibbon did not marry. Her book *De l'Allemagne*, however facile and unoriginal, had great vogue, because it opened to its readers the wonderland of German thought and poetry. It made Carlyle first acquainted with Goethe, Schiller and others who were to be the chief enthusiasm of his early manhood.

Weary of teaching, Carlyle returned with his friend Edward Irving (afterwards the famous preacher) to Edinburgh, and gradually drifted into miscellaneous writing. Already he had begun to suffer—perhaps through early privations—from the dyspepsia which was to trouble the rest of his life with the attendant evils of melancholy and depression. He made a beginning of literary activity with articles contributed to Sir David Brewster's *Edinburgh Encyclopaedia*, and entered enthusiastically upon a study of the German writers. An essay on Goethe's *Faust*—really instructive for its day—appeared in *The New Edinburgh Review* for April 1822. But his first serious task as an interpreter of German literature was an excellent *Life of Schiller*, which appeared serially in

The London Magazine and came out as a book in 1825. While writing the *Schiller*, he turned to Goethe and produced the translation called *Wilhelm Meister's Apprenticeship* (1824). This was followed by four volumes entitled *German Romance* (1827), which included stories by Musäus, Fouqué, Tieck, Hoffmann and Richter, as well as *Wilhelm Meister's Travels*. In the same year (1827) he had begun to write the outstanding series of essays on German literature contributed to *The Edinburgh Review, The Foreign Review* and *The Foreign Quarterly Review*, and now collected in the *Critical and Miscellaneous Essays*.

To a man of Carlyle's immense industry and stern frugality all this work represented a kind of success. But for one great event in his life we must go back a few years. The influence of Irving had helped him to become a tutor to Charles Buller in 1822, and he thus learned to know something of the social world above his own. He grew familiar with London, and visited Paris. In 1821 Irving introduced him to Jane Welsh of Haddington, and the acquaintance led to love and to their marriage in 1826. After a short residence in Edinburgh, the young couple took up their abode at Craigenputtock amid the solitudes of the Dumfriesshire moors, and there Mrs Carlyle, born to grace a *salon*, spent the next six years in poverty and solitude.

The influence of German literature, and especially of Goethe, upon Carlyle was considerable, but can easily be exaggerated. Carlyle was born with an original creative mind, which, like many other creative minds, needed at first the guidance of example. He called Goethe his master; but actually there were very few points of contact. Goethe could not have understood Carlyle's spiritual distress; Carlyle could not have understood Goethe's amorous facility. Goethe obsequiously sought the society of princes; Carlyle, dutifully apologizing for his age, sat down in the presence of Queen Victoria, who was prepared to let him stand. There was no threatening voice of democracy in Weimar to disturb the serenity of Goethe; Carlyle could never forget "the condition-of-England question". Novalis, the theme of perhaps the most beautiful of his German essays, taught him more than Goethe, and he found inspiration in Fichte's political thought. Carlyle's real gain from Germany was romance mingled with philosophy. His critical essays are all touched with romance. He sought the man in the work and endeavoured to expound the creative personality. His essays are thus a landmark in English criticism. They show, of course, the limitations of that method. Carlyle was a sympathetic interpreter of his German masters and of Burns; he was a less sympathetic interpreter of Scott, Heine, Wordsworth, Coleridge and Lamb. On the other hand, Carlyle was eminently fair to the eighteenth century, especially to writers so far from his sympathies as Diderot and Voltaire. His essays are marred by excesses of manner, but they deserve reading.

The most astonishing of the books written by Carlyle under the influence of German romance is *Sartor Resartus*, which, after failing in *Fraser's Magazine*, appeared as a book first in New York in 1836 and then in London in 1838. America revealed Carlyle to England as it was afterwards to reveal De Quincey. Contemporary readers could make as little of *Sartor* as they could of *Sordello*. Like some other books of its kind it is slightly the worse for its machinery—

the elaborate discussion of an imaginary Philosophy of Clothes written by an imaginary German Professor of Things-in-General; but the reader, whether of *Sartor* or of *A Tale of a Tub*, must learn to look beyond the mere device. *Sartor* owed a little to his affectionate study of Jean Paul Richter; but essentially it is a record of his own spiritual adventures, which had already found expression in a crude, verbose unfinished autobiographical novel, *Wotton Reinfred*. Its extraordinary blend of wild humour, spiritual sincerity and imaginative contemplation makes *Sartor Resartus* a unique book in English literature.

In 1833 the Carlyles left their Scottish wilderness and in 1834 came to the house in Cheyne Row, Chelsea where they spent the rest of their lives. Refusing the temptations of ephemeral and remunerative work, Carlyle laboured unremittingly at his *French Revolution*. And, as if the struggles to produce the book were not enough, the manuscript of the first volume was accidentally destroyed in the early part of 1835, when in the hands of John Stuart Mill. *The French Revolution. A History* was published in 1837; and though recognition came slowly, it came definitely, and the book remained in general demand for over a century, in spite of all variations in historical fashions. Carlyle's fashion being entirely his own, *The French Revolution* resembles no other history. It is an epic in prose, flashing with the lightning and reverberating with the thunder of stormy events. You feel that something is really happening and that the course of the world has taken a new direction. Setting out from a conviction that "the history of the world is the biography of great men", he produced both a thrilling story and a collection of marvellously vivid portraits.

The years from 1837 to 1840 were occupied by lectures, the fourth and last series of which, published in 1841 under the title *On Heroes, Hero-Worship, and the Heroic in History*, was the most successful. It elucidates, with the help of picturesque and contrasting portraits, the cardinal doctrine of Carlyle's romantic creed of individualism, namely, that greatness lies in the exercise of the "heroic" virtues—in the power to renounce, coupled with the will to achieve. Believing that the working-classes were both misled and exploited by the quack-radicalism of his time, Carlyle wrote a little book, *Chartism* (1840), to assert his belief that "the condition-of-england question" would be solved, not by radical doctrines of universal suffrage and political economy, but by honest service and submission to natural leadership. More successful as literature is *Past and Present* (1843), which reiterates the demands for duty, responsibility, and just dealing, and incorporates a delightful picture of the past drawn from the chronicle of Jocelin of Brakelond. Seven years later, Carlyle again essayed the *rôle* of political prophet in his *Latter-Day Pamphlets* (1850), which made him many enemies and estranged some old and excellent friends like Mill and Mazzini. Carlyle's wholehearted denunciation of philanthropy, in particular, appeared to an eminently philanthropic age as the utterances of a misanthrope. *Latter-Day Pamphlets* must be read historically as a counterblast to the serious revolutionary disturbances abroad in 1848. Before *Latter-Day Pamphlets* came the welcome re-appearance of Carlyle as a historian in *The Letters and Speeches of Oliver Cromwell* (1845). The task of rehabilitating the great Protector was peculiarly fitted to Carlyle's gifts, and he has left us an unchallengeably great historical portrait. Another memorable portrait—this time of a forgotten figure—the

Life of John Sterling (1851), contains some of Carlyle's most trenchant writing, notably the often quoted pen-portrait of Coleridge.

The most ambitious of Carlyle's works had still to come, *The History of Friedrich II of Prussia, called Frederick the Great*. The first volume appeared in 1858, the sixth and last in March 1865. This enormous work, which exhausted the energy of its author, must be called a failure, in spite of many wonderful pages. The test is simple: industrious historians do not use it for instruction, and ordinary readers do not use it for pleasure. It is read neither in Germany nor in England. The formula of the *French Revolution* and *Heroes*, applied to a vaster canvas with an overwhelming multitude of details, here breaks down. In 1865 Carlyle became Lord Rector of his own university and delivered his address *On the Choice of Books*. But his triumph ended in tragedy. Before he got back to London, the news reached him that his wife had been found dead in her carriage when driving in Hyde Park. The light of his life had gone out and his creative career was over. *The Early Kings of Norway* (1875) has little of the old fire and strength. Disraeli offered him a title which he declined.

To his own time Carlyle presented the difficulty that he could not be politically labelled. He was an aristocratic radical, deeply interested in the welfare of the people, but believing that the way of salvation lay in duties, not in rights. He was the implacable foe of the mechanical radicalism of Bentham and of the kind of political economy ("the dismal science") which, in an industrial age, concerned itself with figures and not with souls. It was, significantly, to him that Dickens dedicated *Hard Times*. His idealism was an impracticable creed, but idealism, after all, is not meant to be practicable; its true purpose is to leaven the practice of life. And his influence was enormous: not only on Ruskin— "Carlyle was the revered Master," said Emerson, "Ruskin the beloved disciple" —but on all those they were to affect both in England and New England.

After the death of his wife, Carlyle discovered that he had been self-absorbed and had failed in some of the domestic virtues. Dyspeptic geniuses are "gey ill to live wi". Knowing how deeply he had loved, he heaped upon himself bitter reproaches which his biographer James Anthony Froude took far too literally. Jane Welsh had a gift for writing letters. But the chief interest of her correspondence (published 1883) is that it is written by the wife of Carlyle.

II. THE TENNYSONS

Alfred Tennyson (1809–92), the most representative and the most popular poet of Victorian England, was the fourth son of the rector of Somersby in Lincolnshire. His two elder brothers, Frederick and Charles, had very personal poetical gifts which the greater glory of Alfred tended to obscure. They were all men of singular physical beauty and strength, dark and stalwart, and through them ran a vein of ultra-sensitiveness and melancholy. Educated at home and at Louth Grammar School not far away, Tennyson, unlike Wordsworth, Coleridge, Byron, Keats and Shelley, developed intense domestic and national affections, and was always to be, not wholly for the benefit of his poetry, in close sympathy with the moral and political perplexities of the nineteenth-century Englishman. Tennyson went to Cambridge, and his associates, including Arthur Henry Hallam, Gladstone's most intimate friend at Eton, were young men of high and strenuous seriousness, strangers alike to the revolutionary hopes that intoxicated the youthful Wordsworth, and to the reactionary spirit of "blood and iron" against which Byron fought and over which Shelley lamented. The era of conservative reform, of Canning and Peel, of attachment to English institutions combined with a philanthropic ardour for social improvement, had begun. Of Tennyson, as of Carlyle, it may be said that though his mind was liberal his heart was conservative. As in politics, so in religion. He shrank from extremes, and never reached the kind of certitude that wings the words and imposes assent.

Tennyson began, as a poet should, by trying to discover the style and measures in which he could best express himself. *Poems, by Two Brothers* (1827), containing work by all three, is in value entirely negligible. At Cambridge he won the Chancellor's prize with *Timbuctoo* in 1829, and in 1830 published his *Poems, Chiefly Lyrical*. They attracted no attention. It was the *Poems*, dated 1833, that announced the heir of Keats and the successor of Wordsworth. The volume actually appeared in 1832; and so such familiar "Victorian" poems as *Œnone, The Dream of Fair Women, The Palace of Art, The Lotus Eaters* and *The Lady of Shalott* belong to the year of the Reform Bill. The Tennyson of 1830 and 1832 was no older than the Keats of 1817 and 1818; and if he was less murderously attacked it was not because the intentions of reviewers were more benevolent, but because critical utterances had become more civilized. Angered by ribald and obtuse derision he put forth nothing further till the great *Poems. By Alfred Tennyson*, 2 vols. (1842), which first revealed his full poetic stature and aroused the highest expectations of his friends. To drastic revisions of the poems named above were added *Ulysses, The Vision of Sin, Sir Galahad, Morte d'Arthur* and *Locksley Hall*, many familiar shorter poems, and *Of Old sat Freedom on the Heights* with its companions in the stanza to be made famous by *In Memoriam*.

The volumes of 1842 contained little, either in theme or content, unforeshadowed in the volume of 1833. The unmistakable advance was to be found in the poet's mastery of his craft. As a metrical artist Tennyson is with the greatest, and he combined with his metrical skill a careful attention to the musical value of vowel and consonant unparalleled since Milton, Pope and Gray. His aim, both in composition and in revision, was to match movement with mood. But as well as a delicate ear he had a vivid and curious eye, and he divined that a picture presented with extraordinary precision and relevance of detail may contribute potently to the communication of a state of feeling—the whole secret of Pre-Raphaelitism. The outcome of the severe and continuous discipline to which Tennyson submitted his art was a verse of such extraordinary variety and melody that its beauty sometimes became its own end and beguiled him from his fuller purpose.

The poems of 1842 showed clearly that Tennyson had mastered his decorative, musical style, and that his poetry had gained in substance, in dramatic insight, and in power of feeling. The question for his anxious admirers was whether this advance would continue; and the first reply was a disappointment; for *The Princess*, first published in 1847 but revised and re-revised in 1851 and

1853, presented a poor story told with elaborate avoidance of simplicity. In its conceits and mellifluous periphrases the fundamental faults of "poetic diction" seemed to have returned. Tennyson's own hope, encouraged by admiring friends like FitzGerald, was to be what he himself called a "sage-poet" like Dante or Goethe; but Tennyson, though a poet of their quality, was not a poet of their quantity; and in striving for larger effects he lost point without gaining breadth. What makes *The Princess* memorable is not its feeble story or its feebler thesis, but its beautiful lyrical interludes added to the third edition.

In 1850 Tennyson published the poem upon which he had been at work since the untimely death of Arthur Henry Hallam in 1833. Called simply *In Memoriam A. H. H.* it appeared to offer the poet the great theme he needed. Not merely irrevocable and inexplicable loss, but the shadow cast by death and the larger hope of light beyond the shadow must move the poet's song; and it is not to be denied that Tennyson was thus moved. The evidence is on the face of the poem. The style is pure, direct, noble, and free from the diffused prettiness that had disfigured *The Princess*. To this the verse contributed, the celebrated stanza which had been casually used by Ben Jonson and Lord Herbert of Cherbury, but which Tennyson made so entirely his own that we now call it by the name of his poem. And yet the poem disappointed and still disappoints. Its main defect, when judged by the standard of the highest examples, is that it remains a collection of poetical observations and does not cohere into a great creative utterance. To such an utterance Tennyson was never to attain. The separate lyrics, some weak and some assured, some valiant and some self-deceiving, have all a genuinely poetic quality. The best of them touch the topmost heights of Victorian poetry and will be treasured for their expression of mood in picture and music long after the puzzled philosophy of the whole has been forgotten.

Tennyson succeeded Wordsworth as Poet Laureate in 1850, and his first official poem was the fine *Ode on the Death of the Duke of Wellington* (1852), a bold and successful metrical experiment, which would have astonished its subject. The titular piece in *Maud and Other Poems* (1855) employs an even bolder variety of metrical forms to tell in monodrama a story of tragic passion. The poem has real power and its measures appear the natural forms for their purpose. But once again Tennyson succeeds in detail and fails in large design. Yet nowhere else has Tennyson expressed such intensity of passion with such felicity of utterance. *Maud* is rich in lyrics poignant or lovely and in the magical touches of description which no other English poet has excelled; but it disconcerted both those who wanted comfortably sweet poems like *The Gardener's Daughter* and those who were prepared to acclaim the poet as the laureate of a spacious period. He had, too, his own solicitings. Once more he addressed himself to the composition of a large work, and once more this took the form in which alone his genius could work at ease, a series of poems each with its own mood of feeling; and we know the result as *Idylls of the King*. Tennyson had been early attracted by the stories of Malory, and his first experiment, *Morte d'Arthur*, had appeared in 1842 as a fragment of Homeric epic. The poems were issued at intervals between 1857 and 1885, and appeared complete in 1889. In the stories as Tennyson tells them, the epic style of the first *Morte* is abandoned for the more leisurely beauty of the idyll. The blank verse is uniformly melodious and skilfully paragraphed, but it has the vital defect of unsuitability for narrative. It is too static. It pauses to be beautiful. Further, the reader is left uncertain whether his attention is to be engaged by the tale or by some vague and obvious allegory. The truth is that Tennyson had no great gifts either as a teller of tales or as an inventor of allegory. His personal addition to the stories of the Round Table is neither purpose nor vision, but something purely poetical—something that a producer of genius gives to a play—a creative setting or dramatic significance which connects the stories and gives to the series a power over and above the charm of the separate tales. From the bright youth and glad springtide of *Gareth and Lynette* we pass gradually to the mists and winter-cold of the end, and as we read we "know the change and feel it". In his pictures of mood Tennyson succeeds to admiration; in his characters he fails. No memorable figure emerges from any of the poems. Arthur, usually considered the greatest failure, is no greater failure than Lancelot or Guinevere. The objection that Tennyson has made his characters Victorian is merely ignorant. Tennyson had as much right to make Arthur and Lancelot Victorian as Shakespeare had to make Hamlet and Macbeth Elizabethan. Tennyson's characters fail not because they are Victorian but because they are not alive. *Idylls of the King*, once the most popular of Tennyson's works, must now take a more lowly place. The strong, epical *Morte d'Arthur* of 1842 exposes the vaguely religious and timid aspiration of the rest.

The same defects and the same compensation can be found in the rustic idyll which gives its name to the volume published in 1864, *Enoch Arden, etc.*, a tragedy of village life recalling in many of its details Crabbe's *The Parting Hour*. Tennyson's advance towards dramatic truth is shown more clearly in two poems which accompany *Enoch Arden*, the dialect ballads *The Grandmother* and *The Northern Farmer—Old Style*. The latter is the first successful expression of a gift for caustic satire to which he might have given freer play with advantage to his permanent, if not his immediate, popularity.

Of Tennyson's dramas it may be said briefly that they are not dramatic. In *Queen Mary* no single character arrests and dominates our interest, and the hero of *Harold*, as of many later plays, resembles Hamlet without being Hamlet. The strongest in interest and the most impressive in performance is *Becket*. Tennyson's plays came upon the stage with every chance of success; but they are muffled in their own wordiness and have no quality of permanence.

In *Lucretius* (1868), *The Revenge: A Ballad of the Fleet* (1878), the startling *Ballads and Other Poems* of 1880, *Tiresias, and Other Poems* (1885), *Locksley Hall Sixty Years After* (1886), *Demeter and Other Poems* (1889), *The Death of Œnone, Akbar's Dream and Other Poems* (1892), we find Tennyson revealing the same metrical cunning as in the romantic creations that filled the two volumes of 1842. The utterance is still perfect. But the magic of youth is gone; gone, too, is the early strain of hopeful contemplation which has tempted shallow critics to apply the inappropriate epithet "complacent" to the troubled, sensitive soul of Tennyson. Now and then we have outbursts of strong patriotism, but in general the poet's mind circles ever round one theme, the pathos of man doomed to wander between a faith that is rooted in fear, and a widening knowledge that dispels the fear but leaves him without hope. Tennyson was not able to expel, though he could subdue, the ghosts which haunted him. His lyrical gift never deserted him; and at the age of eighty the poet of *Tears, idle tears* could write *Crossing the Bar*, perfect in music and in feeling.

Tennyson was not a seer, as some of his friends thought him. He had not the mental stature of a "sage-poet". He was a great sensitive soul, full of English prejudices, but also with an English conscience, anxious to render a good account of the talent entrusted to him, and to make art the handmaid of duty and faith. But the days are gone when people could turn to Tennyson for his "teaching". He survives as a master of poetic speech tuned to the note of his age. In 1884 he accepted a peerage from his friend Gladstone. His *Life* was written in 1897 by his son Hallam, the second Lord Tennyson, who later became Governor-General of Australia. The best modern biography is that written in 1950 by his grandson, Sir Charles Tennyson.

Alfred Tennyson was not the only poet of his family. His fame at first over-shadowed, and now has lent interest to, the work of his brothers Frederick and Charles. Frederick Tennyson (1807–98) lived much out of England. He was a great reader, a student of art and a passionate lover of music. His first volume of poems *Days and Hours* was published in 1854. Thereafter, he published nothing until 1890, when he issued a long volume of blank verse idylls called *The Isles of Greece*, followed in 1891 by a volume of classical stories, *Daphne and Other Poems*. He was deeply interested in metaphysical problems and sometimes he lost himself in a Swedenborgian mist. There was a touch of the mystic in Frederick Tennyson; and his strange unequal poems are the expression of a solitary soul.

Charles Tennyson (1808–79) took the name of Turner on succeeding to some property. The greater part of his life was spent as vicar at Grasby in Lincolnshire, where he cultivated his delicate meditative verse, writing sonnets on incidents in his daily life, public events, and theological topics. The best are inspired by aspects of natural scenery and simple incidents, and have the charm of felicitous workmanship and delicate feeling. *Letty's Globe* is a delightful example of his talent.

III. THE BROWNINGS

It was the odd fate of some famous Victorian writers to make strongly contrasted pairs. No pair could be more unlike than Tennyson and Browning. Tennyson belonged by birth, education and inclination to the "church and classics" tradition. Browning belonged by birth and upbringing to strong and independent nonconformity. Tennyson is numbered in the glorious company of Cambridge poets; school and college played no part in the life of Browning. The swarthy foreign-looking Tennyson disliked "abroad" and was scarcely ever out of England. Browning, a familiar type of Englishman in appearance, made Italy his second home and was something of a good European.

Robert Browning (1812–89) was born in Camberwell, the son of a clerk in the Bank of England. His father, an unusual man, allowed the boy unchecked reading in a large and comprehensive library and encouraged his diversity of interests. Side by side with his precocious literary omnivorousness went, from early childhood, careful training in music; and the Dulwich Gallery, not far away, became a beloved haunt of his childhood. The first book he bought with his own money was Ossian, and his first composition was naturally something in that seductively imitable manner. But his real teachers were Byron and Shelley. If we do not clearly understand that Browning was an ardent, and almost the first, disciple of Shelley we shall miss the secret of his first inspiration. When he was twelve years of age, a collection, under the title *Incondita*, was made of his "Byronic poems", and this was seen by W. J. Fox, editor of *The Monthly Repository*, who did not forget the boy poet. *Queen Mab* made him "a professing atheist and a practising vegetarian". With some difficulty, his mother secured for him others of "Mr Shelley's atheistical poems"; and, apparently, through *Adonais* he was led to Keats. His more regular studies ranged from the classics to medicine.

The wholesome confusion of Browning's youth is clearly apparent in his earliest published poem, *Pauline*, which appeared anonymously in January 1833, when its author was twenty years old. It is probably the most consummate poem of its length ever written by a youth. What astonishes the reader who considers the age of the writer is the assurance with which the delineation of a poet's soul is attempted, together with an equal assurance in the use of language. It was a work of almost infinite promise; but though a few choice spirits were attracted by it, the public at large ignored it. In 1833 Browning visited Russia and applied unsuccessfully for a diplomatic post in Persia. During the next year he contributed poems to *The Monthly Repository;* and then in 1835, before he was quite twenty-three, appeared *Paracelsus*, in vision and in apprehension the most profound of his youthful poems, which gained him the notice of Wordsworth, Dickens, Landor and Carlyle. He was now an accepted poet.

Browning's first two poems had shown that his expectations from his readers were very high. To follow his leaping thoughts and eager utterance was not easy, and he sometimes failed to give the clue. This defect was to be a perpetual hindrance to the appreciation of his third ambitious poem, *Sordello*, upon which he at once began work. But that work was interrupted by a request from Macready for a play. Browning, glad of a chance to show character in action, responded with *Strafford*, which was produced at Covent Garden on 1 May 1837. Browning's main defects as a dramatist are clearly apparent in it. The characters, however complex, are all simple in the sense that they remain always in one condition of mind. Situations and dramatic moments abound; but genuine dramatic movement is wanting. Apparently more vital than most literary plays, these have the radical defect of all such productions: they expatiate, they do not proceed. The characters are explained by the author; they do not explain themselves. After *Strafford* Browning returned to his third "soul-history"—the poem we know as *Sordello* (1840). Abandoning the blank verse of *Pauline* and *Paracelsus*, the poet chose the heroic couplet as his form; but it helped him as little as it had helped Keats in *Endymion*. *Sordello* remains uncompromisingly difficult reading. Its radical defect is, simply, that the reader cannot follow the author, and the fault is the author's. The unknown Guelph and Ghibelline characters, the obscure psychology and the exclamatory utterance are, so to speak, merely cast at the reader to be scrambled for. The story of the triumph and the ultimate failure of a poet untrue to his real self could never have been simple, but it need not have been made gratuitously difficult. Browning credited the public with his own darting intelligence, and so fastened upon himself from the beginning a reputation for obscurity which he never lived down.

To gather materials for *Sordello* Browning visited Italy and at once conceived a passionate love for that beautiful land. He was at work on two tragedies for the stage—*King Victor and King Charles* and *The Return of the Druses*; but the finest immediate fruit of his Italian journey was the exquisite collection of dramatic scenes and lyrics that we know as *Pippa Passes*. Here invention and execution are both simple and lively; yet it did not escape the charge of obscurity. It was long believed that Pippa's little refrain "God's in his Heaven, All's right with the world'', appropriate to her upon her one whole day of joy, represented Browning's own considered view of the universe. Moxon, the publisher, thought that Browning might have a better chance with the public if his new works were issued cheaply in parts. Accordingly between 1841 and 1846 appeared a series of astonishing poetical pamphlets to which the simple-hearted Browning gave the title *Bells and Pomegranates*, supposing that the public would recall Exodus XXVIII and understand. The public did nothing of the kind; but resolutely believed that *Pippa*, which appeared as Part (i) (1841), was another *Sordello* designed to mystify and tease. The remaining seven parts of *Bells and Pomegranates* were these: (ii) *King Victor and King Charles* (1842); (iii) *Dramatic Lyrics* (1842); (iv) *The Return of the Druses* (1843); (v) *A Blot on the 'Scutcheon* (1843); (vi) *Colombe's Birthday* (1844); (vii) *Dramatic Romances and Lyrics* (1845); (viii) *Luria* and *A Soul's Tragedy* (1846). All were "dramatic"; for all are plays except the two collections of lyrics and romances, and these are specifically called "dramatic" by the poet himself, as being (in his own words) "so many utterances of so many imaginary persons". The question naturally arises whether Browning is really dramatic either in play or in lyric. Compared with Shakespeare, he is not. Of Shakespeare's creations we can never say, "Here is the author himself"; of Browning's we can never say, "Here the author is not". Browning could not take an objective view of any character. Such is the intensity of his personal interest that it pervades not only the *dramatis personae* but the world in which they live. The outer world is not genuinely outer. It is an arranged world, with Browning, the "producer", everywhere energetic. In the dramatic lyrics the insistent personality of the poet may be a gain; in the plays it is an impediment to success, and they have failed to hold a place on the stage.

It was at the end of this, the first period of his poetic life, that he met and married the fellow poet who is now chiefly remembered as his wife. Elizabeth Barrett Moulton Barrett (1806–61)—six years older than her husband—was born at Coxhoe Hall, Durham, the eldest of eleven children of Edward Moulton Barrett, a West Indian planter. An accident in her early girlhood was the occasion, if not the cause, of her being treated as an incurable invalid by her father, who was an outstanding example of the patriarchal tyrant. The Barrett family had settled in Wimpole Street, and it was here that Browning first saw Miss Barrett in 1845, after a correspondence founded on their admiration for each other's gifts. In the end they decided to marry, and Elizabeth had to escape from her father, in whose inflexible programme the marriage of his eldest daughter had no place. The two poets were married in 1846 and departed for Italy, where at Casa Guidi in Florence they made their home. *The Battle of Marathon* (1820), Elizabeth Barrett's juvenile poem in Popesque couplets, was succeeded in 1826 by *An Essay on Mind and other Poems*, a volume which bears the stamp of Pope in its title but nowhere in its contents. Then in 1833 came *Prometheus Bound*, a poor translation from Aeschylus, which the translator tried to improve in a second version (1850). *The Seraphim and other Poems* appeared in 1838, the two volumes of *Poems* following in 1844. Such was the tale of her work when Browning came into her life. The influence of her love is felt at once in the forty-four sonnets fancifully called *Sonnets from the Portuguese*. They exhibit a new intensity of feeling combined with economy of utterance very remarkable in a writer who had hitherto sprawled, even in her sonnets. The *Sonnets from the Portuguese*, first printed in *Poems* (1850), were over-valued in their day for sentimental reasons; but even with the inevitable abatement of personal interest they remain the most generally profitable part of her large production.

Of the journeys made by the Brownings only one needs record, that in the summer of 1855 when they brought to England the manuscripts of *Men and Women* and *Aurora Leigh*, not yet completed. Elizabeth finished her poem at the end of the year and it was published in 1857. It is her most ambitious and most original work, a serious attempt at a "novel-poem", that is, a creation with the form and spirit of a poem and the matter of a contemporary novel. Mrs Browning deliberately refused to retreat to romantic antiquity and sought humanity in the drawing-rooms of her own age. That was entirely praiseworthy. Unfortunately she had no gifts of construction, and the novel-poem succeeds neither as novel nor as poem. But it was a courageous attempt; and much about the passions and aspirations of Victorian women can be learned by those willing to explore its eleven thousand lines.

Italy reacted very differently upon the two poets. Browning was interested in the artistic past, Elizabeth in the political present. Herself but lately escaped from a tyrant, she was profoundly moved by the agitation for freedom; and of the publications of her later life two are entirely Italian and political in theme— *Casa Guidi Windows* (1851) and *Poems before Congress* (1860). They disagreed about Napoleon III. Elizabeth defended him; Robert distrusted him. They agreed to write about him, and *Poems before Congress* represented Elizabeth's view. When Napoleon annexed Nice and Savoy Robert destroyed what he had written and expressed his opinion, unmistakably if obscurely, some years later in *Prince Hohenstiel-Schwangau*. The interest of *Casa Guidi Windows* and *Poems before Congress* is now entirely historical. Neither they nor the post-humous *Last Poems* (1862) added to Elizabeth's literary reputation. She died suddenly in 1861 and was buried in Florence. A tablet on the walls of Casa Guidi expressed the gratitude of the city for her advocacy of Italian freedom. Elizabeth Barrett Browning is, in many ways, a pathetic figure. Eager-hearted and sincere, moved by noble impulses, and gifted with a poet's vision, she was denied any power of command over her material. Few close students of poetry have learned less from example. Her work, save in the *Sonnets from the Portu-*

guese, is chaotic, luxuriant, improvident. Yet for many years and for many people the poet Browning meant Elizabeth, not Robert. When Wordsworth died in 1850, the *Athenaeum* suggested her as Poet Laureate. She will be remembered as a figure of romantic story—better understood in the *Letters of Robert Browning and Elizabeth Barrett* (1899) than in Virginia Woolf's novel *Flush* or Rudolf Besier's play *The Barretts of Wimpole Street*—and as the writer of a few short poems, among them *The Cry of the Children*, that searing and unanswerable accusation. It is right to remember that the first and fiercest exposure of the price paid for Victorian commercialism came from a woman poet writing only seven years after the accession of the Queen.

We return to Robert. Only two publications of verse marked this period— *Christmas Eve and Easter Day* (1850) and *Men and Women* (1855). He also wrote at this time an attractive essay on Shelley, by way of introduction to certain letters which were afterwards found to be fabrications. *Christmas Eve and Easter Day* probably indicates some influence from Elizabeth's devout Christian faith, and certainly illustrates Browning's lifelong interest in religious experience. The original *Men and Women* of 1855 is as rich a collection of poems as any produced in the Victorian age; and we may justly regret that it was afterwards broken up by the author and dispersed. An adequate conception of Browning's genius can be more readily gained from these fifty varied and energetic poems than from any other part of his work. The collection contains some of his best-loved pieces and ends with *One Word More*, his unique tribute to his wife. Less agreeably inspired by Elizabeth is *Mr Sludge, the Medium*, published later in *Dramatis Personae*. A celebrated American medium, David Douglas Home, had impressed Elizabeth by his spiritualistic manifestations. Browning was alarmed and gave voice to his feelings in verse. *Mr Sludge* is a great creation. It is not a portrait of Home; it is any or every humbug. Sludge is the greatest of Browning's magnificent casuists, who themselves are new figures in poetic literature.

After the death of Elizabeth, Browning came to London and never returned to Florence, nor did he visit Italy again till 1878. He lived at first in retirement, but thought that such a life was unmanly, and in 1863 began to frequent society. He became a familiar figure in London life, although, except for a very few friends, all women, none ever saw of Browning more than "a splendid surface". He was now at the height of his powers. Rarely is his poetic work so uniformly impressive as in *Dramatis Personae* (1864); and *The Ring and the Book* (1868–9) is the most magnificent of all his achievements, in spite of its inequalities. Browning had begun to consider this old murder story in 1860, but he put it aside in the year of his sorrow. He now resumed his work upon it. The telling of a story from several different points of view appealed to Browning. His gift of multivariety and his old delight in describing "soul-states" could display themselves fully in the different narratives. *The Ring and the Book* exhibits, as very long works invariably do, the poet's strength and weakness—his sense of tragedy, his immense pity, his mere cleverness and his love of jargon. To discuss in the abstract whether a story should be told in this fashion is useless. All that matters is whether the result succeeds. The best parts of *The Ring and the Book* succeed; the worst parts could not succeed in any form of story-telling.

Browning having won what seemed like a reward of popularity proceeded to squander it. He ventured into the classics, and published *Balaustion's Adventure; including a Transcript from Euripides* in 1871. *Aristophanes' Apology; including a Transcript from Euripides: being the Last Adventure of Balaustion* followed in 1875. Balaustion herself is delightful. The Hercules in the first poem and the Aristophanes in the second are magnificent; but the "transcripts" are quite bad; and the *Agamemnon of Aeschylus* (1877) is merely eccentric. Even more unpopular were *Prince Hohenstiel-Schwangau* (1871), *Fifine at the Fair* (1872), *Red Cotton Night-Cap Country or Turf and Towers* (1873) and *The Inn Album* (1875). Browning bantered his critics in *Pacchiarotto and how he worked in Distemper* (1876), which tells the whimsical tale of the artist who tried to reform his fellows. *La Saisiaz and the Two Poets of Croisic* followed in 1878; *Dramatic Idyls* in 1879–80; *Jocoseria* in 1883; *Ferishtah's Fancies* in 1884; and *Parleyings with Certain People of Importance in their Day* in 1887. The last revived at seventy-five memories of his boyhood's industrious happiness in his father's library. In all these volumes readers found less of the poet and more of the crabbed mannerist in style. Tennyson remained mellifluous to the end. Browning became more wilfully cacophonous. But the persistence of his creative gift is evident in some lovely lyrical interpolations.

Browning visited Italy several times in his last years, and lived in a house at Asolo, the little castled town of Pippa. His last volume, named from it *Asolando: Fancies and Facts*, and dated 1890, was published on 12 December 1889, the day on which he died at the Rezzonico Palace in Venice. He had not expected death, but, to the last, was full of projects, his courage unabated, his enterprise not weary; and his last words, the great *Epilogue* with which he closed the collected gleanings of his genius, fitly expressed the faith which made his life heroic. Browning is one of the most original of Victorian poets. So complete is the success of his "dramatic lyrics"—the poems spoken, as it were, in character— that he may be called the inventor, and, indeed, the proprietor, of that form. There was in him a curious strain of Renaissance curiosity and medieval pedantry and his utterance is at times almost deliberately crabbed. His enduring strength lies in his lyric intensity, his grasp of character and his power of transmuting "soul-states" into vivid and energetic poetry. In *The Poetry of Barbarism* (1900) Santayana compared him with Whitman; in *Mesmerism*, an early poem published in 1909, Ezra Pound expressed his own debt to "Old Hippety-Hop o' the accents...Clear sight's elector."

IV. MATTHEW ARNOLD, ARTHUR HUGH CLOUGH, JAMES THOMSON

Eminent alike as poet and critic, Matthew Arnold holds a place of singular distinction among Victorian writers. His poetical work is smaller in volume and narrower in range than that of his two great contemporaries, but it reflects, more clearly than the poetry of either, the collapse of faith that was a tragedy in many sincere lives of the period. Like Browning, Arnold was a man of the world; but, unlike Browning, he kept the world out of his poetry. It is in his

critical prose writings that we discover the shrewd observer of men and movements, sensitive to all "play of the mind", wherever and in whomsoever he
found it. When, at an early period in his literary career, he abandoned poetry
for prose, he at once came into touch with a wider public. His poetry exhibits
some of Gray's reluctance "to speak out"; but his prose has a sense of freedom,
and even of gaiety. He had his reward. He preached as insistently as Carlyle; but
he preached like a man of this world; and though some of his readers found it
difficult to endure the Olympian air of superiority affected by a critic who took
the whole conduct of life for his province, few could resist the charm of prose
discourses cast in a delightfully fresh and individual form and delivered with a
disarming, if delusive, air of innocent candour. Much of Arnold's social, political
and religious criticism has lost its point; but his literary criticism will live as long
as the best of its kind. Only Dryden, Coleridge and Eliot, poets like himself,
share his pre-eminence.

Matthew Arnold (1822–88) was the eldest son of Thomas, the headmaster of
Rugby. That he owed much to his father is clear; but his character and temperament developed in a strongly individual way. From Rugby he passed to
Oxford in the full tide of the Tractarian movement. Though fascinated by
Newman's personal charm, he stood coolly aloof from all the ecclesiastical
alarums and excursions. Matthew Arnold was never the man to lose his all,
even at Oxford, in a cause already lost; but Oxford, whatever its faults, was
always to him a permanent bulwark against the raw and vulgar. From the
worldly point of view, his subsequent career was prosaic and unspectacular.
Something brilliant in the public service—perhaps in diplomacy—might have
been predicted for him. But Lord Lansdowne, to whom he had been private
secretary, made him an inspector of elementary schools; and that was all the
public promotion he ever obtained. However, he was the greatest man who
became an inspector of schools, and that inconspicuous calling has shone in his
lustre ever since. Actually, nearly all Arnold's best poetry was written during the
busiest years of his school inspectorate. The work did him good. He loved
children, he took an interest in the work of teachers, and in the course of his
journeys met many of the English types—"populace, Philistines and barbarians"
—whom he was to use in his writings. What may be called his official works—
Popular Education in France (1861), *A French Eton* (1864), *Schools and Universities
on the Continent* (1868), *Special Report on Elementary Education Abroad* (1888),
and *Reports on Elementary Schools* (1889)—still have a place of their own in the
literature of education. His influence was entirely beneficent and his demands
were thoroughly practical. Educational, though unofficial, was *A Bible Reading
for Schools* (1872), a selection of chapters from Isaiah designed to make the
Bible attractive as great literature. To the years of his earlier official activity
belong the critical discourses *On Translating Homer* (1861) and *The Study of
Celtic Literature* (1867), based on his allocutions from the chair of poetry at
Oxford which he held for ten years (1857–67).

His poetical publications begin with such *juvenilia* as the Rugby prize poem
Alaric at Rome (1840) and the Oxford prize poem *Cromwell* (1843). His first
formal appearance was modestly made with *The Strayed Reveller, and other
Poems, by A.* (1849). His second collection, *Empedocles on Etna, and other Poems,*

by A. (1852), was withdrawn, like the first. In 1853, however, he published boldly, under his own name, a new volume with a preface defining his views upon some of the objects and functions of poetry. This volume included many of the poems already printed in its two predecessors, together with such notable additions as *Sohrab and Rustum* and *The Scholar-Gipsy*. In 1855 appeared *Poems by Matthew Arnold, Second Series*, a volume with only two new poems, but containing a further instalment of republications. In 1858 appeared *Merope, a Tragedy*, and in 1867 *New Poems*—the last of his separate volumes of verse. After that date came nothing but occasional pieces—the elegy on Stanley, and the three exquisite "animal" poems, *Geist's Grave, Poor Matthias* and *Kaiser Dead*, which are among the very best of their unusual kind.

A survey of Arnold's poems brings into prominence two outstanding facts —the early maturity of his genius, and his steadfast adherence throughout to certain very definite ideals of poetic art. He took his stand upon the classics and upon the practice of those moderns touched by the high seriousness of classical example. The Greeks, Goethe, Wordsworth—these are the prime literary sources of Matthew Arnold's poetical inspiration. Perhaps the most original poem in the 1849 volume is *The Forsaken Merman*, which is remarkable alike for its pathos and its metrical skill. In his picture of the Merman waiting forlorn outside the church which he could not enter, Arnold drew, no doubt unconsciously, a picture of his own religious state. The preface to the 1853 volume deserves careful reading, as it is Arnold's first published "essay in criticism". He rejects decisively the doctrine that a poet must "leave the exhausted past, and draw his subjects from matters of present import". Here is sounded the first note of his battle-song against the Philistines. But in spite of Arnold's own warm feeling for the classics, *Merope*, a tragedy in the Greek manner, is a frigid failure. On the other hand *Sohrab and Rustum* is both the most Homeric and the most successful of his narrative poems. The outstanding new contribution to the 1853 volume is *The Scholar-Gipsy*, which, with the later *Thyrsis*, his elegy on Clough, shows the poet in his richest mood of lyric invention and reflective feeling. Another pair, *Stanzas in Memory of the Author of Obermann* and the later *Obermann Once More*, gives us the most intimate revelations of his troubled soul. With them may be named *Stanzas from the Grande Chartreuse* (1855), another personal revelation. No one who has ever felt deeply about ultimate things can read it without emotion. *Rugby Chapel*, in memory of his father, and *A Southern Night*, lamenting the death of his brother, are both deeply and quietly moving. Matthew Arnold did not write the verses of a man of letters. His faultiest poems exhibit the faults of poems, not the failures of poetical exercises. The peculiar charm of his best work lies in its intensity of feeling and restraint of utterance. He is as free from sentiment as from excess of diction. He suffered deeply from the malady of his time because his firm sincerity could abide no self-deception; and he attracts us because we are made to feel both his spiritual yearning and his intellectual fortitude. His range is small; but within its limits he attains perfection.

Matthew Arnold's prose writings were the work of his middle and later years. They deal with the general fabric of English civilization and culture in his day; and they are all directed against national insularity and provincialism of mind. The main body of his literary criticism is to be found in the slight but attractive lectures *On Translating Homer* (1861), and *The Study of Celtic Literature* (1867), and in the two volumes entitled *Essays in Criticism* (1865, 1889). Here, for the first time, we encounter the verbal weapons used in a lifelong campaign against the "Philistines". We hear of "the best that is known and thought in the world", "the free play of the mind", "flexibility of intelligence", "prose of the centre", "criticism of life" and other phrases destined, by reiterated use, to become familiar. Arnold had learnt much from French prose, especially from Renan and Sainte-Beuve. To French poetry his ear had never been opened, and he made in this, as in other matters, no pretence. He charged the great Victorian public with complacent vulgarity. He declared that the end and aim of all literature is a criticism of life, that poetry itself is a criticism of life. These unusual claims not only puzzled the public, but irritated the literary dunces, who, as Leslie Stephen has put it, were "unable to distinguish between an epigram and a philosophical dogma". The public, however, appeared to like being provoked by Arnold, and he was led to the composition of the book called *Culture and Anarchy* (1869), which may be termed his central work in criticism other than literary. It has endured remarkably well. *Friendship's Garland* (1871), a series of satirical letters, is the most Puckish of his attacks on the great British public. The later *Mixed Essays* (1879) and *Discourses in America* (1885) should not be overlooked. Of his theological writings, *St Paul and Protestantism* (1870), *Literature and Dogma* (1873), *God and the Bible* (1875) and *Last Essays on Church and Religion* (1877), little need be said, as they were tracts for the times and have lost much of their point. Matthew Arnold's best prose is as certain of survival as his best poetry. It is a fulfilment of his own ideals of order and lucidity, with the added graces of ease, elegance and persuasiveness.

Their common connection with Rugby and Oxford, and the commemoration of their Oxford friendship in *Thyrsis*, link the names of Matthew Arnold and of Arthur Hugh Clough (1819–61), a saddened soul with cloistral instincts and sceptical convictions. Most of Clough's poetry is the record of the spiritual and intellectual struggles into which he was plunged by the religious unrest of the time. His best and most memorable poem was the first to be printed, *The Bothie of Toper-na-Fuosich* (1848), afterwards called *The Bothie of Tober-na-Vuolich*. He had already written short poems, some of which have lasted very well, and these appeared in *Ambarvalia* (1849). During a visit to Rome in 1849, Clough composed his second hexameter poem, *Amours de Voyage*, and in the following year at Venice he began *Dipsychus*. The works recorded here, together with other lyrics, of which the group entitled *Songs in Absence* is the most notable, constitute the sum of Clough's poetical productions. He remains the poet of *The Bothie*, which owes much of its success to his free and happy use of the long line. *The Bothie* proves that, whatever may happen to English hexameters when they are earnestly used, they are a delightful vehicle for serio-comic verse.

From a poet of perplexity we may fitly pass to a poet of despair, James Thomson (1834–82), usually distinguished from the earlier James Thomson by the initials "B.V.", representing "Bysshe Vanolis", a name under which he wrote. He took the first name from Shelley and the second from Novalis. His life was hard, and his later years were darkened by poverty and ill-health, largely due to insomnia and intemperate habits. The two separate volumes published just before his death, *The City of Dreadful Night and Other Poems* (1880) and *Vane's Story and Other Poems* (1881) contain the bulk of his verse. *The City of Dreadful Night*, which first appeared in his friend Charles Bradlaugh's *National Reformer* in 1874, cannot sustain the reputation it once had, but its best passages remain Thomson's most impressive achievement.

V. THE ROSSETTIS, WILLIAM MORRIS, SWINBURNE, FITZGERALD

In 1848, a few young artists and men of letters united to oppose the conventional or academic approach to art, and, as an act of homage to the simple sincerity of the early Italian painters, called themselves "the Pre-Raphaelite Brother-hood". The purely pictorial side of the movement is not our concern; but it happens that one of the group, Dante Gabriel Rossetti (1828–82) was remarkable both as painter and as poet, and through the force of his personality came to be regarded as the leader of the revolt. The name of the "brotherhood" unfor-tunately suggested some imitation of medievalism; actually its work was entirely modern, and was medieval in nothing but sincerity of spirit. Rossetti, indeed, had a pronounced idiosyncrasy of style that made imitation impossible to him. The general aim of the movement found an ardent champion in Ruskin, who defended both its works and its spirit. The brotherhood endeavoured to express its purpose in a magazine *The Germ: Thoughts towards Nature in Poetry, Literature and Art*, and defined its creed as "an entire adherence to the simplicity of art". The first number appeared in January 1850, the fourth and last in April. It is, in its interest, almost entirely a Rossetti production. Apart from Rossetti's curious story *Hand and Soul*, which is strangely like his paintings, the prose of *The Germ* is negligible. Its literary importance is mainly due to the eleven poems by Rossetti himself and the seven lyrics by his sister Christina. Some of these were "trial proofs"—*The Blessed Damozel*, for instance, being revised later.

About 1850 Rossetti met the beautiful Elizabeth Eleanor Siddal, who became his wife in 1860. In 1861 he published his first volume, *The Early Italian Poets*, rearranged later as *Dante and his Circle* (1874). This was a series of translations, including a prose version of *La Vita Nuova*, from Dante and the poets of his time. Meanwhile Rossetti had contributed to *The Oxford and Cambridge Maga-zine* in 1856 *The Burden of Nineveh* and a new version of *The Blessed Damozel*. Other poems written during this period were copied into a manuscript book, which, when his wife died tragically in 1862, was buried with her. Rossetti himself became a victim of chronic insomnia, and found his end in an overdose of narcotic. *Poems by D. G. Rossetti*, his first volume of strictly original poetry, was published in 1870. Most of its contents had lain undisturbed in his wife's grave since 1862; but he yielded to entreaty and consented to their disinterment. His last volume, *Ballads and Sonnets*, appeared in 1881. That the quantity of his verse is not very large may be in part explained by his laboriousness in composition and his equal laboriousness in revision. All his work exhibits a marked strain of the sensual and the mystic—a sense of the flesh and a sense of the spirit. The extremes are naturally more evident in his pictures than in his writings. *The Blessed Damozel*—the poem, not the picture—is almost perversely fascinating, because it has every quality of a mystically religious creation, except religious conviction. It is a triumphant attempt to figure forth the indescribable and transmit a vision of the beyond; and the triumph is secured, not by dim suggestion, but by a daring use of almost trivial detail. In this respect Rossetti is a descendant of the Keats who wrote *The Eve of St Agnes* and *The Eve of St Mark*—the latter of which might be called a pre-Raphaelite poem by anticipation. But Rossetti was not a poet of one style. He could achieve something of the swiftness and vigour of the ballad in *The White Ship* and *The King's Tragedy*. He could blend the romantic with the supernatural in *Sister Helen* and *Rose Mary*. He could be at once ironical and strangely sincere, as in *The Burden of Nineveh*. He could make poems of purely suggestive music, as in the sonnets of *The House of Life*. He does not always succeed; but when he does succeed he is unique.

Rossetti's two prose tales, *Hand and Soul* and the unfinished *Saint Agnes of Intercession*, have a moving "other-worldly" quality. None of his work in any form of art offers the least justification for the pseudonymous attack made upon him and Swinburne by Robert Buchanan in an article called *The Fleshly School of Poetry*, to which Rossetti replied contemptuously in *The Stealthy School of Criticism*. The incident has, at this date, little importance. The work of Rossetti as a translator is hardly less remarkable than his original poetry. His versions of Villon are good, and he ventured also into German. But he would be assured of fame if he had produced nothing more than his volume derived from the friends and precursors of Dante. In his own writings Rossetti displayed an elaborately poetic diction, which Keats had with supreme mastery brought back into English verse.

The power of Rossetti's personality is attested by his influence over the impetuous William Morris (1834–96). Morris's early enthusiasm for the Middle Ages appeared likely to lead him into the Church; but the reading of Ruskin's chapter "The Nature of Gothic" in *The Stones of Venice* (1853) changed the current of his whole life, and after a tour among the churches of France in 1855, he and his friend Edward Burne-Jones decided to abandon their intention of taking orders and to devote themselves to art. At first, Morris studied architecture; then, under the influence of Rossetti, he turned with ardour to painting. In 1859 he married Jane Burden, whose strange exotic beauty is immortalized in many of Rossetti's pictures; and his desire to make a worthy home led him to the activities that ended in the foundation of the celebrated firm of decorative artists, which he controlled from 1861 to his death, and which revolutionized public taste in fabrics and furniture. There was no longer a strict choice between beautiful old things and hideous modern things. Even though public taste may have gone beyond the ideals of Morris, it was his work and teaching that made any advance in domestic crafts both possible and practical. The famous products of his Kelmscott Press, begun in 1891, have been criticized by later printers; but it was Morris himself who showed them the possibilities of beauty in a modern book. The tendency of the best practice since Morris—for instance, in the work of Eric Gill—has been an attempt to combine the "book beautiful" with the "book useful". Morris's revolt against the hideous products of commercialism led him to revolt against the hideousness of commercial life itself, and he became a passionate Socialist. The extraordinary fact about Morris as a writer is that most of his long works are *parerga*. After a hard day's work in office or workshop, he found relaxation in the composition of epic poems and prose romances.

His earliest writings are among his most remarkable. As Rossetti found himself in *The Germ*, so Morris found himself in *The Oxford and Cambridge Magazine* (1856), which he conducted materially and artistically for twelve months. The *Magazine* is important almost solely for the few contributions by Rossetti and the several in prose and verse by Morris. *The Hollow Land*, *The Story of the Unknown Church*, and others are semi-mystical prose narratives that clearly point to the later romances. Four of the five poems written by Morris for *The Oxford and Cambridge Magazine* appeared in the volume called *The Defence of Guenevere and other Poems* (1858). With all its defects of crudity, this collection contains the most original poetry that Morris wrote. The now familiar pieces show us a spirit intoxicated with the romance of the past and striving after a perfect transmission of its beauty. In *The Life and Death of Jason* (1867), his next volume, inspired by Chaucer he has become a teller of tales, though his manner is not Chaucer's, but follows the looser style of the metrical romances. In his next poetical publication, *The Earthly Paradise* (1868–70), the teller of tales is even more apparent; for the sad and simple thesis of aged wanderers seeking for a fabled earthly paradise and coming to rest in a nameless city allows the narration of twenty-four stories. Twelve of the stories, told by elders of the city, come from classical sources; the other twelve, told by the wanderers, are derived chiefly from medieval Latin, French and Icelandic originals, with gleanings from Mandeville and *The Arabian Nights*. There is great variety both in the telling and in the effect. Some of the tales are thin and unmomentous, others are tense and vigorous. Its masterpiece is *The Lovers of Gudrun*, a version of the *Laxdaela Saga* in heroic couplets. In spite of its occasional failures and flatnesses *The Earthly Paradise* remains a fine achievement of narrative art. The interludes of the months have a special attractiveness.

Love is Enough (1873), a morality, has not been popular. The narrative poet returns in *The Aeneids of Virgil* (1876) which reads as if it had been translated from an Icelandic original. But after a small volume of actual Icelandic translations Morris showed his power again as a poetic teller of tales in *The Story of Sigurd the Volsung and the Fall of the Niblungs* (1877). The main theme is magnificently handled; the episodes follow one another with unfailing vigour and freshness; and in the climax of the story the poet rises to the height of his power. After *Sigurd*, Morris practically abandoned poetry, save for his translation of the *Odyssey*, and his last original book of verse was the collection of lyrics and ballads, *Poems by the Way*, issued from the Kelmscott Press in 1891.

The extent of Morris's prose is equally astonishing. His Socialist propaganda was marked by two romances, *A Dream of John Ball* (1888), and the Utopian *News from Nowhere* (1891). In 1889 he essayed pure romance with a prose story *The House of the Wolfings*. This was followed in 1890 by *The Roots of the Moun-*

tains and in 1891 by *The Story of the Glittering Plain*—first of the Kelmscott Press books. *The Wood beyond the World* came in 1895 and *The Well at the World's End* in 1896. Two more romances were published posthumously, *The Water of the Wondrous Isles* (1897), the most fairylike of the series, and *The Sundering Flood* (1897), completed less than a month before his death. The prose of these stories is at first a little disconcerting in its archaism. But the style was as natural to Morris as the style of *The Faerie Queene* was to Spenser, and, after the first discomfort, is just as readable. What one misses in all the tales of Morris, whether in prose or in verse, is a touch of the wholesome, saving, Dickensian "commonness" of Chaucer.

Morris was a lifelong propagandist; his love of the beautiful work of the past, material and imaginative, stood for him in the place of religious fervour, and his whole strength of purpose was dedicated to the reconstitution of modern life upon conditions that would bring beauty back to all men. Like Ruskin and Carlyle, Morris can be numbered with the saints who in the days of triumphant commercialism strove unweariedly against its crimes.

Algernon Charles Swinburne (1837–1909) announced his allegiance to Rossetti in the dedication of his first book—*The Queen Mother and Rosamond* (1860), two poetical dramas written in elaborate blank verse. Swinburne, born in London of an old Northumbrian family, was, as befits the son of an admiral, a lover and singer of the sea. At Eton and Oxford he developed his love of poetry, and when he came into association with the Rossetti circle it was with a taste already formed for many kinds of verse. He was a good classic, and his poetical patriotism was bestowed equally upon ancient Greece and Elizabethan England. His sympathy with republican freedom was learned from Landor and Shelley and, last but not least, from Victor Hugo, who shared with Shakespeare the shrine of his lifelong idolatry. With all his metrical originality, Swinburne was in substance an "echo" poet; and there was no writer who so completely furnished him with inspiration as Victor Hugo. He began with youthfully daring atheism and youthfully outspoken republicanism; and he never quite grew up. His convictions were always passionate and always literary. It is a curious fact that no influence coloured the language of the atheistic republican so richly as the sacred literature, biblical and liturgical, of the religion whose professors were the objects of his tireless invective.

Atalanta in Calydon and *Chastelard* in 1865 and *Poems and Ballads* in 1866 won Swinburne both celebrity and notoriety. *Chastelard*, the first of his three plays upon the life of Mary Queen of Scots, is a romantic drama in the style of his two earlier works. *Atalanta*, classical in subject, is an attempt to reproduce the characteristic forms of Greek drama in English verse. The avowed atheism of *Atalanta* might pass unchallenged, as long as it was partly veiled in the decent obscurity of its antique setting; but *Poems and Ballads* shocked most readers by its open flouting of conventional reticence. Here indeed were *fleurs du mal* flagrantly planted on English soil! The apparition of Swinburne shamelessly chanting his songs of satiety gave respectable England the dreadful sensation of finding Tannhäuser hymning the joys of Venus in the glazed courts of the Great Exhibition. And the curious fact is, that as Rossetti's religious poems had everything except religious conviction, so Swinburne's sensual poems had everything except sensual conviction. But the new metres captured the young, who chanted the music of *Dolores* without quite knowing what it was all about.

Sagacious friends tried to divert the poet's ecstasies to other channels. He was persuaded to be active in the cause of Italian freedom. All the elements needed to excite him were there—the Papacy, the Austrian Empire, and, above all, Napoleon the Little, dearest enemy of Victor Hugo. And so the ardent poet whose hymns of lust and satiety had dazzled the young turned suddenly and sang the praises of Mazzini and Garibaldi in *A Song of Italy* (1867). *Songs before Sunrise* (1871) was a collection of poems written during the final struggle for Italian freedom. It includes much of Swinburne's best work, the majestic *Hertha*, the lament for captive Italy in *Super Flumina Babylonis* and the apostrophe to France in *Quia Multum Amavit*. *Songs of Two Nations* (1875) continued his fierce political strains. But there is no conviction in his ardours. A sudden jolt would have made him write as hotly on the other side. It would be difficult to maintain that his poems of liberty are better than his poems of lust. After the achievement of Italian hope in 1870 and the fall of Napoleon III, which he hailed with savage delight, Swinburne had leisure for other interests. In the length and rhetoric of *Bothwell* (1874), sequel to *Chastelard*, he followed the example of Hugo's *Cromwell*. As *Bothwell* followed *Chastelard*, so *Erechtheus* (1876) followed *Atalanta* with equal eloquence and with closer relation to the spirit of Greek tragic form. The lyric choruses of *Erechtheus*, less enchanting than those in *Atalanta*, have a more constant loftiness and majesty. A second series of *Poems and Ballads* (1878), as musical as the first, was more chastened in matter. *Studies in Song* and *Songs of the Springtides*, in 1880, were full of love of the sea, the prevailing passion of the poet's later verse. As if he had become aware of his own excess in utterance, he turned to parody, and in the anonymous *Heptalogia: or The Seven Against Sense* (1880) produced gravely elaborate burlesques of Tennyson, Browning, Rossetti, Patmore and others, as well as himself. His touch was a little too heavy for perfect parody; and of his own *Nephelidia* it may be said that he was always capable of writing some of its lines in poems not intended to be amusing.

Most admirers of Swinburne felt that the *Tristram of Lyonesse* volume, published in 1882, was the crown of his mature work. The title-piece is, like Morris's *Jason*, a long narrative in couplets; but with the kind of music that Morris could (and perhaps would) not have made. *Tristram of Lyonesse* is Wagnerian. It is a glorification of bodily passion. In form it is a marvellous study in the use of the couplet; in substance it is most permanently successful in its sea passages. That it is verbose, excessive, extenuated and monotonous can hardly be denied. The same volume also contained the series of sonnets on the Elizabethan dramatists, sometimes uncritical in enthusiasm but always memorable in expression. *A Century of Roundels* (1883) is remarkable as an exhibition of poetical dexterity which makes much of a slight metrical form. In 1881 Swinburne concluded with *Mary Stuart* the trilogy begun with *Chastelard* and continued with *Bothwell*. After *A Midsummer Holiday* (1884), he returned to drama in *Marino Faliero* (1885), a subject which he felt had been handled unworthily by Byron. *Locrine* (1887), his next drama, was an original experiment in which each scene was presented in rhymes of a recurring stanza-form; it is more intricate than dramatic. Two years later came the third series of *Poems and Ballads* (1889). In its lighter pieces and especially in such ballads as *The Jacobite's Lament* there is much of the accustomed freshness of spirit; but there are signs of flagging energy; nor did the poet recapture his inspiration in the later volumes, *Astrophel* (1894), *A Tale of Balen* (1896), *A Channel Passage* (1904) and the plays, *The Sisters* (1892), *Rosamund Queen of the Lombards* (1899) and *The Duke of Gandia* (1908). A surprising development was the sudden flaming of "Imperialism", at the time of the South African War, in a poet hitherto dedicated to republicanism.

In addition to his poetry, Swinburne published from 1868 onwards several volumes of literary criticism. His *Essays and Studies* and *Miscellanies* bear striking testimony to his knowledge and love of poetry and his scholarly insight. Of his numerous monographs and essays upon individual writers, *A Study of Shakespeare* takes the first place. His criticism, however, was too much charged with the white heat of enthusiasm to be always judicious. A specially notable volume is the study of Blake, first published as long ago as 1868, a warm and generous appreciation of a poet who is sometimes thought to be a modern discovery. Swinburne even wrote a novel which appeared serially and pseudonymously in a forgotten weekly during 1877 and was republished as *Love's Cross Currents: A Year's Letters* (1905). It has a faint suggestion of Meredith and is quite readable. Swinburne was not a great critic, but his essays contain passages of great criticism.

Swinburne was always true to himself as a poet. Receptive of manifold influences, classical, English and foreign, he reproduced them in a style wholly individual. He was fearless in the poetic proclamation of his ideals of liberty and justice, and tireless in the metrical ingenuity with which he fashioned his astonishing fluency into poetic forms both musical and memorable.

The first number of *The Germ* contained, as well as Rossetti's *My Sister's Sleep*, two lyrics by his sister Christina Georgina Rossetti (1830–94), which gave evidence of clear and quite original genius. Unlike her brother, whose sympathy with religion was merely artistic, and still more unlike Swinburne, whose attitude was openly hostile, Christina Rossetti was, to the end of her life, a devout Christian, finding the highest inspiration in her faith, and investing Anglican ideals of worship with a mystical beauty. Her volumes of verse, beginning with *Goblin Market and Other Poems* in 1862 and ending with *New Poems* collected in 1896 by her brother William Michael, are rich in devotional feeling. Her religious ecstasy is moving rather than winning, and she presents as much of the difficulty as of the beauty of holiness. Her sequences of sonnets, *Monna Innominata* and *Later Life*, are filled with a sense of the claims of divine love over human passion. Readers of *Sonnets from the Portuguese* should never omit to read the different story of *Monna Innominata*. The woman in Christina Rossetti is most delightfully apparent in *Sing-Song, a Nursery Rhyme Book* (1872). It is difficult to find any who can contest her claim to be the finest of English poetesses.

To the group of poets here considered may be added Arthur O'Shaughnessy (1844–91), friend of Rossetti. His volumes, *An Epic of Women* (1870), *Lays of France* (1872) (founded on the lays of Marie de France) and *Music and Moonlight*

(1874) abound in Swinburnian stanza forms, though the story of *Chaitivel* in *Lays of France* borrows the delightful measure of Samuel Daniel's *Ulisses and the Syren*. "We are the music-makers" and a few other pieces deserve a place in the anthologies, where alone O'Shaughnessy is likely to survive.

Edward FitzGerald (1809–83) is remarkable as a poet who has won immortality by translations. Apart from his charming prose dialogue, *Euphranor* (1851), and his letters, which are among the very best in our language, he wrote scarcely any original work. He was independent in the worldly sense, and as a kind of hermit in Suffolk was independent in every other sense. One of his friends was Bernard Barton, the friend of Charles Lamb, and with Barton's daughter he contracted a marriage which was immediately repented. Yet another friend was the Reverend George Crabbe, grandson of the poet, whose works he strove to make more widely known by his *Readings in Crabbe* (1883). The two great events in his life were the study of Spanish and the study of Persian. From the study of Spanish came first *Six Dramas of Calderon* (1853), very free translations in blank verse and prose in which he attempted to adapt a foreign author to English thought. Then followed *The Mighty Magician* and *Such Stuff as Dreams are made of* (1865), with which he took such liberties that the result is neither Spanish nor English. The study of Persian led FitzGerald to begin a version of *Salámán and Absál* of Jámí, and in 1862 he completed *A Bird's Eye View of Faríd-Uddín Attar's Bird-Parliament*. These, however, were mere experiments. The true kindling of his genius came when he read the *Rubáiyát* or aphoristic quatrains of Omar Khayyám, the astronomer-poet of Persia. Over these he brooded with delight, and then produced in 1859 what is, in effect, an English poem of seventy-five quatrains based upon selections and combinations of the original stanzas. Later editions revised the expression and extended the length. But the book may be said to have been concealed rather than published. Eminent Orientalists have protested against English devotion to an inferior Persian poet. They have missed the point. No English reader cares about the Persian poet, and other attempts to present Omar have gained no success. English readers care only about FitzGerald's Omar, which is an English poem with Persian allusions. Its bold scepticism proved singularly attractive, when at last the poem was allowed to become generally known; but, apart from its matter, the Augustan beauty and perfection of phrase and the supple grace of melody and rhythm have earned it a permanent place among the masterpieces of English poetry. Its stanza was a novelty which others, like Swinburne in his *Laux Veneris*, were not slow to borrow. In an age when scepticism was sorrowful and reluctant, FitzGerald was frank and undismayed. He faced boldly what had to be faced and put lamentation and complaint resolutely behind him. Though the end was Death, was there not Life? There is comfort as well as courage in his song.

VI. GERARD MANLEY HOPKINS AND LESSER POETS OF THE MIDDLE AND LATER NINETEENTH CENTURY

In volume XIII of the original *Cambridge History of English Literature*, a volume first published in 1916, the poetry of Gerard Manley Hopkins is mentioned in a footnote to the chapter on "Lesser Poets of the Middle and Later Nineteenth Century" contributed by George Saintsbury. Earlier, in the revised third edition of his own *History of Nineteenth Century Literature* (1901), Saintsbury had referred to "the remarkable talents of Mr Gerard Manley Hopkins, which could never be mistaken by any one who knew him, and of which some memorials remain in verse"—the reference being to some extracts from a few of Hopkins's poems which had been printed in Alfred H. Miles's *The Poets and the Poetry of the Nineteenth Century* (1891–7) and in two anthologies by H. C. Beeching (1895). In so cautious a manner was one of the greatest poets of the century introduced to the public.

The exaggerated caution was due to Hopkins's literary executor Robert Bridges, the future Poet Laureate, who later included a few of his friend's verses in his wartime anthology *The Spirit of Man* before editing the first edition of the *Poems* in 1918—nearly thirty years after the author's death. Exasperation at this unnecessary delay must be tempered by recognition of the fact that Bridges kept for eventual publication, not only the poems (which in some cases might otherwise have been lost altogether) but the letters of his friend—including some pretty severe criticism of Bridges's own work, which a lesser man might well have destroyed. *The Letters of Gerard Manley Hopkins to Robert Bridges*, together with the correspondence to Dixon, Patmore and others (1935, 1938, 1955), are comparable in their picture of the development of a poet's mind to those of Keats.

It is to Blake, of course, rather than to Keats, whom we must go in order to find even a faint parallel to the case of Hopkins as regards tardy recognition. Blake was better known to his contemporaries than Hopkins was to his, but the full recognition of his genius came a good many years after his death, some of his poems remaining in manuscript till late Victorian times. Indeed, we may say without much reservation that just as the Victorians discovered one of the greatest poets of the late eighteenth century, so the twentieth century discovered the poems and letters of the man who in several respects is the greatest poet of the Victorian age. It must be accounted a pity that acute critics like Saintsbury had so little opportunity of reading these poems, but perforce had to form their appreciation, extremely generous in the circumstances, from a few paltry extracts, "like the proverbial reconstruction," as Saintsbury well put it, "of a fossil beast from a few odd bones."

The simile in another sense, in the light of our greater knowledge, was not the happiest that could have been used. For it is not simply the fact that Hopkins, by the accident of his tardy publication, happens to be the "newest" of the Victorians that makes him, on the whole, the most living voice among their poets. Think for a moment what so much of Victorian poetry consists of: of what Yeats, speaking of Morris, called a "dream world...the antithesis of daily life", either vaguely medieval, as in much of Tennyson and Rossetti, or vaguely Renascence, as in much of Browning. Only a minority of Victorian verse (only a minority, as he afterwards recognized, of the early, Victorian verse of Yeats himself) escapes from this escapism; only occasionally are most other Victorian poets able to do what Hopkins does at his best: that is, make great poetry out of the very tensions, the very frustrations, of their time and place; only occasionally, as in Matthew Arnold's *Dover Beach*, do Hopkins's elders and contemporaries speak with the living voice—what he called "the current language heightened"—that was his intention and in some cases his achievement. In this strength and vigour of idiom, as much as in any Sprung Rhythm which he re-employed, does his originality reside.

The prime reason for the excessive caution of Robert Bridges probably lay, nevertheless, in these "sprung and outriding rhythms", which Hopkins himself may have made too much of. When he uses most successfully his extra-metrical or counterpoint effects, they are nearly as unobtrusive as in the later Shakespeare and should no more than in *The Tempest* or *The Winter's Tale* need the attention of special typographical marks. When prosody comes in at the door, poetry is apt to fly out of the window, and Hopkins may have been mistaken in consider-ing it necessarily a virtue that his poems were the first since the time of *Piers Plowman* to employ Sprung Rhythm, which he held to be "the nearest to... the native and natural rhythm of speech", as "the governing principle of the scansion." It can, at any rate, be said that where he is least successful his com-parative failure is due to his being too much concerned with this governing principle of scansion and not enough with the experience which should govern the whole.

One other thing distinguishes him from most of the other Victorian poets, and that is the relative paucity of his work, which is about equal in bulk as well as in genius to *The Temple* of George Herbert, both very slender volumes compared with the collected poems of Tennyson, Browning, Mrs Browning, Arnold, Swinburne, Morris or Meredith. To get a partial explanation for this fact we must turn briefly to the life.

Gerard Manley Hopkins (1844–89) was born at Stratford, Essex, and educated at Highgate School and Balliol College, Oxford, where he was the pupil of Jowett and Pater and began his lifelong friendship with Bridges. The Oxford Movement was, in one sense, over, with the secession to Rome of its leader Newman the year after Hopkins's birth, but the Oxford of the eighteen-sixties remained a centre of religious controversy and inquiry, with the High Church party, led by Pusey, defending the Anglican *via media* against Rome on the one side and liberalism on the other. Hopkins himself became a Puseyite, despite the rival attractions of the humanism of Matthew Arnold and the new aestheti-cism of Pater—to say nothing of his own lifelong feeling for art and nature which led him to believe at one time that he might become a professional artist, like two of his brothers. But his was not a spirit which could be satisfied for very long with a compromise, with anything less than an absolute authority to which he could owe obedience, and in 1866, while still an undergraduate, he was received by Newman into the Roman Catholic Church. For a few months after graduation he taught at Newman's Oratory School at Edgbaston, and then in 1868, at the age of twenty-four, took the decisive step of his life and entered the novitiate of the Society of Jesus.

How this affected his poetry is best told in his own words, in the oft-quoted letter of 1878 to his friend Canon Dixon. He had been writing verse since his schooldays, but on becoming a priest he burnt, as he thought, all he had written —though a few pieces survived—and "resolved to write no more, as not belonging to my profession, unless by the wish of my superiors." This intended sacrifice may not have been necessary, even allowing for a strict interpretation of the *Spiritual Exercises* of St Ignatius Loyola, for if the Jesuit is supposed to devote all his intellect and will to the service of Christ it is a most Puritan reading of the instruction to imagine that it means giving up the practice of such Christian poetry as Hopkins was to write. He said himself, in one of his sermons, that the poet and his works are creatures of God, and Dixon expostulated with him: "Surely one vocation cannot destroy another: and such a Society as yours will not remain ignorant that you have such gifts as have seldom been given by God to man." Furthermore, he had read Herbert at Oxford and must have known that the rector of Bemerton managed to combine the writing of some of the most impressive poetry of the seventeenth century, admittedly published only after his death, with the utmost diligence in his duties. That Hopkins was eventually able to do the same—whether as parish priest, teacher at Stonyhurst (1882–4) or Professor of Greek at University College, Dublin (1884–9)—was partly due to a chance remark of his own rector in 1875. "For seven years I wrote nothing but two or three little presentation pieces which occasion called for. But when in the winter of '75 the *Deutschland* was wrecked in the mouth of the Thames and five Franciscan nuns, exiles from Germany by the Falck Laws, aboard of her were drowned I was affected by the account and happening to say so to my rector he said that he wished some one would write a poem on the subject. On this hint I set to work and though my hand was out at first, produced one." When, however, he offered *The Wreck of the Deutschland* to the Jesuit magazine, *The Month*, the editor refused it, a fate which was afterwards to overtake another of Hopkins's poems on a similar subject, *The Loss of the Eurydice* (1878). That the Jesuits did not fail eventually to recognize the genius of one of their greatest Englishmen in modern times is proved by the request to Bridges of the Rev. Joseph Keating, S. J. in 1909 to be allowed to publish a complete edition of Hopkins—a request, however, which was refused by Bridges, presumably because his own edition was in active preparation.

Whether Hopkins would have written more poetry had he not become a Catholic priest is a question which is really irrelevant. He might have been as prolific as Browning if he had remained a layman, but we should not have had the poetry which he actually wrote, nearly all of which springs, directly or indirectly, from his ministry. (The importance of the *Deutschland* episode is that after it he "felt free to write.") It is as impossible to imagine the Hopkins we know a lay poet as Blake or Byron a member of the Society of Jesus. The fact that some of his finest poetry springs from his "wrestling with (my God!) my God" only emphasizes his kinship with Herbert; it is not a sign that he would have been greater as a poet, though perhaps happier as a man, if he had become an artist or a man of letters instead of a Jesuit priest.

The poetry remains, a matter of a mere hundred pages or so, but the best of it as infinitely re-readable as the best of Blake or Herbert. Not that there is any absolute consensus of opinion as to which are Hopkins's best poems, any more than with most other poets. He himself described *The Windhover* as "the best thing I ever wrote", and this powerful poem, written in 1877, about the "dapple-dawn-drawn" kestrel, dedicated "To Christ our Lord", has remained a favourite with many readers, together with *The Wreck of the Deutschland* and *Felix Randal* (1880). Probably the best of Hopkins, in the main, is to be found where he is most simple—simple in structure, though often profound enough in meaning. In this view, such poems as *God's Grandeur*, *Spring and Fall* and that early impressive poem *The Habit of Perfection* (1866) are among the best, while such poems as *The Leaden Echo and the Golden Echo* and *Spelt from Sibyl's Leaves* seem to be not entirely successful experiments. In this view, too, the pre-eminently great Hopkins is to be found in such late sonnets as *Carrion Comfort*, "No worst, there is none..." and above all *Justus quidem tu es, Domine* ("Thou art indeed just, Lord...")—sonnets which are profoundly moving, alike to the Christian and the non-Christian reader, in the same way, sometimes in detail, as the *Love*, *The Collar*, *The Flower* and the *Affliction* of George Herbert. Such poems (written *c*. 1885–9) are surely the final answer to those who have regretted Hopkins's vocation. They were "written in blood", doubtless, but so after all were some of the poems of Keats; like Herbert's, they record both the struggle with God and the victory in acceptance of what the poet conceives to be God's will. A lay Hopkins might have given the world more poems as great as *Spring and Fall*, but he could not have had the poignant experiences of the soul which resulted in the triumph, both in life and in art, of these late sonnets. While Pre-Raphaelites like Rossetti were toying with religious emotions mainly for their aesthetic value, Hopkins was undergoing the reality, and as an inevitable consequence his poems work at a deeper level than most of theirs. From this point of view, the metrical licences and the "metaphysical" wit are, like Donne's and Herbert's, the mere tools of expression, the ropes and pulleys by whose aid Hopkins, more steeply than any other poet of his period, ascended the mountains of the mind.

The pioneer study of Hopkins in F. R. Leavis's *New Bearings in English Poetry* (1932) remains the best account. The centenary of his birth inspired *Gerard Manley Hopkins* (1944) by a group of American critics associated with *The Kenyon Review* and a two-volume work *Gerard Manley Hopkins: A Study of Poetic Idiosyncrasy in Relation to Poetic Tradition* (1944–9) by W. H. Gardner of the University of Natal who succeeded Bridges and Charles Williams as editor of the Oxford *Poems* (4th edition, with N. H. MacKenzie, 1966) and edited the Penguin selection of the poems and prose (1953). A fellow-Jesuit, G. F. Lahey, wrote Hopkins's Life in 1930.

The *Letters* (edited by Claude Colleer Abbott) have been mentioned; it is to the *Note-Books and Papers* (first published 1937, now contained in the enlarged *Journals and Papers*, 1959) that we must turn in order to discover that, however exceptional Hopkins was, he was nevertheless in some ways of his time and place. The *Journal* in particular, which he kept during the "silent years" 1866–75, shows us a student of nature whose remarkable eye for detail significantly recalls Ruskin rather than Wordsworth. It is a painter's eye as much as a poet's which we see at work here, and in this conjunction Hopkins, no mean draughtsman himself, can be said to be one of the greatest of those associated in some measure, though not in his case personally, with the Pre-Raphaelites, the only one perhaps to apply at all consistently in the field of poetry the principles of the Brotherhood in art. We should not forget that the Brotherhood, to which Hopkins's friend Dixon belonged, owed its initial impulse (in England) to a remark of Keats cited by Rossetti. Writing to his brother William in 1848, Rossetti said that he had been reading Houghton's *Life and Letters of Keats*, then just published: "Keats seems to have been a glorious fellow, and says in one place (to my great delight) that, having just looked over a folio of the first and second schools of Italian painting, he has come to the conclusion that the early men surpassed even Raphael himself!" In poetry, it was mainly the lesser, the fanciful, the more obviously charming side of Keats that the Pre-Raphaelites went on to explore, and in some cases to exploit, but if for the moment we include Hopkins among them (as he might well have been among them in other circumstances) the picture they present is rather different. A very minor artist compared with Rossetti or Holman Hunt, a very minor critic of art and culture compared with Morris (to say nothing of Morris's mentor Ruskin), Hopkins in poetry was fitted to be Keats's successor more than those who actually succeeded Keats among the Pre-Raphaelites and their associates. Even as early as *The Habit of Perfection*, however, Hopkins was a Keats with a difference, a difference more radical and original than that revealed in the early poems of Tennyson. If later generations find Victorian poetry, for all its customary charm and occasional greatness, lacking in many of the virtues of the first Romantics or of the early seventeenth century, then a partial explanation must lie in the fact that it was truncated at both ends: by, in the first place, the death of Keats in 1821—his exact contemporary Carlyle lived till the eighteen-eighties—and in the second place by the non-publication of Hopkins, Keats's true successor. A Keats with an averagely-long life (not to mention a Byron and a Shelley surviving with him) and a longer-lived Hopkins with an averagely-large readership—"What I want," he wrote to Bridges, "to be more intelligible, smoother, and less singular, is an audience"—would have given Victorian poetry that stiffening of intelligence it required and might have rendered superfluous the reaction against the nineteenth century which took place in the nineteen-twenties.

Such speculations are of interest in literary history primarily because we cannot see a period like the Victorian as it mostly saw itself. Any original work, whether published at the time or not, is bound to alter the perspective by which we see other works. In T. S. Eliot's well-known words in his essay on *Tradition and the Individual Talent* (1919): "What happens when a new work of art is created is something that happens simultaneously to all the works of art which preceded it. The existing monuments form an ideal order among themselves which is modified by the introduction of the new (the really new) work of art among them." No one today can see Victorian poetry without Hopkins, however much without him it actually was. Our feelings about Hopkins, our judgment of his relative worth, must inevitably affect our feelings about the other Victorian poets—however much we agree that poets do not compete with one another, that any poet of distinction has his own particular virtues. If we see Hopkins as, in many ways, the chief figure, the main living voice against a background of Victorian knights in armour, then inevitably we must see even Tennyson himself, the great representative poet of his age, as in most of his work a relatively minor writer. If, on the other hand, we see Hopkins as an interesting but minor poet (which is the view of some critics, including, it would appear, T. S. Eliot), then our estimate of Tennyson, Browning, Arnold, Swinburne or Meredith is likely to be enhanced rather than the reverse. The Victorians themselves, by their fuller appreciation of Blake, saw the poetry of Blake's time differently from the way his contemporaries saw it—though as late as 1880, when Matthew Arnold took the "roll of our chief poetical names" he omitted Blake but included Scott, Campbell and Moore. The Edwardians discovered the poetry of the seventeenth-century mystic Thomas Traherne (first published 1903–10), and if Traherne had been a poet of the stature of Donne or Marvell then the whole of the poetry of the seventeenth century might have had to be reconsidered.

"The effect of studying masterpieces," wrote Hopkins to Bridges, "is to make me admire and do otherwise. So it must be on every original artist to some degree, on me to a marked degree." Partly because his greatest successors, Yeats and Eliot, were themselves poets of a high degree of originality, partly because he was published too late to influence them in their receptive period, the main effect of Hopkins in the creative field was not a very fortunate one. His more obvious singularities were found to be only too imitable, so we had the spectacle, not for the first time in English literary history—one thinks of Milton and the eighteenth century—of many of the minor poets of the nineteen-thirties and after employing the outward show of a great poet in verse that was not really suited to the employment at all. In the critical field, the effect of studying Hopkins is a certain bias against the conventional in language and rhythm, a bias which has to be allowed for, here as elsewhere, when we come to consider the poets who sometimes succeeded him in practice but who were mostly published long before.

In the first place we must allow for this natural bias when we turn from Hopkins himself to his intimate and much loved friend Robert Bridges, born the same year as Hopkins, 1844, but who lived until 1930, when the greatest poet of the next generation, T. S. Eliot, had already written *The Waste Land* and *Ash Wednesday*. Taking up literature professionally in 1882, after practising medicine in London, Bridges had the advantage over Hopkins of attaining publication in his lifetime, but for some years shared his friend's obscurity so far as the general reading public was concerned. His verse dramas on classical themes (1883–94) won him a reputation among scholars—Hopkins found his *Return of Ulysses* "a fine play", though (like other plays of the kind) unreal in character and too archaic in language—but it was not until the *Shorter Poems* of 1896 that he first began to be at all widely known beyond university circles. Even as late as 1913, when he succeeded Tennyson's successor Alfred Austin as Poet Laureate, the more popular newspapers complained that no one had ever heard of him—which was perhaps another way of saying that, compared with

Kipling, "the Poet Laureate of the British Empire", Bridges (like Austin in 1896) was still known to very few readers. He never attained to Kipling's enormous popularity, among readers of many different kinds, any more than any other poet of the period who aimed at something higher than Kipling genuinely achieved, but in his old age his long poem *The Testament of Beauty* (1929) went through many editions and gave rise to commentaries on the poet's philosophy of life. The main value of the *Testament* is rather in the field of scholarly reflection than, strictly, in the field of poetry. As we should guess from his controversies with Hopkins, all the truth in which may not have been on the one side (it is a pity that both sides of the correspondence have not survived), Bridges was inclined to the conventional in poetic diction, though he sometimes experimented in metre. He is more readable in the best of his shorter pieces, whether in the 1896 collection or the *New Verse* of 1925, than in the verse plays or in most of the lengthy *Testament*. One of the best short pieces is, fittingly, the introductory sonnet to his dead friend, and his "plumage of far wonder and heavenward flight", prefaced to his edition of Hopkins in 1918. Hopkins's own opinion of an earlier set of sonnets *The Growth of Love* (1876), expressed in a letter to Dixon—"In imagery he is not rich but excels in phrasing, in sequence of phrase and sequence of feeling"—is a fair criticism of the best of the later work also.

Dixon himself—Richard Watson Dixon (1833–1900)—was educated at Oxford, where with his friends Morris and Burne-Jones he became a member of the Pre-Raphaelite Brotherhood and with Morris projected *The Oxford and Cambridge Magazine*. After his ordination in 1858, he taught for a while at Highgate School, where Hopkins was a pupil. He was Canon of Carlisle 1868–75 and became an ecclesiastical historian (see p. 671) of the first rank. *Mano* (1883), a "Poetical History" in *terza rima*, is his most ambitious work in poetry, but he is more convincingly himself in his lyrics, especially those in *Christ's Company* (1861).

A less intimate friend and correspondent of Hopkins was Coventry Patmore (1823–96), whose collected volume of *Poetical Works* (1886) Hopkins called "a good deed done for the Catholic Church and another for England, for the British Empire." Patmore had started with contributions to the Pre-Raphaelite *Germ*, but had first come into prominence with the domestic epic *The Angel in the House* (1854–6), which was a great popular success but described by *Blackwood's Magazine* as "the spawn of frogs", with unrepentant references by the reviewer to "the life into which the slime of the Keatses and Shelleys of former days has fecundated." More original than this apotheosis of Victorian married love was the book of odes *The Unknown Eros* (1877), on the whole Patmore's most impressive work.

The bibliography bearing the title "Lesser Poets of the Middle and Later Nineteenth Century" in volume XIII of the original *Cambridge History* extends to fourteen pages of close print. This is partly because it includes verse written by those better remembered today by their prose writings, such as the medievalist Sebastian Evans, the novelists Mrs Clive and George Macdonald, the critic Frederic Myers, the "compleat angler" Thomas Westwood, and the biographer William Sharp—who wrote neo-Ossianic prose and verse under the pseudonym "Fiona Macleod". Most of these, and many others—over two hundred in all—are included in the twelve volumes of Alfred Miles's *Poets and Poetry of the Nineteenth Century*, one of the features of which is the memoir prefaced to each poet by one of the leading critics of the time. Thus in the volume entitled *William Morris to Robert Buchanan*, including selections from poets born between 1834 and 1841, Morris is introduced by Keats's editor H. Buxton Forman, Roden Noel by John Addington Symonds, Swinburne by Arthur Symons, Wilfrid Blunt by Richard le Gallienne.

We can continue our own briefer survey by considering three figures of importance in their day, dissimilar in almost every respect, yet each representing a grade or stage of popular reading and critical response. These are Macaulay, Tupper and Philip James Bailey. Macaulay's *Lays of Ancient Rome* (1842), enjoyed by generations of schoolchildren, are not only good poetry of their kind, they have the merit (belonging to the best of their class) of leading into liking for better poetry still. Martin Tupper (1810–89) and his *Proverbial Philosophy*, first published in 1838 and steadily enlarged till the final edition of 1876, lie at the other extreme of the literary scale. Neither in form nor in matter does that once celebrated book approach the nature of poetry; yet it sold in unbelievable numbers, both in Britain and America, and its "vaguely rhythmical, but quite unmetrical, stave", as Saintsbury says, was "pretty certainly not without influence on Whitman." Readers admired Tupper because he was homely and appeared to be scriptural; readers, from Tennyson down, admired Philip James Bailey (1816–1909) and his *Festus*—first published 1839 and like Tupper's work steadily enlarged till 1889—because he was ambitious and appeared to be profound. *Festus* is a long verse drama written in imitation of Goethe's *Faust*: the first scene is laid in Heaven, the first speaker is God. The poverty of its intellectual content is matched by the poverty of its poetic expression. The passages once quoted with admiration are mostly "purple patches" in the strictest sense—very purple and very patchy.

Bailey and Tupper had rivals in the production of "near-poetry". There were verbally excessive writers like Alexander Smith and Sydney Dobell who formed, with Bailey, what Aytoun called the "spasmodic school". There were political poets like Ebenezer Jones and Ernest Jones. There were slightly agitated writers like the painter William Bell Scott and the physician Thomas Gordon Hake who, after showing "spasmodic" signs, became, as it were, outside Pre-Raphaelites later. And throughout the century there were poets of largely-forgotten large-scale works like Sir Lewis Morris (1833–1907) with his *Epic of Hades* (1877).

Ernest Jones (1819–69), like many other political rebels, was of good birth and liberal education. He became an ardent Chartist and suffered two years' imprisonment for his inflammatory speeches. *The Song of the Lower Classes* is the most vigorous (if also the most unconsciously aristocratic) poem in his *Songs of Democracy* (1856–7). His namesake and fellow-Chartist Ebenezer Jones (1820–60) had a harder life. *Studies of Sensation and Event* (1843), admired by Browning and Rossetti, show an unmistakable lyric faculty, never to be fully developed during the short and troublous time allowed him.

Alexander Smith (1830–67) and Sydney Dobell (1824–74) suffered much, like Ebenezer Jones, through ill-health and misfortune; but both had greater opportunities of showing the best that was in them. Smith's *Life Drama* and Dobell's *Balder* appeared in 1854, followed by Dobell's *England in Time of War* (1856) and Smith's *City Songs* (1857), containing some of his best poems. Dobell's more mature work is still marked by the excesses of verbiage that earned the name "spasmodic". His one remembered lyric is part of a longer poem and is generally called *Keith of Ravelston*.

Consideration of the "spasmodic school" leads us naturally to William Edmonstoune Aytoun (1813–65), the Scottish lawyer and man of letters by whom that term was invented. The Victorian age had one clear mark of greatness: it was not afraid to laugh at itself. The century had begun well with the bards of *The Anti-Jacobin*. Three years after the accession of Queen Victoria came the first series of *The Ingoldsby Legends. Punch* was founded in 1841. *Bon Gaultier* appeared in 1845 and Lear's *Book of Nonsense* in 1846. Numerous "Bohemians", as Prowse called them, carry us on to *Alice* (1865) and Gilbert's *Bab Ballads* (1869), and thence to the work of Calverley and J. K. Stephen. Its light verse alone would make the Victorian era notable. Aytoun's best–known work is his *Lays of the Scottish Cavaliers* (1849), "near-balladry" rather than "near-poetry", indebted inevitably to Scott. His more durable work was of the comic or serio-comic kind. *Firmilian: or the Student of Badajoz. A Spasmodic Tragedy* (1855) is a burlesque of the whole spasmodic school, reaching back to Bailey and the Byronists and forward, by anticipation, to the Brownings. *The Book of Ballads. Edited by Bon Gaultier* (1845) was the joint work of Aytoun and his future biographer Sir Theodore Martin.

Percival Leigh (1813–89) in *Punch* and William Jeffery Prowse (1836–70) in *Fun* are excellent representatives of periodical light verse. Mortimer Collins (1827–76), a better scholar than either, left some charming love-poetry as well as satiric verse like *The British Birds*, with its title after Aristophanes. The first great writer of nonsense verse, Edward Lear (1812–88), was a traveller, a painter, and a teacher of drawing to Queen Victoria. For the grandchildren of his patron the Earl of Derby he composed and illustrated *A Book of Nonsense* (1846) —the verses being in the delightfully concise form mysteriously called the "Limerick", now always associated with his name. In both limericks and longer poems like *The Owl and the Pussy-Cat*, Lear combines sense and nonsense, after the specially English fashion, in a way never known before and excelled only by his successor Lewis Carroll. Another "laureate of the nursery" (actually so called in the *Dictionary of National Biography*) was William Brighty Rands (1823–82), author of *Lilliput Lectures* (1871).

Frederick Locker, afterwards Locker-Lampson (1821–95), was one of the few English writers who have devoted themselves wholly to what is called *vers de société*. Most of it is found in *London Lyrics* (1857) and in the delightful and too little known collection of prose and verse called *Patchwork* (1879).

A remarkable group is formed by those who derived the substance and the spirit of their light poems from the social and academic traditions of the older universities. Charles Stuart Calverley, born Blayds (1831–84), was educated at Harrow, Oxford and Cambridge. A disastrous accident accounts for his comparatively early death and the comparatively small quantity of his work. His

Verses and Translations (1862) and *Fly Leaves* (1866) had a vogue which continued till the eighteen-nineties. His light verse, whether parody or original, remained for years the standard by which all such efforts were usually tried. Like Calverley in spirit and in the physical misfortune that produced decay and early death was James Kenneth Stephen (1859–92) of Eton and Cambridge, whose *Lapsus Calami* and *Quo Musa Tendis?*, both published in 1891, are the nearest approach to Calverley in the essentials of their kind. Light verse, either original or burlesque, continued to flourish, notably in the contributions to *The Oxford Magazine* and elsewhere by the classical scholar Alfred Denis Godley (1856–1925) and the novelist and critic Arthur Quiller-Couch (1863–1944) and in the work of Owen Seaman (1861–1936), long editor of *Punch*. Seaman's *Battle of the Bays* (1896) contained pieces in the style of contemporary poets imagined as competing for the vacant laureateship. The subsequent election of the very minor poet (but accomplished journalist) Alfred Austin (1835–1913) to succeed the great Tennyson proved, once again, that fact can be stranger than fiction.

A very different kind of "university wit" was Charles Lutwidge Dodgson (1832–98), universally beloved as "Lewis Carroll". Educated at Rugby and Oxford, he took deacon's orders in 1861 and from 1855 to 1881 was mathematics lecturer at Christ Church. That his vein was mathematical and not classical differentiates him at once from the Calverley-Stephen kind of humour; there is something of the manipulation of symbols in his logical absurdity and the nonsensical preciseness of his humour. Some, indeed, of his collegiate and private skits were actually mathematical in form, and it is fitting that the mathematically-trained poet and critic William Empson should have written one of the best modern accounts of his work in *Some Versions of Pastoral* (1935). Carroll's *Alice in Wonderland* (1865) and *Through the Looking-Glass* (1871), originating in stories told to little girls, have become an enduring part of English "nonsense literature" appealing to all ages. It is the verse of his books that is our immediate concern, and most remarkable verse it is, whether it takes the form of the inspired jargon of *Jabberwocky*, the Wordsworthian parody of the White Knight's song, or the transmutation of plain sense into pure nonsense of *The Walrus and the Carpenter*. Less popular than it deserves to be is *The Hunting of the Snark* (1876).

The fairy tales of the scholar and folk-lorist Andrew Lang (1844–1912) were almost as popular as *Alice* with children in Victorian times and afterwards. In verse Lang is mainly remembered, with William Ernest Henley (1849–1903), as a student of French poetry who tried to emulate his models in English. The title of his *Ballads and Lyrics of Old France* (1872) indicates his characteristic archaic bias, but Henley, interestingly enough, was a student of contemporary French art as well, his striking *Hospital Verses* (1875) making him what may be termed the first "French impressionist" in English poetry. Like Toulouse Lautrec, he was a cripple from boyhood, his most famous poem being the pardonably bragging stanzas of *Out of the Night* where he proclaims himself "master" of his fate, "captain" of his soul.

Charles Montagu Doughty (1843–1926) concealed rather than published the record of his Eastern adventures in the deliberately archaic prose of *Travels in*

Arabia Deserta (1888). The same qualities and defects can be found in his massive contributions to poetry, beginning with *The Dawn in Britain* (1906) and *Adam Cast Forth* (1908) and ending with *Mansoul* (1920), works which resemble primitive statuary in their disdain of normal scale and proportion. In his deliberate difficulty of speech, in his vague and unfamiliar mythology, Doughty placed in the path of understanding obstacles which few readers have cared to surmount.

Another notable traveller in the East, Wilfrid Scawen Blunt (1840–1922), was as modern in his outlook as Doughty was archaic. With many advantages of birth and position, he took an anti-imperialist view of British government, his *Ideas about India* (1885) anticipating to some extent the views of E. M. Forster. His verse—*Love Sonnets of Proteus* (1880) and *The Seven Golden Odes of Pagan Arabia* (1903)—is as individual in tone as his prose *Diaries*.

In the opening poem of *Responsibilities* (1914), Yeats refers affectionately to his early years in London, to the

> Poets with whom I learned my trade,
> Companions of the Cheshire Cheese...

The "Cheshire Cheese" was the London public-house where meetings of the Rhymers' Club were held. They produced two volumes of verse: *The Book of the Rhymers' Club* (1892) and a second book in 1894. Yeats's "companions" included Ernest Dowson (1867–1900) and Lionel Johnson (1867–1902) and among the poems printed were such well-known pieces as Yeats's *Lake Isle of Innisfree*, Johnson's *By the Statue of King Charles at Charing Cross* and Dowson's "*Non sum qualis eram bonae sub regno Cynarae*", with its haunting refrain "I have been faithful to thee, Cynara! in my fashion", a poem which in its singular music and sense of nostalgia is a kind of epitome of the whole *fin de siècle* mood of the "aesthetic" or "decadent" poets which resulted in so many early deaths from despair and dissipation and so many late conversions to the discipline of the Roman Catholic Church. The two volumes of *Fleet Street Eclogues* (1893–5) by John Davidson (1857–1909) were part of a conscientious, if self-conscious, attempt to supply the "blood and guts" which Davidson thought most of the Rhymers lacked. His later verse includes a series of *Testaments* (1901–8), in one of which, *The Testament of a Man Forbid*, he comforts "used-up workers", prostitutes, etc. with the reflection: "You are the dung that keeps the roses sweet"—a sentiment which Dowson might well have endorsed. Maurice Lindsay's *Selection* from Davidson's poems (1961) has a preface by T. S. Eliot and an essay on his fellow Scots poet by Hugh McDiarmid.

Francis Thompson (1859–1907) was as pronounced a believer as Davidson was a doubter. He was a "born Catholic", not a convert like Hopkins or like Dowson, Johnson, Wilde, Beardsley, Henry Harland, "Baron Corvo", and other aesthetes of late Victorian and Edwardian times. He wrote both mystical verse and songs in nostalgic praise of the cricket of his native Lancashire. Settling in London, he suffered from poverty and ill-health for many years, but in the early eighteen-nineties he was befriended by the poet Alice Meynell (1847–1922) and her husband Wilfrid, who shared his enthusiasm for the mystical poetry of the seventeenth century and arranged the publication of his *Poems*, including the famous "Pindaric", *The Hound of Heaven*, in 1893. Later works were *Sister Poems* (1895) and *New Poems* (1897). A collected edition was published in 1913, with a memoir by Wilfrid Meynell. Alice Meynell's own poetry dates from *Preludes* (1875) to the *Collected Poems* of 1923.

None of the minor poets of the Victorian age—with the possible exception of Sir Edwin Arnold (see p. 737) with his poem on the life and teaching of the Buddha *The Light of Asia* (1879)—is still remembered for any large-scale work. Most inevitably survive by a few lyrics made familiar in anthologies, particularly in the magnificent *Golden Treasury* (1861) compiled originally by Francis Turner Palgrave (1824–97), dedicated to Tennyson and completed with his assistance. The later editions, one of which was edited by the poet and art-historian Laurence Binyon (1869–1943), added not only Tennyson himself and the other chief Victorian poets but such lyrics as Caroline Norton's *I do not love thee!*, Lord Houghton's *The Men of Old*, Sir Francis Doyle's *The Private of the Buffs*, Alfred Domett's *A Christmas Hymn*, Charles Mackay's *Tubal Cain*, Jean Ingelow's *High Tide on the Coast of Lincolnshire*, W. J. Cory's *Heraclitus*, and Alexander Smith's *Barbara*, besides American lyrics by Bryant, Emerson, Longfellow, Holmes and Whitman and the poem by the early Victorian George Darley which Palgrave originally included by mistake in his seventeenth-century section. Later anthologies, such as Ernest Rhys's *New Golden Treasury*, the English Association's *Poems of To-Day* and Harold Monro's *Twentieth Century Poetry*, included lyrics by some of the minor Victorian and Edwardian poets like William Watson, Henry Newbolt, Lord Alfred Douglas, Mary Coleridge, Charlotte Mew, and Thomas Sturge Moore (1870–1944)—brother of the philosopher G. E. Moore and friend of Yeats. *W. B. Yeats and T. Sturge Moore: Their Correspondence 1901–37* (1953) spans the Edwardian and the Georgian era and reflects the change in poetry and criticism from the time of the poets' youth.

"All but the greatest poetry of the period," as Saintsbury truly wrote, "is an echo, though a multifarious and often a beautiful one"; and the chief characteristic of the period is its "too general *literariness*". In these circumstances, there could have been worse fates for a minor poet than to be remembered in the anthologies of Palgrave and his successors, particularly at a time when so much of the age's intelligence and creative ability went into prose.

VII. THE PROSODY OF THE NINETEENTH CENTURY

As we have seen (p. 499), the metrical practice of Pope and his followers was reduced to a system by Bysshe who maintained that English verse was to be strictly measured by syllables. Ossian, the *Reliques*, Blake and Chatterton mark a definite departure from this formula. The chief metrical lesson of the *Reliques*, namely the artistic success of occasional three-syllabled feet in the ballad lines, was learned by Chatterton and Blake, but not by poets generally till we reach *The Ancient Mariner* of 1798. Johnson's parody "I put my hat upon my head" leaves the old ballads unscathed; but it catches exactly the pusillanimous sing-song of eighteenth-century ballad imitation. Chatterton saw the light and followed it; Blake saw it and followed it more boldly; and Burns, who inherited his freedom from Scottish song, set the new tune of verse running in the heads of all his readers.

It is difficult for people unread in prosodic history to understand the refusal of the eighteenth-century ear to accept the principle of substitution. We recognize at once the beauty of the variation in—

> The king sits in Dunfermline town,
> Drinking the blood red wine;

but there was a time when that sounded irregular, and therefore faulty—when the ear expected the mechanical regularity of this:

> The king sat in Dunfermline town,
> And drank the blood red wine;

and was irritated when it received something different, even though the difference here is not in the number of syllables, as it is in a variation like the third and fourth lines of the same stanza:

> O where will I get a skeely skipper
> To sail this new ship of mine.

The correct eighteenth-century versifier complained that such lines were "licentious" and "rustic", that they lacked "smoothness" and "numbers", and that they had the "rudeness of a Scottish song". To us the substitution of a three-syllabled foot for a two-syllabled foot and the replacing of an "iamb" with its "rise" by a "trochee" with its "fall" are neither faults nor anomalies, but the touches that transmute metre into rhythm. In listening to Chatterton and Blake and Coleridge we must not take these things for granted; we must make an imaginative retreat in audition, and hear the liberties of the new poetry as they first fell upon ears attuned to the regularity and smoothness practised by the poets who came after Pope, and prescribed by the theorists who formulated the principles they expected the poets to practise. But the end of the century saw many signs of revolt against mechanical regularity. The older poets, especially Spenser and Milton, steadily regained popularity and new writers ventured upon experiments which sometimes sheltered themselves behind classical authority. Southey's "sapphics" annoyed the Anti-Jacobins as much by their form as by their matter. Southey is not usually considered an innovator in prosody; yet the free rhymeless stanzas of *Thalaba* (to name nothing else) can be taken as a bold declaration of metrical independence.

The major poets of the nineteenth century went ahead without any theories of prosody. One of the landmarks of English metrical study, Guest's *A History of English Rhythms* (1838), appeared at the very time of the new era in poetry marked by Tennyson's *Poems* of 1842 and Browning's *Bells and Pomegranates* (1841, etc.); but there is no evidence that either poet knew anything about Guest. The whole of nineteenth-century poetry is anti-Bysshe in every particular. The great poets said what they had to say without pausing for explanation or defence; and their metrical achievements were magnificent. Speculations upon prosody abound; but they are the work of scholars or of poets below the first rank.

Wordsworth, who argued much about diction and little about prosody, used many forms well. The great *Immortality Ode* is a study in beautiful metrical freedom, and the great passages of blank verse are individual in style and rich in formal variety. But Wordsworth's supreme contribution to poetic form is the rediscovery of the sonnet, scarcely used since the time of Milton. The eighteenth century was curiously shy of the sonnet, which seemed to offer many invitations to "correctness"; but its dangers were evident and the narrower plot of the couplet was felt to be safer. Pope would attempt an ode, but not a sonnet.

Coleridge was certain to be interested in prosody; and whether the famous introductory note to *Christabel* be a satisfactory account of the *Christabel* metre or not, the statement itself remains one of the most important in the history of the subject. But it is odd that he should have said so little more. His actual experiments show that his natural ear, assisted by his study of Shakespeare, had made him thoroughly conscious of that principle of substitution which strikes the difference between the old prosody and the new, and which *The Ancient Mariner* and *Christabel* were to make familiar to the next three generations.

From Scott one would not expect prosodic study; yet he, too, makes illuminating remarks, e.g. in the Introduction to *The Lay of the Last Minstrel*; and as to practice he stands almost in the first rank. He was greatly interested in the unpublished specimens of *Christabel* he had seen. The ballads, which he knew by ear rather than by sight, had preserved in the north the principle of substitution which seemed to have been forgotten in the south, and they were the model for his own utterance. *Proud Maisie* is a supreme variation of the ballad stanza, and *Bonnie Dundee* a bold demonstration of what could be done with anapaests.

Byron, usually undervalued as a poet, is also undervalued as a prosodist. The expressed admirer and champion of the eighteenth century, he carried some of its merits into the nineteenth. He fails in none of the metres he attempted—certainly not in blank verse or the heroic couplet. His Spenserians are naturally (and allowably) Byronic; as a personal use of this form it would be difficult to surpass the best stanzas of *Childe Harold*. But Byron's greatest metrical triumph is, assuredly, to be found in the octaves of *Beppo* and *Don Juan*. For light narrative and satiric running commentary, as well as for description of the kind required, Byron's *ottava rima* cannot be excelled and certainly has not been equalled.

The prosodic variety of Shelley is immense; there is, perhaps, hardly a poet who has written so consummately in so large a number of measures. But the curious fact is that he begins, even in his larger works, with imitation before he finds himself. *Queen Mab* follows *Thalaba*; the blank verse of *Alastor* is Wordsworthian; *The Revolt of Islam* begins with a touch of *Childe Harold*, and even *Adonais* does not entirely escape a suggestion of Byron. It is in the more lyrical forms that he offers the perfect results of emancipated prosody. If we meet with what seem to be occasional failures we have to remember that many of his poems were prepared for publication by another hand.

Keats, unlike Shelley, was not a poet who caught at a mere suggestion from another, but a diligent worker from models. In the couplets of *Endymion* he may have followed Hunt, but it is probable that he had also read Chamberlayne's

Pharonnida. Knowing that he had been excessive, he set to work upon a corrective study of Milton and Dryden, with *Hyperion* and *Lamia* as the result. The octaves of *Isabella* show less definite following; but *The Eve of St Agnes* has evidently profited from a study of Spenser, and the singularly beautiful *Eve of St Mark* has clearly gone back to the quiet coolness of Gower. In a study of this kind there is nothing inimical to creative originality. *La Belle Dame sans Merci* is, like *Proud Maisie*, a triumphant variation of the ballad measure, and the management of the larger odes is simply consummate.

The prosodic practice of the new school of poets did not fail to arouse the wrath of the critical. The *Quarterly* reviewer disclosed his abject critical incapacity in the single sentence which condemns *Endymion* because "there is hardly a complete couplet enclosing a complete idea throughout the book". Writers on prosody in the early years of the century are all unimportant. Edwin Guest alone deserves attention as the first historian of English rhythms in any sense worthy of the title. He knew the whole range of English poetry from Caedmon to Coleridge and could cite any part of it for his purpose. Unfortunately he makes arbitrary assumptions and has strange prepossessions. Guest, in fact, as George Saintsbury said, was "indefatigable in collecting and arranging examples, not trustworthy in judging them"; and his book *The History of English Rhythms* (1838; revised by Skeat, 1882) has probably done as much harm as good.

Prosodic practice flowed smoothly and prosperously during the nineteenth century; but prosodic theory remained contentious. The poets, apparently, failed in reading each other's poems. Even Coleridge "could hardly scan" some of Tennyson's verses; he thought the younger poet "did not very well know what metre is", and wished him "to write for two or three years in none but well known and correctly defined" measures. Yet there is nothing in the Tennyson of 1833 rebellious to the principles embodied in *The Ancient Mariner* and *Christabel*. Even after the volumes of 1842 an acute critic could be found denouncing the Hollyhock song ("A spirit haunts the year's last hours") as outlandish, ear-torturing, and altogether metrically indefensible and unintelligible.

The nineteenth century concerned itself considerably with the English hexameter. As we have seen, Stanyhurst attempted hexameters in a translation of Virgil I–IV as long ago as 1582, and unimportant poets had made essays in that metre during the seventeenth and eighteenth centuries. The translations from the German by William Taylor of Norwich carried the experiment into the nineteenth century; and it was revived in Southey's *A Vision of Judgment*, and later in Clough's *Bothie*, Longfellow's *Evangeline* and Kingsley's (but not Hopkins's) *Andromeda*. The panting prosodists toiled after the poets and tried to explain, or explain away, the various attempts at hexameters. Whether the English language lends itself readily to the hexameter can be proved only by a poet in his practice, and not by any prosodist in his theory. There is no great English poem in that metre. *Andromeda* would be no better in any other form. A brief technical explanation may serve to make clear some of the difficulties. Greek prosody depended upon "quantity", "length", or "duration" of syllables. A "long" (–) was equal to two shorts (⌣⌣). Thus a dactyl (–⌣⌣) was the equivalent of a spondee (--) and one could take the place of the other. Latin prosody was taken over from the Greek, and, for a short period, the classical Latin poets used quantitative measures. Medieval Latin, like modern Greek, ignored quantity. A syllable was "long by nature" if it contained a long vowel, as in "lēgēs"; a syllable was "long by position" if a vowel was followed by two consonants, as in "ars". There were other rules, but they need not trouble us here. English words clearly have quantity. Thus in "lever" the first syllable is long and the second short. In "ever" both syllables are short. In "banker" the first syllable is long and the second short. In "bankrupt" both syllables are long—"bankrupt" is a "spondee" (--). But the English ear is not trained to notice and employ quantity in English, as it is trained to notice and employ quantity in Greek or Latin. A Latin hexameter line contained six feet, the "type" being five dactyls *plus* a final spondee, thus:

$$| - \cup \cup | - \cup \cup | - \cup \cup | - \cup \cup | - \cup \cup | - - |$$

Here is a famous line of this pattern:

> Quadrupedante putrem sonitu quatit ungula campum.

Spondees, being the equivalent of dactyls, could be substituted for them, but usually a dactyl was retained in the fifth foot. The last syllable was "common". Now if the word-stress coincides with the metrical shape in the last two feet (as in the line given above) we get what has been called the "strawberry jam-pots" ending. In Latin, with the quantities clearly recognizable, this can be avoided; in English, with the quantities scarcely recognizable and the stresses insistent, this can hardly be avoided. The writer of English hexameters is there-fore in a difficulty. If he gives us line upon line of "strawberry jam-pots" he risks monotony; if he tries to avoid the "strawberry jam-pots" by variation of stress or of foot he risks metrical unintelligibility. An English reader can make a fair shot at a line like this, even though at first it seems a little odd:

> Fell by slumber opprest unheedfully into the wide sea;

but a line like this he will probably fail to read correctly:

> In so far as unimpeded by an alien evil.

The radical trouble with English hexameters, quantitative or accentual, is that they tend to break up and rearrange themselves into a different kind of metre. Almost any line of Kingsley's *Andromeda* can be read in this way:

> × Skil | ful with nee | dle and loom | and the arts | of the dy | er and weav | er

Can such a line be regarded as a hexameter? Is it very different from a line like this?

> Glory to Man in the highest, for Man is the master of things.

But Swinburne never supposed that the substitution of "all things" for "things" would turn his line into a hexameter. The most important of later attempts at quantitative hexameters can be found, with an illuminating discussion of the question, in *Ibant Obscuri* (1916) by Robert Bridges. But some of his lines, even with the oddities of spelling that he used later in *The Testament of Beauty*, refuse to sound really English. Bridges, as we know from his correspondence with Hopkins, was an ardent prosodist, and his tract, *Milton's Prosody* (1893), enlarged later, is one of the little books that must be read by every student of poetry. Much discussion of the hexameter in English is rendered uncritical by the curious classical "snobbery" affected by some scholars during the nineteenth century and later—a mistaken loyalty that compelled them to proclaim the inferiority of English to the classical languages. It is a humorous commentary on the claims of the hexameter to be taken seriously that the only really enjoyable English poem in that kind is Clough's *Bothie*. In other words, the metre, whether regarded solemnly as the dactylic hexameter of Homer and Virgil or accepted more genially as a native arrangement of stresses, appears to find its appropriate place as a medium of serio-comic or mock-heroic matter. And there we must leave it.

In the considerable prosodical literature of the latter half of the century there is very little of permanent interest. Much of it is special pleading for some personal view of writing. Of great value on the associated side of sound-values are the works of Henry Sweet in phonetics and the monumental treatise of Alexander J. Ellis on English pronunciation. Another work of special interest is the *Shakespearean Grammar* of E. A. Abbott, which discusses Shakespeare's versification somewhat rigidly. Useful surveys can be found in J. B. Mayor's *Chapters on English Metre* and *A Handbook of Modern English Metre*. Among later prosodists is T. S. Omond, whose *Study of Metre* (1903), *Metrical Rhythm* (1905) and *English Metrists in the Eighteenth and Nineteenth Centuries* (1907) are among the books which should be read by all students of verse-structure. Exceedingly useful on the historical side are two foreign handbooks, *A Short History of English Versification* by Max Kaluza (1911) and *A History of English Versification* by Jakob Schipper (1910). The standard and necessary treatise, delightful to read and delightful even to differ from, is *A History of English Prosody* (1906–10) by George Saintsbury, with its wealth of illustration and *obiter dicta*.

The supremacy of Tennyson and Browning during the nineteenth century is attested as much by their immense prosodic variety as by their poetic achievement. William Morris is as remarkable for the variety of his poetic forms as for the extent of his production. "Run-on" couplets, heroic or octosyllabic, in the style of the old romances, were used for his poetic stories. In *Love is Enough*, he tried a bolder but less successful archaism by reviving alliterative and rhymeless movements; but later, in *Sigurd the Volsung*, he refashioned the old rhymed fourteener into a really splendid metre for narrative purposes. In metrical virtuosity (as distinguished from rhythmic mastery), it may be doubted whether Swinburne has ever had a superior. Swinburne's *Dolores* stanza, Tennyson's *In Memoriam* stanza and FitzGerald's *Omar* stanza, to whatever extent anticipated, have been definitely added to English metres by those poets. The Sprung Rhythm used, or re-used, by Hopkins in many of his poems is explained in detail in the Author's Preface to the 1918 and subsequent editions.

VIII. NINETEENTH-CENTURY DRAMA

Of nineteenth-century drama it may be said that though it is important in the history of the theatre, it scarcely concerns the history of literature. Much of it belongs to the region of the penny novelette. If original, it manufactured an artificial world unvisited by any gleams of intelligence; if adapted from work originally intelligent, it removed or overlaid the intelligence as a hindrance to success. The larger figures in literature whose work includes acted plays are considered in their own place. We are concerned here with those whose theatrical compositions are their chief claim to notice.

The theatre of Congreve and Sheridan appealed to an educated public; but there was always an uneducated public that wanted amusement of the cruder kind; and that kind of public rapidly increased during the nineteenth century. As a public institution, the theatre was still under the control of the Court, and the only recognized establishments were the "patent" houses, Drury Lane and Covent Garden, and the theatre in the Haymarket. These were insufficient for the public. The patent houses, especially Drury Lane, were enlarged till any play not of the roaring kind was engulfed; and other theatres furtively struggled into existence by the simple expedient of pretending not to be theatres, but "places of entertainment". Not till 1843 did the Theatre Regulation Act legalize the position of "illegitimate" houses. An immovable obstacle to the development of later drama as a serious criticism of life was the power of the Lord Chamberlain, unchallengeable and irresponsible, to forbid the perform- ance of any play on the grounds of alleged immorality, blasphemy or sedition. This power, conferred by the Licensing Act of 1737 as a political retort to Fielding (see p. 421), was capriciously used to suppress plays that were challeng- ingly serious, when light entertainments reaching the extreme of lubricity were allowed. The plays of the nineteenth century are therefore, in general, unim- portant either as literature or as drama. Tragedy lost its greatness and multiplied its excesses. Romance coarsened into elaborate make-believe. Comedy loosened into loud farce and boisterous horse-play. What was new was a homely, crude melodrama, very moral, very sententious, and entirely unreal. Nevertheless, tragedy was a favourite exercise with men of letters. Wordsworth had already tried his hand; Coleridge, Godwin, Lord Byron, Mary Russell Mitford, Disraeli and others, composed tragedies, some of which were produced upon the stage, while others remained polite exercises in a literary form.

The three most famous writers of stage tragedy in the first part of the century were Richard Lalor Sheil (1791–1851), like Sheridan a politician; Charles Robert Maturin (1782–1824), an Irish clergyman; and Henry Hart Milman (1791–1868), Dean of St Paul's (1849). Sheil's chief plays are *Adelaide* (1814), *The Apostate* (1817) and *Bellamira* (1818), the last perhaps the best. One line from *The Apostate*,

This is too much for any mortal creature,

tells most of the truth about Sheil as a writer of plays. The influence of the German tragic romance of horror (typified by Schiller's *The Robbers*) went to the making of Maturin (see p. 507), whose three tragedies—*Bertram; or, The*

Castle of St Aldobrond, Manuel and *Fredolfo*—were produced in London in the years 1816 and 1817. There was a strain of poetry in Maturin, but he has now only the interest of curiosity. Milman is of a higher order than either Sheil or Maturin. *Fazio*, acted in 1818, is good drama if not good tragedy, and had a long stage life. *The Fall of Jerusalem* (1820) and *The Martyr of Antioch* (1822) are both founded upon a legitimately conceived struggle between two passions or ideas. *Belshazzar* (1822) contains some good lyrics. James Sheridan Knowles (1784–1862) takes an honourable place in the history of nineteenth-century drama as the author of sincere if rather ingenuous plays owing nothing to German extravagance or to feats of wild and whirling verbiage. His chief tragedies and comedies—*Caius Gracchus* (1815), *Virginius* (1820), *William Tell* (1825), *The Hunchback* (1832) and *The Love Chase* (1837)—had genuine success on the stage and are not intolerable to read. The tragedies of Richard "Hengist" Horne (see p. 534), *Cosmo de' Medici* (1837), *Gregory VII* (1840) and *Judas Iscariot* (1848) were literary rather than dramatic. His one genuine success was a short piece, *The Death of Marlowe* (1837). Once acted with some success were the now forgotten *Ion* (1835) and *Glencoe* (1840) of Sir Thomas Noon Talfourd, the biographer of Lamb.

The tragedies we have mentioned were all attempts to write in the manner of past centuries. John Westland Marston (1819–90)—father of the blind lyric poet Philip Marston, friend of Swinburne and Thomson—was the first writer of his time to attempt a poetical tragedy of contemporary life, *The Patrician's Daughter* (1842). Marston was a mystic, a poet and a scholar; and he showed courage in writing what was so near to a political play as *The Patrician's Daughter*, with its opposition between the haughty, heartless world of high society and the meritorious life of the poor. Marston's other tragedies in verse, *Strathmore* (1849) and *Marie de Méranie* (1850), were the last of their kind that deserve consideration.

The pressure of public demand for entertainment caused brisk dramatic activity during much of the century. Comedy, farce, extravaganza, burlesque, opera and melodrama were vamped up from any handy materials by practised hands. Scott, Dumas and Dickens were eagerly drawn upon, for no copyright then protected the unhappy authors of novels from the depredations of theatre hacks. Plays were liberally interspersed with songs and dances, in order that they might call themselves "entertainments" and so evade both the Lord Chamberlain and the lessees of the patent theatres. The special dramatic form evolved to fit the mid-nineteenth-century audience was melodrama, a term borrowed from the French. Whatever part music had played in melodrama soon vanished, and the name stood, and still stands, for plays of a peculiarly stagey kind. Melodrama divided human nature into the entirely good and the entirely bad. It was in its way a "criticism of life" as understood in the age of the French Revolution, Parliamentary Reform, Chartism, and the Corn Laws. It allied itself boldly with the democratic against the aristocratic. To be rich and well-born was, almost inevitably, to be wicked; to be poor and humble was a guarantee of virtue. To be a baronet was to be doomed to a life of crime. Hero, heroine and villain, comic and virtuous retainers, heavy father (with Scriptural curses), fading and ultimately dying mother, dishonest solicitor juggling with title-deeds and marriage-lines—these and similar figures were expected from any melodrama that desired success. The morals were unexceptionable. Virtue was sumptuously rewarded and vice punished with poverty or prison.

Isaac Pocock (1782–1835), the author of *The Miller and his Men*, took the subject of his innumerable melodramas from French or German drama and English novels. Edward Ball (1792–1873), afterwards Fitzball, was an equally prolific purveyor of borrowed plots. William Thomas Moncrieff (1794–1857) was for a time manager of Astley's Circus, to which he furnished one very successful equestrian drama, *The Dandy Family*, and won fame by supplying Drury Lane with a romantic melodrama called *The Cataract of the Ganges; or, The Rajah's Daughter*, in which real horses and a real waterfall appeared. With the dramas of Douglas William Jerrold (1803–57) we come to work not wholly unreadable. The most famous of his plays is *Black-ey'd Susan; or, All in the Downs*, which was founded upon the ballad by John Gay. The dramas of John Baldwin Buckstone (1802–79), most of them written for the Adelphi Theatre, are the origin of the familiar term, "Adelphi melodrama". They are extravagantly turgid and sentimental; but they are well constructed. Both *The Green Bushes* (1845) and *The Flower of the Forest* (1849) kept the stage till the end of the century.

The writer who gave melodrama the definite form that was to distinguish it completely from the drama of serious interest was Dionysius Lardner Bourcicault (1820–90) who shortened his name to Dion Boucicault. By all the rules he should have failed. Neither his plots nor his incidents are original. His characters are fixed theatrical types. But he had a sure instinct for what actors could deliver and audiences accept with conviction; moreover he could add to his fables what the unsophisticated took for romance. And so his three Irish dramas, *The Colleen Bawn* (which had a second life as Benedict's opera *The Lily of Killarney*), *Arrah-na-Pogue* and *The Shaughraun*, though belonging to the late Fifties and Sixties, lived on to the age of Shaw and Wilde. The Boucicault type of melodrama was carried on in the Adelphi plays of George R. Sims and Henry Pettitt and in the Drury Lane plays of the Augustus Harris regime, though these harked back to the "real horses" and "real water" of Moncrieff.

The next playwright to show distinctive merit was Tom Taylor (1817–80), who wrote melodrama suitable for polite society, as well as "costume" dramas. Very little of his work is original; but in *Plot and Passion* (1853), *Still Waters Run Deep* (1855), and *The Ticket-of-Leave Man* (1863) he proved himself a capable playwright. His one famous comedy is *Our American Cousin* (1858), with the popular character, Lord Dundreary—a comedy which once had a tragic ending, being the play at whose performance in Washington in 1865 John Wilkes Booth assassinated Abraham Lincoln. Taylor's romantic "costume" plays, all founded upon other men's work, had great success. The best of them was *Twixt Axe and Crown* (1870). In the field of historical drama, his eminence was shared by William Gorman Wills (1828–91). For Wills, historical truth had no existence. His Oliver Cromwell in *Charles I* (1872) and his John Knox in *Marie Stuart* (1874) are almost farcical in the intensity of their villainy. Wills is further remembered for his adaptations *Olivia* and *Faust*—the last a mere pantomime caricature of Goethe—in which he owed his theatrical success to the genius of Irving, which sometimes shone brightest in the worst plays.

The comedy of the period, for the most part, is as unconvincing as the serious drama. Almost the only attempt to carry on the tradition of English high comedy was a feeble work of Boucicault's youth, *London Assurance* (1841). Sheridan Knowles, in *The Hunchback* (1832) and *The Love Chase* (1827), was more original than Boucicault, but his plots are as confusing as Congreve's. The nineteenth-century public liked to be thrilled by melodrama, but it also liked to be tickled by crude humour, and innumerable one-act farces were produced to be played, in the lavish fashion of the time, either as "curtain-raisers" or as "after-pieces". Adelphi "screamers" became, under J. B. Buckstone, as famous as Adelphi melodramas. One of the earliest and best of the farce-writers was John Poole (1786–1872), most famous as author of *Paul Pry* (1825), in which several actors (including J. L. Toole) found a suitable field for their comic talent. Indeed, without a natural comedian most of the farces are worthless and cannot be read with patience. The one outstanding exception is *Box and Cox*, adapted from the French by John Maddison Morton (1811–91), though it reads like an original work. Whether in Morton's farce *Box and Cox*, or in the Burnand-Sullivan opera *Cox and Box*, the pair of lodgers must be reckoned as part of the national mythology. James Robinson Planché (1796–1880), the historian of costume, is specially associated with the rise and development of burlesque and extravaganza. The gods and goddesses of Greece and Rome offered him many opportunities for spirited and topical fun.

Nicholas Nickleby gives us glimpses of the theatre in the early part of the century. The best short view of the English stage in the Sixties can be found in Pinero's comedy *Trelawny of the Wells*. Pinero, once a "utility" actor, had first-hand knowledge of what he sets forth. The sketches of the old-time "mummers" are perfect; but the main theme of the play is the coming of Thomas William Robertson (1829–71), called "Tom Wrench" in *Trelawny*. To the middle of the nineteenth century, the drama remained wholly stagey and spoke a language altogether its own. Robertson was really a "new" dramatist. Incurably old-fashioned as much of his work now seems, its naturalness of theme and simplicity of diction were revolutionary and were much resented by the orotund spouters of "platform" drama, who could find "nothing to get their teeth into". A new kind of actor had to be found for what was called the "cup and saucer" comedy of Robertson, and he was fortunate in being taken up by the Bancrofts, who produced *Society* in 1865, and brought the English stage into some relation with simple and normal life. The adventure prospered, and in quick succession came *Ours* (a play of the Crimean War) in 1866, *Caste* in 1867, *School* in 1869, and others of less interest. *Caste*, the best of the series, though it evades rather than solves the problems of caste implicit in the story, has genuine dramatic interest and feeling, and introduces some excellent sketches of character. The influence of Robertson did not produce further Robertsons, but it prepared the public for better plays than his own. Both Henry James Byron (1834–84) and James Albery (1838–89), author of *The Two Roses*, in which Irving made his first great success, and adapter of *The Pink Dominoes*, in which Wyndham played with brilliance, followed Robertson. Albery had a natural gift for comedy which he failed to use fully: circumstances were too much for him. Byron was clever, but had not the genuine feeling of Robertson. His comedies, *Our Boys* (1875) and *Uncle Dick's Darling* (1869), were resoundingly popular and often revived. With the naturalistic plays came an attempt at naturalistic scenery instead of the cataclysmic scenes of melodrama.

The Bancrofts made comedy fashionable, and the Robertson period was followed by what may be called a French period, when the better-class theatres based their productions on French plays, especially those of Sardou and Dumas *fils*. Sardou was an ingenious fabricator of "well-made" plays such as *Diplomacy* (1878); Dumas was more serious, and attempted some "criticism of life" of a narrowly limited kind. The fashionable comedies began to be increasingly artificial and concerned with the unimportant conventions and the sham emotions of "Society".

A unique place in the history of the English stage is held by William Schwenck Gilbert (1836–1911). His earlier pieces were burlesques of no importance. To his second period belong *The Palace of Truth* (1870), *The Wicked World* (1873), *Pygmalion and Galatea* (1871), and *Broken Hearts* (1875). These plays are all founded upon a single idea, that of unaware self-revelation by characters under the influence of some supernatural interference. The satire is shrewd, but not profound; the young author had not learned to make the best use of his curiously logical fancy. His prose plays, such as *Sweethearts* (1874), *Dan'l Druce* (1876), *Engaged* (1877) and *Comedy and Tragedy* (1884), are incurably old-fashioned and lead nowhere. No one could predict from them *The Bab Ballads* (1869), a collection in the right line of English humorous verse, still less the famous series of comic operas (nearly all of them set by Sir Arthur Sullivan) beginning with *Trial by Jury* in 1875 and ending with *The Grand Duke* in 1896. Gilbert was a metrical humorist of a very skilful order, and he raised the quality of burlesque or extravaganza to a height never reached before. In some respects he was "common": he has moments that can only be called vulgar. The peculiarity of Gilbert's humour is a logical and wholly unpoetical use of fantasy. He carries out absurd ideas, with exact logic, from premise to conclusion. To the mind of an old-fashioned high-school headmistress he joined the fantastic logic of a fairy world. That he has given us the self-explanatory epithet "Gilbertian" is a tribute to his originality.

The last two decades of the nineteenth century saw a gradual rise in the general level of acted plays. Robertson and adaptations of contemporary French drama had brought "Society" back to the theatre; but the player rather than the play was sometimes the attraction. Irving, Wyndham and the Bancrofts were fashionable actors and drew audiences for pieces of almost any quality. Still, plays were written, and two new authors began to attract attention, Henry Arthur Jones (1851–1929) and Arthur Wing Pinero (1859–1934). From the beginning there was evident in Jones a strain of the grandiose and the hortatory. His first London play, *A Clerical Error*, was acted in 1879; but his real success came with *The Silver King* (1882), which raised melodrama almost to the level of art. It remains his best play. *Saints and Sinners* (1884), *The Middleman* (1889), *Judah* (1890), and *The Dancing Girl* (1891), were all strong, heavy, and utterly stagey. Jones even attempted a blank-verse tragedy, *The Tempter* (1893), a most pretentious piece of fustian, and an equally pretentious religious play, *Michael and his Lost Angel* (1896). Pinero was more modest. He was an actor, and began with light comedies that could be easily performed. *The Magistrate* and *Dandy Dick* can still amuse. His first outstanding success was *Sweet Lavender* (1888), a lush sentimental comedy owing more than a little to the Temple scenes of *Pendennis*. In *The Profligate* (1889) he chose a more serious theme, but destroyed the whole effect of his story by surrendering to the popular demand for a happy ending. Indeed, the stage-work of Jones, Pinero and such less notable people as Sydney Grundy (1848–1914) had no artistic importance and made no contribution to the criticism of life. Their plays were theatrical inventions in which theatrically conceived figures behaved, at theatrical crises, in the expected theatrical manner. The literary counterpart of the popular play was not the novel, but the novelette. No contemporary English writer of the first rank paid any attention to the theatre. What shook the English stage into some recognition of its artistic ineptitude was the tremendous impact of Ibsen with his relentless, unsentimental criticism of life and his revealing exhibition of the dramatic possibilities in the actual lives of commonplace people in commonplace circumstances. Several attempts had been made to introduce Ibsen to the English public, but his plays did not become generally known till William Archer (with some assistance) translated the bulk of his work. In 1891 The Independent Theatre, founded by J. T. Grein, began its activity, and produced the work of Ibsen and other serious Continental dramatists on the English stage. It is difficult for a reader of today to understand the violence of execration with which Ibsen was greeted by the accredited critics of drama and the general playgoing public. "Muck-ferreting dog" was among the gentler terms applied to him. The prosecution of all concerned in the production of his plays was loudly demanded. But, detested as he was, Ibsen made it impossible for English playwrights to go on with their theatrical deceptions. Jones developed his unexploited vein of serious comedy and produced more reputable work in *The Liars* (1894) and *The Case of Rebellious Susan* (1897). Pinero made a bold attempt at stating social problems in *The Second Mrs Tanqueray* (1893), *The Benefit of the Doubt* (1895), *Iris* (1901), *Letty* (1903) and *His House in Order* (1906). But they appeared to express a conviction that the only problem for the theatre was that concerning women who had made, or were contemplating, breaches of the Seventh Commandment. Moreover, the plain fact is that, while Ibsen is a great writer, Jones and Pinero had no existence as men of letters. The one play of Pinero with genuine life is *Trelawny of the Wells* (1898), which, despite a muddled ending and some failure of character, is sincerely written and has actual relation to life. As we have already indicated, its theme is the passing of the old melodrama of the Sixties and the coming of a new dramatist, with the reactions of the change upon the lives of a group of players.

A brilliant interlude in the Jones-Pinero period was the sudden emergence as playwright of Oscar Wilde (1858–1900), who, in *Lady Windermere's Fan* (1892), *A Woman of No Importance* (1893) and *An Ideal Husband* (1894) showed that he could write with insolent ease and polished utterance better bad plays than the regular purveyors of dramatic fare could produce with their most laboured efforts. They could still be revived as period pieces and they can still be read for their sallies of wit. Wilde reached the height of his achievement in *The Import-ance of Being Earnest* (1895), the perfection of artificial comedy, produced in the year of his tragic downfall. It is one of the two best comedies written since the time of Sheridan. The other, *Arms and the Man* (1894) by Bernard Shaw, leads naturally to a consideration of that dramatist, whose main work, however, reaches forward to the next century and must be reserved for later discussion.

Still another pleasing interlude was provided by the brief but definite success of Stephen Phillips (1868–1915) as a writer of poetical plays. Phillips had come into notice with his early publications *Christ in Hades* (1896) and *Poems* (1897). He seemed to be a new and original voice in the post-Tennysonian chorus, and some of his metrical irregularities aroused equal applause and reprobation. He was so far in the news as a poet that he was asked by George Alexander to write a play, and *Paolo and Francesca* (printed 1899, acted 1902) had great success. Herbert Beerbohm Tree then secured from him *Herod* (1901) and *Ulysses* (1902). But either the poet's inspiration failed or the actor's curious megalomania intervened unfavourably, for the two plays, successful dramatically, were less sincere as poems. They approached the region of grand opera and suggested Meyerbeer and *Le Prophète*. *The Sin of David* (1904) was poor, and *Nero* (1906) was almost pure Meyerbeer. Only the first three are important. Today they seem feeble and futile, but they cannot be entirely ignored. Phillips succeeded where Tennyson and Browning had failed—he put poetry of a kind on the stage and made it popular. *Paolo and Francesca* is the best of his plays. It is full of the lush diction which, at the end of the nineteenth century, seemed the proper idiom of poetic drama; but it could be spoken on the stage, and it could give an audience the sensation of hearing something that was beyond mere prose and brought an echo from the shores of old romance. Phillips provided an agreeable and successful interlude in the dead days of the drama.

The last decade of the century had better critics than writers of drama. William Archer (1856–1924) and Arthur Bingham Walkley (1855–1926), as well as Bernard Shaw, discussed plays in essays of the critical kind that later journalism had seldom a place for. Archer's work is preserved in *The Theatrical World*, 5 vols. (1894–8), and Shaw's in *Dramatic Opinions and Essays*, 1894–8, 2 vols. (1907). Both are readable for their own sake and invaluable as sources for the dramatic history of the decade. Walkley's *Playhouse Impressions* (1892) and *Drama and Life* (1937) are excellent.

IX. THACKERAY

It is a little saddening to examine the row of Thackeray's works and to find that of this long and once famous line only three, *Vanity Fair* and *Esmond*, with *Pendennis* lagging far behind, remain in the general repertory of "the great variety of readers". By a select body of Thackerayans everything he wrote can be read. By a larger body of serious readers, the *Roundabouts*, the *Sketches*, the *Lectures*, *The Rose and the Ring*, the *Burlesques*, the *Ballads* and the rest of the novels will not be overlooked. Nevertheless, to the greater number Thackaery is the author of two or perhaps three novels. The versatility of his invention as

novelist, essayist, humorist, rhymester and draughtsman makes him less easy
to judge than more homogeneous writers. His feebler work obstructs his best.
At once satirist and sentimentalist, he combined two points of view and, in
both capacities, he worked with a refinement that does not make for general
popularity.

William Makepeace Thackeray (1811–63) was born near Calcutta, the son
of a "collector"—the important office held by the great Jos Sedley. Thackeray
was another of our writers with a homeless childhood, for his father died in
1815, and his mother soon remarried. The small boy of six was sent to England,
and when the ship called at St Helena he saw Napoleon walking in the garden
of Longwood. He attended various schools, the last being Charterhouse ("Grey-
friars"), then in London, and entered Trinity, Cambridge, which he soon left
without achieving anything but the friendship of Tennyson, FitzGerald and
other seriously inclined young men. From Cambridge he passed to Weimar,
began to read law in the Middle Temple, and then made a home in Paris,
where he gained acquaintance (and lost money) with a shady, shabby-genteel
set of wasters, who furnished him with material for later sketches. Thereafter
he began to inhabit the Bohemian world of letters, writing and drawing in
various papers and magazines, and using many pseudonymns. *Pendennis*, though
not strictly autobiographical, contains many traces of these earlier years. Much
of his early journalism will be found in the various collections bearing the
names of *Yellowplush*, *Major Gahagan*, *FitzBoodle* and *Titmarsh*. *Catherine*, *by
Ikey Solomons junior* (1839–40) was an attempt to ridicule "with solemn sneer"
the romantic burglars, highwaymen and murderers of Lytton and Ainsworth.
A Shabby Genteel Story, which appeared in *Fraser* during 1840, is the precursor
of the later *Philip*. In this year occurred the greatest calamity of Thackeray's life.
He had felt able to marry in 1836; four years later his wife became insane and
they were separated for ever. She outlived him by nearly thirty years. Their
eldest daughter Anne Thackeray, Lady Ritchie (1837–1919) wrote novels and
reminiscences; their youngest, Harriet, married the critic Leslie Stephen.

The pseudonym "Michael Angelo Titmarsh", which was assumed by the
author of *The Great Hoggarty Diamond* (1841), and had been first used in 1840
for *The Paris Sketch Book*, also appeared in 1841 on the title-page of *Comic Tales
and Sketches* as the name of the editor of *The Yellowplush Correspondence*, *Major
Gahagan* and other previously published stories. In *Fraser* of June 1842 Thackeray
took the name George Savage Fitz-Boodle for the *Confessions* of this middle-
aged clubman. Fitz-Boodle, as "editor", began to supply *Fraser* in 1844 with
the remarkable work called *The Luck of Barry Lyndon*, Thackeray's most substantial work of fiction before *Vanity Fair*. It is a very able piece of work. With
it may be mentioned *The Irish Sketch Book* (1843), notable for its observation of
a people in whom the novelist found an abundance of material. Thackeray's
earliest *Punch* contributions (1842) are unimportant. Not until he hit upon the
parodies known as *Punch's Prize Novelists* (1847) did he find the right vein.
Other famous burlesques are *A Legend of the Rhine* (1845), *Barbazure* and the
inimitable *Rebecca and Rowena* (1850). A tour to the East in 1844 produced the
Notes of a Journey from Cornhill to Grand Cairo (1846). During 1846 and the
beginning of 1847 he wrote for *Punch* the papers entitled *The Snobs of England*,

by one of themselves, afterwards published as *The Book of Snobs*. But while the *Snob* papers were approaching completion, the monthly numbers of *Vanity Fair* were beginning to appear from the office of *Punch*.

On the covers of *Vanity Fair* (1847–8) Thackeray used his own name. His protean changes of pseudonym had obscured the real man, and it was not until the new novel was well advanced in its serial course that popular interest was aroused. Much of the work that Thackeray had produced during the ten years preceding *Vanity Fair* was purely fugitive. But he had acquired practice in a style which he was to use with perfection in his later books. That Thackeray loved the eighteenth century is clear; he had a natural affinity with the period of the essayists. Moreover, in Fielding's tolerant view of life he found the closest response to his own appreciation of generosity and hatred of meanness. His long apprenticeship to journalistic character-sketches gave him command over the *dramatis personae* of his great story. There is not a failure in it; and its greatest strength lies, not in its deservedly famous incidents, but in its entirely homogeneous life, uncoloured by inappropriate sentiment and undiverted to the delusive comfort of any "happy ending".

The objective and impartial nature of Thackeray's character-drawing, clear to every reader of *Vanity Fair*, is continued, though with less success, in *Pendennis*, the first number of which was published in November 1848. There must have been strong temptation to optimize the character of a hero whose early career bears so close a resemblance to Thackeray's own; but the temptation is resisted, and Pendennis, though likeable, is frequently irritating. The success of the book lies in its wealth of minor characters—if such triumphs as the Captain, the Major and Morgan can be called minor. Among the women, Blanche is unfailingly amusing, Laura is too good to be true.

In *The History of Henry Esmond*, published in 1852, Thackeray applied his powers to a drama of the Queen Anne period, with a wide knowledge of its social and literary history and a natural liking for its idiom of speech. The book triumphs over a major difficulty of form—a narrative in the first person by its grave and modest hero, and over a major difficulty of incident—the transfer of the hero's love from a daughter to her mother. The general texture is even richer and more rewarding than in *Vanity Fair*, and the ending, which avoids a conventional close, is a moving piece of drama.

The rest of Thackeray's own story is disappointing. From Christmas to Christmas appeared the series of books beginning in 1847 with *Mrs Perkins's Ball* and ending with the ever-delightful *The Rose and the Ring* in 1855. He yielded in 1851 to the temptation of lecturing and produced, as a result, *The English Humorists of the Eighteenth Century*, which is satisfying neither as literature nor as criticism. The celebrated peroration to the lecture on Swift, beginning "Only a woman's hair", showed that Thackeray could out-Dickens Dickens himself in lush sentimentality. A second series of lectures, *The Four Georges*, delivered in 1855 and 1856, remains unprofitable as history or as literature.

Thackeray, like Balzac and Dumas, carried over some of his characters from one book into another, and *The Newcomes* (1853–5) is ostensibly edited by Pendennis, domesticated with his Laura. Once a great favourite, *The Newcomes* finds few enthusiasts today. The celebrated death scene of the Colonel is now as disconcerting as the death scenes of Little Nell and Paul Dombey. Nor do other of the principal characters succeed. Barnes Newcome is as incredible a villain as Ralph Nickleby, and Mrs Mackenzie's unresting malignity is more tiresome than convincing. On the other hand, Ethel is one of Thackeray's best female characters, and Lady Kew the most perfectly drawn of his shrewd and cynical old women of the world. Colonel Newcome is Thackeray's attempt to transmit in character the ideals which were in the minds of serious young poets and artists of the day; unfortunately the Colonel, unlike Mr Weller, a father of different ideals, never really rose out of the pages to live a genuine life of his own. *The Virginians* (1857–9) is a chronicle of the descendants of Henry Esmond. It commits the crime of being uninteresting and the blunder of reviving Beatrix as Baroness Bernstein, raddled, decayed and horrible. She points no moral and she disadorns the tale. Authors really have duties to the characters they have brought into the world.

The first number of *The Cornhill Magazine* (January 1860) under Thackeray's editorship contained the first instalment of *Lovel the Widower*, a short story in his early manner, and the first of *Roundabout Papers*, a set of discursive essays, often charming, but not in the front rank of their kind. Thackeray's last complete novel, *The Adventures of Philip*, was contributed to *The Cornhill* of 1862. For the subject he returned to the characters of *A Shabby Genteel Story*; but the tale tells us nothing new and presents no truly memorable invention. Thackeray's last work of fiction, *Denis Duval*, was left unfinished at his death. Like *Esmond*, it is historical, though its period is that of the French, not the English, Revolution. The fragment recovers much of the old charm, mellowed and enriched, and so the last work that came from Thackeray's hand leaves us with happy memories of his best achievements. Thackeray, like Dickens, died quite suddenly. That each should have left a highly promising unfinished story makes the parallel of their lives curiously complete.

Thackeray was never a "crusader" and propounded no problems. His range of character is limited compared with that of Dickens, and the sentiments and actions of his people are far more restrained by the usual conventions; he kept closely to the world he knew, and did not, like Dickens, create a vast world of fantasy. His sense of human littleness and his preoccupation with the ways of snobbery do not endear him to the great multitude of readers; but when the cynical author, genuinely moved, trembles on the brink of tears, he is irresistible. Like Fielding, he saw that in life it is hard to draw a clear line between vice and virtue, but that it is not hard to know the difference between moral geniality and moral meanness. This kindly understanding is transmitted in prose not, indeed, free from mannerisms and imperfections, but endowed with a flexibility that responds to every demand, and suffused with a personal charm that brings writer and reader into unstrained communication. It should be added that Thackeray's humorous verse is excellent of its kind and that the general Thackerayan gospel of life is summed up in the lightly serious stanzas called *The End of the Play*.

X. DICKENS

The first clear fact about Dickens is the immense and enduring popularity of his work. For this unique popularity there must be some reasons. The most important are easily found. The first is that, with the exception of Shakespeare, there is no greater example of creative force in our literature. Every figure the creative finger of Dickens touched came alive, from Mr Pickwick's cabman to Mr Wegg's hoarse charioteer. The stock objection that Dickens's creations are not characters but caricatures can at once be answered: Where there is no character there can be no caricature. Caricature is an artistic excess of character. Vitality, exuberance, idiosyncrasy—these are the notes of Dickens's characters. They are sometimes more lively than life itself, and they are never forgotten. That is the first reason for his popularity. The second is his humour. The great humorists of the world can be counted on the fingers of a single hand, and Dickens is of that choice company. The third is the sheer abundance and variety of his invention. We have in Dickens, then, an astonishing combination of creative vigour, unstaled humour and abundant variety. His world-wide popularity is certain of endurance. Nevertheless some general charges are seriously made against him and must be considered.

The first charge is that he sacrificed art to pamphleteering. Boz was called "the Inimitable"; and as long as the Inimitable is at work, all is well. But Dickens, like many other great Victorians, was acutely and honourably conscious of "the condition-of-England question". That our most popular novelist devoted some of his talent to the exposure of oppression and injustice is a great piece of luck. But good intentions never made a work of art, and in this strange world of ours art will live when good intentions are forgotten. Dickens never ceased from mental fight, nor did the sword sleep in his hand, and sometimes the Crusader obstructed the Inimitable. The Inimitable made a hungry workhouse boy ask for "more", the Crusader made an old woman struggle melodramatically against pauperdom. The vital question is not which of these two is a finer document in social criticism, but which comes home to the heart. Everyone remembers Oliver Twist; nobody remembers Betty Higden. Dickens has thus put a severe handicap on his own popularity by adulterating art with pamphleteering. Had the Crusader got control, the novels would be hastening to oblivion. Fortunately the Inimitable prevailed. But we must not hesitate to admit that Dickens, in the interests of philanthropy, sometimes falsified his values and ceased to be an artist. Another charge is that Dickens had a strong histrionic bent: that, living in the age of melodrama, he sometimes introduced into his books figures that mean nothing off the transpontine boards. Among these are minor villains like Monks, Gride and Gashford, moving dimly in the greenish light of melodramatic gloom and never entering the real world of Dickens, because the creative finger has never touched them. These must be frankly accepted as blunders, hard to forgive, though fortunately easy to forget. The common charge of sentimentalism and lush pathos can be admitted. Excess of sentiment is part of the price that has to be paid for sensitiveness. That Dickens wrote sincerely in the tone of his period is evident from the tidal wave of tears that washed over the British islands and across the Atlantic when Little Nell died. We do not like the tremulant pathos of Dickens; but our forbears did.

No great creative artist ever had a more unpromising birth and upbringing. Charles Dickens (1812–70) was born in Portsmouth. His father was a dockyard clerk, and a transfer to Chatham made the child familiar with the neighbouring Rochester and its ancient appeal. A further transfer to Somerset House brought the family to London, where, after living in a sordid suburb, the acutely sensitive child became painfully familiar with another great national institution, a debtors' prison, the Marshalsea, to which the father was consigned. To the privations and humiliation of dire poverty was added the degrading experience, at the age of twelve, of potting and labelling blacking in a small factory with which some member of the family was connected. The release of the father led to a reconsideration of the family position. Dickens's father proposed to send Charles to school; but his mother was in favour of his return to the blacking pots. This was the deepest wound made in his young soul, the one cruelty that he never forgot. But the father prevailed, and the boy was released from the indignities that had wounded his eager spirit. It is a point for high admiration that Dickens nowhere writes with a sense of resentment, and never indulges in self-pity. The chapters in *David Copperfield* are the sole record in a story of his tragedy, though David was far better off than Dickens ever was. For Dickens there was no beneficent Betsey Trotwood, no transfer to a great school and no entry into a dignified profession. Dickens passed from a shabby school to a boy clerk's job in a solicitor's office, taught himself shorthand, became a reporter for several papers, and, in that sense, entered the House of Commons. It is often forgotten that Dickens's frequent gibes at "Government" came from a man thoroughly familiar with parliamentary procedure.

Dickens got his first literary enthusiasm from an intense and excited reading in childhood of the great classics of fiction, original or translated. So he was early prepared to write. His reportership gave him a hold on the fringe of literature, and he soon fastened that hold on the garment itself. He had plenty of material. He had the observing eye and the experiencing nature. His travels as a reporter made him familiar with places and people, with coaches and inns, where, as Cervantes tells us, all adventures should begin. Like many great originals, he got his first impulse from others. Very inferior work will sometimes give the born writer his cue. He reads something, and says inwardly "I could do that", and proceeds to do it, till he does better. Dickens's first aim was the right one, though apparently, and only apparently, a lowly one, namely, to produce what editors would print and readers enjoy. From the very beginning he was himself, and continued to be himself to the end. This self-sufficiency, in the best sense, did not necessarily bring with it the counterbalancing gift which idiosyncrasy requires—the gift of self-discipline and self-criticism, and we have to deplore some examples of arrogance, cocksureness and doubtful taste, and some undue indulgence in "tricks and manners". These defects do not arise from "defective education" or "humble origin", they are the defects of great qualities, the seamy side of intense originality. Very many writers, poets as well as novelists, have had small powers of self-discipline and self-criticism, and have obstinately gone on writing what everyone, save the authors, knew to be inferior work.

The very earliest of his writings deserve consideration. The *Sketches of Young Gentlemen, Sketches of Young Couples* and *The Mud-fog Papers*, never reprinted by Dickens himself, are good samples of journalism, with a certain touch of individuality in them which might come to something or might not. What came immediately is not the great novels, but the *Sketches by Boz*, which themselves promise something more. They indicate the arrival of a writer whose competence is unquestionable and whose note of authority causes a hush of expectation. Not much good is gained by seeking for resemblances to Leigh Hunt or Theodore Hook. The fact is that Dickens, Thackeray and other "sketch" writers were all trying to reach the same kind of public. Dickens's first sketch, *A Dinner at Poplar Walk*, retitled *Mr Minns and his Cousin*, was published in December 1833. After that he wrote numerous tales and sketches, and in a year or two had enough from which to make two selections, *Sketches by Boz. Illustrative of Every-day Life, and Every-day People* (1835) and a second series (1836). The full title is worth notice. Thus, in his twenty-third year, Dickens was moderately well-known as the author of journalistic or magazine contributions, and no more. What happened next is like a fairy tale. Publishers are nothing if not imitative. The success of the "Jorrocks" sketches of Surtees made Messrs Chapman and Hall believe that some humorous letterpress written to accompany humorous sporting pictures might also be successful. Dickens was asked to add the written matter to the pictures, because his "Boz" sketches in *The Monthly Magazine* were recalled and there was a chance that he had the journalistic invention desired. The work so casually conceived was to become one of the world's comic masterpieces. The first monthly number appeared in April 1836 and bore on its wrappers the title, *The Posthumous Papers of the Pickwick Club, Containing a Faithful Record of the Perambulations, Perils, Travels, Adventures and Sporting Transactions of the Corresponding Members. Edited by Boz*. One specimen of the verbose titles then thought humorous will suffice. The new venture did not begin well. Dickens was writing to order and had not found himself. The earlier chapters are stiff, crude and unrewarding; but with the cab journey from Goswell Street to the Golden Cross we enter an entirely new world and are never shut out of it until Death performs the ungracious office and leaves the story of *Edwin Drood* half told. There is no book like *Pickwick* anywhere; it is a Rabelaisian fairy-tale, with a stout little man in tights and spectacles as the presiding genius. In nothing does *Pickwick* more clearly foreshadow what was to come than in its creation of a world, which, like the different Gilbertian world, is this familiar world, with a curiously refracting atmosphere that makes the values unfamiliar. Dickens is not always true to his own fantasies, and disconcerts us at times by dragging in "economic" beings from the statistical world of Blue Books and Reports. In *Pickwick* there is very little confusion of the planes, save in the final "happy endings", and in some of the intercalated stories, which are thoroughly bad, always excepting, of course, the delightful bagman's tales. Certain other characteristics of Dickens are clearly seen in *Pickwick*—his power (to use the Aristotelian phrase) of rendering impossibility probable or not improbable, his creation of real conversation, and his power of imparting, not indeed the complexity, variety and depth of life, but a certain "external intensity" of it. *Pickwick* is a triumph of the curious and difficult process that we may call realism disrealized. That its vast and vigorous world, with its three hundred characters and twenty-two inns, was created by a young man of four-and-twenty is one of the miracles of art.

The immense success of *Pickwick* made Dickens his own man for ever. He could now write just what he liked, and it is very interesting to notice what he liked. The humorist vanishes, and in the almost contemporary *Oliver Twist* (1837–8) and *Nicholas Nickleby* (1838–9) we behold the crusader with wrongs to set right, the journalist with evils to expose, the philanthropist with causes to proclaim, and the melodramatist with villains to denounce. Dickens at once put the extravaganza of *Pickwick* behind him, and at no time did he make any attempt to repeat his resounding success in that manner. This is a point over-looked by those who think of him as more a showman than an artist. *Oliver Twist* is, by general consent, in the lower rank of Dickens's novels. Oliver himself, save in his one sublime moment, is uninteresting. Indeed, only the "bad" characters, and not all of those, are really memorable. Bumble has given a deathless name to something which is often with us, which is likely to be still more with us, and which, under whatever alias, is always certain to be evil. Fagin is such a masterpiece of grotesque fantasy that we are inclined to resent the terrible realism of his end. Tremendous in parts, feeble in others (and those standing for virtue), *Oliver Twist* fails to be properly successful, though the workhouse chapters remain singularly impressive.

The faults of *Oliver Twist* reappear in *Nicholas Nickleby*; but the book is on a very much larger scale; it is more varied in scene and character, and almost all the new elements are sheer gain. The horrors of Dotheboys Hall are not too heavily exploited and are enlivened with excellent comedy. Mrs Nickleby is the hen-brained silly woman of all times and places. Out of mere absence of under-standing Mrs Nickleby is as ready to consign her daughter to an evil marriage as Mrs Dickens was to consign her son to the blacking factory. To modern readers the most repellent character is Smike. The one thing that may not be done artistically to a mentally deficient youth is to make him romantic, and this Dickens tries hard to do. Mr Crummles and those about him remain, like all the best things in Dickens, joys unspeakable and inexhaustible for ever; and they are not ill-seconded by the Mantalinis, the Kenwigses and the delightful Newman Noggs. The book regains and displays that abundance which only the greatest "makers" in verse and prose possess.

What Dickens "liked to do" next was to commit a blunder, as he soon recognized. To us, who accept the "omniscient narrator" of our fiction as an unnoticed part of the machinery, there seems something odd in the anxiety of the older novelists to account for the way in which they got their information. Collections of letters, edited memoirs, discovered manuscripts and so forth had all been used. Dickens tried the device of "Master Humphrey's Clock", inside the case of which the members of a club placed their manuscripts. Worse still, he attempted to revive, not *Pickwick* itself, but a post-Pickwickian Pickwick and Sam Weller. The inset tales of *Master Humphrey's Clock* (1840–1) go back to the level of the old *Sketches*. Only two full-length tales, *Barnaby Rudge* and

The Old Curiosity Shop, belong to the Clock—the latter story still embarrassed in the beginning by the horological machinery; and then, like the celebrated timepiece in the Victorian music-hall song, Master Humphrey's stopped short, never to go again; nor did Dickens make any more attempts to manufacture "machinery" of narration or to re-introduce old characters.

The Old Curiosity Shop (book form 1841) is remarkable for the fact that the two most prominent and disputable characters, Nell and her grandfather, could be almost cut out of the book, except as terms of reference. Nell, whose death made continents weep in one generation and scoff in the next, is one of the Dickens characters in some need of revaluation. Those who, from report, think of Little Nell as a Dickensian angel-child perishing in Dickensian effulgence should really read the story, and discover Nell Trent. Nothing can be done with the grandfather, whose habit, gambling, is realistic, and whose character, antiquarian, is fantastic. But almost all the other characters are superb—the showmen, Mrs Jarley, the Brasses, Quilp, and above all, Mr Swiveller and the Marchioness, the last a triumphant example of what the Inimitable could do for the oppressed when the Crusader did not impede him.

Barnaby Rudge (book form 1841) is an interesting example of what Dickens "liked to do". Indeed, he made two attempts at historical fiction, and then desisted. Some obvious reasons for his failure are alleged: he did not know enough; but what he needed could easily have been acquired: he was not interested in the past; but he wrote *A Child's History of England*, and his sense of the past was strong. The most probable reason is that his large manner was cramped by the strict limits of space and time. Neither of the historical tales can be called unsuccessful; but neither is deeply loved by the true Dickensian. Thackeray was never more truly himself than in *Esmond*; we have to search for Dickens in *Barnaby Rudge* and *A Tale of Two Cities*. *Barnaby Rudge* contains much excellent matter and a few Dickensian characters—is the world not full of Tappertits? Its most elaborate efforts (such as Sir John Chester) are the least successful. A most curious demonstration of the artistic truth of the Dickensian world is this, that whereas *Pickwick*, which is an extravaganza of unrelated scenes, appears to be a whole thing, *Barnaby*, which is elaborately planned and closely written, seems to be a collection of incidents.

In 1842 Dickens paid a long-contemplated visit to America—the first of the tours abroad, which became frequent and exercised a great influence on his work. This particular voyage produced *American Notes* and *Martin Chuzzlewit*. The *American Notes* (1842) have lost much of their face value. As a book it is fairly amusing, but it lacks the peculiar fantastic attraction of the novels. It is not really unkind; but only excessive flattery would have been acceptable. Much more severe is the criticism contained in *Martin Chuzzlewit* (parts 1843–4), which contains a fair number of failures—or at least of unsuccesses. Tom Pinch is mere sentimentalism; Mark Tapley is rather tiresome. But the worst blunder is Mercy Pecksniff, who is first proffered as a grotesque for our laughter, and next proffered as a tragic woman for our tears. The countervailing recompense, however, is enormous. Mrs Gamp, "Todgers's", Betsy, Bailey, and the rest of a whole army of minor figures display the true Dickensian abundance.

The year 1843 gave us *A Christmas Carol*, first of the endearing Christmas books, which continued annually with *The Chimes, The Cricket on the Hearth, The Battle of Life* and *The Haunted Man*, and only ceased when the establishment of *Household Words* changed them to shorter Christmas stories which, in that paper and in *All the Year Round*, were scattered over the rest of the writer's life. The claim that Dickens created the popular notion of Christmas as a season of enlarged heart and waistcoat cannot be maintained. Washington Irving had written *Bracebridge Hall* when Dickens was still at the blacking factory. Moreover, those who think that Dickens preached nothing but a gospel of hearty feeding at Christmas have evidently left unread the four uncomfortable and disturbing stories that follow the *Carol*. What Dickens did in the five Christmas stories was to indulge in some moral stock-taking at the traditional season of good will; and what he claimed in them was the right of all, even of the poorest, to enjoy themselves in their own way, undeterred by economists, statisticians and professional philanthropists. It has been charged against Dickens that he was equally ready to denounce, in the name of humanity, those who left things alone, and, in the name of liberty, those who tried to make things better. The charge is too abstract to carry conviction. Everything depends upon the kind of "letting alone" and the kind of "making better". There are plenty of middle courses between Bourbonism and Bolshevism. What Dickens is solidly against, from his first book to his last, is the tendency to brigade a population, either into submerged masses for neglect or into intimidated masses for improvement. He is, to use the old-fashioned word, an out-and-out individualist, denying the right of Scrooge to grind the humanity out of Cratchit, and affirming the right of Cratchit to squander his money on goose and gin at the Christmas season. The continued popularity of the Christmas books owes much to the general instinct that more is meant than meets the ear. The general instinct is right. They are wonderful fables.

Between the first and the last of the Christmas books Dickens did much other work. *Pictures from Italy* (1846) can be dismissed as unimportant. *Dombey and Son* (the usual abbreviation of a thirteen-word title) appeared in parts during 1847–8. It marks a change in manner, for it is Dickens's first attempt at painting actual modern society. Much of it is unsuccessful. How could there be any convincing tragedy with such a pasteboard figure as the over-dentured Carker in the *rôle* of villain? But many of the humorous characters have all the old success. Cousin Feenix, though absurd, is a true-blue aristocrat. Even the unfortunate little Paul is an engaging, elfin creature, in spite of the disconcerting excess of the death scene. His conversation with the ever-delightful Toots about the sea is like an accusing parody of the sentimentalist by the Inimitable. *Dombey* is, by general consent, remitted to the lower rank among the novels. After *Dombey* the inexhaustible man not only began writing *David Copperfield* but undertook the new and very important adventure of editing *Household Words*, a weekly periodical which very soon justified its title and which, with its sequel, *All the Year Round*, he carried on till his death. These contained, thenceforward, a great deal of his own work, and they enriched popular literature with a great deal of good work by many other writers.

David Copperfield did not appear in *Household Words*, but in the old monthly form (1849–50). It is written with a curious tenderness, for there is in it something of what the young Dickens was, and something of what the young Dickens wanted to be. Yet it contains no accusation against the world—indeed, it is the sweetest of all the stories. That it is one of the few really great English novels cannot be denied except by the perverse. The abundance of life and vitality, the range of characters, the close-knit texture of the story and the high quality of the writing can hardly be paralleled. There is no "crusading", but there is, unfortunately, some melodrama. Does one really care much about what happened to Little Em'ly at any time? Steerforth never gets beyond an admiring schoolboy's idea of a fine fellow. But the failures are forgotten in the successes. Micawber takes his place with Falstaff; and after Micawber comes a whole world of memorable creatures like the stars of heaven for multitude. *David Copperfield* is Dickens's most varied, most serious and most firmly sustained effort.

In the spring of 1852 Dickens began *Bleak House* (parts 1852–3), a rather grave book which is very variously received. Dislike for the heroine (a dislike far from universal) is not a convincing excuse for disliking the book. And for once, the chief crusading *motif*—that against the law's delays—is used as art and not as pamphlet. Much of the story and many of the characters are attractive in spite of the gloom of the underworld and the brooding air of crime. Even Poor Jo is not too grossly sentimentalized. For whatever faults it possesses *Bleak House* has abundant recompense, and it takes high rank in the opinion of many whose views deserve respect.

Next in chronological order comes *A Child's History of England* (three volumes, 1852, 1853, 1854) which had, no doubt, a life of its own in the domestic circle, and should have been confined there. *Hard Times. For these Times* (1854, after appearance in *Household Words*) is not one of the books that have been popular, except for the Sleary group and Mr Gradgrind (ever useful in political speeches). But Louisa is interesting as an attempt at the character of a real live girl of the nineteenth century. Part of the book is mere crusading, and refuses to come to life as art. To some the novel has seemed Dickens's most conspicuous failure, but Ruskin thought it "in several respects the greatest he has written".

Now for the first time comes a pause in the astonishing stream of production. Perhaps editorial work became an impediment, perhaps domestic infelicity checked the natural outflow. Not till the end of 1857 did the first part of *Little Dorrit* appear, to be completed in 1858. This is a book that can easily be misjudged. A single reading leaves an impression of dullness. A second reading shows that what seemed dullness is a rather unusual homogeneity. The shadow of the Marshalsea broods over it, and the "Fall of the House of Clennam" intensifies the gloom. There is some crusading and some melodrama; but the tale is so well-ordered and so enriched with subsidiary figures, that its faults cease to tease, and it becomes as re-readable as any but the very best.

Two important events belong to this period. In 1859 Dickens ended *Household Words* and began *All the Year Round*, on rather more literary lines. It continued till his death. But he also began those celebrated readings from his works, which, by all report, were so intensely dramatic that they rapidly consumed what was left of his vitality. In *All the Year Round* he led off with *A Tale of Two Cities* and the papers afterwards collected as *The Uncommercial Traveller* (1861), a singularly rich volume, which has never had the popularity it deserves. *A Tale of Two Cities* owes something to Carlyle's *French Revolution* and something to the old melodrama *The Dead Heart*. The story is well-plotted and closely woven, and has a romantic "hero with a weakness", who never fails to appeal to a female auditory. The adventures of the book in forms other than the novel have been extensive. Many people who do not care for the rest of Dickens like it greatly; many who are enthusiastic about Dickens refuse to give it a second reading. It is the least Dickensian of all the tales. On the other hand, *Great Expectations* (1860–1) is undoubtedly Dickens, and some of it both new and of the best. Pip is even better than David. Estella is an attractive attempt at a hitherto unattempted kind of heroine; but unfortunately there is too little of her. All the humorous characters are of the richest vintage, and are all natural relief in a well-knit story with some very tense moments.

The Christmas numbers of *Household Words* and *All the Year Round* contain some of Dickens's best shorter works, including the exquisite *Holly-Tree* story of juvenile love. *Our Mutual Friend* (parts 1864–5), was the last novel he completed. For reasons difficult to understand this fine novel had to fight its way through indifference and positive dislike to its present assured popularity. Few of its predecessors are so rich in exuberant character. The surprising new feature in *Our Mutual Friend* is the moving romance of Eugene and Lizzie, lightly but beautifully touched.

Only the familiar practice of prophesying after the event can detect fatigue and failing powers in *Our Mutual Friend*; and the last tale of all, *The Mystery of Edwin Drood* (1870), begins superbly. As usual, the part of the story that has attracted most attention is that which was never written, and one is compelled to conclude that the public likes its stories and its symphonies unfinished. All the "continuators" seem to have overlooked the fact that what matters most is not the story but the way Dickens tells the story. Edwin Drood and Denis Duval, consorting in the paradise of literary creations, must often smile at the efforts of lesser mortals to wield the weapons of their masters.

Dickens was lucky in his sudden death. He was spared the decay of Scott and the dotage of Swift. Popular as he always was, he seems to be arriving at a new and more rational popularity. The danger is that some of his faults may be construed as virtues, and that he may be exalted for his pamphleteering. But, as we have said, at no time, past or present, did propaganda or philanthropy alone make a work of art. The wicked Fagin lives in our affections; the good Riah, meant as a deliberate apology to Jewry, fails to move us.

The prose of Dickens offers examples of almost every excellence in an immense range of effects. Dickens's sense of words is exquisite and his genius in coining names unsurpassed. Perhaps the most remarkable quality in his work, apart from its miraculous variety, is the ever-present touch of fantasy, as if the pen that wrote in prose were moved by some impulse from the spirit of poetry. And so characters that seem almost as far from real existence as Ariel or Caliban have genuine and enduring life. Such is the unity in his immense variety that the whole collection of works can be read and re-read as one vast human comedy, ranging from the expansive fun of *Pickwick* to the haunting tragedy of *Drood*. With Shakespeare, Dickens is the most English of writers, and, like

Shakespeare, he has conquered the world. The faults of Dickens are the faults of the English character; his virtues are the virtues of the English character; and these in their richest abundance he has expressed with an exuberant fertility of device, a daemonic energy of creation and a vast universal charity to which there is only one parallel in literature.

The Life of Charles Dickens (1872–4) by his intimate friend John Forster remains the best biography, though to be supplemented on some points by later works such as those by Hugh Kingsmill (1934), Jack Lindsay (1950), Edgar Johnson (1952) and K. J. Fielding (1966). Three volumes of *Letters*, edited by Walter Dexter, were included in the Nonesuch Dickens (1937–8); a twelve-volume Pilgrim Edition, containing some 12,000 letters, was edited by Humphry and Madeline House, in collaboration with Graham Storey and others, in 1965– . The first critical edition of the novels, the Clarendon edition (1966–), was edited by Kathleen Tillotson and John Butt. Among the critics who have written memorably on Dickens are Gissing, Chesterton, Santayana, Eliot, Orwell, Leavis and Edmund Wilson.

XI. THE POLITICAL AND SOCIAL NOVEL: DISRAELI, CHARLES KINGSLEY, MRS GASKELL, GEORGE ELIOT

Of the men and women named above, the first three represent the social and political movements of a period, and the fourth supplements them by providing a background of scene and reflection. The "condition-of-England" question had become increasingly acute. Country, under the two-fold attack of Free Trade and industrial competition, was being beaten into bankruptcy, and Town, swollen by the success of factory production, was enlarging into a spawning mass of insanitary slums inhabited by discontented operatives. At the other extreme of the social scale, the great estates of titled and historic landlords were being bought up by the new commercial magnates, who had yet to learn that property means duty and not merely opportunity. In circumstances such as these was born "the condition-of-England" novel, the novel that is "historical" in the sense of responding to impulses derived from political and social conditions. Dickens, as we have seen, was deeply moved by the social evils of his day; but the essentially fantastic, non-realistic nature of his genius gave him success in characters rather than in causes. When he tried to embody causes in characters he often failed. The prophet of this period (roughly 1830–60) was Carlyle, who, politically Liberal as he was, denounced equally the soulless philosophy of Benthamite radicalism and the soulless arithmetic of commercial economics. Harriet Martineau tried to blend economics and fiction in her once celebrated *Illustrations of Political Economy* (1832–4) and *Illustrations of Taxation* (1834)— confessed hybrids of directly didactic purpose in narrative form. Her two novels, *Deerbrook* (1839) and *The Hour and the Man* (1841), are not economic in any sense. She is better remembered by her short tales for the young, collected under the title *The Playfellow* (1841). The popularity of *The Crofton Boys*, *The Settlers at Home* and *Feats on the Fiord* was long maintained.

The most remarkable attack on the new industrialism with its accompanying pauperization was made, not by any solemn revolutionary, but by the vivacious dandy who became Prime Minister—Benjamin Disraeli (1804–81), once called "the Younger" in recognition of his learned father, Isaac, author of the *Curiosities of Literature* and other agreeable works. Nothing that Disraeli ever did, said or wrote was devoid of self-consciousness; but we must beware of supposing, as many have supposed, that self-consciousness is another name for insincerity. Few people suspected the indomitable courage and inexorable tenacity of the insolent, over-dressed dandy who thought he could capture a dull House of Commons by witticisms. Disraeli's life is as great a romance as any to be found in his stories. In the history of English literature he is the one astonishing instance of an author who became Prime Minister of England and went to the House of Lords with a title taken from his first novel. He began, as Dickens began, with many disadvantages, not the least being that he was born a Jew, though baptized in childhood. He was never at a public school or university, till then the normal training ground of most English statesmen. The earliest education he received was that which, like Vivian Grey, he found for himself in his father's library. During much of his life he was burdened by debt; but he made "the grand tour" and found, like Napoleon, that the East is a career. Among the most remarkable passages in his novels are the pictures which reproduce the humours as well as the splendours of the Orient. In a brief consideration of Disraeli's literary achievement we must at once dismiss *The Revolutionary Epick* (1834, reissued 1864) and *Count Alarcos, a Tragedy* (1839). The former (far from unreadable) shows that he admired the sentiments of Byron and the allegories of Shelley; the latter shows nothing but what may be called "common form" in literary tragedy—opera without music. But we should not forget, in estimating the prose compositions of Disraeli, that he wrote and published ambitious verse, and that both Shelley and Byron contributed to the formation of his mind. His definite political writings are few and unimportant. *The Vindication of the English Constitution* (1835), which enunciated with extraordinary gusto his views on the three estates of the realm, was followed by *Letters of Runnymede*, which, after appearing in *The Times*, were published anonymously in 1836 with a brief congenial diatribe, *The Spirit of Whiggism*. Much more important is the life of his patron, *Lord George Bentinck: A Political Biography* (1852), in which principles rather than personal details take first place. The book is remarkable for a glowing chapter on the destiny of the Jewish race, which has nothing to do with the subject and which is sublimely excused in the opening of the next chapter.

Disraeli's earliest novel, *Vivian Grey* (1826), is a young man's book, wild and melodramatic; but it contains some good sketches of character and some brilliant sallies of wit. The story—left half-told—is not constructively political, though it moves easily among political intrigues. *The Young Duke* (1830) embodies some pungent political criticism, but deals almost exclusively with the world of fashion. *Contarini Fleming* (1832), "the psychological romance", is a Disraelian attempt at a *Wilhelm Meister*. *Alroy* (1833) and *The Rise of Iskander* (1835) are historical, or quasi-historical, romances of a more or less conventional type. *Henrietta Temple*, which rightly calls itself "a Love Story", and *Venetia* (both 1837), have nothing to do with political or social problems. The latter contains a very good portrait of Byron and a very bad portrait of Shelley.

So far, Disraeli's novels hardly entitle him to a place among "political and social writers" in the serious sense, in spite of their political flavour and their brilliant society scenes. He becomes a new person, however, with what is called his "Young England" trilogy, *Coningsby, or The New Generation* (1844), *Sybil, or The Two Nations* (1845) and *Tancred, or The New Crusade* (1847). Disraeli's solution of the "condition-of-England" problem resembles the homespun remedy of Cobbett made brilliant and aristocratic. It is a return to some imagined medievalism—always a handy and attractive proposal. England was to be saved neither by the old Toryism nor the new Radicalism, but by a new Toryism that accepted the new conditions but assimilated them to the old traditions. The Crown must govern, the Church must inspire, the Aristocracy must lead, the Commons must construct. The watchword must be, "the few for the many, not the many for the few". There must be no more political scheming of greedy landowners exploiting an impoverished peasantry. These views are set forth persuasively in brilliant character sketches, dazzling society functions and a glitter of epigrammatic fireworks. Given though he was to hyperbole and excess, there is, nevertheless, a fine quality in Disraeli's best work. The vividness, subtle humour and attractive lightness of his general prose style reached their height in *Coningsby* and *Sybil*; but the more earnest note in the writing of *Tancred* and *Lothair* deserves both attention and admiration. These books, with the much later *Endymion*, show his genius for depicting the conflict of great ideas. In general effect of characterization the novels of Disraeli may be called Winterhalter translated into literature. Everyone is beautified; but the colours are brilliant and remain fresh. Few writers have excelled Disraeli in depicting brilliantly attractive young men and women. But his "Young England" programme came to nothing; and the last two novels, *Lothair* (1870) and *Endymion* (1880), are full of politics, indeed, but have abandoned a constructive purpose. *Lothair* exhibits Disraeli's strong interest in religion, and *Endymion* depicts the rise and success of a great political adventurer, with Louis Napoleon as model.

Disraeli's brilliant pictures of contemporary life and manners have enduring interest, and his blend of social wit, politics, race, religion and romance is altogether his own. The mingling of western romance with "Asian mystery" lent itself to parody; but it could be parodied successfully because it succeeded. Disraeli's novels were regarded by some nineteenth-century critics as a joke. The joke has outlasted the critics. Disraeli has never ceased to find readers. No other novelist has approached him in ability to use politics as the matter or the background of novels. What he might have written had he not entered Parliament in 1837 and fought his way implacably through the warfare of politics till he became Prime Minister in 1868 is a matter for speculation. What remains of him in literature affords no evidence of a sense of frustration.

The life of Charles Kingsley (1819–75) was, in outward circumstances, as simple and modest as the career of Disraeli was world-embracing in its renown. Yet each dealt, after his own fashion, with the same social problems—the peasant, the operative, the landlord, the mill-owner, how they were to live in peace and grow towards a shared and beneficent prosperity. Kingsley was, in spirit as in fact, a country parson, an honest, limited, hasty, impulsive man, without the least personal ambition. He drew his first social inspiration from Carlyle; but in 1844 he met Frederick Denison Maurice, who soon became "the Master" to him and a band of fellow enthusiasts. His actual first publication was a drama in prose and verse, *The Saint's Tragedy*, which appeared in the year of the Chartist fiasco. Kingsley, Maurice and other devoted, chosen spirits took up the cause of the over-worked, under-nourished men, women and children, who in fetid homes and filthy factories wore away their short lives in the sacred cause of commercial prosperity. Kingsley's placard to the "Workmen of England" posted up two days after the Chartist fiasco, his papers signed "Parson Lot" in *Politics for the People*, his contributions to *The Christian Socialist*, *The Journal of Association* and *The People's Friend*, and his numerous tracts and pamphlets, of which the most famous was *Cheap Clothes and Nasty*, preached the doctrine that salvation must be sought, not in Acts of Parliament, but in personal striving for improvement. Socialist as he was willing to be called, Kingsley was the most pronounced advocate of individual judgment. Neither the teetotal movement nor the agitation for the rights of women could reckon him among its champions. He thought sanitary reform more important than either. The first of his novels to be planned was *Yeast, a Problem* (1851), though *Alton Locke* (1850) was published a year sooner. Both are well-intentioned pamphlets in the form of stories. *Yeast* began to appear in *Fraser's Magazine* in the fateful year of revolutions, 1848, but the proprietors took fright, induced Kingsley to cut it short and refused to publish its successor. *Yeast* is far less successful than *Alton Locke*, but neither is a really successful novel, and even as pamphlets they are vague, unvital and inconclusive. *Alton Locke, Tailor and Poet* can still be read for its social facts, but is never likely to attract most readers of fiction.

For a moment the crusader rested, and began in 1851 the publication, once more in *Fraser's Magazine*, of *Hypatia, or New Foes with an Old Face* (1853). *Hypatia* is not Kingsley's most popular novel, but it is his finest in conception and in construction. The scene is Alexandria at the period of the downfall of the Western Empire, and the novelist's purpose is to depict the antagonism between an aggressive church and a decrepit state, and the tragedy of a noble philosophical faith without regenerative power. One of the "new foes with an old face" is scepticism, an attitude of mind which Kingsley also treated in an essay under the title *Phaethon, or Loose Thoughts for Loose Thinkers* (1852), one of the freshest and brightest of his lesser productions. In *Hypatia* Kingsley is honestly fair to all parties; and the real tragedy he presents is the church's rejection of an alliance with grace and beauty and its acceptance of asceticism as the symbol of righteousness.

In 1855 was published the most successful of all his novels, *Westward Ho! or the Voyages and Adventures of Sir Amyas Leigh, Knight, of Burrough in the County of Devon, in the reign of Her Most Glorious Majesty Queen Elizabeth*. The book breathes the spirit of martial heroism and naval enterprise typified by the Elizabethan age and the county of Devon, and it is animated by an aggressive patriot-

ism, and a still more aggressive Protestantism. Kingsley seemed unable to think
of a Roman Catholic except as a kind of villain. This instinct led him into the
accusation of mendacity that produced Newman's *Apologia*. Newman was open
to serious charges, but not to that charge, and he might have been attacked in
several ways, but not in that way. Newman was a scrupulously exact writer;
Kingsley was the kind of bluff Christian who believed that anything beyond
plain Yes or No was an attempt to tamper with the truth. Of *Westward Ho!*,
now relegated to the juvenile department, it is hardly necessary to say anything.
Though not as notable a literary performance as *Hypatia*, it is an excellent tale
of its kind.

In *Two Years Ago* (1857) Kingsley once more returned to contemporary life,
and endeavoured to show that suffering calls out from man the great virtues of
faith, hope and self-sacrifice—the kind of spiritual giving which is the only way
of receiving. The story, in spite of its vivid Crimean and cholera episodes, does
not hold the attention. Kingsley's last completed novel, *Hereward the Wake*,
was not published till 1866. It is a work of much vigour and freshness, and hardly
inferior to *Westward Ho!* in the picturesque vividness of its setting; but it has
never been really popular, perhaps because the story is a "foregone conclusion",
and too remote for interest. Apart from his solitary tragedy Kingsley wrote a
fair quantity of verse, the most ambitious being *Andromeda*, a good piece of
story-telling in the hexameters already discussed (p. 610). Everybody knows
some of his shorter pieces such as *The Last Buccaneer* and *The Sands of Dee*. His
lectures as Regius Professor of Modern History at Cambridge hardly concern
the history of literature. A visit to the West Indies in 1869 gave him the inspiration of *At Last* (1871).

It is one of the numerous ironies of literary history that Kingsley, who strove
nobly for social righteousness, should survive as the author of a novel of religious
history, as the author of a story for schoolboys, but chiefly as the author of tales
for children. *The Heroes* (1856) and *The Water-Babies, a Fairy Tale for a Land-
Baby* (1863) have never lost their public and deserve their success. With Kingsley
should be mentioned his philanthropic associate Thomas Hughes (1822–96),
now remembered almost solely for *Tom Brown's School Days* (1857) and its
more purposive and less spontaneous successor, *Tom Brown at Oxford* (1861).

The third of our "social" novelists, Elizabeth Cleghorn Stevenson (1810–65),
a beautiful Chelsea girl who married William Gaskell, high-minded Unitarian
minister of Manchester, brought to her work neither Disraeli's exotic genius
nor Kingsley's crusading spirit, but a clear, shining creative soul that shed light
into some very dark places; and her pictures of the social horrors that made the
Thirties and Forties in England a perpetual shame endure because her first aim
was to tell a story and not to exploit grievances. Most of her girlhood was spent
with relatives at Knutsford in Cheshire, and most of her adult life in Manchester.
The first was to be scene of her best-loved book, the latter was to be the inspiration of her strongest. Mrs Gaskell's impulse to write came naturally from her
knowledge of the lives led by the Manchester factory-hands, and her first
model was Crabbe. *Mary Barton, a Tale of Manchester Life* (1848) is another
famous book published in the Chartist year, though it depicts the life of a period
ten years earlier. It is the first "labour" novel—the first novel that finds its

central conflict between those who, in hard times, are cut short in "things for show" and those who have to stint in "things for life". It is a powerful and disturbing book—so disturbing in its day that the political economists fell upon it and proved by science how wrong it all was. It has not ceased to be disturbing. Mrs Gaskell's remedy—the bringing about of a good understanding between masters and men—had only just begun to be applied in the period with which *Mary Barton* deals; but even to these beginnings she pays a tribute. The book, as might be expected from a first effort, was in places crude and melodramatic. Its story has been summed up as "seven deathbeds and a murder". It is both powerful and fair; and if it proved nothing economically, it proved that the writer was a born story-teller. The success of *Mary Barton* brought Mrs Gaskell into association with the great writers of her day, especially with Dickens, who showed her, as a writer in *Household Words* and *All the Year Round*, the highest consideration and regard. A remarkable tribute to the purity of her creative gift is that contact with Dickens never once tempted her into imitation. And indeed, after *The Moorland Cottage* (1850), a simple story, she produced from contributions to *Household Words* her most original, most popular, and most exquisite book, the prose idyll that we know as *Cranford* (1853). This intimate record of a few ordinary lives in a Cheshire village combines humour and pathos with an irresistible touch of delicate understanding and it has taken unquestioned rank as one of our minor prose classics.

Ruth (1853) suddenly returns to problems—this time moral, not social; and for its time it was courageously outspoken. More important is *North and South* (1855), which returns to the matter of *Mary Barton*, though the manner is not the same. Like its companion it is a moving and powerful story. From this strong effort of creation Mrs Gaskell turned aside to a kind of literature in which she was a novice, and wrote her *Life of Charlotte Brontë* (1857), a book which so completely fills its essential purpose that no later treatment of the theme will ever supersede it. With her natural honesty she had included domestic details which (the Brontë father being still alive) were resented; and, indeed, not all her information was well-founded. But in substance the book is as true as it is good, and its hostile reception checked for a time her desire to write. With *Sylvia's Lovers* (1863) she not only found herself again, but found a new setting for her genius in the wild Yorkshire coast which here serves as a background to a domestic drama of extraordinary power. In striking contrast is its successor, *Cousin Phillis* (1865), which tells exquisitely the story of a broken heart, without any circumstances of storm-swept tragedy. It is one of the loveliest books of its kind. Mrs Gaskell's last story, *Wives and Daughters* (1866), left on the very edge of completion when death took her in full enjoyment of her powers, is in many ways her best. Her humour, already shown in *Cranford*, had now mellowed into a delicious softness, and even in depicting the serious conflicts through which the souls of men and women have to pass she had learnt the value of "the subdued colouring—the half-tints of real life"—which George Eliot had desiderated in *Ruth*.

In Mrs Gaskell's hands the social novel developed into a form of fiction which she made entirely her own. She knew instinctively how to subdue controversial matter to the service of art; and the peculiarity of her contribution to the great "condition-of-England" discussion is this, that though her social novels do not present us with characters that we recall as readily as we recall the characters of *Cranford*, they do put vividly before us a figure that stands for a period, "the operative", which she was the first to use genuinely for artistic creative purposes in English fiction.

The fourth of our novelists is social in a different sense. If Mrs Gaskell gave us the first of the operatives, George Eliot gave us the last of the yeomen. Her tales call up before us the farms that Constable had painted and the countrymen that Morland had drawn. Mary Ann Evans (1819–81) spent her early years in a rural home on a great estate of which her father was agent. When quite young, she was compelled by circumstances to assume the charge of her father's house and acquired singular self-reliance and self-control. She never ceased to read and study, and her acquirements became both deep and extensive. Her sincerity of mind led her through many absorbing spiritual experiences, including a period of devotion to ascetic ideals, intensified by the example of an aunt, whose religious enthusiasm was to suggest later the character of Dinah Morris. The religious inquirer, unless overcome by fear, does not stand still; and when circumstances caused the Evans family to move near Coventry and Miss Evans herself to become acquainted with the unorthodox Charles Bray, author of *The Philosophy of Necessity* (1841), and his brother-in-law Charles Hennell, author of *An Inquiry concerning the Origin of Christianity* (1838), the sometime evangelical and ascetic began to move towards free thought in religion, and presently took over from the Hennells a translation of Strauss's *Life of Jesus critically examined* (1846), then the last word in unorthodoxy. From that time Miss Evans became a figure in "advanced" circles. Chapman, the publisher of Strauss, had acquired *The Westminster Review* from Mill, and Miss Evans became the actual, though not the acknowledged, editor. She lodged with the Chapmans, and met many of the figures in "advanced" thought, including Herbert Spencer, who introduced her to George Henry Lewes, a man of considerable gifts. Attracted by his extraordinary intellectual vivacity and quickness of sympathy, she made an unofficial "marriage" with him. His own home had for some time been broken up, and on his three sons she bestowed the fullest maternal affection. He showed to her unsurpassable devotion, and watched over her literary labours with unremitting care. This spiritual or intellectual marriage transformed Mary Ann Evans into George Eliot.

Besides translating Ludwig Feuerbach's *Essence of Christianity* (1854)—the only work of "Marian Evans" published under her name—she was heavily engaged wtih the *Review*. Lewes himself was working at his *Life of Goethe* (1855). One day he discovered a story which she had written during 1856 in the intervals of journalistic business—*The Sad Fortunes of the Rev. Amos Barton*. He insisted on its being brought to light; and it began to appear in *Blackwood* in January 1857, and was followed, in the course of the same year, by *Mr Gilfil's Love Story* and *Janet's Repentance*. All three bore the signature "George Eliot"— a name chosen almost at random. The completed work, *Scenes of Clerical Life*, appeared in 1858. Thackeray thought the author a man; but Dickens was sure of the woman. Both great novelists were warm in their admiration, as also were Bulwer Lytton, Anthony Trollope and Mrs Gaskell. In *Amos Barton* there is some abruptness in the sequence of incidents, and in *Janet's Repentance*, the most powerful of the tales, the construction is not sound; but in *Mr Gilfil's Love Story* there is scarcely a fault, and it remains one of the best English short stories. The whole book clearly showed that a new writer with true creative genius had arrived.

The appearance of *Adam Bede* in 1859 satisfied the high expectations aroused by the *Scenes*. It is a great story, and it succeeds by daring to be simple. The keynote of the story—the belief that the divine spirit which works in man works through man's own response to its call—dominates the narrative from first to last. In Adam's own words, "it isn't notions sets people doing the right thing— it's feeling". What no one could have expected from the prophetess of *The Westminster Review* was the large Shakespearean humour that accompanies the presentation of the tragedy. Mrs Poyser is part of the national mythology. The book bears upon it the character of its day, but in religious feeling rather than in social stirrings. It was an age still faintly lit by the afterglow of Methodism and hardly touched by the new fires of revived ecclesiasticism. With the creative spirit still strong in her, George Eliot at once began a new story. *The Mill on the Floss* (1860) may not be the greatest of its author's novels, but it was that into which she poured most abundantly the experiences of her own early life. Like its predecessor, *The Mill on the Floss* is rich in character and description, but it is more ample in scope and scale. *Silas Marner*, which followed in 1861, is smaller in scale than its predecessors, but it is smaller in no other respects. Silas, Eppie and the company at the Rainbow engage our interest as keenly as any of the characters in the larger works. The tenderness of fancy and humour and the strong simplicity of invention make *Silas Marner* a perfect story.

"I began *Romola* a young woman; I finished it an old woman." So said the author herself. It was published in 1863, only two years after *Silas Marner*; but into those two years George Eliot had put the intensity of many. Perhaps *Romola* might be more permanently endeared to us if the author had laboured less and had written with a larger creative freedom. The historical reconstruction of Medicean Florence is magnificently arranged; the tragedy of Savonarola is fitly narrated; the minor figures are sketched with divining insight. Only the central human tragedy fails to touch our deepest convictions. Tito is almost too bad; Romola is almost too good. Romola is both more than human and less than human, and she cannot take her place in our hearts with Maggie or Dorothea.

George Eliot's next novel, called *Felix Holt, the Radical* (1866), was based partly on the life of the Christian Socialist poet Gerald Massey and is the only political story she attempted. It is not one of her great successes, though it contains some admirable things such as the preliminary sketch of rural England into which the railways were first beginning to penetrate and much of the Transome story later on. With *Middlemarch, a Study of Provincial Life* (1871–2) George Eliot happily returned to her first and best manner—the relation of domestic tragedy and comedy set in the English scene. *Middlemarch* is a great piece of constructive art, in which the three main stories are far more successfully interwoven than the two stories in *Felix Holt* or in *Daniel Deronda*. In amplitude of scene, character and humour *Middlemarch* is as great as any novel in the language and it is difficult to disagree with John Buchan when he called it "the greatest novel of the Victorian age", a verdict supported on the whole by later critics like Virginia Woolf. *Daniel Deronda* (1876) was the last of George Eliot's novels and has never been widely popular. Although Henry James liked it, it disappointed her admirers at the time. In Daniel himself we are curiously reminded of Disraeli and his visions, and the "racial" ending is rather forced.

George Eliot attempted no more fiction. She felt that the labour of long creative work was beyond her, and the death of Lewes in 1878 removed her watchful adviser. The romance of her life continued to the very end, when in 1880 she married John Walter Cross, an old and devoted friend, who became the editor of *George Eliot's Life as related in her Letters and Journals* (1886), still the best biography. *The Impressions of Theophrastus Such*, not published till 1879, is a series of essays of a kind that failed to liberate her best qualities. George Eliot is often oppressive when she speaks in her own person; but she quickens miraculously into life when she speaks through her characters. The verse of George Eliot is not an important part of her work. *The Spanish Gypsy*, *The Legend of Jubal* and *Armgart* may interest enthusiasts, but will very improbably find general readers. Some of the shorter pieces are better known. But George Eliot is not in essence a poet. Her fame rests upon her novels; and her place in English fiction is secure. In command of pathos, humour and tragedy, she is excelled by no English writer of her time.

XII. THE BRONTËS

It is a matter for regret that the three Brontë sisters (as well as the brother and the father) have been "taken up" by enthusiasts of many kinds with theses to maintain, theories to propound, cases to prove and even personal interests to serve. The range of *Bronteana* includes details, not merely about the family, but about everybody who can be shown to have had any kind of association with any member of it. Most of this extraneous matter is totally devoid of literary value and should be ignored. The story of the Brontës in literature is so far peculiar that it must begin with the father (1777–1861), who came from Co. Down in Ireland with the unpromising name of Patrick Prunty or Brunty, which he happily changed to Brontë—perhaps with a glance at Nelson's Sicilian dukedom. A later Mr Shandy might amuse himself with speculating whether Charlotte Prunty would ever have achieved the fame of Charlotte Brontë or whether Emily Brunty could have written *Wuthering Heights*. By some means, the Irishman got himself into St John's College, Cambridge, in 1802, and, after holding minor clerical posts, became perpetual curate of Haworth, in a wild and lonely moorland district of Yorkshire, and there remained till his death. He had married in 1812 and by 1822 his wife was dead and he was left with six children, Maria, Elizabeth, Charlotte, Patrick Branwell, Emily Jane and Anne, of whom the eldest was eight and the youngest not yet two years of age. Natural disposition aggravated by poverty and misfortune had made him almost as gloomy and silent as the graves that neighboured the melancholy house. The children roamed the moors, and amused themselves with writing. They got some instruction from the father, and when they had grown beyond him the elder girls were sent to a cheap, subsidized boarding-school for the daughters of clergymen. Of this institution it is enough to say that it killed Maria and Elizabeth, that it nearly killed Charlotte, and that it served as the model for Lowood in *Jane Eyre*. When Charlotte was nearly fifteen she was again sent to a boarding-school. A little later, Charlotte returned as a kind of teacher, with Emily and Anne as pupils. Charlotte was unhappy in her work, and left it after a year or two. Emily also tried school-teaching and failed. Branwell was growing into a sinister consumer of the meagre family resources. The three girls, after trying the life of governesses in private families, thought they could do better in a school of their own. But some knowledge of foreign languages was indispensable, and in February 1842 the two elder sisters, aged, respectively, twenty-five and twenty-three, went as pupils to the Pensionnat Heger in Brussels. There Charlotte found herself attracted by Constantin Heger, a man of thirty-three, with considerable gifts and a powerful personality. The death of the aunt who kept house brought the girls back to Haworth. Emily took over the household duties, and Charlotte went back to Brussels in 1843 to teach English in the Heger establishment. But the arrangement failed. Heger had attracted her both as a man and as the expounder of life and literature, and in a year she was home again, very unhappy. To her beloved professor Charlotte then wrote the four letters first completely printed in 1913. They are, as we should expect, full of deep feeling honourably expressed. Heger was firmly silent, and she found relief in authorship.

In 1846, Charlotte (1816–55), Emily (1818–48) and Anne (1820–49) united in producing *Poems by Currer, Ellis and Acton Bell*. The volume was not success-ful. Charlotte then embodied some of her experiences in a novel, *The Professor*, which was rejected. But the effort was not wasted. It gave her practice. Though she was a born writer, she had to learn her technique, and especially the transcen-dental technique which converts a recital of facts into a creation with a life of its own. In *Jane Eyre* by "Currer Bell" (1847) Charlotte Brontë found herself. Naturally, she chose a story of unhappy experience and troubled love. One difficulty in the book is capable of explanation. How came the "good" Rochester to plan deliberate bigamy? It is possible that Charlotte had met a somewhat similar story by Le Fanu, published in a magazine in 1839, and had found in it the starting point of her own invention, which presently developed in its own different way; for the important fact is that, according to Jane's understanding, the bigamous intentions of Rochester were "honourable", even tragically honourable—he was not proposing a union of "shame", and Jane could respond with full outflow of feeling. Jane seemed to her time so much the modern woman that even Mrs Gaskell, herself a pioneer, was a little shocked by what may be called the positiveness of her love. *Jane Eyre* is a unique Victorian book because in it purity becomes passionate and outspoken. Gone is the "man's woman"; here is woman herself, confronting man on equal terms. In a sense, *Jane Eyre* is the first modern novel, the first to envelop the life of a plain, ordinary woman with romance. The voice of free insurgent woman, free to feel and to speak as she feels, first comes clearly into modern literature out of the remote Haworth parsonage.

The other sisters were writing, too; for in 1847 appeared *Wuthering Heights* by "Ellis Bell" with a bound-in "third volume" called *Agnes Grey* by "Acton Bell"—all novels of the period were expected to be in three volumes. *Wuthering Heights* was long a kind of battle ground for the contentions of those who declared that it is the equal of *King Lear* and those who declared that it is full of wasteful and ridiculous excess. The book is unique. There was nothing like it before, there has been nothing like it since, there will be nothing like it again; for the combination of high imagination with pure ignorance—in the fullest literal sense of the words—will not be found in any woman of a later generation. The wickedness of *Wuthering Heights* appals us because it is pure wickedness, free from any taint of the flesh. The passion is fierce and consuming, but it is not physical. Indeed, of all the books by the Brontë sisters we may say that, out of the innocence of the heart, the mouth speaketh. Into the question whether *Wuthering Heights* owed anything in any way to Branwell Brontë this is not the place to enter. The matter has small intrinsic importance, and attracts chiefly those whose interest in literature is unliterary. Anne's qualities have been underrated because she is less vehement than her sisters; but *Agnes Grey* is a moving personal record and *The Tenant of Wildfell Hall* shows clear signs of undeveloped strength and fine observation. But time and experience were denied her. Branwell drugged himself to extinction in 1848. Before that year closed Emily too was gone. Anne herself died in the next year. Charlotte was alone.

Shirley (1849) was begun in the first excitement of success; it was finished in utter bereavement. Unlike *Jane Eyre*, *Shirley* is not easy to read. Its beauty is of the rarer, more difficult kind. After visits to London, where she received much appreciation and encouragement, Charlotte found recuperation, and her temperament underwent some steeling. She then took up the theme she had essayed in *The Professor*. *Villette* (1853) is a remembrance of Brussels, but the story is told by an artist, not by a sufferer. To compare *Villette* with *The Professor*, published in 1857 after her death, is to see the difference between material transformed and material merely used. But material still counts for too much; and though *Villette* is brilliant and a work of genius, it does not entirely escape the defects of a personal record. It was the last of Charlotte's books. Two chapters of a novel called *Emma* were all that she left. She had married her father's curate, A. B. Nicholls in 1854, and in 1855 she was dead before she was thirty-nine, when happiness seemed at last to be coming. The old man at Haworth lived on in his implacable loneliness.

Of the poems by the three sisters only those of Emily have intrinsic importance. She has quiet strength and fine metrical music, though she, like the other two, failed to carry her inspiration throughout a whole poem, except in such short pieces as *The Old Stoic*, *Remembrance* and the so-called *Last Lines*. But her poems have what her one unique novel has, character, strong, gripping, inescapable. Whether the intenser poems are read as impersonally as we read the novel, or whether they are taken as intimations of some personal crisis undisclosed, they are clearly the outpourings of a rare and ardent spirit.

XIII. OTHER NOVELISTS

Edward George Earle Lytton Bulwer (1803–73), who took the additional name of Lytton on succeeding to the Knebworth estate and was created Baron Lytton of Knebworth in 1866, continued, in the midst of numerous social, editorial and political activities and disastrous matrimonial quarrels, to produce quantities of fiction, verse, drama and miscellaneous prose until his death. His versatility was extraordinary and he had a keen sense of what the public was going to want. His first novel, *Falkland*, appeared in 1827. His second, *Pelham, or The Adventures of a Gentleman* (1828), bears some resemblance to the contemporary *Vivian Grey* in its excesses and its more impudent qualities. Both are supreme examples of what might be called the dandiacal-Byronic style in fiction. In Lytton's next batch of novels we encounter the interesting criminal. *The Disowned* (1829) and *Lucretia* (1846) use as incidents the crimes of Fauntleroy and Wainewright; and *Paul Clifford* (1830) and *Eugene Aram* (1832) make heroes of the highwayman and the murderer. Lytton's next profitable venture was the historical novel—*The Last Days of Pompeii* (1834), *Rienzi* (1835), *The Last of the Barons* (1843) and *Harold* (1848). His skill in construction and invention is heavily handicapped, however, by the diction he chose to use as the appropriate vehicle of historical narrative. Of the humour and magnanimity of Scott he has no trace. After crime and history came the occult—*Zanoni* (1842), *A Strange Story* (1862), and the short tale *The Haunted and the Haunters* (1859) in which everything is satisfactory but the explanation. Another interesting group is formed by his pleasantly garrulous novels of quiet daily life— *The Caxtons* (1849), *My Novel* (1853) and *What will he do with it* (1858). In 1871 Lytton broke new ground with *The Coming Race*, an interesting forerunner of the now numerous descriptions of some future perfection of "planned" government and social order. Supremacy reposes upon that *desideratum* of all dictators, an intangible, irresistible force, here called "Vril". The book was published a year before Butler's satirical *Erewhon*—a curious coincidence, if it be a coincidence. Lytton concluded his long line of inventions with *Kenelm Chillingly* (1873) and *The Parisians* (1873), picturing the feverish political and social activities in England and the Paris of the Second Empire. Even in an age of voluminousness, Lytton was extraordinarily fertile. To his novels must be added a great mass of epic, satirical and translated verse, much essay-writing, pamphleteering and a number of successful plays, three of which are theatrical classics, *Richelieu* (1838), *The Lady of Lyons* (1838) and *Money* (1840). Had he concentrated his powers Lytton might have taken a more considerable place in the history of literature. But, like his son Edward Robert Bulwer, first Earl Lytton, who wrote extensive verse-novels under the name of Owen Meredith, he was ruined by a fatal facility of production. Yet, rhetorical and excessive as he may appear to later generations, he cannot be scoffed out of existence. His talent was various and his invention copious. Some parts of his work will always attract, and deserve to attract, some kinds of readers. More than that is not given to many.

Anthony Trollope (1815–82) is a "lesser" novelist only by comparison with the giants. After a wretched boyhood and youth, of which he gives some glimpses in his *Autobiography* and in *The Three Clerks* (1858), he entered upon a doubly prosperous career as a civil servant in the Post Office and as a man of letters. Of his sixty novels the best are to be found among the tales of "Barset", a county as genuinely a part of English literary geography as the more heavily-soiled Wessex of Hardy. Two Irish stories, *The Macdermots of Ballycloran* (1847) and *The Kellys and the O'Kellys* (1848), and *La Vendée* (1850), were out of accord with his natural aptitudes, which resembled those of Thackeray, on whom he wrote in the English Men of Letters series. The real Trollope begins with *The Warden* (1855), a "scene from clerical life", and develops in its successors, *Barchester Towers* (1857), *Dr Thorne* (1858), *Framley Parsonage* (1861), *The Small House at Allington* (1864) and *The Last Chronicles of Barset* (1867). In these we get a perfect picture of English provincial life, with the middle or upper middle classes as its main figures, the boundaries of the greater world being indicated by the Palace of the Bishop of Barchester and the Castle of the Duke of Omnium. Trollope is less successful than Disraeli in his political novels, of which *Phineas Finn* (1869) may be taken as the type. *Can You Forgive Her?* (1864) and *Orley Farm* (1868) are representative of his social, discursive and domestic manner. Trollope was a man of strong prejudices. He disliked the crusading spirit of Dickens (caricatured in *The Warden*); he disliked "intruders" into normal society (his hand is heavy on Obadiah Slope); and he disliked, in general, whatever did not accord with his Palmerstonian views of England. His foremost concern is with people; and the people in his books come to our notice in the natural fashion of acquaintanceship, hardening or mellowing with time. His popularity was checked for a time by his delightfully frank *Autobiography* (1883), which disappointed his admirers because it refused to strike affected poses, and spoke of literary work as something that could be done regularly by the clock at the rate of two-hundred-and-fifty words every fifteen minutes. Later generations have liked him the better for it. Trollope's writing is lucid, harmonious and completely successful in narrative and dialogue. He endures and is likely to endure, as a thoroughly representative English novelist and the social historian of a period. His books are numerous; and most of them are not only readable, but perpetually re-readable. He has worn better than most of his contemporaries.

Charles Reade (1814–84), playwright and novelist, was at all points the opposite of Trollope. He was no improviser of pleasant stories. He was always a fighter. He took up causes. He attacked abuses. He made almost every novel a document, fortified by authorities. He turned novels into plays and plays into novels—usually preferring the former course as he could then more easily pursue his imitators by legal process, for which he had a limitless appetite. His first novel *Peg Woffington* (1853) was made from his play *Masks and Faces* (1852). *Christie Johnston* (1853), his most idyllic story, delineates life in a Scottish fishing village, and appears to have no stage counterpart. Reade was deeply in sympathy with the impulse towards realism which was at work in fiction in the middle of the century, and in his methods anticipated Zola. His documentary novels are not all of one kind. There are, first, those in which he makes use of his knowledge, Defoe-like in its intimacy, of trades and occupations; such are *The*

Autobiography of a Thief (1858), *Jack of all Trades* (1858) and *A Hero and a Martyr* (1874). Secondly, there are stories of philanthropic purpose; in these Reade sweeps aside Godwin's theories and Lytton's sentiment, replacing them by fact irrefutably established and by fierce denunciation. The ghastly cranks and collars and jackets of *It is never too late to mend* (1856) were things he had seen in the gaols of Durham, Oxford, and Reading. He could cite precedent for every single horror of the asylum scenes in *Hard Cash* (1863); on all the other abuses which he attacked—"ship-knacking" in *Foul Play* (1869), "rattening" in *Put Yourself in his Place* (1870), insanitary village life in *A Woman Hater* (1877)—he wrote as an authority on scandals flagrant at the moment. Pitiless, insistent hammering at the social conscience is the method of these novels, which remind us at times of Victor Hugo, at times of Eugène Sue and at times of *Uncle Tom's Cabin*. Reade's habit of challenging attention by capitals, dashes, short emphatic paragraphs, and so forth, accentuates the general impression of urgency and anticipates the devices of modern journalism. But his novels, however documentary, are masterly as narratives, and contain scenes of "actuality"—fire, flood and shipwreck—that are as thrilling in print as they would be on the stage. The greatest triumph of his documentary method is the historical novel, *The Cloister and the Hearth* (1861), enlarged from the first version tamely entitled *A Good Fight*, which, as it does not contain Denys, omits one of his greatest creations. The remoteness of the scene helps to mitigate Reade's indignant crusading, but even here he is "out" against one abuse, the celibacy of the clergy, to which he recurred in *Griffith Gaunt* (1866).

Some novelists are remarkable for their use of a formula or pattern which enables them to give consistency and continuity to their work. Thus, Mary Russell Mitford (1787–1855) may be said to have created a literature of place in *Our Village*, published in five volumes between 1824 and 1832. The scene was Three Mile Cross, where she supported her reprobate father for the last twenty years of his life; the village is near Reading, the country town of her *Belford Regis* (1835). Her inmost desire was to write ambitious tragedies in verse such as her *Rienzi* (1828); happily, the art of Jane Austen taught her to work upon a miniature scale. She brushes lightly over her small world; places, people, especially children, seasons, sports, and atmosphere are touched into bright and graceful animation. Her one regular novel, *Atherton* (1854), is of small account.

Margaret Oliphant (1828–97), excellent and overdriven author of innumerable books, wrote several of her novels as *Chronicles of Carlingford*—*Salem Chapel* (1863), *The Rector and the Doctor's Family* (1863), *The Perpetual Curate* (1864) and *Miss Marjoribanks* (1866)—the best of which, *Salem Chapel*, is an excellent study of life in the atmosphere of a dissenting chapel. Another region which Mrs Oliphant's art explored was the unseen world. *A Beleaguered City* (1880) and *A Little Pilgrim in the Unseen* (1882) are most successful adventures in a kind of writing that appears to solicit failure. Setting and place serve Mrs Oliphant well, again, in the stories of her native land, which follow in the established tradition of Susan Ferrier, Galt and Moir. Her Scottish tales, from *Margaret Maitland* (1849) to *Kirsteen* (1890), are excellent. To the mere volume and miscellaneous nature of her work, undertaken in a heroic effort to provide for a family fated to disaster, must be set down Mrs Oliphant's failure to win a place nearer to George Eliot and Mrs Gaskell.

George Macdonald (1824–1905), poet, mystic and novelist, had many gifts, but never quite attained to success. *David Elginbrod* (1863) and *Robert Falconer* (1868) portray the folk of the Moray country with sureness and sympathy. His powers are best revealed in his various fairy tales, in which he shows a fertile invention and a deft poetical handling of the inverted causes and sequences and proportions of that world; and so he seems most likely to survive as a writer for children.

The whole century, from Maria Edgeworth onwards, was remarkable for the number of writers who, in books and magazines, contributed to the entertainment of children. Some have already been mentioned; a few others must be honourably, if briefly, named. Mrs Margaret Gatty (1809–73) edited *Aunt Judy's Magazine* from 1866 to her death and published *Aunt Judy's Tales* (1859) and *Aunt Judy's Letters* (1862). But her principal work is the delightful *Parables from Nature* in five series (1855–71). Her daughter, Mrs Juliana Horatia Ewing (1841–85), produced many slim volumes that the young of her time thought both good to read and good to look at, for among her numerous illustrators were George Cruikshank and Randolph Caldecott. She had a wide range and knew how to capture the affections of any normal children from "six to sixteen". Typical examples of her work, other than that for the very young, are *Mrs Overtheway's Remembrances* (1866), *A Flat Iron for a Farthing* (1870), *The Brownies* (1871), *Six to Sixteen* (1872), *Jan of the Windmill* (1872), *Lob Lie-by-the-fire* (1873), *Jackanapes* (1879) and *Daddy Darwin's Dovecot* (1881). Mrs Maria Louisa Molesworth (1839–1921) is remembered for *Tell Me a Story* (1875), *Carrots* (1876), *The Cuckoo Clock* (1877) and *The Adventures of Herr Baby* (1881) —all books with real charm. But the classics, both among books for children and among books of nonsense, are *Alice's Adventures in Wonderland* (1865) and *Through the Looking-Glass* (1871), to the completeness of which the illustrations by Sir John Tenniel contributed so much that the stories hardly seem the same with other pictures even by eminent hands. The author, "Lewis Carroll", i.e., Charles Lutwidge Dodgson (1832–98), has already been mentioned for his verse. *Sylvie and Bruno* (1889) and *Sylvie and Bruno Concluded* (1893) are much less successful and have never been loved like the *Alice* books. Lewis Carroll's academic skits are the prey of collectors and his text books are now forgotten. The *Alice* books and *The Hunting of the Snark* are the result of pure inspiration working as inexplicably as unexpectedly in a shy and spinsterish mathematical tutor. A later writer who scored many successes in books for and about children is E. Nesbit, Mrs Hubert Bland. From her numerous volumes we select for mention *The Story of the Treasure Seekers* (1899), *The Wouldbegoods* (1901), *The New Treasure Seekers* (1904) and *The Railway Children* (1906). In her Bastable children E. Nesbit shows real understanding of juvenile minds. Several beloved magazines, from *Chatterbox* to *The Monthly Packet* with *The Boy's Own Paper* (1879–1967) coming happily between, competed on the Victorian juvenile shelf (and on the shelves of several generations of children afterwards) with the splendid tales of adventure written by R. M. Ballantyne (see p. 747), W. H. G. Kingston, G. A. Henty and the Irish-American novelist Mayne Reid, with

Anna Sewell's *Black Beauty* and with the post-Hughes type of school story begun by Talbot Baines Reed (who reacted against *Tom Brown* and Dean Farrar's *Eric*) and continued into the early twentieth century by Warren Bell, Gunby Hadath and P. G. Wodehouse. While the twentieth cannot match the nineteenth in the field of juvenile literature, a century which has produced, for different ages, Beatrix Potter, Kenneth Grahame, A. A. Milne and Frank Richards is not to be despised. There were other writers whose work, not written for the young, nevertheless attracted them. Some of these will be mentioned later. We now return to the general account of Victorian novelists.

William Black (1841–98), a long-popular writer, who brought the Highlands home to the circulating libraries of the south, was most successful in depicting the clash between the Scottish character and alien temperaments. This is the main theme of such books as *A Daughter of Heth* (1871) and *A Princess of Thule* (1874). Place and history both lend glamour to the *Lorna Doone* (1869) of Richard Doddridge Blackmore (1825–1900), whose other stories, such as *Springhaven* (1887) and *Perlycross* (1894) hardly deserve the oblivion that seems to have enveloped them. History, political and spiritual, is the theme of *John Inglesant* (1880), the only important book of Joseph Henry Shorthouse (1834–1903), which tells of the Civil War in England and of the uprising and suppression of the Molinists in Rome. The spiritual progress of the hero is described with deep sympathy.

Current moral, religious and domestic ideals, reflected in books such as Charlotte Yonge's *The Heir of Redclyffe* (1853), Mrs Craik's *John Halifax, Gentleman* (1857) and Thomas Hughes's *Tom Brown's School Days* (1857) illustrate the diversity of the exhortations to which the mid-Victorian era submitted; but there were mockers as well as enthusiasts. The standard of rebellion was raised chiefly by two writers, George Alfred Lawrence (1827–76) and "Ouida", Louise de la Ramée (1839–1908). *Guy Livingstone* (1857), Lawrence's most characteristic book, is laughable in its florid satanism. The historical innovation which Lawrence effects is the endowment of the super-humanly immoral person with heroic qualities and social aplomb. Muscular blackguardism here replaces muscular Christianity. Ouida gained success in more than one region of invention. Her high society world of splendid male animals (Guardsmen), heroic in sport and war, and affecting languor and boredom in the thick of conflict, proved singularly attractive to readers. The *vivandière* Cigarette, in *Under Two Flags* (1867), comes near to poetry in her last ride and death, as does the deserted Italian child Musa of *In Maremma* (1882) in her innocence, devotion and suffering. Though her flamboyant style is now a "period piece", Ouida's outspokenness, rebellious instinct and cosmopolitanism played some part in widening the scope of the novel.

This larger range of the novel now began to include the novel of crime, in which the interest lay not in retribution but in detection. The publication in France of Vidocq's *Mémoires* in 1828–9 (Poe's three detective stories are much later) stimulated the production of such inventions. An early example in England is *Paul Ferrol* (1855) by Mrs Archer Clive. But the chief master of this art in England is William Wilkie Collins (1824–89), the contemporary of Émile Gaboriau in France. In Wilkie Collins the unravelling of the skein of crime is the work, not of the hand of the law, but of some person with a compelling interest in the elucidation. Sometimes there is no crime, but only a mystery. The same skill is lavished on both; and Wilkie Collins has never been excelled as a contriver of complicated plots. His first outstanding success, *The Dead Secret* (1857), was followed by the unsurpassed "thriller", *The Woman in White* (1860). Other successes are *No Name* (1862), *Armadale* (1866), *The Moonstone* (1868) and *The Law and the Lady* (1875). Wilkie Collins has the power of generating an atmosphere of foreboding, and of imparting to natural scenes a desolation which suggests depression and horror of spirit. The beginnings of his books are sometimes so tremendous that the conclusion fails to maintain the level. This is true, for instance, of *Armadale*. The main defect of the Wilkie Collins method is an abuse of machinery—not indeed of the machinery of detection, but of the machinery of narration. We get diaries, papers, memoirs, confessions, and so forth, which, designed to give verisimilitude, end in giving tedium.

Of the stream of novels poured out during the latter half of the century to satisfy the demands of a growing multitude of readers no description can be given here. We may usefully notice, however, a few of the lesser novelists, who, beginning in the nineteenth century, worked on into the twentieth, and, for some special qualities, have left memories that still linger.

Mary Elizabeth Braddon (1837–1915) became the mother of the twentieth-century novelist, W. B. Maxwell. She had already written poems and stories when popular success came with the thrilling *Lady Audley's Secret* (1862), the perfect circulating library novel of its time. Miss Braddon is historically interesting as a manufacturing novelist called into existence to supply the demand of a vast public for thrills combined with a kind of commonplace romance. It is perhaps worth notice that her first successful book was almost exactly contemporary with the immensely popular *East Lynne* (1861) by the older writer Mrs Henry Wood (1814–87) and with Rhoda Broughton's *Cometh up as a Flower* (1867).

A brief and unusual career in fiction was that of William Frend De Morgan (1839–1917) who, at the end of a busy artistic life, produced in his sixty-seventh year his first novel *Joseph Vance* (1906). This was followed by *Alice-for-Short* (1907), *Somehow Good* (1908), *It never can happen again* (1909) and others of steadily decreasing interest. De Morgan had some creative power in the plastic arts and seems to have undergone a curious diversion of his activity towards fiction. His originating power was not great. He went back to old memories and poured out into his ill-organized, easy-going stories all that had grown in his mind after a distant absorption of Dickens, Thackeray and Trollope. He is a strangely belated Victorian of the old type. His contemporary Richard Whiteing (1840–1928) was another example of late flowering. After a notable career in journalism he produced in 1888 *The Island*, an ironic social fantasia of great merit but small popularity, and eleven years later a kind of realistic sequel, *Number 5 John Street* (1899), which became a popular success. It is an arresting picture of social insurgence at the time of the Queen's Diamond Jubilee. Both books have interest as criticism of accepted values in life. A line of notice should be given to James Payn (1830–98), an industrious and pleasing writer who scored at least a century of novels, the most famous being *Lost Sir Massingberd*

(1864) and to the prolific W. E. Norris (1847–1925) whose numerous well-devised novels maintained the tradition of Trollope. Walter Besant (1836–1901) alone or in collaboration with James Rice produced many novels of which the best is *All Sorts and Conditions of Men* (1882). Besant helped to found the Society of Authors in 1884 and was its first chairman.

Romance in the cruder sense was provided by Stanley Weyman (1855–1928) who in *A Gentleman of France* (1893) and *Under the Red Robe* (1894) neatly reduced the matter of Dumas to the dimensions of circulating-library readers. The numerous novelistic melodramas of Hall Caine must rest unnamed.

Romance of another kind came from Arthur Conan Doyle (1859–1930), a doctor who became a prolific writer of fiction and ended as an exponent of spiritualism. *The White Company* (1891), *Micah Clarke* (1889), *The Refugees* (1893) and *Rodney Stone* (1896) still appeal to a juvenile auditory; but Doyle's great feat was to add the fascinating detective Sherlock Holmes and his ingenuous interlocutor Dr Watson to the mythology of the western world. Baker Street still keeps the glamour their residence shed upon it. Holmes first appeared in *A Study in Scarlet* (1888); but this was a mere preliminary sketch for the better Holmes of *The Sign of Four* (1889) and a long series of short stories collected as *Adventures* (1891) and *Memoirs* (1893) of the hero, with another long story, *The Hound of the Baskervilles* (1902) following later. Thereafter Doyle, unmindful of an author's duty to his creations, did his best to write Holmes out of existence by putting him into some very feeble and exhausted stories; but the successful Holmes continues to live and the failures are forgotten. No useful purpose is served by trying to derive Conan Doyle from earlier writers of detective fiction. The qualities that endear Sherlock Holmes and Dr Watson to a wide world of admirers were his own invention. Simplification, not complication, is the life of a detective story; and Doyle, like Poe, found the short story the best medium for his work. The *differentia* of Doyle's work is that he made the detective not merely an agent in romance, but its hero.

Still another purveyor of romance was "Anthony Hope" Hawkins (1863–1933), inventor of Ruritania, a kingdom lying remotely on the skirts of the former Germany and Austria as they look eastwards. Here are enacted the adventures described in *The Prisoner of Zenda* (1894) and its sequel *Rupert of Hentzau* (1898). His contemporary, Israel Zangwill (1864–1926), found romance of a different kind in the life of East-End Jews. *The Children of the Ghetto* (1892) is typical of his work, which, within its small range, showed humour and insight.

A "regional" novelist of another sort is Eden Phillpotts (1862–1960) whose literary home (though not native to him) is Devonshire. *The Children of the Mist* (1898), *The Human Boy* (1899) and *The Secret Woman* (1905), with some lighter plays, especially *The Farmer's Wife* (1916), show humour or strength and should be taken as representative of an enormous productiveness. Adjacent to Devonshire is the "Delectable Duchy" of Cornwall, annexed as his demesne by "Q" (A. T. Quiller-Couch), who began with a thrilling invention, *Dead Man's Rock* (1887), attracted the juveniles with *The Splendid Spur* (1889) and exploited the humours and tragedies of "Troy" (Fowey) in *The Astonishing History of Troy Town* (1888), *The Mayor of Troy* (1905) and other stories. A large variety of tales showed the gifts of a born story-teller and the touch of a true man of letters.

A romantic writer of the more traditional kind was Maurice Hewlett (1861–1923), who sought sedulously for the beauty which had strangeness and delivered it with elaborately antique diction. He had already written the Pateresque *Earthwork out of Tuscany* (1895) when he attained celebrity with *The Forest Lovers* (1898), which carried neo-medievalism almost to the verge of caricature. *Richard Yea-and-Nay* (1900) had more substance but as much ornament. Hewlett's artistic sincerity was beyond question; but it took the unhappy form of a conviction that literature must be always literary. He seemed to be a victim of the prevalent end-of-the-century fever for the verbal gesticulations then called "style"—the elaborate avoidance of the simple, of which Meredith was the great exemplar and Stevenson the avowed prophet.

One exceptional person, entirely outside the main stream of romance, is William Hale White (1829–1913), who as "Mark Rutherford" delineated a noteworthy phase of English life, the deep disturbance of provincial Dissent by the theological growth of the more sincere ministers beyond the understanding of their congregations. The perplexity and misery of the pastors are revealed with insight and sympathy in *The Autobiography of Mark Rutherford* (1881), *Mark Rutherford's Deliverance* (1885), *The Revolution in Tanner's Lane* (1887), and *Catherine Furze* (1894). Emotional sincerity, descriptive power and critical restraint distinguish the work of this singular writer, whose work, never popular, will continue to attract those whose feelings about ultimate things lie deep.

The end of the nineteenth century witnessed a remarkable outburst of novel writing by women. For this there were two obvious reasons: the generation of women that had profited by higher education had been reached and the "position-of-women" question had been newly and searchingly raised. Mary Wollstonecraft's *Vindication*, a century old, was now ancient history. *Jane Eyre* (1847) was hardly recognized as a declaration of emotional independence for women; Mill's *Subjection of Women* (1869) was indeed recent enough to be still in the minds of advanced political thinkers; but the active liberator of the moment was Ibsen, whose "new" women, Lona, Nora, Ellida and Rebecca, had set new standards of freedom. Women had long been knocking at the door of professions hitherto closed to them as the preserves of men; now the whole social relation of woman to man became the subject of scrutiny; and so novels were not merely written by women, they were written about women. A world that is accustomed to the free competition of women with men in the professions, the arts, the sports and the other activities in which free competition is possible, must beware of supposing that this freedom is of long duration. Till the end of the nineteenth century woman was still, by a convention accepted by the majority of women themselves, the weaker vessel needing the strength of protective man. Ignorance, material, economic, political and biological, was forced upon woman as part of her womanly charm; but it was not called ignorance: it was called innocence. The most implacable opponents of the courageous women who forced their way into the medical profession were the other women. A woman who became a doctor had publicly forsaken her womanliness. She was not "nice". She had repudiated the professional innocence that was the chief asset of a marketable bride. It is not surprising, then, that most of the novels written by women at this time sounded a note of revolt.

The most impressive woman writer of the time, Mary Augusta Arnold (1851–1920), afterwards Mrs Humphry Ward, stood aloof from the conflict, which she regarded wth disapproval. Her considerable intellectual gifts and her capacity for serious thought did not prevent her from being thoroughly conservative in her view of women. All her novels are stories of conflict; but she never sets any of her heroines to fight for the independence of women. She was already a practised writer when *Robert Elsmere* (1888) attained notoriety for its discussion of religious doubts. Actually there is nothing sensational in it. It marks almost the last point at which incertitude about the Christian miracles could provide material for a tragic conflict. All her stories are really "about" something: they propound problems and attempt a serious "criticism of life" —a phrase here specially appropriate, for its inventor, Matthew Arnold, was Mrs Humphry Ward's uncle. But of her famous kinsman's humour, grace, and celerity of mind she had no trace. Her books, all solidly earnest, relieved their readers from any reproach of wasting their time on trifles. They are well-constructed and seriously written. They have, indeed, some of the highest virtues of fiction; but the highest of all virtues, readability, they have not. Because Mrs Humphry Ward was a learned woman and a novelist she has been mentioned with George Eliot. The association of the two names is completely uncritical. George Eliot, even in her least inspired efforts, belongs to a world of creative energy in which Mrs Humphry Ward had no part.

The women writers concerned with the "position-of-women" question were far below the level of Mrs Humphry Ward in every respect. "Sarah Grand" (Mrs M'Fall) wrote the book of her day in *The Heavenly Twins* (1893), but had already attacked the "sex-question" in *Ideala* (1888) and returned to it in *The Beth Book* (1897). Sour and inharmonious sex-relation is the main theme of the stories in *Discords* by the writer who called herself "George Egerton". The contemporary *A Yellow Aster* (1894) by "Iota" (Mrs Caffyn) deals with differences about the bringing up of children. A much more uncompromising feminist was Elizabeth Robins (at first disguised as "C. E. Raimond") who showed in *The Magnetic North* (1904) that she had some power as an original novelist telling a strong tale of hardship and endurance. But *The Convert* (1907) was a novelistic tract presenting a case for women's suffrage and "*Where are you going to...?*" (1912) an unabashed and undisguised pamphlet in which "white slavery" was exploited to influence legislation against sexual offences. *The Woman who Did* (1895), a story of a woman who believed conscientiously that the fact of marriage was possible without the tie of wedlock, was written by a man, Grant Allen (p. 744 below), but it could easily have passed as the work of a woman. All the books named above were indications of that insurgence of women which was to develop later into the open violence of the suffragist agitation.

Other women writers were not definitely pamphleteers. Mrs Harrison, who called herself "Lucas Malet" and inherited a talent for story-telling from her father, Charles Kingsley, first gained popular success with *The Wages of Sin* (1891), which might have been written by a man, and then strayed into the abnormal with *The History of Sir Richard Calmady* (1901). Fame of a different kind attended the brilliant, unhappy woman who called herself "John Oliver Hobbes" (1867–1906)—in life Mrs Reginald Craigie. *Some Emotions and a Moral* (1891) and *A Sinner's Comedy* (1892) were slight productions admired for their audacity of theme and their vivacity of utterance. More serious were *The School for Saints* (1897) and its sequel *Robert Orange* (1902), which introduced Disraeli among the characters. In these, religious disturbance is the main pre-occupation, and they reflect the spiritual or emotional conflict which led the author herself into the Roman Church. Wit was the main attraction of *Concerning Isabel Carnaby* (1898) by Ellen Thorneycroft Fowler, and sentimental pathos drew crowds of readers for *Ships that pass in the Night* (1893) by Beatrice Harraden. Both were ambitious writers with "ideas"; but their other works did not succeed in any sense. Of "Marie Corelli" (Mary Mackay) no more need be said than that the pretentious treatment of lofty themes by the illiterate for the illiterate was in itself a sidelight on the period, and, so far, worthy of mention. The quality of this egregious and once enormously popular writer can be tested by the curious in a single specimen of her work, *The Sorrows of Satan* (1895).

Rather later in time come two writers of much higher level, M. P. Willcocks, author of *The Wingless Victory* (1907) and *A Man of Genius* (1908) and May Sinclair, author of *The Divine Fire* (1904) and *The Combined Maze* (1913), the latter a moving exposition of the harsh pressure of the divorce laws upon the honest life of a poor London clerk. Both these women had considerable intellectual powers, which they used, though not always artistically, in their stories.

The writers here selected arbitrarily for notice exhibit tendencies rather than specific achievement, and indicate the general spirit of an age. The end of the nineteenth century was the period of the "new woman", and the faded fiction of those years does not lack a touch of heroism. It is an ignorant view that sees in the War of 1914–18 the liberation of fiction from the restraints and conventionalities of Victorianism. That liberation can be dated as far back as *Jane Eyre* and as far forward as *The Story of an African Farm* (p. 762 below) and the free thought that its influence stimulated. While most of the men writers (with the great exception of Hardy) were pursuing romance for its own sake, the women were making romance a vehicle for realism. Absurd and antiquated as some of them now appear, they deserve the honour due to pioneers. They blazed the trail that their successors followed with ease and they prepared the minds of a large public for the novel of ideas.

XIV. GEORGE MEREDITH, SAMUEL BUTLER, THOMAS HARDY, GEORGE GISSING

The writers named above, though completely Victorian in birth and upbringing, represent a rejection of the normal Victorian values in faith and life. George Meredith (1828–1909) was partly Welsh by birth and was educated at the Moravian school at Neuwied. He was never quite the complete Englishman. His grandfather was a successful tailor (the "great Mel" of *Evan Harrington*), a fact about which he seemed unduly sensitive. Meredith, at first articled to a solicitor, drifted towards literature, and made a literary union by marrying a widowed daughter of Peacock. The marriage was not successful; and the early association with Peacock influenced Meredith in ways curiously unfavourable to his development. What in Peacock was naturally fantastic became in Meredith elaborately fantasticated; and Peacock's native economy of style became in Meredith an artificially oracular allusiveness. Meredith's first volume, *Poems* (1851), containing pieces of high promise and actual merit, gained very little recognition. His first prose works, *The Shaving of Shagpat* (1856) and *Farina* (1857), are remarkable as showing his extraordinary power of fantastic invention and his equally extraordinary power of concealing his thought in verbal flourishes. A loose grouping of the subsequent novels can be usefully given at once. *The Ordeal of Richard Feverel* (1859), *Evan Harrington* (1861), *Emilia in England* (1864)—the title was changed to *Sandra Belloni* in 1887—and *The Adventures of Harry Richmond* (1871), all deal with the upbringing of well-born youth to the state of "capable manhood". *Rhoda Fleming* (1865) differs from them in giving prominence to figures of the yeoman class, who, in the earlier novels, are subsidiary. In *Vittoria* (1867)—the sequel to *Emilia*—*Beauchamp's Career* (1875) and, to a less degree, in *The Tragic Comedians* (1880) the novelist takes a wider sweep of vision over the world of politics in England and Germany and of high national aspiration in Italy. The short stories, or, rather, the short novels, *The House on the Beach* (1877), *The Case of General Ople and Lady Camper* (1877) and *The Tale of Chloe* (1879) are not important. *The Egoist* (1879) stands apart, not only from contemporary novels, but from Meredith's own fiction, in its originality of attitude and technique, the clues to which are disclosed in the essay *On the Idea of Comedy and the Uses of the Comic Spirit* (1877). The four novels *Diana of the Crossways* (1885), *One of our Conquerors* (1891), *Lord Ormont and his Aminta* (1894) and *The Amazing Marriage* (1895) have in common a chivalrous advocacy of women compromised in honour and in pride by male despotism. The early-written and unfinished *Celt and Saxon*, published in 1910, has resemblances to *Diana of the Crossways*, especially in its criticism of the English temperament. Throughout his career, from the publication of his first poem, *Chillianwallah*, in *Chambers's Journal* (1849), Meredith continued the writing of verse without winning any but the smallest body of admirers. In 1862 appeared *Modern Love*, the poet's tragic masterpiece; it is a series of fifty "sonnets" each containing four quatrains. The volumes called *Poems and Lyrics of the Joy of Earth* (1883), *A Reading of Earth* (1888) and *A Reading of Life* (1901), in which Meredith sets forth his cult of "earth", stand high in the tradition of Victorian metaphysical poetry. *Ballads and Poems of Tragic Life* (1887), *The Empty Purse* (1892), *Odes in Contribution to the Song of French History* (1898) and the *Last Poems* of 1909 all contain work elaborately thought and elaborately wrought, but encumbered with difficulties not inherent in their substance.

Meredith began to write at a time when Dickens, Thackerary, Browning and Tennyson were at the height of their powers and when George Eliot was hardly known; but he cannot be affiliated to any of his contemporaries or predecessors. He is in every sense an eccentric. The society he depicts is almost feudal in its caste feeling; the attitude to the wonderfully attractive women depicted is almost medieval. Only occasionally, when historical events are involved, is it possible to infer a date or period in the action of his novels. The process of intellectualization in art, which at times injured the work of Browning, is in Meredith so fully developed as to become a mere vanity of display. And this deliberate and mocking remoteness is intensified by his ruthless reinterpretation of the moral idea. He was a Pagan, deriving all things from the earth. Blood, brain and spirit are the names given to the successive stages in the process of life. Spiritual valiancy, tried in passionate ordeals of love, friendship and patriotism—that is the final goal; the "warriors of the sighting brain" are the ideal type. These are the ideas expressed in some of Meredith's richest poems, and implicit in his representation of human relations and conflicts. But familiarity with the prose and verse of Meredith can be attained only at a cost which few readers are willing to pay. He is oracular, allusive, aphoristic, figurative, fantastic. Though he could write an exquisite poem like *Love in the Valley*, though he could write a lovely prose idyll like the meeting of Richard Feverel and Lucy, though he could tell a thrilling story like the revolutionary singing of Vittoria at La Scala, he chose generally to deter his readers by wilful and injurious excess of verbal tricks and manners. One is oddly conscious of a sense of inferiority concealing itself in display. The moving tragedy of such stories as *An Amazing Marriage* and *One of our Conquerors* is impaired by the incessant gesticulations of the author. The poems, strong, original, intrepid, suffer from the intense compression of their utterance. Meredith was a great metrical experimenter. He has devised some wonderful stanza forms and has brought some difficult lines to success. It is curious that the tune of certain poems will linger in the ear when the words that hold it have vanished. Even to the sonnet he gave a strong individual note. In all his work Meredith remained fanatically true to his own ideals of matter and expression. Disdaining popular approval, he sought to give the world nothing but his best, and was content to be a drudge for years in order to be free from the demands of the market for fashionable goods. His artistic sincerity, integrity and courage are as unimpeachable as they are inspiring. *George Meredith* (1956) by the Australian novelist-critic Jack Lindsay is perhaps the best modern study of his work.

Samuel Butler (1835–1902) was the grandson of a celebrated namesake who was headmaster of Shrewsbury and Bishop of Lichfield and the subject of an over-lengthy biography by Butler himself. His father, too, was a clergyman, and Butler was intended for the church. At Cambridge he did well in classics and pursued his interest in music. In 1859, abandoning his intention of taking orders, he went to New Zealand and successfully managed a sheep-run. Returning to England in 1864, he settled for the remainder of his life in Clifford's Inn. He dabbled in painting and was occasionally "hung" at the Royal Academy exhibitions. *Erewhon*, based on earlier articles, was published in 1872. Its immediate successor, *The Fair Haven* (1873), provides an ironical setting for the matter of his pamphlet, *The Evidence for the Resurrection of Jesus Christ*, written in 1865. He had begun, about 1872, *The Way of all Flesh*; but it was laid aside, worked over for several years, and posthumously published in 1903. His books of scientific controversy include *Life and Habit* (1877), *Evolution Old and New* (1879), *Unconscious Memory* (1880), *Luck or Cunning* (1887), and *The Deadlock in Darwinism* (1890). Several Italian holidays led to the publication of *Alps and Sanctuaries of Piedmont and the Canton Ticino* (1881). It is characteristic of Butler as a critic that he loved Handel fanatically and belittled all other composers. An intention to compose a Handelian piece on the subject of Ulysses led him to read Homer carefully, and the result was a conviction that the *Odyssey* was written by a woman, and that the ten years' voyage of Ulysses was nothing but a circumnavigation of Sicily. These views he expressed in a delightful volume, *The Authoress of the Odyssey* (1897). He also made prose translations, in a vigorous homely idiom, of the *Iliad* (1898) and of the *Odyssey* (1900). In 1899 appeared *Shakespeare's Sonnets, reconsidered and in part re-arranged,* combating the view that the poems were academic exercises, and contending that "Mr W. H." was a plebeian of low character. Butler's critical works exhibit the kind of originality that rejoices in differing from everybody else; but fortunately it is not necessary to agree with Butler in order to enjoy him. A selection from his manuscript collections appeared in 1912 under the title *The Note-Books of Samuel Butler.* It is, in many respects, the most attractive and rewarding of his writings. Butler was an original but overweening writer. He deliberately sought to play the part of *enfant terrible* and then complained that he was not taken seriously. His criticism of Darwin was sound; but it did not entitle him (as he seemed to hope) to be hailed as a pioneer in science. He had made no investigations and no discoveries; he had examined very acutely the evidence; he accepted the facts, but disputed the conclusion, and gave to "cunning" and "unconscious memory" the place that "natural selection" gave to "luck". But the value of Darwin's researches (to say nothing of Darwin's achievements in other realms of investigation) remained unaffected by Butler's attacks. His true cause of complaint was that there was some reluctance and some disingenuousness shown in admitting the force of his criticism. The feud between Butler and the Darwinians hardly concerns literature. *Life and Habit,* his major contribution to the controversy, continues to live as an excellent example of clearly presented argument touched with a literary charm beyond the hopes of most writers on science. It should be added that some of Butler's suppositions anticipate modern explorations of the unconscious. The first book in which he challenged destructively the current values in morals and religion was *Erewhon* (1872), a satirical "Nowhere", in which disease is a crime, crime a misfortune, religion a banking system, and education the suppression of originality. With singular prophetic insight the Erewhonians banish machines from their republic on the ground that they will evolve, and then become the masters of their makers. And in a sense, Butler proves his own thesis; for in *Erewhon Revisited* (1901), an ill-advised sequel, the machinery of his satire overwhelms its interest. Butler had a strain of the genius of Swift, not least in his capacity for writing plain prose, over which he took great pains (spending half a lifetime in writing and re-writing his *Note-Books*), though, characteristically, he held up to derision all who took pains with their writing, protesting that he did no such thing. Much of the success of his novel *The Way of All Flesh* lies in its personal essayistic touches, in its casual satire and in its humorous asides. Its criticism of the relations between parents and children is deep and searching; but neither in vision nor in execution has it the qualities of a great creative novel. A juster conception of Butler's capacity is to be derived from *Alps and Sanctuaries*, in which appreciation of people and place blends with the acid flavour of his wit to produce a travel book inimitable in its idiosyncrasy. The same spirit is at play in his shorter essays, some of the best of which, in miniature or at length, can be found in the *Note-Books*. That Butler had genius is not to be denied; but it was largely a sterile genius. As a humorist and satirist, expressing himself in lucid, personal prose, he takes high place; but for the more richly creative qualities of a writer one looks to him in vain. *Butleriana* (1932) and the *Letters between Samuel Butler and Miss Savage* (1935) complete the picture of an acrimonious and at times curiously provincial character. His life was written in 1919 by his intimate friend Henry Festing Jones; the most judicious modern study is *Samuel Butler and "The Way of All Flesh"* (1947) by G. D. H. Cole.

Thomas Hardy (1840–1928) forms with George Meredith one of those remarkable pairs of opposites who divided the suffrages of Victorian readers. Nothing could be more unlike the resplendent, glittering fabric of Meredith, adorned with gallant figures, than the simple homespun of Hardy, wrought with sad sincerity of soul. He was born near Dorchester in rather poor circumstances, and received the beginnings of his education in local schools. Thence he passed to London, and studied in the evenings at King's College. From 1856 to 1861 he was the pupil of an ecclesiastical architect, and from 1862 to 1865 he worked under Sir Arthur Blomfield, drawing and surveying many old churches since restored out of recognition. Hardy was a prizeman of the Royal Institute of British Architects and of the Architectural Association, and his first publication was an article in *Chambers's Journal* (1865) entitled "How I built myself a House". It is not fanciful to find evidence of Hardy's architectural disposition in the careful planning of his books, and it is quite safe to find in his study of old parish churches the nourishment of his native interest in local associations. In Hardy always, as in Meredith rarely, the sense of time and place is very strong. He re-created in literature the characters of his own native Wessex and he moved at ease in the period of the Napoleonic wars, of which he had learned details from survivors. Like Meredith, Hardy began with poetry, though he published no early collection. Some of his first poems appeared many years later, others were transposed into passages of the novels; but he was always a poet in spirit. His first published novel was *Desperate Remedies* (1871), and this was followed in regular succession by *Under the Greenwood Tree* (1872), *A Pair of Blue Eyes* (1873), *Far from the Madding Crowd* (1874), *The Hand of Ethelberta* (1876), *The Return of the Native* (1878), *The Trumpet-Major* (1880), *A Laodicean* (1881), *Two on a Tower* (1882), *The Mayor of Casterbridge* (1886), *The Woodlanders* (1887), *Tess of the D'Urbervilles* (1891), *Jude the Obscure* (1896), and *The Well-Beloved* (1897). There were also collections of lesser tales. A short view of Hardy's special qualities can be gained from a reading of *Tess, Jude, The Mayor of Casterbridge, The Return of the Native*, and *Far from the Madding Crowd*. Never overlooked, and increasingly recognized as a sincere writer with an unflinchingly honest view of life, Hardy was read and admired by a large following of thoughtful persons. Late in his career he attained fierce notoriety by the publication of *Tess*, with its challenging sub-title *A Pure Woman*; he then infuriated the protectors of the proprieties by the crude, gratuitous realism of *Jude*, and puzzled even his admirers by the rather incredible plot of *The Well-Beloved*, which appeared to show symptoms of exhausted powers. Hardy's *Tess* came out in the Ibsen period, and current opinion charged both these stern moralists with deliberate outrage against the decencies of life. Few epithets of disgust were left even for *Jude*. Partly in contempt for the assaults of indignant sentimentality in England upon books that would have aroused no murmur of protest in any centre of Continental culture, and partly because he felt that he had no more to say in the form of prose fiction, Hardy returned to his first love, poetry, and published *Wessex Poems* (1898), *Poems of the Past and Present* (1902), *Time's Laughing-Stocks* (1909), *Satires of Circumstance* (1914), and *Moments of Vision* (1917), in which there was as little concession to sentimental ideas of form and theme as in the later novels. The suspicion of exhausted power aroused by *The Well-Beloved* was completely dispelled when the most astonishing of Hardy's works began to appear in 1904—*The Dynasts*, an epic-drama of the Napoleonic wars in Europe. This was completed by further instalments in 1906 and 1908. Readers and critics were a little puzzled and disconcerted when the first instalment appeared. They were shown only part of the picture; its vastness of design and mastery of execution could not be discerned till the whole was displayed. As poetry, drama and history *The Dynasts* is a great and enriching contribution to literature. The deliberately unadorned blank verse dialogue serves its own purpose well and forms a perfect setting for the choral odes and the imaginative prose connections. There is no trace in it of the "debased Elizabethan" common in literary tragedy. The idiom of *The Dynasts* and indeed of the poems generally is Hardy's own. His poetry, on whatever scale, offers few allurements of verbal grace or metrical felicity, but it has pure lyric inspiration, the vision of a poet and the veracity of an undeluded mind. His prose is so completely without manner as to appear sometimes without distinction. In prose and verse alike, Hardy abjured the current sentimental attitude to life, love and religion. His interpretation of existence is not a "reading of earth" in the mystical Meredithian sense, but it is an interpretation of earthly facts. The most impressive character in his novels is not a person, but a place, Egdon Heath, timeless, immemorial, and unmindful of the human life that flutters briefly upon its ancient bosom. Though he tells us, in Aeschylean phrase, that the President of the Immortals had ended his sport with Tess, Hardy had no belief either in Immortals or in President. A complete fatalist, from the first movements of his novels to the last workings of destiny in *The Dynasts*, Hardy saw man living, loving, labouring and perishing against a background of remote, indifferent, implacable forces, themselves unconscious and uncontrolled. He seemed drawn to the darker side of truth, and appeared to turn the balance against hope, because his artistic veracity forbade him to propagate delusions about a happy issue out of human afflictions. As far apart in spirit as in time from the great Greek writers, he had their view of man as born to endure that which was to befall him; and he expressed his faith in creations that often rise to the dignity of tragedy. His novels, gravely sincere, but unequal and sometimes unconvincing, gave distinction to the closing years of the nineteenth century; his poems are among the most considerable written in the twentieth.

From Hardy to George Gissing (1857–1903), another Victorian rebel and realist, is a descent to a lower level of creative apprehension. Gissing began at Owens College, Manchester, a promising academic career that was cut short by several misfortunes, including an ill-starred marriage. Indeed, he seemed born to encounter mischances in life, and it is fitting that he became the chronicler in fiction of lives in which success had no part. His first novel, *Workers in the Dawn*, was published at his own expense in 1880. He endured great poverty and hastened his end by deliberate privation. He was determined to live a literary life and refused to touch journalism in any form. His more important books are *The Unclassed* (1884), *Isabel Clarendon* (1886), *Demos* (1886), *Thyrza* (1887), *The Nether World* (1889), *New Grub Street* (1892), *Born in Exile* (1891) and *The Odd Women* (1893). There are several later volumes that add nothing to what he had already said. When he could follow his heart and write what he wished, he set to work upon a novel of Roman history, *Veranilda* (1904), which he did not finish, and which is no more successful or important than Wilkie Collins's *Antonina*. Three books outside the department of fiction are *Charles Dickens: A Critical Study* (1898), *By the Ionian Sea* (1901), and *The Private Papers of Henry Ryecroft* (1903). He made a second unfortunate marriage, and his life was cut short by persistent ill-health. In form the novels of Gissing are Victorian; in matter they reject the current themes and beliefs. That he was influenced by the art of the French realists is clear, but he was in no sense a follower of any school. He was the first English novelist of importance to consider seriously the psychology of sex, and in certain characters he shows without concealment the furtive, unlovely side of amorousness. Though he was a close student and admirer of Dickens he had no touch of the master's creative energy or fantasy. Dickens (when he was not crusading) could depict the lives of the poor as rich in idiosyncrasy and humorous vitality; Gissing, who was bred in the north, saw nothing in poverty but a squalid, mirthless waste on the outskirts of hideous commercialism; and he pictured it without pity and without sympathy. The novels that depict a higher level of suburban society have the same kind of hopelessness. His books are stories of defeat without dignity. Yet he was not himself without avenues of escape from the dismal world in which for a great part of his career he worked and studied. He had the instincts and equipment of a scholar and could rejoice in classical poetry and the scenes it calls to mind. He had a sound appreciation of Dickens, who has brought comfort and courage to many lives. His monograph on Dickens was the first sound critical study of that master by a fellow novelist. It disposed finally of the heresy that Dickens's characters are mere caricatures; it did justice to his skill in the presentation of various types of women; and it set true value on his style, demonstrating in it the salutary element drawn from the eighteenth century. The most pleasing, though not the most important, of Gissing's books is *The Private Papers of Henry Ryecroft*—part diary, part essays, part confessions. *By the Ionian Sea* must be the most joyless holiday book ever written. Gissing is the uncompromising historian of the seamy side of later-day Victorian England; yet in spite of his careful, seriously intended work, he does not take rank with the greater novelists, because he had imperfect apprehension of man's sheer vitality even in circumstances that invite surrender to despair. He had considerable influence in his last years, and many stories of mean lives in mean streets—for instance Arthur Morrison's *Tales of Mean Streets* (1894) and *A Child of the Jago* (1896)—owed their existence to his example. Gissing's own life, very transparently disguised, is drawn in *The Private Papers of Henry Maitland* (1912) by Morley Roberts, author, among other books, of *The Western Avernus* (1887), a remarkable record of "toil and travel in further North America".

EMPIRE AND AFTER: FROM THE
NINETEENTH TO THE TWENTIETH CENTURY
IN BRITAIN AND OVERSEAS

I. PHILOSOPHY FROM MILL TO RUSSELL

About the middle of the nineteenth century English philosophy had reached its lowest ebb. The general public had ceased to be occupied with speculative thought and gave attention mainly to political theory. Three writers can be honourably named as contributing to an intellectual revival, the greatest of them not a philosopher in the usual sense. Carlyle, through his wrestlings with the ultimate meaning and value of life, affected the thought of his time as Coleridge had affected the thought of an earlier generation; and Sir William Hamilton and John Stuart Mill, in their various discussions of the mind and its problems, gave philosophy once more an honoured place in the national culture. Before it could succeed, philosophy had to overcome not merely public indifference but its own current form. The Benthamite creed regarded the great problem of man's nature and life as solved; ethical principles had been finally settled, and nothing remained but their application to different situations. Political and social theory had been divorced from any principle save that of utility. The poor might suffer inconvenience; but philosophical Radicalism accepted calmly its own consequences.

The economic doctrines characteristic of the Utilitarian school were elaborated by a writer who was not a member of it, and who was attracted neither by philosophy nor by social theory. This was David Ricardo (1772–1823), a prosperous business man, whose interest in economic study, aroused by a reading of Adam Smith, was attested by a pamphlet on the currency (1809). With the encouragement of James Mill—who was himself engaged on the *History of British India* which was to bring him a high post in the service of the East India Company—he then produced his chief work, *Principles of Political Economy and Taxation* (1817). Ricardo was less concerned with the nature and causes than with the distribution of wealth. This distribution has to be made between the classes concerned in the production of wealth, namely, the landowner, the capitalist, and the labourer; and Ricardo seeks to show the conditions which determine the share of each. Here his theory of rent is fundamental. Rent is the price which the landowner is able to charge for the special advantages of his land, and it rises as the margin of advantage spreads. Naturally this doctrine leads to a strong argument in favour of free and unrestricted imports; otherwise rent will be artificially high. Adam Smith believed that the interests of the country gentleman harmonized with that of the mass of the people; Ricardo showed that the rent of the land rises with the increasing need of the people.

This opposition of interests seemed to him the result of inevitable law. He took no account of other than economic motives in human conduct, and he may be said to have invented the fiction of the "economic man", though he did not use the phrase. His doctrines, relentlessly scientific and inhuman, led to the later reaction against private ownership. The *Political Economy* (1821) of James Mill (1773–1836) reduces Ricardo's doctrines to text-book form, and states them with the concise and confident lucidity which distinguished the author. But Mill did not limit himself to economics. He endeavoured to determine the best form of political order by deductive reasoning; and his method was severely criticized by Macaulay in the *Edinburgh Review*. Mill's chief philosophical work was, however, his *Analysis of the Phenomena of the Human Mind* (1829), in which he laid a psychological foundation for the Utilitarian superstructure. In general, Mill followed the "associationism" of Hartley.

Sir William Hamilton (1788–1856), once highly regarded, though always acutely criticized, has not maintained his former reputation. His *Discussions on Philosophy and Literature, Education and University Reform* (1852) contained articles previously published. He prepared an edition of Reid's *Works* (1846), which he illustrated with elaborate appended Notes, chiefly historical. *Lectures on Metaphysics and Logic* appeared posthumously in four volumes (1858–60). Hamilton's influence was great. Since the time of Descartes, Continental thought had had little effect upon English philosophy. Leibniz and even Spinoza were hardly more than names. The doctrines of Locke, Berkeley and Hume had entered into the European tradition; but the reaction which they produced, and which began with Kant, was for long ignored in England. One or two enthusiasts, following the lead given by Coleridge, tried to make Kant known, but their efforts were not widely successful. Hamilton's cosmopolitan learning broke in upon British philosophy and freed it from the narrowness both of the Scottish academic teachers and of the English disciples of Bentham. Hamilton devoted much ingenuity to an elaborate modification of the formal doctrine of traditional logic, and his view was hailed as the greatest logical discovery since the time of Aristotle. It is known as "the Quantification of the Predicate". Hamilton's own expositions of it are incomplete. The clearest accounts of his views have to be sought in *An Essay on the New Analytic of Logical Forms* (1850), by his pupil, Thomas Spencer Baynes, and in *An Outline of the Laws of Thought* (1842), by William Thomson, afterwards Archbishop of York. Two contemporary mathematicians, Augustus De Morgan, ingenious author of a *Budget of Paradoxes* (1872), and George Boole, went even further than their master; and the latter's treatise entitled *An Analysis of the Laws of Thought* (1854) laid the foundations of the modern logical calculus. Another doctrine associated with Hamilton is the "philosophy of the conditioned", the value of which is not easy to estimate, owing to the difficulty of stating the exact sense in which he held his favourite doctrine of the relativity of human knowledge. The theological results of Hamilton's philosophy of the conditioned and the relativity of human knowledge were worked out thoroughly by Henry Longueville Mansel (1820–71), Dean of St Paul's, in his *Metaphysics* (1860), in his *Philosophy of the Conditioned* (1866), and especially in his famous Bampton lectures, *The Limits of Religious Thought* (1858).

John Stuart Mill (1806–73), son of James, is the most interesting figure in nineteenth-century English philosophy. From his earliest years he was subjected to a rigid system of intellectual discipline; but the philosophical father failed to observe that the boy had not only a mind, but a body and a soul; and something like tragedy followed later, when the body began to break under the long strain of intellectual exertion and the soul began to suffer from emotional starvation. The story is told in Mill's intensely interesting *Autobiography*, posthumously published in 1873. After many months of despair, he began to understand that "among the prime necessities of human well-being" is "the internal culture of the individual". In the poems of Wordsworth he discovered exactly what he needed. The older fanatics of the Utilitarian faith thought he was lost, especially when Carlyle called him "a new mystic"; but he was a loyal son and disciple, and though he did not become a mystic he became human. No one had fuller appreciation of Bentham's great constructive faculties; but Mill had insight into regions beyond the vision of Bentham. The most considerable of Mill's books is *A System of Logic* (1843), in which he works out a theory of evidence in harmony with the principles of the empirical philosophy. A later and more comprehensive discussion of his philosophical views can be found in his *Examination of Sir William Hamilton's Philosophy and of the Principal Philosophical Questions Discussed in his Writings* (1865), a work that shows Mill's powers at their most mature stage. In particular, his doctrines of the external world and of the self attracted great attention, though there is nothing fundamentally original in them: they derive from Berkeley and Hume. Matter, in one of his phrases that became famous, is "permanent possibility of sensation". Mill's sole contribution to the fundamental problem of ethical theory was his small volume *Utilitarianism* (1863). On the political side his most important book is *Principles of Political Economy* (1848), which has been variously regarded as an improved Adam Smith and as a popularized Ricardo. But it has breadth and vision, and in spite of his adherence to the maxim of *laissez faire*, Mill recognized the possibility of modifying the system of distribution, even to the extent of a leaning towards the socialist ideal, which became more discernible as his life advanced. Better known and more generally read are his shorter works, *Thoughts on Parliamentary Reform* (1859), *Considerations on Representative Government* (1861), *On Liberty* (1859) and *On the Subjection of Women* (1869). The essay *On Liberty*, the most popular of all his works, is an eloquent defence of individualism. *On the Subjection of Women* states a convincing case for rights now conceded. *Three Essays on Religion* (1874) appeared after his death. In these essays, as well as in his *Auguste Comte and Positivism* (1865), Mill showed signs of moving from his early agnosticism towards some form of theism. Apart from their intrinsic value, the writings of John Stuart Mill deserve study as the revelation of a perfectly sincere and intellectually honest mind that followed truth wherever it led.

A reaction is shown in the work of William Stanley Jevons (1835–82), whose *Theory of Political Economy* (1871), *Pure Logic* (1864), and *Principles of Science* (1874) indicate some divergence from the philosophical position of Mill. George Grote, the historian of Greece, deserves mention here not only for his works on Plato and Aristotle, but also for some independent contributions to

ethics, published together under the title *Fragments on Ethical Subjects* (1876). He
had little sympathy with Mill's "mystical" tendency. In this respect he agreed
with Alexander Bain (1818–1903), who had assisted Mill in some of his works,
especially the *Logic*. Bain's own pre-eminence was in psychology, to which his
chief contributions were two elaborate books, *The Senses and the Intellect* (1855)
and *The Emotions and the Will* (1859). His influence as psychologist and educationist, once considerable, has now faded.

Religious philosophy in England was stimulated by the work of three men,
Frederick Denison Maurice (1805–72), John Henry Newman (1801–90) and
James Martineau (1805–1900). Maurice's influence was due more to his personality than to his books; and he was a social reformer and religious teacher rather
than a philosopher. John Henry Newman was still less of a philosopher, though
his *Grammar of Assent* (see p. 557) propounds a theory of the nature and ground
of belief, and suggests the existence of an "illative sense". The *Essay on the
Development of Christian Doctrine* (1845) does not anticipate evolutionary theory.
Development, as Newman himself defines it, is certainly not evolution. Of
greater importance in philosophy was James Martineau, to whom reference has
already been made (p. 562). He was eighty years old, or upwards, when his
chief books appeared—*Types of Ethical Theory* (1885), *A Study of Religion* (1888),
and *The Seat of Authority in Religion* (1890). The first is still a classic of its kind.

The publication of Darwin's *Origin of Species* in 1859 marks a turning-point
in the history of modern thought. Men were compelled to re-adjust their views
of creation, just as, centuries before, men had been compelled to re-adjust their
views of the solar system by the doctrines of Copernicus and Galileo. Though
Darwin was not in any sense the discoverer of the evolutionary idea, he was the
first to make it an accepted view of life by the convincing force of his patient
investigations. The acknowledged leader of the evolutionary movement in
philosophy was Herbert Spencer (1820–1903), a railway engineer with lifelong
mechanical interests. His early writings show that he was working towards a
theory of evolution before he had any knowledge of Darwin's researches, the
results of which were still unpublished. Then, in 1860, he issued his "Programme
of a System of Synthetic Philosophy", to the elaboration of which he devoted
his life. In regular succession came *First Principles* (1862), *Principles of Biology*
(1864–7), *Principles of Psychology* (1870–2), *Principles of Sociology* (1876–96) and
Principles of Ethics (1879–92). Spencer also produced such smaller works as
Education (1861), *The Classification of the Sciences* (1864), *The Study of Sociology*
(1872), *The Man versus the State* (1884) and *Factors of Organic Evolution* (1887).
Spencer's idea of philosophy is a system of completely co-ordinated knowledge
—a "synthetic" system. His elaboration of this scheme approaches completeness,
and, in this respect, he stands almost alone among modern writers; no other
English thinker since Bacon and Hobbes had even attempted anything so vast.
Spencer displayed much ingenuity in fitting organic, mental and social facts
into his mechanical framework, and built his system as he might have built a
bridge. He set the greatest store upon his work in ethics, and *The Data of
Ethics* (1879) remains one of his most attractive essays.

No other philosopher of the time sought to rival Spencer's attempt at a
reconstruction of the whole range of human thought. But George Henry Lewes

(1817–78) had great versatility and was known as essayist, novelist, biographer, and expositor of popular science. His philosphical publications began with *The Biographical History of Philosophy* (1845–6), which, with all its defects, remains an attractive and readable work. After an interval, he produced volumes entitled *Comte's Philosophy of the Sciences* (1853) and *Aristotle: a Chapter from the History of Science* (1864). More original is the constructive thought in *Problems of Life and Mind*, the first two volumes of which, entitled *The Foundations of a Creed*, appeared in 1874–5, and the fifth and final volume in 1879. The association of Lewes with George Eliot has been noted elsewhere (p. 636). Possibly his most enduring work is not philosophical but biographical, the *Life and Works of Goethe* (1855). Lewes was interested in the theatre, and both his critical essays and the tract *On Actors and Acting* (1875) retain their interest. He is a remarkable instance of a highly gifted man willing to sacrifice his own ambitions in order to serve one whose gifts he believed to be greater.

Thomas Henry Huxley (1825–95), the distinguished zoologist and advocate of Darwinism, made many incursions into philosophy, and always with effect. He was a master of expository and argumentative prose, and did for Darwinism the apostolic work that Darwin could not do himself. Of his many works we may cite *Zoological Evidences for Man's Place in Nature* (1863), *On the Physical Bases of Life* (1868), *Lay Sermons* (1877) and *Hume* (1879). There was insight, courage and some over-confidence in the writings of William Kingdon Clifford (1845–79); but he did not live long enough to develop his talents. *Seeing and Thinking* (1879) is the one memorable book he produced. Among those who approached philosophy from the literary side special mention should be made of Leslie Stephen (1832–1904). His *History of English Thought in the Eighteenth Century* (1876) is penetrating and usually just in its estimate of the philosophers and their work. A further stage of the same history, *The English Utilitarians* (1900), was completed towards the end of his life. His own independent contribution is given in *The Science of Ethics* (1882). Walter Bagehot's *Physics and Politics* (1869) is an application of the evolutionary idea to political society. This delightful book, with which we may name *The English Constitution* (1867), *Lombard Street* (1873), and *Economic Studies* (1880), exhibits the brilliance of a wittily critical but hardly a constructive mind. Two philosophers who saw that evolution was not an "open sesame" to the secrets of philosophy and yet owed small allegiance to the idealist movement of their own times were Henry Sidgwick (1838–1900) and Shadworth Hodgson (1832–1912). Sidgwick's reputation as a philosophical writer was made by his first book, *The Methods of Ethics* (1874). He afterwards published smaller treatises on political economy and on politics. Shadworth Hodgson's life was an example of rare devotion to philosophy. In the first period of his activity he published three books: *Time and Space* (1865), *The Theory of Practice* (1870) and *The Philosophy of Reflection* (1878). In the course of years he attained to new ideas and recast his system as *The Metaphysic of Experience* (1898). Hodgson may be called a materialist, for he held that the only real condition known to us is matter, though it is itself conditioned by something which is not material, and which is beyond our investigation.

The latter half of the nineteenth century was marked by the work of a number of writers who were influenced by the German speculation variously called "neo-Kantian", "Hegelian" or "neo-Hegelian", though its English exponents described it simply as "idealism". The first important work of the new movement was *The Institutes of Metaphysic* (1854) by James Frederick Ferrier (1808–64), professor at St Andrews. After his death many of his papers were collected as *Lectures on Greek Philosophy and other Philosophical Remains* (1866). More important was *The Secret of Hegel* (1865) by James Hutchison Stirling (1820–1909). Although he wrote many books afterwards—the best being a *Text-book to Kant* (1881)—*The Secret of Hegel* remains his greatest work. What Stirling meant by the "secret" of Hegel was presumably the relation of Hegel's philosophy to that of Kant. The influence of Hegel was shown by a number of academic writers, especially in Oxford and Glasgow. Of these one of the earliest and, in some respects, the most important, was Thomas Hill Green (1836–82), who, as editor of Hume, was able to show that Mill and Spencer had not advanced beyond the earlier philosopher. He appealed to "Englishmen under five-and-twenty to close their Mill and Spencer and open their Kant and Hegel"; and this appeal marks an epoch in English thought during the nineteenth century. Green's academic lectures were gathered in his collected *Works* (three volumes, 1885–8). His greatest book, *Prolegomena to Ethics*, appeared in 1883. Of the numerous writers who represent a type of thought similar to Green's in origin and outlook we can mention here only William Wallace (1844–97) and the brothers John Caird (1820–98) and Edward Caird (1835–1908), whose major works are cited in the larger *History*. The most important and original philosophical writer of his time was Francis Herbert Bradley (1846–1924) whose achievement has been differently viewed: sometimes as being the finest exposition of idealism, sometimes as marking its dissolution. His first philosophical work, *Ethical Studies* (1876), presented brilliant criticism of conventional ethical ideas. His *Principles of Logic*, published in 1883, broke new ground and exposed the defects of empirical logic with subtlety and severity. His next and most widely read book, *Appearance and Reality* (1893), has probably exerted more influence upon philosophical thinking in English-speaking countries than any other treatise of its time. A later volume, *Essays on Truth and Reality* (1914) deals in great part with controversies which belong to the twentieth century. Bradley was a master of philosophical prose, and he has left at least a tradition, if not a school.

On the fringe of philosophy stands the engaging figure of Arthur James Balfour, afterwards Earl of Balfour (1848–1930), who gave up to politics very great suppleness and tenacity of mind. He attracted attention as a writer with *A Defence of Philosophic Doubt* (1879), a book which was never taken quite seriously, because its title appeared faintly flippant. The *Foundations of Belief* (1895), *Theism and Humanism* (1915) and *Theism and Thought* (1925) were later excursions into philosophy; but they contributed nothing to current thought. Balfour was critical rather than constructive, and wrote mainly to clear his own mind. A more powerful mind was that of Richard Burdon, afterwards Viscount, Haldane (1856–1928), eminent as jurist, statesman and philosopher. Haldane had resources of mind and character which placed him far above the illiterate politicians who sought to drive him from public life. He had studied philosophy in Germany, "his spiritual home", and began his literary career with a translation of Schopenhauer's *The World as Will and Idea* (1883–6). His original studies in absolute and relativist philosophy are contained in a series of deeply thought works, *The Pathway to Reality* (1903), *The Reign of Relativity* (1921), *The Philosophy of Humanism* (1922) and *Human Experience* (1923). Haldane's extraordinary mind worked both profoundly and rapidly, and his books must be wrestled with before they yield their reward. The most impressive of the later neo-Hegelians was John M'Taggart Ellis M'Taggart (1866–1925), pupil of Henry Sidgwick and James Ward (1843–1925), the latter a considerable writer, whose article *Psychology* in the *Encyclopaedia Britannica* long retained standard rank. M'Taggart at Cambridge attracted many disciples and his work still occupies the thought of expositors. His contribution to written philosophy is to be found in *Studies in Hegelian Dialectic* (1896), *Studies in Hegelian Cosmology* (1901), *Some Dogmas of Religion* (1906), *A Commentary on Hegel's Logic* (1910) and *The Nature of Existence* (1921–7). M'Taggart is not an easy writer to understand, nor, where he is understood, does he convince all readers that the principles he elaborates are valid. He managed to combine atheism with a belief in the survival of the human spirit. The vogue of his teaching was in part due to a singularly attractive personality. Like Macaulay he had an unlimited appetite for novel-reading.

Schopenhauer and Nietzsche, though both widely read, never became the objects of academic consideration in England. There were fervent English disciples of Benedetto Croce and Henri Bergson; but they failed to establish their masters in permanent esteem. The most important development of thought after "idealism" was "pragmatism", a "new name for some old ways of thinking", specially associated with the American philosopher William James, brother of Henry James the novelist. The general reader, if he wishes to understand subsequent developments in this ever more specialized field, cannot do better than study the last four chapters—on Bergson, James, John Dewey, and Logical Analysis—in *The History of Western Philosophy* (1946) by the most eminent of British philosophers of the twentieth century, Bertrand Russell (b. 1872), who in the course of a long and distinguished career (fittingly rewarded by a Nobel Prize in 1950) had earlier put the general public in his debt by his classic *Problems of Philosophy* (1911). Russell's own philosophy is quoted and discussed, together with that of G. E. Moore, Croce, Santayana, Whitehead, Sartre, Wittgenstein, and others, in Morton White's *The Age of Analysis* (1955), a volume in the Mentor philosophy series, New York, which also includes Herbert Kohl's *The Age of Complexity* (1965), taking us on from Russell to A. J. Ayer, Gilbert Ryle, John Austin and Rudolf Carnap and including a section on "Philosophers as Novelists and Novelists as Philosophers" and "A Collect of Philosophy" by the American poet Wallace Stevens. The relations between philosophy and literature, estranged for a while, appear now to be coming closer.

II. HISTORIANS, BIOGRAPHERS AND POLITICAL
ORATORS FROM MACAULAY TO CHURCHILL

1. *Writers on Medieval and Modern History*

The antiquarians of the eighteenth century showed great enthusiasm in collecting the ancient documentary records which are the materials of history; the writers of the nineteenth century made notable use of these materials. In a sense, the first important historical compositions of the age were the novels of Scott, for they taught historians how to depict in narrative the colour of local scenes, the vividness of common life, and the human qualities of great, remote personalities. The lesson was not lost, and it was reinforced by two scholarly movements of the age. One was the beginning of historical criticism, arising from a study, in the records, of national institutions; the other was the beginning of social history, arising from a study, scarcely attempted before, of the economic influences under which nations develop. To this latter study the revolutionary movements of 1830 and 1848–9 gave natural impetus. The former impulse led some writers to dwell with emphasis upon the Germanic origin of the English people, simply because the records had become available. People forgot that England was for over four centuries part of the Roman Empire. Of that long period there are very few records, and it is always easy to suppose that where there are no records there were no events.

The first historian of the Germanic invaders was Sharon Turner (1768–1847) who, having his enthusiasm kindled in youth by the *Death-Song of Ragnar Lodbrok* in Percy's *Five Pieces of Runic Poetry*, devoted his maturer studies to the Cottonian manuscripts in the British Museum, and produced his *History of the Anglo-Saxons from the Earliest Period to the Norman Conquest* between 1790 and 1805. To this he added *The History of England from the Norman Conquest to 1500* (1814–23) and, later, histories of the reign of Henry VIII (1826) and of the reigns of Edward VI, Mary and Elizabeth (1829). The earliest volumes were the best, and inspired scholars like Thorpe and Kemble to make further researches. Sharon Turner was antiquarian rather than historian. He did not write well; but he was a real pioneer, and the first to teach his fellow-countrymen something valuable about their immigrant forefathers. Contemporary with Sharon Turner was John Lingard (1771–1851), whose *Antiquities of the Anglo-Saxon Church* was published in 1806. Lingard was a Roman Catholic, a man of such liberal views that his most violent opponents were those within his own church. Lingard's *History of England from the First Invasion of the Romans to the Accession of William and Mary* (1819–30) achieved a remarkable success. His work is so scrupulous that it lacks the intensity of spirit and the animation of personality which alone can transform historical composition into literature, and he is now not much read. But he is still useful.

Henry Hallam (1777–1859) approached the Middle Ages in a more critical spirit. Easy circumstances enabled him to take his time about both reading and writing, and it was not till 1818 that his first book appeared. In this work, *A View of the State of Europe during the Middle Ages*, he surveyed the course of European history during ten formative centuries and exhibited the severely judicial qualities that made Mignet call him "the magistrate of history". Its successor, *The Constitutional History of England from the Accession of Henry VII to the Death of George II* (1827), remained for a long time the standard treatise on its subject. Hallam was a Whig of the "finality" school. He distrusted the multitude, and could hardly have been the historian of later constitutional reform. *The Constitutional History* was, at a later date (1861–3), adequately continued by Sir Thomas Erskine May, who had made a name for himself by his standard work, *The Rules, Orders and Proceedings of the House of Commons* (1854). Hallam's last important book, the *Introduction to the Literature of Europe during the Fifteenth, Sixteenth and Seventeenth Centuries* (1837–9), forsakes politics for literature and lays open the treasures of a well-stored mind. But though the matter is fascinating, the style is arid, and the book is for utility rather than for delight. Of another Whig historian, Sir James Mackintosh (1765–1832), whose revolutionary *Vindiciae Gallicae* (1791) had challenged Burke, and whose subsequent "apostasy" (as it was viewed) provoked the bitter resentment concentrated in the six lines of Lamb's acrid epigram, it is not necessary to say more than that his *History of England* (1830), his unfinished *History of the Revolution in England in 1688* (1834) and a *Dissertation on the Progress of Ethical Philosophy, chiefly during the 17th and 18th Centuries* (1830) caused more excitement than they seem now to be worth. He was carefully reviewed by Macaulay, who superseded him as a historian, and to whom we now turn.

Thomas Babington Macaulay (1800–59), the son of Zachary Macaulay (1768–1838), a pillar of the anti-slavery movement, passed to Trinity College, Cambridge, after education in private schools. Though he served the state for many years with honesty and dignity, Macaulay was in his heart, from first to last, a man of letters and a passionate lover of books. His first compositions show clearly that he had the instincts of a historian; but before he could engage in the long and unprofitable labours of research, he was compelled by unexpected poverty to earn a living and attain to some kind of independence. The most obvious source of income lay in contributions to periodical literature. With other brilliant young men he began writing for *Knight's Quarterly Magazine* (1823), a new venture that did not last long. His father, who expected something solid, decorous and serious, was hurt and even alarmed by the young man's outbreak into verse (*Ivry* and *The Armada*, for instance) and had to be mollified. Macaulay then turned to *The Edinburgh Review* and at once made himself famous by a single article, the *Milton*, which appeared in the number for August 1825. It announced the arrival of a new critic with a note of authority, a style of great distinction, and an extraordinary power of capturing and holding the attention of readers. These gifts were pre-eminent in Macaulay to the end of his life. So much interest was excited by Macaulay's *Edinburgh* articles that the author was welcomed in eminent Whig society and found the way to political life open to him. He entered Parliament in 1830, and held minor offices with distinction. The turning-point of his life came when he was offered a seat on the Supreme Council of India. Though this meant exile from England he decided to accept the post, feeling sure he could save enough to make himself independent. The years from 1834 to 1838 were therefore spent in India, where he did work of characteristic honesty and thoroughness (see p. 736 below). After returning to

England he became M.P. for Edinburgh in 1839 and took office as Secretary for War (1839–41). From 1846 to 1848 he was Paymaster-General; but after an electoral defeat at Edinburgh in 1847 he withdrew from political life. Edinburgh repented, however, and re-elected him in 1852. In 1857 he was raised to the peerage.

From 1825 to 1844 Macaulay contributed to *The Edinburgh Review* the long series of articles first collected in America as *Critical and Miscellaneous Essays* (1841–4). The value of such a body of writing of course varies greatly, but the *Essays* remain permanently readable and have opened to many eager young minds the great treasures of history and literature. An essay by Macaulay is eminently a thing of its own kind, with its own unrivalled excellences. Some subjects he should have left alone; but, in general, Macaulay's blend of history, biography and literary enthusiasm is entirely and successfully his own creation.

The long conceived historical work did not easily come to birth. It was begun about 1839 after his return from India, but even then was interrupted by the characteristic eagerness which produced the *Lays of Ancient Rome* (1842). When the first two volumes of *The History of England* appeared in 1848, Macaulay was past his maturity and must have known that the completion of his plan was a dream never to be realized. The third and fourth volumes appeared in 1856, and by that time he was a stricken man awaiting the end. The fifth volume appeared in 1861, after his death, and leaves the story on the very eve of the great Queen Anne period which he would have described as no other ever could. Macaulay's *History*, fragment though it is, remains a landmark of English historical literature, and takes rank with our other great historical classic, *The Decline and Fall of the Roman Empire*. Macaulay was peculiarly fitted for the literary research required in the composition of history. The historians who confine themselves to purely historical material leave half their tale untold. Macaulay's vast general reading enabled him to paint pictures of English life and society full of colour and variety, and to produce a gallery of vividly drawn portraits unequalled by any other English historian. Macaulay's *History* remains one of the most triumphant literary masterpieces of the Victorian age.

It is both fortunate and appropriate that the biography of Macaulay should have been written (1876) by a member of his family with the gifts of a literary historian. Sir George Otto Trevelyan (1838–1928) was the son of Macaulay's much loved sister Hannah, and became the father of yet another distinguished historian, George Macaulay Trevelyan (who in turn wrote *his* Life). His public career as a statesman was like his uncle's, honourable and useful. Beginning with lighter works, he found his true subject in the period of the American Revolution. *The Early History of Charles James Fox* (1880) was followed by *The American Revolution* (1899–1907), the story being completed by *George III and Charles Fox* (1912–14). To a command of material he added a gift of arresting narrative that places him among the few historians who can be read for pleasure.

Sir Archibald Alison (1792–1867) was like Macaulay in being both essayist and historian, but like him in no other way. Of his *History of Europe during the French Revolution* (1833–42) with its continuation *The History of Europe from the Fall of Napoleon to the Accession of Napoleon III* (1852–9) someone has said that it was written to prove that Providence was on the side of the Tories. Alison's once great reputation has dwindled into that of a safe writer who may be taken for granted without being read.

Sir Francis Palgrave (1788–1861), son of Meyer Cohen and father of the anthologist, became a Christian on his marriage in 1823 and took the name by which he is now known. His contribution to historical study is that of an enthusiast for the national records. In 1831 he brought out a *History of the Anglo-Saxons*, and in the following year *The Rise and Progress of the English Common-wealth*, covering the same period. In 1834 he published *An Essay on the Original Authority of the King's Council*. In 1837 he produced the more popular *Truths and Fictions of the Middle Ages: the Merchant and the Friar*. His chief work, *The History of Normandy and of England*, appeared between 1851 and 1864. Palgrave's interpretation of history was both original and audacious. He held that the Germanic kingships derived naturally from the Roman imperial idea, but that, in England, the free judicial institutions of the Germanic communities prevented the Roman tradition from leading to absolutism, and called forth the beginnings of our peculiar constitutional freedom. These "imperialist" views were attacked by the "Germanist" school of writers, who appeared to have better evidence; but the work of Palgrave has been undervalued.

John Mitchell Kemble (1807–57) may be called the first of the Germanist school. After studying at Göttingen under Jakob Grimm, he edited the *Anglo-Saxon Poems of Beowulf* (1833–7) and the *Codex Diplomaticus Aevi Saxonici* (1839–48). His best-known work, *The Saxons in England* (1849), written at a time when the foundations of existing European governments seemed falling to ruin, declared that England owed her pre-eminence among nations, her stability and her security, to the principles and institutions bequeathed by the Teutonic invaders.

The most vigorous exponent of the Germanist view was Edward Augustus Freeman (1823–92), who followed Kemble, and would not hear of Palgrave's paradox as to the kinship between the Romanized Celts and the English invaders. To Freeman the Germanic invasions meant extirpation. Always an eager controversialist as well as a voluminous writer, he is better remembered by his great *History of the Norman Conquest* (1867–76) than by his attacks and defences. That the Germanic invasions made England, and that the Norman Conquest left its free national life in all essentials unchanged, remained the cardinal doctrines of Freeman's life and teaching.

The close association of Freeman and Stubbs was long a theme of academical jest. William Stubbs (1825–1901), successively Bishop of Chester and of Oxford, made his mark as a historical writer nearly a decade later than his friend. His principal achievement in the department of ecclesiastical history was *The Councils and Ecclesiastical Documents of Great Britain and Ireland*, edited by him in conjunction with A. W. Haddan (1871–8). In 1870, Stubbs first came before a wider public by arranging and editing *Select Charters and other Illustrations of English Constitutional History* (to the reign of Edward I). This book was followed, in 1874–8, by *The Constitutional History of England in its Origin and Development*, which was long accepted as the standard work on its subject.

Closely associated by friendship with Stubbs and Freeman was John Richard

Green (1837–83), a historian of the same Germanist convictions, but of very different powers. His physical delicacy would always have prevented him from being one of the long-distance athletes of history. He formed the intention of becoming the historian of the Church of England. This plan he changed from time to time with characteristic eagerness. Then he was attacked by consumption and knew that whatever he had to do must be done quickly. His ideas steadily cleared, and the result was the famous book we know as *A Short History of the English People* (1874), which attained a success unprecedented since the days of Macaulay. The deserved popularity of this book, the first history of England to deal comprehensively with the development of the people, is due to narrative and descriptive power of very high order, and to unusual sympathy with the whole interests of the nation, artistic and literary as well as political and economic, and especially with the life of the poor in all periods. The larger work, *A History of the English People* (1877–80), was expanded from the more popular book. Aided by his gifted wife, Alice Stopford, he produced *The Making of England* (1882) and *The Conquest of England* (1883)—the latter completed by her.

Brief mention only can be given to certain historians who illuminated special aspects of their subject. Sir Henry Maine (1822–88), in *Ancient Law* (1861) and in *Village Communities in the East and West* (1871), based on his knowledge of life in India, showed his command of legal and political problems. James Edwin Thorold Rogers (1823–90), in *A History of Agriculture and Prices in England from 1259–1793* (1866, etc.) and in *Six Centuries of Work and Wages* (1884), provided an invaluable economic survey. Frederic Seebohm (1833–1912) produced two volumes that are historical classics, *The Oxford Reformers* (1867) and *The English Village Community* (1882). Frederic William Maitland (1850–1906) reinterpreted and almost re-created English legal history in a number of specialist works, particularly the *History of English Law before the Time of Edward I* (1895) written in conjunction with Sir Frederick Pollock.

The next outstanding name that meets us is that of James Anthony Froude (1818–94). Though he came to regard Carlyle as his master, he had begun to write under the influence of Newman, and never quite lost the ecclesiastical note. His *History of England from the Fall of Wolsey* (1856–69), first intended to reach to the death of Elizabeth, closes with the dissipation of the Spanish Armada. A celebrated article (1852) called *England's Forgotten Worthies* foreshadows the sympathies and the antipathies of the *History* in the phrase that describes James I as "the base son of a bad mother". That a work which offended many and startled more should have had such a popular success is a fact explicable only by the literary power of the author. Froude, like Macaulay before him, had creative narrative genius. His study of original documents was most assiduous; but he presented his matter in a literary, rather than a historical, spirit. His style is all but irresistible to those who enjoy the union of felicity of form with wealth of colouring; it is almost infuriating to those who feel that he is making the worse seem the better cause. The assaults upon the *History*, led by Freeman, were many and fierce. The true charge against Froude lies, not in his neglect of authorities, but in something like a perversion of them. He does not inspire full belief. Froude was undoubtedly sincere in his view of Henry VIII as a hero; but it was his constant misfortune to appear disingenuous in advocacy. His later works—*The English in Ireland in the Eighteenth Century* (1872–4), *Caesar* (1879), *The Divorce of Catherine of Aragon* (1891), *The Spanish Story of the Armada* (1892) and *The Life and Letters of Erasmus* (1894) neither increased nor diminished the reputation created by the *History*. Among Froude's miscellaneous works may be named *Oceana*, a delightful but provocative record of a tour overseas, the volumes of collected essays called *Short Studies in Great Subjects* (1867–82), full of excellent matter, and, chief of all, his life of Carlyle, which, with all its errors of taste and judgment, tells part of the truth about its subject.

Passing from Froude to Samuel Rawson Gardiner (1829–1902) we pass from Tudor to Stuart history, and from the brilliant historical artist to the assiduous historical artisan. The first two volumes of Gardiner's great *History of England from the Accession of James I* appeared in 1863 and the work was issued steadily in successive instalments until 1882, after which it was revised and reissued in ten volumes, as *The History of England from 1603 to 1640*. Later came the continuation, the *History of the Great Civil War* (1886–91) and the *History of the Commonwealth and Protectorate* (1894–1901). Gardiner's fame rests upon the solid substance of his work.

A remarkable historical writer was Goldwin Smith (1823–1910). His work took a strongly political tone, and in *The Empire* (1863) he advocated the separation of the British colonies from the mother-country and their establishment as independent states. In 1866 he resigned his Oxford chair and transferred himself, with his political aspirations and disappointments, first to Cornell University, in the United States, and thence, in 1871, to Toronto, where he continued his intense journalistic activity. He could not keep the spirit of political controversy out of anything he wrote; and, in truth, that spirit was part of his genius. His works were both numerous and various. Books like *Jane Austen* (1890) and *Guesses at the Riddle of Existence* (1897) represent the less provocative aspects of a strange character.

Sir John Robert Seeley (1834–95) first became famous (see p. 561) as the anonymous author of *Ecce Homo* (1865). His standpoint as a historical teacher and writer was clear to himself from the first. In the opening sentence of his most successful work, *The Expansion of England* (1883), he declares that history, "while it should be scientific in its methods, should pursue a practical object". This practical object was practical politics; and he set himself the task of training the statesmen of the future. His purely historical works (e.g. *Life and Times of Stein*, 1878) failed to establish themselves permanently; but *The Expansion of England* became a bible of politics. Imperialism, the very opposite system to that cherished by Goldwin Smith, was here shown to be the ideal which should guide the government of the British Dominions.

The History of the War in the Crimea (1863–87) by Alexander William Kinglake (1809–91), author of the brilliant and delightful *Eothen* (1844), was based on the papers of the Commander-in-Chief Lord Raglan, and was at once an apologia and an exhaustive treatment of its subject. Its splendid literary qualities have failed to give it a place in the general reading of the public, perhaps because the subject (like that of Carlyle's *Frederick*) is now thought insufficiently attractive for such lengthy discussion. A famous story of an earlier war is Sir

William Napier's *History of the War in the Peninsula* (1828–40), a fine example of its kind.

Among nineteenth-century historians of Scotland, precedence must be accorded to Patrick Fraser Tytler (1791–1849), whose *History of Scotland* (1828–43) was first suggested to him by Scott. The *History of Scotland* (1867–70) by John Hill Burton (1809–81) is worthy, but not easily readable. Burton is much more enjoyable in lighter efforts, such as *The Book-Hunter* (1860) and *The Scot Abroad* (1862). The most attractive of Scottish historians is Andrew Lang (1844–1912), whose gift of narrative and charm of style carried him safely over the wide range of his *History of Scotland from the Roman Occupation* (1890–7). Lang excelled in the historical monograph, such as *Pickle the Spy* (1897), with a dash of mystery in the subject; but he was most at home on the doubtful ground between history and legend, and so the most popular of his many productions was the *Life and Death of Jeanne D'Arc* (1908).

Of ecclesiastical historians during this period the most notable was Mandell Creighton (1843–1901), Bishop of London, whose *History of the Papacy during the Period of the Reformation* (1882–94) is the chief of his many works. Richard Watson Dixon's *History of the Church of England from the Abolition of Roman Jurisdiction* (1878–1902) is marked by the attractive character of its author, who was poet and divine as well as historian. Bare mention is all that can be given to *The English Church in the Eighteenth Century* (1878) by John Henry Overton, *The History of the English Church* (1901, etc.) edited by William Richard Stephens and William Hunt, and the more biographical *Lives of the Archbishops of Canterbury* (1860–76) by Walter Farquhar Hook.

Henry Thomas Buckle (1821–62) in his *History of Civilization in England* (1857, 1861) showed the touch of genius that fits a theme to an age; for he applied to history the methods which Darwin was applying to nature, and he followed Comte in his search for natural laws in the world of humanity. The book is a mere fragment; but it helped to place the treatment of historical problems on a broader basis.

William Edward Hartpole Lecky (1838–1903), born and educated in Ireland, composed the earliest of his works under the influence of Buckle. The anonymous *Leaders of Public Opinion in Ireland* (1861) attracted less attention than it deserved. Much more successful was the *History of the Rise and Influence of the Spirit of Rationalism in Europe* (1865), severely critical of theological dogmatism and its inevitable product, persecution. *The History of European Morals from Augustus to Charlemagne* (1869) dealt with the same field of philosophical inquiry in the same spirit. Lecky turned next to political history, and was moved by Froude's anti-Irish calumnies to make some vigorous rejoinder. But *A History of England in the Eighteenth Century* (1878–90) was not designed controversially. *Democracy and Liberty* (1896) took Lecky back into the sphere of political philosophy. *The Map of Life* (1899) is more aphoristic and, perhaps on that account, more popular. Lecky, who was at first a Liberal, became a strong Unionist, and was M.P. for Dublin University from 1895 to 1902. Though not a great narrative artist, Lecky wrote very well, and exhibited in every aspect of his work the fine quality of a richly endowed mind.

Of later writers who have made additions to historical literature we can mention only a few outstanding names. The tragedy of Lord Acton (1834–1902), most learned historian of his time, is that he wrote no great historical work. Essays, notes, addresses, letters, and his famous inaugural lecture on the study of history (1895) are all that remain. Even *The Cambridge Modern History* which he planned, contains nothing from his pen. The problem of his personal life was how to reconcile the principle of liberty, to which he was passionately attached, with submission to the authority of the Roman Church, of which he was a devout member. Of the history of liberty, which he desired or hoped to write, nothing exists. He is the most striking example of great gifts nullified by absence of the creative impulse, and he remains a tradition, a mystery and a legend.

To omit the name of Sir Adolphus William Ward (1837–1924) would be unbecoming in a volume based upon *The Cambridge History of English Literature*, of which he was joint editor with Alfred Rayney Waller. His services to university education in history were outstanding. In solidity and variety of learning few scholars excelled him. Of his numerous works the best is *English Dramatic Literature to the Death of Queen Anne* (2nd ed. 1899).

James, afterwards Viscount, Bryce (1838–1922) was publicist, statesman, historian, traveller and jurist, and served his country with high distinction as Ambassador to the United States. His first historical publication, *The Holy Roman Empire* (1864), was the enlargement of an Oxford prize essay, and it quickly took rank, both at home and abroad, as a classic of its kind. Another standard work, especially in the country of which it treats, is *The American Commonwealth* (1888), much revised in the edition of 1920. *Studies in History and Jurisprudence* appeared in 1901. Works like *Impressions of South Africa* (1897) and *South America* (1912) belong to the debatable ground where travel, history and politics meet; but the African book has strong historical interest as a broad and sagacious view of a country on the eve of a great conflict. Like some other great Victorians, Bryce was a man of wide interests which ranged from botany to mountaineering.

At the other extreme lies the work of John Horace Round (1854–1928), who was intensely narrow, contentious by choice, and provocative even as an interpreter. *Geoffrey de Mandeville* (1892), *Feudal England* (1895) and *The Commune of London* (1899) were severely critical of generally accepted ideas about medieval history. *Studies in Peerage and Family History* (1900) and *Peerage and Pedigree* (1910) destroyed some ancient and agreeable legends of descent in noble families.

A reaction against the dehumanized economic doctrines of Ricardo led to an examination of the social problems created by the violent expansion of industry and commerce at the beginning of the nineteenth century. In a trilogy of studies, *The Village Labourer 1760–1832* (1911), *The Town Labourer 1760–1832* (1917) and *The Skilled Labourer 1760–1832* (1919), John Lawrence Hammond (1872–1949) and his wife Lucy Barbara Bradby (1873–1961), interpreted, in sound, unexcited writing, the conditions of a celebrated "age of unexampled progress". *The Rise of Modern Industry* (1925) and *The Age of the Chartists* (1930) carry the story into a later period. The study of economic history, new at the beginning of the nineteenth century, was sensibly advanced by these excellent writers at the beginning of the twentieth.

The collection and dissemination of materials for the study of economic history and government rather than the literary creation of historical narrative is honorably associated with the names of another famous pair, Sidney Webb, Lord Passfield (1859–1947) and his wife Beatrice Potter (1858–1943). *The History of Trade Unionism* (1894), *Industrial Democracy* (1897), *Problems of Modern Industry* (1898), *English Local Government* (1906–22) and *English Poor Law History* (1927–9) are all works that must be known to the student of modern history. The Webbs, more humanely moved, resembled in their devotion and in their power of inspiration the very different school of Bentham and his disciples a century earlier. They were the great expositors of a new science, sociology. Beatrice Webb's *My Apprenticeship* (1926) and *Our Partnership* (1948) are autobiographies of outstanding human appeal.

Herbert Albert Laurens Fisher (1865–1940) and George Macaulay Trevelyan (1876–1962) wrote in the great historical tradition. Fisher's command of matter and utterance can be discerned equally in his short *Napoleon* (1913) and his long *History of Europe* (1935), the first a masterpiece of historical miniature and the second a masterpiece of extended survey. Trevelyan, son of Sir George Otto Trevelyan, supports with distinction the perilous burden of two historical names. Of his writings those of largest appeal are the Garibaldi trilogy— *Garibaldi's Defence of the Roman Republic* (1907), *Garibaldi and the Thousand* (1909), *Garibaldi and the Making of Italy* (1911), and the Queen Anne trilogy— *Blenheim* (1930), *Ramilies and the Union with Scotland* (1932), *The Peace and the Protestant Succession* (1934). The *History of England* (1926) tells, within the limits of a single volume, a rich and vivid story with clear command of narrative. *English Social History* (1942) is the best work in its field since J. R. Green.

The outstanding contribution of the mid-twentieth century to historical literature is *A Study of History* (10 vols., 1934–54) by Arnold Joseph Toynbee (b. 1889), author of various studies of ancient and modern affairs, especially in the near and the far East. *A Study of History* is perhaps the greatest single-handed historical achievement since *The Decline and Fall*. Toynbee is concerned with the decline and fall, not of one empire, but of all the great civilizations known to record. Alike in narrative power, in command of vast material and in challenge of interpretation, this *Study* takes indisputably high rank among English works of historical literature.

The most impressive achievement of co-operative labour is the great series of Cambridge Histories—*The Cambridge Ancient History*, *The Cambridge Medieval History* and *The Cambridge Modern History*, the forty volumes of which contain a vast library of valuable monographs with bibliographies and illustrative matter. The growth of the whole Western world from its rise in the East is here fully displayed.

2. Biographers and Memoir-Writers

Biography, like portrait-painting, has always flourished in England. Of the several biographies belonging to the early part of the nineteenth century the best is Lockhart's *Scott*, one of the greatest examples of its kind, now supplemented by H. J. Grierson's *Sir Walter Scott* (1938). Scott's own *Life of Buonaparte*, written in the midst of pain, sorrow and ruin, is a failure. Byron's autobiographical memoirs were destroyed by solemn advisers, but Moore's life of his friend appended to Byron's *Letters and Journals* (1830) will never be entirely superseded, in spite of obvious shortcomings.

The biographical form of composition was adopted by William Roscoe (1753–1831) in his chief historical works. Roscoe combined business with humanism in a most engaging fashion. His first important work the *Life of Lorenzo de' Medici* appeared in 1796. Its unqualified success was not fully repeated in his *Life of Leo X* (1805), which covered dangerous ground and displeased English enthusiasts for the German Reformation. It is, however, a delightful book, still valid as a picture of Medicean Rome. A later and less attractive phase of the Renaissance was discovered to English readers by the *Isaac Casaubon* (1875) of Mark Pattison (1813–84); but it was in his own outspoken and uneasy *Memoirs* (1883) that Pattison made the most striking addition to our biographical literature. The *Essays in Ecclesiastical Biography* (1849) and the *Lectures on the History of France* (1852) by Sir James Stephen, a distinguished administrator, have pronounced qualities. Stephen had strong religious convictions (see p. 559), and detested the sociological view of history. There is unusual power of historical imagination in his work. Of his sons, Sir James Fitzjames Stephen was an eminent judge and writer, and Sir Leslie Stephen (pp. 675, 678) an eminent essayist and biographer.

The highly popular *Lives of the Queens of England* (1840–8) by Agnes and Elizabeth Strickland was followed by similar volumes of royal interest written by the same authors. Mrs Mary Anne Everett Green, who, previously, under her maiden name Wood, had published *Letters of Royal Ladies of Great Britain* (1846), produced the *Lives of the Princesses of England* (1849–55), and the *Life and Letters of Queen Henrietta Maria* (1857). Mrs Green did very valuable work in research and edited numerous volumes of the *Calendars of Domestic State Papers* at the Record Office. Another biographer of royalty was Sir Theodore Martin (1861–1909), whose *Life of the Prince Consort* (1875–80) was written by Queen Victoria's desire. Besides other works, Martin wrote a memoir (1900) of his wife, the beautiful actress Helen Faucit.

Lord Campbell's *Lives of the Lord Chancellors* (1846–7) and *Lives of the Lord Chief Justices of England* (1849–57) were said to have added another terror to death. The *Lives of Lord Lyndhurst and Lord Brougham*, which followed (1860), filled the cup of remonstrance to overflowing. Far more attractive are the pen-and-ink portraits of the Scottish bench and bar published in *Memorials of His Time* (1856), by Lord Cockburn, biographer of Lord Jeffrey (1852).

The most ambitious biography produced in the mid-Victorian age was David Masson's *Life of Milton, narrated in Connection with the Political, Ecclesiastical, and Literary History of his Time* (1859–80). The full title of the book must be given to indicate its range. Everything Milton wrote is here taken into account. That these six massive volumes will ever be frequently read as a whole may be reasonably doubted; but they are indispensable for reference. Later views of Milton take account of matters beyond Masson's range. John Forster, by his *Life and Times of Oliver Goldsmith* (1854), his *Life of Walter Savage Landor* (1869) and his *Life of Charles Dickens* (1872–4), took a place in the first rank of English biographers. Forster had his personal foibles, but his literary life was one of generous purpose, and his friendship was valued by some very famous men. *The Life and Correspondence of Thomas Arnold* (1844) written by his former pupil Arthur Penrhyn Stanley (1815–81), afterwards Dean of Westminster, is an excellent example of Victorian biography in its pieties and in its suppressions. That Stanley gave Arnold sole credit for educational reforms initiated by others can hardly be denied; nevertheless Arnold accomplished a great work at Rugby. Stanley really knew his own headmaster, and his evidence, combined with that of Thomas Hughes, cannot be resisted.

The *Life of Gladstone* (1903) by John (Viscount) Morley is a political monument, and presents for our admiration the heroic form of a great public figure. To students of history it is a necessary book; but its lack of the warmer human feelings will keep it from being loved for its own sake. Misfortune attended the preparation of a life of Disraeli. It was not till 1910 that the first volume appeared written by W. F. Monypenny, whose task was completed by G. E. Buckle, a former editor of *The Times*.

The last years of the nineteenth century were specially rich in biographical production. This was eminently the age of brief monographs, typified by the "English Men of Letters" Series, which combined criticism with biography in a sane, revealing fashion, and whose authors included Trollope on Thackeray, Stephen on Johnson and Henry James on Hawthorne. Pre-eminent among biographical works stands the great *Dictionary of National Biography*, founded in 1882 by George Smith. It was edited by Leslie Stephen, a man by all endowments of mind entirely fitted for the enterprise. He was succeeded by Sidney Lee, the biographer of Shakespeare.

Among the numerous memoir-writers of the nineteenth century Charles Cavendish Fulke Greville (1794–1865) is by far the best. *The Greville Memoirs*, first published between 1874 and 1887, and issued complete in 1938, contains shrewd comment on the course of English politics and society from the accession of George IV to the year 1860 and remains among the choicest examples of its kind. Greville had genuine insight into character, and his collection is already a classic. *The Croker Papers* (1884), published long after John Wilson Croker's death (1857), tells us something of political history in the first decades of the nineteenth century. Entirely delightful is *The Creevey Papers*, published in 1903, about seventy years after the death of the writer. Thomas Creevey, himself unimportant, seemed to know everybody, and had an instinct for recording the very things that later generations like to know. His story of Waterloo is as good as fiction.

A novel form of political memoir was that of *Conversations with M. Thiers, M. Guizot and other distinguished persons during the Second Empire* (1878), recorded by the well-known economist Nassau William Senior (1790–1864). These volumes had been preceded by *Journals kept in France and Italy* (1871), and by *Correspondence and Conversations with A. de Tocqueville* (1872), who pronounced Senior's the most enlightened of English minds. The earlier *Journals, Conversations and Essays relating to Ireland* (1868) are full of lively interest. Other works in this kind range from the intensive interest of Crabb Robinson's *Diary* (with the later additional selections) to the pleasant garrulity of Grant Duff's *Notes from a Diary*. Hardly to be ranked as "memoirs", yet full of personal illumination, are the volumes of Queen Victoria's letters, invaluable as material and intensely interesting as a revelation of a figure that, politically and domestically, dominated the greater part of a wonderful century.

3. *Political Orators*

The great age of English political oratory seemed to have passed away with the fatal year (1806) which removed both Pitt and Fox from the scene of their conflicts. Times were changing. The long oratorical "set piece" adorned with quotations from the classics began to sound as antiquated as the plays of Shakespeare in the age of Dryden. But the old tradition lingered. Among the masters of eloquence at the beginning of the nineteenth century were William Wilberforce, the apostle of abolition, and, indeed, of any crusade which had the welfare of mankind as its object; William Windham, a schoolfellow of Fox and a follower of Burke; Samuel Whitbread, the defender of the Princess of Wales; Thomas, Lord Erskine, less famous as a political orator than as an advocate; and George Tierney, a complete politician, formidable in debate and master of a colloquial manner.

Greatest among the orators of the new age was George Canning (1770–1827), in whose speeches imaginative power and wit are sustained by scholarship and magnanimity. The outstanding figure of Canning's later years was Henry, Lord Brougham (1778–1868) whose extraordinary gifts were nullified by some grave defect of character. His arrogance and aggressive omniscience were insupportable. "If Brougham only knew a little law", said O'Connell of the Lord Chancellor, "he would know a little of everything." In the debates on the Reform Bill, Macaulay's renown as an orator was first established. Among his later speeches, those on the question of copyright are notable as having not only influenced but actually determined legislation. Macaulay's speeches are less read than they deserve to be. Outside parliament, the Reform Bill campaign was carried on in innumerable speeches, among which those of Henry ("Orator") Hunt should be mentioned. With the Irish, oratory appears to flourish as a natural gift. Among the successors of Grattan, William Conyngham Plunket, afterwards Lord Plunket, was probably the most finished speaker. But by far the most renowned of all Irish orators was Daniel O'Connell. His wit, his ardour, his impudence, his piety, were racy of the soil to which he belonged, and, though he held his own against the foremost debaters of the House of Commons, he was at his best in his native surroundings, in law courts or city hall, or facing the multitudes at Limerick or on Tara Hill. The third in the triad of great Irish orators who strove, though not always in concord, for the welfare of their country, was Richard Lalor Sheil, already mentioned as a dramatist. Sir Robert Peel was a good, rather than a great speaker. Edward Stanley, fourteenth Earl of Derby, was called by Bulwer Lytton in *The New Timon* "the Rupert of debate" because of his impetuous eloquence. Disraeli had, as one would expect from his novels, great imaginative gifts and power of sarcasm, never better exhibited than when he was at bay. Inseparably linked together in political history are the great Radical names of Richard Cobden and John Bright, memorable for their crusade against the Corn Laws. Cobden was a self-taught speaker; but eloquence was the native gift of Bright. His mind was steeped in the Bible, and in his loftier flights he seemed to be breathing the atmosphere of the Old Testament.

During much of his very long political life, William Ewart Gladstone (1809–98) seemed to be the voice of England. When he spoke out in public oration or in published pamphlet, Europe as well as England listened seriously. Two later political orators who had the grand manner were Lord Rosebery and Herbert Henry Asquith, afterwards Earl of Oxford and Asquith (1852–1928). Rosebery, with a natural endowment of opulence had, fortunately, a controlling gift of style that saved him from excess. Asquith commanded, as by native right, the sonorous idiom of Burke. Unfortunately he could not command Burke's creative fullness of mind, and his printed work, like that of his great rival David Lloyd George, is comparatively empty. Stanley Baldwin, afterwards Earl Baldwin, having unexpectedly emerged from political mediocrity to become Prime Minister, seemed to become the typical Englishman, saying what that sometimes muddled person believes that he thinks, but saying it with a felicity that reminded his hearers of the prose style of his cousin Rudyard Kipling.

Oratory was only one of the gifts of the many-talented Sir Winston Spencer Churchill (1874–1964), statesman, soldier, author, painter, whose published works include a novel *Savrola* (1900), biographies of his father *Lord Randolph Churchill* (1906) and his ancestor *Marlborough: His Life and Times* (1933–8), autobiography in *My Early Life* (1930), histories of the two world wars *The World Crisis* (1923–9) and *The Gathering Storm, Their Finest Hour*, etc. (1948–54) and *A History of the English Speaking Peoples* (1956–8), besides numerous volumes of speeches of which the most notable were those delivered to Parliament or broadcast to the nations during the grim early years of the Second World War. It was as much in recognition of these speeches as for his literary gifts that he was awarded the Nobel Prize for Literature in 1953.

III. CRITICAL AND MISCELLANEOUS PROSE FROM BAGEHOT AND RUSKIN TO JEFFERIES AND STURT

The critical and miscellaneous prose of the period is vast in extent and diverse in kind. A brief survey is all that can be attempted here, and we may properly begin with a writer born in the first year of the nineteenth century. Abraham Hayward (1801–84) made a very good prose translation of *Faust*, and he was interested in Stendhal at a time when that fascinating writer was hardly known in England. Hayward could draw a good biographical sketch, but he had no critical power, and his *Essays*, collected in five volumes (1858–74), have not retained their interest. A serious attempt to enunciate critical principles was made by Eneas Sweetland Dallas (1828–79) whose oddly and unhappily named book *The Gay Science* (1866) may be classed without hesitation among the really valuable contributions to criticism. It is lucid in thought and in style; and it is, in a true sense, fundamental. Only two of the proposed four volumes were written, for the incurable English distrust of system condemned the book to oblivion. *The Gay Science* is psychological, and anticipates much later thought, especially in the region of what is now called the unconscious, which lies, Dallas believed, at the root of all art. Aristotle's theory that art is imitation, he tells us, "has transmitted an hereditary squint to criticism"; what art does, is not to imitate what any eye can see, but, rather, to bring into clear vision what is first apprehended only by "the hidden soul". We need not here defend Aristotle's view of "imitation". It is enough to say that Dallas's discussion of art moves clearly and convincingly in the region of ideas, and deserves to be better known.

Walter Bagehot (1826–77) and Richard Holt Hutton (1826–97) were contemporaries and friends. Hutton was a literary critic with strong theological convictions. To purely aesthetic considerations he was a little insensitive, and his many critical studies are not now of much value. For over thirty years he was one of the editors of *The Spectator*, which, under his direction, exerted a powerful influence upon serious minds. The fame of Hutton has waned; but the spirit of Walter Bagehot burns as brightly as ever. He, too, was an editor; but his paper was *The Economist*, which had influence, indeed, but not in the realm of letters. Bagehot was better known in his day as economist and publicist than as literary critic; but it is the critic who now survives. *Lombard Street*, *Physics and Politics* and *The English Constitution* have lost much of their textbook value; but they remain eminently readable through their uncovenanted wealth of wit and wisdom. In fact, the best parts of them belong to criticism. In Bagehot's more regular critical essays, the keen incisive phrases, the humour, the penetrating analyses of character and the touches of philosophy, give an impression almost of greatness. But the impression is not abiding. There is no discernible critical faith such as gives consistency to the writings of Matthew Arnold; and for this reason the posthumously published *Literary Studies* and *Biographical Studies* have never taken the rank to which they seem entitled.

Sir Leslie Stephen (1832–1904) was a "muscular freethinker". His earliest acknowledged volume was the collection of mountaineering sketches called *The Playground of Europe* (1871). *Essays on Free Thinking and Plain Speaking*, which followed in 1873 marked a fundamental change of belief, for Stephen had taken orders in 1855. His philosophical studies are mentioned on p. 662. Biography, in the "English Men of Letters" series and the great *Dictionary*, claimed most of his working life. *Hours in a Library* (1874–9) and *Studies of a Biographer* (1898–1902) show his capacity as an essayist. The fine study called *An Agnostic's Apology* (1893) reveals Stephen as a rationalist, and contains the penetrating study *Newman's Theory of Belief*. With Stephen may be mentioned Richard Garnett, long connected with the British Museum, who collected some of his papers as *Essays of an Ex-Librarian*. The most original of his works is *The Twilight of the Gods* (1888), a collection of singular tales in which he shows grim, sardonic humour. As Stephen's literary talents descended to his daughter Virginia Woolf, so Garnett's descended to his son Edward, critic and dramatist, and grandson David Garnett the novelist.

Theodore Watts, afterwards Watts-Dunton (1832–1914) attained his greatest fame in anonymity. His periodical essays and the long article on poetry in the *Encyclopaedia Britannica* gave him a great reputation which had almost vanished by the time he chose to publish anything. The chief interest of his novel *Aylwin* (1898), apart from a study of Rossetti, lay in its gipsy element—an element strong in the work of his younger contemporary Francis Hindes Groome (1851–1902), the author of *In Gipsy Tents* (1880) and *Gipsy Folk Tales* (1899).

Community of interest brought both of these writers into touch with George Borrow (1803–81), who first gave gipsies a citizenship in English literature, though his knowledge of them, as of many other things, seems to have been more extensive than exact. In a loose sense Borrow might be called a scholar, since he knew many languages, and spoke and wrote them freely. *The Zincali or an Account of the Gipsies of Spain* (1840) is the first clear indication of Borrow's special interest. That this wild and gusty person should have become an agent entrusted by the British and Foreign Bible Society with the distribution of the Scriptures in the Peninsula sounds like an incident in a picaresque romance; and, in fact, *The Bible in Spain* (1843), his own story of the adventure, belongs to that order of literature. *Lavengro* (1851) and its continuation *The Romany Rye* (1857) are such a blend of romance and autobiography, that to say where literal truth ends and imaginative truth begins would have puzzled the author himself, but need not puzzle the reader, who has nothing to do but enjoy books that are unique in English literature for the sense they convey of intimate contact with adventurous, lawless life. In *Wild Wales* (1862) Borrow shows the same qualities, as far as the more topographical matter allows. Essentially, he is a man of the open air; and few have equalled him in the art of transporting the reader from the restraints of civilization into the freedom of nomadic life. His formless books—like those of John Cowper Powys—are held together by sheer force of the pervading personality.

Returning to the main stream of Victorian criticism, we may note three typical figures, Henry Duff Traill (1842–1900), Edward Dowden (1843–1913) and William Ernest Henley (1849–1903). Of these the first and last gave much of their energy to literary journalism. Traill survives in the essays collected as *The New Fiction* (1897), and the "dialogues of the dead" called *The New Lucian* (1884) which attempt a bold criticism of the thought of their day. Dowden, a product of Trinity College, Dublin, was, like Traill, a critic with academic training. His first book was his best—*Shakspere: a Critical Study of his Mind and Art* (1875), a thoughtful interpretation, written in lucid and attractive style, which struck a new note in Shakespearean study. Dowden's one other book of importance is the *Life of Shelley* (1886). Henley had no academic leanings, and wrote constantly in an attitude of defiance, even when there was no provocation. Perhaps his greatest service to the prose of his age was the lesson of incisiveness taught to a generation apt to lose itself in words.

Henley was a critic of pictorial art as well as of literature, and from him it is natural to step backwards to the greatest of all writers of the kind in the Victorian period. The works of John Ruskin (1819–1900) are bewildering in their number, in their enigmatic titles, in their extremes of style, and in their variety of subject; but with all their contradictions they exhibit an almost formidable consistency of spirit. Ruskin received a sheltered education in a wealthy home. He was intended for the evangelical ministry and his parents hoped to see him a bishop. There was a vast difference between the arid, practical education of John Stuart Mill and the humane, artistic, literary and religious education of Ruskin. Yet both revolted. Mill moved towards poetry and mysticism. Ruskin became a heretic in religion and a revolutionary in economics and politics.

Like Macaulay, Ruskin was a writer from his childhood. His prose style was founded on the Bible, which he had read constantly with his mother. At Oxford he wrote verse, and is among the several famous writers who began as winners of the Newdigate. That he paid attention to his prose is evident from the style of his earliest pieces. The germ of *Modern Painters* is to be found in an indignant essay he wrote at seventeen in defence of Turner against a ribald criticism in *Blackwood*. The first volume of the work itself appeared in 1843. Seventeen years were to pass before it was completed. The long journeys, year after year, through France to Switzerland and Italy not only furnished materials for it, but opened up ever new vistas. *The Seven Lamps of Architecture* (1849) and *The Stones of Venice* (1851-3) were both by-works, undertaken and carried through while the major enterprise was still on hand. All three were designed to teach. *Modern Painters* was conceived in a mood of "black anger" at the ignorance and insensitiveness of England; the author felt that he had an apostolic call to dispel the ignorance and to pierce the insensitiveness. Though Ruskin disappointed the episcopal hopes of his parents, he was all his life a preacher. In 1850, he intervened on behalf of the Pre-Raphaelites, as, in 1843, he had intervened on behalf of Turner. He became an ardent lecturer, and—like Morris after him—preached beauty in all the ugly centres of industrialism. Ruskin was now near the great dividing line of his work and life; and he crossed it when, in 1860, he published both the last volume of *Modern Painters* and the essays afterwards (1862) known by the title *Unto this Last*.

There is nothing strange in the transformation of the writer on art into the writer on economics. Ruskin wanted art to have all the qualities we sum up in the great word "righteousness". Still more he wanted life to have righteousness. He was shocked by showy insincere art; he was shocked by the inhuman economic doctrines of Ricardo and the Utilitarians; he was shocked by the poverty and misery which were the price exacted by commercial prosperity; he was shocked by the contented ugliness of the lives led by the swarming people and their masters. He had already vigorously protested in *The Seven Lamps of Architecture* against the uselessness of much of the toil to which the working classes were condemned. When the essays forming *Unto this Last* began to appear in *Cornhill*, they aroused such indignation that Thackeray the editor stopped them; and when the essays forming *Munera Pulveris* began to appear in *Fraser*, they aroused such indignation that Froude the editor stopped them. Triumphant commercialism was in power and refused to let itself be criticized. Ruskin could never be persuaded that he was a revolutionist. He hated the word. His enemies called him a Socialist. He called himself an old-fashioned Tory of the school of Homer and Walter Scott and his acknowledged master was Carlyle.

Ruskin's appointment to the Slade Professorship in Fine Art at Oxford in 1869 gave him a chance to preach his ideals to the young, and he inspired his students (who included Oscar Wilde) to undertake the practical work of road-making. The variety of his interests and the extent of his labours were prodigious. After *Unto this Last* (1862) on economics had come *Sesame and Lilies* (1865) on literature, *The Crown of Wild Olive* (1866) on work, traffic and war, *The Ethics of the Dust* (1866) on crystallization, *The Queen of the Air* (1869) on Greek myths of cloud and storm. In 1871 he began *Fors Clavigera*, a periodical issue of letters (ninety-six in all) addressed to the working men of England. The collection is an astonishing exhibition of the multifariousness of the writer's mind and of his genius in the presentation of his matter. But his exhaustive labours and fiery enthusiasm broke down his health, and after 1878 he was never the same man. He was re-elected to the Slade professorship in 1883, but resigned in the next year. In his latter days he produced what is the most charming and certainly not the least enduring of his works, *Praeterita* (1885-9), half-spoken, rather than written, for we seem to hear the very voice of the old labourer calmly and happily reviewing his life. Ruskin died in the last year of the century which he had done as much as any man to ennoble: he was fittingly commemorated by Ruskin College, Oxford, founded in 1899 by the American historian Charles A. Beard to provide education in the social sciences for working-men.

The prose of Ruskin exhibits all resources of the language. In his first great works the Biblical eloquence is resolutely sought, and though writing in that kind was natural to him at this stage of his growth, it is read with some sense of strain. He came to dislike his own early style as he moved in maturity towards simplicity. His failure to give the current hard-faced commercialism a conviction of its sin sometimes made him peevish and petulant, but seldom impaired his writing. It is in the prophetic admonitions of *Modern Painters* that we can see most clearly the defects of an imperious temper, not in the patient argument and quiet beauty of *Unto this Last*, the disciplined reasonableness of *Fors Clavigera*, and the charming garrulity of *Praeterita*. More beautiful prose than that of *Unto this Last* the nineteenth century can hardly produce; nor did it produce a writer whose general influence was more beneficent. Art, to Ruskin, was the expression of man's delight in the forms and laws of the world. He asserted intrepidly the serious claims of art in an age of base commercialism. A painting, to him, was not something commercially produced, and commercially acquired, to be stuck on the walls of an ugly house to give it an "art finish". It was an expression of the spirit. That spirit he assiduously sought and declared. He taught the English people almost everything they now know about pictures. He revealed the sincere Primitives and abolished the pretentious Eclectics. He gave to England the freedom of Italy, and made its galleries, palaces and churches as familiar as Trafalgar Square. He revealed, however wilfully, the nature of Gothic, and made the glory of the French cathedrals a general possession. No one ever declared so clearly that art is a possession and an expression of a whole people, and not a costly privilege of the rich or a fancy of the coteries. Further, he humanized economics, and showed that righteous art and righteous polity must go hand in hand. It was the conviction that, while life without industry is guilt, industry without art is brutality, which drove Ruskin to examine the kind of industry by which the modern world escapes guilt, only to fall into brutality. The intense humanity which inspires all Ruskin's work, political and aesthetic alike, can never become antiquated.

Nearly all subsequent aesthetic criticism in England and America is derived from Ruskin. Benjamin Robert Haydon (1786-1846) stands quite apart. Though a far older man than Ruskin, Haydon, as the author of printed works, comes after him. Haydon and Barry were to Ruskin examples of "bad" artists, animated by desire for the kind of "greatness" which is really inflation and which merely appears great to indolence and vanity. Posterity has fully confirmed this judgment. But Haydon's delightful *Autobiography*, posthumously edited (1853), is unaffected by the worthlessness of his paintings. Anna Brownell Murphy, afterwards Mrs Jameson (1794–1860), also Ruskin's senior, published her *Handbook to the Public Galleries of Art in London* in 1842. Her later works on art, however, were strongly influenced by Ruskin, who met her in Venice, and refers to her with gentle humour in *Praeterita*. Mrs Jameson's other books, *Memoirs of the Early Italian Painters* (1845), *Sacred and Legendary Art* (1848), *Legends of the Monastic Orders* (1850), *Legends of the Madonna* (1852) and *History of Our Lord as exemplified in Art* (1864) were much read by those who found Ruskin's demands too high for them.

It was in Ruskin's own university that the aesthetic school took root, though its flowers and its fruit were not precisely what he would have desired. The disciples never gave that weight to ethics which the master desired, and, as time went on, they paid it less rather than more attention. Of this group, John Addington Symonds (1840–93) may be described as an outlying member, and his principal work, *Renaissance in Italy* (1875–86), illustrates the weakness of the school to which he belonged. It is lacking in unity and completeness, not only because it dwells upon art and passes lightly over other factors in the history of the period, but because in the treatment of art itself emphasis is laid upon the emotional element at the expense of the intellectual. The other works of Symonds have the same defects, and his prose is self-conscious, over-elaborated and diffuse. More original, in all respects, was Walter Horatio Pater (1839–94), who was influenced by Ruskin but was utterly unlike him in spirit. Ruskin, bowed with sorrows, remained unconquerably optimistic, and laboured with even excessive hopefulness at schemes of social regeneration. Pater retired from the dust of social conflict and became an artistic Benedictine, with his literary labour as a kind of rite. The conclusion of his *Studies in the History of the Renaissance* (1873) is, in the highest degree, significant. Its teaching is that, to beings like men, beings under sentence of death, but with a sort of indefinite reprieve, the love of art for art's sake is the highest form of wisdom. Pater was the most scrupulous of literary artists. He strove to make each sentence bear its full weight of duty, and the defect of his prose is not, as some appear to think, that it becomes a kind of poetry, but that it becomes a kind of science. Indeed, until it is understood as science it cannot be understood as beauty. Every word, almost every syllable, is part of a formula; and so the prose of Pater is inevitably slow—a perpetual *Adagio*. His romance, *Marius the Epicurean* (1885), is sadly attractive, but leads to no conclusion of comfort. How could it? There was no comfort to offer, and Pater was too gravely sincere to offer delusions. *Imaginary Portraits* (1887), *Appreciations* (1889), *Plato and Platonism* (1893), and the posthumous *Miscellaneous Studies* (1895), *Greek Studies* (1895) and *Gaston de Latour* (1896) repeat the manner and the message of his earliest volume. Pater's studies in character and essays in literature and art embody no faith and no exact knowledge of the Ruskinian kind. He is nearer to Wordsworth in his consciousness of the heavy and the weary weight of all this unintelligible world, and he sought to lighten "the burthen of the mystery", not by resorting to the ministrations of nature, but by exact and studious contemplation of man in some state of spiritual sensation or of the artistic creations in which man externalizes the inner apprehension. A writer so dedicated can never be submerged; but it is difficult to believe that his public will ever be large or that his doctrine of "art for art's sake" will ever be a working creed.

While Pater represented the aesthetic movement in its most earnest phase, Oscar Wilde (1856–1900) gave utterance to its principles in the language of persiflage. In verse and in prose, in lyrics and in essays often bright with raillery and occasionally weighted with thought, e.g. in *Intentions* (1891), he showed a remarkable talent. *The Ballad of Reading Gaol* (1898) and the unconvincing *De Profundis* (1905) are the product of his tragic overthrow; but his one clearly surviving work is *The Importance of Being Earnest* (1895), a comedy of genius.

With the writers just considered, it is appropriate to name William Hurrell Mallock (1849–1923), whose once famous book *The New Republic, or Culture, Faith, and Philosophy in an English Country House* (1877) presents, under thin disguises, Ruskin, Jowett, Matthew Arnold, Walter Pater and other figures of the day, and sets them discussing the problems that specially interest them. Despite the glance at Plato in the title, the book is an experiment in the Peacockian manner without the penetrating Peacockian humour, and except as a commentary (not free from malice) on the moral discontents of the age it has no enduring value. *The New Paul and Virginia, or Positivism on an Island* (1878) did not repeat the success of *The New Republic*. Mallock, who was a nephew of Froude, took himself very seriously as a thinker and felt called to oppose democracy, socialism, and other levelling tendencies, in a number of volumes that have not retained their interest. His *Memories of Life and Literature* (1920) may serve as a footnote to the discussions of his day.

Among later writers on art and life a reputable place is taken by Violet Paget (1856–1935), known as "Vernon Lee", who interpreted to English readers both Italian art and Italy itself, the country of her long residence. Her early works, from *Studies of the Eighteenth Century in Italy* (1880) to *Renaissance Fancies and Studies* (1895), are akin in spirit to Pater. But her style and thought cleared and took their own note. *Genius Loci* (1899), *The Enchanted Woods* (1904) and such later studies as *The Handling of Words* (1923) and *The Poet's Eye* (1926) show genuine character and vision and prove that she was not a mere echo of the Pater period but grew with her times and faced the problems of her age.

Contemporary with Pater and Symonds was Henry Austin Dobson (1840–1921), a writer on art and letters, but in a totally different spirit. After monographs on Hogarth, Fielding, Bewick, Steele and Goldsmith, he began the sketches known as *Eighteenth Century Vignettes*, published in collections between 1892 and 1896. That Dobson had sound understanding of part of the eighteenth century cannot be denied; that he always caught its touch and style in his own prose cannot be maintained.

An interesting figure of the "aesthetic" period is Arthur Symons (1865–1945), who wrote largely on every kind of art. He is often derivative: he echoed Pater in prose and Baudelaire in verse. But his book *The Symbolist*

Movement in Literature (1899) retains its importance as a pioneer study of a movement that was to change its character radically during the twentieth century and his translations from Mallarmé, as Yeats acknowledged, influenced the "elaborate form" of many of the poems in his friend's *Wind Among the Reeds* and *The Shadowy Waters*.

Of the authors who came into literature from the world of politics, the most important in his day was John, afterwards Viscount, Morley (1838–1923). He spent many years in "the higher journalism" as editor of *The Fortnightly Review* and *The Pall Mall Gazette*, but continued the composition of works such as *Voltaire* (1872), *Rousseau* (1873), *On Compromise* (1874) and *Diderot and the Encyclopaedists* (1878). Morley was editor of the first and best series of the "English Men of Letters" monographs, to which he contributed a study of Burke, and of the "Twelve English Statesmen" series, to which he contributed a volume on Walpole. His interpretation of the French writers was instructive to his age, but is not now satisfying. Morley's prose is always that of a publicist. In manner it is clear and pleasantly touched with allusion; in matter it keeps close to the surface and presents no difficulties of profundity.

There was more native genius for literature in another Liberal statesman, Archibald Philip Primrose, Earl of Rosebery (1847–1929), although his performance, in every respect, fell tragically short of his high promise. His speeches (as we have noted earlier) were in the great tradition, and his *Pitt* (1891) was perhaps too deliberately of Pitt's own oratorical period in style. The longer books, *Napoleon, the Last Phase* (1900) and *Chatham, his Early Life and Connections* (1910), are more considerable. They exhibit historical vision in substance and easy eloquence in utterance. After Disraeli and Churchill, Rosebery is the most literary of our Prime Ministers.

Slight in substance but unfailing in charm are the essays of another Liberal statesman, Augustine Birrell (1850–1933), whose best qualities were lost in politics. His small volumes, *Obiter Dicta* (1884), *Essays about Men, Women and Books* (1894), *In the Name of the Bodleian* (1906), *More Obiter Dicta* (1924) and others of less note appear to have little solidity, but they have what is ultimately more precious than mere weight, the genuine grace, personality and sincerity that separate true essays from fluent imitations. Yet another Liberal politician, Herbert Woodfield Paul (1853–1935), out of whose various studies in literature, history and biography, two volumes of essays emerge, *Men and Letters* (1901) and the less good *Stray Leaves* (1906), might be called the last of the Whig essayists; and in this department of writing the Whigs had the best of it. The contemporary Tory, Charles Whibley (1862–1930) was joint editor of the delightful *Tudor Translations* and author of the essays contained in such volumes as *A Book of Scoundrels* (1897). His *Musings without Method*, contributed regularly to *Blackwood's Magazine* for many years, was a long-sustained flow of ultra-Tory journalism. George Wyndham (1863–1913), a romantic and even tragic figure in Unionist politics, came very agreeably into literature with editions of North's *Plutarch* and Shakespeare's *Poems*, and a volume of collected papers called *Essays in Romantic Literature* (1919), posthumously published.

From these writers who belonged to the world of affairs, let us turn to those who come from the world of books—the scholars, editors and literary historians.

In a volume devoted to a study of English literature it would be ungrateful to leave unmentioned the name of Henry Morley (1822–94), who, in the eleven volumes of his unfinished *English Writers* (1887–95), and in several comprehensive series of reprints, such as Cassell's National Library (1886, etc.), the Universal Library and the Library of English Literature did more than any man of his time to make books of world-renown familiar to the new public created by the spread of education.

Thomas Wright and F. J. Furnivall have already been mentioned (pp. 568–9). The Philological Society, of which Furnivall was secretary, gathered much material now incorporated in *A New English Dictionary on Historical Principles*, conveniently called *The Oxford Dictionary* (1884–1928), of which the first editor was Sir James Augustus Murray (1837–1915). *The Concise Oxford Dictionary* (1911) was based on the larger work and was edited by Henry Watson Fowler (1858–1933) and his brother F. G. Fowler. The former later produced *A Dictionary of Modern English Usage* (1926), a classic work of lexicography whose second edition (1965) was revised by Sir Ernest Gowers. A wonderful contribution to the study of words was made in *The English Dialect Dictionary* edited by Joseph Wright (1855–1930), who was sent to manual labour at the age of six and yet made himself one of the great philological scholars of the time. Henry Bradley (1845–1923), like Joseph Wright a self-taught scholar, became one of the editors of *The Oxford Dictionary*, wrote many valuable essays, and produced one small book, *The Making of English* (1904), which is a classic. Walter William Skeat (1835–1912), another great student of language, edited numerous volumes, some with Richard Morris (1833–94), and is specially memorable as the authoritative editor of Chaucer and *Piers Plowman*. Arthur Henry Bullen (1857–1920) edited a series of the old dramatists and produced his delightful *Lyrics from the Song Books of the Elizabethan Age* (1886), first of a long line of similar collections.

The Irish scholar Stopford Brooke (1832–1916) (see p. 2) wrote with native grace of manner various theological and critical volumes, but is remembered specially for *A History of Early English Literature* (1892) and the illuminating *Primer of English Literature* (1876) which surveys a thousand years of creative work in a hundred and fifty justly proportioned pages. William John Courthope (1842–1917) edited Pope and produced in six volumes a *History of English Poetry* (1895–1909) which discusses literature as austerely as if it were jurisprudence. Less important is Sir Edmund William Gosse (1849–1928), whose facility in writing did not atone for shallowness of judgment and frequent inaccuracy. He is entitled to remembrance less as critic and historian than as the apostle of modern Scandinavian literature in England (especially as the first herald of Ibsen) and as the author of *Father and Son* (1907), a study in the clash of temperaments, when the religious discords of the post-Darwinian period could tragically sunder the generations of serious families. Samuel Butler and Robert Louis Stevenson were other examples of this severance.

Three scholars on the heroic scale of learning may be named together, George Saintsbury (1845–1933), William Paton Ker (1855–1923) and Oliver Elton (1861–1945). Saintsbury was wide and discursive rather than profound and precise. His foible of omniscience was so transparently ingenuous as to be attractive rather than offensive. He had what few scholars seem to possess, an immense vitality of enjoyment, and he invited the world to share his hearty preferences. To the large vision of a critic he added the bright, short view of a journalist, and combined, in a degree almost unique, scholarship with popular appeal. Of his immense variety of writings the most important are *A History of Criticism* (1900–4), *A History of English Prosody* (1906–10), *A History of English Prose Rhythm* (1912) and *A History of the French Novel* (1917–19), which are not really histories, but vast miscellanies lightly held together by chronology. They do not always command assent—and the *Criticism* is now superseded by the work of more modern scholars like René Wellek, W. K. Wimsatt Jr and Cleanth Brooks—but they attract by the vigour of their personal vitality and their wealth of illustration. Miscellanies on a small scale are *Notes on a Cellar Book* (1920), three *Scrap Books* (1922–4), and *A Letter Book* (1922). Saintsbury is always exhilarating to read, for he transmits his opinions with gusto. His gnarled and knotty style, with large assertions complicated by instant qualifications and sub-qualifications—"complaints, undoubtedly, are, sometimes, made" that he was overfond (as here) of the comma—is really conversational in texture. It was easier to hear than to read. Ker, more formidably endowed, was not popularly communicative. If he ever desired a large audience—the supposition is improbable—he took no pains to secure one. He had plenty of wit and humour of the sardonic kind, but it was reserved for a few. His major contributions to scholarship are *Epic and Romance* (1896), *Essays on Medieval Literature* (1905), *The Art of Poetry* (1923) and the posthumous *Collected Essays* (1925), and *Form and Style in Poetry* (1928). They are full of illuminating critical judgments illustrated with ease from a wide range of reading in ancient and modern literature, including the classical literature of northern Europe. Elton, least generally known of the three, was not the least gifted. His six volumes entitled *A Survey of English Literature* (1912–28), covering the period between 1730 and 1880, have encyclopedic range. One of the most attractive of his books is the biography of a great and overlooked scholar, Frederick York Powell (1850–1904), editor and translator of *Corpus Poeticum Boreale* (1881), a full and invaluable collection of ancient northern poetry.

Small in quantity but fine in quality is the work of Andrew Cecil Bradley (1851–1934), whose *Commentary on "In Memoriam"* (1901), *Shakespearean Tragedy* (1904) and *Oxford Lectures on Poetry* (1909), touched by the Hegelian spirit, appealed to the public as readable philosophic explanations of familiar literary phenomena. Bradley's Shakespearean criticism was the most widely read after Dowden's, and in spite of the reaction to his "character"-istic approach by such later critics as Eliot, Knights and Leavis, it still remains impressive.

John William Mackail (1859–1945) has to his credit an excellent biography of William Morris (1899) as well as some equally excellent critical essays, including the delightful and illuminating *Latin Literature* (1895), *The Springs of Helicon* (1909) *Lectures on Poetry* (1911), and *Studies of English Poets* (1926); but his fame is most firmly established by his translations, especially *Select Epigrams from the Greek Anthology* (1890).

Two critics who add to the gaiety if not to the gravity of criticism are Sir Walter Raleigh (1861–1922), a Cambridge man who became professor at

Oxford, and Sir Arthur Quiller-Couch (1863–1944), an Oxford man who became professor at Cambridge. In both the personal charm and influence exceeded the mere baggage of acquisition. Raleigh's books are slight in substance. *Stevenson* (1895) and *Style* (1897) appealed to their own generation; *Milton* (1900) and *Wordsworth* (1903) are more substantial but do not endure as vital interpretations. *Shakespeare* (1907) is as good as any small book on a vast subject can be. It marks a reaction against romantic criticism. Raleigh's finest constructive work is embodied in *Six Essays on Johnson* (1910). Quiller-Couch brought to the criticism of literature the practical understanding of a skilled craftsman in fiction and the light touch of an accomplished parodist in verse (see pp. 604, 647). His important works are those embodying his Cambridge lectures—*On the Art of Writing* (1916), *Shakespeare's Workmanship* (1917), *Studies in Literature* (three series, 1918, 1922, 1929), *On the Art of Reading* (1920) and *Charles Dickens and Other Victorians* (1925). In none of these volumes is there any approach to philosophical criticism; but neither is there mere facile preference or impressionism. Literature is consistently presented, with convincing enthusiasm and creative understanding, as something for hearty, rational, disciplined enjoyment by normal human beings, and this, in a sense, is the best philosophy of literature. To condemn the criticism of Quiller-Couch because it is not ponderous or pretentious is itself bad criticism.

Among the miscellaneous essayists and writers, several of note belong to Scotland. The unhappy Hugh Miller (1802–56), a self-taught, old-fashioned student of science, wrote *The Old Red Sandstone* (1841) and *My Schools and Schoolmasters* (1854). The two brothers Robert and William Chambers are remembered chiefly as the founders of *Chambers's Journal* and of the great publishing house bearing their name. Robert, the gifted brother, had however created a sensation by his anonymous *Vestiges of the Natural History of Creation* (1844), which prepared the way for a popular understanding of Darwin. Best remembered of several John Browns is the doctor (1810–82), whose essays are collected as *Horae Subsecivae*, and whose literary creations include the dog Rab and the child prodigy Marjory Fleming (1803–11), admired by Scott. Alexander Smith, the "spasmodic" poet, survives as a prose writer in *Dreamthorp* and *A Summer in Skye*. The much-derided Samuel Smiles (1812–1904), an admirable worker in the public service, wrote several useful biographies besides the celebrated *Self-Help* (1859), *Character* (1871), *Thrift* (1875) and *Duty* (1880), which are much better books than those who mock at self-help, character, thrift and duty appear to suppose.

Most famous of Scottish essayists is Robert Louis Stevenson (1850–94). It was not until the publication of *Treasure Island* as a separate volume in 1883 that Stevenson attained popularity as a writer of fiction; but, prior to that, he had written and published many essays and some fantastic stories like those in *The New Arabian Nights* (1882). The records of personal experience which are embodied in *An Inland Voyage* (1878) and in *Travel with a Donkey in the Cevennes* (1879) are essentially essays. Fugitive papers were gathered into volumes, intimate and confidential, as in *Virginibus Puerisque* (1881) or critical, as in *Familiar Studies of Men and Books* (1882). Other volumes, akin in spirit and substance, were added in later years, among them *Memories and Portraits* (1887) and

Across the Plains (1892). *Treasure Island* made Stevenson successful and directed the current of his subsequent efforts. It was followed by a series of romances—*Kidnapped* (1886), with its sequel *Catriona* (1893), *The Black Arrow* (1888) and *The Master of Ballantrae* (1889); by the fabulous *Strange Case of Dr Jekyll and Mr Hyde* (1886) and the wildly farcical *The Wrong Box* (1889); and towards the end by various South Sea sketches, the unfinished *Weir of Hermiston* (1896) and *St Ives* (1897), the last completed by "Q". In these romances Stevenson is at his best, like Scott, when he is dealing with his native land. The essays, with a few exceptions, have worn rather badly. Like Meredith, whom he admired not wisely but too well, Stevenson is scarcely ever simple, and at times approaches the condition of manner without matter. The reason for this was not his confessed discipline of "playing the sedulous ape" to other writers, for that way of study is ancient, honourable and profitable; indeed that is the way in which, consciously or unconsciously, all writers begin. His too celebrated "style" was due to a love of pose together with an ingrained artificiality of the kind that made him wear long hair and velvet coats. Stevenson retained a belated boyishness, and not till he wrote the unfinished *Weir of Hermiston* did he show signs of attaining to restraint and self-command.

Andrew Lang (1844–1912), already named (p. 671) among the historians, was the most various miscellaneous writer of his time. Folk-lore, the occult, history, the Homeric question, literary criticism—in all he was active. Under such conditions, it was scarcely possible to be quite first-rate in any department; but Lang never failed to make himself interesting and some of his lighter work has charm. He collaborated with S. H. Butcher in a translation of the *Odyssey* and with Walter Leaf and E. Myers in a translation of the *Iliad*. His collections of essays include *Letters to Dead Authors*, *Books and Bookmen* and *Letters on Literature*. The numerous multi-coloured volumes of fairy-tales and other stories for children are still treasured.

Two rolling stones, both of whom gathered moss, as the elder hinted in the title of one of his books (*Moss from a Rolling Stone*, 1887), were Laurence Oliphant (1829–88) and Lafcadio Hearn (1850–1904). Oliphant's first important publication, *The Russian Shores of the Black Sea* (1853), caused him to be consulted when the Crimean War broke out. He knew Japan while it was still in the medieval stage. In the literary sense his most valuable work was the satiric novel *Piccadilly* (1870), which shows him as a penetrating critic of the society of his time. Lafcadio Hearn (see further below, p. 930) was a literary "impressionist" and recorded in various volumes, especially *Glimpses of Unfamiliar Japan* (1894), his impressions of a country of which he became a citizen, and in which he married a native wife, but of which his knowledge remained superficial.

While Oliphant and Hearn found their literary capital in the distant and unfamiliar, the sphere of Richard Jefferies (1848–87) was the fields and the hedgerows around us. His task was to show that the unfamiliar lay near at hand. He belongs to the class of field naturalists like White of Selborne, but Jefferies was wider in his range. *The Game-Keeper at Home* (1878) and *Wild Life in a Southern County* (1879) belong to the Selborne tradition, but *Hodge and his Master* (1880) deals with the human element in the spirit of Cobbett, while *After London* (1884) and *Amaryllis at the Fair* (1886) are novels of great imaginative power. His story of a boy, *Bevis* (1882), somehow missed popularity. A certain vein of poetry is present in all the works of Jefferies. It is specially rich in *Wood Magic* (1881), and gives charm to the fine spiritual autobiography, *The Story of My Heart* (1883). His life was admirably written by the poet Edward Thomas in 1909.

Jefferies was English to the core; William Henry Hudson (1841–1922) was born in South America and grew up amid the exotic life of a remote and brutal continent. He did not come to England till 1869 and did not become a British subject till 1900. In one respect only does Hudson resemble Jefferies, namely in his smouldering resentment at the crimes of "civilization". His autobiography *Far Away and Long Ago* (1918) gives the essential feelings rather than the facts of his life, and it is, in many respects, the book most necessary to an understanding of the author. With this of course go such works as *The Naturalist in La Plata* (1892) and *Idle Days in Patagonia* (1893). To the English scene he brought an extraordinarily vivid creative interpretation and poured out his impressions in the moving pages of *A Shepherd's Life* (1910), his second essential book. Of similar character are *Nature in Downland* (1900), *Hampshire Days* (1903), *The Land's End* (1908) and *Afoot in England* (1909). Hudson's sensitive, but totally unsentimental, understanding of bird-life finds expression in several books, especially *British Birds* (1895), *Birds and Man* (1901), *Adventures among Birds* (1913), and *Birds in Town and Village* (1919), an enlargement of his first book on birds originally published in 1893. Hudson adopted a plastic form of fiction in *The Purple Land that England Lost* (1885), the curious *A Crystal Age* (1887), the enigmatic *A Little Boy Lost* (1905), the exquisite *Green Mansions* (1904) and the vivid sketches *El Ombú* (1902).

South America forms a link between W. H. Hudson and Robert Bontine Cunninghame Graham (1852–1936), who was as much at home in that continent as in Spain, Scotland and England. An aristocrat by birth, a *hidalgo* in appearance, and a social rebel by act and instinct, he refused classification in life as in literature. Much of his writing hovers between the essay, the story and the impressionistic sketch; but there is no indecision about its character. Unfortunately he chose to lavish much of his skill upon the history of South American adventurers and dictators who cannot be made interesting to English readers even by the most picturesque of writers. Cunninghame Graham's first important book was *Mogreb-el-Acksa* (1898), a vivid account of a frustrated journey in Morocco when the interior of that tourist-haunted land was still inaccessible. *A Vanished Arcadia* (1901), the best of the semi-historical books, tells the story of the Jesuit settlement in Paraguay. Some of Cunninghame Graham's work has already lost its interest; but the best of his sketches have the qualities of permanence.

In the English tradition of Cobbett and Jefferies, and probably the last great writer in that tradition, was "George Bourne", i.e. George Sturt (1863–1927), who came from a family of Surrey wheelwrights, In *The Bettesworth Book* (1901), *Memoirs of a Surrey Labourer* (1907), and *Lucy Bettesworth* (1913) we are shown, without the falsification either of idealism or of realism, the life of the working poor. *Change in the Village* (1912) offers a more general account of country life. *William Smith* (1920) and *A Farmer's Life* (1922) show us revealing pictures of rural England in the form of family history—the persons concerned being Sturt's own forbears. Unquestionably his finest book is *The Wheelwright's Shop* (1923) which gives genuine artistic life to the story of a craft, the workers and the products. *A Small Boy in the Sixties* (1927) is autobiography which tells also the story of time and place. Sturt depicts with feeling and understanding the rural scene, with the high lights thrown upon the human rather than upon the natural elements in the picture.

IV. THE GROWTH OF JOURNALISM

The transition, towards the end of the seventeenth century, from the circulated manuscript "newsletter" of reported gossip, or the small pamphlet of "special intelligence" purchased by a few subscribers, to a regularly issued periodical sheet like *The London Gazette*, with a distinctive name and a regular supply of varied news, marks the true beginning of the modern newspaper. In the opening years of the eighteenth century, interest in the newspaper had become so general that the Stamp Act of 1712 was resisted as a blow to cheap reading (see p. 470). Children, it was alleged, would be deprived of the means of learning to read. The tax was not removed; but statesmen began to recognize that newspapers might be useful to them, and, as we have seen, Harley called in Defoe to provide journalistic propaganda. Then, as now, one great problem of newspaper production was distribution, and so the growth of journalism in the eighteenth century was stimulated by John Palmer's establishment of regular stage coaches. But there were hindrances as well as helps. Parliament was hostile to reporting, and its displeasure was felt even by provincial newspapers, some of which had by this time established themselves. *The Newcastle Courant* began in 1711, *The Liverpool Courier* in 1712, *The Leeds Mercury* in 1720 and *The Manchester Gazette* in 1730. There were many others.

The history of journalism in the nineteenth century is the history of the rapid growth of a reading public, a growth affecting all forms of printed matter. At the beginning of the century the newspapers sought to appeal to a select public; by the end of the century newspapers were competing to secure the largest and least critical public. The early select papers appealed only to man, the political animal; the later popular papers appealed to the whole family, men, women, boys and girls. With the gradual widening of appeal there came, naturally, a softening of the worst asperities of political journalism. No respectable newspaper would now descend to the language of *The Times* when it told "Mr Babbletongue Macaulay" that "he was hardly fit to fill up one of the vacancies that have occurred by the lamentable death of Her Majesty's two favourite monkeys". Dickens's sketch of Eatanswill journalism was written from the experience of a practical newspaper man. But there was much else besides political scurrility. Papers sought the co-operation of reputable writers. Coleridge, Hazlitt, Leigh Hunt, G. H. Lewes and John Forster were all journalists. The arts were taken seriously. To Irving's production of *Macbeth* in 1888 *The Times* gave between seven and eight thousand words of notice. In 1938 such a production would have received a thousand words in the "better" papers, and five hundred in the "popular" papers. Serious criticism of the arts, like serious discussion of politics, disappeared from all but the best papers, and even those were not generous in space. Verbatim reports of important speeches, once a feature of Victorian newspapers, were rarely given in later years. On the other hand, the older papers had nothing resembling the "magazine" pages of modern journals.

Competition for the "largest circulations" during the nineteenth century led to marvellous developments in printing. In 1814 John Walter, the second of that name, made history by showing that, with the aid of steam, newspapers could be printed at the rate of 1100 copies an hour. Today the modern newspaper printing machine is one of the wonders of the world. Less admirable is the growth of fierce commercialism. Newspapers must not only pay their way, they must make "big money" and must therefore, at any cost, succeed. Success of that kind has to be paid for, and the "largest circulations" pitch their appeal very low. The result is not that readers suffer deterioration in taste or feelings, but simply that they do not take their papers seriously. Success has to be found too by the extinction of rivals; and a curious fact of the modern world is that as the number of readers has increased, the number of newspapers has decreased. Thus in 1895 the Londoner had nine evening papers to choose from; in 1935 he had three, in 1965 only two. No one will have the hardihood to assert that these survived through any special fitness: they were in every respect inferior to their vanished rivals. *The Echo, The St James's Gazette, The Pall Mall Gazette, The Globe*, and *The Westminster Gazette* had qualities to which later evening papers could make no pretence; and they were crushed out of existence by brute forces that had nothing whatever to do with journalism. Another modern development was the increased dependence of newspapers upon advertisements. Advertisers are not philanthropists. They require value for their money, and the papers must not offend them. If a time should come when advertisements ceased and costs of production rose we might have to revert to the old four-page sheet. For half of the century the papers were unfettered. There was no censorship of any kind. The tax of a halfpenny a sheet imposed by the Act of 1712 was increased, and in 1815 was four pence. Seven pence was then the usual price of a paper. But in 1836 the duty was reduced to a penny, and in 1855 it was abolished.

Some account of *The Times*—the finest thing of its kind in the world—will illustrate the development of newspapers generally during the century. It was founded by John Walter in 1785 as *The Daily Universal Register*, a title which, in 1788, gave place to *The Times*. It was the first newspaper to be printed by steam-power (1814); it was the first to send special correspondents abroad; it was the first to commission one of its staff, W. H. Russell, as a war-correspondent; it was the first to print what is known as a Parliamentary sketch or leading article; it was the last to oppose the abolition of the stamp and paper duty; it was the last to lower its price to a popular level and the last to print news instead of advertisements on the front page. The first John Walter was its first editor; the second called in the aid of John Stoddart, who was replaced in 1817 by Thomas Barnes, the first of two editors whose fame has never been excelled. Barnes was succeeded in 1841 by John Thaddeus Delane, who reigned till 1877 and made *The Times* a power not merely in England but in Europe. His public prestige was increased by his wisdom in refusing personal publicity. At no time in the Victorian age was it supposed that ownership of a newspaper conferred any right of dictatorship in public affairs.

The most serious rival of *The Times* was *The Morning Post*, which had a continuous history from 1772 to 1937, when it was extinguished for reasons other than journalistic, and merged in *The Daily Telegraph*, which, established in 1855, became the organ of the "great middle classes" and proclaimed its views in a flamboyant style that made it a constant theme of Matthew Arnold's irony. *The Morning Chronicle* ran from 1769 to 1862 and numbered among its reporters the young Charles Dickens, who, much later, undertook the charge of a new Liberal paper, *The Daily News* (1842), but retired after seventeen numbers and was succeeded by John Forster. Another Liberal paper, *The Daily Chronicle*, established in 1877, was in later years absorbed by *The Daily News*, the new production being called *The News Chronicle* (later still incorporated in *The Daily Mail*). Of the vanished evening papers perhaps the most remarkable was *The Pall Mall Gazette*, founded in 1865 by Frederick Greenwood, a great journalist and publicist. He was succeeded by John Morley, who in his turn was succeeded by W. T. Stead, the kind of writer inseparable from "sensations". Stead's exposure of social evils gave him both fame and notoriety, and his stormy career found an appropriate end in the wreck of the "Titanic". *The Echo*, founded in 1868, was the first of London's modern halfpenny papers. Its note was Liberal seriousness. On the other hand, *The Star*, founded in 1888 (and seventy years later incorporated in *The Evening News*), aimed at Radical gaiety that was almost impudence, and found two brilliantly appropriate contributors in A. B. Walkley on drama and George Bernard Shaw on music. The "pink" *Globe*, founded in 1803, and the "green" *Westminster Gazette*, founded in 1893, had such a strong hold on the affections of readers that their extinction seemed calamitous. Gone for ever was the end-of-the-day friendliness that the old evening papers seemed to exhale. Acrimony was now thrust upon us.

The serious "weeklies" played an important part in the life of Victorian readers. Of these the most important was *The Spectator*, founded in 1828 as an organ of "educated Radicalism". *The Saturday Review*, founded in 1855, attained a position of authority which its later years made rather incredible. Two famous "Society" papers were Yates's *The World* and Labouchere's *Truth*. The former was notable for its serious discussion of the drama and music by William Archer and George Bernard Shaw in articles of outstanding merit. *Truth* specialized in the exposure of fraud. Literature and kindred arts were notably served by *The Athenaeum* founded in 1828. Its supremacy was unsuccessfully challenged by *The Academy*, which, after an attempt to save itself by a change of style, collapsed. *The Athenaeum* itself failed to maintain its existence and disappeared into *The Nation*, an organ of advanced Liberalism, which, in its turn, was absorbed by *The New Statesman*, an organ of constructive Socialism. In 1897 *The Times* began to issue a weekly called *Literature*, the place of which was taken in 1902 by *The Times Literary Supplement*. In the twentieth century it became more and more difficult for any serious weekly to maintain a successful existence. The newspapers, and especially the better Sunday newspapers, could provide more diversified matter of the same kind at a much lower price.

Illustrated papers are no new thing. *The Times* had an illustration of Nelson's funeral car, and *The Observer* in 1820 was using illustrations so well that it may be called the first of illustrated papers. But the true vogue of the illustrated weekly set in with *The Illustrated London News* (1842) and *The Graphic* (1869). The quality of the artists and of the reproduction made these weeklies Victorian institutions. *The Queen*, *The Illustrated Sporting and Dramatic News*, *The Field*, and *Country Life* extended illustration to more special regions of appeal. A great change came when the reproduction of photographs was made possible. Though this abolished the special charm of artist and engraver, the gain was great. *The Graphic* was able in 1890 to issue *The Daily Graphic*, the first serious attempt at an illustrated daily; but technical methods developed so rapidly that soon every daily paper had its illustrations, some of great beauty. Increased facilities of production and distribution made it possible for the London papers to invade provincial regions which once possessed their own cherished papers, and one by one most of the local journals perished. The outstanding survivor was *The Manchester Guardian*, later called *The Guardian* with its main office in London. A full description of Victorian journalism would have to take some account of such remarkable products as *The London Journal*, *The Family Herald*, *The Sporting Life* ("*Pink 'Un*"), *Pick-me-up*, *Tit-Bits*, and *Ally Sloper's Half-Holiday*. No survey of the kind can be attempted here.

The most important journalistic event in the last years of the nineteenth century was the reappearance of the halfpenny morning paper. Till then, no ordinary working man or poorly paid clerk regularly bought a morning paper. The year 1892 saw the first attempt to capture this public by the issue of *The Morning* and *The Morning Leader*. The former had a short life; the latter endured for several years, and was then "absorbed". What was needed to give the halfpenny paper a secure life was a combination of journalistic and commercial genius; and this was found in Alfred Harmsworth, later Lord North-cliffe, whose *Daily Mail*, issued in 1896, was the outstanding success of the early twentieth century. Harmsworth, through *The Daily Mail* and the numerous other ventures in which he became concerned, definitely changed the English newspaper for better and for worse. The old journalism recorded news; the new journalism found news, and, if necessary, made news—not, indeed, by invention, but by falsification of values. *The Daily Express*, *The Daily Mirror* and *The Daily Herald*, which successfully challenged *The Daily Mail* in circulation figures, first appeared respectively in 1900, 1903 and 1912. *The Sun* replaced *The Daily Herald* in 1964.

The War of 1914–18, with its financial and social reactions, caused many changes in the world of journalism. Some periodicals perished, some were shattered and never recovered. The halfpenny papers became penny papers; but in character they were halfpenny papers still. The effects of the War of 1939–45 were not entirely beneficial either. Apparently the spread of education had produced a population unwilling to read anything more than large-type headlines, short paragraphs, and alluring captions to pictures. But that was only part of the truth. Never before was there such a plentiful supply of good cheap literature, which must have found a public, or it would not have existed. The tendency towards narrow concentration of proprietorship and the ruthless extinction of independent rivals could not be regarded without alarm. But journalism itself had now to reckon with powers unforeseen and unpredictable—the films, broadcasting, television. It was the competition of television advertising that led to the number of newspapers in New York (of all places) being reduced by the nineteen-sixties to a number below that in London. If the process spreads and continues, then the title of this section will have to be altered to "The Growth and Decline of Journalism".

V. UNIVERSITY JOURNALISM

The *differentia* of university journalism is that it is written by the young for the young. Austere dons may unbend in witty and frolicsome contributions; but the prevailing note is that of youth—youth with the privileges of manhood and none of its responsibilities. A further peculiarity is that university journalism is—or was—written by the scholarly for the scholarly. Intellectual high spirits used to find their most characteristic expression in classical parody and light verse. Here, Cambridge could show a long line of masters from Prior and Praed to Thackeray, Calverley and J. K. Stephen. Oxford was more serious and more prolific in prophets, but could claim first-rate professors of the sportive mood in Andrew Lang, A. D. Godley, A. T. Quiller-Couch and W. P. Ker. Calverley who belonged to both universities was the leading master, and had many disciples.

The credit of having been the first enduring university organ belongs to *The Cambridge Review*, which was started in 1879. It had solid qualities, but it had also its humours, as the selections in *The Book of the Cambridge Review* (1898) clearly proved. In the Nineties, *The Granta* started as a light commentator on Cambridge affairs, and absorbed some of the humour which would have found a place in the *Review*. The wayward genius of J. K. Stephen, already an accomplished rhymer in his Eton days, shone in both periodicals.

The Oxford Magazine, which was started in 1883, secured a recognized position as a commentator on university affairs. Resembling *The Cambridge Review* in general, it differed in being the organ of the don. The pieces in *Echoes from the Oxford Magazine: being reprints of Seven Years* (1890) and *More Echoes* (1896) formed a collection hard to match for cultured fun. These volumes were strong in that humour which comes from imitating in English the style and manner of an ancient author. As *The Cambridge Review* was supplemented by *The Granta*, *The Isis* was started in 1892 as a light-hearted variant on the sobriety of *The Oxford Magazine*.

Conditions in Scotland differed so widely from those prevailing in Oxford and Cambridge, especially in the matter of corporate collegiate life, that the resultant journalism did not make so general an appeal. The first magazine proper of Aberdeen, *The King's College Miscellany* (1846), was serious. *Alma Mater*, also of Aberdeen, began its existence in 1883 and is thus six years senior to *The St Andrews College Echoes*, and *The Glasgow University Magazine* (1889), and four to the Edinburgh *Student* (1887). *The University Maga*, the happiest of early efforts in Edinburgh academic journalism, ran for twenty-four weekly numbers beginning in 1835. Not until 1887, when *The Student* began its career, was it possible to establish an Edinburgh university journal with a reasonable chance of permanence. The Edinburgh university of Carlyle's time, for instance, was an intensely independent and fiercely individualistic society, with no common meeting-place, no common activities, and no sport. In such conditions a students' magazine could not prosper. The university of Edinburgh includes among its academic writers R. L. Stevenson, whose essay entitled "A College Magazine" relates the brief fortunes of *The Edinburgh University Magazine*—one of several efforts bearing that title.

The Dublin University Review, which started in 1885, was a sound and serious production with a shorter life than the earlier *Dublin University Magazine* (see p. 717). It had a far wider scope than English periodicals of the sort, and even included nationalist politics. It was a pioneer, too, in including poetry in the original Irish, the first specimens of Irish type seen in a modern review. The oddly named *Kottabos* is, however, the cream of Irish academic wit and scholarship. It was started by R. Y. Tyrrell in 1868, and appeared three times a year, for thirteen years. Its fortunes and revival are recorded in *Echoes from Kottabos* (1906). The contributors included Edward Dowden, Oscar Wilde, and Standish O'Grady. The "kottabos" was a game favoured by Athenian young men which depended on the skilful throwing of wine from a cup—a title thus peculiarly apt to Irish university life, if we can believe James Joyce and others.

VI. CARICATURE AND THE LITERATURE OF SPORT

Though caricature, in its purely pictorial sense, is beyond the scope of the present survey, we may remark that the relations of caricature and literature are very close. The famous pamphlet ascribed by Swift to Arbuthnot, *Law is a Bottomless Pit, or The History of John Bull* (1712), was a fertile source of figures for draughtsmen. For instance, it popularized, if it did not originate, the personification of England as John Bull. The pictures of William Hogarth (1697–1764) are a kind of literature: they must be read as well as seen. After Hogarth, the next memorable caricaturist is James Gillray (1757–1815), whose savage and brutal inventions appealed to the taste of his age. Hogarth had helped to win for the artist copyright in his own engravings (1735), and the way was thus opened for profitable association between publisher and illustrator. In this connection, honourable mention should be made of John Boydell the printseller, who brought out his famous illustrated edition of Shakespeare in 1802, and employed for his purpose the favourite artists of the day.

Most celebrated among the publishers who extended the relations between art and literature was Rudolph Ackermann (1764–1834), a German, who established lithography in England as a means of reproduction and used the process in his monthly publication, *The Repository of Arts, Literature, Fashions, Manufactures* (1809–28). Ackermann turned to the caricaturists for illustrations to books, and among the earliest of his publications was Bunbury's *Academy for Grown Horsemen...by Geoffrey Gambado, Esq.* Henry William Bunbury (1750–1811), sportsman, caricaturist and writer, was already known for his admirable chalk-drawings of scenes in real life. The book is an early example of the literature of sport, and it was the first of the humorous books for which Ackermann's publishing house became famous. Among the artists working in London was a young man, Thomas Rowlandson (1756–1827), who had given up serious portrait-painting for caricature. Someone suggested to him a series of plates representing a country curate travelling about England. Gilpin had made illustrated travel books popular. Ackermann therefore approved the idea and engaged William Combe to write the letterpress. William Combe (1741–1823) had begun his literary career with *The Diaboliad* (1776). Its successors, *The Diabolady* and *The Anti-Diabo-lady* are equally spirited. The travelling curate was named Dr Syntax, and the work was done, by both artist and author, under extraordinary conditions. One drawing at a time was sent to Combe, then a man of sixty, and confined for debt in the King's Bench prison. The result was a set of thirty plates accompanied by nearly ten thousand lines of verse. Under the title *The Tour of Dr Syntax in Search of the Picturesque*, the joint work of Rowlandson and Combe was published first in *The Poetical Magazine* (1809) and then as a volume in 1812. Its popularity was so great that it at once found imitators; and Ackermann, finding the collaboration profitable, set the pair to work upon other productions. *The Second Tour of Doctor Syntax in Search of Consolation* appeared in 1820 and *The Third Tour of Doctor Syntax in Search of a Wife* in 1821.

The most celebrated exploiter of the "picturesque" was William Gilpin (1724–1804), a clergyman, who in 1782 published his *Observations on the River Wye and several parts of South Wales*. The fashion for illustrated books of travel owed much to him. He had found a profitable formula and worked it out. His next *Observations* (1786) viewed "the Mountains and Lakes of Cumberland and Westmoreland". This was followed by *Observations relative to Picturesque Beauty made…on several parts of Great Britain; particularly the Highlands of Scotland* (1789); and after this came further volumes of "Observations" or "Remarks" on almost all the rest of England.

Illustrated books of travel were among the most successful publications of Ackermann. For his great work of 1821–6, *The World in Miniature*, the earlier of the 637 plates were the work of Rowlandson, and the others of William Henry Pyne, who was both artist and writer. Pyne and Combe together wrote the text of Ackermann's important publications, the histories of *Westminster Abbey* (1812), of *The University of Oxford* (1814) and of *The University of Cambridge* (1815). Rowlandson and Combe were again associated with one of Ackermann's most valuable works, *The Microcosm of London* (1808, etc.).

A different kind of microcosm of London was Pierce Egan's *Life in London; or, The Day and Night Scenes of Jerry Hawthorn, Esq. and his elegant friend Corinthian Tom, accompanied by Bob Logic, the Oxonian, in their Rambles and Sprees through the Metropolis*, a work which began to appear in July 1821, in shilling numbers. For his illustrations Egan went to two brothers, Robert and George Cruikshank. George Cruikshank, the younger and abler, had already maintained the succession from Gillray and Rowlandson as a political caricaturist. Egan's book suited the taste of the time, when a "fast" life had become a conscious aim. Egan himself was a "sporting" man who did not sport. The candid rogues of great picaresque fiction would be ashamed to own Corinthian Tom or Bob

Logic for their kin. But the work is interesting as a revelation of current coarse life and language. Egan was a master of the "flash", and was able to furnish the slang phrases to his new edition (1823) of Francis Grose's *Classical Dictionary of the Vulgar Tongue* (1785), which itself had a new edition in 1963, edited by that *rara avis* among etymologists, Eric Partridge. Imitations of *Life in London* were swift and frequent. One of these, *Real Life in London*, was published in sixpenny numbers in 1821, with excellent illustrations by Heath, Alken, Dighton, Rowlandson and others. An offshoot of *Life in London* was *The English Spy: An Original Work, Characteristic, Satirical and Humorous* (1825), illustrated with many coloured plates, mostly by "Robert Transit" (i.e. Robert Cruikshank), and written by "Bernard Blackmantle", a pseudonym for Charles Molloy Westmacott. *The English Spy* attempts to do for many places in England what *Life in London* and *Real Life in London* had done for the metropolis. The title owed something to Ned Ward's *The London Spy* (see p. 403). In or about 1823, a young artist named Theodore Lane brought to Pierce Egan a series of designs representing theatrical life, and round them Egan wrote *The Life of an Actor* (1824). In 1828 Egan brought out *The Finish to the Adventures of Tom, Jerry and Logic, in their Pursuits through Life In and Out of London*, with illustrations by Robert Cruikshank. It was a kind of moral atonement. Tom is killed, Logic dies, and Jerry settles down.

Among the books on life in London during this period one deserves special notice, *A Book for a Rainy Day, or Recollections of the Events of the Years 1766–1833* (1845) by John Thomas Smith, an artist, who had written a vivid and malicious life of his father's master, the sculptor Nollekens. Smith spent his life in close touch with the artistic and literary life of London, and his *Rainy Day* is one of the most entertaining and trustworthy memorials of his time.

Within twelve hours of the appearance of *Life in London*, the title, the names and the story were seized upon by James Catnach (1792–1841), who put forth a twopenny broadside entitled *Life in London: or, the Sprees of Tom and Jerry, attempted in cuts and verse*. Catnach had long been providing for the poor the highly seasoned fare that Egan was providing for the rich. The son of a north-country printer who, at Alnwick, had issued volumes illustrated by the wood-cuts of Bewick and Clennell, Catnach set up as a printer of popular literature in Seven Dials in the year 1813, and held his own even against the older business of Pitts, hard by. In those days, when newspapers cost sevenpence, Catnach performed an important service for the working classes. He printed and sold illustrated books for children, some at a farthing, some at a halfpenny, some at a few pence; and very good, in their way, they were, with their simple renderings of famous fairy stories, their moral lessons and improving or amusing verses. To Catnach's flysheets one may turn for information about all the turbulent life of the London streets. But chiefly he was known for his exploitation of crime. Those were the days of highwaymen and of public executions. Catnach's sheets, each with portrait, last confession and woeful ballad, sold enormously.

Catnach had no monopoly of crime stories. *The Observer* (later so respectable) flourished on illustrated details of crime. Those were the days, too, of *The Newgate Calendar*. The original series, *The Newgate Calendar; or, Malefactors' Bloody Register*, published in or about 1774, contained in its five volumes notorious crimes from 1700 to the date of publication. Between 1824 and 1826, Andrew Knapp and William Baldwin, attorneys-at-law, issued in four volumes *The Newgate Calendar, comprising Interesting Memoirs of the Most Notorious Characters*; and in or about 1826 they issued in six volumes *The New Newgate Calendar*, which consisted of their original series much enlarged. It was read (mainly by the respectable) almost out of existence. Crime, as a literary titillation, is not, as some suppose, a discovery of the modern intellectual.

Pierce Egan has another distinction. He was the first of sporting journalists. His special line was "the fancy", as pugilism and its followers were called. Thanks to the pleasure taken in the prize-ring by the Prince of Wales and his brothers, pugilism was the most fashionable of amusements. One of Hazlitt's best essays, *The Fight*, describes the great contest between Hickman and Neate. George Borrow (himself a man of his hands) acclaimed "the bruisers of England" in a memorable chapter of *Lavengro*. Of the general interest in sport the great illustrated work of the artist and antiquary Joseph Strutt, *Glig-Gamena Angel-Deod, or The Sports and Pastimes of the People of England from the earliest period* (1801) is a sign. Egan was not the first to write of pugilism; but he had a way with him. He was the inventor of the florid Corinthian style which called the sun "Old Sol" and which long spoke in football journalism of "the visiting custodian" who "literally hurled himself at the leather". In 1824 he began editing a weekly paper, *Pierce Egan's Life in London and Sporting Guide*, which later developed into the more famous sporting journal, *Bell's Life in London*. Egan's *Book of Sports and Mirror of Life* (1832) is a valuable compilation; but his most successful work on sport was the illustrated book, *Boxiana; or, Sketches of Antient and Modern Pugilism, from the days of the renowned Broughton and Slack, to the Championship of Crib*, issued at various dates between 1818 and 1829.

Hunting, like pugilism, became a favourite theme of literature. Peter Beckford's *Thoughts on Hunting* (1781) and *Thoughts upon Hare and Fox Hunting* (1796) are held to have laid the foundations of hunting as a regularized sport. Another book of great influence was *The British Sportsman* (1812) by Samuel Howitt. Among the earliest successors of Bunbury was Henry Alken, who did excellent sporting pictures between 1816 and 1831. His *National Sports of Great Britain, The Analysis of the Hunting Field*, and others, deserve the popularity they achieved. Alken was commended specially for ability to draw English gentlemen, as Cruikshank could not. He was presently associated with someone who could write like a gentleman. "Nimrod", whose name was Charles James Apperley (1779–1843), was a man of education, a country squire and a genuine sportsman. He is best known by two books, *The Life of a Sportsman* (1842), and *Memoirs of the Life of John Mytton* (1837), both of which were illustrated with coloured engravings by Alken. *The Life of a Sportsman* contains a pleasant account of country life in days when sport was no longer confused with debauchery. The *Memoirs of the Life of John Mytton* performed a difficult task with fidelity and tact. Apperley had to write the life of a man who, while he was one of the most heroic sportsmen that ever lived, was also drunken, diseased and insane; and he performed the task with admirable judgment.

Most famous of sporting writers in the nineteenth century is Robert Smith Surtees (1803–64), a Durham squire, who started in 1831, with Ackermann the younger, *The New Sporting Magazine*, which he edited till 1856. Here first appeared the comic papers which in 1838 were published in a book under the title of *Jorrocks's Jaunts and Jollities*. Jorrocks, "the renowned sporting Citizen of St Botolph Lane and Great Coram Street", was a real creation, and he was further exploited in *Handley Cross, or the Spa Hunt* (1843), which was enlarged into *Handley Cross, or Mr Jorrocks's Hunt* (1854) with pictures by John Leech. Then came *Hawbuck Grange* (1847), illustrated by "Phiz" (Hablot Knight Browne); *Mr Sponge's Sporting Tour* (1853), *Ask Mamma, or The Richest Commoner in England* (1858), illustrated by Leech, and *Mr Facey Romford's Hounds* (1865), illustrated by Leech and Browne. It was the success of Surtees that made Chapman and Hall look for an author to write letterpress for Seymour's pictures of Cockney sportsmen. They found Dickens, and *Pickwick* was born. Surtees is a comic writer of a broad and hearty humour which rejoices in personal oddities, yet does not lack the lighter touches. He was careless in construction, but he had a natural gift of fun and lavished it with abounding energy. Surtees was fortunate in the assistance of two young artists who were then carrying on the succession of Alken and George Cruikshank. Both John Leech and H. K. Browne were keen sportsmen and good artists; and though Leech never learned to draw a horse, both men were comic draughtsmen of inventiveness and humour. Browne found good material in the novels of another sporting writer, Francis Edward Smedley (1818–64), a cripple with a taste for sporting literature. Smedley wrote three novels of high spirits and rapid comedy, *Frank Fairlegh* (1850), *Lewis Arundel* (1852) and *Harry Coverdale's Courtship* (1854–5), of which the first long maintained its popularity. Two other famous novelists of sport were George John Whyte-Melville (1821–78), who ventured also into history, and Henry Hawley Smart (1832–93), a soldier of the Indian Mutiny, whose many stories include some still readable.

The old and neglected art of wood-engraving was revived towards the end of the eighteenth century by the genius of Thomas Bewick (1753–1828), who thus brought into being a means of illustration in black and white very useful to the periodical press. Books with Bewick's illustrations are justly valued. In the early years of the nineteenth century, *The Observer*, *Bell's Life in London*, and other papers employed the revived process. The first important illustrated book on cricket was *Felix on the Bat* (1845), written by "N. Felix" (Nicholas Wanostrocht) and illustrated by no less an artist than George Frederic Watts. *Wisden's Cricketing Almanack* began its career in 1864.

The cruder humours of the Regency began to sweeten during the reign of Queen Victoria, and her influence, together with the new possibilities of cheap illustration, served to bring into existence a civilized comic journalism of which *Punch* is the great exemplar. George Cruikshank issued for some years after 1835 his *Comic Almanack*, to which eminent authors contributed; and Thomas Hood had founded his famous *Comic Annual* in 1830. Gilbert Abbott à Beckett (1811–56), a barrister who became a police magistrate, started in 1832 an illustrated comic journal entitled *Figaro in London*, which was illustrated by Robert Seymour and after him by Robert Cruikshank. He was succeeded in the editorship of *Figaro* by Henry Mayhew (1812–87), novelist and philanthropist, best known for his *London Labour and the London Poor* (1851–62). Douglas

Jerrold's *Punch in London* was a predecessor of *Punch*. *Punch* itself may be said to have crept quietly into being. Several people had an idea that something like the Paris *Charivari* ought to succeed. Ebenezer Landells, a wood-engraver, seems to have been the originating spirit; but the first real move was made by Henry Mayhew and Mark Lemon, a publican turned dramatist. The first number appeared on 17 July 1841. To the influence of Henry Mayhew has been ascribed the geniality of tone which differentiated *Punch* from the Paris *Charivari*; but the dominant note was soon struck by a contributor to the second number, Douglas William Jerrold (1803–57), a dramatist and wit who had already made a success with his play, *Black-ey'd Susan*. Jerrold's work gave *Punch* its tone. Here appeared, in 1843, *Punch's Letters to his Son*; in 1845, *Punch's Complete Letter-writer*; and *Mrs Caudle's Curtain Lectures*, which was issued as a book in 1846. Like Dickens, Jerrold had an instinctive sympathy with the poor. Thackeray began his connection with *Punch* with *Miss Tickletoby's Lectures on English History*. In *Punch*, too, appeared his *Diary of Fitz-Jeames de la Pluche*, his *Snobs of England*, and his *Punch's Prize Novelists*. In *Miss Tickletoby's Lectures* some have seen the germ of *The Comic History of England* (1847)—itself the germ of Sellar and Yeatman's *1066 And All That* (1930)—and *The Comic History of Rome* (1852), written by Gilbert Abbott à Beckett, and illustrated by John Leech. Besides these two prolonged efforts of humour, à Beckett wrote a brilliant piece of parody, *The Comic Blackstone*, illustrated by George Cruikshank and John Leech. Thomas Hood began to contribute to *Punch* in 1843, and for the Christmas number of that year wrote *The Song of the Shirt*. Mark Lemon (1809–70), who soon became sole editor, remained in wise and genial control for twenty-nine years. He was succeeded by Shirley Brooks, who began the *Essence of Parliament*. After Brooks came Tom Taylor, after Taylor came F. C. Burnand, and after Burnand came Owen Seaman, who was succeeded by E. V. Knox and Malcolm Muggeridge. Among the early artists should be mentioned Richard ("Dicky") Doyle, whose delightful cover (with his monogram) was long in use. Perhaps the crowning glory of *Punch* was the succession of great black-and-white artists —John Leech, John Tenniel, Charles Keene, George du Maurier and Linley Sambourne. *Punch* had many rivals—*Fun* and *Judy* were both excellent; but they failed to survive. *Punch* continued to prove a faithful mirror of the changing times.

VII. THE LITERATURE OF TRAVEL
AND MOUNTAINEERING

The literature of travel ranges between the insistent personality of Sterne's *Sentimental Journey through France and Italy* and the rigid impersonality of Baedeker's *Guides*. Too much personality makes the reader overlook the travel; too much topography makes the reader forget the person. The writer of a successful book of travel must (in several senses) take the reader with him. Of the many books of travel written since the age of *North-West Fox* (see p. 157), only a very few can be mentioned here.

William Dampier (1652–1715), sailor, buccaneer, privateer and explorer, gives us the earliest travel-books of the period. His *Voyages* appeared in four volumes between 1697 and 1709. Dampier was an excellent writer, full of picturesque and unemphatic detail. At one time he was pilot to Captain Woodes Rogers, who wrote *A Cruizing Voyage round the World* (1712), the most famous passage of which describes the finding of Alexander Selkirk on Juan Fernandez in 1709. George Anson (1697–1762), afterwards Admiral and Lord Anson, made his famous voyage round the world in 1740–4. The excellent book known as his *Voyage round the World* (1748) was compiled by his chaplain R. Walter. The wreck of the "Wager", one of Anson's ships, on a desolate island off southern Chile, produced several narratives. The most notable of these was written twenty-six years after the event by Admiral John Byron, nick-named "foul-weather Jack", who had sailed as a young officer in the "Wager". Byron's *Narrative* (1768) is a well-told story, which possesses a special literary interest in the use made of it by the admiral's more famous grandson for his description of the storm and shipwreck in *Don Juan*.

Several voyages of exploration in the Pacific during the reign of George III were described in readable and interesting narratives by their commanders, Wallis and Carteret (1766–8), James Cook (1768–71, 1772–5, 1776–9) and George Vancouver (1791–5). The account of Cook's first voyage which has been most often published was compiled by John Hawkesworth from the journals of Cook and of Joseph Banks, who accompanied the expedition as botanist; and most people will probably find this compilation more readable than Cook's own narrative, and will also find Banks's journal more interesting than Cook's account. Cook shows a more practised hand in the livelier and easier narrative of his second and third voyages, the last story being cut tragically short by the death of the great navigator at the hands of savages in the Sandwich Islands.

The literature of maritime discovery is continued in Arctic and Antarctic voyages accomplished and related by John Franklin, William Parry, John Ross, James Ross and Francis McClintock during the first part of the nineteenth century. These narratives present thrilling stories of resource, daring, endurance and brilliant achievement in strange and terrible surroundings. One of the most moving of all Polar records is the *Journal* (1913) of Robert Falcon Scott, in which the last entry was made by the dying hand of the writer as he sank under the buffets of storm and frost on his return journey from the South Pole.

The narratives of land travel in the eighteenth century contain, generally, a less interesting story and less readable matter than the maritime records. The object of the writers is, usually, to impart both information and improving reflections. The prevailing dislike of mountains, of uncultivated lands and of Gothic buildings was unfavourable to the sympathetic spirit of travel. The various *Tours* (1769, etc.) of Thomas Pennant at home and Bishop Pococke's *Description of the East* (1743–5) belong to topography rather than to literature. Personality almost overpowering is the note, however, of James Bruce, laird of Kinnaird (1730–94), whose *Travels to Discover the Sources of the Nile*, published in five large volumes (1790), tells a tale so variously romantic, that some people (including Dr Johnson) refused to believe it. It was Bruce who made people really aware of Abyssinia, a country in which his name remained a legend for many years. A contemporary of Bruce was Edward Daniel Clarke, who had all the high spirit and zest of a true traveller; but these qualities appear not so much in his eleven volumes of *Travels in Europe, Asia and Africa* (1816–24), as in the diaries and letters quoted in the biography of Clarke (1824) by his college friend Bishop Otter. Clarke's friend and correspondent, J. L. Burckhardt (1784–1817), a Swiss by birth, but by adoption a Cambridge man and, in some sort, an Englishman, won an enduring reputation by his extensive travels in Asia and Africa and by his faithful descriptions of Oriental life. His *Travels in Nubia* (1819), *Travels in Syria and the Holy Land* (1822) and *Travels in Arabia* (1829) were all published posthumously.

The farthest East found an observer in Sir John Barrow, who accompanied Lord Macartney in the first British embassy to China in 1792. But the reader should turn, not to Barrow's formidable quarto volumes *Travels in China* (1804) and *A Voyage to Cochin-China* (1806), but to his *Auto-biographical Memoir*, published in 1847. Barrow was for forty years under-secretary to the Admiralty, and distinguished himself as supporter and historian of Arctic exploration. The tale of Oriental travel is continued by Sir John Malcolm, who published, in *Sketches of Persia* (1828), an account of his journey as envoy to the Shah from the East India Company.

Curiously characteristic of the Victorian period is the earnestness with which men of normally sedentary habit (like W. P. Ker) made difficult and dangerous mountain ascents and recorded their exploits with an air of nonchalance. *The Alpine Journal* contains much excellent matter, some of which was extracted in the two series of *Peaks, Passes and Glaciers* (1859, 1862). Individual classics of mountaineering are Leslie Stephen's *The Playground of Europe* (1871), Edward Whymper's *Scrambles among the Alps* (1870), with its deathless story of the Matterhorn tragedy, John Tyndall's *The Glaciers of the Alps* (1860), and A. F. Mummery's *My Climbs in the Alps and Caucasus* (1895). What may be called a sub-alpine book is Samuel Butler's *Alps and Sanctuaries*. The successful assaults on Mount Everest and its neighbours have produced some remarkable books, notably by Frank Smythe, John Hunt, the New Zealander Sir Edmund Hillary and the poet-climber Wilfrid Noyce (1917–65) who also wrote *Scholar Mountaineers* (1950) about some of his predecessors mentioned above.

In the nature of things the tale of travel introduced a strong personal note. Perhaps the extreme example is Byron's *Childe Harold*. Alexander von Humboldt's narrative of travels in tropical South America, translated into English in 1814–21, had a personal character that deeply influenced later observers. In 1825 appeared Charles Waterton's *Wanderings in South America*, a most entertaining and vivacious record of adventurous and unconventional travel. One may open this book at any page and be sure of entertainment. Waterton afterwards turned his Yorkshire park into a kind of museum of living creatures. At the age of eighty-three he was still climbing trees and rising daily at 3 a.m.

The war of South American independence and the accompanying political revolution in the early years of the nineteenth century produced a number of descriptions of travels in that continent. Noteworthy is Captain Basil Hall's *Journal on the Coasts of Chile, Peru and Mexico* (1824). Pre-eminent, however, is Darwin's *Journal* (1839) of his voyage in the "Beagle", not only for its place in the history of science, but also for its qualities as a quietly readable record of travel. Another important South American book is *Travels on the Amazon and*

Rio Negro (1869) by Darwin's fellow scientist, Alfred Russel Wallace; but *The Malay Archipelago* (1869) by the same excellent writer and thinker is even better. Associated with Wallace was Henry Bates, a tireless, patient observer, author of *The Naturalist on the River Amazons* (1863).

The most remarkable example of a guide-book that turned into literature is Richard Ford's *Handbook for Travellers in Spain* (1845), which combines sympathy with superiority in a most attractive fashion. Its contemporary, *The Bible in Spain* (1843) by George Borrow, contains little about Spain and less about the Bible, but a great deal about gipsies and low life in certain parts of the Peninsula. Ford and Borrow are complementary and should be read together.

The Near East produced some books of singular fascination. In 1844 appeared two Eastern narratives, *The Crescent and the Cross* by Eliot Warburton, an Irish barrister, and *Eothen* by his college friend Kinglake, of the English bar, afterwards historian of the Crimean War. Warburton who perished in the "Amazon", burnt at sea in 1852 on the way to the West Indies, had at first the greater success; but his book, with its slightly melodramatic and self-conscious tone, cannot be compared with the easy and scholarly *Eothen*, which is, perhaps, the best book of travel in the English language. Kinglake, like Ford, had keen sympathy and understanding, but is always the English gentleman abroad. The same English good-breeding is found in *The Monasteries of the Levant* (1849) by Robert Curzon, afterwards Lord Zouche, who visited the Near East to examine and collect ancient manuscripts.

Foremost among nineteenth-century travellers stands Sir Richard Burton (1821–90). A man of cosmopolitan education and tastes, soldier, linguist, and Oriental scholar, he has recorded the strenuous activities of his crowded life in many volumes recounting travels in Asia, Africa, and South America. Of his books on the East the most important are *Pilgrimage to El-Medinah and Mecca* (1855–6) and the translation of *The Arabian Nights*, annotated with curious knowledge.

A more leisurely picture of Eastern life is found in *A Year's Journey through Central and Eastern Arabia in* 1862–3 by William Gifford Palgrave. Very startling is the *Travels in Arabia Deserta* (1888) by Charles Montagu Doughty (1843–1926), who chose to adopt for his astonishing story of hardships and endurance an elaborately archaic Elizabethan prose which intensifies the fierce light and heat of the desert, but which also intensifies the difficulty of enjoyment; and so a book bearing clear marks of greatness (one of the favourite books of Lawrence of Arabia) has never gained popularity. It is an epic poem in antique prose. An Eastern travel-book of a very different order is *A Popular Account of Discoveries at Nineveh* (1851) by Austen Henry Layard, who was a restlessly energetic wanderer of cosmopolitan tastes and habits. In his old age, after a varied diplomatic and parliamentary career, Layard wrote a charming book called *Early Adventures in Persia, Susiana and Babylonia* (1887).

The exploration of Africa during the nineteenth century produced a multitude of volumes, recording much heroic effort and achievement. David Livingstone must come first. His two books, *Missionary Travels in South Africa* (1857) and *Expedition to the Zambesi* (1865), contain the plain straightforward story of a strenuous life devoted to missionary work and scientific observation. They are clear, well-written records, rather than personal narratives. And, in general, this is true of other works concerning African travel. Most of them are more notable for what they relate than for their manner of relating it, though Burton's *The Lake Region of Central Africa* (1860) expresses the virile and aggressive personality of that untiring traveller. Speke's *Journal of the Discovery of the Source of the Nile* (1863) is a fine record of exploration. Among those whose lives were sacrificed to their passion for Africa there are two outstanding figures, W. Winwood Reade (1838–75) and Mary Kingsley (1862–1900). Reade, a nephew of the novelist, published his vivid *African Sketchbook* in 1873. Two years later he died from the effects of his share in the Ashanti campaign. Winwood Reade is the author of one other famous book, *The Martyrdom of Man* (1872), a pessimistic general sketch of history which has been an inspiration to many readers. Though it is "out of date" in some matters of fact, it can never lose its value. It is a book of genius. Mary Kingsley, whose father and two uncles were all notable voyagers and authors, travelled for scientific observation. In 1900 she died at Simon's Town of enteric fever, caught in tending Boer prisoners. Her *Travels in West Africa* (1897), though marred in places by overlaboured humour, is very good at its best. The Welsh-American Sir Henry Morton Stanley (1841–1904) wrote the travel best-sellers of the nineteenth century in *How I found Livingstone* (1872) and *In Darkest Africa* (1890).

Of South Sea travel the best general accounts are those of Stevenson in several volumes, including the *Vailima Letters* recording his life in Samoa. The growth of the British oversea dominions has produced many books of which the interest is political rather than literary. Froude's *Oceana*, mentioned on p. 670, is an exception in its literary qualities.

The literature of travel expresses something inherent in the character of the British, who may change their skies, but never their souls, and can make themselves a home in any region of the globe. In more recent years, when everyone travelled, many books were compiled to gratify the writers or to adorn the catalogues of publishers, but with them came occasionally some rare volume like Belloc's *Path to Rome* (1902), H. M. Tomlinson's *The Sea and the Jungle* (1912), Norman Douglas's *Old Calabria* (1919) or Freya Stark's *Southern Gates of Arabia* (1936), and we recognized the spirit that moved in *Eothen* and *The Bible in Spain*.

VIII. THE LITERATURE OF SCIENCE

1. Physics and Mathematics

The brilliant achievements of British mathematicians, astronomers and physicists under the influence of Isaac Newton were followed by a long period of comparative inactivity. Native science was out of touch with European movements. Newton, in his *Principia*, had confined himself to geometrical proofs because their validity was unimpeachable; and, his results being novel, he did not wish the discussion as to their truth to turn on the methods used to demonstrate them. But his followers, long after the principles of the calculus had been accepted, continued to employ geometrical proofs. Thus, during the last seventy years of the eighteenth century British mathematical science was in a backwater. But there were some philosophers of outstanding ability. The investigations of Colin Maclaurin, of Thomas Simpson, of John Michell, of Henry Cavendish, of Joseph Priestley and of Sir William Herschel advanced in many ways both the progress of research and our knowledge of natural phenomena. In practical applications of science the early years of the nineteenth century were notable for the invention of the steam-engine, the modern forms of which can be dated from the improvements introduced by James Watt, Richard Trevithick and Henry Bell. With the nineteenth century came a new era. In its early years the use of analytical methods was introduced into the mathematical curriculum at Cambridge, which was recognized as the principal school of mathematics. By 1830 the fluxional and geometrical methods of the eighteenth century had fallen into disuse. At the laboratories of the Royal Institution in London, Thomas Young was preparing the way for the acceptance of the undulatory theory of light, and we may associate with him the names of Count Rumford and Sir David Brewster. At the same time John Dalton in Manchester was studying the expansion of gases. General interest was shown by the formation of societies and the growth of popular lectures. The year 1831 saw the foundation of the British Association for the Advancement of Science, which still carries on its valuable work. Mention should be made of William Whewell's *History of the Inductive Sciences* (1837) which put together in a readable form the leading facts in the history and growth of science. Hardly less important were the twenty-seven volumes of *The Penny Cyclopaedia* (1833–43).

The most notable physicist at the beginning of the Victorian period was Michael Faraday (1791–1867), who in 1831 began those investigations on electricity which revolutionized industrial science. His earliest electrical work related to induced currents, and the main result of his labours is the modern dynamo. It is difficult to overrate Faraday's abilities as an experimen al philosopher. He was followed at the Royal Institution by John Tyndall (1820–93), whose lectures did much to excite and maintain general interest in physical questions. Before the first half of the century had closed Sir Charles Wheatstone had not only suggested the use of spectrum analysis and invented stereoscopic instruments, but had brought electric telegraphy into practical use. The continuation and extension of Faraday's work naturally fell into the hands of mathematicians. In the mid-century we find half a dozen mathematicians—De Morgan, Hamilton, Sylvester, Adams, Cayley and Smith—whose researches make that period memorable. Augustus De Morgan was the oldest. With him we may associate George Boole, the creator of certain branches of symbolic logic. Sir William Rowan Hamilton has many claims to eminence, but is best known by his introduction of quaternions as a method of anlysis. James Joseph Sylvester wrote much on the theory of numbers and higher algebra. Three investigations in theoretical astronomy are specially connected with the name of John Couch Adams of Cambridge. The first is his discovery in 1846 of the planet Neptune; the second is his discussion of the secular acceleration of the moon's mean motion; the third is his determination of the orbit of the Leonid shooting stars. Arthur Cayley discussed many subjects in pure mathematics. Henry John Stephen Smith did brilliant work in the theory of numbers and Sir George Howard Darwin, great son of a greater father, distinguished himself by work on the origin of the moon and the causation of tides.

It was the good fortune of the Cambridge school to produce in the Victorian period some of the greatest physicists of the century. Of these four are outstanding—George Green, Sir George Stokes, Sir William Thomson (Lord Kelvin) and Clerk-Maxwell. George Green was a self-educated man who came to Cambridge in middle life, and in the few years before his death had made valuable researches which profoundly impressed Stokes and Kelvin. Sir George Gabriel Stokes did a mass of varied and valuable work in optics, hydrodynamics, and geodesy, as well as in pure mathematics. Sir William Thomson, Lord Kelvin, was a man of so many interests that it is difficult to give any brief account of them. He possessed an almost intuitive power of realizing fundamental principles. Electromagnetics, hydrodynamics, elasticity, and thermodynamics were some of the subjects on which he wrote, and his papers on energy and entropy were of far-reaching importance. Throughout his life he endeavoured to give science a practical application. He made submarine cabling possible. He was a keen yachtsman and took up the problem of compasses. He seemed to touch nothing that he did not make more practical. James Clerk-Maxwell, applying mathematical demonstration to the ideas of Faraday, showed that light consists of transverse waves of the same medium as that required for the explanation of electric and magnetic phenomena. Further researches in mathematical physics are associated with the names of Lord Rayleigh, Sir Joseph John Thomson and Sir Joseph Larmor. Some of Clerk-Maxwell's assumptions remained unsupported; but a few years later his main theory was established by the researches of Hertz, and the results of the experiments led to the introduction of wireless telegraphy. The question of the conduction of electric discharges through liquids and gases had been raised by Faraday. It was now taken up seriously, and various types of rays, cathode rays, Röntgen rays, etc., were discovered. These researches led to new views on the constitution of matter.

The work in physics of the Victorian period completely revolutionized the subject, and, both on its theoretical and its practical sides, far exceeded in value that previously done in any period of similar extent. The twentieth century began with Planck's "quantum" theory of the propagation of energy. Then came the Michelson-Morley investigation into the velocity of light, showing that there was no fixed frame of reference for the measurement of cosmic motion. The first promulgation of Einstein's theory of relativity followed; and the physical concepts that had seemed as firm as the earth itself began to grow insubstantial. The sweet simplicity of the gravitational pull sank into an antiquated superstition. Euclidean space was to be regarded as a mere local and temporary convenience of definition, not as a condition of the universe. No more could we think of "space" and "time" as separate entities: we were compelled to think in terms of a "space-time" continuum. The idea was not entirely new. Readers of C. H. Hinton's *What is the Fourth Dimension?* (1884) had been invited to consider "some stupendous whole, wherein all that has ever come into being or will come co-exists". More startling, because more popular and intelligible, was the first scientific fantasia of H. G. Wells, *The Time Machine* (1895), in which it is claimed that "any real body must have extension in *four* dimensions"; that "there is no difference between Time and any of the three dimensions of Space except that our consciousness moves along it"; and that this motion of our consciousness in one direction has led to a distorted view of Time. A later book, *An Experiment with Time* (1927), by J. W. Dunne, cited the well-known "irrationality" of time in dreams, and propounded a theory of "serialism" which, apart from any question of its validity (it was severely criticized by the philosopher C. D. Broad in the *Proceedings of the Aristotelian Society*), disconcerted those who had thought of time merely as something measured on the circumference of a clock-face or along a graduated line. These works, which in no derogatory sense may be called popular, were as symptomatic of a changing view of the universe as the treatises of the great investigators. Alice, in continual perplexity about her varied extensions in Space, i.e. about her changing universe, and the Mad Hatter, convinced that Time was not "It" but "Him" (and therefore dimensional), may be taken as parables in anticipation.

Among the older philosophical men of science, Sir Oliver Lodge (1851–1940) not only did work of great importance in the study of the ether, but presented views of psychical belief that the generation of Huxley and Tyndall would have regarded as superstitiously unscientific. In volumes such as *Electrons* (1923), *Atoms and Rays* (1924) and *Ether and Reality* (1925) Lodge dealt with the atomic structure of electricity and passed into wider speculations. Much of his later work dealt with the borderland between the physical and the psychical world. *Evolution and Creation* (1926), *The Survival of Man* (1927), *Beyond Physics* (1930) and *The Making of Man* (1934) have the peculiar interest that attaches to the speculations of a scientific mind about things unseen.

Sir Joseph John Thomson (1856–1940), Master of Trinity, made profound researches into the nature of the atom and contributed to the discovery of the electron. His first great book, *Elements of the Mathematical Theory of Electricity and Magnetism*, had appeared in 1895; his later works, *The Corpuscular Theory of Matter* (1905), *The Electron in Chemistry* (1923) and *Beyond the Electron* (1925) take us into the new world of physical speculation. Sir William Henry Bragg (1862–1942) contributed to our knowledge of light and radiation, and in *The Universe of Light* (1933) showed the possibility of a reconciliation between the corpuscular and the wave theories.

A great contribution to the philosophy of mathematics was made by Bertrand, afterwards Earl, Russell (see p. 664) and Alfred North Whitehead (1861–1947) in *Principia Mathematica* (1910–13). Whitehead passed from *Principia Mathematica* to *Introduction to Mathematics* (1919), which presents mathematics as the foundation of exact thought in the study of natural phenomena, and to *An Enquiry Concerning the Principles of Natural Knowledge* (1919), which showed the necessity of emphasizing the connection rather than the separation of space and time. *The Concept of Nature* (1920) presents ultimate physical ideas. In 1922 came *The Principle of Relativity* and in 1926 *Science and the Modern World*, perhaps his most important work. The breadth of Whitehead's constructive mind is exhibited in such books as *Religion in the Making* (1927), *Process and Reality* (1929), *Adventures of Ideas* (1933), *Nature and Life* (1934) and in numerous essays and addresses on a wide range of subjects. Whitehead and his "philosophy of organism" hold an important place in the thought of the early twentieth century.

The new approach to astronomy was attractively shown in the works of Sir James Jeans (1877–1946), who had in a high degree the gift of making abtruse discussion intelligible to the ordinary studious reader. *The Stars in their Courses* (1931) and *Through Time and Space* (1934) were both based on popular addresses. *The Universe Around Us* (1929) and *The Mysterious Universe* (1930) presented general views of cosmology in the light of modern physical theory. *The New Background of Science* (1934) was a philosophical discussion of recent research and discovery. *The Mathematical Theory of Electricity and Magnetism* (1925) and *Atomicity and Quanta* (1926) were more technical studies.

Sir Arthur Eddington (1882–1944), director of the Observatory at Cambridge, brought to the problems of space and time a mind of great power in conception and of great lucidity in expression. *Space, Time and Gravitation* (1921) was an outline of the general relativity theory. *Stars and Atoms* (1927) showed how the new knowledge of atoms and radiation helps the study of astronomy. More important in philosophical interpretation were *The Nature of the Physical World* (1928) and its sequel *New Pathways in Science* (1935).

The Expanding Universe (1933) was perhaps the most notable of all Eddington's more popular works, since supplemented in the light of more recent observations by such books as Fred Hoyle's *Frontiers of Astronomy* (1955) and Raymond A. Lyttleton's *The Modern Universe* (1956). Both Sir Harold Spencer-Jones, Astronomer Royal 1933–55, and Sir Bernard Lovell, Director of Jodrell Bank, have written books for the intelligent non-specialist. Spencer-Jones's *Life on Other Worlds* (1940) should be read as a sober complement, or contrast, to the science fiction which in the mid-twentieth-century beginnings of the Space Age naturally outdid the wildest fantasies of Jules Verne and H. G. Wells —though it must be recorded that at least two distinguished scientists, the British astronomer Hoyle and the Russian-born American biochemist Isaac Asimov, have written science fiction themselves. Lovell's books include *Radio Astronomy* (1952) and the 1959 Reith Lectures, *The Individual and the Universe*. "The science of the universe" is the subject of H. Bondi's *Cosmology* (1952) and of an absorbing little book *Rival Theories of Cosmology* (1965) by Bondi, Lyttleton, W. B. Bonnor and G. J. Whitrow.

Modern physical theory ranges from the telescopically vast to the microscopically minute. The great researches of Ernest, afterwards Lord, Rutherford (1871–1938) were in part embodied in *Radioactivity* (1904), afterwards expanded into *Radiations from Radioactive Substances* (1930). The New Zealander Rutherford was a giant in the laboratory and is regarded as the greatest experimental physicist since Faraday. Amongst those who have written on the atom are Frederick Soddy in *The Interpretation of the Atom* (1932), Edward Neville da Costa Andrade in *The Structure of the Atom* (1927) and George Gamow in *Atomic Energy in Cosmic and Human Life* (1947). The useful Pelican book *Atomic Energy* (1950), edited by J. L. Crammer and the German-born R. E. Peierls, has contributions by such international authorities as Sir John Cockcroft, the American physicist Philip Morrison, the Austrian physicist Otto Robert Frisch, the German physicist Hans A. Bethe and the Australian mineralogist C. E. Tilley.

2. Chemistry

Chemistry has always busied itself with the changes in material things. Some of these changes were so startling that, paradoxically, the earlier chemists began to seek for the unchanging. The history of alchemy is the history of a particular branch of the universal quest, the quest of the absolute. In the later years of the eighteenth century, between 1770 and 1790, chemistry changed rapidly from an empirical art to an experimental science. The man who made the great transformation was Antoine Laurent Lavoisier, a Frenchman of such beneficent eminence that he was naturally guillotined during the Revolution. After the days of Lavoisier, chemists began to concentrate their attention on the changes that happen during combustion. At the end of the eighteenth century and the beginning of the nineteenth we find some outstanding names. Priestley and Cavendish investigated the phenomena of combustion. Black was the first chemist to make an accurate, quantitative examination of a particular, limited, chemical change, and, by so doing, to give clearness to the expression "a homogeneous substance". The atomic theory was Dalton's gift to science. Williamson and Frankland added the molecule to the atom. Graham and Faraday worked on the borderland between chemistry and physics. The investigations of Davy touched and illuminated every side of chemical progress.

Joseph Priestley (1733–1804), theologian, educationist and intrepid liberal reformer, is mainly remembered by his remarkable scientific work. Self-taught in science, under the influence of Benjamin Franklin, he published *The History and Present State of Electricity* (1767) recording new researches, and later discovered the oscillatory electrical discharge, almost entirely overlooked by subsequent investigators. His discovery, or isolation, of ten new gases, including oxygen (as it was afterwards called), led to the revolution in chemistry of which Lavoisier was the outstanding figure. Priestley's preference, after much wavering, for the "phlogiston" theory of combustion as a simpler explanation of the facts than Lavoisier's has unduly discredited his memory. Yet Priestley, though regarding speculation as "a cheap commodity", was a pioneer in scientific theory, of which he thought the object was "to comprise as much knowledge as possible in the smallest compass". Henry Cavendish is associated with "inflammable air" (hydrogen) as Priestley is with "dephlogisticated air" (oxygen). He exploded accurately measured volumes of dephlogisticated air (oxygen) and inflammable air (hydrogen), and found that water was the sole product of the change when the volumes were as one to two. He could not explain what he had done, because he insisted on making the facts uphold the phlogistic theory; but he had, in fact, determined the quantitative volumetric composition of water. Joseph Black is associated with "fixed air" (carbon dioxide), which he found was given off from magnesium carbonate. He laid the foundations of quantitative analysis and worked out the theory of latent heat. John Dalton (1766–1844), a quiet, simple Quaker, gave chemistry a new tool when he published *A New System of Chemical Philosophy* in 1808. Many of Dalton's predecessors, both chemists and physicists, had used, in a vague and general manner, the Greek conception of the atomic structure of matter. Dalton showed how the relative weights of atoms could be determined. Incidentally he investigated colour blindness (from which he suffered) and this defect was long known as "Daltonism". An Italian chemist, Avogadro, brought into science the notion of a second order of minute particles, thus supplementing the conception of atom by that of molecule. Alexander Williamson endeavoured to determine the relative weights of molecules by purely chemical methods, though his methods proved to be less satisfactory than the physical methods of Avogadro. Sir Edward Frankland (1825–99) applied the notion of equivalency to the atoms of elements, and arranged the elements in groups, the atoms of those in any one group being of equal value in exchange. The great industry of making aniline colours is an outcome of the notion of atomic equivalency introduced by Frankland into chemical science. Humphry Davy (1778–1829), the friend of Wordsworth and Scott, was the most brilliant of English chemists. He isolated the hitherto unknown metals potassium, sodium, calcium, barium, strontium and magnesium, and proved that "oxymuriatic acid" is not an acid, but a simple substance, which he named "chlorine" from its colour. He investigated the relations between chemical affinity and electrical energy, and his researches into the behaviour of "firedamp" led to the invention of the miner's safety lamp. Among the earlier physical chemists a high place is taken by Thomas Graham, who established the fundamental phenomena of the diffusion of gases and of liquids, and distinguished between crystalloids and colloids.

Electrochemistry, the study of the connections between chemical and electrical actions, has been productive, in recent years, of more far-reaching results than have been obtained in any other branch of physical chemistry. Faraday did much of the pioneer work. To him we owe the fundamental terms of electrochemistry. The separation of a salt into two parts by the electric current he called "electrolysis"; the surfaces from which the current passes he named "electrodes"; the substance liberated at the electrodes he called "ions". He distinguished the intensity of electricity from the quantity of it, and indicated the meaning of each of these factors. The results established by Faraday have led to the conception of atoms of electricity, a conception which has been of great service in advancing the study of radioactivity. His Diaries were fully published in 1932–3.

At the time of the foundation of the Royal Society in 1660 chemistry was a conglomeration of more or less useful recipes and a dream of the elixir. Today, chemistry is becoming an almost universal science, passing across the frontiers to physics in one direction, and to biology in another. And by strange revolution the ancient dream of a universal, absolute substance can no longer be dismissed with a smile, as some of the so-called elements are in danger of having their independence destroyed by resolution. Chemistry has become the creative ally of commerce, and many products of the laboratory are now among articles of general utility. A great deal of revolutionary work has also been accomplished in the study of nutrition. Chemistry shades into biochemistry, and some researches that might be considered as belonging to chemistry may be regarded as mainly biological. Possibly the greatest recent advance is the discovery of the mysterious vitamins, or accessory food-factors, our knowledge of which we owe mainly to the researches of Sir Frederick Gowland Hopkins (1861–1947).

3. Biology

"The Royal Society of London for Improving Natural Knowledge", one of the oldest scientific societies in the world, and certainly the oldest in the British Empire and Commonwealth, was formally founded in 1660 and received its royal charter of incorporation two years later. The word "natural", as used in the charter, was deliberately opposed to "supernatural", the aim of the Society being, at any rate in part, to discourage divination and witchcraft. Of Harvey and his contemporaries something has already been said (see p. 374); a few words should be added about their immediate successors. The recent invention of the microscope had given a great impetus to the study of the anatomical structure of plants and, later, of animals. Thus helped, Nehemiah Grew (1641–1712) was able to pursue his study of plant-anatomy. His most interesting contribution to botany was the discovery that flowering plants, like animals, have male and female sexes. The study of botany was further aided by John Ray (1627–1705), who made a classification of plants which remained in use till it was gradually replaced by the Linnaean system. Ray has other claims on our notice. With Francis Willughby he began methodical investigations of animals and plants in all the accessible parts of the world. He has been called the founder of natural history as a scientific study. His greatest single improvement was the division of the herbs into monocotyledons and dicotyledons. Robert Hooke (1635–1703), curator of experiments to the Royal Society, was a man avid of fame. His work in astronomy is specially remarkable. Newton owed something to him, but Hooke was anxious to claim personal priority for almost every advance made in his time. His "Microscopicall Observations" fascinated Pepys. During much of the eighteenth century the study of the anatomy of plants made little progress; but there was a real advance in our knowledge of plant physiology. One of the pioneers was Stephen Hales (1677–1761), who showed that the air might be a source of food for plants and connected the assimilative function of leaves with the action of light. He was not less remarkable as an investigator of animal physiology, and was the first to measure the blood-pressure, and the rate of flow in the capillaries. He was, further, a man of "many inventions", especially in the fields of ventilation and hygiene.

The most important activity of the eighteenth century was the formation of public museums. Various collections had found a home in great private mansions, in coffee-houses, and in the homes of surgeons and apothecaries. Now public libraries were being established, and in many of these botanical, geological and especially zoological specimens found a home. The British Museum received its charter in 1753. The nucleus of the University Museum at Cambridge was formed in 1728. John Tradescant established in South Lambeth a museum which was acquired in 1659 by Elias Ashmole and which, transferred to Oxford, became the present Ashmolean Museum. The collection of John Hunter developed into the great museum of the Royal College of Surgeons. Botanic Gardens were founded, during the seventeenth century, at Oxford, Edinburgh and Chelsea. Cambridge followed in 1759, and in 1765 the greatest of all, Kew Gardens, was founded. In 1783 Sir James Edward Smith secured, from the mother of Linnaeus, for a thousand guineas the entire Linnaean collections; and in 1788 the Linnaean Society was founded and produced a revolution in scientific literature by issuing "Transactions" instead of treatises. Other "single science" societies were formed—the Horticultural in 1803, the Geological in 1807, the Zoological in 1826 and the Botanic in 1839.

Great advance was made in our knowledge of the flora and fauna of the British dominions beyond the seas by the work of Sir Joseph Banks (1744–1820) and his secretary Robert Brown (1773–1858). Brown was the first to observe the cell-nucleus. In the early part of the nineteenth century, improvements in the microscope were demonstrating very clearly that all living organisms, whether plant or animal, consist either of a single cell or a complex of cells, and that they all began life as a single cellular unit. Another great advance, largely due to Brown, was the replacing of the Linnaean system of classification by the more natural groups.

Modern geology in Great Britain begins with James Hutton, who published his *Theory of the Earth* in 1795, and used strictly inductive methods in investigation. He "saw no occasion to have recourse to the agency of any preternatural cause in explaining what actually occurs". William Smith (1769–1839), the "father of English Geology", became interested in the structure of the earth's crust, at first, from a land-surveyor's and engineer's point of view. He was one of the earliest to recognize that each of the strata he studied contains animal and plant fossils peculiar to itself, by which it can be identified. Belief in a universal deluge was firmly held by most geologists during the first half of the nineteenth century. But *The Principles of Geology* (1831, 1832, 1833) by Sir Charles Lyell marks a transition. Lyell discredited orthodox "catastrophic" teaching about the age and creation of the earth and established the modern view that the earth was gradually shaped by causes still in operation. Lyell's first volume was carefully studied by Darwin during the voyage of the "Beagle". In his turn Lyell was converted by Darwin's *Origin of Species* (1859) and investigated the evidence in favour of the early existence of man. Sir Roderick Impey Murchison, who had fought in the Peninsular War, was attracted to science by Davy and became an eager and enthusiastic geologist. In 1831 he began his real life's work, a definite inquiry into the stratification of the rocks on the border of Wales. The result of his labours, published in 1839, was the establishment of the Silurian system and the record of strata older than any hitherto described in these islands. Later, with Adam Sedgwick, he established the Devonian system. On the zoological side, one of the most productive morphological anatomists of the nineteenth century was Sir Richard Owen. Following on the lines of Cuvier, he was particularly successful in reconstructing extinct vertebrates.

Among marine biologists of eminence was Edward Forbes, who was the first to investigate the distribution of marine organisms at various depths in the sea. The custom of naturalists to go on long voyages was still maintained. Joseph Hooker accompanied Sir James Ross in the "Erebus" on his voyage in search of the south magnetic pole; Huxley sailed on the "Rattlesnake" and laid the foundation of his remarkable knowledge of the structure of marine animals; Darwin sailed on the "Beagle" (1831–6) and was thus enabled to form his theory of the structure and origin of coral-reefs. The invention of telegraphy indirectly brought about a great advance in our knowledge of deep-sea fauna. It was necessary to survey the routes upon which the large oceanic cables were to be laid, and, by the invention of new sounding and dredging instruments, it was becoming possible to secure samples of the bottom fauna as well as of the sub-stratum upon which it existed. The most important attempt to solve the mysteries of the sea was that of H.M.S. "Challenger", which was despatched by the Admiralty at the close of the year 1872. But though much of interest was discovered, the depths of the ocean did not render up creatures either ancient or unknown.

By far the most important event in the history of biology in the nineteenth century was the publication of *The Origin of Species* (1859), a book which changed the intellectual outlook of the world. There were several British evolutionists before Darwin, amongst whom may be mentioned Charles Darwin's grandfather Erasmus Darwin, and some even hinted at natural selection. Above all, Robert Chambers, whose *Vestiges of Creation* (1844) remained anonymous until after his death, strongly pressed the view that new species of animals were being evolved from simpler types. Two lines of thought about evolution must be carefully distinguished; first, that, by some means, new forms of life are derived from pre-existing forms; and second, that this change of old forms into new must be the result of some discoverable process or processes. The first of these lines of thought had been accepted by many writers. Darwin's great merit was that he conceived a process by means of which this evolution in the organic kingdom could be explained. The theory of natural selection through the survival of the fittest was formed almost at the same time, at two far ends of the earth, by Charles Darwin and Alfred Russel Wallace, each of whom honourably gave credit to the other. It is difficult now to conceive the horror with which the doctrine of evolution filled the minds of the orthodox, who were certain that rejection of a belief in the creation of the universe by six divine acts on six days of a single week destroyed the foundations of religion and morality. Not all men of science accepted the evolutionary view. Owen was unconvinced; but in Hooker on the botanical side, in Huxley on the zoological side, and in Lyell on the geological side Darwin found three of the ablest intellects of his time as champions. Like all great observers in all ages Darwin made mistakes. Perhaps if he had used the term "natural rejection" instead of "natural selection" some unnecessary criticism might have been avoided. Darwin was a modest man and did not suppose that he had said the last word about the origin of species; but in his simple and almost religious way he said a first word of such power that the year 1859 still marks an epoch in the history of thought.

After Darwin came Mendel and Weismann with their researches into heredity and the transmission of acquired characteristics. The English apostle of Mendel was William Bateson (1861–1926), author of *Materials for the Study of Variation* (1894) and *Mendel's Principles of Heredity: a Defence* (1902), in which he used the term "genetics". *Problems of Genetics* followed in 1913. The posthumous *Essays and Addresses* (1928) revealed Bateson's command of lucid, expository prose.

Numerous attractive volumes came from Sir John Arthur Thomson (1861–

1933), the most important being *Life: Outlines of General Biology* (1931) written in collaboration with Sir Patrick Geddes (1854–1932), a vigorous, active thinker, whose many interests extended from zoology to town-planning. The same pair had produced *The Evolution of Sex* (1899) and *Evolution* (1922). Thomson alone wrote a long series of volumes, some dealing with specific biological problems, some touching the relations of science and religion, and some more popular descriptive works in general natural history. Among them may be named *The Control of Life* (1921), *What is Man?* (1924), *Science and Religion* (1925), *Concerning Evolution* (1925), *Heredity* (1926), *Scientific Riddles* (1932) and *Purpose in Evolution* (1932). There was greater depth in Thomson than one would expect from such ready productiveness.

Two notable names, properly considered together, are those of John Scott Haldane (1860–1936) and John Burdon Sanderson Haldane (1892–1964), father and son, members of a remarkable family, the elder being a brother of Lord Haldane and of Elizabeth Sanderson Haldane, the latter of whom combined valuable public service with published studies in the life and writings of Descartes. J. S. Haldane's work in biology was both philosophical in interpretation and practical in its application. *Organism and Environment* appeared in 1917, *The New Physiology*, a collection of varied addresses, in 1919 and *Human Experience* in 1926. More important in its presentation of thought is *The Sciences and Philosophy* (1929). *The Philosophical Basis of Biology*, a consideration of ultimate questions raised by modern research, followed in 1931 and *The Philosophy of a Biologist* in 1935. J. B. S. Haldane, like his father, united power of research with ability to present large general views. His *Possible Worlds* (1928) and *The Inequality of Man* (1932) ranged from history to Mahatma Gandhi, and *The Causes of Evolution* (1932) subjected the Darwinian hypothesis to critical re-examination. His essays appeared in journals ranging from *Nature* to *The Rationalist Annual*, from *The Daily Worker* to *The Proceedings of the Royal Society*. He ended his life working in India. His *Animal Biology* (1927) was written in collaboration with Sir Julian Huxley (b. 1887), author of *Essays of a Biologist* (1923), *Essays in Popular Science* (1926), *Religion without Revelation* (1927) and *Evolution: The Modern Synthesis* (1942). The literary talent of the Huxley family, descending from Thomas, the great Darwinian zoologist, to Leonard, scholar and man of letters, and thence to the brothers Julian and Aldous, is a remarkable case that should interest students of heredity.

Sir Francis Galton (1822–1911), author of *Hereditary Genius* (1869) and *Inquiries into the Human Faculty and its Development* (1883), founded the branch of biological study which he called "eugenics". He was a great authority on meteorology, and, in another sphere of research, organized the study of human finger-prints. He is thus the father of modern criminal detection. His follower and biographer, Karl Pearson (1857–1936), author of *The Grammar of Science* (1892), gave us the statistical biological method known as "biometrics".

The researches of Sir Arthur Everett Shipley (1861–1927) are indicated in the title of his best-known book, *Pearls and Parasites* (1908). *The Minor Horrors of War* (1915) and *More Minor Horrors* (1916) are further studies in parasitology and the spread of disease. Sir Ronald Ross (1857–1932) rendered invaluable service to the human race by his researches into the carrying of malaria by mosquitoes. His scientific investigation was touched by the imaginative spirit that expressed itself in his *Poems* (1928) and other works in literature.

The study of geology was notably advanced by William Johnson Sollas (1849–1936) in *The Age of the Earth* (1905) and *Ancient Hunters* (1911), and the study of botany by Sir Frederick Keeble (1870–1952), author of *Plant-Animals: a Study in Symbiosis* (1910) and by Sir Albert Charles Seward (1853–1941), author of *Plant Life through the Ages* (1931), *Plants, What They Are and What They Do* (1932), and editor of some valuable composite volumes.

Man as both the creator and the creature of his own myths attracted some very notable writers. Sir Edward Burnett Tylor (1832–1917) in his *Primitive Culture* (1871) made anthropological research familiar to the general reader. A writer of far wider range was Sir James George Frazer (1854–1941), whose original treatise on comparative religion grew into the numerous volumes of *The Golden Bough* (1890, etc.), equally remarkable for its vast assembly of facts and its unusual charm of presentation. Few men of such learning have written more attractively. Besides numerous other works in his special subject, Frazer produced an elaborately edited translation of Pausanias in six volumes (1898) and various literary essays and selections that reveal a mind as sensitive to poetry as to science. A later view of man's developing civilization was presented by Sir Grafton Elliot Smith (1871–1937), an Egyptologist and anatomist of Australian birth, who, in *The Ancient Egyptians and the Origin of Civilization* (1923), propounded the doctrine that civilization had its origin in Egypt and was gradually diffused, even to America and Japan, by bands of traders. *Human History* (1934) discusses further the development of local culture. Among other writers on man in nature and in social history may be named Sir Arthur Keith (1866–1955), whose major works include *The Human Body* (1912), *The Antiquity of Man* (1915), and *A New Theory of Human Evolution* (1948).

Nothing would more astonish the materialist philosophers of the last four decades of the nineteenth century than the changed attitude of scientific speculation towards the intangible element in human aspiration. With the advance of research into regions undreamed of—including research into dreams themselves by Freud and his followers and research into what J. B. Rhine has called "extra-sensory perception"—there has come a lessening of the confident agnosticism and materialism that marked the period of Huxley and Tyndall. That is one side of the extraordinary progress of science during the twentieth century. There is a less comforting side. In Butler's Erewhon, machines were rigorously suppressed on the ground that they were bound to evolve and destroy their makers. Butler's Darwinian jest was nearer to truth than he knew, for man is now in the ignominious predicament of seeking ways of escape from the terrors of his own inventions. It was not a satirist or moralist, but a great engineer and physicist, Sir Alfred Ewing, author of works on magnetic induction and thermodynamics, who, in his presidential address to the British Association in 1932, deplored that progress in physical science has given to man powers which he is at present morally unfitted to use.

IX. ANGLO-IRISH LITERATURE AND THE IRISH LITERARY REVIVAL IN THE AGE OF SYNGE AND YEATS

For the purposes of this chapter, Anglo-Irish literature means the work of Irish writers treating (mainly) of Irish themes in the English language. It does not mean ancient, medieval or modern Irish literature written in Latin or in Irish. The elaborately trained Irish bards preserved many old legends; and some of the stories and the style of their telling lived on in the memory of the Irish people, colouring their way of speech and their way of feeling. Perhaps the radical difference between the Irish and the English is that they have different mythologies. There are few traces of any direct connection between native Irish literature and English after the missionary period. Spenser had first-hand knowledge of Ireland; but his description of the country is so hostile that he was unlikely to have felt any interest in the native poetry.

Matthew Arnold, in the lectures collected as *The Study of Celtic Literature*, considers Shakespeare full of Celtic magic in his handling of nature. Arnold's general thesis, courageously propounded in the days when the German school of history was in the ascendant, is that there was no such incredible event as the extermination of the British by the invading Teutons during the fifth and sixth centuries; there was slaughter, but there was also mingling; and the result was a leavening of the dull, efficient German by the lighter, imaginative Briton. And so Arnold declares that there is a Celtic element in the English nature, as well as a Germanic element, and that English poetry got its turn for style possibly from this Celtic element, its turn for melancholy probably from this Celtic element, and its turn for natural magic certainly from this Celtic element. But that Celtic element is native, and has not been derived from Wales or Scotland or Ireland.

Of English (and American) hospitality to Celtic story, style and spirit the immense vogue of Ossian is sufficient proof. (Jefferson tried to learn Gaelic in order to read "the original text"). Had there been an Irish Macpherson in the eighteenth century, he would have been welcomed as warmly. But there was no interpreter of Ireland to England. The greatest of Irish-born writers, Swift, had little Irish about him. The first writer of modern Irish who had literary renown was Geoffrey Keating (1570?–1644?), poet and historian of Ireland; but English people were ignorant of him and his work. Till the age of Synge and Yeats, Anglo-Irish literature meant, if it meant anything, literature in the English tradition written by people who happened to be Irish by birth or residence. Swift, Sheridan and Shaw are Irish writers, but they belong almost entirely to the English tradition.

There are few instances of a hereditary talent so persistent as that of the Sheridan stock. Richard Brinsley Sheridan inherited his poetic tastes from his mother, his dramatic bent from his father, and his sense of style from his grandfather, the intimate of Swift. His own brilliant wit descended to his son Tom Sheridan, father of Caroline Sheridan, afterwards Mrs Norton, and of Helen Sheridan, Lady Dufferin. From the Sheridan stock, too, descends the Le Fanu talent; for Alice, Richard Brinsley Sheridan's sister, a clever writer of verse and plays, was grandmother of Joseph Sheridan Le Fanu. Sheridan Knowles, the popular actor and dramatist, is yet another offshoot from the Sheridan family. Joseph Sheridan Le Fanu (1814–73) was a novelist with a mastery of the mysterious and supernatural that imposed itself upon his times and still retains something of its power. He is seen at his best in *The House by the Churchyard* (1863), *Uncle Silas* (1864), and *In a Glass Darkly* (1872), as well as in shorter stories. His drama *Beatrice* has hardly survived; but there is life in his stirring ballads, *Shamus O'Brien* and *Phaudrig Crohoore*.

Le Fanu, however, was a mere incident of the mid-century and he is read for his mysteries, not for his nationality. To trace the general course of history we must return to the closing years of the eighteenth century when Irish parliamentary independence was drawing to an end and when Irish separatism was encouraged by the French Revolution to acts of violence. The Act of Union (1800) closed the Irish Parliament, but it did not silence the eloquence of the courts or the wit of private assemblies, nor did it lessen the activities of the nationalists. Notable among the last was William Drennan (1754–1820), a founder of the Society of United Irishmen (1791). His *Letters of Orellana* (1785) appealed to the Irish sympathies of Ulster and his rousing poems gained him the renown of an Irish Tyrtaeus. It was Drennan who gave currency to the popular phrase, "The Emerald Isle". Apart from the patriotic poems of Drennan and such national folk-ballads as *The Shan Van Vocht* and *The Wearing of the Green*, there was a revival of interest in Irish native poetry and music, evidenced by the publication of Charlotte Brooke's *Reliques of Irish Poetry* (1789), the holding of the Granard and Belfast meetings of Irish harpers (1792), and the consequent issue of Edward Bunting's first and second collections of *Ancient Irish Music* (1796, 1812), which inspired Moore's *Irish Melodies*. But these movements were interrupted by political agitations, and Dublin lost more and more of its prestige as a capital. The services rendered to the Irish cause by the songs of the expatriated Tom Moore have not always been rightly valued by some of his ungrateful countrymen. The *Irish Melodies* aroused in England far more interest and sympathy than could ever have been compelled by acts of legislation or of rebellion.

But not all the Irish writers had definite political intentions. Caesar Otway (1780–1842) founded and conducted the *Dublin Penny Journal* and *The Irish Penny Journal*, joined Bishop Singer in producing *The Christian Examiner*, and wrote admirable vignettes of Irish natural beauty in *Sketches in Ireland* (1827), *A Tour in Connaught* (1837) and *Sketches in Erris and Tirawley* (1841). Some notable writers were associated with *The Dublin University Magazine*. William Maginn (1793–1842) has earned an unsavoury reputation for his onslaughts in *Blackwood* upon Shelley and other poets. He was the typical hard-living "Bohemian" journalist. It was probably Maginn who suggested to William Hamilton Maxwell (1792–1850), another Trinity College graduate, the writing of military novels. The most effective result was the *Stories of Waterloo* (1829). Maxwell was a great sportsman, if a poor parson, and his *Wild Sports of the West* (1832) deserved the popularity it attained. Charles Lever (1806–72), as a young man, sat at Maxwell's feet, but soon surpassed his master in popularity. Most of his earlier work, like that of Maxwell, appeared in *The Dublin Univer-*

sity Magazine, which he edited when it was in its prime; and in its pages his spirited military novels were first published. *Harry Lorrequer* (1840), *Charles O'Malley* (1841), *Jack Hinton the Guardsman* (1843) and its followers all have the same formula, and helped to create the tradition of the "typical" Irishman as a wild, hilarious, devil-may-care young man overflowing with inventive energy and animal spirits. Lever held posts abroad and was consul at Trieste when he died. His later works, such as *The Daltons* (1852), *The Martins of Cro' Martin* (1859) and *A Day's Ride* (1864) show a quieter, more finished manner and a much greater mastery of the novelist's art; but they never had the popularity of his more facile works. There is merit in the undervalued stories of Samuel Lover (1797–1868)—*Rory O'Moore* (1836) and *Handy Andy* (1838)—and some charm in the poems contained in his *Songs and Ballads*.

The treatment of national stories was first raised to the level of an art by Thomas Crofton Croker (1798–1854) in his *Fairy Legends and Traditions of the South of Ireland*, a set of folk-tales full of charm, published anonymously in 1825. William Carleton and the brothers John and Michael Banim followed Crofton Croker with what Douglas Hyde describes as folk-tales of an incidental and highly manipulated type. William Carleton (1794–1860) absorbed old songs and stories from his father and mother and forgot nothing he had learned. Poverty prevented Carleton from becoming a priest, so he made his way to Dublin and obtained employment from Caesar Otway on *The Christian Examiner*, to which he contributed thirty sketches of Irish peasant life, afterwards collected and published (1832) in a volume entitled *Traits and Stories of the Irish Peasantry*. The success of the book was great and immediate. A second series appeared in 1833, and a kindred volume, *Tales of Ireland*, was issued in 1834. These stories and sketches, which alternate humour with melancholy, are very faithful to the Irish peasant life they depict. Challenged by critics who doubted his ability to write a connected narrative, Carleton replied with *Fardorougha the Miser* (1839), a powerful and sombre story. Other novels by Carleton are *Valentine McClutchy* (1845) and *The Black Prophet* (1847).

Patrick Kennedy (1801–73) was a genuine writer of Irish folk-tales. His *Legendary Fictions of the Irish Celts* (1866), *The Banks of the Boro* (1867), *Evenings in the Duffrey* (1869) and *The Bardic Stories of Ireland* (1871) were put on paper much as he heard them when a boy in his native county Wexford. Kennedy is a true story-teller, animated and humorous. A different kind of humorist was Francis Sylvester Mahony (1804–66), better known as "Father Prout". He was a Jesuit, but abandoned the clerical calling. Mahony was a learned and witty essayist and wrote much for the magazines. His contributions to *Fraser* were collected as *The Reliques of Father Prout* (1836). The one piece of Mahony's known to all is *The Bells of Shandon*. The brothers Banim, John (1798–1842) and Michael (1796–1874), are best known by their joint work, *Tales of the O'Hara Family* (1825). John's life was unhappy and unfortunate. He produced a tragedy, *Damon and Pythias*, at Covent Garden, and wrote a series of clever satires called *Revelations of the Dead*. Michael Banim was the best of brothers. He helped John materially and claimed no share in their joint work. Though the elder, Michael outlived John by thirty years, during which period he produced *Father Connell* (1842), one of his best novels. *The Croppy* (1828) is a characteristic earlier work. Gerald Griffin (1803–40) wrote much in a short lifetime, and takes high rank as author of *The Collegians* (1829), the best Irish novel written in the nineteenth century, and the source of the best known Irish play of the period, Boucicault's *The Colleen Bawn*.

The celebrated Countess of Blessington (1789–1849) was associated with Count d'Orsay, Lord Byron and Dickens. Her novels are never likely to be read again; but her dubious *Journal of Conversations with Lord Byron* (1832) retains the interest of its subject. Sydney Owenson (Lady Morgan, 1783–1859) wrote a once celebrated novel, *The Wild Irish Girl* (1806); some of her other books aroused the ire of Croker and the *Quarterly*. Mary Shackleton, afterwards Mrs Leadbeater (1758–1826), poet and friend of Burke, is still remembered for her *Cottage Dialogues of the Irish Peasantry* (1813), intended as an appeal on behalf of that suffering class, and *The Annals of Ballitore from 1768 to 1824* (1862), a life-like record of the doings and sayings, droll and pathetic, of the folk of a village during a period that included the rebellion of 1798. Marmion Savage (1803–72), an oddly attractive writer, gained popularity with two novels, *The Bachelor of the Albany* (1847) and *Ruben Medlicott* (1852); but his *Falcon Family* (1845), a satire on the leaders of the Young Ireland party, is the best known and the ablest of his stories. Annie Keary (1825–79), daughter of an Irish clergyman, wrote several novels of which *Castle Daly* (1875) and *A Doubting Heart* (1879) are the best. She also wrote, in collaboration with her sister, a Scandinavian story, *The Heroes of Asgard* (1879), long popular with young readers. Jane Francisca Wilde—"Speranza"—(1826–96), wife of Sir William Wilde the surgeon, and mother of Oscar Wilde, wrote *Ancient Legends, Mystic Charms, and Superstitions of Ireland* (1887) and *Ancient Cures, Charms and Usages of Ireland* (1890) which are well-meant but show more enthusiasm than knowledge.

Eminent among Irish scholars is George Petrie (1786–1866), artist, archaeologist, musician and man of letters, who inspired many others to national research. His two archaeological works, the *History and Antiquities of Tara Hill* (1839) and the *Inquiry into the Origin and Uses of the Round Towers* (1845), are masterpieces of reasoning, and his descriptive sketches have a charm as wistful and delicate as his own water-colours. Petrie's collection of Irish traditional songs and tunes, taken down by himself from the peasants, appeared in 1855, and first gave currency (for instance) to the now popular "Londonderry Air". Of outstanding importance as the source of much knowledge were the lectures given by Eugene O'Curry (1796–1882), who was one of Newman's professors at the ill-fated Catholic University in Dublin. They were published as *Lectures on the Manuscript Materials of Ancient Irish History* (1861). Among other scholars may be named William Stokes (1804–78) and his daughter Margaret (1832–1900), authors, respectively, of a *Life of George Petrie* (1868), and *Early Christian Architecture in Ireland* (1878); and, most versatile of all, Patrick Weston Joyce (1827–1914), who contributed Irish folk-songs and notes on Irish dances to a later edition of Petrie's *Ancient Music of Ireland*. Other works of his on Irish music have already been named (see p. 569) His *Social History of Ireland* is written with a direct simplicity that at once engages the attention of the reader, and his *Old Celtic Romances*, a series of free translations from old Irish folk-tales, inspired Tennyson's *Voyage of Maeldune*.

We must now go back to writers who were the precursors of the extraordinary revival of Irish literature in the later years of the nineteenth century; and we must draw a distinction between the national writers and the nationalist writers —between those whose instinct was creative and those whose interest was political. First among the definitely nationalist writers is Thomas Osborne Davis (1814–45), the son of parents of strictly Unionist principles and with very little Irish blood in his veins. His strong independence of view attracted the attention of Charles Gavan Duffy, the young Catholic editor of a Belfast national journal. The two men became friends and their association led to the establishment of *The Nation*, from which sprang what was soon known as the "Young Ireland" movement. At first, Davis was opposed to the introduction of verse into *The Nation*; but he saw the possibilities of the poetic appeal, and in early numbers appeared two of his finest lyrics, *My Grave* and the *Lament for Owen Roe O'Neill*. Much of his verse however was smothered in its political purpose and only rarely did he give his poetic spirit freedom. His *National and Historical Ballads, Songs and Poems* appeared in 1846. Duffy himself also wrote verse; but two other contributors to *The Nation* had clearer poetic gifts, Denis Florence MacCarthy and Thomas D'Arcy McGee. MacCarthy's translations of Calderon's dramas were accepted as standard works of the kind; and his *Shelley's Early Life from Original Sources* made known the poet's efforts for the improvement of Irish government.

Thomas D'Arcy McGee (1825–68) went to America at seventeen, but returned to work with Duffy on *The Nation*. There is a mystical splendour about his poem *The Celts*, and *The Sea-divided Gaels* might serve as a pan-Celtic anthem. McGee's career was extraordinary. After the failure of the Young Ireland rebellion in 1848 he escaped to America, passed into Canada, entered the Canadian parliament and rose to office. His views gradually changed, and from being a leader of Irish separatism he became an advocate of the federal idea. Having denounced Irish disloyalty, he was marked down; and the Irish patriotic poet was shot by patriotic Irish assassins. Hardly less remarkable was the career of Charles Gavan Duffy (1816–1903). After being concerned in Irish revolutionary politics, he emigrated in 1856 to Australia. Here he rose to be premier of Victoria, was knighted, and returned to this country to become a leading figure in the Irish Literary Societies of London and Dublin. His most enduring work is *The Ballad Poetry of Ireland* (1843). The most gifted poet connected with *The Nation* was James Mangan (1803–49), who called himself James Clarence Mangan, a writer of genius whose life is a sorry tale of misery, misfortune and vice. Mangan's versions of German poetry in *Anthologia Germanica* (1848) are sometimes so free as to bear small resemblance to the originals; and he wrote poems of his own as translations from non-existent authors. But whatever their origin, there is poetical quality of a kind in some of Mangan's so-called "eastern" poems. He knew no eastern language; he did not even know Gaelic. His songs in *The Poets and Poetry of Munster* (1849) were based on prose versions. He anticipated Poe in his use of a repeated and varied refrain, an effect found in his loveliest lyric, *Dark Rosaleen*, which was a long time in reaching its final form.

Sir Samuel Ferguson (1810–86), already mentioned (p. 569), first showed his real quality as an Irish nationalist poet by his elegy on Davis; but his sympathy with the Young Ireland poets and patriots was not extended to their successors. In 1864 appeared his *Lays of the Western Gael*, a small volume of great importance, for its first poem, *The Tain-Quest*, with some shorter pieces, made familiar the names Fergus, Cuchulain, Conor, Maev, Deirdra and other figures of Irish legend, and its versions from the Irish included *The Death of Dermid*, *Deirdra's Farewell to Alba* and *Deirdra's Lament for the Sons of Usnach*—the spellings are those used by Ferguson. In 1872 followed *Congal*, a fine poetic story of the last heroic stand by Celtic paganism against the Irish champions of the Cross. The *Poems* of 1880 maintained his reputation as a singer of Irish themes. Ferguson was a fine Irish scholar and brought to his work a fullness of knowledge beyond the reach of the more genuinely inspired Mangan. Timothy Daniel Sullivan (1827–1914), long editor of *The Nation* in its latest phase of political existence, wrote stirring narrative poems entitled *The Madness of King Conchobar* and *The Siege of Dunboy*, and collaborated with Robert Dwyer Joyce (1836–83) in an English rendering of the beautiful early Irish *Story of Blanaid*; but it was as a writer of patriotic Irish songs and ballads that Sullivan made his special mark. *God Save Ireland*, though not an inspired poem, has done useful service as a national anthem. The Fenians, who succeeded the Young Ireland patriots, relied upon weapons other than literary, though R. D. Joyce, C. J. Kickham and Ellen O'Leary, all Fenians, achieved some distinction as writers of verse.

William Allingham (1824–89), though he was born in Ireland and wrote Irish poems that became popular in Ireland itself, was not really an Irish poet. His literary affinities were with the English Pre-Raphaelites, and he had no marked feeling for Irish thought and speech. Aubrey de Vere (1814–1902) is a more serious figure and takes rank with Ferguson as an early singer of Irish themes. *Inisfail, A Lyrical Chronicle of Ireland* was published in 1862, *The Legends of St Patrick* in 1872, and *The Foray of Queen Maeve and Other Legends of Ireland's Heroic Age* in 1882. Aubrey de Vere had strong Irish political sympathies which he had expressed as early as 1848 in *English Misrule and Irish Misdeeds*. But just as Allingham was a Pre-Raphaelite, so Aubrey de Vere was a Wordsworthian. He used the matter of Ireland, but he used it to make English poetry. He was not moved, as Ferguson was, to bring back to Ireland the heroic strains of the native song. Nevertheless he is entitled to a place among the pioneers.

There is a touch of the national "bull" in the fact that the father of modern Irish poetry wrote in prose. The awakening of Ireland to a creative sense of its epic past came from Standish O'Grady (1846–1928), the Herodotus and prose Homer of his country. The first volume of his *History of Ireland: The Heroic Period* appeared in 1878; the second, *History of Ireland: Cuculain and his Contemporaries*, followed in 1880. Between them came the essay, *Early Bardic Literature* (1879), pleading for general recognition of Ireland's contribution to the literature of the world. The world had a complete excuse for its ignorance; it had been waiting for O'Grady. People cannot become familiar with a literature that is inaccessible, and, when accessible, written in a language known to few. More than a century earlier the world had eagerly accepted Macpherson's sophistication of the Ossian story; but there had been no Irish Macpherson. O'Grady's conception of history was epic, not scientific. He had stories to tell, and he told them with the fervour and ingenuousness of a bard. To the historical imagina-

tion of Geoffrey of Monmouth he joined the romantic ardour of Malory, and
he is the father of the Cuchulain legend as Geoffrey is the father of the Arthurian
legend. That Geoffrey's sources, unlike O'Grady's, are not now forthcoming is
a mere accident of difference. The pedants gravely assured O'Grady that his was
no way to write history, and he tried to be more subdued in the *History of
Ireland: Critical and Philosophical*, Vol. 1 (1881); but the significant facts are
first, that romance would keep breaking in, and next, that no more of the work
was written. O'Grady's political writings, excellent of their kind, do not concern us. The born teller of stories turned naturally from history to fiction, and
in *Red Hugh's Captivity* (1889) produced a novel of Elizabethan Ireland; but he
was over-conscious of the claims of history, and a sequel, *The Flight of the Eagle*
(1897), gains from its greater imaginative freedom. *The Bog of Stars* (1893)
contains short stories of the same period. *The Coming of Cuculain* (1894), *In the
Gates of the North* (1901) and *The Triumph and Passing of Cuculain* (1920) tell
over again, for a larger audience, the stories of the *History*. O'Grady was both
the inspirer of a literary revival and the generous friend of all who shared in it.
He should be distinguished from his older contemporary, Standish Hayes
O'Grady (1832–1915), an Irish scholar of less creative gifts.

The influence of O'Grady's work spread widely. Poets were moved to sing
of new themes; scholars were moved to recover the fast-vanishing folk-tales
of the peasants. Not only had there been no Irish Macpherson, there had been
no one to do for Ireland what John Francis Campbell (1825–85) had done for
Scotland in the four volumes of his *Popular Tales of the West Highlands* (1860–2).
But interest in the folk-stories revived. The Irish language, the dying tongue of
illiterate peasants, frowned upon by the church as heathen and despised by
Society as contemptible, was now thought to be worth not merely saving but
reviving. No movement is ever simple, and the first stirring of interest in Gaelic
song was discernible before O'Grady was even grown out of boyhood. George
Sigerson (1839–1925), doctor and historian, had published as long ago as 1862
Poets and Poetry of Munster, Part II—Part I having been prepared by Mangan in
1849. Mangan had done no more than put into the poetic speech native to his
genius the prose versions of old songs supplied by John O'Daly the publisher.
He knew no Irish. Sigerson was a scholar, and sought to make something more
than a mere popular song book. He strove earnestly to revive an active interest
in native Irish poetry. By 1897, when he published the elaborate and learned
Bards of the Gael and Gall, with its careful metrical renderings of Irish songs and
poems, both the legends and the language of Ireland were matters of established
enthusiasm.

From belief in the necessity of reviving Irish to belief in the necessity of driving
out English was, naturally, a short step; and presently there arose the patriots
who declared that English was an exhausted and foreign language, and that
no literature worthy of Ireland could be written in anything but Irish. Further
we were assured that all the beauties of rhyme, rhythm and metrical invention
in post-classical European poetry were derived from the literature of Ireland.
These excesses are common form in any period of intense revivalism. The
enthusiasts for the Irish language got most of their knowledge from Douglas
Hyde (1860–1949), later President of Eire, who published in 1889 a book of

folk-tales in the original language and applied a powerful mind to the advocacy of its claims. For English readers the interest of his work begins with *Beside the Fire* (1890), containing tales from the earlier book with renderings into an Anglo-Irish idiom. This was followed by *Love Songs of Connacht* (1893), with the Irish similarly translated. Later came *Songs ascribed to Raftery* (1903) and *The Religious Songs of Connacht* (1906). Hyde did for the poetry of Connacht what Sigerson had done for the poetry of Munster. A work of more general interest was *A Literary History of Ireland* (1897) which presented to English readers the almost totally unknown story of native Irish literature. Upon the value of Douglas Hyde's work in Gaelic we can offer no opinion. His normal English prose has little charm and his verse-renderings of Irish poems are not always themselves poems. But in the literal translations appended to some of his poetic versions there is at times a singular beauty of the kind that we now associate with the plays of Synge—the beauty of English touched to an appealing strangeness by the Gaelic way of speech, with its different tenses and its different run of the sentence. And being founded upon speech, this is a genuine idiom, and not an artificial literary device. That the movement for the revival of Irish as a medium for national literature should take a political turn was to be expected; but we are here concerned only with language as a means of artistic expression.

The new enthusiasm led to the formation of several leagues and societies, and even to some actual co-operation—with the usual dissensions and schisms. But a volume called *Poems and Ballads of Young Ireland* (1888) was a visible sign of early agreement, for it contained work by several writers, including George Sigerson among the older and William Butler Yeats (1865–1939) among the younger. The lesser contributors gained no great addition of fame and do not call for mention here; Yeats was to become the most notable figure in the revival. He began writing as the heir of Spenser and Shelley, and his first slender volume, *Mosada, a Dramatic Poem* (1886), had nothing Irish about it; but this and other early verses gave intimations of an original poetic gift. Movements do not create poets; they sometimes discover poets. The Irish movement was fortunate in attracting a young poet of singular charm and character; the poet was fortunate in finding early in life his true direction. He was not, like Allingham, Aubrey de Vere and some of the contributors to *Poems and Ballads of Young Ireland*, a writer with a formed English and classical habit. Though he drastically revised his work he did not change its character. He had little to unlearn; and his first important volume of poems, *The Wanderings of Oisin*, published in 1889, adopted easily the national note and set the pattern for the rest of his work. Some of the latest Yeats is implicit in the earliest, particularly in the field of the drama. Yeats's earliest verse took dramatic form; and his next important publication was *The Countess Kathleen and Various Legends and Lyrics* (1892) in which the principal work is a play. A recollection of this fact should prevent the supposition that Yeats was diverted to the stage by the Irish Literary Theatre movement. His early wanderings in Sligo among the Irish peasants who retained in their memories a store of tales and songs had interested him in the literature that is spoken. Yeats, in spirit, was always a bard, and thought of poetry as something chanted, not as something printed. *The Countess Kathleen*, though dramatic in theme and form, is not, even as revised, a theatrical piece; it is a poem that can be dramatized. Between *The Wanderings of Oisin* and *The Countess Kathleen* came a curious pseudonymous volume, *John Sherman and Dhoya* (1891), the first piece a short novel and the second an expanded legend. *John Sherman* is not an important contribution to the fiction of its time, but, as usual in a first story by a writer not strongly inventive, there is some autobiographical revelation. Then followed a delightful collection of Irish sketches and stories called *The Celtic Twilight; Men and Women, Dhouls and Fairies* (1893), written in limpid and expressive prose. Thus from the beginning the career of Yeats as a writer was equally proportioned between poems, plays and prose; and from the beginning his own essential character appears. Those who trace his mysticism and symbolism to the influence of other writers have evidently omitted to read his own early works. That Yeats found affinities with certain writers in French (see the important chapter on the poet in Edmund Wilson's *Axel's Castle*) need not be questioned; the point is that he was not made by those affinities. Symbolism and mysticism were in the air: the author of *The Wild Duck* was a symbolist; the author of *Pelléas et Mélisande* was a mystic. It was inevitable that Yeats should become an editor of Blake and that a volume of imaginative essays should be called *Ideas of Good and Evil* (1903); it was inevitable that the kind of mysticism and symbolism natural to him should grow into a pre-occupation with certain forms of occultism, and that he should write the prose studies found in *The Secret Rose* (1897), *The Tables of the Law* (1897) and *The Wind among the Reeds* (1899); but his mysticism was always cloudy: there is no evidence in his work of Blake's intense and insistent vision.

Yeats's poems were published in numerous slim green volumes which at intervals were revised and collected. The two volumes of *Poetical Works* (1906–7) included the lyrical and dramatic poems mentioned above with such later additions as the one-act drama *The Land of Heart's Desire* (1894), which had a run in London, and *The Shadowy Waters* (1900). The eight volumes of *Collected Works in Verse and Prose* (Stratford-on-Avon, 1908) included the poems *In the Seven Woods* (Dublin, 1903) and the essays *Discoveries* (Dublin, 1907). *Plays for an Irish Theatre* (1913), some of which were written with the assistance of his friend Lady Gregory, included the prose play *Cathleen ni Houlihan* (1902), which was performed by the Irish Dramatic Company and which was his first real theatrical success, besides the morality play *The Hour Glass* (New York, 1904) and the "heroic farce" *The Green Helmet* (1910). The first volume of Macmillan's *Collected Edition* came out in 1922; the last was the important volume called *Autobiographies* (1926), containing *Reveries over Childhood and Youth* (1915) and *The Trembling of the Veil* (1922), reminiscences which, with the later *Dramatis Personae* (1935)—all included in the New York *Autobiography* (1938)—must be read and pondered over, by any reader who wishes to get to the heart of the poet's mystery and desires to understand how Yeats could be at once a poet of the Irish literary revival and a poet for the whole English-speaking world, a poet who was in one lifetime the younger contemporary of his English friend Morris and the elder contemporary of his American friend to whom he offered the volume of essays *A Packet for Ezra Pound* (Dublin, 1929). As we follow his long career through the pages of the Macmillan *Collected Poems* (1950), we see how he left the mood and the idiom of the late nineteenth century behind him and developed his own distinctive style as early as the poems collected in *The Green Helmet* volume of 1912 and *Responsibilities* (1914). Many of the poems in these two volumes, and most of the contents of *The Wild Swans at Coole* (1917), *Michael Robartes and the Dancer* (1920), *The Tower* (1928) and *The Winding Stair* (1933), take us out of the hypnotic dream-world of the Celtic Twilight into a daylight world, sometimes of bitter regret, but always of honesty and courage. Some individual poems in these volumes—such as *The Second Coming*, *Byzantium*, *Leda and the Swan* and the epigram on the critics who damned Synge's *Playboy*—are widely acknowledged to be among the finest achievements of the early twentieth century, as *Innisfree* and *Mongan* were among the finest achievements of the late nineteenth. It is not often that a poet thus spans the generations, growing in stature with what are to others the declining years.

Yeats is the greatest poetical figure of the age: a transitional age, as it may come to be regarded, between Morris and Pound, Swinburne and Eliot, being himself responsible for much of the ease of the transition. He had his own vision of man and the world and he spoke with distinctive, original authority. He owed much to Ireland, as Ireland owed much to him, but that he was a world poet as well as an Irish was recognized in 1923 when he was awarded the Nobel Prize for Literature and again on his death in 1939, which inspired verses by Auden in America, A. J. M. Smith in Canada, George Barker and Kenneth Allott in England. His most percipient critics and commentators have been drawn from an equally cosmopolitan field: Leavis, Eliot (quoted p. 855), Norman Jeffares, Frank Kermode in England, Wilson and Richard Ellman in America, the Indians Balachandra Rajan and V. K. Narayana Menon, besides fellow-Irishmen like Frank O'Connor and Louis MacNeice and Celtic neigh-bours from Scotland like David Daiches and G. S. Fraser. The centenary of his birth in 1965 produced books, papers and special numbers in nearly every country of the world, including Nigeria and Korea. His Life was admirably written in 1943 by J. M. Hone. His published letters include those to Dorothy Wellesley (1940), Florence Farr (1941), Sturge Moore (1953; p. 606 above) and Katherine Tynan (1955).

With Yeats it is natural to consider his contemporary George William Russell (1867–1935), who wrote poems, painted pictures, sought truth in Theosophy, edited *The Irish Homestead* (1904–23) and *The Irish Statesman* (1923–30), and laboured unselfishly to show Ireland how to become self-supporting and self-respecting. He was a practical mystic. Theosophy—with Madame Blavatsky, inspired by Tibetan Mahatmas, as its prophetess—attracted some earnest young men in Dublin, including Yeats, Russell and William Kirkpatrick Magee ("John Eglinton"). The mystical movement went parallel with the national movement, and both had in common the quest for the powers behind pheno-mena—for the Celtic deities were as esoteric as the Hindu. In 1892 a monthly magazine *The Irish Theosophist* began to appear, and to it and its successors a constant contributor was George William Russell, who in 1894 published his first volume of poems, *Homeward: Songs by the Way*, with the signature "A. E." It was followed by *The Earth Breath* (1897) and *The Divine Vision* (1903). These and some later poems were first collected in 1913. *Gods of War* (1915) was an outcry of bewilderment provoked by the European disaster. Other volumes appeared at intervals, notably *The Candle of Vision* (1918) and *Midsummer Eve* (1928). A. E.'s prose includes an address to the Fellows of the Theosophical Society (1894), much political writing, mainly defensive of the Irish co-operative movement, and many essays and sketches, some of which were collected in *Imaginations and Reveries* (1915), which also contains *Deirdre*, first acted in 1902 and printed in 1907, a tragedy in exquisite prose scarcely touched by the Anglo-Irish idiom. The best of A. E. is to be found in his first three volumes of verse, and in them the careful reader can trace both the deepening of his faith and the development of his power of communication. The note of A. E.'s work is to be found in a motto from the *Bhagavad-Gita* prefixed to one of the early poems, "I am Beauty itself among beautiful things". To him the soil of Ireland, once trodden by the ancient deities, was holy ground. The Celtic allusions in his works are few; yet the feeling of Ireland is as strong in the twenty lines of *A Call of the Sidhe* as in whole volumes of other people's work. His pantheism is sometimes reminiscent of Emerson—more than one poem suggests *Brahma*—and his intensity of faith is akin to the spirit that inspires Emily Brontë's *Last Lines*.

Of the other Dublin Theosophists the only one calling for notice is "John Eglinton", i.e. William Kirkpatrick Magee (1868), who wrote verses which survive imperfectly in anthologies, and a few collections of prose which show an international rather than a national spirit. *Two Essays on the Remnant* (1895) and *Pebbles from a Brook* (1901) deal with the "intangibles" of criticism. They are not easy reading, for they say more than the quiet, finely turned prose seems to imply; but they present critical ideas of general validity and diagnose acutely the spiritual distress of the age. *Bards and Saints* (1906) appears a little more concrete and shows signs of waning confidence. *Anglo-Irish Essays* (1917) is slighter in substance and worth; but *Irish Literary Portraits* (1935) contains some almost sardonically realistic sketches of Yeats, A. E. and Moore, and should be read as a corrective supplement to Moore's own *Hail and Farewell*. His finely touched memoir of A. E. appeared in 1937. John Eglinton has attracted less attention than some of his contemporaries; but among those who have written much, he seems to be the one who should have written more. He has in prose something of A. E.'s spirit in verse.

The numerous lesser poets of the revival cannot be discussed in detail. The anthologies will present as much as need be known of Katherine Tynan, Nora Hopper, Dora Sigerson and "Moira O'Neill". More important are Yeats's successors in the "Celtic Daylight" mood, particularly F. R. Higgins (1896–1941), Austin Clarke (b. 1896) whose *Collected Poems* came out in 1936 and *Later Poems* in 1961, Patrick Kavanagh (b. 1905) the self-educated poet of *A Soul for Sale* (1947), and Donagh MacDonagh (b. 1912) who has written both ballads for reading and ballad-comedies for the stage, notably *Happy as Larry* (1946) which was included in Martin Browne's *Modern Verse Plays* (1957).

The influence of the Irish revival was specially felt in the theatre. At the beginning, however, the Irish dramatic movement was not specifically Irish, but was part of that general revolt of educated people against conventional commercial drama which led to the formation of Antoine's Théâtre Libre in

Paris (1887) and J. T. Grein's Independent Theatre Society in London (1891). It is scarcely a paradox to say that the father of the Irish dramatic revival was Ibsen. In *Impressions and Opinions*, published in 1891 and containing articles written before that date, George Moore, moved by the Paris performance of Ibsen's *Ghosts*, had demanded an English equivalent to the Théâtre Libre, which would produce works of real dramatic art as distinguished from popular after-dinner entertainments. And specially he demanded a Théâtre Libre for original plays, and not merely for translations. The Independent Theatre Society of London, when it came, produced a play by Moore and a play by Shaw; but in the main it depended upon versions of Ibsen. Yeats was anxious for a similar organization in Ireland, and, as it happened, there was an unacted Irish Ibsen, in the person of Edward Martyn, a landowner with creative dramatic gifts. Through the efforts of Lady Gregory and Yeats the faith of others was kindled, and the Irish Literary Theatre was duly born in 1899 and began its work with Yeats's *The Countess Kathleen* followed by Martyn's *The Heather Field*. It endured for three years—a longer period than the fundamentally diverse views of the management would have led a cynical observer to predict. For historical convenience we continue the story of the theatre without reference to the dramatists. The Irish Literary Theatre was an association for the production of great plays in Ireland; it was not a society for the production of Irish plays acted by Irish players. A specifically Irish theatre was the creation, not of any literary society, but of two actors, W. G. Fay and his brother F. J. Fay, who were training Irish amateurs to use their ears and their voices in the rare art of beautiful speech on the stage. They made a modest public beginning in 1902 as The Irish National Dramatic Company, with A. E.'s *Deirdre* and Yeats's *Cathleen ni Houlihan*. Yeats, with his bardic instincts responsive to poetic speech, saw in this company the beginnings of genuine national drama; Moore and Martyn, still thinking in larger terms, saw in it the end of their desires for a nationalized international drama. Yeats, A. E. and Lady Gregory gave their support to the Fays, and in 1902 The Irish National Dramatic Company drew the more active spirits from The Irish Literary Theatre and became The Irish National Theatre Society. The providential emergence of Synge in the next year established the artistic success of the new venture. Commercially it was insecure. Persons not devoid of humour may like to observe that The Irish Literary Theatre was inspired by a Norwegian, Ibsen, and that The Irish National Theatre was maintained by an Englishwoman, Emily Horniman, who, from 1904 to 1910, gave it a home of its own in the Abbey Theatre and subsidized it generously. We may now return to the dramatists.

Edward Martyn had published in 1899 two plays, *The Heather Field* and *Maeve*, which are studies in Ibsen's symbolism with an Irish setting. Moore, who wrote an introduction to the volume, was convinced of Martyn's Ibsenism; but there is no challenge, as in some of Ibsen's plays, to current moral values; instead there is an intimation of impalpable forces behind apparent fact, as in *The Wild Duck* and *Rosmersholm*. Both plays are beautifully imagined and beautifully written. Two further pieces by Martyn, *The Tale of a Town* and *The Enchanted Sea*, appeared in 1902. The first, rewritten by George Moore for stage performance as *The Bending of the Bough*, is a municipal satire, recalling

An Enemy of the People; the second returns to the note of symbolic suggestion discernible in *The Lady from the Sea*. Later plays, *Glencolman* (1912) and *The Dream Physician* (1914) show no extension of scope in the dramatist's art. Martyn, who kept to the highroad of European tradition, has never had the popularity that accrued to those who followed the by-paths of "peasant drama"; but his work for the stage is some of the best that the Irish revival produced. He followed artistic truth where he saw it, and through various organizations patiently and unselfishly sought to make his country aware of the larger dramatic world. With A. E., Edward Martyn holds an honourable place in the Irish movement as a lover of Ireland entirely free from self-seeking, or desire of notoriety, or passion for personal exploitation.

The National Theatre Society, or the Abbey Theatre, as it was afterwards generally called, had given the prose farce *A Pot of Broth*, written by Yeats with the obvious assistance of Lady Gregory—Yeats being not naturally inclined to the farcical; and in the next year (1903) it gave *The King's Threshold* and *The Shadowy Waters*, more genuine products of Yeats's own gifts. But by a singular piece of good luck, the new national dramatic venture and a new national dramatic genius seemed to be born together. John Millington Synge (1871–1909) had lived among the islanders of the west and grew to know their life and spirit and speech. Though his sketches contained in *The Aran Islands* were not published till 1907, they represent his years of apprenticeship to the interpretation of peasant life. Encouraged by Yeats, Synge turned to playwriting, and the one-act piece *The Shadow of the Glen* was produced by the National Theatre in 1903. This play, hotly resented by the patriots as an insult to the pure women of Ireland, revealed in its short compass the special qualities of Synge: his sense of the stage, his extraordinary power of dramatizing a nation in his characters, and his natural command of the Gaelicized English, which, used almost casually by Hyde, became, under his own shaping care for the substance and rhythm of prose speech, a new literary language, appropriate to his matter, and succeeding, like a kind of poetry, by its intrinsic beauty. Synge had found at once the style for which Yeats was always seeking. *Riders to the Sea*, which followed in 1904, with poor fisher folk for its characters, and the commonplace incident of death by drowning as its theme, attains to the dignity of great tragedy. *The Tinker's Wedding* (1908), written much earlier, is a not very prosperous comedy; but *The Well of the Saints*, produced in 1905, is a highly original, racy, yet imaginative and poetic treatment of a theme that Maeterlinck would have made tenebrously sentimental, the restoration of sight to a pair of blind beggars and their final rejection of the doubtful blessing. It is, in every sense, a beautiful invention. Synge, already famous, became notorious when *The Playboy of the Western World* was produced in 1907. The patriots found in Synge's characters and incidents an insult to the Irish nation, an attack upon Irish religion, a slander upon Irish men and an aspersion upon Irish women; and they expressed their disapproval in noisy violence that carried the author's name far into the intelligent world outside. *The Playboy* is as much and as little of an insult to Ireland as *Don Quixote* is to Spain. It is at once comedy, satire, tragedy, parable and prose-poem, and like other great plays it delivers general truth in its particular story. *The Playboy* is a masterpiece of dramatic art because it is simply a piece of dramatic art. It is not a comedy of ideas, it propounds no problem, it attempts no propaganda. It exists in itself and for itself as purely as a lyric poem. Whatever message it has is part of the uncovenanted profit that comes from any artistically sincere criticism of life. The career of Synge came to an end with *Deirdre of the Sorrows*, the third and most memorable of contemporary plays on that theme. In it his language has become almost too beautiful. Nothing more could be done with the Anglo-Irish idiom, which, like the poetic idiom of Shakespeare, fell into the hands of imitators, and became a stage speech as artificial as the heroics of mid-Victorian melodrama. But Synge must not be blamed for the crimes committed in his name. His brief contribution of six plays made the Irish dramatic movement important not merely to Ireland but to the whole western world.

A notable figure in the Irish revival has already been named, Augusta Persse, Lady Gregory (1859–1932), whose home at Coole became a nest of poets. She directed the efforts of Yeats towards popular drama and collaborated with him. Her first important book, *Cuchulain of Muirthemne* (1902), tells over again in a simple Anglo-Irish idiom the stories more imposingly narrated by O'Grady and more learnedly collected in *The Cuchullin Saga in Irish Literature* (1898) by Eleanor Hull. *Gods and Fighting Men* (1904) is a second volume of the same kind. Lady Gregory's first play, *Twenty-five* (1903), is not important; but *Spreading the News*, acted in 1904 and printed later in *Seven Short Plays* (1911), set a successful pattern for its numerous successors—a humorous situation with the comedy heightened by quaint turns of talk. *The Workhouse Ward* is a perfect specimen of the kind. *The Gaol Gate* almost touches tragedy. Lady Gregory gave to her variety of the Anglo-Irish idiom the name of "Kiltartan", and into it she translated successfully some of Molière's comedies. Of her six *Irish Folk-History Plays* (1912), *Grania*, *Kincora* and *Dervorgilla* are tragedies, and *The Canavans*, *The White Cockade* and *The Deliverer* "tragic-comedies"—comedies in texture with a tone of satirical bitterness. The theme of *The Image*, the statue of a non-existent hero, has been treated more farcically by "George Birmingham". Lady Gregory's Kiltartan dialect is amusing in the comedies; in a poetic tragedy like *Grania* it lacks the transfiguring touch that Synge gave to the speech of *Deirdre*. She is at her best in the lighter one-act pieces. *Poets and Dreamers* (1902) is a beautiful narrative volume and *Our Irish Theatre* (1913) is the story of an important movement told by one of its leading spirits.

But the classic account of the Irish revival is that given with exquisite malice and mordant ingenuousness by George Moore (1852–1933) in *Hail and Farewell* (1911–14). Moore meddled with the Irish theatre to no one's advantage, not even his own; for *The Bending of the Bough* (1900) is Edward Martyn's *The Tale of a Town* and *Diarmuid and Grania* (1901) is Yeats adapted by his collaborator. But Moore had an artist's eye for the human oddities of the principal figures in the movement and an unrivalled power of conveying the sting of caricature in apparently friendly portraiture. Martyn and A. E. emerge not merely with credit but with charm; the rest are all a little ridiculous. De Quincey among the Lake Poets was not more ingenuously malicious. Much of Moore's own work barely touches the Irish movement and is cosmopolitan rather than Hibernian. He belonged to three countries: born in the west of Ireland, he was educated—

as he tells us in *Confessions of a Young Man* (1888)—in the cafés and studios of Paris, then spent forty years as a leading figure in the literary life of London, the scene of *Conversations in Ebury Street* (1924) and the unfinished *Communication to My Friends* (1933). His novels (p. 866 below) are among the most notable of those influenced by the theory and practice of Flaubert and Maupassant.

The one contemporary of Synge who seemed likely to attach his name memorably to the Irish theatre was Padraic Colum (b. 1881). His *Broken Soil* was produced in 1903, the year of *The Shadow of the Glen*, and was printed later as *The Fiddler's House*. *The Land* (1905) dramatizes one tragedy of Ireland, the draining away of its vigorous life by emigration. *Thomas Muskerry* (1910) is the bitter story of a workhouse master brought down to pauperdom by those whom he has befriended. *The Destruction of the Hostel*, performed semi-privately in 1910 and published in 1913, forsakes normal Irish life for the age of legend. Padraic Colum, as the dates will show, was not a follower or imitator of Synge. He was an original writer with his own expressive style; but his plays never had power enough to force their way into the wider theatrical world. William Boyle began well with *The Building Fund* (1905) but failed to maintain its level in *The Eloquent Dempsey* (1906), *The Mineral Workers* (1906) and *The Family Failing*. Lennox Robinson (1886–1958) touched domestic tragedy in *The Clancy Name* (1908), and Irish political history in *The Dreamers* (1915). *The White-headed Boy* (1917) is delightful as comedy and as satire. *The Lost Leader* (1918) failed to call up Parnell and *The Big House* (1926) intended more than it achieved. Of George Fitzmaurice, Seumas O'Kelly, T. C. Murray and R. J. Ray merely the names can be recorded. George Shiels ("George Morshiel" b. 1886) of Ulster wrote several popular comedies, the best being *The New Gossoon* (1930) and *The Jailbird* (1936). *The Passing Day* (1936) is more serious.

Unlike the other Irish writers of his time, Edward John Moreton Drax Plunkett, Lord Dunsany (1878–1957), ignored the Celtic deities and, like Blake, invented his own myths. *The Gods of Pegana* (1905), *Time and the Gods* (1906), *The Sword of Welleran* (1908), *A Dreamer's Tales* (1910) and *The Book of Wonder* (1912) are narrative creations rich in fancy but without any deep imaginative foundation. Gods must be human if they are to be divine. Dunsany's dramatic work began in 1909 when *The Glittering Gate* was produced at the Abbey Theatre. *King Argimenes* followed in 1911. These, with *The Gods of the Mountain*, *The Golden Doom* and *The Lost Silk Hat*, were published in *Five Plays* (1914). Four others appeared in 1917 as *Plays of Gods and Men*. All are brief—so brief as to be little more than symbolical anecdotes. In *The Gods of the Mountain* seven jade deities stalk heavily into a city and turn to jade the seven rascals who have been prosperously impersonating them, with the result that doubters are convinced that the transfigured impostors were veritable gods. But the substance of the play is too light to carry so tremendous a jest. The music of Mozart can make the arrival of one statue terrible; the prose of Dunsany cannot carry seven. There is variety in his matter, but not in his method. In *The Lost Silk Hat* symbolism is expressed in terms of farce; and in *The Flight of the Queen* the life of a hive is dramatized with delicate fantasy. The mind of Dunsany is poetical. He is essentially a maker of fairy-tales, and chooses to people his fables with figures terrible, grotesque, or fantastic. But his inventions fail to achieve the momentum of enduring creations: his words have not the force of his fancies. He is a curiously original and solitary figure among the dramatists of his time.

Ulster also had its dramatic movement; but it found no Yeats or Synge, and its productions are difficult to assess carefully, as some of the plays were not printed and were rarely performed out of Ireland. The Ulster Literary Theatre made a modest start in 1902 by performing some of the Dublin pieces; in 1904 it had begun to find its own dramatists, most of whom chose to write under assumed names, and some of whom acted as well as wrote. The first in order of date is "Lewis Purcell", i.e. David Parkhill, whose municipal satire *The Reformers* was produced in 1904. Other pieces by him are *The Enthusiast* (1905) and *The Pagan* (1906). The latter, printed in 1907, presents a clash between Christianity and Paganism in sixth-century Ulster, but treats the situation with satirical humour. With *The Enthusiast* was played *The Little Cowherd of Slainge* by Joseph Campbell (Seosamh Mac Cathmhaoil), a poet of delicate feeling. The piece is in prose, and, though not dramatically powerful, it is remarkable as the one early Ulster play that has a poetic spirit. Most important of the northern dramatists is "Rutherford Mayne", i.e. Samuel Waddell, whose *Turn of the Road* was acted in 1906. Not all the Ulster plays were produced in Ulster. Rutherford Mayne's most popular piece, *The Drone*, was first performed in Dublin (1908) but was given at Belfast in a lengthened form a year later. Belfast, however, produced *The Troth* (1909), *The Captain of the Hosts* (1910), *Red Turf* (1911), *If* (1914), *Neil Gallina* (1916) and *Industry* (1917). *The Phantoms* (1923) had its first performance in Dublin. *The Turn of the Road* dramatizes the struggle between an artistic temperament and the respectable Protestant prejudices of the province. *The Drone* is more universally Irish in presenting the figure of "a grand talker" escaping from fact and defeating the practical folk in the end of all. It is the most considerable of the Ulster plays. *Red Turf* is a brief serious treatment of the Irish passion for land. *Neil Gallina*, a revision of *The Captain of the Hosts*, is a tragedy, with Death, the Captain, triumphing over the human combatants. Rutherford Mayne is an original writer owing nothing to Synge, with whom he is sometimes uncritically paired, no doubt because *The Drone* is a kind of Ulster *Playboy*. The humorous or satirical note of the Ulster Theatre is most definitely sounded by "Gerald Macnamara", i.e. Harry Morrow, whose *Suzanne and the Sovereigns*, written in collaboration with Lewis Purcell, was produced in 1907. The "Sovereigns" are William of Orange and James II, who are represented as really fighting for the possession of "Suzanne", a non-existent girl of surpassing beauty. It is an effective satire on the Ulster animosities. *The Mist that Does Be On the Bog* (1909) and *Thompson in Tir-Na-N'Og* (1912) satirize the "peasant drama" and the Gaelic movement. Both proved obstinately popular. Other plays by Gerald Macnamara include *The Throwbacks* (1917), a satirical sketch of the Irish past, *No Surrender* (1928), a satirical excursion into the Irish future, and *Who Fears to Speak* (1929), a satirical caricature of a revolutionary club in 1797. The plays of Gerald Macnamara have no great importance, but they are evidence of a cheerful spirit not afraid of laughing at certain Irish solemnities. "Lynn Doyle", i.e. Leslie Montgomery, contributed *Love and the Land*, an agrarian comedy, and *The Lilac Ribbon*, a domestic comedy. Quite apart from Ireland in theme is *The Spoiled Buddha* (1915), a satirical religious comedy of Japan by Helen Waddell, sister of Rutherford Mayne, and now better known as the author of *The Wandering Scholars*. For the Ulster Theatre George Shiels wrote his earliest comedies, *Away from the Moss* (1918) and *Felix Reid and Bob* (1919). St John Ervine (b. 1883) is an Ulster playwright by birth rather than by conviction. *Mixed Marriage* (1911) and *The Orangeman* (1913) present with power the tragedy of religious bigotry. *The Magnanimous Lover* (1912) has religious cant as its basis of action, but that evil is not peculiar to Ulster or to Ireland. *John Ferguson* (1915) is a melodramatic story of the struggle between a religious family and a ruthless money-lender. Its tragedy is accidental rather than essential. The only play by St John Ervine produced by the Ulster Theatre is *The Ship* (1924), a tragedy that is rather buried in the excess of its story. Ervine's later dramatic works belong to the English commercial theatre. Even the best of his earlier plays seem to exploit local life dramatically rather than to grow from it naturally.

Sean O'Casey (1884–1964) stands apart from the national movement. His first success, *Juno and the Paycock* (1926), a tragi-comedy of the Dublin slums, forms a satirical companion picture to *The Playboy*. Its hero is an urban and elderly waster living greedily on his own facile eloquence and the flattery of his hanger-on. He is a bitter symbolical figure in spite of the farcical comedy in his presentation. *The Shadow of a Gunman* (1923) and *The Plough and the Stars* (1926) follow a similar pattern. *The Silver Tassie* (1929) and *Within the Gates* (1934) pursue symbolism more directly and less happily. They are defeated by excess of pattern and insecurity of diction. Nevertheless O'Casey (see further, p. 908) has the curious Irish gift of presenting tragedy in figures that English writers would make merely squalid and repulsive.

That the most popular form of literary art, the novel, did not at first greatly attract the Irish writers can be explained by the bardic nature of their work. Legends and poems are for recitation; plays are for performance; novels are for private leisurely reading. O'Grady himself wrote stories, but they are not his best work. Other Irish writers who chose the novel as their vehicle cannot be related to any movement, and some of them are not intrinsically important. George Moore is as little an Irish novelist as Bernard Shaw is an Irish dramatist. One exception is the Hon. Emily Lawless (1845–1913), whose real sympathy with the Irish, though not of the kind approved by the nationalists, expressed itself both in poems and in stories. *Hurrish* (1886) is a serious tale of the Land League days, too veracious to please political minds, and her historical tales *With Essex in Ireland* (1890) and *Maelcho* (1894) proved more acceptable. The poems in her volume *With the Wild Geese* (1902) are good without attaining to any memorable felicity. Jane Barlow (1860–1917) the poet of *Bogland Studies* (1892) wrote many tales of Irish rural life which have the interest of their setting, but no other special merit. *Irish Idylls* (1892) is a good example of her pleasant gifts.

No better humorous sketches of Irish provincial life have been written than the series of tales by Violet Martin ("Martin Ross", 1865–1915) and her cousin Edith Œnone Somerville (1861–1949). *Some Experiences of an Irish R.M.* (1899), *Further Experiences of an Irish R.M.* (1908) and *In Mr Knox's Country* (1915) form a trilogy conveying with complete conviction the characters of men, women, horses and dogs, and depicting with quiet beauty the soft scenes of the south-west. The point of view is that of the "gentry" and so the tales are not in favour with some of the patriots; but the aspects of life chosen for description are rendered with fine artistic restraint and sympathetic comprehension.

There is real originality and even genius in *The Charwoman's Daughter* (1912), *The Crock of Gold* (1912) and *The Demi-Gods* (1914) by James Stephens (1882–1950). The first is a humorous idyll of the Dublin slums, the second and third carry an impish spirit into the realms of fantasy. The poems of Stephens are slight in substance, but have the character and charm of his prose. In both forms of writing he is original and follows no master. Later works have not shown evidence of developing power, and his earliest work is still the best.

The Irish literary revival was justified by its faith and its works. That there was a national as well as a nationalist spirit to be expressed in literature was clear in the *Irish Melodies* of Tom Moore, who is still the nearest approach to Burns that Ireland has produced. By being artistically true to itself the Irish movement produced works of literature when Scotland was expressing itself in commercially popular novels flavoured with odours from the kailyard. In its days of creative activity the Irish revival directed the gifts of Yeats and inspired the genius of Synge. It re-discovered the Celtic mythology. It made a triumphantly successful revolt against the theatre of social sham and moral humbug. It produced plays which were unlike any written before and which showed that tragedy might wear the rags of a beggar as greatly as the robes of a queen.

That the immense influence of Irish dramatists and poets upon the twentieth-century literature of the English-speaking world is not apparently equalled by their novelists is due partly to the fact that it is more difficult with Irish-born novelists than with Irish-born poets or dramatists to decide who should be included among "Irish writers" and who not. Synge and Yeats, by common agreement, are at once Irish figures and world figures, but James Joyce (1882–1941; p. 877) and Samuel Beckett (b. 1906; pp. 880, 912), not to mention Elizabeth Bowen from County Cork and James Hanley and Iris Murdoch from Dublin, are harder to pin down. An exception should perhaps be made of the Irish short story which, though as likely to have appeared originally in *The New Yorker* or *The London Magazine* as in Seumas O'Sullivan's *Dublin Magazine* or Peadar O'Donnell's *Bell*, does appear to be a distinctive species, almost as Irish as Synge or Yeats. The novelists James Hanley, Liam O'Flaherty and Séan O'Faoláin are among the masters here; another is Frank O'Connor, the pen-name of the Cork-born Michael O'Donovan (1903–66), whose stories have been collected in such volumes as *Bones of Contention* (1936) and *The Common Chord* (1947). O'Connor's World's Classics anthology *Modern Irish Short Stories* well illustrates their wide range of expression from the time of George Moore, Daniel Corkery, Somerville and Ross, and the young Joyce of *Dubliners* (1914) to the post-Independence era of O'Flaherty, O'Faoláin, Elizabeth Bowen and Mary Lavin. The author of *The Playboy of the Western World*, no less than Senator Yeats, would have approved of the fact that, though the official language of the Poblacht na hÉireann is now Irish, English is still recognized as a second official language.

X. ANGLO-INDIAN LITERATURE AND THE
ENGLISH LITERATURE OF INDIA, PAKISTAN
AND SOUTH-EAST ASIA

Before the Indian Independence Act of 1947, Anglo-Indian literature meant three different but related things. It meant, in the first place, the literature produced during the seventeenth, eighteenth, nineteenth and early twentieth centuries by a small body of British administrators, soldiers and missionaries who, during the working part of their lives, were residents in a remote and exotic sub-continent to which, in spite of every effort of love and duty, they could never, they often felt, in any real sense belong. This Anglo-Indian literature, whose highest achievement in the nineteenth century was in some of the work of Rudyard Kipling, was written for the public at home as much as for the British in India. To say that its interest for the modern reader is largely historical is not really to belittle it, for its best authors were themselves aware of their lonely position in a long historical process, aware of the great age of India, of the heavy burden of the past and the unrealized possibilities of the future. Anglo-Indian literature meant also the literature written in English by Indians themselves, many of whom had been educated both in India and in England and who had thus the advantages of a cosmopolitan view. And finally it meant the literature written by those like the poet Henry Louis Vivian Derozio—author of *The Fakeer of Jungheera* (1828)—who were Eurasian by blood, Anglo-Indian in the literal sense.

Since Independence, the pukka Sahibs have retired in good order to their bungalows called "Poona" or "Lucknow" in Cheltenham, Bournemouth or Tunbridge Wells: like Othello, they "have done the state some service, and they know't." But the English language they took with them to India has remained behind, still a potent force throughout India, Pakistan and Ceylon and to a lesser extent in Burma and the adjoining countries in South-East Asia. In a sub-continent with thirteen "recognized languages" and where Sir George Grierson in his *Linguistic Survey of India* (1898–1928) described no less than 179 languages and 544 dialects, English as a link language, though spoken by a small minority, has some of the advantages which Latin possessed in the European Middle Ages. To the pre-Independence, pre-Partition Anglo-Indian literature must therefore be added the literature in English written since 1947 by Indians, Pakistanis, Ceylonese and others. Within the limits of a few pages, we shall endeavour here to trace the principal periods and authors in this long history, bearing in mind, as we have said, that this history is itself but an episode in the whole lengthy book of India.

Anglo-Indian literature begins with the letters, preserved by Purchas (p. 156 above), of the Jesuit missionary Thomas Stephens or Stevens (c. 1549–1619) who went to Goa in 1579 and was the first Englishman to settle in India. Ralph Fitch, a London merchant, travelled in India and the East in 1583–91 and the lively description of his adventures, preserved by Hakluyt and Purchas, was very useful to those who sought to promote the English East India Company. For a hundred years after the Company in 1600 had received its charter from Queen

Elizabeth, Anglo-Indian literature meant, simply, books of travel, like the *Journal* of Sir Thomas Roe, ambassador of James I at the court of the Mogul Emperor Jahangir, whom he calls in Miltonic cadence "the Great Mogoar, King of the Orientall Indyes, of Condahy, of Chismer, and of Corason." William Methold in his *Relations of the Kingdome of Golchonda* (1626) describes his experiences in south India. William Bruton's *Newes from the East Indies* (1638) relates how the English obtained their first footing in Orissa in 1632. John Fryer in his *New Account of East India and Persia* (1693) throws light on the contemporary politics of western India. Though less brilliant than their French contemporaries of the seventeenth century—such as François Bernier, author of *Travels in the Moghul Empire* (1671; trans. 1893)—these early Anglo-Indian writers have a characteristic distinction which is often wanting in their successors. They have been well served, and well quoted, in Ram Chandra Prasad's excellent book *Early English Travellers in India* (Delhi, 1966).

The greater part of the eighteenth century was, in a literary sense, uneventful. The chief name is that of Robert Orme (1728–1801), who during a varied official life gathered the knowledge which enabled him to become one of the greatest of Anglo-Indian historians in his *History of the Military Transactions of the British Nation in Indostan* (1763–78). His contemporary Alexander Dow produced a *History of Hindostan... translated from the Persian* (1768–72). John Zephaniah Holwell, a survivor of the tragedy, wrote a *Narrative of the Deplorable Deaths of the English Gentlemen who were suffocated in the Black Hole* (1758). The modern student can supplement these accounts by a reading of Indian historians like Ram Gopal, whose book *How the British occupied Bengal* came out in 1964. The same year saw the first volume, from the Princeton University Press, of the novelist Khushwant Singh's *History of the Sikhs*, covering the period 1469–1839 (completed 1967 by *Vol. II: 1839–1964*). The change from eighteenth-century "Nabob" to nineteenth-century "Sahib" is recorded in two excellent books: T. G. Percival Spear's *The Nabobs: A Study of the Social Life of the English in Eighteenth-Century India* (1932) and Hilton Brown's *The Sahibs: The Life and Ways of the British in India as Recorded by Themselves* (1948).

The closing years of the Indian career of Warren Hastings saw the real birth of English literature and literary studies in India. *Hicky's Bengal Gazette*, the first newspaper of British India, was founded at Calcutta by James Augustus Hicky in 1780. Sir William Jones (1746–94) was already an Oriental scholar when he went to India in 1783 as Judge of the Supreme Court. He founded the Bengal Asiatic Society, became the first great English Sanskrit scholar, translated Kalidasa's masterpiece *Shakuntala* and wrote elaborate "oriental" poems of his own. Garland Cannon's biography *Oriental Jones* was published at New Delhi in 1964 by the Indian Council for Cultural Relations. Jones's work was carried on by the Scots poet and orientalist John Leyden (1775–1811; p. 498), that "lamp too early quenched", as Scott lamented. Leyden lived in the East from 1803 to his death and was the first of that long line of Anglo-Indian writers who expressed in verse the common feelings of British exiles in what Sir Alfred Lyall was to call (in the poem of that name) "the Land of Regrets".

The first two decades of the nineteenth century were marked by other signs of literary advance. James Tod pursued in Rajputana the researches which he ultimately gave to the world in his classic *Annals and Antiquities of Rajasthan* (1829–32), a work richer in romance than most epics. Mark Wilks made history in Madras and wrote it in his impartial and critical *Historical Sketches of the South of India* (1810–17). Sir John Malcolm also took part in many of the events he described in such important works as *A Sketch of the Political History of India* (1811). That the mem-sahibs were equally active in the literary field was proved by Eliza Fay's *Original Letters from Calcutta* (1817) and by Mary Martha Sherwood's children's story *Little Henry and his Bearer* (1815).

Macaulay was in India from 1834 to 1838, and his controversial Minute on education resulted in the adoption in 1835 of the English language as the basis for all higher education in India—a measure previously advocated by the Bengali reformer and scholar Ram Mohan Roy (1772–1833). After the Independence Act of 1947, the debate on the wisdom or otherwise of Macaulay's Minute naturally resumed with added point. Macaulay certainly cared little for the languages, religions and literature of India; on the other hand, there was both cultural and commercial gain in having a common link-language for the scholar of Karachi and the merchant of Madras. The Hindu College was founded at Calcutta in 1816 for the instruction of Indians in English and it was followed by other foundations, many of which developed into universities. The adoption of English had the unexpected and desirable result of revivifying the vernaculars. Stimulated in part by English literature and Western knowledge, Bankim Chandra Chatterji, the first graduate of Calcutta University, created modern Bengali fiction. His younger contemporary, Romesh Chunder Dutt (1848–1909), Prime Minister of Baroda, wrote in both Bengali and English. His English novels and his *Lays of Ancient India* (1894) show impressive command of the language. Michael Madhu Sadan Dutt (d. 1873) lives by his Bengali poems rather than his *Captive Ladie* (1849), which tells in English verse the story of Prithwi Raj, King of Delhi. Toru or Tarulata Dutt (1856–77) was the daughter of Govind Chandra Dutt, who himself wrote English verse and contributed to *The Dutt Family Album* (1876). She was in close contact throughout her short life with both Indian and European culture, as is evident in her French novel, *Le Journal de Mlle D'Arvers*, in her *Sheaf Gleaned in French Fields* (1876) and in her *Ancient Ballads and Legends of Hindustan* (1882).

Meanwhile, both before and after the rising of 1857 and the subsequent taking over by the British Crown of the powers and responsibilities of the East India Company, the stream of Anglo-Indian literature in its British meaning flowed on unimpeded till its culmination in the work of Rudyard Kipling. There were historians like James Grant Duff, who wrote a *History of the Mahrattas* (1826); Mountstuart Elphinstone, whose *History of India* (1841), like Sir William Hunter's uncompleted *History of British India* (1899), is among the classics of its time; and Sir John Kaye, who founded *The Calcutta Review* in 1844. There were scholars of Islamic culture like Sir Henry Miers Elliot, who wrote *A History of India as told by its own Historians* (1867–77), and Sir William Muir, who wrote *The Life of Mahomet* (1858–61). And there were novelists and story-writers like William Browne Hockley, whose best book was *Pandurang Hari* (1826) but who is better known for his *Tales of the Zenana* (1827); Philip Meadows Taylor, author of the celebrated *Confessions of a Thug* (1839); and

Matthew Arnold's brother, William Delafield Arnold, whose *Oakfield; or Fellowship in the East* (1853) is a stern moral protest against the dissipation of the Anglo-Indian community and its disregard of native interests. Lighter, more satirical novelists included John Lang, author of *The Wetherbys* (1853) and *The Ex-Wife* (1859), and Henry Curwen, editor of *The Times of India*. Some of these looked forward to the first satirical stories of Kipling, as did also the American novelist Francis Marion Crawford (1854–1909), who went to India in 1879 and became editor of *The Indian Herald* at Allahabad and whose novel *Mr Isaacs: A Tale of Modern India* (New York, 1882) is a story of a diamond-merchant in Simla.

Of the pre-Kipling poets, the most re-readable are Sir Alfred Lyall (1835–1911) and Sir Edwin Arnold (1832–1904). Lyall founded the new university of Allahabad and wrote the important work *The Rise and Expansion of the British Dominion in India* (1893). In such poems as *Meditations of a Hindu Prince* and *The Amir's Message*—and other poems afterwards collected in *Verses Written in India* (1889)—he broke new ground by having as his spokesmen sympathetic examples of the old, pre-British India. Edwin Arnold was principal of Deccan College, Bombay. After his return to England he wrote *The Light of Asia* (1879), a long poem on the life and teaching of the Buddha whose modern admirers included T. S. Eliot. The lighter side of Anglo-Indian verse was shown in *Lays of Ind* (1875) by "Aliph Cheem" (Walter Yeldham) and in Thomas Francis Bignold's *Leviora: being the Rhymes of a Successful Competitor* (1888). The miscellaneous prose of the period includes two once-celebrated satires, *The Chronicles of Budgepore* (1870, 1880) by Iltudus Prichard and *Twenty-One Days in India, being the Tour of Sir Ali Baba* (1878–9) by George Robert Aberigh-Mackay. Pleasanter reading was provided by Sir Henry Stuart Cunningham's *Chronicles of Dustypore* (1875) and Edward Hamilton Aitken's *Behind the Bungalow* (1889). The effects of the change from the old method of selecting officials to the new were first noted in *The Competition Wallah* (1864) by Sir George Otto Trevelyan (1838–1928; p. 667), a nephew of Macaulay. There was thus a good deal of varied literature in India, written by different kinds of literary wallahs over tiffin, before the popular genius of Rudyard Kipling made Mrs Hauksbee, Private Ortheris, Gunga Din and "the road to Mandalay" the common property of the whole English-speaking world.

The literary reputation of Kipling has gone through three phases, the third of which is likely to be the most lasting. The first phase, one of enormous popularity and esteem—though there were always dissenting voices such as Oscar Wilde's—lasted the greater part of his life and reached its apogee in 1907 when he was awarded the Nobel Prize for Literature. He had refused the Laureate-ship in 1895. The second phase, lasting from the nineteen-twenties to the forties or fifties, was one of steadily decreasing reputation, as it became realized how much Kipling had taken for granted and what gaps there were in his appreciation of the land of his birth. The third phase looks at him more tolerantly, but also more historically, though here we have the partial exception of the distinguished Indian writer Nirad C. Chaudhuri, who in his *Continent of Circe: being an essay on the peoples of India* (1965) considers Kipling to be "the only English writer who will have a permanent place in English literature with

books on Indian themes, and who will also be read by everyone who wants to
know not only *British* India but also *timeless* India." Kipling would have been
grateful for the latter avowal, for in his more sensitive moments he did not
regard himself simply as "the Poet Laureate of the British Empire" or the
prose laureate of the British Raj, but as "the two-sided man" of the poem of
that title in *Kim*, who could drink "a health, my brothers" to

> Wesley's following, Calvin's flock,
> White or yellow or bronze,
> Shaman, Ju-ju or Angekok,
> Minister, Mukamuk, Bonze...

Despite irreverent references in the *Barrack-Room Ballads* to "the Widow at
Windsor", Kipling was a loyal subject of the Queen-Empress, who was nevertheless conscious of the immensity of the pre-British Indian past and the curious
way that past was always present. To some extent, this consciousness of Kipling's
was inherited.

Rudyard Kipling (1865–1936) was born in Bombay, the son of John Lockwood
Kipling (1837–1911), a Methodist minister's son who had become a professional
artist. The elder Kipling was a designer and an architectural sculptor, curator of
the Central Museum and principal of the School of Art at Lahore, an acknowledged authority on Indian crafts and customs, and author of that delightful
book, *Beast and Man in India* (1891). Kipling's mother, also of a Methodist
minister's family, had artistic connections of her own, notably with Morris and
the Pre-Raphaelites. One of her sisters married Edward Burne-Jones, another
Alfred Baldwin, father of the future Conservative statesman. Kipling thus
inherited not only, from his father, a feeling for the cultural past of India but
also, from his mother, a great deal of Pre-Raphaelite artistic sensibility, his
violent reaction from which early in life made him perhaps exaggerate his own
tendency towards the more Philistine virtues. At the United Services' College
in England, he "read a good deal", as he tells us in his unfinished autobiography
Something of Myself (1937): "Emerson's poems; and Bret Harte's stories" as
well as Browning (his favourite poet) and Donne. Poor sight prevented him
following a career in the Indian Army, like his friend, the future Major-General
Dunsterville, the boyhood hero of *Stalky and Co.* (1899) and himself the genial
author of *Stalky's Reminiscences* (1928). So when Kipling returned to Lahore in
1882, it was not as one of the soldiers or administrators he lauded in *The White
Man's Burden*—in *The Five Nations* (1903)—but as sub-editor of *The Civil and
Military Gazette*. He had already appeared in print as the youthful poet of
Schoolboy Lyrics (1881), which was followed by *Echoes; by Two Writers* (1884),
a volume of parodies written with his sister Beatrice. But it was his training as a
journalist on *The Gazette* which created him as a writer, a fact (commoner with
American writers than with British) which he always gratefully acknowledged.

Maturity of a kind came early to Kipling, and he soon reached a point
beyond which he never grew. *Quartette*, the Christmas Annual (1885) of *The
Gazette*, contained two of his later collected tales, as well as other pieces in prose
and verse (by all four Kiplings) never reprinted. The official skits called *Departmental Ditties* (1886) showed the first clear symptoms of a characteristic
manner in verse—a manner, however, which (as Kipling himself pointed out)

had a long tradition of Anglo-Indian light verse behind it, going back to the early years of *The Bengal Gazette*. Kipling was now, in a sense, quite "set", and in quick succession came collections of stories, already printed in *The Civil and Military Gazette* or elsewhere, beginning with *Plain Tales from the Hills* (1888) and continuing the same year with six slim volumes in Wheeler's Indian Railway Library: *Soldiers Three, The Story of the Gadsbys, In Black and White, Under the Deodars, The Phantom Rickshaw* and *Wee Willie Winkie*. In 1890 followed *The City of Dreadful Night*, about the underworld of Calcutta, and in 1891 *The Smith Administration*, where he writes of those Englishmen in India "who live down in the plains and do things other than writing futile reports." These early books achieved immediate popularity in India and became almost as quickly known in Britain and America. The acrid stories of married flirtations among the "Sahibs" and the humorous stories of broad adventures among the "Tommies" proved equally popular, and the style, which combined vividness of descriptive journalism with terseness of cynical epigram, caught the fancy of the public. With his notebook always at hand, and with his curiosity about the ways of machines, Kipling in these early stories was akin to Zola, whom he had read in the original at Lahore at a time when he was still untranslated.

Kipling had unquestionably succeeded with the short story. Could he build on a larger scale? *The Light that Failed*, a *nouvelle* first contained in *Lippincott's Monthly Magazine*, Philadelphia (January 1891), evaded rather than answered the question, which was answered much more satisfactorily in *Kim* (1901), probably his best prose work, though he himself gave the palm to *Just So Stories for Little Children* (1902), a vein of juvenile writing which he continued in *Puck of Pook's Hill* (1906). His best volumes of verse, on the whole, are *Barrack-Room Ballads* (1892) and *The Seven Seas* (1896).

As was almost inevitable in a popular writer of such early fame, Kipling in his later work tended to repeat his old successes. The majority of the work by which he will be remembered belongs to the nineteenth century: from *Plain Tales* to *Kim*. And the majority of it belongs to India, whether written there or in America. The "timeless India" which Chaudhuri speaks of is particularly obvious in *The City of Dreadful Night*, in *Kim*, and on a different level in the two *Jungle Books* (1894–5), books which introduce our children to the India of animal life, with Mowgli the wolf-child—who had first appeared in *Many Inventions* (1893)—as the focus of attention.

When dealing with adults rather than with children, animals or machines, Kipling's understanding is limited. If he saw much, he divined little. Despite his sympathetic treatment of both Hinduism and Islam—as Professor Sajjad Husain of the University of Dacca points out in his valuable study *Kipling and India* (1965)—he was so deeply imbued with the prejudices of most of his fellow-Englishmen in India that he could see no justification for the transfer of responsibility from British to Indian hands. Kipling's chief service to India is not that he made it understood, but that he made it interesting to a large general public who had never before given it serious attention. There is more sensitive treatment of some aspects of India in lesser writers like Mrs Steel, Mrs Penny and Mrs Bell ("John Travers"), not to mention later and greater writers like E. M. Forster.

On the other hand, as was pointed out by George Orwell—who was himself born in India, served in the Indian Imperial Police 1922–8 and wrote *Burmese Days* (1934)—what Kipling wrote about "the long-service, mercenary army of the late nineteenth century", as of what he wrote about "nineteenth-century Anglo-India", is "not only the best but almost the only literary picture we have. He has put on record an immense amount of stuff that one could otherwise only gather from verbal tradition or from unreadable regimental histories." And his defence of the private soldier, however condescending in its carefully dropped aspirates, must be put to his credit. The Victorians were too apt to take their army for granted, particularly the ordinary soldier who was lauded in theory—if not often as naïvely as in Hopkins's poem about "our redcoats, our tars"—but despised in practice; one recalls the miner in *Sons and Lovers* "almost ashamed" to go to his public house after he had learnt of his son's enlistment. Kipling's defence, in *Tommy* and other verses—"We aren't no thin red 'eroes, nor we aren't no blackguards too"—was as shrewd as it was necessary, the line "makin' mock o' uniforms that guard you while you sleep" being one of the most telling of his frequently telling phrases. If some of his higher poetical flights, like *Recessional* (1897)—that self-satisfied appeal for national humility— make curious reading today, Kipling still lives as an original verse-writer in the best of the *Barrack-Room Ballads* and his other soldier's songs.

The *Ballads* originally appeared in *The National Observer*, *Macmillan's Magazine*, *The St James's Gazette* and *The Athenaeum*. When he collected them in 1892, Kipling dedicated the book to his American brother-in-law Wolcott Balestier, who had collaborated with him in *The Naulahka: A Story of East and West* (1891). At his Vermont home in 1892–6 Kipling produced some of his most characteristic work, including the *Jungle Books* and *Captains Courageous*. American fascination with British India goes back as far as Whittier's *Relief of Lucknow*, but it was Kipling's ballads and stories which won over so many American writers to the creed of the White Man's Burden and "the manifest destiny" of the Anglo-Saxon race. The young Frank Norris was among the American writers who began to talk of "the Anglo-Saxon's birthright" and found himself dancing, as he said, to the pipe of the "little bespectacled colonial", to whose song, he insisted, "we must all listen." Kipling was also among the favourite writers of H. L. Mencken, and Jack London copied out by hand some of the stories of the man whom he called his "British idol" when he was too poor to buy the book. In his days of prosperity, London continued to glorify the "great race-adventure of the Anglo-Saxon", the "salt of the earth", who were destined, he believed as firmly as Kipling, to rule the brown, the red, the yellow and the black races—for, of course, their own good. More liberal ideas, in America as in Britain, gradually ousted the first popularity of this most famous of Anglo-Indians, who had had the good sense to marry an American girl and who had settled for a while in New England. But long after Kipling had died in 1936 in his "Sussex by the sea", American interest in him revived in a less enthusiastic but more scholarly form. *Kipling in India* (1966), by Louis L. Cornell of Columbia University, is one of the typically judicious studies which have come from the West, studies which can be usefully compared with those by Orwell in England and by Chaudhuri and Husain in India and Pakistan. In

Kipling studies, the celebrated "twain" have met more easily than he envisaged in his *Ballad of East and West*.

The contrast comes in when we turn from Kipling to his successors in Anglo-Indian literature. "One may as well begin"—not, indeed, with Helen's letters to her sister in the opening chapter of E. M. Forster's *Howards End*, but with the letters the author himself wrote home from the Central Indian state of Dewas Senior in his two periods as secretary to the Maharajah, the first in the years 1912–13, the second in 1921. These letters, so remote from all that Kipling stood for, form the main part of the book *The Hill of Devi* (1953), which apart from its own intrinsic interest is valuable as one of the sources of Forster's master-piece, *A Passage to India* (1924), the novel in which England said goodbye for ever to Kipling's simplified views of Anglo-India and where a liberal mind saw the tragic irony, as well as the incidental humour, of the lack of contact between East and West. That Forster's views were not simply his own, but were shared by other Anglo-Indians of his generation, is proved by his dedication of *The Hill of Devi* to Sir Malcolm Darling, author of *The Punjab Peasant in Prosperity and Debt* (1925) and *Apprentice to Power: India 1904–8* (1966), one of those enlightened liberal administrators who had succeeded the generally more con-servative officials of Kipling's time. Another was Leonard Woolf, whom we associate mainly with Bloomsbury and the Hogarth Press, but who served in the Ceylon Civil Service 1904–11, encouraged Forster to complete *A Passage to India* when the author, as he confessed, "felt only distaste and despair" over the opening chapters, and himself wrote *The Village in the Jungle* (1913), a sensitive study in fictional form of the life of a rural community in South Ceylon. Another Anglo-Indian of liberal outlook was the poet and scholar Edward Thompson (1886–1946), who wrote *An Indian Day* (1927) and *A Farewell to India* (1930) and who was the chief English interpreter of the great Indian poet and philosopher Rabindranath Tagore (1861–1941). Tagore himself wrote in both Bengali and English, sometimes translating his own works, notably the collection of lyrics *Gitanjali* and the verse play *Chitra*. His Bengali novel *Binodini* (1902) is generally regarded as the first modern novel by an Indian author; it was translated into English (Honolulu, 1965) by his biographer Krishna Kripalani, secretary of the Indian National Academy of Letters. Like his follower, the philosopher-president Sir Sarvepalli Radhakrishnan, author of *The Philosophy of Rabindranath Tagore* and *Eastern Religions and Western Thought* (1939), Tagore was desirous of establishing a new relationship between Western education and Eastern philosophy and founded at Santiniketan, Bolpur, a school and international university to that end. He resigned his knighthood in 1919 in protest against British repression of his countrymen. Men like Forster, Darling, Woolf and Thompson—like, before them, the poet and traveller Wilfrid Scawen Blunt, author of *Ideas about India* (1885)—were as strongly in favour of Indian self-government as most of Kipling's generation were against it. It was partly owing to their influence, on the British side, that the transference of power was carried out so peaceably in 1947.

On the Indian side, the chief influence for peace was, of course, that of Mohandas Karamchand Gandhi (1869–1948), who preached Hindu-Moslem unity, civil disobedience and a return to the traditional rural virtues and who became widely revered as the Mahatma or Great Sage. Though he naturally favoured the resurgence of the Indian languages rather than any further increase in the use of English—he wrote his autobiography *The Story of my Experiments with Truth* in his native Gujarati—Gandhi owed much of the world sympathy for his cause to his own skilful use of the English tongue, as did his colleague and successor Jawaharlal Nehru (1889–1964), first Prime Minister of India and author of *Glimpses of World History* (1939) and *Discovery of India* (1946). Nehru's *Autobiography* (1936) can be compared with *Friends Not Masters: A Political Autobiography* (1967) by Ayub Khan, President of Pakistan. The Muslim poet and philosopher Sir Muhammad Iqbal (1875–1938)—whose major poetic work, the *Javidnama*, was translated by A. J. Arberry in 1966— was described by Forster as "one of the two great cultural influences of Modern India". As President of the Muslim League in 1930 he advocated the creation of a separate Muslim state in North-West India and subsequently helped to convert to the idea of Pakistan the founder of that country, Mohammed Ali Jinnah (1876–1948). The most impartial and scholarly account of the period for the British or American reader is probably Percival Spear's *Oxford History of Modern India: 1740–1947* (1965).

Anglo-Indian literature in the old British sense naturally disappeared with the transfer of power in 1947 and the subsequent creation of the independent countries of India, Pakistan, Ceylon and Burma. But Englishmen continued to write about the East; and some Americans, too, from Louis Bromfield to John Berry and Allen Ginsberg. In the Meadows Taylor tradition was John Masters, whose series of historical novels began with *Nightrunners of Bengal* (1951), about the period of the Indian Mutiny, and included *The Deceivers* (1953) about the Thugs and the near-contemporary *Bhowani Junction* (1954), set in India at the time of Partition. This was also the period and place of *The Scarlet Sword* (1951) by H. E. Bates, some of whose other novels, such as *The Jacaranda Tree* (1949), are set in Burma. The continuance of English as the medium of higher education meant the replacement all over the East, from West Pakistan to Singapore, of English governors, civil servants or advisers by English or American university lecturers and professors. The devoted careers of the former can be studied in such excellent books as Darling's *Apprentice to Power*, John Cameron's *Our Tropical Possessions in Malayan India* (1865; repr. 1966 with introduction by Professor Wang Gungwu of the University of Malaya); Charles Burton Buckley's *An Anecdotal History of Old Times in Singapore* (Singapore, 1902; Kuala Lumpur, 1966); Maurice Collis's biography (1966) of Sir Stamford Raffles (1781–1826); Victor Purcell's *Memoirs of a Malayan Official* (1965) and Sir Robert Reid's *Years of Change in Bengal and Assam* (1966). Some of the latter have emulated Forster and Leonard Woolf by embodying their experiences in fictional form, like D. J. Enright in Thailand and Anthony Burgess in Malaya and Borneo.

The most interesting work, however, has been in the field, not of Anglo-Indian literature, but of what may be termed Indo-Anglian or Indo-British literature and its counterparts in the adjoining countries: that is, the literature in the English language produced since 1947 by Indians, Pakistanis and others, who have emulated the skill and power of the best of their predecessors in the

British past such as the poetess and Congress Party leader Sarojini Naidu (1870–1949), the subject of an excellent biography (1966) by Mrs Padmini Sengupta; the poet Manmohan Ghose (1867–1924); the novelist of the *purdah*, Cornelia Sorabji; and the novelist and story-writer, both in English and Urdu, who most impressively spans the imperial past and the independent present, Ahmed Ali, author of *Twilight in Delhi* (1940) and *Ocean of Night* (1964), who since Partition has lived in Pakistan. Among Ali's most interesting contemporaries and successors, of both Muslim and Hindu background, may be mentioned his novelist friend Raja Rao, author of *Kanthapura* (1938) and *The Serpent and the Rope* (1960); Mulk Raj Anand (b. 1905), who wrote *Coolie* (1932), *Untouchable* (1935) and other novels and stories of peasant life; R. K. Narayan, whose dry, ironic humour, as of a South Indian E. M. Forster, is seen in *The Man-Eater of Malgudi* (1963), *The Sweet-Vendor* (1967) and other novels; Sudhindra Nath Ghose (b. 1899), author of *Cradle of the Clouds* and *The Flame of the Forest*, who like Toru Dutt writes in both English and French; and Ruth Prawer Jhabvala, whose picture of cosmopolitan cultural life in modern Delhi in *A Backward Place* (1966) can be contrasted with that of the traditional Muslim life of pre-1914 Delhi in Ali's masterpiece. To which we may add the Sikh novelist Khushwant Singh, already mentioned for his history, and the Tibetan novelist Tsewang Pemba, whose *Idols on the Path* (1966) traces in fictional form the history of his country from the British expedition of 1904, under Sir Francis Younghusband, to the Chinese invasion of 1950.

Indian poetry, since Independence, has not on the whole been so impressive as Indian fiction. Among the names most known in the West are those of Dom Moraes and the poet-critic Nissim Ezekiel, associate editor of the Calcutta quarterly *Quest* and editor of the P.E.N. symposium *Writing in India* (Bombay, 1966). The stranger to modern Indian poetry in English can get some impression of prevailing trends from a reading of the Indian sections in Margaret O'Donnell's *Anthology of Commonwealth Poetry* (1963) and P. L. Brent's *Young Commonwealth Poets* (1965). Brent's anthology includes some of the best work of both Moraes and Ezekiel, besides separate sections on Pakistan and Ceylon and on Wong Phui Nam and other poets of Malaysia. Modern Malaysian literature can itself be sampled in Oliver Rice's and Abdullah Majid's *Modern Malay Verse* (1963) and in T. Wignesan's *Bunga Emas: An Anthology of Contemporary Malaysian Literature, 1930–63* (1964). There was a special "Singapore and Malaysia Number", edited by Edwin Thumboo, of the Madras monthly *Poet* in 1966. Tom Harrison's *Borneo Writing* (Kuching, 1966) is a publication of *The Sarawak Museum Journal*.

Indian and Ceylonese criticism, both of literature and society, has done some useful work in the hands of such writers as Nirad Chaudhuri, the critic-novelist Balachandra Rajan, the critic and dramatist E. F. C. Ludowyk, and the art critic and educationist Ananda Coomaraswamy (1877–1947), who taught both in India and America and whose nephew, the Ceylonese poet M. J. Tambimuttu, became well known in England during the Second World War and after by his editing of the journal *Poetry London*. We may add the name of the Trinidadian novelist V. S. Naipaul (p. 932 below), whose visit to the India of his ancestors produced the disturbing and controversial book *An Area of Darkness* (1964).

In Pakistan, the number of works written in English continued to be much smaller than those in the two national languages, Bengali and Urdu. Among the most interesting of their recent writers in English, in both verse and fiction, have been Zulfikar Ghose, author of *The Loss of India* (1964) and the novel *The Contradictions* (1966), and Mehdi Ali Seljouk, whose sketches entitled *Corpses* (1966) are an ironic commentary on his Preface, in which he tells of his own sufferings in that tragic India–Pakistan conflict which Gandhi had forecast as the inevitable result of Partition.

The non-Asian reader can best find his way about the literature thus briefly mentioned if he follows up his reading of Bhupal Singh's *Survey of Anglo-Indian Fiction* (1934) and K. R. Srinivasa Iyengar's P.E.N. Book *Literature and Authorship in India* (1943) by a study of the latter author's *Indian Writing in English* (1962) and the relevant sections and essays in *The Journal of Commonwealth Literature*, edited by Arthur Ravenscroft, a joint venture of the University of Leeds and Heinemann Educational Books, whose first number appeared in September 1965. (The fifth number, July 1968, gave special attention to English writing in India and Pakistan.) Particularly valuable to the British or American reader are the sections on countries not so well known for their English literature as India itself, such as Yasmine Gooneratne's contributions on Ceylon and Lloyd Fernando's and T. Wignesan's on Malaysia and Singapore. The "road to Mandalay" and beyond is thus as well covered in literature and criticism as Kipling could have desired, if some of the opinions expressed would have staggered him.

XI. ENGLISH-CANADIAN LITERATURE

Like the literature of all countries which began as colonies of Europe and proceeded gradually to independence, the English literature of Canada, even more than the French literature of the *Canadiens*, must be accepted as a fact without seeking too precisely for a definition. Not all English-Canadian writers are Canadian (or British) by birth, and some who are Canadian by birth do not write of Canada at all. The nineteenth-century poet William Henry Drummond was born in Ireland; but everybody thinks of him as a Canadian writer. The historian Goldwin Smith (see p. 670) was born in England; yet though he lived in Toronto for forty years and edited *The Canadian Monthly* 1872–4, he remained almost completely English and is not usually regarded as a Canadian writer except by adoption. Grant Allen (1848–99) was born at Kingston, Ontario, but was educated at Oxford and after a period as Professor of Logic at Queen's College, Jamaica, returned to England, not to Canada, to take up his literary career. He was a man of wide interests and besides being a novelist (see p. 649) wrote on history and science. The economist and humorist Stephen Leacock (p. 748 below) is one of the best known of Canadian writers; yet he was born in England, studied for a time at the University of Chicago, seems to have regarded the United States as well as Canada as virtually part of the British Empire—if an errant part—and as late as 1933, in his critical biography *Charles Dickens: His Life and Work*, writes "we English" as if the Atlantic Ocean and the Confederation of Canada did not exist.

Canadian literature naturally began late. The intrepid men and women who were making a new country, whether they came from England or Ireland, Scotland or France, were not given to the making of books. In general, they were well satisfied with literary imports from Europe and felt little need for local products. Nevertheless, local work, both in English and in French, began slowly to appear. *The Literary History of Canada* (1965), edited by Carl F. Klinck and others for the University of Toronto Press, goes back to the eighteenth century, to the time of the first Canadian novelist, Mrs Frances Brooke (1724–89), who was the wife of the chaplain to the garrison of Quebec. Some extracts from her novel, *The History of Emily Montagu* (1769), open the first volume, *Early Beginnings to Confederation*, of A. J. M. Smith's anthology *The Book of Canadian Prose* (1967–), by the same scholar and poet who was responsible for *The Oxford Book of Canadian Verse* in 1960. Klinck collaborated with Guy Sylvestre and Brandon Conron in the bilingual biographical and bibliographical dictionary *Canadian Writers—Écrivains Canadiens* (1964). In 1965 appeared the English translation of the *History of French-Canadian Literature* by the French-Canadian scholar Gérard Tougas.

The first original Canadian writer in English was perhaps the author of *Sam Slick*, often wrongly assumed to be, like Sam himself, the countryman of Artemus Ward and Mark Twain. Thomas Chandler Haliburton (1796–1865) was in fact born in Nova Scotia and rose to be a Judge of its Supreme Court. His literary work began with histories of his native province, originally called Acadia. His *Sam Slick* papers first appeared in 1835 as contributions to Joseph Howe's newspaper *The Nova Scotian*. They were published in book form as *The Clockmaker; or the Sayings and Doings of Sam Slick of Slickville* (Halifax, 1837), a second and third series following in 1838–40. American humour, Artemus Ward wrote, has its source in *Sam Slick*, where the shrewdness of a Yankee clockmaker is contrasted with the inertia of Haliburton's own "bluenose" compatriots. There is thus a comic tradition running from Judge Haliburton to Stephen Leacock on the northern side of the border, and more significantly from Haliburton to Ward and Twain on the southern. In view of the immense influence of the United States on later Canadian literature, this early influence in the other direction is worth noting.

The first Canadian poetry was naturally "colonial", heavily indebted to the poetry of the mother country, from the time of the appropriately-named Oliver Goldsmith (1794–1861)—a grandnephew of his great namesake— to the mid-century generation of Charles Sangster (1822–93), author of *The St Lawrence and the Sanguenay* (1856), the sonneteer and dramatic poet Charles Heavysege (1816–76), and the "Canadian Burns" Alexander McLachlan (1818–96), who were followed by the Irish-born Isabella Valancy Crawford (1850–86). In *The Rising Village* (1825) the Canadian Goldsmith wrote of the hardships of pioneer life in late-eighteenth-century poetic diction inspired inevitably by his namesake's *Deserted Village*. *Love's Forget Me Not*, the first poem in Isabella Crawford's collected volume of 1905, has been described as a poem in the Brontë tradition without the tragic power that lifts the best of Emily's verse above the Victorian commonplace. Her *Malcolm's Katie* (Toronto, 1884) is one of the first poems to be distinctively Canadian in expression.

Archibald Lampman (1861–99) was the first consistently Canadian poet. As Pelham Edgar wrote: "With Wordsworth, Keats and Arnold on one's shelves, one does not draw inspiration from Sangster and Heavysege"; but Lampman is "in a different category from his predecessors" and can be regarded "as the poet who, under the necessary conditions of imitation, was as Canadian as circumstances would allow." His friend and fellow-poet Duncan Campbell Scott (1862–1944), author of *New World Lyrics* (1905), told the brief story of Lampman's life in the memoir prefixed to his collected poems. He was born in Ontario, of a family of Dutch loyalists who had migrated from Pennsylvania at the time of the American Revolution. His first volume, *Among the Millet* (1888), was as much inspired by his own intense love of nature as by his reading of Keats and Wordsworth. The title of his second volume, *Lyrics of Earth* (1896), indicates his continued, Meredithian interest in natural themes. But his mood was changing. General problems of society were beginning to occupy his mind, and the poems posthumously published show the new direction of his sympathies. Lampman at his best is musical and expressive. *Morning on the Lièvre*, from his first volume, is singled out by Pelham Edgar as "wholly free" from his abiding weakness of monotony "and reproduces with vigour and cunningly contrived detail a characteristic Canadian scene." The same "exquisite lyric" is described by a modern Canadian critic, the poet A. W. Purdy, as "surely the earliest genuine poem written in Canada."

Lampman and Scott were the best of the "Confederation Poets", poets who set out to create a body of distinctively Canadian poetry and who included Major Roberts, Wilfred Campbell, Charles Mair, and Bliss Carman (1861–1929). Carman wrote *Low Tide on Grand Pré* (1893), later emigrated to the United States, and in 1927 edited the first *Oxford Book of American Verse*. George Frederick Cameron (1854–85) died before he had reached the full measure of his powers. The Indian poetess Pauline Johnson, author of *The White Wampum* (1895), had a genuine lyric gift within a limited range. Marcus Van Steen's critical biography, *Pauline Johnson: Her Life and Work*, was published in Toronto in 1965.

William Henry Drummond (1854–1907) found his most rewarding theme in the lives of the French settlers. While still a boy he came into contact with the *habitant* and the *voyageur* and listened to their thrilling tales of backwoods life. From one of them he heard the tragic story which he was to tell again in verse in *The Wreck of the Julie Plante*. Drummond achieved the considerable feat of transmitting the peculiarities of his characters in a language other than their own. His poems are contained in four volumes, *The Habitant* (1897), *Johnny Courteau* (1901), *The Voyageur* (1905) and *The Great Fight* (1908). Drummond depicts the homely lives and sentiments of the French-Canadian peasant without false glamour and with no touch of caricature. "Dans son étude des Canadiens-français," wrote the French-Canadian poet and critic Louis Fréchette (1839–1908), "jamais la note ne sonne faux, jamais la bizarrerie ne dégénère en puérilité burlesque." The *habitant* tales of William McLennan, whose *Songs of Old Canada* (1886) were translated from the French, are an interesting prose counterpart of Drummond's verse.

Nineteenth-century and early twentieth-century Canadian poetry was mainly known to the British public through the medium of anthologies, from L. V. Burpee's *Flowers from a Canadian Garden* to Wilfred Campbell's *Oxford Book of Canadian Verse* (1912), which preceded A. J. M. Smith's. The same public knew the soldier-poet John McCrae (1872–1918) by his one memorable poem, *In Flanders Fields*, and appreciated the Kiplingesque verses and stories of the Lancashire-born Robert W. Service (1874–1958), who wrote of rough frontier and mining life in British Columbia and the Yukon in *Songs of a Sourdough* (1907) and *The Trail of '98* (1910). The poems of Major Sir Charles Roberts (1860–1943) were less well known in England than his magnificent stories of animal life, such as *The Kindred of the Wild* (1902), which shared the same fascinated readership, from youth up, as the animal stories of Marshall Saunders and E. Thompson Seton.

Inevitably, too, Canadian fiction and Canadian fact tended to merge in the mind of the average British reader, brought up as he was on the stories of Robert Michael Ballantyne (1825–94), the Scotsman—nephew of Scott's publishers—whose personal experiences in the Hudson Bay Company in 1841–7 produced *The Young Fur Traders, Ungava*, and other novels for boys which could be read as much for their factual information as for their fictional adventure. This typically Victorian recipe of instruction through entertainment was continued by a clergyman, the Rev. Charles Gordon, "Ralph Connor" (1860–1937), who wrote romantic novels like *The Sky Pilot* (1899) based on his missionary experiences in the Canadian backwoods of Alberta and Manitoba. We have only to compare such fiction as Ballantyne's and Connor's with the accounts of the explorers, from Samuel Hearne's *Account of a Journey to the North-West* (1795), Sir Alexander Mackenzie's *Voyages from Montreal* (1801), George Heriot's *Travels through the Canadas* (1807) and the American Alexander Henry's *Travels and Adventures in Canada* (1809), to the end of the nineteenth century, to realize that the British or urban American reader, while not being put in possession of all the facts, was on the other hand not being seriously misled. Even *The Seats of the Mighty* (1896) and the other romantic historical novels of Sir Gilbert Parker (1862–1932) have a certain basis in Canadian history, if duly corrected and demythologized by a study of more sober historians from Heriot and Parkman to William Kingsford and G. M. Wrong. Born in Ontario, Parker travelled widely, editing a paper in Sydney and visiting the South Sea Islands and Egypt, "moved always," as he wrote in the foreword to *Donovan Pasha* (1905), "by deep interest in the varied manifestations of life in different portions of the Empire." His admitted tendency towards anachronism and "disregard of photographic accuracy" was justified by him on the score of having deliberately "sacrificed superficial exactness while trying to give the more intimate meaning and spirit." One of the last of the strongly imperialist novelists, Parker has by now a minor historical importance of his own.

Mrs Brooke appears to have been the only eighteenth-century Canadian novelist, but the early nineteenth century produced John Richardson's *Wacousta* (1832), which was followed by *The Canadian Crusoes* (1852) by Mrs Catherine Traill, sister of the poet Susanna Moodie (1803–85), whose attractive book of reminiscences *Roughing it in the Bush* appeared the same year. The best of the later nineteenth-century novelists was probably William Kirby (1817–1906), whose most ambitious work, *Le Chien d'Or; or The Golden Dog*, was published in 1877. The most widely popular of early twentieth-century novelists and story-writers were Lucy Montgomery, Mrs Macdonald, who wrote *Anne of Green Gables* (1908); the poet Marjorie Pickthall (1883–1922) who won contemporary acclaim for both her songs and her stories; and Mazo de la Roche, chronicler of the Whiteoak family of Jalna. *Fruits of the Earth* (1913) by Frederick P. Grove is a good example of the more realistic Canadian fiction of the period. The best work of the humorist Stephen Leacock (1869–1944) is contained in *Sunshine Sketches of a Little Town* (1912) and *Arcadian Adventures with the Idle Rich* (1914) rather than in his *Literary Lapses* (1910), *Nonsense Novels* (1911), *Moonbeams from the Larger Lunacy* (1915), and their numerous successors, where his pleasant humour could not always endure the process of attenuation to which it was increasingly subjected. Professor of Economics and Political Science at McGill University, Montreal, Leacock's more serious works include *Elements of Political Science* (1906), *The Unsolved Riddle of Social Justice* (1920), *My Discovery of England* (1922) and *Our British Empire* (1940), besides valuable critical biographies of Dickens and Mark Twain. He owed much to Twain, as Twain at first owed much to Haliburton and Ward, and he shared Twain's gift for public speaking, his uproarious lectures at McGill being predictably very popular with his students. His unfinished autobiography, *The Boy I Left Behind Me* (1946), is now supplemented by Ralph L. Curry's *Stephen Leacock: Humorist and Humanist* (1959). Donald A. Cameron's critical study of his work was published in Toronto in 1967.

The more recent Canadian literature of the twentieth century is connected with the growth of literary studies, if not always as intimately as in the founding of *The McGill Fortnightly Review* in 1925 by the poet-critics Frank R. Scott and A. J. M. Smith, which marked the beginning of the "Montreal Group" of writers who were influenced particularly by the poetry of Yeats and the criticism of Eliot. Among them, but standing somewhat apart by theme and background, is Abraham Klein, born in Montreal in 1909 of an orthodox Jewish family, a poet whose work from *Hath Not a Jew* (1940) to *The Rocking Chair* (1948) and *The Second Scroll* (1951) makes him, in the opinion of A. W. Purdy and other good judges, one of the four leading Canadian poets of the mid-twentieth century. The most senior of these four was E. J. (Ned) Pratt (1883–1964) who was born in Newfoundland. His first important book was *Newfoundland Verse* (1923); his *Collected Poems* appeared in 1944. Earle Birney, born in Alberta in 1904, taught at the Universities of Utah, Toronto and Oregon and for nineteen years was Professor of English at the University of British Columbia. His first book was *David and Other Poems* (1942). His verse-drama *Trial of a City* came out in 1952 and *Selected Poems* in 1966. Irving Layton was born in Rumania in 1912, his family emigrating to Montreal while he was a child. He wrote for many years without attracting much attention, but when his collected poems were published in 1959 under the title of *A Red Carpet for the Sun*, the red carpet for the poet, too, was spread out by critics in both Canada and the United States.

The most famous Canadian writer of fiction in the mid-twentieth century was Morley Callaghan, born in Toronto in 1903 of Irish descent, described by

Edmund Wilson in *The New Yorker*, as late as 1960, as "perhaps the most unjustly neglected novelist of the English speaking world." While still a student, Callaghan worked part-time for *The Toronto Daily Star* and in 1923 got to know its European correspondent, Ernest Hemingway, who encouraged him in his writing. Callaghan's first collection, *A Native Argosy*, published in New York in 1929, contained two *nouvelles* and fourteen short stories, most of which had appeared in print before, one of them in *transition*, Parisian organ of the cosmo-American *avant garde* (p. 880 below). *That Summer in Paris* (1963) looks back upon this period and includes Callaghan's reminiscences of Hemingway and Scott Fitzgerald. Among his early novels were *A Broken Journey* (1932) and *Such is My Beloved* (1934). His second collection, *Now That April's Here* (1936), includes stories written between 1929 and 1935, "tales very full of human sympathy," wrote Wyndham Lewis in the Toronto journal *Saturday Night*, "a blending of all the events of life into a pattern of tolerance and mercy." Perhaps the best of his later work is *A Passion in Rome* (1961), a novel set in the Eternal City at the time of the death of Pope Pius XII and described by Brandon Conron, author of the critical study *Morley Callaghan* (1966), as "the most complex of Callaghan's works...a searching appreciation of the mystery and power of the Christian tradition."

In *The Loved and the Lost* (1951) Callaghan touches on what is perhaps the most significant theme in modern Canadian literature, the existence of the two cultures of English and French Canada, which itself is but the most obvious instance in a whole complex of isolations of one group, creed or colour from another, each trying to "belong" to a Canada that seems more and more an abstraction rather than a reality. This was observed by Lord Tweedsmuir when he was Governor-General in Ottawa in 1935–40. In Janet Adam Smith's biography *John Buchan* (1965) he is quoted as reporting to King George VI that "Canadians know uncommonly little about their own country, and the result is that each part is apt to feel isolated from the rest." Since Buchan's time, many novels and critical works have been devoted to some aspect or other of this overriding theme, such as Hugh MacLennan's *Two Solitudes* (1945), Gabrielle Roy's *Bonheur D'Occasion* (1945; trans. 1958), Gwethalyn Graham's *Earth and High Heaven* (1960), Mordecai Richler's *The Incomparable Atuk* (1963) and Edmund Wilson's *O Canada: An American's Notes on Canadian Culture* (1967), a typically acute study by the most eminent of American literary and social critics which first appeared in *The New Yorker* in 1964. The non-Canadian reader who has not had the opportunities of a Buchan or a Wilson to judge for himself can best find his way across the thin ice of this Canadian problem—a kind of Canadian Apartheid which has produced as much literature as the South African species—by coupling with the reading of Wilson's book a reading of an illuminating article by Catherine Rubinger, "Two Related Solitudes: Canadian Novels in French and English", which appeared in the "Canadian" issue of *The Journal of Commonwealth Literature* (July 1967).

This issue, commemorating the centenary of Canadian Confederation and including excellent articles by Canadian scholars on Leacock, Irving Layton, Morley Callaghan, and English-Canadian poetry since 1867, is a welcome reminder that the literary criticism and scholarship of Canada, in both English and French, has matched their finest achievements in creative literature. The generation of Pelham Edgar (1871–1948) and W. H. Blake (1861–1924) was succeeded by the generation of F. R. Scott (b. 1899) and A. J. M. Smith (b. 1902), in turn supplemented by the writings of younger critics like Northrop Frye, author of *Anatomy of Criticism* (1957), and Marshall McLuhan, author of *Understanding Media* (1964). Some of the best Canadian criticism has appeared in their coast-to-coast literary journals such as the Vancouver quarterly *Canadian Literature*, edited by George Woodcock; *The Dalhousie Review*, edited by C. L. Bennet at Halifax, Nova Scotia; *Queen's Quarterly* of Kingston, Ontario; Louis Dudek's *Delta* from Montreal; the bilingual *Culture* from Quebec; *The Canadian Forum* and *The Tamarack Review* from Toronto; and *The University of Toronto Quarterly*.

One thing remains constant, and that is the difficulty of deciding who is (or who is not) a Canadian writer. Saul Bellow (b. 1915), one of the most admired of modern American novelists—author of *The Adventures of Angie Marsh* (1953), *Henderson the Rain King* (1959) and *Herzog* (1965)—was born in Quebec but educated in Chicago and is usually regarded as belonging to the United States, like the French-Canadian beatnik novelist Jack Kerouac. One of the most admired of West Indian novelists, Austin C. Clarke (see p. 932), emigrated to Toronto from his native Barbados and in his novel *The Meeting Point* (1967) wrote about the problems of West Indian immigrants in Canadian cities—an aspect of the overall problem referred to above. Perhaps the most curious instance is that of the Englishman Malcolm Lowry (1909–57) who lived in China, Russia, the West Indies and Mexico before settling in 1939 near Vancouver. His masterpiece, *Under the Volcano*, a partly autobiographical novel about a dipsomaniac in Mexico, was begun in 1934 and rewritten several times before it was published in 1947. At his death, a few million words of manuscript were found at his Vancouver home, including some of the stories in the collection entitled *Hear us, O Lord from Heaven Thy Dwelling Place* (1962) to which he was putting the finishing touches when he died. Like Scott Fitzgerald, Lowry could write of the over-hung half-world of the dipsomaniac from personal experience, his most memorable character being the Geoffrey Firmin of *Under the Volcano* who drowns himself in liquor and drugs and who also appears in one of the stories in *Hear us, O Lord*. Lowry's *Selected Poems*, edited by Earle Birney, were published in 1962 and he is included in both Smith's *Oxford Book* and Ralph Gustafson's *Penguin Book of Canadian Verse* (1958; rev. 1967). His *Selected Letters*, edited by Harvey Breit and Mrs Margerie Bonner Lowry, appeared in 1966.

XII. THE LITERATURE OF AUSTRALIA AND NEW ZEALAND

The earliest literature of Australia and New Zealand differs from that of the hardly less remote outposts of England and Scotland in early Anglo-Saxon times in being more accessible to the non-specialist reader and in being in general much more readable. But just as in *Beowulf* and "all our early national poetry" (see above, p. 3), "the allusions are Continental or Scandinavian", so the early literature of Down Under is inevitably indebted to English traditions and to some extent to English-born writers like Henry Kingsley and Marcus Clarke in Australia and Alfred Domett and Samuel Butler in New Zealand. And just as English literature in its earliest days is primarily interesting to the modern reader in its gradual growth away from Europe, so the literature of the Southern Continent and its neighbouring Dominion becomes more and more interesting as it becomes more and more individual, eventually creating a new literature of its own from a combination of British, American and native sources.

The fact that the earliest Australian poets and novelists were mostly convicts transported from England may seem less hurtful to Australian dignity if it is remembered that Tucker's denunciation of the convict system in *Ralph Rashleigh* was an indictment of British justice, not Australian; if it be recalled, too, how many famous writers, from Cervantes to Cobbett, spent part of their lives in prison, mostly as victims of even greater injustice; and if it is realized that Dame Mary Gilmore's famous tribute to the pioneers in her poem *Old Botany Bay*:

> I was the conscript
> Sent to hell
> To make in the desert
> The living well...

has a literary as well as a general application. Michael Massey Robinson was an English attorney, transported to Botany Bay soon after the penal colony was founded in 1788, who wrote a number of odes for special occasions which were published in Australia's first newspaper, *The Sydney Gazette*, founded in 1803 under the editorship of George Howe. Another early convict-poet, Francis Macnamara ("Frank the Poet"), wrote *The Convict's Tour of Hell* and other songs inspired by the traditional Irish ballads of his homeland. The first Australian novel was the thinly-disguised convict autobiography *Quintus Servinton* (Hobart, 1830–1) by Henry Savery, which was followed by the colonial reminiscences, half-autobiography, half-fiction, of Charles Rowcroft (*c.* 1781–1850) in *Tales of the Colonies* (1843) and Alexander Harris (1805–74) in *Settlers and Convicts* (1847). James Tucker (*c.* 1808–66) was a convict transported in 1827 whose novel *Ralph Rashleigh, or The Life of an Exile; by Giacomo Di Rosenberg* (written *c.* 1845, first published 1929) did not enjoy an authentic text (or a probably correct attribution) till Dr Colin Roderick's edition of 1952. This novel gives a picture of early colonial times, particularly of the iniquities of the degrading convict system, which is evidently written from bitter personal experience and which can be favourably compared, from the point of view of authenticity if not literary merit, with later books on the same theme like Caroline Leakey's *The Broad Arrow* (1859), Marcus Clarke's *For the Term of His Natural Life* (1874), Price Warung's *Tales of the Convict System* (1892) and William Hay's *Escape of the Notorious Sir William Heans* (1918). The Chartist John Frost, who was transported to Tasmania in 1839, was later pardoned and wrote his *Horrors of Convict Life* after his return to England in 1856.

In poetry, Robinson and Macnamara were succeeded by Charles Lamb's friend Barron Field (1786–1846) who became Judge of the Supreme Court of New South Wales and privately published in 1819 his *First Fruits of Australian*

Poetry, containing the oft-quoted lines beginning "Kangaroo! Kangaroo! Thou spirit of Australia..." As a poet, Field was an excellent Judge. *The Sydney Gazette*, which had published Robinson, also printed *Australasia* (1823), a poem submitted for the Chancellor's Medal by the future Australian statesman William Charles Wentworth (1793–1872) while a student at Cambridge. Ironically enough, this poem by an Australasian (Wentworth had been born on Norfolk Island) was placed only second, the prize going to W. M. Praed, the Old Etonian writer of light verse (see p. 533) who had never seen the Pacific. While Wentworth turned from poetry to journalism and politics—he was to be chiefly responsible for the founding of Sydney University in 1852—the Australian-born poet Charles Tompson published in Sydney in 1826 his *Wild Notes from the Lyre of a Native Minstrel*, the best volume of Australian verse before the time of Harpur and Kendall.

The decade 1840–50, preceding the rush to the gold-diggings, was an important period in the history of Australian poetry. The development of New South Wales brought an increase in the number of newspapers, and the newspapers, as in the comparable period of American growth, gave opportunities for the publication of verse as well as sketches and short stories. Sir Henry Parkes (1815–96) emigrated to Sydney from Birmingham in 1839, worked as a farm labourer before resuming his old trade of ivory turner and in 1850 founded *The Empire* newspaper as an organ of Australian liberalism. He wrote verse himself and in the days of his political eminence—he became Prime Minister of New South Wales and one of the chief instigators of the Australian Federal Commonwealth, founded in 1901 after his death—materially assisted other poets, including Henry Kendall. The earliest of his own five volumes of verse was published in 1842; the best is *Murmurs of the Stream* (1857). The first distinctively Australian poet, though still influenced far too much at first by such English masters as Milton and Wordsworth, was Charles Harpur (1813–68), son of convict parents, whose earliest book was *Thoughts: A Series of Sonnets* (1845). He came in time to trust more in himself and his own surroundings, becoming the first native Australian writer to give a worthy imaginative representation of the Australian scene, for instance in his poem *The Creek of the Four Graves* and his play *The Bushrangers* (1853). *The Tower of the Dream* (1865) contains some of his best verse.

The gold rush of the fifties brought to Australia a few men of intellectual attainments, as the gold rush of the sixties and the nineties brought to California and the Klondike writers like Bret Harte and Jack London. Richard Henry Horne (p. 534 above) changed his second name to the more virile "Hengist" as a compliment to his new surroundings, writing an *Australian Autobiography* to preface his lively *Australian Facts and Prospects* (1859). James Lionel Michael concealed his own autobiography in the long narrative poem *John Cumberland* (Sydney, 1860) and was the first to discover the literary talents of Henry Kendall (1839–82), who was employed by him as clerk and amanuensis. On his advice, some of Kendall's first poems were sent to Parkes, who printed them in *The Empire* and who was later to secure for the poet a position as Inspector of Forests. Later poems appeared in *The Athenaeum*, the first English periodical to give any recognition to Australian poetry. Kendall's first volume, *Poems and*

Songs (1862), included a narrative poem about the explorers Burke and Wills, who had died so tragically in 1861 on their way home from their pioneer journey into Central Australia: the theme also of a well-known poem by Adam Lindsay Gordon. Kendall's second volume, *Leaves from the Australian Forests* (1869), contained a poem to the memory of Harpur, to whom he always acknowledged a debt, besides such memorable verses as the spring poem *September in Australia* and *The Song of the Cattle Hunters*. Although he lived both in Sydney and in Melbourne, where he became a member of the Yorick Club, of which Marcus Clarke was one of the founders, Kendall's strength as a poet lies in his sensitive, Swinburnian treatment of the forest country in Victoria and New South Wales he knew so well. The *Leaves* and his third volume, *Songs from the Mountains* (1880), contain his best and most influential work.

Kendall in some respects is perhaps more the "national bard" of Australia (in these early years of Australian poetry) than his friend and contemporary Adam Lindsay Gordon (1833–70), who was far more widely recognized as such in England as well as Australia and whose celebrity led to his bust being placed in the Poets' Corner of Westminster Abbey in 1934. Where Harpur and Kendall were Australian born and bred, Lindsay Gordon, a Byronic figure descended from two famous Scottish families—and connected with both a Duke of Gordon and with the Lady Anne Lindsay (see p. 497) who wrote *Auld Robin Gray*—was born in the Azores, educated in England, and did not see Australia till he arrived in Adelaide in 1853 at the age of twenty. He spent, however, the remainder of his short life in his adopted country, becoming a police-trooper, a horse-trainer, a livery-stable keeper, a steeplechase rider and a member of the South Australian House of Assembly before he shot himself by Brighton beach near Melbourne at the age of thirty-seven. Gordon expressed memorably several sides of Australian life, particularly the Australian passion for sport and for horses—the latter passion still strong in the age of the combustion engine. Seeing sport as the best thing in life, Gordon gave dignity to its treatment; the rhythm of horse-hoofs seems to beat in most of his poems. His best work is contained in *Sea Spray and Smoke Drift* (1867) and in *Bush Ballads and Galloping Rhymes* (1870), a volume dedicated to Major Whyte-Melville, the historical and sporting novelist he so greatly admired. Many of Gordon's poems first appeared in journals like *Bell's Life in Victoria*, *The Australasian* and Marcus Clarke's *Colonial Monthly*. *How we beat the Favourite* is his most famous racing poem; it was written during the same month, January 1869, as *The Sick Stockrider*, the best known and the most impressive of his dramatic lyrics.

"What's become of Waring?" the doyen of the dramatic lyric inquired; and the answer was that Browning's friend "Waring", Alfred Domett (1811–87), had gone to the Antipodes, like Mrs Browning's friend and collaborator "Hengist" Horne. Domett lived in New Zealand from 1842 to 1871 and became Prime Minister for a short time (1862–3) before returning to England to complete his longest and most ambitious poem, the Anglo-Maori epic *Ranolf and Amohia* (1872). He was not the first to write of the Maoris. The artist Augustus Earle (1793–1838), some of whose Maori paintings can be seen in Wellington, wrote *A Narrative of a Residence in New Zealand* (1832), one of the best accounts of the country and its inhabitants in the years before colonization. Frederick

Edward Maning (1812–83) went from Tasmania to New Zealand in 1833, married a Maori wife and wrote the classic work *Old New Zealand* (1863), which together with Edward Jerningham Wakefield's *Adventure in New Zealand* (1845), Sir George Grey's *Polynesian Mythology* (1855) and Samuel Butler's *A First Year in Canterbury Settlement* (1863)—we may perhaps add Butler's article "Darwin among the Machines" (the germ of *Erewhon*) which appeared in *The Christchurch Press* the same year—virtually completes the literary picture during the first colonial period. The poet of the national anthem, *God Defend New Zealand*, who also gave the title-deeds to the deity in the poem *God's Own Country*, was Thomas Bracken (1843–98), who wrote of Maori life in such poems as *The March of Te Rauparaha*. The second colonial period merges gradually into the early modern or first independent period—New Zealand became a Dominion in 1907—in the work of New Zealand-born writers like the poet Eileen Duggan, the poet and journalist Jessie Mackay (1864–1938), who wrote a *Maori War Song*, and the poet, economist and statesman William Pember Reeves (1857–1932), friend of Shaw and the Webbs, whose historical work *The Long White Cloud* (1898) is the classic description of his native country. It was left to an Englishman, William Satchell, who emigrated to New Zealand in the eighteen-eighties, to write in *The Greenstone Door* (1914) what is reckoned by Alan Mulgan (*Literature and Authorship in New Zealand*) "the most ambitious and probably the best story of Anglo-Maori relations." Maoris have their own cultural traditions, and their own quarterly magazine in *Te Ao Hou* (Wellington), but they have also contributed to English literature themselves. Among New Zealand writers of Maori or part-Maori stock may be mentioned the distinguished anthropologist Dr Peter Buck (Te Rangi Hiroa), author of *Anthropology and Religion*, etc., who became Director of the Bishop Museum, Honolulu, and Professor of Anthropology at Yale, and the modern poet Hone Tuwhare (b. 1922), whose *No Ordinary Sun* (Auckland, 1965) made an impression in England as well as New Zealand. Kath Walker's *We Are Going* (Brisbane, 1964), the first volume of verse published by an Australian aborigine, lamented the passing of the aboriginal tribes and pleaded for greater understanding of them on the part of white Australians. While it is true that there has never been in Australia the enthusiasm for the aborigines shown by New Zealand writers, from Maning and Domett onwards, towards the Maoris, a number of Australian writers from D. H. Lawrence's collaborator Mollie Skinner to Rex Ingamells (1913–55), founder of the Jindyworobak movement, have emphasized the value of aboriginal culture and tradition.

A younger contemporary of Browning's "Waring" and Mrs Browning's "Hengist" was James Brunton Stephens (1835–1902), who emigrated to Queensland from Scotland in 1864. His *Convict Once* (1871) is a narrative poem of some melodramatic power, but his popularity rests chiefly on his humorous poems *My Chinee Cook*, *To a Black Gin* and *Universally Respected*, vigorous sketches in verse which made him the Bret Harte of Australia and whose tradition was maintained in the free and easy rhymes of common life written by John Farrell and his successors. Stephens in his more prophetic vein, notably in *The Dominions of Australia: A Forecast* (1877), was succeeded by George Essex Evans (1863–1909), who emigrated from London to Brisbane in 1881, contributed poems to *The Queenslander* and wrote *Australian Symphony, Queen of the North* and other patriotic pieces—which, however, have not escaped criticism from later Australian critics as relying too much upon "old-world" attitudes and idiom.

A rival to both Kendall and Gordon as the "national bard of Australia" is the author of *Waltzing Matilda,* Andrew Barton ("Banjo") Paterson (1864–1941), the *Banjo of the Bush* of Clement Semmler's biography (1967). Paterson was the foremost of the "Bush Balladists" associated with *The Bulletin,* founded at Sydney in 1880 by J. F. Archibald and John Haynes, drawing its readers and contributors from both Australia and New Zealand, and perhaps best known to English readers through D. H. Lawrence's half-admiring, half-sardonic comments in *Kangaroo* (1923). Lawrence refers to "the pink page" of the "Bully". This was, of course, the Red Page, the literary page of *The Bulletin* founded and edited by Alfred George Stephens (1865–1933), first of a long line of distinguished Australasian critics and scholars whose contemporaries and successors include the classical scholar and translator Gilbert Murray (1866–1957; p. 904), Professor of Greek at Oxford 1908–36, President of the Society of Australian Writers 1952–7; Walter Murdoch (b. 1874) of *The Melbourne Argus* and the University of Western Australia; the New Zealand philologist Eric Partridge (b. 1894); G. A. Wilkes, first professor of Australian Literature in the University of Sydney; the New Zealand-born poet and dramatist Douglas Stewart (b. 1913) who edited the Red Page 1941–61; and the poet-critic Geoffrey Dutton (b. 1922), general editor of the Melbourne series *Australian Writers and Their Work.* To that series John Hetherington contributed the booklet on Norman Lindsay (b. 1879), who was the chief cartoonist on *The Bulletin* for many years, the author of some amusing satirical novels, and father of the critic and novelist Jack Lindsay and the historical novelist Philip Lindsay. The short-lived polemical journal *Vision* (1923–4), largely inspired by Norman Lindsay and edited by Jack Lindsay, Frank Johnson and Kenneth Slessor, meant a great deal to some of the best of the Australian poets of the early twentieth century, including Slessor himself and the poet-artist Hugh McCrae (1876–1958) whose first verse and drawings were contributed to *The Bulletin.*

Paterson's "bush ballads" and his longer narrative poems like *The Man from Snowy River* (1895) had predecessors in the anonymous verses by "Cockatoo Jack" and other legendary persons which were repeated around camp-fires by the billabong, in shearers' huts on lonely farms, and in other places far removed from city life and the luxury of print. Paterson himself collected some of these verses in his *Old Bush Songs* (1905) and the New Zealander Douglas Stewart, co-editor of a later collection, *Australian Bush Ballads* (1955), believes they are "the most distinctively national" poetry Australia has produced. Besides the "bush ballads" of Paterson and Henry Lawson, *The Bulletin* printed the *Rhymes from the Mines* (collected 1896) of Edward Dyson and the sea ballads of E. J. Brady, as well as poems by the Irish-born aesthetic poet Victor Daley, author of *Wine and Roses* (1905), by Barcroft Boake, whose *Where the Dead Men Lie* (1897) is in the Adam Lindsay Gordon tradition, and by C. J. Dennis, best known during the war as the author of *Songs of a Sentimental Bloke* (Sydney, 1915), which sold thousands of copies in Australia and New Zealand.

Henry Lawson (1867–1922), whose father was a Norwegian seaman named Larsen, stands out among his contemporaries because of his almost equal distinction in the "bush ballad" and the short story. It is not to be wondered at that the two should be connected, that the story as well as the ballad should be a distinctive feature of both Australian and New Zealand literature, as it was of American literature in a comparable period of its history—though the New Zealand ballad was a tame thing compared with the Australian and the American. The camp fire lends itself to stories, whether verse or prose, short or tall, and traditions which arise naturally through oral means can be maintained in print long after the camp fire has gone out for ever. *The Bulletin* encouraged the short story as well as the ballad: Dyson wrote many of each, notably about the miners in the Ballarat district of Victoria, and Lawson's first book was *Stories in Prose and Verse* (1894). The directness and the democratic sentiments of his *Ballad of the Drover*, *Faces in the Street* and other typical verses, are repeated in the finest of his stories contained in such volumes as *While the Billy Boils* (1896) and *Joe Wilson and His Mates* (1902). A collected edition of *The Stories of Henry Lawson*, edited by Cecil Mann, was published in three volumes in 1965. An Australian Mark Twain in his humour and in his democratic feelings, Lawson was indebted to some extent, as Twain was, to the example of Bret Harte. He has had as strong an influence upon the course of Australian and New Zealand fiction (he lived in both countries) as Twain upon American. He not only stands pre-eminent among most of his contemporaries—who included Barbara Baynton and Steele Rudd in Australia and Arthur Adams in New Zealand—his influence is seen in the stories of later generations, from the time of Ernest ("Kodak") O'Ferrall, another *Bulletin* writer, to the more sophisticated days of Gavin Casey, Alan Marshall, Hal Porter and Peter Cowan. The links between Lawson and his successors, as well as the differences in outlook and idiom between their writing and his, can best be discovered by the non-Australian reader through the various anthologies devoted to this typically Australian form of literature, for instance *Australian Short Stories*, edited by George Mackaness, and the World's Classics volumes of the same title, the first series of which (1951) was edited by the critic Walter Murdoch and the novelist Henrietta Drake-Brockman, the second (1964) by Brian James, the pen-name of John Tierney, who interestingly enough was born (1892) in the same small town in New South Wales as Lawson himself and whose family were intimately associated with Lawson's.

That the one internationally famous New Zealand writer, Katherine Mansfield—the pen-name of Kathleen Mansfield Beauchamp (1888–1923)—should also be a writer of short stories, and indeed one of the leading exponents of the art in early twentieth-century literature, is some proof in itself of the truth of C. K. Stead's contention in the second series (1966) of the corresponding *New Zealand Short Stories* in the World's Classics—the first series (1954) was edited by the novelist D. M. Davin—that "the short story in New Zealand has had for a long time a special place. It has been recognized, not as a novelist's by-product, or as the promise of a novel, but as a form in its own right by which a talent may fully declare itself." Certainly Katherine Mansfield's considerable, Chekhovian talent thus fully declared itself, particularly in those stories—such as *At the Bay* and the title-story in *The Garden Party and Other Stories* (1922) and *Prelude* and *The Little Girl* in *Something Childish and Other Stories* (1924)—which reveal, in the words of the New Zealand critic Ian A. Gordon, "a kind of *recherche du temps perdu*, a remembrance of things past in a distant dominion." Katherine Mansfield was born in Wellington, but spent most of her short life in England and Europe, never returning to her native land. But the death of her brother in France in 1915 awakened memories: "In my thoughts I range with him over all the remembered places." She was determined in the short future that remained to her—like her friend Lawrence, she was a victim of consumption—to write of New Zealand: "I want," she said, "to make our undiscovered country leap into the eyes of the Old World...I want to write about my own country till I exhaust my store." In so doing, she achieved her greatest successes in her peculiarly demanding form of art. "Without ceasing to belong to the country that bred her," Ian Gordon concludes in his booklet *Katherine Mansfield* (1954), "she is one of the few writers so far who have in any worthy way repaid something of the debt that the Commonwealth owes to the literature of England."

Reviewing *Bliss and Other Stories* (1920) in *The Freeman*, New York, the American poet and critic Conrad Aiken put his finger on the outstanding quality of Katherine Mansfield when he headed his notice "The Short Story as Poetry". Such an individual form is not likely to have so clear a succession as Bret Harte's or Lawson's, whose more simple, more direct, often more sentimental kind of story is as closely related to the ballad as Katharine Mansfield's to the lyric. In her New Zealand successors—novelists and story-writers like Jane Mander, Jean Devanny, James Courage, John Mulgan, Frank Sargeson, Janet Frame— we are as often reminded of the directness and simplicity of Lawson as of the subtlety of her more sophisticated art. The future of fiction in both countries may well lie, as here, in a fruitful blending of the two traditions.

The history of the novel in Australia naturally proceeded first of all from "colonial" to "commonwealth". Charles Kingsley's younger brother Henry Kingsley (1830–76) spent five years in Australia (1853–8) and on his return home wrote the vigorous romance *Geoffry Hamlyn* (1859) which, though founded on Kingsley's own varied Australian experience, can hardly be considered a novel of Australian origin or appeal; the aim of the chief characters is to make enough money in Australia to retire on to England. *Clara Morison* (1854) by the Scottish-born Catherine Helen Spence (1825–1910) is more genuinely an Australian novel, but the first clear advance was made by Gerard Manley Hopkins's old schoolfellow Marcus Clarke (1846–81) and by Thomas Alexander Browne (1826–1915) who wrote under the name of Rolf Boldrewood. Clarke's *For the Term of His Natural Life* (1874)—first serialized in *The Australian Journal* —deals historically with the same theme that Tucker and Savery had dealt with from personal experience; it is well documented and vividly written and remains the classic picture of a penal settlement. Boldrewood was a squatter, a magistrate and a commissioner of goldfields and knew thoroughly the life he described in *Robbery Under Arms* (1888), the story of the bushranger Captain Starlight— first serialized in *The Sydney Mail* in 1881—and in his numerous other novels, which include *The Squatter's Dream* (1890).

The next landmark was provided by Joseph Furphy (1843–1912), who wrote under the name of Tom Collins. His novel, *Such is Life: Being Certain Extracts from the Life of Tom Collins* (1903), was sent in 1897 to A. G. Stephens, who rightly thought it a classic of its kind but advised revision and shortening. This was no easy thing to do, for the novel is the *Tristram Shandy* or *Moby-Dick* of Australian literature, with no formal plot and with many digressions and philosophical reflections which are an integral part of the book. In his *Australian Literature* (Seattle, 1929), the American critic C. Hartley Grattan described it as "a primary document for any student of Australian attitudes." Not only Australians, though, will approve of Collins's severe, but on the whole just, attitude to "colonial" novelists like Kingsley with their heroes "of the croquet lawn" called "Captain Vernon de Vere (or words to that effect)".

An account of the genesis of *Such is Life* is given in the biography *Joseph Furphy: the Legend of a Man and His Book* (1944) which Miles Franklin (1879–1954) wrote in collaboration with Kate Baker. Herself a novelist of distinction, whether or not she is also the writer of *Up the Country* (1930) and other novels written under the mysterious pseudonym "Brent of Bin Bin", Stella Miles Franklin was one of several Australian women writers who came into prominence during the first twenty or thirty years of the twentieth century. The others include the poet and journalist Mary Gilmore (1865–1962), the novelists Henry Handel Richardson and Katharine Susannah Prichard (b. 1883), and D. H. Lawrence's collaborator in *The Boy in the Bush* (1924), Mollie L. Skinner, who probably wrote the greater part of that novel and also *Black Swans* (1925) and a volume of sketches *Men Are We* (1927) about the aborigines of Western Australia. Henry Handel Richardson was the pen-name of Ethel Florence Richardson (1870–1946) of Melbourne, who married John G. Robertson, professor of German at London University, and in her almost life-long exile from her native land resembled Katharine Mansfield. Her fiction, however, is not of the short, Mansfield kind. Like other Richardsons of the novel (Samuel and Dorothy), she wrote at great length, particularly in her trilogy *The Fortunes of Richard Mahony* (1917–29), which has been called the first tragedy in Australian literature. She lived up to the "Handel" of her pseudonym in being one of the few writers able to use music successfully as a theme in fiction, notably in *Maurice Guest* (1908), based on her own experiences as a student of music in Germany.

That the novel was slow to mature in both Australia and New Zealand, in comparison with the short story, was partly due to the presence of journals and the relative absence of publishers. The journals printed occasional serials as well as short stories, and *The Bulletin* not only published *Such Is Life* but in the late twenties promoted a novel competition, prizes in which were won by Katharine Susannah Prichard with *Coonardoo* (1929) and Vance Palmer with *The Passage* (1930), both novels among their writers' most distinguished works. For many years, though, the novelist in Australia and New Zealand, owing to the smallness of the population, had to rely far too much on the London or New York publisher, who with the best will in the world was not always qualified to pronounce on the merits of works with so distant a background.

From "colonial" to "commonwealth", from "commonwealth" to "cosmopolitan": that, in brief metaphor, is the history of the novel in Australia and may even be regarded as the over-all summary of Australian literature in general—and (with the substitution of "dominion" for "commonwealth") also the over-all summary of the literature of New Zealand. The critic and essayist Walter Murdoch, in a conversation reported in John Hetherington's *Forty-Two Faces: Profiles of Living Australian Writers* (1963), saw three main developments in Australian writing: "First it was crudely imitative of English writing. Then for a time it was dominated by *The Bulletin* school. Now it has caught up with modern culture; it has become civilized." The patronage of literature in both countries began to change from weekly papers like *The Bulletin* to the English departments of the universities and to literary periodicals, some of them government or university sponsored, like C. B. Christesen's *Meanjin Quarterly* (founded 1940 at Brisbane) and S. Murray-Smith's *Overland*, both now in Melbourne, R. G. Howarth's *Southerly* and James McAuley's *Quadrant* in Sydney, Geoffrey Dutton's and Max Harris's *Australian Letters* in Adelaide, Noel Hoggard's *Arena* in Wellington and Charles Brasch's *Landfall* in Christchurch. The setting of most novels and stories began to change from the bush or the outback to the big city or the suburbs, and writers began to realize that "antipodean" is a relative term, that England is as much Down Under in regard to Australia and New Zealand as they are to England. As the United States recovered from what Edgar Allan Poe (p. 801 below) described as "the first hours of our novel freedom", so Australian literature, followed to some extent by the literature of New Zealand, recovered from its period of commonwealth defiance, finding it could stand on its own feet with no need either of English association or nationalist assertion. "Bush Balladists" like Lawson and Patterson, and poets militant like Bernard O'Dowd (1866–1953) and William Baylebridge (1883–1942), gave way gradually in public esteem to poets of greater variety and sophistication, who themselves were as varied in outlook as the philosophical poet Christopher Brennan (1870–1932), who was influenced by Mallarmé and the French symbolists, the remarkable, self-educated lyric poet Shaw Neilson (1872–1942) and the poets mentioned above, first associated with Lindsay's *Vision*, like Hugh McCrae, Kenneth Slessor and their immediate followers, the best of whom were probably Robert FitzGerald (b. 1902) and the poet-novelist Kenneth Mackenzie (1913–55) from Perth. In the novel itself, Furphy was soon followed by more cosmopolitan or sophisticated novelists like Henry Handel Richardson, Louis Stone, Katharine Susannah Prichard, William Hay…"I don't know about Furphy," concluded Walter Murdoch. "When *Tom Collins* first came out I was tremendously struck with it; it was so aggressively Australian. Perhaps that is the very quality that goes against it today."

At the same time, the movement has not been entirely away from the past or away from the native soil. The interest (often the intensely critical interest) of both Australian and New Zealand writers in the history and tradition of their own countries—seen in novels like Nellie Scanlan's *Pencarrow* series (1932 etc.), Brian Penton's *Landtakers* (1934), Miles Franklin's *All That Swagger* (1936), Xavier Herbert's *Capricornia* (1938) and Eleanor Dark's *The Timeless Land* (1941), in plays like Douglas Stewart's *Ned Kelly* (1943) and Frank Sargeson's *A Time for Sowing* (1965), in poems like Kenneth Slessor's *Five Visions of Captain Cook* (1931), R. A. K. Mason's *No New Thing* (1934), A. R. D. Fairburn's

Dominion (1938), Allen Curnow's *Landfall in Unknown Seas* (1942) and Robert FitzGerald's *Wind at Your Door* (1959)—this abiding interest is as much a feature of Australasian literature in the mid-twentieth century as the more overtly "cosmopolitan" fiction of Australia's greatest modern novelist Patrick White (b. 1912), one of whose own novels, *The Tree of Man* (1956), has been described as "a two-generation saga" of Australian life. While the most impressive of White's younger contemporaries, Randolph Stow (b. 1935), has set all his novels, from *A Haunted Land* (1956) onwards, firmly in the landscape and tradition of Western Australia.

The opinion of many of their most respected critics is, however, that the literature of Australasia is still in its "infancy". Certainly no Australasian novelist has yet won a Nobel Prize for Literature to match Lord Rutherford of Nelson's in physics, nor have their poets reached a height on the slopes of Parnassus comparable to Sir Edmund Hillary's on Everest. Yet it seems to a reader Down Under—that is, in England—that the development outlined above is a pretty lusty infancy that in the later twentieth century will come more and more to influence the older literatures of the English-speaking world. By the nineteen-sixties, this literature was being studied, not only in Britain, but in many other countries. Dr Joachim Schulz published his *Geschichte der Australischen Literatur* at Munich in 1960; in 1962 there was an Australian number of *The Texas Quarterly*; during the same year Professor John Matthews, the Australian-born Director of the Institute of Commonwealth and Comparative Studies at Queen's University, Ontario, published his comparative study of Australian and Canadian literature in his book *Tradition in Exile*; and in 1964 there was an all-Australian number of the Bombay journal *The Literary Criterion*, edited by Professor C. D. Narasimhaiah of Mysore. The non-Australian reader or student cannot do better than start with John K. Ewer's admirable "selective survey", *Creative Writing in Australia* (1945; rev. 1962) or Geoffrey Dutton's scholarly *Literature of Australia* (1964), and then follow up his particular interests with the aid of such more detailed works as Morris Miller's *Australian Literature* (1940), H. M. Green's *History of Australian Literature* (1961), Judith Wright's *Preoccupations in Australian Poetry* (1966), the Australian Poets series published by Angus and Robertson—from Harpur and Kendall to A. D. Hope and Austin Dobson's granddaughter Rosemary Dobson—and anthologies like *Poetry in Australia* (1965) edited by T. Inglis Moore and Douglas Stewart, *The Penguin Book of Modern Australian Verse* (1961) edited by R. G. Howarth, Kenneth Slessor and John Thompson, John Manifold's *Australian Song Book* and Russel Ward's *Australian Ballads* (1965) from the same publishers, and Walter Murdoch's *Oxford Book of Australasian Verse* (1918) which covers both countries. Alan Mulgan's P.E.N. Book, *Literature and Authorship in New Zealand* (1943), with M. H. Holcroft's *The Deepening Stream* (1940) and Allen Curnow's *Penguin Book of New Zealand Verse* (1960), likewise lead to the more extensive surveys by E. K. McCormick in *New Zealand Literature* (1959) and Joan Stevens in *The New Zealand Novel 1860–1960* (1962). "Infancy", perhaps; but pretty well documented and anthologized! It may well be the task of future Australasian critics and literary historians to separate, even more than they have already, the Antipodean wheat from the Antipodean chaff.

XIII. SOUTH AFRICAN LITERATURE IN ENGLISH

The history of South African literature in the English language divides itself pretty easily into three periods. The first covers the greater part of the nineteenth century; the second runs from the Boer War of 1899–1902, through the creation of the Union in 1910, to the First World War of 1914–18; the third covers the literature written since the nineteen-twenties. The outstanding authors of the first period are Thomas Pringle in verse, Bishop Colenso in prose, and Olive Schreiner and Rider Haggard in fiction; the second period seems at first glance to be the preserve of writers, soldiers and politicians who were *in* rather than *of* South Africa, Uitlanders like Kipling, Gandhi, Baden-Powell, Buchan and Edgar Wallace, but it also includes Smuts and the early work of poets like Arthur Cripps and Charles Murray who made South Africa their home; the third period is by far the richest, with writers such as Sarah Gertrude Millin, Pauline Smith, Stuart Cloete, Roy Campbell, William Plomer, Alan Paton, the Rhodesian novelist Doris Lessing, and several others of varying racial background, who have all achieved, to greater or lesser degree, an international reputation.

The most important early name in South African literature is that of a Scotsman, Thomas Pringle (1789–1834), called by South African critics the father of their poetry. When Kipling whose Boer War ballads are reprinted in *The Five Nations* (1903) was asked what South African poetry there was besides his own, he had to reply: "As to South African verse, it's a case of there's Pringle, and there's Pringle, and after that one must hunt the local papers", a pardonable exaggeration of the truth, so far as poetry in the English language was concerned. There was also, of course, Cape-Dutch verse, as Kipling added: "F.W. Reitz's *Africaanse Gedigte*, songs and parodies in the Taal, which are very characteristic." As a later South African poet, R. C. Russell, puts it: "There do not appear to have been any poets of note between Pringle's time and the generation which has just passed away"—that is, between the eighteen-thirties and the end of the century.

Pringle was already a distinguished man of letters before he saw South Africa. He was editor of *The Edinburgh Monthly Magazine*, the parent of *Blackwood's*, and his first volume of poems was published in 1819. The same year he emigrated to Cape Town, being appointed government librarian. He was dismissed from this office in 1823 after a violent quarrel with the Governor, having, in the opinion of his friend Sir Walter Scott, made "the mistake of trying to bring out a whig paper in Cape Town." He returned to London in 1826 and became secretary to the Anti-Slavery Society, working closely with Wilberforce and Clarkson. His second volume of verse, *Ephemerides* (1828), was followed by his *Narrative of a Residence in South Africa* (1834), a striking passage in which, as Tennyson recorded, suggested the famous lines in *Locksley Hall* about the "hungry people" and the "lion creeping nigher". The same year Pringle fell ill from his labours in the anti-slavery cause; he died in London at the early age of forty-six.

The characteristics of his poetry are a love of freedom, a hatred of oppression, and a warm feeling for the people and nature of his adopted land. "A knightly soul unbought and unafraid" was the verdict of a later South African poet, Vine Hall, and Pringle has always been valued in South Africa, as much for his radical, independent spirit as for his poetry, the best of which includes *The Bechuana Boy, Lion Hunt, The Ghona Widow's Lullaby* and *Afar in the Desert*. The last-named poem, reckoned by Coleridge to be one of the most perfect lyric poems in the language, was translated into Taal or Cape Dutch (the earlier Afrikaans) as *Ver in de Wildernis* by the F. W. Reitz mentioned above, the Boer poet and statesman who was President of the Orange Free State in Kipling's time. The anthology *Klaas Gezwint en Zijn Paert* (1884) contained some of Pringle's poems and A. G. Bain's *British Settler's Song*, as well as the *Volk's Liederen*, many of which were clever parodies in Cape Dutch of famous English and Scottish poems, such as the title-piece *Klaas Gezwint* (from *Tam o' Shanter*) and *Die Boer zijn Zaterdag Aand* (from *The Cotter's Saturday Night*). Edward Heath Crouch's *Treasury of South African Poetry and Verse* (1907) included Pringle and Pringle's friend and contemporary John Fairbairn, whose poems he placed above his own, and their principal successors such as E. B. Watermeyer (1824–67), whose lines about "the land I dwell in Dutch and English plough" suitably prefixed the Anglo-Dutch anthology of 1884.

Pringle's love and respect for the native African was shared by Bishop Colenso of Natal (1814–83), whose radical theological doctrines, and the consequent persecution of their author, have been noted above on p. 561. He was a much greater man than his off-handed treatment by Matthew Arnold might suggest. Another "knightly soul unbought and unafraid", Colenso in 1875 exposed the corruption of some of the British colonial officials and their ill-treatment of his African congregations. In 1879 he denounced the Zulu War. He was a man of many parts, called by the Zulus "Sobantu" or "father of the people." Besides writing sermons, theological works and textbooks on mathematics, he used his knowledge of the language to compose a Zulu dictionary and grammar, translated into Zulu parts of the Bible, and taught printing to his pupils. His earlier works include *Ten Weeks in Natal* (1854). His daughter, Frances Colenso (1849–87), shared his anti-imperialist views and was joint-author of a *History of the Zulu War* (1880).

The most remarkable book produced by South Africa during the nineteenth century was *The Story of an African Farm: a Novel by Ralph Iron* (1883), a realistic picture of Boer life in which the girl Lyndall, closely imprisoned in the strictest of conventions, religious and moral and domestic, nevertheless attains to independence of belief and action. This deceptively quiet little book achieved world fame and became one of the chief weapons in the struggle for women's rights during the last years of the nineteenth century. Its author was discovered to be Olive Schreiner (1855–1920), sister of the statesman William Schreiner, Prime Minister of Cape Colony during the Boer War. She wrote nothing else of great importance, though a later novel, *Trooper Peter Halkett* (1897), about Rhodes and Rhodesia, would have pleased the Colensos by its anti-imperialist spirit.

The novelist who first made the English reading public familiar with the kopje and the veld was Sir Henry Rider Haggard (1856–1925) who went to

Natal in 1875 and returned to his native Norfolk in 1881. His first book was *Cetewayo and his White Neighbours* (1882), but it was by his romantic novels that he won popularity. The first of these, *King Solomon's Mines* (1885), was the result of a wager between Haggard, who said he could write a better boys' story than *Treasure Island*, and his brother, who said he couldn't. Most of the succeeding novels—*She, Allan Quatermaine*, etc.—were written for adults, but they are mainly found today on the juvenile shelf. Haggard had a romantic view of Africa and a paternal attitude towards the Africans. He was an authority on agriculture, and his *Rural England* (1902) shows how anxious he was that the farm-worker, whether in Norfolk or Natal, should have a fair deal. Like Colenso, he admired the Zulus, but mainly for their martial qualities. Many of us first read of the exploits of the Zulu Napoleon, Chaka (c. 1783–1828), in the stirring pages of *Nada the Lily*. This can now be compared with *Chaka*, a novel by Thomas Mofolo (1877–1948) of Basutoland, which was translated into English in 1931, and with the South African novelist Daphne Rooke's *Wizards' Country* (1957).

Haggard's friend Kipling was not at his best in his South African phase. He did not know the country with the intimacy he knew India, and *Stellenbosh, Piet, Two Kopjes*, and the rest of his Boer War verses, have only a period interest today. One of the troopers drafted to South Africa was Edgar Wallace (1875–1932), who was to become the most successful writer of thrillers the world has ever seen. Margaret Lane's *Edgar Wallace: The Biography of a Phenomenon* (1938) is among the most fascinating biographies of the twentieth century. While in South Africa, Wallace wrote soldiers' songs and stories, in the manner of Kipling, and later used his knowledge of West Africa in *Sanders of the River* (1911) and other romantic novels. The hero of Mafeking, Robert Baden Powell (1857–1941)—son of the Oxford theologian and mathematician Baden Powell whose liberal views were considered as dangerous as Colenso's—lives in history by his *Scouting for Boys* (1908) and his creation of the Boy Scout Movement. His book owed much to Kipling, but the Boy Scouts developed into an international, post-Kipling movement, which had the further admirable object of encouraging a love of the outdoor life in the youth of big cities. Lord Baden-Powell (as he became) had learnt this love himself in India and Africa, the origin of the Scouts being partly due to his observation of the methods of Indian and African trackers of big game. Also in South Africa during this period was the Indian leader Gandhi, who served as a stretcher-bearer on the British side in the Boer War. A barrister in Johannesburg from 1893, Gandhi first practised his technique of passive resistance or "Satyagraha" (truth-force), later so potent a weapon in India, on behalf of his fellow-Indians in South Africa, securing an agreement in 1914 with General Smuts, then Minister for Defence.

Jan Christiaan Smuts (1870–1950), the chief architect of the Union, was its Prime Minister in 1919–24 and again in 1939–48. He wrote on his country's problems in *A Century of Wrong* (1900); on international affairs in *The League of Nations: A Practical Suggestion* (1918); and on his personal philosophy in *Holism and Evolution* (1926). The first four volumes of *Selections from the Smuts Papers*, edited by Sir Keith Hancock and Jean van der Poel, appeared in 1966. The Union was aided, on the British side, by "Milner's young men", young graduates of Oxford who in South Africa in 1902–5 assisted the High Commissioner, Lord Milner, to heal the wounds of war. They included John Buchan (1875–1940), later Governor-General of Canada, who used his African experiences to good effect in his famous romance *Prester John* (1910) and Lionel Curtis (1872–1955), who wrote much on Commonwealth affairs, notably in *The Problem of the Commonwealth* (1916) and *The Protectorates of South Africa* (1935). Arthur Shearly Cripps (1869–1952), also of Oxford, became a missionary in South Africa and wrote verse of traditional quality in *Pilgrimage of Grace* (1912) and *Africa* (1939), besides stories in *Lion Man* (1928). *The Centenary Book of South African Verse* (1925, rev. 1945) was edited by Francis Carey Slater, the poet of *The Sunburnt South* (1908) and *The Karoo* (1924). A *Critical Survey of South African Poetry in English*, by G. M. Miller and Howard Sergeant, was published in Cape Town in 1957.

Smuts's "century of wrong" has been followed by a century which began with much promise in the Union of 1910 but which has increasingly disturbed liberal thinkers, particularly after the doctrine of Apartheid pursued by the post-Smuts, post-Hofmeyr Nationalist Government which created the Republic of South Africa in 1961. It is impossible to keep politics out of a discussion of twentieth-century South African literature because so many of the best writers, mostly but not exclusively on the liberal side, deal with questions which have a political bearing. Smuts's biographer, Sarah Gertrude Millin (b. 1889), was the outstanding South African novelist of the inter-war period, notably in *God's Stepchildren* (1924), a novel about the racial problem written with that combination of humane feeling and practical grasp of realities so characteristic of the best South African literature. Later novels by Mrs Millin included *Mary Glenn* (1925) and *The Sons of Mrs Aab* (1931). She wrote "an explanation of South Africa" called *The South Africans* (1926, rev. 1934) which remains one of the best accounts of that troubled land. Her dramatic adaptation of *Mary Glenn*, entitled *No Longer Mourn*, was produced in London in 1935.

Pauline Smith's stories in *The Little Karoo* (1925) and her novel *The Beadle* (1926) were acclaimed by Arnold Bennett and other critics as the most sensitive interpretations of South African life since Olive Schreiner. Stuart Cloete, in his novels *Turning Wheels* (1937) and *Watch for the Dawn* (1939), did much to enlighten the more insular of Rooineks on the part played by the Boers in the history of their country. Roy Campbell (1902–57), born in Natal, joined with William Plomer, born 1903 in the Transvaal, in editing the literary journal *Voorslag* ("Whiplash"). Both have been cosmopolitan in their lives and writings. Campbell once described himself in *Who's Who* as "horse merchant", mentioning poetry merely as his "recreation". His "recreation" nevertheless produced *The Flaming Terrapin* (1924), *Adamastor* (1928), the satirical *Georgiad* (1931), and later volumes such as *Talking Bronco* (1940) and *Sons of the Mistral* (1941), which includes the early poem *Poets in Africa*, "cursed with sense and hearing" and "doubly cursed with second sight." *Flowering Rifle* (1939) was a poem written at the front during the Spanish Civil War, in which Campbell served with Franco's Nationalist forces. He continued to talk bronco in his autobiography, suitably entitled *Light on a Dark Horse* (1951). Plomer's first novel, *Turbott Wolfe* (1926), has been compared with Forster's *Passage to India* in its disturbing effect upon the complacent reader. It was naturally less mature than Forster's masterpiece, being the work of a young man who, in his own later words, "was attempting to reach by a short-cut what can only become even visible by taking an arduous road"; but the South African scene never looked quite the same after *Turbott Wolfe*, as Anglo-India never really survived Forster's *Passage*. Plomer's later books include *I Speak of Africa* (1927) and a judicious biography (1933) of Cecil Rhodes (1853–1902), the British imperialist who gave his name to Rhodesia and founded the Rhodes Scholarships at Oxford for students from the Commonwealth, the United States and Germany. Plomer's *Selected Poems* appeared in 1940. His autobiography *Double Lives* (1943) has both a South African and a cosmopolitan interest.

More recent South African and southern African literature is particularly strong in the field of realistic fiction, usually with political implications, as in Alan Paton's *Cry, the Beloved Country* (1948) and in novels written during the nineteen-fifties and sixties by Nadine Gordimer, Peter Abrahams, Dan Jacobson, Kenneth Mackenzie, Richard Rive, Jack Cope and others. Paton, who was Hofmeyr's biographer, founded the South African Liberal Party with the publisher Leo Marquard, author of *The Peoples and Policies of South Africa* (1959). Rhodesia (formerly Southern Rhodesia), besides the novels of the South African-born Ronald Leavis, has produced Doris Lessing's *The Grass is Singing* (1950) and her novel-sequence *Children of Violence* which began with *Martha Quest* (1952). The Scottish novelist Naomi Mitchison used her experience of tribal life in Botswana (formerly Bechuanaland) in her novel *When We Become Men* (1965). Peter Lanham's *Blanket Boy's Moon* (1953) was based on an original story by A. S. Mopeli-Paulus, chieftain of Basutoland, who also collaborated with Miriam Basner in *Turn to the Dark* (1956). The Rev. James Jolobe, born in Cape Province, translated his own Xhosa poems into English in *Poems of an African* (1946). His long poem *Thuthula* is one of the most impressive poems in *A Book of African Verse* (1964), edited by John Reed and Clive Wake. Ulli Beier's anthology *Black Orpheus* (1964)—based on the Nigerian magazine of the same name (see p. 935)—includes contributions from South African writers like Alex La Guma and Bloke Modisane as well as from African and Afro-American writers in other parts of the continent and the world. Modisane was one of the writers associated—together with Can Themba, Henry Nxumalo, Ezekiel Mphahlele and others—with the Johannesburg magazine *Drum* when it was edited by Anthony Sampson from 1951 to 1955. The break-up of this multi-racial group of writers, under the pressure of Apartheid, is recorded in *Home and Exile* (1966) by Lewis Nkosi, himself an exile in America.

The many books on political questions—or *the* political question—include Ndabaningi Sithole's *African Nationalism* (1959). *No Easy Walk to Freedom* (1965) was the sad but truthful title Ruth First gave to her collection of articles and speeches by the imprisoned Nelson Mandela, president of the African National Congress in the Transvaal. Mandela's belief in "a democratic and free society in which all persons live together in harmony and with equal opportunities" is the voice of one powerful tradition in South African life and literature, to which, in their differing historical contexts, Pringle and Colenso, Gandhi and Mrs Millin, Plomer and Paton and Mopeli-Paulus, have all borne witness.

XIV. EDUCATION

An extraordinary fertility of invention in the means of mechanical production
and transport produced, at the end of the eighteenth century and the beginning
of the nineteenth, what is commonly called the Industrial Revolution. Into
details of the changes included under that name we are not called upon to enter.
But we shall not understand the spirit of nineteenth-century literature, in its
widest sense, without some knowledge of the "condition-of-England" question
and of the attempts to combat manifest social evils by some measure of intellectual civilization. Many of the changes had been rapid. Population increased;
great urban communities arose in the midlands and in northern England; there
was a general movement away from the rural districts; a hitherto unwonted
aggregation of capital altered the scale of industrial operations. While wealth
increased, so, also, did poverty. It would be difficult to parallel in the previous
history of England the wretched and degraded condition of the workers
during the last years of the eighteenth and the first decades of the nineteenth
century. The state did nothing at all for the minds or bodies of the industrial
population. Such educational provision as charity, parish or Sunday schools
offered was both meagre and unsuitable. It was in every sense a beggarly contribution. The desperate plight of parents and the unsparing employment of
children in mills and factories would have made the offer of a complete provision little more than a mockery. Yet these very conditions of ignorance and of
moral degradation stirred the hearts of reformers to attempt their alleviation by
some form of instruction. The bodies of the poor seemed past help. Could
anything be done for their minds?

England lagged far behind its Continental neighbours. France and Germany
had begun to move a whole generation earlier, and had faced at once the
fundamental "religious question". Education had been almost entirely an
ecclesiastical activity; but the relations of church and state had changed, and
the modern state was unwilling to leave the upbringing of the young entirely
to the church. In France Rousseau had altered the whole current of thought
about the teaching of children. The expulsion of the Jesuits in 1767 struck the
first great blow at the kind of instruction which, for some two and a half
centuries, had been general throughout Europe. Prussia had initiated reforms
that made her the model for the German people. As early as 1763 Frederick
had decreed compulsory instruction and the provision of primary schools.
A little later Prussian schools other than primary passed from ecclesiastical
control, and in 1789 the first advance was made towards the evolution of the
modern German university. Although much of this educational activity was
inspired by the teaching of an Englishman, Locke, the history of English
education during this period is a sorry tale of obstruction and animosity. The
admissions to Oxford and Cambridge fell steadily in numbers. The Church of
England stood in the gates of those ancient foundations and denied their
benefits to any who would not subscribe to the Thirty-Nine Articles. The
struggle was not between religion and secularism, but between one form of
religion and other forms of religion; and the history of English educational

reform is a prolonged story of sectarian obstruction. At the public schools, the studies and the method of education remained in substance what they had been. In all, the life was brutal and turbulent. Not till after the time of Arnold did the public schools become civilized. For girls of the middle classes, such education as existed was almost entirely domestic; for girls of higher social standing, education meant nothing but the acquisition of pretentious and useless "accomplishments".

The eighteenth century exhibits no more sincere exponents of Locke's educational ideas than the Edgeworths of Edgeworthstown. The literary monuments of their activity are the work of Richard Lovell Edgeworth and his daughter, Maria; but the initial movements were due to Richard's mother, Jane Lovell. Richard married the first of his four wives before he was one-and-twenty; his first child was born two years after the publication (1762) of Rousseau's *Émile*. From the age of three this son was brought up for five years on Rousseau's system, with results that did not entirely satisfy the father. It was at this time that Edgeworth's college friend, Thomas Day (in later years author of *Sandford and Merton*)was superintending, at the age of twenty-one, the education of two orphan girls with the purpose of marrying one of them. He married neither. Edgeworth conducted his educational experiments, as we may call them, in the bosom of his family, which was ample, for he was married four times and had eighteen children. He studied educational methods on the Continent and met Pestalozzi himself. Edgeworth proposed (1809) a scheme of "secondary" schools (the word is his) to be established throughout the country under the management of a private association—a more practical scheme than that suggested in Joseph Lancaster's *Improvements in Education* (1803). With his second wife, Honora Sneyd, Edgeworth wrote *Harry and Lucy* (1778), which, undertaken as a supplement to Mrs Barbauld's writings, itself became the originator of *Sandford and Merton*. Honora Edgeworth, anticipating later discoveries, declared that education was an experimental science, and began in 1776 to keep a register of observations concerning children, upon which her husband was still engaged nearly twenty years after her death. That record guided Maria Edgeworth in writing the collection of tales for children which she called *The Parent's Assistant* (1796); it formed the basis of fact beneath the theory applied in *Practical Education* (1798), the joint work of herself and her father, and the most considerable book on its subject produced in England between John Locke and Herbert Spencer. Its reiterated recommendation of play and of spontaneous activity in general, as agents of instruction, is an anticipation of Froebel. As evidence of the care bestowed by Edgeworth on teaching the rudiments of English to children, it may be noted that he devised (and published in *A Rational Primer*) a set of diacritical marks to make the alphabet phonetic. *Professional Education* (1809) is the work of Richard Edgeworth alone. If it were written today it would probably be called "Vocational Education". A quite unmerited neglect has fallen upon the educational writings of the Edgeworths, who taught principles which were later accepted in England as revelations when presented by German or American or Italian authors.

The numerous utterances of Wordsworth upon education, in *The Prelude* and *The Excursion*, contain very sound doctrine, especially in their recollections of what children found delightful and in their repudiation of mere "useful knowledge". Coleridge, Lamb and Wordsworth—like Dickens after them— were agreed in a passionate defence of the fairy-tales despised by the utilitarians. In any consideration of the minds of children, the divining experience of a poet's creative spirit is worth much more than the theories of pseudo-scientists who manufacture their own data.

Two books belonging to the close of the eighteenth century deserve mention, *Liberal Education* (1781) by Vicesimus Knox and Joseph Priestley's *Miscellaneous Observations relating to Education* (1778), the latter of which contains an anticipation of the first chapter of Herbert Spencer's *Education* so close in thought and phrase as to suggest Spencer's familiarity with the work. Knox is valuable for his account of current abuses as well as for his constructive suggestions. No subject had greater interest for the reformers than the mother-tongue, the teaching of which had usually been sacrificed to the teaching of the classical languages. The difficulty was the absence of means and standards. The classical languages were fixed, and there was a traditional technique of teaching them. In English there was no tradition and no technique. A belief—expressed by Swift, for example (see p. 391)—gradually established itself that the English language could be fixed and secured against changes. In other words, a living language was expected to behave as if it were dead; and in this spirit grammar books treated English as if it were a kind of Latin. Most famous, or notorious, of such books was the *English Grammar* (1795) of the American Quaker, Lindley Murray, who was the chief, though not the only, begetter of that formal treatment of its subject which long made English grammar the least profitable of school studies. What Murray did was to apply the apparatus of Latin grammar to a language of entirely different behaviour. This process had the semblance of that methodical systematization which educationists had long been seeking, and the book became disastrously popular and authoritative. The revolt, a century later, against the teaching of English grammar was not really a revolt against grammar, but a revolt against the artificial aridities imposed upon English. In Scotland the quest for a method in teaching the living language ended in the emergence, not of grammar books, but of the Scottish school of "rhetoric" and of some famous works which expressed its principles, the most notable being the *Elements of Criticism* (1762) by Henry Home, Lord Kames, *The Philosophy of Rhetoric* (1776) by George Campbell, and the *Lectures on Rhetoric and Belles Lettres* (1783) by Hugh Blair. These writers and lecturers did good by asserting the importance of the emotions in the production and in the enjoyment of literature. The Scottish school laid great stress on the value of public speaking and reading, a matter about which Vicesimus Knox and Richard Edgeworth were both emphatic. William Enfield's *The Speaker* (1774), a long-popular anthology of recitations from the standard writers, was intended to be associated with the Scottish teaching of rhetoric. But it did greater service than that: it gave many young people their first acquaintance with poets, as we know from the frequent references to it in autobiographies such as those mentioned on p. 470.

To the modern mind, which expects "the State" to do everything for everybody, it is a little surprising that advanced thinkers at the end of the eighteenth century were antagonistic to the interference of the state with education. Priestley, Paine and Godwin were all against the establishment or maintenance of schools by the state. Mary Wollstonecraft stood almost alone in her readiness to accept the French conception in full. The effect of this suspicion is clearly discernible in the whole history of English national education. There has been no such difficulty in Scotland, where the principle of national education was fully accepted and where the so-called "religious question" was boldly faced. Elementary education passed beyond the range of merely academic discussion on the appearance of Joseph Lancaster's *Improvements in Education* (1803). Lancaster proposed the establishment of a society, "on general Christian principles", that is, on undenominational principles, for the provision of schools, and the instruction of teachers. The Church was alarmed, and the matter became political. Lancaster's "undenominational" system was taken up by the Whigs as a guarantee of religious liberty and opposed by the Tories as an attack on the Church. In 1811, therefore, "The National Society for Promoting the Education of the Poor in the Principles of the Established Church" was founded. The rival organization was "The British and Foreign School Society" (1814), the successor of the Royal Lancasterian Institute and Lancaster's Committee founded in 1808. "National" and "British" schools (so named from the supporting societies) were set up and continued their rival existence without serious competition, till the appearance of the "Board" schools created by the Act of 1870. A famous pioneer in education was Robert Owen (1771–1858), the social reformer, who established at his New Lanark cotton-mills an adult evening-school, a day-school for children whose ages ranged from six to ten, and an infant-school for little ones of a year old and upwards. The fame of New Lanark spread all over the world. But Owen, like other great pioneers, knew nothing of compromise, and his determined opposition to any form of organized religion frightened his partners, who in 1824 brought the Lanark experiment within the system of the British and Foreign School Society. However, Owen had accomplished more than he supposed. He had established the infant-school; and this important branch of educational activity was fostered by the Infant School Society (1824) and its superintendent, Samuel Wilderspin, who wrote *On the Importance of Educating the Infant Poor* (1824).

Lord Brougham, who had been educated in Scotland, and admired the system that made the parish school a step towards the college, vigorously promoted educational advance in England, though almost every good cause he took up suffered as much as it gained from his advocacy. In association with George Birkbeck and other reformers he helped to create the London Mechanics' Institution, out of which grew Birkbeck College. Furnivall, Hughes, Kingsley, Ruskin and others were moved to found and support the Working Men's College in 1854. Later years saw such further developments as Ruskin College, and the University Tutorial classes of the Workers' Educational Association. Yet another activity with which Brougham was connected was the Society for the Diffusion of Useful Knowledge, founded in 1827. The Society's publications (most of them issued by Charles Knight) included *The Penny Magazine* (1832–7), *The Penny Cyclopaedia* (1832, etc.), *The Library of Entertaining Knowledge* and *The Library of Useful Knowledge*. Brougham was also active in supporting the foundation of the new secular "University of London", as it was called, established in Gower Street in 1828. Religious contentions once more nearly destroyed an excellent proposal, first made by Thomas Campbell the poet, and the Church, stung into action by the successful creation of a college in which no form of religion was taught, hastened to found a rival Anglican institution. This second institution received its charter as King's College, and was opened in 1831. The older college did not receive its charter till 1836, when it was re-named University College, the title "University of London" being given to a new examining corporation. London remained without a real university until 1900.

A new tone was set in the public schools by Samuel Butler at Shrewsbury and Thomas Arnold at Rugby. Oxford and Cambridge, strongly entrenched behind the ancient college foundations, long resisted any kind of reform; there was no Honours School of English Language and Literature at Oxford till 1893 and no English Tripos at Cambridge till 1917. The principle of undenominational education embodied in the university of London was extended to Ireland in 1844–9 by the foundation of Queen's Colleges at Belfast, Cork and Galway and their incorporation as Queen's University in the next year, notwithstanding strong Catholic protests. The hierarchy determined to establish a Catholic university in Dublin and placed John Henry Newman at its head. Here were delivered the discourses which Newman afterwards collected as *The Idea of a University*. But as everybody concerned appeared to have different intentions, the Catholic University failed, for reasons that had nothing to do with education.

Shortly before Parliament, in 1833, voted £20,000 per annum in aid of schools for the people, John Arthur Roebuck unsuccessfully moved a resolution in the Commons in favour of universal compulsory education, the professional training of teachers, and the appointment of a Minister of Education. Over seventy years were to pass before that policy was made even partially effective. The Government attempted some form of control by appointing inspectors of schools; but the great extension of the franchise in 1867 made the question of public education acute, and at last, in 1870, a Bill was introduced to provide for public elementary education in England and Wales, and this was passed after six months of contentious debate. The Act did not touch the "National" and "British" schools; but it empowered School Boards to provide undenominational schools which should be inspected in secular subjects only. It did not attempt to settle the religious dispute; it kept the dispute alive; but, with all its faults, the Education Act of 1870 was immensely important, because the English state then for the first time assumed direct responsibility for public education as a national need. This responsibility was at first confined to elementary instruction; but its extension was unavoidable. It would be ungrateful to mention the first Education Act without a tribute to Ruskin, whose unwearied advocacy had prepared the public mind for the acceptance of free compulsory education as a national duty. Another honourable name is that of Matthew Arnold, whose service in the cause of education cannot be valued too highly. As an inspector he sought to give life to the bare bones of elementary education and he preached unceasingly the necessity of an organized scheme of liberal secondary education. Our middle classes, he declared again and again, were the worst educated in the world. Arnold died before any of the sane and creative reforms for which he pleaded were effected; but that they were at last effected is due to his patiently reiterated demands. Arnold's official educational writings still remain excellent and valuable reading. Of numerous other works on education only a few of special interest can be mentioned here. Among the most conspicuous was Herbert Spencer's *Education, Intellectual, Moral and Physical* (1861). Spencer's book is largely Rousseau's *Émile* in nineteenth-century English guise. With very obvious faults, it remains a striking contribution to its subject and much of its doctrine has been absorbed into modern practice. John Stuart Mill's *Inaugural Address* to the university of St Andrews on being installed Lord Rector in February 1867, while not neglecting the controversies of the hour, raises the discussion about education to a level which controversies seldom reach. Mill's *Inaugural Address* and Newman's *Idea of a University*, when made mutually corrective, portray ideals of individual attainment which it is hard to imagine irrelevant at any stage of human civilization. Edward Thring's *Theory and Practice of Teaching* (1883) is a series of disconnected chapters full of shrewd observation and practical hints expressed in a rugged yet epigrammatic style, quite stimulating to read. It carries the authority of the man who made Uppingham a great school.

The advance in the education of girls and women may be traced back to the early activities of the Governesses' Benevolent Institution, founded in 1843. Queen's College, parallel to King's College, was founded in 1848; and the relationship between King's College and Queen's College was repeated between University College and Bedford College for Women by the foundation of the latter in 1849. In 1869 Cambridge and London universities instituted examinations for women. Emily Davies then started the college at Hitchin which, in 1873, was removed to Girton; in 1869 courses of lectures were begun in Cambridge, and this activity led to the foundation of Newnham College. The Girls' Public Day School Company was founded in 1872 and The Maria Grey Training College in 1878. The university of London threw open its degree examinations to women in 1878, Cambridge opened the Triposes to them in 1881, and three years later Oxford allowed women to pass the examinations of certain of its Schools. Colleges for women had been instituted at Oxford in 1879. It will be seen that Tennyson's "sweet girl graduates" of *The Princess* (1847) were a long time in attaining actual existence.

The creation of universities out of provincial colleges was formally effected in more recent years—Manchester and Liverpool in 1903, Leeds in 1904, Sheffield in 1905, Bristol in 1909 and others since. The University of London Act of 1908 led to the restoration of its teaching function and the possibility of unifying the higher education of the metropolis. Wales preceded England in the organization of secondary education. The Welsh Intermediate Education Act of 1889 gave the principality a scheme which filled the gap between public elementary schools and her three colleges, Aberystwyth, Cardiff, and Bangor; and the system was completed by the incorporation of these colleges as the University of Wales in 1893.

The English Schools Boards had been feeling their way towards secondary education by the establishment of Pupil-Teacher Centres, Higher Grade

Schools, and so forth; but the position was cleared by the Cockerton judgment (1901), which declared that any public expenditure upon education other than elementary was unlawful. The way was thus cleared for new action; and the general policy long before indicated by Matthew Arnold and reiterated by the Bryce Commission of 1894 was at length embodied in the Board of Education Act of 1899 and the Education Acts of 1902–3. A thousand years after the death of King Alfred, the English state had at last consented to accept responsibility for national education in all its branches.

XV. CHANGES IN THE LANGUAGE SINCE SHAKESPEARE'S TIME

In a general view of the fortunes of the English language since Shakespeare's time, one of the first things to strike an observer is the world-wide expansion of its use. At the beginning of the seventeenth century English was, with few exceptions, confined to England. The exceptions were Ireland, where English colonization had begun in the previous century, and Scotland, where literary English was already influencing the speakers of a tongue descended from the old Northumbrian dialect. Even today English does not completely occupy the whole of the United Kingdom: in 1951 about 2,000 people in Scotland could speak Gaelic only; in 1955 about 48,000 people in Wales could speak only Welsh. Outside the British Isles, the language followed the flag, and is spoken all over the Commonwealth and former British colonies, and it possesses a vigorous life and literature among many millions in the United States of North America. (A writer in *Life* magazine in 1962 estimated that 300 million of the world's population—about one in ten—used English as their primary language and another 300 million understood it in some degree.) In these large regions of the world, as well as in the small regions of the mother country, the spoken language varies in sound and in actual vocabulary; but the printed language of standard and current literature is everywhere the same. To discuss the changes which the last three centuries have made in that language is impossible in a volume like the present. All we can do is to give, under the three divisions of pronunciation, grammar and vocabulary, a few examples of such changes.

1. Pronunciation

Any person of moderate education can read without difficulty a play in the First Folio edition of Shakespeare dated 1623. The differences in orthography are slight, and whole sentences may occur in present-day spelling. But if such a person could be taken back to a Shakespearean performance at the Globe Theatre, he would be puzzled by the differences in sound. Some words he would fail to understand, and the performance as a whole would strike him as the effort of a company drawn from some remote provincial region where "standard English" had failed to penetrate. We, for instance, give *week* and *weak* the same sound. Once they were different. An Irishman still tends to give the latter word its old pronunciation *wake*. Pope rhymes *days* with *ease*—just as the traditional Irishman is supposed to pronounce *easy* as *aisy*. To say *ile* for *oil* is to our ears vulgar, dialectical or comic; but Dryden rhymes *choice* and *vice*, Pope rhymes *join*, *line*, and *divine*, and there are still elderly people who pronounce *point* as *pint*. Shakespeare requires *o-ce-an* as a trisyllable, and *passion* can be found still earlier spelt as *passyoun*. In older English the *-tion* termination must often be given its French value and not be reduced to the modern monosyllabic *-shon*.

In recent times one of the most noteworthy developments has been the loss of *r* as a trill. Once "the dog's letter", so called from its snarling sound, it is now lost medially before other consonants, and finally, in most cases, except in combinations where a vowel sound follows. In a phrase like *far, far away*, a southern speaker will pronounce the two words *far* differently. Often the *r* merely determines the value of the vowel it follows—we do not know how to pronounce *e*, but we know how to pronounce *er*, even though the *r* is not sounded. Phonetic changes do not necessarily make a language better or worse in its essential character of an instrument to reveal our thoughts; but they may spoil old rhymes, even though they admit new ones, and they may obscure other effects. When *chivalry* is sounded with initial *sh* (as if the word were a recent importation from France) instead of *tch*, the alliterative effect in Campbell's "And charge with all thy chivalry" is ruined. Changes in the fall of syllabic stress may also tend to spoil the rhythm of old lines. Such words as *re-vén-ue*, *ob-dúr-ate*, and *con-tém-plate* were pronounced as written here till quite recent times.

Modern spelling is marked by two features; fixity and dissociation from the spoken language. Phonetic representations are few, and even these vary in pronunciation in different parts of the country. On the whole, we spell by the eye, not by the ear. The ear helps little in a language where one sign may represent several sounds, as *ch* in *which*, *chemistry*, *machine*, and *i* in *pick*, *pike*, *pique*; or where one sound may be represented by a variety of signs, as *o* in *go*, *oath*, *dough*, *sow*, *sew*, and *k* in *call*, *keen*, *deck*, *chaos*, *quoit*. A fixed printed symbol is translated into different sounds in Glasgow, Galway, Wales, Bloomsbury, Peckham, Virginia, California and New York—a fact often forgotten by the advocates of scientific phonetic spelling. Fixed spelling has sometimes modified pronunciation, as in words like *backward*, *forward*, *Edward*, where, in the seventeenth century, the *w* sound was regularly dropped. Dickens makes the driver of Mr Wegg call his donkey *Eddard*; Shakespeare spelt *bear-ward* as *berrord*, and sailors still say *forra'd*. In some words letters were inserted as a clue to the etymology. In certain instances this insertion has not affected the pronunciation, as *b* in *doubt*; *c* in *scent*, *victuals*; *g* in *foreign*; *l* in *salmon*; *s* in *island*; in others, the letter has gradually come to be pronounced, as *c* in *perfect*, *verdict*. Milton uses both *perfet* and *perfect*. *Fault* was pronounced without the *l* sound right into the eighteenth century. Pope rhymes it with *ought*, *thought*. At the present day, *solder* and *sawder* are both heard. The word *ache* is very curious. Originally the noun *ache* and the verb *ake* differed in spelling and in pronunciation, like *speech* and *speak*. For both words *ache* we now have the spelling of the noun and the pronunciation of the verb. But the old distinction must be remembered for the sake of certain puns. Thus Thackeray says: "(She) never wanted medicine, certainly, for she never had an *h* in her life."

2. Grammar

The story of English grammar is a story of simplification, of dispensing with grammatical forms. Though a few inflections have survived, yet, compared with Old English, the present-day language has been justly designated one of lost inflections. It is analytic, not synthetic. One "good riddance" is the disappearance of grammatical gender from nouns, adjectives and most pronouns. Verb forms like *cometh*, regularly used in the Bible of 1611, were replaced by forms like *comes*. The simpler forms, at first colloquial, found their way into poetry for metrical or euphonic reasons. Thus, Sir Henry Wotton writes "That *serveth* not another's will", and, a little lower in the same poem, "Who *envies* none that chance doth raise". For a time the custom prevailed of writing -*eth* and saying -*s*; so that in 1643 among lists of words "alike in sound and unlike in writing", we find *rites, rights, wrights, righteth, writeth,* and "Mr *Knox* he *knocketh* many *knocks*". Steele protests against *pardons* and *absolves* for *pardoneth* and *absolveth*; and Addison regrets the multiplication of hissing sounds due to the use of -*s* for -*eth*. The later poets revived -*eth*, and, indeed, sometimes over-used it. The -*ed* of verbs was shortened in pronunciation to '*d*, though the spelling was unaltered. The poets used both forms (shortening *ed* into *t*, as in *washt*, when possible). The old texts of Shakespeare usually distinguish between the long and short forms; modern texts often do not. Thus we now find printed in some editions,

Hugged and embraced by the strumpet wind,

where the first word is "hugg'd" and the third "em-bra-ced". The second person singular of verbs and the pronouns *thou* and *thee* have gradually vanished from normal language, and though we have gained in simplicity, we have lost the advantages of the Continental second person singular. Subjunctive forms have almost entirely vanished, and with them part of the imperative. We no longer say, "Break we our watch up". Gone, too, is the so-called "ethical dative", familiar in Shakespeare, as in "Knock me at this gate and rap me well". The distinction between *dog* and the genitives *dog's, dogs'* is not a true inflectional difference but a spelling device, which we could quite well do without. The '*s* and *s*' do not occur in the old texts of Shakespeare, and do not appear to have been regularly used before the eighteenth century. The '*s* showing elision, as in "That dog's lively", is more defensible.

A tendency towards condensation has robbed us (except in poetry) of the emphasis conferred by double negatives and double comparatives. Condensation has also allowed a much larger use of attributive nouns than the old grammarians would have liked. We are quite used to *Empire products* and *press notices*, and we can even speak without ambiguity of a *loose leaf note book manufacturer*. Hyphens sometimes give a sense of unity to compound epithets as in *the condition-of-England question*. These uses exhibit one aspect of the freedom with which in English any part of speech can be used as any other part of speech. We not only have a *garage* for cars, but we *garage* the cars in it. We make a room *tidy* or we *tidy* a room. We not only *sit down*, but colloquially, we have *a sit down*.

Oddly enough, there is no marked tendency for strong verbs to become weak. We now generally say *crowed* instead of *crew*, and we always say *climbed* instead of *clomb*; but on the other hand we say *dug*, when Shakespeare, Milton, and the Bible never say anything but *digged*. Within the strong conjugation, numerous changes have been made. In the sixteenth and the seventeenth century, there was a general movement towards supplanting the form of the perfect participle by the form of the past indicative. Shakespeare used *mistook* for *mistaken*, *drove* for *driven*, *wrote* for *written*. In Purcell's *Dido and Aeneas*, Nahum Tate the librettist has the precious couplet, "Our plot has took, The Queen's forsook." In present-day English the original participles have, as a rule, been restored.

We have secured regularity in the use of pronouns, often wildly irregular in Elizabethan English. *Who, which*, and *that*, as relatives, have now fairly clear differences, and we distinguish clearly between nominative and accusative, except in such admitted colloquialisms as *Who is that for?* and *It's me*. The most valuable addition to the language is the word *its*. This form does not occur at all in the Bible of 1611; it does not occur in plays by Shakespeare printed in his lifetime; it occurs very seldom in Milton. At first a colloquialism, it appeared in print (as far as we know) for the first time in Florio's *Worlde of Wordes* (1598); but by 1660 it was so well established that the old *his* or *it* seemed strange. Shakespeare's "It had it head bit off by it young" is often thought a misprint. We have gained the indispensable *its*; we have not yet acquired a singular pronoun of the third person, common gender, and are reduced to saying, with pedantic accuracy, "*each* did *his or her* best", or with cheerful inaccuracy, "*Each* did *their* best". Careful writers endeavour to find safety in the plural.

The auxiliaries *shall* and *will* established their present use during the seventeenth century, but only in England. To this day Scotsmen and Irishmen find it difficult to follow the usage that seems instinctive to Englishmen. The uses of *do* as an auxiliary have settled down. In the seventeenth century *write* and *do write*, *wrote* and *did write* were used without grammatical difference, as in the text "*Rejoice* with them that *do rejoice* and *weep* with them that *weep*". This unemphatic *do* became a poetic fashion and its indiscriminate use led to the making of many weak lines. The Bible of 1611 uses *doth* and *doeth* without any distinction. The nineteenth century made *doest*, *doeth*, the verb of full meaning, *dost*, *doth*, the auxiliary. The verb *do* is now the common auxiliary in negative and interrogative forms, and it is used idiomatically in constructions like "Swallows never build here now". "Yes they *do*."

A noticeable feature of the English verb is its wealth of tenses, whereby precise and accurate expression is given to many shades of meaning. Forms like *I am writing* existed long ago; but it was well into the seventeenth century before the current distinction arose between *I am writing*, the actual present, and *I write*, the present of general application or of habit. The corresponding passive forms in *-ing* were much later in origin than the active, and at first met with fierce opposition. Constructions like "The house is being built" and "Rabbits were being shot in the field" have not been traced further back than the last decade of the eighteenth century. The adaptability of the English passive may be seen in the fact that, not content with a construction like "A book was given him", the language has devised "He was given a book".

3. *Vocabulary*

During the last three centuries or more, the vocabulary of English has displayed the characteristic marks of a living tongue—words have become obsolete, words have altered in meaning, words have been created. In addition, many words have been borrowed, and the borrowing has been world-wide. To display the changes by examples would need the space of a small dictionary. Shakespeare uses many beautiful and expressive words that we have lost. He also uses words like *let* (hinder), *secure* (unwatchful), *censure* (judgment), *conceit* (imagination), which we keep, with a different meaning.

Modern necessities tend sometimes to give a limited specific meaning to a word of general application—*train, negative, film, broadcast,* are instances, and slang may distort desirable words like *blooming, balmy, fabulous.* We have gained many words from proper names: *sandwich* and *boycott* remain necessary; *hansom* is now merely historical; *gamp* was scarcely needed; *bowdlerise* and *spoonerism* illustrate the ease with which new coinages can be made. American periodicals and films have given to some words and phrases an international currency. The curious fact about some of these phrases is their verbosity. We do not become more efficient in word or in deed by "facing up to" a fact instead of "facing" it.

The two chief methods of word-making—composition and derivation—are extensively employed in modern English. It is sometimes asserted that English has lost the power of composition and has, in that respect, become enfeebled. The claim will not bear a moment's examination. A language that can borrow freely has no need to resort to clumsy compounds—a *perambulator* (even when called a *pram*) is better than the *pushwainling* of misguided enthusiasts like William Barnes; but, in actual fact, English can make new compounds as readily as it wishes. Some of them shock the pedants, whose emotion, however, is not insupportable. Leaving aside the compounds that abound in all the poets, we find modern coinages, sometimes frank hybrids like *superman*, that we cannot do without. A word like *absent-minded*, i.e. adjective *plus* noun *plus -ed*, represents an inexhaustible source of supply. Even a journalistic coinage like *suffragette* expressed in a single word something that would have needed a whole phrase of description. Abbreviations like *bus, cab, taxi, phone, recap* make their way firmly into the language. "Back-formations" represent another source of supply— the verbs *sulk* (from *sulky*), *stoke* (from *stoker*), *swindle* (from *swindler*), *spring-clean* (from *spring-cleaning*), *resurrect* (from *resurrection*), *frivol* (from *frivolous*), are all modern coinages, some permanently established, some colloquial.

War, travel, exploration, commerce and politics have constantly increased the national vocabulary. A word like *camouflage* was unknown before the 1914 War. There is, indeed, hardly a language of the world that has not contributed something to our stock of speech. The coinages of science belong to their own place; but some of these gradually come into current use. Mere babes now babble of *ideologies*.

The beautiful reiterations of the Prayer Book–"We have *erred* and *strayed*", "We *acknowledge* and *confess*", "He *pardoneth* and *absolveth*"—illustrate a peculiar kind of richness in English, the shades of meaning attaching to words that seem almost alike. This is specially seen in the signification of some foreign borrowings. Besides *man* and *manly*, we have *human* and *humane*; besides *king* and *kingly*, we have *royal* and *regal*; in addition to *length* we have *longitude*; in addition to *height*, we have *altitude*. Fanatics who want to evict "foreign" words in favour of something they suppose to be "pure English" are complicators, not simplifiers, of the language. Pure English is not plain English. A "farspeaker" is not a simpler thing than a "telephone"—which at least lends itself to abbreviation. At all periods there has been opposition between the plain style and the adorned style. Each has its merits and its defects. The plain style tends to become bare and inexpressive, the adorned style tends to become gaudy and unintelligible. Some of the Elizabethans deliberately endeavoured to beautify prose. In the first half of the seventeenth century we meet with various devices to enrich literary style, exemplified in verse by the "conceits" of Donne, Crashaw and other metaphysical poets, and in prose by the antitheses and tropes of Bacon, the quaintness of Burton and Fuller, and the ornate splendour of Taylor, Milton and Browne. The Royal Society appointed a committee to improve the language; but nothing was done. What a committee or an academy could not do was done by a great writer, Dryden, who showed how great prose and great poetry could be written in a conversational manner. The Royal Society, anticipating Wordsworth, preferred "the language of artisans, countrymen and merchants before that of wits"; but L'Estrange and the mob of pamphleteers showed the depths to which that kind of "native easiness" could descend. Swift, Steele and Addison sought to improve the language by dignifying the plain style. Addison desiderated "something like an Academy, that by the best authorities and rules drawn from the analogy of languages shall settle all controversies between grammar and idiom". Swift, more mistakenly, in his *Proposal for correcting, improving and ascertaining the English Tongue* (1712) believed there should be some method of "*ascertaining* and *fixing* our language for ever". Johnson, in the preface to his *Dictionary*, acknowledged with his usual common sense that language was something not to be fixed by any lexicographer or academy, but urged the duty of individual responsibility in maintaining a high standard.

One remarkable experiment in the twentieth century should not be passed without notice, the development by C. K. Ogden and I. A. Richards from 1926 to about 1940 of what was called B.A.S.I.C. (British-American-Scientific-International-Commercial) or "Basic" English, which reduces the number of essential words to 850, but keeps to normal English constructions. Winston Churchill declared his support for its international use in a speech at Harvard, and in 1947 the copyright was purchased by the British government. Basic English begins at once with a clear foundation in meaning. The foreigner who has mastered Basic has still much to learn, but he need have nothing to unlearn.

There is much looseness in the use of English, but there is not the least sign of decay. Exhausted minds will always periodically discover that English is an exhausted language and that we must find salvation by writing in some kind of dialect. To all the objections of pedantry, preciousness and provincialism the final answer is the spectacle, presented in this volume, of a mighty and puissant language perpetually renewing its youth and passing from the compass of one small island to become the native speech of vast territories far across the seas.

CHAPTER XV

THE LITERATURE OF THE UNITED STATES
OF AMERICA FROM THE COLONIAL PERIOD
TO HENRY JAMES

I. THE COLONIAL PERIOD

The literature of North America is older than the U.S.A. To say nothing of any transatlantic contributions to the Norse sagas of pre-Columbian Viking explorers in the eleventh century, or of Welsh explorers in the twelfth, it is evident from references in Elizabethan literature that English writing in or about America dates back to the times of Sir Walter Ralegh, Richard Hakluyt, George Sandys and Captain John Smith. "*Fruitfullest Virginia*" is mentioned by Spenser in the *Faerie Queene*; the Red Indian princess Pocahontas, heroine of Smith's *Generall Historie of Virginia, New-England and the Summer Isles* (1624) and later the wife of John Rolfe, comes into Ben Jonson's *Staple of Newes*; Richard Rich's poem *Newes from Virginia* (1610) may have suggested some scenes in *The Tempest*; and there is even a personal connection with Shakespeare himself in the fact that Henry Wriothesley, Earl of Southampton, to whom Shakespeare dedicated *Venus and Adonis* and *Lucrece*, was later treasurer of the Virginia Company in a neglected period of its fortunes and, in the words of a contemporary Virginian account quoted by the British historian A. L. Rowse in his biography *Shakespeare's Southampton: Patron of Virginia* (1966), helped "to recreate and dip it anew into spirit and life."

Despite these not inglorious connections, one or two aspects of which we have glanced at in Chapter IV and afterwards, and despite its throwing up some very interesting writers during the period of its growth, American literature for long had to suffer a note of apology in the writings of both British and American critics. As late as 1879 we find Henry James, in his excellent study of Hawthorne in the "English Men of Letters" series, speaking of his subject as "the writer to whom his countrymen most confidently point when they wish to make a claim to have enriched the mother-tongue," adding that, "judging from present appearances, he will long occupy this honourable position." James went on to say that "our author must accept the awkward as well as the graceful side of his fame; for he has the advantage of pointing a valuable moral." This moral to James is that "the flower of art blooms only where the soil is deep, that it takes a great deal of history to produce a little literature, that it needs a complex social machinery to set a writer in motion. American civilization has hitherto had other things to do than to produce flowers, and before giving birth to writers it has wisely occupied itself with providing something for them to write about. Three or four beautiful talents of trans-atlantic growth are the sum of what the world usually recognizes, and in this modest nosegay the genius of Hawthorne is admitted to have the rarest and sweetest fragrance."

No critic today, whether British or American, would write of American literature in quite that tone, though it was a tone common enough in both America and Europe for the greater part of the nineteenth century, if not always taken to the extreme of Sydney Smith's bland inquiry in 1820—"In the four quarters of the globe, who reads an American book, or goes to an American play, or looks at an American picture or statue?"—or de Tocqueville's equally emphatic opinion in *Democracy in America* (1835): "The inhabitants of the United States have then, at present, properly speaking, no literature." Improperly speaking, they had, of course, by 1835 the novels of Cooper, the sketches of Irving, the poems of Bryant, the first lectures and essays of Emerson.

Everyone can accept part of what James said. American literature in the seventeenth and eighteenth centuries, for obvious non-literary reasons, produced no Milton or Dryden, no Swift or Johnson. The American literature of the colonial period, and for some time afterwards, with only a limited number of exceptions, is of historical rather than literary importance: there was no Bunyan or Marvell (though there was a Roger Williams) to counter Cotton Mather, no Blake or Burns (though there was a Benjamin Franklin) to succeed the Quaker founder of Pennsylvania. Although America can claim a part in both Paine and Cobbett, there was no Wordsworth pondering by the shores of the Great Lakes, Coleridge did not after all emigrate in the spirit of Thomas Chatterton to "the Susquehannah down in the Delaware country" along whose banks Cooper's Deerslayer had hunted "a hundred times", and it was George Keats, not John Keats, who did eventually settle in Louisville, Kentucky. But the contrast cannot fairly be extended much beyond the period of the American Revolution and the Napoleonic Wars, for when we come to the Victorian age in England, and the contemporary period in the United States, while the British contribution is still much the greater as regards the quantity of distinguished writing in every field (for most of the period the British reading public was larger than the American), as regards quality, as regards literature of permanent worth, the two countries, to all intents and purposes, are equal. Fenimore Cooper, it is true, looks back to the pre-Victorian Scott, but for the Victorian Dickens, America has Mark Twain; for George Eliot, Henry James himself; for Hardy, Hawthorne; for Tennyson, Longfellow; for Browning, Whitman; for Carlyle, Emerson; for Ruskin, Thoreau; for Thackeray, Howells; for Hopkins, Emily Dickinson; for Emily Brontë, Melville; for Butler, Henry Adams; for Kipling, Poe; for Wells, Jack London; for Gissing, Dreiser...It would be rash to place one achievement, in the period *c.* 1840–1910, much above the other, and in fact we are not usually tempted to do so. For the whole privilege of being born into the English language resides precisely in the fact that we can read both Dickens *and* Mark Twain, both Melville *and* Emily Brontë, with the spice of unfamiliarity—unfamiliar Yorkshire to a New Yorker, unfamiliar Missouri to a Londoner—added to the common literary and linguistic heritage. We are too busy, and too contented, reading both literatures to find time to compare unfavourably one with the other.

When James wrote his study of Hawthorne in 1879, Mark Twain had still to produce his masterpiece *Huckleberry Finn*. But Melville had written *Moby-Dick*, Whitman *Leaves of Grass*, and Thoreau (whom James praises judiciously) his *Walden, or Life in the Woods*. And a mere mention of these four works is enough for us to question the "valuable moral" that James saw Hawthorne as pointing for American literature. There is a core of truth in James's observation, in the sense, as we have said, that American literature in its first two centuries was of historical rather than literary importance, that the makers of a country had to produce a civilization before they could write about it, but nevertheless the truth is only a partial one. James was making the unwarrantable assumption that the only valuable literature was the kind he wrote himself, the kind Hawthorne wrote before him in *The Marble Faun*. Whereas a mention of *Moby-Dick*, *Walden*, *Leaves of Grass* and *Huckleberry Finn* proves that the real moral of American literature in the nineteenth century, a moral that the twentieth century has taken to heart, is that literature develops not only from a settled urban society, as James assumed, but that the more primitive life of the frontier, the forest, the village, the plantation, the river, the ocean...can itself produce great writing. We shall see, in the course of this chapter, that the Hawthorne-James strand in United States literature is only one strand in the American knot, that Mark Twain, Herman Melville and other writers created strands quite as valuable in themselves and even more authentically "American", as distinct from "British" or "European". With the advantage over James of a greater perspective, including the reading of both his own and Mark Twain's later works, we can see now that it was natural and inevitable that this should be so.

Not all the early settlers were Puritans or Separatists: there were Anglicans in Virginia, Roman Catholics in Maryland, and Pennsylvania was settled predominantly by Quakers and Deists. And not all the colonists by any means came to America because of religious persecution at home, whether in Britain or on the Continent of Europe. Yet the popular notion of the prevailing colonial culture as being that of the "Pilgrim Fathers" who landed from the *Mayflower* at Plymouth, Massachusetts, in 1620—often confused as they are with the more numerous Puritans (including the ancestors of Hawthorne and T. S. Eliot) who settled around Salem on Massachusetts Bay ten years later— has a certain poetical truth. "Let it not be grievous unto you," some of their Separatist brethren had written to the Pilgrims from England, "that you have been instrumental to break the ice for others. The honour shall be yours to the world's end." The Puritan strain was only one of the fruitful contrasting strains in American colonial culture, but it was on the whole the predominant one, and a feature of its predominance was the leading place given to theology and religious controversy in American colonial literature. Even the verse is primarily theological, from the metaphysical poetry of Edward Taylor (*c.* 1644–1729), not published till 1937–9, to the more homely rhymes of Captain Edward Johnson, Michael Wigglesworth (whose *Diary* has been published under the sub-title of *The Diary of a Seventeenth-Century Puritan*) and Anne Bradstreet (1612–72) whose *Works* were reprinted at Harvard in 1967 and who is the subject of *Homage to Mistress Bradstreet* by the modern American poet John Berryman.

Mostly read now in short poems or extracts in anthologies, the American colonial poets of the seventeenth and early eighteenth centuries are evidence of the influence of Milton and other contemporary English poets rather than of any distinctively American culture. New England poetry, as Milton might have put it, was but Old England verse writ large.

The prose writers, too, are mainly known today from the anthologies or from extracts quoted by historians of the United States or of American culture from George Bancroft to Admiral Morison, Perry Miller and Professor Louis B. Wright. This is not to belittle them, for their importance is primarily historical, like so many of the English writers of an earlier age. The Pilgrim Fathers produced no *Pilgrim's Progress*, but the Yorkshireman William Bradford (1590–1656), who in 1621 succeeded John Carver as governor of Plymouth Colony, left behind him a *History of the Plymouth Plantation* (begun *c.* 1630, not published till 1856) which shows many of Bunyan's sturdy Puritan virtues, if scarcely a trace of his humour. And this history, like the *Journal* (*c.* 1630–49) of John Winthrop and other early writings, was compiled, we must not forget, in conditions and under stresses that must have made Bedford Jail seem like a castle in the Delectable Mountains. The more sinister side of Puritanism, the side Hawthorne was later to recall in his classic fable *The Scarlet Letter*, was seen in the contrasting careers and writings of those apostles of toleration and intolerance, Roger Williams (*c.* 1600–83) and Cotton Mather (1663–1782). Williams, a Welshman, emigrated to New England in 1631, but was banished four years later for his opposition to the Salem theocracy. He founded the colony of Rhode Island in 1636 on a basis of democracy and complete religious freedom—in much the same spirit as the Catholic Lord Baltimore when he founded Maryland in which "province", ran its earliest law, "no person professing to believe in Jesus Christ shall be in any ways troubled, molested, or discountenanced for his or her religion, or in the free exercise thereof." In 1639 Williams established the first Baptist church in America. Among his writings are a *Key into the Language of America* (1643), *The Bloudy Tenent of Persecution for Cause of Conscience* (1644) and *The Bloudy Tenent yet more bloudy by Mr. Cotton's Endeavour to wash it White in the Blood of the Lamb* (1652).

Cotton Mather—so named after his grandfather, Williams's antagonist John Cotton whose death inspired a well-known poem by Benjamin Woodbridge—was the son of Increase Mather, pastor of the North Church, Boston for sixty years. The elder Mather was also president of Harvard, the first American university which had been founded at Cambridge, Massachusetts, in 1636 and named in honour of its chief benefactor John Harvard, son of a butcher in Shakespeare's Southwark. Increase Mather, whose name would have delighted Ben Jonson, wrote more than a hundred books and pamphlets, including a *History of the War with the Indians* (1676), but was surpassed in this respect by his son, who wrote more than three hundred. Cotton Mather's notoriety rests on his incitement of the persecutors before and during the Salem witchcraft mania in 1692–3, his justification for the persecution being given in such works as his *Memorable Providences relating to Witchcraft and Possessions* (1685) and *Wonders of the Invisible World* (1692), books which would have impressed King James I. Cotton Mather's *Magnalia Christi Americana* (1702) is a massive, undigested, rhetorical history of New England Puritanism during the first century of its existence.

Its second century is chiefly memorable for the remarkable career and writings of the theologian Jonathan Edwards (1703–58), the subject of a celebrated essay in Leslie Stephen's *Hours in a Library*. Born in Connecticut, Edwards was educated at Yale University, New Haven, in his native State: the third oldest American university, after Harvard and William and Mary (1693), being founded in 1701 and named after its chief benefactor Elihu Yale, the Bostonian who had entered the service of the East India Company and had become governor of Madras. Edwards became minister at Northampton, Massachusetts, gradually exchanging his early liberal views (which some have seen as an anticipation of Emerson) for a passionate conviction of the truth of the Calvinist doctrines of human depravity, original sin and predestination of the elect. Depressed by what he considered the worldliness of his parishioners, and refusing to allow communion to those who were not consciously converted, he resigned his ministry in 1750 and became a missionary to the Indians in a remote village in the Berkshire Hills in Western Massachusetts. Edwards is regarded as the last and greatest of American Puritan divines, among America's most original thinkers in metaphysics, and with his exact contemporary John Wesley (who was in Georgia 1735–8) perhaps the last notable descendant of St Augustine. His writings include *Freedom of Will* (1754) and *Original Sin Defended* (1758).

It is a relief to turn from these sinister or hell-fearing aspects of Puritanism to the truly more "friendly" writings of the American Quakers in the late seventeenth and early eighteenth centuries. We have seen something of them already in our mention (pp. 346–7) of William Penn, founder of Pennsylvania, and the New Jersey mystic John Woolman (1720–72), who was one of the first preachers to speak and write against the institution of Negro slavery and whose *Journal* was warmly recommended by Lamb. The Quakers have given America some of her most attractive writers, from Woolman in the eighteenth century to John Greenleaf Whittier and Bayard Taylor in the nineteenth and Logan Pearsall Smith in the twentieth. Whitman, the most American of American poets, and Fenimore Cooper, the creator of the Redskin in American fiction, were both of Quaker ancestry, as was also Thomas Paine of Norfolk, the *Citizen Tom Paine* of Howard Fast's novel, the Englishman who by his pamphlet *Common-Sense* became one of the heroes of the American Revolution.

II. REVOLUTION AND ROMANCE

At first glance it seems a curious thing that the period of the American Revolution in politics should have been immediately succeeded by a period in American literature when the newly independent United States was influenced, as hardly before or since, by the romantic literature of England and Europe. "The accepted way of declaring literary independence of Britain," as Robert Spiller of the University of Pennsylvania well puts it in his *Cycle of American Literature* (1955), "was to write something on an American theme as nearly as possible in the manner of a favorite British author." The classical Augustan writers like

Addison and Pope were laid under contribution by Joel Barlow and others, as well as contemporary or near-contemporary writers like Scott, Horace Walpole —whose *Castle of Otranto* suggested Brockden Brown's "Gothic" novels— and Sheridan, whose comedies suggested to Royall Tyler his witty play *The Contrast* (1787), in which for the first time American characters appeared on the American stage.

The paradox, however, is more apparent than real. The American Revolution was not just a quarrel between a stubborn group of colonists on one side of the Atlantic and a complacent, high-handed king and government on the other. As was made even clearer when the French Revolution followed it—albeit to the alarm of some of the American "rebels" like Washington and Adams as well as of some of their British supporters like Burke—the American Revolution was part of a general, international movement, analogous in some respects to the Renascence and the Reformation, a movement moreover in which some of the leading ideas had come from British sources. Benjamin Franklin (1706–90), the former printer's apprentice who pleaded the cause of the American colonists in England in 1765 and was one of the signatories of the Declaration of Independence eleven years later, was a man of the eighteenth-century Enlightenment, the Voltaire of his country, who had early been converted to the ideas of Locke and the English Deists. Addison and Swift had been his acknowledged models when he founded in Philadelphia in 1733 the first annual volume of *Poor Richard's Almanack*, part of his success coming, as to Swift for his Partridge, from his unmerciful ribbing of his chief competitor, one Titan Leeds, who published *The American Almanack* in the same city. A many-sided genius, Franklin by his researches into electricity and cognate matters had been elected a Fellow of the Royal Society, like the Virginian planter and diarist William Byrd of Westover before him. His *Autobiography* and *Letters*, both published posthumously, convince us of his share in that combination of enlightened patriotism and true international feeling so characteristic of the political and literary leaders of the American Revolution and which we find, in their different ways, in men so dissimilar as the Englishman Paine, the Frenchman Lafayette, the West Indian-born Alexander Hamilton, and the first three presidents of the United States: George Washington and Thomas Jefferson of Virginia and John Adams of Massachusetts.

On the other side of the Atlantic, there was far more support for the colonists among literary men in Britain than there was antagonism towards them. Although Johnson shocked Boswell by a typical home-thrust at what we may perhaps call, in Churchillian phraseology, "the soft under-belly" of the axioms which Franklin and others had put forward—asking in *Taxation no Tyranny* (1775) "How is it that we hear the loudest *yelps* for liberty among the drivers of negroes?"—Boswell and Wilkes were more typical of the English feeling at the time, while among the younger generation no less a poet than Blake supported his friend Paine with *America:A Prophecy* (1793), a somewhat obscure poem in which George Washington, Franklin and King George III mix freely with such mythical characters as Urizen and Orc. There were changes of feeling about France among some of the romantic poets, notably Wordsworth and Coleridge, after the French Revolution had been followed by the Terror and the Napoleonic Wars, but in regard to America not even the deplorable conflict of 1812–14—when opinion was divided among Americans as well as British and the States of Connecticut and Massachusetts refused to contribute either money or men—not even this unhappy episode, in which the British captured and burnt the capital city of Washington, while the Americans took Toronto, could affect the general sympathy with the United States that was common to most of the English poets and their readers. The Romantics of the Regency were, after all, as much the heirs of the eighteenth-century Enlightenment as Franklin and Jefferson themselves, and it was not only the youthful Coleridge who thought longingly of America as a country where democratic ploughboys drove "tinkling teams" of horses "o'er peaceful freedom's undivided dale." The disappointment of English liberals over the development of France from Revolution to Empire only strengthened their fellow-feeling for America. There were plenty of patriotic poems written in England during the wars against Napoleon, notably by Wordsworth in 1802–7; no English poet felt an urge to celebrate the burning of the White House by a British army in 1813.

The leaders of the American Revolution, though sometimes men of letters, are naturally more prominent in political than in literary history. Probably their most interesting name in literature, after Franklin, is that of Thomas Jefferson (1743–1826), who was largely responsible for the noble wording of the Declaration of Independence in 1776 and was afterwards, successively, Governor of Virginia, Minister to France, Secretary of State, and third President of the Republic. His writings range from neo-Deist philosophy to *A Summary View of the Rights of British America* (1774). His *Notes on the State of Virginia* (Paris, 1784) was an answer to a series of questions put by the secretary of the French legation at Philadelphia and, like Crèvecoeur's *Letters from an American Farmer* (1782), is regarded as one of the best surviving studies of American civilization at the end of the eighteenth century. His political and social philosophy, based on a belief in mankind's fundamental goodness, can be compared with less optimistic views expressed by his political opponents Alexander Hamilton, James Madison and John Jay in *The Federalist* (1787–8).

John Adams (1735–1826), who succeeded Washington and preceded Jefferson as President of the young Republic, is less remarkable for his own writings— the chief of which, his *Defence of the Constitution of the United States*, was published in London in 1787—than for his founding of almost as numerous a family in American cultural history as the family in Hebrew history or legend founded by the original Adam in the Book of Genesis. John Adams, the second President, begat John Quincy Adams (1767–1848), the sixth President, who in his turn begat the diplomatist Charles Francis Adams (1807–86) who edited his grandfather's works, whose *Diary* was published for the first time in 1965, and who in his turn begat the historian, man of letters and autobiographer Henry Adams (1838–1918)... And the days of John Adams—it is tempting Biblically to conclude—were ninety years. And he died. But not before he had seen his son John Quincy Adams succeed Jefferson, Madison and John Monroe as the sixth President of the United States.

Revolution was followed by Romance; the soldier, the statesman, the pamphleteer gave way to the man of letters. Not entirely so, of course. Washington

Irving was Minister to Spain, Fenimore Cooper consul at Lyons, and Philip Freneau (1752–1832), "the poet of the Revolution", wrote his best lyrics, such as *The Wild Honeysuckle* and *The Indian Burying Ground*, early in life and after 1800 largely gave up poetry for political satire and propaganda. But neither Irving nor Cooper attained his international reputation as a diplomatist, while for every European reader who had heard of Freneau, Timothy Dwight, Joseph Stansbury, Jonathan Sewall, Mercy Warren, Francis Hopkinson, Joel Barlow or Joseph Rodman Drake, a hundred had heard of William Cullen Bryant—though admittedly the Bryant of the early nature poems rather than the Bryant who later helped to found the Republican Party. It was Irving, Cooper and Bryant who first gave American literature a place in the sun. If it was partly reflected glory, from Goldsmith in the case of Irving, from Scott with Cooper, from Wordsworth with Bryant, we must in each case distinguish what was frankly borrowed (the borrowings across the Atlantic were by no means all one way) from the distinctively American contribution. Cooper, in particular, gave us at his best a genuine American novel, even if Irving gave us mainly an Anglo-American sketch and Bryant an Anglo-American poem.

Washington Irving (1783–1859) was born in New York of Scottish and Cornish ancestry. Nearly a third of his life was spent in Europe: two early years, 1804–6, in Italy, France, England and Holland; seventeen years, 1815–32, mostly in Germany, France, Spain and England; besides another four years, 1842–6, as Minister to Spain. His first essays were published in *Salmagundi* (1807), a short-lived venture in New York on the pattern of Addison's *Spectator*, Irving's own contributions, however, being more in the style of his beloved Goldsmith, whose biography (1849) is one of the most attractive achievements of his closing years. In true eighteenth-century style, Irving—like that other lover of the eighteenth century, Thackeray, after him—wrote some of his most characteristic works under various facetious pseudonyms. For instance, *A History of New York from the Beginning of the World to the End of the Dutch Dynasty* (1809), a good-humoured satire on the original Dutch settlers of what was then called New Amsterdam, is supposedly written by "Diedrich Knickerbocker", while the work which brought him international fame, *The Sketch-Book* (1819–20), is supposedly written (or "drawn") by "Geoffrey Crayon, Gent." The essays and stories in this once celebrated collection—as popular in Britain as in America and translated into most European languages—have not worn particularly well, with the significant exception of the famous tales (perhaps adapted from German originals) of *Rip Van Winkle* and *The Legend of Sleepy Hollow*, two early examples of American folk-lore which have long been added to the universal heritage of mankind. *The Sketch-Book* was followed by a sequel by the same "Geoffrey Crayon" entitled *Bracebridge Hall* (1822), in which Irving lovingly recalls his first Christmas visit to an old English country house.

A trip to the American West in 1833 bore fruit in *A Tour on the Prairies* (1835) and *The Adventures of Captain Bonneville* (1837). But Irving's later works are mostly in the historical and biographical fields, including a *Life of Columbus* (1828) and a five-volume *Washington* (1855–9). His own life was written by his nephew Pierre Munro Irving in 1862–4; Van Wyck Brooks's magnificently detailed study *The World of Washington Irving* (1944) sets the man in his time, the time of the slow growth of a specifically American literature. He was not the greatest figure in his period, but he was the most representative. He was the first "mid-Atlantic" man of letters, whose descendants include Henry James, George Santayana and T. S. Eliot. He was the ideal cultural ambassador of America to Europe, of Europe to America. "He is just the man he ought to be," wrote Dickens on first meeting him; and it is not difficult to see how his genial works and personality helped pave the way for later American writers to the hearts and minds of British readers. In his native city, *The Knickerbocker Magazine* (1833–65) maintained his style and influence.

That James Fenimore Cooper (1789–1851) is "the American Scott" is a literary equation that seems more and more true the closer we examine it. A good deal of Scott has faded, particularly those pseudo-medieval novels like *Ivanhoe* which Mark Twain was later to blame, somewhat unfairly, for the factitious elements in the culture of the Southern states. Where Scott is still very impressive is in his novels of the more recent past, where he was able to build upon the living memory of elderly relatives and friends to whom he had listened in boyhood. And it is precisely here that Fenimore Cooper, too, is impressive. He remarks himself, in the very first paragraph of *The Deerslayer*, that "the history that most abounds in important incidents soonest assumes the aspect of antiquity. In no other way can we account for the venerable air that is already gathering around American annals. When the mind reverts to the earliest days of colonial history, the period seems remote and obscure...and yet four lives of ordinary duration would suffice to transmit, from mouth to mouth, in the form of tradition, all that civilized man has achieved within the limits of the American Republic."

From mouth to mouth... Just as the young Walter Scott listened eagerly to the memories of those elders who had known at first hand the '15 and the '45, so the young James Cooper—who was later to insert the "Fenimore" from his mother's maiden name—listened eagerly to the tales of Indians like Chingachgook told by his father Judge William Cooper, who had founded Cooperstown in upstate New York and was himself the author of *A Guide in the Wilderness* (1810). As Scott used his own knowledge of Scotland, Scottish ballads, Scottish history, to supplement his elders' memories, so Cooper was to supplement his father's tales with his own knowledge of the terrain, his own consummate woodcraft, and his reading of pioneer writings like those of the Moravian missionary Heckewelder. Cooper, wisely, did not go very far back: there are no seventeenth-century American novels to match Scott's medieval romances, though he did write a novel about Columbus and a trilogy about Renascence Europe intended to dispel the glamour of feudalism. "The incidents of this tale," he tells us in *The Deerslayer*, "occurred between the years 1740 and 1745"; and *The Deerslayer*, though not written till 1841, is the first episode in the series of novels known generically as the *Leather-Stocking Tales*, with their central character the backwoodsman and homespun philosopher Natty Bumppo, also known as "Deerslayer", "Leather-Stocking" and "Hawkeye". Natty's story—he is a mere youth in *The Deerslayer*—is continued in *The Last of the Mohicans* (1826), *The Pathfinder* (1840), *The Pioneers* (1823) and *The Prairie* (1827). Obviously, from the discrepancy between the order of the story and the order of composition, Cooper did not have the full plan in mind from the beginning; but it is equally plain that Natty is a character based on originals known to the novelist in boyhood and that after he had begun *The Pioneers* he must have realized that he had found the ideal subject for which he had been seeking. He had begun with a novel of domestic life in England called *Precaution* (1820): which is as if Jane Austen had tried her hand at a novel of Red Indian life on the Western frontier of the United States. But his second novel, *The Spy* (1821), is a romance of the Revolution set in New York, and seldom afterwards did he stray from his native ground.

Like Scott, Cooper had an immense international fame, his novels, particularly the *Leather-Stocking Tales*, being translated not only into most European languages but even into Persian and Turkish. He wrote *The Prairie* in Paris, and in the eighteen-thirties and forties, Van Wyck Brooks tells us in *The Dream of Arcadia* (1958), "was so famous...that every novel he produced was published simultaneously in thirty-four European cities. Castles were placed at his disposal and he found his name known in country inns and post-offices in small Italian towns..." He created the Redskin and the Paleface for the literature of the world and his influence was seen for more than a century in Western novels and films. Cooper was also the first American juvenile classic, the *Leather-Stocking Tales* being the first of a series of novels, including Melville's *Typee*, Twain's *Tom Sawyer*, Harris's *Uncle Remus*, Louisa Alcott's *Little Women*, the Canadian Marshall Saunders's *Beautiful Joe*, John Habberton's *Helen's Babies*, Kate Wiggin's *Rebecca of Sunnybrook Farm*, Jack London's *The Call of the Wild*, and the Canadian wild-life stories of Major Roberts and Thompson Seton, a series of juvenile classics in which North America handsomely repaid the debt owed by her children to *Robinson Crusoe, Gulliver, Ivanhoe, Old St Paul's, David Copperfield, Alice, The Swiss Family Robinson, Struwwelpeter*, the fairy tales of Grimm and Andersen, and other productions of British and European story-telling genius. The writer of this chapter read *Beautiful Joe* at so tender an age he did not even realize that it was American. But American it is, as surely as *Black Beauty* is English, and he pays it here a passing salute.

When Cooper died in 1851, as when Irving died in 1859, a poem of lament and eulogy was written by William Cullen Bryant (1794–1878), "the American Wordsworth" not only in this national, "laureate" way, but in his early religion of Nature, in his impressive span of years, and in the fact that he was both poet and critic and wrote his poems, as Wordsworth the *Lyrical Ballads*, according to his own critical theories. Bryant was born, like Hawthorne, of the earliest New England stock and grew up in a little town in western Massachusetts among those Berkshire Hills to which Jonathan Edwards had retired to preach to the Indians and where Hawthorne was to write *The House of the Seven Gables* and Melville *Moby-Dick*. Like Pope, Bryant lisped in numbers for the numbers came, and at the age of thirteen published a satirical poem called *The Embargo*. His most famous poem, the strongly-Wordsworthian *Thanatopsis*, was begun in his teens and frequently revised before its publication in 1817. Almost all the lyrics by which he is best known—for instance, *The Yellow Violet, A Walk at Sunset, The Evening Wind, To a Waterfowl*—were the product of his early life, written or begun mostly between the years 1815 and 1830.

They are poems of nature, in which an eye as keen as Cooper's (Cooper sometimes quotes him in the novels) is wedded to the Wordsworthian philosophy and the Wordsworthian form. He found moral lessons, as Wordsworth had found them in the Lake District, in the natural beauties of Massachusetts—including the natural beauty of the girl, "the fairest of the rural maids", he later married. "Bard of the river and the wood," Whitman called him in *Specimen Days in America*, "ever conveying a taste of open air, with scents as from hay-fields, grapes, birch-borders...here and there through all...touching the highest universal truths, enthusiasms, duties—morals as grim and eternal, if not as stormy and fateful, as anything in Aeschylus." But Bryant was also a lawyer by training and a journalist who edited *The New York Evening Post* from 1829 to his death in 1878. He became the leading liberal editor of his day, helped to found the Republican Party in 1854, and was a leading advocate of the abolition of slavery. In his case, the career of the American man of letters, so recently begun, almost came full circle, if not precisely to the revolutionary and the pamphleteer, at any rate to the politician and the party editor. The moral element which Whitman remarked in Bryant's poetry was part of the man himself; no more than Whitman or Whittier could Bryant rest content with literary fame while the contradiction at the heart of America's boasted freedom incurred the criticism of her closest friends.

III. EMERSON, HAWTHORNE AND NEW ENGLAND

The literary history of the United States is intimately connected with its geographical expansion. Like Topsy in *Uncle Tom's Cabin*, if sometimes with some deliberate assistance, the States "just growed" from the original thirteen in 1790—comprising, in order of admission, Delaware, Pennsylvania, New Jersey, Georgia, Connecticut, Massachusetts, Maryland, South Carolina, New Hampshire, Virginia, New York, North Carolina and Rhode Island—to fifty in 1959 with the admission of Alaska and Hawaii. The American flag shows accordingly thirteen stripes and fifty stars, and American frontier literature, whether contemporary or nostalgic, kept pace with "the star-spangled banner" of Francis Scott Key's song (there were already eighteen stars at the time the song was written in 1814) by constantly shifting its ground: from Natty Bumppo's Delaware and upper New York frontier about 1750 to Huckleberry Finn's Mississippi frontier a hundred years later, and from Huck's Mississippi frontier in 1850, after the expeditions of Frémont and Carson, and their successors, to the Pacific and the Mexican frontiers by the seventies and eighties. The original "striped" States of Old Glory remained for many years, however, the main centres of population, education and industry—including the industries of writing books and publishing them. Philadelphia had had one moment of international glory with Benjamin Franklin in the eighteenth century, and New York had produced Irving and Cooper in the eighteen-twenties, to the delight of America and Europe alike. Now, in the period *c.* 1830–40, the literature of the United States began to centre—or began to centre again—on those northeastern Atlantic States which Captain John Smith in 1614 had christened New

England, though it was a New England rather different in outlook from the original Puritan (or mainly Puritan) States of the seventeenth century. The most important names here are Emerson, Hawthorne, Thoreau, Margaret Fuller, Longfellow, Whittier, Holmes, Lowell, and the four historians: George Bancroft (1800–91) who wrote the *History of the United States* (1834–85); J. L. Motley (1814–77) whose most famous work is his *Rise of the Dutch Republic* (1856); W. H. Prescott (1796–1859) who wrote the *Conquest of Mexico* (1843) and the *Conquest of Peru* (1847); and Francis Parkman (1823–93) who devoted himself to the rise and fall of the French dominions in America in a series of volumes from *The Pioneers of France in the New World* (1865) to *Montcalm and Wolfe* (1884). The centre of this New England centre was Boston, "the American Athens", and more particularly a little town in Massachusetts, some twenty miles west of Boston itself, a town well named Concord, a town which had been founded by one of Emerson's own Presbyterian ancestors.

"Well named Concord" because it was the fine achievement of the New England school of writers, when all fair criticisms have been made of them, to reconcile the Puritan idealism of their forbears with the very different demands of the nineteenth century. Some of them were immensely accomplished persons: Emerson was versed in theology, philosophy, literature, science; Longfellow was professor of Modern Languages and Literature at Harvard for close on eighteen years and translated or adapted from German, French, Spanish, Italian and Swedish; the partially-blind Prescott studied like another Gibbon for his life's work in Spanish history; Margaret Fuller, later the Marchioness Ossoli (1810–50), who was called "the Yankee Corinne" after the romance of Madame de Staël, began to read Virgil and Ovid at six and was studying music, philosophy, Italian, French and German before she was twenty; Holmes was professor of Anatomy and Physiology at Dartmouth, New Hampshire, besides essayist, novelist, biographer, poet; Lowell succeeded Longfellow at Harvard and was poet, essayist, editor, besides barrister and ambassador... For the Puritan pulpits of many of their ancestors, these new New Englanders substituted the lecturer's chair or the editorial desk. What they lacked in holy orders, they more than made up for in the international size of their congregation. Like Carlyle, Ruskin and Matthew Arnold in old England, they gave to the nineteenth century what the nineteenth century particularly wanted: some kind of moral certainty to take the place of the old theological certainties whose grip for many was being loosened by developments in the natural sciences. If for younger generations they later became themselves a generation to be superseded —"Every hero," as Emerson remarked, "becomes a bore at last"—that does not really affect the value of their achievement for their own time, still less the part of it which is of permanent and not simply historical importance. The young T. S. Eliot treated Emerson with lofty patronage, but some of his own forbears must have been among the kind of Unitarians in whose households the young, radical Emerson first began to think for himself.

Ralph Waldo Emerson (1803–82) was the son of William Emerson, minister of the First Unitarian Church in Boston. He was educated at Harvard and in 1829 became pastor of the Second Unitarian Church, apparently destined for a career in "public preaching and private influence" (as he himself puts it in his

Journals) very similar to that of his father and grandfather. But his times were not theirs, and even the very mild orthodoxy of Unitarianism—to which such celebrated preachers as William Ellery Channing the elder, author of *The Moral Argument against Calvinism* (1820), had moved from their earlier Congregational faith—even this mild orthodoxy began to seem to the young Emerson a bar to his lifelong belief in complete personal integrity, whatever the cost in spiritual and mental suffering. To these trials was added the death of his first wife in 1831, after only two years of marriage; and the following year, after a controversy with his congregation over a sermon on the Lord's Supper, he resigned his ministry and sailed for Europe with the twofold intention of trying to forget his private sorrow among fresh surroundings and of finding time to think things out. His *Journals* for these years do not go into any great personal detail—he was no Boswell or William Byrd in any sense—but we know that he visited Carlyle at Craigenputtock in 1833 and that henceforth the Scottish prophet was to be his lifelong friend and mentor. The *Correspondence of Emerson and Carlyle*, originally edited by Charles Eliot Norton in 1883, had a fine new edition by Joseph Slater at the Columbia University Press, New York, in 1965.

The return of Emerson from Europe began the most important years of his life: the period of trial was over, the period of fulfilment was about to begin. In 1834 he moved to Concord, the home of his ancestors, with his second wife, Lydia Jackson of Plymouth, and there he remained with his growing family— as his son's book *Emerson in Concord* (1889) faithfully records—until his death nearly fifty years later. "What is called a warm heart, I have not," he had noted in his *Journals* with characteristic honesty, but it cannot have been altogether an accident that the first period of his important production should have followed closely upon his domestic happiness. He was a preacher now without a pulpit, but he soon found his proper role in the public sphere by becoming one of the earliest and most successful practitioners of what Dickens was to find a peculiarly American institution: the lecture on cultural matters delivered with ministerial earnestness and at great length to crowded and attentive audiences in all sorts of places and under all sorts of conditions. The prose-poem *Nature* (1836), in which Emerson summarized his early philosophical views and looked forward to "a poetry and philosophy of insight and not of tradition", was followed by his famous Phi Beta Kappa address at Harvard on *The American Scholar* (1837), which has been variously described as "a declaration of American intellectual independence" and "a courageous blast at formalism and tradition in learning and literature." The *Address before the Divinity Class, Cambridge*, which followed at Harvard a year later, defined his own position in regard to the church of which he had been a minister and was a plea for the individual conscience against all creeds, bibles and churches, setting up the soul of each individual person as the supreme judge in spiritual matters. So far had New England come from the theocracy of Salem, so far in so short a space of time from the Calvinism of Jonathan Edwards, even from the Unitarianism of the elder Channing.

The early views of Jonathan Edwards had something in common, nevertheless, with Emerson's, as we have noted, and Dr Channing's nephew, William Ellery Channing the younger, became a member, with his sister-in-law

Margaret Fuller, the educationist Bronson Alcott (father of Louisa), Henry Thoreau, Elizabeth Peabody and her sister Sophia who married Hawthorne, George Curtis, future editor of *Harper's Weekly*, the poet and essayist Jones Very, the poet and painter Christopher Pearse Cranch, and others, of the Transcendental Club, an informal group of Boston and Concord neighbours who met at Emerson's home to discuss abstract questions and in particular the new German idealism, originating with Kant, which in Britain had profoundly influenced not only Coleridge but Emerson's friend and correspondent Carlyle. In *American Notes* (1842) Dickens observes that "there has sprung up in Boston a sect of philosophers known as Transcendentalists. On inquiring what this appellation might be supposed to signify" (another century had the same kind of trouble over the name Existentialist), "I was given to understand," Dickens continues, "that whatever was unintelligible would be certainly transcendental. Not deriving much comfort from this elucidation, I pursued the inquiry still further, and found that the Transcendentalists are followers of my friend Mr Carlyle, or I should rather say, of a follower of his, Mr Ralph Waldo Emerson." The sect, concludes Dickens, "has its occasional vagaries...but it has good healthful qualities in spite of them...And therefore, if I were a Bostonian, I think I would be a Transcendentalist." Emerson (whom Henry James calls "the man of genius of the moment...the Transcendentalist *par excellence*") was the main mover behind their quarterly magazine "for literature, philosophy and religion" called *The Dial* (1840–4), edited first by Margaret Fuller and then, after her departure for New York and Italy, by Emerson himself. Some of his own contributions were reprinted in his *Essays*, First and Second Series (1841, 1844), which are among his most widely read books. Dickens found much in the first volume that he thought "dreamy and fanciful", but "much more that is true and manly, honest and bold."

In 1847 Emerson revisited Britain to give the lectures on *Representative Men*, published in 1850. On his return he delivered at Boston in 1848 the series of lectures published in 1856 as *English Traits*, a kind of riposte to Dickens's *American Notes* in which Emerson casts a friendly but critical eye on his late hosts, admiring British common sense and their "bias to practical skill" but deploring their limitations in philosophy and their general tendency (despite Coleridge and Carlyle) to "shrink from a generalization." That Emerson never so shrank himself is proved by nearly all his work, in particular the later volumes like *The Conduct of Life* (1860) and *Society and Solitude* (1870). How much of his prose work survives in a literary and not simply an historical sense is a question as difficult to answer as in the somewhat parallel cases of Carlyle and Ruskin. His status as "Sage of Concord" and "monumental figure in American literature" tends to cover up his originality and radicalism, but even when we allow for this, we are still seeing him mainly in historical perspective. Probably some of his heavier prose will remain largely unread, while attention is directed to comparatively lighter works such as *English Traits* and *Representative Men*, to the *Journals and Notebooks*, first published 1910–14 and re-edited in a handsome Harvard edition 1965– , and to the *Poems*, where he seems the chief forerunner of Whitman, whose *Leaves of Grass* he was among the first to salute. Emerson, incidentally, was one of the first American poets, with Bryant, Holmes and others, to be included in the enlarged, post-Palgrave editions of the *Golden Treasury*, where his striking poem *Brahma* must have made his poetry first known to many British readers of a younger generation. There are not many poets since the seventeenth century who have thought successfully in verse, and most of them are poets like Emerson and Matthew Arnold whose main work has lain in prose. Oliver Wendell Holmes once called the New England school, to which he himself belonged, "the Brahmins", a nickname which has been extended to include intellectual workers in general, particularly of the more favoured social classes. Perhaps the answer to the question asked in this paragraph about Emerson's literary survival can be found, *mutatis mutandis* and with a pinch of mortal salt, in the third stanza of his most famous poem:

> They reckon ill who leave me out;
> When me they fly, I am the wings;
> I am the doubter and the doubt,
> And I the hymn the Brahmin sings.

Whosoever would be a man, Emerson had said, must be a non-conformist. None took this advice more to heart than his disciple and fellow-Transcendentalist Henry David Thoreau (1817–62), born of Jersey-Scots stock in Concord itself. Where Emerson theorized, Thoreau put his ideas into practice, notably in his Walden Pond venture in 1845–7 and in his day's imprisonment in Concord Jail in 1846 for refusing to pay his poll tax to a government that supported the Mexican War. After graduating at Harvard in 1837, Thoreau had opened with his brother John on the principles of Bronson Alcott what would now be called a "progressive school", Concord Academy, in which the emphasis was laid, in a manner that would have won the approval of his contemporary Ruskin and his successors William Morris, John Dewey, A. S. Neill and Bertrand Russell, less on desk-learning than on learning through doing, exploring nature rather than books. Thoreau and his brother were years before their time and their school, like Alcott's Temple School at Boston, was not very successful in commercial terms. He then tried lecturing and writing, contributing essays and poems to *The Dial* and following Emerson's lead in first entering observations in his *Journals* (started in 1837 and eventually totalling thirty-nine notebooks of daily jottings), preparing a lecture from them, and then revising the lecture into an essay suitable for print. This was, of course, sound advice from Emerson at the time, but literary tastes change and the twentieth century, more interested in the daily jottings than the formal essays, perhaps more interested in the personality than the writer, has published fourteen volumes of the original *Journals*, with scholarly notes. There is also available a complete edition (nearly 2,000 pages) in two volumes, besides several useful selections.

From 1841 to 1843 Thoreau lived in Emerson's house, serving his guide, philosopher and friend as a general handyman. Then, in 1845, he began to put into practice the ideas he had been committing to the privacy of his *Journals* and which he had been meditating upon in his lonely walks in the woods around Concord. Carlyle and Emerson were the origin of most of these ideas, but Thoreau was himself an original mind, in nothing more so than in his long-meditated resolve to be a "transcendentalist" in life as well as in theory, showing here a streak of "Yankee cussedness" which to say the least was un-Emersonian and which Harvard should have suppressed but luckily did not. Thoreau, like Lizzie Borden in the song, took an axe—and in March 1845, with the help of Hawthorne, Curtis and a few other friends, began to build himself a log-cabin on the wooded edge of Walden Pond, about two miles south of Concord. He lived alone there, a combination of Robinson Crusoe and Natty Bumppo, from July 1845 until September 1847, when he rejoined the Emerson household for a while, when Emerson himself was lecturing in Europe.

These two years by Walden Pond were the most important in Thoreau's life, both in themselves and in the work they produced. In his little new log-cabin, made with the sweat of his own brow—while Longfellow, for instance, in his comfortable study at Harvard, was writing poems about the "honest sweat" of other people—Thoreau meditated, Thoreau fished, Thoreau read, Thoreau wrote... He wrote, to begin with, much of his book *A Week on the Concord and Merrimack Rivers*, an account of a trip he had made in 1839 with his brother John in a home-made boat from Concord up into New Hampshire. This book was published in 1849, the author having to pay the cost of printing out of his meagre earnings as whitewasher, gardener, fence-builder and the other occasional jobs he had again taken up after he returned from Walden Pond. He also wrote there his essay on Carlyle and what was afterwards his most popular book: *Walden, or Life in the Woods*, published in 1854. This is at once his self-justification for his seemingly eccentric mode of living and an indictment of the busy commercial world of the mid-nineteenth century, an indictment whose relevance has only increased with the years. Emerson had taught the supreme value of the individual soul; but what were most men's lives like in practice, Thoreau asked, and he did not shrink from some honest and uncomfortable answers. Emerson, the minister's son, had preached from the lecture platform the doctrines of Transcendence to packed rows of applauding disciples; Thoreau, whose family trade was making lead-pencils not sermons, lived a life of "transcendence" over the comforts of nineteenth-century civilization, "Emerson's independent moral man made flesh" as Henry James called him, putting into practice Wordsworth's "plain living and high thinking." He had not inherited Emerson's eloquence from a long line of pulpiteers. But Walden Pond was his audience, and he addressed the calm waters in the stately periods of an orator, enlivened by aphorisms such as "A man is rich in proportion to the number of things he can let alone" and "I have learned that the swiftest traveller is he that goes afoot", aphoristic bait which it would have taken a dull fish indeed not to grasp. He made two brief excursions from his log-cabin during 1846: one, the first of three visits to Maine described in the posthumous collection *The Maine Woods* (1864); and secondly, his day in Concord Jail for refusing to pay his poll tax, which episode resulted in his essay *On the Duty of Civil Disobedience*, a classic protest against governmental interference with individual liberty which is said to have formed the basis for Gandhi's passive resistance movement in South Africa and India (pp. 741, 763 above) many years later. This was first delivered as an oration to the Concord Lyceum in 1848, then recast as an essay in the opening (and final) number of

Elizabeth Peabody's *Aesthetic Papers* (1849), a venture which it was hoped would succeed *The Dial*.

Thoreau died in early middle age, twenty years before his mentor Emerson. Apart from his contributions to *The Dial* and its even shorter-lived successor, and two abolitionist pamphlets *Slavery in Massachusetts* (1854) and *A Plea for Captain John Brown* (1860)—the Brown whose soul went marching on—he saw only two works of his in print in his lifetime: *Walden* and the *Week*, neither of which sold many copies or made much stir. But he has had, like the John Brown of the famous song, an ample posthumous revenge. Not only were five books published in the sixties by his family and friends: the essay *Life Without Principle* (1863) and four books of travel edited from his notes: *Excursions* (1863), *The Maine Woods* (1864) already mentioned, *Cape Cod* (1865) and *A Yankee in Canada* (1866); but the steady growth of interest in *Walden*, making it, like Melville's *Moby-Dick*, a twentieth-century as much as a nineteenth-century classic, led to a renewed interest in the *Civil Disobedience* essay and a demand, which was met, for a complete edition of the *Journals*. Thoreau seemed to many twentieth-century critics, in Europe, Asia and Africa as well as America, to speak to the modern world with more contemporary an accent than his master Emerson or than those fellow New Englanders like Longfellow, Whittier, Holmes and Lowell, whose writings were so much more popular in their time than his. The last laugh does indeed appear to be the Hermit of Concord's in his little log cabin at the wooded edge of Walden Pond.

Thoreau's poetry, like Melville's, is a minor part of his work. At the same time, it must in fairness be compared, not so much with the massive collected poems of such "professional" poets as Longfellow and Whittier, as with what actually remains of them in most people's adult reading. No one who recalls the reading of his childhood and youth will have any other feelings than gratitude and respect for both Henry Wadsworth Longfellow (1807–82) and John Greenleaf Whittier (1807–92). The mere writing down of their full names seems in itself an exercise in affectionate recollection. They were exact contemporaries, Longfellow born in Maine, Whittier of a poor Quaker family in Massachusetts. Longfellow's splendidly-tuned *Song of Hiawatha* (1855), a poem which had a new lease of life in the musical setting by the Afro-English composer Samuel Coleridge-Taylor, as *The Golden Legend* (1851) had been set to music by Liszt; Whittier's stirring ballads of *Barbara Frietchie* and *The Relief of Lucknow*; Longfellow's *Hesperus*, *Excelsior*, *Village Blacksmith* and *Psalm of Life*, poems first read in childhood of which everyone still obstinately recalls isolated lines; both men's compassionate anti-slavery poems: these are a few of the more obvious highlights as we turn over the pages of their voluminous collected editions. Longfellow translated or adapted freely from many languages, old and new; and Baudelaire repaid the compliment by imitating two of Longfellow's poems in *Les Fleurs du Mal*. Apart from *Hiawatha*, his large-scale works have not worn particularly well, but it is interesting to notice, remembering Cooper's words in the first paragraph of *The Deerslayer*, how many of their themes are historical. Thus *Evangeline* (1847) is a story in hexameters about the early French settlers in Acadia (Nova Scotia), while *The Courtship of Miles Standish* (1858), like the *New England Tragedies*, *John Endicott* and *Giles Corey of the Salem Farms*, and like Whittier's *Mabel Martin*, goes back to the early days of the Puritan settlers in Massachusetts and can therefore be compared, not altogether unfavourably in certain respects, with Hawthorne's masterpiece *The Scarlet Letter*. One of Hawthorne's Puritan ancestors is a leading character in *Giles Corey*.

History, in its widest sense, was the common link between all these new New Englanders, Thoreau included. "I aspire to be acquainted," he says in the third chapter of *Walden*, "with wiser men than this our Concord soil has produced"; and thus in the intervals of shaping logs he read Homer and Aeschylus and recommended Zoroaster to the "solitary hired man on a farm...who has had his second birth...and is driven as he believes into silent gravity and exclusiveness by his faith." A less exclusive culture than the Puritan will breed a greater liberality and tolerance: so far as any one phrase can sum it up, this was the Gospel of these new apostles, whether Thoreau himself in *Walden*, his master Emerson in his lectures, Longfellow and Whittier in many of their poems, Holmes and Lowell in much of their writing. It was in this spirit that Longfellow turned from French and German to write the *Song of Hiawatha*, that Lowell put an epigraph from Aeschylus to his poem *A Chippewa Legend*, that the Boston historian Francis Parkman rode westwards to the lands of the Sioux and wrote *The Oregon Trail* (1849) before settling down on his eight-volume history of the French dominions in America. If they were occasionally "exclusive" in their very inclusiveness, too proud of their own lack of pride, and generally too complacent for even their admirers' comfort—Melville wrote to Evert Duyckinck: "I could readily see in Emerson, notwithstanding his merit, a gaping flaw. It was the insinuation that had he lived in those days when the world was made, he might have offered some valuable suggestions" —there were not lacking within their own ranks several witty commentators to hold them up to gentle ridicule. Of these Holmes and Lowell, with the Hawthorne of *The Blithedale Romance*, are the most important—though we must not forget the almost incredible fact that "Western humour" had its birth in "the Modern Atkins", as Artemus Ward called it, in a comic weekly called *The Carpet Bag* published in Boston by the humorist B. P. Shillaber, whose character Mrs Partington is a Yankee version of Mrs Malaprop. *The Carpet Bag* was widely read and quoted in the West, including Mark Twain's home town of Hannibal, Missouri, and one number of this Boston weekly in the year 1852 had the distinction of printing the very first published sketches of both Mark Twain and Artemus Ward.

The Dial, we have seen, ran for only four years, while its intended successor failed after only one number. But *The Atlantic Monthly*, founded in Boston in 1865 by James Russell Lowell (1819–91) and Oliver Wendell Holmes (1809–94) —often called "Dr Holmes" to distinguish him from his almost equally famous son and namesake "Mr Justice Holmes"—was still with us a century later and has published all the leading American writers, including the first efforts of Sarah Orne Jewett and its future editor W. D. Howells and under Howell's shrewd guidance both Henry James and Mark Twain. Holmes and Lowell were born "in the right place", at Cambridge, Massachusetts, Lowell having the further Brahmin distinction of being the son of a minister. Both were educated "locally" at Harvard, and gained, with Longfellow, their first literary renown as the "trio" of "Cambridge poets". Holmes took up medicine, Lowell pursued a career as poet, man of letters, journalist. His *Biglow Papers* (1846) grew out of a satiric poem in the Yankee dialect that denounced the pro-slavery party and the conduct of the government at the outbreak of the war with Mexico; a second series was written during the Civil War. With Charles Eliot Norton he edited *The North American Review*, 1863–7, and in later life was Minister to Spain (like Irving) and afterwards to Britain. Holmes was less of a public figure, but even more prolific in various literary forms including fiction and biography. He is remembered chiefly for the essays which first appeared in *The Atlantic* and were then reprinted in the volumes *The Autocrat of the Breakfast Table* (1857–8), a favourite book of Mark Twain's, and its successors *The Professor at the Breakfast Table* (1858–9) and *The Poet at the Breakfast Table* (1872). These witty, whimsical essays, interspersed with poems, are unique in American literature and indeed in the English language. A touch of Lamb perhaps, a breath of Irving, but fundamentally "Dr Holmes" himself, who proved, more than the comparatively humourless Emerson was able to do, and more than the comparatively caustic Thoreau was willing to do, that the doctrine of Humanity with a capital aitch was not inconsistent with ordinary humane feeling and a genial, man-of-the-world humour that could laugh with human vanities and failings as well as at them.

The greatest of the new New Englanders we have kept to the last, for while Hawthorne may not have been quite the exceptional figure in all American literature that Henry James took him to be, there is no doubt that he is among the greatest American novelists of the nineteenth century and the only one of this group of New Englanders who was primarily a literary artist rather than a preacher or a propagandist. The propaganda, of course, was very much needed, at its best both high-minded and effective, and occasionally, as we have seen, there was a poem like *Hiawatha* where the author was not concerned with any message but was creating a work of art, however limited in intention, for his own enjoyment and that of his readers. Emerson and Thoreau had cast a critical eye on the Puritan tradition, endeavouring to keep and extend what was valuable and to destroy what they felt was harmful to the progress of civilization. This, like Ruskin's and Matthew Arnold's in Britain, was "propaganda" in its very loftiest sense: a job crying out to be done and being done as well as humanly possible. There still remained room for the literary artist, to look at that Puritan tradition more dispassionately and at the same time to take a cool look at the reformers themselves and perhaps to come to some implied conclusions much more radical than the genial satire of Holmes and Lowell could produce. Hawthorne filled that role to perfection, first in *The Scarlet Letter* and *The House of the Seven Gables*, secondly in *The Blithedale Romance* and *The Marble Faun*.

He began with some advantages. Nathaniel Hawthorne (1804–64) was, as we have noted, of the earliest (or, to be pedantically precise, the second earliest) New England stock, born in Salem, the town where the notorious witch trials had taken place at the end of the seventeenth century and personally connected with the persecutors through his direct ancestor Judge William Hathorne (so spelt), that "grave, bearded, sable-cloaked and steeple-crowned progenitor" the traditional curse on whose family was the basis for the story of *The House of the Seven Gables* and whom Hawthorne evokes in the introductory chapter of *The Scarlet Letter*: that "soldier, legislator, judge" who had "all the Puritanic traits, both good and evil" and who was "a bitter persecutor; as witness the Quakers, who have remembered him in their histories, and relate an incident of his hard severity towards a woman of their sect, which will last longer, it is to be feared, than any record of his better deeds, although these were many." Judge William's persecuting spirit descended to his son Colonel John Hathorne (the Magistrate in Longfellow's tragedy) who "made himself so conspicuous in the martyrdom of the witches" in 1692 that "their blood may fairly be said to have left a stain upon him." This stain Hawthorne seeks to expunge in the writing of *The Scarlet Letter* and *The House*, as he had sought to expunge the whipping of the Quaker women ordered by Judge William through the writing of his story *The Gentle Boy*. "The present writer, as their representative, hereby take shame upon myself for their sakes, and pray that any curse incurred by them...may be now and henceforth removed." Hawthorne recognizes, however, that "either of these stern and black-browed Puritans would have thought it quite a sufficient retribution for his sins" that their descendant should have been a novelist. "A writer of story-books!" he imagines "one gray shadow" of his forefathers murmuring to the other: "Why, the degenerate fellow might as well have been a fiddler!" "Let them scorn me as they will," Hawthorne wryly concludes, "strong traits of their nature have intertwined themselves with mine." The Pilgrim Fathers, we have said, produced no *Pilgrim's Progress*; but through their "degenerate" descendant the Salem Fathers did produce in the end *The Scarlet Letter*, a moral fable bearing a strong relation to Bunyan's masterpiece. The relation may indeed have been too strong in one respect, if we agree with Henry James that the symbolism, so essential but so unobtrusive in Bunyan, is in Hawthorne sometimes overdone.

Between these Puritan forefathers in the seventeenth century and Nathaniel Hawthorne in the nineteenth there stood some generations of a different if related breed. Salem was for many years a noted seaport, and both the father and the grandfather of the novelist were sea-captains—of the type, we can imagine, of Melville's Captain Peleg rather than his Captain Bildad or Captain Ahab. Men of action had thus crossed the otherwise Puritan introspection of the novelist's ancestry, and though Hawthorne was anything but a man of action himself, a certain salty common sense can be found in his writings, whether he is imagining the Salem of his "steeple-crowned progenitors" or casting a satirical eye upon what he calls (as his father would have called before him) the "impractical schemes" of "the dreamy brethren of Brook Farm."

To become a captain in the merchant service requires a long apprenticeship, but no longer, Hawthorne found, than to become a novelist. He was not, like his college friend Longfellow, "a born writer", one to whom words came easily. After his return to Salem from Bowdoin College, Brunswick, Maine, where he had graduated in 1825, he spent twelve years in seclusion and growing frustration as he struggled to master his craft. His first novel, *Fanshawe* (1828), was unsuccessful, but some of the short stories which he was contributing to various magazines and literary journals in Britain and America happened to gain the favourable attention of the London *Athenaeum* and a volume of them was issued under the title *Twice-Told Tales* (1837), which had a fair measure of success. A second series followed in 1842, the year of his marriage to Sophia Peabody, younger sister of the Elizabeth who was to print Thoreau's *Civil Disobedience* essay in the first (and last) number of *Aesthetic Papers*. He had met the Peabody sisters, with Thoreau and other Transcendentalists, in 1838; he was later to join for a while the Brook Farm community at West Roxbury, near Boston, the community which was to serve as a model for that in *The Blithedale Romance*.

Brook Farm was an attempt to put into practice the Transcendentalist theories of Carlyle and Emerson and Fourier's principle of the *phalange*. It was a less individualistic experiment than Thoreau's was to be at Walden Pond: an experiment indeed in communal living, like some others of the time, a "family" in which "brothers" and "sisters" ploughed fields, milked cows and cooked their own meals, and in their leisure hours read books, held discussions and contributed to their own journal, *The Harbinger*. It was founded in 1841 by George Ripley, until then a pastor in Boston. Margaret Fuller, who seems to have been the model for Zenobia in *The Romance*, and Emerson himself, were among the frequent visitors to the community, in which Hawthorne lived for a year, doing his share of the manual work but, like his hero Miles Coverdale, not taking part a great deal in the discussions, an outside observer rather than a full member of the brotherhood.

Through the influence of the historian Bancroft, then Collector of the port of Boston, Hawthorne had served for two years in the Boston Custom House before going to Brook Farm and he was soon, as he tells us in the introductory chapter to *The Scarlet Letter*, to serve another term in the same profession, this time, 1846–50, in the Custom House of his native town. The period from leaving Brook Farm to joining the customs staff at Salem had been mainly spent in Concord, where he wrote stories for children and also the sketches and stories contributed to *The Democratic Review* of Washington which formed the volume called *Mosses from an Old Manse* (1846). The period in the Salem Custom House itself produced *The Scarlet Letter* (1850), his masterpiece as well as his most popular work, some points of which we have already noticed.

There is no doubt about the distinction of this novel. All the long years of apprenticeship had paid off: Hawthorne had now obtained his master's certificate. Customs in the commercial sense he had, of course, been dealing with, as Chaucer and Burns before him. But before Salem was a thriving seaport, it was a theocracy, with its own rigid Puritan customs. Before the jaunty caps of the sailors there had been the steeple-crowned heads of Puritan judges, whose word was law, who were in absolute authority. Woe betide any person who strayed from their narrow path of virtue, like the unfortunate Hester Prynne who is commanded to wear a scarlet letter A—standing for Adultery—upon her guilty bosom. Hawthorne's theme is sin and its consequences, but treated in an imaginative, ironical, psychological rather than theological manner, a manner that would itself have seemed sinful to his sable-hearted ancestors. We see Hester and her child Pearl as dispassionately as any Puritan judge, but the same eye of the literary artist is turned upon her accusers, upon her cowardly lover the

Reverend Arthur Dimmesdale, upon the curious and sinister figure of the wronged husband, Roger Chillingworth. There is the usual small cast, typical of Hawthorne and contrasting with Dickens: Hester, Pearl, Dimmesdale and Chillingworth make up almost the entire novel, much as Hephzibah Pyncheon, Clifford, Phoebe, Judge Pyncheon and Holgrave do *The House of the Seven Gables* and (even more deliberately) the four characters Miriam, Hilda, Kenyon and Donatello whose names constitute the titles of the first and last chapters of *The Marble Faun* and who have that novel virtually to themselves. *The Scarlet Letter* is a strange tale, a disturbing allegory: "densely dark", as Henry James well puts it, "with a single spot of vivid colour." It has engaged the attention of some of the acutest minds in American criticism, from James to F. O. Matthieson, Mark Van Doren, Lionel Trilling, Harry Levin and Marius Bewley.

The last-named critic has pointed out, in the British review *Scrutiny*, the debt to Hawthorne of Henry James himself, a point also raised by Murray Krieger, of the University of Illinois, in the Signet Classic edition of *The Marble Faun*. The debt is not to *The Scarlet Letter* nor to its happier but on the whole weaker successor, the story of the decline of the Pyncheon family, *The House of the Seven Gables* (1851); nor, of course, to the charming books for children that succeeded the Pyncheons: *The Wonder Book* (1851) and *Tanglewood Tales* (1853). The debt is to *The Blithedale Romance* (1852) and to Hawthorne's last completed novel, *The Marble Faun* (1860)—first published in Britain under the title *Transformation*—a novel which was the product of his years in Liverpool as American consul (which also produced the volume of sketches of English life and character called *Our Old Home*) and of his travels in Italy. The *Blithedale Romance*, as we know from his study of Hawthorne, interested James very much: it was the sort of treatment of New England Puritanism and Transcendental reform that he was himself to be engaged with in some of his own novels and stories, particularly, as Mr Bewley says, in *The Bostonians*. (It was widely believed in shocked Boston, despite James's fervent denials, that Miss Birdseye in that novel had been based on Hawthorne's sister-in-law Elizabeth Peabody.) While we have only to read through a few pages of *The Marble Faun* to find ourselves in that world of American tourists in European art galleries, and that "international situation", which is even more obviously James's province. Neither the *Romance* nor the *Faun* is an altogether successful novel: James improved immensely on what Hawthorne left him—even if Hawthorne improved little on that episode of the Protestant girl seeking the comfort of the Catholic confessional that he borrowed, curiously, from Charlotte Brontë's *Villette*. But the relationship means that a third outstanding merit must be added to the two we have already put to Hawthorne's account. Not only did he write, in *The Scarlet Letter* and *The House of the Seven Gables*, the masterpieces in fiction of the new New England school, while putting the Transcendentalists into perspective in *The Blithedale Romance*; but in that novel and *The Marble Faun* he was to be the link between the Puritanism of old New England and the most eminent and the most cosmopolitan of his late-nineteenth-century successors. To reach back to the Bunyan period with one hand and forward to Henry James with the other was no common achievement, as when all is said the achievement of the new New Englanders in general was no ordinary one.

IV. POE AND THE SOUTH

There was one contemporary of Emerson and Hawthorne who, though born in New England, belongs fundamentally to the South. Edgar Allan Poe (1809–49) was one of the first critics to greet Hawthorne the short-story writer, hailing him in 1842 as the finest practitioner of the art. Just as Hawthorne, as we have said—though the novelist rather than the story-writer—is the link between the Puritan seventeenth century and the cosmopolitan fiction of Henry James, so Poe links the eighteenth century, partly of Swift but more of Sterne, Beckford and the Gothic romance of Horace Walpole, not only with the detective stories of Conan Doyle and his twentieth-century followers, but with the lives and writings of the French symbolists of the nineteenth century and with the decadents of the *fin de siècle* school and their Dadaist successors of the twenties. If the "gentle reader" (as Walpole would have called him) has ever wondered why Sherlock Holmes or Philo Vance shows such a remarkable knowledge of black-letter volumes or other esoteric pursuits, or why Des Esseintes, the hero of Huysman's novel *A rebours*, sleeps by day and stays up all night, the answer will be found in the stories of Edgar Allan Poe. Seldom in the history of literature has one writer owed so much to the past, while at the same time, by his own originality, influencing so wide a variety of his successors. Baudelaire as well as Conan Doyle, Mallarmé as well as Kipling, Huysmans and Aragon as well as Jules Verne, Dostoevsky as well as H. L. Mencken's friend and colleague Willard Huntington Wright who wrote his Philo Vance detective stories under the pseudonym S. S. Van Dine.... None of these writers would have been quite the same without the example of Poe. And we cannot imagine Poe, despite his strong streak of the pioneer, without the example of Scott and Byron and those lofty heroes and heroines of Gothic romance who tickled the wit of Jane Austen but whom many readers besides Poe and Brockden Brown took more seriously.

The life of Edgar Allan Poe is a Tale of Mystery and Imagination that would have puzzled the "peculiar analytic ability" of his own character C. Auguste Dupin, a "young gentleman", it will be recalled, "of an excellent—indeed of an illustrious family." Whether Poe's brief existence had more in it of the tragic or the comic depends on the point of view. Life is "a comedy to those who think," Walpole had written, "a tragedy to those who feel." It was, on the whole, a tragedy to Poe himself, although it cannot be denied that his life had in it some elements of tragi-comic irony which if put down in a novel would be regarded as altogether too far-fetched.

The first ironic thing Poe did was to be born in Boston, Massachusetts. Any less likely birthplace for the future author of *The Fall of the House of Usher* would be hard to imagine. Nor did Poe choose his parents with quite that degree of circumspection which might have been expected of the creator of Roderick Usher, C. Auguste Dupin, William Legrand, and the rest of his heroes of ancient, if sometimes impoverished, stock. Both his parents were professional actors, and though Poe could hardly have known them personally, for he was left an orphan in early childhood, his own gifts for elocution and impersonation, as well as the histrionic nature of many of his stories and poems, must have been to some extent inherited. He was more fortunate, from his own aristocratic point of view, with his foster parents, for he was brought up by the childless wife of a wealthy Scottish merchant of Richmond, Virginia, named John Allan, whose name he afterwards inserted in his own. He was educated by Allan, first like his character William Wilson at a school in "a large Elizabethan house in a misty-looking village of England" and afterwards at Thomas Jefferson's newly-opened University of Virginia at Charlottesville. Quarreling with his guardian over some gambling debts, Poe in 1827 absconded to Boston, published there *Tamerlane and other Poems*, enlisted in the artillery in South Carolina and actually rose to be sergeant-major before Allan procured his discharge and sent him, in 1830, to West Point Military Academy. After less than a year he was dismissed for neglect of duty and giving up hope of regaining the favour of his guardian—after his first wife's death Allan married again and when he died left nothing to his adopted son whom in fact he had never legally adopted—Poe went to Baltimore to seek out his father's family. He found his aunt making a scanty living as a seamstress, supporting not only herself but her bedridden mother and her invalid daughter Virginia, the cousin whom in 1836, at the age of thirteen, Poe was to marry and who died in her early twenties.

If Poe had been idle at times—the evidence is conflicting—both at university and at West Point, from 1832 to the end of his short life he more than made up for it by his desperate and ill-paid attempts to make a living by writing, a dogged and determined effort interspersed with occasional bouts of dissipation and lordly extravagance. A third edition of his *Poems* (1831) had contained such well-known pieces as *Israfel*, *To Helen*, *The City in the Sea* and *The Lake*; but there was not much money in poetry and Poe turned largely to prose, writing stories and sketches and reviewing books—often very justly, as in the case of Hawthorne, and with a sense of the importance of literary criticism that was, as Bayard Taylor said, a new thing in American literature. Poe believed that the time was now ripe for discrimination: "We have at length arrived at that epoch when our literature may and must stand on its own merits or fall through its own defects. We have snapped asunder the leading-strings of our British Grandmamma, and, better still, we have survived," Poe continued, though the author of *Martin Chuzzlewit* may not altogether have agreed, "we have survived the first hours of our novel freedom—the first licentious hours of a hobbledehoy braggadocio and swagger. At last, then, we are in a condition to be criticized." Poe was no Dr Johnson or Matthew Arnold, but he had definite views of his own on the nature of poetry, of satire, of allegory, and besides writing well on Hawthorne, Bryant, Dickens and other American and European novelists and poets, his "tomahawk" qualities, as Bayard Taylor called them, though they were sometimes "buried" in deference to his Southern prejudices when fair poetesses of Virginia or Kentucky were in question, were on the whole a great improvement upon previous journalistic habits of indiscriminate praise.

He made many enemies by his candour, but he also had influential friends. He was encouraged and assisted by the veteran statesman William Wirt, by the wealthy Baltimore lawyer and novelist John Pendleton Kennedy—author of

Swallow Barn (1832) and *Horse-Shoe Robinson* (1835)—and by the Georgia poet
Thomas Holley Chivers. And in 1833 he won a much-needed hundred-dollar
prize for his story *Manuscript Found in a Bottle*. The first of his macabre tales,
Berenice, was accepted in 1835 by *The Southern Literary Messenger* of Richmond,
Virginia, a journal of which he became assistant editor and chief reviewer for
two years. In 1837 he was in New York, where he wrote *The Narrative of
Arthur Gordon Pym*, and then, a year later, he settled for a while in Philadelphia,
where he collected his *Tales of the Grotesque and Arabesque* (published 1840),
wrote for the *The Gentleman's Magazine*, became literary editor (1841–2) of its
successor *Graham's Magazine*, and won a second prize of a hundred dollars for
his story *The Gold-Bug*, whose scene is laid in Sullivan's Island, near Charleston,
South Carolina, where he had been stationed as an artilleryman in 1827.

In 1844 he returned to New York, where his poem *The Raven*, printed in
The Evening Mirror in 1845, became widely read and quoted on both sides of
the Atlantic, an accession of fame which had, like the poem, a background of
"unmerciful Disaster" in the slow decline and death of his "child-wife" and
cousin Virginia—wasted away by some "mysterious" disease (in her case
consumption aggravated by poverty and semi-starvation) like his heroines
Madeline of Usher, Berenice, Ligeia and Eleanora. The brief remainder of Poe's
life, a "decadent" and *fin de siècle* existence in the bustling, commercial America
of mid-century, can be as briefly told. He attempted suicide in 1848, and had
an attack of delirium tremens in June 1849. He recovered for a while in Richmond and became engaged to a lady of means, but was ill-treated—or too well
treated?—by a party of electioneering roughs on a visit to Baltimore in October
1849 and died in Baltimore hospital a few days later. The author of *Tamerlane*
had come to a Marlovian end.

Of the many stories Poe wrote, some are poor, dashed off in a hurry and now
forgotten, but most are well known through various collections usually called
Tales of Mystery and Imagination. The volume of that title in Nelson's Classics,
edited by John Buchan, contains thirteen stories; Padraic Colum's edition of
the same title in Everyman's Library contains forty-five. Sometimes Poe speaks
with the very accent of Swift, as in his story *Some Words with a Mummy*, where
his character Mr Gliddon "could not make the Egyptian comprehend the term
'politics', until he sketched upon the wall, with a bit of charcoal, a little car-
bunkle-nosed gentleman, out at elbows, standing upon a stump, with his left
leg drawn back, his right arm thrown forward, with his fist shut, the eyes
rolled up towards Heaven, and the mouth open at an angle of ninety degrees."

But more often it is a later eighteenth century that Poe reminds us of. Stories
like *The Fall of the House of Usher* sent a shiver down the spines of the nineteenth
century, but like Walpole's *Castle of Otranto*, which had the same chilling
success a hundred years before, they are hardly re-readable in the twentieth
century without an occasional smile at their absurd theatrical effects. All seems
played out on a melodramatic stage, with backcloths of sombre magnificence
and pale, Hamlet-like heroes flinging casements wide open to the storm. Poe's
mother had played Cordelia, but it is not the Elizabethan so much as the Victorian drama, or its American counterpart, of which Poe's tales of horror most
often remind us—though we must not forget that before the Civil War there

were plenty of "Gothic" mansions in Virginia and Maryland and many "Gothic" heroes too. Fortunately, that was only one side of Poe; there were other sides much more interesting and even more influential. In some stories, he anticipated the dream-psychology of Freud and the dream-literature of Kafka; in others, he invented the detective story.

To the temperament of an actor and a *raconteur* (his grandfather had come from Ulster) Poe added a life-long interest in problems of logic, cryptography and criminal detection, a bent of his mind which is seen to perfection in *The Murders in the Rue Morgue* (1841), *The Mystery of Marie Roget* (1842), *The Gold-Bug* (1843) and *The Purloined Letter* (1845). Nine-tenths of the detective fiction of the late nineteenth and early twentieth centuries stems from these stories. Sherlock Holmes is an upright British version of Poe's Dupin, retaining Dupin's scorn of the professional police and his aristocratic langour when not actually engaged upon a case. In Dupin, of course, two sides of Poe came together. He is the languid aristocrat, though of Paris not Virginia, that Poe wanted to be and had reason to believe he would actually be if and when his guardian made him his heir. At the same time, Dupin had Poe's own remarkable analytic ability, an ability seen in practice throughout his life, for instance in his accurately predicting to the astonished Dickens the whole plot of *Barnaby Rudge* from a reading of the first few chapters—as doubtless he could have predicted the outcome of *Edwin Drood* had he lived to 1870. This combination of romance with analysis led to Poe's Dupin having two distinct offshoots: to the latter we owe the long line of amateur sleuths, solving problems that baffle the professional police, created by such writers as Conan Doyle, E. C. Bentley, G. K. Chesterton, S. S. Van Dine, Ernest Bramah, and a host of others; to the former we owe, as we have noted, some characteristic traits of the French symbolist movement from Baudelaire to Mallarmé, of the *fin de siècle* aesthetes of the type of Joris-Karl Huysmans and Villiers de l'Isle-Adam, and of the Dadaists in Zürich, Paris and New York in the nineteen-twenties. Here, of course, the influence of Poe's prose is bound up with the influence of his poetry.

Longfellow, we saw, was imitated by Baudelaire in two poems in *Les Fleurs du Mal*: a rather dubious compliment, come to think of it, from the dissipated Parisian author of *Flowers of Evil* to the respectable New England author of *A Psalm of Life*, who could not have expected his footprints on the sands of time to give renewed heart to that particular shipwrecked brother. Longfellow, however, was a mere episode in Baudelaire's poetry: it was, naturally enough, not the author of *Un Psaume de Vie*—with his "L'Art est long et le Temps est fugitif..." (to quote Baudelaire's own translation in his notes to *Les Fleurs du Mal*)—but the author of *Le Palais hanté* and *A Hélene*, as forlorn and shipwrecked a brother-poet as even Baudelaire could have imagined, who became one of his lifelong passions. He came to revere Poe as the most striking example of the pure artist misunderstood and persecuted by the philistine public of the nineteenth century. Poe had been translated into Russian as early as the late eighteen-thirties and no less a novelist than Dostoevsky had written of his "fantastic realism." Now Baudelaire translated the tales—*Histoires extraordinaires* (1856–65) —into French; and Poe's critical writings, which he also translated, no less than the deliberately dream-like and overtly "musical "poetry of *Annabel Lee* and *Ulalume*, helped to create not only the *Fleurs du Mal* but the whole poetry of the Symbolist Movement from Baudelaire and Théophile Gautier to Mallarmé and Yeats. To Emerson Poe was "the jingle man", but Yeats considered him "always and for all lands a great lyric poet". In his sonnet on Poe, Mallarmé speaks of the need to give "un sens plus pur aux mots de la tribu", a phrase often quoted by Ezra Pound and which recalls Poe's own criticism of his American contemporaries Longfellow, Rodman Drake and Fitz-Greene Halleck. If Poe, who regarded "the indefinite" as "an element of the true poesis" and constantly sought "the unknown—the vague—the uncomprehended", is regarded as a greater poet in France than he commonly is either in Britain or America, it is none the less true that he gave something to French poetry which French poetry was to digest and transform and give again to Anglo-American poetry through Yeats and T. S. Eliot. In his native country, his chief follower in both poetry and criticism was his fellow-Southerner Sidney Lanier (1842–81) of Georgia, who wrote *The Science of English Verse* (1880) on Poe's principles of poetic composition and who, fittingly enough, was both a poet and a musician.

It was the *Histoires extraordinaires* which deeply affected the extraordinary histories of some of the French decadents at the end of the nineteenth century, both in their writings and in their lives, which like Poe's own were intimately connected, if not in reality, then in imagination. *The Murders in the Rue Morgue* might seem a curious place to find the genesis of Huysmans's novel *A rebours* (1884), as well as of Doyle's *A Study in Scarlet* (1888), but there is no doubt about the indebtedness of each. "It was a freak of fancy in my friend," says Poe's narrator of Dupin, "to be enamoured of the Night for her own sake; and into this *bizarrerie*, as into all his others, I quietly fell; giving myself up to his wild whims with a perfect *abandon*." The two friends accordingly stay in all day in their closely-shuttered house and when night falls they sally forth into the streets of Paris, "roaming far and wide until a late hour." Similarly, Des Esseintes, the noble hero of *A rebours*, cultivates refined and bizarre situations—*bizarrerie* for *bizarrerie*'s sake—including (of course) sleeping by day and staying up all night. The interesting pallor so engendered must have made Des Esseintes as well as Dupin even more aristocratic than before—at least in the opinion of their creators. Nobody seems to have told Poe or Huysmans or Villiers de l'Isle-Adam (the hero of whose *Axel* has "a paleness almost radiant") that many of the *hoi polloi*—bakers, printers, nurses, transport workers, and others—have frequently to sleep by day and stay up all night, too, so there does not seem anything particularly aristocratic about it.

It is, none the less, the aristocratic illusion (and the aristocratic element of the dilettante) that associates the Boston-born Poe with the literature of his adopted State of Virginia and with the South generally. Perhaps "illusion" is too strong a word, though it was implied at least in this very connection by Mark Twain, when in a celebrated chapter of his *Life on the Mississippi* (1883), he blamed the romances of Walter Scott for perpetuating the bogus "cavalier" elements in Southern speech, Southern customs, Southern literature. Twain was writing in the generation after Poe's, and in a polemical vein, but he was, like Lincoln, a Southerner (or South-Westerner) himself and there does appear to be something in his suggestion that but for this imitation Scott-land in the Southern States, the South could have produced, or could have continued to produce, as many notable writers as the North. "Cavalier ideals" went back, of course, to the original Royalist settlers in Virginia, Maryland and the Carolinas in the seventeenth century, whose impressive culture could still be seen, up to and after the Revolution, in the lives and writings of such Southerners as Byrd, Jefferson, John Taylor, John Randolph, and Poe's patron William Wirt. Charleston could boast the oldest theatre in the country, where Otway's *The Orphan* was performed in 1736, and many of the old Southern gentry were not only chivalrous in their dealings with their slaves, compared with the brutality of their successors which so shocked foreign observers like Dickens, but were enthusiastic patrons of literature, music and painting. The fault lay in the perpetuation of the "ideal" after the reality had disappeared, though one must not withhold all sympathy from a defeated cause and can readily understand how the South, after the Civil War, tended to turn from the shabby realities of the present to the cultural glories of the past. Mark Twain singled out, as exceptions to the general nostalgic rule—though only partial exceptions, as we shall see—the novelist George Washington Cable and the creator of "Uncle Remus", Joel Chandler Harris; and referred to "three or four widely known literary names" (presumably Poe, Cable, Harris and himself) who had either been born in the South or were connected with it. But "the South ought to have a dozen or two—and will have them when Sir Walter's time is out."

This prophecy was to come true during the twentieth century, though presumably due to other factors besides a decline in the popularity of *Ivanhoe* among Kentucky colonels and Virginian merchant knights. In the century of Faulkner, James Branch Cabell, Tennessee Williams, Edgar Lee Masters, O. Henry, Thomas Wolfe, Erskine Caldwell, H. L. Davis, Allen Tate, Robert Penn Warren, Carson McCullers, and numerous other Southern-born writers of distinction in various fields, the South became as well represented as the North in post-Twain American literature. But in the nineteenth century Poe and (in the following generation) Mark Twain himself—who was as much a Westerner as a Southerner—do tend to stand out, partly at any rate because of the comparative mediocrity of their nearest Southern rivals. Poe died in early middle age, perhaps before he had accomplished all that he could have accomplished; and the Maryland poet Edward Coote Pinkney, whom he quotes at length in his essay *The Poetic Principle*, died (like Joseph Rodman Drake of New York) at the very early age of twenty-five. We must pass over here the various Southern belles or ducklings whom Poe's Virginian chivalry led him to glorify as swans. But among their male rivals, both in Poe's generation and Mark Twain's, there were several writers of considerable talent, one or two of whom are still highly esteemed.

Of these, the most popular, both in the North and in the South, both in America and Britain, was Joel Chandler Harris (1848–1908), the Georgia-born printer and journalist whose character "Uncle Remus" first appeared in the pages of *The Atlanta Constitution* in 1879. In book form, *Uncle Remus: His Songs and his Sayings* (1880)—with its successors *Nights with Uncle Remus, Uncle Remus and His Friends*, etc.—became one of the best sellers of the late nineteenth century and its author was described by Mark Twain, a connoisseur of American idiom, as "the only master" of Negro dialect. Plantation dialect had been written down before, of course, in Poe's *Gold-Bug*, Judge Longstreet's *Georgia Scenes* (1835) and other stories and sketches by Southern writers, but mostly *de haut en bas*, in a spirit of kindly humour or condescension. Chandler Harris, a shy genius like that other children's favourite Lewis Carroll, was the first white writer to understand the "humour of the underman", to listen to and remember and retell the stories (some of them with a long African ancestry; see p. 933 below) which old Negroes like "Uncle Remus" used solemnly to recount to their assembled "nephews", black and white, while he was himself a child just before the Civil War: stories about Brer Rabbit and other talking animals whose stratagems enabled them to survive in a hostile world, stories whose human application was clear to the more sensitive adult reader. There is much more to *Uncle Remus*, as there is much more to *Alice*, than meets the innocent eye. H. L. Mencken, indeed, quoting in his second series of *Prejudices* (1920) "the last bard of Dixie", J. Gordon Coogler:

> Alas, for the South! Her books have grown fewer—
> She never was much given to litera-ture...

refers to a Georgian who "once upon a time" published some books "that attracted notice." But "immediately it turned out that he was little more than an amanuensis for the local blacks—that his works were really the products, not of white Georgia, but of black Georgia." A point of view which, despite its characteristic polemical nature, Harris would have been the first to admit had a core of truth in it. (While he was editing his *Uncle Remus's Magazine*, 1900–8, the Negro author Dr William DuBois, who wrote *The Souls of Black Folk*, 1903, etc., was teaching economics and history at Atlanta University, 1896–1910.)

At the same time, Harris would not have agreed with Mencken—a next-generation Southerner, born of German stock at Baltimore in 1880—that when he was writing "*as* a white man, he swiftly subsided into the fifth rank." The creator of "Uncle Remus" cannot really be considered in simple, political terms: he saluted the Negro, particularly the Negro slave of the old regime, for his humour and his courage, but he respected some of the white masters, too, and was by no means enamoured of the post-war situation in the South, the rule of the Yankees and the carpet-baggers. His policy as editor under Henry Grady on *The Atlanta Constitution* was to reconcile not only the interests, but the feelings, of the South and the North. Primarily a journalist as he was, Harris shared some of Mark Twain's artistic sensibility: he realized, no less than the author of *Huckleberry Finn* and *Pudd'nhead Wilson*, that the Southern way of life was no simple paradox, able to be resolved immediately by political action.

The writer whom Mark Twain coupled with Harris as one of the "very few Southern authors who do not write in the Southern style"—that is to say, in the "old inflated style" which Twain was attacking—was George Washington Cable (1844–1925), who used the Creole dialect in his novels and stories with as much care as his friend Harris used the dialect of the Georgian plantations. (As, indeed, Mark Twain used in *Huckleberry Finn*, as he tells us in a foreword,

"the Missouri negro dialect, the extremest form of the backwoods South-
Western dialect, the ordinary 'Pike-Country' dialect, and four modified
varieties of this last"; and as minor Southern writers like Thomas Nelson Page
and Richard Malcolm Johnstone were careful to distinguish Southern Negro
speech from Eastern Virginian and Eastern Virginian from Middle Georgian.)
Born in New Orleans, Cable's first Creole sketches appeared in *Scribner's
Magazine* in 1873 and were later collected and developed in *Old Creole Days*
(1879), the first of a series of stories and novels in which he goes back, like
Harris and Twain, to the pre-Civil-War period of his boyhood, or occasionally,
as in *The Grandissimes* (1880)—a novel about the period 1800–20 when the
Louisiana territories were bought from Napoleon and Florida from Spain—to
the days of his grandfather's boyhood, more in the spirit of Cooper, "the
American Scott" (as we have seen) in an unpejorative sense. A grand-niece of
Cooper, Constance Fenimore Woolson (1840–94), the subject of one of Henry
James's *Partial Portraits*, went to live in the South from her native New Hampshire and wrote some of her best stories about post-Civil-War life in Florida
and South Carolina.

With writers like Harris and Cable, the South came of age again, beginning
to realize that it had no need, with all its colourful past and present—however
drab the superficial present in comparison with the nostalgic past—to borrow
a brush from the medieval Scott or the Byron of *Childe Harold*. Poe's kindly
Baltimore patron John Pendleton Kennedy (1795–1870), one of whose numerous
"Virginian cousins" was the John Esten Cooke who wrote the famous Southern
romance *The Virginia Comedians* (1854), helped Thackeray in the American
chapters of *The Virginians*, a novel heavily indebted to the view of Southern life
which Mark Twain was to attack. But other writers from the South, from the
time of Harris of Georgia and James Lane Allen of Kentucky up to the time of
Winston Churchill (1871–1947) of Missouri—almost the exact contemporary
of his famous British namesake—did sometimes attempt to learn the lesson of
the *Leather-Stocking Tales* and temper their Southern romanticism with comparatively sober realism. "Ship me somewheres South of Harpers," a Southern
Kipling might have written, "where the best is like the worst"—as in the novels
of William Gilmore Simms (1806–70), son of a poor Irish storekeeper in
Charleston, South Carolina, whose idealizations of the Southern aristocracy
are literally bound up with his vigorous and realistic observations of a wide
variety of more humble life in the Carolinas, Tennessee, Kentucky, West
Virginia, Alabama and Mississippi. Some of Simms was the kind of artificial
romance Twain was attacking; but Cable, one of the writers he singled out for
praise, was a friend of the Charleston novelist and wrote an admirable life of
him. "Mr Simms has abundant faults," said Poe, but "he has more vigour,
more imagination, more movement, and more general capacity than all our
novelists (save Cooper) combined."

Twain did not like Cooper, either, perhaps because he associated him, in a
bad sense, with the influence of his *bête noire* Sir Walter and that extensive feudal
territory called Scott-land which was found, to his disgust, on both sides of the
Atlantic. Disagreeing with President Lincoln, who whimsically credited the
Civil War to the authoress of *Uncle Tom's Cabin*—"So you're the little woman

who made the book that made the great war"—the creator of Huck and Jim blamed the author of *Waverley* for it. "It seems a little harsh towards a dead man to say that we never should have had any war but for Sir Walter; and yet something of a plausible argument might, perhaps, be made in support of that wild proposition. The Southerner of the American Revolution owned slaves; so did the Southerner of the Civil War; but the former resembles the latter as an Englishman resembles a Frenchman. The change of character can be traced rather more easily to Sir Walter's influence than to that of any other thing or person."

More than a century after Gettysburg, this still remains a debateable point. Certainly Jefferson shared Mark Twain's dislike of the feudal elements in Scott and his admiration for *Don Quixote* for its debunking of chivalry. But the difference between the old agrarian order of Jefferson's time and the plantation economy which Twain and Harris knew in boyhood cannot be estimated primarily in literary terms, even with a writer so popular as Scott was in the South and who inspired the duels and tournaments which had long died out in Britain. The "cotton snobs", the *nouveau-riche* cotton planters who bred slaves for the market and even re-opened the long-abandoned slave trade, had succeeded the comparatively liberal regime of Jefferson's time, as Calvinism, which was giving place to Unitarianism in New England, had largely succeeded in the South to the old aristocratic Deism and free-thought. Ministers of religion began to cite the Scriptures in support of slavery, as university professors began to cite the classics. Scott was possibly less important than Carlyle, for while the younger Carlyle of *Sartor Resartus*, the friend and inspirer of Dickens, was the writer loved in New England, the more authoritarian Carlyle of *Frederick the Great* was the man esteemed and quoted in the South.

At the same time, as Herman Melville wisely said, "this thing"—slavery—"was planted in their midst"; the Southern whites were the "fated inheritors", not the originators, of the evil—however much they are to be blamed for its extension. Economics, not literature, was the over-riding factor. The Southern literary myth, from the time of Kennedy, Cooke, Simms and William A. Caruthers to the time of Margaret Mitchell's *Gone With the Wind*, was a bold front, consciously or unconsciously intended to cover up some pretty shabby realities. There is a valid comparison with the myth of "Merrie England" so obstinately fertile in Britain from Elizabethan times up to the times of Morris and Chesterton, and with the more superficial aspects of the literature of the British Empire in the late nineteenth century. Poe and Kipling are brothers "under the skin." It is perhaps best to follow Whitman and Melville, those haters of slavery, in their valiant attempt, after the Civil War, to understand, not simply to condemn, the South. We need, in fact, to show greater understanding of the complicated Southern position, where economic factors shade into social, social into literary and religious, than Poe showed of the ancient world of philosophy and slavery, of civilization and crucifixion, when he lamented "the glory that was Greece" and "the grandeur that was Rome."

V. WHITMAN, MELVILLE AND THE CIVIL WAR

The Civil War of 1861–5 was not only the great dividing line in American history, it can also be considered, with a fair approximation to the truth, the great divide in American literature. "The worlds before and after the Deluge," wrote the poet and critic Edmund Clarence Stedman in 1873, "were not more different than our republics of letters before and after the late war." Southern writers like Simms seemed irretrievably "pre-war" to the literary tastes of the sixties and seventies, and some of the New England writers like Longfellow began to share in their eclipse. Emerson as well as Poe belonged now to the old order; Whitman as well as Mark Twain belonged to the new. The New York of Whitman was, of course, a new New York well before the Civil War: the commercial capital of the nation began to supersede Boston as the literary capital as early as the fifties, as Boston had begun to supersede the old New York of Irving and Cooper twenty years before that. A certain degree of continuity nevertheless obtained. Emerson, as we have seen, had been among the first to salute the arrival of the poet of *Leaves of Grass* in 1855, the Brahmin of Brahmins heralding "the bard of American democracy." And there were other New England "harbingers" who, as early as the late forties, began to take a hand in the new order itself. When Brook Farm was disbanded in 1847, its founder George Ripley, continuing *The Harbinger* in New York till 1849, had joined the staff of *The New York Tribune* under Horace Greeley and had helped, with Margaret Fuller, George Curtis, Charles Dana and other former Transcendentalists, Brook Farmers and *Harbinger* contributors, to give *The Tribune* its great importance and influence during the war, when it was one of the most zealous supporters of the Union cause against the eleven Confederate States of the South. Dana was to become assistant Secretary of War under Lincoln and, after the war, the editor and part owner of *The New York Sun*. When Lincoln was assassinated in 1865—by a fanatical actor named John Wilkes Booth who might have stepped out of a story by Edgar Allan Poe—Whitman lamented his "Captain" in a poem read and admired (and wept over) all over the world. But Whitman had an earlier skipper: he described Emerson as "the original true Captain" who had discovered the shores of "the moral American continent." While editor of *The Brooklyn Eagle* in the forties, the young Whitman had reprinted some of Margaret Fuller's essays from *The Tribune*. On the other side, no less a New Englander than Thoreau, the Hermit of Concord, described the *Leaves of Grass* as a "trumpet-note ringing through the American camp"—a figure of speech that was later to have a more literal meaning.

One of the features of the new literary world was the prominent place given in it to newspapers and newspapermen, both journalists and printers. Where Boston, Concord and West Roxbury had been mostly clerical or donnish in background, the New York of Whitman and Melville, and indeed the greater part of the new literary America in general, tended to have printers' ink upon their fingers at an early age. An amazing number of writers contemporary with Whitman worked for a time, as Whitman did himself, in printing shops. They include, besides Whitman in New York, such future poets, novelists and critics as Stedman in Connecticut, Bayard Taylor in Pennsylvania, Mark Twain in Missouri, Bret Harte and Henry George in California, Richard Watson Gilder in New Jersey, Horace Greeley in Vermont, "Uncle Remus" Harris in Georgia, William Dean Howells in Ohio, Artemus Ward in Massachusetts, Edward Eggleston and Ambrose Bierce in Indiana... It was a natural step from composition in the printing sense to composition in the literary, from setting up other people's words to writing your own, as natural a step as that taken in New England when preachers descended from the pulpit to become lecturers at the lyceum. It was natural, too, that a literary world largely composed of journalists and ex-journalists should have succeeded a literary world of lecturers and scholars after a civil war in which newspaper correspondents like the poet Stedman of *The New York World* had become almost as important as soldiers. There was both gain and loss, as in the war itself. We cannot imagine Emerson, Hawthorne or Poe in the new order; we cannot imagine Whitman or Mark Twain, or even Melville, in the old. When they salute each other, as they sometimes did, it is over an unbridgeable gulf.

Whitman and Melville... They were born in the same year, both of Dutch-British ancestry, one in New York itself, the other thirty miles away on Long Island. They spent much of their lives in their native or neighbouring city and died within a year of each other. They shared the same love of the sea, the same admiration for what the aristocratic Melville called "the kingly commons" and what the carpenter's son Whitman called the "nobility" of ordinary people. They both wrote memorably of the Civil War and its aftermath, particularly of the fundamental issues involved. They even had the same powerful physique and much the same preference for the simple life over the sophisticated. One would have thought they must have spent much of their time in each other's company. Yet there is no record of their ever having met, except in the columns of *The Brooklyn Eagle* when Whitman reviewed *Typee* and *Omoo*. They must have passed each other in the New York streets as ships pass in the night. Melville knew Hawthorne, Whitman Hawthorne's friend Longfellow, but the author of *Moby-Dick* knew not, apparently, the author of *Leaves of Grass*. It is as if Shakespeare and Ben Jonson, or Dickens and Thackeray, had been strangers all their lives in literary London. In that bustling city of New York, with its bohemian and journalistic flavour, there was apparently no Horace Greeley, Bayard Taylor or other notability of the time to introduce Ishmael to the Democratic Bard or the Democratic Bard to Ishmael. "Herman, I want you to meet Mr Whitman"; "Walt, do you happen to know Mr Melville?" It should all have been so simple, yet the introduction, apparently, never took place. The poet who saw in *Salut au Monde* "the whale-crews of the South Pacific and the North Atlantic" never saw the whaler who wrote of Captain Ahab and of his chase in the "Pequod" of the mightiest Leviathan of them all. Despite the temptation, therefore, to treat of Whitman and Melville together, we shall have to take them separately, as they lived. They are great enough, when all fair criticisms have been made of them—and they are open to criticism on several accounts—to stand on their own feet. Either, it will be agreed, would have made the New York of the fifties and after one of the principal stepping-stones in the progress of American literature.

Walt Whitman (1819–92) was born at West Hills on the north shore of Long Island, about thirty miles from New York, the family moving to Brooklyn when the future poet was four years old. His father, who named two of his other sons Thomas Jefferson and Andrew Jackson, was a radical-minded carpenter from New England who had known Paine and who subscribed to *The Free Inquirer*, edited by Robert Owen's son Robert Dale Owen who had emigrated from Glasgow to help in the New Harmony community in Indiana. Whitman's mother was of Dutch Quaker ancestry, and he felt he owed more to her than to anyone else. If his lifelong radical convictions came from his father, and from the books on his father's shelf, perhaps indeed it was a poet's version of the Quaker "inner light" that led Whitman in the *Leaves of Grass* to abandon most of the conventional themes and all the conventional measures which had served earlier poets.

Though he said he preferred "loafing and writing poems", he could have claimed, with Cobbett, that he did not remember a time when he was not earning his own living. Errand-boy, clerk, printer, teacher in country schools, then in 1846 editor of *The Brooklyn Eagle*. He wrote stories "with a moral" for the magazines, spoke at meetings, and joined William Cullen Bryant of *The Evening Post*, not only in most of the reforms advocated by that veteran nature poet, but in rambles through the countryside around Brooklyn. Whitman himself was country-bred, but he had early made the acquaintance of the busy streets of New York: he was a "lover of populous pavements", as he puts it in the autobiographical poem *Starting from Paumanok*—"Paumanok" being the Indian name for Long Island, as "Mannahatta" for Manhattan, "city of ships, my city." Thus he was well fitted, from childhood, for his life's work in poetry, to write of America and Americans, of ploughmen, miners, mechanics, sailors, ironworkers, clerks, shipbuilders, "the country boy", "the athletic American matron", poems "of occupations" addressed to "Male and Female!... American masses!...Workmen and Workwomen!" And he became even more fitted when in 1848 he visited the South and the West, served for a while on *The New Orleans Crescent* and picked up the French words and phrases he was afterwards so fond of using—not always correctly, as when in *Night and Death* he walks by himself on the prairie after supper and exclaims: "How plenteous! How spiritual! How *résumé!*"

Whitman next followed his father's business of carpenter and builder at Brooklyn, and then in 1862, after the battles of Bull Run, volunteered to nurse the Union wounded in the field, at the same time acting as correspondent for *The New York Times*. One of his brothers, Lieutenant-Colonel George Whitman of the 51st New York Veterans, was wounded at Fredericksburg in the December of that year, and the poet of *Drum-Taps* was soon nursing him and his fellow-soldiers, both Union and Confederate, both Northerner and Southerner, in the hospital at Washington. It is said that by the end of the war in 1865 Whitman had personally ministered to more than 100,000 men from all parts of the United States, as he himself describes in poems—among his best and most thoughtful work—like *The Wounded*, *A Sight in Camp*, *A Grave*, *The Dresser*, *A Letter from Camp* and *Hymn of Dead Soldiers*. His experiences during the war aged Whitman—he caught an illness on duty which disabled him for six months—but they made him a more mature, less innocently optimistic, writer. He received a clerkship in the Department of the Interior at Washington at the end of the war, but was dismissed when it was learnt that he was the author of "an indecent book" called *Leaves of Grass*—whose outspokenness shocked not only government officials. In 1873 Whitman left Washington for Camden, New Jersey, where he lived, often in poverty, till his death nearly twenty years later. His Canadian friend, the physician R. M. Bucke, wrote his biography (1883) with his assistance, while a younger disciple Horace Traubel made extensive notes of his conversation for the three volumes of *With Walt Whitman in Camden* (1906–14).

The first edition of *Leaves of Grass* (1855), with its well-known portrait of the poet in his slouch hat and open-necked shirt, was set up by Whitman himself on a press he had borrowed from some printer friends. This recalls Blake in its combination of art and craft, and the poems themselves, particularly the passages with Biblical overtones, remind us sometimes of the Prophetic Books. There is no doubt, however, about Whitman's originality: both his strength and his weakness spring fundamentally from the fact that he was a new voice, speaking in a new idiom of "immediate days", "current America". George Santayana, comparing him with Browning in the essay "The Poetry of Barbarism" in *Interpretations of Poetry and Religion* (1900), criticizes, fairly enough, his "abundance of detail without organization" and his "wealth of perception without intelligence" which spoil his "wonderful gift of graphic characterization" and "occasional rare grandeur of diction." It must be admitted that Whitman's lists of cities, States, rivers, jobs tend to become as boring as his frequent exclamation marks. (His early admirer Emerson complained that he had "expected him to make the songs of the nation but he seems content to make the inventories".) But it is not much use contrasting him (as Santayana tends to do) with Homer or Dante or any of the "classics". Homer, Dante and Shakespeare Whitman had declaimed to the seagulls on the then lonely beaches of Coney Island, but when he came to write poetry himself he knew he must abandon classical models and speak in new measures of "spar-makers in the spar-yard" and the "brisk short crackle of the steel driven slantingly into the pine." In his natural exuberance at having found a new field for poetry, he ploughed too hard and too often—and, in the opinion of his more Puritan contemporaries, unearthed a good deal that would have been better covered up. He was more appreciated, at first, in Britain than in his native country which he had done so much to exalt. An edition of *Poems by Walt Whitman*, selected and edited by William Michael Rossetti, dedicated to William Bell Scott, and with epigraphs from Swedenborg, Carlyle and Robespierre, was published in London in 1868 and had a great success, not only with the Pre-Raphaelites and their followers. The applause in Britain, however, was not entirely uncritical. In his Prefatory Notice Rossetti quotes "a friend" (probably Swinburne) who, while a great admirer of Whitman, complains justly of his "bluster": "He is in part certainly the poet of democracy; but not wholly, *because* he tries so openly to be, and asserts so violently that he is—always as if he was fighting the case out on a platform." This acute criticism applies particularly to some of the original *Leaves of Grass* and to the poems which Rossetti named "Chants Democratic", far less so, however, to the war poems *Drum-Taps* which Whitman added to the 1867 edition of the *Leaves* and which Rossetti also included in his London edition. Whitman continued to revise and embellish his *Leaves* till the final edition of 1891-2. The original ninety-four pages had grown to over four hundred.

In his dedicatory address at Gettysburg on 19 November 1863, Abraham Lincoln—like Whitman, the son of a carpenter—reaffirmed the faith of Jefferson that "government of the people, by the people, for the people, shall not perish from the earth." Fittingly enough, for the author of *O Captain! My Captain!* and *President Lincoln's Funeral Hymn*—the fine poem beginning "When lilacs last in the door-yard bloomed"—that was also the overriding theme of Whitman's principal prose work, *Democratic Vistas* (1871), where the poet of democracy tried to come to terms with the corrupt post-war world of Jay Gould, Daniel Drew and other financiers whose activities were shortly to inspire *The Gilded Age: A Tale of Today* (1873), the novel in which Mark Twain collaborated with Charles Dudley Warner of *The Hartford Courant*. The poet of *Leaves of Grass*—"On no occasion did he laugh," remembered Moncure Conway, "nor indeed did I ever see him smile"—could not take Twain's broadly humorous view. But he realized, as much as Twain and Warner, that the post-war, post-Lincoln decade was one of political opportunism and business greed, where poverty was growing side by side with wealth. He wrote *Democratic Vistas* to "admit and face these dangers", but he faced them in the spirit of "father Abraham" and of those earlier "founding fathers", Jefferson and Paine, who had meant so much both to Lincoln and himself. He kept his faith in America, in the fundamental decency of ordinary people; he welcomed the ever-increasing waves of immigrants, feeling that the continental republic, now stretching from coast to coast—and from 1869 linked by railroad from New York to San Francisco—had room for all races, could absorb all elements. If he was, in the short run, more naïve than Twain—or Melville—his was the longer view that had eventually its justification. For the "dreadful decade" of the seventies was later to be looked back upon with the national shame it deserved, and some at any rate of Whitman's optimistic prophecies were to come true.

In her essay *American Literature* (1846), Margaret Fuller, Marchioness Ossoli—who four years later was to be drowned with her husband and child not far from Whitman's Long Island—foretold the arrival of a mighty genius in the Western world. Whether Whitman was that genius depends on our estimate of his importance in the literature of the nineteenth century. He is almost certainly the greatest American poet of the century: only Emerson, Poe and Emily Dickinson have a possible claim to superiority, and of these Emerson and Poe are probably greater in their prose writings than in their verse. Where Bryant, Longfellow, Whittier, Holmes and Lowell—not to mention such admirable minor poets as those Civil War opponents Julia Ward Howe of the *Battle-Hymn of the Republic* and Henry Timrod of the *Ode in Magnolia Cemetery*—where such poets are mostly conventional in theme and treatment, Whitman is nothing if not original. And where they lack successors of any great importance, Whitman's influence was great on some of the American poets of the twentieth century like Sandburg and Lindsay, as on poets in Australia and Africa, and is seen even where it has been denied, for instance in T. S. Eliot, who thinks

Whitman was "a great prose writer" who was mistaken in asserting that "his great prose was a new form of verse", but whose own "hermit-thrush" lines in *The Waste Land* are unconsciously indebted to the "shy and hidden bird... solitary the thrush, the hermit withdrawn..." in the *Lincoln Hymn*. Most of Santayana's criticisms can be accepted, provided we do not lose sight of Santayana's praise.

When the British critic Robert Buchanan visited Whitman at Camden in 1885, he tried to see Melville as well, for he agreed with the poet James Thomson that the two Americans had much in common. But though he knew that Melville was somewhere in New York, no one he asked "seemed to know anything of the one great imaginative writer fit to stand shoulder to shoulder with Whitman on this continent." Buchanan had to leave for home without having had the satisfaction of meeting the author of *Moby-Dick*.

Forty years before there would have been no such difficulty. For Melville was world famous as the author of *Typee* (1846) and *Omoo* (1847), as the sailor who had "lived among the cannibals", when Whitman was hardly known at all beyond limited circles in Brooklyn and New York. The history of Melville's reputation is one of the most curious in American literature, even more curious in some respects than Thoreau's or Emily Dickinson's. Early fame, followed by relative indifference—and this at a time when he had published his masterpiece *Moby-Dick*—followed by almost complete obscurity so far as New York was concerned, though London, as we have seen, was more appreciative. This obscurity lasted until his death and for many years afterwards: Henry James does not mention him in his study of Hawthorne, although he must have known that the two novelists were personal friends and were neighbours for a time in the Berkshire Hills. Then, in the nineteen-twenties, there was a revival of interest both in America and Britain: *Moby-Dick* was added to the World's Classics series in 1920, with a highly appreciative introduction by Viola Meynell; Professor Raymond Weaver published the first full-length American study, *Herman Melville, Mariner and Mystic* (1921); Princeton University published some previously uncollected material in *The Apple-tree Table, and Other Sketches* (1922); *Billy Budd*, that brief masterpiece written during the last few months of Melville's life in 1891, was added with various other stories, essays, reviews and poems to the Standard Edition in sixteen volumes (1922–4); and when Morley's "English Men of Letters" series was continued by Messrs Macmillan in 1926, under the general editorship of J. C. Squire, *Herman Melville* by John Freeman was the opening—and excellent—volume. Since the twenties, *Moby-Dick* and Melville in general have engaged the most serious attention of many of the most distinguished critical minds in America and Europe, and in the operatic version (1951) by the British composer Benjamin Britten *Billy Budd* has had a new lease of life. "Mariner and Mystic": the emphasis now lies on the latter; Melville is no longer world famous as the sailor who had lived among the cannibals, still less as the boys' author of emasculated versions of *Typee* and *Omoo*—versions, however, which were admirable for their purpose and where many of us first made the acquaintance of the author of *Moby-Dick*.

Herman Melville (1819–91) was born in New York, as we have noted, and was, like Whitman, of mixed Dutch-British origin—like so many New Yorkers and Long Islanders—but, unlike Whitman, of aristocratic or near-aristocratic stock on both sides. His father was descended from a John Melville of Carnbee who had been knighted by James VI of Scotland and, more immediately, from an Allan Melville, son of a Scots clergyman, who had emigrated from Fife in 1748 and become a merchant at Boston. Melville's mother was the daughter of General Gansevoort, a hero of the War of Independence whose services were officially honoured by Congress. The novelist inherited the robust Gansevoort physique, but not much else; for his father's business affairs did not prosper and when he died in 1832, he left his widow and eight children in comparative penury—as Melville records in that curious blend of fiction and autobiography *Redburn: His First Voyage, being the Sailor-boy Confessions and Reminiscences of the Son-of-a-Gentleman in the Merchant Service* (1849). We cannot take this book *au pied de la lettre*, any more than some of Whitman's semi-autobiographical poems like *A Word out of the Sea* or *Longings for Home*. The truth in Melville, as in Whitman, is as often symbolic as literal. There is no doubt, however, that Melville in 1837, at the age of eighteen, perhaps inspired by the "wonderful Arabian traveller" (as he calls him) John Lloyd Stephens, made his first voyage from New York to Liverpool on the "St Lawrence" with a cargo of cotton from the Southern plantations to the Lancashire mills; and there is no doubt that he shipped as a common sailor, like Fenimore Cooper in 1806 after his expulsion from Yale and like R. H. Dana in 1835 who was to describe his voyage round Cape Horn in his famous book *Two Years before the Mast* (1840). It was not the mast which troubled the robust Melville, though the life of a green apprentice sailor, scarcely more than a cabin-boy, was naturally a hard one; it was the very mixed society of the gloomy forecastle that shocked his sensitive soul, as it was again to be shocked when he saw the miserable slums of Liverpool. Cockroaches, rats, syphilis (not to mention robbery and murder) throve in the forecastle of the "St Lawrence", as in some other ships in which the now hardened Melville was to serve. None of these things had much entered the experience of Emerson or Longfellow, or even of Thoreau or Whitman; but Melville saw the worst early in life and was able to value more strongly the contrasting virtue of a Jack Chase, the hero of *White Jacket*, or of some of the Polynesians he was to praise in *Typee*.

On his return to America, Melville taught for a while in country schools, like Whitman, but in 1841 sailed for the South Seas on the whaler "Acushnet" from New Bedford, Massachusetts: the whale-fishery centre so vividly described in *Moby-Dick*. After fifteen months of hardship, where the tyranny of the captain was as unbearable as the food, Melville deserted while the ship lay off the chief port of the Marquesas and escaped inland with his shipmate Richard Tobias Greene (afterwards an editor in Buffalo), the "Toby" of *Typee*. His treatment by the cannibals he described as "an indulgent captivity"—though he was naturally rather afraid he was being kept in good condition for a certain purpose —but it was ended when he was taken off Typee by an Australian whaler, in which he served in her voyage to Tahiti, as described in *Omoo*. From Tahiti, or perhaps from Honolulu—accounts differ—Melville then joined the crew of an American warship, the "United States", the "Neversink" of *White Jacket* (1850), where he had as shipmate the original of the man to whom he was to dedicate *Billy Budd* in the closing months of his life: "Jack Chase, Englishman, wherever that great heart may now be, here on earth or harboured in paradise."

There was much to bear on the "United States", particularly the naval practice of flogging for trivial offences which Dana had brought to the notice of the public in *Two Years before the Mast*. Melville's own descriptions of the practice in *White Jacket*—where Jack Chase's intervention with the well-named Captain Claret saves the narrator from being one of the victims—had a great influence in the eventual abolition of corporal punishment in the American Navy.

Melville returned home in 1844. He was still only twenty-five, but he had packed a life-time of varied experience into his last seven years, an experience he was to draw upon for his writing during the long remainder of his life, whether in fictionalized autobiography like *White Jacket* or in that master-work of the imagination, *Moby-Dick*. The first two books he wrote were, as we have noted, semi-fictional accounts of his adventures in the South Seas. The basis in both books was fact; the details were sometimes coloured by the novelist's imagination. *Typee* (dedicated to Melville's future father-in-law Justice Shaw of Massachusetts) was published in London in 1846 in Murray's "Colonial and Home Library", publication in New York preceding it the same year. With its sequel of the year after, *Omoo*, it received a mixed reception in both countries, praise being unstinted as regards the narrative, but deep offence being given in some quarters because of Melville's criticism of the ill-effects of Christian missionaries and other well-meaning persons on the unfortunate South Sea islanders. In the twentieth century, after the investigations of anthropologists like W. H. R. Rivers, author of *The History of Melanesian Society* (1915), and Margaret Mead, author of *Coming of Age in Samoa* (1928), no intelligent reader would have found fault with Melville's criticisms. But this was 1846–7, when it was almost universally taken for granted that the effects of western civilization upon redskins and brownskins (not to mention blackskins) could be nothing but good ones. That such people as inhabited Typee could have a culture that was, on some points, superior to the practice, if not the ideal, of civilized countries like France and the United States was considered preposterous. And this indignant reaction had two contrasting results on Melville's future work and reputation.

First, *Typee* itself was reissued in 1849 in an emasculated version which cut out most of the author's criticisms. And this version, being considered more suitable for young people, is the one most of us have read in youth and was indeed reprinted many times both in Britain and America, the full text not being available again till the collected edition of 1922. Secondly, Melville was provoked to write *Mardi: And a Voyage Thither* (1849), a satiric romance owing something to Swift and Rabelais where the author, under a thin Polynesian disguise, is able to scoff at the hell-fire preaching of the missionaries and to forecast truly that the savannahs of the Southern States "may yet prove battlefields." It was no accident, either, that among the characters of *Moby-Dick* were to be the dignified and courteous cannibal Queequeg and the gigantic negro Daggoo, of such a size that "a white man standing before him seemed a white flag come to beg truce of a fortress."

The history of *Moby-Dick* itself—*Moby-Dick; or The Whale* (1851)—is very interesting. Melville's original plan seems to have envisaged a tolerably straightforward narrative, drawing to a large extent on his personal experiences in the "Acushnet". What created the "whale of a book" we know, with all its digressive "by-products", from this simple tale of adventure, was in the first place the intensive reading Melville is known to have indulged in about this time—he re-read Shakespeare and also the masters of digression like Rabelais, Burton, Sterne, De Quincey—and secondly his meeting with Hawthorne, who was living at Lenox in the Berkshire Hills while Melville was at Pittsfield near by. Until then Melville had not mixed a great deal with his fellow American writers, apart from the circle of his family friends Evert and George Duyckinck, for whose New York weekly journal *The Literary World* he had reviewed Hawthorne's *Mosses* and *Scarlet Letter* and Parkman's *Oregon Trail*. Hawthorne himself had reviewed *Typee* in *The Salem Advertiser* and had read Melville's later works. So the two writers met in a spirit of cordial admiration for each other's very different genius. They had something in common in their connection with the sea, but Hawthorne the former customs official, the son and grandson of Salem-based mariners, was "a sadder and a wiser man" than the younger Melville, whose early experiences of hardship and squalor on board ship seem not yet to have fundamentally affected his more buoyant nature. He could, however, respond to the "great power of blackness" in Hawthorne which he had noted when reviewing *Mosses from an Old Manse* for *The Literary World*, a power, he recognized, which "derives its force from its appeal to that Calvinistic sense of Innate Depravity and Original Sin, from whose visitations, in some shape or other, no deeply thinking mind is always and wholly free."

This "great power of blackness" was inserted in the simple adventure story of the hunt for the white whale, which became, as Melville worked upon it, less of a romance of the sea and more of an allegory of the whole human condition. Like all great works of literature—like *Hamlet*, like *Paradise Lost*, like *The Pilgrim's Progress*, like *Gulliver*, like *Wuthering Heights*—*Moby-Dick* is readable on several different levels, ideally on all these levels at once. It *is* "a simple adventure story of a chase after a white whale" (a whale which had bitten off more than it could chew: *videlicet*, the left leg of Captain Ahab); it is that, certainly, in the sense that the *Pilgrim* is a simple adventure story of a hero with a Christian name who fights giants and dragons, and that *Gulliver*, as Dr Johnson so clearly stated, is a tale "of big men and little men". But there are other levels to Melville's masterpiece, which make it, in John Freeman's words, "a parable of an eternal strife...an allegory of the ancient war between spirit and sense" or, as D. H. Lawrence saw it in his chapter on Melville in *Studies in Classic American Literature* (1923), a parable of a conflict in which Moby Dick (so spelt by Melville throughout: the hyphen is in the title only) is a symbol of "the deepest blood-being of the white race...hunted by the maniacal fanaticism of our white mental consciousness...hunted by monomaniacs of the idea." Into the hold of the "Pequod", into the belly of the White Whale, can drift all manner of interpretations, any number of allegorical meanings. The critical literature now surrounding *Moby-Dick* presents as fearful an aspect as Captain Ahab to the second mate Stubb, when that worthy rashly suggests that the

Captain's ivory heel might make less din if it were suitably padded. "Am I a cannon-ball, Stubb," roars Ahab, "that thou wouldst wad me that fashion? But go thy ways; I had forgot. Below to thy nightly grave; where such as ye sleep between shrouds, to use ye to the filling one at last. Down, dog, and kennel!"

As that short quotation makes apparent, *Moby-Dick* succeeds in spite of the appalling risks which Melville took in the way of deliberately heightened melodramatic language, not to mention sheer absurdity and digressions of enormous length upon cetology and cognate matters. By every known rule of writing, *Moby-Dick* should be the failure which most contemporary reviewers thought it to be; actually, it holds the reader throughout its one hundred-and-thirty-five chapters from the very first sentence—"Call me Ishmael"—to the moment when Ahab goes down with his ship. There is plenty of time on a voyage: that is the reason why sailors are often such great readers. It is not every day that we sight a whale, and meanwhile we can descend into the ship's library of Melville's imagination and refresh our whaleless hours with disquisitions on every subject under the sun. *Moby-Dick* succeeds better than *Tristram Shandy* in making its digressions tidy and ship-shape: there is something of advantage, even in the literary world, in having the training of a sailor. And Melville does not keep us too long under hatches: "Enter Ahab; to him, Stubb" and we are once again in action.

Moby-Dick is, among other things, a masterpiece of humour: perhaps, with *Huckleberry Finn*, that inland voyage, the most sustained piece of humorous writing that America has produced. The critical fashion of the mid-twentieth century has been to dwell on the darker, more "existentialist" side of the work. That is certainly there, as we have noted; but unless we are blind to the more genial aspects, to the humour of incongruity and exaggeration, we shall not take the "power of blackness" as covering all. There are many episodes in *Moby-Dick* which Dickens himself could not have bettered for humorous observation. One such meets us even before we go on board the "Pequod", when Ishmael attends the Whaleman's Chapel in New Bedford and observes how Father Mapple mounts "hand over hand" into the pulpit "with a truly sailor-like but still reverential dexterity", being careful to draw up his rope-ladder when he is safely "on deck". As for Captain Ahab himself: well, he is no doubt an "existentialist" character, if we are determined to be gloomy or have a thesis to prepare, but he seems to the writer of this chapter to be also one of the most successful humorous creations in the language. If he is a Lear on the starboard side, he is a Falstaff on the port; and we cannot read some of the speeches Melville puts into his mouth without a smile of delighted recognition.

Critical opinion has had more than a century to digest *The Whale*—as the novel was called in its first London edition—and it is easy enough now to smile at some of the sneers which it originally provoked. On the whole, the contemporary reviews make sad reading. The London *Examiner* compared the last pages to *Tom Thumb the Great*, while *The Athenaeum* considered that the author had only himself to blame "if his horrors and his heroics are flung aside by the general reader as so much trash belonging to the worst school of Bedlam literature, since he seems not so much unable to learn as disdainful of learning the craft of an artist." There is, of course, some truth in the latter criticism, which a novelist-critic like Henry James might have put more circumspectly. But Jamesian standards, however applicable to most serious fiction, do not really apply to "loose", "humorous" fiction like *Don Quixote, Joseph Andrews, Tristram Shandy, Martin Chuzzlewit, Moby-Dick* or *Huckleberry Finn*. Such fiction can afford many lapses of literary taste, many passages of "Bedlam", many absurdities; the author can even change his mind half-way through (as Mark Twain did in *Pudd'nhead Wilson*) or (like Cervantes) forget whether at the moment Sancho Panza has lost Dapple or recovered him. Humorous fiction, and *Moby-Dick* comes into this general category, is not constructed on a definite plan, but is inspirational, the author "making it up" as he goes along and introducing some of his best passages, or (like Dickens) some of his best characters, on the spur of the moment. "Call me Ishmael," Melville begins and from that time onward we are at the mercy of the glittering imagination of this bright-eyed Mariner. We cannot really expect him to be a Jane Austen or a Henry James as well.

Moby-Dick rests for ever on the crest of Melville's wave. His subsequent fortunes can be discussed more briefly. His disappointment at the public reception of his masterpiece was tempered by Hawthorne's whole-hearted approval, judicious praise from the friend and the master whom beyond all others Melville was anxious to please. "A sense of unspeakable security is in me at this moment, on account of your having understood the book." But his general disillusionment is mirrored in his next novel, the semi-autobiographical *Pierre* (1852), and in most of his later fiction like *Israel Potter* (1855)—dedicated to "a private of Bunker Hill who for his faithful services was years ago promoted to a still deeper privacy under the ground"—and *The Confidence-Man* (1857), a satirical fantasy about a journey down the Mississippi from St Louis to New Orleans which, suitably enough, anticipates some of the criticism of *The Gilded Age*. The Civil War produced the poems collected as *Battle-Pieces and Aspects of the War* (1866), in which year Melville obtained the post of Inspector of Customs which he held till his retirement in 1885. He died in his native city of New York six years later, having completed towards the end of his life that brief masterpiece *Billy Budd* which he had dedicated to his early friend and shipmate "Jack Chase": a story of the mutiny at the Nore in 1797, "a story", says Melville, "not unwarranted by what happens in this incongruous world of ours—innocence and infamy, spiritual depravity and fair repute." It is probably Melville's best work after *Moby-Dick*, and with *Benito Cereno*—the best story in *The Piazza Tales* (1856)—the most profound treatment of a naval theme before Conrad.

The first poem in *Battle-Pieces* is called *Misgivings* (1860), and the trend of the whole volume is towards Melville's realization that this fratricidal conflict had come about through the contradiction of slavery existing within a free republic: "the world's fairest hope linked with man's foulest crime." Melville is no great poet, except in some of the prose of *Moby-Dick*; but the tragedy of the Civil War did not require the genius of a Shakespeare to produce poetry that has the inevitable pathos and sublimity of the theme: the minor talent of a Whittier, a Julia Ward Howe, a Henry Timrod could match the hour. And in this company Melville can hold his own. He never produced a stirring *Battle-Hymn* to rival Mrs Howe's. But Timrod's *Ode on the Confederate Dead at Magnolia Cemetery, Charleston* (1867) is equalled by Melville's simple lines on Grant's costly victory in Tennessee in April 1862:

> Now they lie low,
> While over them the swallows skim
> And all is hushed at Shiloh.

VI. MARK TWAIN AND THE WEST

Before we enjoy ourselves talking about Mark Twain, we might have a word or two with Mark Tapley. Readers of *Martin Chuzzlewit* will recall the famous scene in the office of the Eden Settlement where the agent Zephaniah Scadder shows the ingenuous Martin and the sceptical "Co" a plan of "the thriving city of Eden"—probably meant for Cairo, Illinois, that "dismal swamp" at the confluence of the Mississippi and the Ohio which had so shocked Dickens in *American Notes*. Martin observes to Scadder that there does not seem much scope for a new architect like himself, with all these banks, churches, factories and hotels already built, and is surprised to learn that there is not a single architect in the whole town. "The soil being very fruitful," comments Mark Tapley, "public buildings grows spontaneous, perhaps." At which the indignant Scadder offers his hands for symbolic examination—"Air they dirty, or air they clean, sir?"—an invitation which Mark naturally declines.

Millions of readers, British and American, must have laughed at this episode, even if they felt more like crying when Martin and Mark eventually arrive at the cluster of log houses on "the hideous swamp"—"the waters of the Deluge might have left it but a week before"—that is the thriving city of Eden in reality. Yet, though Dickens in *Chuzzlewit* was true to the facts as he had witnessed them in *American Notes*, the last laugh was really on him—and it was not very long delayed. "Public buildings" did not spring up "spontaneous" in the West any more than they did anywhere else, but by comparison with the normal growth of a town or a village in England, the term was not a great exaggeration. If we read the careful, detailed chapter "The West: 1830–1840" in Van Wyck Brooks's *World of Washington Irving*, we shall be able to put Dickens into proper historical perspective and even find some grudging admiration for scoundrels like Zephaniah Scadder. "In the visions of the auctioneers," writes Brooks, "the country was covered with mills and factories, described in their printed circulars as already existing... Large towns appeared on many a broadside where the visiting eye could only find a hickory stump in the middle of the public square, but, as often as not, within a year, the square was a reality, and the town...too." Not quite "spontaneous", but Mark Tapley would not have needed to emulate the twenty years' sleep of Rip van Winkle to be amazed at the growth of "Eden", Illinois, from swamp to city—though it remains true that many so-called "cities" and "towns" in mid-century America would have been called villages anywhere else.

In one of these mushroom towns or villages on the Mississippi, during the very period when Dickens was visiting the United States and recording his impressions, there was living a red-haired, rather under-sized boy, a combination of his own Tom Sawyer and a juvenile Pudd'nhead Wilson, who was to become to America what Dickens was to England: her national humorist. Though actually born a few miles west of the river, at the little town of Florida, Missouri, whence his parents had migrated from their home states of Virginia and Kentucky, Samuel Langhorne Clemens, "Mark Twain" (1835–1910) is always rightly connected with the river town of Hannibal, the steamboat stop above St Louis and about three hundred miles above "the thriving city of Eden"—past which, without knowing it, Huck and Jim float on their raft in the fog, finding peril for Jim in the slave-owning South instead of freedom along the Ohio. In Hannibal, Missouri—the St Petersburg of *Tom Sawyer*, the Dawson's Landing of *Pudd'nhead Wilson*—young Clemens whitewashed a fence or two like Tom, fell in love with a series of Becky Thatchers, saw a man shot in the street by a frontier gentleman of the type of Dickens's Mr Hannibal Chollop, heard (as he tells us) "a Negro drayman, famous for his quick eye and prodigious voice" shout "S-t-e-a-m-boat a-comin'!", saw the steamer "Waverley", "Marmion" or "Lady of the Lake"—Clemens could never get away from Sir Walter—move cautiously into the shore, and perhaps heard the cry of the leadsmen in shallow water, "M-a-r-k twain!...M-a-r-k twain!"—meaning "by the mark two fathoms"—a cry he was later to make into a pseudonym as loved the world over as "Boz" or "Lewis Carroll".

Although on a map of the United States Missouri does not look particularly "southern", in Mark Twain's youth it was technically part of the South, the slave-owning Southern way of life having penetrated the Mississippi Valley and reached as far north as the country of Tom Sawyer and Huckleberry Finn, though in the Civil War Missouri did not join the Confederate States. The Clemens family were rather poorly off: Mark Twain always spoke of himself as a man of the people and his friend William Dean Howells justly called him "the Lincoln of our literature." Yet the family and their relations owned a little land and a few slaves, including the Uncle Dan'l who was the young Sam's particular ally in childhood and whom he later affectionately recalled as the Nigger Jim whom Huck (against all the rules of his Southern upbringing) helps escape from bondage. Huck knows he is doing wrong, that he is inviting eternal damnation for his defiance of religion and morality in daring to help a slave to freedom, instead of doing the Christian thing and claiming the reward for handing him over to his rightful owner. Particularly does his conscience prick him when the grateful Jim talks about enlisting the aid of an Abolitionist to steal his two children, who are slaves somewhere else. "Here was this nigger," reflects Huck, "which I had as good as helped to run away, coming right out flat-footed and saying he would steal his children—children that belonged to a man I didn't even know; a man that hadn't ever done me no harm." The irony of *Huckleberry Finn*, though at that later date it did not arouse the fury in the South caused by Mrs Stowe's *Uncle Tom's Cabin* thirty years before—when the editor of *The Southern Literary Messenger* (Poe's old paper) told the reviewer that he would like "the review as hot as hell-fire, blasting and searing the repu-

tation of the vile wretch in petticoats who could write such a volume"—
Twain's irony no doubt contributed to the fact that his masterpiece won its way
into popular approval against a good deal of criticism in influential quarters.

The young Clemens, then, sat at the feet of Uncle Dan'l, as the young Harris
sat at the feet of "Uncle Remus": he listened spellbound to the tall stories told
so solemnly in the quarter and filed them away in his mind for future use.
Like Stephen Foster, he listened, too, to the Negro songs and spirituals familiar
to a later generation through the magnificent organ voice of Paul Robeson. He
agreed with Melville, who in *Benito Cereno* was to write of the cheerfulness and
harmony of the Negro race, "as though God had set the whole Negro to some
pleasant tune". In later life, he not only created the commanding figure of
Roxy, the slave heroine of *Pudd'nhead Wilson*, but put his beliefs into practice
(as part of the reparation "due from every white man to every black man") by
helping two Negro students through college...

One wishes one could end there. But though literature has much to its credit
in this issue of Negro slavery—not least in the intrepid career of William Lloyd
Garrison, editor of *The Liberator*, and in the deaths in the Civil War of the poet
and story-writer Fitz-James O'Brien and the novelist Theodore Winthrop, a
descendant of John Winthrop the Puritan governor of Massachusetts—there
was another side. The eminent statesman from South Carolina, John Calhoun,
used all his considerable gifts of oratory in defence of slavery and gave as good
as he got in his frequent battles of words against his political opponents Henry
Clay and Daniel Webster. And when the Ku Klux Klan was founded in
Tennessee in 1865 and began its career of terrorism, its "chief justice" was the
poet Albert Pike of Arkansas and its "grand chaplain" another poet, the Roman
Catholic priest Father Abram Ryan, who had written songs for the Confederate forces.

Emerson had prophesied in *The Dial* in 1843 that the future of American
literature would not lie wholly in the East. "Our eyes will be turned westward,"
wrote the Sage of Concord, "and a new and stronger tone in literature will
be the result." He rightly saw as "genuine growths" such flourishing plants as
"the Kentucky stump-oratory, the exploits of Boone and David Crockett, the
journals of Western pioneers..." He might have added "Western humour",
which had part of its origin, as we have noted, in his own New England: in
the Boston comic weekly, *The Carpet Bag*, which in 1852 was to throw both
Artemus Ward and Mark Twain on to an unsuspecting American public—
which has never been quite the same since.

Mark Twain had left school at twelve when his father died and had been first
a printer, then a river pilot: thus fulfilling a boyhood dream, for as he tells us in
Life on the Mississippi (1883) "there was but one permanent ambition" among
the Tom Sawyers of his day and "that was, to be a steamboatman." They had
other transient ambitions, such as to be a clown in a circus and "now and then
we had a hope that if we lived and were good, God would permit us to be
pirates. These ambitions faded out, each in its turn; but the ambition to be a
steamboatman always remained."

The outbreak of the Civil War in 1861 disrupted the river traffic and after a
fortnight as a Confederate irregular (during which it rained all the time) Twain

deserted and followed his brother to the West. He tried silver-mining in Nevada, an experience he was to describe in his book *Roughing It* (1872), and then became a journalist in Virginia City and afterwards in San Francisco, with a brief assignment to the Hawaiian Islands in the Pacific. He saw much of Artemus Ward in Virginia City, as he was to see much of Bret Harte in San Francisco. Charles Farrar Browne, "Artemus Ward" (1834–67), whose Boston *début* Twain had shared in 1852, had become the best-known American humorist while Twain had been learning to be a river pilot. He was read by Lincoln at cabinet meetings and before his short life was ended by consumption was famous in Britain as well as America through *Artemus Ward, His Book* (1862) and its equally hilarious successors *Artemus Ward among the Mormons* (1866) and *Artemus Ward in England* (1867). It was Ward who urged Twain to publish *The Celebrated Jumping Frog of Calaveras County and Other Sketches* (1865) and it was Ward the platform humorist, with his melancholy appearance and his poker-faced wit, whom Twain was to follow in his successful career as travelling comic lecturer, sometimes in company with his fellow-humorists Josh Billings (Henry Wheeler Shaw) and Petroleum V. Nasby (David R. Locke), a trio of "Western" comedians (though two of them had come from the East) who could have made a good living in the mortuary business.

This, of course, was part of the Western technique (and the Southern Negro technique) of telling the tallest of stories with the utmost gravity of expression. The "exploits" of Daniel Boone of Kentucky and Davy Crockett of Tennessee which Emerson mentions, though sufficiently remarkable in reality, had become deliberately exaggerated as they passed from mouth to mouth and from tavern to tavern till they rivalled those of the legendary lumberjack Paul Bunyan. Colonel Crockett himself had written down some of his adventures, with a little help from others; but it was the Western love of the tall story and the practical joke that credited him with feats like wading the Mississippi, leaping the Ohio and hugging a bear out of breath, though he was never credited, as Paul Bunyan was, with using a pine-tree as a shaving-stick. As a sort of second string to Western exaggeration, there was the equally solemn habit of Western under-statement, as when the citizen of Eden in *Martin Chuzzlewit*, slowly dying in a fever-ridden swamp, admits the country is "moist perhaps, at certain times." Both habits Mark Twain was to exploit to the full in his lectures and books.

But though Twain succeeded Artemus Ward as the national humorist of America, and though he always venerated the memory of his predecessor and spoke gratefully of his early debt to him and to Bret Harte, the two writers—as distinct from the two platform entertainers—were not much alike. Ward, like Billings and Nasby, and somewhat like the later Chicago humorist Finley Peter Dunne, creator of Mr Dooley, owed much of his appeal to simple tricks like "frontier" or "farmer's" spelling and malapropisms meant to puncture complacency or pomposity—as when he described Boston as "the Modern Atkins"—and this kind of homespun humour (as Shakespeare and Sheridan knew) can only be bearable if taken in small doses. Twain was not above using every comic device that came to hand: he could barely open his mouth without making some wisecrack like "I would rather decline two drinks than one German adjective" or—when charged eight dollars for a trip on the Sea of

Galilee—"Do you wonder now that Christ walked?" But this was only the surface comedian, "the wild humorist of the Pacific Slope", as he was described after his journalistic success in California, the Twain we mainly find in *The Innocents Abroad* (1869). The mature Twain went deeper, as we have already seen in regard to *Huckleberry Finn*. Twain at his best is the American Dickens, as profoundly moved as Dickens was at the tragi-comic spectacle of life, sharing Dickens's sense of the high importance of comedy, his fellow-feeling for the outcast and oppressed, sometimes—it must be admitted—his sentimentality. And just as even Dickens's greatest works are to some extent weakened by passages which a more careful artist like Henry James would have expunged, so Mark Twain has no real masterpiece without serious flaws.

We have described *The Adventures of Huckleberry Finn* (1884) as his masterpiece, and so indeed it is. Yet it is a masterpiece that does not leave a wholly satisfactory impression. In a sense, it is two books in one, and perhaps that is what is wrong with it. The beginning and the end carry on from the admirable boys' book *The Adventures of Tom Sawyer* (1876), but the middle chapters, particularly the wonderful chapters where Huck and Jim float down the Mississippi on their raft, are more than boys' reading, though a sensitive boy would understand some of it. The "adventure" aspect is done to perfection, as only Mark Twain could have done it; but when Huck and Jim pass "Eden" in the fog, they not only drift remorselessly ever deeper into Southern territory, but also ever deeper into Southern and Western institutions. Some of these institutions are more civilized than others. The blood-feud between the Grangerfords and the Shepherdsons introduces us to an aspect of frontier life which Dickens had criticized in *American Notes* and which, though more prevalent in Arkansas and further west than in Missouri, the young Clemens had seen something of back home in "St Petersburg". The false conception of "honour" comes out more clearly from Huck's bewildered observations than from Dickens's shocked protests. The episode of Colonel Sherburn follows, and once again a man is murdered in cold blood—or rather in hot blood, for Boggs, "the best-naturedest old fool in Arkansaw", is very drunk at the time he challenges the proud Colonel. The "king" and the "duke" provide some welcome light relief, but even here Twain's eye is not fixed entirely on their comic qualities. The scene at the camp-meeting, where the lecherous old "king", pretending now to be a converted pirate, hugs and kisses "the prettiest kind of girls, with the tears running down their cheeks", is not unrelated to other camp-meetings which Mark Twain had observed and which featured equally lecherous evangelists of greater clerical standing, the primitive prototypes of Sinclair Lewis's *Elmer Gantry*. The "king" and the "duke" inevitably go too far: they have a good run for their money, but in the end are run out of town themselves, tarred and feathered, "astraddle of a rail." Another good old Southern or Western custom, but "it made me sick to see it," says the tender-hearted Huck; "I was sorry for them poor pitiful rascals... It was a dreadful thing to see. Human beings *can* be awful cruel to one another." Which more or less ends the adult part of the book before we are once again with Tom Sawyer and his boyish pranks and mystifications.

Twain's second masterpiece, *The Tragedy of Pudd'nhead Wilson, and the*

Comedy, Those Extraordinary Twins (1894), is even more obviously divided into two parts, partly it would seem by deliberate design. This book has provoked the most varied reactions: "the masterly work of a great writer," says F. R. Leavis truly; and "an absurd and unholy mixture of tragedy and farce," says Van Wyck Brooks—equally truly. The best parts are among the finest of Mark Twain's achievements: the creation of Roxana, the majestic slave, who was only one-sixteenth black, "and that sixteenth did not show"; the author's bold handling of the "forbidden" theme of miscegenation; the neatly ironic ending, where the Governor pardons Tom and the creditors sell him "down the river": all this is done with masterly, deceptive ease. But what are we to say of the rest? Even if we take Twain's explanation with a grain of salt, suspecting that there is more here than meets the eye, the "crossing" of a tragic theme with a farcical is still very much to be deplored. The novel is Mark Twain's *Changeling* in more than one sense, and perhaps he had the Elizabethan play in mind when he decided to mix Roxy's story with the story of the twins, with Pudd'nhead Wilson, the Sherlock Holmes of Dawson's Landing, as the link. If he had ever written a completely satisfactory novel, apart from the boys' classic *Tom Sawyer*, we might more readily believe that the apparent muddle is really a subtle way of paralleling the major theme with the minor, of balancing one irony against the other. But, as it is, the author's note of apology cannot be ignored: "The reader...has been told many a time how the born-and-trained novelist works; won't he let me round and complete his knowledge by telling him how the jackleg does it?" We know that he was uncertain at first about what he intended to do in *Huckleberry Finn*, whether he should simply continue the boys' story begun in *Tom Sawyer* or introduce more adult issues. Perhaps he got into similar confusion over *Pudd'nhead Wilson* and took in the end the only way out. If, on the other hand, we are the victims of a dead-pan, practical joke in the best traditions of the Western frontier, that, too, would not be entirely unexpected in the author of *The Celebrated Jumping Frog*, *The Stolen White Elephant* (1882) and *A Connecticut Yankee in King Arthur's Court* (1889)—which last-named book was an attempt to lay the elusive ghost of Sir Walter Scott, and all his medieval trappings, once and for all.

Mark Twain is the one great genius of the West, but by no means the only Western or Mid-Western writer of the period who is still worth reading. There was, indeed, a remarkable variety of literature being produced in the Western and Mid-Western states during the Twain half-century, *c*. 1860–1910, from the stories of Bret Harte and Ambrose Bierce to the novels of Jack London, from "the poet of the people", James Whitcomb Riley, to Ina Coolbrith, "the Sappho of the Western sea", who was a niece of the Mormon prophet Joseph Smith. The *Pike County Ballads* (1871) of Henry Adams's friend John Hay and *The Hoosier Schoolmaster* (1871) and *The Faith Doctor* (1891) of Hay's and Riley's fellow writer from Indiana, Edward Eggleston, can be compared or contrasted with the Oregon poet Joaquin Miller's *Songs of the Sierras* (1871) and *Songs of the Desert* (1875), both of which had a great vogue in England, and *My Reminiscences as a Cowboy* (1930) by the Irish-born journalist Frank Harris (1856–1931), better known for his equally unreliable *My Life and Loves* (1923–7). General Lew Wallace wrote *Ben Hur* (1880) while he was Governor of New Mexico, a region later associated with Mary Austin, Willa Cather, Mabel Dodge Luhan and D. H. Lawrence. The "Western novel" of cowboys on the purple sage, whose later practitioners included the British favourite Zane Grey—and which goes back in some degree to Fenimore Cooper—had perhaps its most distinguished exponent in Owen Wister, author of *The Virginian* (1902). Just as Cooper based his Natty Bumppo on backwoodsmen he had known, so even the most romantic and far-fetched of "Westerns" was indebted to some extent to the real-life exploits of Wild West heroes (and showmen) like "Buffalo Bill" Cody. The West without the glamour and the show, but with the genuine excitement left in, can best be read about in Andy Adams's *Log of a Cowboy* (1903) from Texas to Montana and in H. L. Davis's novel covering the same period in Oregon *Honey in the Horn* (1935).

We have called Mark Twain the American Dickens. His friend and associate in San Francisco, Francis Bret Harte (1836–1902), had the enviable distinction of being praised by Dickens himself. "Not many months before my friend's death," writes Forster in his biography, "he had sent me two *Overland Monthlies*, containing two sketches by a young American writer, far away in California, *The Luck of Roaring Camp* and *The Outcasts of Poker Flat*, in which he had found such subtle strokes of character as he had not anywhere else in later years discovered...I have rarely known him more honestly moved." Harte was to return the compliment (then unknown to him) in his famous poem *Dickens in Camp* (1870), where he expresses his sorrow at the news of Dickens's passing, records an incident around a camp-fire in the Sierras when a haggard band of gold-diggers momentarily forget their "race for wealth" in listening to "the book wherein the Master had writ of Little Nell", and offers this symbolic "spray of Western pine" to go with the English oak and holly on Dickens's grave.

Dickens's judgment was very sound. These early stories by Bret Harte, published in *The Overland Monthly* which he had helped to found in San Francisco in 1868—it also printed Mark Twain, the economist Henry George, the philosopher Josiah Royce, and R. L. Stevenson's friend Charles Warren Stoddard—are not only among Harte's best work but are notable, historically, as the original character-studies of the soon-to-be-passing world of the mining camps, of gentlemanly gamblers, of lucky strikes, which were to have such an enormous influence upon later fiction and films. Harte was first to become famous, however, by a poem called *Plain Language from Truthful James* (1870) which was quoted throughout the United States under the title of its refrain "The Heathen Chinee". This dialect poem about a bland Oriental who beats two indignant Western cardsharpers at their own game was reprinted all over the English-speaking world and is no doubt among the "many things" in Harte to which Kipling handsomely acknowledged a debt. It is difficult now, when we turn up the poem in, for example, the World's Classics *Book of American Verse*, to recapture the astonished delight of 1870, perhaps because— or *For Simla Reasons* (to quote the title of Harte's own parody of Kipling)— "the Poet Laureate of the British Empire" improved so much upon Harte in this particular field. The best of Harte's stories—from *The Luck of Roaring Camp* (1868) to *Snowbound at Eagle's* (1886)—are certainly superior to his verse, with the possible exception of some poems he wrote about the Civil War. Sometimes he outdid Dickens in sentimentality, yet Henry Adams linked him with Whitman in his realistic treatment of sex.

Ambrose Bierce (1842–c. 1914), son of a poor farmer of Horse Cave Creek, Meigs County, Ohio, succeeded Bret Harte as literary dictator in San Francisco after Harte had gone to live in England. His stories about the Civil War, *Tales of Soldiers and Civilians* (1891)—called in the British edition *In the Midst of Life* —are the most authentic account of the war in prose before Stephen Crane's imaginative masterpiece *The Red Badge of Courage* (1895). Crane, unlike Bierce, did not write from personal experience, because he was not born till 1871, ending his brief consumptive existence in 1900. But he had studied records and pictures and, like a lesser Flaubert—or a lesser Manet (V. S. Pritchett well calls him "a brilliant impressionist")—could enter imaginatively into experiences he had not personally known—as in *The Red Badge* and his first story *Maggie: A Girl of the Streets* (1892)—with as much conviction as when he was writing from personal and recent experience, as in *The Open Boat* (1897), based on his shipwreck off Florida on the way to Cuba as a war correspondent. Two of the best of his stories, *The Blue Hotel* and *The Bride Comes to Yellow Sky* (1898), were the fruit of his Western trip to Nevada and Texas. Most of Bierce's work recalls Poe rather than Harte or Crane, particularly where he follows the supernatural and "horrible" Poe as in some of the stories in *Can Such Things Be?* (1893). In Bierce at such times the Western "tall tale" becomes involved in all sorts of Southern gloom and melodrama, what he himself called "the sun and shadow land of fancy." It was perhaps fitting that in 1914, at the age of seventy-one, he should have mysteriously disappeared on a secret, Poe-like mission to Mexico. The professional police were baffled, almost as in a detective story, and there was no C. Auguste Dupin to tell us the simple solution to the mystery.

The writer who succeeded Mark Twain as the most widely-read Western novelist in the world was born in San Francisco with even less material prospects than Bierce had in Ohio. Jack London (1876–1916) was the natural son of a music teacher and a wandering astrologer and quack doctor of the common Western type from whose lower reaches Twain drew his shabby and lecherous "king" in *Huckleberry Finn*. The young London sold newspapers like any future millionaire, worked in a cannery, raided oyster-beds, sailed before the mast, became a tramp, spent nights in jail and one term at the University of California, and then in 1899 joined the gold-rush to the Klondike, the scene of his first book of stories *The Son of the Wolf* (1900), where he had experiences even wilder than those Twain had recorded in *Roughing It* and Harte had observed in *The Luck of Roaring Camp*. A distinctively American combination of the "husky" and the "intellectual", the outdoor and the reading man, like Melville whose books he so admired, like Cooper and Whitman, like Ambrose Bierce and "Teddy" Roosevelt, like Hemingway later on, Jack London had early learnt to fend for himself, as his animal heroes have to do in *The Call of the Wild* (1903) and *White Fang* (1906), novels which still remain the best of their kind. London is a cruder writer than Melville, as Kipling is a cruder writer than Dickens; but this "Kipling of the Klondike", even more than his Anglo-Indian prototype, had had experiences which do not often come the way of literary men. His more imaginative writing is best seen in that neglected novel of prehistoric man *Before Adam* (1906), which was based to some extent on his study of Darwin.

Before writing *Maggie: A Girl of the Streets*, Stephen Crane, son of a Methodist minister and just out of college, had lived for a while, in the spirit of Zola, among the slum-dwellers of New York. It was easier for Jack London some years later to vanish for weeks into the slums of the East End of London: he had simply to act the part of an American sailor, as he had once been. The book he wrote afterwards, *The People of the Abyss* (1903), was partly inspired by these personal experiences, partly by a reading of that influential work *Progress and Poverty* (1879), which its author Henry George (1839–97) had helped to set up in print in Jack London's native San Francisco. He was soon to read and ponder more revolutionary works still. Marx and Nietzsche, in roughly equal proportions, are behind that startling forecast of a totalitarian future, *The Iron Heel* (1907). As George Orwell pointed out, it is not all loss, even from a literary point of view, when a writer has sufficient crudity in himself to understand the less civilized movements of mankind. In his role of prophet, Jack London was shrewder than his astrologer father, in one case unhappily so: in his semi-autobiographical novel *Martin Eden* (1909) he forecast his own suicide seven years before that tragic event.

VII. CHICAGO, NEW YORK AND HENRY JAMES

Ernest Hemingway's oft-quoted remark in *The Green Hills of Africa*, that "all modern American literature comes from *Huckleberry Finn*", has a good deal of truth in it. Hemingway need not even have stressed the "modern", for the influence of Mark Twain in general, both before and after he had written *Huckleberry Finn*, was seen very early, years before his death. *The Story of a Country Town* (1883) by E. W. Howe, a newspaper editor in Kansas, has many of the down-to-earth qualities inculcated by Twain and by Twain's intimate friend William Dean Howells. Twain himself praised this unglamorized portrait of "arid village life", saying "I have seen and lived it all." To Hamlin Garland (1860–1940), son of a Wisconsin farmer, Mark Twain was "the largest and most significant figure in American literature" and he followed the significance, if not the humorous largeness, in some of his own novels and stories of farm life on the prairie such as *Main Travelled Roads* (1891), *Prairie Folks* (1893) and *A Son of the Middle Border* (1917). Twain's realistic view of Southern and South-Western life was inherited and developed by two women novelists born in Virginia, Ellen Glasgow (1874–1945) and Willa Cather (1876–1947). To Twain's rejection of Southern "chivalry" for its unrealistic aspects Ellen Glasgow added her own rejection for its unwritten code of masculine supremacy: the basic theme of most of her novels from *The Descendant* (1897) to *Barren Ground* (1925). Willa Cather moved from Virginia to Nebraska, and afterwards to Wyoming, Colorado, Arizona and New Mexico. She wrote both of the South of her childhood and of the West and South-West of her adolescence and maturity in *April Twilights* (1903), *The Song of the Lark* (1915) and later novels of which the most widely read was *Death Comes for the Arch-*

bishop (1927), a novel about New Mexico in the eighteen-fifties. For a time she was in New York, being managing editor of *McClure's Magazine* from 1906 to 1912.

It was not so much New York, of course, as Chicago, "the capital of the Middle West", where Mark Twain found so numerous a group of admirers and, to some degree, inheritors. Chicago, Illinois, like a greater "Eden", had mushroomed "spontaneous" in about thirty years from a frontier village to a metropolis, and it was already clear by the time the World's Fair was held there in 1893 that it was soon going to rival New York and Boston not only in trade but in art and letters. Hamlin Garland had as little doubt about it as H. L. Mencken later on, when the Sage of Baltimore called Chicago "the literary capital of the United States" and praised the new writers like Theodore Dreiser and Ring Lardner who were using "the American language"—high praise from a critic who, despite the more typical bluster of his series of *Prejudices* (1919–27) made an enduring contribution to the culture of his country in precisely that field, in the volumes of *The American Language* (1918–48). In *Crumbling Idols* (1894)—published the same year as Frederic J. Turner's famous essay *The Significance of the Frontier in American History*—Garland observed with satisfaction that "the literary supremacy of the East" was passing away and that the inheritance by rights ought to pass to Chicago and the upper Mississippi valley, the valley where Mark Twain had been born. But this was a different Mississippi valley from the one Twain had grown up in, a new America, far more cosmopolitan than the old. Many of the more recent immigrants to such states as Illinois, Indiana, Wisconsin, Minnesota, Iowa, and North and South Dakota, were of Scandinavian or German extraction, like the Norwegian-American economist Thorstein Veblen (1857–1929) who wrote the influential *Theory of the Leisure Class* (1899), the Swedish-American poet and biographer Carl Sandburg (1878–1967) and the German-American novelist Theodore Dreiser (1871–1946). Sandburg followed Whitman as the bard of American democracy in *Chicago Poems* (1916) and *Slabs of the Sunburnt West* (1922), in his biography of Lincoln (1926–39) and in his only novel *Remembrance Rock* (1948), where he returns in imagination to the founding fathers (and mothers) of the country in the seventeenth century. Some of Sandburg's poems first appeared in the influential Chicago monthly *Poetry: A Magazine of Verse*, which Harriet Monroe had started in 1912 and which was to print some of the first work of Robert Frost, Robinson Jeffers, Amy Lowell and its European editor Ezra Pound. Whitman was also the main inspiration, and *Poetry* the first voice, of Vachel Lindsay (1879–1931) who early adopted a wandering life through the Mid-West and South-West, supporting himself by lectures, by reciting his own verse, and by doing a succession of odd jobs in the spirit of Thoreau. His *Rhymes to be Traded for Bread* (1912), whose "strange beauty" and "earnest simplicity" were praised by Yeats, followed by *Congo and other Poems* (1914) and *Chinese Nightingale* (1917), can be contrasted with the *Spoon River Anthology* (1915) by his sceptical Chicago contemporary Edgar Lee Masters (1869–1948) where a Whitmanlike idiom is made to serve a most un-Whitmanlike purpose in describing the frustrated lives of a small town's inhabitants. Spoon River followed the Tilbury Town of *The Children of the Night* (1897) by the Maine poet Edwin Arlington

Robinson (1869–1935) and was itself the precursor of Sherwood Anderson's Winesburg in his stories *Winesburg, Ohio* (1919) and Sinclair Lewis's Gopher Prairie, Minnesota, in his novel *Main Street* (1920).

Theodore Dreiser was concerned with the big city, with cities like Chicago and their effect upon recent immigrants like his own family. Lesser novelists like Henry Blake Fuller, Robert Herrick and Frank Norris, author of the prose epic of wheat *The Octopus* (1901) and its successor *The Pit* (1903), had written of the realities of Chicago finance, the struggles of farmer against capitalist, of capital against labour, as Upton Sinclair did more simply in *The Jungle* (1906), a pamphleteering novel about the appalling conditions of the workers in the stockyards, a novel which shocked the nation and which Jack London truly described as the *Uncle Tom's Cabin* of wage-slavery. What gives Dreiser greater significance as a novelist than Norris or Sinclair is his greater concern with the individual, though the impersonal forces so vividly portrayed in *The Octopus* and *The Jungle* are well adapted to the novelists' purpose. Dreiser saw deeper, perhaps because he had suffered more acutely, both in himself and in observing the struggles of his parents and his brothers and sisters. He was to embody their story and his own in a series of semi-autobiographical novels stretching from *Sister Carrie* (1900)—suppressed for "immorality", reissued 1907—through *Jennie Gerhardt* (1911) and *The Financier* (1912) to *An American Tragedy* (1925) and *Dawn* (1931), in which he looks back to his childhood. A more cheerful Dreiser is seen in *A Hoosier Holiday* (1916), where he describes his return in middle life to the Indiana of his birth. Dreiser is the American Balzac or Zola rather than the German-American Twain, but he shared both Zola's and Twain's lifelong concern for the victims of a competitive economic structure, even if his obsession with the tragic irony of fate was not often lightened by Twain's contrasting sense of ironic comedy.

So far, then, can we see the truth, or the partial truth, in Hemingway's observation, from the period of the 'eighties to the period of the Chicago literary renascence *c.* 1894–1915. It could be extended, of course, this general influence of Mark Twain, to include later writers like Sinclair Lewis, Sherwood Anderson, Hemingway himself, John Steinbeck, John Dos Passos and that modern novelist of Chicago, James T. Farrell (p. 884 below) who shared his predecessor Dreiser's Balzacian or Zolaesque aims. It could be extended also to include Southern and South-Western writers like William Faulkner and Erskine Caldwell, who to some extent have carried on from Twain, Ellen Glasgow and Willa Cather in trying to present a picture of Southern life that is at once fair to the facts and real to the feelings. Their over-all symbolism is perhaps the raft on which Huck and Jim float for ever down the Mississippi, white and black bound by history together and endeavouring to come to terms with their proximity. It was in 1901 that the Negro educationist, Booker Taliaferro Washington (1856–1915), wrote his classic work *Up from Slavery*. Twain's *Huckleberry Finn* is the nearest to a white man's corresponding "Up from Slave-Owning"—a more difficult ascent from a greater degradation—unless we give that credit to Eugene O'Neill's *Thirst* (1914) or *The Emperor Jones* (1920), plays which themselves owe something to Mark Twain as well as to Jack London.

But, taking "modern American literature" as a whole, Hemingway's observation, fertile as it is, is evidently only partly true. T. S. Eliot, born on the banks of the Mississippi, and Ezra Pound, born in Idaho, are not "Western" writers in any other sense—except perhaps in Pound's fondness for "frontier" spelling ("kulchur", "Rooshins", and so on)—and obviously owe more to the example of Henry James, Emily Dickinson, Henry Adams, George Santayana, not to mention Confucius, Dante and Laforgue, than they do to Mark Twain. A truer version of Hemingway's observation would be to say that a good deal of American literature in the twentieth century derives ultimately either from *Huckleberry Finn* or from *Washington Square*, from one of the two great American writers at the close of the nineteenth century who seem to have divided the country's critical allegiance between them in a kind of literary civil war "West" versus "East"—Vachel Lindsay described the Chicago literary renascence as a "Western movement"—who seem at first glance to have nothing in common save their greatness, to exist at the opposite poles of thought and creation.

Yet even this account, while much nearer the truth than Hemingway's observation, is not completely true. We dropped a hint just now when we referred in passing to Twain's intimate friend William Dean Howells (1837–1920), the eminent literary critic who succeeded Lowell and James T. Fields as editor of *The Atlantic Monthly* in 1871 and whose essays in *The Atlantic* and in *Harper's Monthly*, New York, together with some of his own novels such as *Indian Summer* (1886) and *A Hazard of New Fortunes* (1889), were a great influence upon the naturalism of the Chicago school. "Let fiction cease to lie about life," he wrote in an essay about Mark Twain; "let it portray men and women as they are, actuated by the motives and the passions in the measure we all know." Regarding the contemporary novel in England as in a state of decline ever since Jane Austen—which criticism would have greater validity had Dickens and Emily Brontë, for example, been trying to do what Jane Austen did to such perfection—Howells was devoted to Balzac and Turgenev and most of all to Tolstoy. His tastes in practice were, however, wider than his critical theories might suggest: not only Mark Twain *and* Henry James, but Emily Dickinson, Stephen Crane, Thorstein Veblen, Frank Norris, Hamlin Garland, Robert Frost, the Negro poet Paul Lawrence Dunbar (1872–1906)… all found in Howells a judicious welcome and in many cases he was among the first critics to realize, as with Crane and Dunbar, a writer's promise from his first efforts. His birth in a small town in Ohio, roughly equidistant from Henry James's New York and Mark Twain's Missouri, may have fitted him to be both the model for Strether in *The Ambassadors*—an anecdote of his provided the germ of that novel—and the equally warm friend (and counsellor) of the writer whom he affectionately remembered in *My Mark Twain* (1910). He printed both writers in *The Atlantic*, and in January 1875 they occupied the same number, James with an instalment of his first novel *Roderick Hudson*, Twain with *Old Times on the Mississippi*. Though the wisecracking Twain once said that he would "rather be damned to John Bunyan's heaven" than read *The Bostonians*, in his more serious moments he respected James's writing, though he naturally felt no urge to alter his own very different style of composition or his own very different way of thinking, which owed more to Paine and to Paine's successor, "the great agnostic", as he was called in the Middle West, Colonel Robert G. Ingersoll (1833–99), than to Swedenborg, Emerson or any of the French or British masters at whose feet the young Henry James sat. James, on his side, may well have thought that he would rather be damned to Tom Sawyer's heaven than read *Huckleberry Finn*, but through their common friend Howells he must have learnt some degree of puzzled respect for the touch-and-go methods of Mark Twain.

Two different kinds of cosmopolitan faced each other at this juncture in American literary affairs. There was the Chicago kind we have glanced at, whose position can be roughly stated as independence of Europe, however many of their poets, novelists and critics were of recent European origin. Mark Twain, for all his travels in Europe and his great love for England—a love that was returned—was fundamentally on the Chicago side in their natural assumption that the continental United States, with writers of every racial origin among them, was now a match for Europe as a whole and should not any longer need to be dependent on the older civilization, particularly in Britain (as some British critics themselves were the first to agree.) The nation, as Randolph Bourne later put it, was becoming "transnational", the natural inheritor of many different literary traditions from which could come a distinctively American literature of its own. Among these Chicago cosmopolitans there were some university men, such as the poet and dramatist William Vaughn Moody (1869–1910), a teacher at the new University of Chicago who used prose in his plays dealing with contemporary problems. But many of them, like Dreiser and Moody's friend Garland, had started working early in life and had mixed, as Twain had, with all sorts and varieties of people from an early age. Moody himself had some connection (or "confluence") with Twain, being the son of a steamboat captain on the Ohio.

The other kind of cosmopolitan, seen at its finest in Henry James, was a more leisured kind, based on New York and New England, having a more intimate contact with Europe either through the older universities in the East or through early travel to Britain, France, Italy and Germany. They were the inheritors of the older New York of Irving and the older New England of Emerson, as the cosmopolitans of Chicago and the Mississippi were the inheritors of Whitman and Whitman's hero Abraham Lincoln, the "prairie-lawyer, master of us all", as Vachel Lindsay called him. One would hesitate to divide the two kinds of cosmopolitan according to wealth or social status, or indeed according to extrovert and introvert—there being so many kinds of introspection—but generally speaking, allowing for exceptions on either side, the Chicago-Mississippi kind were humbly born, like Dreiser, while the Eastern kind, like Henry James and Edith Wharton, were comparatively wealthy.

The founders of the James family in America were largely self-made men of predominantly Ulster and Scots descent. The novelist's Irish grandfather, William James of Albany, enjoyed such commercial success in that city that a street is still named after him. He married three times, Henry James senior (1811–82), the Swedenborgian philosopher and friend of Emerson, being the son of the third marriage. The novelist, Henry James junior (1843–1916), was born in New York and during his last years in England wrote of his family background and early life in three autobiographical sketches: *A Small Boy and Others* (1913), *Notes of a Son and Brother* (1914) and the unfinished *The Middle Years* (1917), collected together under the rather misleading title of *Autobiography* (1957). This is misleading in the first place because it is mainly the early years which are dealt with—luckily, the later years are well covered by the *Letters* (1920, 1956)—and in the second place because, as the title of the second of the sketches implies, there is nearly as much about the father, Henry senior, and about the elder brother William James (1842–1910), who became Professor of Philosophy at Harvard and author of the influential work *The Varieties of Religious Experience* (1902), as about James himself. Nevertheless, something of the early life emerges: the Irish-American background, the prosperous descendants of self-made men becoming a new aristocracy in Albany, New York City, and Boston; the highly individualistic education, which sent the brothers from school to school, from tutor to tutor, from country to country, on a pre-arranged plan of their father's, which was at any rate more humane and liberal than the notorious plan of the elder Mill; the rather solitary existence of the young Henry amidst a crowded home life and a constantly changing experience abroad; the tremendous eloquence of Henry senior, which his sons longed to emulate... there could have been many worse preparations for the kind of writer James was to become.

The kind of writer he first became can be studied in the back numbers of *The North American Review*, the New York *Nation* and *The Atlantic Monthly*, which accepted his first stories and articles in the eighteen-sixties and later employed him as correspondent in Europe. To a modern eye some of his first stories seem romantic and melodramatic to an absurd degree, and even as late as 1884 he wrote, from London, two stories for *The New York Sunday Sun*, one of which, *Georgina's Reasons*, Leon Edel in *Henry James: The Middle Years* (1963)— the second volume in that excellent biography—frankly describes as "a strange unmotivated sensational little story, written in some misguided belief that this was what newspaper-readers wanted." Both stories were syndicated across the American continent, just as if Henry James had been Mark Twain or Artemus Ward, and one journal in the Wild and Woolly West gave the "sensational little story," the following un-Jamesian headlines:
"*GEORGINA'S REASONS!* HENRY JAMES'S LATEST STORY. A WOMAN WHO COMMITS BIGAMY AND ENFORCES SILENCE ON HER HUSBAND! TWO OTHER LIVES MADE MISERABLE BY HER HEARTLESS ACTION!" But this, of course, was not the James we know, whose first collected volume *A Passionate Pilgrim and Other Tales* (1875) shows how far he had advanced towards psychological subtlety even in his first decade. It was in the same year, 1875, that he left America virtually for good, settling first in Paris, where he saw something of Flaubert and Turgenev, and then in London, which he found "interesting, inspiring, even exhilarating." It partly inspired his first period as a novelist, from *Roderick Hudson* (1876) to *Washington Square* and *The Portrait of a Lady* (1881), a period which includes the novels *The American* (1877) and *The Europeans* (1878) as well as *Daisy Miller* (1879) and other stories and his fine study of Hawthorne which we quoted earlier in this chapter. James was supremely well qualified to undertake the main work of

this period, which was to be the theme of some of his later work also: to interpret the "international situation", as he came to call it—and which had earlier, as we have seen, engaged the attention of Hawthorne—so subtly and impersonally that the reader could not tell whether the book in question was written by an American with knowledge of England and the Continent or by an Englishman with knowledge of both American and European life. These first novels are not only very interesting for the masterly manner in which the "situation" is explored in all its possibilities, they are the easiest of James to read—a point of some importance when one considers the involved style of so much of the later work—and they include perhaps his chief masterpiece in *The Portrait of a Lady*, where the international theme is itself transmuted into tragedy.

The middle period runs roughly from *The Bostonians* (1886)—coupled by F. R. Leavis with *The Portrait* as "the two most brilliant novels in the language" and whose relationship to Hawthorne has been observed—and *The Princess Casamassima* (1886) nearly to the end of the century and includes two other impressive works in the *nouvelles*—"the dear, the blessed *nouvelle*" as he called that shorter form in which he and his friend Conrad did so much of their best writing—*The Spoils of Poynton* (1897) and *What Maisie Knew* (1898). The latter in particular is one of those seemingly slight affairs which no writer but James could have developed into anything so much out of the common run. His statement of the fundamental theme, in his preface, reveals an inquirer into the human heart in the true line of succession from George Eliot's *Middlemarch*: "No themes are so human as those that reflect for us, out of the confusion of life, the close connection of bliss and bale, of the things that help with the things that hurt, so dangling before us for ever that bright hard metal, of so strange an alloy, one face of which is somebody's right and ease and the other somebody's pain and wrong." The style of *Maisie* is not of the easiest: there we may well sigh for the lucidity of *Middlemarch*. But on the whole this study of corruption through the eyes of innocence is a commanding performance, probably with *The Bostonians* the masterpiece of the middle period, as *The Portrait* is of the early and *The Wings of the Dove* of the late. This middle period is a crowded one (some critics, ignoring dates, include *The Portrait* within it), the time perhaps when James was most easily in control of his material, before there set in that painfully explanatory style, foreshadowed in *Maisie*, which makes the last novels, for all their undoubted genius, so difficult at times to follow. It includes, for instance, not only his most celebrated *nouvelle*, the ghost story *The Turn of the Screw* (1898), but some of his best short stories—such as the ironic (and ambiguous) *Lesson of the Master* (1892)—on a favourite theme of his, the literary life in an age of increasing commercialization. It includes also that unsuccessful period of play-writing which ended in 1896 with his retirement to Rye, in Sussex, his home for the rest of his life.

The experience in writing for the stage, unprofitable as it was in the commercial sense, was not without some considerable influence on his style and procedure as a novelist in these later years. He had always been remarkably surefooted on the most perilous slopes of speech; now he began to write his novels, as Flaubert had written *Madame Bovary*, from what he called "a really detailed scenario, intensely structural, intensely hinged and jointed preliminary frame", and dialogue, so prominent a feature already in such an early novel as *The Europeans*, became all important to him. (At precisely the same time as James was thus endeavouring to get the dramatic virtues into the novel, Bernard Shaw was trying to get the virtues of the novel into the drama.) *The Awkward Age* (1899) is written almost entirely in dialogue—though dialogue, it must be added, of a kind that has seldom been heard outside the imagination of the author. (It would have been interesting to have had Mark Twain's considered opinion of it.) Largely a failure as a novel, and almost as unreal in a different way as *Georgina's Reasons*, it is nevertheless, from the purely technical point of view, a remarkable piece of writing. The rest of the later novels, with the partial exception of *The Wings of the Dove* (1902), can be described in the words James used of America when he revisited his native land two years after that novel was published: "interesting, formidable, fearsome, and fatiguing." To come to these novels first of all is to take the risk of being put off James for ever; it is better to approach these Becher's Brooks of fiction after a successful clearing of such lesser hurdles as *The Spoils of Poynton* or *What Maisie Knew*. Part of the reason for the difficulty of most readers over *The Sacred Fount* (1901), *The Ambassadors* (1903) and *The Golden Bowl* (1904) must lie in the fact that these last novels were dictated to an amanuensis; the voice we hear painfully explaining the furthest reaches of the obvious is the voice of James as recorded in countless anecdotes of his conversation during these last years: a voice like the chimneys of Dickens's Coketown, "out of which interminable serpents... trailed themselves for ever...and never got uncoiled." We cannot avoid the conclusion that his method, to some extent, defeated his intentions, which were, of course, to put the reader in possession of the facts of the situation without the slightest risk of ambiguity. If the reader can master the highly metaphorical and allusive procedure, then he can enjoy the result, particularly perhaps in *The Wings of the Dove*, that last fine tribute to the dead cousin Minny Temple to whom, as he himself put it to Ford Madox Ford with whimsically conscious under-statement, he was "most tenderly attached." Critics have not been wanting who see *The Ambassadors* and *The Golden Bowl* as also among the masterpieces of James's work; but *The Ivory Tower* (1917) has found few readers, not altogether because it was left unfinished at the author's death. The story may lack a conclusion, but the dialogue and the stage directions, as it were, are so very "finished" as to be almost unbearable.

It is a pity, on the whole, that James should have ended his career like this, that among the unconscious "lessons of the master" should have been the warning that subtlety can overreach itself, and, like ambition, fall on th' other. Those modern critics who see him as the Shakespeare of the novel (it is a measure of his undoubted greatness that the comparison is not even more of a contrast) have to ask themselves why his last period should have been so different from Shakespeare's last period: the tragi-comedies so profound in meaning, yet so simple in structure. Shakespeare, of course, had his audience to think of, whereas James, after his disappointments in the realms of the sensational story and (more seriously) in the theatre, seems to have resigned himself to the fact that his work would never be popular in his lifetime but could nevertheless be "finished" to a T for the benefit of posterity. That unpredictable generation, however, has mostly preferred the early and middle work, while giving to the later, with the partial exception of *The Wings of a Dove*, the sort of distant respect which in practice leaves the volumes unread upon the shelf.

Henry James was the first Anglo-American writer of importance, the precursor of other American writers of varying stature who spent most of their lives in England. These include Logan Pearsall Smith (1865–1946) from New Jersey, who wrote in *Trivia* (1902) and *More Trivia* (1921) two of the most re-readable little books in light literature and in *Words and Idioms* (1925) one of the most judicious studies of the English language. Two of his sisters maintained the transatlantic links, Mary Logan Smith by marrying the American art historian Bernhard Berenson (1865–1959), who spent most of his life in Italy, Alys Pearsall Smith by becoming the first wife of the British philosopher and mathematician Bertrand Russell. Other writers who followed Henry James to England included Mrs Pearl Craigie from Boston, who wrote novels under the name of John Oliver Hobbes (see p. 650); Henry Harland (1861–1905; p. 898) who edited *The Yellow Book*; besides later writers like Hilda Doolittle ("H.D."), Mrs Aldington, from Bethlehem, Pa., and T. S. Eliot, fleeing from Irving Babbitt, Cousin Harriet, and *The Boston Evening Transcript*.

But James is Anglo-American in a deeper sense than by virtue of the fact that he spent much of his life in London and Sussex, that he became a British subject a year before he died, and that his novels and stories frequently record the impact of England upon Americans or America upon English people. In his work we find a double inheritance: one stemming from Hawthorne and the Puritan ethos of New England, the other from Jane Austen and the later George Eliot. Even James, of course, great as he is in many ways, was not heir to all the ages of the English and American novel. Although in his autobiographical sketches he writes reverently and movingly of the creator of *Copperfield* and gives him the name of Master with equal conviction of capital initial to George Eliot herself—he had had the privilege of meeting both Masters personally— what we may loosely call the "outdoor" or "masculine" tradition in the British novel, from Defoe, Fielding and Smollett to Scott and Dickens, affects his work much less specifically than the "drawing-room" or "feminine" tradition of Richardson, Jane Austen and certain chapters in the later George Eliot. Nor is there much connection, save in the theme, so differently handled, of "innocents abroad", between James and that more consciously American tradition we have been discussing, whose masterpiece is *Huckleberry Finn*, and which seems to some American critics to be the only genuine native tradition, James in this view being a European or a cosmopolitan novelist rather than an American and the influence on him of Balzac, Flaubert and Turgenev being stressed. "The historian of fine consciences" was the tribute of that other cosmopolitan novelist, Joseph Conrad, and there is little to add or to detract from that characteristically just appreciation.

James had his moments of comparative popularity in his lifetime, for instance after his friend John Buchan became partner in Thomas Nelson in 1907 and put *The American* (followed by *Roderick Hudson*) into the famous Sevenpenny Library—along with Wells, Mark Twain, Jack London, Conan Doyle, W. W. Jacobs, Conrad, Gissing, Frank Norris, Sir Gilbert Parker, Booth Tarkington,

Hall Caine, Quiller Couch, and Mrs Humphry Ward—as "an example of the best work of one who is regarded with justice as among our greatest living novelists" and as "one of the most perfect examples of Mr Henry James's remarkable art." In general, though, he did not become widely read till many years after his death, his gradual rise to fame being partly due to the insistence of literary critics like F. R. Leavis in England and Edmund Wilson, F. O. Matthiessen and Lionel Trilling in America. There followed a natural tendency to overpraise an author who had been before so seriously underestimated, a tendency to be applauded rather than the reverse, for the critics were far more just to James than were Wells and E. M. Forster, even if we recognize the core of truth in Wells's and Forster's too severe remarks.

There is even a core of truth in Ambrose Bierce's catty reference to "Miss Nancy James", if we see James as the American Jane Austen, as we saw Mark Twain as the American Dickens. To call a male novelist "feminine" in the sense in which Jane Austen is feminine is neither obnoxious nor Freudian: it merely defines the novelist's sphere of interest. We cannot imagine Henry James, any more than we can imagine Jane Austen, serving before the mast like Dana and Melville, joining the army like Poe and Tolstoy, digging for gold like London and Harte, navigating a river like Thoreau and Twain, setting up type like Howells and Henry George, hunting big game like Cooper and Turgenev, farming the land like Cobbett and Garland, building a house like Whitman and Hardy, or in fact doing anything very much save conversing in drawing-rooms, partaking of afternoon tea on the lawn ("the implements of the little feast" are whimsically described on the first page of *The Portrait of a Lady*), dining out in the best society and escorting ladies (or being escorted by gentlemen) around art galleries or to the theatre... This, of course, is putting the matter in extreme form, for the sake of the necessary emphasis; we know, in fact, that Jane Austen was pretty busy in various domestic pursuits and wrote *Pride and Prejudice*, as Virginia Woolf puts it, "stealthily under cover of a creaking door"; we also know that Henry James was debarred from leading an active life by an accident to his back in boyhood, curiously paralleling the childhood accident which left his father with only one leg. But we cannot imagine James being very different in outlook even if he had been as robust as his brother William. There is a revealing phrase in his *Hawthorne* when he says that "in the United States, in those days, there were no great things to look out at (save forests and rivers)...." The exceptions, thus parenthesized, provide the material for a good deal of American literature and art: for all of Audubon, for most of Cooper, for a good deal of Twain, Thoreau, Bryant, Parkman, Whitman, and scores of others. The world of nature, so important in American literature, was closed to Henry James and he takes hardly more interest in the daily concerns of the majority of mankind. Men hardly come into Henry James, any more than they do in Jane Austen, save in domestic or courtly relation to women: virtually the only exceptions are writers and painters. Jane Austen, it has been well said, was too wise to follow the gentlemen, even in imagination, when once they had left the drawing-room or the dining-table: she kept to what she knew, unlike some other women novelists such as Charlotte Brontë and Ouida. Henry James did not follow the gentlemen much either, except to the studio or the novelist's desk. He knew women, and he saw men largely through women's eyes. He hardly deals at all with men when they are together in male company, men without women. But all this is not nearly such a disadvantage as it might seem at first glance. For the one fatal weakness in nearly all the Victorian male novelists, particularly Dickens and Thackeray, is in their romantic treatment of women: most of their heroines are as unreal as Scott's or Tennyson's medieval knights. The lifelong bachelor James—perhaps partly through the influence of the French novelists—seems to have known so much more about the female character than any of these husbands and fathers who had greater opportunities for observing it. He could even deal, in *The Bostonians*, and with what admirable delicacy, with the difficult theme of female homosexuality or lesbianism. Dickens could no more have created an Olive Chancellor than James a Mrs Gamp.

The New York which James knew, the New York he evokes in *Washington Square*, was not the city of Whitman and Melville. Still less was it the new New York of Greenwich Village and Harlem, or of any of the twentieth-century manifestations he described in *The American Scene* (1907). His New York was the older, upper-class New York of his friend and fellow-cosmopolitan Edith Wharton (1862–1937), who as the youthful poet Edith Newbold Jones had written verses admired by Longfellow and printed at his recommendation in *The Atlantic Monthly*. This well-named "up-town New York" of fashion and snobbery, "in all its flatness and futility", as she once put it, was recalled by Mrs Wharton in *The House of Mirth* (1905), *The Age of Innocence* (1920), and other shrewdly written novels and stories. A different Edith Wharton is seen in *Ethan Frome* (1911), a moving little novel, recalling Hawthorne rather than James, about the frustrations and the pathos of country life in a village with the symbolic name of Starkfield, situated somewhere among those Berkshire Hills in Western Massachusetts where an earlier New Yorker had written *Moby-Dick*.

That it was not really necessary to spend most of one's life in Europe, in order to follow the Emerson–Hawthorne tradition in American literature rather than the Whitman–Twain tradition, was proved by the minor poet Frederick Goddard Tuckerman (1821–73) whose *Poems* (1869) were praised by Emerson and modern critics like Witter Bynner and Yvor Winters and who spent nearly all his life in his native Massachusetts; by the Maine novelist Sarah Orne Jewett (1849–1909), whose *Country of the Pointed Firs* (1896) is a masterpiece of local colour and history; and above all by the poet Emily Dickinson (1830–86) who hardly left her native town of Amherst, Massachusetts, except for brief visits to Boston, Philadelphia and Washington and one year at Mount Holyoke College when she thought she had a call to enter the service of the Church. Emily Dickinson is one of the small number of women poets whose verse, at her rare best, is worthy of comparison with that of her male contemporaries, female literary genius having gone far more often into the novel. She wrote what a mystical Jane Austen—if we can imagine such a paradox—might have written had her lot been cast in Calvinist New England in the mid-nineteenth century instead of Anglican old England in the Regency. A sceptical Emerson, with an economy of style that was to have a deep and lasting influence on the American poetry of the twentieth century, her strange little verses in sober quatrains with short lines and with a particular kind of surprise masked by a certain level tone of voice, her verses were nevertheless often based on the rhythms and cautionary tales of her Calvinist childhood, particularly those of Isaac Watts. This is part of the reason why she sometimes reminds us, disconcertingly, of Lewis Carroll, whose parodies of Watts are as successful as his parodies of Wordsworth. "Faith is a fine invention," she once said, for those fortunate enough to find it. For those who live in doubt, the habit of microscopic self-analysis may prove useful:

> I measure every Grief I meet
> With narrow, probing, Eyes—
> I wonder if It weighs like Mine—
> Or has an Easier size...

Such poetry totters on the edge of the sublime and occasionally falls over into the sort of verse the White Rabbit or Humpty Dumpty might have declaimed. It was, on the whole, a risk worth taking, for she was exploring on her own account, without much help from others, that almost extinct tradition of expressing the deepest feelings of the soul in terms of wit which we vaguely call "metaphysical" and which had hardly been expressed in America since the early New England days of Edward Taylor and Anne Bradstreet.

The history of the publication of this "Emily in Wonderland" curiously parallels that of her younger contemporary—and greater poet—Hopkins in England. There was even an admiring editor, the Rev. Thomas Wentworth Higginson, who like Bridges with Hopkins wanted to smooth out her ambiguities and "improve" her for print. A reasonably complete edition of her poems did not become available till the centenary volume of 1930, though Conrad Aiken's edition of 1924, with its percipient introduction, had much to do with establishing her twentieth-century reputation. A further volume, *Bolts of Melody*, was published in 1947; and it was followed by the Harvard editions of *The Poems* (1955) and *The Letters* (1958), both edited by Thomas H. Johnson, in which the senior university of the United States paid as scholarly a tribute to Emily Dickinson as the senior university of England had previously paid to Hopkins.

When Edmund Clarence Stedman, late of *The New York World*, produced his *American Anthology* in 1900—he had previously edited *Poets of America* (1886)—he included Emily Dickinson as well as some poems from Stephen Crane's *The Black Riders* (1895) which had been written under her influence, as well as other new poets like Robinson and Moody among more conventional writers like Aldrich and R. H. Stoddard. The period *c.* 1900-15 opened a time of stock-taking among American critics and historians, a time for looking back as well as forwards, a time for re-assessment of American traditions and ways of life. This was the period of some of the best work of Henry Brooks Adams (1838–1918) who wrote that remarkable book, half-autobiography, half-philosophy of history, *The Education of Henry Adams*, which was privately printed in 1907 and posthumously published in 1918 by his former pupil at Harvard, Henry Cabot Lodge, the future Republican statesman. Rather like Carlyle in *Past and Present*, Adams intended the *Education* as a deliberate contrast to his studies of the thirteenth century, *Mont Saint-Michel and Chartres* (privately printed 1904;

revised for publication 1913), with their famous and influential contrast of "the Virgin and the Dynamo". At the same time the Spanish-American philosopher and man of letters George Santayana (1863–1952) was teaching the history of philosophy at Harvard and writing some of his most influential books, notably *Interpretations of Poetry and Religion* (1900) and *The Life of Reason* (1905–6). These two great American figures were very different in personal background. Adams was in the New England Puritan tradition in general and in the Adams dynasty in particular, as he wryly confesses in the oft-quoted second paragraph of the *Education*:

Had he been born in Jerusalem under the shadow of the Temple and circumcised in the Synagogue by his uncle the high priest, under the name of Israel Cohen, he would scarcely have been more distinctly branded.

Santayana, the future author of that ironic fictional study of New England frustration *The Last Puritan* (1935)—perhaps based to some extent on Henry Adams and his friends and relatives—was the kind of good-tempered, sceptical, sophisticated Catholic whose theology is not unfairly summarized in the saying apocryphally attributed to him: "There is no God, and the Virgin Mary is His Mother." Nevertheless, different as they were personally, they both presented to their pupils a background of historical tradition wider even than that urged on a previous generation of New Englanders by Emerson, Longfellow and Thoreau. The Civil War and the post-war Industrial Revolution had come between the two generations, and the scepticism about the modern world which both Adams and Santayana fostered—reinforced as it was by the ostensibly opposed New Humanism of Irving Babbitt and the New Original Sin preached by Paul Elmer More in the New York *Nation*—had an immense influence on such spokesmen of the coming age as T. S. Eliot.

From 1915 to 1918 many Americans were to go to Europe on a different and unhappier errand from that of Henry James or Henry Adams, and some of them, including Alan Seeger (1888–1916), the author of the sadly prophetic lines:

> I have a rendezvous with Death
> At some disputed barricade...

were not to return. Others more fortunate, like Hemingway, Dos Passos, E. E. Cummings, Harry Crosby, Malcolm Cowley, were to stay in Europe or return to it and were to contribute to the cosmopolitan literature of an age that was no longer either "English" or "American" in a purely national sense but can more accurately be considered, as we do in fact consider it in the following chapter, as the mid-twentieth-century literature of the English-speaking world. Both kinds of cosmopolitan we have glanced at, the Chicago and the New York, the West and the East, together with the more international view of history inculcated in New England by Santayana and Henry Adams, played their part in this development, a development which seems, looking back, to have been inevitable, to have been the ultimate horizon, beyond all frontiers, towards which American writers as different as Franklin and Cooper, as Poe and Whitman, as Emerson and Mark Twain, had been moving steadily all along.

CHAPTER XVI

THE AGE OF T. S. ELIOT:
THE MID-TWENTIETH-CENTURY
LITERATURE OF THE
ENGLISH-SPEAKING WORLD

I. INTRODUCTION: LOOKING BEFORE AND AFTER

The first sentence of this book was an indication that the language and the literature of one nation would be destined eventually to be international, that "English literature" would become "literature in English", ceasing to belong merely to England or the British Isles but taking in the literatures of the Commonwealth, the United States and other countries which had formerly some colonial tie with Britain. The last two chapters have seen this "manifest destiny" being realized. We have seen, in chapter XIV, how the literatures of Australia and other far-flung portions of empire have proceeded from colonial to commonwealth, from commonwealth to cosmopolitan, how the English literatures of India and South Africa have taken a somewhat similar course, how the Irish literary revival associated with Synge and Yeats has come to influence the twentieth-century literature of the whole English-speaking world. And in chapter XV we have traced the main events in the literature of the United States of America from the seventeenth to the early twentieth century, finding here too a progress from colonial to independent, from independent to cosmopolitan. As we arrive in our final chapter, with the ground-work and some of the details already thus prepared, it will come as a surprise to no one that the accent throughout will be upon the world which speaks English, not upon the nation which had the privilege of having spoken and written it in the first place. Prophecy is as dangerous in literary matters as in political, and in this instance they may well be connected, but we are running no great risk of having to eat our English words when we say that literature in the English language is likely to become more and more cosmopolitan the further the twentieth century proceeds towards its own manifest destiny in the twenty-first. If the accent of mid-twentieth-century English literature is so clearly international, the accent—or the varying accents—of late-twentieth-century English literature is hardly likely to be less so.

The international, cosmopolitan nature of "English literature" meets us now at every turn. We pick up, for instance, a recent issue of *The Times Literary Supplement*, the chief literary organ of the United Kingdom, published in London. We open it at random and our eye is caught by a notice of the current number of the American *Literary Review*. No doubt the matters under discussion chiefly concern the literature of the United States? But no: this particular issue of *The Literary Review*, with Professor Desmond Pacey as guest editor, is a special number devoted to "modern Canadian writing in all its major forms" and in both English and French. The London reviewer welcomes this special number, but reminds us that this is the second, not the first, non-Canadian magazine in America to have an all-Canadian number, the Argentinian journal *Sur*, under the editorship of Victoria Ocampo, having previously run an issue entirely devoted to Canadian literature. So merely by opening a copy of *The Times Literary Supplement*—which itself makes a practice of having an occasional number devoted to Commonwealth or European literature—we have crossed the Atlantic Ocean, not only to New York and Toronto, but to Quebec and Buenos Aires. We must therefore add to our prospect of an English-speaking world an English-studying world also, with some return of compliment in English-speaking Canada to French-Canadian literature and among English-speaking South Africans to literature in Afrikaans. We must take a Johnsonian view, including not only speakers and writers of English from Wales to New South Wales, from Perth to Perth, but also students of English all over the globe whose mother-tongue may be Peruvian-Spanish or Straits-Chinese. All the modern European languages are to some extent international, but the language of Shakespeare has penetrated even further than the languages of Cervantes, Camoens or Molière. Only the languages of music and mathematics, and the religious literature of Israel in both its Jewish and its Christian forms, have had a comparable spread.

The increasing cosmopolitanism of literature in the English language is connected with the rise of English studies in the higher education of the mid-twentieth century. If we glance through the list of contributors to *The Journal of Commonwealth Literature*—with its own detailed references to Commonwealth articles and reviews in *The Times Literary Supplement*, *The New Statesman*, *The London Magazine*, *The South Atlantic Quarterly* (South Carolina), *African Forum* (New York), *Transition* (Uganda), *Présence Africaine* (Paris), etc.—we shall find the names of West Indians who teach in Nigeria, Australians who teach in South Africa, Englishmen who teach in India, Indians who teach in Canada, Canadians who teach in Africa, Africans who teach in California, New Zealanders who teach in England, Welshmen who teach in Egypt... Never, in the history of the language used by Sir Winston Churchill in his famous war-time tribute, has so much literature been taught to so many students by so many lecturers of such different nationalities in so many different parts of the world. In the field of literary research, indeed, the progress of writing can scarcely keep pace with the avalanche of scholarship. As the budding Ph.D. searches desperately for a subject that has not yet been covered—the Neo-Houyhnhnm Element in the Later Work of Nat Gould being a field of study now pretty well exhausted—it is all to the good perhaps that literature continues to be produced in so many more places than before. While creative literature remains even one step ahead, there is no danger that the definitive work of scholarship on the early poetry of young Mr Smith from Alabama or Zululand will be published in advance of Mr Smith's first slim volume.

"English literature" in this final chapter will concern the writings of authors of so varied or so ambiguous a nationality as Conrad and Eliot, Pound and Joyce, Beckett and Auden, Naipaul and Achebe. We have mentioned, in chapter xiv, some of the writers of the mid-twentieth century we should other-wise have been mentioning here for the first time, for there were obvious reasons of economy and comprehension why, for example, we should have taken the history of philosophy from Mill right on to Russell and why the English literatures of India, Canada, Australasia and South Africa should not be need-lessly divided into two sections each when their progress from colonial to independent, from independent to cosmopolitan, could be seen more easily in one. We left poetry in an interesting condition: in chapter xiii with Hopkins and his contemporaries and immediate successors in Victorian–Edwardian Britain, in chapter xiv with Yeats and the Irish literary revival, in chapter xv with *Poetry* and the Chicago literary renascence. Now we must look at Anglo-American poetry in the age of Eliot and Pound, covering chiefly the period from the nineteen-twenties to the sixties. Then we must discuss the novel in Britain and America in the age of Lawrence and Joyce, for we left fiction too in an interesting position: with Hardy, Meredith, Butler and Gissing in England and with Henry James and Edith Wharton in, as it were, mid-Atlantic. English drama, which since the time of Farquhar has always been largely Irish drama, we left in the capable hands of Wilde, Synge and Yeats, with some brief pre-liminary mention of Shaw and the Irish-American dramatist Eugene O'Neill. Criticism and culture we left with Ruskin and Morris in England, and with Henry Adams and George Santayana in the United States, so these topics also must be brought up to date before we close on a suitably Commonwealth-cosmopolitan note by briefly considering the English literatures of the West Indies and the former colonial territories of Africa, literatures which have largely been the creation of mid-twentieth-century independence.

Although we shall be discussing some earlier writers like Conrad and Hous-man, the period covered by this chapter is essentially 1918–65: "the Age of T. S. Eliot", in so far as any one writer can give his name to a period of half a century and of such a wide geographical extent. Eliot's twin status as both the leading poet and the leading critic of the period—"the Dean of English letters" as Ezra Pound well called him—no less than his Wordsworthian span of years and his Jamesian position in the exact centre of the Atlantic Ocean, gives him the edge in this respect over his nearest rivals for the honour, such as the English-man Lawrence, who lived in Germany, France, Italy, Australia and the United States and who died in 1930, or the Irishman Joyce, who lived in France, Italy and Switzerland and died in 1941. Eliot achieved between the years 1935 and 1965 a degree of eminence and authority in Anglo-American literary life given to no writer since the days of Dryden and Johnson; and as chapter viii of this volume is fittingly named after the author of the *Essay on Dramatic Poetry* and chapter x after the author of the *Lives of the Poets*, so the present chapter must seem to many of us misnamed if it does not commemorate the author of *The Sacred Wood*.

II. ANGLO-AMERICAN POETRY IN
THE AGE OF ELIOT AND POUND

During the nineteenth century a recurring theme among American critics was the subservience of American poetry to British and the time-lag that occurred between poetic fashions in London and Edinburgh and those in New York and Boston. Neither complaint was as justified as was often thought, but in so far as there was some truth in it, the situation in the early twentieth century can be said to be the exact reverse. Hopkins being unpublished and virtually unknown, and the early poetry of Yeats from 1886 to 1910 being not far removed in subject and technique from the poetry of Morris and the Pre-Raphaelites, it is to Harriet Monroe's founding of *Poetry: A Magazine of Verse* in Chicago in 1912 (see p. 829 above) that we can most effectually date the beginnings of twentieth-century poetry in the English-speaking world. There was in England, of course, a publisher and editor of nearly the same name. And in the same year, 1912, Harold Monro founded in London *The Poetry Review* and joined with Edward Marsh in producing the first volume of the highly successful *Georgian Poetry*. Where America had the lead over England can be seen, retrospectively, in their contrary attitude to the early poetry of Eliot. *The Love Song of J. Alfred Prufrock* was offered to Harold Monro but rejected, in spite of a strong plea in its favour by the Anglo-American poet-critic Conrad Aiken, then living in Sussex. Subsequently, the *Love Song* and most of the poems which afterwards appeared in the *Prufrock* volume found a home in Chicago in Harriet Monroe's magazine. Thus what can be called the Monroe Doctrine of publishing the best of the more revolutionary poets like Pound and Eliot, together with the best of the more traditional poets like Edwin Arlington Robinson and Robert Frost, proved of greater benefit to the future of poetry in the English language than the more conservative attitude adopted by Monro and Marsh. When Ezra Pound, the European editor of *Poetry*, had first settled in London in 1908, he had confidently expected to find more room to breathe, in a poetical sense, than he had found back home in New York, Chicago or his home state of Idaho. But he was to be speedily disillusioned, finding England poetically "as dead as mutton" and turning in some nostalgia to Chicago again —if only the Windy City could refresh itself by a breath or two from Paris— for the particular literary renascence he and Eliot were to advocate.

In America, as we have noted (p. 832), there was still a certain rivalry between the American-based cosmopolitan—who argued with some truth that the continental America of the twentieth century, with its varying racial background, was itself as international as could ever be desired—and the Atlantic-facing cosmopolitan who either lived abroad or hankered after European standards of culture and behaviour. Both kinds contributed to *Poetry*, Sandburg and Lindsay as well as Eliot and Pound, but on the appearance of Eliot's *Waste Land* in 1922 there were not wanting voices in America to deplore the poet's use of his great gifts in defending a thesis which appeared to strike particularly at the traditional beliefs of his native land. Pound's friend William Carlos Williams (1883–1963), to whom he had dedicated his *Ripostes* in 1912 and who wrote most of his own poetry around the life of his New Jersey home, called the publication of *The Waste Land* "the great catastrophe", all the more a betrayal of the Whitman–Lincoln tradition—which nevertheless was to be continued in such notable works as Stephen Vincent Benét's *John Brown's Body* (1928) and Hart Crane's *The Bridge* (1930)—because of the very genius of its composition. Writing more in sorrow than in anger, Williams saw Eliot and Pound as having finally forsaken America and cannot have been much surprised when in 1927 Eliot joined the Anglican Church and in 1935 Pound began persuading himself that Mussolini and Jefferson were much the same kind of person.

In England, the leading influences behind the conservative attitude of Harold Monro and Edward Marsh were probably those of Robert Bridges (1844–1930; p. 600) and the author of the attractive and popular *Shropshire Lad*. Alfred Edward Housman (1859–1936) was a classical scholar of European eminence, successively Professor of Latin at University College, London, and from 1911 at Cambridge, who wrote lyric poetry as a rare accomplishment rather than as a vocation. As he himself put it, with characteristic bluntness: "I am not a poet by trade: I am a professor of Latin." In contrast to Yeats, who is remarkable in modern times for the length and radical nature of his development and who was the one poet great enough, and professional enough, to take in his stride the poetic revolution initiated by Pound and Eliot, the later verse of Housman, published with some earlier pieces in 1922, in the posthumous volume of 1936 and in the memoir (1937) by his brother, the dramatist Laurence Housman, is scarcely distinguishable from the lyric sequence *A Shropshire Lad*, published in 1896 and mostly written 1890–5. His virtues and his limitations seem both to have set in early, though the *Shropshire Lad* itself—refused by several publishers and finally printed at the author's expense—had to wait for recognition till well after the Boer War and did not attain the fullness of its reputation till the period of the First World War. "Among people who were adolescent in the years 1910–25", George Orwell has recorded, "Housman had an influence which was enormous... In 1920, when I was seventeen, I probably knew the whole of the *Shropshire Lad* by heart." (As a later adolescent generation knew by heart most of Eliot's *Poems 1909–25*.) Orwell goes on to say that this appeal was due partly to the adolescent nature of the verse itself: "All Housman's themes are adolescent—murder, suicide, unhappy love, early death. They deal with the simple, intelligible disasters that give you the feeling of being up against the 'bedrock' facts of life... Housman stood for a kind of bitter, defiant paganism, a conviction that life is short and the gods are against you, which exactly fitted the prevailing mood of the young; and all in charming fragile verse that was composed almost entirely of words of one syllable."

There is more to Housman than this, as Orwell recognizes; but the criticisms that most of him is in the same tune, and that the self-pity is pervasive, are basically sound. It was in London, we must remember, not in Shropshire, that he wrote the *Lad*: compared with his senior contemporary Thomas Hardy (1840–1928; p. 654), and with his junior contemporaries Edward Thomas and Robert Frost, he was hardly a countryman; but the limitation had its corresponding strength. For Housman expressed for many readers the townsman's nostalgia for the countryside, later to be one of the dominating themes of the *Georgian*

Poetry anthologies. He expressed it memorably in such poems as *Loveliest of trees* and *Into my heart an air that kills* and by the nostalgic use of English place-names—"on Wenlock Edge", "in summer time on Bredon"—which still remain, to thousands of people, part of the genuine attraction of the countryside in a later age of motor travel. The fact that he writes mostly in nostalgic vein means that he is sometimes betrayed into mere sentimentality, but at his best his apparently simple verse is truly poignant. Like some of the minor Elizabe-thans—and the comparison would have pleased the author of *The Name and Nature of Poetry*, a lecture he delivered at Cambridge in 1933—he has been well served by composers, among those inspired by his verse to produce some of their own most characteristic music being Butterworth, Ireland, Gurney and Vaughan Williams. The monotony of his cadence is a limiting factor, but it corresponds pretty well to the limited truth of his vision of life. Compared with Yeats and Hardy at their best, he seems a minor poet, but he is one of those relatively minor figures who have great influence, alike on the ordinary reader and on other poets. His impact on *Georgian Poetry* is evident enough, though he always refused to allow the sequence of the *Shropshire Lad* to be dismembered for purposes of anthology. Among later poets whose reading of the *Lad* meant a difference to them can be singled out the many-talented John Masefield (1878–1967), poet, dramatist, novelist, essayist, critic, whose early life embraced periods as a sailor and as a barman in a New York saloon, who succeeded Bridges as Poet Laureate in 1930, and whose *The Everlasting Mercy* (1911) and *The Widow in the Bye-Street* (1913) reveal a kind of Christianized Housman allied to an impressive command of verse narration. Housman's more general influence has been acutely noted in W. H. Auden, the leader of the Marxist school of the nineteen-thirties whose later verse had itself so great an influence on some of the most characteristic of the younger poets writing in Britain and America after the Second World War.

If Housman was known to thousands of poetry-lovers during the first quarter of the century, then his contemporary Rudyard Kipling (1865–1936; p. 737) must have been known to millions, most of whom would not have described themselves as poetry-lovers at all. In his Introductory Essay to *A Choice of Kipling's Verse* (1941) Eliot describes him as a great verse-writer rather than a great poet. It would be difficult perhaps to define either term, but the distinction is useful if we have our eye on the best of Kipling, which certainly could not have been written by any ordinarily-talented versifier, and then compare this best with the best poetry of a Hopkins, a Hardy or a Yeats. Another useful distinction is between great poetry of the latter sort, which is serious poetry able to command the utmost attention of our mind and spirit, and the sort of relatively "light verse", light in quality though often deadly serious in intention, which the first quarter of the century rather specialized in. Some of this light verse owed a great debt to Kipling himself, from Masefield's *Salt-Water Ballads* (1902) and Sir Henry Newbolt's *Songs of the Sea* (1904) down to the verses of army life written by the young Edgar Wallace in South Africa. But other writers of light verse were more original, notably Hilaire Belloc, E. C. Bentley and G. K. Chesterton in Edwardian and early Georgian days, and that belated Edwardian, John Betjeman, after the Second World War.

Chesterton's *The Wild Knight and Other Poems* (1900) and such later verses as the address to Lord Birkenhead entitled *Anti-Christ, or the Reunion of Christendom* (1914) and *Wine, Water and Song* (1915) are among the best light verse of the period. The last-named, originally part of the novel *The Flying Inn* (1914), contains the famous ballad about the rolling English road which surely entitles Chesterton to the rank of "great verse-writer" as much as any of Kipling's.

The characteristics of a great deal of such verse are a striking of lofty attitudes on the part of the writer, combined with a calculated onslaught upon the emotions of the reader, particularly those simplified, crowd-pulling emotions which do not always stand up to a more cool-headed examination. One has the sense, as Orwell put it of verses like Kipling's *Mandalay*—and he could as justifiably have cited verses like Chesterton's *Donkey, Lepanto* or *Ballad of Saint Barbara*—"of being seduced by something spurious, and yet unquestionably seduced." What Coleridge might have called "a willing suspension of intelligence" is required of the reader. Where poetry of the order of Hopkins's last sonnets or Yeats's *Second Coming, Leda and the Swan* and many of the poems in *The Winding Stair* (1933) requires the utmost attention, the most alert response, the verse of a Kipling or a Chesterton—or, in a slightly different way, a Dylan Thomas or an "Ern Malley"—needs to be read with the more sensitive faculties lulled, the imagination half-asleep. To this end the hypnotic rhythm helps: the reader could hardly accept otherwise the sometimes questionable attitudes which are forced upon him.

Chesterton was among the writers represented in the first volume of *Georgian Poetry* (1912), compiled, as we have noted, by Sir Edward Marsh, friend and biographer of Rupert Brooke, and published by Harold Monro (1879–1932) of *The Poetry Review* and Poetry Bookshop, which also published Charlotte Mew, F. S. Flint and other poets. Further volumes appeared in 1915, 1917, 1919 and 1922, the poets represented numbering nearly forty in all, ranging from Masefield to D. H. Lawrence, from James Stephens (1882–1950; p. 737) to Edmund Blunden and Robert Graves. Those who appeared in each of the five volumes, and who were most typical of the spirit of the anthology, were the Welsh poet W. H. Davies (1871–1940), whose adventures in the United States had inspired his *Autobiography of a Super-Tramp* (1908), the dramatist John Drinkwater, Wilfrid Gibson (1878–1962), Walter de la Mare, and Monro himself. But Lawrence, Gordon Bottomley (1874–1948) and Lascelles Abercrombie (1881–1938) appeared in each of the first four volumes, so must logically be considered almost as typical. Lawrence, whose chief contribution to literature, it will be agreed, lies in the novel, is nevertheless one of the most striking and original of the relatively minor poets of the period. He published a good deal of verse throughout his life, most of it, directly or indirectly, autobiographical, from *Love Poems and Others* (1913) and *Amores* (1916) to the satirical *Nettles* (1930); among the best of the individual poems are *Virgin Youth, Ballad of Another Ophelia*, the nostalgic *Piano, Song of a Man who has Come Through* ("...not I, but the wind..."), *The Ship of Death* and some of the verses in the collection *Birds, Beasts and Flowers* (1923). The poetry of Walter de la Mare (1873–1956) spans the half-century, from *Songs of Childhood* (1902) to *Winged Chariot* (1951); an original and attractive talent, one of the modern masters of the short lyric.

of which he wrote upwards of eight hundred, as well as a minor master of the short story, de la Mare's best work includes *The Listeners and Other Poems* (1912) —containing the famous *All That's Past*—and the long lyrical poem *The Traveller* (1946).

Even from this brief survey it will be seen that Georgian poetry was not all of one kind, that it could range from the calculated sentiment of Chesterton to the simple sincerity of de la Mare, from the winsome warblings of Davies to the more subtle rhythms of Lawrence. (A good selection is the Penguin *Georgian Poetry*, 1962, edited by the poet-critic James Reeves.) It would not appear that Marsh or Monro had any conscious critical aim; their avowed intention was simply to introduce to a wider public the poetry being written at the time, and in this at any rate they were successful, the volumes being deservedly popular (the third sold nearly 20,000 copies), if in contrast to *Poetry* (Chicago), to repeat our comparison, they do not appear to have led anywhere in particular. Coming as they did before the poetic revolution initiated by Pound and Eliot had got properly under way, and before the later, astringent poetry of Yeats—for instance, in *The Tower* (1928)—the volumes seem in retrospect scarcely more momentous than the collection for boys and girls, *Poems of To-Day*, issued in 1915 by the English Association—which interpreted "today" in so elastic a fashion as to include some of the later Victorians like Stevenson, Meredith and Lionel Johnson. But *Georgian Poetry* was truly representative of its period, the first publications of Pound and Eliot having reached before 1922, both in England and the United States, only a very small public indeed.

Before we go on to discuss this poetic revolution, which was post-war in effect though Eliot and Pound had written their first poems before 1910, we must glance briefly at those poets whose careers were cut short by the war itself. "There died a myriad," wrote Pound in *Mauberley*, "and of the best, among them"; and these best included the poets Rupert Brooke (1887–1915), Julian Grenfell (1888–1915), Charles Sorley (1895–1915), Edward Thomas (1878–1917), T. E. Hulme (1881–1917), Arthur Graeme West (1891–1917), Isaac Rosenberg (1890–1918) and Wilfred Owen (1893–1918), besides the Canadian poet John McCrae (1872–1918; p. 747), the American poet Alan Seeger (1888–1916; p. 840) and Jean Verdenal (1889–1915), "mort aux Dardanelles", the college friend to whom Eliot dedicated his *Prufrock*. Brooke became the most popular of the British war-poets, largely because of his Housman-like poem *The Old Vicarage, Grantchester* (1913), his patriotic reaction to the outbreak of war ("Now, God be thanked Who has matched us with His hour") and his prophetic sonnet *The Soldier*, written shortly before his death in the Gallipoli campaign. Henry James, who contributed a preface to Brooke's *Letters from America* (1916), saw in him the perfect embodiment of British youth, but complained: "Why *need* he be a poet? Why need he so *specialize*?" Certainly Owen, Rosenberg and Thomas had more to offer the post-war mind, and Hulme's *Speculations* (1924) were as much an influence upon the religious thought of Eliot as his few poems upon the Imagist movement associated with him, Pound and the Aldingtons from 1909 to 1917. Owen's *Insensibility*, *Exposure* and *Strange Meeting* ("I am the enemy you killed, my friend") and Rosenberg's *Break of Day* and *Dead Man's Dump* are among the best poems to come out of the trenches; Thomas's *Poems* (1917) and *Last Poems* (1918) are among the most original and most poignant of those whose inspiration was mainly of pre-war country days, "taking the aspect of the past on the eve of a long farewell" as Walter de la Mare put it, with unconscious prophecy, when he reviewed the 1917 volume in *The Times Literary Supplement*.

Thomas is distinguished from most of the Georgians, though akin to Lawrence, de la Mare and Blunden among them, by a greater particularity in his treatment of nature, as befitted the biographer of Richard Jefferies. In this sense, he is nearer to Hopkins and to Frost than to Yeats or Eliot. It was, in fact, Robert Frost (1874–1963), who had arrived in England from New Hampshire in 1912, who by his friendship and example persuaded Thomas to take up poetry again after some years of reviewing and miscellaneous authorship. The two poets had much in common, and if we owe it to New England that Thomas was able to produce his *Poems* and *Last Poems* before his early death, Frost in turn owed much to England, to the encouragement and enthusiasm of Thomas, Gibson and Abercrombie, which enabled him to publish in London his first two books of poems *A Boy's Will* (1913) and *North of Boston* (1914) and become for a while better known in Britain than in the United States. The future poet of *New Hampshire* (1923) and *A Further Range* (1936) owed nearly as much to Thomas and his friends as Thomas owed to him, a pleasing episode in Anglo-American literary history which is recorded in the first part of Lawrance Thompson's fine biography, *Robert Frost: The Early Years, 1874–1915* (1967).

The simple patriotism of Rupert Brooke was answered during the war by the more realistic poems of Siegfried Sassoon (1886–1967), notably in *The Old Huntsman* (1917) and *Counterattack* (1918), by some of the poems of West and Sorley, and by such post-war literature in prose and verse as Sir Herbert Read's *Naked Warriors* (1919) and *In Retreat* (1925), C. E. Montague's *Disenchantment* (1922), Edmund Blunden's *Undertones of War* (1928), Robert Graves's *Goodbye to All That* (1929), David Jones's *In Parenthesis* (1937) and some of the most characteristic work of Ford Madox Ford, Sir Compton Mackenzie, Charles Morgan, R. H. Mottram, Sir Osbert Sitwell, and Henry Williamson, the best parts of whose lengthy autobiographical novel-sequence *A Chronicle of Ancient Sunlight* (1951, *et seq.*) are those dealing with the Western Front. Owen's *Poems* were published in 1920; a fuller edition, with memoir by Edmund Blunden, came out in 1933, and a further edition, with some more unpublished poems, was edited by Cecil Day Lewis in 1963. The three volumes of *Journey from Obscurity: Wilfred Owen 1893–1918* (1963–5), subtitled *Memoirs of the Owen Family*, by his brother, the artist Harold Owen, give a remarkable, detailed picture of the poet's life. A collected edition of his letters was edited by Harold Owen and John Bell in 1967. Rosenberg's poems and letters, particularly interesting as being those of a largely self-educated private soldier, were edited by Gordon Bottomley and D. W. Harding in 1937.

The situation in England in the nineteen-twenties was roughly as follows. The greater part of the poetry-reading public were still "Georgian" in outlook, were still thinking of such poets as Masefield, whose *Reynard the Fox* dates from 1919, as the most modern of the moderns, were still venerating the young Yeats of *Innisfree* and lamenting the death of Rupert Brooke in terms that would not have been excessive if applied to Keats. But a small minority were reading the early poetry of Eliot and his mentor Pound, were looking for the first time at the poems of "the magnificent Gerard Manley Hopkins" (as Harold Monro was writing by 1929), were understanding that the Yeats of *Responsibilities* (1914), *The Wild Swans at Coole* (1919) and *Michael Robartes and the Dancer* (1921) was an even greater poet than the Yeats of the eighteen-nineties, and were realizing that the loss of Owen, Thomas and Rosenberg was more damaging to the future of English poetry than the loss, bad as it was, of the more conventional Brooke. For many years this minority remained a minority, in Britain as in America, despite the advocacy of Eliot and Pound themselves, of their associates Wyndham Lewis and Ford Madox Ford, of Edmund Wilson's *Axel's Castle: A Study in the Imaginative Literature of 1870–1930* (1931) and F. R. Leavis's *New Bearings in English Poetry: A Study of the Contemporary Situation* (1932). But gradually its point of view prevailed among the majority of the younger generations of poetry readers—so gradually, though, that a second world war was to follow the first before the poetic revolution was to become established in anything like public favour.

The characteristics of the new school of Pound and Eliot are best seen, to start with, by contrast with the current school of *Georgian Poetry* (in most of its aspects), *Poems of To-Day* and their associated writers. That, after all, was how it first appeared to the contemporary English reader—and, with national differences, to many readers in the British Commonwealth and the United States. Into the world of Kipling, Masefield, Bridges, Brooke... there appeared Eliot's early poems and his *Waste Land* and the *Hugh Selwyn Mauberley* of Ezra Pound. The difference was a striking one: where the poetry of the Georgians was consciously English, full of nostalgia for the countryside in spring, the life of the village, the open road, the inn at twilight—"the clock at Grantchester, the English rook" as Auden was to put it—the poetry of the new school was consciously cosmopolitan and allusive, the nostalgia it invoked was for the city, the crowded streets, the life of offices and bars and flats, the prostitutes at eventide. *Reynard the Fox*, Kipling's *Sussex*, Belloc's *South Country*, Drinkwater's *Mamble*, had given place to the "typist home at teatime" and "Sweeney addressed full length to shave." And where most of the Georgians were in the tradition, or on the last legs, of the English romantic verse of the nineteenth century—though that was not how they saw themselves, "the intention" of *Poems of To-Day* being "to represent mainly those poetic tendencies which have become dominant as the influence of the accepted Victorian masters has grown weaker, and from which the poetry of the future, however it may develop, must in turn take its start"—the early verse of Eliot was based partly on his reading of Laforgue and the other French Symbolists, partly on his study of the later Elizabethan dramatists and the Metaphysical poetry of the seventeenth century. For perhaps the first time since Wordsworth and Coleridge, a poet's critical work and his work in poetry were two closely related aspects of the same activity.

There was not lacking, however, at least one link between the old and the new. The poetry of Eliot and Pound was read chiefly by a small minority of the reading public of the younger generation in the years succeeding the war, and this same generation more generally, as we have seen, was reading the *Shropshire Lad*. Whether the two publics overlapped much one cannot be sure, but there are certain characteristics of Housman that are by no means absent in the earliest verse of Eliot. *Prufrock and Other Observations* can be regarded, from the sociological angle, as a more sophisticated, more cosmopolitan version of the adolescent themes so dear to Housman. "Restless nights in one-night cheap hotels" may have succeeded "the blue remembered hills", but the note of self-pity at the end of *The Love Song of J. Alfred Prufrock*—"I do not think that they will sing to me"—is not very distant from the unhappy love-affairs celebrated in the *Shropshire Lad*. The achievement of Eliot of course—to which we must now turn in more detail—is that his development from *Prufrock* to the *Four Quartets* is only less radical than the development of Yeats from *Crossways* and *The Rose* to *The Tower* and *The Winding Stair*. Whereas Housman, as we have noted and as is admitted by his warmest admirers, hardly developed at all from the virtues and the limitations of the *Shropshire Lad*—"that voice", as Edmund Wilson says in his essay on Housman in *The Triple Thinkers* (1952), which, once sped on its way, "so quickly pierced to the hearts and minds of the whole English-speaking world and which went on vibrating for decades."

Thomas Stearns Eliot (1888–1965) was born at St Louis, Missouri, on the banks of that mighty river associated in Anglo-American literature with *Martin Chuzzlewit* and *Huckleberry Finn*. His origins, however, lay further east: he was descended on both sides from Puritan families of the early settlements, his ancestor Andrew Eliot having gone to Massachusetts in 1670 from the Somerset-shire village of East Coker—which gives its name to the second section of the *Four Quartets*—and his mother being a descendant of the Isaac Stearns who was one of the original settlers of the Bay Colony in 1630. The shocked surprise of these Puritan forebears if they had known that one of their descendants was to proclaim himself in 1927 "royalist in politics and anglo-catholic in religion" would have been exceeded only by that of the Puritan settlers in general had they known that Boston in the twentieth century was to become the most Roman Catholic city of the United States. How much of Eliot's scorn for the Puritan and humanist mind, expressed ironically in his early verse and more straightforwardly in his later prose writings, was due to a natural reaction from the ethos of his ancestry is an interesting question. It can at any rate be said that a reaction of this sort is by no means rare in modern times: just as the grandson and the namesake of Bishop Butler of Lichfield wrote *The Fair Haven* and *The Way of All Flesh*, so in our own time we have seen the sons of zealous agnostics go into monasteries and the daughters of clergymen become subscribers to the Rationalist Press Association. For those who accept uncritically all Eliot's debatable views on the Puritan and liberal tradition, it is worth noting that he was himself the product of the Puritan and humanist culture of three centuries.

The cosmopolitan nature of his education—at Harvard, at the Sorbonne, in Germany and at Oxford—was nearly as varied as that of William and Henry James, if not as deliberately so. In 1915 he finally settled in England, working first as a schoolmaster and then for eight years in a bank in the City of London. It is a pleasing paradox that, just as it needed the Polish mariner Conrad to give us the most memorable view in our literature of the Port of London and the

English merchant navy in late Victorian times, so it needed the American bank-clerk Eliot to present most memorably for us the London of the early nineteen-twenties. Forster had asked in *Howards End*: "Who can explain Westminster Bridge Road or Liverpool Street in the morning...?" In *The Waste Land* Eliot came nearest to explaining, if not these thoroughfares, then the crowd that "flowed over London bridge...and down King William Street" and the "public bar in Lower Thames Street...where fishermen lounge at noon."

His first volume of verse, *Prufrock and Other Observations*, was published in 1917, most of the poems, as we have observed, having first appeared in the Chicago magazine *Poetry*. This was followed in 1919 by *Poems*, hand-printed by Leonard and Virginia Woolf at the original Hogarth Press in Richmond, Surrey. The *Ara Vos Prec* volume of 1920—the title comes from the *Purgatorio*, Canto XXVI—incorporated the contents of these two little books with a number of additional poems, including *Gerontion*, his most impressive achievement up to that time. He had been assistant editor of *The Egoist* 1917–19 and had contributed to it some of the finest of his early criticism, including the famous essay on *Tradition and the Individual Talent*. Now in 1922 he founded *The Criterion*, in the first number of which—simultaneously with its appearance in *The Dial*, New York—appeared his poem *The Waste Land*, dedicated to Ezra Pound, "il miglior fabbro", and published in volume form the next year. *Poems 1909–25* (1925), containing all the poems mentioned with the addition of *The Hollow Men*, completes the first phase of his poetic career and more or less coincides with his first impact upon the general reading public.

As we have already suggested, the *Poems 1909–25* fitted as snugly into the pockets and minds of the adolescents of the nineteen-thirties as had the *Shropshire Lad* into those of their predecessors. Where Housman was so easily remembered because of his simple tune and his words of one syllable, Eliot was remembered mainly because his early verse—as the legendary old lady said of *Hamlet* —is so "full of quotations". It is one of the most obvious differences between Eliot's early verse and his late that the earlier is full of phrases which stick, willy nilly, in one's memory. "Time for you and time for me", "I have seen the moment of my greatness flicker", "Full of high sentence, but a bit obtuse", "The burnt-out ends of smoky days", "An old man in a dry month", "A dull head among windy spaces", "Beyond the circuit of the shuddering Bear", "April is the cruellest month", "I will show you fear in a handful of dust": such phrases, and there are many of them, have the "inevitability of great poetry" and a like inevitability attends the movement—virtually the blank-verse movement of the later Shakespeare and the Jacobean dramatists—of such extended passages as the close of *Portrait of a Lady*, the "After such knowledge ..." passage in *Gerontion*, and the ending of the first part of *The Waste Land*. Such passages seemed to show that the style of Shakespeare, Middleton and Tourneur could indeed be used by a modern poet in verse that was as dramatic to read if not fitted in itself for the modern theatre.

The criticism that Eliot's poems had first to bear was, of course, that he is "full of quotations" in another sense: that is, full of reminiscences of other poets, particularly Dante, Shakespeare and the Jacobean dramatists, which sometimes extend as far as actual quotations without the inverted commas, for instance "Those are pearls that were his eyes" from *The Tempest* in *The Waste Land*. It is perhaps to be regretted that Eliot should have added notes to this poem, listing his borrowings, for one point of such reminiscences is that they should be immediately recognized by the reader without any assistance; they add a further dimension to the poem, though if one misses all of them one can still understand it in most of its aspects. The majority are successful in their context, though Eliot's habit, from *Ash Wednesday* onwards, of quoting freely from the Bible and Prayer Book became a little mechanical—as it became a mere trick of fashion in his numerous imitators. We can be grateful that *Gerontion* was written in the poet's comparatively unregenerate days—during the period that produced that superb poem about the True Church and the hippopotamus—so that the reference to "Christ the tiger" was not inevitably followed, as it might well have been later on, by the stock quotation from Isaiah: "And with his stripes we are healed."

Most of the reminiscences in the early poems and *The Waste Land* are used to point the contrast between the modern world and the ideal heroic world of literature and the arts, for instance in *Burbank with a Baedeker*, *Sweeney among the Nightingales*, and the "Game of Chess" and "Fire Sermon" sections of *The Waste Land*. (And, of course, in Pound's *Mauberley*.) As literature itself, the contrast is often very convincing—"fishing in the dull canal...round behind the gashouse, musing upon the king my brother's wreck..." etc.—but historically it is less admissible. One cannot legitimately compare the literature or the art of one period with the stark reality of another, though all through European literature writers have been doing so. The literary value of *The Waste Land* is not in question: it is clearly the masterpiece of Eliot's first phase, as the *Four Quartets* are of the second. But we may doubt whether the disgust with the realities of the modern world, and the nostalgia for the past, not in its own kind of disgusting reality but as abstracted in literature and art, is anything more than a traditional literary device.

The second phase of Eliot's poetry began with his reception into the Anglican Church in 1927: during the same year he became a British subject. It is essentially, that is to say, a phase of religious poetry—linking up with his experiments in poetic drama from *The Rock* and *Murder in the Cathedral*—as the first phase may be said to have been, in retrospect, comparatively humanist. Although there are signs in the early work of Eliot's profound interest in Christianity—in *Gerontion* and in *Mr Eliot's Sunday Morning Service* with its fine lines about "the unoffending feet"—it is a general, non-theological interest, the ending of *The Waste Land*, a poem significantly owing much to Frazer's *Golden Bough*, being a Hindu, not a Christian, benediction. The change is first seen coming in *The Hollow Men*, with its truncated refrain "For Thine is the Kingdom", and in *Journey of the Magi* (1927), first of the poems contributed to the "Ariel" pamphlets published by the firm of Faber in which Eliot had been a partner since 1925. The changed manner becomes explicit in *Ash Wednesday* (1930), a poem in which the slight Shakespearean echoes—retained in the contemporary *Marina* —give place gradually to the influence of Dante, taking on new power and point by virtue of the poet's own conversion to Christian orthodoxy. The despair of *The Hollow Men* has now given place to what the poet conceives to be resignation to God's will, in which, echoing Dante and Ezekiel, is "our peace... even among these rocks." The poem is a haunting one, where the images of the Lady, the garden and the turning of the stairs are remote enough, yet finally as memorable as the more tangible images of *The Waste Land*. From the point of view of Eliot's development as a poet, the fundamental difference of this poem from the earlier one is what requires to be stressed. His personal conversion aside, it is the mark of a great poet like Eliot that he can develop in this radical way, as Yeats and Pound developed and as Housman and Frost comparatively did not. "The standard set by Shakespeare,"Eliot wrote in his essay on John Ford (1932), "is that of a continuous development from first to last, a development in which the choice both of theme and of dramatic and verse technique in each play seems to be determined increasingly by Shakespeare's state of feeling, by the particular stage of his emotional maturity at the time." Something of this high standard was maintained by Eliot himself, which is not the same thing, of course, as suggesting that *Ash Wednesday* and the *Four Quartets* are necessarily better poems than *Gerontion* and *The Waste Land*—any more than *Coriolanus* and *The Tempest* are necessarily greater plays than *King Lear* and *Measure for Measure* because they were written at a later stage of Shakespeare's development.

Four Quartets was published as a whole in New York in 1943, the first British edition following the year after. But the poem had been a long time in its creation, and its various parts had been published separately from 1936 to 1942. Each part is named after a place: *Burnt Norton* (first printed in 1936 in *Collected Poems 1909–35*) from an old country house in Gloucestershire; *East Coker* (1940) from the village near Yeovil whence Eliot's Puritan ancestors had emigrated to the New World from the Anti-Christ of Anglo-Catholicism; *The Dry Salvages* (1941) from some islands off the coast of Massachusetts known to the poet from his boyhood; and *Little Gidding* (1942), probably the best poem in the sequence, from the village in Huntingdonshire where George Herbert's friend Nicholas Ferrar (who saw to the publication of *The Temple*) established his "Protestant nunnery" in the seventeenth century, best known to modern readers (see above, pp. 311, 645) through J. H. Shorthouse's novel *John Inglesant*. These are meditative poems, in which Eliot thinks aloud on a number of associated matters: problems of national history, including the war during which three of the poems were written; personal problems concerning his development as a poet; the problems the modern poet in general has to face, in particular that of finding a vocabulary in which an affirmation of belief could be made. "Trying to learn to use words," he says, for example, in *East Coker*, "and every attempt ...a wholly new start, and a different kind of failure." The poems are closely connected with each other, key phrases being repeated and set in new contexts. The general context, of course, is Christian— "The hint half guessed, the gift half understood", he writes in *The Dry Salvages*, "is Incarnation"—and the sequence suitably ends with a vision of the religious life and controversy of the seventeenth century, in which Milton appears as well as Charles I and Nicholas Ferrar. Nothing could well be more removed from *Prufrock* and *The Waste Land*, yet it is the same poet speaking and echoes of the early work do momentarily occur—as do echoes of *Sweeney Agonistes* (1932) in *The Cocktail Party* (1950). Some of us may miss the vigour and the irony of the younger Eliot and feel that the rhythmic movement of the *Quartets*, though distinguished, is a little slow and inclined at times to an almost pulpitarian solemnity. There may have been a mutual influence here between Eliot and the verse of his friend and fellow-Anglican Charles Williams (1886–1945), for instance in *Taliessin through Logres* (1938). What matters, however, is the whole achievement of Eliot in poetry, of which the *Quartets*, apart from the experiments in poetic drama (see below, p. 909), were the last distinguished work. From *The Love Song of J. Alfred Prufrock* to *Little Gidding*: it is a long journey, and one can only be grateful for the varied experiences enjoyed by the way.

Hopkins, as we have noted, was published too late to influence Eliot; nor was he affected in any great measure by the poetry of Yeats. In his Yeats Lecture at the Abbey Theatre, Dublin, in 1940 (reprinted in the volume *On Poetry and Poets*, 1957), he himself gave some reasons for this: "When I was a young man ...just beginning to write verse, Yeats was already a considerable figure in the world of poetry, and his early period was well defined. I cannot remember that his poetry at that stage made any deep impression upon me.... The kind of poetry that I needed, to teach me the use of my own voice, did not exist in English at all; it was only to be found in French. For this reason the poetry of the young Yeats hardly existed for me until after my enthusiasm had been won by the poetry of the older Yeats; and by that time—I mean, from 1919 on— my own course of evolution was already determined."

So we have the remarkable fact that three out of the four greatest poets of the modern age in the English language—Hopkins, Yeats, Eliot—wrote almost entirely without awareness of one another; with which we can contrast the strong associativeness of most of the century's lesser poets, particularly those in well-propagated "movements", whose characteristic work can be fathered on to any member of the group with perfect propriety. The originality expected of a great poet was in the case of Hopkins, Yeats and Eliot reinforced by the accidents of time and place; Hopkins was almost entirely original, even to a fault, as he acknowledged—though he did owe something to his study of *Piers Plowman* and Welsh verse—while Yeats's early debt to his "companions of the Cheshire Cheese" (see p. 605 above) was, like Eliot's debt to Pound, only the starting point for an intensely original development. We can, none the less, say of Eliot in conclusion what he himself ends his lecture by saying of Yeats: that he is one of those few poets "whose history is the history of their own time, who are a part of the consciousness of an age which cannot be understood without them."

We can best understand the importance of Ezra Pound, the fourth of the great poets of the modern age, who was born in Idaho in 1885, by looking first of all at the passage in the *Purgatorio* (Canto XXVI, verses 112 *et seq.*) which Eliot quoted in the dedication to *The Waste Land*. Dante mentions to the spirit of Guido Guinicelli of Bologna (we use Thomas Okey's prose translation in the Temple Classics) "your sweet ditties, which so long as modern use shall last, will make their very ink precious." But the modest Guido will have none of Dante's flattery: "O brother," he says, pointing to a spirit in front, "this one

whom I distinguish to thee with my finger" *fu miglior fabbro del parlo materno,*
"was a better craftsman of the mother tongue."

A better craftsman than himself in the English language, as Arnaut Daniel
was than Guido in the Provençal: that was Eliot's opinion of the author of the
modern *Cantos*, and that it was not just a friendly gesture of personal indebtedness can be seen if we follow up the clue by closing the *Purgatorio* and opening
the volume in which the craftsman from the Far West—*il miglior fabbro dell'
Idaho*—first became widely known to the poetry-reading public in England:
the *Selected Poems of Ezra Pound*, edited with an introduction by T. S. Eliot,
published in 1928 and reprinted in Faber paper-covered editions in 1948, with
a postscript by the editor. This volume conveniently gathered together most
of the early poetry of Pound up to and including *Mauberley*, consisting of
generous selections from earlier out of print slim volumes like *A Lume Spento*
(Venice, 1908), *Personae* (1909), *Ripostes* (1912), etc., besides the whole of *Hugh
Selwyn Mauberley* (1920). Eliot's introduction—he had previously written
Ezra Pound: His Metric and Poetry (New York, 1917)—again lays the stress on
the craftsman: "This book would be, were it nothing else, a text-book of
modern versification." We follow Pound, as it were, from the nineties onwards,
reminding ourselves that Quiller-Couch included two of his earliest poems in
the *Oxford Book of Victorian Verse* and that his *Ballad of the Goodly Fere* had the
even rarer distinction of being reprinted (according to Malcolm Cowley) in a
publication called *The International Sunday School*. "It was the first of the
masculine ballads in the genre that Masefield would afterwards exploit, and
Pound might have exploited it himself... Instead he had gone to England in
1908 and started a new career."

Pound began in the tradition of Browning, the Pre-Raphaelites and the early
Yeats, and re-reading some of the early verse—for example, *La Fraisne*, *Vil-
lonaud for this Yule*, *Mesmerism* (the complimentary poem to Browning quoted
above on p. 584), and *Sestina: Altaforte* ("...you whoreson dog, Papiols,
come!")—one wonders now why their modest degree of success, sardonically
glanced at in a later poem *Salutation the Second*, was not more pronounced.
"You were praised, my books," reflects this later Pound, "because I had just
come from the country; I was twenty years behind the times, so you found an
audience ready." The "Victorian" Pound threw off his Pre-Raphaelite cloak
and put to more modern use the technical lessons he had learnt from Browning
and the early Yeats of the "Cheshire Cheese". He made a pact with Walt
Whitman. He came to recognize that it was Whitman, with all his faults, who
"broke the new wood." They had, after all, "one sap and one root"—"let
there be commerce between us."

From this time forward, Pound was twenty years before the poetic times
rather than twenty years behind them—so he found no audience ready. But,
like the hero of *Mauberley*, he rejected the kindly advice of people like Mr Nixon
(said to be modelled on Arnold Bennett) to "give up verse, my boy, there's
nothing in it." From about 1910 onwards Pound was connected with various
poetic causes, which he had a disconcerting habit of leaving behind him just
when his colleagues were drawing breath after catching him up. The doctrine
of Imagism claimed his allegiance, as it did that of the philosopher-poet T. E.

Hulme, Hilda Doolittle ("H. D.") and her husband Richard Aldington, John Gould Fletcher from Arkansas, future poet of the Agrarian school, and the Boston poetess Amy Lowell (1874–1925)—of the great Lowell family—who edited *Some Imagist Poets* (1915) and wrote *Tendencies in Modern American Poetry* (1917). But Pound soon became dissatisfied with the modest scope of this movement towards precision of language and the use of clear, hard images, deeply influenced as it was—and as Pound continued to be—by contemporary translations of Chinese and Japanese verse. The Imagists produced some memorable slight pieces, notably by Hulme and Mrs Aldington and in some of the epigrammatic verses in Pound's *Lustra* (1916). But from about 1917 Pound was in close contact in London with Eliot, the two men deciding (as Pound later put it in *The Criterion* in his staccato, punning prose) that "the dilution of *vers libre*, Amygism, Lee Masterism, general floppiness, had gone too far and that some counter-current must be set going. Parallel situation years ago in China…" And, of course, in France before Gautier and Baudelaire. Eliot and Pound agreed, in fact, that the "remedy" was "rhyme and regular strophes", as in Gautier's *Émaux et Camées* and the *Fleurs du Mal*. "Results," concluded Pound succinctly: "poems in Mr Eliot's *second* volume…also *H. S. Mauberley*. Divergence later."

The process of events cannot have been quite so clear-cut as that, but Pound undoubtedly gives the gist. The inevitable "divergence" from Eliot, which did not affect the mutual esteem of the two men, was only partly poetic in character. As Eliot drew closer to the Anglican Church, and Pound to Mussolini, they found themselves having less and less in common—although both continued to write for A. R. Orage's *The New Age* (1907–22) or its successor *The New English Weekly* (1932–49) based upon the Social Credit theories of the Anglo-Canadian economist Major Douglas. Pound's personal "purgatorio" can be lightly touched on here, before his and Mauberley's "two dusts with Waller's shall be laid"—for Pound, like Waller, has "reformed our numbers" and his political idiosyncrasies must inevitably seem less important as the years go by. Anti-Semitism is a disease that has affected many otherwise healthy minds, from Cobbett to Belloc and from Chesterton to Eliot—who in *Gerontion* speaks rather contemptuously of "the jew" (with a small "j") who has been "spawned in some estaminet of Antwerp." The Fascist dictators of the nineteen-thirties found some support among British and American writers, including Wyndham Lewis, if mostly as a reaction from the Communist views of other writers like Auden. Where Pound differed was in maintaining his pro-Fascist outlook up to and during the Second World War, while Eliot was fire-watching in the Blitz on London (as described in *Little Gidding*), Wyndham Lewis was making a public recantation of his approving words about Hitler, and writers in general, Marxist and anti-Marxist, were serving together in some branch of the armed or unarmed forces. Not for nothing was Pound born in the Far West: he has the stubbornness associated with the Western farmer of pioneer legend and (to a lesser extent) with the army mule. He continued doggedly to assert that Mussolini was in the Jeffersonian tradition, that Franklin D. Roosevelt was in the pay of world-Jewry, etc. Broadcasting these extravagances from Rome during the war, he was naturally arrested for treason in 1945 after the Allied victory. Judged "insane" by a merciful court (who had perhaps been reading certain passages in the *Cantos*), he was confined to a mental hospital until 1958. On his release, he returned to Italy and resumed work on what Eliot had called "the only 'poem of some length' by any of my contemporaries that I can read with enjoyment and admiration."

The *Cantos* referred to were begun in London about 1918, continued in Paris and Italy, and published in instalments from 1919 to 1960. Despite the approval of Eliot, and of other discerning critics like Ford Madox Ford, Wyndham Lewis, Allen Tate, William Carlos Williams and Carl van Doren, the *Cantos* have not found favour with everyone. *The Waste Land* succeeds despite its occasional obscurity and parade of scholarship; *Mauberley* is stiffer going and most readers will have been grateful at one time or another for the elucidation provided by critics like Leavis in *New Bearings* and Donald Davie in Boris Ford's *Modern Age* (1961), but on the whole the poem is worth the effort required. The *Cantos*, like some of the more obscure poems of E. E. Cummings and Marianne Moore, do not so often reward us. Dante is not so much the comparison that springs to mind as Pound's old favourite Browning, this time the later Browning of *The Ring and the Book* and *Red Cotton Night-Cap Country*, poems in which the poet's undoubted genius for striking expression fights a frequently losing battle against his extravagance, his love of jargon and display. Pound's world-wide "kulchur", recommended in his *How to Read* (1931), *ABC of Reading* (1934) and *Guide to Kulchur* (1938), has a field-day in the *Cantos*, with its allusions to Confucius and Ovid and its all-star cast from Dante down. This side of Pound—the "Burbank with a Baedeker"—is perhaps seen to better advantage in *Cathay* (1915) and *Homage to Sextus Propertius* (1934), free translations or paraphrases that bring their remote periods up to date with greater conviction. The old humour, missing from most of the *Cantos*, is ever present in the *Letters* (1954), which show again how intimate a contact Pound has always had with most of what was worth while in contemporary Anglo-American poetry. His professional attitude was of immense benefit to his contemporaries and successors in the United States, such poets as Williams, Cummings, Hart Crane, Robinson Jeffers, Wallace Stevens, Marianne Moore, whether or not they agreed with his orientation towards the European past. As Marcus Cunliffe well puts it in his chapter on "The New Poetry" in his *Literature of the United States* (1954): "Pound rendered invaluable service to such contemporaries, not by his wild denunciations of America, but by demonstrating that the professional poet, if he had the courage to renounce popular favour, could come out of Moscow, Idaho, and yet take the whole world for his province."

In one of his contributions to *The Egoist* in 1918, Eliot reviewed the third volume of *Georgian Poetry* and *Wheels: A Second Cycle* under the Shavian title "Verse Pleasant and Unpleasant". The subsequent careers of the later Georgians and the original free-wheelers do not, however, altogether support the distinction. Easily the best of the poets who contributed to the third volume of *Georgian Poetry*, and continued to publish verse up to the nineteen-sixties, was Robert Graves (b. 1895), whose *Collected Poems* appeared in 1965. Graves may possibly be mistaken in thinking his poetry more important than his prose writings—which include the historical novels *I, Claudius* (1934) and *King Jesus* (1946) and, with Joshua Podro, *The Nazarene Gospel Restored* (1953)—but no one could call his verse merely "pleasant" in the innocuous sense that might be applicable to some of the early Georgians. He is, rather, the most distinguished follower in verse of his old friend Thomas Hardy. On the other hand, while one recognizes that the Sitwells' anthology *Wheels* (1916–21) was designed as a deliberately sophisticated counterblast to early Georgian innocuousness, that haunting poem *The Sleeping Beauty* (1924), together with the best of the later verse of Dame Edith Sitwell (1887–1965)—in the *Collected Poems* of 1957— surely deserves the epithets "pleasant" or "attractive" in as complimentary a sense as could be applied to the art criticism and travel books of Sacheverell Sitwell or the five-volume autobiography (1945–50) of Sir Osbert. Many readers at the time would have described the reviewer Eliot's poetry, rather than the poetry reviewed, as "unpleasant", largely because of the unfamiliar accent and technique. Only the year before, in fact, *The Times Literary Supplement* had shaken its head kindly but gravely over *Prufrock*, deploring "the purely analytic treatment...untouched by any genuine rush of feeling." Neither Graves nor Edith Sitwell has been a technical innovator of the order of Eliot or Pound, though each has produced, throughout a long career, successful poems in which an original imagination has found the right expression for its use. The question now to be asked is whether Eliot's successors of a younger generation, the poets who started writing in England in the late nineteen-twenties or early thirties, were innovators of a high order like himself and Pound or comparatively conventional practitioners, "amateurs of genius" in the British tradition, like Graves and the Sitwells.

The question was answered at the time, and in the most flattering sense, by the poets themselves, for example in Cecil Day Lewis's *A Hope for Poetry* (1934) and Louis MacNeice's *Modern Poetry* (1938), both of which contained a spirited defence of the new school of W. H. Auden, Stephen Spender, Day Lewis, MacNeice and their associates—first nicknamed "the Pylon Poets" after an image in an early poem of Spender's—against the older school of Yeats and Eliot. But though their alleged subject was poetry, most of the arguments used by Day Lewis and MacNeice to persuade the public that the poets of *New Signatures* (1932) were the valid successors of the old, were political or sociological. The literary decade of the nineteen-thirties was pre-eminently Marxist in outlook, when most of the younger poets—with some notable exceptions like William Empson and Ronald Bottrall—adopted extreme left-wing views and unfortunately adopted with them that confusion between literary and political values characteristic of Marxists like Trotsky in his *Literature and Revolution* (1917) and which can best be studied in its British aspects in Day Lewis's symposium *The Mind in Chains* (1937), whose contributors included the novelist Rex Warner, author of *The Wild Goose Chase* (1937) and *The Aerodrome* (1941), and the South African-born sociologist Charles Madge, co-founder of Mass Observation the same year. Mostly drawn from the more comfortably-off classes, with an abstract enthusiasm for "the workers" only matched by their profound ignorance of the English people—which, unlike their contemporary George Orwell, they took no steps to remedy—the Marxist poets genuinely hoped that their writings might have the popular appeal they felt, with some justice, was lacking in most of the poetry of Yeats, Eliot and Pound. But in fact their own work was esoteric, appealing mainly to their own small group, "popular" only in the sense that Marxism became the latest fashion in literary circles in London and the universities. There was much to be said, however, for holding extreme views at this time, for it was the period of unemployment and semi-starvation in the industrial districts of Britain, of the rise to power on the Continent of the Fascist and Nazi dictatorships, of civil war in Spain. It was the period, in short, of Orwell's *Road to Wigan Pier* and *Homage to Catalonia*, in which that most honest of Socialists and most unusual of Old Etonians recorded his experiences in the Britain of the slums and the dole and in the international forces fighting in Spain. Some fought there who did not return, notably the Cambridge poet John Cornford (1915–36), the critic Ralph Fox (1900–37), author of *The Novel and the People* (1937), and the philosopher Christopher Caudwell—Christopher St John Sprigg (1907–37)—who wrote *The Crisis in Physics, Illusion and Reality* and *Studies in a Dying Culture*, all published posthumously.

The comparative worth of the Marxist poets is best seen, not during the Marxist decade itself so much—when even their best poems, such as Auden's *Spain* and Spender's *Vienna*, seemed journalistic efforts compared with Eliot's *Ash Wednesday* or Yeats's *Winding Stair*—as afterwards, when the red nineteen-thirties gave way to the solidarity of the Second World War and the poets, their Marxism modified or evaporated, went their several ways to the Home Guard, the Fire Service and the Ministry of Information. Auden himself, who had joined the Communist Party about 1932, left it in disgust in 1939 after the signing of the Nazi-Soviet Pact, and Warner, Day Lewis, Madge and others also left the party about this time. The approach of war, according to *1st September 1939*, Auden's poem on the subject (with its memorable, oft-quoted line: "We must love one another or die"), found him sitting "in one of the dives on Fifty-Second Street" in New York City, "uncertain and afraid", where formerly all had seemed so certain and straightforward. This characteristic honesty was shared by Day Lewis, who admitted in *An Italian Visit* (1953) that "We who 'flowered' in the Thirties" were "an odd lot", but "still there is hope for us"—though it must be said, with every respect, that this hope in 1953 had nothing much to do with the beliefs once expressed in the influential *Hope for Poetry* in 1934.

These poets were grossly overpraised in the nineteen-thirties, not least by each other—Auden was freely compared with Byron, Spender with Shelley—and by a natural reaction they have perhaps been underrated since. A truer comparison is surely with the Georgians, if we do not fall into the similar mistake of either overpraising or underrating these predecessors too. The young Auden of the thirties can be compared with the Rupert Brooke of the same age: the Marxist poems with the no less innocent patriotic sonnets, both being based to some extent on memories of their schooldays, and Auden's sophisticated light verse, very attractive at its best, with Brooke's excellent mock-heroic *Heaven*. Stephen Spender (b. 1909) can be compared with Wilfrid Gibson, social consciences of two generations expressed in poetry whose deep sincerity makes up for its comparative lack of originality. Gibson, as he wrote, felt "the heartbreak in the heart of things". He became a social worker in the East End of London—the rough equivalent of joining the Communist Party in 1932—and served in the ranks in the 1914 war, as Spender served in Civil Defence throughout the London Blitz and wrote the official book on the subject, *Citizens in War—and After* (1945). The many-talented Cecil Day Lewis (b. 1904), poet, critic, novelist, translator from French and Latin—notably of Paul Valéry's *Le Cimetière marin* (1946) and Virgil's *Aeneid* (1952)—and detective-story writer under the pseudonym "Nicholas Blake", can be compared either with the poet and novelist John Masefield, whom he succeeded as Poet Laureate in 1968, or with the poet and actor-dramatist John Drinkwater. And Michael Roberts (1902–48), editor of *New Signatures* (1932) and *New Country* (1933)—compare the *New Numbers* (1914) by Brooke, Gibson, Drinkwater and Abercrombie—and author himself of *The Modern Mind* (1937) and *T. E. Hulme* (1938), can be compared with his predecessor in enthusiasm and encouragement, Harold Monro.

Although some of the later work of Spender has proved popular, in both verse and prose—he was co-editor with Cyril Connolly of the magazine *Horizon* 1940–1 before starting *Encounter* in 1953—most critics are agreed that Wystan Hugh Auden (b. 1907) remains the chief figure, the former leader of the nine-teen-thirties whose poetry since—Protestant Episcopalian instead of Marxist, under the influence of Charles Williams rather than Freud—has not often been bettered by any other poet of his generation. In 1945 he became an American citizen, England being the gainer in a transatlantic deal which exchanged the author of *Look, Stranger* (1936) for the author of *The Waste Land*. His later poetry includes *Another Time* (1940), *New Year Letter* (1941), *For the Time Being: A Christmas Oratorio* (1944), *The Age of Anxiety: A Baroque Eclogue* (1947), *Nones* (1951), *The Shield of Achilles* (1955), *Homage to Clio* (1960) and *About the House* (1966). His development as a poet has not been of the radical nature of Yeats or of Eliot, to both of whom, in a superficial sense, he owes much; on the other hand, he has long been, like another transplanted English-man, Aldous Huxley, in prose, among the most intelligent of the writers who have chronicled the reactions of a sensitive—if sometimes too "knowing"—mind to the events and ideas of their time. In this sense, the public nature of his work, so emphasized by his admirers in the thirties in contrast to the private nature of much of Yeats's and Eliot's, has been well justified. Some of his criti-cism, contributed to *The New Republic* and other journals, was reprinted in *The Dyer's Hand* (1963). *The Enchaféd Flood, or The Romantic Iconography of the Sea* (1951) was based upon lectures he gave to the University of Virginia in 1949. *Making, Knowing and Judging* was his inaugural lecture as Professor of Poetry at Oxford in 1956. In 1967 he gave the first series of T. S. Eliot Memorial Lectures at the University of Kent.

The most original British Marxist poet of the nineteen-twenties and thirties wrote some of his best work not in English at all but in Scots. Yeats is as much a world poet as an Irish, but Hugh McDiarmid, the pen name of Christopher Murray Grieve (b. 1892), belongs more exclusively to Scotland, not only because he was one of the founders of the Scottish Nationalist Party and the editor of *The Voice of Scotland*, but because he was the leader of

what Denis Saurat called the Scottish Renascence, the contemporary school
of Scottish poetry which has turned its back upon the Anglo-Scots tradition
and is trying to make contact again with the older, more robust tradition
of Henryson, Dunbar, Burns and the Scottish ballads. An English critic
can only be dimly aware of the difficulties involved—though he can now
follow John MacQueen's and Tom Scott's *Oxford Book of Scottish Verse* (1967)
from Dunbar and Henryson to McDiarmid and Norman Cameron—and should
not, in any case, presume to express his Sassenach opinion while critics like
Edwin Muir in his *Scott and Scotland: The Predicament of the Scottish Writer*
(1936), John Speirs in *The Scots Literary Tradition* (1940) and McDiarmid himself in *Contemporary Scottish Studies, The Present Condition of Scottish Arts and
Affairs*, etc., and in his autobiographies *Lucky Poet* (1943) and *The Company
I've Kept* (1966), have debated the question from intimate knowledge. Among
the positive achievements in Scots and English can be reckoned McDiarmid's
Sangschaw (1925)—virtually the start of the new movement—with the same
author's *A Drunk Man Looks at the Thistle* (1926), *First Hymn to Lenin and Other
Poems* (1931) and *A Kist of Whistles* (1947); Douglas Young's *A Braird O
Thristles* (1948), which contains *The Kirkyaird by the Sea*, a version of Valéry's
poem which can be compared with Day Lewis's English version; and the
Poems in Scots by William Soutar, whose brief life, much of it stoically spent in
illness of a paralytic nature, ended in 1943.

From the point of view of poetry, Soutar was possibly the most serious
casualty of the war years; for compared with the war of 1914–18, the Second
World War of 1939–45 was not too hard upon our literary future. Again "there
died a myriad, and of the best, among them", and inevitably these best again
included poets as well as plumbers, writers as well as underwriters. But the poets
who were killed in this new and even more terrible war were poets of promise,
like Sidney Keyes (1922–43), Alun Lewis (1916–44) and Keith Douglas (1920–
44), rather than poets of accomplishment such as Owen, Rosenberg and Edward
Thomas. Comparison of Keyes's *Collected Poems* (1945) with Rosenberg's, or
Lewis's *Raiders' Dawn* (1942) and *Ha! Ha! Among the Trumpets* (1945) or
Douglas's *Collected Poems* (1951) with Owen's *Poems*, supports the contention
—though it must be added that no one can tell, when a poet is killed thus early,
whether his future career might not have been among the major achievements
of the present age.

Generally speaking, it is the relatively minor poets of a period who are apt
to be compared by their admirers with the indisputably great. One would not
immediately recognize, for instance, the identity of the eighteenth-century poet
who was described by one admirer as "the greatest genius that England has
produced since the days of Shakespeare", by another as a poet who "must rank,
as a universal genius, above Dryden, and perhaps only second to Shakespeare",
and who was compared by other enthusiasts with Homer and Milton. The
name of this universal genius was not Pope or Blake but—Thomas Chatterton.
Similarly, one would not immediately recognize the identity of the twentieth-
century poet of whose future one admirer wrote that "we might yet find that
we had in our midst a poet worthy to be classed with Dante, Shakespeare or
Milton, and not merely with Hölderlin, Rimbaud or Hart Crane." The name

of this other universal genius was not Yeats or Eliot but—Dylan Thomas (1914–53). The easiest way of seeing the absurdity of such comparisons is to remember that logically they work both ways and to envisage our congratulating the shade of Shakespeare on attaining a rank even greater than Chatterton's or patting Dante on his ghostly back for having achieved the lofty eminence of Dylan Thomas. We might also remember that, as Shakespeare or Milton is considered roughly equal to Chatterton, and Dylan Thomas roughly equal to Milton or Shakespeare, then logically Thomas must be roughly equal to Chatterton.

Fortunately for the critical respect of the twentieth century, the extravagant language used by some of Dylan Thomas's admirers (not by himself) was by no means the unanimous opinion of his readers. Indeed, few poets of the century have caused more disagreement, the most curious feature of which was that admirers and critics were apt to use the same words in defence of their contrary opinions. For instance, one admirer speaks enthusiastically of "the turmoil of his imagery", which is much the criticism made by his severest critics of his characteristic lack of imaginative organization, of his emotional incoherence. The disagreement, in short, touches on fundamental questions of poetic art, and it must be regarded as in some sense a compliment to Thomas, whose literary gifts were never in doubt, that he does raise such fundamental questions.

His debt to Hopkins, obvious enough, should not be stressed, for Hopkins himself owed something to that traditional Welsh verse which may be presumed to form part of the cultural background of every Welsh poet, whether English-speaking or bilingual. Thomas's gift of the gab in poetry is also a native inheritance, characteristic of a great deal of modern Anglo-Welsh literature, from J. C. Powys, Caradoc Evans and Rhys Davies to Vernon Watkins and Gwyn Thomas—a characteristic that at times is wonderfully impressive, particularly in humorous form, but at other times can become more mechanical in conception and comparatively boring to read. Those "voters" (as Gwyn Thomas calls the inhabitants of the modern world) who had the misfortune to be born the wrong side of the Severn, could get something of this characteristic Celtic flavour from the pages of Keidrych Rhys's *Wales* and Gwyn Jones's *Welsh Review*.

Dylan Thomas first aroused the attention of the poetry-reading public by his *Eighteen Poems* (1934) and *Twenty-Five Poems* (1936), containing verse which in its romantic rhetoric made a welcome change from the more feeble of the Marxist poetry being produced at this time. Later volumes included *The Map of Love* (1939), the mock-Joycean autobiography *Portrait of the Artist as a Young Dog* (1940) and *Deaths and Entrances* (1946), which most of his admirers see as the highest point of his work. His most popular production, and perhaps in certain humorous aspects his best, is *Under Milk Wood: A Play for Voices*, commissioned for broadcasting by the B.B.C. and published posthumously in 1954 after his sudden death on a lecture tour in the United States. His *Collected Poems* came out in 1952 (Everyman edition, 1966). His *Letters* (1957) to his fellow Welsh poet Vernon Watkins (1906–67) give his own views on what he was trying to do in poetry; the book by his widow, Caitlin Thomas, *Left-over Life to Kill* (1957), can be compared or contrasted with the memoirs of his greater namesake Edward: Helen Thomas's *As It Was* (1926) and *World Without End* (1931). *The Life of Dylan Thomas* by Constantine FitzGibbon came out in 1965.

The obscurity of some of his verse has provoked much argument, the usual line of defence being that in poetry it is more important to establish a pattern of words than to establish communication with one's readers. It can be granted that occasionally one likes a poem before one fully understands it, mainly because of the beauty of the words or the movement. But Thomas is surely the first poet in English literature whose most-admired poems are sometimes as difficult to understand as they are painful to read. "The minimum requirement of good poetry," according to Eliot—who nevertheless published some of Thomas's first poems in *The Criterion*—"is that it should have the virtues of good prose." Most of Eliot's own work has this minimum requirement; most of Thomas's has not. His comparatively few comprehensible poems reveal a pleasing romantic gift, but his reputation has been mainly built on his incomprehensible poems, which must appeal to readers who mistake deliberate ambiguity of utterance for profundity of meaning. Like Edward Thomas, he died before he was forty and it is not certain that he would have become even more obscure had he lived; perhaps the "young dog" of the mock-Joycean autobiography would have reversed the career of the Joycean "artist", by proceeding from obscurity to literature instead of the other way round. Compared, at any rate, with the verse of some of his numerous imitators in the nineteen-forties—particularly in the so-called "New Apocalyptic" movement anthologized in *The New Apocalypse* (1939) and *The White Horseman* (1941) and whose images were certainly a revelation—the most incomprehensible and turgid of Thomas's poems are models of dazzling clarity.

It was Australia which most upset the apple-cart of this new Spasmodic School. In England, the enthusiasts for Dylan Thomas included Edith Sitwell and Herbert Read, his harshest critics included Robert Graves and Geoffrey Grigson, who had printed some of his earliest poems in *New Verse*. Among poet-critics of a younger generation, G. S. Fraser's persuasive little study in the Writers and Their Work series, *Dylan Thomas* (1957)—Fraser had written *Apocalypse in Poetry* to explain the new movement led by Henry Treece (1911–66)—can be set against David Holbrook's uncompromising *Llareggyb Revisited* (1962) which does not leave Thomas's admirers much room to manoeuvre.

But it was Australia which unseated these White Horsemen once and for all —and as early as 1944. In that year the first poems of "Ern Malley" were printed in the autumn issue of the Adelaide *avant-garde* magazine *Angry Penguins*, edited by Max Harris. These poems contained striking lines and passages —"The black swan of trespass on alien waters", "The swung torch scatters seeds In the umbelliferous dark", etc.—of which Thomas himself might have been proud and which would have slipped unnoticed into *Poetry London*, as they did in fact into *Angry Penguins*. But "Ern Malley", the Australian New Apocalyptic, had not only died young: he had never really existed. The whole of his tragic life work—collected with commentary in *Ern Malley's Poems* (1961)—was produced in one afternoon by two Australian poet-critics, James McAuley and Harold Stewart, as a deliberate imitation of "the whole literary fashion as we knew it from the works of Dylan Thomas, Henry Treece and others" and which they feared, with reason, was invading Australasia as well as America. "We opened books at random," they confessed, "choosing a word or a phrase haphazardly. We made lists of these and wove them into nonsensical sentences... We deliberately perpetrated bad verse..." Unfortunately, they confessed to their deception far too early, before admirers had had time to compare Malley with Dante, before Malley's greatest poems were in all the current anthologies, before Edith Sitwell had introduced a judicious selection, before Malley was being set for school examinations along with Shakespeare and Dylan Thomas... The importance of the episode, nevertheless, remains: after 1944, no editor of an *avant-garde* magazine could be absolutely certain that he had not a second Malley hidden away among his honest perpetrators of bad verse. It was as well for such editors that the *avant-garde* changed course again in the nineteen-fifties. A neo-romanticism, combining surrealist techniques with apocalyptic visions, had succeeded in the early nineteen-forties to the Marxist exhortations of the thirties; now that reaction was itself to be reacted against in the sparer, leaner poetry of the fifties written by Philip Larkin, the critic D. J. Enright, the novelists Kingsley Amis and John Wain, and other minor poets. Possibly the most enduring minor poetry of the Eliot-Pound era will prove to have been written among those whom it is more difficult to fit into any of these categories or their American equivalents. One thinks of poets like Bottrall and Empson in England, R. S. Thomas in Wales, Edwin Muir (1887–1959) in Scotland, Austin Clarke in Ireland, Judith Wright and A. D. Hope in Australia, Derek Walcott in the West Indies, Robert Lowell and Theodore Roethke (1908–63) in the United States, Abraham Klein and Irving Layton in Canada... Most of these poets, as well as some of those mentioned previously, are still writing at the present time, so they will not concern literary history, save in a tentative fashion, till criticism has had a chance to digest their work.

No one could call the cultural climate of the twentieth century a favourable one for the production of poetry. Yet the number of our practising poets has been enormous. Harold Monro's *Chapbook* once devoted an entire issue to "A Bibliography of Modern Poetry" covering the period 1912–20: the poets named ran to over a thousand! Since then, publication has become more difficult. The magazines devoted to poetry have done good work against heavy commercial odds, none more so than Harriet Monroe's *Poetry* in Chicago, which has completed more than a century of existence. In England the chief successors to *The Chapbook* (1919–25) were Geoffrey Grigson's *New Verse* (1933–9) and *Poetry London* (1939–49) edited by the Ceylonese poet M. J. Tambimuttu, which printed some of the most "Malleyable" of the New Apocalyptics besides better things like the editor's own *Ceylonese Love Songs*. The "machine-culture" of our times has had its incidental benefits, privileges denied to former ages—if we make an exception of Lord Tennyson, intoning *The Charge of the Light Brigade* for Mr Edison's phonograph in 1890. Some of our best poets, including Yeats and Eliot, have recorded their poetry for posterity or broadcast it over the B.B.C. wavelengths. The radio has itself provided a new field for poetry, in the verse drama specially written for broadcasting, among the most successful writers of which was Louis MacNeice (1907–63), himself a producer of such drama. Whether these new opportunities have now become comparatively lost through the newer advent of television, or whether television will eventually prove a worthy successor to radio in this field (as it has done in prose drama in the plays of Harold Pinter and others), it is still perhaps too early to say.

The only clear test of poetry is survival, and one way of testing survival—particularly during a period in which too many poets are chasing too few publishers—is through anthology. While not forgetting the salutary warning of Robert Graves and Laura Riding in their *Pamphlet against Anthologies* (1928), it is a useful exercise to look through the various anthologies of twentieth-century verse through the years in order to discover which poets have kept their place and which have become "redundant". Yeats and de la Mare are probably the only poets to have held their own since 1915—at any rate, in most British anthologies. Hopkins, Eliot and Pound have been consistent in both England and America since Monro's *Twentieth-Century Poetry* (1929), but some of the Marxist poets, featured in such strength in Michael Roberts's *Faber Book of Modern Verse* (1936; revised by Anne Ridler 1951), have fallen by the wayside since the war. (The third edition of the Faber book, 1965, has a supplement chosen by Donald Hall which includes his fellow American poets Robert Lowell, William Carlos Williams and John Berryman.) How many of the younger poets, so prominent in more recent anthologies like *Poems of To-Day: Fourth Series* (1948), Kenneth Allott's *Penguin Book of Contemporary Verse* (1950), Elizabeth Jennings's *Anthology of Modern Verse* (1961) and Alfred Alvarez's *The New Poetry* (1962; enlarged 1966), will still be prominent in the anthologies of the year 2000 is an interesting question. Perhaps, by 2018, the most prominent place will be given to a contemporary of ours we have never even heard of and who, like another Hopkins, will be published to our posthumous confusion by our more discerning descendants.

III. THE NOVEL IN BRITAIN AND AMERICA
IN THE AGE OF LAWRENCE AND JOYCE

The relations between English and American literature, closer today than ever before, first came into significant focus through the personal life and artistic career of the author of *The Ambassadors*, whose own ambassadorial importance in this respect has been touched on in the final section of the previous chapter. James's theory of the Commanding Centre, of the unifying element in the work of art, was supremely well illustrated in his own novels, from first to last, as it was in the best work of his friend and fellow Anglo-American novelist Edith Wharton. In Britain, there were a number of other novelists, notably George Moore (1852–1933; p. 729), Arnold Bennett (1867–1931) and Somerset Maugham (1874–1965), who followed a similar theory drawn less from James himself than from Flaubert and Maupassant—who in the preface to *Pierre et Jean* (1881) had insisted that "the realist, if he is an artist, will seek to give us not a banal photographic representation of life, but a vision of it that is fuller, more vivid and more compellingly truthful than even reality itself." Novels like Moore's *A Mummer's Wife* (1885) and *Esther Waters* (1894), Bennett's *Anna of the Five Towns* (1902), *The Old Wives' Tale* (1908), *Clayhanger* (1910), and

Riceyman Steps (1923), Maugham's *Liza of Lambeth* (1897), *Of Human Bondage* (1915), *The Moon and Sixpence* (1919), *Cakes and Ale* (1930) and *The Razor's Edge* (1944)—and the solitary masterpiece of George Douglas, *The House with the Green Shutters* (1901)—novels like these prove how important such a discipline was to writers of less distinctive genius than James who nevertheless at their best are related to him rather than to their contemporary Wells by reason of their serious concern for the art of fiction. Though they also wrote much that was frankly of a commercially popular nature, the relevant passages in Maugham's *The Summing Up* (1938) and the *Letters of Arnold Bennett* (1966 *et seq.*) show how seriously these novelists took their best work, some of which was equally popular with more discerning readers.

We should beware, however, of supposing that works of this kind, however distinguished, are the only valuable creations of the English or American novel (as distinct from most of the French.) We have only to remember Dickens and Mark Twain to see that this is by no means the case. What, we may ask, would James have made of *Martin Chuzzlewit*, if he and not Dickens had thought of the subject? We can be sure that in James's hands it would have been a masterpiece of construction, with the study of selfishness and hypocrisy the centre of attention—as it was meant to be in Dickens—but there would have been no artistic necessity for such characters as Sairey Gamp and Young Bailey (to say nothing, so to speak, of Mrs Harris), or for the side-splitting Columbian episodes, and it is precisely in these characters and episodes that the genius of *Chuzzlewit* mainly resides. A *Chuzzlewit* without Mrs Gamp, a *Copperfield* without Micawber, a *Little Dorrit* without Flora and Mr F.'s Aunt: such would have been the probable result had a James been in Dickens's shoes, and most readers will be very thankful that an exchange like this is only imaginary. A Dickens pouring the full force of his sentimentality into *What Maisie Knew* or *The Wings of the Dove* would have been a spectacle hardly more distressing.

Nor can there be any rigid distinction between what is commonly called "the novel of ideas", as written by such novelists as Wells and Aldous Huxley, and the novel of more artistic value such as those we have mentioned. We rarely have a contrast as clear as that between Peacock and Jane Austen or between Wells and Henry James. Most often it is a question of degree, not of absolute distinction, "congenital" novelists—as Huxley well calls them—like Forster and Lawrence being also men of ideas, and novelists of ideas like Wells and Huxley sometimes approaching close to the novel conceived as a work of art. The distinction we make in this chapter—taking first the "congenital" novelists from Conrad to Cary, afterwards the novelists of ideas from Wells to Orwell—is therefore for purposes of convenience mainly, one of those necessary abbreviations or approximations to truth (like "influences", "movements" and so forth) without which literary history, at any rate in a small compass, could scarcely be written.

The Irishman Yeats and the Americans Eliot and Pound we have conceived to be the greatest English poets of the twentieth century. The Pole Josëf Teodor Konrad Nalecz Korzeniowski (1857–1924) has a claim to be considered the greatest English novelist of the period between James and Lawrence, as well as perhaps the most remarkable figure in the whole history of English literature.

Born at Berdiczew, in one of the Ukrainian provinces of Poland long under Tsarist rule, he became a French sailor at seventeen, an English master mariner at twenty-nine, and under the name of Joseph Conrad one of the greatest of English novelists at forty-five. He learned French before English, beginning his first novel *Almayer's Folly* (1895) on the endpapers of a copy of *Madame Bovary*. Not that this first exotic excursion, nor his second effort, *An Outcast of the Islands* (1896), has much in common with Flaubert's masterpiece (being more akin to the first version of *La Tentation de Saint Antoine*). But we are entitled to stress, as he himself did, the profound influence of the French masters, including the Russian novelist Turgenev, on his literary career, which held till it was replaced, in his own view, by the influence of Henry James from about 1903 onwards. So obviously original an author could afford to remind his readers that he was well in the European tradition, and if *Almayer* and the *Outcast* did not at once bring him into the circle of the great, they were the first decisive step and real greatness lay not far ahead.

For it was his third novel. *The Nigger of the "Narcissus"* (1897; first serialized in W. E. Henley's *New Review*) that gave him his first indisputable claim to classic rank. That it is one of his finest stories few will deny, and it is significant that it was based on personal experience—less so than such stories as *Typhoon* (1903) and *The Shadow Line* (1917) but much more so than his previous, too romantic work. The "Kipling of the South Seas", to quote an early reviewer, gave place to the great Conrad, the literary artist, first in *The Nigger* and *Lord Jim* (1900), then in those deeply moving and impressive *nouvelles*, *Heart of Darkness* and *The End of the Tether*, in the collected volume *Youth* (1902). *Heart of Darkness*, perhaps the finest short novel in the language, is drawn from his experiences as captain of a river steamer in the Belgian Congo in 1890—when, incidentally, the manuscript of *Almayer's Folly* was nearly lost overboard.

Conrad is rightly regarded as the best writer about the sea and seamen who has ever lived, a much better novelist than the still underrated Marryat, who in Polish translation was one of the enthusiasms of his youth and one of the causes of his desire to become an English sailor. As Henry James (forgetting Melville) once said to him, no one before Conrad had ever known, for the purposes of literary art, what he had known. But he disclaimed the classification, "sea-story writer", and justifiably so, for some of his best work is not about the sea at all. His most ambitious novel *Nostromo* (1904), highly organized in the James manner and "the most anxiously meditated," he tells us, "of the longer novels", is a political novel (first serialized in *T.P.'s Weekly*) set in an imaginary South American republic; *The Secret Agent* (1907) is a Dickensian study, dedicated to H. G. Wells, of an anarchist plot in London; *Under Western Eyes* (1911) takes place in Russia and in that refuge for revolutionaries, Switzerland. One of Conrad's reflections here has gained an even greater truth with the passage of time: "The scrupulous and the just, the noble, humane and devoted natures; the unselfish and the intelligent may begin a movement—but it passes away from them. They are not the leaders of a revolution. They are its victims." We might almost be reading Koestler's *Darkness at Noon* or Achebe's *A Man of the People*.

Conrad's epigraph to *Youth*, from *Grimm's Tales*—"...but the Dwarf answered: 'No, something human is dearer to me than the wealth of the world'"

—can be applied to himself. What Santayana said of Dickens (in *Soliloquies in England*, 1922) may be said of him, that he had "a vast sympathetic participation in the daily life of mankind." The combination of that Dickensian quality with the intensely serious idea of the novel as a work of art—which he drew from the French and Russian masters, from his first source of encouragement Edward Garnett (whose wife Constance translated the Russians into English), from Henry James and from Ford Madox Ford, his collaborator in *The Inheritors* (1901) and *Romance* (1903)—this rarest of combinations produced his unique fiction, probably the best in English of the early twentieth century and equal to the best in any other language.

His last works are not, on the whole, so impressive as his earlier ones, from *The Nigger* to *Under Western Eyes*. They include *Chance* (1911), the novel which first brought him wide popularity both in England and the United States; *Victory* (1915), where he returns more maturely to the Malaya of his first fiction; *The Rescue* (1920); and *The Rover* (1924), appropriately dedicated— "this tale of the last days of a French brother of the Coast"—to his French friend and biographer G. Jean-Aubry, editor of *The Life and Letters of Joseph Conrad* (1927). Conrad's incidental weaknesses are obvious enough: sometimes, particularly in these last works, his perception of human nature degenerates almost into melodrama, sometimes his wisdom is perfunctory. That other fine novelist, E. M. Forster, speaks of his noble obscurity: "The secret casket of his genius contains a vapour rather than a jewel"—a criticism, it must in justice be added, which has sometimes been applied to the critic's own work.

Edward Morgan Forster (b. 1879) is the finest survival in literature, as Bertrand Russell in philosophy, of that liberal, humanist tradition of the early twentieth century against which some of the most acute intelligences of our time have directed their powers of denigration. While we continue to read Forster and Russell, the humanist tradition is in no danger of being altogether superseded, though like other traditions it may require modification or revision from time to time. For all Forster's impatience with Conrad, the author of *The Shadow Line* is himself in the same tradition: in a note to that *nouvelle* he speaks of the supernatural as "but a manufactured article, the fabrication of minds insensitive to the intimate delicacies of our relation to the dead and to the living... Whatever my native modesty may be, it will never condescend so low as to seek help for my imagination within those vain imaginings common to all ages and that in themselves are enough to fill all lovers of mankind with unutterable sadness."

Most of Forster's novels were written before Conrad wrote those words: in fact, as long ago as from 1905 to 1910. Yet, significantly enough, his novels, save in superficial details, do not appear "dated" in the least, which phenomenon we can put down partly to the surprising strength of the humanist tradition, attacked as it has been from Christian orthodoxy on the one side and from Marxist orthodoxy on the other—and frequently written off by both—partly to Forster's preoccupation with those problems of morality and personal relationships which are not of an age but for all time. There seems little doubt that he will be read as eagerly in the year 2000 as he is in 1968 and as he was in 1910; compared not only with Wells, most of whose novels were confessedly built on current issues, but with Conrad's friend John Galsworthy (1867–1933), whose *Forsyte Saga* (1906–21), good as are the early, less sentimental parts—it deservedly won him the Nobel Prize for Literature in 1932—becomes more and more of historical rather than strictly literary interest, Forster today seems modern, as modern as his younger contemporaries Lawrence and Joyce. He has never been a widely popular author, but the number of his readers through the generations may well prove greater than Galsworthy's massive public, mainly restricted as it was to a single generation.

Forster was born in London, partly of Welsh stock, partly of the "Clapham" ancestry mentioned above on p. 559 and which he describes in his "domestic biography" *Marianne Thornton: 1797–1887* (1956). He was educated at Tonbridge School and King's College, Cambridge, where he came under the influence, directly or indirectly, of the philosopher G. E. Moore and formed a friendship with the scholar and humanist Goldsworthy Lowes Dickinson, author of *The Greek View of Life* (1896), whose biography he wrote in 1934. After leaving Cambridge—which he was to return to in 1946 as an Honorary Fellow of King's—he lived for a time in Italy, the background of his first and third novels, *Where Angels Fear to Tread* (1905) and *A Room with a View* (1908). Between these two studies of an "international situation" somewhat different from James's—among the ironies of the theme being the contrast between the Italy of reality and the Italy of English imagination—was published *The Longest Journey* (1907), a novel of English life perhaps the most autobiographical of the three and despite some characteristically fine passages probably Forster's only failure of importance, though it remained the author's favourite work: "the least popular of my five novels," he wrote in 1965, "but the one I am most glad to have written." Then followed the first of his two undoubted masterpieces, *Howards End* (1910), a novel as great as any written during the twentieth century and which reveals new subtleties with each successive reading. The theme is again one of contrast, this time between two families, the half-German Schlegels, who are interested in literature and music and who in general stand for the spiritual values the author himself stands for, and the Wilcoxes, the practical, unimaginative business people who nevertheless have in one member of the family, the first Mrs Wilcox, a woman instinctively respected by the most arty-crafty and "delightful" of the Schlegel circle. The rest of the Wilcoxes are not spared by the author, any more than he had spared similar unimaginative characters in *Where Angels Fear to Tread* and *The Longest Journey*; yet when Mrs Wilcox dies Margaret Schlegel marries Henry Wilcox—and it is this event, inevitable as it seems when once the theme of the novel has been properly understood, which some of Forster's most percipient critics have construed as a weakness. In fact, the strength of the novel lies exactly here, in Forster's realization of the less admirable side of the Schlegels, personified by the deliberately "impetuous" Helen and the comic prig Tibby, and the corresponding more admirable side to the Wilcoxes, personified mainly by the dead woman and symbolized by her house Howards End which she leaves to Margaret on her death-bed. The marriage follows inevitably from this realization, which is Margaret's as well as the author's. "Only connect!" is the key-phrase: "connect the prose in us with the passion...and the beast and the monk, robbed of the isolation that is life to either, will die." Without the criticized marriage, it is doubtful whether the novel could have held together at all.

The Schlegels and the Wilcoxes are equally well observed; the one weakness of the novel—devastatingly exposed, from intimate knowledge, by Frank Swinnerton in *The Georgian Literary Scene* (1935)—lies in the character of Leonard Bast, where the author perhaps depended more on hearsay than on personal experience. It is part of a general weakness, not restricted to Forster alone, but inherent in the very ethos of what has come to be called "the Bloomsbury group"—comprising the daughters of Sir Leslie Stephen, Virginia Woolf and Vanessa Bell, with their husbands the editor and publisher Leonard Woolf and the art critic Clive Bell, and their friends the artist and critic Roger Fry (of the great Quaker family), the painter Duncan Grant, the "biographical novelist" Lytton Strachey, the literary critic Desmond MacCarthy, the economist Maynard Keynes, the philosophers Moore and Russell, the historian G. M. Trevelyan and the novelist Forster, to name the leading lights. They had many of the virtues which we find expressed in Forster's novels, their chief weakness being a social complacency which irritated D. H. Lawrence among others and which indeed finds little justification in the cultural history of England, to say nothing of Scotland or the United States. They were remarkably sure of their position as the self-appointed leaders of English culture—one of the points later satirized by Wyndham Lewis in *The Apes of God* (1930)—which partly accounts for their condescending treatment, both in life and in fiction, of those whom they felt to be less favoured people. Lawrence was a writer most of them—apart from Forster himself—never fully appreciated, and when Forster smiles at the favourite authors of Leonard Bast he is passing an unconscious judgment on his own cultural standards. For Leonard was reading the "wrong" writers, not by literary standards so much as by fashionable ones: Ruskin, Borrow, Jefferies, Stevenson, Thoreau... by the standards of Bloomsbury 1904–10 were considered very much *vieux jeu* and enthusiasm for them could only be smiled at as evidence of a lack of breeding. But the rest of the reading public did not agree with Bloomsbury, as was proved when J. M. Dent and Ernest Rhys started their famous Everyman's Library in 1906 and some of Leonard's favourite authors sold in their thousands and keep on selling. Ruskin and Thoreau, Borrow and Jefferies, can indeed be criticized for their incidental weaknesses, and like most authors some of their work has lasted better than others; but Margaret and Helen, and their creator Forster, were not applying the standards of culture but those of fashionable taste—which, like the fashions in women's costume they so much resemble, are liable to alter every season.

Some of the essays in Forster's *Abinger Harvest* (1936) are spoilt by a similar complacency, so much at odds with his usual admirable perception. For instance, in *Notes on the English Character* he writes of his own class, the upper-middle class: "They gained wealth by the Industrial Revolution, political power by the Reform Bill of 1832; they are connected with the rise and organization of the British Empire; they are responsible for the literature of the nineteenth century." Responsible for nineteenth-century literature? We can only say so if we ignore, not only the publishers of humble birth like the Macmillans and Cassell, but the contributions of writers like Blake, Burns, Crabbe (one of

Forster's favourite authors!), Paine, Cobbett, Godwin, Gifford, Hogg, Clare, Lamb, Hunt, Keats, Carlyle, Mill, Dickens, George Eliot, Mark Rutherford, Thomson, Gissing, Hardy, Barnes, Jefferies... and the literature thus truncated (with the additional omission of writers like Whitman and Twain in the United States) would hardly be the literature of the nineteenth century as we know it.

It was in 1912 that Forster went to India for the first time, and in 1914 he began work on an Indian novel which was to prove his second undoubted masterpiece. But the novel was delayed by the war, which took him to Alexandria, and he paid a second visit to India in 1921 before resuming it. *The Hill of Devi* (1953), in which he records his Indian experiences, is valuable both as history and as a source-book for *A Passage to India* (1924; p. 741 above)—which at this date has itself a double interest as an historical as well as a literary work. This most famous of Forster's novels portrays post-Kipling but pre-Partition India, the sub-continent at a transitional stage in her existence. Full of Forster's characteristic ironic humour, the novel is nevertheless fundamentally a tragedy, in which the failure to "connect" and the related failure to establish human relationships between the British and the Indians, leads to more momentous results than a similar failure in *Howards End* or *Where Angels Fear to Tread*. If *Howards End* remains on the whole his best novel, *A Passage to India* is certainly, from several points of view, his most important work.

Forster has never been a prolific writer. Besides the books mentioned, he has published two volumes of short stories, *The Celestial Omnibus* (1914) and *The Eternal Moment* (1928); the Clark Lectures at Cambridge, *Aspects of the Novel* (1927); a book of collected essays with the highly characteristic title *Two Cheers for Democracy* (1951); and a few other miscellaneous works. Of his style, the most important thing to observe is that it owes little or nothing to the example of James, Conrad or any other novelist who had tried to raise fiction from what they thought the careless habits of the eighteenth and nineteenth centuries. Forster's is a style at once colloquial and reflective; he thinks nothing of commenting upon the action as it proceeds, as though he were a Fielding, a Thackeray or a Samuel Butler. Where Conrad, in *Lord Jim*, *Heart of Darkness* and *Chance*, uses Marlow as a mouthpiece, Forster is usually content to use himself, though he does use Margaret to some extent in *Howards End* and the character Fielding in *A Passage to India*. The opening of *Howards End* is characteristic of his style in its simplicity and apparent carelessness: "One may as well begin with Helen's letters to her sister..." The novelist who is most akin to Forster here is, curiously enough, D. H. Lawrence—the Lawrence of the lesser novels like *Kangaroo*, the unfinished *Mr Noon* (written 1921; published in *A Modern Lover*, 1934) and *The Lost Girl*, which opens: "Take a mining townlet like Woodhouse, with a population of ten thousand people..." and continues for pages in that colloquial strain, with interludes of personal reflection.

When James in *Notes on Novelists* (1914) gave his opinion on the most promising of the younger practitioners in England, he omitted Forster altogether and, in a famous mixed metaphor, confessed he found Lawrence "hang in the dusty rear" behind "the boat" of Hugh Walpole, Compton Mackenzie and the dramatic critic turned novelist Gilbert Cannan (the Mr Gunn of *Fanny's First Play*.) Possibly James was correct at the time, according to his own limited conception of the novel's function, but for most readers today Forster and Lawrence, together with Joyce and Virginia Woolf, have proved much more important than Cannan, Mackenzie and Walpole—whose "fresh play of oar" in *The Duchess of Wrexe* (1914) James singled out for attention. Walpole's *Mr Perrin and Mr Traill* (1911) and *Fortitude* (1913), besides *The Duchess*, are certainly novels out of the common run, as are Sir Compton's *Carnival* (1912) and *Sinister Street* (1913–14); but they are not in the same class as *Howards End* or *Sons and Lovers*. While Cannan's translation of Romain Rolland—which seems to have inspired the translation of Proust by C. K. Scott-Moncrieff—is perhaps more valuable than any of his own fiction, including *Round the Corner* (1913), the novel praised by James.

David Herbert Lawrence (1885–1930) was born at Eastwood, Nottingham-shire, the son of a miner, and was educated at Nottingham University College, where he qualified as a teacher. He taught at Croydon till 1913, when he had to resign because of illness, and thenceforward he devoted himself to literature. Much of his poetry, we noted, is autobiographical, and some of his novels, too, are based pretty directly on personal experience in many parts of the world. His first novel, *The White Peacock* (1911), was begun when he was only twenty, so it is not surprising that it should be in certain respects—like its successor *The Trespasser* (1912)—a comparatively immature performance, though the tragedy of the young farmer George, particularly in the closing chapters, would not have disgraced the pen of Hardy himself, from whom this best part of the novel mainly derives. The weakness of the *Peacock* is best seen by contrast with Lawrence's first masterpiece *Sons and Lovers* (1913), which is much more directly autobiographical. The Morel family here are the Lawrence family only faintly disguised, and the domestic tragedy is very similar to that of the Lawrences in real life; whereas in the *Peacock* all the "family" characters have taken a step up in the social scale and in doing so have lost whatever reality they might otherwise have had. (The hero Cyril, for example, calls his mother "the mater", a mode of address which would have startled Mrs Lawrence in her miner's cottage in Hell Row.) *The White Peacock* is romantic, almost Meredithian; *Sons and Lovers* is realistic, and the first half of it at any rate is among the best things Lawrence ever wrote.

It had a decided success when it was first published and a lesser man might have gone on to repeat the success in slightly different forms. A writer of the stature of Lawrence, however, is always looking for fresh ways in which to present his maturing experience, and his next novel, *The Rainbow* (1915), is as different from *Sons and Lovers* as *Sons and Lovers* from *The White Peacock*. That it is in itself one of his most impressive novels few readers will deny, but in conjunction with its sequel *Women in Love* (1921) it gives perhaps a less satisfactory impression. Lawrence thought at one time of calling the novels "*Women in Love* Part One and Part Two", so intimate a connection did he intend, but about the merits of the sequel (begun soon after *The Rainbow* was finished) the most diverse opinions have been held. Some have seen it as a sad falling-off from *The Rainbow*; others, notably F. R. Leavis in *D. H. Lawrence: Novelist* (1955), as one of his supreme masterpieces. It will be sufficient here simply to record the difference of opinion over what is, in any case, Lawrence's most ambitious undertaking, in which he portrays a wider variety of English life than he had ever done before.

The post-war Lawrence is, in general, less impressive than the pre-war. For the first time his novels, with the exception of the comparatively light-hearted work *The Lost Girl* (1920)—begun, however, before the war—become difficult to get through. *Aaron's Rod* (1922), *Kangaroo* (1923), *The Plumed Serpent* (1926), *Lady Chatterley's Lover* (1928): all contain admirable things amidst a mass of windy rhetoric. Virginia Woolf's opinion in *The Common Reader* (1925)— "Mr Lawrence, of course, has moments of greatness, but hours of something very different"—is very inadequate as a judgment of Lawrence in general, but only an exaggeration of the truth in regard to the novels just mentioned. The greatest work of this period is, significantly, not a full-length novel at all, but the very moving *nouvelle*, *The Man Who Died*, not published in England till 1931, after his own death. Like George Moore's *The Brook Kerith* (1916), it takes as a starting-point the revolutionary idea about the Crucifixion originally developed by Renan and in Samuel Butler's *The Fair Haven*.

Lawrence's first fiction to be published was in the shape of short stories contributed in 1909 to Ford Madox Ford's *English Review*, and he continued to produce stories of varying length, from mere sketches to *nouvelles*, during the rest of his life. In this field, he gained rather than lost with the years. If his post-war novels are verbose, that criticism cannot be made of such *nouvelles* as *The Fox* (1923) and *St Mawr* (1925) or the best stories in *England, My England* (1924), *The Woman Who Rode Away* (1928) and *The Lovely Lady* (1932).A prolific writer for publication—his work includes poems, plays, travel books, essays, criticism, besides the novels and stories—he was also a prolific letter-writer, with a wide range of correspondents. His *Letters*, which form one of the most valuable autobiographies of modern times, were admirably edited by Aldous Huxley in 1932. A more extensive collection, not however superseding Huxley's, was edited in 1962 by Harry T. Moore of the University of Southern Illinois, who also wrote what is probably the best of the numerous biographies of Lawrence: *The Intelligent Heart* (1955).

The story the *Letters* present, though full of incidental humour, is in essence a tragic one. For Lawrence's life was an unending and courageous struggle against two things: his own ill-health—like Keats, Stevenson and the Brontës, he was consumptive—and the prudery of the public. A pioneer in the serious treatment of sexual themes, he inevitably came up against those self-appointed guardians of public morals, the pundits of the popular press, who have always preferred smoking-room stories. *The Rainbow* was the first of his novels to incur their wrath and they succeeded in having it withdrawn soon after publication. May Sinclair and Arnold Bennett were the only two writers to make any public protest against this malicious censorship, but in her biography *The Savage Pilgrimage* (1932) Catherine Carswell records that the review written by Walter de la Mare for *The Times Literary Supplement* was "long and largely favourable, but it was still in proof when the prosecution took place, and so was never published." Thenceforward the hunt was on, *Women in Love* being greeted with the headlines A BOOK THE POLICE SHOULD BAN: LOATHSOME STUDY OF SEX DEPRAVITY: MISLEADING YOUTH TO UNSPEAKABLE

DISASTER, one reviewer writing: "I do not claim to be a literary critic, but I know dirt when I smell it, and here is dirt in heaps—festering, putrid heaps which smell to high Heaven." A LANDMARK OF EVIL was their reaction to *Lady Chatterley*: "the bearded satyr and world-famous novelist, who has prostituted art to pornography." And once again they were successful in their attack, only an expurgated version of the novel being allowed to be published in England until 1960. It has to be added, however, that if Lawrence had lived to a normal old age, he would have found himself as revered a literary figure as Swinburne or Hardy, some of whose work provoked nearly as much indignation among Victorian reviewers. And he would have found himself wealthy beyond the dreams of Arnold Bennett, if he had lived to draw the massive royalties from the Penguin edition of *Lady Chatterley*, the film rights from *Sons and Lovers*, and all the other rights from radio, television, paperbacks and school editions.

One other thing can be said. Lawrence was the contemporary of his distinguished namesake Thomas Edward Lawrence (1888–1935), best known as Lawrence of Arabia, whose most notable work, *The Seven Pillars of Wisdom* (1926), coupled with the almost legendary nature of his career, led Bennett and other critics to compare seriously with the novelist as a literary force. The answer to that confusion was made by Colonel Lawrence himself shortly before he changed his name and rank to Aircraftman T. E. Shaw—and incidentally became the original of Private Meek in Bernard Shaw's *Too True to be Good*. "It's a sin against decency and proportion," he wrote—see *The Letters of T. E. Lawrence*, edited by David Garnett (1938)—"for Arnold Bennett to let the unhappy likeness of our names bracket us publicly. If I could have published *Revolt in the Desert* (1927; the abbreviated version of *The Seven Pillars*) under any other name, I'd have left D. H. L. in his sole use... Lawrence, for this generation, is D. H. L., an infinitely greater man than all of us rolled together."

James's views on the younger generation of novelists, which we have referred to, were expressed in 1914 when he was himself over seventy. Five years later, one of the younger generation in person, who like James was a notable critic as well as a novelist, gave a much more penetrating view in an essay on *Modern Fiction* afterwards included in *The Common Reader*. This is one of the most important essays on the twentieth-century novel ever written, and its author Virginia Woolf (1882–1941), whom we have briefly mentioned in relation to Forster and the Bloomsbury Group, is herself important partly because she had the courage in creative work of her convictions in criticism. She began by expressing her dissatisfaction with the novels of the three most popular writers of the day: Wells, Bennett and Galsworthy. "No single phrase will sum up the charge of grievance which we have to bring against a mass of work so large in its volume and embodying so many qualities, both admirable and the reverse. If we tried to formulate our meaning in one word, we should say that these three writers are materialists." More specifically, of Bennett: "His characters live abundantly... but it remains to ask... what do they live for? More and more they seem to us, deserting even the well-built villa in the Five Towns, to spend their time in some softly padded first-class railway carriage... and the destiny to which they travel... becomes more and more unquestionably an eternity of bliss spent in the very best hotel in Brighton." Of Wells: "He is a materialist from sheer goodness of heart...in the plethora of his ideas and facts scarcely having leisure to realize...the crudity and coarseness of his human beings...Nor, profoundly though we respect the integrity and humanity of Mr Galsworthy, shall we find what we seek in his pages."

From these novelists who "spend immense skill and immense industry making the trivial and the transitory appear the true and the enduring," Virginia Woolf sought "to define the quality which distinguishes the work of several young writers, among whom Mr James Joyce is the most notable." She must also have been thinking of Dorothy Richardson (1873–1957), whose *Pointed Roofs* (1915) and *Backwater* (1916) were the first instalments of a twelve-part autobiographical sequence of novels with the general title of *Pilgrimage* (1938). With the previously unpublished thirteenth section, *March Moonlight*, the whole *Pilgrimage* was reprinted in 1967 with an illuminating introduction by the novelist-critic Walter Allen.

The famous phrase, "stream of consciousness", was originally applied to Dorothy Richardson by the novelist-philosopher May Sinclair. But the words were not entirely hers: she was paraphrasing William James of Harvard, the philosopher brother of Henry James, who had spoken of the "stream of thought"; and among James's most brilliant pupils at Radcliffe had been the future novelist Gertrude Stein (1874–1946), friend of Joyce in Paris. The plot, as it were, thickens; and a place on the graph must certainly be found for the extraordinary Miss Stein, whom we shall be meeting later on in connection with Hemingway and the post-war American exiles in Europe. In *The Autobiography of Alice B. Toklas* (1933)—her own autobiography, but written as if by her secretary and confidant—Gertrude Stein records how the first chapters of her novel *The Making of Americans* were published in 1924 in Ford Madox Ford's *Transatlantic Review*, though the novel had been written as far back as 1906–8. "So for the first time," she says with characteristic modesty, "a piece of the monumental work which was the beginning, really the beginning of modern writing, was printed, and we were very happy."

Inevitably, as Henry James's theories with Henry James's novels, the novelist whom Virginia Woolf's essay casts most light on is not Joyce or Gertrude Stein, nor even Dorothy Richardson, so much as herself. Beginning with comparatively conventional novels like *The Voyage Out* (1915) and *Night and Day* (1919), she progressed in accordance with her own theories through the only partially successful *Jacob's Room* (1922) and *Mrs Dalloway* (1925) to the much more satisfying *To the Lighthouse* (1927), the novel in which theory is at last successfully wedded to practice, to create an impressive work of art. "Examine for a moment," she had said, "an ordinary mind on an ordinary day" receiving "a myriad impressions... Let us trace the pattern...which each sight or incident scores upon the consciousness." It is a poet's task, rather than a novelist's, as commonly understood, but Virginia Woolf's later novels, such as *The Waves* (1931) and the posthumous *Between the Acts* (1941), are more consciously poetic than *To the Lighthouse* and not nearly so successful. *To the Lighthouse* is a novel, and on the whole a memorable one; it owes something to her vivid memories of her father Leslie Stephen, the original of Mr Ramsay, and—as has been unkindly remarked—it is the only one of her novels in which anything happens. The short poetic chapter showing the passage of time has been severely criticized—not least by the author (see *A Writer's Diary*, 1953)—but it is more successful in its context than the interludes of prose-poetry in *The Waves*.

Most of Mrs Woolf's novels are on a small scale; to James or Conrad they would have been little more than *nouvelles*. This was partly, one suspects, in reaction from the often overblown productions of H. G. Wells; partly because the theory in itself, despite the contemporary examples of Dorothy Richardson, Gertrude Stein and Proust's *A la recherche du temps perdu* (1913–27), seemed to demand what reviewers call a small canvas. Could the "stream of consciousness" become a flood without the risk of drowning the reader? *Pilgrimage* was one answer (or thirteen answers); *Ulysses* was another.

In Victorian times, in the heyday of the three-volume novel—when many novelists wrote for serial publication and padded out their numbers against the clock—*Ulysses* would not have been considered so very much longer than normal. The legend of its gigantic length—many admirers, forgetting *Don Quixote*, *Clarissa Harlowe*, *War and Peace* and *A Glastonbury Romance*, believe it to be the longest novel ever written—has this truth behind it: it is by far the longest novel in one volume where the stream-of-consciousness technique is adhered to throughout. ("I try," Joyce explained, "to give the unspoken, unacted thoughts of people in the way they occur.") *Ulysses* is an artistic whole, whose action takes place on a single day in a single city: 16 June 1904 in Dublin. Whether it is a complete success is a different matter, the most eminent critics being as unsure of their verdict as the most ordinary reader. When Mrs Woolf mentioned Joyce in the essay quoted, she had only a fragment of *Ulysses* to go by, the part then appearing in *The Little Review*, New York; and her opinion, that it was "undeniably important" and that "in contrast with those whom we have called materialists, Mr Joyce is spiritual", was "hazarded", as she said, "rather than affirmed." When some years later, after the whole of the work had appeared, she wrote *How it Strikes a Contemporary*, she was more definite in her judgment, though much less sympathetic: "*Ulysses*," she wrote, "was a memorable catastrophe—immense in daring, terrific in disaster."

James Joyce was born in the same year as Virginia Woolf, 1882, and died the same year, 1941; his background, however, was about as different as it could be. Where Mrs Woolf succeeded to a liberal humanist culture of the English upper-middle class, Joyce was born in Dublin of Irish Catholic lower-middle-class stock, his father being a rate collector and the family background being similar to that of the Dedaluses in *A Portrait of the Artist* and *Ulysses*. He was educated at Jesuit colleges and at University College, Dublin. After leaving Ireland in 1902, he studied medicine for a while in Paris, where he met Synge and was the first person to read *Riders to the Sea*, which he was later to translate into Italian. From 1904 to 1915 he was a teacher of languages in Trieste, later living in Zürich and again in Paris. *Chamber Music* (1907) was his first publication: "a suite of songs," as he described them to one of his composers, "and if I were a musician I suppose I should have set them to music myself." These were followed by *Dubliners*, a book of realistic stories begun in 1904, rejected by

forty publishers and finally published in 1914; the best is the moving *nouvelle*
called *The Dead*, in which the name of the chief character and the symbolism of
the snow were suggested by a story of Bret Harte's. Then in 1916 came Joyce's
first masterpiece, *A Portrait of the Artist as a Young Man*, written 1904–14 and
first printed in serial form in *The Egoist* 1914–15. Praised by both Wells and
Mrs Woolf, in point of style it forms a transitional stage between the realism
of *Dubliners* and the symbolism of *Ulysses*. It is a novel in its own right, but
can also be regarded as the entrance-hall to *Ulysses*, Stephen Dedalus, as closely
based upon the author as Paul Morel upon Lawrence in *Sons and Lovers*, being
the hero of the *Portrait* and the Telemachus of its successor. In retrospect, it seems
a pity that the two novels were not conceived as one, for a prior knowledge of
the *Portrait* is much more essential to an understanding of *Ulysses* than a prior
knowledge of the *Odyssey*. But one can see how the separation came about.
Joyce, often thought to be precocious, was in fact a slow developer: he had to
start with his realistic sketches of Dublin, then proceed with his autobiographical
novel, before he could envisage the gigantic scheme that was to illumine Dublin
and his own life, and so much else, in one symbolic whole.

   Ulysses, which first saw the light, as we have mentioned, in some passages
serialized in Margaret Anderson's *Little Review* in New York in 1918–20, was
published as a volume in Paris in 1922, for many years remaining banned for
obscenity in Britain and the United States. Alfred Noyes, the Georgian poet
and biographer of Voltaire, was one of the distinguished men of letters who
supported the ban, explaining to a lady at dinner that if he were to quote
certain extracts from *Ulysses* the lady would never speak to him again. But
there are passages from many authors, including Voltaire, Rabelais, Chaucer,
Shakespeare, Swift—not to mention the Old Testament—which no man would
repeat to a woman, or indeed to another man, unless they were on familiar
terms. (And what occasion would normally arise for the repetition?) The
passages Noyes was thinking of, and which formed the chief reason for the
banning, are mostly contained in the last section of the novel, where Molly
Bloom's thoughts in bed are presented in all their naked glory, as uninhibited as
they are unpunctuated. The lack of punctuation is probably a mistake, for while
it is easy enough to write without commas and stops—school children do it
every day—in order to read Mrs Bloom (or Mrs Finching in *Little Dorrit*) the
reader has to supply the commas and stops for himself. For short stretches, as in
Little Dorrit—or even as in Beckett's *Godot*, where Lucky has only two pages of
unpunctuated speech—this is amusing enough; but there are fifty pages of
Molly without a single punctuation mark until the final full stop, and this—
in a different sense from Alfred Noyes's—is too much for most readers to bear.

   Ezra Pound wrote in *Le Mercure de France* that Joyce had succeeded in *Ulysses*
where Flaubert had failed in *Bouvard et Pécuchet*: that is, in presenting the Average
Man. There can be no doubt that this was part of Joyce's intention; but the
scene of the novel is Dublin, and if Joyce had wanted to make his Ulysses the
average Dubliner he would surely have made him an Irishman, and a Catholic
Irishman at that. But Leopold Bloom (whose father, born Virag, had come
from Hungary) is a Jew, and a Jew in Ireland—as Mr Deasy indicates before we
meet Bloom for the first time—is about the most un-Average Man Joyce could

possibly have thought of. In the scene at the cemetery, he is good-humouredly patronized by Simon Dedalus and the rest of the mourners—each of whom, far more than Bloom, has a claim to be considered the Average Dubliner (several of them, in fact, made an earlier appearance in *Dubliners*). And this leads on to a more important question: what sort of a novel *Ulysses* really is.

The consensus of opinion today replies that, fundamentally, *Ulysses* is a comic work—using the term "comedy" in its very widest sense. There is a good deal to be said for this: not only are there many incidental passages of comic invention—like the famous scene in the lying-in hospital, where the prose-style ranges from Anglo-Saxon to the most modern forms of cosmopolitan slang—Bloom and Molly can be considered great comic characters, comparable with Falstaff and the Wife of Bath. And Joyce himself remarked on one occasion that the book is meant "to make you laugh". Yet Bloom is a Jew among Gentiles, as Stephen is an artist among Philistines, and the novel is a sequel, however gigantic a sequel, to the *Portrait*, which no one has ever called a comic work. There is something to be said for describing *Ulysses* as a comic epic in prose, like *Tom Jones*; there is also something to be said for calling it, fundamentally, a tragedy: the tragedy of loneliness. In certain respects a comic figure, Bloom is more truly a figure of pathos; he is wretched, not only because his wife is unfaithful to him, but because his son has died in infancy, as Stephen is wretched because he has refused his mother's dying wish. These two isolated figures—never more isolated than when in company—wander about Dublin, eventually meeting in a brothel, the traditional refuge from loneliness, whence Bloom takes Stephen home with him. It is difficult not to feel that their meeting is the intended climax of the novel and that Mrs Bloom, like Simon Dedalus, is an altogether subsidiary character. Homer's Ulysses wandered a mere twenty years; Joyce's belongs to the race which has been wandering for two thousand. No novelist who had conceived his theme entirely in terms of comedy could have made his Ulysses a Jew in a Catholic city and his Telemachus a poet in a Philistine society.

The style of *Ulysses* has been the subject of numerous learned theses in England, France and the United States. What has mostly been ignored is that Joyce owes part of his apparent originality to typographical, not literary, methods. It would be a useful exercise to "translate" a typical page of *Ulysses* into ordinary English typography, then to put into Joycean shape a typical page of *Sons and Lovers* or *A Passage to India*. On the whole, however, the novel triumphs over these tricks of typography so dear to Joyce's heart, as it does over the occasions when the reader is nearly drowned in the flood of Bloom's consciousness; and it triumphs, like other great novels, partly because of the human theme, partly because the author's prose style, at its best, is that of a genuine and original artist. But it was a near thing; and the trap Joyce so narrowly avoided in *Ulysses*—of finding his technique more important than the purpose which should have used it—claimed its predestined victim in *Finnegans Wake*.

This was the fruit, much of it carried with great labour from the Dead Sea, of Joyce's later years, when he had become the idol of the cosmo-American intelligentsia in Paris, France, centred around the reviews *transition* and *Transatlantic Review*, both of which printed parts of the *Work in Progress* (as it was

long called) from 1924 to 1938. Separate sections of the work were later published in book form: *Anna Livia Plurabelle* (1928), *Tales Told of Shem and Shaun*
(1929), *Haveth Childers Everywhere* (1930), etc., and the whole work *Finnegans
Wake* in 1939—completed under great difficulty, Joyce being now more than
half blind. To understand *Finnegans Wake* entirely the reader needs a mental
equipment and a personal life very similar to the author's: not only an extensive
and peculiar knowledge of Dublin and of Irish history, legend, slang and folk-
lore, but some little acquaintance with French, German, Italian, English and
the language of dream-psychology. But any cosmopolitan Irishman, living in
Europe and dreaming of Dublin, should be able to understand parts of it, and
the rest of the reading public, "yung and easily freudened", can enjoy the music
of some of the incomprehensible passages, the ingenious parodies of *Macbeth*—
"For a burning would is come to dance inane. Glamours hath moidered's lieb
and herefore Coldours must leap no more. Lack breath must leap no more…"
—the circular, gramophone-record structure of the book, where the last sentence runs straight into the first (a trick which that other Irishman, the author
of *Tristram Shandy*, would have envied), and above all the completion, in this
"record" of the unconsciousness of a single night ("allspace in a notshall"), of
the scheme of *Ulysses*, which was the record of the consciousness of a single day.
Joyce once advised his readers to devote their whole life to the understanding
of his works, a suggestion which reminds us that he was born in the same city,
and had kissed the same stone, as Bernard Shaw—who once recommended his
public to read all his plays "at least twice over every year for ten years"—and
was anxious to pull the same number of Anglo-Saxon legs.

The Letters of James Joyce were edited by Stuart Gilbert in 1957 and continued
(1966) in two further volumes by Richard Ellmann of North-Western University, Illinois, who also wrote, in 1959, the best of the several biographies of
Joyce. Among the introductions to an author who certainly requires some elucidation, mention can be made of Edmund Wilson's chapter in *Axel's Castle*
(1931), Harry Levin's *Critical Introduction* (1941), Eliot's *Introducing Joyce* (1942),
L. A. G. Strong's *The Sacred River* (1949)—a sensible account by a fellow Irish
novelist—and J. I. M. Stewart's pamphlet in the British Council's Writers and
Their Work series, with the same critic's chapter on Joyce in *Eight Modern
Writers* (1963), the final volume of *The Oxford History of English Literature*.
Ezra Pound's pioneer essays on Joyce, contributed 1914–22 to *The Dial* and
other journals, are reprinted in *Polite Essays* (1937) and *Literary Essays of Ezra
Pound* (1954).

But it was the Parisian review *transition*, edited by Eugene Jolas and Elliot
Paul, which not only published parts of what was to become *Finnegans Wake*
but also discussions by various influential critics, including Samuel Beckett,
which were reprinted in the breathlessly-named volume *Our Exagmination
round his Factification for Incamination of Work in Progress* (1929). Samuel Beckett,
born 1906 in Joyce's native city of Dublin, was for a time his secretary in Paris
and in certain respects can be regarded as his chief successor. Most of his writing,
including the famous play *En attendant Godot* (1952)—*Waiting for Godot* (1954)
—was originally written in French, then translated by the author into English,
so it is doubtful whether, even in this cosmopolitan age, Beckett belongs

entirely to English literature, though he belongs here more than the French novelist Julian Green, born of American parentage in Paris in 1900, whose chief works include *Minuit* (1936). That theme of loneliness, which we noticed as one of the aspects of *Ulysses* and which is obviously one of the major themes of the modern urban world, has been exploited in full measure by Beckett, both in his drama (see below, p. 912) and in his novels, for instance in *Malone meurt* (1951)—*Malone Dies* (1956)—which is the death-bed soliloquy of an old and helpless man who is sick and tired of life, though being an Irishman he keeps on talking about it. As Vladimir and Estragon observe to each other in *Waiting for Godot*: "To have lived is not enough for them. They have to talk about it." Compared with Joyce, Beckett's humour is rather bleak; his stream of consciousness often dries up before it gets properly under way and among his lonely, miserable, uprooted characters with Irish names like Murphy and Molloy he has no "cultured all-round man" like (we have his own word for it) Leopold Bloom. The more lively side of Joyce, with some of the naughty words, was better continued by the American novelist Henry Miller in his *Tropic of Cancer* (1934), a novel about the seamier side of artistic life in cosmopolitan Paris between the wars whose seediness is to some extent redeemed by the obstinate vitality of the author. An ambitious, relatively successful attempt to view the Joycean stream of consciousness through the space-time spectacles of Einstein was made by Miller's English friend Lawrence Durrell (b. 1912) in the four novels known collectively, from their place of origin, as the Alexandria Quartet: *Justine* (1957), *Balthazar* (1958), *Mountolive* (1958) and *Clea* (1960).

Henry Miller, born of German parentage in New York in 1891, was the last notable figure among the group of American writers who settled in Paris for longer or shorter periods during the nineteen-twenties and thirties and whose archetype and universal great-aunt, who had said "America is my country and Paris is my home town", was Gertrude Stein, from Pittsburgh, Pa., who had been in France since 1902. It was Miss Stein, speaking to Hemingway, who called her fellow-expatriates of the post-war years "the lost generation", meaning principally those American writers like the novelists Hemingway and Fitzgerald and the poets E. E. Cummings and Archibald MacLeish, whose young lives had been deeply affected by the 1914–18 war and its disillusioned aftermath and a few of whom, like D. H. Lawrence's friend the poet Harry Crosby, who committed suicide in 1929, never really recovered from it. Their exploits have been recounted in numerous memoirs, notably Malcolm Cowley's *Exile's Return* (1934), Samuel Putnam's *Paris Was Our Mistress* (1947), Sylvia Beach's *Shakespeare & Company* (1959), the Canadian novelist Morley Callaghan's *That Summer in Paris* (1963) and Hemingway's *A Movable Feast* (1964), besides in Gertrude Stein's autobiography and her *Paris, France* (1940), in Ford Madox Ford's semi-fictional reminiscences and in Douglas Goldring's *The Last Pre-Raphaelite* (1948) and Frank MacShane's *Life and Work of Ford Madox Ford* (1965), more reliable records than Ford's own of the achievements of the editor of *The Transatlantic Review*, who did almost as much as H. L. Mencken and George Jean Nathan, editors of *The Smart Set* and *The American Mercury*, to encourage the lost generation to find their feet.

On the whole, these writers merited such ample documentation, for among them we find some of the chief figures in the American literature of the twentieth century. F. Scott Fitzgerald (1896–1940) belongs particularly to "the jazz age", as he called it, which he embodied in novels like *This Side of Paradise* (1920) and *The Beautiful and the Damned* (1922) and in collections of stories like *Flappers and Philosophers* (1920) and *Tales of the Jazz Age* (1922). His finest novel is undoubtedly *The Great Gatsby* (1925), a story of the love and death of a wealthy bootlegger, a novel symbolic of the period in American life which came to an end in the Wall Street crash of 1929. The best of Fitzgerald's later work is the novel *Tender is the Night* (1934), with its title after Keats.

That tradition, of coming to literature by way of newspaper reporting, which has always been so strong in America, gained new strength in the work of Hemingway and Dos Passos, some of whose earliest stories, written in their leisure hours, appeared in Ford's *Transatlantic Review*. Sinclair Lewis (1885–1951) had used his journalist's eye to great effect on many different aspects of American life, in gently satirical novels from *Main Street* (1920) and *Babbitt* (1922)—the novel which gave a new word to the language—to *Arrowsmith* (1925) and *Elmer Gantry* (1927), to name the chief, and had been justly rewarded in 1930 by becoming the first American to receive the Nobel Prize for Literature, an honour he accepted, he said at Stockholm, on behalf of a whole generation of American writers—five of whom (Eugene O'Neill, Pearl Buck, Faulkner, Hemingway, Steinbeck) were later to receive the same distinction. ·

There was this amount of truth in Sinclair Lewis's characteristic modesty, that his naturalistic technique had been to some extent anticipated by Sherwood Anderson (1876–1941) in the stories collected in *Winesburg, Ohio* (1919), stories of a typical small American town as seen through the eyes of a young reporter, and that this technique was to be transformed to more serious purpose still in the best work of Hemingway, Dos Passos and James T. Farrell. After serving with an ambulance unit on the Italian front in 1918, Ernest Hemingway (1898–1961) had worked as a correspondent in Europe for *The Toronto Star* and the International News Service. He arrived in Paris in 1922, bearing a letter of introduction from Sherwood Anderson to Anderson's mentor Gertrude Stein and was soon finding his first stories rigorously blue-pencilled by such indefatigible exponents of the laws of literary art as Miss Stein, Ezra Pound and Ford Madox Ford. His tough, matter-of-fact, confidential, Midwestern style first appeared in *Three Stories and Ten Poems* (Paris, 1923), in the collection of stories *In Our Time* (New York, 1925) and in his first novel *The Sun Also Rises* (1926), whose narrator-hero, like the author at the time, is an American newspaperman working in Paris. Hemingway remained a journalist all his life (he had started on *The Kansas City Star* at the age of nineteen), but he was a journalist with a difference, a journalist who had sat at the feet of Gertrude Stein and whose tough prose style was consciously as well as unconsciously "American" and "twentieth-century". In *A Farewell to Arms* (1925) he looked back on his experiences on the Italian front. In *Death in the Afternoon* (1932) he glorified the bull-fighting which Lawrence had regarded with a less romantic eye in *The Plumed Serpent* and whose sentimental sadism Max Eastman was to analyse. *For Whom the Bell Tolls* (1940) is perhaps Hemingway's best novel and certainly among the best literature to come out of the Spanish Civil War. The most impressive of his later work is the *nouvelle* about a Cuban fisherman, *The Old Man and the Sea* (1952).

Hemingway was the first novelist in Anglo-American literature who might as easily have won a Lonsdale Belt in the Noble Art as a prize for literature in the Nobel Trust. The difficulty of separating the man from the legend lies in the fact that the man partly created the legend, partly was created by it. The strain of keeping up with the myth of the regular guy must have contributed to the depression of Hemingway's last years and his probable suicide. To this extent, he was a victim of his own publicity, and inevitably, too, in his later writing there came to be a degree of artifice in what was at the start, when all fair criticisms have been made, a genuine distinction.

The finest single achievement in the tradition of American naturalist fiction, of which Anderson and Sinclair Lewis had been the twentieth-century pioneers, belonged not to Hemingway but to John Dos Passos with his trilogy *U.S.A.* (1938). Dos Passos, born in Chicago in 1896, had served in the U.S. Army Medical Corps before becoming a freelance correspondent in Spain and the Near East. His "farewell to arms" had been written earlier than Hemingway's, and more bitterly, in *One Man's Initiation* (1920) and *Three Soldiers* (1921). From the East, via Paris, he returned home, both literally and in literature, achieving in *Manhattan Transfer* (1925) and the three novels in the *U.S.A.* trilogy—*The Forty-Second Parallel* (1930), *Nineteen-Nineteen* (1932) and *The Big Money* (1936)—what is at once a portrait in depth of a great nation and a running commentary on that nation's history since the beginning of "the American century". To achieve this feat, Dos Passos resorted to some "tricks of the trade" which would probably not have occurred to a writer without practical journalistic experience and which were in the main highly successful in *U.S.A.*, if not so successful when repeated, in more conventional terms, in later novels like *Midcentury* (1961). The passages of Joycean prose-poetry which are mere epigraphs to chapters in *Manhattan Transfer* are transformed in *The Forty-Second Parallel* and its successors into a device called "The Camera Eye" in which a disembodied, Whitmanesque intelligence reflects on affairs both in close-up and at long range. Similarly, the newspaper headlines and the snatches of popular songs that occasionally interrupt the fictional narrative of the earlier book are given a central importance in the trilogy in the device called "Newsreel" in which headlines like NATION GREETS CENTURY'S DAWN and LUTHERANS DROP HELL FOR HADES are interspersed with choruses from Broadway all the way from *Alexander's Rag Time Band* to *My Blue Heaven*. And the interwoven stories of the fictitious characters, drawn from all classes and occupations, are now interspersed with potted biographies of real people like Edison, Henry Ford, Randolph Bourne and Thorstein Veblen—Veblen who like Socrates asked dangerous questions and drank the bitter drink "in little sips through a long life."

The achievement here is a panorama of fact and fiction which owes much to *Ulysses* for its initial inspiration but which has been made into a truly original work of literary art, a picture mainly of urban America and in particular of the skyscraper city of New York. The Chicago of the twentieth century was covered in even more detail, and with much greater autobiographical, Dreiser-

like intimacy, by James T. Farrell (b. 1904) in a series of novels of which the
most famous is the *Studs Lonigan* trilogy—*Young Lonigan* (1932), *The Young
Manhood of Studs Lonigan* (1934), *Judgment Day* (1935)—and which was continued in *A World I Never Made* (1936), *No Star is Lost* (1938) and later novels
and stories featuring Danny O'Neill, Eddie Ryan and other semi-autobiographical heroes, to form an American counterpart to the *Comédie humaine* of
Balzac or the *Rougon-Macquart* of Zola. Henry James would have shuddered at
the all-inclusive nature of these American novelists' preoccupations and sighed
for less raw material, more artistic selection. While the criticism is one to bear
in mind while reading the less rewarding pages of Dos Passos and Farrell—not
to mention Thomas Wolfe—it might be argued that it should apply to *Ulysses*
as well and that when the whole intention is so plainly Balzacian or Zolaesque,
late-Jamesian standards are irrelevant. What matters is whether Dos Passos
and Farrell do give us the overall impression of New York and Chicago that
they intend, and the answer of most readers would be that, on the whole, they do.

Criticizing some twentieth-century notions of freedom, D. H. Lawrence
once exclaimed: "Thank God I am *not* free, any more than a rooted tree is
free!" It would be easy to criticize the critic, pointing out that Lawrence himself in adult life hardly stayed long enough in one place to cast a shadow, let
alone put down roots. But there were many valid reasons for Lawrence's
peregrinations, and in general we find that some of the best work in both American and British fiction during the twentieth century has been achieved either by
those like Joyce who wandered in body but whose spirit remained at home or
by those who hardly left home at all.

We find this particularly, in American fiction, when we turn from novelists
of the urban north like Dos Passos and Farrell to novelists of the more rural
south and south-west like Faulkner, Steinbeck, Caldwell and Thomas Wolfe of
North Carolina (1900–38)—the title of whose first and best novel, *Look Homeward Angel* (1929), might be called the prayer of them all. John Steinbeck, born
in 1902 in California, took his native soil as the background for his most
impressive work, including that wonderful story *Of Mice and Men* (1937) and
his masterpiece *The Grapes of Wrath* (1940), an epic account of the struggles of
a farming family during the Depression of the thirties. Erskine Caldwell, born
in Georgia in 1903, described from intimate knowledge the back lands of the
cotton country in *Tobacco Road* (1932) and *God's Little Acre* (1933) and the
racial conflicts of the South in *Trouble in July* (1940). Poet and critic as well as
novelist—associated with the Regionalist and Agrarian movement of Ransom,
Tate, Fletcher and Donald Davidson—Robert Penn Warren, born in Kentucky
in 1905, has written both of the Southern present, as in the political novel *All
the King's Men* (1946), and of the Southern past, as in *Band of Angels* (1956),
where a girl brought up white is discovered to be the daughter of a Negro slave
woman and is shipped down river to be sold for 2,000 dollars—a variant on the
story Mark Twain told in *Pudd'nhead Wilson* and before him J. T. Trowbridge
in *Neighbor Jackwood*.

But William Faulkner (1897–1962) of Oxford, Mississippi, is the pride, if the
slightly baffling pride, of American Southern fiction in the twentieth century,
writing almost exclusively from *Sartoris* (1929) to *The Reivers* (1962) of Yok-

napatawpha County, Mississippi, in a series of novels and stories which though masterly at their best are sometimes as difficult to get the hang of as the name Yoknapatawpha is difficult to spell or pronounce. There is no deeper South than Faulkner's, and if it is partly his own invention, as we do not feel that Mark Twain's South ever is, the results—particularly in some of the novels of the late twenties and early thirties like *The Sound and the Fury* (1929) and *Light in August* (1932)—are worth the effort of comprehension involved. *Sartoris* was the first of the series in which Faulkner described the decline of two representative families of the Old South and the rise of the unscrupulous Snopes family, a theme he continued in *The Sound and the Fury*, on the whole his best novel, though one of the most difficult to grasp at first reading. Comparatively simpler going is provided by *As I Lay Dying* (1930), by *Requiem for a Nun* (1951), a novel partly in dramatic form which was adapted for the stage by Albert Camus, and by some of the short stories in *Go Down, Moses* (1942). Faulkner described his novels in his Nobel Prize speech in 1949 as "a life's work in the agony and sweat of the human spirit." The reader, particularly the non-American reader, who does not wish to sweat too much himself for Faulkner's meaning can find great help in Malcolm Cowley's introduction to *The Portable Faulkner* (1946) and Cleanth Brooks's *William Faulkner: The Yoknapatawpha Country* (1964), an enlightening piece of criticism published by the Yale University Press.

What Thomas Wolfe once told Scott Fitzgerald—that "a great writer is not only a leaver-outer but also a putter-inner"—would have disturbed Henry James by its implications but would have been enthusiastically endorsed by a British novelist who spent half his life in America and shared Wolfe's passion for autobiography. Just as Wolfe's heroes, whether called Eugene Gant or George Webber, are unmistakeably Thomas Wolfe himself, so the heroes of John Cowper Powys (1872–1963), whether named John Crow, Wolf Solent or another, are unmistakeably aspects of John Cowper Powys himself, who once retorted to his brother Llewelyn's remark that revision should cut *down*—"the shorter the better"—by the Wolfe-like assertion: "No, no! the *more* the better!"

A whole family of novelists must be a rare phenomenon, yet two examples have occurred in Britain during the last hundred years. The half-Irish, half-Cornish Brontë sisters, whose paternal grandfather was an illiterate peasant farmer called Branty or Brunty, have been succeeded in our time by the Anglo-Welsh Powys brothers, sons of the Vicar of Montacute—not far from Eliot's East Coker—and descended on their mother's side from the family of Cowper and Donne. The brother just mentioned, John Cowper Powys, spent half his life in the United States as a lecturer on English literature, travelling all over the country and writing his novels in trains and hotels—as he records in his *Autobiography* (1934), the book which may well outlive most of his auto-biographical fiction. He was a magnificent lecturer, speaking for hours without a note, seldom knowing when he started what he was going to say next: a Coleridge re-born, though none of his published criticism—from *Visions and Revisions* (1915) to *Obstinate Cymric* (1947)—has anything like Coleridge's power of thought. But the superb gift of expression which served him so well in lectures, in private conversation and letters—see *The Letters of John Cowper*

Powys to Louis Wilkinson (1958)—was a mixed blessing for a novelist. He wrote as he spoke, with hardly a pause for reflection, dreaming with a pen in his hand of his beloved Dorset and Somerset as his train sped through the snows of Wisconsin or the cotton-fields of Faulkner's Mississippi. Like the young Dickens, the young J. C. Powys at school and at home was both a voracious reader and a ready spinner of yarns himself, making up characters and stories as he went along. The gift never left him, but it makes his novels, highly readable as they mostly are—among the best are *Wolf Solent* (1929), *Weymouth Sands* (1934) and *Maiden Castle* (1936)—prolix and repetitive, often strangely empty, full of unconscious reminiscences of other novelists' work. Once the spell has worn off, it is difficult to take them entirely seriously. The apparent exception, which proves the rule, is *A Glastonbury Romance* (1932), a novel which brings the Grail legend up to date and which does have a suitable ending, to round the whole thing off, in the famous scene where the Mayor of Glastonbury, John Geard, floats down the river to his death. But even this novel, much longer than *Ulysses*, is fatally marred by a total lack of revision, by the author's determination to put everything in.

What John Cowper Powys lacked, the power of self-criticism to add to his enviable gifts of expression and invention, was attained by two of his brothers: the novelist and fabulist Theodore Francis Powys (1875–1953) and the essayist and philosopher Llewelyn Powys (1884–1939). Llewelyn was the best critic of the three, both of his own and his brothers' work; his revision of Theodore's first novel *Mr Tasker's Gods* (written 1916–17, first published in New York 1924) was as clearly to Theodore's advantage as it was against the theory and the practice of John Cowper. Neither Theodore nor Llewelyn had the eldest brother's fluency; both began hesitantly, as can be seen from Theodore's first stories and his *Soliloquies of a Hermit* (1918) and from Llewelyn's *Ebony and Ivory* (begun 1913, published 1923), stories and sketches of his native Dorsetshire and of his farming life in Kenya before the war. But both brothers could learn from their comparative failures: the hesitant Theodore of *Mr Tasker* and the *Soliloquies* was to become the masterly fabulist of *Mr Weston's Good Wine* (1927), while Llewelyn's first *Ebony* sketches were to be followed by the far more convincing *Black Laughter* (1924), an evocation of the African scene which remains among his best books.

Llewelyn was not primarily a novelist, though he did write one novel, *Apples Be Ripe* (1930), besides an "imaginary autobiography" *Love and Death* (1939), completed just before his own death after years of courageous struggle against consumption. He is better known for his essays on country life, like *Earth Memories* (1934) and *Dorset Essays* (1935), and for his philosophical works like *The Pathetic Fallacy* (1930) and *Impassioned Clay* (1931). His *Letters* were edited by Louis Wilkinson in 1943, with an introduction by Llewelyn's widow Alyse Gregory, formerly managing editor of *The Dial* in New York. *The Life of Llewelyn Powys* (1946) by Malcolm Elwin is one of the best biographies of our time.

The Dorset downs of Theodore Powys are as central to his novels and stories as the Yorkshire moors to *Wuthering Heights* and at his best he can be seriously compared with Emily Brontë as well as with his Dorsetshire predecessor Thomas

Hardy. But his masters are Bunyan and the Bible, and he gives a Biblical twist
to the Dorsetshire vernacular to produce what is at once a recognizable feature
of country speech in this district of England and a medium for the "eternal
verities" of Love and Death. No writer of our time has owed so much to Christian legend as T. F. Powys; he is as steeped in the Bible as that other parson's
son Samuel Butler, but unlike Butler he puts his intimate knowledge to profoundly serious though very unorthodox use. His work is all of a piece, from
his first publication *An Interpretation of Genesis* (1908) to the latest of his stories.
His best work includes the short stories originally called *Fables* (1929; reprinted
under the title *No Painted Plumage*, 1934); the *nouvelles, The Left Leg* (1923) and
The Only Penitent (1931; reprinted in *Bottle's Path*, 1946); and the novels *Mr
Weston's Good Wine* (1927) and *Unclay* (1931). The two novels and the *Fables*
are among the finest achievements of their kind that the twentieth century has
produced.

His symbolism is as simple as Bunyan's and as profound: a well of clear water
compared with the extensive shallows of the *Glastonbury Romance. The Ass and
the Rabbit*, in *Fables*, is an allegory of the Creation; *The Left Leg* of the Incarnation, not in the orthodox account but more in that of Blake's *Everlasting Gospel*.
God takes human form in the tinker Jar in *The Left Leg, The Only Penitent,
Unclay* and *The Two Thieves* (1932), and again in Mr Weston, the wine-trader,
whose Good Wine, fundamentally the same wine, is served in two strengths:
the Light Wine, which is Love, and the Dark Wine, which is Death. The Dark
takes on flesh in *Unclay*, where John Death loses his scythe, as Time stops for a
while in *Mr Weston*. Where Theodore Powys differs most profoundly from
orthodox Christian belief is in regarding death as the natural and desirable end
and immortality as not only a mistaken idea (as Llewelyn was also to argue)
but as undesirable in itself. He agrees with Forster that "death destroys a man,
but the idea of death saves him"; with Wordsworth's Margaret that "the good
die first, and they whose hearts are dry as summer dust burn to the socket";
and with Blake that priesthood began by "choosing forms of worship from
poetic tales... Thus men forgot that All Deities reside in the Human breast."
In *Soliloquies of a Hermit* Powys expressed his belief that the most beautiful
things in life are the things that die and that part of their beauty lies in their
transience; immortality is the unenvied lot of the stones of the field. At the end
of *The Only Penitent*, Tinker Jar comes to confess his sins to the vicar of Maids
Madder: "I crucified my son," he says: "I destroy all men with a sword. I cast
them down into the pit, they become nothing." In the spirit of FitzGerald's
Omar, Mr Hayhoe asks: "Is that last word true?...Then, in the name of Man,
I forgive your sin; I pardon and deliver you from all your evil...and bring
you to everlasting death."

The first and best critic of the Powys brothers was their intimate friend Louis
Wilkinson ("Louis Marlow", 1881–1966), who established his recognition of
Theodore's artistic superiority over John Cowper as early as his dialogue
Blasphemy and Religion (New York, 1916) and continued to find evidence for it
in his memoirs *Welsh Ambassadors* (1936) and *Seven Friends* (1953). A critical
biography dedicated to Wilkinson is *The Powys Brothers* (1967) by Kenneth
Hopkins, the best of the more recent studies of the family in general. Wilson

Knight's *The Saturnian Quest* (1965) gives reasons for treating J. C. Powys as
seriously as Knight has so well treated Shakespeare. The best critical accounts
of Theodore are William Hunter's pamphlet *The Novels and Stories of T. F.
Powys* (1930) and H. Coombes's judicious study *T. F. Powys* (1960).

With T. F. Powys the boundary might appear to have been crossed between
the novel conceived as a work of art and the novel of ideas. But Powys, it will
be agreed, is first and foremost a literary artist. The true novelists of ideas are
those like Wells, Huxley, Orwell and Koestler whose characteristic work is built
upon or against the ideas current at the time of writing and who run the risk of
becoming dated as soon as the ideas cease to be current. The literary artist in
fiction puts down deeper roots than the novelist of ideas; the beliefs behind his
work are the fundamental moral or spiritual views of mankind rather than the
ideas we read about in the newspapers. Conrad, Forster, Powys, Myers: these
rather than Butler, Wells, Huxley and Orwell give the humanist position its
greatest depth in human feeling; as it is perhaps to some of the later work of
Graham Greene and Evelyn Waugh, rather than to G. K. Chesterton or C. S.
Lewis, that we should go to find any comparable depth of feeling—if it exists
at all in modern fiction (as it exists in the poetry of Eliot)—on the Christian side.

Leo Hamilton Myers (1881–1944) was the son of F. W. H. Myers, friend of
George Eliot and one of the founders of the Society for Psychical Research, and
was educated at Eton and Cambridge. His first novel was the Forsterian study of
family life called *The Orissers* (1923)—where the family house Eamor plays
much the same symbolic role as Howards End in Forster's novel—which was
followed by *The "Clio"* (1925). But Myers's most important work is the
sequence of novels dealing with the India of the Mogul emperor Akbar: *The
Near and the Far* (1929; later the title for the whole sequence, 1943); *Prince Jali*
(1931); *The Root and the Flower* (1934); and *The Pool of Vishnu* (1940). In the
preface to the last-named, Myers explained his intention in going so far back,
his hope being that we might understand better "from the distant vantage-
ground" of sixteenth-century India "the social and ethical problems that force
themselves upon us at the present time."

In that hope he was, at any rate, partly justified. The conversation between the
Guru and Mobarek in *The Pool of Vishnu*, for instance, is of the most urgent
contemporary significance as well as one of the perennial debates of mankind.
The Guru, who is the author's spokesman, represents the traditional humanist
faith; Mobarek, whose name might have been Eliot or Christopher Dawson,
Maritain or Berdyaev or Thomas Merton, represents the idea of the Church
and the claims of authority. The antagonists are well matched, and it is perhaps
the lack of an opponent of Mobarek's calibre that makes *Strange Glory* (1936),
in which the character Wentworth is the spokesman for Myers, a slighter work
on the whole than the best parts of the Indian sequence.

The spiritual and moral problems of those who take, like Mobarek, an orthodox religious position, are developed in the later work of two converts to the
Roman Catholic faith, Graham Greene (b. 1904) and Evelyn Waugh (1903–66).
In both writers, a distinction can be made between their lighter work—Greene
calls some of his "entertainments"—and their serious fiction. Greene's lighter
work is of the "thriller" variety, in which the technique of the cinema plays a

great part; the best of these novels is *Stamboul Train* (1932). The later, more serious fiction, foreshadowed by *Brighton Rock* (1938), is of a specifically religious nature, and includes *The Power and the Glory* (1940)—the tale of the "whisky priest" in Mexico which is among his most impressive novels—*The Heart of the Matter* (1948), *The End of the Affair* (1951) and *A Burnt-Out Case* (1961). Waugh's lighter work, for instance *Decline and Fall* (1928) and *Vile Bodies* (1930), is sophisticated comedy, in which the influence of Aldous Huxley has been skilfully blended with that of Ronald Firbank. The best of his later, more serious work is undoubtedly *Brideshead Revisited* (1945)—"an attempt to trace the divine purpose in a pagan world"—where we are reminded less of Huxley or Firbank than of the war-novels of Ford Madox Ford. The criticism of *Brideshead Revisited*, and of Waugh's snob-Catholicism in general, made by "Donat O'Donnell" (Conor Cruise O'Brien) in the Dublin monthly *The Bell* in 1947 is very severe but on the whole not unjustified.

With Greene and Waugh can be mentioned their younger contemporary William Golding (b. 1911), whose first and most famous novel *Lord of the Flies* (1954) was a deliberate attempt to bring Ballantyne's *Coral Island* up to date, to probe deeper than Ballantyne into the recesses of the human heart, to prove—as Golding wrote in his volume of essays *The Hot Gates* (1965)—that "man produces evil as a bee produces honey." Although in 1966 a party of youths were actually rescued from a coral island after being marooned there for more than a year—and had behaved themselves in co-operative, Ballantyne fashion instead of misbehaving as Golding imagined—*Lord of the Flies* remains a useful parable for the times, as does Golding's second novel *The Inheritors* (1955), the best novel about primitive man since Jack London's *Before Adam*. Golding's later work includes *Pincher Martin* (1956) and *The Spire* (1964).

Greene in his later work has been influenced to some extent by Henry James, but he ignores a good deal of the best fiction of the twentieth century when he says, while writing of François Mauriac, that "With the death of James, the religious sense was lost to the English novel, and with the religious sense went the sense of the importance of the human act." Unless we give to "religious" the restricted sense of "orthodox Christian"—and James was by no means orthodox himself—the statement is not true. "Religious", in the widest sense, is what the best work of Forster, Lawrence, T. F. Powys and Myers surely is; it is certainly not true that "the sense of the importance of the human act" is something that distinguishes James and Mauriac from Conrad, Forster or Lawrence. It is even less true that we are more aware of this importance in Greene, Waugh, Charles Williams, C. S. Lewis and William Golding than we are in their humanist predecessors and contemporaries. "The sense of the importance of the human act" we certainly find in *The Power and the Glory*, *Brideshead Revisited* and *Lord of the Flies*; but it is at least equally present in *The Rainbow*, *A Passage to India*, *Mr Weston's Good Wine*, *The Near and the Far*, and the best novels of Joyce Cary.

It is with Joyce Cary (1888–1957) that we end our survey of the novel proper before going on to discuss more briefly the novel of ideas. Cary is a particularly good choice with which to end, for if ever there was a novelist concerned with the work of art, and not in the least with his personal views, it is Cary. He came to literature late in life, after serving from 1918 to 1932 as resident magistrate in a remote region of Nigeria. His first novels, *Aissa Saved* (1932), *The African Witch* (1936) and *Mister Johnson* (1939), are based on his Nigerian experiences. His most popular novel is *The Horse's Mouth* (1944), with its Joycean hero Gully Jimson—who had been seen through the eyes of Sara Munday in an earlier novel *Herself Surprised* (1941). These two novels, with the related story of the lawyer Wilcher in *To be a Pilgrim* (1942), are probably Cary's most striking achievement. Their chief weakness is inseparable from the use (or the over-use) of the first-person narrative; we feel on occasion, as we do in the mystery stories of Wilkie Collins, that Cary's characters are altogether too fluent, too conscious of their own idiosyncrasies, to be quite real. A more serious weakness in his fiction as a whole is best seen in his last novel *The Captive and the Free* (1959)—which, however, was unrevised by the author and edited by a friend after his death. It becomes evident from this novel that it is possible to be too detached, to envisage a theme in which detachment is a weakness rather than a strength. Cary has been called "the Protestant answer to Graham Greene", but we feel at the close of *The Captive and the Free* that neither the claims of supernatural religion nor the arguments against it have had justice done to them.

There can be no rigid distinction, we said, between what is commonly called "the novel of ideas" and the novel of more purely literary value. It is a question of degree, not of absolute distinction in kind. Most of Forster's novels were contemporary with Wells's early-middle period, and it is puzzling at first to account for the fact that the Margaret of *Howards End*, for example, seems much more alive today than Ann Veronica Stanley or the Margaret of *The New Machiavelli*. Perhaps it is because Margaret Schlegel (like the feminist characters in *The Bostonians*) is so much more than the sum of her opinions, whereas Ann Veronica, without the Condition-of-Woman question, hardly exists at all. In the novel of ideas, the ideas are apt to come first and human characters are then created to give expression to them. It is not surprising, therefore, that what usually survives are not the characters but the opinions, if increasingly of historical interest. Literary creation is of many different kinds, and writers who are imaginative in one field are not necessarily so in others. No one could call writers like Wells and Huxley unimaginative, but their imagination, their power of invention, is in the realm of ideas rather than of persons, their characters being often embodiments of their thoughts or thinly-disguised autobiography on the most literal level. Imaginative insight into other people, the creation of individuals and their relationships, is by no means unknown among these writers but it is not usually their strongest point.

Connected with this is the fact that the novelist of ideas is not usually a novelist alone. Generally speaking, it is the "congenital" novelist, as we should expect, who devotes himself to the novel in the sense that a painter of genius devotes himself to his art, his non-fictional work—like James's plays, Lawrence's travel books, Joyce's poems—being comparatively unimportant; whereas the novelist of ideas is often a writer of many other things as well, things which may well stand in equal value to his novels, and whose opinions may be expressed in fictional or non-fictional form entirely as the mood takes him or the opportunities arise.

The satirical novel is one form of the novel of ideas, and few ages have needed the stroke of satire more than the twentieth century. If our satires, from *Mr Clutterbuck's Election* to *The Apes of God*, from *Brave New World* to *Animal Farm*, are not great enough to be universal, like *Gulliver*, they have influenced our thinking and in some cases our actions. The present age, furthermore, has been increasingly an age of specialization, and the novel of ideas has been one way, and not the least admirable, of conveying to a larger public the knowledge that would otherwise have remained the province of the specialist or at most of the comparative few who, like the novelist himself, have sufficient specialized knowledge to be able to pass some of it on.

We have begun with general observations, because the difference between the novel of ideas and the novel proper has not been at all widely understood. Proceeding now with the chief novelists of the kind in roughly chronological order, we begin with the greatest and the most widely read, Herbert George Wells (1866–1946), son of the Kent professional cricketer Joseph Wells and educated under Aldous Huxley's grandfather Thomas Henry Huxley at the Royal College of Science. His writing career extends from 1893 to 1945 and he wrote over a hundred books. In this prodigious output he is typical of the species who, like his own Mr Britling, has "ideas about everything...in the utmost profusion" and proceeds to pour them out in an unending stream of novels, essays, pamphlets and so forth. Luckily, there is fairly general agreement as to which of Wells's works have survived the years and which have not. Nearly everyone agrees that most of the middle and later works, including *Mr Britling Sees It Through* (1916), are rather like Mr Britling's conversation: a monologue rapidly tending to become a bore. Even with a liberal sprinkling of dots—the trademark of Wells is as certainly "..." as Aldous Huxley's is "inevitably, semi-colon"—the pages seem over-encumbered with words, as their creator with ideas. It is as well to remind ourselves that one of the chief virtues of the early Wells is his splendid economy.

His first scientific romance, *The Time Machine* (1895; p. 706 above), is a case in point. It is the length of the French *nouvelle*, which suits Wells down to the ground. Many of his later, lengthier works would have been the better for the concentration he gave to this one—he rewrote it six times in seven years before it was published—and to the best of his short stories from *The Stolen Bacillus* (1895) to *The Country of the Blind* (1911; first printed in *The Strand Magazine*). It was this economy of style, allied as it was to his powers of imagination, out-doing Jules Verne in Verne's own sphere, that gave him such a reputation in France—where the fortunes of the great publishing house, the *Mercure de France*, were largely founded on the immense sales of his early scientific stories—and thus was partly responsible for his earning a world reputation earlier in life than any English writer since Dickens.

Comparison with Dickens as a literary artist is no longer possible, though one can understand its being made in the first flush of enthusiasm for such admirable social comedies as *Love and Mr Lewisham* (1900), *Kipps* (1905)—the novel which James considered his masterpiece—*Tono-Bungay* (1909) and *The History of Mr Polly* (1910). All these are highly enjoyable, but they are light-weight Dickens and compared with the almost contemporary *Sons and Lovers* (1913) of D. H. Lawrence there is a condescension of the author towards his characters that makes one doubt whether the full personality is engaged. The consensus of critical opinion today, that these novels will outlive the best of the scientific romances, may yet turn out to be false.

In his correspondence with Henry James—see *Henry James and H. G. Wells* (1958) edited by Leon Edel and Gordon N. Ray—Wells accepts the name of "journalism" for most of his writing, whether in fictional or non-fictional form: "I had rather be called a journalist than an artist." In *Boon* (1915) he satirized the literary artist of the James–Ford type, as in *The New Machiavelli* (1911) he had satirized the sociologist of the type of the Webbs. His humility, however, in his controversy with James, is no less striking than his acuteness (some of his criticisms of James's novels were to be endorsed by Forster in *Aspects of the Novel*). We must not forget the comparative situations of the two men at the time: Wells with an international reputation, his works translated into every language in the world, James with a reputation among a minority of the reading public in England and the United States. Wells's failure to appreciate James at his full value must be offset against his shrewd placing of his own works.

Probably he even exaggerated the dependence of his novels upon the occasion of their composition. We can agree that *Ann Veronica* (1909) is almost entirely of historical interest now; that *The Wheels of Chance* (1896) and most of *Tono-Bungay* have a period rather than a literary importance; that *The War in the Air* (1908) has been superseded by the more horrible reality. But *The Country of the Blind*, *The Time Machine*, and some others of the stories and scientific romances—such as *The Invisible Man* (1897) and *The First Men in the Moon* (1901)—are not dependent for their value on any period interest and approach to the status of a work of art of a decidedly original kind. The "idea" remains the dominant factor, but it involves the moral idea of the novel proper and the whole personality of the author is more engaged. From such a mass of ore the true gold may appear a meagre crop, but it is surely more just to look at the matter from the opposite angle. Given Wells's astonishing productivity, and his frank estimate of his writings as mainly journalism of the moment, it is remarkable how much survives in the literary sense. That any should survive at all is a tribute to the fundamental seriousness that was not the least of his many gifts. It was a tragic irony that he should have died during a black period of the world's history—*Mind at the End of its Tether* (1945) to quote the title of his last book—and not have survived to see the beginnings of that Space Age he had prophesied so long before.

To the Socialism of Wells and Shaw, the "Chesterbelloc"—a fearsome engine of war comprising Hilaire Belloc (1870–1953) and Gilbert Keith Chesterton (1874–1936)—opposed the contrasting ideal of Distributism, a theory owing something to Cobbett. In Belloc's *The Servile State* (1912) and in the contributions of Belloc and both G. K. and Cecil Chesterton to *The New Witness* (edited by Cecil Chesterton till his untimely death in the First World War) we have journalism of a brilliance to match that of Wells and Shaw, the best of which still repays reading. Belloc's political novels were allied efforts and—if we grant their anti-Semitism to be in the nature of an unconscious boomerang—they wear on the whole remarkably well. Sometimes set in the future, presumably to avoid actions for libel, they are the nearest twentieth-century equivalents to the novels of Disraeli. Like him, Belloc speaks from experience, though he never attained the political eminence of his predecessor. The links between high finance and Parliament are the main theme of these novels, from *Mr Clutterbuck's Election* (1908) and *A Change in the Cabinet* (1909) to *Mr Petre* (1925) and *The Postmaster-General* (1932)—a theme which has not yet become entirely of historical interest. Some of them were illustrated by G. K. C., whose own novels can best be considered along with his essays. The opening of *The Napoleon of Notting Hill* (1904), for example, could be an intro-duction to a work of fiction or a work of non-fiction with equal plausibility; while there are many essays in the various collections—from *The Defendant* (1901) to *The Well and the Shallows* (1935)—which could quite easily have developed into novels had the author seen fit. The title of one such collection, *Tremendous Trifles* (1909), would do for a general description of the novels. Chesterton usually begins with something apparently trifling or commonplace and then extracts a paradoxically important meaning out of it; this is his main method in fiction and non-fiction alike. As light entertainment, the end justifies the means: *The Club of Queer Trades* (1905) and some of the *Father Brown* stories (1911–35) stand high in their field. But how does such a method serve, in the more serious literary sense?

It serves pretty well so long as the joke, so to speak, is not taken too far. Even more than Wells, Chesterton suffers in proportion to the length of his fiction—which in style owes a great debt to Stevenson's *Dr Jekyll and Mr Hyde* and *New Arabian Nights*. The *nouvelle* was the ideal length for Wells; the novels of G. K. C. can be described not unfairly as short stories padded out to novel length. The first few chapters are nearly always the best, the later development being attended with a sense of strain. This is even more true of *Manalive* (1912) and *The Flying Inn* (1914) than of the early *Napoleon* and *The Man who was Thursday* (1908). The initial idea is good, and promises well for the length of a short story; but it is padded out to a size and an importance it simply will not bear, as in the essays a paradox that would serve as material for a paragraph is often stretched to bursting-point over half-a-dozen pages. It is as if Hans Andersen had made a novel in three volumes of the story of the ugly duckling.

After 1918, though Wells, Belloc and Chesterton continued to be as prolific as before, they were no longer in tune with the mood of the younger generation. The influence of Aldous Huxley (1894–1963) on the generation growing up in the nineteen twenties and thirties was very similar to theirs upon the pre-war public, and as with Chesterton it is difficult to remember, looking back, whether a particular idea was expressed in one of Huxley's novels or in one of his collec-tions of essays, so fundamentally alike are the majority of his writings. In the essays, of course—from *On the Margin* (1923) to *Themes and Variations* (1950)—it is Huxley in person who addresses us, while in the novels he speaks with a variety of opinions under the guise of the different characters. But this is not an absolute distinction, for Huxley, like Auden, has always owed much to the ideas of others. Some of the essays in *Do What You Will* (1929) owe an evident debt to his conversations with D. H. Lawrence, the original of the character Rampion in *Point Counter Point* (1928). The early novels—*Crome Yellow* (1921),

Antic Hay (1923), *Those Barren Leaves* (1925)—owe something to Norman Douglas's *South Wind* (1917) and Wyndham Lewis's *Tarr* (1918). Their method is that of Peacock, whose recipe for the novel of ideas has been brought up to date and to some extent improved upon. Ideas in the "congenital" novelists are enacted rather than discussed; in Huxley, as in Peacock, there is often no organic connection between what is said, sometimes at enormous length, and what happens, sometimes very perfunctorily.

It was in *Point Counter Point* that Huxley not only developed the distinction referred to between the novel of ideas and the "congenital" novel, but tried himself to develop from the one into the other. It was a brave attempt, and the novel remains his most ambitious. If the undertaking was only a partial success, we could be thankful in the main, for it meant that the later Huxley—from *Brave New World* (1932) to *Ape and Essence* (1949) and *Brave New World Revisited* (1958)—was mostly the old Huxley, his talk as stimulating as ever, his social comedy as entertaining. His admirers in his native England—he lived in California from 1947 to his death—could only hope that he would continue to give us his "uncongenital" novels, not minding overmuch whether they were inferior as works of art to the best of D. H. Lawrence.

The novel proper is based upon personal experience, however imaginatively handled; but ideas are impersonal and therefore the novelist whose province lies therein can set his scene either in the present or in the future, entirely as he feels inclined. Novels of warning like *The Time Machine* or *Brave New World*, or of political satire like *The Postmaster-General*, are as fitted to be set in the mythical future as cloak-and-dagger melodramas in the mythical past. They are not exempt, however, on that account from the critical attention paid to novels set in the present, particularly if they contradict, as Orwell's *Nineteen Eighty-Four* does, the author's previous observations.

The impact of George Orwell—the pen-name of Eric Blair (1903–50)—upon the generation of the nineteen-forties was similar to that of Huxley in pre-war days. He had observed of the prophecies of the American sociologist James Burnham that they are suspect because "at each point Burnham is predicting a continuation of the thing that is happening" (*Second Thoughts on James Burnham*, 1946; reprinted in *Shooting an Elephant and Other Essays*, 1950). As a prophecy *Nineteen Eighty-Four* is suspect for the same reason, because it assumes that certain aspects of the Soviet regime in 1948, when the novel was written, would set the pattern for the whole world within the next forty years. Furthermore, by including England among the Communist tyrannies of the near future, Orwell was contradicting the perceptive observations he had made of the English people in *The Road to Wigan Pier* (1937), *Inside the Whale* (1940) and *The Lion and the Unicorn* (1941)—strikingly original books where he had dispelled the Marxist myth that there was a "proletariat" in England avid to follow the lead of their Communist betters and had stressed instead the thoroughly "bourgeois" nature of the English people. In *Nineteen Eighty-Four* (1949) all this is suddenly changed: the bourgeois English people become "proles" after the Marxist pattern and all power is in the hands of just the kind of "comrade" whose pitiful nonsense the author had exposed. If Chesterton had written *Crux Ansata* or Wells *The Everlasting Man*, it could not have been more of a *volte-face*.

As a prophecy, *Nineteen Eighty-Four* cannot be taken seriously; as a satire on the present, it makes some very good points, particularly the conception of Newspeak, a development of the essay *Politics and the English Language* which originally appeared in *Horizon* and which is reprinted in *Shooting an Elephant*. But *Nineteen Eighty-Four* lacks the neatness of *Animal Farm* (1945), which is content to do a small thing well and which contains one immortal phrase in the slogan ALL ANIMALS ARE EQUAL BUT SOME ANIMALS ARE MORE EQUAL THAN OTHERS.

Orwell is one of those writers who should be read as a whole, and unfortunately it is quite easy to do this. He died in early middle age, of the same disease that cut short the careers of D. H. Lawrence and Llewelyn Powys, and his books number a mere fifteen—as compared with Belloc's one hundred and fifteen. His novels, like Chesterton's and Huxley's, can best be appreciated if they are read along with his essays. Much of his work is autobiographical, and where he does not speak from personal experience his touch is apt to falter. *Burmese Days* (1934) is much less amusing than *Coming Up for Air* (1939), but it is more authentic. Orwell had served in Burma from 1922 to 1927; he knew relatively little about the thoughts and emotions of a commercial traveller. George Bowling is one of those characters of Orwell's, like Gordon Comstock in *Keep the Aspidistra Flying* (1936), who are supposed to be of the common stock—the name Comstock might almost be an anticipation of Newspeak— but who are really very much out of the ordinary, a kind of composite figure of the ordinary man as seen by Orwell and Orwell himself. This accounts for the sense of unreality which occasionally pulls the reader up short in Orwell's novels, when the private opinions of the author are placed in the mouth of a character whose counterpart in real life would probably express himself very differently. For instance, Bowling says: "I'm what you might call the typical Boots Library subscriber, I always fall for the best-seller of the moment (*The Good Companions, Bengal Lancer, Hatter's Castle*—I fell for every one of them) ..." A Bowling in real life might well have belonged to that excellent circulating library (which served booklovers from 1899 to 1966) and might well have enjoyed such widely-read books by Priestley, Yeats-Brown, Cronin, etc., but it is Orwell himself who introduces the pejorative implications of "fell for every one of them". The literary critic has taken over for a while from the commercial traveller—through an incidental weakness not easily avoidable by the novelist of ideas.

"Heavens, how we laughed!" wrote John Middleton Murry in *The Adelphi*, reflecting on the impact of H. G. Wells upon his generation. The exclamation might well be echoed by critics of a later generation in regard to Huxley and Orwell. For in general it is the novelist of ideas rather than the "congenital" novelist who has maintained the humorous tradition in English fiction in our time. In their novels and essays alike, they have often a deliberately exaggerated mode of expression, which is one of the classic features of English humour in the eighteenth and nineteenth centuries—as well as of "Western" humour in the United States and "bush" humour in Australia and New Zealand. They are novelists with a purpose, but the pill of their propaganda is sweetened by laughter, so much so indeed that if a modern Thackeray should ever write an

"English Humorists of the Twentieth Century" he would surely give a much higher place to them than to professional humorists (grateful as we are to them too) like Jerome K. Jerome, W.W. Jacobs, P. G. Wodehouse or James Thurber.

He would also include, we believe, those "eminent fictorians" who are the modern masters of the biographical novel. Lytton Strachey (1880–1932) is the chief figure, and a modern Thackeray would surely recognize that Strachey cannot be seriously considered either a biographer or a novelist, either an historian or a writer of fiction, but rather some curious species between the two —which we can call either "biographical novelist" or "fictorian" (to coin a word by the method of Lewis Carroll). Strachey was one of the original Bloomsbury Group, as we have noted: to him Virginia Woolf dedicated her *Common Reader* and he is appropriately prominent in the pages of *The Bloomsbury Group* (1954) by the Canadian scholar J. K. Johnstone, the best study of Bloomsbury that has appeared. Strachey's first book was *Landmarks in French Literature* (1912), a contribution to that excellent popular series, the Home University Library (see p. 928 below), written at the same time and during the same summer holiday as his friend G. E. Moore's *Ethics*, published in the same series the same year. *Eminent Victorians* came out in 1918 and was a spectacular success. It was followed by *Queen Victoria* (1921)—where, as has been well said, he came to scoff and remained to pray—and *Elizabeth and Essex* (1928).

Eminent Victorians is undoubtedly his best work as well as the work which has caused all the fuss, both in contemporary eulogy and subsequent criticism. Considered as serious biography, these studies of Cardinal Manning, Florence Nightingale, Dr Arnold and General Gordon certainly leave something to be desired; and Dr Arnold himself, in his *Christian Life* (1845), had already passed the final judgment on Strachey's passion for the eighteenth century and patronizing contempt for the Victorian age: "There are few stranger and sadder sights than to see men judging of whole periods of the history of mankind with the blindness of party-spirit, never naming one century without expressions of contempt or abhorrence, never mentioning another but with extravagant and undistinguishing admiration."

We have to realize, however, in the first place, what book it was, and what kind of book, which so influenced the writing of *Eminent Victorians* and to which that work is indebted both in its general tone and in some of its characteristic tricks of style. That book was Samuel Butler's novel *The Way of All Flesh* (1903; p. 653 above), which contains in the character of Theobald Pontifex a portrait of the author's father Canon Butler that bears much the same relation to the real Canon as Strachey's portraits of Manning, Newman, Dr Arnold, etc., to those more eminent Victorians. It remains to ask what precisely that relation implies.

The truth about any historical figure, especially one of recent date, is bound to be seen differently according to our own individual beliefs. No Christian reader today can accept Strachey's account of the Oxford Movement, though if he is broad-minded enough he may admit that Strachey at times comes nearer the truth than some more sober historians. The truth for him, however, is contained in Dean Church's *History* or in Christopher Dawson's characteristically excellent work *The Spirit of the Oxford Movement*. But is it contained therein for those who share Butler's and Strachey's disbelief in the supernatural? We can hardly think so, any more than an agnostic reader can quite disbelieve in the portrait of Canon Butler painted by his unfilial son. Theobald Pontifex is a caricature of Canon Butler, as Strachey's Manning, Newman, Pusey, Gordon and the rest are caricatures of their originals. But in literature, as in art, caricatures have an element of truth in them. No one disputes this in the case of Sir Max Beerbohm's drawings in *The Poet's Corner* (1904) and *Rossetti and his Circle* (1922), and it is in that context, not in the context of serious biography, that *Eminent Victorians* should be placed. Strachey's account of the genesis of the Oxford Movement, of the Vatican Council which established the infallibility of the Pope, and similar highlights, are surely comic writing on a very high level, comedy containing at least part of the historical truth. If we want a different account from different premisses, Church or Dawson can supply it, without really affecting, except to the most bigoted reader, the comic truth of Strachey's version. It is possible, after all, both to venerate the teaching of William Morris and to delight in the absurd caricatures of him drawn by Max Beerbohm.

With *Eminent Victorians* we can consider five lesser-known works of the same species: *Ancient Lights* (1911), *Thus to Revisit* (1921), *Return to Yesterday* (1931), *It was the Nightingale* (1934) and *Mightier than the Sword* (1938; called *Portraits from Life*, 1937, in U.S.A.) by Ford Madox Ford (1873–1939), already frequently mentioned in this chapter as Conrad's collaborator, James's friend, novelist in his own right, and founder and editor of *The English Review* in London and *The Transatlantic Review* in Paris. Born Ford Hermann Hueffer, grandson of the Pre-Raphaelite painter Ford Madox Brown and original (in outward appearance) of Morton Densher in James's *Wings of the Dove*, Ford was a many-talented writer, his seventy-odd works including novels—notably *The Good Soldier* (1915) and the Tietjens war series from *Some Do Not* (1924) to *Last Post* (1928)—besides criticism, verse and biography. The five books first mentioned are of the reminiscent type, for which Ford had a particular flair, and parts of them must be among the most comical writing of the twentieth century. The sketches of Swinburne in the care of Watts-Dunton, the reminiscences of the later James, the picture of Belloc arguing about Sussex with W. H. Hudson at the Café Royal... such things may exasperate the serious biographer in their mixture of truth and invention, but they may well outlive most of the more sober works of their irrepressible author.

A similar fortune may await the autobiographies of Ford's friend, that even more multifarious writer Percy Wyndham Lewis (1884–1957), who was novelist from *Tarr* (1918) and *The Childermass* (1928) to *Self Condemned* (1954); short story writer from *The Wild Body* (1927) to *Rotting Hill* (1951); satirist in prose with *The Apes of God* (1930) and in verse with *One Way Song* (1933); social critic and philosopher in *The Art of Being Ruled* (1926) and *Time and Western Man* (1927); literary critic from *The Lion and the Fox* (1927) and *Men Without Art* (1934) to *The Writer and the Absolute* (1952); not to mention founder and editor of three short-lived reviews: *Blast* (1914–15), *The Tyro* (1924) and *The Enemy* (1927–9). But Lewis was also a considerable painter and draughts-man, whose fine portrait of Ezra Pound is in the Tate Gallery, whose art criti-

cism includes *The Caliph's Design* (1919) and *The Demon of Progress in the Arts*
(1954) and whose drawings of Pound, Eliot, Joyce and others illustrate the first
of his biographical rhapsodies *Blasting and Bombardiering* (1937), which was
followed by *Rude Assignment* (1950). It is difficult to decide, unless one is a critic
of both art and literature like Lewis himself, whether these brilliant drawings or
the accompanying text are the more amusing (or the more libellous). Like
Ford, Lewis is inclined to be a tough writer; but whereas Ford's toughness, his
admiration for the soldierly qualities, was a conscious reaction from his Pre-
Raphaelite childhood, Lewis's seems to have been born with him in his father's
country of the United States. In literary history, he had the misfortune, like
Ford (and like George Moore), to be the intimate friend of some of the greatest
writers of the century, his memoirs of whom may outlive most of his own
works. But, like Ford again, he must have been a man and a writer well worthy
of that intimate friendship. His courageous struggle against poverty and blindness in his later years—see *The Letters of Wyndham Lewis* (1963) edited by
W. K. Rose—should impress even those most embittered by some of his
earlier literary and political opinions.

  We end with the peculiar case of an early twentieth-century novelist whose
posthumous fame is largely due to a biography which is, in a sense, a better
novel than any which he wrote himself. The self-styled Baron Corvo, Frederick
William Rolfe (1860–1913) belongs, like Beerhohm, "to the Beardsley period",
contributing his first stories to Henry Harland's *Yellow Book* (1894–7) in company with Henry James and George Moore among the writers and Beardsley
and Sickert among the illustrators. His thwarted desire to become a priest found
compensation in his novel *Hadrian the Seventh* (1904), in which the hero Rose
in similar circumstances defeats his detractors in the Church and is miraculously
elected Pope. In this novel and in that successor to Gissing's *New Grub Street*,
Nicholas Crabbe (not published till 1958), Rolfe revenges himself for slights, real
and fancied, by exercising his talent for invective. The amount of truth in these
caricatures of ecclesiastics and publishers must be small; they are too monotonously abject to carry conviction. Rolfe himself must have been one of the most
unpleasant and conceited writers who have ever lived (contrast him with Hopkins, for example, or even with that amiable diabolist, the "Reverend"
Montague Summers), and yet in the biography or biographical novel by
A. J. A. Symons, *The Quest for Corvo* (1934), he becomes in the end a sympathetic, even an impressive figure. Symons it was who started the Corvine cult,
which at the time of writing has a surprising number of adherents on both sides
of the Atlantic.

  It would have needed much greater space than we had at our command to
treat at all fully of the fiction of the twentieth century, the most popular reading
of the modern age. Inevitably we have had to be selective, both in authors and
in argument, discussing among the dead only those novelists who seem to us
most important, with some others of mainly historical interest, and treating of
living novelists—most of whom have not yet completed their work—only in
a comparatively few cases. Whole areas of fiction, we realize, have gone virtually
unexplored. We should have liked, for instance, to have considered what we
may term, with no great pejorative implications, the "eccentric" or "man-

nered" novelists, writers like Ronald Firbank, Ivy Compton-Burnett and Henry Green; the novelists who have written most acutely of childhood or adolescence, like Richard Hughes, Rebecca West, Forrest Reid, L. P. Hartley, Carson McCullers, J. D. Salinger; the novelists who have written most knowledgeably of the traditional English life of town and countryside, like Robert Tressell, Adrian Bell, A. G. Street; the novelists and story-writers of Scottish life, like Eric Linklater and Lewis Grassic Gibbon and of Irish life, like Seán O'Faoláin, Liam O'Flaherty, James Hanley, Frank O'Connor, Elizabeth Bowen, F. L. Green; the "serial" novelists like C. P. Snow and Anthony Powell, who are perhaps our nearest modern equivalents to the Victorian Trollope, as the South African-born Angus Wilson may be our nearest modern equivalent to Thackeray; the masters of the American short story, from O. Henry to Dorothy Parker and William Saroyan; the "sociological" novelists like Truman Capote, John O'Hara, Nathaniel West, Colin MacInnes; the novelists who have written most memorably of politics or the human results of political events, like the Hungarian-born Arthur Koestler, whose later novels have been written in English, and the Nigerian novelist Chinua Achebe (see p. 936 below); the "picaresque" novelists like the New Zealander Frank Sargeson, the Canadian-born Saul Bellow, and the Russian-born Vladimir Nabokov, whose *Lolita* is as pure in intention as Defoe's *Roxana*; the American Negro novelists like James Baldwin, Ralph Ellison, Richard Wright; the American Jewish novelists like Bellow, Henry Roth, Edward Lewis Wallant, Norman Mailer and Bernard Malamud, whose creative achievement in mid-century American fiction has been equal to the achievement of such critics as Harry Levin and Leslie Fiedler in regard to the American past... Distinguished novels continue to be written, and it would be easy to mention a dozen living novelists who may perhaps be among the classics, major or minor, to future generations. The example of Henry James in 1914 must, however, give us pause: where so great a man as he went so far astray, lesser critics may well hesitate to rush in.

Regular reviewers of current fiction, like the writer of the present chapter, are perhaps not the best placed to see the wood of literature for the trees and saplings. A reading of fifty to a hundred novels every year might even be supposed to jade the appetite for fiction altogether. What it does do is to make one aware of two things. First, it makes one aware of the world-wide nature of fiction in the English language today, when a reviewer in England (for example) is as likely to receive the latest Patrick White from Australia, the latest Wilson Harris from the West Indies or the latest Vladimir Nabokov from the United States as the latest Graham Greene from his native country. We have considered some aspects of this world-wide literature in chapter xiv and shall consider them further when we come to the literatures of the West Indies and the new African states. Secondly, such reading makes one aware of the high level of technique in the modern novel—save in those cases where novels have been written with deliberate carelessness to conform to some anti-literary doctrine. The pioneers, like James, Joyce and Virginia Woolf, have not lived in vain in this limited respect, though it may be many years before a succession of notable novels comparable to those published between 1880 and 1940 once more enriches our literature.

IV. THE OLD DRAMA AND THE NEW

The dramatic criticism, and the translations from Ibsen, of William Archer (1856–1924) have been mentioned in chapters XIII and XIV (pp. 618, 692). Here it is proposed to consider the principal work of his last years, *The Old Drama and the New* (1923), in relation both to Eliot's criticism of it and to Eliot's part in the abortive poetic drama of the twentieth century, the paradoxical situation arising of the "new drama" becoming the old and the "old drama" becoming for a while the new. This, we believe, is to sum up an important aspect in the complicated relationship between literature and the twentieth-century theatre in as little space as possible.

Eliot's criticism of *The Old Drama and the New*, which he rightly calls a "brilliant and stimulating book", is contained in *Four Elizabethan Dramatists* (1924) and *A Dialogue on Dramatic Poetry* (1928), both reprinted in *Selected Essays*. Archer's book was a defence of Ibsen and other modern dramatists against those writers like Yeats who preferred the old drama of the Elizabethans. Archer took the war into the enemy's camp by reconsidering the Elizabethans themselves, pointing out the absurdity of many of their conventions, such as the soliloquy and the aside, and what he thought the general lack of humanitarian feeling in their work. He did not include Shakespeare in his castigation, but he did include those dramatists like Webster and Tourneur who had been highly praised in the introductions to the original Mermaid series of 1887–9 by Havelock Ellis and his co-editors. Eliot's criticism of the book falls into three parts: first, that Archer was wrong "in having attacked the minor figures of Elizabethan drama and not having understood that he was obliged to attack Shakespeare as well"; secondly, that he made the error "of supposing that the dramatic merit of a dramatic work could be estimated without reference to its poetic merit"; and thirdly, that "he gains his apparent victory over the Elizabethans for this reason, that the Elizabethans themselves admit the same criteria of realism... Their great weakness is the same weakness as that of modern drama, it is the *lack* [our italics] of a convention."

It would have been interesting to have had a full-scale debate on the subject between the veteran critic Archer, supporter of the new drama, and the young poet-critic Eliot, defender of the old. But Archer died the same year as Eliot published the first of his criticisms (and several years before Eugene O'Neill in *Strange Interlude* put to fresh use the Elizabethan convention of the aside), and a debate between Eliot and Archer's intimate friend Bernard Shaw, who held much the same views, never took place. It might have been mere talking at cross-purposes, so different were the preoccupations of the two men, but it is one of those debates between men of different but equal calibre—like the missing controversy between Henry James, trying to write his novels in dramatic terms, and Shaw, trying to write his plays in terms of the novel—which we can only regret did not occur. In criticism, Eliot's is much the stronger position; in play-writing itself, Shaw's is an achievement in prose drama which Eliot's in poetic drama did not nearly equal, let alone surpass. In the case of both men, the criticism and the play-writing are intimately connected.

One figure in the controversy most of us in English-speaking countries must reluctantly discard. We cannot really discuss Ibsen in Archer's translations or in Shaw's *The Quintessence of Ibsenism* (1891) as we discuss Webster or Tourneur, who wrote in our native language and whose work does not provide an "ism" to be debated separately. On the other hand, we can discuss Shaw himself, despite the curious fact that to the end of his life Archer never believed that Shaw could write a play of any importance. For us, in retrospect, Shaw is the most eminent prose dramatist of the century, with the single obvious exception early on—not really an exception at all—of his fellow-Irishman John Millington Synge (1871–1909), whose *Collected Works* (poems, plays, prose) we can now read in the fine new edition in five volumes (1962–8) under the general editorship of Robin Skelton. The curious case of Synge has been properly discussed in relation to the Anglo-Irish literary movement (pp. 728–9 above), and it is not necessary here to do more than confirm and emphasize the impression given, that Synge's plays—particularly *Riders to the Sea* (1904), *The Well of the Saints* (1905) and *The Playboy of the Western World* (1907)—are not merely unique in the Irish literary movement but also in the whole history of English drama. That Synge is the early twentieth century's greatest dramatist in the English language seems as certain as that his opportunities—except possibly in Africa, where the plays of Wole Soyinka and J. P. Clark have something of his blend of tradition and originality—will not again occur in the modern world. His plays are in prose, but the prose to modern urban ears is a kind of poetry, based as it was on the speech of Irish peasants and fisherfolk, still at the beginning of the twentieth century living spiritually in the pre-industrial age; and it enables the dramatist to achieve effects of tragedy and comedy unknown to English drama since the time of the Elizabethans. John Masefield's *The Tragedy of Nan* (1908), dedicated to Yeats, was the best attempt to do with English characters what Synge had done with Irish; but it was an impossible task, and the play on the whole, despite some moving moments, is a failure. Trying to get back as much as possible to pre-industrial speech, Masefield has to set his play in the past (in 1810) and his Herefordshire shepherd-folk, lacking the contemporary reality of Synge's Irish peasantry, inevitably become rather artificial characters. His Gaffer has some of the functions of the Greek chorus, commenting on the action as it proceeds, but there is something precious about his language— "The horn. The horn. Gold hoofs beating on the road..."—connected no doubt with Masefield's preface, where he speaks of "that power of exultation" in the Renascence dramatists "which comes from a delighted brooding on excessive, terrible things."

The achievement in prose drama of George Bernard Shaw (1856–1950) can most readily be appreciated if we consider first of all the state of the London theatre in the eighteen-nineties, the enfeebled melodramatic and farcical traditions he had to break away from. If the best drama of today is both worth seeing on the stage and reading as literature, we owe the fact primarily to the work of Shaw in drama and criticism, only secondarily to the achievements of Yeats, Synge and Oscar Wilde. In *Widowers' Houses* (1892) he dealt with slum landlords, in *Mrs Warren's Profession* (1894) with prostitution, in a style at once witty and penetrating. In *Arms and the Man* (1894) he suggested that the romantic heroism of the soldier was a mere invention of civilians; in *The Philanderer* (1893), *Candida* (1895) and *You Never Can Tell* (1897) he dramatized respectively the "new woman" of the pseudo-Ibsenites, the marriage of a Socialist parson, and the "new parent" and the old. All these plays can fairly be criticized for incidental weaknesses, but they were so very much superior to the average "commercial play" of the period that it seems incredible that they gained their first real fame, not on the boards—*Mrs Warren* was actually banned by the censor—but by the publication in 1898 of the two volumes of *Plays Pleasant and Unpleasant*. Shaw is probably the only dramatist in the world's history who became famous in print first, then in the theatre afterwards; and this reversal of the usual procedure had itself a profound influence on the dramatic literature of the twentieth century.

Shaw was convinced that the modern dramatist had to compete in realism with the modern novelist. (He had himself started with the novel, in what he afterwards referred to as "novels of my nonage", written 1879–83). Where the Elizabethans could simply say "another part of the field" and leave it at that, the modern dramatist had to set his scene in the utmost detail as well as give the actors the utmost help in the speaking of his lines. Thus every scene in a play by Shaw is commonly introduced by paragraphs of preliminary explanation, setting the scene and describing minutely both the outward appearance and the mental habits of the characters; and he seriously thought that Shakespeare, whom he admired for his poetry, for what he well called the "orchestration" of his language, was a lesser dramatist for being without such preliminary paragraphs. That the poetry itself carries all the dramatic weight required was as inconceivable to Shaw as to Archer, who in *The Old Drama and the New* admired some of the poetry of the Elizabethans, as it were in isolation, refusing to credit its dramatic value.

Shaw's own idea of the poetic character was a very romantic one, like his idea of the artist personified in the character Dubedat in *The Doctor's Dilemma* (1906). The poet Marchbanks in *Candida* is rather an absurd creation, the legendary poetical type caricatured in Gilbert's *Patience* (1881) in the character Bunthorne, that "greenery-yallery, Grosvenor Gallery, foot-in-the-grave young man." When we come to Shakespeare himself, as seen by Shaw in *The Dark Lady of the Sonnets* (1910), we understand more clearly Shaw's notion of the Elizabethan drama. This one-act play has considerable charm and wit, like most of Shaw's writings, but the character of Shakespeare is one that could only have been invented by someone like Shaw who combined a deep appreciation of music—he was music critic to *The Star* 1888–9 and *The World* 1890–4—with a total misconception of the art of dramatic poetry. His Shakespeare carries a notebook about with him and when anybody utters in conversation a "strain of music" he jots it down for future use. The Beefeater, for example, exclaims: "Angels and ministers of grace defend us!" and down it goes in Shakespeare's "tablets" for future use in *Hamlet*. The limited truth behind this misconception is, of course, that Shakespeare's language, like that of the Authorized Version of the Bible, was based upon the common speech of the time; but what Shaw failed to realize is that poetic drama is not drama with poetry added to it but a distinct species of its own in which the drama and the poetry are one and the same thing. This was realized, not only by those of the persuasion of Yeats and Eliot, but by Harley Granville-Barker (1877–1946), who gave Shaw his first real stage success in 1904–7 at the Royal Court Theatre, Sloane Square—the same theatre, incidentally, which from 1956 was to become the home of the English Stage Company and was to see the first performances of some of the leading plays of the fifties and sixties. Granville-Barker's own plays have not lasted so well as Shaw's—the best are *Waste* (1907; banned from public performance till 1936) and *The Madras House* (1910)—but his *Prefaces to Shakespeare* (1927–45) and his masterly contribution to *A Companion to Shakespeare Studies* (1934), which he edited with G. B. Harrison, give us the rewarding view of one who combined experience as an actor-manager and a practising playwright with an understanding of dramatic poetry. The more gifted Shaw never to the end of his long working life understood the fundamental difference between his kind of drama and the Elizabethan.

This was Shaw's great weakness; his great strength lies in a mastery of comic invention which bears comparison with the best of Congreve, Wycherley, Sheridan and Oscar Wilde. There is, in fact, nothing superior to Shaw in English dramatic comedy (Synge alone excepted) since the time of Shakespeare and Ben Jonson, who have, as it were, an extra dimension in their comedy precisely because they are dramatic poets.

Only one of Shaw's plays, *The Doctor's Dilemma*, is described as a tragedy, and while this play has its moving as well as its witty moments and must be counted on the whole among his successes, the misconception involved in the character of Dubedat robs it of the ultimate significance the author intended. (Shaw reserved his romantic ideas for poets and artists; he would not have tolerated them in composers.) *Widowers' Houses* and *Mrs Warren's Profession* are problem plays, like Galsworthy's *Silver Box* and the plays written for Emily Horniman's Gaiety Theatre, Manchester, by Charles McEvoy, Stanley Houghton and Allan Monkhouse, which inevitably, like the contemporary "novels of ideas" they resemble, have become dated today by the very virtue of currency, allied to compassion, which gave them their initial impact. In general, those of Shaw's plays which survive on the stage, and are likely to survive in the future, are plays like *You Never Can Tell* and *Pygmalion* (1916) in which the comedy triumphs over the ideas which originally gave rise to it. This is not the same thing, of course, as a perversion of the original intention, like that which has transformed two of Shaw's least sentimental comedies into sentimental operettas or musical comedies: *Arms and the Man* into *The Chocolate Soldier* and *Pygmalion* into *My Fair Lady*.

Luckily, Shaw—like Shakespeare—is a dramatist to be read as well as seen, and some of his most ambitious plays, such as *Man and Superman* (1903), *Major Barbara* (1905), *Back to Methuselah* (1921) and *Saint Joan* (1924), gain a good deal by being read, with their prefaces, instead of (or after) being performed. Shaw the historian, of course, who was first seen in *The Man of Destiny* (1896), *The Devil's Disciple* (1897) and *Caesar and Cleopatra* (1898), needs to be taken with as liberal a helping of Irish salt as Shaw the philosopher, and these plays—like the dramas of his "second nonage" from *Too True to be Good* (1934) to *Far-Fetched Fables* (1950)—mostly survive because of their incidental virtues of wit or comedy. The entire *Man and Superman* is a play to read; as a stage drama, the comedy on earth is separable from the massive conversation-piece in hell and has generally been performed without it. The entire *Back to Methuselah* sequence—or "metabiological pentateuch"—has been performed several times (notably by Sir Barry Jackson's company at Birmingham in 1923), but the production takes the best part of a week, so here again the play is one to be read, preferably with the preface, the best and wittiest summary of the Darwinian controversy ever written. Shaw's determination to rival the novel in detailed setting and characterization helps the more ambitious plays to be read as literature; it is the less ambitious comedies that are likely to have the greater future upon the stage.

The original of Cusins in *Major Barbara* was the eminent Australian-born Greek scholar Gilbert Murray (1866–1957), author of *Five Stages of Greek Religion* (1925), whose translations of Euripides—from *Hippolytus* (1904) to *The Bacchae* (1908)—had greater success in the theatre than any of their predecessors in the eighteenth and nineteenth centuries and made Euripides as familiar to the Edwardian playgoer as Ibsen, Shaw, Barrie or Galsworthy. Their success is a fact of theatrical history; whether they are equally successful as English literature is more doubtful. Eliot's stringent criticism in the essay *Euripides and Professor Murray* (1918) made the points that the actors were often struggling against Murray's verse and that as a poet the translator was "merely a very insignificant follower of the pre-Raphaelite movement." The critic who was to complain of the lack of convention in English drama was evidently well disposed towards the Greek; but "Greek poetry will never have the slightest vitalizing effect upon English poetry if it can only appear masquerading as a vulgar debasement of the eminently personal idiom of Swinburne... And it is inconceivable that anyone with a genuine feeling for the sound of Greek verse should deliberately elect the William Morris couplet, the Swinburne lyric, as an equivalent."

The contrast between Murray's theatrical success and Eliot's literary criticism of the plays can partly be explained in terms of the different generations addressed. The Victorian age in poetry, including dramatic poetry, did not really come to an end until the nineteen-twenties; to the generation of Murray, Archer and Shaw the verse of Swinburne and Morris was not "the fluid haze" it appeared to Eliot, but rather the most modern of modern poetry, which a Marchbanks might have written. To select it as the best equivalent to the Greek was therefore not a miscalculation to Murray's generation, but the obvious choice. Yeats was to translate Sophocles into modern *prose*, but not till 1928; the only alternative to Murray's Euripides that Eliot mentions are the choruses translated by the American imagist poet Hilda Doolittle, Mrs Aldington, who wrote under the initials "H. D." One can agree with most of Eliot's strictures while being doubtful whether he or Ezra Pound could have produced translations from the Greek as popular with an Edwardian audience as Murray's were. Translations on Eliot's principles might well have been incomprehensible to the followers of Ibsen, Shaw and Archer before 1920.

There is no other prose dramatist of the early twentieth century—Synge again excepted—to match Shaw for his overall achievement. Even those plays where his comic genius gets bogged down by windy rhetoric, farcical incident or empty paradox—plays like *John Bull's Other Island* (1904), *Getting Married* (1911), *Misalliance* (1914), *Androcles and the Lion* (1916), *Heartbreak House* (1919) and *The Apple Cart* (1930)—even these plays contain many moments of superb comedy and are better worth seeing or reading than most other plays of the period. *John Bull's Other Island* was written for the Abbey Theatre at Yeats's request, but it did not go down particularly well in Dublin with the more fervently patriotic followers of the Celtic Renascence. At an earlier performance in London, however, it is recorded that King Edward VII laughed so much his chair gave way beneath him: which must, at any rate, have been the greatest Irish victory over the British monarchy since Nell Gwyn seduced Charles II... Of the numerous biographies and criticisms of G. B. S., the two worst are probably by G. K. Chesterton (1909) and Frank Harris (1931), the three best by Hesketh Pearson (1942), St John Ervine (1956) and Ivor Brown (1966). His *Collected Letters*, edited by Dan H. Laurence, were published in 1966–8.

The novelist John Galsworthy (1867–1933; p. 870 above) was Shaw's chief rival in the problem play, of which his best include *The Silver Box* (1906), *Strife* (1909), *Justice* (1910), *Loyalties* (1922) and *The Forest* (1924). A passionate concern for social and racial justice—he was the obvious and admirable choice for first president of the P.E.N. world association of writers in 1921—was not allied in Galsworthy with anything like Shaw's powers of comic invention and sheer gift of language. And therefore his plays, while still often moving, have not very much of permanent literary interest to fall back upon, when once the problems they discuss have ceased to be current, as is the case with most of them today.

The dramatic situation in the United States in the early years of the twentieth century was even less hopeful than it had been in Britain before the advent of Shaw, Wilde and Synge in the period 1890–1905. Luckily, there were Irishmen in America, too, and it was largely due to one great Irish-American dramatist, Eugene O'Neill (1888–1953), that the United States from about 1915 began quickly to catch up with Britain and in the twenties and thirties began to surpass her. It was a period of great experiment in American drama, and if some of the experiments were less successful than others, that does not affect the immense value of the initiative.

O'Neill was a dramatist born, not made. Like Poe, whose sense of fatality some of his plays remind us of, he was the son of a professional actor of "the old school"—which was even "older" in the United States than in Britain. The dramatist who was to lead the American theatre away from its old ways knew those ways intimately from boyhood. The young O'Neill occasionally toured with his father, playing small parts; his autobiographical drama *Long Day's Journey into Night* (1940) gives us an insight, not only into the individual lives of the O'Neill family, but into a period in American theatrical history which was not to survive the impact of his own first plays and those of his rivals.

But O'Neill knew more than the life of the theatre. Such plays as *The Moon of the Caribbees* (1916) and *The Hairy Ape* (1921) were not mere theatrical experiments: they were based on his own personal experience of life at sea and on shore in many different parts of the world, both as a sailor (inspired by the example of Jack London) and as a newspaper reporter. His first plays, like *Bound East for Cardiff* (1914), were a pretty direct transcript of his own adventures from the time he left Princeton University to the time of his serious illness at the age of twenty-four, when the threat of tuberculosis put an end to his roving life and sent him back to the theatre.

A theatre now, however, with a difference. For things had been moving in Europe, and though the United States had been even slower than Britain in catching up with the theatrical times, when things once started moving in America, the American reputation for hustle, for getting a move on, was not belied. O'Neill was not the only budding American dramatist who had read widely in recent European drama and was feeling dissatisfied with American efforts. The nineteenth century in drama in the United States was like the Victorian drama in England—only more so. It was the great age of the actor, from the Booths to the Barrymores, from Mrs David Poe to James O'Neill, the age too of the dramatized novel, like *Uncle Tom's Cabin*, which enjoyed as immense a success as a stage melodrama as it had as a book. But the new century saw some faint stirrings of life. Appropriately-named New Theatres opened in Chicago in 1906 and New York in 1909. In 1912 the English actor-manager Maurice Brown founded the Little Theatre in Chicago. As early as 1905 G. P. Baker had started his course in play-writing and production at Harvard that was to grow into the "47 Workshop", with which O'Neill for a short time—as well as more conventional dramatists like S. N. Behrman, Sidney Howard and Philip Barry—was to be associated.

But it was the advent of the company of American actors and authors known as the Provincetown Players that first put American drama firmly into the twentieth century. Their avowed intention was to "give American playwrights a chance to work out their ideas in freedom", and in their brief span of life, from 1915 to 1929, first in Provincetown, Massachusetts, then in Greenwich Village, New York, they amply fulfilled their intention, putting on not only most of O'Neill's plays, from *Bound East for Cardiff* to *Strange Interlude*, but plays by many other new American dramatists, including the first plays of Susan Glaspell, Edna Ferber and the poets E. E. Cummings and Edna St Vincent Millay. O'Neill also became one of the founding members in 1918 of the Theatre Guild, New York, a company founded to put on plays considered to be of dubious commercial value, to stand little chance of production on Broadway. It was this company that first performed the entire *Back to Methuselah* sequence in 1922 as well as O'Neill's *Mourning Becomes Electra* (1930) and *Ah, Wilderness!* (1933).

Poe and Mark Twain came together in Eugene O'Neill, and with an element too of Jack London's open-necked radicalism—as different from Shaw's as the Wobblies were different from the Webbs—he launched the American drama of the twentieth century on its own distinctive path. O'Neill did not have Shaw's strictly literary ability: his plays need performance, in addition to reading, to reveal their strength. But otherwise he dominates the American drama of the early twentieth century as Shaw does the British, and the two men have in common, not only a desire to put the actor back in his rightful place as subordinate to the dramatist, each having a part with the director and the designer in a dramatic whole—a desire also seen in this period of the American theatre in the founding in 1916 of *The Theatre Arts Monthly* and in 1938 of the Playwrights' Company—but a constant urge to experiment, to use to the full the freedom of the dramatist thus obtained. Shaw "tried everything once": he has the widest range of any English dramatist since Ben Jonson. Similarly, O'Neill —partly in reaction from the conventional settings of his father's day—sets the first scene of *The Hairy Ape* in "the firemen's forecastle of a transatlantic liner", the opening of *All God's Chillun Got Wings* (1923) in "a corner in lower New York, at the edge of a coloured district" where "three narrow streets converge." O'Neill ranges from the rural tragedy of *Desire Under the Elms* (1924) to the domestic comedy of *Ah, Wilderness!*; from the rise and fall of the Negro boss of a West Indian island in the expressionist, Poe-like play *The Emperor Jones* (1920) to a stage variant on the Joycean–Woolf "stream of consciousness" in *Strange Interlude* (1926), in which the characters speak aloud their "asides", their conscious or unconscious thoughts. He adapted a Greek theme to the tragic aftermath of the American Civil War in the trilogy *Mourning Becomes Electra*; and could turn back to the realism of *Anna Christie* (1920) in a late play *The Iceman Cometh* (1939), whose scene is a Bowery saloon. Altogether, allowing for those incidental weaknesses of crudity and melodrama which are unavoidable in an experimental programme, it is an impressive achievement, not surpassed as a whole by any later American dramatist, though individual plays, like Elmer Rice's *Adding Machine* (1923), *Street Scene* (1929) and *Judgment Day* (1935), Tennessee Williams's *Streetcar Named Desire* (1947) and Arthur Miller's *Death of a Salesman* (1949) and *View from the Bridge* (1955), may be deemed superior to some of his. What Poe did for the American short story, what Mark Twain did for the American novel, O'Neill did for the American theatre. It was never the same again after O'Neill, as the British theatre of Victorian times never survived, fortunately, the shocking impact of Synge on the one hand and Shaw on the other. These three Irishmen were the essential liberators, to whom most of their contemporaries and successors on both sides of the Atlantic were and are indebted.

The other chief dramatists in prose who won fame in the O'Neill–Shavian era can most easily be considered in a small compass like ours if we choose one or two typical examples of their work. Whether *Peter Pan* (1904) is typical of Sir James Matthew Barrie (1860–1937) is, of course, questionable; his plays for adults have much of the whimsicality of *Peter* and of the sentiment which made his novels the precursors of the "Kailyard School" of Scottish fiction, but three of them at least—*The Admirable Crichton* (1902), *What Every Woman Knows* (1908) and *Dear Brutus* (1917)—have a tougher reasonableness beneath their slight dramatic grace. The plays of Somerset Maugham (1874–1965; p. 866 above) will not, we believe, survive as long as the best of his novels. A very professional writer, in fiction and drama alike, he keeps a high level by commercial standards, if he seldom rises above it. Those of his plays which are most worth attention from the literary point of view include *Our Betters* (1915) and *For Services Rendered* (1932).

Some dramatists of the period, on both sides of the Atlantic, won fame by what may be termed "anthology pieces": that is, plays which have so often been collected in omnibus volumes or mentioned in encyclopaedias, as well as performed by every repertory company, that they come to be considered, fairly or unfairly, as typical of their work. Alfred Sutro's *Walls of Jericho* (1904), Stanley Houghton's *Hindle Wakes* (1912), Harold Brighouse's *Hobson's Choice* (1916), C. K. Munro's *At Mrs Beam's* (1922), Sutton Vane's *Outward Bound* (1923), Frederick Lonsdale's *Last of Mrs Cheney* (1925), R. C. Sherriff's *Journey's End* (1929), Noel Coward's *Private Lives* (1930), Marc Connelly's *Green Pastures* (1930), Robert Sherwood's *Petrified Forest* (1935), Terence Rattigan's *French Without Tears* (1936), Thornton Wilder's *Our Town* (1938), Moss Hart's and G. M. Kaufman's *Man who Came to Dinner* (1939) and William Saroyan's *Time of Your Life* (1939) are cases in point, most of the plays mentioned belonging less to literary than to theatrical history, like the plays of J. B. Priestley (b. 1894)—such as *Time and the Conways* (1937) and *Johnson over Jordan* (1939) —the novelist who most brilliantly succeeded Sutton Vane and Elmer Rice in the drama of ideas. Priestley in turn leads on to some extent to the drama of Harold Pinter, there being the same relation between his *Dangerous Corner* (1932) and Pinter's *The Basement* (1966) as between Vane's *Outward Bound* and Sartre's *Huis-clos*—itself the model for Pinter's *Caretaker* (1960). The early work of Sean O'Casey, whose masterpiece remains *Juno and the Paycock*, has been mentioned above on p. 732; his later, more socialistic plays include *The Star Turns Red* (1940), *Red Roses for Me* (1943), *Purple Dust* (1945)—perhaps the best of his later work—and *Oak Leaves and Lavender* (1946). Ireland produced another notable dramatist in Denis Johnston (b. 1901), who wrote *The Moon in the Yellow River* (1931) and *A Bride for the Unicorn* (1933), besides a dramatist of great potential in Brendan Behan (1923–64), author of *The Quare Fellow* (1954) and *The Hostage* (1958; first written in Irish). The mantle of J. M. Barrie descended appropriately upon the Scottish shoulders of James Bridie, the pen-name of O. H. Mavor (1888–1959), whose gently satirical plays include *Tobias and the Angel* (1931) and *A Sleeping Clergyman* (1933).

The majority of the plays so far mentioned in this chapter belong, in Archer's definition, to the "new drama" of the twentieth century, drama in modern prose, however symbolically handled, with no Elizabethan nonsense about it. But the new in every sphere of life has a fatal tendency for becoming the old almost as soon as its novelty has been defined. To the generation of Eliot and Pound, neither Shaw nor Gilbert Murray seemed particularly new, the former's ideas being as elderly as Samuel Butler and the Fabian Society, the latter's poetry the last dying gasp of the Pre-Raphaelites. In their search for a new drama, they envisaged a return to the Greeks in a spirit opposite to Murray's and they were reading the Elizabethans as Synge and Yeats had read them, not like Shaw. At the same time, it is important to realize that there is nothing new in a revival of poetic drama: poetic drama is constantly being revived, it exists in a perpetual state of convalescence. The poets of the nineteenth century, from Wordsworth and Byron to Stephen Phillips and Robert Bridges—and in the United States from Longfellow to William Vaughn Moody—almost all tried their hand at the drama, mostly for reading rather than acting, though two or three of Phillips's had a stage success. Of the Georgian poets, Abercrombie and Bottomley, Masefield and Noyes, all wrote poetic drama, and in John Drink-

water (1882–1937) appeared a poet with knowledge of the stage as an actor—
a combination peculiarly rare in the country of Shakespeare. Drinkwater, who
became manager of the Birmingham Repertory Theatre, wrote poetic dramas
such as *Rebellion* (1914) and *The God of Quiet* (1916) before winning success as
an historical dramatist in prose with *Abraham Lincoln* (1918). James Elroy
Flecker (1884–1915) won a posthumous reputation with the Oriental melodrama *Hassan*, produced in 1923 with incidental music by Delius. Unkindly
compared with *Chu Chin Chow*, some of its verse at any rate is worthy of the
music it inspired.

We must keep this background in mind—and also remember the poetic
drama in the United States from Moody and Wallace Stevens to Maxwell
Anderson, Robert Frost, Archibald MacLeish and Robert Lowell—if we are
to see in perspective the Eliot–Fry revival of poetic drama which may be said
to have originated in Ashley Dukes's founding of the little Mercury Theatre
in London in 1933 and the production there in 1935–6 of Eliot's *Murder in the
Cathedral*, first produced at the Canterbury Festival by E. Martin Browne,
who subsequently directed all Eliot's plays. Eliot himself always took a modest
view of the importance of this latest revival of poetic drama; speaking in 1959,
he said that he and his fellow poet-dramatists were somewhat in the position
of a Kyd or a Peele, with perhaps a Marlowe, even a Shakespeare, to come in
the future after their preliminary work was over. One would have greater
faith in the comparison did one not suspect that a similar belief was held by
Phillips, Masefield, Drinkwater and Flecker—in the preface to *The Tragedy of
Nan* Masefield indeed says something very similar—and still we have only
Kyds and Peeles, with Marlowes, not to mention Shakespeares, as far off as
ever! It is better perhaps to forget about the Elizabethans altogether and to
compare the Eliot–Fry revival of poetic drama (*c.* 1935–55) with the numerous
other revivals that preceded it.

Forgetting Shakespeare is, in fact, the first principle of the modern poetic
dramatist, as Eliot pointed out. In his Harvard lecture on *Poetry and Drama*
(1951) he made some valuable observations based on his own experience in the
theatre. Speaking of the first conception of *Murder in the Cathedral*, he says that
he was "only aware at this stage that the essential was to avoid any echo of
Shakespeare, for I was persuaded that the primary failure of nineteenth-century
poets when they wrote for the theatre…was not in their theatrical technique,
but in their dramatic language." Accordingly, Eliot went back a hundred years
further, to the versification of *Everyman* (*c.* 1500), which has the advantage of
being comparatively unfamiliar to a modern audience. The chorus, however,
is in the Greek manner, and the prose speeches of the Knights after the murder of
Becket are in the manner of Shaw in general and of *Saint Joan* in particular.
Does the play survive this juxtaposition of three distinct dramatic styles? For
its limited purpose, the answer is evidently yes; and fortunately the purpose was
less limited than in the contemporary dramas of Auden and Isherwood. But
Eliot himself recognized that the play was a dead-end, so far as the future
writing of poetic drama was concerned. A play for a particular purpose—not
unlike Charles Williams's *Thomas Cranmer*, which succeeded Eliot's in the
Canterbury Festival in 1936, and Ronald Duncan's religious masque *This*

Way to the Tomb (1945)—*Murder in the Cathedral*, despite its superior points, could not hope to solve the problems of speech in verse which the modern poetic dramatist has to face. Eliot's next play, *The Family Reunion* (1939), is therefore his most important, if not his best, because it was here that he solved some of the outstanding problems facing him.

One is embarrassed in discussing Eliot's plays by the fact that in the Harvard lecture mentioned he himself discussed them better than anyone else can hope to do. The chief point to observe is that in *The Family Reunion* Eliot first worked out the contemporary verse idiom he afterwards continued to employ, with minor variations, in *The Cocktail Party* (1950), *The Confidential Clerk* (1954) and *The Elder Statesman* (1958). This is a type of verse in which the rhythm is close to that of ordinary modern English, closer even than in Eliot's first dramatic experiment, *Sweeney Agonistes: Fragments of an Aristophanic Melodrama* (1932): a type of verse, in Eliot's own words, which is "capable of unbroken transition between the most intense speech and the most relaxed dialogue." In *The Cocktail Party* he laid down for himself "the ascetic rule to avoid poetry which could not stand the test of strict dramatic utility: with such success, indeed, that it is perhaps an open question whether there is any poetry in the play at all." This is one self-criticism capable of a wider interpretation; another is Eliot's dry remark that in writing *The Cocktail Party* he "tried to keep in mind that in a play, from time to time, something should happen."

These are undoubtedly the twin weaknesses, not only of Eliot's own plays, but of the poetic drama of recent times in general. Quite half of *The Cocktail Party* and a good deal of *The Family Reunion* could have been written in prose and no audience would have noticed the difference: so far to the other extreme has gone Eliot's determination to avoid Shakespearean echoes. Even more important than this lack of poetry in these poetic dramas is their lack of drama: not enough happens. (The weaknesses are, of course, closely connected.) In Shaw's plays, even the most conversational, like *Getting Married* or *Back to Methuselah*, something is always happening or about to happen. In this respect Shaw is far more Shakespearean than Eliot. It is true there is a murder in the *Cathedral*, but that was "given" and in none of the later plays has the poetry, supposedly stripped bare for dramatic action, been found capable of any action beyond the most ordinary kind. When we think of the constant *movement*, in Shakespeare and Shaw alike, the main criticism that Eliot, like most of his Victorian and Georgian predecessors, has to bear is that his plays are too static. The problem of dramatic movement in relation to modern verse idiom is one that Eliot has by no means solved. The difficulties are enormous, and it is probable that where Eliot, despite the unaffected modesty of his self-criticism, has failed, no other poet of the twentieth century is likely to succeed.

The Left-wing verse (or verse-and-prose) drama of the nineteen-thirties was contemporary with *Murder in the Cathedral* and *The Family Reunion*, but by reason of its political currency at the time now appears comparatively dated. The three best were written by W. H. Auden in collaboration with the novelist Christopher Isherwood (b. 1904), author of *Mr Norris Changes Trains* (1935), *Goodbye to Berlin* (1939) and the autobiography *Lions and Shadows* (1938), whose post-Marxist career has, like Auden's, embraced citizenship of the United

States, but in combination with the Oriental mysticism of California rather than the episcopal Christianity of New York, influenced by the *Bhagavad Gita*, which he translated in 1947 with Swami Prabhavananda, rather than, like Auden, by the *Christianity and Power Politics* (1940) of the American theologian Reinhold Niebuhr. Their first play, which seems in retrospect scarcely more than an undergraduate charade, was *The Dog Beneath the Skin* (1935). Equally orthodox in its Marxism but much more dramatic in its action was *The Ascent of F6* (1936), on the whole the best play produced at the Group Theatre in London. It was followed by *On the Frontier* (1938). In these plays there was not much attempt to meet the problems of dramatic poetry. Louis MacNeice's *Out of the Picture* (1937) and Stephen Spender's *Trial of a Judge* (1938) were commendably more ambitious in this respect, but they lacked the theatrical qualities of the best scenes of Auden and Isherwood. Altogether, the Left-wing drama of the thirties, a kind of dramatized version of the contemporary pamphlets sponsored by the Left Book Club, was a disappointing movement from the point of view of literature. We must constantly bear in mind, however, the immense difficulty of writing poetic drama or verse-and-prose drama in our time, which the attempt of these dramatists to promulgate Marxist ideas on the stage— more realistically done by Clifford Odets at the Group Theatre in New York —could hardly have lessened. It would have needed a combination of Shaw and Eliot, or O'Neill and Pound, to have succeeded where Auden, Isherwood and their associates comparatively failed.

Such a combination may be as far off as ever, but we had at any rate in Christopher Fry (b. 1907) a dramatist whom Shaw and Eliot influenced in about equal proportions. Fry himself described Eliot as his master, but in reality he had two masters, and this perhaps was the most encouraging thing about him. Like Drinkwater, he combined poetic talent with a practical knowledge of acting and production—a practical experience shared by some of the best of the prose dramatists, like Pinter, Osborne, John Whiting and the Australian dramatist Ray Lawler, who largely succeeded him in public favour and fashionable esteem during the nineteen-fifties and sixties. Eliot is the main influence behind *The Boy with a Cart* (1939), *The First Born* (1946), *The Lady's Not for Burning* (1949) and *A Sleep of Prisoners* (1951); Shaw's influence predominates in that entertaining one-act play *A Phoenix too Frequent* (1946) and perhaps also in *Venus Observed* (1950), *The Dark is Light Enough* (1954) and *Curtmantle* (1961). If Fry's verse is more on Dylan Thomas's level than on Eliot's—the *Cathedral*, as it were, restored in "decorated" style—he has the compensating advantage over Eliot of commanding much more dramatic movement; we feel with Fry that here is a dramatist who has no need, like Eliot, to remind himself that in a play something should happen: like Synge and Shaw, he starts from that assumption.

Eliot is a great poet who did not quite manage the immensely difficult task of writing poetic drama of the same quality as the best of his non-dramatic work; a somewhat parallel case is the Yeats of *The Death of Cuchulain* and *Purgatory* (1939), plays influenced by the Noh drama of Japan. Fry is a minor poet who has nevertheless learnt from Shaw and his own stage experience how to write plays which are more dramatically alive than Eliot's. The required combination of poetry and drama that makes great dramatic poetry like Shakespeare's, where the drama is inseparable from the poetry, is easy enough to envisage but seems virtually impossible to write in modern English. However much credit we give to Shakespeare individually, we shall be foolishly derogatory of modern dramatists if we fail to recognize what advantages Shakespeare and his rivals possessed in Elizabethan English. The language of the Authorized Version of the Bible was based on similar speech (an advantage which Professor C. H. Dodd and his co-translators of the New English Bible of 1961-8 had to do without) and if in addition Shakespeare and his principal rivals were great poets, it is certain that George Abbot, Lancelot Andrewes and their associates were not. Considering the immense difficulties facing them, the limited dramatic achievements of Yeats, Eliot, Anderson, Frost, Auden, Fry... are worthy of some literary as well as theatrical applause. If we compare them with their nineteenth-century and Georgian predecessors—and this is the fairest comparison that can be made —we can hardly say that they represent a decline. Eliot's *Murder* is an improvement in the main upon Tennyson's *Becket*, as Yeats's *Purgatory* upon his own *Countess Kathleen* (1892) and Maxwell Anderson's *Winterset* (1935) upon Longfellow's *New England Tragedies*; and Fry's success in the theatre of the nineteenforties was not less justified than Phillips's or Flecker's in their time.

The "new drama" of the nineteen-fifties, which eventually superseded in public favour the "old drama" of Eliot and Fry, was not the "new drama" of William Archer which formerly "superseded" the "old drama" of the Elizabethans. It was mainly a prose drama, certainly, but with symbolic overtones reminiscent of the more "expressionist" prose dramas of O'Neill, and in the plays of John Arden, such as *Serjeant Musgrave's Dance* (1959), with prose alternating with verse. It owed less to Ibsen than to the German dramatist Bertolt Brecht, less to Shaw than to the French philosopher-dramatist Jean-Paul Sartre and the Rumanian-born French dramatist Eugene Ionesco. It was preeminently a "post-war" drama, both in the sense that such typical crests of the "new wave" as John Osborne's *Look Back in Anger* (1956) and the Jewish trilogy (1958-60) by Arnold Wesker were essentially protests against the social and spiritual chaos engendered by the Second World War, and in the sense that Beckett, and to some extent Harold Pinter, had connections with the Dadaist movement of 1916-24, which was itself partly a protest against the chaos of the 1914 war, partly an extension of that chaos, and which was to become the father (or, in justified pun, the "dada") of both Surrealism and the Theatre of the Absurd.

Whether Samuel Beckett (b. 1906; p. 880 above) belongs to French or to Anglo-Irish drama is still as controversial a question as whether his play *En attendant Godot* (1952)—*Waiting for Godot* (1954)—is a work of great profundity or a profoundly boring experience. Probably it has elements of both boredom and profundity, as Beckett himself is both a French and an Anglo-Irish writer. In *Godot* that theme of loneliness we observed both in *Ulysses* and in Beckett's own novels is reinforced by the neo-Existentialist philosophy of the cosmic absurdity of man's lot. There is genuine pathos in *Godot*, and genuine simplicity: the setting is not even the Elizabethan "another part of the field" but (Act I) "A country road. A tree. Evening" and (Act II) "Next Day. Same Time.

Same Place." Plot and character are virtually—even self-righteously—absent: there is something of the fanaticism of Pascal and Kierkegaard about Beckett's artistic puritanism, as there is about Sartre's philosophy. We know now, at any rate, what *Hamlet* looks like without the Prince of Denmark—not to mention without the King of Denmark, the Queen of Denmark, the Majesty of buried Denmark, Ophelia, Laertes, Horatio, etc. Never before has the Second Grave-Digger had so much light cast on him.

Against the genuine pathos and simplicity, and the genuine comedy—which, however, owes more to "business" than to the actual text of the play—must be set some pretty serious deficiencies. There is too much reliance altogether on ambiguous dialogue which can bear a dozen different meanings—some commentators have even seen a profound Christian meaning in the play—or no meaning at all. It is the easiest thing in the world to gain by such means a spurious reputation for profundity. The commonest stage-direction is "silence", which even with the frequent variation, "long silence", seems a very boring way of expressing boredom.

Fortunately, we do not need to go as far back as Vladimir's "million years ago, in the nineties" to get a parallel both to Beckett's theory and to Beckett's practice. The theory is contained in the Dada Manifesto of 1916, which announced: "Order = disorder; ego = non-ego; affirmation = negation: all are supreme radiations of an absolute art... Art is a private matter; the artist does it for himself; any work of art that can be understood is the product of a journalist."

The practice can be read about at length in that amusing chapter, "The Death of Dada", in Malcolm Cowley's *Exile's Return* (1934). The new artist, writes Cowley, "might, for example, make an arrangement of watch springs, ball bearings and kitchen matches, and photograph it (like Man Ray); he might clip illustrations out of old mail-order catalogues, shuffle them into an ingenious design and exhibit them as a painting (like Max Ernst, who later sold such pictures at a stiff price)... he might have his poems printed in the typography of advertisements for nerve tonics and cancer cures (like Tristan Tzara), or invent a new system of punctuation (like E. E. Cummings)..." Or he might, of course, write a tragi-comedy in two acts called *Waiting for Godot* which dispenses with such crude conventions as plot, character and style, or a novel of fourteen pages called *Imagination Dead Imagine* (1966) which its publishers solemnly describe as "a work of fiction from which the author has removed all but the essentials, having first imagined them and created them. It is possibly the shortest novel ever published. It may well be numbered among the greatest."

Beckett's second play, *Fin de partie* (1957)—*Endgame* (1958)—concerns a number of characters who live in dustbins. The well-named *Happy Days* (1961), written in English and first performed in New York, concerns a woman who is buried alive until in the last act only her head is visible. *Play* (1963), first performed in Germany, has three characters, their heads protruding from urns, who speak only when a shaft of light hits their face, the whole text (for some obscure Dadaist reason) being played through twice—but not three times—in twenty minutes. One would not deny the limited interest, more theatrical than literary, of such curiously old-fashioned *avant-garde* productions, which must remind elderly play-goers of the post-war theatre of the nineteen-twenties in Russia and Germany as well as in the United States. In such plays the director is more important than either the actors or the playwright, and Beckett's strictly literary value is less than O'Neill's and much less than Synge's or Shaw's. The wheel has come full circle, and it is the director who has superseded the old actor-manager in stealing the thunder of the dramatist.

Max Ernst, we must not forget, sold his "mail-order" pictures "at a stiff price", and *Waiting for Godot* was a great popular success throughout the world. In general, the dramatists of the "new wave" have been able to ride on the crests of public approval almost from the start. Not for them the ten years' obscurity endured by Shaw, the censorship of certain plays suffered by Shaw and Granville-Barker, the storm of protest from outraged citizens that greeted Synge's *Playboy of the Western World*. These new "play-boys" have themselves taken the western world by storm, so we should beware of comparing them with those earlier dramatists who had to bear the hostility of the public until they eventually overcame it. A truer comparison is with those dramatists of the past, like Galsworthy and Maugham, who in their day gave the public what it wanted. At the same time, we cannot say, any more than with the poetic drama of Eliot and Fry, that this fashionable "new drama" in prose represents any serious decline compared with older fashions. There is as much dramatic meat to chew upon in Osborne and Wesker as in Galsworthy, Maugham or Harold Brighouse, as much dry humour in Pinter as in Barrie. At the close of the nineteen-sixties, the future of such British dramatists is awaited with as much interest as that of Arthur Miller and Edward Albee in the United States, Ray Lawler and Patrick White in Australia, Wole Soyinka and J. P. Clark in Nigeria... The pioneers of twentieth-century drama—those three great Irishmen, Synge and Shaw and O'Neill—have not had a successor of equal genius, but on the whole they have not been unworthily followed.

V. CRITICISM AND CULTURE

We have not yet said much in this chapter about the conditions of culture under which, or against which, the poems, novels and plays we have discussed came to be written. The methods of big business in the literary and theatrical worlds, the growth of advertisement, the "book of the week" publicity in the popular newspapers, the taking over of most of the smaller publishers in London and New York by a few big concerns, the tremendous popularity of crime stories among all sections of the reading public, the decline in the bookshop sales of some kinds of bound book and the corresponding growth of the paperback, the struggle for survival of the serious quarterlies, monthlies and weeklies, the competition and the influence of the cinema, the radio and television: these are a few of the matters which the critic in the mid-twentieth century is forced to take into account in his consideration of contemporary literature. By and large, it is the less serious writers who swim with the commercial tide, the more serious who battle against it. Few great novelists of our time, and even fewer poets and dramatists, have managed to win recognition without a struggle against the accepted ideas of the public. The controversies concerning Lawrence and Joyce are only an exaggeration of a prevailing twentieth-century trend. The growth of the reading public and the loss of homogeneity which has made at least three fairly distinct literary publics—highbrow, lowbrow and middle-brow—out of what was virtually one in the time of Dickens: these changes affect literature at its source, and their results, though possibly not so striking in post-war years as they were in the nineteen-twenties and thirties—the chief danger now being a kind of popular-highbrow culture based on mass publicity and social values—are still sufficiently with us. We are bound to assess the literary critics of our time, not entirely by their powers in literary criticism alone, but by the extent of their awareness of the matters we have glanced at. The best critic of the Victorian age, Matthew Arnold, was as much a critic of society as he was of literature. Probably we shall not go far wrong if we inquire which of the critics of the mid-twentieth century are most like Arnold, while recognizing that critics totally unlike him may also have a right to our esteem. There are three in Britain—the greatest born in America—who seem to stand high above their contemporaries, and it is significant that each of them is not only a critic in himself but, like Falstaff in wit, the cause of criticism in others: they were each the founders and editors of literary reviews, the centre of a chosen field of culture in which they stand supreme. These writers are T. S. Eliot himself, founder and editor of *The Criterion*; John Middleton Murry, founder and editor of *The Adelphi*; and F. R. Leavis, chief founder and editor of *Scrutiny*. Each of these reviews has now ceased publication, though they have been reprinted in their entirety in volume form.

We begin naturally with Eliot, whose criticism has been closely associated with his poetry and whose justification for naming the modern age in this chapter rests nearly as much on his *Sacred Wood* and *Selected Essays* as on his *Waste Land* and *Four Quartets*. He gives us a starting point when he observes in his essay on Arnold in *The Use of Poetry and the Use of Criticism* that "From time to time... it is desirable that some critic shall appear to review the past of our literature, and set the poets and the poems in a new order. This task is not one of revolution but of readjustment..." or what Leavis was to call revaluation. Arnold was one such critic, like Dryden and Johnson before him, and no one has a better claim to the distinction in the mid-twentieth century than Eliot himself. When speaking of his own poetry (pp. 851-5 above), we noted that the early verse was partly built on the poet's study of the French symbolists and of the later Shakespeare and the lesser Elizabethan dramatists; he has, as it were, repaid the debt incurred by making these writers more intelligible to the modern public through such essays as the ones on Baudelaire (1930), *Shakespeare and the Stoicism of Seneca* (1927), Ben Jonson (1919) and Cyril Tourneur (1931). This is not, of course, in the case of the Elizabethans, to supersede altogether the introductions to the original Mermaid series of 1887-9, for which we remain grateful to that many-talented man Havelock Ellis (1859-1939) and his associates, for Eliot reminds us that "no generation is interested in Art in quite the same way as any other; each generation, like each individual, brings to the contemplation of art its own categories of appreciation." For us, his studies of the Elizabethans— mostly contributed to *The Times Literary Supplement* under the editorship

(1902–38) of Sir Bruce Richmond—are as potent an experience as were those of Lamb, Coleridge, Swinburne and Ellis for their own time. Eliot's debt in his poetry to the tradition of wit in the seventeenth century has again been amply repaid by his critical essays on Marvell, Dryden and the Metaphysical Poets.

His first critical essays and reviews were contributed 1917–22 to *The Egoist, The Athenaeum* (edited by Middleton Murry) and *The Times Literary Supplement*. The first of his critical books, *The Sacred Wood: Essays on Poetry and Criticism* (1920), was drawn from these contributions, which include *Tradition and the Individual Talent* (1917), *Euripides and Professor Murray* (1918; p. 904 above) and the essays on Marlowe, *Hamlet*, Ben Jonson, Massinger, Blake and Swinburne. *The Criterion* was founded in 1922 and did not cease publication till 1939, by which time Eliot had contributed nearly a hundred Commentaries as well as articles and reviews. It did not have the circulation it deserved, largely because the price at which it had to be published was far too high for most of the public for which it was designed. It had, however, as Eliot said with justified complacency, "a definite character and cohesion, although its contributors were men holding the most diverse political, social and religious views. I think also that it had a definite congeniality with the foreign periodicals with which it associated itself"—such as *La Nouvelle Revue Française* and *Die Neue Rundschau*. In a phrase that would have won the approval of Matthew Arnold, "we could take for granted," said Eliot, "an interest, a delight, in ideas for their own sake, in the free play of intellect." If *The Criterion* had the incidental failings inseparable from an ambitious undertaking, its dissolution in 1939 created a vacancy in London which Cyril Connolly's *Horizon* (1940–50) could only partly fill. Although *Horizon* published some of the best work of George Orwell, and other contributions of equal value from a wide range of contributors, it lacked the critical seriousness of *The Criterion* and is more justly to be described, both in its literary and its pictorial aspects, as *The Yellow Book* of the culture-hungry forties. We must in fairness own, however, that in 1968 we could do with a flourishing *Horizon* as well as a flourishing *Criterion*, *Adelphi*, *Scrutiny*, *Life and Letters*, and all the other literary reviews which have given up the ghost in recent times. Those still in existence in London in 1968—the revived *Cornhill Magazine*, *Encounter*, *The London Magazine*, to name the chief—follow *Horizon* and John Lehmann's *New Writing* (1936–46) rather than *The Criterion* and do not in any case make up for those that have been lost.

Eliot followed *The Sacred Wood* by a slimmer volume of critical essays *Homage to John Dryden* (1924), containing besides the title-essay the essays already mentioned on Marvell and the Metaphysical Poets, both among his very finest critical achievements. The next volume was the first in which his Anglo-Catholic preoccupations began to permeate—some would say, undermine—his literary criticism: *For Lancelot Andrewes: Essays on Style and Order* (1928), the recipient of the title being the Jacobean divine and Bishop of Winchester who was one of the translators of the Authorized Version of the Bible. Then followed *Dante* (1929), an impressive study which must be one of the best things ever written about its subject in English and which is connected with Eliot's *Ash Wednesday*, the poem composed during the same period. *Thoughts after Lambeth* (1931) was a pamphlet on Church affairs afterwards included in the important volume of *Selected Essays* (1932), containing the best of his work up till that date; it was enlarged in 1934 and again in 1951 and must be considered on the whole the most influential body of criticism published during the present century.

The second phase of Eliot's criticism is relatively unbuttoned, a considerable portion of it consisting of lectures delivered to various scholarly audiences on both sides of the Atlantic. It opens with the volume we quoted to begin with: *The Use of Poetry and the Use of Criticism* (1933), incorporating lectures delivered at Harvard. *After Strange Gods: A Primer of Modern Heresy* (1934) similarly embodied lectures at the University of Virginia. This has been the most widely attacked of all Eliot's criticism and the author's own feeling of dissatisfaction with it led to its being left permanently out of print. Some of his remarks in this book on "heretics" like Hardy and Lawrence were unworthy of his critical reputation, though possibly congruent with his theological views at the time. *The Idea of a Christian Society* (1939), originally lectures at Cambridge, was a much more impressive work, which together with *Notes Towards the Definition of Culture* (1948) gives us the most reasoned statement of his later cultural position. Between these two important books come several minor works of criticism: *The Music of Poetry* (1942), the W. P. Ker Memorial Lecture at Glasgow University; *The Classics and the Man of Letters* (1942), the Presidential Address to the Classical Association; *What is a Classic?* (1945), an address to the Virgil Society; and *Milton* (1947), a lecture to the British Academy. The last of these created the most controversy, for Eliot had written on Milton before, in *A Note on the Verse of John Milton*, contributed to *Essays and Studies of the English Association* in 1936, and what he said now seemed to contradict what he had said earlier. In general, Eliot was at some pains during the nineteen-forties and fifties to dissociate himself from those who had taken seriously his critical pronouncements of the twenties and thirties, explaining in the words of *Prufrock*: "That is not what I meant at all. That is not it, at all." It appeared now, not only that he was more conservative in his opinions than we had thought him, but that he had *always* been more conservative. Some people were relieved; others were as puzzled as the citizens of Orwell's Oceania when they were informed that they had always been fighting Eurasia, not Eastasia as they had imagined. Eliot was not, after all, the "literary Bolshevik" whom Dean Inge had rebuked, but on the contrary the bluest of academic Tories, fond of Milton, Tennyson and Kipling, who could scarcely open his mouth in public without tearing yet another leaf from the ruined choirs of the sacred wood. Whether his original observations or his later denials will cut more ice with the future remains to be seen.

It was, we observed, John Middleton Murry (1889–1958) who published some of Eliot's earliest criticism while he was editor of *The Athenaeum*, 1919–21. Other contributors included Santayana, Virginia Woolf, Herbert Read and Aldous Huxley. Murry himself contributed to many literary journals, including *The Criterion*, but his name will always be associated with one in particular: with *The Adelphi* (1923–55), of which he was the founder and which he edited for the majority of its career. (Other editors included Sir Richard Rees, Henry Williamson and George Godwin.) Like *The Criterion*, *The Adelphi* published some of the most distinguished writers of the century, from Lawrence to Eliot, but it is important less for the prestige of its contributors than for the merits of its platform. From the first it adopted—like *Scrutiny* and like *The Southern Review* in the United States—a very critical attitude to the "machine" culture of the modern age, coming eventually (in Murry's case) to reinterpret the earlier protests of Carlyle, Thoreau, Ruskin and Morris in the light of an unorthodox Christianity based as much on Rousseau, Blake, Dostoevsky, Lawrence and Albert Schweitzer as on the New Testament. Murry became convinced that the most satisfactory answer to the ills of the modern world lay in a revived agriculture, which must not be so much the traditional agriculture of English history, with its hierarchy of classes, as a democratic community, on the lines of Brook Farm, New Harmony and other communities of the kind in the United States (see pp. 798, 811 above.) With that courage of his convictions so characteristic of him, Murry put his idea into practice, *The Adelphi* during the period of the Second World War being run as the organ of a pacifist farming community in Suffolk. Some of its best work was done at this time, particularly notable being the editorials—we had almost said the sermons—of Murry himself. (The later volumes in Henry Williamson's novel-sequence *A Chronicle of Ancient Sunlight* give some intimate glimpses of this pacifist farming community.) Those who regret the older Murry of more purely literary criticism have not much more of a leg to stand on than those Victorian readers who said Ruskin should stick to art and not meddle with economics.

Murry's platform was perhaps shaky on several points, but our recognition of this need not prevent a sincere admiration for his work as a whole. He is one of those writers, like Orwell and Edmund Wilson, who are intensely readable, whatever the subject of their writings may be; and this is partly due to the sheer force of character behind them. His literary criticism, often inseparable, like that of Sainte-Beuve, from interpretative biography, includes *Fyodor Dostoevsky* (1917), *Aspects of Literature* (1920), *The Problem of Style* (1922), *Countries of the Mind* (1922, 1931), *Keats and Shakespeare* (1925), *William Blake* (1933) and *Swift* (1954). His other works include his autobiographies *The Evolution of an Intellectual* (1920) and *Between Two Worlds* (1934); his *Life of Jesus* (1926); and his socio-religious criticism *The Necessity of Pacifism* (1937), *Heaven and Earth* (1938), *The Betrayal of Christ by the Churches* (1940), *Adam and Eve* (1944) and *The Free Society* (1948). His first wife was "the New Zealand Chekhov", Katharine Mansfield (1888–1923; p. 756), author of some of the best short stories of our time, whose *Journal* (1927) and *Letters* (1951) he edited. Some of Murry's work still remains uncollected from journals, which is also the case in regard to Eliot and Leavis.

Frank Raymond Leavis (b. 1895) and *Scrutiny: A Quarterly Review* (1932–53) are subjects impossible to separate. Leavis himself, of course, has always insisted on the collaborative nature of *Scrutiny*; and this is true enough, in three different senses. In the first place, *Scrutiny* was the product of collaboration between Dr Leavis and Mrs Q. D. Leavis, author of that pioneer study of popular culture *Fiction and the Reading Public* (1932): a man-and-wife partnership not uncommon in literary history, of which other notable examples are John Richard and Alice Stopford Green, Sidney and Beatrice Webb, J. L. and

Barbara Hammond, H. M. and Nora Chadwick, Leonard and Virginia Woolf, Robert S. and Helen Lynd, and G. D. H. and Margaret Cole. In the second place, *Scrutiny* was the product of collaboration between Leavis and his co-editors, who included L. C. Knights, D. W. Harding, Denys Thompson (later editor of *The Use of English*), H. A. Mason and the music critic Wilfrid Mellers. In the third place, *Scrutiny* was the product of collaboration between Leavis and his pupils at Downing College, Cambridge, many of whom became contributors in their turn.

But the common factor in these three kinds of collaboration was Leavis himself, without whom we cannot imagine *Scrutiny* existing, any more than we can imagine *The Criterion* without Eliot or *The Adelphi* without Murry. What made *Scrutiny* on the whole such an important journal was the critical genius of its editor and the academic revolution in the teaching of English of which he was the central figure. The term "academic" may be questioned, since it was the academic mind of the early nineteen-thirties against which Leavis and his associates had at first to fight, since moreover none of the founders of *Scrutiny*, as Leavis himself once put it, was "of any academic importance." But the paradox is more apparent than real: in the first place, the fight against the old-style academic, still in the nineteen-thirties living spiritually in the nineteenth century, was in the main a successful one (though no revolution, in either culture or politics, ever goes quite the way the originators hoped and a certain amount of compromise is inevitably involved); and secondly, of the editorial board of *Scrutiny*, L. C. Knights soon became Professor Knights (eventually succeeding Quiller-Couch and Basil Willey at Cambridge), D. W. Harding Professor Harding, and Leavis himself began that teaching career at Downing College (soon to be the official address of *Scrutiny*) upon which his reputation in university circles partly rests. By the late thirties almost the entire contents of the journal were being written by dons and schoolmasters, and the academic footnote began to blossom at the bottom of the page, though not without some raising of eyebrows on the part of original subscribers. By the late forties *Scrutiny* was no longer the Cambridge equivalent to a "metropolitan literary review" but an increasingly academic journal in which criticism of criticism (like the essay with the awesome subtitle, "Reflections on Mr Ford's Rejoinder") took much of the space formerly occupied by reviews of current poems and novels.

This history of *Scrutiny*, though in some respects a sad one, seems nevertheless, in retrospect, inevitable, for the great strength of Leavis and his associates lay from the start in their appeal to the younger generation of dons, students and schoolmasters who were reading the literature of the twenties and thirties and who were disgusted with the puerilities of current academic criticism, based as it largely was on the outmoded attitudes of the late nineteenth century. Inevitably, when the editors of *Scrutiny* themselves succeeded to important academic positions, the journal changed its character and became less interesting to the general serious reader and more strictly of benefit to the university public. What did not change, and could hardly have changed with Leavis still in charge, was the high standard of literary criticism; and that, after all, was the important thing, to which the change from free-lance to academic was entirely secondary.

The strong points and the weak points of *Scrutiny*, as compared with other notable literary reviews in Britain, the Commonwealth and the United States, are now widely recognized. Its great strength was admirably summarized by the American literary and dramatic critic Eric Bentley—who was to edit a volume of selections *The Importance of Scrutiny* (New York, 1948)—in an article in *The Kenyon Review* in 1946: "Richards wrote *Practical Criticism* but *Scrutiny* was practical and criticized. Cleanth Brooks wrote notes for a new history of English poetry but in essay after essay *Scrutiny* accumulated a new history *in extenso*. Burke and Ransom extended the boundaries of critical discussion but *Scrutiny* actually occupied the territory and issued new maps."

That was truly as well as wittily said: the strength of *Scrutiny* lay above all in its literary criticism. Its acknowledged weakness was in the field of creative literature, in which—apart from a few poems by Ronald Bottrall, Richard Eberhart and others—it hardly competed at all with *The Adelphi* or *The Criterion* (which had their own critical weaknesses). Most literary reviews of the twentieth century have tried to combine criticism with creation, on the pattern of the great reviews of the eighteenth and nineteenth centuries. The first number (December 1908) of Ford Madox Ford's *English Review*, for example, printed stories by Henry James, Galsworthy and H. G. Wells (the opening chapters of the serial *Tono-Bungay*), a poem by Hardy, articles by Conrad, W. H. Hudson, W. H. Davies and H. W. Nevinson, a translation of Tolstoy by Constance Garnett, and reviews by Conrad and others. Later numbers printed contributions, both creative and critical, by Yeats, Lawrence, Pound, Edward Thomas, Wyndham Lewis, Eden Phillpotts, Norman Douglas, Granville-Barker, Belloc, H. M. Tomlinson, Gilbert Cannan, etc., besides the editor Ford and his sub-editor Douglas Goldring. The first number (June 1928) of Desmond MacCarthy's *Life and Letters* printed Hardy, Beerbohm, Santayana, Clive Bell, later numbers Edith Wharton, Somerset Maugham, Logan Pearsall Smith, Aldous Huxley and Richard Hughes (whose novel *A High Wind in Jamaica* was serialized). Most other London literary reviews, from Sir John Squire's *London Mercury* (1919–34) to John Lehmann's *New Writing* and Connolly's *Horizon*, have pursued a similar course, their weakness in literary criticism being balanced by their strength in other fields. Both Lehmann's *New Writing* and *Life and Letters* (1928–50) in its last years (under the editorship of Robert Herring) made a point of printing contributions, not only from Britain and the United States, but from Europe and the Commonwealth. Herring's *Life and Letters* published entire issues devoted to India, New Zealand, the West Indies, etc., and can therefore be considered the principal British pioneer in a field of culture which today is regarded as of growing importance and of which the leading British organ is *The Journal of Commonwealth Literature* (p. 744 above)—an enterprise from the same stable of the University of Leeds as *A Review of English Literature*, founded by Laurence Brander and edited by A. Norman Jeffares.

The *Review*, like F. W. Bateson's *Essays in Criticism*, Margaret Willy's *English* (the magazine of the English Association) and the University of Hull's *Critical Quarterly* (edited by C. B. Cox and A. E. Dyson), follows *Scrutiny's* practice of publishing mainly critical or educational articles, with an occasional poem. But most of the leading literary reviews in the Commonwealth and the United States during this century have been more like *The Criterion* than like *Scrutiny*: that is, they have published literary criticism (occasionally on as high a level as *Scrutiny's* best) together with fiction, poetry, drama, etc., and have regarded their creative function as seriously as their critical. This applies, for example, in the United States to *The Dial* in its New York days (1916–29), whose editors included Conrad Aiken, Randolph Bourne and Marianne Moore and which printed, says Hart (*Oxford Companion to American Literature*), "virtually all the distinguished authors of the period." It applies also to Van Wyck Brooks's *Freeman* (1920–4); to *Hound and Horn* (1927–34), whose editors included R. P. Blackmur and Yvor Winters and which published work by Eliot, Pound, Gertrude Stein and Kenneth Burke; to *The Southern Review* from Louisiana (1935–42, revived 1965) whose editors have included the poet and novelist Robert Penn Warren; to Allen Tate's *Sewanee Review* from the University of the South in Tennessee; to John Crowe Ransom's *Kenyon Review* from Kenyon College, Ohio; and *The Hudson Review*, New York; as well as to the leading Commonwealth reviews such as Geoffrey Dutton's *Australian Letters* (Adelaide), C. B. Christesen's *Meanjin Quarterly* (Melbourne), James McAuley's *Quadrant* (Sydney), Charles Brasch's *Landfall* (Christchurch) and C. L. Bennet's *Dalhousie Review* (Halifax, Nova Scotia). None of the editors of *Scrutiny*, though a few of the contributors, had written either poetry or fiction, whereas it was and is the practice of most other literary reviews throughout the English-speaking world to have editors who are poets or fiction-writers as well as critics.

At the same time, it would be uncritical to repeat here, what is sometimes asserted, that the only critics worth attention are those who are themselves creative artists, that in regard to poetry we should listen exclusively to poet-critics like Dryden, Johnson, Coleridge, Arnold, Yeats, Pound, Eliot, Graves, Auden, Shapiro, etc.; in regard to fiction exclusively to novelist-critics like Howells, James, Forster, Lawrence, Virginia Woolf, Wyndham Lewis, Graham Greene, Robert Penn Warren... This may be generally true. Yet there are a fair number of exceptions in the past, notably Hazlitt in England and Sainte-Beuve in France, neither of whose non-critical work is of prime importance. In the present age we have Murry (whose verse can be disregarded) and Leavis, who are probably not as great in criticism as Eliot at his best, but who nevertheless must rank not far below him. (We pass over without comment the critical aberrations of some eminent creative artists, like Byron in *Don Juan*, James in *Notes on Novelists*, Yeats in *The Oxford Book of Modern Verse*.) Much of Murry's criticism is connected with his views on society and religion; much of Leavis's with his revolutionary opinions on university education in English. Beginning in 1930 with the pamphlet *Mass Civilization and Minority Culture*—earning him the uncomprehending criticism of a whole generation of Marxists—Leavis published his first important work, *New Bearings in English Poetry*, in 1932. This was the pioneer study of Hopkins, Eliot and Pound, to which (with Edmund Wilson's chapter on Eliot in *Axel's Castle*, 1931) all subsequent criticism of these poets is indebted; and it was introduced by a discussion of Victorian and Georgian poetry which carried the entire study over a period of a hundred years. With the companion work, *Revaluation: Tradition and Development in English Poetry* (1936), the whole of English poetry from Donne to Eliot was reconsidered, a large number of the reconsiderations having since become accepted, or at least arguable, in the most conservative quarters. Leavis's most important work on the function of university education in English, connected closely, as always, with his practical experience, is *Education and the University* (1943). *For Continuity* (1933), *The Common Pursuit* (1952) and "*Anna Karenina*" *and Other Essays* (1967)—the last-named containing a notable study of Mark Twain—are the equivalent to Eliot's *Selected Essays* and among the few critical volumes of our time that can stand the comparison.

The one obvious gap in the criticism of Eliot—he has written very little about the novel—has been filled increasingly in recent years by other critics, not least by Leavis himself in *The Great Tradition* (1949) and *D. H. Lawrence: Novelist* (1955), the two books together forming a "revaluation" of English fiction similar to that he had undertaken with poetry. Not that *The Great Tradition* itself escapes criticism. A view of tradition in the English novel that relegates Dickens to an appendix and dismisses *Wuthering Heights*, in horticultural language, as a "sport", seems suspect to start with. The essay on *Hard Times* is probably the best ever written on that neglected novel, and Leavis's opinion of Dickens's language—"The final stress may fall on Dickens's command of word, phrase, rhythm and image: in ease and range there is surely no greater master of English except Shakespeare"—is as memorable as it is true. Yet a Dickens who had written only *Hard Times* would not have been the great novelist he is, and there is surely a critical confusion in Leavis's view of "the novel as dramatic poem" combined with the relegation to an appendix of the novelist whose use of language is only bettered by our supreme dramatic poet.

The *Scrutiny* group were neither the earliest nor the only distinguished contributors to what John Crowe Ransom called "the New Criticism". Besides Eliot's *Sacred Wood* (1920), Murry's *Problem of Style* (1922), Edwin Muir's *Transition* (1926) and some of the literary articles in A. R. Orage's political weekly *The New Age* (1907–22), there was the short-lived but influential review *The Calendar of Modern Letters* (1925–7), edited by Edgell Rickword and Douglas Garman, which produced three volumes of selections: *Scrutinies* I and II (1928–31), edited by Rickword, and *Towards Standards of Criticism* (1933), edited by Leavis. There were also the influential books of I. A. Richards (b. 1893) of Cambridge and Harvard, whose *Principles of Literary Criticism* (1924) and *Practical Criticism* (1929) also preceded *Scrutiny* in date and—like *Hound and Horn* and the early work of Ransom, Blackmur, Tate and Winters in the United States—to some extent prepared the way for it. The difference between Richards's more theoretical criticism and Leavis's more practical can perhaps best be seen in a comparison of the former's *Coleridge on Imagination* (1934) with the latter's *Mill on Bentham and Coleridge* (1950). Richards won world fame through his association with the originator C. K. Ogden in the development of Basic English (see above, p. 777). In literary criticism his most distinguished follower is the poet William Empson (b. 1906), whose critical work includes *Seven Types of Ambiguity* (1930), *Some Versions of Pastoral* (1938), *The Structure of Complex Words* (1951) and *Milton's God* (1961)—the last-named a contribution to the modern Miltonic controversy which has involved arguments, from widely differing points of view, by Eliot, Leavis, Tillyard, C. S. Lewis and A. J. A. Waldock. In Shakespearean criticism, to which Eliot, Murry, Leavis, Empson, L. C. Knights, M. C. Bradbrook and D. A. Traversi have each contributed some impressive work, the highest place must surely go to George Wilson Knight (b. 1897), author of *The Wheel of Fire* (1930) and *The Imperial Theme* (1931), whose influence on *Scrutiny* critics and others has been profound.

We give chief attention here to Eliot, Murry and Leavis because they are, by and large—with Edmund Wilson, R. P. Blackmur and a few others in the United States—the critics of the post-1918 era who have produced the most distinguished body of work, the principal successors in our time to Matthew Arnold and Leslie Stephen. The critical writings of Leslie Stephen's daughter Virginia Woolf have been discussed in relation to her novels (p. 875 above) and there is no need here to do more than confirm the impression already given, that the best essays in *The Common Reader* (1925) are among the classic criticism of the age. Her *Collected Essays*, edited by Leonard Woolf, were published in four volumes in 1966–7. Forster's *Aspects of the Novel* (1927), Edwin Muir's *Structure of the Novel* (1929), Walter Allen's *English Novel* (1954) and V. S. Pritchett's *Living Novel* (1947) and *Working Novelists* (1965) are critical works by novelist-critics not unworthy to be classed with Mrs Woolf's. Most of Pritchett's criticism originally appeared in *The New Statesman*, some of it under the literary editorship of Raymond Mortimer, whose own best work is probably his well-named *Channel Packet* (1942), essays on English and French literature. *The New Republic* and *The New Yorker* have published some of the best work of America's most distinguished "home-based" critic, Edmund Wilson (b. 1895), a critic of the stature of the Anglo-American Eliot and the Englishman Leavis, a critic moreover who has followed Emerson and Arnold in being both a critic of literature and a critic of society. The United States, to our common profit, has produced a fair number of these "philosophical" or "moral" critics, as they might loosely be called: critics who have taken the whole world for their province, who have turned from literature or art to mankind in general, in his history or in his essence. The names of Santayana, Henry Adams, Lewis Mumford, Perry Miller, Yvor Winters, Lionel Trilling... come to mind. We have already mentioned three of Wilson's best books: *Axel's Castle* (1931) and *The Triple Thinkers* (1952; p. 851 above), essays originally contributed to *The New Republic* (of which he was associate-editor 1926–31), *The Atlantic Monthly*, *Hound and Horn*, *Partisan Review*, etc., besides the more recent *O Canada* (1967; p. 749), an assignment from *The New Yorker*, where he discusses the two cultures, British and French, of the Dominion. *To the Finland Station* (1940) is a study of Marxism; *The Wound and the Bow* (1941) and *Classics and Commercials* (1951) reprint essays ranging from Dickens to Sherlock Holmes. *Patriotic Gore* (1962) is a study of the literature of the American Civil War.

Some of George Orwell's essays have been mentioned (p. 894) with his novels. In literary criticism, which in Orwell's case is always closely connected with social and political criticism, his best work includes the essays on Dickens, Henry Miller and Boys' Weeklies in *Inside the Whale* (1940), on Koestler, P. G. Wodehouse and Kipling in *Critical Essays* (1946) and on Tolstoy in the posthumous collection *Shooting an Elephant* (1950), which also reprints a selection from "I Write as I Please", the weekly column he contributed to *Tribune*.

The critical work of Robert Graves is, like Orwell's, as original as his other books. It includes *A Survey of Modernist Poetry* (1927) and *A Pamphlet against Anthologies* (1928), with the American poet Laura Riding, and *The Crowning Privilege* (1955). The last-named reprints *The Common Asphodel* (1949), together with the Clark Lectures of the title and essays on Ezra Pound and E. E. Cummings. The final Clark Lecture, entitled "These be your Gods, O Israel!", presents the neo-Georgian case against Eliot, Pound and the later Yeats with all the bluff conviction, and the regimental wit, of an old soldier of the Somme who is going to stand no nonsense from any post-Georgian recruit. In recent years Graves is less convincing as a critic-poet than as a scholar-poet who has specialized in anthropology. One would, of course, need to be an anthropologist oneself in order to discuss at all adequately *The White Goddess: A Historical Grammar of Poetic Myth* (1948; revised and enlarged 1952), but it is evidently a learned work and perhaps an important one also. The Goddess of the title is the traditional figure of the Muse, who recurs often enough in *The Crowning Privilege* for the reader to suspect where Graves's primary interest now lies. *The White Goddess* is hard going in places and cannot be compared, for unfailing clarity allied to scholarly distinction, with Sir James Frazer's abridged one-volume edition of *The Golden Bough* (1922), a feat of literature almost as remarkable in its way as the writing of the original work—which itself remains a permanent classic, despite the contributions of contemporary or later scholars and anthropologists like Jane Harrison, W. H. R. Rivers, Lord Raglan, A. C. Haddon, Bronislaw Malinowski and Margaret Mead, which have either modified Frazer or sometimes come to radically different conclusions. The one-volume *Bough* came out the same year as Eliot's *Waste Land*, which acknowledged a debt to the third edition in twelve volumes (1911–15) as well as to Jessie L. Weston's book on the Grail legend *From Ritual to Romance* (1920). Literary critics of several generations have been indebted to Sir Herbert Grierson (1866–1960) for his edition of Donne (1912), his anthology of *Metaphysical Poets: Donne to Butler* (1921) and his *Cross-Currents in the Literature of the Seventeenth Century* (1929); to the studies of English folksong by Cecil Sharp (1859–1924; p. 93); to G. R. Owst's *Literature and Pulpit in Medieval England* (1933); to the Shakespearean scholars mentioned in chapter v; to classical scholars like Sir Maurice Bowra, who has also written *The Heritage of Symbolism* (1943); and to literary historians of the calibre of Basil Willey, author of *The Seventeenth Century Background* (1934) and *The Eighteenth Century Background* (1940).

To the ranks of distinguished historians who are also men of letters (p. 671 above) we must add the name of Christopher Dawson (b. 1889), whose *Spirit of the Oxford Movement* (1933) has been mentioned in connection with Strachey's *Eminent Victorians*; his other works include *The Making of Europe* (1932), *Medieval Religion* (1934)—a volume containing his excellent essay on *Piers Plowman*—and *Religion and Culture* (1948). It is to Dawson, and to the studies of monastic life of Dom David Knowles, we should surely send those Protestant and agnostic readers who rely too much on H. G. Wells's *Outline of History*, as it is to George Gordon Coulton (1858–1947) we should send those Catholic readers who have swallowed whole the view of the Middle Ages propagated by Belloc and Chesterton. Coulton's works include his translation of Salimbene, *From St Francis to Dante* (1906), *Chaucer and his England* (1909) and his massively-documented *Five Centuries of Religion* (1923–36). One of the later works of Trevelyan, *English Social History* (1942; p. 673), is a book as interesting to the general reader as to the student of history or literature, a compliment that can also be paid to G. M. Young's *Victorian England* (1936), C. V. Wedgwood's *The King's War* (1955) and *The King's Peace* (1958) and some of the studies of Elizabethan England by A. L. Rowse and Sir John Neale. One of the most widely-readable of the later works of Herbert Butterfield, author of the influential *Whig Interpretation of History* (1931), is his *Origins of Modern Science* (1949). Hugh Trevor-Roper, author of numerous learned studies, mainly of the sixteenth and seventeenth centuries, reached a wider public with his *Last Days of Hitler* (1947). The autobiographical volume *Acquaintances* (1967) by Arnold Toynbee (p. 673) tells how on "one autumn morning in the year 1909" while he was an undergraduate at Oxford he found himself having breakfast with an unexpected visitor who announced himself briefly as "Bernstein". Many readers have since shared Lewis Bernstein Namierowski's scholarly conversation in the books he has written under his naturalized British name, Sir Lewis Namier: for instance *The Structure of Politics at the Accession of George III* (1929), *England in the Age of the American Revolution* (1930 etc) and *In the Margin of History* (1939).

To philosophers who are also of literary importance (see p. 663 above) we must add the name of R. G. Collingwood (1889–1943), author of *The Principles of Art* (1937) and *The New Leviathan* (1942), whose autobiography appeared in 1939. Bertrand Russell (p. 664) waited till he was over ninety before he started his own autobiography, the first part of which was published in 1967. To the ranks of those scientists like Jeans and Eddington who have managed to convey specialized ideas in unspecialized language we have added (p. 708) the names of Hoyle, Gamow and others who are to a new generation what Jeans and Eddington were to their fathers. Popular science has its dangers of over-simplification and philosophical naïvety, but those literary critics who condemn it altogether are guilty of a misconception. Most of them are no more capable of reading specialized works on physics or astronomy than the most illiterate man in the street, for the simple reason that their knowledge of Shakespeare and Henry James is not matched by a corresponding knowledge of physics or higher mathematics. For most of them, as for the public in general, it is a choice between complete ignorance of the latest scientific researches or a reading of the popular works of Jeans, Eddington, Hoyle and Gamow (or of "novels of ideas" based upon them). To suppose that there is any medium between the two is an academic fallacy: literary appreciation can exist on many different levels, but physics and mathematics are exact sciences, which you either understand or you don't. We may not all be interested, for example, as to whether or why the universe is expanding, but we must all have wondered from time to time why the sky is dark at night. A reading of Raymond Lyttleton's *The Modern Universe* (1956)—which has a suitable epigraph from Edgar Allan Poe—will convince us of the intimate connection between the two, but the reader unversed in science who can understand this book will not be able to understand *The Stability of Rotating Liquid Masses* (1953), to name a specialist work by the same author.

It was not far from the cloistered peace of Downing College, Cambridge, that Rutherford and Cockcroft split the atom (as Mark Twain might have put it) as that blamed atom had never been split before. An early, non-radio-active dust has now settled on the once-celebrated controversy between Dr Leavis of Downing and the scientist-turned-novelist C. P. Snow (later Lord Snow) over the cultural split of the twentieth century in which the achievements of Rutherford, Cockcroft and their colleagues were merely one item on the scientific side. The main documents in the controversy—Snow's Rede Lecture, *The Two Cultures and the Scientific Revolution* (1959), and Leavis's Richmond Lecture at Downing, *The Significance of C. P. Snow* (1962)—seem in retrospect, in their talking so much at cross purposes, to exemplify Snow's principal assertion, that the literary and the scientific cultures have never before been so divided. At the same time, there is no doubt that Leavis was able to show up several weak points in Snow's argument, particularly over his attitude to Ruskin, Morris, Lawrence and other opponents of the Industrial Revolution, who were much more constructive in their criticism than Snow seems to have recognized.

Snow's strong point lay, nevertheless, in his insistence on the dangers of too great a divorce between the scientific and the literary worlds. Most literary men will agree that Snow was right in maintaining that the self-impoverishment is not all on the one side, that men of letters should take more interest in scientific achievements, as scientists should be better acquainted with literature. But the emphasis lies on the "achievements", the results, not on the technique. Snow is demonstrably wrong when he suggests that the ability to describe the Second Law of Thermodynamics (or any other technical ability) is "the scientific equivalent" of the ability to comprehend a play by Shakespeare. There is no literary equivalent of the Second Law. The nearest would be a knowledge of poetic technique or prosody, a perfectly legitimate study (see above, pp. 45, 127, etc.) but one by no means essential to the understanding of *King Lear*. The character Tibby in *Howards End* takes along a copy of the score to a performance of Beethoven's Fifth; but Forster does not imply that Tibby, with his ability to read a score, appreciates Beethoven more deeply than other listeners who cannot read a note. A knowledge of brushwork is not the necessary preliminary to an appreciation of Rembrandt. Snow can only criticize literary men if they take no interest in the results of science, including the social sciences like sociology and anthropology. Whether there are living beings on other worlds (for example) is a question of human, as well as scientific, importance: the layman can appreciate that excellent book, *Life on Other Worlds* (1940), without knowing any of the complicated scientific techniques by means of which Sir Harold Spencer-Jones reaches his tentative conclusions. Mathematics itself has a human, as well as a technical, interest—as we realize when we read G. H. Hardy's *Mathematician's Apology* (1940), to whose 1967 reissue Snow himself contributes a foreword. It is scientific classics like Hardy's *Apology* or J. W. N. Sullivan's *Limitations of Science* (1930) that the literary man should be more often aware of, besides (according to his individual interests) revolutionary books in a particular field, like Eliot Howard's *Territory in Bird Life* (1920); books which summarize revolutionary achievements, like Rona Hurst's *The Loom of Life* (1964) about the break-through in genetics; histories of science like Butterfield's book mentioned and J. D. Bernal's *Science in History* (1954)... If the literary man reads some books of this kind, he will be as well acquainted with the scientific culture of the twentieth century as he can ever hope to be; he can safely leave both the First and the Second Laws of Thermodynamics to the specialist.

The main author of the present volume, George Sampson (1873–1950), was for many years in Matthew Arnold's profession of Inspector of Schools. He was a member of the Departmental Committee on the Teaching of English in England and his *English for the English* (1921) is a pioneer work on the subject, still relevant to the debate, sometimes revived, on whether English should supersede Greek and Latin as the basis of a humane education in English-speaking countries in modern times. Leavis takes the argument a stage further in his *Education and the University* and part of his case against Snow in his Richmond Lecture rests on his conviction that the study of English literature can indeed form a centre for the humanities in the modern world comparable to the study of the classical languages in the past. The more interests that can be allied to such a centre, of course, the better—and these would include scientific interests, though probably not, as we have said, of any technical order.

Arnold considered his own time an age of criticism rather than creation, an opinion shared of hers by Virginia Woolf, who thought that by comparison with the period 1800–21 (also Arnold's standard of comparison) the period 1900–21 had little to show for itself. Both critics were probably mistaken, as we look back at them now with all the advantages of a retrospective view. Arnold was thinking mainly of poetry, and we can still agree that the Victorian age, particularly without Hopkins, is no match for the age of Blake, Burns, Wordsworth, Coleridge, Byron, Shelley and Keats. But in fiction we regard the best novels of Arnold's time, whether in England alone or including the United States, as at least equal in value to Jane Austen and Scott. "If we ask for masterpieces" in the period 1900–21, wrote Mrs Woolf sadly, "where are we to look?" She need have looked no further, many of us will now reply, than her friend Forster's *Howards End*, to say nothing of *The Wings of the Dove*, *Heart of Darkness*, *Nostromo*, *Sons and Lovers*, *The Rainbow*, *A Portrait of the Artist*, *Riders to the Sea*, *The Playboy of the Western World*, *Responsibilities*, *Gerontion*, and *The Golden Bough*. It is our more recent period, since about 1930, which looks barren of major works, compared with the period 1900–30; but this, too, may be an illusion, to be corrected in due course by later generations. What makes criticism of our contemporaries so difficult is itself a difficult question, the answer to which we may search for in vain in *The Common Reader*, *The Common Pursuit*, *The Principles of Literary Criticism*, *The Sacred Wood* or the numerous works of Wyndham Lewis, Edmund Wilson or Sir Herbert Read. We can, at any rate, take warning by the examples of Arnold and Mrs Woolf, and resist the temptation to describe the present period, since 1930 or since 1945, as pre-eminently one of criticism and scholarship, not creation. If an Arnold could be mistaken in this matter, we may certainly be mistaken ourselves. For

Matthew Arnold, according to one of the weightiest boomerangs thrown by Lytton Strachey, "mistook his vocation... He *would* be a critic." With the same irritating lack of self-knowledge, Dickens *would* be a novelist and Shakespeare a poet.

Strachey himself, nevertheless, contributed to the Home University Library (founded 1911) not the least excellent of that excellent series: which from 1966 has been given a new lease of life by the Oxford University Press under the title of Opus Books, reprinting the best of the original contributions, like Strachey's and Russell's, together with new books like Godfrey Lienhardt's *Social Anthropology*. We may fittingly conclude our brief survey of criticism and culture by reminding ourselves that not everything in our present state is to be deplored. It is easy to criticize the B.B.C., for example, but considering their primary duty to the general public, in the way of news, light music, sport and so forth, minority interests have not been neglected, particularly since the advent of the Third Programme (Radio 3) in 1946. The B.B.C., indeed, has taken over some of the functions of the pre-1914 serious newspaper, such as *The Westminster Gazette* in the days of J. A. Spender and *The Manchester Guardian* in the early years of C. P. Scott. We glanced at the more sombre aspects of publishing, but here, too, there is a brighter side to chronicle. The established series of reprinted classics, old and new, like Everyman's Library, the World's Classics, the Thinker's Library, etc., obtained a new rival in 1937, when the first flight of Pelicans settled on the bookstalls next to their elder cousins of the Penguin species which had taken up their breeding grounds there two years before. Such twentieth-century classics as Roger Fry's *Vision and Design*, Constant Lambert's *Music Ho!*, R. H. Tawney's *Religion and the Rise of Capitalism*, Beatrice Webb's *My Apprenticeship*, Sir Leonard Woolley's *Digging up the Past*, Eileen Power's *Medieval People*, Helen Waddell's *The Wandering Scholars*, and many others already mentioned in the course of this chapter, became available to the poorest student, and specially commissioned works, similar to those in the Home University Library, began to follow the classics in this series—some of them, like Susan Stebbing's *Thinking to Some Purpose* and Nikolaus Pevsner's *Outline of European Architecture*, now of classic rank themselves. The story of the various offshoots of Penguin Books, from Puffins to Peregrines, from E. Nesbitt to W. Empson, is too well known to need lengthy mention, but we must note two points: first, that there is a pleasing continuity in the fact that Sir Allen Lane of Penguin Books is a nephew of, and was first apprenticed to, the John Lane of the Bodley Head (and *The Yellow Book*) who was largely responsible, with Elkin Matthews and William Heinemann, for the disappearance of the Victorian three-volume library novel at a guinea-and-a-half in favour of the one-volume novel at six shillings, with beneficial results for literature and popular culture; and secondly, that literature of the most serious sort, including criticism, retains an honourable place in current Penguin activities—as it does in the current programmes of their many rivals in Britain and the United States: Signet and Mentor Paperbacks, Harper Torchbooks, Cambridge Paperbacks, Faber Paper-Covered Editions, Papermacs from Macmillan, the Fontana Library from Collins, to name a few of the most notable among them. One of the best editions of Hopkins is in Penguin, besides an eighteen-volume D. H. Lawrence, Eliot's

Selected Poems and *Selected Prose*, and a *Guide to English Literature* by critics of the *Scrutiny* school. There is very little in the entire range of literature covered by this book—from *Beowulf* to *Godot*, from folksongs to genetics—that is not obtainable in paperback form from Penguin or one of its rivals, so massive has been the revolution since that July day in 1935 when Allen Lane produced his first ten Penguin titles. The best-selling Penguin of them all is not a detective story, as might be imagined, but E. V. Rieu's translation of Homer's *Odyssey*, which by 1959 had sold a million copies. If the mid-twentieth-century reader tends to borrow books from the local library instead of buying them at the local bookshop, he buys paperbacks more than ever, including the most serious titles in criticism, history, philosophy and science. This is still minority culture in a mass civilization, but a minority who can buy a million Homers may in time leaven the mass.

VI. THE LITERATURE OF THE WEST INDIES AND THE NEW AFRICAN STATES

1. West Indian Literature

The first West Indian writer was, of course, Columbus, who

> from his after-
> deck watched heights he hoped for,
> rocks he dreamed, rise solid from my simple water...

to quote some memorable lines from a modern West Indian poet, Edward Brathwaite, in his *Rights of Passage* (1967). But Cristoforo Colombo (*c.* 1446–1506), whom the Spaniards called Cristóbal Colón, did not write in English when he informed the King of Spain that he had landed on some islands off the coast of India. So the letters of the unsuspecting discoverer of the New World cannot really be considered part of the literature of the West Indies as we know it today, which belongs in English, as it does in French, almost entirely to the twentieth century.

At the same time, there is a greater historical depth to West Indian literature —which includes here, as it usually does, the literature of Guyana—than might at first be imagined. In the first place, an astonishing variety of British and American writers—not to mention notorious slavedrivers like Mrs Browning's father—were either born in the West Indies, or the adjacent South American coast, or spent part of their lives there. The literature of Guyana goes back to the book by Sir Walter Ralegh (*c.* 1552–1618; p. 152 above) with the magnificent Elizabethan title *The Discoverie of the large, rich and bewtiful Empyre of Guiana, with a relation of the Great and Golden Citie of Manoa* (1596). The novelist and dramatist Mrs Aphra Behn (1640–89; pp. 351, 357) spent her girlhood in Ralegh's "rich and bewtiful Empyre", then under Dutch rule. Her most famous novel, *Oroonoko, or the History of the Royal Slave* (*c.* 1678), owes much to her memories of plantation life in Surinam and is the first expression in English literature of sympathy for the oppressed Negro slaves who had been brought from Africa to America for the benefit of Europeans. These Europeans included William Beckford senior, Lord Mayor of London, who was born in Jamaica in 1709 and whose vast fortune was inherited by the author of *Vathek* (p. 504) and helped to build the wasteful Folly at Fonthill. The bawdy dramatist Mrs Behn, whose plays were no better than they should be, thus anticipated Clarkson, Wilberforce and the Quakers in their protests against the shameful traffic documented for our own age by Dr Eric Williams, Prime Minister of Trinidad, in *Capitalism and Slavery* (1944; new ed. 1964 with foreword by Sir Denis Brogan), Daniel Mannix and Malcolm Cowley in *Black Cargoes* (1963) and James Pope-Hennessy in *Sins of the Fathers* (1967).

More than a hundred years of misery were to elapse between the date of Mrs Behn's novel and the time when the House of Commons set up a select committee to look into the slave trade—to the distress of people like Boswell who thought an inquiry of this sort a monstrous invasion of the liberty of the subject. Dr Johnson, whose servant Francis Barber was born in Jamaica—and addressed by him in a letter ending "your affectionate Sam. Johnson"—once proposed a toast at Oxford "to the next insurrection of the negroes in the West Indies." But Boswell thought it morally wrong "to abolish a status which in all ages God has sanctioned." It never seems to have occurred to Boswell that the liberty he championed on behalf of Corsica and the American colonies was the same passion that led to so many revolts by West Indian slaves against their European oppressors.

In 1812 Matthew Gregory Lewis ("Monk Lewis", 1775–1818; p. 507) inherited from his father two large estates in Jamaica. "To better the condition of his slaves there," says *Chambers's Biographical Dictionary*, "good-hearted, lachrymose, clever little 'Mat' forsook the society of the Prince Regent, Byron, and all his other great friends, and made the two voyages, in 1815–17, which furnished materials for his one really valuable work, the posthumous *Journal of a West India Proprietor* (1834)... On his way home he died of yellow fever..." The poet and hymn-writer James Montgomery (1771–1854; p. 536) spent part of his childhood in Barbados, where his father was a missionary. His reminiscent volume, *The West Indies and Other Poems* (1809), went through five editions by 1818. Religion and yellow fever are two of the subjects most discussed by Lady Nugent in her *Journal of a Residence in Jamaica* (1839). She was equally shocked by the absence of morals in the country and by the prevalence of mosquitoes which led to so many early deaths.

The "poet of the American Revolution", Philip Freneau (1752–1832; p. 785), spent part of his early life as secretary to a wealthy planter on the island of Santa Cruz, where in 1776 he wrote the romantic *Beauties of Santa Cruz* and the satirical *Jamaica Funeral*, a bitter attack on the hypocrisies of the colonial Church. The American statesman Alexander Hamilton (1757–1804; p. 784) was born in the Leeward Islands, the illegitimate son of a Scottish merchant; the first appearance in print of the future author of *The Federalist* was a letter in the local newspaper describing a West Indian hurricane. The artist and naturalist John James Audubon (1785–1851) was born in Haiti and educated in France before he went to the United States and won international fame for his *Birds of America* (1827–38). Lafcadio Hearn (1850–1904; p. 688) lived in Martinique in 1887–9 and recorded his impressions in *Two Years in the French West Indies* (1890). His novel of the same year, *Youma*, is based on an actual occurrence in the slave rebellion on the island in 1848—the same island of Martinique which was to be the birthplace of Aimé Césaire, the apostle of *Négritude* in twentieth-century Paris and the poet of *Cahier d'un retour au pays natal* (1939). James Anthony Froude (1818–94; p. 669) visited the West Indies in 1886–7 and published in 1888 *The English in the West Indies*, perhaps the first historical account of any value since Edward Long's pioneer *History of Jamaica* (1774).

It was Long who first mentioned the almost legendary career of the learned slave Francis Williams, a compatriot and a contemporary of Dr Johnson's Francis Barber. Williams was sent home to England to be educated, returned to Jamaica as a schoolmaster, and spent his leisure hours thereafter in the composition of Latin odes. But here, when we turn from the European plantocracy or their visitors to the West Indian natives or forced immigrants, the early historical picture is not so clear and indeed is the subject of some controversy among West Indian authorities themselves. Jamaica in the eighteenth century had, at any rate, a Francis Williams to prove that the illiteracy of the majority of his compatriots was due to lack of opportunity rather than to incapacity— which was also proved by the careers of the American Negro poets Jupiter Hammon (*c*. 1720–1800) and Phillis Wheatley (*c*. 1753–84) and the ex-slave from Nigeria, the author of *Equiano's Travels* (p. 936 below) and later on by the career of Edward Wilmot Blyden (1832–1912). Blyden was born in the Danish West Indian island of St Thomas, his father being a tailor of Nigerian slave ancestry. He was helped by American Presbyterians, became associated with the American Colonization Society, and himself emigrated to Liberia in 1851, subsequently becoming Professor of Classics at Liberia College, Liberian Ambassador in London, Agent of Native Affairs in Lagos, Director of Mohammedan Education in Sierra Leone, and the author of numerous essays and lectures some of which have been collected under the title of *Christianity, Islam and the Negro Race*. His varied and controversial career is the subject of a careful study by Hollis R. Lynch, *Edward Wilmot Blyden: Pan-Negro Patriot* (1967), published by the Oxford University Press in their West African History series.

The Guyanese novelist and critic O. R. Dathorne, in an important article "The Writers of Guyana "(*Times Lit. Suppl.*, 26 May 1966) and in the introduction to his anthology *Caribbean Narrative* (1967), traces Guyanese literature back to the early nineteenth century, mentioning for example an earlier anthology (1931) by the dramatist and critic N. E. Cameron which collected verse from the eighteen-thirties onwards. "Simon Christian Oliver, a village schoolmaster, had written in 1838 about freedom from slavery"—a "public poetry" which Dathorne sees as characteristic of a good deal of Guyanese literature, then and now. "Later in the century Egbert Martin was to discover romantic landscapes", and Dathorne finds the traditional *mystique* of the jungle in twentieth-century Guyanese novelists like Wilson Harris and Edgar Mittelholzer.

The picture, both in Guyana and in the Indies, becomes much clearer when we leave the nineteenth century behind and come to the early twentieth. We meet, for instance, the impressive figure of the poet and novelist Claude McKay (b. 1890) who emigrated from his native Jamaica to the United States in 1912 and whom readers of Van Wyck Brooks's monumental *Makers and Finders* series will remember meeting before in the Harlem chapter of *The Confident Years*. McKay was one of the discoveries of Frank Harris—who, like Ford Madox Ford, was always discovering unknown writers or asserting afterwards that he had done so. McKay became an editor of Max Eastman's Marxist paper *The Liberator*, "as well as the outstanding 'contact man'", adds Brooks, "between the Greenwich Villagers and the 'Mecca of the New Negro', the Negro metropolis, Harlem." He first won attention by his *Songs of Jamaica* (1912) and a further volume of poems *Harlem Shadows* (1922). His forceful novels began with *Home to Harlem* (1928), the story of a Negro soldier's return from France to America in 1918 and of his learning from a Haitian waiter of the glories and miseries of his African past; and continued with *Banjo* (1929) and *Banana Bottom* (1933). *A Long Way from Home* (1937) is the aptly-titled autobiography of a career that took the author from Jamaica to New York, from Alabama to Marseilles.

McKay is one of the most interesting and re-readable of the West Indian writers of the early twentieth century, of the generation which also produced Marcus Garvey, George Padmore and Herbert De Lisser, author of the Jamaican folk-story *The White Witch of Rosehall* (1929). But it is, of course, the West Indian writers of the post-war generation, the writers who mostly began in the nineteen-forties or fifties, who have done even more than McKay, De Lisser and other pioneers to put forward West Indian literature on equal terms with the literature of the rest of the English-speaking world. Columbus would not have been surprised to learn that among the foremost of these writers is an Indian: the novelist and critic V. S. Naipaul, born 1932 in Trinidad, whose grandfather came from Uttar Pradesh and who in novels like *The Mystic Masseur* (1957) and *A House for Mr Biswas* (1961) gave a picture of the Hindu community in the West Indies which for humour combined with nostalgic tenderness reminded many English reviewers of Dickens. Trinidad also produced Samuel Selvon, a novelist with a wicked sense of humour and a Naipaulian ear for dialect, whether he is writing of his native island, as in *Turn Again Tiger* (1959) and in the story he contributed to Dr G. R. Coulthard's excellent anthology *Caribbean Literature* (1966) or whether he is describing the tragi-comic problems of the West Indian community in London, as in *The Housing Lark* (1965).

Trinidad, however, does not have a monopoly of modern West Indian literature—even of modern West Indian humour, as witness Louise Bennett and Andrew Salkey in Jamaica and Edgar Mittelholzer in Guyana. The most impressive aspect of mid-twentieth-century West Indian literature is, in fact, the way in which every part of this far-flung archipelago, from the coast of South America to all the "islands at anchor in the west"—to quote the Barbadian poet George Lamming—has contributed to it. Barbados has produced, not only Lamming, but the white West Indian poet and novelist Geoffrey Drayton, author of the semi-autobiographical novel *Christopher* (1959), and the novelist Austin C. Clarke (see above, p. 750), who wrote *The Survivors of the Crossing* (1964) and who emigrated to Canada in 1956. The tiny island of St Lucia, in the Windwards, has produced the poet and dramatist Derek Walcott, author of

In a Green Night, Tales of the Islands, etc., who is regarded by many good judges as the best West Indian poet of his generation. Jamaica, the largest and most populous of the former British West Indies, has produced, among others of note, the novelist Roger Mais (1905–55), whose three novels *The Hills were Joyful Together* (1953), *Brother Man* (1954) and *Black Lightning* (1955) were reprinted in one volume in 1966; the Canadian-born novelist John Hearne (b. 1926), author of *Voices Under the Window* (1955), *Stranger at the Gate* (1956), etc.; the poets George Campbell and A. L. Hendriks; and the Panama-born Andrew Salkey, whose retelling of the Jamaican folk-story of Anancy the giant spider—"the kind of spider with heaps of shoulder-muscles, a black-hairy chest and a night-black frighten-children beard on his chin"—will be recalled from the *Black Orpheus* anthology (1964) and will remind American and British readers of the equally ambiguous tales of *Uncle Remus* and West African readers of the traditional stories of their country, like the one where the ground-squirrel by strategy defeats the lion: a tale included in H. A. S. Johnston's *Selection of Hausa Stories*, 1966, in the Oxford Library of African Literature.

Guyana, formerly British Guiana, has produced the impressive, brooding, Faulknerian novels of Wilson Harris—*Palace of the Peacock* (1960), *The Secret Ladder* (1963), *Heartland* (1964), *The Eye of the Scarecrow* (1965), etc.—besides the poems of A. J. Seymour, editor of the literary journal *Kyk-over-al*, and the books of Jan Carew, author of *Black Midas* (1958), and E. R. Braithwaite, whose *To Sir, With Love* (1959) describes the problems of a West Indian teacher in a London school. The career of the Guyanese novelist and poet Edgar Mittelholzer (1909–65) was tragically cut short by his own hand. Among his dozen books, *A Morning at the Office* (1950) and *My Bones and My Flute* (1955) have a sure place of their own in modern West Indian literature. The cosmopolitan nature of that life and literature is brought home to us by the former novel, in which the office of Essential Products Ltd has an English chief accountant, an East Indian assistant, a West Indian secretary, a Chinese typist and a Portuguese switchboard operator...

The majority of the post-war writers named above are still writing at the present time (1968), either in their native West Indies or in Africa, Britain, Canada or the United States. Their careers are by no means finished, their place in the literary history of the twentieth century by no means settled. If we may risk any general reflection at this very early stage, it is one that concerns the novelists in particular, who have sometimes been criticized by the more cosmopolitan or sophisticated West Indian critics for relying too much on "local colour". It is the natural ambition, of course, of any serious novelist, to have the universal appeal of the poet or the philosopher. But, of European novelists, few are more "universal" in their best work than Tolstoy, Dickens and Joyce; yet each is intimately associated with a certain period and a certain place: Tolstoy with nineteenth-century Russia, Dickens with Victorian London, Joyce with Dublin in 1904. Naipaul, Harris, Clarke, Salkey and other West Indian novelists who may one day come to be regarded as among the mid-twentieth-century's classic writers, major or minor, will not find themselves considered by posterity as any less universal in their appeal because they are so closely associated with the colour and the speech (to say nothing of the colourful speech) of Trinidad, Guyana, Barbados and Jamaica. Such writers, novelists and poets alike, have brought a new idiom, in every sense, to literature in the English language, as their calypso-singing compatriots have brought a new rhythm to popular music and their cricketers a new vitality to sport. Many British and American readers will echo the hope of the Guyanese novelist and historian Christopher Nicole in his book *The West Indies: Their People and History* (1965): "African in its heritage, European in its culture, the West Indies forms a unique bridge between two extremes, at worst a mediator, but at best an example and even a guide."

2. African Literature

The connection between the West Indies and Africa is of profound importance, both historically and symbolically. The historical aspect is given, for instance, in the book by Christopher Nicole just quoted and in *The Sociology of Slavery* (1967) by the Jamaican novelist and sociologist Orlando Patterson, in which the author goes in great detail into the origin of the various tribes who were sold by African kings to European merchants and shipped across the Atlantic from the West African coast. The symbolic aspect is the subject of an excellent article by the Guyanese novelist and critic O. R. Dathorne, "Africa in the Literature of the West Indies", in the opening number (September 1965) of *The Journal of Commonwealth Literature*. Dathorne speaks with particular authority on this controversial question, being a lecturer at the University of Ibadan, Nigeria, who was born and bred in Guyana. His novel *The Scholar-Man* (1964) reflects his own experiences, in its "subtle appreciation", to quote Fernando Henriques in the same number of *The Journal*, "of the remoteness for the West Indian of things African"—remoteness, none the less, that has itself a symbolic importance for the West Indian of African or part-African ancestry like Derek Walcott, who in his well-named poem *A Far Cry from Africa* asks himself:

> How choose
> Between this Africa and the English tongue I love?
> Betray them both, or give back what they give?
> ...How can I turn from Africa and live?

Dathorne does not deny the non-African elements in the West Indies, which we have seen for ourselves above when speaking of V. S. Naipaul, Edgar Mittelholzer and Geoffrey Drayton. But he goes into Walcott's dilemma in sympathetic detail, considering both the remoteness from Africa in time and distance and the strong symbolic pull which he illustrates from literature and incidentally from his own career. He quotes the views (often conflicting) of Sartre, Naipaul, Salkey, Lamming, F. G. Cassidy (author of *Jamaica Talk*), the South African novelist Ezekiel Mphahlele, the Ghanaian sociologist W. E. Abraham, among many others—to which we could add the discussion of this and related topics in Gerald Moore's and Ulli Beier's introduction to their *Modern Poetry from Africa* (1963)—and comes to the undogmatic conclusion that as "even the Africans cannot agree about the identity of West Indians", it is "scarcely surprising that West Indians themselves are divided about whether there is or is not an African presence. But it is from this ambiguity and from an attempt to reconcile the paradoxes, that some worthwhile literature has been written"—not least Dathorne's own novel *The Scholar-Man* and the article quoted, whose lengthy and scholarly argument is but briefly summarized here.

There are other contacts between modern Africa and the West Indies besides Dathorne's and Walcott's. One of the best South African novelists, Peter Abrahams (p. 765 above), whose father came from Ethiopia to the Transvaal, has himself emigrated to Jamaica, become editor of *The West Indian Economist* and has written his later novels, for example *This Island Now* (1966), about West Indian life. Dathorne lists two other West Indian writers besides himself who have crossed the Atlantic in the other direction: Denis Williams from Guyana and the Nigerian-born Jamaican novelist Neville Dawes, author of *The Last Enchantment*, who has returned to his native continent. Another Jamaican novelist, V. S. Reid, a pioneer in several aspects of West Indian writing, set one of his best novels, *The Leopard* (1958), in East Africa. He was able to do this before he had actually visited the country: a remarkable illustration of Dathorne's argument about Africa's symbolic importance for the West Indian writer.

The history of South African (and southern African) literature in the English language has been briefly summarized in chapter xiv (p. 761 above). There we had occasion to mention, as also here, the Nigerian literary magazine *Black Orpheus*, founded in 1957 by the German scholars Ulli Beier and Janheinz Jahn (the latter also editor of the anthology *Schwarzer Orpheus*, Munich, 1964), which made a policy of publishing not only West African writers but also writers from East and South Africa, the West Indies, the United States and elsewhere who were of Negro or part-Negro origin. It is from this magazine (now edited by J. P. Clark) and the anthology (1964) drawn from its pages, and from other anthologies like Peggy Rutherfoord's *Darkness and Light: An Anthology of African Writing* (1958), Langston Hughes's *African Treasury* (1960) and *Poems from Black Africa* (1963), Richard Rive's *Modern African Prose* (1964), John Reed's and Clive Wake's *Book of African Verse* (1964), Ellis Ayitey Komey's and Ezekiel Mphahlele's *Modern African Stories* (1964), David Cook's *Origin East Africa: A Makerere Anthology* (1965), Anne Tibble's *African English Literature* (1966), Paul Edwards's *Through African Eyes* (1966) and Mphahlele's *African Writing Today* (1967)... it is from such sources that many British and American readers, young and old, have been first introduced to the literature of modern Africa. There is no need to be ashamed of such an easy introduction to a difficult art, for modern African literature is nearly as young as the independent, former-colonial States it helped to bring into being, and just as statesmen and men of commerce have taken a little time to adjust themselves to the new situation in politics and economics, so the average reader or student in Britain, the United States and elsewhere needs a little persuasion before he comes to terms with this striking new literature. He has probably known of Africa before only by the romances of Rider Haggard and John Buchan, by the accounts of missionaries, explorers and anthropologists, or at best by the far-seeing masterpiece of Winwood Reade, *The Martyrdom of Man* (1872; p. 704 above), where the author, attempting to write the history of Africa alone, found himself writing the history of the world, so intimate a connection did he find, from ancient times onwards, between Africa and Asia, Africa and Europe, Africa and America.

None of these books is without value for either the general reader or the student of African affairs, provided a varying degree of toleration is allowed for, for outmoded beliefs and prejudices. But apart from Reade's history and such more modern works as Llewelyn Powys's *Black Laughter* (1925), Geoffrey Gorer's *Africa Dances* (1935) and the Nigerian novels by Joyce Cary, they all suffer, to a greater or a lesser degree, from being written from a European angle, without much attempt to enter imaginatively into what Africa means to the African. It is part of the purpose, implied or explicit, of this new African literature of the mid-twentieth century, whether in English, French or Portuguese—the French came first—to correct this view, to give the reader of European origin an insight into African life as seen by Africans themselves, in the spirit of McKay's *Home to Harlem* and the Ghanaian historian J. C. de Graft-Johnson's *African Glory: The Story of Vanished Negro Civilizations*. This is, of course, only part of their purpose, but it is an important one, for historical reasons. The most untravelled of New Yorkers or Londoners can now learn a little neighbourliness by having on his bookshelf a few volumes of this new African literature, as well as West Indian, to rub shoulders with his Dickens or Mark Twain. The Trinidadian Naipaul already rubs shoulders with Dickens in a Pickwickian sense, and the author of *Huckleberry Finn*, with its carefully-differentiated South-Western dialects, would have been the first to applaud the achievement of Amos Tutuola, the Nigerian author of *The Palm Wine Drinkard*.

Tutuola's *Drinkard* (so spelt), published in 1952, "was the first West African novel," says Rive, "to make any impact on the English reading public." But it was the first of a good many. Besides later novels by Tutuola himself, some of them even more peculiar in their humour, philosophy and syntax—such as *My Life in the Bush of Ghosts* (1954) and *Simbi and the Satyr of the Dark Jungle* (1955)—the nineteen-fifties saw the emergence of two other Nigerian novelists of stature in Cyprian Ekwensi and Chinua Achebe (b. 1930), both of whom have since achieved international recognition. To some extent, they complement each other; and the stranger to Nigerian literature cannot do better, we believe, than read them together: Ekwensi's *People of the City* (1954) or *The Drummer Boy* (1960) with Achebe's masterpiece *Things Fall Apart* (1958), for example, or Ekwensi's *Burning Grass* (1962) with Achebe's *Arrow of God* (1964). Achebe's satirical novel, *A Man of the People* (1966), which so sadly forecast the political upheavals in the Federation and the civil war in which the poet Christopher Okigbo was among the Nigerians killed, can be compared with the novel loosely based on the rise and fall of the president-philosopher Nkrumah, *The Gab Boys* (1967), by the Ghanaian novelist and journalist Cameron Duodu, formerly editor of *Drum* in Accra.

Most of these novels are obtainable in Heinemann's African Writers series, of which Achebe himself is the editorial adviser. The series covers Africa as a whole and includes, for instance, *Weep Not, Child* (1964) and *A Grain of Wheat* (1967) by the Kenyan novelist and dramatist James Ngugi, novels and stories by Lenrie Peters from Gambia and Alex La Guma from South Africa, besides Paul Edwards's edition of *Equiano's Travels*—a selection from the Nigerian ex-slave Olaudah Equiano's *Interesting Narrative* (1789)—which we mentioned in connection with his contemporary Francis Williams of Jamaica. This recent upsurge of African writing would have pleased Equiano, Williams and Francis Barber, and Dr Johnson would have been equally pleased to find that the Press of his own University of Oxford is playing its part in the publication of African literature, old and new, in friendly rivalry with the University Presses of Cambridge and Harvard and such other publishers as Heinemann, Longmans, Penguin and André Deutsch. This modern African literature is very like the West Indian in its geographical extent. Nigeria must bear the palm—or tap the first of the palm-wine—for having produced the novelists Tutuola, Ekwensi and Achebe, the poets Gabriel Okara and Christopher Okigbo (1932–67), and the dramatists Wole Soyinka (b. 1935) and J. P. Clark (mentioned briefly above, pp. 901, 914), besides the journal *Black Orpheus* from Ibadan which did so much to bring together African writers from all parts of the continent and the world. But less populous countries than Nigeria have contributed their quota, in both poetry and fiction. A mere thumbing-through of Reed-and-Wake (*A Book of African Verse*) throws up, for example, David Rubadiri from Malawi, Aboiseh Nicol from Sierra Leone, Albert Kayper Mensah from Ghana, Dr S. D. Cudjoe from Togoland... "with a more larger list of sceptres" both in English and French literature than space allows us to mention here. While Richard Rive (*Modern African Prose*) chooses his selection from eight South African writers, four Nigerian, two each from Kenya and Sierra Leone, and one each from Ghana, Guinea and Mozambique. To which we could add several writers in English from Ethiopia, the Egyptian novelist Waguih Ghali, and Okot p'Bitek from Northern Uganda, whose *Song of Lawino* (Nairobi, 1967) has been translated into English by the poet himself from the original Lwo, the language of the Acoli people, much as the Rev. James Jolobe (p. 765 above) translated into English his own Xhosa poems in *Poems of an African* (1946). A truly continental literature: "Africa," as Can Themba says, "speaking to Africa and to the world." In the Whitmanesque idiom of the Nigerian poet Sam Epelle: "greetings to all Afric's lands... to lands of yams and palms... to Sahara, Kalahari, Nile, Niger, Congo, Zambesi... lands of strong men with heads raised high..."

Boswell might have found such an African literature difficult to credit, but Dr Johnson, as we have indicated, would not have been so surprised. "I am very well satisfied with your progress," he writes to Francis Barber, who did not have the educational advantages enjoyed by many modern Africans (though he had more than some of them). "Let me know what English books you read for your entertainment. You can never be wise unless you love reading." The wisdom and the entertainment are now being returned in full measure. Eliot wrote that haunting poem *The Journey of the Magi*, beginning with a phrase adapted from a sermon by Lancelot Andrewes: "A cold coming we had of it ..." A modern African poet, David Rubadiri from Malawi, has adapted Eliot's adaptation, thinking of the "hot coming" of European explorers like Stanley in his poem *Stanley meets Mutesa*, which appears in several anthologies, including Reed-and-Wake's and David Cook's. The poem opens with complaints about "the heat of the day" and "the chill of the night", but ends triumphantly when after a moment's hesitation "the tall black king" greets Stanley with the words *Mtu Mweupe karibu* (white man, you are welcome):

> The gate of polished reed closes behind them
> And the west is let in.

There will be time in the future for a critical *Lives of the Poets* or a *Sacred Wood* on this mid-century upsurge of poetry, fiction and drama, where Africa confronts the West as formerly the West had confronted Africa. Some African critic, or student of African literature, will provide it, some scholar of the calibre and experience of the German Ulli Beier, the Englishman John Reed, the Guyanese O. R. Dathorne, the South African Ezekiel Mphahlele... The ordinary British or American reader can only be deeply impressed by this unexpected addition to the literature of his native tongue, following as it did so swiftly upon the heels of the almost equally unexpected upsurge of modern West Indian literature. We hardly anticipated, some of us hardly deserved, such a bonus, but we will enjoy it in the same spirit of "common wealth" as Africans and West Indians enjoy Shakespeare and Dr Johnson, Whitman and T. S. Eliot. The critical discrimination will be the business of a future generation.

In our end is our beginning... Readers of the opening chapters of this book will have noticed a certain parallel between the position of African and West Indian literature in the mid-twentieth century and that of English literature in its early years. Britons may have been slaves to Rome, and Anglo-Saxons to Danes and Normans, during these early centuries, as later they enslaved others of African birth, but English literature grew out of these centuries of oppression, in more than one sense, as West Indian and African literatures have grown out of European oppression in modern times. The debt of these modern literatures to the literature of Shakespeare and Dr Johnson is no heavier than the debt of English literature to Greece, Rome and the Continent of Europe. A blend of English tradition and foreign influence produced much of the best of the literature of England in the past, as we do not doubt that West Indian and African traditions, blended with that English literature, will produce much of the best of their writing in the future.

INDEX

A full index to this volume would be of impracticable length. Entries have been almost entirely limited to authors or works discussed or cited; casual allusions are ignored. Individual works are not usually entered unless they are by unknown or little known authors, except in the case of a few works of historical interest like *Gorboduc*. Where an author is known almost equally by his real name and by his pseudonym (e.g. Dodgson–Carroll, Clemens–Twain), we have adopted the procedure of Bateson and Watson (in works mentioned on p. 571) and entered him under both. Where there are several entries under one name the main references are indicated by heavier type. A single entry can be presumed to be the main reference. The list of contents will serve as a brief subject index.